1995

(* INDICATES DATE OF REIGN OR TERM OF OFFICE)

THIS HISTORY DEVOTES MUCH MATERIAL TO EXPLAINING THE LIVES AND DAILY PRACTICES OF <u>WOMEN</u> IN OUR WESTERN CIVILIZATION — CERTAINLY THIS REGARD FOR EXPLAINING THE DAILY LIVES OF WOMEN IN THIS HISTORY, IS MORE THAN I AM USED TO IN OTHER HISTORIES OF WESTERN CIVILIZATION. BUT IT ALSO REFLECTS A SPECIAL INTEREST IN AMERICAN SOCIETY AT THE TIME IN WHICH IT WAS WRITTEN.

NO WONDER DR. JOY KOPP CHOSE IT AS HER TEXT AS THE INSTRUCTOR OF WESTERN CIVILIZATION FOR HER CLASSES AT EAST CENTRAL COLLEGE,

1991

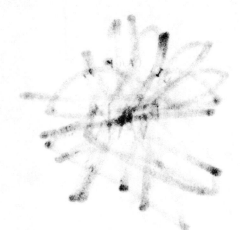

The Challenge of the West

The Challenge of the West

PEOPLES AND CULTURES
FROM THE STONE AGE TO THE GLOBAL AGE

1995

Lynn Hunt
University of Pennsylvania

Thomas R. Martin
College of the Holy Cross

Barbara H. Rosenwein
Loyola University Chicago

R. Po-chia Hsia
New York University

Bonnie G. Smith
Rutgers University

D. C. Heath and Company
Lexington, Massachusetts   Toronto

Address editorial correspondence to:

D. C. Heath and Company
125 Spring Street
Lexington, MA 02173

Acquisitions Editor: James Miller
Developmental Editor: David Light
Production Editor: Janice Molloy
Designer: Henry Rachlin
Photo Researcher: Rose Corbett Gordon
Art Editor: Diane Grossman
Production Coordinator: Charles Dutton
Permissions Editor: Margaret Roll
Map Coordinator: Patricia Wakeley

International Standard Book Number: 0–669–12162–2

Library of Congress Catalog Number: 94–75072

10 9 8 7 6 5 4 3 2 1

ABOUT THE AUTHORS

Lynn Hunt, Annenberg Professor of History at the University of Pennsylvania, received her B.A. from Carleton College and her M.A. and Ph.D. from Stanford University. She is the author of *Revolution and Urban Politics in Provincial France* (1978), *Politics, Culture, and Class in the French Revolution* (1984), and *The Family Romance of the French Revolution* (1992); she is also the editor of *The New Cultural History* (1989) and the co-author of *Telling the Truth About History* (1994). She has been awarded fellowships by the Guggenheim Foundation and the National Endowment for the Humanities and is a Fellow of the American Academy of Arts and Sciences.

Thomas R. Martin, Jeremiah O'Connor Professor in Classics at the College of the Holy Cross, earned his B.A. at Princeton University and his A.M. and Ph.D. at Harvard University. He is the author of *Sovereignty and Coinage in Classical Greece* (1985) and collaborated on *Perseus 1.0: Interactive Sources and Studies on Ancient Greece* (1992), which was named the EDUCOM Best Software in Social Sciences (History) in 1992. He has received fellowships from the National Endowment for the Humanities and the American Council of Learned Societies and is councilor of the American Numismatic Society.

Barbara H. Rosenwein, professor of history at Loyola University Chicago, earned her B.A., M.A., and Ph.D. at the University of Chicago. She is the author of *Rhinoceros Bound: Cluny in the Tenth Century* (1982) and *To Be the Neighbor of Saint Peter* (1989), and co-author of *Saint Maïeul, Cluny et la Provence: Expansion d'une abbaye à l'aube du Moyen Age* (1994). She has received fellowships from the Guggenheim Foundation and the National Endowment for the Humanities.

R. Po-chia Hsia, professor of history at New York University, received his B.A. from Swarthmore College and his M.A. and Ph.D. from Yale University. He is the author of *Society and Religion in Munster, 1535-1618* (1984), *The Myth of Ritual Murder: Jews and Magic in Reformation Germany* (1988), *Social Discipline in the Reformation: Central Europe 1550-1750* (1989), and *Trent 1475: Stories of a Ritual Murder Trial* (1992). He has been awarded fellowships by the Woodrow Wilson International Center for Scholars, the National Endowment for the Humanities, the Guggenheim Foundation, and the Mellon Foundation.

Bonnie G. Smith, professor of history at Rutgers University, earned her B.A. at Smith College and her M.A. and Ph.D. at the University of Rochester. She is the author of *Ladies of the Leisure Class* (1981), *Confessions of a Concierge: Madame Lucie's History of Twentieth-Century France* (1985), and *Changing Lives: Women in European History Since 1700* (D. C. Heath, 1989). She has received fellowships from the Guggenheim Foundation, the Davis Center of Princeton University, and the American Council of Learned Societies.

PREFACE

Many American universities introduced Western civilization courses after World War I. Their intent was to explain what the United States had in common with its western European allies, that is, to justify American involvement in a European war. The emphasis on defending a shared tradition of Western values gained in urgency during World War II, but since the 1960s, and especially since the end of the Cold War, the wisdom of this approach has come into question. Even if everyone agreed on the purposes of teaching and learning about Western civilization, however, no one person or even team of authors could possibly master every field of scholarship and every national history that rightly enters into such an account. It is all the more important, therefore, to explain how we authors approached our task and what we hoped to accomplish.

The title of this book, *The Challenge of the West*, tells much about its general orientation. We focus on the contributions of a multitude of peoples and cultures to the making of Western values and traditions. But it is important to keep in mind that in the overall perspective of recorded human time, the very idea of the West is of recent vintage. It emerged as an idea in the fifteenth century, when the West began to dominate other areas of the globe through trade and colonization. The modern idea of the West as a trans-Atlantic entity—Europe and its colonial offshoots in North America—sharing common values and modes of social and political organization acquired distinctive meaning only at the end of the nineteenth century, when the United States joined the western European powers as a major industrial and colonizing force. Our task as authors has been to recount and analyze the evolution of these values and forms of organization, from the ancient ideas of community and individual responsibility to the modern forces of science and industry. We have consistently tried to place the West's emergence in a larger, world context, recognizing that it was not inevitable or predetermined but rather an unexpected, even surprising development.

As it secured technological and economic advantages, the West inevitably *challenged* other cultures, even dominated many of them for a time and destroyed some altogether. But in the late twentieth century, the West in turn faces challenges from other cultures and distinctively different modes of social and political organization in the rest of the world. To understand the West's ascent to dominance and the present-day challenges to that hegemony, it is imperative to set the history of the West's own internal unfolding into the context of its relations with the other cultures of the world. We consequently return again and again to the theme of Western relationships—economic, military, and cultural—with the wider world.

Peoples and cultures appear in the plural in our title because we want to emphasize the variety of groups, ethnicities, cultures, and nations that have played important roles in making the West. Cultures are whole ways of life, not always neatly confined within the state boundaries or standard chronologies of traditional history. Historians now pay increasing attention to the continuities and long-term trends in ordinary people's lives in the past. The age at which young people marry, the number of children they have, the houses they live in, the clothes they wear, and the ways they read and entertain themselves have all provided significant clues to the attitudes, values, and actions that shaped the West. They cannot replace the history of wars, changes of rulers, and shifts in political alignments, but they help to put those political events into a broader, more meaningful context.

The original, early-twentieth-century conception of Western civilization was much more narrow. Historians defined Anglo-American political institutions—representative, constitutional government and a free-market society—at the core of Western values. The Western civilization course effectively offered training in the history of diplomacy, warfare, and past politics for the next generation of leaders of the "free world." In 1919 one such course was described as creating "a citizen who shall be safe for democracy."

This view has a relatively long lineage, going back to eighteenth-century European writers who took for their model English religious tolerance (in fact limited to Protestants), freedom of the press, and constitutional monarchy (even when only a small proportion of adult men had the vote). The English agricultural expert and essayist Arthur Young, for example, offered a map of liberty in 1772:

> Asia is by the best accounts despotic throughout. . . . Africa comes next, and what misery involves that vast country! . . . In Europe itself, what disproportion between liberty and slavery! Russia, Poland, the chief of Germany, Hungary, Turkey, the greatest part of Italy, Spain, Portugal, France, Denmark and Norway. The following [free countries] bear no proportion to them, *viz* the British Isles, Sweden, Holland, Switzerland, and the Germanic and Italian states. And in America, Spain, Portugal and France, have planted despotism; only Britain liberty.

There is much in this picture that we would agree with still today. The English did indeed pioneer our modern Western conceptions of religious tolerance, freedom of the press, and constitutional government. Our sense of the geography of freedom, however, is both broader and more nuanced.

Historians today devote much more of their attention to the countries that did not follow the English model but developed their own distinctive routes, and to the groups—slaves, indigenous peoples, workers, women, immigrants—who labored in supposedly free societies without enjoying the guarantees of liberty until very recently. By pushing further and further back into the past, to the once derided "Dark Ages" of medieval times, to Greek and Roman precedents, back even to the very earliest settlements known in prehistoric times, historians of the West have revealed all the surprising turns, the routes not taken, and the alternatives once available and then lost as humans collectively made the decisions that have led us to where we are today. We go back in time so far not just to trace the emergence of the entity later known as the West but also to learn and to satisfy our curiosity about how peoples and cultures in the past organized themselves and experienced their worlds.

As democracy has expanded in meaning to include different religious groups, women as well as men, workers as well as employers, immigrants as well as natives, and peoples of all races and ethnicities, so, too, the history of what counts in the West has grown more capacious. We have tried to incorporate the history of once subordinate groups into our general narrative, showing how the struggles of daily life and ordinary people also helped to shape the Western past. We see these aspects not as colorful anecdotes or entertaining sideshows but rather as significant determinants of social and political relations. *Peoples* means *all* the people.

As Cold War barriers have broken down and the boundaries of the European Economic Community have expanded, the idea of Europe itself has changed. As a consequence, we make every effort to include Russia and eastern Europe in our story. It is hard to avoid the temptation of seeing eastern Europeans as "backward," "unfree," and certainly not Western like the rest of us, much as Arthur Young viewed them in the 1700s. But just as the West has begun to incorporate all its own peoples, so, too, it must confront its other geographical half—eastern Europe and Russia. Understanding the history of eastern Europe and its relationship to the West is one small step toward a meeting of cultures, perhaps even toward true integration that will render Young's version truly obsolete.

We have tried to present our account in a straightforward chronological manner. Each chapter covers all of the events, people, and themes of a particular slice of time; thus the reader will not be forced to learn about political events in one chapter and then backtrack to the social and cultural developments of the period in the next. We have followed this pattern from the very beginning, where we discuss the roots of Western civilization in prehistory and in the ancient Near East, to the very end, where we ponder the transforming effect of globalization on the idea of the West.

We believe that it is important, above all else, to see the interconnections—between politics and cultures; between wars and diplomacy, on the one hand, and everyday life, on the other; between so-called mainstream history and the newer varieties of social, cultural, and women's history. For this reason, we did not separate intellectual and cultural life or women's and social history into distinct chapters or sections. We have tried to integrate them chronologically throughout.

History will always be an interim report; every generation rewrites history as interests change and as new sources are discovered or known ones are reinterpreted. We have tried to convey the sense of excitement generated by new insights and the sense of controversy created by the clash of conflicting interpretations. For history is not just an inert thing, lying there in moldering records to be memorized by the next generation of hapless students. It is constantly alive, subject to pressure, and able to surprise us. If we have succeeded in conveying some of that vibrancy of the past, we will not be satisfied with what we have done—history does not sit still that long—but we will be encouraged to start rethinking and revising once again.

Special Pedagogical Features

A range of useful study aids has been built into *The Challenge of the West.* Each chapter begins with a vivid anecdote that draws readers into the atmosphere and issues of the times and raises the chapter's major themes; the chapters conclude with brief summaries that tie together the thematic strands and point the readers onward. At the beginning of each chapter readers will find a list of important dates that introduces some of the key actors, events, and trends of the period. Timelines interspersed throughout the text give students a chronological overview of particular themes and processes. At the end of each chapter are carefully chosen bibliographies, first, of source materials ranging from political documents to novels, and second, of up-to-date interpretive studies that will aid those wishing to seek in-depth treatment of particular topics.

The text's full-color design features nearly 400 illustrations, including examples from material culture, the history of architecture, iconography, painting, cartoons, posters, and photography. The images come not only from Europe and the United States but also from Russia, Africa, and Asia. The illustrations combine well-known classics that are important for cultural literacy with fresh images that document, in particular, the lives of ordinary people and women. The text also contains more than 200 maps and graphs. Each chapter includes large maps that show major developments—wars, patterns of trade, political realignments, and so on—as well as smaller "spot" maps that immediately aid the student's geographical understanding

of issues ranging from the structure of Old Kingdom Egypt to the civil war in Yugoslavia.

Supplementary Program for *The Challenge of the West*

An extensive ancillary program accompanies *The Challenge of the West.* It is designed not only to assist instructors but to develop students' critical-thinking skills and to bolster their understanding of key topics and themes treated in the textbook. In the supplements as in the textbook, our goal has been to make teaching and learning enjoyable and challenging.

Students will find a valuable tool in *Studying Western Civilization: A Student's Guide to Reading Maps, Interpreting Documents, and Preparing for Exams,* by Richard M. Long of Hillsborough Community College. The guide includes helpful aids such as chapter outlines and summaries, vocabulary exercises, and a variety of self-tests on the chapter content. It also features primary-source excerpts (selected by the text authors) with interpretive questions, as well as map exercises to build geographical understanding of historical change. A two-volume set of documents provides students and instructors alike with hundreds of primary references, ranging from the classics of Western political, legal, and intellectual history to the freshest sources on social, cultural, and women's history.

The *Instructor's Guide,* prepared by Sara W. Tucker of Washburn University, includes annotated chapter outlines, lecture suggestions, and a wealth of teaching resources. The annotated chapter outlines are available on disk as the *Instructor's Toolkit.* D. C. Heath is also making available to adopters a Western civilization videodisc with 2,100 images that is barcoded, captioned, and indexed for classroom use.

Rounding out the supplementary resources are the *Computerized Testing Program,* which allows instructors to create customized problem sets for quizzes and examinations, and the accompanying printed *Test Item File.* More than 4,000 questions, prepared by Denis Paz of Clemson University and Jachin Warner Thacker of Western Kentucky University, are available in this testing program. Finally, we have produced a transparency set with some 100 full-color maps.

Acknowledgments

We first want to acknowledge the outstanding efforts and unstinting support of many people at D. C. Heath and Company in the development of this textbook. We thank History editor James Miller; developmental editors David Light, Debra Osnowitz, and Pat Wakeley; production editor Janice Molloy; designer Henry Rachlin; photo researchers Rose Corbett Gordon and Martha Shethar; production coordinator Charles Dutton; and permissions editor Margaret Roll.

Numerous colleagues around the country read and commented on the chapters, often at great length and with great insight. Here we thank those who contributed formal written reviews:

Dorothy Abrahamse, California State University, Long Beach; **Jeremy Adams,** Southern Methodist University; **Meredith Adams,** Southwest Missouri State University; **Thomas Adriance,** Virginia Polytechnic State University; **Kathleen Alaimo,** Xavier University; **James Alexander,** University of Georgia; **Kathryn Amdur,** Emory University; **Glenn J. Ames,** University of Toledo; **Susan Amussen,** Connecticut College; **Abraham Ascher,** City University of New York; **Achilles Avraamides,** Iowa State University; **James Banker,** North Carolina State University; **George Barany,** University of Denver; **John Barker,** University of Wisconsin, Madison; **Kenneth Barkin,** University of California, Riverside; **H. Arnold Barton,** Southern Illinois University; **Barrett Beer,** Kent State University; **Rodney Bell,** South Dakota State University; **Martin Berger,** Youngstown State University; **Patrice Berger,** University of Nebraska; **David Bien,** University of Michigan; **Rebecca Boehling,** University of Maryland, Baltimore County; **Donna Bohanan,** Auburn University; **Gordon Bond,** Auburn University; **Marilyn J. Boxer,** San Diego State University; **Jay Bregman,** University of Maine, Orono; **William Brennan,** University of the Pacific; **Renate Bridenthal,** City University of New York, Brooklyn College; **Jon Bridgman,** University of Washington; **E. Willis Brooks,** University of North Carolina; **Peter Brown,** Rhode Island College; **Paul Burns,** University of Nevada, Las Vegas; **Thomas Burns,** Emory University; **Stanley Burstein,** California State University, Los Angeles; **June K. Burton,** University of Akron;

Carter Carroll, College of DuPage; **Jack Censer,** George Washington University; **Paul Chardoul,** Grand Rapids Junior College; **William Chase,** University of Pittsburgh; **Anna Cienciola,** University of Kansas; **Henry Clark,** Canisius College; **Catherine Cline,** Catholic University of America; **Marilyn Coetzee,** Denison University; **Gary Cohen,** University of Oklahoma; **William Cohen,** Hope College; **Susan Cole,** University of Illinois; **John J. Contreni,** Purdue University; **John Conway,** University of British Columbia; **Marc Cooper,** Southwest Missouri State University; **Ruth Schwartz Cowan,** State University of New York, Stony Brook; **Marvin Cox,** University of Connecticut; **Guy S. Cross,** Pennsylvania State University; **Paige Cubbison,** Miami-Dade Community College; **Robert V. Daniels,** University of Vermont; **Elinor M. Despalatovic,** Connecticut College; **Barbara Diefendorf,** Boston University; **Jeffrey Diefendorf,** University of New Hampshire; **John Patrick Donnelly, S.J.,** Marquette University; **Seymour Drescher,** University of Pittsburgh; **Katherine Fischer Drew,** Rice University; **Lawrence Duggan,** University of Delaware; **Chester Dunning,** Texas A&M University; **Evelyn Edson,** Piedmont Virginia Community College; **Geoffrey Eley,** University of Michigan; **Barbara Engel,** University of Colorado; **Amanda Eurich,** Western Washington University; **Barbara Evans Clements,** University of Akron; **John Evans,** University of Minnesota; **Theodore Evergates,** Western Maryland College; **Steven Fanning,** University of Illinois at Chicago; **Diane Farrell,** Moorhead State University; **Joanne Ferraro,** San Diego State University; **Arthur Ferrill,** University of Washington; **Elmar Fetscher,** University of Central Florida; **Monte Finkelstein,** Tallahassee Community College; **Robert Finlay,** University of Arkansas; **Nels W. Forde,** University of Nebraska; **John Freed,** Illinois State University; **Linda Frey,** University of Montana; **Ellen Friedman,** Boston College; **James Friguglietti,** Eastern Montana College; **Stephen Fritz,** East Tennessee State University; **James A. Funkhouser,** Edison State Community College; **Alison Futrell,** University of Arizona; **Alan Galpern,** University of Pittsburgh; **James Gentry,** College of Southern Idaho; **Bentley B. Gilbert,** University of Illinois at Chicago; **John Gillis,** Rutgers University; **Kees Gispen,** University of Mississippi; **R. Edward Glatfelter,** Utah

State University; **Abbott Gleason,** Brown University; **Penny Gold,** Knox College; **Richard Golden,** Clemson University; **Walter Gray,** Loyola University Chicago; **John Guilmartin,** Ohio State University; **James W. Hagy,** College of Charleston; **Charles Hamilton,** Simon Fraser University; **Barbara Hanawalt,** University of Minnesota; **Sarah Hanley,** University of Iowa; **Janine Hartman,** University of Cincinnati; **John Headley,** University of North Carolina; **David Hendon,** Baylor University; **Gerald Herman,** Northeastern University; **Holger Herwig,** University of Calgary; **Walter Hixson,** Michigan State University; **J. H. Hoffman,** Creighton University; **Daniel Hollis,** Jacksonville State University; **Blair Holmes,** Brigham Young University; **Rodney Holtzcamp,** College of DuPage; **David Hood,** California State University, Long Beach; **Jeff Horn,** Stetson University; **Donald Howard,** Florida State University; **David Hudson,** California State University, Fresno; **James W. Hurst,** Joliet Junior College; **John Hurt,** University of Delaware; **William Irvine,** Clendon College, York University; **Matthew Jaffe,** Antelope Valley Community College; **Barbara Jelavich,** Indiana University; **Carol Thomas Johnson,** University of Washington; **Yvonne Johnson,** Collin County Community College; **Richard Kaeuper,** University of Rochester; **Susan Karant-Nunn,** Portland State University; **Donald Kelley,** University of Rochester; **Joseph Kett,** University of Virginia; **William Keylor,** Boston University; **Joseph Kicklighter,** Auburn University; **Raymond Kierstead,** Reed College; **Carla Klausner,** University of Missouri, Kansas City; **Paul Knoll,** University of Southern California; **John Kohler,** Clayton State College; **Rudy Koshar,** University of Wisconsin, Madison; **Cynthia Kosso,** Northern Arizona University; **Z.J. Kostolnyik,** Texas A&M University; **Richard Kuisel,** State University of New York, Stony Brook; **P. David Lagomarsino,** Dartmouth College; **Ira M. Lapidus,** University of California; **David Large,** Montana State University; **Ann C. Lebar,** Eastern Washington University; **Helen Lemay,** State University of New York, Stony Brook; **Richard Levy,** University of Illinois at Chicago; **Richard Long,** Hillsborough Community College; **David Longfellow,** Baylor University; **Carolyn Lougee,** Stanford University; **William Lubenow,** Stockton State College; **J. Ter-**

race Lyden, St. Meinrad College; **Joseph Lynch,** Ohio State University; **Michael J. Lyons,** North Dakota State University; **Richard Mackey,** Ball State University; **Thomas Mackey,** University of Louisville; **Anne MacLennan,** Dawson College; **J.P. Madden,** Hardin Simmons University; **Sally Marks,** Rhode Island College; **Benjamin Martin,** Louisiana State University; **Ralph Mathisen,** University of South Carolina; **Margaret McCord,** University of Tampa; **Wade Meade,** Louisiana Technical University; **Meredith Medler,** St. Cloud State University; **Paul Michelson,** Huntington College; **James Mini,** Montgomery Community College; **Robert Moeller,** University of California; **Anthony Molho,** Brown University; **Michael Monheight,** University of South Alabama; **A. Lloyd Moote,** University of Southern California; **Marjorie Morgan,** Southern Illinois University; **Gordon Mork,** Purdue University; **Edward Muir,** Hagley Museum & Library; **John Kim Munholland,** University of Minnesota; **James Murray,** University of Cincinnati; **Philip Naylor,** Marquette University; **John Newell,** College of Charleston; **Gerald Newman,** Kent State University; **Martha Newman,** University of Texas, Austin; **Donald Niewyk,** Southern Methodist University; **Janet Nolan,** Loyola University Chicago; **Robert Nye,** Rutgers Center for Historical Analysis; **Dennis O'Brien,** West Virginia University; **Mary O'Neil,** University of Washington; **Robert Oden,** Dartmouth College; **Walter Odum,** Eastern Kentucky University; **Jeanne Ojala,** University of Utah; **William Olejniczak,** College of Charleston; **Richard Olson,** St. Olaf College; **Aristides Papadakis,** University of Maryland, Baltimore County; **Thomas Pesek,** Washington State University; **Dolores Peters,** St. Olaf College; **Michael Phayer,** Marquette University; **Ruth Pike,** Hunter College; **Linda Piper,** University of Georgia; **Jeremy Popkin,** University of Kentucky; **Johannes Postma,** Mankato State University; **Thomas Preisser,** Sinclair Community College; **Richard Price,** University of Maryland; **Anne Quartararo,** United States Naval Academy; **Hugh Ragsdale,** University of Alabama, Tuscaloosa; **Samuel Ramer,** Tulane University; **Orest Ranum,** Johns Hopkins University; **Marion Rappe,** San Francisco State University; **Norman Ravitch,** University of California, Riverside; **Charles Rearick,** University of Massachusetts, Amherst; **Virginia Reinberg,**

Boston College; **Kathryn Reyerson,** University of Minnesota; **Peter Riesenberg,** Washington University; **Harry Ritter,** Western Washington University; **John Roberts,** Lincolnland College; **Ronald Ross,** University of Wisconsin, Milwaukee; **Robin Rudoff,** East Texas State University; **Julius Ruff,** Marquette University; **Roland Sarti,** University of Massachusetts, Amherst; **Benjamin Sax,** University of Kansas; **Kenneth Schellhase,** Northern Michigan University; **Wolfgang Schlauch,** Eastern Illinois University; **R.A. Schneider,** Catholic University of America; **Robert Schnucker,** Northeast Missouri State University; **Sally Scully,** San Francisco State University; **Paul Seaver,** Stanford University; **David Sefton,** Eastern Kentucky University; **Kyle Sessions,** Illinois State University; **William Sewell,** University of Michigan; **Neil Shipley,** University of Massachusetts, Amherst; **Jane Slaughter,** University of New Mexico; **J. Harvey Smith,** Northern Illinois University; **Patrick Smith,** Broward Community College; **Ronald Smith,** Arizona State University; **Paul Spagnoli,** Boston College; **Elaine Spencer,** Northern Illinois University; **Jonathan Sperber,** University of Missouri, Columbia; **Zeph Stewart,** Center for Hellenic Studies; **Gale Stokes,** Rice University; **Gerald Strauss,** Indiana University; **Richard Sullivan,** Michigan State University; **Frederick Suppe,** Ball State University; **Francis Roy Swietek,** University of Dallas; **Edith Sylla,** North Carolina State University; **Emily Tabuteau,** Michigan State University; **William Tannenbaum,** Missouri Southern University; **Timothy Teeter,** Anne Arundel Community College; **Carol Thomas,** University of Washington; **Jason Thompson,** Western Kentucky University; **James Tracy,** University of Minnesota; **Sara Tucker,** Washburn University; **William Tucker,** University of Arkansas; **John Tuthill,** Georgia Southern University; **Gloria Tysl,** Illinois Benedictine College; **Ted Uldricks,** University of North Carolina, Asheville; **Johannes Ultee,** University of Alabama; **Raymond Van Dam,** University of Michigan; **Emily Vermuele,** Harvard University; **Robert Vignery,** University of Arizona; **Mack Walker,** Johns Hopkins University; **Sue Sheridan Walker,** Northeastern Illinois University; **Allan Ward,** University of Connecticut; **Bernard Wasserstein,** Brandeis University; **John Weakland,** Ball State University; **Robert Wegs,** University of Notre Dame; **Lee Shai Weissbach,** University of Louisville; **Eric Weitz,** St. Olaf College; **Robert Welborn,** Clayton State College; **Charlotte Wells,** University of Northern Iowa; **Peter Wells,** University of Minnesota; **Joseph Werne,** Southeast Missouri State University; **Victor Wexler,** University of Maryland; **Stephen D. White,** Wesleyan University; **Mary Wickwire,** University of Massachusetts, Amherst; **Ronald Witt,** Duke University; **Charles Wood,** Dartmouth College; **Neil York,** Brigham Young University; **Gordon Young,** Purdue University; **Reginald Zelnick,** University of California, Berkeley.

Professor Rosenwein especially wishes to thank Charles Brauner, Zouhair Ghazzal, Charles Radding, and Ian Wood for their assistance.

Professor Hunt extends special thanks to Caroline Bynum, Margaret Jacob, Sheryl Kroen, and Thomas Laqueur.

L.H
T.R.M.
B.H.R.
R.P.H.
B.G.S.

CONTENTS

PART

I

*The Emergence of the West, from
Earliest Times to* A.D. *567*   *1*

CHAPTER

1

The First Civilizations in the West   *3*

CHAPTER

2

*New Paths for Western Civilization,
c. 1000–500* B.C.   *37*

CHAPTER

5

*The Rise and Fall of the Roman Republic,
c. 800–44 B.C.*   *147*

CHAPTER

6

*The Roman Empire,
44 B.C.–A.D. 284*   *187*

CHAPTER
7

*The Fragmentation and Transformation
of the Late Roman Empire,
284–568*   225

The Reorganization of the Roman
Empire   226

The Christianizing of the Empire   231

New Patterns of Life   241

PART
II

*The Quickening of the West,
568–1560*   *266*

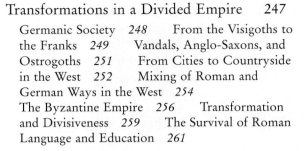

CHAPTER
8

*The Heirs of the Roman Empire,
568–756*   *269*

Byzantium: A Christian Empire Under
Siege   270

CHAPTER
13

*The Collapse of Medieval Order,
1320–1430*   *437*

CHAPTER
14

*Renaissance Europe,
1430–1493*   *469*

CHAPTER
15

The Struggle for Faith and Power,
1494–1560   *501*

PART
III

The Take-off of the West,
1560–1894   *538*

CHAPTER
18

New Societies and the Early Enlightenment,
1690–1740   *611*

CHAPTER
19

The Promise of a New Order,
1740–1787   *645*

CHAPTER
20

*The Age of Revolutions,
1787–1799*   *679*

CHAPTER
21

*Napoleon, the Restoration,
and the Revolutionary Legacy,
1799–1832*   *711*

CHAPTER
22

*Industrialization, Urbanization,
and Revolution,
1832–1851*   *747*

CHAPTER
23

*Politics and Culture of the Nation-State,
1851–1871*   *781*

CHAPTER
29

Technology, Social Change, and Challenges to Western Dominance, 1962–1979   *1009*

CHAPTER
30

The West and the New Globalism, 1979–Present   *1041*

MAPS, CHARTS, AND GRAPHS

The B.C/A.D. System for Reckoning Dates

"When were you born?" "What year is it?" We customarily answer questions like this with a number, such as "1978" or "1995." Our replies are usually automatic, taking for granted the numerous assumptions Westerners make about dates. But to what do numbers such as 1978 or 1995 actually refer? In this book the numbers used to specify dates follow the system most commonly utilized in the Western secular world. This system reckons the dates of solar years by counting backward and forward from the putative date of the birth of Jesus Christ, nearly two thousand years ago.

Using this method, numbers followed by the abbreviation B.C., standing for "before Christ," indicate the number of years counting backward from the birth of Jesus. The larger the number after B.C. the earlier in history is the year to which it refers. The date 431 B.C., for example, refers to a year 431 years before the birth of Jesus and therefore comes earlier in time than the dates 430 B.C., 429 B.C., and so on. The same calculation applies to numbering other time intervals calculated on the decimal system: those of 10 years (a decade), of 100 years (a century), and of 1,000 years (a millennium). For example, the decade of the 440s B.C. (449 B.C. to 440 B.C.) is earlier than the decade of the 430s B.C. (439 to 430 B.C.). "Fifth century B.C." refers to the fifth period of 100 years reckoning backward from the birth of Jesus and covers the years 500 B.C. to 401 B.C. It is earlier in history than the fourth century B.C. (400 B.C. to 301 B.C.), which followed the fifth century B.C. Because this system has no year "zero," the first century B.C. covers the years 100 B.C. to 1 B.C. As for millennia, the second millennium B.C. refers to the years 2000 B.C. to 1001 B.C., the third millennium to the years 3000 B.C. to 2001 B.C., and so on.

Because B.C. indicates dates reckoned backward, adjectives such as "early" or "late" when applied to decades, centuries, or millennia B.C. refer to higher and lower numbers, respectively. For example, the two early decades of the fifth century B.C. are the 490s B.C. and the 480s B.C. The 420s B.C. is a late decade of the same century. The year 506 B.C. is a

date in the late sixth century B.C. The date 2966 B.C. is in the early third millennium B.C. Similarly, the first quarter of the eighth century B.C. covers the twenty-five years from 800 B.C. to 776 B.C., whereas the second half of the same century consists of 750 B.C. to 701 B.C.

To indicate years counted forward from the birth of Jesus, numbers are preceded by the abbreviation A.D., standing for the Latin phrase *anno Domini* ("in the year of the Lord"). The date A.D. 1492, for example, translates as "in the year of the Lord 1492," meaning 1492 years after the birth of Jesus. Writing dates with A.D. following the number, as in 1492 A.D., makes no sense because it would amount to saying "1492 in the year of the Lord." It is, however, customary to indicate centuries by placing the abbreviation A.D. after the number. Therefore "first century A.D." refers to the period from A.D. 1 to A.D. 100. For numbers indicating dates after the birth of Jesus, of course, the smaller the number, the earlier the date in history. The fourth century A.D. (A.D. 301 to A.D. 400) comes before the fifth century A.D. (A.D. 401 to A.D. 500). The year A.D. 312 is a date in the early fourth century A.D., and A.D. 395 is a date late in the same century. When numbers are given without either B.C. or A.D., they are presumed to be dates after the birth of Jesus. For example, "eighteenth century" with no abbreviation accompanying it refers to the years A.D. 1701 to A.D. 1800.

No standard system of numbering years, such as the B.C./A.D. method, existed in antiquity. Different people in different parts of the world identified years with varying names and numbers. Consequently, it was difficult to match up the years in any particular local system with those in a different system. Each city of ancient Greece, for example, had its own method for keeping track of the years. The ancient Greek historian Thucydides therefore faced a problem in presenting a chronology for the war between Athens and Sparta, which began (by our reckoning) in 431 B.C. To try to explain to as many of his readers as possible the date the war had begun, he described its first year by three different local systems: "the year when Chrysis was in the forty-eighth year of her priesthood at Argos, and Aenesias was overseer at Sparta, and Pythodorus was magistrate at Athens."

A monk named Dionysius, who lived in Rome in the sixth century A.D., invented the system of reckoning dates forward from the birth of Jesus. Calling himself "Exiguus" (Latin for "the little," or "the small") as a mark of humility, he contributed to chronological reckoning by placing Jesus' birth 754 years after the foundation of ancient Rome. Others then and now believe his date for Jesus' birth was in fact several years too late. Many scholars today figure that Jesus was born in what would be 4 B.C. according to Dionysius's system, although a date a year or so earlier also seems possible.

Counting backward from the putative date of Jesus' birth to indicate dates earlier than that event represented a natural complement to reckoning forward for dates after it. The English historian and theologian Bede in the early eighth century was the first to use both forward and backward reckoning from the birth of Jesus in a historical work, and this system gradually gained wider and wider acceptance because it provided a basis for standardizing the many local calendars used in the western Christian world. Nevertheless, B.C. and A.D. were not used regularly until the end of the eighteenth century.

The system of numbering years from the birth of Jesus is not the only one still used. The Jewish calendar of years, for example, counts forward from the date given to the creation of the world, which would be calculated as 3761 B.C. under the B.C./A.D. system. Years are designated A.M. (an abbreviation of the Latin *anno mundi,* "in the year of the world") under this system. The Islamic calendar counts forward from the date of the prophet Muhammad's flight from Mecca, called the *Hijra,* in what would be the year A.D. 622 under the B.C./A.D. system. The abbreviation A.H. (standing for the Latin phrase *anno Hegirae,* "in the year of the Hegira," or "after the Hegira") indicates dates calculated by this system. Today the abbreviations B.C.E. ("before the common era") and C.E. ("of the common era") are often used, especially in Biblical studies, in place of B.C. and A.D., respectively, to allow the retention of numerical dates as reckoned by the B.C./A.D. system without the Christian ref-

erence implied by this system. Anthropology commonly reckons distant dates as "before the present" (abbreviated B.P.).

Finally, historians often label time by ages, eras, and other designations that people living in those periods would not have used. People living in the Stone Age, for example, did not refer to themselves as "Stone Age people." These historical labels can have various inspirations. The term *classical Greece,* for example, refers to the period from the Greek wars with Persia early in the fifth century B.C. to the death of Alexander the Great in 323 B.C. The label *classical* comes from art history and is meant to indicate a positive value judgment about the quality of the art of this time period. The term *Carolingian Age* refers to the period A.D. 751–987 and comes from the name of a prominent ruler, Carolus (Latin for "Charles"). The term *colonial America* in turn refers to the period in the seventeenth and eighteenth centuries before American independence, when British colonial government was in place. Terms such as *Stone Age, Bronze Age,* or *Iron Age* refer to the material used to make the most important tools in a given stretch of time.

These labels for periods of time are coined to make helpful generalizations about history, but we must remember that they are usually reflections of hindsight and potentially misleading if taken as indications of the ways people in the past may have viewed their own times. Today, for example, we routinely designated the year 323 B.C. as the end of what we call the Classical Age in Greek history and the beginning of the three centuries we refer to as the Hellenistic period—modern terms implying that the earlier period was better and finer than the later. But we cannot assume that Greeks alive in 323 B.C. would have agreed that it marked a watershed in their history or that the years before that year were necessarily better than after or should be called "classical." Likewise, today we might well ask whether we still live in the Iron Age or have moved into the Polymer Plastics Age.

Key to Symbols
✳   period of reign, term in office
✴   site of major battle

Before Civilization

The history of Western civilization is the story of what it has meant to live in the societies that first took shape in the ancient Near East, around the Mediterranean Sea, and in northern Europe. Eventually this story includes the New World of the Americas and the impact of Western civilization all over the globe. In telling this story, historians set themselves tasks that sound deceptively simple: to discover how people in these societies organized, supported, reproduced, and governed themselves; to understand what they thought about their world; and to search for reasons why the conditions of life and people's attitude toward life and death changed over time. To attempt these tasks requires the study not only of social, economic, and political history but also of religion, philosophy, literature, science, and art. Textbooks have often addressed these topics separately, yet they all *interact* to constitute the history of human culture, the complex sum of assumptions, traditions, and ideals that we rely on to guide our everyday lives. Because humans have the unique ability, through language, to pass their cultural heritage from generation to generation, the past inevitably influences the present. In this book we will look for the roots of that influence, paying special attention to the interplay between social and cultural changes and political power.

Our story of Western civilization's roots begins tens of thousands of years ago, in the Stone Age, so named because the people of the time had only stone, in addition to bone and wood, from which to fashion tools and weapons; they had not yet discovered the use of metals. Nor did these earliest humans know how to cultivate their own food. When the technology of agriculture was

Venus of Willendorf
This Late Paleolithic statuette is characteristic of "Venus figurines" discovered at many European prehistoric sites. These figurines probably expressed a recognition of the importance and uncertainty of human fertility.

developed about ten thousand to twelve thousand years ago, humans experienced enormous changes and began to affect their environment in unprecedented ways. This transformation opened the way to the creation of cities and of political states (people living in a definite territory and organized under a government with leaders, officials, and judges). These new forms of human organization first appeared in the ancient Near East.* They evolved gradually and emerged at such distant places as India, China, and the Americas—whether through independent development or some process of mutual influence, we cannot say. The early cities and states of the ancient Near East, the Mediterranean island of Crete, and Greece exerted a profound impact on the course of Western civilization. The development of writing and metallurgy further transformed life. Despite regional differences in their circumstances, early peoples had in common the challenge of forging a sustainable and satisfying way of life under conditions strikingly different from those experienced by their predecessors, before the invention of agriculture.

---

*The meaning of the term *Near East,* like *Middle East,* has changed over time. Both terms originally reflected a European geographic point of view. During the nineteenth century, *Middle East* usually meant the area from Iran to Burma, especially the Indian subcontinent (then part of the British Empire); the *Near East* comprised the Balkan peninsula (today the territory of the formerly united Yugoslavia, Albania, Greece, Bulgaria, Romania, and the European portion of Turkey) and the eastern Mediterranean. The term *Far East* referred to the Asian lands that border the Pacific Ocean.

Today the term *Middle East* usually refers to the area encompassing the Arabic-speaking countries of the eastern Mediterranean region, Israel, Iran, Turkey, Cyprus, and much of North Africa. Ancient historians, by contrast, commonly used the term *ancient Near East* to designate Anatolia (often called Asia Minor, today occupied by the Asian portion of Turkey), Cyprus, the lands around the eastern end of the Mediterranean, the Arabian peninsula, Mesopotamia (the lands north of the Persian Gulf, today Iraq and Iran), and Egypt. Some historians exclude Egypt from this group on strict geographic grounds because it is in Africa, while the rest of the region lies in Asia. In this book we will observe the common usage of the term *Near East,* that is, to mean the lands of southwestern Asia and Egypt.

The Paleolithic Period

From fossil remains, anthropologists have identified a long period of development before the emergence of people with the same anatomical characteristics as humans of today. Many modern authorities date the most distant human ancestors several million years in the past and place their origin in sub–Saharan Africa, from where they moved out into the Near East, Europe, and Asia hundreds of thousands of years ago. The human type called *homo sapiens,* the immediate ancestor of the modern type (called *homo sapiens sapiens,* an anthropological term that means "wise, wise human being") first appeared several hundred thousand years ago in Africa in the Paleolithic (Greek for "Old Stone") period. The Stone Age can be divided roughly into an older period, the Paleolithic, whose beginnings extend at least four hundred thousand years into the past (some estimates say seven hundred thousand), and a more recent period, the Neolithic ("New Stone") period, which began about ten thousand to twelve thousand years ago.

The Spread and Organization of Paleolithic Peoples

Humans in the Paleolithic period lived a radically different life from the settled existence most of us now take for granted: they roamed all their lives, moving around because they had to find their food in the wild. Although they knew a great deal about their environment, they had not yet learned to produce their own food by growing crops and raising animals. Instead they hunted wild game for meat, fished in lakes and rivers, collected shellfish if they could, and gathered wild plants, fruits, and nuts. Because they had to survive by hunting and gathering their food, we refer to these early humans as *hunter-gatherers. Homo sapiens sapiens* was the last of a long line of populations to live by hunting and gathering, the way of life that characterized human experience for by far the greatest span during which humans have inhabited the earth.

Some of the African *homo sapiens* population migrated into the rest of the world at least one hundred thousand years ago, such as the type known as *homo sapiens Neanderthalensis,* so named because archaeologists have found their remains in Germany's Neanderthal valley. *Homo sapiens sapiens* apparently began to leave Africa about forty-five thousand to forty thousand years ago, during the last part of the Paleolithic period. They first moved into Asia and Europe and later into the Americas and Australia, transversing then–existent land bridges. When *homo sapiens sapiens* first appeared in Asia and Europe, they encountered *homo sapiens* populations that had migrated much earlier. How *homo sapiens sapiens* came to replace completely these earlier peoples such as the Neanderthals remains unknown. Although humans by this time had developed spoken language, the invention of writing still lay tens of thousands of years in the future. These early hunter-gatherers therefore left no documents to tell us about their lives, and archaeologists and anthropologists who study prehistory, the period before written records, must rely on other sources of information.

We cannot say for certain why some hunter-gatherers left Africa in the Paleolithic period yet others stayed. Periodic, extended fluctuations in climate that made the plains of Africa more arid may have influenced migration. Persistently drier conditions would have driven some local game animals north in search of moisture, and some of the mobile human populations who hunted them would have followed. No evidence exists, however, to explain how people at the time would have decided whether to migrate.

Archaeological discovery of objects left at early human campsites has revealed much about the lives of hunter-gatherers of different anthropological types. Anthropologists have even been able to speculate about the lives of ancient hunter-gatherers from comparative studies of certain modern populations because a few small groups of people, such as the !Kung San who inhabit the Kalahari Desert in southern Africa, still live by hunting and gathering. Thus, archeology and anthropology allow us to reconstruct some outlines of the life of Paleolithic hunter-gatherers. They probably banded together in groups of about twenty-five individuals who hunted and foraged for food that they shared with each other. Because women of childbearing age had to nurse their young, they would have found it difficult to roam far from their camp. They and

A Modern Hunter-Gatherer
This woman gathering food from wild plants in Africa exemplifies the only way human beings could support themselves before the invention of agriculture. Women's responsibilities for small children meant that they could not roam as far from home as men did on their hunts.

the smaller children gathered food closer to home by foraging for edible plants and catching small animals. The plant food they gathered constituted the bulk of the diet of hunter-gatherer populations. Men probably did most of the hunting of large and sometimes dangerous animals, which often took place far from camp. Prehistoric groups thus tended to divide their main labor—finding food—between men and women.

Because both men and women made an essential contribution to the group's support, these prehistoric bands perhaps did not divide power and status according to gender. In fact, early hunter-gatherer society (the organization of their communal relationships with one another) may have been largely egalitarian; that is, all adults, regardless of gender, may have shared decision making about the group's organization and actions. Furthermore, hunter-gatherers lacked laws, judges, and political institutions in the modern sense. Nevertheless, differences in prestige probably existed among some ancient hunter-gatherers. Modern hunter-gatherer groups, for example, sometimes observe prestige differences according to gender, such as assigning greater value to the meat hunted by men than to the plant food gathered by women, despite the latter's greater contribution to the continuing sustenance of the group. Older people likely enjoyed higher social status in ancient hunter-gatherer populations because of their greater knowledge. Their age also set them apart in an era when most people died of disease or accidents before they were thirty.

Recent archaeological discoveries of Paleolithic graves containing weapons, tools, animal figurines, ivory beads, and bracelets show not only that humans in the Old Stone Age attached special, perhaps religious, significance to death but also suggest that they recognized social differences among individuals based on other grounds. We can surmise that persons buried with such elaborate care and expenditure enjoyed superior wealth, power, or status. These rich burials may indicate that some Paleolithic groups organized themselves into *hierarchies,* social systems that ranked certain people as more important than others. One important component of the story of early Western history is the evidence for *social differentiation,* the marking of certain people as wealthier, more respected, or more powerful than others in their group.

The Knowledge and Beliefs of Hunter-Gatherers

Paleolithic hunter-gatherers did not roam randomly in their search for food. Each group tended to stay within its own territory. If they behaved anything like modern hunter-gatherers, they ranged over an area that averaged roughly sixty miles across in any one direction. Because no one had yet domesticated oxen or horses or built wheeled vehicles for transport, hunter-gatherers had to walk everywhere and to carry their belongings with them, under their own power. Although this constant exercise kept them in robust condition, they counted on their knowledge as well as their strength. For example, they planned ahead for cooperative hunts at favorite spots, such as river crossings, where they were likely to find large game animals. They also established their camps in regular locations that past experience had shown to be particularly good spots for gathering wild plants. They sought shelter from the weather in caves or rough dwellings made from branches and animal skins. Occasionally they built more elaborate shelters, such as the domelike hut found in western Russia that was constructed from the bones of mammoths. Nevertheless, although hunter-gatherers might return year after year to the same places where they had found food in the past, their temporary dwellings could never become permanent homes. They had to move in order to survive.

Their mobility and skill at hunting constituted only part of the store of knowledge that Paleolithic people assembled. Over time they developed considerable skill at shaping tools such as hammers and blades from stone, wood, and bone. Almost everything these people possessed they either found or made in the area covered by their wanderings. When they encountered other bands, however, hunter-gatherers could exchange goods. Whenever possible they bartered with each other for attractive objects. The objects exchanged in this way could travel great distances from their point of origin: for example, seashells used as jewelry made their way inland through repeated swaps from one group to another. Such exchanges, known from at least the late Paleolithic period, foreshadowed the development of international trade that would later forge far-reaching connections among distant parts of the world.

Prehistoric humans had many skills that their ancestors had passed down to them. Their forebears taught them how to make tools and how to fashion ornaments to wear on the clothing they created from animal skins. Their knowledge of making fire proved essential for survival during the extended winters of periodic ice ages, when the

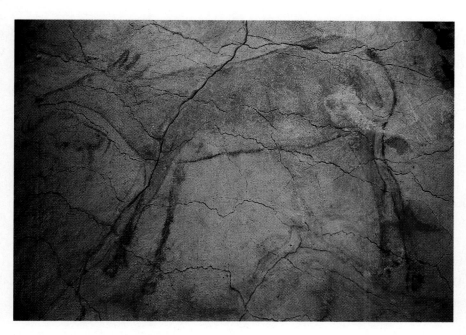

Paleolithic Painting
This deer was one of an entire herd painted on the ceiling of a cave in Altamira, Spain, about fifteen thousand years ago. Prehistoric people often painted the animals they hunted.

northern European glaciers moved much farther south than usual. The coldest part of the most recent Ice Age, for example, started about twenty thousand years ago and created a harsh climate in much of Europe for nearly ten thousand years. Their control of fire also helped hunter-gatherers survive by cooking foods. Cooking was an important technological innovation because it made edible and nutritious food out of some plants, such as wild grain, that were indigestible when raw.

But the skills of these hardy people went beyond mere survival. They sculpted statuettes of human figures, presumably for religious purposes. For example, tiny female statuettes (called Venus figurines by modern archaeologists after the Roman goddess of sexual love), sculpted with extra-large breasts, abdomens, buttocks, and thighs, have turned up in excavations of Paleolithic sites all over Europe. The exaggerated features of these female figurines suggest that the people to whom they belonged had a special set of beliefs and probably community rituals about fertility and birth. The care with which they buried their dead—the corpses decorated with red paint, flowers, and seashells—conveys a concern with the mystery of death and perhaps some belief about an afterlife. The late Paleolithic cave paintings found in Spain and France show the artistic ability of the hunter-gatherer populations of early Europe and also hint at their religious beliefs. Using strong, dark lines and earthy colors, artists of this period painted on the walls of caves that were apparently set aside as special places and not used as day-to-day shelters. The paintings, which depict primarily large animals, suggest that these powerful beasts and the dangerous hunts for them played a significant role in the life and religion of these prehistoric people. We still do not understand the significance of many of their beliefs, such as the meaning of the signs (dots, rectangles, and hands) that they often drew beside their paintings of animals.

Despite their varied knowledge and technological skills, prehistoric hunter-gatherers lived precarious lives dominated by the relentless search for something to eat. Survival was a risky business at best. Groups survived only if they learned to cooperate effectively in securing food and shelter, to profit from technological innovations like the use of fire and tool making, and to teach their children the knowledge, beliefs, and social traditions that had helped make their society viable. Paleolithic history matters in the story of Western civilization because successful hunter-gatherers passed on to later societies these traits that comprised their strategy for survival in a harsh world.

The Neolithic Period

Compared with the enormous length of time humans lived exclusively as hunter-gatherers, the origins of our modern way of life are relatively recent. Daily life as we know it depends on agriculture and the domestication of animals, developments that began about ten thousand to twelve thousand years ago. These radical innovations in the way humans acquired food caused fundamental changes in the ways they lived.

Neolithic Origins of a Modern Way of Life

Precisely how people learned to sow and to harvest crops and to raise animals for food remains a mystery. Recent archaeological research indicates that it took several thousand years to gain this knowledge. The process began in southwestern Asia when the climate there became milder and wetter than it had been in the preceding period. This favorable change in the weather promoted the growth of fields of wild grains in the Fertile Crescent, an arc of relatively well-watered territory bounded by desert and mountains, which stretched from modern Israel northward across Syria, and then southeast down to the plain of the lower stretches of the Tigris and Euphrates rivers in what is now southern Iraq. The hunter-gatherer populations who then inhabited the Fertile Crescent began to gather more and more of their food from these now easily available and increasingly abundant stands of wild cereal grains. The ample food supply in turn promoted fertility, which led to population growth, a process that might have already begun as a result of a milder climate. The more people that were born, the greater the corresponding need to exploit the food supply efficiently to feed these new, hungry mouths. Perhaps thousands of years of repeated trial and error were necessary before humans in the Fertile Crescent learned to plant part of the seeds from one crop to produce another crop. Because Neolithic women, as foragers for plant food, had the greatest knowledge of plant life, they probably played the major role in the invention of agriculture and the tools needed to practice it, such as digging sticks and grinding stones. For a long time, they did most of the agricultural labor, while men continued to hunt.

During this same period, people also learned to breed and herd animals for food. The sheep was the first animal domesticated as a source of meat, beginning about 8500 B.C. (The dog had been domesticated much earlier but was not principally used as a meat source.) The domestication of animals had become common throughout the Near East by about 7000 B.C. In this early period of domestication some people continued to move around to find grazing land for their animals, living as what we call *pastoralists.* They may have also cultivated small, temporary plots from time to time when they found a suitable area. Others, relying increasingly on growing crops, kept small herds close to their settlements. Thus men, women, and children alike could tend the animals. The earliest domesticated herds seem to have been used only as a source of meat, not for so-called secondary products such as milk and wool.

Once Neolithic hunter-gatherers in the Fertile Crescent learned how to grow crops and raise animals, tremendous changes in human life ensued. Called the Neolithic, or somewhat loosely, agricultural, revolution, these changes laid the foundation for the way of life we today regard as normal. For example, to raise permanent crops, people had to cease roaming and settle in one location. Farming communities thus began to dot the landscape of the Fertile Crescent as early as 10,000 B.C.; they shared the region with more mobile pastoralists. Moreover, parents needed to have more children to practice agriculture effectively. Much larger than the fleeting settlements of Paleolithic hunter-gatherers, villages of farming families boasted permanent houses built from mud-bricks. The earliest houses were apparently circular huts, such as those known from Jericho in Palestine (the region at the southeastern corner of the Mediterranean, where modern Israel is located). Perhaps two thousand people lived at Jericho around 8000 B.C. Their huts formed a haphazardly arranged settlement without formal streets, and it stretched over about twelve acres. The village's most striking feature was the massive fortification wall around its perimeter. Three meters thick, the wall was crowned with a stone tower ten meters in diameter, which even included an internal flight of stairs.

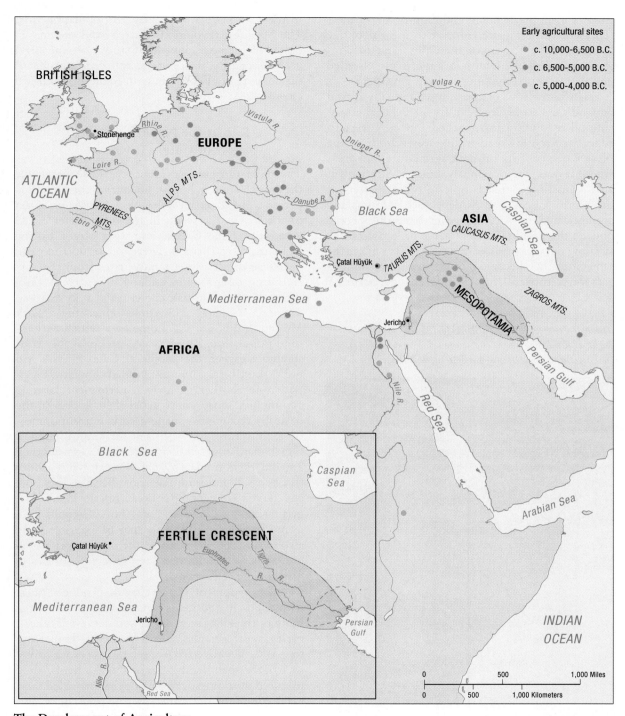

The Development of Agriculture

This walled, permanent community of farmers represented a dramatic contrast to the Paleolithic hunter-gatherers' way of life. This kind of constructed environment with its large, densely settled population was something entirely new.

The knowledge of agriculture gradually spread beyond the Fertile Crescent. By 4000 B.C. the agricultural revolution had reached Europe's western edge. Farmers slowly migrating westward from the Near East probably brought agriculture into areas where it was not previously known, although it also seems likely that people in other regions of the world independently developed farming and domesticated animals. However Neolithic people outside the Fertile Crescent came to know of this startling new way to live, their lives were never the same after they became farmers instead of hunter-gatherers. Above all, fundamental changes occurred in the way people responded to population flux. The Neolithic revolution clearly shows the importance of demography—the study of the size, growth, density, distribution, and vital statistics of the human population—in understanding historical change.

Life in the Neolithic Village of Çatal Hüyük

The most intriguing evidence yet discovered for the vast changes in human life during the Neolithic period comes from an archaeological site northwest of the Fertile Crescent, in the region later called Anatolia by the Greeks and Asia Minor by the Romans (now Turkey). There, on an upland plain near a river, a massive mound rises from the surrounding open countryside. Known to us only by its modern Turkish name, Çatal Hüyük (pronounced "Chatal Hooyook," meaning "Fork Mound"), this site was home to a settled agricultural population. By 6500 B.C., and probably considerably earlier, the people at Çatal Hüyük had built mud-brick houses nestled chock-a-block with one another to form a permanent farming community. They constructed their houses in the basically rectangular shape used in current domestic architecture, but with one striking difference: they had no doors in their outer walls. Instead they entered their homes by climbing down a ladder through a hole in the flat roof. Because this hole also served as a vent for smoke from the family fire, getting into a house at Çatal Hüyük could be a grimy business. But the absence of exterior doors also meant that the walls of the community's outermost houses could serve as a general fortification wall for the settlement.

The people of Çatal Hüyük produced their own food. In the fields stretching out below the mound, the villagers planted and harvested wheat, barley, and vegetables such as field peas. To increase the yield, they diverted water from the nearby river to irrigate their fields. Beyond these fields, they pastured the domesticated cattle that provided their main supply of meat and, by this time, hides and milk. (Sheep and goats were the norm elsewhere in the Near East as the principal domesticated animals.) They still hunted, too, as we can tell from the paintings of hunting scenes, reminiscent of the cave paintings of much earlier times, they drew on

Tower in the wall of Neolithic Jericho
Built around 8000 B.C., the stone wall around Jericho in Palestine is one of the earliest such defenses known.

the walls of some of their buildings. Unlike hunter-gatherers, however, these villagers no longer depended on the hit-or-miss luck of the hunt or risked being killed by wild animals to acquire meat and leather. At its height, the population supported in this way probably numbered as many as six thousand.

The diversity of occupations practiced at Çatal Hüyük marked another significant change from the past and hinted at the economic complexity of later societies. Because the community could produce enough food to support the village without everyone having to work in the fields or herd cattle, some people could develop crafts as full-time occupations. Craft specialists continued to fashion tools, containers, and ornaments using traditional materials—wood, bone, hide, and stone—but they now also worked with the material of the future: metal. So far, archaeologists are certain only that metalworkers at Çatal Hüyük knew how to fashion lead into pendants and to hammer naturally occurring lumps of copper into beads and tubes for jewelry. Because traces of slag have been found on the site, however, the workers may also have begun to develop the technique of smelting metal from ore. This tricky process—the basis of true metallurgy and the foundation of much modern technology—required temperatures of 700 degrees centigrade. Other workers at Çatal Hüyük specialized in weaving textiles; the scraps of cloth discovered there are the oldest examples of this craft ever found. Like other early technological innovations, metallurgy and the production of cloth apparently also developed independently in other places.

Trade also figured in the economy of this early village. Through trade, the people of Çatal Hüyük acquired goods, such as shells from the Mediterranean Sea to wear as ornaments and a special flint from far to the east to shape into ceremonial daggers. The villagers could trade for these prized materials by offering obsidian, a local volcanic glass whose glossy luster and capacity to hold a sharp edge made it valuable. The trading contacts the villagers negotiated with other settlements meant that their world was not made up merely of isolated communities. On the contrary, they already seem to have started down the path of economic interconnection among far-flung communities—a pattern familiar in our world today.

The nearby volcano that rendered obsidian proved in the end to be as dangerous as it had been profitable. Çatal Hüyük never recovered from a volcanic eruption that destroyed it, probably about a thousand years after its foundation. A remarkable wall painting suggests that the people of Çatal Hüyük regarded the volcano as an angry god whom they needed to propitiate, and shrines found by excavators show how much their religious beliefs meant to the villagers. They outfitted these special rooms with representations of bulls' heads and female breasts, perhaps as symbols of male and female elements in their religion. Like the hunter-gatherers before them, they sculpted figurines depicting amply endowed women who perhaps represented goddesses of birth. This evidence of their fascination with the secrets of life and fertility finds its mirror image in the evidence of their deep interest in the mystery of death: skulls displayed in the shrines and wall paintings of vultures devouring headless corpses. We cannot tell whether the village had priests or priestesses with special authority for religious matters, just as we cannot know precisely what sort of political organization the villagers had. We can feel confident, however, that the people of Çatal Hüyük had some sort of social and political hierarchy. The need to plan and regulate irrigation, trade, and the exchange of food and goods between farmers and crafts producers presumably created a need for leaders with more authority than was required to maintain order in hunter-gatherer bands. Furthermore, households that were successful in farming, herding, crafts production, and trade generated wealth surpluses that distinguished them from others whose efforts proved less fortunate. In short, the villagers did not live in an undifferentiated, egalitarian, or leaderless society.

The equality between men and women that may have existed in hunter-gatherer society had also disappeared by the late Neolithic period. The reasons for this shift remain unclear, but they perhaps involved gradual changes in agriculture and herding over many centuries. Farmers began to use plows pulled by animals sometime after about 4000 B.C. to cultivate land that was more difficult to sow than the areas cultivated in the earliest period of agriculture. Men apparently operated the plows, perhaps because plowing required more physical strength than digging with sticks and hoes. Men also predominated in tending the larger herds that had become more common now that grazing animals such as cattle were kept as sources of milk and sheep were raised for wool. The herding of a community's animals tended to take place at a distance from the home settlement because new grazing land had to be found continually. As with hunting in hunter-gatherer populations, men, free from having to nurse children, took on this task. Women probably became more tied to the central settlement because they had to bear and raise more children to support agriculture. The responsibility for new labor-intensive tasks also fell to women. For example, they now turned milk into cheese and yogurt and made cloth by spinning and weaving wool. However the transition occurred, the predominance of men in agriculture in the late Neolithic period and the accompanying changes in the lives of women apparently led to women's loss of equality with men.

Permanent homes, large families, relatively reliable food supplies from agriculture and animal husbandry, specialized occupations, and hierarchical societies in which men have held the most power have characterized Western history from the Neolithic period forward. For this reason the broad outlines of the life of Neolithic villagers might seem so familiar to us as to be unremarkable. But their way of life probably would have astounded the hunter-gatherers of the earlier Paleolithic period. The Neolithic revolution marked a turning point in human history. Now that farmers and herders could produce a surplus of food to support other people, specialists in art, architecture, crafts, religion, and politics could multiply as never before. Hand in hand with these developments came an increasing social differentiation and a division of labor by gender that saw men begin to take over agriculture and women take up new tasks at home. These developments reflected the apportionment of power in the society. The surpluses created by the Neolithic revolution opened the way to the development of Western civilization as we know it.

The Challenge of the West

Cloth Merchants, Roman Relief

The Emergence of the West, from Earliest Times to A.D. 567

REC:
TAPE

What do we mean by *Western civilization*? Historians use *Western* in this context to refer mainly to the history of Europe. The term *Europe* comes from the ancient Greeks, who gave that name to the Greek mainland; it means "[the place of] the setting of the sun." The Greeks referred to regions east of them as "the place where the sun rises," and they judged themselves very different from the inhabitants of those areas. Thus the notion of a distinctive Western civilization arose from the interaction of peoples in the ancient Near East and Greece. But what exactly is *civilization*? Historians define the concept not by making value judgments but by examining the level of complexity of human activity. Thus they see the embryo of civilization in the momentous changes of twelve to fourteen thousand years ago, when the development of agriculture produced the first farming communities. The material needs of such communities—for irrigation, tools, and defense—led to an increasing division of labor and an accelerating tendency to value some people more than others.

By around 3000 B.C., the ranking of people to construct a social hierarchy had grown more complex as farming settlements in the Near East swelled into large cities. We can certainly say that civilization had begun by this time. In politics, the growth of hierarchy culminated in the development of monarchical government. The idea of a supreme ruler seemed natural—a reflection of the superiority of gods to humans. The need to ensure divine favor by proper performance of religious rituals on behalf of the ruler and the whole community created another source of complexity. Furthermore, the invention of writing and the development of metallurgical technology led to more specialized jobs.

Deeply influenced by their Near Eastern and Egyptian neighbors, the first European civilizations emerged in the eastern Mediterranean, especially on the island of Crete and the Greek islands and mainland. About three thousand years ago, a period of crisis profoundly disrupted these civilizations and their older counterparts to the east. The Near East recovered faster from these disasters than Greece, and the Assyrians soon built a great empire from Mesopotamia to Syria in the tradition of their forerunners.

Having regained their prosperity by about 750 B.C., the Greeks created a new form of political and social organization that would prove enormously significant for Western civilization: the democratic city-state, or *polis*. Although ancient Greek democracy coexisted with slavery and excluded women from politics, it introduced the radically new principle of including the poor as citizen-participants alongside the rich. The Greeks, however, never created political unity: it was left to Rome to become the political master of the Mediterranean. The Romans had no real technological advantage over those whom they came to dominate. But unlike the Greeks, who only rarely admitted outsiders to full membership in the city-state, the Romans assimilated others into their society. This characteristic allowed the Romans to organize a political domain greater than any the Western world had seen.

Roman rule's vast expansion took place during the Republic, a state that in theory was governed by the people but in practice was dominated by a few upper-class families. The leaders of these families brought down the Republic by engaging in civil wars; what emerged was a monarchy disguised as an improved republic, which we call the Roman Empire. For the first two centuries of this new system, the Roman emperors presided over relative peace. Cities prospered and grew, and the needs of huge urban populations significantly expanded interactions across the Mediterranean world. Civil wars, combined with epidemics and other natural disasters, dramatically weakened the empire in the third century. A century later the emperor Constantine instituted the most striking change in the period—and the most enduring legacy for later Western civilization—when he made Christianity the official state religion.

By the end of the fourth century A.D., the Roman Empire struggled to accommodate large numbers of Germanic peoples from northern Europe seeking safety and prosperity inside Roman territory. Peoples in and outside the empire had long interacted along its frontier zones, but now conflict between the old-time inhabitants of the empire and the newcomers periodically erupted into violence. These intense changes overwhelmed Roman governmental institutions in the western half of the empire in the fifth century and led to the creation of kingdoms that were ruled by newcomers but populated by old and new inhabitants. These new states, constructed from Germanic and Roman traditions, would be the connection between antiquity and medieval Europe. The eastern half of the empire, by contrast, maintained its traditional identity, which combined Greek and Near Eastern populations, and it endured politically for another thousand years as what we call the Byzantine Empire. The legacies of ancient times to later Western civilization were thus transmitted through two distinct channels, stemming from the western and the eastern halves of the former Roman Empire.

Around 2600 B.C. a king named Gilgamesh ruled the city of Uruk (today Warka, Iraq). Gilgamesh became a legendary figure in ancient Mesopotamia ("the land between the rivers"), the great plain of the Tigris and Euphrates rivers where Western civilization first emerged and settlers built the earliest cities. The *Epic of Gilgamesh* spun a tale of heroic adventures that took Gilgamesh to the ends of the earth. The ultimate goal of his quest was immortality. By diving to the bottom of the sea and seizing the magic plant of rejuvenation, Gilgamesh gained the secret of eternal life. But as he and his boatman traveled home with their treasure, misfortune struck:

> *. . . they stopped for the night. Gilgamesh saw a pool whose water was cool, and went down into the water and washed. A snake smelt the fragrance of the plant. It came up silently and carried off the plant. As it took it away, it shed its scaly skin. Thereupon Gilgamesh sat down and wept. . . . He spoke to Ur-shanabi the boatman: "For what purpose, Ur-shanabi, have my arms grown weary? For what purpose was the blood inside me so red? I did not gain an advantage for myself. . . . I shall give up, and I have left the boat on the shore." . . . They reached Uruk the sheepfold. Gilgamesh spoke to . . . the boatman: "Go up on to the wall of Uruk, Ur-shanabi, and walk around, inspect the foundation platform and scrutinize the brickwork! Testify that its bricks are baked bricks, and that the Seven Wise Ones must have laid its foundations! One square mile is city, one square mile is orchards, one square mile is claypits, as well as the open ground of [the goddess] Ishtar's temple. Three square miles and the open ground comprise Uruk."*

The First Civilizations in the West

Cuneiform Tablet
Mesopotamian scribes wrote using pointed sticks to make wedge-shaped marks (cuneiform) on soft clay tablets, which were preserved by baking. This earliest form of writing developed as Western civilization became more urbanized and more economically and socially complex.

When Gilgamesh concedes defeat in his quest for immortality, he consoles himself with thoughts of Uruk, which he describes with pride. His finely built city gives meaning to his life in the end.

To Gilgamesh, Uruk represented the pinnacle of his life's achievement. To people today, cities can also be a source of pride, a measure of human accomplishment—a symbol of civilization even. In fact, modern notions of what "civilization" means usually include the development of cities as an integral characteristic. Other attributes usually deemed essential for a society to be called "civilized" include the ability to write and keep written records, the use of a formal set of laws enforced and regulated by a hierarchical political organization, a developed system of agriculture, and the capability to build large structures. Using these criteria, we find evidence of the first civilizations in southwestern Asia and Egypt as early as the fourth and third millennia B.C. These earliest civilizations developed in the Bronze Age, which followed the Neolithic Age in the late fourth millennium. During that era, crafts producers first learned to combine copper with tin to make the metal alloy bronze, a material that revolutionized the production of luxury goods, tools, and most of all weapons. This technological innovation made people eager to acquire supplies of metal, by force if necessary. Through trade, contacts made in travel, and perhaps migration, these early civilizations of the ancient Near East significantly influenced the development of the civilizations that later emerged on the Mediterranean island of Crete and in Greece.

The First Civilizations in the Near East

More than any other single factor, living in cities has traditionally been associated with the concept of civilization. Historians usually reserve the term *city* for densely populated settlements with special features such as fortified walls, major buildings used for religious and political purposes, and a complex political administration. Because some and occasionally all of these elements appeared in embryonic form in early Neolithic villages, such as Jericho and Çatal Hüyük, the growth of cities

> ### IMPORTANT DATES
>
> **c. 3500 B.C.*** First cities established and writing developed in Sumer
>
> **c. 3100–3000 B.C.** King Menes unites Upper and Lower Egypt
>
> **c. 3000 B.C.** Stone temples constructed on Malta
>
> **c. 2600 B.C.** King Gilgamesh rules the city of Uruk in Sumer
>
> **c. 2575 B.C.** Great Pyramid of Cheops constructed at Giza in Egypt
>
> **c. 2350 B.C.** Sargon establishes the Akkadian empire
>
> **c. 2200 B.C.** Earliest Cretan palaces constructed
>
> **c. 1792–1750 B.C.** Reign of Hammurabi, king of Babylon
>
> **Early fifteenth century B.C.** Reign of Queen Hatshepsut of Egypt
>
> **c. 1400 B.C.** Earliest Mycenaean palaces constructed in Greece
>
> **c. 1285** Battle of Egyptian King Ramesses II with the Hittites at Kadesh in Syria
>
> **Early or mid-thirteenth century B.C.** Exodus of the Hebrews from Egypt
>
> **c. 1200 B.C.** Disturbances across the eastern Mediterranean region

proper seems to have been an evolutionary rather than a revolutionary process. The first cities truly worthy of the name were built in Mesopotamia.

The Earliest Cities: Sumer

Urban settlements large enough to be called cities had emerged in southwestern Asia by about 3500 B.C.† Most of these early cities clustered in Mesopotamia. Cities first emerged there in the alluvial land at the southern end of the plain, where the hot weather and fertile soil made for good farming conditions when river water was diverted to the

---

*The abbreviation c., standing for the Latin *circa*, means "approximately" and is used to indicate dates about which some uncertainty exists.

†Most dates in ancient Near Eastern history must be regarded as tentative because our evidence simply does not allow precision.

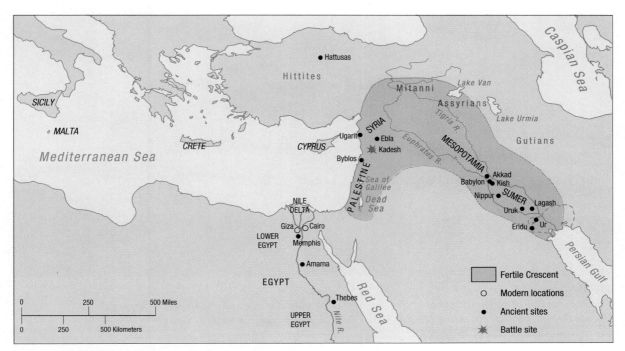

The Early Civilizations of the Near East and Egypt

fields via a complex system of irrigation canals that made up for the scarcity of rainfall. By 3000 B.C. the Sumerians, the people from the southern Mesopotamian territory called Sumer, dominated this part of the Fertile Crescent. They established sizable cities there, such as Uruk (the Erech of the Bible), Eridu, and Ur, which grew up around great temples built of mud-brick and whose control extended to the agricultural land outside the cities. This geographical arrangement—an urban center exercising political and economic control over the countryside around it—is often called a *city-state*. In later Greek history the city-state is associated with self-governance by an assembly of male citizens. Assemblies of male citizens probably decided major issues under the leadership of a council of elders in the earliest Mesopotamian cities, too, but this feature waned as strong monarchies developed. Although we do not know the precise organization of early Sumerian city-states, we do know that they saw themselves as separate political entities and regularly squabbled with one another.

The Sumerians' prosperity stemmed from the surpluses yielded by their farms and their development of trade routes to exchange these surpluses for materials not available in their locale. Through hard work and ingenuity, they grew plants and raised animals on the rich soil of their river plains, where summer temperatures often reached 120 degrees and canals diverted water for irrigation. The strongly flowing rivers required careful attention because they tended to change course unpredictably, causing devastating floods—an ironic danger in the desert. The Sumerians traded their surpluses of grain, vegetable oil, woolens, and leather for products such as metals, timber, and precious stones. Sumerian sea trade regularly reached as far east as India. Technological innovation also strengthened the early Mesopotamian economy: around 3000 B.C. the wheel was invented in a form sturdy enough to be used on carts. The ability to transport loads on wheeled vehicles greatly aided the Sumerians in agriculture and commerce.

By about 2500 B.C. most Sumerians inhabited walled cities populated with twenty thousand or more residents, some many more. Their mud-brick houses consisted of rooms grouped around an open court. Most people lived in only one or two rooms, but the wealthy constructed two-story dwellings that had a dozen or more rooms. But rich and poor

The Ziggurat of Ur
The massive size of ziggurats (temples) like this one at Ur indicated the importance of the worship of the gods in ancient Mesopotamian culture. For the scale, notice the size of the car compared to that of the ziggurat.

alike suffered the ill effects of a domestic water supply often contaminated by sewage. No system of waste disposal existed beyond the pigs and dogs who scavenged in the streets and open spaces where garbage was unceremoniously dumped.

Inside the cities' walls, the great temple-towers (ziggurats) soared as high as ten stories, emphasizing the centrality of religion to the Sumerians. They viewed the gods as their absolute masters to whom they owed total devotion. The Sumerians demonstrated their religious devotion most visibly by giving their gods tremendous material support. The revenues from numerous fields and the toil of gangs of semifree laborers supported the ziggurats and their religious activities, which were supervised by powerful priests and priestesses. These priests and priestesses also administered the gods' considerable property. The priest or priestess of the city's chief divinity, which differed from place to place, enjoyed extremely high status.

Although the temples and their support systems predominated in the economy of Sumerian cities, some private households also held significant power. Like the temples, wealthy households derived income from the agricultural land they controlled. Also like the temples, private individuals could own slaves. Slavery existed in many forms in the ancient Near East, and no single description of the social and legal position of slaves can cover all the permutations. People became slaves by being captured in war, by being born to slaves, by voluntarily selling themselves or their children because they were too impoverished to survive on their own, or by being sold under duress to satisfy debts they could not otherwise pay. Foreigners enslaved as captives in war or in raids dispatched to acquire slaves had an inferior position compared to citizens who fell into slavery to pay off debts. Children whose parents dedicated them as servants to the gods, although counted as slaves, could rise to prominent positions in the temple administrations. In general, however, slavery was a state of near-total dependency on other people and legal exclusion from most normal social relations; most slaves worked without compensation and lacked almost any legal rights.

Although slaves sometimes formed relationships with free persons and frequently married each other and had families, they had no guarantee that their family members would not be sold. Slaves in the most inferior position could be bought, sold, beaten, or even killed by their masters—they counted as commodities, not as people. Slaves worked in domestic service, craft production, and

Royal Finery from Ur
Women from the royal court of Ur in Sumer wore elaborate jewelry of gold and lapis lazuli. This head-dress was found in a royal tomb containing the bodies of sixty-eight women similarly outfitted.

farming, but their economic significance compared to that of free workers in early Mesopotamia is still disputed. Free persons appear to have performed the majority of state labor as a kind of corvée service (paying a tax with labor rather than money). Under certain conditions slaves could be manumitted (set free), for example, by the provisions of their masters' wills or by purchasing their freedom from the earnings they could sometimes accumulate. Manumission, however, remained only a faint possibility for most slaves.

The complex, hierarchical political organization—what we would call the state—of Sumerian cities directly affected their economy. In theory the gods ruled Sumerian cities, a notion that made the state a theocracy (government by gods) and gave the priests and priestesses a say in secular affairs. By about 2700 B.C., however, the state as it existed in Sumerian cities had a supreme temporal, or worldly, ruler—a king—with a council of older

men as his advisers. Diverse factors contributed to the emergence of this highly structured political organization: the similarity to the rule of the divine world by a chief god, the increasing need for supervision of the cities' complex economic systems, and above all the necessity of having a military commander to lead the defense of the community against raiders and rivals eager to seize its riches, its land, and its water supply.

As befitted his status, a Sumerian king and his family lived in an elaborate palace that rivaled the scale of the great temples. It served as the secular administrative center for the city and its surrounding territory. Another major function of the king's palace was to store the enormous wealth the royal family accumulated. The Sumerian state demanded that a significant portion of its economic surplus be dedicated to displaying the superior status of its royal leaders. Archaeological excavation of the immense royal cemetery in Ur, for example, has revealed the dazzling extent of these riches. The rulers of Ur took with them to their graves spectacular possessions crafted in gold, silver, and precious stones. These graves also yielded grislier evidence of the exalted status of the king and queen: the bodies of the servants and retainers who were sacrificed to serve their royal masters after death.

The spectacle of wealth and power that evidently characterized Sumerian kingship suggests just how great the gap between the upper and lower ranks of Sumerian society had become. The days of relative equality between men and women were also long gone. Patriarchy—domination by men in political, social, and economic life—was already established in these first cities. Although a Sumerian queen was respected because she was the wife of the king and the mother of the royal children, the king ruled. The high priestess of the city's patron god owed most of her elevated status to her relationship with the king, with whom she celebrated the annual religious ritual of the sacred wedding during the New Year holiday. This reenactment of a mythological story of the marriage of the goddess Inanna and the god Dumuzi supposedly ensured successful reproduction in the city's population that year.

The Sumerians were the first people to develop a system of writing based on nonpictorial symbols. Some scholars think people used small tokens to represent quantities of items before the invention

Earliest pictographs 4000 B.C.	Denotation of pictographs	Pictographs in rotated position	Cuneiform signs c. 1900 B.C.
	head and body of a man		
	head with mouth indicated		
	bowl of food		
	mouth and food		
	stream of water		
	mouth and water		
	fish		
	bird		
	head of an ass		
	ear of barley		

Sample of Sumerian Cuneiform

tokens, which obviously prevented these balls from becoming permanent records. People eventually avoided this particular problem by representing the number of tokens inside the ball with an equivalent number of marks scratched on the outside. These marks symbolically represented the number of objects. A natural next step in the process of using symbols to express meaning was drawing small pictures on clay tablets to represent objects. At first these pictographs symbolized concrete objects only, such as a cow. Eventually the pictographs and signs came to represent the sounds of spoken language. Sumerian writing was not an alphabet, in which a symbol represents the sound of a single letter, but a mixed system of phonetic symbols and pictographs that represented the sounds of entire syllables and often stood for entire words.

The Sumerians' fully developed script is now called *cuneiform* (from *cuneus,* Latin for "wedge") because of the wedge-shaped marks impressed into clay tablets to record spoken language. Other peoples in this region subsequently adopted cuneiform to write their own languages. For a time, writing was largely a professional skill mastered by only a few men and women, known as scribes, and was used mostly in accounting. Eventually, writing was used for other purposes, above all to record the culture's stories, previously preserved only in memory and speech. Thus written literature began. The world's oldest poetry by a known author was composed by Enheduanna in the twenty-third century B.C. She was a priestess, prophetess, and princess, the daughter of King Sargon of Akkad. Her poetry, written in Sumerian, praised the life-giving goddess of love, Inanna (or Ishtar). Some later princesses, who wrote dirges, love songs, lullabies, and prayers, continued the Mesopotamian tradition of royal women as authors. The number of literate women and men in the general population was probably quite small. By 2000 B.C., Mesopotamians in various places had begun to record their myths, such as the epic of Gilgamesh. Stories about Gilgamesh had circulated orally for centuries, but now they were permanently recorded in cuneiform.

The evolution of writing had a tremendous impact on the organization of society as well as on the forms of literature. Powerful men such as kings, priests, and wealthy landowners could control their workers even more strictly because they could keep

of writing. Food producers, for example, might need to verify the amount of grain, the number of animals, or the quantity of some other commodity they were having someone else deliver. They would therefore seal the appropriate number of tokens in a clay ball to prevent tampering. Unfortunately, this method of accounting had a critical flaw: the receiving agent had to shatter the ball to check the number of items delivered against the number of

precise track of who had paid, who still owed, and the amounts of debt. A scribal administrative class developed and began to keep documents. Most significantly, writing provided a powerful new tool for passing on a culture to later generations.

Bronze Age Metallurgy

About the same time cities emerged in Mesopotamia, crafts producers there and in other areas of the Mediterranean world developed advanced techniques for working with bronze, lead, silver, and gold. Devising innovative ways to alloy metals at high temperatures, smiths fashioned new luxury goods and better tools for agriculture, construction, and warfare. Most revolutionized by this new technology was the field of weaponry. Pure copper weapons, which had been available for some time, had offered few advantages over stone weapons because they easily lost their shape and edge. Bronze, with its strength and ability to hold a razor edge, enabled smiths to produce durable and deadly metal daggers, swords, and spearheads. Weapons of bronze soon became standard equipment for every prosperous man in the Bronze Age. Cities without metal ore had to develop trade contacts or conquer territories with mines.

Bronze Age smiths could also create daggers and swords that were far more than utilitarian implements for hunting and war. The sometimes lavish decorations added to these weapons displayed the owners' wealth and status. Such weapons also underscored the division between men and women in society, because they signified the masculine roles of hunter and warrior that had emerged long ago in the division of labor of hunter-gatherers. The development of metallurgy had other social consequences as well. People's desire to accumulate wealth and to possess status symbols stimulated demand for metals and for the skilled workers who could create these coveted articles: lavishly adorned weapons for men; exquisitely crafted jewelry made from exotic materials, such as imported ivory, for both women and men. Growing numbers of craftspeople swelled the size of Bronze Age settlements. Greater availability of such items made even more people want them. People began to question whether they were paid appropriately for their labor. They now expected to acquire wealth in metal, not just in foodstuffs, animals, or land.

The Akkadian Empire

Weaponry played such a large role in Mesopotamia's history because the cities there constantly battled one another for control. Historical documents reveal that the city of Kish achieved political supremacy in the so-called Early Dynastic Period during the middle of the third millennium B.C. In about 2350 B.C., however, a new power emerged when Sargon, the ruler of Akkad, north of Sumer, declared himself supreme, and eventually dominated the region militarily. Sargon was Akkadian, not Sumerian. The Akkadians were one of the peoples we call Semitic based on the characteristics of their language. The Sumerians were a non-Semitic people; their language seems to have been unique to them. But aside from using different languages, the Akkadian and Sumerian cultures appear to have been identical. From Sargon's records of his career as a commander and ruler, we learn that he launched campaigns of conquest far to the north and south of his homeland, building by force the first empire (a political unit that includes a number of territories or peoples ruled by a single sovereign leader) recorded in history. A poet of about

The Akkadian Empire

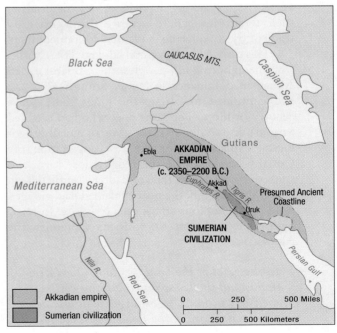

2000 B.C. attributed Sargon's success to the favor of the god Enlil: "to Sargon the king of Akkad, from below to above, Enlil had given him lordship and kingship."

Sargon's energetic grandson, Naram-Sin, continued the family tradition of military expeditions to conquer distant lands. By 2250 B.C. he had severely damaged Ebla, a large city whose site has only recently been discovered in what is now Syria, over five hundred miles from Naram-Sin's home base in Mesopotamia. Archaeologists have unearthed many cuneiform tablets at Ebla, some of them in more than one language. These discoveries may mean that Ebla had thrived as an early center of learning.

Although Sargon and Naram-Sin warred so aggressively partly because success in battle proved their worthiness to rule, they also harbored other motives for their imperialism. The Akkadian conquerors wanted a reliable supply of metal. Effective weapons required bronze, which necessitated acquiring copper and tin. We still do not know where the Mesopotamians obtained the tin they needed to make bronze. Tin is not found in the Near East today; the closest source appears to be in what is now Afghanistan, far to the northeast. The Mesopotamians may have imported tin from there by caravan. Because of the increasing dependency on metals from the Bronze Age on, ancient states lacking deposits of raw materials in their territories had to acquire them either by trade or by conquering lands that contained them.

This early Akkadian empire did not last. Attacks from neighboring hill peoples, the Gutians, ended Akkadian dominance in Sumer around 2200 B.C. and continued to plague the kings there for a century or more. The same poet who had credited Sargon's rise to divine favor gave an equally theological explanation for the vast devastation the Gutians—a people, he sneered, "whose form and stuttering words are that of a dog"—inflicted on Sumer. Naram-Sin, the poet explained, had enraged Enlil by his impious attack on a holy site. In retribution the god sent the Gutians to punish the Akkadians:

In the gates of the land the doors stood deep in dust, all the lands raised a bitter cry on their city walls. . . . The large fields and acres produced no grain, the flooded acres produced no fish, the watered gardens produced

no honey and wine. . . . The people droop helplessly because of their hunger.

Mesopotamian Mythology and Early Laws

This description of the plight of Sumer near the end of the third millennium B.C. reveals how precarious human life remained despite the development of complex, urban, and literate societies. The myths preserved in Mesopotamian literature reveal a belief in the gods' awesome power over humans and in the limits of human control over the circumstances of life. The themes of Mesopotamian mythology not only lived on in their own poetry and songs but also powerfully influenced the mythology of distant peoples, most notably the Greeks in later times.

ENUMA ELISH

A long narrative poem, the *Epic of Creation,* tells the Mesopotamian version of how all things came into being. A violent struggle among the gods supposedly created the universe. The poem depicts these primeval deities as unruly and violent. The first two gods, the female Tiamat and the male Apsu, have a blazing argument when Apsu threatens to get rid of their four generations of descendants because their incessant noise keeps him from sleeping. Eventually the fearsome male god Marduk—"four were his eyes, four were his ears; when his lips moved, fire blazed forth"— becomes the supreme deity by destroying Tiamat, her army of snaky monsters, and the gods allied with her in a gory battle. Marduk then fashions human beings out of the blood of Tiamat's chief monster. He creates people not to honor or love them but to demand that they serve and entertain their divine masters.

The *Epic of Gilgamesh* relates the adventures of Gilgamesh (whom we met on his quest for immortality at the beginning of the chapter). This popular poem has numerous versions (none complete, unfortunately) in different Near Eastern languages. In the Mesopotamian story, Gilgamesh is a tyrant who enthusiastically beds all the young women of Uruk and orders the young men to construct a temple and walls for the city. When the city's distressed inhabitants implore the mother of the gods to give them a rival to Gilgamesh, she creates the man of nature, Enkidu. After a wrestling match that ends in a draw, Enkidu and Gilgamesh become friends instead of enemies and set out to conquer Humbaba (or Huwawa), the ugly giant of the Pine Forest. The two comrades also defeat the Bull of Heaven after Gilgamesh offends the goddess Ishtar, but the gods doom Enkidu to die not long after this moment of triumph. In despair over human frailty, Gilgamesh sets out, as we saw, to find the secret of immortality, only to have his quest foiled by a thieving snake. He subsequently realizes that immortality can come only from great achievements and the memory they perpetuate.

The late Sumerian version of the Gilgamesh Epic includes a description of a cataclysmic flood that covers the earth. The gods send the flood to Mesopotamia, but one man is warned of the impending disaster and told to build a boat. He then loads his vessel with his relatives, other humans skilled in crafts, his possessions, domesticated and wild animals, and "the seed of all living things, all of them." After a week of torrential rains he and his passengers disembark to repopulate and rebuild the earth. This story is a striking predecessor to the later Biblical account of the flood and the story of Noah's ark.

The early civilizations of Mesopotamia tenaciously faced the constant challenges posed by social and political existence. They created the earliest recorded sets of public regulations and laws aimed at improving society, at least as defined by the rulers. Uruinimgina,* for example, a ruler of the city of Lagash in the twenty-fourth century B.C., promulgated the earliest known directives for reforming society and government. He sought to strengthen his own position as the central authority by weakening the powers of rich landowners and winning popular support by protecting the poor against unjust seizure of their property. His reforms subsequently influenced the famous set of written laws of Ur-Nammu, king of Ur in the late twenty-second century. Ur-Nammu expressed a commitment to, in his words, "the principles of truth and equity," under which "the orphan was not delivered up to the rich man; the widow was not delivered up to the mighty man; the man of one shekel [a small unit of value] was not delivered up to the man of one mina [a much larger unit of value]." This official concern with protecting the less powerful from exploitation introduces a

moral dimension to law that recurs in later codes, such as that of Hammurabi of Babylon.

But even the comfortable inhabitants of walled cities had only limited protection from disaster, sickness, and starvation. According to the cuneiform poem that records his death, Ur-Nammu himself died fighting the Gutians, "abandoned on the battlefield like a crushed vessel."

The Old Kingdom of Egypt

Africa was home to the other great Near Eastern civilization of the third millennium B.C.: Egypt, a fertile region that snaked along the banks of the Nile River. The region's population included a diversity of people, whose skin color ranged from light to very dark. A significant proportion of ancient Egyptians, especially in Upper Egypt, would perhaps be regarded as black by the standards of modern racial classifications, which ancient people did not observe. Except in the delta of the Nile near the Mediterranean Sea, where the great river fanned out into several channels and swamps, the habitable territory of Egypt encompassed only the lush fields extending several miles away from the river on either side for about seven hundred miles from north to south. This

Old Kingdom Egypt

narrow strip was fertile because late every summer the Nile, swollen by melting snow from the mountains far to the south, overflowed its banks for several weeks to months. This annual inundation enriched the soil with nutrients from the river's silt and prevented the accumulation of harmful deposits of mineral salts. Because of the dark color of this ribbon of fields, the Egyptians called their country the "Black Land." Immediately beyond this fertile strip stretched vast, nearly impassable deserts (the "Red Land"). So abrupt is the transition between these two areas that even today a person can stand with one foot in the Black Land and one in the Red Land. The deserts protected the Egyptians from attack except through the Nile delta and from the Nile valley on the southern frontier with Nubia. The surpluses that a multitude of hard-working farmers produced in the lush Nile valley made Egypt prosperous. Date palms, vegetables, grasses for pasturing animals, and grain grew in abundance. From their ample supplies

---

*His name was formerly read on cuneiform tablets as "Urukagina."

The Harvest in Egypt
This Egyptian painting depicts agriculture along the fertile banks of the Nile River. Techniques of harvesting and winnowing grain (separating the edible core from the inedible chaff) have changed little in many parts of contemporary Egypt.

Preparing Grain in the Traditional Way
Some people today still use the method of winnowing grain that ancient Egyptians used: throwing it into the air by hand so the breeze can blow the light chaff away from the heavier core.

of grain the Egyptians made bread and beer, their favorite beverage. Like the Sumerians, who brewed eleven different types, the Egyptians relished beer.

Despite the relative geographic isolation their surrounding mantle of desert gave the Egyptians, they had contacts with southwest Asia and felt the influence of Sumerian civilization. The Egyptians may have learned about writing from the Sumerians, but they wrote in their own scripts rather than cuneiform. For the most formal texts they used an ornate pictographic script known as *hieroglyphs* (Greek for "sacred carving or writing"). Both Sumerian and Egyptian life centered around religion. The Egyptians worshipped a great variety of gods, who were often represented in art and literature as creatures with both human and animal features. The priests who administered the temples, sacrifices, and festivals of the various Egyptian gods

gained a preeminent place in the social and political life of Egypt, second only to the kings and queens who ruled Egypt after its unification.

Twenty-five hundred years of Egyptian royal dynasties began when King Menes (sometimes identified as Narmer) united the previously separate territories of Upper (southern) Egypt and Lower (northern) Egypt around 3100–3000 B.C. Menes' reign culminated a long process of the centralization of power. Egyptian political history thereafter revolves around the waxing and waning of a strong central authority. At times, for example, the priests or the governors of different regions promoted their own interests at the expense of the king's, causing a decentralization of authority that led to instability. The Egyptians regarded the king as a god in human form, such as the son of the sun god. Because the Egyptians recognized the

The Goddess Sakhmet
*Egyptian legend taught that this lioness-headed deity
had exacted vengeance on the human race when the
gods were angry. She was also regarded as the creator
of the people of Syria, Palestine, and the Libyan desert.*

Hieroglyphic sign	Meaning	Sound value
	vulture	glottal stop
	flowering reed	consonantal I
	forearm and hand	ayin
	quail chick	W
	foot	B
	stool	P
	horned viper	F
	owl	M
	water	N
	mouth	R
	reed shelter	H
	twisted flax	slightly guttural
	placenta (?)	H as in "loch"
	animal's belly	slightly softer than h
	door bolt	S
	folded cloth	S
	pool	SH
	hill	Q
	basket with handle	K
	jar stand	G
	loaf	T

Sample of Egyptian Hieroglyphs

mortality of the reigning king, they probably differentiated the human existence of the individual king and the divine institution of the monarchy. In the Egyptian view the monarchy incorporated the divine force creating harmony and stability, called *ma'at*. Often translated as "truth," or "justice," or "righteousness," *ma'at* expressed the ideal of the beneficent and honorable administration the king as a divine being was supposed to provide his people. Their special religious status distinguished the Egyptian kings from the Sumerian kings, who ruled only as temporal lords in a state devoted to the gods.

Egypt also differed politically from the quarreling city-states of Sumer in its early tradition of unification under one monarch. This central political system gave enormous power to the kings of the so-called Old Kingdom, which lasted from 2686 to 2181 B.C., one of the three major chronological divisions of ancient Egyptian history.* (The Middle Kingdom extended from 2050 to 1786 B.C., the New Kingdom from 1567 to 1085 B.C.) The kings (known by the time of the New Kingdom as *pharaoh,* which means "the Great House," that is, the royal palace and estate) exhibited their authority and resources in their building programs. They built a few cities; their capital, Memphis (south of modern Cairo), grew into a metropolis packed with mammoth structures. But it was outside Memphis that the Old Kingdom kings erected the most stunning manifestations of their might: the pyramids, which served as royal tombs and as the centerpieces of elaborate groups of buildings for royal ceremonies. Although we now know that the pyramids were not the first megalithic (Greek for "of large stones") monuments in the world, they still rank as the grandest. The Old Kingdom monarchs marshaled their resources and population to construct these huge complexes. Imhotep, chief architect of King Djoser around 2650 B.C., became famous for overseeing the construction of the first large pyramid, the Step Pyramid at Saqqara, Egypt's earliest monument built entirely of stone. King Sneferu subsequently had a much larger pyramid built at Dahshur. But king Cheops, around 2575 B.C., commissioned the biggest of them all—the Great Pyramid at Giza outside Cairo. At around four hundred eighty feet high, it stands taller than a forty-story skyscraper. Covering over thirteen acres, its dimensions of roughly seven hundred sixty feet per side required more than two million blocks of limestone weighing on the average two and a half tons, with some as heavy as fifteen tons.

The pyramids and the funerary buildings linked to them were outfitted elaborately to provide the kings with material delights for their existence in the world of the dead. Gilded furniture;

sparkling jewelry; exquisite objects of all kinds, from the domestic to the exotic—the dead kings took it all with them. Archaeologists have even uncovered two full-sized cedar ships buried next to the Great Pyramid; they evidently conveyed King Cheops on his journey into eternity. A hieroglyphic text from around 2300 B.C., addressed to the god Atum, expresses the hope that an Old Kingdom ruler entombed in his pyramid has a secure afterlife: "O Atum, put your arms around King Nefer-ka-Re, around this construction work, around this pyramid. . . . May you guard lest anything happen to him evilly throughout the course of eternity." The kings of Egypt—and presumably their subjects as well—coped with the idea of death as best they could; their lavish preparations for death clearly indicate their strong belief in an afterlife.

Almost all the extant art from ancient Egypt comes from tombs or temples, further testimony to the kings' consuming interest in the afterworld and proper relations with the gods. Egyptian artists of the Old Kingdom excelled in stonework, from carved ornamental jars to massive portrait statues of the kings. These statues invariably represent the subject either standing stiffly with his left leg advanced or sitting on a chair or throne. Artists sculpted the parts of the bodies according to a predetermined set of proportions, and molded the faces into an idealized style that befitted the special religious status of the monarchs. The formalism of this sculpture illustrates how much Egypt's rulers valued order and predictability. The concern for a certain decorum appears in the Old Kingdom literature the Egyptians called *Instructions,* known today as *wisdom literature.* These texts convey precepts for appropriate behavior for high officials. In the *Instruction of Ptahhotep,* for example, the king advises his minister Ptahhotep to tell his son, who will succeed him in office, not to be arrogant or overconfident just because he is well educated and to seek advice from the ignorant as well as the wise.

Even by today's standards the massive pyramid complexes are marvels of engineering and human labor. The effort required to supply workers and materials for such enormous projects, intentionally or not, furthered the organization of a centralized state. Old Kingdom rulers had to develop a stronger government administration just to oversee their great construction projects. Egyptian

---

*The uncertainty that characterizes the chronology of ancient Mesopotamia also pertains to the dates for ancient Egypt, despite the apparent precision implied by the custom of giving specific dates for the reigns of kings, and so on.

The Great Pyramids
The largest of the Egyptian pyramids, built during the Old Kingdom, loomed over the Nile River at Giza. This picture shows the Nile spreading over its banks in one of its annual inundations before the modern Aswan Dam ended them.

society consequently evolved into a more structured hierarchy. The king and queen, whose job included producing children to continue the ruling dynasty, topped the social pyramid. Brothers and sisters in the royal family could marry, perhaps because such matches were believed necessary to preserve the status of the royal line or to imitate the marriages of the gods. The priests and the royal administrators, including the commanders of the army, ranked next in the hierarchy, but their standing was far below the king and queen. The common people, who did all the manual labor, comprised the massive base of this figurative pyramid of free people in Egypt. Free workers built most of the pyramids for wages or as corvée service to the state. Slaves captured in foreign wars served the royal family and the temples in the Old

Kingdom. Privately owned slaves in domestic service did not become common until the Middle Kingdom.

Women in ancient Egypt generally had the same legal rights as men. They could pursue lawsuits, testify in cases, and initiate divorces. Old Kingdom portrait statues vividly express the equal status of wife and husband: each figure is the same size and sits on the same kind of chair. (In New Kingdom art, however, wives appear smaller than their husbands and more relegated to the background.) In general, Egyptian women devoted themselves to private life, managing their households and property, whereas men functioned more in public life. When their husbands went to war or were killed in battle, women often took on the responsibilities their husbands had shouldered, especially concerning the public management of the family's holdings. Some women held government posts, served as priestesses, and practiced medicine.

Producing heirs and preparing for death were not an Egyptian king's only responsibilities. His special status as a religious figure required him to ensure the welfare of his country by following certain rituals. Protocol strictly regulated his every activity, setting a specific time for him to bathe, take a walk, or even make love to his wife. Above all, the king was obliged to marshal the numinous power necessary to make sure the Nile flooded every year. When climate changes beginning around 2350 B.C. caused the annual inundations to shrink and therefore eventually led to famines, the apparent loss of the king's ability to ensure prosperity undermined his political authority and contributed to the breakup of the Old Kingdom. This failure of the kings' efficacy exposed a serious weakness in Egyptian kings' justification of their power: they could not always keep Egypt well fed. Regional governors probably increased their power considerably when these continuing crop failures proved the king could not guarantee the safety of the harvest. These local administrators, who had assisted the kings over the centuries, already had significant power and independence from central authority. When King Peyi II lingered on the throne for over ninety years, the relaxation of royal authority led to the dissolution of the Old Kingdom. The economic chaos and political anarchy that characterized the First Intermediate Period (2181–2050 B.C.) resembled the disruption of society the Gutians had caused in Sumer at about the same time.

The first civilizations of Mesopotamia and Egypt fell for different reasons—the former ravaged by savage neighbors, the latter splintered by rebellious insiders. Archaeological evidence reveals that many settlements in Europe suffered grave damage during this same general period, around 2000 B.C. Although Europe had no cities during this time, the prehistoric societies of Europe had been transformed by a Neolithic revolution. We need to go back in time to trace the history of this metamorphosis and to examine its connection with the evolutionary process that had previously changed the face of the ancient Near East.

Technological and Social Change in Late Prehistoric Europe

At the time the villagers of Çatal Hüyük were already raising their own food, in the seventh millennium B.C., most European peoples still lived as hunter-gatherers. But over the next two to three thousand years, the way of life of many who dwelled in Europe underwent sweeping changes. Some of the same social and technological innovations that marked the Near East's transition to civilization also occurred in Europe. Recent research has caused us to rethink the nature of some of these changes in late prehistoric Europe.

Diffusion and Independent Innovation

Agricultural techniques gradually became known across Europe after their beginnings in the Fertile Crescent. The Neolithic farmers of Europe transformed the landscape of their continent, clearing vast tracts of dense forest. Considering the tools they had available (ax blades fashioned from bone or chipped rocks, wood or bone hoes), their clearing of so much land stands as one of the most remarkable modifications of the natural environment humans have ever accomplished. People began farming all across Europe: in balmier locales near the Mediterranean Sea, such as on the peninsulas formed by Greece and Italy; in upland plateaus nestled against the great east-west chain of mountains that divides southern Europe from the much colder north; in the huge plain of northern Europe that extends east into Russia north of the mountains; and eventually, around 4000 B.C., even on the windswept islands we know as the British Isles. Because the climates of these areas varied as much as their physical features, the kinds of farming undertaken and the crops grown in each region also differed.

What sparked the innovations that transformed Europe in the Neolithic and Bronze Ages? How did European peoples learn to farm and domesticate animals and later to build monumental stone constructions and to use the techniques of copper metallurgy? How much of this knowledge came from Mesopotamia and Egypt, and what, if anything, did the Europeans invent? Until recently most historians believed diffusion of technology answered these questions; they theorized that farmers, herders, architects, and metalworkers migrated to Europe from the Near East, either as settlers or as invaders. With them came the technologies of agriculture, stone construction, and copper metallurgy; that is, these emigrants diffused technological knowledge from the Near East over all of Europe.

New scientific techniques, refined only in the late 1960s, forced historians to reevaluate this diffusion theory. The most important technique, radiocarbon dating, allows scientists to determine the age of prehistoric organic materials found in excavations. By examining the amount of radioactive carbon-14 in ancient bones, seeds, hides, wood, and other materials, laboratory analysts can establish the length of time since the death of the material being tested. Dates obtained in this way have a certain margin of error, but scientists have refined the accuracy of radiocarbon dating by comparing their results with the chronological evidence obtained from counting the internal rings of long-lived trees. These new methods for dating archaeological material have led to a complete reworking of the chronology of Europe in the Neolithic and Bronze Ages. We now know, for example, that farming communities had already appeared in Greece and the mountains immediately to the north (the Balkans) in the early seventh millennium B.C. In this case the idea of migration as a source of cultural change may still hold, because the domesticated grains these communities grew had come from the Near East, probably brought in by migrating farmers. But the domestication of cattle that took place in this region at least as early as in the Near East suggests that the indigenous population of Europe also fostered innovation independently.

Megaliths and Metallurgy

The new dating techniques also reveal that local innovation accounts for the use of megaliths to build monumental structures in Neolithic Europe. Before radiocarbon dating, the pyramids of Egypt were thought to be the earliest megalithic stone constructions. The diffusion hypothesis postulated that migrating Egyptian architects supervised the construction of the large, stone chamber-tombs that are built into the ground along the far western edge of Europe. But radiocarbon dating of materials from these tombs has shown that the earliest of them were built before 4000 B.C., more than a thousand years before the pyramids. It is therefore impossible that the Neolithic inhabitants of western Europe learned to construct megalithic structures from Egyptians. The inhabitants of the Mediterranean island of Malta (south of Sicily) also erected substantial temples of stone before 3000 B.C., obviously without Egyptian advice. These Maltese temple complexes are the earliest freestanding stone monuments in the world. The new dating techniques have also shown that the local population, not visitors from the East, built Stonehenge in what is now southern England. This precisely aligned assemblage of mammoth stones was erected between 2100 and 1900 B.C., possibly to track the movements of the sun and the moon. Although Europeans in the Neolithic Age, or even in the subsequent Bronze Age, had no cities like those of the Near East, they had developed sophisticated megalithic building techniques.

Radiocarbon dates also indicate that Europeans probably did not learn copper metallurgy from Mesopotamian metalsmiths. If Near Eastern smiths had taught Europeans how to smelt copper, we would expect to find evidence that metallurgy began much earlier in the Near East than in Europe. But copper metallurgy developed in various European locations around the same time it did in the Near East. By the fourth millennium B.C., for example, Balkan smiths could cast copper ax heads with the hole for the ax handle in the correct position. Moreover, these smiths of southeastern Europe learned to make bronze in the same period their Near Eastern counterparts did. The Bronze Age therefore started in Europe at roughly the same time as in the Near East. This simultaneous development of metallurgy in such widely separated places can be explained only by independent local innovation.

Our new knowledge of chronology makes explaining the changes in prehistoric Europe even more complicated. Outsiders obviously did not introduce megalithic architecture and metallurgy to Europe. Even though we can still speculate that

Stonehenge
People in southern England erected these megaliths between 2100 and 1900 B.C. most likely to track the different positions of the sun and the moon.

migrating farmers from the Near East were responsible for spreading agriculture throughout Europe, we must also credit Europe's native populations with the capacity to make technological and social innovations independent of outside influence.

The Puzzle of the Indo-Europeans

One of the ongoing debates concerning European prehistory after the Neolithic revolution involves the question of whether peoples collectively labeled as Indo-Europeans migrated to Europe over the course of many centuries and radically changed the nature of its established societies. Some historians hypothesize that the final wave of Indo-European migration became a violent invasion that resulted in the devastation that archaeology reveals occurred in Europe around 2000 B.C. Some believe the Indo-Europeans prompted major changes in European languages, religion, and political organization. And some say these Indo-European newcomers imposed patriarchy on the societies of Neolithic Europe. Deciding whether the scattered evidence for the Indo-Europeans truly means they were responsible for such changes presents an intriguing puzzle of historical interpretation.

The evidence of language reveals that there is a mystery to be solved. Linguists long ago recognized that one ancient language was the ancestor of

most of the major ancient and modern languages of western Europe (including English), of the Slavic languages, of the Persian language of Iran, and of some languages spoken in India. Those who had once spoken the original language (it eventually disappeared, splitting into its many branches) are called Indo-Europeans. Because all who spoke the original Indo-European language died long before the invention of writing, the only traces of that language survive in features of the languages descended from Indo-European. We can tell, for example, that Indo-European had only one word for *night*, which survives in English "night," Spanish "noche," French "nuit," German "Nacht," Russian "noch," Vedic (the type of Sanskrit used in the ancient epic poetry of India) "nakt-," and so on.

Scholars still do not know how the various tongues descended from the original Indo-European language emerged in locations scattered from India to Europe. Perhaps Indo-Europeans migrated to these different regions from their homeland (whose location is unknown). Over time these now separate groups could have developed their own versions of the ancestral language. The words that descended from the original Indo-European vocabulary offer a few hints about the nature of the early Indo-European society. For example, the name of their chief divinity, a male god, survives in the similar sounds of "Zeus pater" and "Jupiter," the names given to the chief god in Greek and Latin, respectively. So we surmise that Indo-European society was patriarchal: the father was not merely a parent but the adult male in charge of the household as well as the public world. Other words indicate that Indo-European society was also patrilocal (the bride joined the groom's family) and patrilineal (the line of descent was traced through the father). Indo-Europeans also had the notion of king, a detail suggesting they had a ranked, socially differentiated society. Scholars usually assume the original Indo-Europeans were also warlike and competitive.

A frequently cited interpretation of the significance of the Indo-Europeans argues that these newcomers transformed what had been an egalitarian, peaceful, and matrifocal (centered on women as mothers) society into a hierarchical, warlike, and patriarchal one. The principal gods of the original Europeans were female, the argument further postulates, but they were now displaced by the male deities of the Indo-Europeans. The major point of this theory is that modern Western culture can find its patriarchal beginnings in this Indo-European onslaught.

This theoretical reconstruction of the way European society became patriarchal remains speculative and controversial. Opponents of the theory argue that we should not even assume the Indo-Europeans moved into the European continent as distinct groups powerful enough to overturn local traditions. Perhaps, even, Indo-European society never differed much from the kind of society that had evolved in late prehistoric Europe. In other words, European patriarchy might have originated in Europe itself, much earlier.

One competing theory suggests that male hunter-gatherers had already started human society on the road toward patriarchy in the Paleolithic Age by stealing women from each other's bands. They may have sought these women to produce children and thereby increase their band's population and strength. In this way men could have dominated women long before the Indo-European invasions supposedly began. The indigenous society of Europe would thus have been patriarchal.

Alternatively, the loss of equality between men and women may have resulted from the changes accompanying the development of plow agriculture and large-scale herding in late Neolithic

Venus Figurine
Archaeologists have discovered small female figures, like this one from Romania, in many Neolithic sites in Europe. Their shape suggests they may have been symbols of human fertility.

Europe. Those who minimize the significance of the Indo-Europeans as a source of cultural change argue further that the Indo-Europeans should not be blamed for the widespread destruction of European sites near the end of the third millennium. Instead, they suggest, exhaustion of the soil, leading to intense competition for land, and internal political turmoil probably caused the devastation.

The significance of the Indo-Europeans in Neolithic Europe remains an unsolved mystery. We know for certain that most members of historical European civilization spoke Indo-European languages, worshipped a male chief god, paid homage to female divinities, and lived in patriarchal societies. But we still cannot be sure how and when these fundamental characteristics of ancient Western society originated.

The First Civilizations in Europe

The first civilizations of Europe arose in the aftermath of the destruction that swept Europe around 2000 B.C. They were created by the early Bronze Age populations of the islands and on the coast of the Aegean Sea, a section of the eastern Mediterranean Sea between Greece and Anatolia (Asia Minor; today the western part of Asian Turkey). These people had advanced technologies, elaborate architecture, striking art, and a marked taste for luxury. They also inhabited a dangerous world whose perils ultimately overwhelmed all their civilized sophistication.

The Palace Society of Minoan Crete

The earliest civilization of the Aegean region emerged on the large island of Crete around 2200 B.C. People had inhabited this large fertile island for several thousand years; the first settlers probably came from nearby Anatolia about 6000 B.C. Like their contemporaries elsewhere in Europe, these pioneers established small settlements near agricultural land. In the third millennium B.C., however, new technological capabilities began to affect Cretan society.

As elsewhere, advances in metallurgy influenced the people of Crete. But the emergence of what is called Mediterranean polyculture—the cultivation of olives and grapes as well as grain in one agricultural system—changed Crete more profoundly. This system, which still dominates Mediterranean agriculture, had two important consequences: the food supply increased, stimulating population growth; and agriculture became diversified and specialized, producing valuable new products such as olive oil and wine. Because old methods were inadequate for storing and transporting these

The Early Civilizations of Greece and the Aegean Sea

commodities, artisans invented and began manufacturing huge storage jars that could accommodate these products, in the process adding another specialized skill to their craft. Craftspeople and agricultural workers, producing their wares using sophisticated but time-consuming techniques, no longer had time to grow their own food or make the goods, such as clothes and lamps, they needed for everyday life. They now bartered the products they made for food and other goods.

Society became increasingly interdependent, both economically and socially, in the palace society of Crete. In the smaller villages of early Neolithic Europe, reciprocity had governed exchanges among the population of self-sufficient farmers. Reciprocal exchange promoted social relationships rather than economic gain: I give you some of what I produce, and you in return give me some of what you produce. We exchange, not because either of us necessarily needs what the other produces, but to reaffirm our social alliances in a small group. Bronze Age society in the Aegean region reached a level of economic interdependence based on redistribution that was far more complex than even the larger Neolithic villages like Çatal Hüyük.

The palace society, named for its sprawling, many-chambered buildings, began to appear on Crete around 2200 B.C. Today this palace society is called *Minoan,* after King Minos, the legendary Cretan ruler known only from Greek myths. The palaces housed the rulers and their menials and served as central storage facilities. The general population clustered around the palaces in houses adjacent to one another. Some other settlements dotted outlying areas. Earthquakes leveled the first Minoan palaces about 1700 B.C., but the Cretans rebuilt on an even grander scale in the succeeding centuries. Accounting records preserved on clay tablets reveal that these new palaces were the hub of the island's economy.

Probably influenced by Egyptian hieroglyphs, the first written records of Crete used a pictographic script to symbolize objects. This system evolved into a more linear form of writing that expressed phonetic sounds. Unlike cuneiform or hieroglyphs, this system was a true syllabary—a character represented the sound of each syllable of a word. The Cretan version of this script, which originated sometime after 2000 B.C., is today called Linear A.

The records kept in Cretan script were lists: accounts of goods received and goods paid out, inventories of stored goods, livestock, landholdings, and personnel. The Minoans kept records of everything from chariots to perfumes. The receipts record payments owed, with any deficits in the amount actually paid—in carefully noted. The records of disbursements from the palace storerooms cover ritual offerings to the gods, rations to personnel, and raw materials for crafts production, such as metal issued to bronzesmiths. None of the tablets records any exchange rate between different categories of goods, such as a ratio stating how much grain was equivalent to a sheep. Nor do the tables reveal any use of bullion as money. (The invention of coinage lay a thousand years in the future.)

The economic system of Minoan Crete appears to have been controlled by the palaces: the king or his representatives decided how much each producer had to contribute and what each would receive for subsistence. Similar redistributive economic systems based on official monopolies, not a market economy, had existed in Mesopotamia for some time. Like them, the logistics of operating the Cretan arrangement were complicated. For example, the palaces' vast storage areas were filled with hundreds of gigantic jars containing olive oil and wine; nearby storerooms were crammed with bowls, cups, and dippers. Scribes meticulously recorded what came in and what went out. This process of economic redistribution applied to craft specialists as well as to food producers, and the palaces' administrative officials set quotas for craftspeople. Although not everyone is likely to have participated in the redistribution system, it apparently dominated the Cretan economy, minimizing the exchange of goods through markets. People in the countryside may have sold goods to one another occasionally. But these small markets never rivaled the palace system. The palaces probably oversaw overseas trade as well.

From all indications this system worked smoothly and peacefully for centuries. Although contemporary settlements elsewhere around the Aegean Sea and in Anatolia had elaborate defensive walls, Minoan Crete had none. The palaces, towns, and even isolated country houses apparently saw no need to fortify themselves against each other. The remains of the newer palaces, such as the one at Knossos—with its hundreds of rooms in five stories, storage jars capable of holding 240,000 gallons, a form of indoor plumbing, and colorful scenes painted on the walls—have led many to conclude that Minoans, at least those who lived in the palace society, were prosperous, peaceful, and contented. The prominence of women in palace frescoes and the numerous figurines of buxom goddesses found on Cretan sites have prompted speculation that Minoan society was a female-dominated culture.

Minoan Contact with Mycenaean Greece

The upper class of Minoan Crete maintained extensive overseas contacts, using another innovation of the third millennium: the longship. Their sea travel in search of trade goods took them not only to Egypt and the other civilizations of the Near East but also to the islands of the Aegean and southern Greece, where another society, the Mycenaean, flourished. Archaeologists have uncovered the Bronze Age site of Mycenae in the Peloponnese (the large peninsula that is southern Greece). Although neither Mycenae nor any other settlement ever ruled Bronze Age Greece as a united state, Mycenaean has become the general term for the Bronze Age civilization of mainland Greece in the second millennium B.C.

Nineteenth-century archaeologists discovered treasure-filled Mycenaean graves. Constructed as stone-lined shafts, these graves contained entombed dead and their golden jewelry, including heavy necklaces festooned with pendants; gold and silver vessels; bronze weapons decorated with scenes of wild animals inlaid in precious metals; and delicately painted pottery that were buried with them. The first excavator of Mycenae thought he had found the grave of King Agamemnon, who commanded the Greeks at Troy in Homer's poem *The Iliad*, but we now know the shaft graves date to the sixteenth century B.C., long before the Trojan War. The artifacts point to a warrior culture organized in independent settlements ruled by powerful commanders who enriched themselves by raiding near and far as well as dominating local farmers.

Another kind of burial chamber, called *tholos* tombs—spectacular underground domed chambers built in beehive shapes from closely fitted stones—marks the next period in Mycenaean society, which began in the fifteenth century B.C. The architectural details of the *tholos* tombs and the style of the burial goods found in them testify to the far-flung contacts Mycenaean rulers maintained throughout the eastern Mediterranean, but particularly with Minoan Crete.

The evidence of contact between the Minoans and the Mycenaeans raises a thorny problem. The art and goods of the Mycenaeans in the middle of the second millennium B.C. display many motifs clearly reminiscent of Cretan design. The archaeologist who excavated Knossos therefore argued that the Minoans had inspired Mycenaean civilization by sending colonists to the mainland, as they undeniably had to various Aegean islands, such as Thera. This "demotion" of Mycenaean civilization offended the excavators of Mycenae, and a debate ensued over the relationship between the two cultures. They were certainly not identical. The Mycenaeans made burnt offerings to the gods; the Minoans did not. The Minoans scattered sanctuaries across the landscape in caves, on mountaintops, and in country villas; the mainlanders did none of this. When the Mycenaeans started building palaces in the fourteenth century B.C., unlike the Minoans they designed them around megarons—rooms with huge ceremonial hearths and thrones for the rulers. Some palaces had more than one megaron, which could soar two stories high with columns to support a roof above the second-floor balconies.

The mystery surrounding the relationship between the Minoans and the Mycenaeans deepened with the startling revelation of documents found in the palace at Knossos, in which a Cretan script had been adapted to Greek—these documents are the famous Linear B tablets, whose pictographic script was based on Linear A. Because these tablets dated from before the final destruction of the palace in about 1370 B.C., they meant that the palace administration had been keeping its records in a foreign language for some time. Presumably this change means that Mycenaeans had come to dominate Cretans, but whether by violent invasion or some kind of peaceful accommodation remains unknown. The Linear B tablets imply that Mycenae had not long, if ever, remained a secondary power to Minoan Crete.

The Zenith of Mycenaean Society

A glimpse of Mycenaean society in its maturity demonstrates the nature of its power. War was clearly the principle concern of those Mycenaean men who could afford its expensive paraphernalia. Contents of Bronze Age tombs in Greece reveal that no wealthy Mycenaean male went to his grave without his fighting equipment. The complete suit of Mycenaean bronze armor found in a fourteenth-century B.C. tomb in the northeastern Peloponnese shows how extensive a warrior's equipment could be. This warrior was buried in a complete bronze cuirass (chest guard) of two pieces (front and back), an adjustable skirt of bronze plates, bronze greaves (shin guards), shoulder plates, and a collar. On his head had rested a boar's-tusk helmet with metal cheekpieces. Next to his body lay his leather shield, bronze and clay vessels, and a bronze comb with gold teeth. Originally his bronze swords had lain beside him, but tomb robbers had stolen them. The expense of these grave goods implies that armor and weapons were so central to a Mycenaean man's identity that he could not do without them, even in death.

Mycenaean warriors could ride into battle in the latest in military hardware—the lightweight, two-wheeled chariot pulled by horses. These revolutionary vehicles, sometimes assumed to have been introduced by Indo-Europeans migrating from Central Asia, first appeared not long after 2000 B.C. in various Mediterranean and Near Eastern societies. The first Aegean representation of such a chariot occurs on a Mycenaean grave marker from about 1500 B.C. Wealthy people evidently desired this new form of transportation not only for war but also as proof of their social status.

The Mycenaeans seem to have spent more on war than on religion. In any case, they did not construct any large religious buildings like the giant temples of the Near East. Although the nature of Bronze Age mainland religion remains largely obscure, many scholars assume the Mycenaeans primarily worshiped the male-dominated pantheon traditionally associated with the martial culture of the Indo-Europeans. The names of numerous deities known from later Greek religion occur in the Linear B tablets.

Bronze Age Mycenaean traders and warriors both journeyed far from home, mainly by sea travel. Mycenaeans established colonies at various locations along the coast of the Mediterranean. Seaborne Mycenaean warriors also dominated and probably usurped the palace society of Minoan Crete in the fifteenth and fourteenth centuries B.C., presumably in wars over commercial rivalry in the Mediterranean. By the middle of the fourteenth century B.C., the Mycenaeans had displaced the Minoans as the preeminent civilization of the Aegean.

The Near East and Greece to the End of the Second Millennium B.C.

The Bronze Age development of extensive sea travel for trading and raiding put the cultures of the Aegean and the Near East in closer contact than ever before. The ease and speed of transportation by water, compared to the difficulty of travel by land in a world largely without roads, encouraged interaction between the older civilizations at the eastern end of the Mediterranean and the younger ones to the west. Minoan and Mycenaean voyagers alike particularly favored visiting Egypt, because they valued exchanging goods and ideas with such a prosperous and complex civilization. The civilizations of Mesopotamia and Anatolia after 2000 B.C. overshadowed those of Crete and Greece: their cities were much larger, and their written legal codes were much more highly developed and extensive. By around 1200 B.C., however, turmoil caused by internal strife and the movements of many peoples throughout the eastern Mediterranean and the Near East seriously damaged the political stability, economic prosperity, and international contacts of the societies of most of these lands.

The Kingdoms of Mesopotamia and Anatolia

The Gutians who had overwhelmed the Akkadian empire near the end of the third millennium B.C. did not set up a lasting political structure. The Third Dynasty of Ur, founded by the Sumerian lawgiver King Ur-Nammu (✳2112–2095 B.C.[*]), reestablished some stability in Sumer by about 2050 B.C. Frequent warfare with rivals for territory, however, fatally weakened the Third Dynasty after about a century. Until after 1000 B.C., Mesopotamia underwent complex and often turbulent changes. Economic difficulties caused by soil pollution may have disrupted political stability in Mesopotamia in the second millennium B.C. The intensive irrigation necessary there had increased the salinity of the fields, hindering production of the agricultural surpluses that could make a state rich. And in Anatolia, to the northwest, the Hittite kingdom arose as a formidable rival to Mesopotamia. No single Mesopotamian state dominated the region in this long period; only after 1000 B.C. did the Assyrians revive their power. Despite its troubles during the early second millennium B.C., Mesopotamia nevertheless experienced the growth of two characteristic features of civilization: private, large-scale commercial enterprise and extensive collections of written laws.

The Assyrians, descended from the Akkadians, lived in the northeastern portion of Mesopotamia. These Semitic people of seminomadic origins freed themselves from Sumerian rule of the Ur III dynasty in the twentieth century B.C. and gained prosperity as an independent kingdom by taking advantage of their geographical location next to Anatolia and establishing trading ties. The various city-states of Anatolia had become the principal source of raw materials such as wood, copper, and silver for the rest of the ancient Near East in the early second millennium B.C. Adapting to their country's lack of natural resources, the Assyrians concentrated on producing woolen textiles to export in return for the raw materials of Anatolia.

Although Mesopotamian societies had traditionally operated mainly under state monopolies in redistributive economic systems, by 1900 B.C. the Assyrian kings allowed private individuals to transact large international commercial deals on their own initiative. Assyrian investors staked traders for a cargo of cloth and travel expenses. The traders then formed donkey caravans to travel the hundreds of miles to Anatolia, where they could make huge profits. After repaying investors' origi-

---

[*]The ✳ indicates date of reign or term in office.

nal investment, the traders split the profits with them. Hired hands received their pay from any profits. This system motivated the participants to maximize profits, and the enormous profits these entrepreneurs could earn reflected the equally large risks of the business. Regulations existed to deal with fraud by the trader as well as losses in transit. The Assyrian domestic economy still centered on a redistributive system similar to those of the Aegean, but this emergent profit-driven international trade foreshadowed the shape of many economies of the later Greco-Roman world.

Attacks by the aggressive kingdom of the Mitanni in Anatolia cost Assyria its prosperity and independence, but strong Assyrian kings fought to recover them by the thirteenth century B.C. King Tiglath-Pileser I (*c. 1114–1076 B.C.) successfully protected Assyria in its frequent wars with the Babylonian kingdom in Mesopotamia, the Phrygians of Anatolia, and the Aramaeans from Syria. But by about 1000 B.C. incessant Aramaean attacks had ground down the power of Assyria, leaving no single state able to dominate the area.

In hierarchical societies such as those of the ancient Near East, social life required official rules. This need for laws became more pressing as the expansion of private trade and property ownership further complicated life in a centralized monarchy. Although we know Sumerian kings promulgated laws as early as about 2400 B.C., King Hammurabi (*c. 1792–1750 B.C.) of Babylon instituted the most famous Mesopotamian laws. His Amorite ancestors, another seminomadic Semitic people, began migrating into Mesopotamia and Syria from 2200 to 2000 B.C. Eventually the Amorites established a powerful kingdom centered in Babylon. After long struggles in the early eighteenth century B.C., Hammurabi became the dominant power in southern Mesopotamia (though he never assembled an extensive empire).

Hammurabi's laws legally divided society into three categories: free men and women, commoners, and slaves. The criteria for differentiating the first two levels of free people remain uncertain, but the terms did express a social hierarchy. An attacker who caused a pregnant woman of the free class to miscarry, for example, paid twice the fine levied for the same offense against a woman of the class of commoners. Among social equals, the principle of

"an eye for an eye" (in Latin *lex talionis,* "law of retaliation") prevailed in cases of physical injury. But a member of the free class who killed a commoner was not executed, only required to pay monetary compensation. Most of the laws concerned the king's interests as a property owner who leased innumerable tracts of land to tenants in return for rent or services. The laws imposed severe penalties for offenses against property, including mutilation or a gruesome death for crimes as varied as theft, wrongful sales, and careless construction. Women had some legal rights in this patriarchal society, although their rights were more limited than men's. They could make business contracts and appear in court. A wife could divorce her husband for cruelty; but a husband could divorce his wife for any reason. The inequality of the divorce laws was tempered in practice, however, because a woman could recover the property she had brought to her marriage, a fact that represented a considerable disincentive for a man to end his marriage.

Although written laws helped prevent the kinds of arbitrary decisions unwritten laws could allow, the major omissions in Hammurabi's laws show that he was not attempting to codify, or systematize, the law comprehensively. For example, criminal law receives less attention than a full codification would require. Furthermore, the documents of the period show almost no evidence that Hammurabi's laws were applied; in practice, penalties were often less severe than the law specified. Common, or unwritten, law presumably governed most of everyday life. Hammurabi's laws publicized a royal ideal; they did not necessarily reflect reality. Why did Hammurabi have his laws written down? He announces his reasons in the prologue and epilogue to his collection: to give all his subjects a chance to have certain knowledge of the rules governing them and to demonstrate his status as a just king before his god and his people. Above all, Hammurabi had his laws inscribed on a polished stone slab in a temple because he wanted to show Shamash, the sun god and god of justice, that he had fulfilled the social responsibility imposed on him as a divinely installed monarch—to ensure justice and the moral and material welfare of his people. That responsibility corresponded to the strictly hierarchical vision of society that characterized all Mesopotamian societies.

The situations and conflicts covered by Hammurabi's laws illuminate many aspects of the lives of city-dwellers in ancient Mesopotamia. Crimes of burglary and assault apparently plagued urban residents. Marriages were arranged by the groom and the bride's father, who sealed the agreement with a legal contract. The husband dominated the household, although the state retained the right to decide cases of disinheritance. The detailed laws on surgery make clear that doctors practiced in the cities.

Information gleaned from archaeological excavations and surviving literature and other documents supplement what we know about the lives of early Mesopotamians. Their cities had many taverns and wine shops, often run by women proprietors, possibly attesting to the city-dwellers' enjoyment of spirits and a convivial atmosphere. Because disease was believed to have supernatural origins, Mesopotamian medicine included magic as well as treatment with potions and diet. A doctor might prescribe an incantation as part of his therapy. Magicians or exorcists offered medical treatment that depended primarily on spells and on interpreting signs such as the patient's dreams or hallucinations. Contaminated drinking water caused many illnesses because sewage disposal was rudimentary (as in most cities until the twentieth century). Relief from the odors and crowding of the streets could be found in the open spaces set aside for city parks. The oldest known map in the world, an inscribed clay tablet showing the outlines of the Babylonian city of Nippur about 1500 B.C., shows a substantial area designated for this purpose.

Mesopotamian achievements in mathematics and astronomy had a profound effect that endures to this day. Mathematical specialists knew how to employ algebraic processes to solve complex problems, and they could derive the roots of numbers. They discovered the system of place-value notation, in which the quantity indicated by a numeral is affected by its place in a sequence. We have also inherited from Mesopotamia the system of reckoning based on powers of sixty that we use in the division of hours and minutes and degrees of a circle. The Mesopotamians used both this sexagesimal system and a decimal system of numeration. Their expertise in recording the paths of the stars and planets across the night sky probably arose from

their desire to make predictions about the future based on the astrological belief that the movement of celestial bodies directly affected human life. Astrology never lost its popularity in Mesopotamia. But the charts and tables compiled by Mesopotamian stargazers laid a basis for scientific astronomy.

The centralized Babylonian administration forged by Hammurabi failed not long after his death, and a decentralized political system characterized Babylonia until about 1460 B.C. At that time the Kassites once again unified it. Some Kassites had first come to Babylon as agricultural workers, but others invaded. The centralized political system the Kassites created endured for 250 years, longer than any other Babylonian dynasty. The Kassites assimilated much of the Mesopotamian culture. Perhaps their willingness to adopt Mesopotamian customs helped prevent revolts by making their rule seem less onerous.

To the northwest of Mesopotamia other important kingdoms thrived in Syria and Anatolia in the middle centuries of the second millennium B.C. Our scanty sources reveal little about the powerful kingdom of Mitanni or the Hurrian people who constituted the majority of its population. From about 1550 to 1350 B.C., Mitanni dominated the region around the northern reaches of the Euphrates River. Then the Hittite king Suppiluliumas I forced it to become a subservient ally of his kingdom in Anatolia. The Hittites, who spoke an Indo-European language but took their method of writing from the Mesopotamians, probably came from the Caucasus area between the Black and Caspian Seas into the highland plateau of central Anatolia and wrested control from the indigenous population by about 1750 B.C. Their capital, Hattusas, grew into an expansive city with straight streets, huge palaces, massive defensive walls and towers of stone, and many sculptures of animals, warriors, and the royal rulers. The Hittite monarchy maintained its rule by forging personal alliances—cemented by marriages and oaths of loyalty—with the noble families of the kingdom. Judging from their appearance in documents, royal letters, and foreign treaties, Hittite queens apparently played a prominent role in public life. Hittite public religion combined worship of deities inherited from the original Anatolian population with those of Indo-European extraction. The king served as high priest, and his ritual purity was paramount. His drinking water had to be strained, for example; once when a hair was found in his water jug, the water carrier was executed.

In the periods during which ties with the nobility remained strong and the kingdom therefore preserved its unity, the Hittite kings aggressively campaigned to extend their power. A Hittite army raided as far as Babylon in 1595 B.C., weakening the Amorite kingdom and contributing to its eventual replacement by the Kassites. Hittites eventually dominated Anatolia and Syria, and in the battle of Kadesh about 1285 B.C. the Hittite king Muwatallis prevented the Egyptian king Ramesses II from recovering Egypt's Syrian possessions. The economic strength of the Hittite kingdom depended on its effective defense of the international trade routes by which it secured essential raw materials, especially metals. Scholars no longer accept the once popular idea that the Hittites owed their imperialistic success to a special knowledge of making weapons from iron, although Hittite craftsmen did smelt iron from which they made ceremonial implements. (Not until after 1200 B.C.—at the end of the Hittite kingdom—did iron objects become common in the Mediterranean world.) The Hittite army did excel in the use of chariots and perhaps this skill gave them the edge in their evident military success. Nevertheless, the unified Hittite kingdom fell in the twelfth century B.C. in the catastrophes that struck eastern Mediterranean societies at that time.

The New Kingdom in Egypt

In Egypt the social order continued to depend on the flooding Nile to bring prosperity and the ability of the royal family to build political unity. The famine and civil unrest of the First Intermediate Period (2181–2050 B.C.) thwarted attempts by the princes of Thebes in Upper Egypt to reestablish political unity. King Mentuhotep II finally reunited Egypt in the Middle Kingdom (2050–1786 B.C.). Gradually the monarchs of the Middle Kingdom restored the divine authority their Old Kingdom predecessors had lost. They pushed the boundaries of Egypt farther to the south and expanded contacts to the northeast in ancient Palestine and Syria and to the northwest in Crete. In the midst of all this activity, the Egyptians retained a warm pride in their homeland, as the vigorous literature of this period demonstrates. The main character of the Middle Kingdom tale *The Story of Sinuhe,* for example, reported that he lived a luxurious life while in Syria: "It was a good land. . . . Figs were in it, and grapes. . . . Bread was made for me as daily fare, wine as daily provision, cooked meat and roast fowl." But the point of the tale was his eagerness to come home to Egypt.

By the Second Intermediate Period (1786–1567 B.C.), nature had again undermined the kings' hold on a unified Egypt: famines caused by irregular Nile floods weakened the population. A people, whose real name is unknown but whom the Egyptians called Hyksos (meaning "Rulers of Foreign Lands"), took advantage of this debilitation and invaded Egypt. These Semites from the Syria-Palestine region had taken over Lower Egypt by around 1670 B.C. Recent archaeological discoveries have emphasized the role of the Hyksos settlers in transplanting elements of their culture to Egypt. These interlopers introduced such innovations as new musical instruments, the olive, and the war chariot and increased Egypt's contact with other states in the Near East.

Eventually, the leaders of Thebes fought once again to reunite their land. Amosis finally won their war of liberation from the Hyksos around 1567 B.C., initiating the New Kingdom (1567–1085 B.C.). The New Kingdom kings, known as pharaohs, no longer brooked local political rivals, such as the provincial governors, although they were prudent enough to acknowledge other powerful monarchs in the world. In fact, the New Kingdom pharaohs regularly exchanged letters on matters of state with their "brother kings," as they called them, elsewhere in the Near East. They also fought campaigns abroad. Wars to the south in Nubia and the Sudan won them access to gold and other precious materials, while the raids into Palestine and Syria by Thutmosis I (died c. 1512 B.C.) gave notice of the Egyptian interest in conquering the coastal lands of the eastern Mediterranean. These fighting pharaohs of Egypt presented themselves as the incarnations of a warrior god, but they also practiced the wiles of diplomacy. Thutmosis III, for example, forged defensive alliances with both the Babylonians and the Hittites in the fifteenth century B.C.

Massive riches supported the power of the New Kingdom pharaohs. Egyptian traders exchanged fine goods such as ivory for foreign luxury goods, such as Mycenaean painted pottery.

The Egyptian kings displayed their wealth most conspicuously in the enormous sums they spent to build temples of stone. Nothing the people of Europe and the Aegean constructed in this period remotely compared to these structures. Queen Hatshepsut of the fifteenth century B.C. renewed this tradition with the great complex at Deir el Bahri near Thebes, which includes a temple dedicated to the god Amon and to her own funerary cult. After the death of her husband, Thutmosis II, Hatshepsut proclaimed herself "female king" as co-regent with her young stepson Thutmosis III. By doing so she shrewdly sidestepped Egyptian ideology, which made no provision for a queen to reign in her own right. The relief sculpture she commissioned to portray the expedition she dispatched to gather myrrh in Punt (probably Somalia, southeast of Egypt) faithfully records the characteristics of the people, flora, and fauna of this land renowned for its spices. This work of art is the first recorded anthropological report of a foreign culture.

As fellow divine beings, the pharaohs had a deep personal interest in the standing of Egypt's legions of traditional gods. The various gods of the Egyptian pantheon oversaw all aspects of life and death, with particular emphasis on the afterlife. The cults of the main gods, who were honored with glorious temples, were integral in the religious life of both the general population and the leaders. The principal festivals of the gods, for example, offered occasions for public celebration. A calendar based on the moon governed the dates of religious ceremonies. (The Egyptians also developed a calendar for administrative and fiscal purposes that had 365 days, divided into 12 months of 30 days each, with the extra 5 days added before the start of the next year. Our modern calendar is based on this civil calendar.)

The New Kingdom pharaohs promoted the state god Amen-Re of Thebes until he overshadowed the other gods. This Theban cult incorporated and subordinated the other gods without denying either their existence or the continued importance of their priests. But the pharaoh Amenhophis IV, known as Akhenaten, went a step further during his reign in the fourteenth century B.C. when he began to tout the cult of Aten, who represented the shining disk of the sun. This new cult excluded the other deities and their supporters, although it perhaps should not be called pure monotheism

Queen Hatshepsut of Egypt
This statue shows Hatshepsut dressed in the distinctive garb of a pharaoh to demonstrate her claim to rule. She had the statue placed in a temple she built outside Thebes.

The Contents of King Tut's Tomb
Egyptian royalty packed their tombs with everything they would need in the afterlife.
Over the years thieves broke into most Egyptian tombs, but Tutankhamun's escaped
detection until an achaeologist opened it in 1922.

(the worship of only one god) because Akhenaten seems not to have denied the divine associations of the king, and the population presumably went on venerating the ruler as before. Chiseling the names of the other, now disgraced deities out of inscriptions and building a new capital for his god at modern Amarna, Akhenaten neglected practical affairs as he obsessively tried to force his new version of official religion on recalcitrant priests and other followers of the traditional cults. He also attempted to imbue royal Egyptian art with more realistic portraiture, even allowing court artists to reveal his own angular face and dumpy physique. Ultimately, his failure to attend to government business left financial distress and a weakened defense as legacies to his successors, such as the boy king Tutankhamun. Akhenaten's religion did not survive his reign.

The pharaohs following Tutankhamun in the thirteenth and twelfth centuries B.C. had their hands full protecting their territories outside

Egypt. They faced heavy competition for control of Palestine and Syria from the Hittites. Pharaoh Ramesses II finally settled the issue by making a sophisticated treaty with the Hittite king around 1269 B.C. and then marrying the king's daughter. Remarkably, both Egyptian and Hittite copies of this landmark in diplomatic history survive. In it the Egyptians and Hittites pledged to be "at peace and brothers forever." Ramesses II continued the pharaonic building tradition with a passion. Fully half the temples remaining in Egypt today come from his reign. The architecture of Egypt's rectangular buildings of stone studded with columns served as a model for the style of the later temples of Greece.

Archaeology does not clearly reveal whether the prosperity of the New Kingdom rulers trickled down to the general free population. The rhythm of the lives of most ordinary people still revolved around the relation between their labor and the annual inundations of the Nile. During the months when the river stayed between its banks they worked their fields along the water's course, rising very early in the morning to avoid the searing heat. Their obligation to work on royal building projects came due when the flooding halted agricultural tasks and freed them to move to workers' quarters erected next to the building sites. Although slaves became more common as household workers in the New Kingdom, mostly free workers doing corvée service labored on the mammoth royal construction projects of this period. Surviving texts reveal that they lightened the burden of their labors by singing songs and telling adventure stories.

Ordinary people devoted much attention to deities outside the royal cults, to gods they hoped would protect them in their daily lives. They venerated Bes, for instance, a dwarf with the features of a lion, as a protector of the household and carved his image on amulets, beds, headrests, and the handles of mirrors. People also continued to spend much time and effort on preparing for the next life. Those who could afford it arranged to have their bodies mummified and their tombs outfitted with all the paraphernalia needed for the journey to their new existence. An essential piece of equipment for a corpse was a copy of the *Book of the Dead,* a collection of magic spells to ward off dangers and ensure a successful verdict in the divine judgment that people believed every soul had to pass to avoid a second death. In the underworld, the dead underwent a mystical union with the god Osiris.

Magic played a large role in their lives, too, as they sought spells and charms from professional magicians to seek relief from disease and injury, ward off demons, smooth the often rocky course of love, and exact revenge on enemies. As with the homage they paid minor deities, these personal dealings with the supernatural probably meant more to their everyday lives than the cults of the major divinities.

Later pharaohs of the New Kingdom had less opportunity for building projects because they had to spend much of their time fighting foreign invaders from all directions. During the twelfth century B.C. this pressure from outside eventually overwhelmed even the heroics of commanders such as the warrior pharaoh Ramesses III. Once again the centralization of authority that gave Egypt its political and military strength dissipated.

Hebrew Origins

The religious rather than the political history of this Semitic people profoundly affected the roots of Western civilization. The enduring influence of the Hebrews (or Israelites, the descendants of Jacob, who was also called Israel) has stemmed above all from the impact of the book that eventually became the Hebrews' sacred scripture—the Hebrew Bible, known to Christians as the Old Testament—on Judaism, Christianity, and Islam. Unfortunately, neither the opening books of the Hebrew Bible nor archaeological research provides a clear picture of the origins of the Hebrews. A reconstruction of the earliest period of Hebrew history depends on limited and controversial evidence.

The Hebrew Bible reports that the patriarch Abraham and his followers left the Mesopotamian city of Ur to migrate to "the land of Canaan" (ancient Palestine). Because other Semitic peoples, such as the Amorites and the Aramaeans, are known to have moved throughout the Fertile Crescent in the early second millennium, the story of Abraham's journey perhaps reflects this era and can be dated about 1800 B.C. When the Hebrews finally reached Palestine (at the southeast corner of the Mediterranean Sea), they continued their traditional existence as seminomads, tending flocks of animals and living in temporary tent settlements. They occasionally planted barley or wheat for a season or two, but they would then move to new pasturage; they never settled down or formed a political state in this period. Political and military power in Canaan resided in the local city-states, kingdoms, and tribes already established there.

Abraham's son Isaac led his people to live in various locations in keeping with the demands of a pastoral way of life and also to avoid further disputes with local Canaanites over grazing rights. Isaac's son Jacob, the story continues, moved to Egypt late in life; Jacob's son, Joseph, brought his father and other relatives there to escape famine in Canaan. Joseph had used his intelligence and charisma to rise to an important position in the Egyptian administration. The Biblical story of the movement of some Hebrews to Egypt represents a crucial event in the early history of the Hebrews; it may reflect a time when drought forced some of the Hebrews, seeking water to save their flocks, to migrate gradually from southwest Asia into the Nile delta of Egypt. They probably migrated during

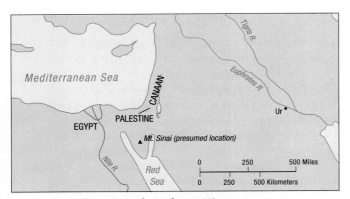

Locations in Early Hebrew History

the seventeenth or sixteenth century B.C. But unlike the Hyksos, who invaded Egypt, these Hebrew immigrants lacked military might. Although they apparently lived peacefully in Egypt for a long time, by the thirteenth century B.C. the pharaohs had conscripted male Hebrews into slave labor gangs for farming and for construction work on the large building projects.

Toward the end of the Bronze Age, groups of Hebrews left Egypt, part of widespread social foment in the Near East that also included displaced people from the cities of Canaan. The Hebrew Bible tells this story in the Biblical book Exodus. The Hebrew deity Yahweh (incorrectly called Jehovah in Christian tradition) instructed Moses to lead the Hebrews out of bondage in Egypt. Yahweh then sent ten plagues to compel the pharaoh to free the Hebrews. When the pharaoh, who may have been Ramesses II in the second half of the thirteenth century B.C., tried to recapture the fleeing Hebrews, Yahweh miraculously parted the Red Sea to allow the Hebrews to escape. When the pharaoh's army tried to follow, the water swirled back together, drowning the Egyptians.

The Biblical narrative of the Exodus then moves to a seminal moment in ancient Hebrew history: the formalizing of a covenant between the Hebrews and their deity, who reveals himself to Moses on Mt. Sinai in the desert northeast of Egypt. The covenant consisted of an agreement between the Hebrews and their deity that, in return for the Hebrew's promise to worship him as their only divinity and to live by his laws, he would make them his chosen people and lead them into a promised land of safety and prosperity. This

binding agreement between the Hebrew people and their deity built on the earlier pledges of the patriarchs Abraham, Isaac, and Jacob, all of which demanded human obedience to divine law and promised punishment for unrighteousness. The Hebrew Bible sets forth the religious and moral code the Hebrews had to follow both in the Ten Commandments (found in 20 Exodus and 5 Deuteronomy), which required the worship of Yahweh; the honoring of parents; and abstention from murder, adultery, theft, lying, and covetousness; and in the other laws described in the Pentateuch, or Torah (the first five books of the Hebrew Bible).

Aside from the Ten Commandments, most of the Pentateuchal laws shared the traditional form of Mesopotamian laws: if someone does a certain thing to another person, then the following punishment is imposed on the perpetrator. They also dealt with similar issues, such as property rights, and even had much content in common with Mesopotamian laws, such as those of Hammurabi. For example, both Hammurabi's laws and Hebrew law considered negligence in the case of the owner of an ox whose animal had gored another person. The owner was penalized only if he had been warned about his beast's tendency to gore, yet done nothing to restrain it. Also like Hammurabi's laws, Hebrew law expressed an interest in the welfare of the poor as well as the rich; but in addition it secured protection for the lower classes and people without power, such as strangers, widows, and orphans. The same law applied to all without regard to their position in the social hierarchy, and the severity of punishments did not depend on a person's social class. Hebrew law furthermore did not allow vicarious punishment—a Mesopotamian tradition specifying, for example, that a rapist's wife be raped or that the son of a builder whose faulty work caused the death of another's son be killed. Women and children had certain legal protection, although their rights were less extensive than men's. For example, wives had less freedom to divorce their husbands than husbands had to divorce their wives, much as in the laws of Hammurabi. Crimes against property never carried the death penalty, as they frequently did in other Near Eastern societies. Hebrew law also protected slaves against flagrant mistreatment by their masters. Slaves who lost an eye or even a tooth from a beating were to be freed.

Like free people, slaves enjoyed the right to rest on the Sabbath, the holy day of the seven-day Hebrew week.

Because the earliest parts of the Hebrew Bible were composed in about 950 B.C., long after the Exodus, their account of the creation of the covenant and the Hebrew laws deals with a distant, undocumented time. Many uncertainties persist in our understanding of the process by which the Hebrews acquired their distinctive religion and way of life, but it seems clear that both took much longer to evolve than the Biblical account describes. The early Hebrews probably worshiped a variety of gods, including spirits believed to reside in natural objects such as trees and stones. Yahweh may have originally been the deity of the tribe of Midian, to which Moses' father-in-law belonged. The form of the covenant with Yahweh conformed to the ancient Near Eastern tradition of treaties between a superior and subordinates, but its content differed from other ancient Near Eastern religions because it made him the exclusive deity of his people. In the time of Moses, Yahweh religion was not yet the pure monotheism it would later become because it did not deny the existence of other gods. Rather, it was monolatry (worshiping one god only). Because in the ensuing centuries some Hebrews worshiped other gods as well, such as Baal of Canaan, it seems that the covenant with Yahweh and fully formed Hebrew monotheism did not emerge until well after 1000 B.C.

The Hebrews who fled from Egypt with Moses made their way back to Canaan, but they were still liable to attack from the Egyptian army. The first documentary reference to their presence in Palestine comes from an inscribed monument erected by the pharaoh Merneptah in the late thirteenth century B.C. to commemorate his victory in a military expedition there. The returning Hebrew tribes joined the Hebrews who had remained in Canaan and had somehow carved out territory for themselves there. The twelve Hebrew tribes remained ethnically, politically, and even religiously diverse from 1200 to 1000 B.C. and lacked a strong central authority. In the twelfth century B.C., they began to suffer depredations from the attacks of raiders from outside Canaan. The presence of these raiders testified to the violent disruptions that had begun to afflict a wide area of the ancient Mediterranean and Near East.

Regional Disruptions

A state of political equilibrium, in which kings corresponded with one another and traders traveled all over the area, characterized the Mediterranean and Near Eastern world of the early thirteenth century B.C. By about 1200 B.C., however, hard times had begun to hit not only small, loosely organized groups like the Hebrews in Canaan, but also major political states. The New Kingdom in Egypt had fragmented; foreign invaders had destroyed the powerful Hittite kingdom in Anatolia; Mesopotamia underwent a period of political turmoil; and the palace societies of the Aegean had disintegrated. Explaining all the catastrophes that occurred in the Mediterranean region from about 1200 to 1000 B.C. remains one of the most difficult puzzles in ancient history.

Egyptian and Hittite records document foreign invasions in this period, some of them from the sea. According to his own account, the pharaoh Ramesses III around 1182 B.C. defeated a fearsome coalition of seaborne invaders from the north, who had fought their way to the edge of Egypt:

> *All at once the peoples were on the move, dispersed in war. . . . No land could stand before their arms. . . . They laid their hands upon the lands as far as the circuit of the earth, their hearts confident and trusting: "Our plans will succeed!" . . . Those who reached my frontier, their seed is not, their heart and their soul are finished forever and ever. . . . They were dragged in, enclosed, and prostrated on the beach, killed, and made into heaps from head to tail.*

These sea peoples, as they are called, comprised many different groups. Some had been mercenary soldiers in the armies of the rulers they then turned against. Some came from far away to raid. And some were Mycenaean warriors who had been displaced by the economic troubles of their homeland, probably looking for more prosperous places to settle. What evidence we have for the history of the sea peoples indicates that no one, unified group pillaged the eastern Mediterranean in a single tidal wave of violence, but rather that many disparate bands wracked the region. A chain reaction of attacks and flights in a recurring and expanding cycle put even more bands on the move. In the end all this turbulence revised the demographic map of the Mediterranean. The reasons for all this commotion remain mysterious, but its dire consequences for Near Eastern and Greek civilization are clear.

The once mighty Hittite kingdom fell about 1200 B.C. when raiders finally cut its supply lines of raw materials and invaders penetrated its borders. The capital city, Hattusas, was razed and never reinhabited, although smaller Neo-Hittite principalities survived for another five hundred years before succumbing to the armies of the Neo-Assyrian kingdom.

Egypt's New Kingdom repelled the sea peoples only through great military effort; the danger at sea created by these raiders left the Egyptian international trade network throughout the Mediterranean in shambles. Power struggles between the pharaoh and the priests also undercut the centralized authority of the monarchy. By the middle of the eleventh century B.C., Egypt had shrunk to its old territorial core along the banks of the Nile. Egypt's credit was ruined along with its international stature. When an eleventh-century B.C. Theban temple official traveled to Phoenicia to buy cedar for a ceremonial boat, the city's ruler demanded cash in advance. Although the Egyptian monarchy continued for centuries after the New Kingdom, continued power struggles between pharaohs and priests, combined with frequent attacks from abroad, prevented the reestablishment of centralized authority. No Egyptian dynasty was ever again an active and aggressive international power.

The calamities of this time also affected the copper-rich island of Cyprus and the flourishing cities along the eastern coast of the Mediterranean Sea. The Greeks later called these coastal peoples the Phoenicians (from the Greek *phoenix* meaning "shellfish"). The inhabitants of cities like Ugarit on the coast of Syria thrived on international maritime commerce and enjoyed a lively polyglot cultural milieu. Although a catastrophic attack by the sea peoples overwhelmed Ugarit and other areas of this region, one of its most brilliant accomplishments survived. In this crossroads of cultures the first alphabet had been developed from about 1700 to 1500 B.C.; its later form eventually became the base of the ancient Greek and Roman alphabets and hence of modern Western alphabets. Using the letters of an alphabet was simpler and more flexible than working with the other writing systems of the

ancient Near East. An alphabetic system with pictures that stood for only one sound had also begun to develop in Egypt around 1600 to 1550 B.C. to write foreign words and names.

Raiders from the north, called Philistines, settled in Palestine and attacked the Canaanites and the Hebrews repeatedly in the eleventh century B.C. (The term *Palestine* was perhaps later derived from the word *Philistine*.) The Hebrew tribes appointed military leaders and legal authorities called judges in an attempt to unify their loose confederation during this period of near anarchy. One of these judges, Deborah, led an Israelite coalition force to victory over a Canaanite army.

The turmoil of this period reached far to the east and to the west of the eastern end of the Mediterranean. A scarcity of sources obscures the course of events in Mesopotamia, but we do know the Kassite kingdom in Babylonia collapsed, and the Assyrians were confined to their homeland. Invasions by the Semitic peoples known as Aramaeans and Chaldeans seem to have devastated western Asia and Syria. The Aramaeans established several small independent states in Syria, foreshadowing their future importance in that area and the later popularity of their language as an international tongue in the Near East.

The Mycenaeans had reached their pinnacle after 1400 B.C. The enormous domed tomb at Mycenae, called the Treasury of Atreus, belongs to this period. Its elaborately decorated facade and soaring roof testify to the confidence the Mycenaean warrior princes had in their power. The last phase of the extensive palace at Pylos on the west coast of the Peloponnese also dates to this time. It boasted glorious wall paintings, storerooms bursting with food, and a royal bathroom with a built-in tub and intricate plumbing. But these prosperous Mycenaeans inhabited a violent world. Ominous signs of danger first appeared during this period of affluence. Linear B tablets from Pylos record the disposition of troops to guard this unwalled site around 1200 B.C. The palace inhabitants of eastern Greece, such as those at Mycenae and nearby Tiryns, now constructed such massive stone walls that the later Greeks thought giants had built them. These fortifications could have protected these coastal palaces against attackers from the sea, who could have been either outsiders or other seafaring Greeks. But the wall around the in-

THE FOUNDATIONS OF CIVILIZATION IN THE WEST

Mesopotamia and Anatolia	Old and New Kingdom Egypt	Europe and the Aegean
c. 3500 B.C. First cities established; writing developed in Sumer; copper metallurgy already known	**c. 3100–3000 B.C.** King Menes unites Upper and Lower Egypt	**c. 5000 B.C.** Substantial houses built in many locations
c. 3000 B.C. Sumerians dominate; the wheel invented for vehicles	**2686–2181 B.C.** Old Kingdom	**c. 4000–3000 B.C.** Copper metallurgy under way in eastern Europe
c. 3000–2500 B.C. Bronze metallurgy under way	**c. 2650 B.C.** Imhotep builds the first pyramid for King Djoser	**c. 3000 B.C.** Stone temples constructed on Malta
c. 2600 B.C. King Gilgamesh rules the city of Uruk	**c. 2575 B.C.** Great Pyramid of Cheops constructed at Giza	**c. 3000–2000 B.C.** Mediterranean polyculture developed
c. 2350 B.C. Sargon establishes the Akkadian empire	**c.1670–1567 B.C.** The Hyksos dominate Lower Egypt	**c. 2200 B.C.** Earliest Cretan palaces constructed
2112–2095 B.C. King Ur-Nammu founds the Third Dynasty of Ur and promulgates set of written laws	**1567–1085 B.C.** New Kingdom	**c. 2100–1900 B.C.** Final phase of construction of Stonehenge
c. 1900 B.C. Private enterprise under way in Assyria	**Early fifteenth century B.C.** Reign of Queen Hatshepsut	**c. 1500–1450 B.C.** Earliest Mycenaean *tholos* tombs built
c. 1800 B.C. Abraham and his family migrate from Ur to Palestine	**Early fourteenth century B.C.** Reign of Akhenaten	**c. 1370 B.C.** Palace of Knossos destroyed
c. 1792–1750 B.C. Reign of Hammurabi, king of Babylon	**c. 1285 B.C.** Battle of Ramesses II with the Hittites at Kadesh in Syria	**c. 1300–1200 B.C.** High point of Mycenaean palace culture
c. 1750 B.C. Hittites begin to establish a kingdom in Anatolia	**c. 1269 B.C.** Treaty of Ramesses II with the Hittites	**c. 1200 B.C.** Disturbances across the Aegean region
c. 1200 B.C. Fall of the Hittite kingdom	**Early or mid-thirteenth century B.C.** Exodus of the Hebrews from Egypt	**c. 1000 B.C.** Destruction of Mycenaean palace culture completed
	c. 1182 B.C. Ramesses III turns back the sea peoples	

land palace at Gla in central Greece, where no foreign pirates could reach, confirms that above all the Mycenaeans had to defend themselves against other Mycenaeans. Never united in one state, the Mycenaeans by the late thirteenth century B.C. fought each other at least as much as they did foreigners.

Internal turmoil and the cataclysmic effects of major earthquakes offer the most plausible explanation of the destruction of the palaces of mainland Greece in the period after 1200 B.C. Jealous rulers regularly battled each other for status and gain. Near constant warfare burdened the elaborate economic balance of the redistributive economies of the palaces, and hindered recovery

from the damage apparently caused by earthquakes. The eventual failure of the palace economies devastated many Mycenaeans, who depended on this redistributive system for their subsistence. The later Greeks remembered an invasion of Dorians (Greek speakers from the north) as the reason for the disaster, but the Dorians who did move to the south most likely came in groups too small to cause such damage by themselves. Indeed, small-scale movements of people characterized this era. Bands of warriors with no prospects at home swarmed the eastern Mediterranean around 1200 B.C.

The damage done to Greek society by the dissolution of the redistributive economies of Mycenae took centuries to repair. Only Athens seems to have escaped wholesale disaster. In fact, Athenians of the fifth century B.C., prided themselves on their unique status among the peoples of classical Greece: "sprung from the soil" of their homeland, they had not been forced to emigrate in the turmoil that engulfed the rest of Greece in the twelfth and eleventh centuries B.C. Other Greeks were less fortunate. Uprooted from their homes, they wandered abroad in search of new territory to settle. The Ionian Greeks, who later inhabited the central coast of western Anatolia, emigrated from the mainland during this period. To an outside observer, Greek society at the end of the Bronze Age might have seemed destined for irreversible economic and social decline, even oblivion. The next chapter shows how wrong this prediction would have been.

CONCLUSION

The basis of our modern way of life arose from the technological and social changes associated with the Neolithic revolution, which began over ten thousand years ago. Over the course of many centuries, hunter-gatherer society transformed into a more settled style of life. People in the Near East learned to farm and domesticate animals for food; such an agricultural system could sustain a growing population and support even more people to work the land. As the knowledge of agricultural technology slowly spread from the Fertile Crescent to the western lands of Europe around 4000 B.C., human society developed well-defined social hierarchies. Marked social differentiation corresponding to differences in wealth and power had now become a standard in Western society, as had a patriarchal social system, in which men dominated political and economic life and exerted power over women in most realms of society.

Beginning about 3500 B.C. the first cities began to develop, in Mesopotamia. Although local conditions inhibited the emergence of cities in some areas, such as Europe, in this early period, societies structured more centrally grew up outside southwestern Asia, especially in Egypt along the fertile banks of the Nile River. These changes started a general trend toward economic specialization and political centralization. The knowledge of writing, which first emerged in the Near East, aided these developments. Written law codes testify to the complex political and legal organization of Mesopotamian society. Mesopotamian and Egyptian accomplishments in art, architecture, astronomy, calculations of calendars, mathematics, and medicine influenced later developments, just as the mythology and the religion of the Hebrews inspired later peoples.

Prehistoric societies in Europe may have been influenced by an influx of Indo-European peoples. The peoples of prehistoric Europe developed technologies, such as megalithic architecture and metallurgy, independently of similar developments in Egypt and the other lands of the Near East. The need to secure raw materials for metallurgy and other commodities not available locally led to the establishment of trade connections throughout the European and Mediterranean worlds. Competition for resources and the desire to appropriate the prosperity of others led to warfare and political takeovers, especially in Mesopotamia and the Aegean. In this latter region, violent strife of this kind probably led to the domination of Minoan civilization by the Mycenaeans. The Mycenaeans lost their civilization because of war and damage from earthquakes. After 1200 B.C. the peace, prosperity, and international trade of the Near East and Greece were shattered during a mysterious period of history characterized by the violent wanderings of raiders like the sea peoples.

Suggestions for Further Reading

Source Materials

Dalley, Stephanie. *Myths from Mesopotamia: Creation, the Flood, Gilgamesh, and Others.* 1989. New, authoritative translations of Mesopotamian myths.

Grayson, A. K., and D. B. Redford, eds. *Papyrus and Tablet.* 1973. A topically arranged selection of translated texts from ancient Egypt and Mesopotamia.

Pritchard, James B. *The Ancient Near East in Pictures Relating to the Old Testament.* 2d ed. 1969. An invaluable anthology that contains many fascinating pictures depicting ancient Near Eastern culture. Comes with a supplement.

———. *Ancient Near Eastern Texts Relating to the Old Testament.* 3d ed. 1969. An indispensable anthology of the literary and documentary evidence for ancient Near Eastern culture. A useful supplement also included.

Interpretive Studies

Aldred, Cyril. *The Egyptians,* Rev. ed. 1984. An illustrated introduction to ancient Egyptian history and culture. (Generally, Aldred's dates for events in Egyptian history have been used in this chapter.)

Baines, J., and J. Malek. *Atlas of Ancient Egypt.* 1980. A superbly illustrated introduction to ancient Egyptian history and culture.

Chadwick, John. *The Mycenaean World.* 1976. A clear introduction to Bronze Age Greece by an authority on Linear B.

Champion, Timothy, Clive Gamble, Stephen Shennan, and Alasdair Whittle. *Prehistoric Europe.* 1984. A demanding presentation of archaeological evidence.

Childe, V. Gordon. *The Dawn of European Civilization.* 6th ed. 1958. A classic work by the most famous "diffusionist." For an excellent discussion of the significance of Childe's work, see Ruth Tringham, "V. Gordon Childe 25 Years After: His Relevance for the Archaeology of the Eighties," *Journal of Field Archaeology* 10 (1983): 85–100.

Ehrenberg, Margaret. *Women in Prehistory.* 1989. A study of women's important contributions to the development of agriculture and of their social status in Europe from the Paleolithic Age to the Iron Age.

Frankfort, Henri, H. A. Frankfort, John A. Wilson, Thorkild Jacobsen, and William A. Irwin. *The Intellectual Adventure of Ancient Man: An Essay on Speculative Thought in the Ancient Near East.* 1946. Reissued with updated bibliography, 1977. Lectures on the myth and thought of the ancient Egyptians, Mesopotamians, and Hebrews.

Gimbutas, Marija. *The Goddesses and Gods of Old Europe, 6500–3500 B.C.: Myths and Cult Images.* New ed. 1984. An updated presentation of the author's views on the matrifocal nature of Neolithic European culture.

James, T. G. H. *An Introduction to Ancient Egypt.* 1979. An excellent guide to the diverse history of ancient Egypt.

Knapp, A. Bernard. *The History and Culture of Ancient Western Asia and Egypt.* 1988. A concise, comprehensive introduction covering prehistoric times to the fourth century B.C.

Kramer, Samuel Noah. *The Sumerians: Their History, Culture, and Character.* 1963. Provides extensive coverage of Sumerian culture.

Lerner, Gerda. *The Creation of Patriarchy.* 1986. A provocative survey of patriarchal ancient civilizations by a feminist historian.

Lesko, Barbara, ed. *Women's Earliest Records from Ancient Egypt and Western Asia.* 1989. A collection of wide-ranging articles and responses on the history of women in ancient Egypt, Mesopotamia, and Israel.

Macqueen, J. G. *The Hittites.* Rev. and enl. ed. 1986. A fast-moving survey of this complex kingdom.

Miller, J. Maxwell, and John H. Hayes. *A History of Ancient Israel and Judah.* 1986. A survey from the end of the second millennium B.C. until the sixth century B.C., with valuable discussions of the difficulties in understanding the earliest history of the Hebrews.

Oates, Joan. *Babylon.* Rev. ed. 1986. Introduces the history and archaeology of Babylonia from the time of Sargon until after Alexander the Great.

Oppenheim, A. Leo. *Ancient Mesopotamia: Portrait of a Dead Civilization.* Rev. ed. completed by Erica Reiner. 1977. A standard work with a helpful appendix on chronology.

Piggott, Stuart. *The Earliest Wheeled Transport from the Atlantic Coast to the Caspian Sea.* 1983. A full treatment of the "technological explosion" that brought to Europe the invention of the wheel and its use in transport, and the domestication of the horse.

Redford, Donald B. *Akhenaten: The Heretic King.* 1984. A revised look at this maverick pharaoh and his monotheistic religion.

Renfrew, Colin. *Before Civilization: The Radiocarbon Revolution and Prehistoric Europe.* 1979. An introduction to the new dating techniques, arguing strongly against the diffusionist explanation of change in prehistoric Europe.

Roux, Georges. *Ancient Iraq.* 2d ed. 1980. Surveys Mesopotamian history from Paleolithic times to the Greco-Roman period.

Sanders, N. K. *The Sea Peoples: Warriors of the Ancient*

Mediterranean, 1250–1150 B.C. Rev. ed. 1985. Reviews the different areas affected by these disparate groups of raiders.

Sarna, Nahum M. *Exploring Exodus: The Heritage of Biblical Israel.* 1986. An interpretative discussion of the period of the Covenant in Hebrew history.

Tigay, Jeffrey H. *The Evolution of the Gilgamesh Epic.* 1982. A comprehensive history of the versions of the Mesopotamian epic poem about Gilgamesh.

Tringham, Ruth. *Hunters, Fishers, and Farmers of Eastern Europe, 6000–3000 B.C.* 1971. Investigates the causes of cultural change, considering both diffusion and indigenous invention.

Vermeule, Emily. *Greece in the Bronze Age.* 1972. A stimulating treatment of this complex subject.

Willetts, R. F. *The Civilization of Ancient Crete.* 1977. Cretan history from earliest times until the eve of the classical period.

According to a story told by the Greek writer Plutarch, around 594 B.C. a foreign king touring Greece visited Solon, the most renowned lawmaker of ancient Athens. At the time, Solon was drawing up a new set of laws at the request of his fellow Athenians, who hoped a revised law code would end the social and political turmoil their self-governing community of free citizens was then experiencing. When the king discovered what Solon was doing, he burst into laughter, saying to the lawmaker, "Do you actually believe your fellow citizens' injustice and greed can be kept in check this way? Written laws are more like spiders' webs than anything else: they tie up the weak and the small fry who get stuck in them, but the rich and the powerful tear them to shreds." Solon replied, "People abide by their agreements when neither side has anything to gain by breaking them. I am writing laws for the Athenians in such a way that they will clearly see it is to everyone's advantage to obey the laws rather than to break them."

This story, like many anecdotes about conversations from the past, may not be historically accurate. But whether or not this particular conversation ever took place is not important. Solon certainly existed and indeed revised the laws of Athens. The point of the story is that it reflects the Greeks' attempts to create systems of law that applied equally to all the free men of the community. In Solon's time the question of whether written laws would promote justice and peace in Athenian society remained unanswered. The earlier political systems of the Near East, though sometimes allowing certain prominent male citizens outside the royal family to participate, had relied on the strong, centralized authority of monarchs.

2

New Paths for Western Civilization, c. 1000–500 B.C.

A Spartan Dancer
This bronze statuette shows the graceful style of Spartan art before it faded away as Sparta developed its regimented way of life, one of the many significant changes in Greek society that took place in the Archaic period.

Solon's Athens exemplified a different type of community that had begun to emerge in Greece around 750 B.C.: self-governing city-states.

Greek city-states contrasted significantly with earlier political and social institutions. They had no traditional monarchy, which still prevailed, for example, in Assyria and other contemporary societies of the Near East; they extended the rights of ordinary citizens, guaranteeing the community's free males, poor as well as rich, a role in state policy making as well as new legal and political rights, and granting women valuable status and additional legal rights; and in some cases they created democratic governments.

To understand the forces behind the advent of Greek city-states in the eighth century B.C. and the momentous consequences for later Western history, we must first trace the political, economic, and social changes that occurred following the great disruptions that characterized the years 1200 to 1000 B.C. The Near East after 1000 B.C. reinstituted the traditional political and social systems of its past: those of monarchy. Although the Hebrews lost their independence in this period, Judaism's transformation into a true monotheistic religion represented a significant development. The enduring power of the Hebrews' religious ideas, which greatly influenced Christianity and Islam, thus joins the novel patterns of life and thought that appeared in the early Greek city-states as the foremost legacies of this period (c. 1000–500 B.C.) to later Western civilization.

> ## IMPORTANT DATES
>
> **Late eleventh century B.C.** Saul becomes ancient Israel's first king
>
> **c. 1000–900 B.C.** Greece experiences severe depopulation and poor economic conditions
>
> **c. 900 B.C.** Neo-Assyrians create an empire
>
> **c. 800 B.C.** Phoenicians begin colonization in western Mediterranean
>
> **776 B.C.** First Olympic Games held in Greece
>
> **c. 750 B.C.** Greeks begin to create city-states
>
> **c. 750–550 B.C.** Greek colonies founded all around the Mediterranean
>
> **604–562 B.C.** Nebuchadnezzar II reigns in Babylon, conquers Judah, destroys the central Hebrew temple in Jerusalem, and exiles most Hebrews to Babylon
>
> **594 B.C.** Athenians appoint Solon to recodify laws to try to end social unrest
>
> **560–530 B.C.** Cyrus founds Persian kingdom
>
> **510 B.C.** Athenian aristocrats and Spartans free Athens from tyranny
>
> **508 B.C.** Cleisthenes begins to reform Athenian democracy

The Early Greek Dark Age and Revival in the Near East

The turmoil during 1200–1000 B.C. weakened or obliterated many city-states and kingdoms in Greece and the Near East. Many of the people who survived suffered grinding poverty. We know little about this period of devastation or the recovery that followed because few literary or documentary sources exist to supplement the incomplete information provided by archaeology. Both because conditions were so gloomy for so many people and because our view of what happened in these years is dim, historians often refer to the era beginning in the twelfth and eleventh centuries B.C. as a Dark Age. The Greeks did not fully regain their strength until about 750 B.C. In contrast, the Near East recovered much sooner, ending its Dark Age around 900 B.C.

The Poverty of the Early Greek Dark Age

The depressed economic conditions in Greece after the fall of Mycenaean civilization typify the desperately reduced circumstances so many people in the Mediterranean and the Near East had to endure during the worst years of the Dark Age. One of the most startling indications of the severity of life in the early Dark Age is that the Greeks apparently lost their knowledge of writing when Mycenaean civilization fell. The Linear B script the Mycenaeans used was difficult to master and probably known only by a few specialists, the scribes who maintained palace records. They wrote only to track the flow of goods in and out of the palaces. When the

Dark Age Greece

redistributive economy of Mycenaean Greece collapsed, the Greeks no longer needed scribes or writing. Oral transmission kept Greek cultural traditions alive.

Later Greeks believed that, following the downfall of the Mycenaeans, a Greek-speaking group from the north—the Dorians—began to invade central and southern Greece. But archaeologists have not discovered any distinctive remains attesting Dorian incursions, and many scholars do not believe these invasions occurred.

Archaeological excavations have shown that the Greeks cultivated much less land and had many fewer settlements in the early Dark Age than at the height of Mycenaean prosperity. No longer did powerful rulers ensconced in stone fortresses preside over several towns and faraway but tightly organized territories, with the redistributive economies they controlled providing a tolerable standard of living for farmers, herders, and a wide array of craft workers. The many ships filled with adventurers, raiders, and traders that had plied the Mediterranean during the Bronze Age had dwindled to a paltry few. Developed political states no longer existed in Greece, and the people eked out their existence as herders, shepherds, and subsistence farmers

bunched in tiny settlements—about twenty people in many cases. The Greek population decreased in the early Dark Age. As the population shrank, less land was cultivated, leading to a decline in food production. The diminished food supply in turn prompted a further drop in the population. These two processes reinforced one another in a vicious circle, multiplying the negative effects of both.

The Greek agricultural economy remained complex despite the withering away of many traditional forms of agriculture. More Greeks than ever before made their living by herding animals. This increasingly pastoral way of life meant that people became more mobile: they needed to move their herds to new pastures once the animals had overgrazed their current location. If the herders were lucky, they might find a new spot where they could grow a crop of grain if they stayed long enough. As a result of this less settled style of life, people built only simple huts and got along with few possessions. Unlike their Bronze Age forebears, Greeks in the Dark Age had no monumental architecture, and they ceased depicting people and animals in their principal art form, the designs on ceramics.

We might assume that the general level of poverty throughout the Greek population in the Dark Age would have resulted in more egalitarian communities. However, archaeologists have recently analyzed contents of graves that suggest that Greek society, perhaps as early as 1050 B.C., had reinstituted a system of social hierarchy. Evidence for this hierarchy shows up clearly in the tenth century B.C. site now known as Lefkandi on the island of Euboea, off the eastern coast of the Greek mainland. There

A Rich Woman's Burial in Dark Age Greece
This burial from the tenth century B.C. dramatically reveals the wealth of some Greeks in the late Dark Age. This woman was buried with her gold jewelry, including an unusual chest ornament.

archaeologists have discovered the richly furnished graves of a man and a woman, who died about 950 B.C. The dead woman wore elaborate gold ornaments that testify to her exceptional wealth. The couple were buried under a building more than one hundred fifty feet long with wooden columns on the exterior. The striking architecture and riches in their graves imply that they enjoyed high social status during their lives and perhaps received a form of ancestor worship after their death. Probably few such wealthy and therefore powerful people lived during this time, but the graves at Lefkandi prove that marked social differentiation had again emerged in the Greek world. Strains in this hierarchical organization later set the stage for the birth of Greece's self-governing city-states.

Resurgent Kingdoms in the Near East

Although the Near East recovered from the devastation of its Dark Age more rapidly than Greece did, no political change comparable to the creation of the Greek city-state occurred. Instead the tradition of centralized authority was renewed. From Anatolia to Egypt to Mesopotamia, kingdoms large and small constituted the most prominent and powerful states, just as in the past. Some of these states were weaker than they had been before the

The Near East

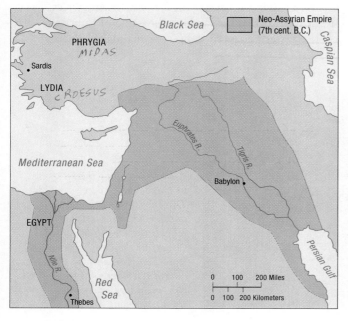

Dark Age—especially Egypt, which had lost its status as an international power. The new Assyrian kingdom, however, put together the greatest territorial empire yet seen in the ancient Near East.

The collapse of the Hittite kingdom in Anatolia had opened the way for the Phrygians, an Indo-European people who had perhaps migrated from Thrace, the spur of the European continent immediately to the west. The Phrygian kingdom's strength derived from the raw materials, especially metals, found in Anatolia. So wealthy did these resources make Phrygia that at the height of the kingdom's prosperity in the eighth century B.C., its ruler, known to the Greeks as Midas, became a legendary figure noted for his hoards of gold. About 695 B.C., however, a northern people called the Cimmerians invaded and destroyed the Phrygian kingdom. Eventually the kingdom of Lydia, in southwestern Anatolia, expanded to control the former territory of the Phrygians. Lydia also became famous for its material wealth, as symbolized by the phrase "as rich as Croesus," which recalls the Lydian king Croesus (✻c. 560–546 B.C.), who bestowed fabulous gifts on religious sanctuaries in Anatolia and Greece. But as before the Dark Age, wealth proved no insurance against disaster. In 546 B.C. the first Persian king, Cyrus, conquered Lydia after Croesus tried to push eastward into Persian territory.

The greatest international power in the Near East during this period was Assyria. Beginning around 900 B.C., the armies of the Neo-Assyrian ("New Assyrian") kingdom drove westward against the Aramaean states in Syria until they finally punched through to the Mediterranean coast. The desire to acquire metals and to secure access to seaborne trade routes to transport these metals probably fueled this enterprise. Eventually the Assyrian kings forced many of the people they conquered to move to Assyria to work on huge building projects in the kingdom's principal cities. So many Aramaeans were transplanted that their language had practically replaced Assyrian as the everyday language of Assyria by the eighth century B.C. Many Aramaeans also rose to prominent positions in the Assyrian army and in government administration. Assyrian imperial government was distinguished by its elaborate and well-organized record keeping, which relied on expert scribes.

Military imperialism pervaded Neo-Assyrian society, which seems to have been dominated by male warriors. Infantrymen provided the backbone of the Assyrian army; trained warriors excelled in the use of technology such as siege towers, battering rams, and swift chariots for carrying archers. Campaigns against foreign lands brought in revenues to supplement the domestic economy, which was based on agriculture, stock raising, and international trade. Conquered peoples who escaped deportation to Assyria had to pay annual tribute, and all citizens were expected to contribute to Assyrian prosperity. When the Phoenicians (who lived on the coast of Syria) eventually came under Assyrian control, they specialized in supplying raw materials and luxury goods such as incense, wine, dyed linens, glasswork, and ivory. So economically valuable did this commerce become to the Neo-Assyrian kingdom that it left the Phoenician cities largely autonomous. The Phoenicians conducted business and settled colonies throughout the Mediterranean, as far west as today's Spain. In 814 B.C. they founded the colony of Carthage in western North Africa, a settlement that grew into a great city. Within a century of its foundation sometime before 750 B.C., the Phoenician settlement on the site of modern Cadiz in Spain had become a city thriving on economic and cultural interaction with the indigenous Iberian population. A Phoenician expedition commissioned by an Egyptian pharaoh completed the first recorded circumnavigation of Africa around 600 B.C.

When not making war, Assyrian men spent much time hunting wild animals, the more dangerous the quarry the better. The king, for example, hunted lions as proof of his vigor and power. Royal lion hunts provided a favorite subject for Assyrian sculptors, who mastered the artistic technique of carving long relief sculptures that narrated a connected story. Although the Assyrian imperial administration devoted much time and energy to preserving documents in its archives, literacy apparently mattered far less to Assyrian males than war and hunting. Only one king is known to have learned to read and write in his youth. Neo-Assyrian public religion, which included deities imported from Babylon, reflected the prominence of war in Assyrian culture. Several cults, including that of Ishtar, the goddess of love, fertility, and war, glorified warfare. The Assyrians' passion for monumental architecture manifested itself in huge temples erected to the gods. The temples' staffs of priests

and slaves grew so numerous that the revenues from temple lands could no longer support them, and the kings had to supply extra funds.

The Neo-Assyrian monarchs pursued an aggressive policy of foreign expansion. Tiglath-pileser III (*744–727 B.C.) extended Assyrian control over portions of Syria-Palestine and conquered Babylon, while Esarhaddon (*680–669 B.C.) added Egypt to the Neo-Assyrian empire, dramatic proof of the weakness that had characterized Egypt since the fall of the New Kingdom. Their vast empire fell, however, when the Neo-Assyrian nobility stopped cooperating with the kings, and Assyria's many enemies combined forces to invade. By 612 B.C. these temporary allies, spearheaded by the newly independent Chaldean dynasty of Babylon, had destroyed the Assyrian capital at Ninevah.

This new Babylonian kingdom took over much of the Neo-Assyrian empire. Like the Aramaeans, who had earlier settled in Babylonia in such great numbers that Aramaean had replaced Babylonian as the common tongue, the Chaldeans of the Neo-Babylonian kingdom were a Semitic people who had originally been seminomads. They absorbed traditional Babylonian culture and preserved much ancient literature like the Gilgamesh Epic and other Mesopotamian myths; they also created many new works of prose and poetry. Educated people read this literature and recited it publicly for the enjoyment of the illiterate. Particularly popular were wisdom literature and texts that prophesied the future. Babylonian advances in astronomy became so influential that the word *Chaldean* came to mean *astronomer* in Greek. As in the past, the primary motivation for observing the stars was the belief that the gods communicated with humans by signs, through such natural phenomena as celestial movements and eclipses, abnormal births, the way smoke curled upward from a fire, and the trails of ants. The interpretation of these phenomena as messages from the gods exemplified the mixture of science and religion characteristic of ancient Near Eastern thought.

The Neo-Babylonian kingdom reached its zenith under Nebuchadnezzar II (*604–562 B.C.). He adorned Babylon with massive buildings, such as the rebuilt temple of the chief god, Marduk; the famous Hanging Gardens (whose original design, perhaps a ziggurat, remains uncertain); and the beautiful city gate dedicated to the goddess Ishtar.

Blue-glazed bricks and lions molded in yellow, red, and white decorated the portal's walls, which were thirty-six feet high. (This gate, reconstructed from the ruins found at Babylon, today stands in a Berlin museum.) Internal strife fatally weakened the kingdom, however, in the reign of Nabonidus (✷c. 555–539 B.C.). He caused a revolt among the priests who championed Marduk by promoting the cult of Sin, the moon god of the Mesopotamian city of Harran, and then retired for ten years to an oasis in the Arabian desert, leaving his son in Babylon to deal with the unrest. Nabonidus finally returned to Babylon, but in a failed attempt to stem an invasion led by the Persian Cyrus, who presented himself as the restorer of traditional Babylonian religion.

The Character of Persian Rule

The kingdom of Persia had taken shape when Cyrus (✷560–530 B.C.) established himself as its first king by overthrowing the monarchy of the Medes. The Median kingdom, centered in what is today northern Iran, had emerged in the late eighth century B.C., and it had joined Babylonia in destroying the Neo-Assyrian kingdom in 612 B.C. Median power then extended as far as the border of Lydia in central Anatolia. The languages of the Medes and the Persians descended from Indo-European; the language of today's Iran derives from ancient Persian. By taking over Lydia in 546 B.C., Cyrus also acquired dominion over the Greek city-states of Ionia (the western coast of Anatolia) that the Lydian king Croesus had previously subdued. Cyrus's son Cambyses conquered Egypt in 525 B.C. The expansion of Persian power under Cyrus and Cambyses set the stage for the great conflict between Persia and Greece in the early fifth century B.C.

When King Darius I (✷522–486 B.C.) ascended to the throne the Persian kingdom, whose ancestral heart lay in southern Iran east of Mesopotamia, covered a vast territory stretching east-west from Afghanistan to Turkey and north-south from inside the southern border of the former Soviet Union to Egypt and the Indian Ocean. Its heterogeneous population numbered in the millions. Darius created a smoothly functioning administrative structure for

The Great King of Persia
This relief sculpture from the palace at Persepolis depicts the proper way to show respect to the Persian king. The larger size of the king and his son behind him symbolizes their greater status.

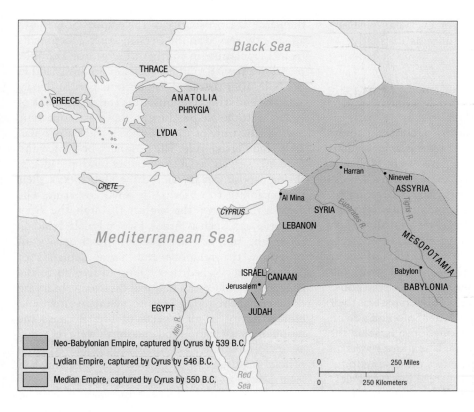

Black Sea

THRACE

GREECE

ANATOLIA
PHRYGIA

LYDIA

CRETE

CYPRUS

• Harran

• Nineveh
ASSYRIA

• Al Mina
SYRIA

LEBANON

MESOPOTAMIA

Mediterranean Sea

Euphrates R.

Tigris R.

ISRAEL CANAAN
Jerusalem •

Babylon •

BABYLONIA

EGYPT

JUDAH

Nile R.

Red Sea

| | Neo-Babylonian Empire, captured by Cyrus by 539 B.C. |
| Lydian Empire, captured by Cyrus by 546 B.C. |
| Median Empire, captured by Cyrus by 550 B.C. |

0   250 Miles
0   250 Kilometers

**Expansion of the
Persian Empire
by Cyrus**

the empire based on Assyrian precedents. Provincial governors (satraps) ruled enormous territories with little, if any, direct interference from the king. Their duties included keeping order, enrolling troops when needed, and sending revenues to the royal treasury. The Persian kings taxed the many different subject peoples of the kingdom in food, precious metals, and other valuable commodities and demanded from them levies of soldiers to staff the royal army. A system of roads and a courier system for royal mail facilitated communications among the far-flung administrative centers of the imperial provinces.

The revenues of its realm made the Persian monarchy wealthy beyond imagination. Everything about the king emphasized his grandeur and his superiority to ordinary mortals. His purple robes were more splendid than anyone's; the red carpets spread for him to walk upon could not be trod by anyone else; his servants held their hands before their mouths in his presence to muffle their breath so that he would not have to breathe the same air as they; in the sculpture adorning his

palace, he appeared larger than any other human. To display his concern for his loyal subjects, as well as the gargantuan scale of his resources, the king provided meals for some fifteen thousand nobles, courtiers, and other followers every day, although he himself ate hidden from the view of his guests. The Greeks, in awe of the Persian monarch's power and his lavish style of life, referred to him as "The Great King."

As absolute autocrats, the Persian kings believed they were superior to all humans. They did not, however, regard themselves as gods, but rather as the agents of the supreme god of Persian religion, Ahura Mazda. Persian religion, based on the teachings of the prophet Zoroaster, was dualistic, perceiving the world as the arena for the ongoing battle between good and evil. Unlike other ancient Near Eastern peoples, such as the Hebrews, the Persians did not sacrifice animals. Fire, kindled on special altars, played an important part in their religious rituals. Despite their autocratic rule, the ancient Persian kings usually did not interfere with the religious practices or everyday customs of their subjects, not even those as distinctive as the Hebrews'.

Israel from Monarchy to Persian Rule

The Hebrews achieved their first truly national organization with the creation of a monarchy in the late eleventh century B.C. Saul became ancient Israel's first king by fighting to limit Philistine power over the Hebrews in Canaan, and his successors David (✱c. 1010–970 B.C.) and Solomon (✱c. 961–922 B.C.) brought the united nation to the height of its prosperity. Israel's national wealth, largely derived from import-export commerce conducted through its cities, was displayed above all in the great temple richly decorated with gold leaf that Solomon built in Jerusalem to be the house of the Hebrews' god, Yahweh. This temple was their premier religious monument. After Solomon's death the monarchy split into two kingdoms: Israel in the north and Judah in the south. The more powerful Mesopotamians later subjugated these kingdoms. Tiglath-pileser III of Assyria forced much of Palestine to become a tribute-paying, subject territory, destroying Israel in 722 B.C. and deporting its population to Assyria. In 597 B.C. the Babylonian king Nebuchadnezzar II conquered Judah and captured its capital, Jerusalem. Ten years later he destroyed its temple to Yahweh and banished the Hebrew leaders and much of the population to Babylon. The Hebrews ever after remembered the sorrow of this exile. Their history from then on was that of a people subject to the political domination of others, save for a period of independence during the second and first centuries B.C.

When the Persian king Cyrus overthrew the Babylonians in 539 B.C., he permitted the Hebrews to return to Palestine, which was called Yehud from the name of the southern Hebrew kingdom Judah. From this geographical term came the name *Jews,* the customary designation for the Hebrews after their Babylonian exile. Cyrus allowed the Jews to rebuild their main temple in Jerusalem and to practice their religion. The priests of the Jerusalem temple, the literal and figurative center of Judaism, became the leaders of the Jewish community. Like other Persian subjects, the Jews were allowed to live as they pleased as long as they did not disrupt

the peace and prosperity of the empire. Some Jews apparently served in the Persian army. Documents from Elephantine in southern Egypt, for example, mention a Jewish military garrison on this island in the Nile, after that land had become part of Persia.

The enduring religious ideas and institutions of Judaism took shape during the postmonarchic period (the time of the prophets), the Babylonian exile, and Persian rule. The prophets, both men and women, served as moral critics and preachers; their purpose was to remind the Hebrews of their responsibility to observe the Sinai covenant. The great prophets of the eighth through the sixth centuries B.C., such as Amos, Hosea, Isaiah, Huldah, Jeremiah, and Ezekiel, taught the necessity of observing the religious and moral demands of Yahweh and warned that failing to live up to the covenant would mean national disaster. Observing the covenant required Jews to maintain ritual and ethical purity in all aspects of life. Because the blood of menstruation and childbirth were regarded as unclean, women were increasingly barred from official positions of authority. The husband had legal power over the household, subject to intervention by the male elders of the community, and only he could initiate divorce proceedings. Marrying non-Jews was forbidden, as was any work on the Sabbath (the holy day of the week). Ethics applied not only to ordinary crimes but also to financial dealings. Taxes and offerings had to be paid to support and honor the sanctuary of Yahweh, and debts had to be forgiven every seventh year.

The prophets assailed their people for falling short of the standards of behavior imposed by the covenant. They interpreted the conquests of the Hebrew kingdoms by the Neo-Assyrians and Neo-Babylonians as divine punishments for worshiping gods other than Yahweh and oppressing the poor. After the destruction of the temple at Jerusalem, the prophets' message turned from doom to hope, with the promise of national regeneration if the people returned to the covenant. An anonymous prophet whose words are recorded in the second half of the book of Isaiah hailed the Persian king Cyrus as an agent of Yahweh who had liberated the people from their exile in Babylon. Some prophets also preached about the coming end of the present world following a great crisis, a judgment by Yahweh, and salvation leading to a new world order. This apocalypticism ("uncovering" of the future), reminiscent of Babylonian prophecy texts, greatly influenced early Christianity later on.

By the Persian period, Judaism had become a monotheistic religion based on the recognition of certain books as authoritative scripture. The identification of sacred texts as the center of Jewish religion proved the most crucial development for the later history not only of Judaism, but of Christianity and Islam as well. These scriptures were assembled by editing earlier Hebrew traditions to form the Torah, the first five books of the Hebrew Bible, which under the Jewish leader Ezra in the fifth century B.C. was recognized as the sacred literature of the Jewish community. The books of the prophets found in the Hebrew Bible were probably also edited at this time and began to be accepted as authoritative.

Although the early Hebrews were never politically, economically, or militarily preeminent in the Near East, their religious ideas greatly influenced the later course of Western history. Through the continuing vitality of Judaism and its impact on the doctrines of Christianity and Islam, the early Jews bequeathed ideas whose effects have endured to this day: the belief in monotheism and the idea, based on the notion of covenant, that nations can have a divinely ordained destiny if they obey the divine will. These religious concepts constitute one of the most significant legacies to Western civilization from the Near East of the first half of the first millennium B.C.

Remaking Greek Civilization

In Greece the Dark Age of depopulation and poverty persisted longer than in the Near East. Although Greek economic improvement is evident as early as about 900 B.C., not until around 750 B.C. did political states, now of a new kind, develop again and the Dark Age end. The history of Greece in these centuries, though often obscure, laid the foundation for the pronounced social, political, and intellectual changes associated with the creation of the Greek city-state. The impact of these changes on Western history has been profound.

THE GREEK DARK AGE

c. 1000 B.C. Almost all important Mycenaean sites except Athens destroyed by now

c. 1000–900 B.C. Greatest depopulation and economic loss

900–800 B.C. Early revival of population and agriculture; iron now beginning to be used for tools and weapons

c. 800 B.C. Greek trading contacts initiated with Al Mina in Syria

776 B.C. First Olympic Games held

c. 775 B.C. Euboeans found trading post on Ischia in the Bay of Naples

c. 750–700 B.C. Homeric poetry recorded in writing after Greeks learn to write again; Hesiod composes his poetry; Oracle of Apollo at Delphi already famous

The Start of Economic Revival

Evidence from burials shows that Greeks in more and more locations had become conspicuously wealthy by about 900 B.C. The hierarchical arrangement of society was evidently spreading throughout Greece, and the few men and women at the pinnacle of society could afford to have expensive material goods placed in their tombs with them. Earlier in the Dark Age the best grave offerings a dead person could expect were a few clay pots. The exceptional contents of rich graves point to significant metallurgical and economic changes already under way by the ninth century B.C.

Two burials from Athens illustrate the changes that occurred in metallurgical technology for war and agriculture, advances that eventually helped end Greece's Dark Age. The earliest grave, from about 900 B.C., consisted of a pit into which a clay pot to hold the dead man's cremated remains was placed. Metal weapons, including a long sword, spearheads, and knives, surrounded the pot. Placing weapons in a male's grave was a burial tradition continued from the Bronze Age; but these arms were forged from iron, not bronze. This difference reflects a significant shift in metallurgy that took place throughout the Mediterranean region during

Model Granary
*Found in a ninth-century
woman's tomb in Athens,
this model imitates the
shape of grain storage
facilities. Its decoration
reflects the geometric
style of Greek art.*

the early centuries of the first millennium B.C.: iron displaced bronze as the principal metal used to make weapons and tools. For this reason historians also refer to the Dark Age in Greece as the Early Iron Age.

The Greeks, like others in the Near East, turned to iron because they could no longer obtain the tin needed to mix with copper to make bronze. The international trading routes once used to bring tin to Greece and the Near East from distant sources had been disrupted in the upheaval associated with the sea peoples and the widespread turmoil that began around 1200 B.C. Iron ore was available locally in Greece and elsewhere throughout the Near East. The Greeks probably learned to smelt iron through contact with people from the island of Cyprus, who in turn had learned it from people in southern Anatolia. Iron eventually replaced bronze in many uses, above all for agricultural tools, swords, and spear points. Bronze was still used for shields and armor, however, perhaps because it was easier to shape into thinner, curved pieces. The lower cost of iron tools and weapons meant that more people could afford them; and because iron is harder than bronze, implements kept their sharp edges longer. Better and more plentiful farming implements of iron eventually helped increase food production, a development reflected by evidence from the second burial.

The second grave, from about 850 B.C., held the remains of a woman and her treasures, including gold rings and earrings, a necklace of glass beads, and an unusual storage chest of baked clay. The necklace was imported from Egypt or Syria, and the style of the gold jewelry was also that of the Near East. These objects reflected Greek trade with the more prosperous civilizations of that region, a relationship whose influence on Greece increased as the Dark Age faded in the next century. The most intriguing object from the burial is the terra-cotta chest, which was painted with intricate, precise, and regular designs. (This style, which modern art historians call Geometric, is characteristic of the late Dark Age.) On its top were sculpted five beehivelike urns that are miniatures of granaries (structures for storing grain). If these models were important enough to be buried as objects of special value, we can deduce that actual granaries and the grain they held were precious commodities. This deduction in turn means that by 850 B.C. agriculture had already begun to recover from the devastation of the early Dark Age. Whether the woman owned grain fields we cannot know, but from her sculpted chest we can glimpse the significance of farming for her and her contemporaries. Increased agriculture production in this period accompanied a resurgence in population. Historians cannot determine whether a rise in population led to the raising of more grain, or whether improve-

	N. Semitic	Attica, Sigeion	Euboia	Boiotia	Thessaly	Phokis	Lokrides and colonies	Aigina, Kydonia	Corinth, Korkyra	Megara, Byzantion	Sikyon	Phleious, Kleonai, Tiryns	Argos, Mycenae	Eastern Argolid	Lakonia, Messenia, Taras	Arkadia	Elis	Achaia and colonies	Aitolia, Epeiros	Ithake, Kephallenia	Euboic W. colonies	Syracuse and colonies	Megara Hyblaia, Selinous	Naxos, Amorgos	Paros, Thasos	Delos, Keos, Syros	Crete	Thera, Kyrene	Melos, Sikinos, Anaphe	Ionic Dodekapolis and colonies	Rhodes, Gela, Akragas	Knidos	Aiolis
Alpha																																	
Beta																																	
Gamma																																	
Delta																																	
Epsilon																																	
Vau																																	
Zeta																																	
Eta																																	
Heta																																	
Theta																																	
Iota																																	
Kappa																																	
Lambda																																	
Mu																																	
Nu																																	
Xi																																	
Omikron																																	
Pi																																	
San																																	
Qoppa																																	
Rho																																	
Sigma																																	
Tau																																	
Upsilon																																	
Phi																																	
Chi																																	
Psi																																	
Omega																																	
Punct.																																	

Phoenician and Greek Alphabets
This chart shows how the Greeks imitated the Phoenician alphabet. The Semitic alphabet appears in the first column of letters, followed by sets of letters used by various groups in Greece.

ments in agricultural technology and the cultivation of more fields spurred population growth by increasing the number of people the land could support. These two developments reinforced one another: as the Greeks produced more food, the better-fed population reproduced faster; and as the population grew, more people could produce more food. The repopulation of Greece in the late Dark Age established the demographic conditions under which the new political forms of Greece were to emerge.

The Social Values of Aristocratic Greek Society

People like the couple from Lefkandi and the woman buried with the granary model at Athens constituted the aristocracy that emerged during the later part of the Greek Dark Age. The term *aristocracy* comes from Greek and means "rule of the best"—"the best" in this case referred to the people with the highest social status and the most wealth and political influence. Although aristocrats in this period seem to have controlled a disproportionate share of their communities' wealth and power, their acceptance into the aristocracy was not based on their resources alone. The key to being a proper aristocrat was to be born into a family that the rest of society considered aristocratic. We can only speculate about the various ways in which families might have originally gained this designation and thus became entitled to pass on their status. Some aristocratic families in the Dark Age might have inherited their status as descendants of the most prominent families of the Bronze Age; some might have made themselves aristocrats during the Dark Age by amassing wealth and befriending less fortunate people who were willing to acknowledge their benefactors' superior status in return for material help; and some might have acquired aristocratic status by monopolizing control of essential religious rituals.

Like the agricultural revival and population growth of the late Dark Age, the aristocrats' code of social values became a fundamental component of Greece's emerging political forms. This code underlies the stories told in the *Iliad* and the *Odyssey,* two book-length poems that first began to be written down about the middle of the eighth century B.C., at the very end of the Dark Age. The Greeks had relearned writing as a result of contact with the literate civilizations of the Near East. Sometime between about 950 and 750 B.C. the Greeks modified a Phoenician alphabet to represent the sounds of their own language; the English alphabet used today is based on this Greek version. The Greeks believed that Homer, a blind poet from the Greek region called Ionia (today the western coast of Turkey), composed the *Iliad* and the *Odyssey.* Although Homer may have been the first to put these poems into the form in which we have them today, countless Greek poets, influenced by Near Eastern epic tales, had sung of these stories for centuries, orally transmitting cultural values from one generation to the next. The behavioral code portrayed in these poems reflects Greek aristocratic values before the rise of political systems based on citizenship.

The primary characters in Homer's poems are aristocrats. The men are warriors, such as Achilles, a hero of the *Iliad.* This poem tells part of the legendary story of a Greek army attack on the city of Troy, a stronghold located in northwestern Anatolia. (Although historians have long believed the Trojans were not Greeks, the poems offer no certain clues to their ethnic identity.) In the *Iliad's* representation of the Trojan War, which the Greeks believed occurred four hundred years before Homer's time, Achilles is "the best of the Greeks" because he is an incomparable "doer of deeds and speaker of words." Achilles' overriding concern both in word and in action is with the eternal glory and recognition he can win with his "excellence" (the best translation for *arete,* a word with a range of meanings). Like all aristocrats, Achilles feared the disgrace of failing to live up to the code of excellence. Under the aristocratic code, failure and wrongdoing produced public shame more than private feelings of guilt.

This quest for excellence was a distinctive feature of the aristocratic code of values presented in Homer's poems, and it was pursued by women as well as men. For an aristocratic woman such as Penelope, the wife of Odysseus, the hero of the *Odyssey,* excellence meant preserving her household and property using her intelligence, beauty, social status, and intense fidelity to her husband. This curatorship required great stamina and ingenuity in resisting the demands of her husband's rivals at home while he was away for twenty years, fighting the Trojan War and then sailing home in a journey fraught with danger. In real life the role of aristocratic women was to develop the excellence that Penelope embodied to set themselves apart from ordinary people. A life not spent trying to attain excellence and the fame that accompanied it was considered contemptible.

Excellence as a competitive value for male Greek aristocrats showed up clearly in the Olympic Games, a religious festival in honor of Zeus, king of the Greek gods. The games were held at Zeus's sanctuary at Olympia, in the northwestern Peloponnese (the large peninsula that forms southern Greece), every four years beginning in 776 B.C. During these great celebrations aristocratic men competed in running events and wrestling as individuals, not on national teams as in the modern

Warriors in Training
Young men in Greece trained for war with sports such as javelin and discus throwing.

Olympic Games. The emphasis on physical prowess and fitness, competition, and public recognition by other men corresponded to the ideal of Greek masculine identity as it developed in this period. In a rare departure from the ancient Mediterranean tradition against public nakedness, Greek athletes competed without clothing. Competitions such as horse and chariot racing were added to the Olympic Games later, but the principal event remained a sprint of about two hundred yards, called the *stadion*. Winners originally received no financial prizes, only a garland made from wild olive leaves and the prestige of victory. In later Greek athletic competitions valuable prizes were often awarded. Admission was free to men; women were barred, on pain of death, but they had their own separate festival at Olympia on a different date in honor of Zeus's wife, Hera. Although we know less about the women's games, literary sources report that virgins competed on the Olympic track in a foot race five-sixths as long as the men's *stadion*. In later times professional athletes dominated international games, including the Olympics. They made good livings from appearance fees and prizes won at various games held throughout Greece. The most famous athlete was Milo, from southern Italy. Winner of the Olympic wrestling crown six times beginning in 536 B.C., he was renowned for showy stunts such as holding his breath until his blood expanded his veins so much that he could snap a cord tied around his head.

The Olympic Games originally centered on showcasing the aristocrats' innate superiority to ordinary people, as the fifth-century B.C. poet Pindar made clear in praising a family of victors: "Hiding the nature you are born with is impossible. The seasons rich in their flowers have many times bestowed on you, sons of Aletes [of Corinth], the brightness that victory brings, when you achieved the heights of excellence in the sacred games." The organization of the festival as an event for all Greek aristocrats—the Olympics were pan-Hellenic, that is, open to all Greeks—nevertheless indicates the trend toward communal activity that was under way in Greek society and politics by the mid-eighth century B.C. The sanctuary at Olympia provided a setting for public gatherings, with surrounding space for crowds to assemble. An international truce of several weeks was declared so that competitors and spectators from all Greek communities could travel to and from Olympia in security; wars in progress were put on hold for the duration of the games.

The arrangements for the Olympic games demonstrate that in the eighth century B.C., Greek aristocratic values of individual activity and the pursuit of excellence were beginning to be channeled into a new context appropriate for a changing society. This new regard for communal interests was another important precondition for the creation of Greece's new political forms.

Religion in Greek Myth as the Voice of the Community

Throughout the history of ancient Greece, religion provided the context for almost all communal activity. Sports events, such as the Olympic Games, took place at religious festivals honoring specific deities. War proceeded according to the signs of divine will that civil and military leaders identified in animal sacrifices and in omens derived from such natural occurrences as unusual weather. Sacrifices, the central event of Greek religious rituals, were performed before crowds in the open air on public occasions that involved communal feasting afterward on the sacrificed meat. Greek religion was based on *myths* (Greek for "stories" or "tales") about the gods and goddesses and their relationships to humans. In the eighth century B.C. the Greeks began to write down their myths. The poetry of Hesiod preserved from this period reveals how religious myths, as well as the economic changes and social values of the time, contributed to the feeling of community that underlay the creation of new political structures in Greece.

Hesiod employed myth to reveal the divine origin of justice. His long poem the *Theogony* ("Genealogy of the Gods") details the birth of the race of gods from primeval Chaos ("void" or "vacuum") and Earth, the mother of Sky and numerous other offspring. Hesiod explained that when Sky began to imprison his siblings, Earth persuaded her fiercest son, Kronos, to overthrow him violently because "Sky first contrived to do shameful things." When Kronos later began to swallow up all his own children, Kronos's wife Rhea (who was also his sister) had their son Zeus depose his father by force in retribution for his evil deeds. These vivid stories, which had their origins in Near Eastern myths like those of the

Woman at Altar
Greek women played a role in public and private religious ceremonies. Here a woman in rich clothing pours a libation onto a flaming altar while carrying a religious symbol in her left arm.

Mesopotamian Epic of Creation, carried the message that existence, even for deities, entailed struggle, sorrow, and violence. Even more significant, however, they showed that a concern for justice had been a component of the divine order of the universe from the beginning.

In his poem *Works and Days,* Hesiod identified Zeus as the fount of justice in human affairs, a marked contrast to Homer's portrayal of Zeus as concerned mainly with the fates of his favorite aristocratic warriors. Hesiod presents justice as a divine quality that will assert itself to punish evil-doers: "For Zeus ordained that fishes and wild beasts and birds should eat each other, for they have no justice; but to human beings he has given justice, which is far the best." Aristocratic men dominated the distribution of justice in Hesiod's day. They controlled their family members and household servants. Others outside their immediate households became their followers by acknowledging their status as leaders. Because these followers were roughly equal in wealth and status among themselves, they needed a figure of stronger authority

to settle their disputes and organize defense against raids or other military threats. In anthropological terms aristocrats operated as chiefs of bands. An aristocratic chief was empowered to settle arguments over property and duties, to oversee the distribution of rewards and punishments, and usually to head the religious rituals deemed essential to the group's security. A chief's power to coerce unwilling members of his band was limited, however. When decisions affecting the entire group had to be made, his leadership depended on his ability to forge a consensus. Hesiod describes how an effective chief exercised leadership: "When his people in their assembly get on the wrong track, he gently sets matters right, persuading them with soft words." In short, a chief could lead his followers only where they were willing to go.

Hesiod reveals that a state of heightened tension had developed between aristocratic chiefs and the peasants (the free proprietors of small farms, who might own a slave or two, oxen to work their fields, and other movable property of value). Their property made peasants the most influential group among the men, ranging from poor to moderately well-off, who made up the bands of followers of aristocratic chiefs in late Dark Age Greece. Assuming the perspective of a peasant farming a small holding, Hesiod insisted that the divine origin of justice should be a warning not to "bribe-devouring chiefs," who settled disputes among their followers and neighbors "with crooked judgments." This feeling of outrage commoners evidently felt at not receiving equal treatment served as yet another stimulus for the gradual movement toward new forms of political organization in Greece.

The Creation of the Greek City-State

During the Archaic Age (c. 750–500 B.C.) the Greeks developed the most widespread and influential of their new political forms, the city-state, or polis. *Polis,* from which we derive our word *politics,* is usually translated as *city-state* to emphasize its difference from what we today think of as a city. As in many earlier states in the ancient Near East,

Archaic Greece

the polis included not just an urban center but also countryside for some miles around that various small settlements occupied. Members of the polis lived both in the central town and also in the surrounding villages. Together these people made up a community of citizens constituting a political state, and it was this partnership among citizens that represented the distinctive political characteristic of the polis. Only men had the right to participate in politics, but women still counted as members of the community legally, socially, and religiously. A particular god or goddess, as, for example, Athena at Athens, presided over each polis as protector and patron. Different communities could choose the same deity as their protector; Sparta, Athens's chief rival in later times, also chose Athena as its patron. The members of a polis constituted a religious association obliged to honor the state's patron deity as well as the community's other gods. The community paid homage and respect to the deities through cults, which were regular sets of public religious activities overseen by priests and priestesses and funded by polis members. Animal sacrifices, the central ritual of a city-state's cults, demonstrated the polis members' respect and piety for their patron.

A polis was independent of neighboring *poleis* (plural form of *polis*), and its citizens were politically unified. Never before had a state been organized on the concept of citizenship for all its free inhabitants, even if, as some scholars think, the Greeks were influenced in the organization of the polis by their contact in the eighth century with the states of Phoenicia. Citizenship was a distinctive organizing concept because it assumed (in theory) certain basic levels of legal equality, essentially the expectation of equal treatment under the law—except for women, whose sexual behavior and control of property were governed by different regulations. But the general legal equality the polis provided did not depend on a citizen's wealth. Because a distinguishing social hierarchy characterized the history of the ancient Near East and

Greece in the Bronze Age and had once again become common in Greece by the late Dark Age, it is remarkable that a notion of legal equality, no matter how incomplete it may have been in practice, became the basis for the reorganization of Greek society in the Archaic Age. The polis remained the preeminent form of political and social organization in Greece until the beginning of the Roman Empire, eight centuries later. The other most common new form of political organization in Greece was the *ethnos* ("league" or "federation"), a flexible form of association over a broad territory that was itself sometimes composed of city-states.

The most famous ancient analyst of Greek politics and society, the philosopher Aristotle (384–322 B.C.), later insisted the emergence of the polis had been the inevitable result of the forces of nature. "Humans," he said, "are beings who by nature live in a polis." Anyone who existed outside the community of a polis, Aristotle only half-jokingly maintained, must be either a beast or a deity. By "nature," Aristotle meant the combined effect of social and economic forces. But the natural world of Greece, especially its geography, also influenced the creation of this radical new way of organizing human communities.

The Physical Environment of the City-State

The ancient Greeks never constituted a nation in the modern political sense because their independent city-states lacked a unifying organization. They identified with each other culturally, however, because they spoke the same language and worshiped the same deities, although with local variations. Their homeland lay in and around the Aegean Sea, a part of the Mediterranean Sea dotted with numerous islands, both large and small, and flanked on the west by the Balkan peninsula and on the east by the coast of Anatolia.

Regardless of where they lived, most Greeks never traveled very far from home; what few long-distance travelers there were went by sea. Overland transport was slow and expensive because rudimentary dirt paths served as the only roads in the predominantly mountainous terrain where most Greeks lived. Greece's rivers were practically useless as avenues for trade and communication because most of them slowed to a trickle during the many months each year of little or no rainfall. The most plentiful natural resource of the mountains of mainland Greece was timber for building houses and ships. Some deposits of metal ore were also scattered throughout Greek territory, as were clays suitable for pottery and sculpture. Various quarries of fine stone such as marble provided material for special buildings and works of art. The uneven distribution of these resources meant that some areas were considerably richer than others.

Although none of the mountains wrinkling the Greek landscape rose higher than ten thousand feet, their steep slopes separated the city-states. Only 20 to 30 percent of the total land area was arable. The scarcity of level terrain in most areas ruled out the large-scale raising of cattle and horses; pigs, sheep, and goats were the common livestock. The domestic chicken had also been introduced from the Near East by the seventh century B.C. The "Mediterranean" climate (intermittent heavy rain during a few months and hot, dry summers) also limited a farmer's options. Because the amount of annual precipitation varied so much, farming was a precarious business of boom and bust. Farmers mostly grew barley, the cereal staple of the Greek diet. Wine grapes and olives were the other most important crops. Wine diluted with water was the Greeks' preferred beverage; olive oil was the main source of fat in their diet and was also used, for example, as a cleaning agent and a base for perfumes.

So jagged was the coastline of mainland Greece that almost all its communities lay within forty miles of the sea. Their proximity to the Mediterranean Sea allowed Greek entrepreneurs convenient access to one another and to potentially lucrative international trade, especially with Egypt and the Near East. But sea travel meant dangers from pirates and storms. Prevailing winds and fierce gales almost ruled out sailing in winter. Even in calm conditions sailors hugged the coast as much as possible and preferred to put in to shore at night for safety. As Hesiod commented, merchants needing to make a living took to the sea "because an income means life to poor mortals, but it is a terrible fate to die among the waves."

By isolating the city-states and making communication difficult, the mountainous geography of Greece contributed to the tradition of independence, indeed of noncooperation, among the city-states. A single island could be home to multiple city-states; Lesbos, for example, had five. Because few city-states controlled enough arable land to support a large population, communities of only several hundred to several thousand people were the rule, even after the rise in the Greek population at the end of the Dark Age. By the fifth century B.C., Athens' population of male citizens numbered in the tens of thousands, but this was a rare exception. Such a large population could be sustained only by the constant importation of food paid for through trade and other revenues.

Economic Revival and Colonization

Some Greeks had emigrated to Ionia as early as the ninth century B.C. Starting around 750 B.C., however, Greeks began to settle much farther from the Greek mainland. Within two hundred years, Greek colonies existed in present-day southern France, Spain, Sicily and southern Italy, North Africa, and along the coast of the Black Sea. Eventually the Greek world encompassed nearly fifteen hundred city-states. (The Greeks established their new form of government wherever they settled.) The revival of international trade in the Mediterranean in this era may have provided the original stimulus for Greeks to venture from their homeland, where the economy was still depressed. Some Greeks with commercial interests, especially in acquiring natural resources such as metal to export back to their lands of origin, moved to foreign settlements, such as those founded in Spain by Phoenicians from Palestine.

Greeks also established trading posts abroad. By 800 B.C. traders from Euboea had already set up commercial contacts with a community on the Syrian coast at a site now called Al Mina. Men wealthy enough to finance risky expeditions by sea ranged far from home in search of metals. The basic strategy of this entrepreneurial commodity trading is described in the *Odyssey,* where the goddess Athena once appears disguised as a metal trader: "I am here . . . with my ship and crew on our way across the wine-dark sea to foreign lands in search of copper; I am carrying iron now." By about 775 B.C., Euboeans, who seem to have been particularly active explorers, had also founded a trading settlement on the island of Ischia, in the Bay of Naples off southern Italy. There they processed iron ore

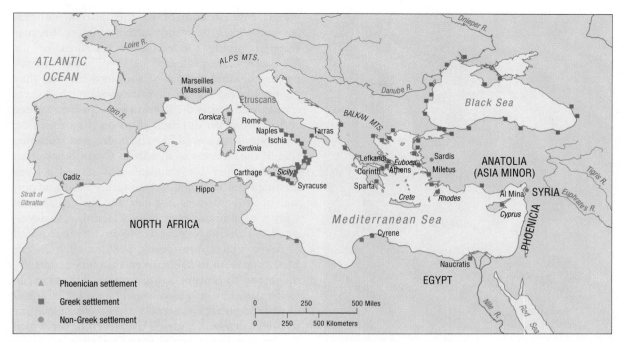

Phoenician and Greek Settlements, c. 800–500 B.C.

imported from the Etruscans, who lived in central Italy. Archaeologists have documented the expanding overseas network of the eighth century B.C. by finding Greek pottery at more than eighty sites outside Greece; for the tenth century, by contrast, only two pots that were carried abroad have been found.

Although commercial interests may have first motivated Greeks to emigrate, the population explosion that had begun in the late Dark Age had by around 750 B.C. caused a severe scarcity of arable land, a condition that induced many more of them to move abroad permanently in the mid-eighth century B.C. Good farming land was the most desirable form of wealth for Greek men, so the shortage caused tension in the male population. Emigration alleviated some of the strain, because landless men often went abroad to acquire their own fields in the new city-states. Sometimes the local inhabitants welcomed the colonists, especially if they settled on previously unoccupied land; sometimes the native peoples greeted them hostilely, and they had to fight for land. Because only males apparently went on these colonizing expeditions, they had to find wives among the locals, either through peaceful negotiation or by kidnapping.

The Greeks' participation in international trade and colonization increased their contact with the peoples of Anatolia and the Near East. They admired and envied these older civilizations for their wealth, such as the gold of the Phrygian kingdom of Midas, and their cultural accomplishments, such as the lively pictures of animals on Near Eastern ceramics, the magnificent temples of Egypt, and the alphabets of the Phoenician cities (which, as we saw, the Greeks adapted for their own use). During the early Dark Age, Greek artists had stopped portraying people or other living creatures, but the pictures they saw on pottery imported from the Near East in the late Dark Age and early Archaic Age inspired them to once again draw figures in their paintings. The style of Near Eastern reliefs and freestanding sculptures also influenced Greek art of the period. Greeks sculpted figures that stood stiffly, staring straight ahead, in imitation of Egyptian statuary. When the improving economy of the later Archaic Age allowed Greeks to revive monumental architecture in stone, many temples for the worship of the gods and goddesses emulated Egyptian architectural designs. In the sixth century B.C. the Greeks began to mint coins,

The Reappearance of Figures in Greek Art
Trading voyages brought Greeks of the Archaic Age into contact with the art of the civilizations of the Near East and led them to reintroduce human and animal figures into their own art. This painted vase from the seventh century B.C. *shows the hero Heracles heading off to battle a monster.*

a technology they learned from the Lydians, who invented coinage in the seventh century B.C. Long after this innovation, however, most economic exchanges involved barter, especially in the Near East. Highly monetized economies took centuries to develop.

Success in competing for international markets affected the fortunes of Greek city-states during this period. Corinth, for example, grew prosperous from ship building and its geographical location,

which gave it control of the narrow isthmus connecting northern and southern Greece. Because shippers plying the east-west sea lanes of the Mediterranean preferred to avoid the stormy passage around the tip of southern Greece, they commonly off-loaded their cargoes and had them transported across the isthmus on a special roadbed and reloaded on different ships on the other side. Small ships may even have been dragged from one side of the isthmus to the other. Corinth became a bustling center for shipping and earned a large income from sales and harbor taxes. Taking advantage of its deposits of fine clay and the expertise of a growing number of potters, Corinth also developed a thriving export trade in fine decorated pottery, which non-Greek peoples such as the Etruscans seem to have prized as luxury goods. By the late sixth century B.C., however, Athens began to displace Corinth as the leading Greek exporter of painted pottery, especially after consumers came to prefer designs featuring the red color for which its clay was better suited than Corinth's.

Greeks always solicited approval from their deities before setting out from home, whether for commercial voyages or colonization. The god most frequently consulted about sending out men to colonize was Apollo in his sanctuary at Delphi, a hauntingly beautiful spot in the mountains of central Greece. The Delphic sanctuary began to win international renown in the eighth century B.C. because it housed an oracular shrine in which a prophetess, the Pythia, spoke the will of Apollo in response to visitors' questions. The Delphic oracle functioned for only a few days over nine months of the year, and demand for its services was so high that the sanctuary operators rewarded generous contributors with the privilege of jumping to the head of the line. Most visitors to Delphi consulted the oracle about personal matters such as marriage and having children. The oracle at Delphi continued as a force in Greek international affairs in the centuries to come.

Aristocrats and Common People in the Rise of the City-State

One insurmountable difficulty in ascertaining the reasons city-states began to emerge in Greece around 750 B.C. is that most of the surviving evidence pertains only to Athens, which because of its large population and extensive territory was not a

Apollo's Temple at Delphi
The sanctuary of Apollo at Delphi, situated high above a dramatic valley, became an internationally famous oracle. Greeks and others sought advice from the oracle on a wide variety of questions affecting their lives.

typical city-state. But by using the information from Athens and various literary sources and other documents, we can draw some general conclusions about how and why the Greeks broke with the traditional form of political organization that depended on a centralized authority and instead gradually instituted the citizen-based city-states.

The economic revival of the Archaic Age and the population growth in Greece evident by the eighth century B.C. certainly gave momentum to the process. Men who acquired substantial property from success in commerce or agriculture could now demand a greater say in political affairs from the hereditary aristocrats. Theognis of Megara, a sixth-century B.C. poet, gave voice to the aristocrats' distress at the opening of new avenues to social and political influence: ". . . men today prize possessions, and noble men marry into 'bad' [that is, nonaristocratic] families and 'bad' men into noble families. Riches have mixed up lines of breeding . . . and the good breeding of the citizens is becoming obscured." The population increase in this era probably came mostly in the ranks of the poor. Such families raised more children to help farm more land, which had been vacant after the depopulation of the early Dark Age. The growing number of poorer folk apparently resented and reacted against the inequitable treatment they received from aristocratic leaders, who sometimes acted as petty kings in their local territory and dispensed lopsided justice to those with less wealth and power.

For the city-state to function as a political institution in which all free men had a share, nonaristocratic men had to insist on equitable treatment, even if aristocrats were to remain in leadership positions and carry out the policies agreed on by the group. The concept of citizenship responded to that demand. Citizenship above all carried certain legal rights, such as access to courts to resolve disputes, protection against enslavement by kidnapping, and participation in the religious and cultural life of the city-state. It also implied involvement in politics, although the degree to which poor men shared political power varied among the city-states. The right to hold public office, for example, could be limited in some cases to owners of a certain amount of property or wealth. Most notably, citizen status distinguished free men and women from slaves and *metics,* foreigners who had limited legal rights and permission to reside in a city-state that was not their homeland. Thus even the poor had a distinction that set them apart from others. Yet despite the legal guarantees of citizenship, social and economic inequality among male citizens persisted in the city-states.

Women's citizenship was crucial because it identified them as a specific group and gave them social status and legal rights denied slaves and metics. Certain religious cults were reserved for citizen women only. Citizen women were legally protected against being kidnapped and sold into slavery. They also had recourse to the courts in disputes over property, but they could not represent themselves—men spoke for them, a requirement that reveals their subordinate legal status. The traditional paternalism of Greek society, with men acting as "fathers" to regulate the lives of women and safeguard their interests as defined by men, demanded that all women have male guardians to protect them physically and legally. Women received no rights to participate in politics. They were not permitted to attend political assemblies, nor could they vote. They could serve as priestesses, however, and they had access to the initiation rights of the popular cult of Demeter at Eleusis, near Athens. This internationally renowned cult may have served as a sort of safety valve for the pressures created by life in Greek city-states, because it promised protection from evil and a better fate in the afterworld for everyone, regardless of class or gender.

The Poor as Citizens

Despite the limited equality of the Greek city-state, especially in practice, this new form of political organization nevertheless represented a significant break with the past. One of the most striking developments in the polis was the extension of at least some political rights to the poor. We cannot be certain why poor men were allowed a say in political matters. For a long time, historians attributed the general widening of political rights in the city-state to a so-called hoplite revolution, but recent research has undermined the plausibility of this theory. *Hoplites* were infantrymen who wore metal body armor, and they constituted the main strike force of the militias that defended each city-state in this period. The hoplites marched into combat shoulder to shoulder in a rectangular formation called a *phalanx.* Staying in line and working as part of the group were the secrets to successful phalanx tactics. In the words of the seventh-century B.C. poet Archilochus, a good hoplite was "a short man firmly placed upon his legs, with a courageous heart, not to be uprooted from the spot where he plants his feet." Greeks had fought in phalanxes for a long time, but until the eighth century B.C. only aristocrats and a few of their nonaristocratic followers could afford the equip-

ment to serve as hoplites. In the eighth century B.C., however, a growing number of men had become prosperous enough to buy metal weapons, especially because the use of iron had made them more readily available. Presumably these new hoplites, because they bought their own equipment and trained hard to learn phalanx tactics to defend their community, felt they should also enjoy political rights. According to the theory of a hoplite revolution, these new hoplites forced the aristocrats to share political power by threatening to refuse to fight, which would cripple the community's military defense.

The theory correctly assumes that new hoplites had the power to demand and receive a voice in politics. But the hoplites were not poor. How, then, did poor men win political rights? If contributing to the city-state's defense as a hoplite was the only grounds for meriting the political rights of citizenship, the aristocrats and the hoplites had no obvious reason to grant poor men anything. Yet poor men did become politically empowered in many city-states, with some variations. All male citizens, regardless of their wealth, eventually were entitled to attend, speak in, and vote in the communal assemblies that made policy decisions for the city-states. The hoplite revolution fails to explain completely the development of the city-state mostly because it cannot account for the extension of rights to poor men. Furthermore, not many men were wealthy enough to afford hoplite armor until the middle of the seventh century B.C., well after the initial formation of the city-state.

No satisfactory alternative or extension to the theory of hoplite revolution as the reason for the rise of city-states yet exists. The laboring free poor—the workers in agriculture, trade, and crafts—contributed to the city-state's economic strength, but it is hard to see how their value as laborers could have been translated into political rights. The better-off elements in society certainly did not extend the rights of citizenship to the poor out of any romanticized vision of poverty as spiritually noble. As one contemporary put it, "Money is the man; no poor man ever counts as good or honorable." Perhaps tyrants (sole rulers who seized power unconstitutionally in some city-states) boosted the status of poor men. Tyrants could have granted greater political rights to poor or disfranchised men as a means of marshaling popular support. Another, more speculative possibility is that the aristocrats and hoplites had simply become less cohesive as a political group, thereby weakening opposition to the growing idea of poor men that it was unjust to be excluded from political participation. According to this view, when the poor agitated for power the aristocrats and hoplites had no united front to oppose them, making compromise necessary to prevent destructive civil unrest.

In any case the hallmark of politics in developed Greek city-states was the practice of citizen men making decisions communally—as a whole in democratic states and to a lesser extent in oligarchies (the Greek word *oligarchy* means "rule by the few"). Aristocrats continued to influence, sometimes dominate, Greek politics even after the emergence of city-states. But the unprecedented political power nonaristocratic men came to wield in city-states constituted the most remarkable feature of the political organization of Greek society in the Archaic Age.

The Emergence of Slavery in Greece

The only evidence of slavery in the Dark Age, which appears in the poetry of Homer and Hesiod, reveals complex relationships among free and unfree people. Some people captured in war evidently became chattel slaves, completely dominated by their masters. Other dependent people described in the poems seem more like inferior members of their owners' households. They lived under virtually the same conditions as their superiors and had families of their own. Slavery apparently had its own dismal hierarchy during this time.

Chattel slavery became widespread in Greece only after about 600 B.C. Eventually slaves became cheap enough that people of even moderate means could afford one or two. But even wealthy Greek landowners never acquired gangs of hundreds of slaves such as those who kept up Rome's water system under the Roman Empire. Maintaining a large number of slaves year-round in ancient Greece would have been uneconomical because the crops cultivated required short periods of intense labor punctuated by long stretches of inactivity. Slaveowners did not want to feed and house slaves who had no work.

By the fifth century B.C. slaves accounted for up to one-third of the total population in some city-states. Even so, most labor was still performed by small landowners and their families themselves, sometimes hiring free workers. (The special system of slavery in Sparta was a rare exception to this situation.) Chattel slaves did all kinds of labor. Household slaves, often women, had the least dangerous existence. They cleaned, cooked, fetched water from public fountains, helped the wife with the weaving, watched the children, accompanied the husband as he did the marketing, and performed other domestic chores. Yet they could not refuse if their masters demanded sexual favors. Slaves who worked in small manufacturing businesses, such as those of potters or metalworkers, and slaves who worked on farms often labored alongside their owners. Rich landowners, however, might appoint a slave supervisor to oversee the work of their field slaves while they remained in town. Slaves who worked in the narrow, landslide-prone tunnels of Greece's few silver and gold mines had the worst lot. Many died doing this dangerous, dark, and backbreaking job.

Many slaves were war captives; others were non-Greeks who pirates or raiders had seized from the rough regions to the north and east of Greek territory. The fierce bands in these areas would also capture and sell each other to slave dealers. Greeks also enslaved fellow Greeks, especially those defeated in war (who were not members of the same city-state as their owners). Rich families prized Greek slaves with some education because they could be used as tutors for children—no schools existed in this period, and few people learned how to read and write.

Some slaves worked as public slaves; they were owned by the city-state rather than an individual. They had a measure of independence, living on their own and performing specialized tasks. In Athens, for example, public slaves eventually certified the authenticity of the city-state's coinage. Temple slaves "belonged" to the deity of the sanctuary, for which they worked as servants. Some female temple slaves served as sacred prostitutes, and their earnings helped support the sanctuary.

Slaveowners could punish, even kill, their slaves with impunity. But beating working slaves severely enough to cripple them or executing able-bodied slaves made no economic sense—in essence the master would be destroying part of his property. For this reason such treatment was probably limited. Under the best conditions, household slaves with humane masters might live lives free of violent punishment. They might even be allowed to join their owners' families on excursions and attend religious rituals. However, without the right to a family of their own, without property, and without legal or political rights, they remained alienated from regular society. In the words of an ancient commentator, chattel slaves lived lives of "work, punishment, and food." Although their labor helped maintain the economy of Greek society, it rarely benefited them. Yet despite the misery of their condition, Greek slaves—outside Sparta—almost never revolted on a large scale, perhaps because they were of too many different origins and nationalities and too scattered to organize. Sometimes owners manumitted their slaves, and some promised freedom at a future date to encourage their slaves to work hard. Freed slaves did not become citizens in Greek city-states but instead mixed into the population of metics. They were still expected to help out their former masters when called upon.

The creation of citizenship as a category to define membership in the exclusive group of people constituting a polis inevitably highlighted the contrast between those included in the category of citizens and those outside it, especially slaves. Freedom from control by others was a necessary precondition to become a citizen with political rights, which in the city-states meant being a free-born adult male. The strongest contrast citizenship produced, therefore, was that between free and unfree. In this way, the development of a clear idea of personal freedom in the formation of the city-state as a new political form may ironically have encouraged the complementary development of chattel slavery in the Archaic Age. The rise in economic activity in this period probably also encouraged the importation of slaves by increasing the demand for labor. In any case, slavery as it developed in the Archaic Age reduced unfree persons to a state of absolute dependence; they were the property of their owners. As Aristotle later put it, slaves were "living tools."

Family Life in the City-State

The emergence of widespread slavery in the city-state made households bigger and added new responsibilities for women, especially rich women, whose lives were devoted to maintaining their

Archaic Elegance in Sculpture
This damaged statue from the late Archaic period shows the elegant and colorful clothing, elaborate hairstyle, and slight smile that distinguished sculptural portraiture of women in this era. The statue would have been dedicated to a divinity.

households. While their husbands farmed, participated in politics, and met with their male friends, wives managed the household (*oikonomia*, Greek for "economics"). They were expected to raise the children, supervise the preservation and preparation of food, keep the family's financial accounts, weave cloth for clothing, direct the work of the household slaves, and see to them when they were ill. Women's work ensured the family's economic

An Ancient Greek Wedding Procession
This painted vase depicts the procession that brought the bride to the groom's house,
the central event in an ancient Greek wedding.

self-sufficiency and allowed the male citizens the time to participate in public life.

Poor women worked outside the home, often as small-scale merchants in the public market that occupied the center of every settlement. Only in Sparta did women have the freedom to participate in athletic training along with men. In all other city-states women engaged in public life solely at funerals, state festivals, and religious rituals. Women could perform public duties in various official cults; for example, women officiated as priestesses in more than forty cults in Athens by the fifth century B.C. Women holding these posts often had considerable prestige, practical benefits such as a salary paid by the state, and greater freedom of movement in public.

When women married they became legal wards of their husbands, as they previously had been of their fathers. Marriages were arranged by men. A woman's guardian—her father, or if he were dead, her uncle or her brother—would commonly betroth her to another man's son while she was still a child, perhaps as young as five. The betrothal was an important public event conducted in the presence of witnesses. The guardian on this occasion repeated the phrase that expressed the primary aim of marriage: "I give you this woman for the plowing [procreation] of legitimate children." The marriage itself customarily took place when the girl was in her early teens and the groom ten to fifteen years older. Hesiod advised a man to marry a virgin in the fifth year after her menarche,* when he himself was "not much younger than thirty and not much older." A legal marriage consisted of the bride moving to her husband's house; the procession to his house served as the ceremony. The woman

brought to the marriage a dowry of property (perhaps land yielding an income, if she were wealthy) and personal possessions that formed part of the new household's assets and could be inherited by her children. Her husband was legally obliged to preserve the dowry and to return it in case of a divorce. Divorce procedures had more to do with power than with law: a husband could expel his wife from his home; a wife, in theory, could leave her husband on her own initiative to return to the guardianship of her male relatives. However, her husband could force her to stay. Except in certain cases in Sparta, monogamy was the rule in ancient Greece, as was a nuclear family (that is, husband, wife, and children living together without other relatives in the same house). Citizen men could have sexual relations without penalty with slaves, foreign concubines, female prostitutes, or willing preadult citizen males. Citizen women had no such sexual freedom, and adultery carried harsh penalties for both parties, except at Sparta.

Greek citizen men placed Greek citizen women under their guardianship both to regulate marriage and procreation and to maintain family property. This paternalistic attitude allowed Greek men to control human reproduction and consequently the distribution of property, an urgent concern in the reduced economic circumstances of the Dark Age. According to Greek mythology, women were a necessary evil. Zeus supposedly created the first woman, Pandora, as a punishment for men in his vendetta against the demigod Prometheus for giving fire to humans. Pandora subsequently loosed "evils and diseases" into the previously trouble-free world by removing the lid from the box the gods had filled for her. Many

* beginning of menstruation

Greek men probably shared Hesiod's opinions about women: he saw the female sex as "big trouble" but thought any man who refused to marry to escape the "troublesome deeds of women" would come to "destructive old age" all alone, with no heirs. In other words, a man needed a wife so he could sire children who would care for him during his waning years and so his descendants would preserve his holdings after his death. Although Greek citizen women were subordinate to men by custom and by law, their lives incorporated social and religious duties essential to the welfare of their own families and of their city-state.

Oligarchy, Tyranny, and Democracy in the City-States

Although the Greek city-states differed in size and natural resources, they shared certain fundamental political institutions and social traditions: citizenship, slavery, the legal disadvantages and political exclusion of women, and the continuing influence of aristocrats in society and politics. During the Archaic Age, however, these common traits mutated in strikingly different ways in the various city-states. In some oligarchic city-states, such as Sparta, only a few men exercised meaningful political power. Tyrants dominated sporadically in other city-states. Tyranny, passed down from father to son, existed at various times throughout the Greek world, from city-states on the island of Sicily in the west to Samos off the coast of Ionia in the east. Still other city-states instituted early forms of democracy ("rule by the people"), allowing all male citizens to participate in governing. Although some assemblies of men had influenced kings in certain early states in the ancient Near East, never had any group of people been invested with the amount of political power the Greek democracies gave their male citizens. The Athenians established Greece's most renowned democracy, in which male citizens enjoyed individual freedom unprecedented in the ancient world. These varied paths of political and social development illustrate the great challenge Greeks faced as they struggled to construct new ways of life during the Archaic Age. In the course of this endeavor they also began to formulate

different ways of understanding the physical world, their relations to it, and their relationships with each other.

The Political Evolution of Sparta

Sparta was an oligarchy in which military readiness overrode all other concerns. During the Archaic Age, this city-state developed the mightiest infantry force in Greece. Spartans were renowned for their self-discipline—a cultural value that manifested their militaristic bent. Sparta's easily defended location—nestled on a narrow north-south plain between rugged mountain ranges in the southeastern Peloponnese, in a region called Laconia—gave it a secure base. Sparta had access to the sea through a harbor situated some twenty-five miles south of its urban center, but this harbor opened onto a dangerous stretch of the Mediterranean whipped by treacherous winds and currents. Thus enemies could not threaten the Spartans by sea; this relative isolation from the sea kept the Spartans from becoming adept sailors. Their interests and their strength lay on the land.

The Peloponnese

The Greeks believed the Spartans emigrated from central Greece and conquered the indigenous inhabitants of Laconia and settled in at least four small villages, two of which apparently dominated the others. These early settlements later joined and formed the core of what eventually became the city-state of Sparta. The Greeks called this process of political unification, in which most people continued to live in their original villages even after one village began to serve as the center of the new city-state, *synoecism*[*] ("union of households"). One apparent result of the compromises required to forge Spartan unity was the retention of two hereditary military leaders of high prestige, the kings. These kings, perhaps originally the leaders of the two dominant villages, served as the religious heads of Sparta and commanders of its army. Their power

* SYNOICISM

to make decisions and set policy was not absolute, however, because they operated not as pure monarchs but as leaders of the oligarchic institutions that governed the Spartan city-state. Rivalry between the two royal families periodically led to fierce disputes. Because having two supreme military commanders paralyzed the Spartan army when the kings disagreed on strategy in the middle of a military campaign, the Spartans eventually decided that the army would be commanded by only one king at a time.

The "few" who made policy in Sparta were a group of twenty-eight men over sixty years old, joined by the two kings. This group of thirty, called the *gerousia* ("council of old men"), formulated proposals that were submitted to an assembly of free adult males. This assembly had only limited power to amend the proposals put before it; mostly it was expected to approve the council's plans. Rejections were rare because the council retained the right to withdraw a proposal when the reaction to it in the assembly foreshadowed a negative vote. "If the people speak crookedly," according to Spartan tradition, "the elders and the leaders of the people shall be withdrawers [of the proposal]." The council could then resubmit the proposal later, after marshaling support for its passage.

A board of five annually elected *ephors* ("overseers") counterbalanced the influence of the kings and the *gerousia*. Chosen from the adult male citizens at large, the ephors convened the *gerousia* and the assembly, and they exercised considerable judicial powers of judgment and punishment. They could even bring charges against a king and imprison him until his trial. The creation of the board of ephors diluted the political power of the oligarchical *gerousia* and the kings; the ephors' job was to ensure the supremacy of law. The Athenian Xenophon later reported:

> All men rise from their seats in the presence
> of the king, except for the ephors. The ephors
> on behalf of the polis and the king on his own
> behalf swear an oath to each other every
> month: the king swears that he will exercise
> his office according to the established laws of
> the polis, and the polis swears that it will pre-
> serve his kingship undisturbed if he abides by
> his oath.

The Spartans demanded obedience to the law; laws were their guide for proper behavior in all matters. When the ephors entered office, for example, they issued an official proclamation to the men of Sparta: "Shave your moustache and obey the laws." The Spartan law-based political system evolved from about 800 to 600 B.C. A Spartan leader named Lycurgus is credited with reforming early Spartan laws, but the dates and nature of his changes remain unknown. The Spartans believed he had consulted the oracle of Apollo at Delphi to receive the laws from the gods. They called the gods' response the Rhêtra ("spoken laws"). Unlike other Greeks, the Spartans never wrote down their laws. Instead they preserved their system from generation to generation with a unique, highly structured way of life based on a particular economic foundation.

The Economic Foundation of Spartan Militarism

The distinctiveness of the Spartans' way of life was fundamentally a reaction to their living in the midst of people whom they had conquered in war and enslaved, but who greatly outnumbered them. To maintain their superiority, Spartan men turned themselves into a society of vigilant soldiers. They accomplished this transformation by radically restructuring traditional family life and enforcing strict adherence to all the laws. Through constant, daily reinforcement of their strict code of values, the Spartans ensured their survival against the enemies they had created by subjugating their neighbors. The seventh-century B.C. poet Tyrtaeus, whose verses exemplify the high quality of the poetry produced before Sparta's military culture began to devalue and exclude such achievements, expressed that code:

> I would never remember or mention in my
> work any man for his speed afoot or wres-
> tling skill, not if he was huge and strong as
> a Cyclops or could run faster than the North
> Wind, nor more handsome than Tithonus or
> richer than Midas or Cinyras, nor more king-
> ly than Pelops, or had speech more honeyed
> than Adrastus, not even if he possessed every
> glory—not unless he had the strength of a
> warrior in full rush.

The supreme male value was martial courage.

Some of the conquered inhabitants of Laconia continued to live in self-governing communities.

These so-called *perioikoi* ("those who live round about") were required to serve in the Spartan army and pay taxes, but they lacked citizen rights. Perhaps because they retained their personal freedom and property, the *perioikoi* never rebelled against Spartan control. Far different was the fate of the conquered people who ended up as *helots* (derived from the Greek word for "capture"). Later commentators described the helots as "between slave and free" because they were not owned by individual Spartans but rather belonged to the whole community, which alone could free them. Helots had a semblance of family life because they were expected to produce children to maintain their population. They labored as farmers and household slaves so Spartan citizens would not have to do such "demeaning" work. Spartan men in fact wore their hair very long to show they were "gentlemen" rather than laborers, for whom long hair was inconvenient.

When the arable land of Laconia, which was held predominantly by aristocrats, proved too limited to support the citizen population of Sparta, the Spartans attacked their Greek neighbors to the west, the Messenians. In the First (c. 730–710 B.C.) and Second (c. 640–630 B.C.) Messenian Wars, the Spartan army captured the territory of Messenia, which amounted to 40 percent of the Peloponnese, and reduced the Messenians to helots. With the addition of the tens of thousands of people in Messenia, the total helot population now more than outnumbered that of Sparta, whose male citizens at this time probably numbered between eight thousand and ten thousand. The Messenians' despair is reflected in their legend of King Aristodemus, who sacrificed his beloved daughter to the gods of the underworld in an attempt to enlist their aid against the invading Spartans. When his campaign of resistance at last failed, in grief he slew himself on her grave. Deprived of their freedom and their city-state, the Messenian helots were ever after on the lookout for a chance to revolt against their Spartan overlords.

In their private lives, helots could keep some personal possessions and practice their religion, as could slaves generally in Greece. Publicly, however, helots lived under the constant threat of officially sanctioned violence. Every year the ephors formally declared war between Sparta and the helots, allowing any Spartan to kill a helot without any civil penalty or fear of offending the gods by unsanctioned murder. By beating the helots frequently, forcing them to get drunk in public as an object lesson to young Spartans, making them wear dogskin caps, and generally humiliating them, the Spartans consistently emphasized the "otherness" of the helots. In this way Spartans erected a moral barrier between themselves and the helots to justify their harsh abuse of fellow Greeks.

Their labor made helots valuable to the Spartans. In addition to farming the plots of land the state allotted to individual Spartan households for their sustenance and working as household servants, by the fifth century B.C., Laconian and Messenian helots alike also accompanied Spartan hoplite warriors on the march, carrying their heavy gear and armor. In the words of Tyrtaeus, helots worked "like donkeys exhausted under heavy loads; they lived under the painful necessity of having to give their masters half the food their ploughed land bore." This compulsory rent of 50 percent of everything produced by the helots working on each family's assigned plot was supposed to amount to seventy measures of barley each year to the male master of the household and twelve to his wife, along with an equivalent amount of fruit and other produce. In all, this food was enough to support six or seven people. Because Spartan men did not have to work their own land, they devoted themselves to full-time training for war. Contrasting the freedom of Spartan citizens from ordinary work with the lot of the helots, the later Athenian Critias commented, "Laconia is the home of the freest of the Greeks, and of the most enslaved."

The Structured Life of Spartans

From childhood on, life in Sparta revolved around military preparedness. Boys lived at home only until their seventh year, when they were sent to live in communal barracks with other males until they were thirty. They spent most of their time exercising, hunting, training with weapons, and being acculturated to Spartan values by listening to tales of bravery and heroism at the common meals presided over by older men. Discipline was strict, to prepare young males for the hard life of a soldier on campaign. For example, the boys were not allowed to speak at will. They were also underfed purposely so they would learn stealth by stealing food. (If they were caught, punishment and disgrace followed immediately.) One famous Spartan tale taught how seriously boys were supposed to fear such failure: having successfully stolen a fox, which he was hiding under his clothing, a Spartan youth died because he let the panicked animal rip out his insides rather than be detected in the theft. By the Classical Age, older boys were dispatched to live in the wilds for a period as members of the "secret band" whose job it was to murder any helots who seemed likely to foment rebellion. Spartan men who could not survive the tough conditions of their childhood training fell into social disgrace and were not certified as Equals, the official name for adult males entitled to full citizen rights of participation in politics and to the respect of the community. Only the sons of the royal family were exempted from this training, perhaps to avoid a potential social crisis if a king's son failed to stay the course.

Each Equal had to gain entry to a group that dined together at common meals, in a so-called common mess, each of which had about fifteen members. The new member was admitted on the condition that he contribute a regular amount of barley, cheese, figs, condiments, and wine to the mess from the produce provided by the helots working on his family plot. Some meat was apparently contributed too, because Spartan cuisine was infamous for a black, bloody broth of pork condemned as practically inedible by other Greeks. Perhaps it was concocted from the wild boars Spartan men loved to hunt, an activity for which messmates were formally excused from the compulsory communal meals. If any member failed to keep up his contributions, he was expelled from the mess and lost his full citizenship rights. The experience of spending so much time in these common messes schooled Sparta's young men in the values of their society. There they learned to call all older men "father" to emphasize that their primary loyalty was to the group and not to their genetic families. There they were chosen to be the special favorites of males older than themselves to build bonds of affection, including physical love, for others at whose side they would have to march into deadly battle. There they learned to take the rough joking of army life for which Sparta was well known. In short, the common mess took the place of a boy's family and school when he was growing

up and remained his main social environment once he reached adulthood. Its function was to mold and maintain his values consistent with the demands of the one honorable occupation for Spartan men: an obedient soldier. Tyrtaeus enshrined the Spartan male ideal in his poetry: "Know that it is good for the polis and the whole people when a man takes his place in the front row of warriors and stands his ground without flinching."

Spartan women were known throughout the Greek world for their relative freedom. Some Greeks thought it scandalous that Spartan girls exercised with boys while wearing scanty outfits. Spartan women were supposed to use the freedom from labor provided by the helot system to keep themselves physically fit to bear healthy children and to raise them as strict upholders of Spartan values. The male ideal for Spartan women appears in the late seventh century B.C. in the work of Alcman, a poet who wrote songs female and male choruses performed at Spartan civic and religious occasions. The dazzling leader of a women's chorus, he wrote, "stands out as if among a herd of cows someone placed a firmly-built horse with ringing hooves, a prizewinner from winged dreams."

Although Sparta deliberately banned money to discourage the accumulation of material goods, women, like men, could own land privately. More and more land came into the hands of women in later Spartan history because the male population declined through losses in war, especially during the Classical Age. Spartan women with property enjoyed special status, because Spartan law forbade dividing the land originally allotted to a family. This law meant that in a family with more than one son, all the land went to the eldest son. Fathers with multiple sons therefore needed to find their younger sons brides who had inherited land and property from their family because they had no brother surviving. Otherwise, younger sons might fall into dire poverty.

With their husbands so rarely at home, women directed the households, which included servants, daughters, and sons until they left for their communal training. As a result, Spartan women exercised more power in the household than did women elsewhere in Greece. Until he was thirty a Spartan husband was not allowed to live with his family, and even newlywed men were expected to pay only short visits to their wives by sneaking into their own houses at night. This Spartan custom was not the only one other Greeks found bizarre. Spartans also had no prohibition against adultery, and, if all parties agreed, a woman could have children by a man other than her husband.

Spartan women were free from some of the restrictions imposed on women in other Greek city-states so they could more easily fulfill their basic function: to produce manpower for the Spartan army. By the Classical Age* the ongoing problem of producing enough children to keep the Spartan citizen population from shrinking had grown acute. Men were legally required to get married, with bachelors subjected to fines and public ridicule. Women who died in childbirth were the only Spartans allowed to have their names placed on their tombstones, a mark of honor for their sacrifice to the state.

All Spartan citizens were expected to put service to their city-state before personal concerns because Sparta's survival was continually threatened by its own economic foundation, the great mass of helots. Because Sparta's well-being depended on the systematic exploitation of these enslaved Greeks, its entire political and social system required a staunch militarism and conservative values. Change meant danger. Although the Spartans institutionalized equality in the form of the common mess, they denied social and political equality to ordinary male citizens, an inevitable inequality in an oligarchy. Whatever other Greeks may have thought of the particulars of the Spartan system, they admired the Spartans' unswerving respect for their laws as a guide to life in hostile surroundings, albeit of their own making.

Tyranny in the City-States

Opposition to aristocratic and oligarchic domination brought the first Greek tyrants to power (although never in Sparta). The most famous early tyrant arose at Corinth around 657 B.C. in protest to the rule of the aristocratic family called the Bacchiads. Under Bacchiad rule in the eighth and early seventh centuries B.C., Corinth had blossomed into the most economically advanced city in archaic Greece. The Corinthians had progressed so far in naval engineering, for example, that other Greeks contracted with them to have ships built. Corinth's strong fleet helped the Bacchiads in founding overseas colonies at Corcyra in northwest Greece and Syracuse on Sicily, city-states that would themselves become major naval powers.

The Bacchiads fell into disfavor despite the city's prosperity, because they ruled violently. Cypselus, an aristocrat whose mother was a Bacchiad, readied himself to take power by becoming popular with the masses: "he became one of the most admired of Corinth's citizens because he was courageous, prudent, and helpful to the people, unlike the oligarchs in power, who were insolent and violent," according to a later historian. Cypselus engineered the overthrow of Bacchiad rule with popular support and a favorable oracle from Delphi. He then ruthlessly suppressed rival aristocrats, but his popularity remained so high that he could govern without the protection of a bodyguard. Corinth added to its economic strength during Cypselus's rule by exporting large quantities of fine pottery, especially to markets in Italy and Sicily. Cypselus founded additional colonies along the sailing route to the western Mediterranean to promote Corinthian trade in that direction.

When Cypselus died in 625 B.C. his son Periander succeeded him. Periander aggressively continued Corinth's economic expansion by founding colonies on the coasts both northwest and northeast of Greek territory to increase trade with the interior regions there, which were rich in timber and precious metals. He also pursued commercial contacts with Egypt, an interest commemorated in the Egyptian name Psammetichus he gave to one of his sons. The city's prosperity encouraged crafts, art, and architecture to flourish. The foundations of the great stone temple to Apollo begun in this period can still be seen. Unlike his father, however, Periander lost popular support by ruling harshly. He kept his power until his death in 585 B.C., but the hostility that persisted against him led to the overthrow of his son and successor, Psammetichus, within a short time. The opponents of tyranny thereupon installed a government based on a board of eight magistrates and a council of eighty men.

Greek tyranny represented a distinctive type of rule for several reasons. Although tyrants were by definition rulers who usurped power by force rather than inheriting it like legitimate kings, they

*500–323 B.C. DEATH OF ALEXANDER THE GREAT

+ BAH·KEE·ADS

The Archaic Temple of Apollo at Corinth
This Doric-style building dating to the sixth century B.C. *is one of the earliest surviving stone temples. The rocky acropolis of Corinth looms in the background.*

too established family dynasties to maintain their tyranny. Also, the tyrants were usually aristocrats, or at least near-aristocrats, who rallied support for their coups among nonaristocrats. In city-states where landless men may have lacked full citizenship or felt substantially disfranchised in political life, tyrants may have garnered backing by extending citizenship and other privileges to these groups. Moreover, tyrants usually preserved the existing laws and political institutions of their city-states.

As at Corinth, most tyrannies needed to cultivate support among the masses of their city-states to remain in power because their armies were composed primarily of commoners. The dynasty of tyrants on the island of Samos in the eastern Aegean Sea, who came to power about 540 B.C., built enormous public works to benefit their city-state and provide employment. They began constructing a temple to Hera meant to be the largest in the Greek world, and they dramatically improved the urban water supply by excavating a great tunnel connected

to a distant spring. This marvel of engineering, with a channel eight feet high, ran for nearly a mile through a 900-foot-high mountain. Later tyrannies in city-states on Sicily similarly graced their cities with beautiful temples and public buildings.

By working in the interests of their peoples, some tyrannies, like that founded by Cypselus, maintained their popularity for decades. Other tyrants experienced bitter opposition from aristocrats jealous of the tyrant's power or provoked civil war by ruling brutally and inequitably. The poet Alcaeus* of the city-state of Mytilene on the island of Lesbos in the northeastern Aegean, himself a rebellious aristocrat, described such strife around 600 B.C.: "Let's forget our anger; let's quit our heart-devouring strife and civil war, which some god has stirred up among us, ruining the people but bestowing the glory on our tyrant for which he prays." Although today the English word *tyrant* labels a brutal or unwanted leader, tyrants in archaic Greece did not always fit that description. Greeks evaluated tyrants based on their behavior, opposing

*AL·SEE·UHS

the ruthless and violent ones but welcoming the fair and helpful ones.

The Early Struggle for Democracy at Athens

Greeks explained significant historical changes, such as the founding of communities or the codification of law, as the work of an individual "inventor" from the distant past. The Athenians traced back the origins of their city-state to a single man. Athenian legends credited Theseus with founding the polis of Athens by the synoecism of villages in Attica, the name given to the peninsula that formed the territory of the Athenian city-state. Because Attica had

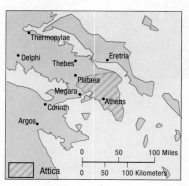

Attica and Central Greece

several ports along its coast, the Athenians were much more oriented to seafaring than were the landlocked Spartans. Theseus made an appropriate mythical founder for Athens: he was described as a traveling adventurer, sailing, for example, to Crete to defeat the Minotaur, a cannibalistic monster, half human and half bull. Theseus embodied the characteristics Athenians valued: courage, adventurousness, and fairness.

Unlike most other important sites inhabited in the Mycenaean period, Athens had not suffered catastrophic destruction at the end of the Bronze Age. Nevertheless, its population shrank in the Early Dark Age, which depressed its economy. By around 850 B.C., however, archaeological evidence shows that the Athenian agricultural economy was reviving. As economic conditions improved in the early Archaic Age, the population of Attica apparently expanded at a phenomenal rate from about 800 to 700 B.C., the free peasants constituting the fastest growing segment of the population. The free peasants evidently began to insist on having a say in making Athenian policies because they felt justice demanded at least limited political equality. Some of these small landowners became wealthy enough to afford hoplite armor, and these men probably pressed the aristocrats who had previously ruled Athens as a relatively broad oligarchy for concessions. Because rivalries among the aristocrats prevented them from uniting to oppose these demands, they had to respond to these pressures to ensure the allegiance of the hoplites, on whom Athenian military strength depended.

By the late seventh century B.C., Athens's male citizens—rich, middle class, and poor—had established the beginnings of a limited form of democratic government. Determining why they moved strongly toward democracy instead of, for example, a narrow oligarchy like Sparta's remains difficult. Two factors perhaps encouraged the incipient democracy at Athens: rapid population growth, and a rough sense of egalitarianism among male citizens that survived the frontierlike conditions of the early Dark Age, when most people had shared the same meager existence. But these conditions affected all of Greece in the Archaic Age. Why then did not all the other city-states evolve into democracies? Perhaps the rapidness of population growth among Athenian peasants gave them greater clout than elsewhere. Their power and political cohesiveness were evident as early as 632 B.C., when they rallied "from the fields in a body," according to a later historian, to foil the attempted coup of an Athenian nobleman named Cylon, who with some other aristocrats had planned to install a tyranny. Influential aristocrats like Solon and Cleisthenes, who later worked to strengthen Athenian democracy for differing reasons, also made democracy more viable at Athens.

The scanty evidence seems to indicate that by the seventh century B.C. all freeborn adult male citizens of Athens could attend open meetings, in a body called the assembly, which elected nine magistrates called *archons* (rulers) annually. The archons, still all aristocrats, headed the government and rendered verdicts in disputes and criminal accusations. As before, aristocrats still dominated Athenian political life—they used their influence to make sure they were elected archons, perhaps by marshaling their traditional bands of followers and by making alliances with other aristocrats. The right of middle-class and poor men to serve in the assembly had only limited value at this time because little business besides electing archons was conducted when the assembly gathered. It probably convened rarely in this period, and then only when the current archons decided it should.

KLĪS·THEN·EEZ

Aristocratic political alliances often proved temporary, however, and rivalries among jealous aristocrats continued under early Athenian democracy. In the aftermath of Cylon's attempted tyranny, an Athenian named Draco was appointed in 621 B.C., perhaps after pressure by the hoplites, to establish a code of laws promoting stability and equity. Unfortunately, Draco's laws further destabilized the political situation; the Athenians later remembered them as having been as harsh as the meaning of his name—"dragon, serpent." (Our word *draconian,* meaning excessively severe, reflects this view.) The well-being of Athens's free peasants deteriorated as well; their circumstances had been eroding slowly for a long time. This condition also undermined social peace. Later Athenians did not know the cause of this economic crisis—only that it pitted the rich against the middle class and the poor.

Many poor Athenians had apparently lost their land to wealthier proprietors by the late seventh century B.C. Athenian farms often operated at subsistence level, and a bad year could mean starvation. Even if crops were abundant in a given year, farmers had no easy way to convert the surplus into imperishable capital they could store to offset future lean years. (Coinage was invented only in the late seventh century B.C., and it did not come into common use for a long time.) To survive, farmers often had to borrow food and seed. When they could borrow no more, they had to leave their land and find a job to support their families, most likely a job working for other, more successful farmers. The more successful farmers, who perhaps employed more effective methods or maybe were simply more fortunate than farmers who failed, could use and eventually buy the land of failed farmers. This process meant that fewer and fewer people gradually controlled or accumulated most of the arable land. The crisis became so acute that impoverished peasants were even being sold into slavery to pay off debts. Finally, twenty-five years after Draco's legislation, civil war threatened to break out. In desperation the Athenians in 594 B.C. gave Solon special authority to revise their laws to deal with the emergency.

As he explains in his autobiographical poetry, Solon tried to steer a middle course between the demands of the rich to preserve their financial advantages and the pleas of the poor to redistribute the land held by wealthy landowners. His famous "shaking off of obligations"—some sort of reduction or cancellation of debts—somehow freed those farms whose ownership had become formally encumbered without, however, actually redistributing any land. He also forbade selling Athenians into slavery for economic reasons and liberated citizens who had become slaves in this way, commemorating his success in verses he wrote: "To Athens, their home established by the gods, I brought back many who had been sold into slavery, some justly, some not. . . ."

Attempting to balance political power between rich and poor, Solon ranked male citizens into four classes according to their income:[1] "five-hundred-measure men" (those with an annual income equivalent to that much agricultural produce),[2] "horsemen" (income of three hundred measures),[3] "yoked men" (two hundred measures), and[4] "laborers" (less than two hundred measures). The higher a man's class, the higher the government office for which he was eligible; laborers were barred from all posts. Solon did, however, reaffirm the right of the laborer class to participate in the assembly. He probably created a council of four hundred men to prepare an agenda for the assembly, although some scholars believe this innovation occurred later than Solon's time. Aristocrats could not dominate the council's deliberations because its members were chosen by lot, probably only from the top three classes. Solon may also have initiated a schedule of regular meetings for the assembly. These reforms added impetus to the assembly's legislative role and thus indirectly laid a foundation for the political influence the laborer class would gradually acquire over the next century and a half.

Solon's classification scheme was another step toward democracy because it allowed for upward social mobility: if a man increased his income, he could move up the scale of eligibility for office. Because income was not directly taxed, ambitious entrepreneurs could make more profit and benefit from what they earned. Solon's reforms gave Athenian male citizens a political and social system far more open to individual initiative and change than that of Sparta.

Equally important to restoring stability in a time of crisis was Solon's ruling that any male citizen could bring charges on a wide variety of offenses against wrongdoers on behalf of any victim of a crime. Furthermore, people who believed a magistrate had rendered unfair judgments against them now had the right to appeal their case to the assembly. With these two measures, Solon involved ordinary citizens, not just the predominantly aristocratic magistrates, in the administration of justice. He balanced these judicial reforms acknowledging the common people, however, by granting broader powers to the "Council which meets on the Hill of the god of war Ares," which we call the Areopagus (meaning "Ares' hill"). Archons became members of the Areopagus after their year in office. This body of ex-archons could, if the members chose to, wield great power, because it judged the most serious cases—in particular, any accusations against archons themselves. Solon probably expected the Areopagus to use its power to protect his reforms as well.

For its place and time, Athens's emerging democracy was remarkable, even at this early stage in its evolution, because it granted all male citizens the possibility of participating meaningfully in making laws and administering justice. But not everyone admired Solon's system. The same king who had scoffed at Solon's lawmaking reportedly also found Athenian democracy ludicrous. Observing the procedure in the Athenian assembly, he expressed his amazement that leading aristocratic politicians could only recommend policy in their speeches, while the male citizens as a whole voted on what to do: "I find it astonishing," he remarked, "that here wise men speak on public affairs, while fools decide them." Some Athenians agreed with the king, and did their best to undermine Solon's reforms. Such oligarchic sympathizers continued to challenge Athenian democracy periodically throughout its history.

Contentiousness among aristocrats, combined with the continued discontent of the poorest Athenians, lay behind the strife in the mid-sixth century B.C. that led to Athens's first tyranny. At this time an Athenian aristocrat named Pisistratus, helped by his upper-class friends and the poor, whose interests he championed, launched an effort to make himself sole ruler by force. He finally established himself securely as tyrant at Athens in 546 B.C. Pisistratus made funds available to help peasants acquire needed farm equipment. He provided employment for poorer men while benefit-

ing Athens, hiring them to build roads and work on such major public works as a great temple to Zeus and fountains to increase the supply of drinking water. His tax on agricultural production, one of the rare instances of direct taxation in Athenian history, financed the loans to farmers and the building projects. He also arranged for judicial officials to go on circuits through the outlying villages of Attica to hear cases, thus saving farmers the trouble of having to leave their fields to seek justice in Athens. Like the earlier tyrants of Corinth, he promoted the economic, cultural, and architectural development of Athens. Athenian pottery, for example, now began to crowd out Corinthian in the export trade.

Hippias, the eldest son of Pisistratus, continued the tyranny after his father's death in 527 B.C. He governed by making certain that his relatives and friends occupied magistracies. But for a time he also allowed his aristocratic rivals to hold office, thereby defusing some of the tension created by their jealousy of his superior status. Eventually, however, the aristocratic family of the Alcmaeonids arranged to have the Spartans send an army to expel Hippias. In the ensuing vacuum of power, the leading Alcmaeonid, Cleisthenes, sought support among the masses by promising democratic reforms when his bitterest aristocratic rival became an archon in 508 B.C. When the rival tried to block Cleisthenes' reforms by calling in the Spartans again, the Athenian people united to force him and his foreign allies out. The conflict between Athens and Sparta ended quickly but sowed the seeds of mutual distrust between the two city-states.

His popular support gave Cleisthenes the authority to begin to install the democratic system for which Athens has become famous, and the importance of his reforms led later Athenians to think of him as a principal founder of their democracy. First he made the villages of the countryside and the neighborhoods of the city of Athens the constituent units of Athenian political organization. Organized in these units, called *demes*, the male citizens participated directly in the running of their government: in deme registers they kept track of which males were citizens and therefore eligible at eighteen to attend the assembly and vote on laws and public policies. The demes in turn were grouped into ten so-called tribes for other political functions, such as choosing fifty representatives by lot from each tribe to serve for one year on the council of five hundred, which replaced Solon's council of four hundred. The number of representatives from each deme was proportional to its population. Most important, the ten men who served each year as "generals," the officials with the highest civil and military authority, were elected one from each tribe. Cleisthenes' reorganization was complex; its general aim seems to have been to undermine existing political alliances among aristocrats in the interests of greater democracy.

By about 500 B.C., Cleisthenes had devised an Athenian democracy based on direct participation by as many adult male citizens as possible. That he could institute such a system successfully in a time of turmoil and that it could endure, as it did, means that Cleisthenes must have been building on preexisting conditions favorable to democracy. As an aristocrat looking for popular support, Cleisthenes certainly had reason to establish the kind of system he thought ordinary people wanted. That he based his system on the demes, most of which were country villages, suggests that some democratic notions may have stemmed from the traditions of village life. Possibly the idea of widespread participation in government gained support from the villagers' customary way of dealing with each other on relatively egalitarian terms: each man was entitled to his say in running local affairs and had to persuade others of the wisdom of his recommendations. Because many aristocrats seem to have preferred to reside in the city, their ability to dominate discussion in the demes was reduced. In any case the idea that persuasion, rather than force or status, should constitute the mechanism for political decision-making in the emerging Athenian democracy fit well with the spirit of intellectual changes rippling through Greece in the late Archaic Age.

New Ways of Thought

Poetry was the only form of Greek literature until the late Archaic Age. The earliest Greek poetry, that of Homer and Hesiod, had been confined to a single rhythm. A much greater rhythmic diversity characterized the new form of poetry, called lyric, that emerged during the Archaic Age. Lyric poems were much shorter than the narrative poetry of Homer or the didactic poetry of Hesiod, and they

encompassed many forms and subjects, but they were always performed with the accompaniment of the lyre (a kind of harp that gives its name to the poetry). Choral poets like Alcman of Sparta wrote songs for groups to perform on public occasions to honor the deities, to celebrate famous events in a city-state's history, for wedding processions, and to praise victors in athletic contests. Lyric poets writing songs for solo performance at social occasions stressed a personal level of expression on a variety of topics. Solon and Alcaeus, for example, wrote poems focused on contemporary politics. Others deliberately adopted a critical attitude toward traditional values such as strength in war. For example, Sappho, a lyric poet from Lesbos born about 630 B.C. and famous for her poems on love, wrote, "Some would say the most beautiful thing on our dark earth is an army of cavalry, others of infantry, others of ships, but I say it's whatever a person loves." In this poem Sappho was expressing her longing for a woman she loved, who was now far away. Archilochus of Paros, who probably lived in the early seventh century B.C., became famous for poems on themes as diverse as friends lost at sea, mockery of martial valor, and love gone astray. The bitter power of his poetic invective reportedly caused a father and his two daughters to commit suicide when Archilochus angrily ridiculed them after the father had ended Archilochus's affair with his daughter Neobule. Some modern literary critics think the poems about Neobule and her family are fictional, not autobiographical, and were meant to display Archilochus's dazzling talent for "blame poetry," the mirror image of lyric poetry as the poetry of praise. Mimnermus of Colophon, another seventh-century B.C. lyric poet, rhapsodized about the glory of youth and lamented its brevity: "no longer than the time the sun shines on the plain." Lyric poets' focus on the individual's feelings represented a new stage in Greek literary sensibilities, one that continues to inspire much poetry today.

Greece's earliest prose literature was written in the late Archaic Age. Thinkers we now usually call philosophers, but who could also be described as theoretical scientists studying the physical world, created Greek prose to express their new ways of thought. These thinkers, who came from the city-states of Ionia, developed radically new explanations of the human world and its relation

Ionia and the Aegean

to the gods and goddesses. Thus began the study of philosophy in Greece. Ionia's geographical location next to the non-Greek civilizations of Anatolia, which had contact with the older civilizations of Egypt and the Near East, permitted Ionian thinkers to acquire knowledge and intellectual inspiration from their neighbors in the eastern Mediterranean area. Because Greece in this period had no formal schools at any level, thinkers like those from Ionia made their ideas known by teaching pupils privately and giving public lectures. Some Ionian thinkers composed poetry to explain their theories and gave public recitations. People who studied with these thinkers or heard their presentations then helped spread the new ideas.

Knowledge from the ancient Near East inspired Ionian thinkers, just as it influenced Archaic Age Greek artists. Greek vase painters and specialists in decorating metal vessels imitated Near Eastern designs depicting animals and luxuriant plants; Greek sculptors produced narrative reliefs such as those of Assyria, and statues modeled on the Egyptian style. Egypt also inspired Greek architects to use stone for columns, ornamental details, and eventually entire buildings.

Information about the regular movements of the stars and planets developed by astronomers in Babylonia proved especially key in helping Ionian thinkers reach their conclusions about the nature of the physical world. The first of the Ionian theorists, Thales (c. 625–545 B.C.), who came from the city-state of Miletus, was said to have predicted a solar eclipse in 585 B.C., an accomplishment implying he had been influenced by Babylonian learning. Modern astronomers doubt Thales actually predicted the eclipse, but the story shows how eastern scientific and mathematical knowledge influenced Ionian thinkers. Working from such knowledge as the observed fact that celestial bodies moved in a regular pattern, thinkers like Thales and Anaximander (c. 610–540 B.C.), also from Miletus, drew the revolutionary conclusion that the physical world was regulated by a set of laws of nature rather than by the arbitrary intervention of divine beings. Pythagoras, who emigrated from Samos to southern Italy about 530 B.C., taught that patterns and relationships of numbers explained the entire world. His doctrines inspired systematic study of mathematics and the numerical aspects of musical harmony.

The Ionian thinkers insisted the workings of the universe could be revealed because natural phenomena were neither random nor arbitrary. The universe, the totality of things, they named *cosmos* because this word meant an orderly arrangement that is beautiful. The order of the cosmos encompassed not only the motions of heavenly bodies but also the weather, the growth of plants and animals, human health and well-being, and so on. Because the universe was ordered, it was intelligible; because it was intelligible, events could be explained by thought and research. The thinkers who deduced this view believed they needed to give reasons for their conclusions and to persuade others by arguments based on evidence. They believed, in other words, in logic (derived from the Greek term *logos*, meaning, among other things, "a reasoned explanation"). This mode of thought represented a crucial first step toward science and philosophy as these disciplines endure today. The rule-based view of the causes of events and physical phenomena developed by these thinkers contrasted sharply with the traditional mythological view of causation. Naturally, many people had difficulty accepting such a startling change in their understanding of the world, and the older tradition explaining events as the work of deities lived on alongside the new approach.

The ideas of the Ionian thinkers probably spread slowly because no means of mass communication existed, and few men could afford to spend the time to become their followers and then return home to explain these new ways of thought to others. Magic remained an important preoccupation in the lives of the majority of ordinary people, who retained their notions that deities and demons frequently and directly affected their fortunes and health, as well as the events of nature. Even though their ideas probably had only a limited effect on the ancient world, the Ionian thinkers had initiated a tremendous development in intellectual history: the separation of scientific thinking from myth and religion. Some modern scholars call this development the birth of rationalism. But it would be unfair to label the myths and religious ways of ancient people irrational if that word is taken to mean "unthinking" or "silly." They realized their lives were subject to forces beyond their control and understanding, and it was not unreasonable to attribute supernatural origins to the powers of nature or the ravages of disease. The new scientific ways of thought insisted, however, that observable evidence had to be sought and theories of explanation had to be logical. Just being old or popular no longer bestowed truth on a story purporting to explain natural phenomena. In this way, the Ionian thinkers parted company with the traditional ways of thinking of the ancient Near East as found in its rich mythology and repeated in the myths of early Greece.

Developing the idea that people must give reasons to explain their beliefs, rather than just make assertions others must believe without evidence, was the most important achievement of the early Ionian thinkers. This insistence on rationality, coupled with the belief that the world could be understood as something other than the plaything of divine whims, gave humans hope that they could improve their lives through their own efforts. As Xenophanes from Colophon (c. 580–480 B.C.) put it, "The gods have not revealed all things from the beginning to mortals, but, by seeking, human beings find out, in time, what is better." Xenophanes, like other Ionian thinkers, believed in the existence of gods, but he nevertheless assigned the opportunity and the responsibility for improving human life to humans themselves.

CONCLUSION

At the start of the Dark Age the future looked bleak in Greece and the ancient Near East. The Near East recovered its political and economic strength more quickly than did Greece, and the Neo-Assyrian kingdom used its military force to build the most extensive empire the region had yet seen—even Egypt, which had never revived as an international power, became part of this empire. The Neo-Babylonian kingdom of the Chaldeans succeeded Assyria as the greatest power in the Near East, but it then fell to the new kingdom of Persia. By 500 B.C., Persia far exceeded even the greatest extent of the earlier Assyrian empire. These kingdoms essentially continued or revived the political and social institutions of their predecessors in the Near East—rule by a strong, centralized authority. The most significant innovations in Near Eastern history in this period occurred in religious history: the consolidation of the Hebrew religion as a true monotheism, whose tenets required Jews to observe strict rules of ethical and ritual purity to maintain their covenant with Yahweh, and the editing of the Hebrew Bible to produce sacred scriptures as the basic texts of Judaism.

The Dark Age truly devastated Greece. The tightly organized redistributive economy and the splendid palaces of the Mycenaean period had been destroyed. Along with them had gone the traditional social and political organization. Much farmland lay vacant or out of cultivation. The population had shrunk to a fraction of its former size. No one, it seems, any longer knew how to write. By around 750 B.C., however, the conditions of life in Greece were strikingly different. The population had grown so rapidly that a shortage of arable land had forced colonists to found new settlements abroad, which were also founded for trade. A developing sense of Greek identity and communal spirit had promoted the creation of pan-Hellenic centers, such as Olympia with its games, and Delphi with its oracle of Apollo. Roused by a desire for the justice that poets taught had the support of the deities, the free peasants of Greece somehow wrested a share of political power from aristocrats and hoplites in Greece's emerging new political form, the independent city-state. The creation of citizenship as the conceptual and organizational basis of the Greek city-state represented a major innovation. The concept of citizenship, though restricted in its political rights to male citizens, emphasized the notion of personal freedom. Chattel slavery contrasted sharply with the ideas of its citizenship. Trade with the Near East once again brought Greeks into contact with the ideas of its civilizations, reintroduced literacy to Greece, and influenced Greek art and mythology.

Geography and the varying courses of local history led to different political and social developments in different city-states in the Archaic Age. Tyrants promoted prosperity in city-states like Corinth. Sparta evolved into an oligarchy and adopted a distinctive way of life designed to exploit a subject population, thereby obligating Spartans to devote all their energies to maintaining their state's military strength. The communal organization of Sparta largely separated men's and women's lives, requiring men to train for war and women to manage both households and farms. Throughout Greece, women were legal wards of their fathers, husbands, or male relatives, with only limited rights of their own. While maintaining their paternalism toward women, Athenian men gradually developed a democracy based on certain egalitarian principles for rich and poor men alike, a revolutionary development for the ancient world.

Equally revolutionary was the change in ways of thought inspired by Ionian thinkers in the Archaic Age. By arguing that the universe was based on laws of nature, which humans could explain through reason and research, they established the conceptual basis for science and philosophy. By their example as well as their theories, they encouraged humans to believe that individual initiative could help "find out what is best." Thus they valued an intellectual freedom that corresponded to the value of political freedom—unequally distributed though it may have been by the exclusion of women and slaves—in the city-state.

It was during the Archaic Age of Greece that the values that have so profoundly affected Western civilization first began to emerge. But the Greek world and its new values would soon face a grave threat from the awesome kingdom of Persia.

SUGGESTIONS FOR FURTHER READING

Source Materials

Barnes, Jonathan. *Early Greek Philosophy.* 1987. An excellent, brief introduction to the Ionian thinkers followed by excerpts in context from them and other early Greek philosophers.

Crawford, Michael, and David Whitehead. *Archaic and Classical Greece: A Selection of Ancient Sources in Translation.* 1983. A collection of excerpts from literature and historical documents with useful introductions and annotations.

Hesiod, *Theogony; Works and Days.* Available in various translations such as one by Apostolos N. Athanassakis, 1983, as well as in the bilingual edition published in the Loeb Classical Library series.

Homer, *Iliad; Odyssey.* Available in various translations such as one by Robert Fitzgerald, 1974, 1961, respectively, as well as in the bilingual edition published in the Loeb Classical Library series.

Rhodes, P. J. *The Greek City States: A Source Book.* 1986. A collection of sources arranged in sections of explanatory narrative.

Sappho. Her poems, many of which survive only in fragmentary form, are available, along with the poems of Alcaeus, in *Greek Lyric I,* 1982, a bilingual edition published in the Loeb Classical Library series. Jeffrey M. Duban, *Ancient and Modern Images of Sappho: Translations and Studies in Archaic Greek Love Lyric,* 1983, includes translations of Sappho, Alcman, Anacreon, Archilochus, and Ibycus.

Interpretive Studies

Boardman, John. *The Greeks Overseas: Their Early Colonies and Trade.* New ed. 1980. A survey of Greek colonization and overseas commerce.

Boardman, John, et al. *The Oxford History of the Classical World.* 1986. Articles on central historical topics as well as Homer, myth and Hesiod, lyric poetry, and philosophy.

The Cambridge Ancient History. 2d ed. Vol. III, Part 3, *The Expansion of the Greek World, Eighth to Sixth Centuries B.C.* 1982. An authoritative survey of Greek history in the Archaic Age.

Cartledge, Paul. *Sparta and Lakonia: A Regional History, 1300–362 B.C.* 1979. A survey beginning in the late Bronze Age with emphasis on geography and the material conditions affecting Spartan history.

Coldstream, J. N. *Geometric Greece.* 1977. Detailed treatment of Greece in the ninth and eighth centuries B.C. with much discussion of artifacts.

Donlan, Walter. *The Aristocratic Ideal in Ancient Greece: Attitudes of Superiority from Homer to the End of the Fifth Century B.C.* 1980. An interpretation of the functioning of concepts such as honor, excellence, and justice in Greek society.

Emlyn-Jones, C. J. *The Ionians and Hellenism: A Study of the Cultural Achievements of Early Greek Inhabitants of Asia Minor.* 1980. An assessment of the art, literature, and philosophy of the Ionians from the eighth to the sixth century B.C.

Finley, M. I. *Ancient Slavery and Modern Ideology.* 1980. A discussion of the nature of ancient slavery as compared to more modern systems of slavery.

———. *Early Greece. The Bronze and Archaic Ages.* Rev. ed. 1981. A brief, readable introduction to Greek history to the dawn of the Classical Age with emphasis on the difficulties of clear interpretation.

———. *The World of Odysseus.* 2d ed. 1965. A standard work on the question of how much history can be found in Homeric poetry.

Finley, M. I., and H. W. Pleket. *The Olympic Games: The First Thousand Years.* 1976. A survey of the history of the games throughout antiquity.

Fitzhardinge, L. F. *The Spartans.* 1980. A well-illustrated survey of Spartan history and society.

Forrest, W. G. *The Emergence of Greek Democracy, 800–400 B.C.* 1966. A provocative classic in the field arguing that developments at Sparta set the stage for the rise of democracy.

Garlan, Yvon. *Slavery in Ancient Greece.* Rev. ed. Translated by Janet Lloyd. 1988. A comprehensive discussion of the varying categories of Greek slavery.

Guthrie, W. K. C. *A History of Greek Philosophy.* Vol. 1, *The Earlier Presocratics and the Pythagoreans.* 1962. The standard, detailed introduction to the Ionian thinkers and other early Greek philosophers.

Hurwitt, Jeffrey M. *The Art and Culture of Early Greece, 1100–480 B.C..* 1985. A detailed treatment of the cultural significance of Greek art before the Classical Age.

Jeffrey, L. H. *Archaic Greece: The City-States, c. 700–500 B.C.* 1976. Political history of the Greek world in the Archaic Age presented geographically.

Morris, Ian. *Burial and Ancient Society: The Rise of the Greek City-State.* 1987. Stimulating, high-level discussion of the archaeological evidence for the social conflicts that provided the context for the rise of the city-state.

Murray, Oswyn. *Early Greece.* 1980. An accessible survey that places archaic Greece in the context of Mediterranean civilization of the time, especially the Near East.

Snodgrass, Anthony. *Archaic Greece: The Age of Experiment.* 1980. An exceptionally stimulating presentation of the Archaic Age as a period of great innovation and change.

———. *The Dark Age of Greece.* 1971. An extensive treatment making the most of the limited evidence available for this period.

Starr, Chester G. *The Economic and Social Growth of Early Greece, 800–500 b.c.* 1977. A brief and readable account of the interdependency of economic and social changes in the Archaic Age.

———. *Individual and Community: The Rise of the Polis, 800–500 B.C.* 1986. A compact survey of the balancing of communal interests and the emerging concept of individual freedom in the Archaic Age.

Swaddling, Judith. *The Ancient Olympic Games.* 1980. A brief, illustrated survey of the history of the games.

Wilbur, J. B., and H. J. Allen. *The Worlds of the Early Greek Philosophers.* 1979. A discussion of the philosophers of early Greece in their historical contexts.

The greatest military danger ever to threaten ancient Greece began with a diplomatic misunderstanding. Fearing the Spartans would again try to intervene at Athens in support of the city's aristocratic faction opposed to democracy, the Athenians in 507 B.C. sent ambassadors to ask for a protective alliance with the king of Persia, Darius I (*522–486 B.C.). The Persian Empire was now the largest, richest, and militarily strongest power in the ancient world. The Athenian emissaries met with a representative of Darius at Sardis, the Persian headquarters in western Anatolia (modern Turkey). When the royal intermediary had heard their plea for help, he replied, "But who in the world are you and where do you live?"

The dynamics of this incident reveal the forces motivating the conflicts that would dominate the military and political history of mainland Greece during the fifth century B.C. First, the two major powers in mainland Greece—Sparta and Athens—remained wary of each other. When the Spartan army had backed Cleisthenes' rival in a power struggle over who would become the leader of Athens, they had been expelled by Athenian soldiers in a humiliating defeat. Spartans began to view Athenians as foes, a feeling reciprocated at Athens after the abortive Spartan interference, during which the Spartan troops had forced some seven hundred Athenian households into temporary exile. Second, the kingdom of Persia had expanded far enough west that the Greeks were becoming aware of its awesome might. Yet neither the Persians nor the mainland Greeks knew much about each other. Their mutual ignorance opened the door to explosive wars.

The Greek Golden Age, c. 500–403 B.C.

New Directions in the Classical Age
The pose of this bronze figure exemplifies the implied motion of the new style developed by Greek artists during the Classical Age. Political and intellectual life also moved in new directions.

Even though one bloody conflict after another raged through Greece in the fifth century B.C., beginning with war against Persia, Athens's international power, economic prosperity, and artistic, literary, and intellectual endeavors flourished during this turmoil-filled century. Athenian accomplishments of the fifth century B.C. have had such an enduring impact that historians call this period a Golden Age. This Golden Age coincided with the beginning of the Classical Age of Greek history, a modern designation that covers the period from about 500 B.C. to the death of Alexander the Great in 323 B.C. During its Golden Age, Athens was the preeminent society in ancient Greece and indeed throughout the Mediterranean basin. (Because we know much more about Athens than about any other place or society in the ancient world during the fifth century B.C., we necessarily focus there.) Unfortunately for the Athenians, their Golden Age ended in the closing decades of the fifth century B.C., as a result of a protracted war with Sparta that ultimately engulfed most of the Greek world. Ironically, a period of such cultural blossoming both ended and began with destructive wars.

Clash Between Persia and Greece

The Athenian ambassadors who had gone to Sardis accepted the customary Persian terms for an alliance by giving tokens of earth and water to the king's representative, thereby indicating Athens's recognition of the superiority of Darius, who acknowledged no one as his equal. The Athenian assembly, although outraged at their envoys' symbolic submission to a foreign power, never overtly repudiated the alliance and therefore unwittingly set in motion a sequence of events that culminated in invasions of mainland Greece by the enormous army and navy of Persia. The Persian kingdom outstripped mainland Greece in every category of material resources, from precious metals to soldiers. The wars between Persia and Greece pitted the equivalent of an elephant against a small swarm of mosquitoes. In such a conflict a Greek victory seemed improbable, to say the least. Equally improbable—given the propensity toward disunity and even mutual hostility of the independent Greek city-

> ### IMPORTANT DATES
>
> **490 B.C.** King Darius sends Persian force against Athens; battle of Marathon
>
> **480 B.C.** King Xerxes leads Persian invasion of Greece; battles of Thermopylae and Salamis
>
> **477 B.C.** Athens assumes leadership of the Greek alliance (Delian League)
>
> **461 B.C.** Ephialtes passes political and judicial reforms to strengthen Athenian democracy
>
> **446 B.C.** Athens and Sparta sign a peace treaty meant to last thirty years
>
> **431 B.C.** The Peloponnesian War begins between Athens and Sparta
>
> **421 B.C.** Nicias* induces Athens and Sparta to sign a peace treaty
>
> **415–413 B.C.** Athenian expedition against Syracuse in Sicily renews the war
>
> **404 B.C.** Athens surrenders to Sparta
>
> **404–403 B.C.** The Thirty Tyrants suspend democracy at Athens and conduct a reign of terror
>
> **403 B.C.** Athenians overthrow the Thirty Tyrants and restore democracy

* NIK·EE·AS

states—was that a coalition of these city-states would unite to repel the common enemy.

The Beginning of the Persian Wars

The most famous series of wars in ancient Greek history—the so-called Persian Wars, which were fought in the 490s B.C. and in 480–479 B.C.—broke out with a revolt in Ionia (the western coast of Anatolia), where the Greek city-states had come under Persian control. The Ionian Greeks had first lost their independence not to the Persians but to the Lydians, who had overpowered them during Croesus's reign (*c. 560–546 B.C.). Buoyed by this success and his legendary riches, Croesus had next tried to conquer territory in Anatolia that had previously been in the Median kingdom, but Cyrus, the Persian king, defeated him and captured his territory.

By 499 B.C., Ionia had rebelled against the tyrannies the Persian kings had installed there, in keeping with their policy of supporting local tyrants who were supposed to keep their city-states loyal to Persia. The Athenian assembly voted to join the city-state of Eretria on the neighboring island of Euboea in sending military aid to the Ionian rebels. Their combined force proceeded as far as Sardis, Croesus's old capital and now a Persian headquarters. After razing much of Sardis, however, the Athenians and Eretrians fled home when a Persian counterattack repelled them, causing them to retreat in disarray. Subsequent campaigns by Persian commanders crushed the Ionian rebels by 494 B.C. King Darius then sent a general, Mardonius, to reorganize the city-states of Ionia into democratic regimes, which Persia now permitted because Darius had seen the problems unpopular tyrannies could cause.

King Darius was furious when he learned that the Athenians had aided the Ionian revolt: not only had they dared attack his kingdom, but they had done so after indicating their submission to him through their alliance. The Greeks later claimed that to keep him from forgetting his vow to punish their disloyalty, Darius ordered one of his slaves to say to him three times at every meal, "Sire, remember the Athenians." In 490 B.C., Darius dispatched a flotilla of ships carrying soldiers that burned Eretria and landed on the northeastern coast of Attica near a village called Marathon. The Persians brought with them the elderly Hippias, exiled son of Pisistratus, expecting to reinstall him as their puppet tyrant of Athens. Because the Persian troops outnumbered the citizen militia of Athenian

The Persian Wars

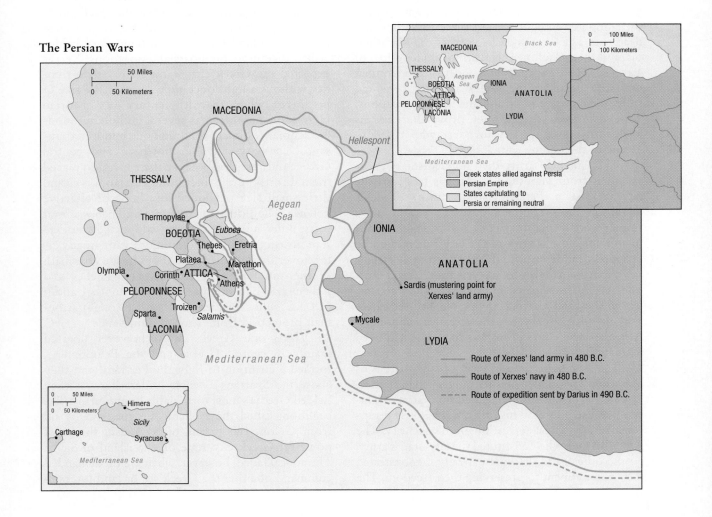

hoplites, the Athenians asked Sparta and other Greek city-states for military help. The Athenian courier dispatched to Sparta became famous because he ran the hundred and forty miles from Athens to Sparta in less than two days. But by the time the battle of Marathon erupted, the only additional troops to arrive were a contingent from the small city-state of Plataea* in Boeotia,† the region just north of Athenian territory, *WHOSE CAPITOL IS THEBES.*

Everyone expected the Persians to win. The Athenian and Plataean soldiers, who had never before seen Persians, grew anxious just at the sight of the Persians' outlandish (to Greek eyes) outfits. Nevertheless, the Athenian generals—the board of ten men elected each year as the civil and military leaders—never let their men lose heart or back down. Carefully planning their tactics to minimize the time their soldiers would be exposed to the deadly arrows of Persian archers, the generals, led by the aristocrat Miltiades (c. 550–489 B.C.), sent their hoplites straight toward the Persian line at a dead run. The Greeks dashed across the Marathon plain in their clanking metal armor under a hail of arrows. Once engaged in hand-to-hand combat with the Persians, the Greek hoplites benefited from their superior armor and longer weapons. After a furious struggle they drove the Persians back into a swamp; any invaders who failed to escape to their ships were killed.

The Athenian army then hurried the twenty-six miles from Marathon to Athens to guard the city against a Persian naval attack. (Today's marathon races commemorate the exploit of a runner who, so the story goes, had been sent ahead to announce the victory to the city, whereupon he dropped dead from the effort.) When the Persians saw the Athenian troops in place, they sailed home. The Athenians rejoiced in disbelief. The Persians, whom they had feared as invincible, had retreated. For decades afterward the greatest honor an Athenian man could claim was to say he had been a "Marathon fighter."

The symbolic importance of the battle of Marathon far outweighed its military significance. The defeat of his punitive expedition enraged Darius because it injured his pride, not because it represented any threat to his kingdom's security. The Athenian men who constituted the city-state's army, on the other hand, had dramatically demonstrated their commitment to preserving their freedom. The unexpected victory at Marathon boosted Athenian self-confidence, and the city-state's soldiers and leaders thereafter boasted that they had withstood the feared Persians on their own, without Sparta's help.

The Great Invasion of 480–479 B.C.

This newly won confidence helped steel the Athenians against the gigantic Persian invasion of Greece in 480 B.C. Darius had vowed to avenge the defeat at Marathon, but it took so long to marshal forces from all over the far-flung Persian kingdom that he died before an attack could be launched. His son, Xerxes I (*486–465 B.C.), therefore led the massive force of infantry and ships that invaded the Greek mainland. So immense was Xerxes' army, the Greeks later claimed, that it required seven days and seven nights of continuous marching to cross the Hellespont strait, the narrow passage of sea between Anatolia and mainland Greece, on a temporary bridge lashed together from boats and pontoons. Xerxes expected the Greek city-states simply to surrender without a fight once they realized the size of his forces, which the fifth-century B.C. historian Herodotus numbered as several million but modern scholars estimate at around one hundred thousand. The city-states in northern and central Greece did just that, *CAPITULATE* because their location placed them directly in the line of the Persian forces, and their small size precluded any hope of effective defense. The Boeotian city-state of Thebes, about forty miles north of Athens, supported the Persian invasion, probably hoping to gain an advantage over its Athenian neighbors in the aftermath of the anticipated Persian victory. Thebes and Athens had become hostile to one another about 519 B.C., when Plataea successfully sought Athenian protection from Theban dominance.

Thirty-one Greek states, however, located mainly in central Greece and the Peloponnese, formed a coalition to fight the Persians, and they chose the Spartans as their leaders because they fielded Greece's most formidable hoplite army. The coalition, called the Hellenic League, sought aid from Gelon, the tyrant of Syracuse, the most powerful Greek city-state on the island of Sicily. The appeal failed, however, when Gelon demanded command of either the Greek sea or land forces in

* PLA·<u>TEE</u>·UH (F&W)   † BEE·<u>O</u>′·SHI″·UH (F&W)

return for his assistance, a price the Spartan and Athenian leaders were unwilling to meet. In this same period, Gelon was battling Carthage over territory in Sicily, and in 480 B.C. his forces defeated a massive Carthaginian expedition at Himera, on the island's northern coast. Some historians have suggested that the Carthaginian incursion into Sicily, and the Persian invasion of mainland Greece were purposely coordinated to embroil the Greek world in a two-front war in the west and the east simultaneously.

The Spartans showed their courage when three hundred of their men led by King Leonidas, along with allies, held off Xerxes' huge army for several days at the narrow pass called Thermopylae ("warm gates") in central Greece. The Spartan troops refused to be intimidated. A Spartan hoplite summed up their attitude by his reputed response to the remark that the Persian archers were so numerous that their arrows darkened the sky in battle. "That's good news," said the Spartan warrior. "We will get to fight in the shade." The pass was so narrow that the Persians could not use their superior numbers to overwhelm the Greek defenders, who were better one-on-one warriors. Only when a local Greek, hoping for a reward from Xerxes, revealed a secret route around the pass was the Persian army able to massacre the Greek defenders, attacking them from the front and the rear simultaneously.

The Athenians soon proved their mettle. Rather than surrender when Xerxes arrived in Attica with his army, they abandoned their city. Women, children, and noncombatants packed their belongings as best they could and evacuated to the northeast coast of the Peloponnese. The Athenian commander Themistocles (c. 528–462 B.C.), purposely spreading misinformation in his characteristically shrewd manner, maneuvered the other, less aggressive Greek leaders into facing the larger Persian navy in a sea battle in the narrow channel between the island of Salamis and the west coast of Attica. Athens was able to supply the largest contingent to the Greek navy at Salamis because the assembly had been financing warship construction ever since a rich strike of silver had been made in Attica in 483 B.C. The proceeds from the silver mines went to the state, and at the urging of Themistocles the assembly had voted to use the financial windfall to build a navy for defense rather than to disburse the

money to individual citizens. As at Thermopylae, the Greeks at the battle of Salamis in 480 B.C. used their country's topography to their advantage. The narrowness of the channel prevented the Persians from using all their ships at once and minimized the advantage of their ships' greater maneuverability. In the close quarters of the Salamis channel, the heavier Greek ships could use their underwater rams to sink the less sturdy Persian craft. When Xerxes observed that the most energetic of his naval commanders appeared to be the one woman among them, Artemisia, ruler of Caria (the southwest corner of Anatolia), he remarked, "My men have become women, and my women, men."

The Greek victory at Salamis sent Xerxes back to Persia, but he left behind an enormous infantry force under his best general and an offer for the Athenians: if they would capitulate, they would remain unharmed and become his overlords of the other Greeks. The assembly refused, the population evacuated again, and Xerxes' general sacked Athens for the second time in two years. In 479 B.C. the Greek infantry headed by the Spartans under the command of a royal son named Pausanias (c. 520–470 B.C.) outfought the Persian infantry at Plataea in Boeotia, and a Greek fleet routed the Persian navy at Mycale in Ionia. The coalition of Greek city-states had thus done the incredible: protected their homeland and their independence from the strongest power in the world.

The Greeks' superior armor and weapons and resourceful use of their topography to counterbalance the Persians' greater numbers help explain their victories on the military level. But what is truly remarkable about the Persian Wars is the decision of the warriors of the thirty-one Greek city-states of the Hellenic League to fight in the first place. They could easily have surrendered and agreed to become Persian subjects to save themselves. Instead, encouraged to resist by the citizens of their communities, they eventually triumphed together against seemingly overwhelming odds. Because the Greek forces included not only aristocrats and hoplites but also thousands of poorer men who rowed the warships, the effort against the Persians cut across social and economic divisions. The Hellenic League's decision to fight the Persian Wars demonstrated courage inspired by a deep commitment to the ideal of political freedom that had emerged in the Archaic Age.

Athenian Confidence in the Golden Age

The struggle against the Persians occasioned a rare instance of city-state cooperation in ancient Greek history. The two most powerful city-states, Athens and Sparta, had put aside their mutual hostility to share the leadership of the united Greek military forces. Their attempt to continue this alliance after the Persian Wars, however, ended in failure, despite the lobbying of pro-Spartan Athenians who believed the two city-states should be partners rather than rivals. Out of this failure arose the so-called Athenian empire, a modern label that accurately describes Athens' new vision of itself after the defeat of the Persians. No longer were Athenians satisfied being co-members of the association of Greek city-states: they fancied a much grander role for themselves.

The Establishment of the Athenian Empire

The victorious Greeks decided in 478 B.C. to continue a naval alliance to attack the Persian outposts that still existed in far northern Greece and western Anatolia, especially Ionia. The Spartan Pausanias, commander of the victorious Greek infantry forces at the battle of Plataea, led the first expedition. But his arrogant and violent behavior toward both his Greek troops and local Greek citizens in Anatolia, especially women, quickly led to disaffection with Spartan leadership among the Greek allies. (This kind of outlaw-conduct became common for Spartan men in powerful positions when away from home; their regimented training apparently left them ill prepared to operate humanely and effectively once they had escaped the constraints imposed by their way of life in Sparta.) By 477 B.C. the Athenian aristocrat Aristides (c. 525–465 B.C.) had persuaded the other Greeks to request Athenian leadership of the alliance against the Persians. Under Athenian direction the alliance took on a permanent organizational structure. Member states swore a solemn oath never to desert the coalition. The members were located predominantly in northern Greece, on the islands of the Aegean Sea, and along the western coast of Anatolia—the areas most exposed to Persian attack.

Most of the independent city-states of the Peloponnese, however, remained in the alliance with the Spartans that they had established long before the Persian Wars. Now Athens and Sparta each dominated a coalition of allies. Sparta and its allies, which modern historians refer to as the Peloponnesian League, had an assembly to set policy, but no action could be taken unless the Spartan leaders agreed to it. The alliance headed by Athens, referred to today as the Delian League because its treasury was originally located on the Aegean island of Delos, also had an assembly of representatives to make policy. Members of the alliance were supposed to share equally in making decisions, but in practice Athens was in charge.

The Athenian representatives came to dominate this "democracy" as a result of the special arrangements made to finance the alliance's naval operations. Aristides based the different levels of "dues" the various member city-states were to pay each year on their size and prosperity. Larger member states were to supply entire triremes (warships) complete with crews and their pay; smaller states could share the cost of a ship and crew or simply contribute cash, which would be added to others' payments.

Over time, more and more Delian League members paid their dues in cash rather than by furnishing warships. It was beyond their capacities to build ships as specialized as triremes (narrow vessels built for speed—they held three banks of oarsmen on each side and had a battering ram attached to the bow) and to train crews in the intricate teamwork required to work the oars (one hundred seventy rowers were needed). Athens, far larger than most of the allies, had the shipyards and skilled workers to build triremes as well as an abundance of men eager to earn pay as rowers. Therefore Athens built and manned most of the alliance's triremes, supplementing the allies' dues with its own contribution. The oarsmen came from the poorest class in society, and their essential contribution to the navy earned them not only money but also additional political influence in Athenian democracy as naval strength became the city-state's principal source of military power.

Because most allies eventually lacked warships of their own, members of the Delian League had no effective recourse if they disagreed with decisions made for the league as a whole by Athens. The

Athenian assembly dispatched the superior Athenian fleet to compel discontented allies to adhere to league policy and to continue paying their annual dues (which because they were compulsory were really "tribute"), thereby becoming the dominant power in the league. As Thucydides observed, rebellious allies "lost their independence," making the Athenians as the league's leaders "no longer as popular as they used to be."

Within twenty years after the battle of Salamis the Delian League had expelled almost all the Persian garrisons that had continued to hold out in some city-states along the northeastern Aegean coast and had driven the Persian fleet from the Aegean Sea, ending the Persian threat to Greece for the next fifty years. Athens meanwhile grew stronger from its share of the spoils captured from Persian outposts and the tribute paid by Delian League members. By the middle of the fifth century B.C., league members' tribute totaled an amount equivalent to perhaps $200 million in contemporary terms (assuming $80 as the average daily pay of an ordinary worker today). For a state the size of Athens (around thirty thousand to forty thousand adult male citizens at the time), this annual income meant prosperity.

The Athenian assembly decided how to spend the city-state's income. Rich and poor alike had a self-interested stake in keeping the fleet active and the allies paying for it. Well-heeled aristocrats like Cimon (c. 510–450 B.C.), the son of Miltiades, the victor of Marathon, enhanced their social status by commanding successful league campaigns and then spending their portion of the spoils on benefactions to Athens. Such financial contributions to the common good were expected of wealthy and prominent men. Political parties did not exist in ancient Athens, and political leaders formed informal circles of friends and followers to support their agendas. Disputes among these aristocratic leaders often stemmed more from competition for public offices and influence in the assembly than from disagreements over policy matters. Arguments about policy tended to revolve around how Athens should exercise its growing power internationally, not whether it should refrain from interfering with the affairs of the other Delian League members to further Athenian interests. The numerous Athenian men of lesser means who rowed the Delian League's ships came to depend on the income they

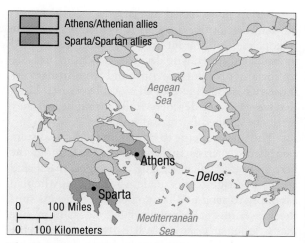

The Delian and Peloponnesian Leagues

earned on league expeditions. Thus alliance was transformed into empire, despite Athenian support of democratic governments in some allied city-states previously ruled by oligarchies. The Athenians believed their conversion from partner to leader was justified because it kept the Delian League strong enough to protect Greece from the Persians.

The Democratic Reform of the Athenian System of Justice

In the decades following the Persian Wars, both the military and political importance of the poorer men who powered the Athenian fleet grew. As these citizens came to recognize that they provided the foundation of Athenian security and prosperity, they apparently felt the time had come to make the administration of justice at Athens just as democratic as the process of making policy and passing laws in the assembly, which was open to all male citizens over eighteen years old. Although at this time the assembly could serve as a court of appeals, the nine archons (annual magistrates of the city-state) and the Areopagus council of ex-archons rendered most judicial verdicts. The nine archons had been chosen by lot rather than by election since 487 B.C., thus making access to those offices a matter of chance and not liable to domination by wealthy aristocrats who could afford expensive electoral campaigns. Filling public offices by lot was considered democratic because it gave all eligible contestants an equal chance. But even

democratically selected magistrates were susceptible to corruption, as were the members of the
Areopagus. A different judicial system was needed
to insulate the men who decided cases from pressure
by socially prominent people and from bribery by
those rich enough to buy a favorable verdict. Laws
that were enacted democratically meant little if they
were not applied fairly and honestly.

The final impetus to reform the judicial system
came from a crisis in foreign affairs. Cimon, the
hero of many Delian League campaigns, marshaled
all his prestige to persuade a reluctant Athenian
assembly to send hoplites to help the Spartans suppress a serious helot revolt in 462 B.C. Cimon, like
many Athenian aristocrats, had always admired the
Spartans, and he was known for registering his
opposition to assembly proposals by saying, "But
that is not what the Spartans would do." His
Spartan friends soon changed their minds about
Athenian assistance, however, and sent Cimon and
his army home. Spartan leaders feared the democratically inclined Athenian soldiers might decide
to help the helots throw off Spartan domination.

This humiliating rejection of their help outraged
the Athenian assembly and provoked renewed
hostility between the two city-states. The disgrace
it brought Cimon carried over to his fellow aristocrats, thereby establishing a political climate ripe
for further democratic reforms. A man named
Ephialtes seized the moment in 461 B.C. and convinced the assembly to pass measures limiting the
power of the Areopagus and, more important, to
set up a judicial system of courts run by male citizens over thirty years old chosen by lot for each
case. The reforms made it virtually impossible to
influence or bribe the citizen jurors because the
jurors for each court were selected only on the day
of the trial, all trials were concluded in one day, and
juries were large (from several hundred to several
thousand). The only official present kept fights
from breaking out. Jurors made up their minds
after hearing speeches by the persons involved. The
accuser and the accused were required to speak for
themselves, although they might pay someone else
to compose the speech they would deliver and ask
others to speak in support of their arguments. A
majority vote of the jurors ruled, and no appeals
were allowed.

The structure of the new court system reflected
the underlying principles of what scholars today

Ostraka
These two ostraka *(inscribed potsherds that were used as ballots in the process of ostracism) were broken from the same pot. The upper piece bore the name of Cimon, the lower one the name of Themistocles.*

call the "radical" democracy of Athens in the mid-
fifth century B.C. This system involved widespread
participation by a cross section of male citizens,
random selection of most public officeholders,
elaborate precautions to prevent corruption, equal
protection under the law for citizens regardless of
wealth, some legal restrictions on citizen women,
and the majority's authority over any minority or
individual. A striking example of majority rule was
a procedure called *ostracism* (from *ostracon*, meaning a "piece of broken pottery," the material used
for ballots). Once a year, at a meeting just for this
purpose, all male citizens were eligible to cast a ballot on which they had scratched the name of one
man they thought should be exiled. If at least 6,000
ballots were cast, the man whose name appeared on
the greatest number was compelled to live outside
the borders of Attica for ten years. He suffered no
other penalty, and his family and property could
remain behind undisturbed. Ostracism was emphat-
ically not a criminal penalty, and men returning
from their exile had undiminished rights as citizens.
Probably no more than several dozen men were
actually ostracized after the first recorded instance
in 488 B.C.; the practice fell into disuse after about
416 B.C.

Ostracism served as a mechanism for blaming
an individual for a failed policy the assembly had
originally approved. Cimon, for example, was ostracized after the disastrous attempt to cooperate with
Sparta during the helot revolt. An ostracism could
also stem from a man's personal eminence, if he
became so prominent that he could dominate the
political scene and thus seem a threat to democracy.
An anecdote about Aristides, who set the original

level of dues for the Delian League members, illustrates this situation. Aristides was nicknamed "The Just" because he was reputedly so fairminded. On the day of the balloting for an ostracism, an illiterate man from the countryside handed Aristides a potsherd and asked him to scratch the name of the man's choice for ostracism on it:

> *"Certainly," said Aristides. "Which name shall I write?"*
> *"Aristides," replied the countryman.*
> *"Very well," remarked Aristides as he proceeded to inscribe his own name. "But tell me, why do you want to ostracize Aristides? What has he done to you?"*
> *"Oh, nothing; I don't even know him,"* sputtered the man. *"I'm just sick and tired of hearing everybody refer to him as 'The Just.'"*

Although Aristides was indeed ostracized in 482 B.C. (though he was recalled in 480 B.C. to fight the Persians), this anecdote may well be apocryphal. Nevertheless, it makes a valid point: the Athenians assumed that the right way to protect democracy was always to trust the majority vote of freeborn, adult male citizens, without any restrictions on a man's ability to say what he thought was best for democracy. This conviction required making allowances for irresponsible types like the illiterate countryman who complained about Aristides. It rested on the belief that the cumulative political wisdom of the majority of voters would outweigh the eccentricity and ignorance of the few.

The Policies of Pericles

This idea that democracy was best served by involving a cross section of the male citizenry received further support in the 450s B.C. when Pericles (c. 495–429 B.C.), whose mother was the niece of the democratic reformer Cleisthenes, successfully proposed that state revenues be used to pay a daily stipend to men who served on juries, in the council of the five hundred, and in other public offices filled by lot. Without this stipend poorer men would have found it difficult to leave their regular work to serve in these time-consuming positions. By contrast, the most influential public officials—the annual board of ten generals, who oversaw both military and civil affairs, especially public finances—

were elected and received no stipend. The assembly elected these generals because their posts required expertise and experience—conditions that random selection could not guarantee. They were not paid mainly because rich men, who had access to the education and resources required to handle this job, were expected to win election as generals. Generals were compensated by the prestige their office carried. The stipend received by other officials and jurors was not lavish, certainly no more than an ordinary worker could earn in a day, but it enabled poorer Athenians to serve in government. Like Cleisthenes before him, Pericles became the most influential Athenian leader of his era by devising innovations to strengthen the egalitarian tendencies of Athenian democracy.

In 451 B.C., Pericles sponsored a law stating that henceforth citizenship would be conferred only on children whose mother and father were both Athenians. Previously, the offspring of Athenian men who married non-Athenian women had been granted citizenship. Aristocratic men in particular had tended to marry rich foreign women, as Pericles' own maternal grandfather had done. The new law enhanced the status of Athenian mothers and made Athenian citizenship more exclusive. The citizens of Athens began to see themselves as part of an elite group.

Pericles initially pursued an aggressive foreign policy against Spartan interests in Greece and against Persian domination of Egypt and the eastern Mediterranean. The disastrous results of the campaigns of the 450s B.C. against Persian territory and the accelerating acrimony with the Spartans convinced the assembly to cease any further expeditions in the eastern Mediterranean after 450 B.C. When operations against Sparta and other members of the Peloponnesian League also failed, Pericles in the winter of 446–445 B.C. engineered a peace treaty with Sparta designed to freeze the balance of power in Greece for thirty years and thus preserve Athenian dominance in the Delian League. Although he remained the most powerful man in Athens during this period, winning election as general fifteen consecutive years beginning in 443 B.C., Pericles had to withstand severe criticism for his policies, both domestic and foreign. His championing of a building program of large temples raised fierce objections over expenses, and his judgment came under attack for a war in 441–439 B.C. with the people of the island of Samos, a valuable Delian League ally. But Pericles soon faced an even greater challenge when relations with Sparta worsened in the mid-430s B.C. over Athenian backing of some rebellious Spartan allies. Corinth, a crucial Spartan ally, threatened to defect to the Delian League unless Sparta acted to prevent Athenian interference with Corinth's own allies. The Spartans finally demanded the Athenians withdraw their embargo of Megara, a Spartan ally, or face war, but Pericles prevailed upon the assembly to refuse all compromises. His critics claimed he was sticking to his hard line against Sparta and trying to provoke a war in order to revive his fading popularity. Pericles retorted that no accommodation to Spartan demands was possible because Athenian freedom of action was at stake. By 431 B.C. the thirty-year peace made in 445 B.C. had been shattered beyond repair. The protracted Peloponnesian War (as modern historians call it) began in that year and ultimately ended the Athenian Golden Age.

The Urban Landscape of Athens

Private homes, both in the city and the countryside, retained their traditional modest size even during Athens' great prosperity in the fifth century B.C. Farmhouses were usually clustered in villages, while homes in the urban center were wedged higgledy-piggledy against one another along narrow, winding streets. The residences of rich people followed the same basic design as other urban homes, which grouped bedrooms, storerooms, and dining rooms around small, open-air courtyards, only on a grander scale. Wall paintings or works of art were not yet common as decorations for private homes. Sparse furnishings and simple furniture were the rule. Sanitary facilities usually consisted of a pit dug just outside the front door, which was emptied by collectors paid to dump the contents outside the city at a distance set by law. Poorer people rented houses or small apartments.

Private patronage funded some public improvements, such as the landscaping with shade trees and running tracks that Cimon paid to have installed in open areas. On the edge of the central market square and gathering spot at the heart of the city, called the *agora*, was the renowned Painted Stoa. *Stoas* were narrow buildings open along one side

whose purpose was to provide shelter from sun or rain. The crowds of men who came to the agora daily to chat about politics and local affairs would cluster inside the Painted Stoa, whose walls were decorated with paintings of great moments in Greek history commissioned from the most famous painters of the time, Polygnotus and Mikon. That one of the stoa's paintings portrayed the battle of Marathon, in which Cimon's father, Miltiades, had won glory, was only appropriate because the building had been paid for and donated to the city by the husband of Cimon's sister, probably with financial assistance from Cimon. The social values of Athenian democracy called for aristocratic men like Cimon and his brother-in-law to provide such gifts for public use to show their goodwill toward the city-state and thereby earn increased social eminence. Wealthy citizens were also expected to fulfill costly liturgies, or public services, such as fully equipping a warship or providing theatrical entertainment at city festivals. To a certain extent this liturgical system for wealthy men compensated for the lack of any regular income or property taxes in ancient Athens.

Athens received substantial revenues from harbor fees, sales taxes, and the "dues" of its Delian League allies. Buildings paid for by public funds constituted the most conspicuous architecture in classical Athens. The scale of these public buildings was usually no greater than the size required to fulfill their function, such as the complex of buildings on the agora's western edge in which the council of five hundred held its meetings and the public archives were kept. Because the assembly convened in the open air on a hillside above the agora, it required no building, just a speaker's platform. In 447 B.C., however, Pericles instigated a great project atop the acropolis, the mesalike promontory at the center of the city, which towered over the agora. Most conspicuous were a mammoth gate building with columns straddling the broad entrance to the acropolis at its western end, and a new temple of Athena to house a huge image of the goddess. These buildings easily cost more than the modern equivalent of a billion dollars, a phenomenal sum for an ancient Greek city-state. Pericles' political enemies railed at him for squandering public funds. The program may have been financed partly from Delian League

The Civic Center of Athens
This model shows the public buildings of the west side of the agora of Athens, the city's physical and governmental center. The two large buildings in the foreground were not built until Roman times.

tributes. Substantial funds certainly came from sales taxes and harbor taxes and from the financial reserves of Athena's sanctuaries, which like those of the other gods throughout Greece received both private donations and public support.

The new temple built for Athena became known as the *Parthenon,* meaning "the house of the virgin goddess." As the patron goddess of Athens, Athena had long had another sanctuary on the acropolis. Its focus was an olive tree regarded as the sacred symbol of Athena, who ensured the economic health of the Athenians. The Parthenon honored Athena in a different capacity: as a warrior serving as the divine champion of Athenian military power. Inside the Parthenon a gold and ivory statue well over thirty feet high portrayed the goddess in

battle armor and holding in her outstretched hand a six-foot statue of the figure of Victory (*Nike* in *NT'KEE* Greek). Like all Greek temples, the Parthenon was meant as a house for its divinity, not as a gathering place for worshipers. In its general design the Parthenon was representative of the standard architecture of Greek temples: a rectangular box on a raised platform, a plan the Greeks probably derived from the stone temples of Egypt. The box, which had only one small door at the front, was fenced in by columns all around. The columns were carved in the simple style called Doric, in contrast to the more elaborate Ionic and Corinthian styles that have often been imitated in modern buildings (for example, in the Corinthian-style facade of the Supreme Court Building in Washington, D.C.).

Architectural Grandeur
This photograph gives
an idea of the size of
the majestic gateway to
the Athenian acropolis
and the dramatic fram-
ing effect it produced
for visitors as they
passed through to-
ward the Parthenon
temple in the distance.

Only priests and priestesses could enter the temple, but public religious ceremonies took place outside.

The Parthenon was remarkable for its great size and elaborate decoration. Constructed from twenty thousand tons of Attic marble, it stretched nearly two hundred thirty feet in length and a hundred feet wide, with eight columns across the ends instead of the six normally found in Doric style, and seventeen instead of thirteen along the sides. Its massive look conveyed an impression of power. Because perfectly rectilinear architecture appears curved to the human eye, subtle curves and inclines were built into the Parthenon to produce an illusion of completely straight lines: the columns were given a slight bulge in their middles, the corner columns were installed at a slight incline and closer together, and the platform was made slightly convex. By overcoming the distortions of nature, the Parthenon's sophisticated architecture and technical refinements made a confident statement about human ability to construct order that was both apparent and real.

Fifth-Century Athens

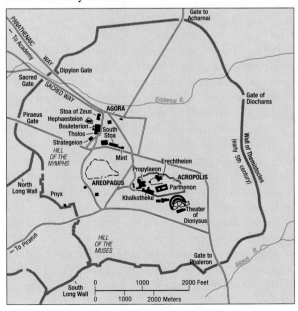

The sculptural decoration of the Parthenon also proclaimed Athenian confidence about their city-state's relationship with the gods. Sculptured panels ran along its exterior above the columns, and tableaux of sculptures appeared in the triangular spaces (pediments) underneath the roof line at either end of the building. Although these decorations were a regular part of the Doric style, the Parthenon also incorporated a unique sculptural feature for a Doric building. A continuous band of figures was carved in relief around the top of the walls inside the porch formed by the columns along the edges of the building's platform. This sort of frieze usually appeared only on Ionic-style buildings. Adding a frieze in Ionic style to a Doric-style temple was a striking departure meant to attract attention. The Parthenon's frieze depicted the Athenian religious ritual in which a procession of citizens paraded to the acropolis to present Athena in her olive-tree sanctuary a new robe woven by specially selected Athenian girls. Depicting the procession in motion, like a filmstrip in stone, the frieze showed men riding spirited horses, women walking along carrying sacred implements, and the gods gathering together at the head of the parade to observe their human worshipers. As usual in the sculptured decoration on Greek temples, the frieze sparkled with shiny metal attachments serving, for example, as the horsemen's reins and with brightly colored paint enlivening the figures and the background.

No other city-state had ever gone beyond the traditional function of temples—glorifying and paying homage to the community's special deities—by adorning a temple with representations of its citizens. The Parthenon frieze made a unique statement about how Athenians perceived their relationship to the gods. Even if the deities carved in the frieze were understood to be separated from and perhaps invisible to the humans in the procession, a temple adorned with pictures of citizens, albeit idealized citizens of perfect physique and beauty, amounted to a claim of special intimacy between the city-state and the gods. Presumably this assertion reflected the Athenian interpretation of their success in helping turn back the Persians, in achieving leadership of a powerful naval alliance, and in amassing wealth that made Athens richer than all its neighbors in mainland Greece. The Parthenon, like the rest of Pericles' building program, honored

The Acropolis of Athens
This rocky promontory, with its three marble temples to the goddess Athena, was the city's religious center.

the deities with whom the city-state identified and expressed Athenian confidence that the gods looked favorably on their empire. Their success, the Athenians would have said, proved that the gods were on their side.

The Message of Sculpture

Like the design of the sculpture on the outside of the Parthenon, the enormous size and expense of the freestanding figure of Athena inside the temple expressed the innovative and confident spirit of Athens in its Golden Age. The statue's creator, the Athenian Phidias, gained such fame that he became a close friend of Pericles and was invited by other Greek city-states to sculpt great statues for their temples. (Phidias's social stature was exceptional,

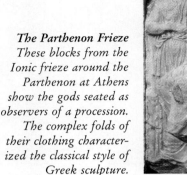

The Parthenon Frieze
These blocks from the Ionic frieze around the Parthenon at Athens show the gods seated as observers of a procession. The complex folds of their clothing characterized the classical style of Greek sculpture.

however. Aristocrats considered most sculptors and artists low status because they labored with their hands. Only the few fortunate talented enough to become famous were welcomed in high society.)

Other Greek artists as well as sculptors experimented with new techniques and artistic approaches in this period, but freestanding sculpture most clearly demonstrates the new and various ways in which the human form was rendered in the fifth century B.C. Such sculptures could be either public (that is, paid for with city-state funds, as were the Parthenon's) or private (paid for by individuals). But Greeks who ordered pieces of private art did not yet use them to decorate the interiors of their homes. Instead they displayed them publicly, for a variety of purposes. Privately commissioned statues of gods could be placed in a sanctuary as a proof of devotion. In the tradition of offering lovely crafted objects to divinities as commemorations of important personal experiences such as economic successes or victories in athletic contests, people also donated sculptures of physically beautiful humans to the sanctuaries of the gods as gifts of honor. Wealthy families would commission statues of their deceased members, especially if they had died young, to be placed above their graves as memorials of their virtue. In every case private statues were meant to be seen by other people. In this sense private sculpture in the Golden Age served a public function: it broadcast a message to an audience.

Archaic statues had been characterized by a stiff posture imitating the style of freestanding Egyptian figures. Egyptian sculptors used this style, unchanged, for centuries. Greek artists, however, had begun changing their style by the time of the Persian Wars, and in the fifth century B.C. new poses became more prevalent in freestanding sculpture, continuing the trend toward movement visible in the sculpture attached to temples. Human males were still generally portrayed nude as athletes or warriors, and females were still clothed in fine robes. But their postures and their physiques were becoming more naturalistic. In the Archaic Age, male statues had been rendered in a uniform pose: striding forward with their left legs, arms held rigidly at their side. Classical Age male statues might have the body's weight on either leg and bent arms. Their musculature was now anatomically correct rather than sketchy and almost impressionistic, as had been the style in the sixth century B.C. Female statues, too, had more relaxed poses and natural clothing, which hung in a way that hinted at the shape of the body underneath instead of disguising it. The faces of classical sculptures reflected an impassive calm rather than the smiles that had characterized archaic figures.

The sculptors who devised these daring new styles preferred to work in bronze, though marble was also popular. Creating bronze statues, which were cast in molds made from clay models, required a particularly well-equipped workshop with furnaces, tools, and foundry workers skilled in metallurgy. Properly prepared bronze had the tensile strength to allow outstretched poses of arms and legs, which could not be done in marble without supports. (Hence the intrusive tree trunks and other such supports introduced in the marble copies made in Roman times of Greek statues in bronze. These Roman copies are often the only surviving examples of the originals.) The strength and malleability of bronze allowed innovative sculptors like the Athenian Myron and Polyclitus of Argos to develop the freestanding statue to its physical limits. Myron, for example, sculpted a discus thrower crouched at the top of his backswing. The figure not only assumes an asymmetrical pose but also seems to burst with the tension of the athlete's effort. Polyclitus's renowned statue of a walking man carrying a spear gives a different impression from every angle of viewing. The feeling of motion it conveys is palpable. The same is true of the famous statue by an unknown sculptor of a female (perhaps the goddess of love Aphrodite) adjusting her diaphanous robe with one upraised arm. The message these statues conveyed to their ancient audience was one of energy, motion, and asymmetry in delicate balance. Archaic statues impressed viewers with their appearance of stability; not even a hard shove seemed likely to budge them. Statues of the Classical Age, by contrast, showed greater range of motion and a variety of poses and impressions. The spirited movement of some of these statues suggests the energy of the times but also reflects the possibility of change and instability.

Continuity and Change in the Golden Age of Athens

Even though the cultural and social life of Athens in the fifth century B.C. underwent unprecedented changes, many central aspects of Athenian society remained unchanged. The result was a mix of innovation and tradition. Tragic drama developed as a publicly supported art form. A new and upsetting (to traditionalists) form of education for wealthy young men with ambitions in public life emerged. Public life remained confined and limited for upper-class women. Women of the poorer classes, however, had more opportunity for contact with the public, male world because they had to work to help support their families. The interplay of continuity and change created a tension that was tolerable until the pressure of war with Sparta strained Athenian society to the breaking point. All these events took place against the background of traditional Greek religion, which permeated public and private life.

Greek Religion in the Classical Period

The Athenians' attitude toward their deities in the mid-fifth century B.C. corresponded to the basic tenet of Greek religion: humans both as individuals and as groups honored the gods to thank them for blessings received and to receive blessings in return. Those honors consisted of sacrifices, gifts to the gods' sanctuaries, and festivals of songs, dances, prayers, and processions. A seventh-century B.C. bronze statuette, which a man named Mantiklos gave to a (now unknown) sanctuary of Apollo to honor the god, makes clear why individuals gave such gifts. On its legs Mantiklos inscribed his understanding of the transaction: "Mantiklos gave this from his share to the Far Darter of the Silver Bow [Apollo]; now you, Apollo, do something for me in return." This idea of reciprocity underlay the Greek understanding of the divine. Deities did not love humans, though in some mythological stories they took earthly lovers and produced half-divine children. Rather they supported humans who paid them honor and did not offend them. Gods whom humans offended retaliated by sending such calamities as famine, earthquake, epidemic disease, or defeat in war.

The greatest difficulty for humans lay in anticipating what might offend a deity. Fortunately, some of the gods' expectations were codified in a moral order with rules for human behavior. For example, the Greeks believed that the gods demanded hospitality for strangers and proper burial for family members and that they punished human arrogance and murderous violence. Oracles, dreams, divination, and the prophecies of seers were all regarded as clues to what humans might have done to anger the gods. Offenses could be acts such as forgetting a sacrifice, violating the sanctity of a temple area, or breaking an oath or sworn agreement made to another person. People believed the deities were especially concerned with certain transgressions, such as violating oaths, but generally uninterested in common crimes, which humans had to police themselves. Homicide was such a serious offense, however, that the gods were thought to punish it by casting a *miasma* (state of pollution) upon murderers and upon all those around them. Unless the members of the affected group purified themselves by punishing the murderer, they could all expect to suffer divine punishment such as bad harvests or disease.

The Greeks believed their gods occasionally experienced sorrow in their dealings with one another, but essentially were immune to tragedy because they were immortal. The twelve most important gods, headed by Zeus, were envisioned assembling for banquets atop Mt. Olympus, the highest peak in mainland Greece. Like the human aristocrats of Homer's stories, the gods resented any slights to their honor. "I am well aware that the gods are competitively envious and disruptive towards humans" is Solon's summary of their nature in one famous (and probably fictitious) anecdote that tells of him giving advice to Croesus before the Lydian king lost his kingdom to the Persians.

To interact with a god, people prayed, sang hymns of praise, offered sacrifices, and presented gifts at the deity's sanctuary. In these sanctuaries a person could honor and thank the deities for blessings and propitiate them when misfortune, taken as a sign of divine anger at human behavior, had struck the petitioner. Private individuals offered sacrifices at home with the household gathered around, and sometimes the family's slaves were allowed to join. Priests and priestesses, who in most cases were chosen from the citizen body as a whole, conducted the sacrifices of public cults. The priests and priestesses of Greek cults were usually attached to a particular sanctuary or shrine and did not seek to influence political or social matters. Their special knowledge consisted in knowing how to perform traditional religious rites. They were not guardians of theological orthodoxy, as are some clergy today, because Greek religion had no systematic theology or canonical dogma, nor did it have any institutions to oversee doctrine.

The ritual of sacrifice provided the primary occasion of contact between the gods and their worshipers. Most sacrifices were regularly scheduled events on the community's civic calendar. Athenians demonstrated their piety toward the deities of the city-state's official cults on the first eight days of every month. For example, they celebrated Athena's birthday on the third day of each month and Artemis's, the goddess of wild animals who was also the special patroness of the Athenian council of five hundred, on the sixth. Artemis's brother, Apollo, was honored on the seventh day. Athens boasted of having the most religious festivals in all of Greece, with nearly half the days of the year featuring one, some large and some small. Not everyone attended all the festivals; hired laborers' contracts specified how many days off they received to attend religious ceremonies. Major occasions such as the Panathenaia festival, whose procession was portrayed on the Parthenon frieze, attracted large crowds of both women and men. The Panathenaia festival honored Athena not only with sacrifices and parades but also with contests in music, dancing, poetry, and athletics. Valuable prizes were awarded to the winners. Some festivals were for women only: one was the three-day festival for married women in honor of Demeter, goddess of agriculture and fertility.

Different cults had differing rituals, but sacrifice served as their focus. Sacrifices ranged from the bloodless offering of fruits, vegetables, and small cakes to the slaughter of large animals. Looking back on fifth-century B.C. Athens, the orator Lysias* explained the necessity for public sacrifice: "Our ancestors handed down to us the most powerful and prosperous community in Greece by performing the prescribed sacrifices. It is therefore proper for us to offer the same sacrifices as they, if only for the sake of the success which has resulted from those rites." The sacrifice of a large animal provided an occasion for the community to assemble and reaffirm its ties to the divine world and, by sharing the roasted meat of the sacrificed beast, for the worshipers to benefit personally from a good relationship with the gods. The feasting that followed a blood sacrifice was especially significant because meat was comparatively rare in the Greek diet. The actual killing of the animal followed strict rules meant to ensure the purity of the occasion. The elaborate procedures required for a blood sacrifice show how seriously and solemnly the Greeks regarded the sacrificial killing of animals. The victim had to be an unblemished do-

* *LÍSÏ·ÚS*

Animal Sacrifice
The sacrifice of large animals was an important Greek religious ceremony. Here, women place garlands on the animals before they are killed to show that they are specially chosen.

mestic animal, specially decorated with garlands and induced to approach the altar as if of its own volition. The assembled crowd maintained strict silence to avoid possibly impure remarks. The sacrificer sprinkled water on the victim's head so it would, in shaking its head in response to the sprinkle, appear to consent to its death. After washing his hands, the sacrificer scattered barley grains on the altar fire and the animal's head and then cut a lock of the animal's hair and threw it on the fire. Following a prayer, he swiftly cut the animal's throat while musicians played flutelike pipes and female worshipers screamed, presumably to express the group's ritual sorrow at the victim's death. The carcass was then butchered, with some portions thrown on the altar fire so their aromatic smoke could waft its way upward to the god of the cult. The rest of the meat was then distributed among the worshipers.

Greek religion also encompassed many activities besides those of the cults of the twelve Olympian deities. Families marked significant moments such as birth, marriage, and death with prayers, rituals, and sacrifices. Greeks honored their ancestors with offerings made at their tombs, consulted seers about the meanings of dreams and omens, and

sought out magicians for spells to improve their love lives, or curses to harm their enemies. Particularly important both to the community and to individuals were hero cults, rituals performed at the tomb of a man or woman, usually famous for performing extraordinary feats in the distant past, whose remains were thought to retain special power. This power was local, whether for revealing the future through oracles, for healing injuries and disease, or for providing assistance in war. The only hero to whom cults were established all over the Greek world was the strongman Heracles (or Hercules, as his name was later spelled by the Romans). His superhuman feats gave him an appeal as a protector in many city-states.

The cult of Demeter and her daughter Kore (or Persephone), headquartered at Eleusis, a settlement on the west coast of Attica, attracted followers from all parts of the world. The central rite of this cult was called the Mysteries, a series of initiation ceremonies into the secret knowledge of the cult. If they were free of pollution (for example, if they had not been convicted for murder, committed sacrilege, or had contact with a birth or death), all free speakers of Greek from anywhere in the world—women and men, adults and children—were eligible for initiation, as were some slaves who worked in the sanctuary. Initiation proceeded in several stages. The main stage took place during an annual festival lasting almost two weeks. So important were the Eleusinian Mysteries that the Greek states observed an international truce of fifty-five days to allow travel to and from the festival even from distant corners of the Greek world. Prospective initiates participated in a complicated set of ceremonies that culminated in the revelation of Demeter's central secret after a day of fasting. The secret was revealed in an initiation hall constructed solely for this purpose. Under a roof fifty-five yards square supported on a forest of interior columns, the hall held three thousand people standing around its sides on tiered steps. The most eloquent proof of the sanctity attached to the Mysteries of Demeter and Kore is that throughout the thousand years during which the rites were celebrated, we know of no one who ever revealed the secret. To this day all we know is that it involved something done, something said, and something shown. It is certain, however, that initiates were promised a better life and a better fate after death. "Richly blessed is the mortal who has seen these rites; but whoever is not an initiate and has no share in them, that one never has an equal portion after death, down in the gloomy darkness" are the words describing the benefits of initiation in the sixth-century B.C. poem *The Hymn to Demeter.*

The Eleusinian Mysteries were not the only mystery cult of the Greek world, nor were they unique in their concern with what lay beyond death. Most mystery cults also emphasized protection for initiates in their daily lives, whether against ghosts, illness, poverty, shipwrecks, or the countless other dangers of ancient Greek life. Divine protection was accorded, however, as a reward for appropriate conduct, not by any abstract belief in the gods. For the ancient Greeks, gods expected honors and rites, and Greek religion required action from its worshipers. Greeks had to pray and sing hymns honoring the gods, perform sacrifices, and undergo purifications. These rites represented an active response to the precarious conditions of human life in a world in which early death from disease, accident, or war was commonplace. Furthermore, the Greeks believed the gods sent both good and bad into the world. As a result the Greeks did not expect to reach paradise at some future time when evil forces would finally be vanquished forever. Their assessment of existence made no allowance for change in the relationship between the human and the divine. That relationship encompassed sorrow as well as joy, punishment in the here and now, and perhaps the uncertain hope for favored treatment both in this life and in an afterlife for initiates of the Eleusinian Mysteries and other similar cults.

The Development of Athenian Tragedy

The complex relationship between gods and humans formed the basis of classical Athens's most enduring cultural innovation: the tragic dramas performed over three days at the major annual festival of the god Dionysus held in the late spring. These plays, still read and produced on stage, were presented in ancient Athens as part of a drama contest, in keeping with the competitive spirit characteristic of many events held in the gods' honor. Tragedy reached its peak as a dramatic form in the fifth century B.C.

Every year, one of Athens's magistrates chose three playwrights to present four plays each at the festival. Three were tragedies and one a satyr play in which actors portrayed the half-human, half-animal (horse or goat) satyrs featured in this more lighthearted form of theater. The term *tragedy*— derived, for reasons now lost, from the Greek words for "goat" and "song"—referred to plays with plots that involved fierce conflict, and characters that represented powerful forces. Tragedies were written in verse and used solemn language; they were often based on stories about the violent consequences of the interaction between gods and humans. The story often ended with a resolution to the trouble—but only after considerable suffering.

The performance of Athenian tragedies bore little resemblance to conventional modern theater productions. They took place during the daytime in an outdoor theater sacred to Dionysus, built into the slope of the southern hillside of Athens's acropolis. This theater held around fourteen thousand spectators overlooking an open, circular area in front of a slightly raised stage platform. To ensure fairness in the competition, all tragedies had to have the same number of cast members, all of whom were men: three actors to play the speaking roles (all male and female characters) and fifteen chorus members. Although the chorus leader sometimes engaged in dialogue with the actors, the chorus primarily performed songs and dances in the circular area in front of the stage, called the orchestra. Because all the actors' lines were in verse with special rhythms, the musical function of the chorus was simply to enhance the overall poetic nature of Athenian tragedy.

Even though scenery on the stage was sparse, a good tragedy presented a vivid spectacle. The chorus wore elaborate, decorative costumes and performed intricate dance routines. The actors, who wore masks, used broad gestures and booming voices to reach the upper tier of seats. A powerful voice and prodigious vocal skills were crucial to a tragic actor because words represented the heart of a tragedy, in which dialogue and long speeches were far more common than physical action. Special effects were, however, part of the spectacle. For example, a crane allowed actors playing the roles of gods to fly suddenly onto the stage, like superheroes in a modern movie. The actors playing the lead roles, called the protagonists ("first competitors"), competed against each other for the designation of best actor. So important was a first-rate protagonist to a successful tragedy that actors were

The Theater of Dionysus at Athens
This theater, cut into the south slope of the Acropolis, held some fifteen thousand spectators for performances in honor of the god Diony-sus. The stone seats, wall, and stage date to the Ro-man period.

assigned by lot to the competing playwrights of the year to give all three an equal chance to have the finest cast. Great protagonists became enormously popular, although unlike many playwrights, they were not usually aristocrats and did not move in upper-class social circles.

The author of a slate of tragedies in the festival of Dionysus also served as director, producer, musi-cal composer, choreographer, and sometimes even actor. Only men of some wealth could afford the amounts of time such work demanded because the prizes in the tragedy competition were probably modest. As citizens, playwrights also fulfilled the normal military and political obligations of Athe-nian men. The best known Athenian tragedians—Aeschylus (525–456 B.C.), Sophocles (c. 496–406 B.C.), and Euripides (c. 485–406 B.C.)—all served in the army, held public office at some point in their careers, or did both. Aeschylus fought at Marathon and Salamis; the epitaph on his tombstone, which says nothing of his great success as a playwright, reveals how highly he valued his contribution to his city-state as a citizen-soldier: "Under this stone lies Aeschylus the Athenian, son of Euphorion . . .

the grove at Marathon and the Persians who landed there were witnesses to his courage."

Aeschylus's pride in his military service illus-trates a fundamental characteristic of Athenian tragedy: it was at its base a public art form, an ex-pression of the polis that explored the ethical quan-daries of humans in conflict with the gods and with one another in a polis-like community. Even though most tragedies were based on stories that harkened back to a time before the polis, such as tales of the Trojan War, the moral issues the plays illuminated always pertained to the society and obligations of citizens in a city-state. In *Antigone* (441 B.C.), for example, Sophocles presented a drama of harsh conflict between the family's moral obligation to bury its dead in obedience to divine command and the male-dominated city-state's need to preserve its order and defend its values. Anti-gone, the daughter of Oedipus, the now-deceased former king of Thebes, clashes with her uncle, the *CREON* new ruler, when he forbids the burial of one of Antigone's two brothers on the grounds that he had been a traitor. This brother had attacked Thebes after the other brother had broken an agreement to share the kingship. Both brothers died in the ensuing battle, but Antigone's uncle had allowed the burial only of the brother who had remained in power. When Antigone defies her uncle by symbolically burying the allegedly traitorous brother by sprinkling dust on his body, her uncle condemns her to die. He realizes his error only when he receives bad omens from the gods. His decision to punish Antigone ends in utter disaster: Antigone hangs herself before Creon can free her, and his son and then his wife kill themselves in despair. In this horrifying story of anger and death, Sophocles deliberately exposes the right and wrong on each side of the conflict. Although Antigone's uncle eventually acknowledges a leader's responsibility to listen to his people, the play offers no easy resolution of the competing interests of divinely sanctioned moral tradition expressed by a woman and the political rules of the state enforced by a man.

A striking aspect of Greek tragedies is that these plays written and performed by men frequently feature women as central, active figures. At one level the depiction of women in tragedy allowed men accustomed to spending most of their time with other men to peer into what they imagined the world of women was like. But the heroines portrayed in fifth-century B.C. Athenian tragedies also served as vehicles to explore the tensions inherent in the moral code of contemporary society by strongly reacting to men's violations of that code, especially as it pertained to the family. The heroines exhibit what Greeks regarded as masculine qualities. Sophocles' Antigone, for example, confronts the male ruler of her city because he deprived her family of its prerogative to bury its dead. Antigone is remarkable in fearlessly criticizing a powerful man in a public debate about right and wrong. Sophocles shows a woman who can speak like an Athenian man.

Sophocles' plays concerned difficult ethical problems in the context of the polis and thus suggest the social and political function of Athenian tragedy. His plays were overwhelmingly popular. In a sixty-year career as a playwright he competed in the drama festival about thirty times, winning at least twenty times and never finishing less than second. Because winning plays were selected by a panel of ordinary male citizens who were influenced by the audience's reaction, Sophocles' record clearly means his works appealed to the many men who attended the drama competition of the festival of Dionysus. (The evidence concerning women's attendance is unclear, but it suggests they could be present.) Their precise understanding of his messages and those of others' tragedies we cannot know, but they must have been aware that the central characters of the plays were figures who fell into disaster from positions of power and prestige. Their reversals of fortune come about not because they are absolute villains but because, as humans, they are susceptible to a lethal mixture of error, ignorance, and *hubris* (violent arrogance). The Athenian empire was at its height when audiences at Athens attended the plays of Sophocles. The presentation of the plays at the festival of Dionysus was preceded by a procession in the theater to display the money Athens received from the tribute of its allies that year. Thoughtful spectators may have reflected on the possibility that Athens's current power and prestige, managed as it was by humans, remained hostage to the same forces that controlled the fates of the heroes and heroines of tragedy. Tragedies certainly appealed to audiences because they were entertaining, but they also had an educational function: to remind male citizens, those who in the assembly made policy for the city-state, that success engendered complex moral problems too formidable to be fathomed casually or arrogantly.

Property, Social Freedom, and Athenian Women

Athenian women exercised power and earned status in both private and public life through their roles in the family and in religion, respectively. Their exclusion from politics, however, meant that their contributions to the city-state might well be overlooked by men. One heroine in a tragedy by Euripides, Melanippe, vigorously expresses this judgment in a speech denouncing men who denigrate women:

Empty is the slanderous blame men place on women; it is no more than the twanging of a bowstring without an arrow; women are better than men, and I will prove it: women make agreements without having to have witnesses to guarantee their honesty. . . . Women manage the household and preserve its valuable property. Without a wife, no household is clean or happily prosperous. And in matters pertaining to the gods—this is our most important contribution—we have the greatest share. In the oracle at Delphi we propound the will of Apollo, and at the oracle of Zeus at Do__dona__ we reveal the will of Zeus to any Greek who wishes to know it.

Euripides' heroine Medea insists that women who bear children are due respect at least commensurate with that granted men who fight as hoplites:

People say that we women lead a safe life at home, while men have to go to war. What fools they are! I would much rather fight in the phalanx three times than give birth to a child even once.

Greek drama sometimes emphasized the areas in which Athenian women contributed to the polis: publicly by acting as priestesses and privately by bearing and raising legitimate children, the future citizens of the city-state, and by managing the household's property. Women had certain property rights in classical Athens, although these rights were granted more to benefit men than to acknowledge women's legal rights. Women could control property, even land—the most valued possession in Greek society—through inheritance and dowry, although they faced more legal restrictions than men did when they wanted to sell their property or give it away as gifts. Like men, women were supposed to preserve their property to hand down to their children. Daughters did not inherit any of their father's property on his death if he had any living sons, but perhaps one household in five had only daughters, to whom the father's property then fell. Women could also inherit from other male relatives who had no male offspring. A daughter's share in her father's estate came to her in her dowry at marriage. A son whose father was still alive when the son married might also receive a share of his inheritance at that time, to allow him to set up a household. A husband legally controlled the property in his wife's dowry, and their respective holdings frequently became commingled. In this sense husband and wife co-owned the household's common property, which was apportioned to its separate owners only if the marriage were dissolved. The husband was legally responsible for preserving

the dowry and using it for the support and comfort of his wife and any children she bore him. A man often had to put up valuable land of his own as collateral to guarantee the safety of his wife's dowry if, for example, she brought to the marriage money or farm animals that he was to manage. Upon her death her children inherited the dowry. The expectation that a woman would have a dowry encouraged marriage within groups of similar wealth and status. As with the rules governing women's rights to inheritances, customary dowry arrangements supported the society's goal of enabling males to establish and maintain households, because daughters' dowries were usually less valuable than their brothers' inheritances and therefore kept the bulk of a father's property attached to his sons.

The same goal shows up clearly in Athenian laws concerning heiresses. If a father died leaving only a daughter, his property devolved upon her as his heiress, but she did not own it in the sense that she could dispose of it as she pleased. Instead (in the simplest case) her father's closest male relative—her official guardian after her father's death—was required to marry her, with the aim of producing a son. The inherited property then belonged to that son when he reached adulthood. This rule theoretically applied regardless of whether the heiress was already married (without any sons) or whether the male relative already had a wife. The heiress and the male relative were both supposed to divorce their present spouses and marry each other, although in practice the rule could be circumvented by legal subterfuge. This rule preserved the father's line and kept the property in his family. The practice also prevented rich men from getting richer by engineering deals with wealthy heiresses' guardians to marry and therefore merge estates. Above all it prevented property from piling up in the hands of unmarried women. At Sparta, Aristotle reported, precisely this agglomeration of wealth took place as women inherited land or received it in their dowries without—to Aristotle's way of thinking—adequate regulations promoting remarriage. He claimed that women had come to own 40 percent of Spartan territory. Athenian men regulated women's access to property and therefore to power more successfully.

Medea's comment that women were said to lead a safe life at home reflected the expectation that

Athenian women from the propertied class would avoid frequent or close contact with men who were not family members or in the family's circle of friends. Women of this socioeconomic level were supposed to spend much of their time in their own homes or the homes of women friends. Women dressed and slept in rooms set aside for them, but these rooms usually opened onto a walled court-yard where the women could walk in the open air, talk, supervise the domestic chores of the family's slaves, and interact with other members of the household, male and female. Here in her "territory" a woman would spin wool for clothing while chatting with women friends who had come to visit, play with her children, and give her opinions on various matters to the men of the house as they came and went. Poor women had little time for such activities because they, like their husbands, sons, and brothers, had to leave their homes, often only a crowded rental apartment, to work. They often set up small stalls to sell bread, vegetables, simple clothing, or trinkets.

A woman with servants who answered the door herself would be reproached as careless of her reputation. And a proper woman left her home only for an appropriate reason. Fortunately, Athenian life offered many occasions for women to get out: religious festivals, funerals, childbirths at the houses of relatives and friends, and trips to work-shops to buy shoes or other domestic articles. Sometimes her husband escorted her, but more often she was accompanied only by a servant and had more opportunity to act independently. Social protocol demanded men to refrain from speaking the names of respectable women in public conver-sations and speeches in court unless practical necessity demanded it.

Because they stayed inside or in the shade so much, rich women maintained very pale complex-ions. This pallor was much admired as a sign of an enviable life of leisure and wealth. Women regularly used powdered white lead to give themselves a suit-ably pallid look. Presumably, many upper-class women viewed their limited contact with men out-side the household as a badge of their superior social status. In a gender-segregated society such as that of upper-class Athens, a woman's primary personal relationships were probably with her children and the other women with whom she spent most of her time.

Men restricted women's freedom of movement partly to avoid uncertainty about the paternity of their children (by limiting their wives' opportunities for adultery) and to protect the virginity of their daughters. Given that citizenship defined the polit-ical structure of the city-state and a man's personal freedom, Athenians felt it crucial to ensure a boy truly was his father's son and not the offspring of some other man, who could conceivably be a foreigner or a slave. Furthermore, the preference for keeping property in the father's line meant that the sons who inherited a father's property needed to be his legitimate sons. Women who bore legiti-mate children immediately earned higher status and greater freedom in the family, as explained, for ex-ample, by an Athenian man in this excerpt from his remarks before a court in a case in which he had killed an adulterer whom he had caught with his wife:

> After my marriage, I initially refrained from bothering my wife very much, but neither did I allow her too much independence. I kept an eye on her. . . .But after she had a baby, I started to trust her more and put her in charge of all my things, believing we now had the closest of relationships.

Bearing male children brought special honor to a woman because sons meant security for parents.

A Greek Woman at the Shoemaker
This Athenian vase shows a woman being fitted for a pair of custom-made shoes by a craftsman and his young assistant. Following Greek custom, the woman did not shop alone but was accompanied by her husband.

***The Pleasures of
a Symposium***
*Wealthy Greek men
frequently joined friends
for a* symposium, *a drinking party usually with
hired female entertainers.
The man at the right is
about to fling the dregs
from his wine cup, a messy
game called* kottabos.

Sons could appear in court in support of their parents in lawsuits and protect them in the streets of Athens, which for most of its history had no regular police force. By law, sons were required to support their parents in their old age. So intense was the pressure to produce sons that stories of women who smuggled in male babies born to slaves and passed them off as their own were common. Such tales, whose truth is hard to gauge, were credible only because husbands customarily stayed away at childbirth.

Men, unlike women, were not penalized for sexual activity outside marriage. "Certainly you don't think men beget children out of sexual desire?" wrote the upper-class author Xenophon. "The streets and the brothels are swarming with ways to take care of that." Men could have sex with female slaves, who could not refuse their masters, or patronize various classes of prostitutes, depending on how much money they wanted to spend. A man could not keep a prostitute in the same house as his wife without offending his wife and her family, but otherwise he incurred no censure or disgrace by paying for sex. The Greeks called the most expensive female prostitutes "companions." Usually from another city-state than the one in which they worked, companions were physically attractive and could usually sing and play musical instruments, which they did at men's dinner parties (to which wives were not invited). Many companions lived precarious lives subject to exploitation and even violence at the hands of their male customers. The most accomplished companions, however, could attract lovers from the highest levels of society and become sufficiently rich to live in luxury on their own. This independent existence strongly distinguished them from citizen women, as did the freedom to control their own sexuality. Equally distinctive was their cultivated ability to converse with men in public. Companions entertained men with their witty, bantering conversation. Their characteristic skill at clever taunts and verbal snubs allowed companions a freedom of speech denied to "proper" women. Only very rich citizen women of advanced years, such as Elpinike, the sister of Cimon, could occasionally indulge in a similar freedom of expression. She once publicly rebuked Pericles for having boasted about the Athenian conquest of Samos after its rebellion. When other Athenian women praised Pericles for his success, Elpinike sarcastically remarked. "This really is wonderful, Pericles, . . . that you have caused the loss of many good citizens, not in battle against Phoenicians or Persians, like my brother Cimon, but in suppressing an allied city of fellow Greeks."

Education, the Sophists, and New Intellectual Developments

Athenians learned the norms of respectable behavior not in school but in the family and in the course of everyday life. Public schools as we know them did not yet exist. Only well-to-do families could afford private teachers, to whom they sent their sons to learn to read, write, perhaps sing or play a musical instrument, and train for athletics and military service. Physical fitness was considered so vital for men, who could be called up for military service from the age of eighteen until sixty, that the city-state provided open-air exercise facilities for daily workouts. Men also discussed politics and exchanged news at these gymnasia. The daughters of wealthy families often learned to read, write, and do simple arithmetic, presumably from instruction at home; a woman with these skills would be better prepared to manage a household and help her future husband run their estate.

Poorer girls and boys learned a trade and perhaps some rudiments of literacy by assisting their parents in their daily work, or if they were fortunate, by being apprenticed to skilled crafts producers. Outside the ranks of the prosperous the level of literacy in Athenian society was low: only a few poor people could do much more than perhaps sign their names. The inability to read did not impede most people, who could find someone to read aloud to them any written texts they needed to understand. The predominance of oral rather than written communication meant that people were accustomed to absorbing information by ear (those who could read usually read out loud), and Greeks were very fond of songs, speeches, narrated stories, and lively conversation.

Young men from prosperous families traditionally acquired the advanced skills to participate successfully in the public life of Athenian democracy by observing their fathers, uncles, and other older men as they debated in the assembly, served as councilors or magistrates, and spoke in court cases. In many cases an older man would choose an adolescent boy as his special favorite to educate. The boy would learn about public life by spending his time in the company of the older man and his adult friends. During the day the boy would observe his mentor talking politics in the agora, help him perform his duties in public office, and work out with him in a gymnasium. Their evenings would be spent at a symposium (a drinking party for men and companions), which would encompass a range of behavior from serious political and philosophical discussion to riotous partying. Such a mentor-protégé relationship commonly included homosexual love as an expression of the bond between the boy and the older male, who would normally be married. Although neither male homosexuality outside a mentor-protégé relationship nor female homosexuality in general were socially acceptable, the homosexual behavior between older mentors and younger protégés was generally considered appropriate, as

long as the older man did not exploit his younger companion physically or neglect his education in public affairs. Athenian society encompassed a wide range of bonds among men, from political and military activity, to training of mind and body, to sexual practices.

In the second half of the fifth century B.C. young men who sought to polish their political skills had access to a new kind of teacher. These teachers were called *sophists* ("wise men"), a label that acquired a pejorative connotation (preserved in the English word *sophistry*) because they were so clever at public speaking and philosophic debates. The earliest sophists practiced in parts of the Greek world outside Athens, but from about 450 B.C. on they began to travel to Athens, which was then at the height of its material prosperity, to search for pupils who could pay the hefty prices the sophists charged for their instruction. Wealthy young men flocked to the dazzling demonstrations these itinerant teachers put on to showcase their eloquence, an ability they claimed they could impart to students. The sophists offered what every ambitious young man wanted to learn: the skill to persuade his fellow citizens in the debates of the assembly and the council or in lawsuits before large juries. For those unwilling or unable to master the new rhetorical skills, the sophists (for stiff fees) would write speeches the purchasers delivered as their own compositions.

The most famous sophist was Protagoras, a contemporary of Pericles, from Abdera in northern Greece. Protagoras emigrated to Athens around 450 B.C., when he was about forty, and spent most of his career there. His oratorical skills and upright character so impressed the men of Athens that they chose him to devise a code of laws for a new colony to be founded in Thurii in southern Italy in 444 B.C. Some of Protagoras's beliefs eventually aroused considerable controversy; one was his agnosticism: "Whether the gods exist I cannot discover, nor what their form is like, for there are many impediments to knowledge, [such as] the obscurity of the subject and the brevity of human life."

Equally controversial was Protagoras's denial of an absolute standard of truth, his assertion that every issue has two, irreconcilable sides. For example, if one person feeling a breeze thinks it warm, whereas another person thinks it cool, neither judgment can be absolutely correct because the wind simply is warm to one and cool to another.

Protagoras summed up his subjectivism (the belief that there is no absolute reality behind and independent of appearances) in the much-quoted opening of his work *Truth* (most of which is now lost): "Man is the measure of all things, of the things that are that they are, and of the things that are not that they are not." "Man" in this passage (*anthropos* in Greek, hence our word "anthropology") seems to refer to the individual human, whether male or female, whom Protagoras makes the sole judge of his or her own impressions.

The sophists alarmed many traditionally minded men, who thought the sophists' facility with words might be used (by them or by their pupils) to destabilize social and political traditions. In a culture like that of ancient Greece, where laws, codes of proper behavior and morals, and religious ideals were expressed and transmitted from generation to generation orally, a persuasive and charismatic speaker could potentially wield as much power as an army of warriors. Many feared people would be swayed by the style of silver-tongued sophists and accept the substance of what they said, which often contradicted the truths commonly held.

Tension Between Intellectual and Political Forces in the 430s B.C.

The teachings of sophists like Protagoras made many Athenians nervous, especially because leading figures like Pericles flocked to hear them. Two related views sophists taught aroused special concern: the idea that human institutions and values were only matters of convention, custom, or law (*nomos*) and not products of nature (*physis*), and the idea that because truth was relative, speakers should be able to argue either side of a question with equal persuasiveness. The first view implied that traditional human institutions were arbitrary rather than grounded in immutable nature, and the second rendered rhetoric an amoral skill. The combination of the two ideas seemed exceptionally dangerous because it threatened the shared public values of the polis with unpredictable changes. Protagoras insisted his doctrines were not hostile to democracy, especially because he argued that every person had an innate capability for "excellence" and that human survival depended on the rule of law based on a sense of justice. Members of the community, he argued, should be persuaded to

obey the laws not because they are based on absolute truth, which does not exist, but because it is expedient for people to live by them. A thief, for example, who might claim he thought a law against stealing was not appropriate, would have to be persuaded that the law forbidding theft was to his advantage because it protected his own property and the community in which he, like all humans, had to live in order to survive.

Protagoras's views were not the only source of disquietude for many Athenian men disturbed by intellectual developments. Philosophers such as Anaxagoras of Clazomenae in Ionia and Leucippus of Miletus propounded unsettling new theories about the nature of the cosmos in response to the provocative physics of the Ionian thinkers of the sixth century B.C. Most people probably thought Anaxagoras's general theory postulating an abstract force he called "mind" as the organizing principle of the universe was too obscure to worry about. But the details of his theory offended those who held to the assumptions of traditional religion. For example, he argued that the sun was in truth nothing more than a lump of flaming rock, not a divine entity. Leucippus, whose doctrines were made famous by his pupil Democritus of Abdera, invented an atomic theory of matter to explain how change was possible and indeed constant. Everything, he argued, consisted of tiny, invisible particles in eternal motion. Their random collisions caused them to combine and recombine in an infinite variety of forms. This physical explanation of the source of change, like Anaxagoras's analysis of the nature of the sun, seemed to deny the validity of the entire superstructure of traditional religion, which explained events as the outcome of divine forces.

Many people feared the teachings of the sophists and philosophers would offend the gods and therefore erode the divine favor they believed Athens enjoyed. Just like a murderer, a teacher spouting sacrilegious doctrines could bring miasma and therefore divine punishment on the whole community. So deeply felt was this anxiety that Pericles' friendship with Protagoras, Anaxagoras, and other controversial intellectuals gave his rivals a weapon to use against him when political tensions came to a head in the 430s B.C. as a result of the threat of war with Sparta. Pericles' opponents criticized him as sympathetic to dangerous new ideas as well as autocratic in his leadership.

*CLAHD·ZO·MEN·EE

Other new ideas also emerged in the mid-fifth century B.C. In historical writing, for example, Hecataeus of Miletus, born in the later sixth century B.C., had earlier opened the way to a broader and more critical vision of the past. He wrote both an extensive guidebook to illustrate his map of the world as he knew it and a treatise criticizing mythological traditions. The Greek historians writing immediately after him concentrated on the histories of their local areas and wrote in a spare, chronicle-like style that made history into little more than a list of events and geographical facts. Herodotus of Halicarnassus (c. 485–425 B.C.), however, built on the foundations laid by Hecataeus in writing his *Histories,* a groundbreaking work in its wide geographical scope, its critical approach to historical evidence, and its lively narrative. To describe and explain the clash between East and West represented by the wars between Persians and Greeks in the early fifth century B.C., Herodotus searched for the origins of the conflict both by delving deep into the past and by examining the cultural traditions of all the peoples involved. He recognized the relevance and the delight of studying other cultures as a component of historical investigation.

New developments in Greek medicine in this period are associated with Hippocrates of Cos, a younger contemporary of Herodotus. Details about the life and thought of this most famous of all Greek doctors are sketchy, but he certainly made great strides in putting medical diagnosis and treatment on a scientific basis. Earlier medical practices had depended on magic and ritual. Hippocrates apparently viewed the human body as an organism whose parts must be understood as part of the whole. Greek doctors characteristically searched for a system of first principles to serve as a foundation for their treatments, but no consensus emerged. Even in antiquity medical writers disagreed about the theoretical foundation of Hippocrates' medicine. Some attributed to him the view, popular in later times, that four elements, called humors (fluids), make up the human body: blood, phlegm, black bile, and yellow bile. This intellectual system corresponded to the division of the inanimate world into four parts as well: the elements earth, air, fire, and water.

Most important, Hippocrates taught that the physician should base his knowledge on careful observation of patients and their response to remedies. Empirically grounded clinical experience,

he insisted, was the best guide to treatments that would not do the sick more harm than good. Hippocratic medical doctrine apparently made little or no mention of a divine role in sickness and its cures, although various cults in Greek religion, most famously that of the god Asclepius, offered healing to petitioners. Hippocrates' contribution to medicine is remembered today in the oath bearing his name that doctors swear at the beginning of their professional careers.

The impact of the developments in history and medicine on ordinary people is hard to assess, but their misgivings about the new trends in education and philosophy definitely heightened the political tension in Athens in the 430s B.C. These intellectual developments had a wide-ranging effect because the political, intellectual, and religious dimensions of life in ancient Athens were so intertwined. A person could discuss the city-state's domestic and foreign policies on one occasion, novel theories of the nature of the universe on another, and whether the gods were angry or pleased with the community every day. By the late 430s B.C. the Athenians had new reasons to worry about each of these topics.

The End of the Golden Age

Tension between Athens and Sparta had peaked by the time a team of Spartan representatives arrived in Athens for diplomatic negotiations in 432 B.C. The Spartan representatives issued an ultimatum stating that war could be averted only if the Athenians revoked their economic sanctions against Megara, a city-state allied to Sparta. Such legalistic wranglings hid the larger issue of power that fueled the hostility between Athens and Sparta. The Spartan leaders feared the Athenians would use their superior long-distance offensive weaponry—the naval forces of the Delian League—to destroy Spartan control over the members of the Peloponnesian League. The majority in the Athenian assembly resented Spartan interference in their freedom of action.

When the negotiations collapsed, the result was the devastating Peloponnesian War, which dragged on from 431 to 404 B.C. and engulfed almost the entire Greek world. The history of the conflict reveals the general unpredictability of war and the consequences of the repeated reluctance of the Athenian assembly to negotiate peace terms instead of simply dictating them. Athens's losses of population and property had a disastrous, although temporary, effect on its international power, revenues, and social cohesiveness.

The Strategy of the Peloponnesian War

The Spartans took an intransigent stance with the Athenians to placate their allies—notably the Megarians and, more important, the Corinthians.

The latter had threatened to withdraw from the Peloponnesian League and form a different international alliance if the Spartans delayed any longer in backing them in their dispute with the Athenians over a rebellious Corinthian ally. In this way the actions of lesser powers nudged the two great powers, Athens and Sparta, over the brink into war.

Most of our knowledge of this decisive war comes from the history written by the Athenian Thucydides (c. 460–400 B.C.), himself a commander in the early years of the war (until the assembly banished him for losing an outpost to the enemy).

Alliances of the Peloponnesian War

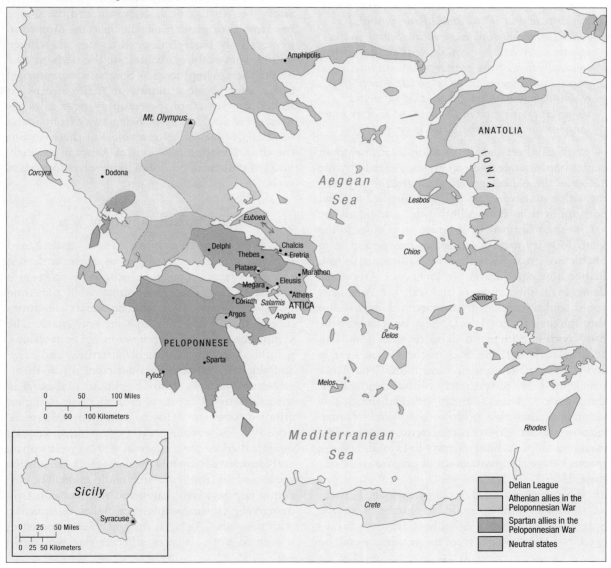

During his exile, Thucydides interviewed witnesses from both sides of the conflict. His perceptive account of the causes and events of the war made his book a pioneering work of history presented as the narrative of great contemporary events and power politics. For example, he revealed that Pericles convinced his fellow citizens to reject the Spartan demands with these arguments:

> If we do go to war, harbor no thought that you went to war over a trivial affair. For you this trifling matter is the assurance and the proof of your determination. If you yield to their demands, they will immediately confront you with some larger demand, since they will think that you only gave way on the first point out of fear. But if you stand firm, you will show them that they have to deal with you as equals. . . . When our equals, without agreeing to arbitration of the matter under dispute, make claims on us as neighbors and state those claims as commands, it would be no better than slavery to give in to them, no matter how large or how small the claim may be.

Athens's fleet and fortifications made its urban center impregnable to direct attack. Already by the 450s B.C. the Athenians had encircled the city center with a massive stone wall and fortified a broad corridor with a wall on both sides leading all the way to the main harbor at Piraeus five miles to the west. Military siege machines of this period were unable to broach such walls. Consequently, no matter how agricultural production of Attica was damaged in the course of the war, the Athenians could feed themselves by importing food by ship through their fortified port. They could pay for the food with the huge financial reserves they had accumulated from the dues of the Delian League and the income from their silver mines. The Athenians could also retreat safely behind their walls if the superior Spartan infantry attacked. From this seemingly invincible position they could launch surprise attacks against Spartan territory by sending their warships behind enemy lines and landing troops before the Spartans could prepare to defend themselves.

This two-pronged strategy, which Pericles devised, was simple: avoid set battles with the Spartan infantry even if Athenian territory was ravaged, and attack Sparta from the sea. In the end, he predicted, the superior resources of Athens would enable it to win a war of attrition. The difficulty in carrying out Pericles' plan was that many Athenians who resided outside the urban center had to abandon their homes and fields to the depredations of the Spartan army when it invaded Attica. As Thucydides reports, people hated coming in from the countryside where "most Athenians were born and bred; they grumbled at having to move their entire households [into Athens] . . . , abandoning their normal way of life and leaving behind what they regarded as their true city." When in 431 B.C. the Spartans invaded Attica for the first time and began to destroy the countryside, the country-dwellers of Attica became enraged as, standing in safety on Athens's walls, they watched the smoke rise from their property as the Spartans torched it. Pericles only barely managed to stop the citizen militia from rushing out despite the odds to take on the Spartan hoplites. The Spartan army returned home after about a month in Attica because it lacked the structure for resupply over a longer period and could not risk being away from Sparta too long for fear of helot revolt. For these reasons the annual Spartan invasions of Attica in the early years of the war never lasted longer than forty days each.

The Unpredictability of War

The innate unpredictability of war undermined Pericles' strategy, especially as an epidemic disease ravaged Athens's population for several years beginning in 430 B.C. The disease struck while the Athenians were jammed together in unsanitary conditions behind their walls to escape Spartan attack. The symptoms were gruesome: vomiting, convulsions, painful sores, uncontrollable diarrhea, and fever and thirst so extreme that sufferers threw themselves into cisterns vainly hoping to find relief in the cold water. The rate of mortality was so high it crippled Athenian ability to man the naval expeditions Pericles' wartime strategy demanded. Pericles himself died of the disease in 429 B.C. He apparently had not anticipated the damage to Athens that the loss of his firm leadership could mean. The epidemic also seriously hampered the war effort by destroying Athenian confidence in their relationship with the gods. "As far as the gods were concerned, it seemed not to matter whether one worshiped them or not because the good and the bad were dying indiscriminately," was Thucydides' description of the population's attitude at the height of the epidemic.

The epidemic hurt the Athenians materially by devastating their population, politically by removing their foremost leader, and psychologically by damaging their self-confidence. Nevertheless, they fought on. In 425 B.C., in fact, their general Cleon won an unprecedented victory by capturing some one hundred twenty Spartan Equals and about one hundred seventy allied troops in a battle at Pylos in the western Peloponnese. No Spartan soldiers had ever before surrendered under any circumstances. They had always taken as their martial creed the sentiment expressed by the legendary advice of a Spartan mother as she handed her son his shield as he went off to war: "Come home either with this or on it," meaning he should return either as a victor carrying his shield or as a corpse carried upon it. By this date, however, the population of Spartan Equals had been so reduced that even the loss of a small group was devastating. The Spartan leaders therefore offered the Athenians favorable peace terms in return for the captives. At Cleon's urging the Athenian assembly refused to make peace.

The lack of wisdom in this decision became clear with the next unexpected development of the war: a sudden reversal in the Spartan policy against waging military expeditions far from home. In 424 B.C. the Spartan general Brasidas led an army on a daring campaign against Athenian strongholds in far northern Greece, hundreds of miles from Sparta. He adroitly meshed diplomacy with brilliant military tactics employing speed and surprise to bring Athens's allies in this crucial region over to Sparta's side. Brasidas's success robbed Athens of access to gold mines and a major source of timber for building warships. (The loss of Amphipolis, an Athenian colony controlling a main route into the interior and its rich resources, was what led the assembly to exile Thucydides—he was the commander in this area.) Cleon then commanded a counterattacking expedition with the aim of recovering Athens's valuable northern possessions. But both Cleon and Brasidas were killed in battle before Amphipolis in 422 B.C., thus depriving each side of its most energetic military leader and opening the way to negotiations. Peace came in 421 B.C.

AM·FIP·OL·IS

when both sides agreed to resurrect the balance of forces just as it had been in 431 B.C. *WHEN THE PEL. WAR BEGAN.*

Still, factions in both city-states clamored for war, and fighting resumed when the brash young Athenian commander Alcibiades (c. 450–404 B.C.) formed a temporary coalition between Athens and Argos, a bitter rival of Sparta for power in the Peloponnese. The coalition disintegrated after being defeated by Sparta's forces at the battle of Mantinea in 418 B.C. The "peacetime war" continued in 416 B.C. when the Athenians besieged the tiny island of Melos, a community sympathetic to Sparta that had taken no active part in the war, and killed the men and sold the women and children into slavery just to demonstrate their strength. In 415 B.C. the war recommenced on a large scale when Alcibiades convinced the Athenian assembly to launch a massive naval campaign against Sicily *& ESP. AGAINST SYRACUSE* to seek its great riches and prevent any Sicilian cities from aiding the Spartans. His aggressive dreams of martial glory appealed especially to young men who had not yet experienced the realities of war. The arrogant flamboyance of Alcibiades' private life and his evident political ambitions had made him many enemies in Athens, and they managed to get him recalled from the expedition's command by accusing him of having participated in a sacrilegious mockery of the Eleusinian Mysteries and being mixed up in the vandalizing of statues called Herms just before his expedition sailed. Herms, stone posts with sculpted sets of erect male organs and a bust of the god Hermes, stood throughout the city as protectors

Mainland Greece and Sicily

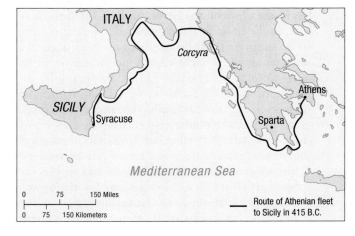

against infertility and bad luck. The vandals outraged the public by knocking off the statues' phalluses. Alcibiades' reaction to the charges was a shock: he deserted to Sparta. The remaining Athenian generals so mismanaged the Sicilian expedition that it ended in total defeat at Syracuse in 413 B.C.

Alcibiades' defection caused Athens enormous trouble because he used his knowledge of the Athenian situation to aid Sparta. On his advice the Spartans established a permanent base of operations in the Attic countryside in 413 B.C. Spartan forces could now raid the Athenian countryside year-round. Twenty thousand slaves working in Athens's silver mines sought refuge in the Spartan camp. An oligarchic coup briefly overturned Athenian democracy in 411 B.C., but Athens soon regained its traditional form of government and fought on, despite the support Sparta now began to receive from Persia. By backing a rebel against the Persian king some five to ten years earlier, Athens had lost any chance for help from King Darius II, who was ready to provide money in return for acknowledgment of his right to control the Greek city-states of Anatolia. Sparta made this concession and received Persian funding. Aggressive Spartan action at sea, with a fleet financed largely by this aid, forced Athens to surrender in 404 B.C. After twenty-seven years of near continuous war, the Athenians were at the mercy of their enemies.

The Spartans resisted the Corinthians' demand for the utter destruction of Athens because they feared Corinth and Thebes might grow too strong if Athens no longer existed to serve as a counterweight. Instead they installed a regime of antidemocratic Athenian aristocrats, who became known as the Thirty Tyrants. These men came from the class of aristocrats that had traditionally despised democracy and embraced oligarchy. Brutally suppressing their opposition, these oligarchs embarked on an eight-month period of terror in 404–403 B.C. The orator Lysias,* for example, reported that their henchmen seized his brother for execution as a way of stealing the family's valuables, even ripping the gold earrings from the ears of his brother's wife. An Athenian democratic resistance movement soon arose, and it seized power from the Thirty Tyrants in Athens after a series of bloody street battles in 403 B.C. Fortunately for the democrats, a split in the Spartan leadership fueled by the competing ambitions of its two most prominent

men had prevented effective Spartan military support for the tyrants. To end the internal strife that threatened to tear Athens apart, the newly restored democracy proclaimed an amnesty, the first known in Western history, under which all further charges and official recriminations concerning the period of terror in 404–403 B.C. were forbidden. Athens's government was once again a functioning democracy; its financial and military strength, however, were shattered, and its society harbored the memory of a bitter divisiveness that no amnesty could dispel.

Response to War in Athens

The Peloponnesian War took its toll on Athens's domestic life as well as its political harmony and international power. It ruined the lives of the many people who lived in the countryside, because the Spartan invaders had wrecked their homes. The crowded conditions in the city led to friction between city-dwellers and the refugees from the rural areas. The economy suffered from the interruptions to agriculture and the loss of income from the silver mines after 413 B.C. Some public building projects were kept going, like the Erectheum temple to Athena on the acropolis, to demonstrate the Athenian will to carry on and also to infuse some money into the crippled economy. But the war had depleted the funds available for many nonmilitary activities. The scale of the great dramatic festivals, for example, had to be cut back. The financial situation had become so desperate by the end of the war that Athenians were required to turn in their silver coins and exchange them for an emergency currency of bronze thinly plated with silver. The regular silver coins, along with gold coins that were minted from golden objects borrowed from Athens's temples, were then used to pay war expenses.

The war caused many men and women to make drastic changes in the way they earned a living. Wealthy families that had money and valuable goods stored-up could weather the crisis by using their savings, but most people had no financial cushion. When enemies destroyed their harvests, farmers used to toiling in their own fields had to scrounge for work as day laborers in the city. Men who rowed the ships of the Athenian fleet could earn regular wages, but they had to spend long periods away from their families and faced death

* Lĭs·ĭ·us

in every battle. Craftspeople and small merchants in the city still had their livelihoods, but their business suffered because consumers had less money to spend. Especially hard hit were many previously moderately well-off women whose husbands and brothers died during the conflict. Such women had traditionally done weaving at home for their own families and supervised the work of household slaves, but the men had earned the family's income by farming or practicing a trade. With no one to provide for them and their children, they were forced to work outside the home to support their families. The only jobs open to them were low-paying occupations traditional for women, such as baby nurse or weaver or some occupations as laborers in such areas as vineyard work, for which not enough men were available to meet the need. Although these circumstances brought more women into public view, they were still not included in Athenian political life.

The stresses of everyday life during trying times were reflected in Athenian comedies produced during the war. Besides tragedies and satyr plays, comic plays were the other main form of dramatic art in ancient Athens. Like tragedies, comedies were composed in verse and had been presented annually since early in the fifth century B.C. They formed a separate competition in the Athenian civic festivals in honor of Dionysus in the same outdoor theater used for tragedies. Women could probably attend, although the evidence for this is ambiguous. Comedies' all-male casts consisted of a twenty-four-member chorus in addition to regular actors. The beauty of the soaring poetry of the choral songs of comedy was matched by the ingeniously imaginative fantasy of its plots, which almost always ended with a festive resolution of the problems with which they had begun. In the *Birds*, by Aristophanes, for example, produced in 414 B.C., two men try to escape the hassles of everyday life at Athens. They run away to seek a new life in a world called "Cloudcuckooland" that is inhabited by talking birds, portrayed by the chorus in colorful bird costumes.

The immediate purpose of a comic playwright was to create beautiful poetry and raise laughs in the hope of winning the award for the festival's best comedy. Much of the humor of Athenian comedy had to do with sex and bodily fuctions, and much of its ribaldry was delivered in a stream of imagi-

The Chorus of a Greek Comedy
The Greek comedies of the fifth century B.C. sometimes sported choruses of actors dressed as animals, such as these horses carrying riders. A musician playing pipes for their dance stands at the left.

native profanity. The plots dealt primarily with current issues and personalities. Insulting attacks on prominent men such as Pericles or Cleon, the victor of Pylos, were a staple. Pericles apparently instituted a ban on such attacks in response to fierce treatment in comedies after the revolt of Samos in 441–439 B.C., but the measure was soon rescinded. Cleon was so outraged by the way he was portrayed on the comic stage by Aristophanes (c. 455–385 B.C.), the only comic playwright of the fifth century B.C. from whose works entire plays have survived, that he sued the playwright. When Cleon lost the case, Aristophanes responded by pitilessly parodying him as a reprobate foreign slave in *The Knights* of 424 B.C. Other well-known men who were not portrayed as characters could come in for insults as sexually effeminate and cowards. Women characters portrayed as figures of fun and ridicule in comedy seem to have been fictional.

Although slashing satire directed against the mass of ordinary citizens seems to have been unacceptable, Athenian comedies often criticized government policies that had been approved by the assembly by blaming political leaders for them. The strongly critical nature of comedy was never more evident than during the war years. Several of

COMEDIES OF ARISTOPHANES PRODUCED DURING THE PELOPONNESIAN WAR (431–404 B.C.)

427 B.C. *Banqueters*

Not preserved; apparently involved an argument between a spendthrift son and his father

426 B.C. *Babylonians*

Not preserved; apparently attacked politicians, leading Cleon to prosecute Aristophanes

425 B.C. *Acharnians*

Comic hero makes peace with Sparta for his family

424 B.C. *Knights*

Attack on Cleon as a deceitful demagogue

423 B.C. *Clouds*

Controversial portrayal of Socrates as an arrogant sophist

422 B.C. *Wasps*

Parody of old men's passion for serving as jurors in Athens

421 B.C. *Peace*

Comic hero flies to the gods on a giant dung beetle to retrieve the goddess Peace

414 B.C. *Birds*

Comic heroes seek quiet life but end up establishing an empire among the birds in Cloud-cuckooland

411 B.C. *Lysistrata*

Athenian and Spartan women ally in a sex strike to compel men to make peace

411 B.C. *Women at the Festival of Demeter*

Women take revenge on the dramatist Euripides for unflattering portrayal of women in his tragedies

405 B.C. *Frogs*

The god Dionysus goes to Hades to bring back the tragedian Aeschylus to teach the Athenians old-fashioned virtue once again

Aristophanes' popular comedies had plots in which characters arranged peace with Sparta, even though the comedies were produced while the war was still being fiercely contested. In *The Acharnians* of 425 B.C., for example, the protagonist arranges a separate peace treaty with the Spartans for himself and his family while humiliating a character who portrays one of Athens's prominent military commanders of the time. The play won first prize in the comedy competition that year.

The most remarkable of Aristophanes' comedies are those in which the main characters are powerful women who compel the men of Athens to overthrow basic policies of the city-state. Most famous is *Lysistrata* of 411 B.C., named after the female lead character of the play. In it the women of Athens join with the women of Sparta to force their husbands to end the Peloponnesian War. To make the men agree to a peace treaty, the women first seize the acropolis, where Athens's financial reserves are kept, and prevent the men from squandering them further on the war. They then beat back an attack on their position by the old men who have remained in Athens while the younger men are out on campaign. When their husbands return from battle, the women refuse to have sex with them. This strike, which is portrayed in a series of risqué episodes, finally coerces the men of Athens and Sparta to agree to a peace treaty.

Lysistrata presents women acting bravely and aggressively against men who seem bent on destroying their family life by staying away from home for long stretches while on military campaign and on ruining the city-state by prolonging a pointless war. In other words, the play's strong women take on what were usually masculine roles in the ancient Greek city-state and assert their collective power to preserve the community's traditional way of life. Lysistrata emphasizes this point in the speech in which she insists that women have the intelligence and judgment to make political decisions: "I am a woman, and, yes, I have brains. And I'm not badly off for judgment. Nor has my education been bad, coming as it has from my listening often to the conversations of my father and the elders among the men." She came by her knowledge in the traditional way, by learning from older men. Her old-fashioned training and good sense allowed her to see what needed to be done to protect the community. Like the heroines of tragedy, Lysistrata is a reactionary; she wants to put things back the way they were. To do that, however, she has to act like a revolutionary. Perhaps Aristophanes was telling Athenian men that all Athenians should find a new vision to preserve old ways, lest they be lost.

CONCLUSION

The Athenians had much to lose in their war with Sparta because the Golden Age of Athens in the fifth century B.C. had been a time of prosperity, political stability, international power, and artistic and cultural accomplishment. Athenians, both men who fought on land and sea and women who kept their households together during the evacuation of 480–479 B.C., had won great glory in the unexpected victory of the Greek alliance against the Persians. This stunning triumph could have occurred, the Athenians believed, only because the gods smiled upon them with special favor and because the Athenians displayed their superior courage, intelligence, and virtue.

Athens's high-handed application of its military prominence soon led to problems, however, as allied city-states unhappy with the new imbalance of power rebelled. Important allies in the Delian League, such as the Samians, were unwilling to take orders in what was supposed to have been a democratically governed alliance. By the time the Spartans threatened war in the late 430s B.C., Athens no longer commanded an alliance of loyal partners on whom it could depend for support.

The dues of the Delian League, in combination with the income from Attica's silver mines, brought Athens previously unimaginable wealth in the Golden Age. The new revenue allowed the Athenians to embark on a spectacular building program and to offer regular employment to thousands of poorer men as trireme rowers. The problematic aspect of this change in the financial fortunes of the Athenians was that it depended on their maintaining hegemony over allies who chafed at their control. Athenians' prosperity led them to act as an imperial power in relation to their fellow Greeks, a policy their opponents called the equivalent of enslavement, the very issue for which Athens had once stood shoulder to shoulder with these same allies against the Persians.

While the Athenians extended their control in the Aegean region, they developed new democratic procedures, which provided greater political participation for rich and poor men alike. Poor men benefited from reforms in the court system that allowed all Athenian men to be involved in dispensing justice. Under the leadership of Pericles, poorer men also gained greater access to political life after stipends became available for jurors and many officeholders. New opportunities to play a role in political life were not extended to women, however. Upper-class women remained restricted to their households, their friends, and their participation in public religious cults. Poorer women helped support themselves and their families, often as small-scale merchants and crafts producers. Legally, Athenian women's control of their own property and their ability to act on their own behalf in matters of law were still restricted. The tension between continuity and change was evident in many of the tragedies written and performed in the fifth century B.C., in which characters engage in intense conflicts concerning their relationship with the gods and with other people.

Further changes helped undermine the new democratic relationship among Athenian men. The additional opportunities for the advanced education of wealthy young men introduced by the sophists certainly made their pupils more skillful participants in Athenian democracy. The techniques of persuasion taught by Protagoras and his fellow teachers of oratory enabled a man to advance his opinions on policy with great effect or defend himself staunchly in court. Because only wealthy men could afford instruction from a sophist, however, this new education worked against the egalitarian principles of Athenian participatory democracy by giving an advantage to the rich. In addition, the relativism of Protagoras and the physical explanation of the universe expounded by philosophers like Anaxagoras struck traditionally minded Athenians as dangerous to the values of the city-state.

The Athenian Golden Age was framed by war. The successful outcome of the Persian Wars had boosted the Athenians to power in Greece and prosperity at home. The Peloponnesian War had quite a different impact on Greece's premier city-state and its jealous competitors and unwilling allies. The pressures of war upset the traditional pattern of life for many people, especially women who were forced to work outside the home for the first time. Among the consequences of the Peloponnesian War was a restructuring of political power in the ancient Greek world.

Suggestions for Further Reading

Source Materials

Aristophanes. *Lysistrata; The Acharnians; The Clouds.* Translated by A. H. Sommerstein. 1973. A lively rendering of three famous comedies from fifth-century B.C. Athens.

Fornara, Charles W. *Translated Documents of Greece and Rome.* Vol. 1, *Archaic Times to the End of the Peloponnesian War.* 2d ed. 1983. A briefly annotated collection of inscriptions, documents, and historical sources.

Grene, David, and Richmond Lattimore, eds. *The Complete Greek Tragedies.* 9 vols. 1953–1991. Translations of all surviving Athenian tragedies of the fifth century B.C.

Herodotus. *The Histories.* Available in various translations such as that of Aubrey de Sélincourt, 1972, as well as in a bilingual edition published in the Loeb Classical Library series. The principal ancient source for the history of the Persian Wars and a compendium of intriguing stories about the interactions of Greeks and other peoples.

Lefkowitz, Mary R., and Maureen B. Fant. *Women's Life in Greece and Rome: A Source Book in Translation.* 1982. Selections from documents and literature on many aspects of women's lives.

Plutarch. *Life of Themistocles; Aristides; Cimon; Pericles.* Available in various translations such as that of Ian Scott-Kilvert, *Plutarch: The Rise and Fall of Athens,* 1960, as well as in a bilingual edition published in the Loeb Classical Library series. Lively biographies of the great men of classical Athens.

Thucydides. *The Peloponnesian War.* Available in various translations such as that of Rex Warner, 1972, as well as in a bilingual edition published in the Loeb Classical Library series. The only surviving fifth-century B.C. account of the development of the Athenian empire (Book 1, sections 89–117) and the principal ancient source for the Peloponnesian War.

Interpretive Studies

Boardman, J., N. G. L. Hammond, D. M. Lewis, and M. Ostwald, eds. *The Cambridge Ancient History.* Vol. IV, *Persia, Greece, and the Western Mediterranean, c. 525 B.C. to 479 B.C.* 2d ed. 1988. An authoritative survey covering the Persian Empire, the Ionian revolt, and the Persian Wars.

Brommer, Frank. *The Sculptures of the Parthenon.* 1979. A magnificent photographic record of the sculptural decoration of the Parthenon, with descriptions.

Burkert, Walter. *Greek Religion.* Translated by John Raffan. 1985. A vast, scholarly catalog of Greek religious practices.

Camp, John M. *The Athenian Agora: Excavations in the Heart of Classical Athens.* 1986. A splendidly illustrated survey of the buildings and monuments of Athens' civic center and their functions.

Cook, J. M. *The Persian Empire.* 1983. A colorful, readable complement to Olmstead's work.

Davies, J. K. *Democracy and Classical Greece.* 1978. A survey of classical Greek history with frequent discussion on the evidence of documents.

De Romilly, Jacqueline. *A Short History of Greek Literature.* 1985. A comprehensive survey including discussions of poetry, philosophy, history, rhetoric, and medical writings.

Dodds, E. R. *The Greeks and the Irrational.* 1951. A stimulating and enormously influential treatment of Greek religion and thought that remains a classic despite some outdated views.

Dover, K. J. *Aristophanic Comedy.* 1972. An introduction to Athenian Old Comedy in general and to the eleven surviving plays of Aristophanes in particular.

Easterling, P. E., and J. V. Muir, eds. *Greek Religion and Society.* 1985. Readable essays on topics including views of life after death, temples, festivals, oracles, and divination.

Ehrenberg, Victor. *From Solon to Socrates.* 2d ed. 1973. A wide-ranging survey of Greek history and civilization in the sixth and fifth centuries B.C.

Finley, M. I. *Democracy Ancient and Modern.* Rev. ed. 1973. A provocative series of lectures that advocate applying the principles of Athenian participatory democracy to modern democracies.

Goldhill, Simon. *Reading Greek Tragedy.* 1986. Introduces the many different approaches modern critics take in interpreting Greek tragedy.

Guthrie, W. K. C. *A History of Greek Philosophy,* Vol.

2, *The Presocratic Tradition from Parmenides to Democritus.* 1965. The standard introduction to Greek philosophy in the fifth century B.C.

———. *A History of Greek Philosophy,* Vol. 4, pt. 1, *The Sophists.* 1971. A thorough discussion of the evidence for the sophists' views.

Joint Association of Classical Teachers. *The World of Athens: An Introduction to Classical Athenian Culture.* 1984. A clearly written handbook arranged topically (originally produced to accompany the Joint Association of Classical Teachers' Greek course).

Kerferd, G. B. *The Sophistic Movement.* 1981. A readable introduction to the thought and the impact of the fifth-century B.C. sophists.

Lacey, W. K. *The Family in Classical Greece.* Rev. ed. 1980. The standard survey of the subject, for a general audience.

McGregor, Malcom F. *The Athenians and Their Empire.* 1987. A detailed introduction to the military and administrative history of the Athenian empire.

Mikalson, Jon D. *Athenian Popular Religion.* 1983. Investigates the religious beliefs and practices of the Athenian people.

Olmstead, A. T. *History of the Persian Empire.* 1948. Still the most comprehensive survey of the subject for the general reader.

Parke, H. W. *Festivals of the Athenians.* 1977. Describes the chief ceremonial occasions of Athens according to their order in the calendar year.

Parker, Robert. *Miasma: Pollution and Purification in Early Greek Religion.* 1983. An extensive treatment of these central themes in Greek life, attributing their importance to a desire for order.

Pollitt, J. J. *Art and Experience in Classical Greece.* 1972. A lively interpretation of the messages conveyed by classical Greek art.

Powell, Anton. *Athens and Sparta: Constructing Greek Political and Social History from 478 B.C.* 1988. A stimulating treatment of the main topics of classical Greek history, including an extensive section on Athenian citizen women.

Robertson, D. S. *Greek and Roman Architecture.* 2d ed. 1971. A detailed survey of the techniques of Greek architecture.

Schaps, David M. *Economic Rights of Women in Ancient Greece.* 1979. Explores the rights and disadvantages of women with regard to property, inheritance, dowry, and commerce.

Sealey, Raphael. *Women and Law in Classical Greece.* 1990. Analyzes women's rights in marriage, property ownership, and questions of inheritance.

Woodford, Susan. *Cambridge Introduction to the History of Art: Greece and Rome.* 1982. A concise introduction to the development of Greek art, especially sculpture, with excellent illustrations and suggestions for further reading.

Wycherly, R. E. *How the Greeks Built Cities.* 2d ed. 1976. Examines the relationship of architecture and town planning to ancient Greek life.

Before going to fight in the Peloponnesian War, an Athenian man named Diodotus had appointed his brother guardian of his three children and left behind a large amount of money and property for their care. The brother happened to be the children's grandfather—their mother was his daughter. After Diodotus was killed in battle, his brother misappropriated much of the funds and eventually claimed he could no longer support the two boys, who would thereafter have to fend for themselves. Their sister was already married, with a dowry from her father's money.

We learn from testimony in a lawsuit brought on the boys' behalf about 400 B.C. by their sister's husband that their mother had done her utmost to dissuade her father from abandoning the boys. She insisted that her father and his friends be brought together so she could address them, saying that her boys' misfortune was so grievous that she must speak out even though she was unaccustomed to speaking in the presence of men. She then asked her father in front of his friends how he could mistreat her children so heartlessly:

> Even if you did not feel ashamed before any person, you should have feared the gods . . . you thought it right to expel these children of your daughter from their own house in worn-out clothes, shoeless, without a servant, without bedding, without cloaks, without the furniture that their father left them, without the money he entrusted to you . . . you are throwing them out to become dishonored and beggars instead of people of means, and yet you feel no fear of the gods nor shame before me, who knows the facts, nor do you remember your brother, but you think money is more important than anything.

Remaking the Mediterranean World, 403–30 B.C.

The School of Plato
This mosaic from Roman times presents an idealized view of Plato's school of philosophy, the Academy, in Athens. Platonism was one of the great legacies of Greece's Golden Age.

This incident, whose outcome is not recorded, illustrates both the continuing importance of family as the center of Greek society and the special pressures war could bring. Families always tried to solve their difficulties among themselves before resorting to legal action, and women played an influential part in this process. But the Peloponnesian War had recently ended and conditions in Athens remained precarious. Children turned out of their homes during such times probably had little chance of surviving, much less prospering. So an ordinary mother took an extraordinary step out of her traditional role to confront her father in front of other males in an effort to save her sons.

Similarly complex interplays of continuity and change characterized Greek history on many levels after the Peloponnesian War. Greek society remained relatively stable at the household level, but a succession of wars among Greece's leading city-states in the wake of the Peloponnesian War weakened their ability to withstand the expansion of the kingdom of Macedonia, the region north of Greece. The success of their monarchy led Macedonians to establish new kingdoms in Egypt and the Near East. The new governments also affected the course of literature, art, and science. Religion and philosophy headed down new paths, too, though many traditional cults and ideas remained popular.

IMPORTANT DATES

399 B.C. Socrates is tried and executed at Athens

359 B.C. Philip II becomes Macedonian king

348 B.C. The philosopher Plato dies

338 B.C. Philip defeats a Greek alliance at the battle of Chaeronea to become the leading power in Greece

336 B.C. Philip is murdered; Alexander takes over as king

334 B.C. Alexander leads an army of Greeks and Macedonians against Persia

326 B.C. Alexander's army mutinies in India

323 B.C. Alexander dies

322 B.C. The philosopher Aristotle dies

306–304 B.C. The Successors of Alexander declare themselves to be kings

did not truly restore the harmony that defeat in war and the dispossession of democratic privileges had shattered. The most prominent casualty of the divisive bitterness of the time was the famous philosopher Socrates, whose trial for impiety in 399 B.C. resulted in a death sentence. The Athenian household—family members and their personal slaves—somehow managed to hold together and survived as the fundamental unit of the city-state's society and economy.

Rebuilding Athenian Society

Many Athenian households lost fathers, sons, or brothers in the Peloponnesian War. Resourceful families found ways to compensate for the economic strain such personal tragedies could create. The writer Xenophon (c. 428–354 B.C.) told of an Athenian named Aristarchus, whose income had severely diminished because of the war and whose household had grown because of the sisters, nieces, and female cousins who had moved in with him. He found himself unable to support a household of fourteen, not counting the slaves. Aristarchus's friend Socrates reminded him that his female relatives knew how to make men's and women's cloaks, shirts, capes, and smocks, "the work considered the best and most fitting for women." Although the women had previously made clothing only for the

The Aftermath of the Peloponnesian War

Strife among prominent city-states vying for power continued to plague Greece in the years following the Peloponnesian War. The losses of population, the ravages of epidemic disease, and the financial hardship brought on by war caused severe difficulties for Athens. Those who had been banished by the Thirty Tyrants fought back and reclaimed Athens as a democracy in 403 B.C. In an attempt to quell social and political animosities wrought by the humiliations and deprivations endured during the brief but vicious rule of the tyrants, both sides agreed to an amnesty forbidding prosecutions for crimes committed during that time. But this measure

family, Socrates suggested they now begin to sell it for profit. Others sewed clothing or baked bread for sale, and Aristarchus could tell the women in his house to do the same. The plan succeeded financially, but the women complained that Aristarchus was now the only member of the household who ate without working. Socrates advised his friend to reply that the women should think of him as sheep did a guard dog—he earned his share of the food by keeping the wolves away from the sheep.

Many Athenian households produced manufactured goods, as did small shops and a few larger enterprises. Among the larger concerns were metal foundries, pottery workshops, and the shield-making company that employed 120 slaves owned by the family of Lysias (c. 459–380 B.C.); businesses bigger than this did not exist during this period.

LĬSĬƏUS

Working Women

This vase shows a woman spinning wool for clothing, which was made at home whenever possible.

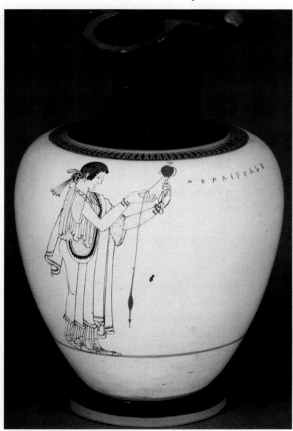

Lysias, an educated metic (resident alien) from Syracuse whose father had been recruited by Pericles to live in Athens, began to earn his living by writing speeches for others after the Thirty Tyrants seized his property in 404 B.C. He wrote the speech the brother-in-law of Diodotus's sons delivered in court. Metics could not own land in Athenian territory without special permission, but they had legal rights in Athenian courts that foreigners without metic status lacked. In return they paid taxes and served in the army when called upon. Lysias lived near Piraeus, the harbor of Athens, as did many metics, who played a central role in the international trade of such goods as grain, wine, pottery, and silver from Athens's mines, commodities that passed through Piraeus. The long walls that connected the city with the port, destroyed at the end of the war, were rebuilt by 393 B.C. at the urging of the great naval commander Conan as part of the Athenian navy's revival. These walls again ensured the safety of traders going in and out of Athens, a signal that trade could resume to prewar levels. Another sign of Athens's recovering economic health was the renewed minting of its famous silver coins to replace the emergency bronze ones created during the last years of the war.

Grain imported through Piraeus was crucial for fourth-century B.C. Athens. Even before the war, Athenian farmers had been unable to produce enough of this dietary staple to feed the population. The Spartan invasions had damaged farm buildings and equipment, making the situation even worse. Sparta had established a year-round base at Decelea near Athens from 413 to 404 B.C., giving their forces ample opportunity to demolish Athenian resources, which they could not do on the short campaigns customary in Greek warfare. The invaders probably even cut down Athenian olive trees, the source of valuable olive oil. These trees took a generation to replace because they grew so slowly. After the war, Athenian property owners worked hard to restore their land and businesses not only to benefit themselves but also to provide for their heirs. Athenian men and women felt strongly that their property, whether land, money, or belongings, should be preserved for their descendants. For this reason, Athenian law allowed men who squandered their inheritance or an inheritance entrusted to them, as did Diodotus's brother, to be prosecuted. The same spirit underlay the requirement that parents ensure

Greek Women at a Fountain
Wearing the standard long robes and hair coverings of their time, women in a Greek city collect water from a large and decorative municipal fountain.

their children's livelihood, either by leaving them income-producing property or training them in a skill.

Most working people probably earned just enough to feed and clothe their families. Athenians usually had only two meals a day, a light lunch in midmorning and a heavier meal in the evening. Bread baked from barley or, for richer people, wheat constituted the main part of their diet. A family bought its bread from small bakery stands, often run by women, or made it at home, with the wife directing and helping the household slaves grind the grain, shape the dough, and bake it in a pottery oven heated by charcoal. Those few households wealthy enough to afford meat from time to time often grilled it over coals on a pottery brazier. Most people ate vegetables, olives, fruit, and cheese as the bulk of their diet; they had meat only at animal sacrifices paid for by the state. The wine everyone drank, usually much diluted with water, came mainly from local vineyards. Water was fetched from public fountains and brought to the house in jugs, a task the women of the household performed or made sure the household slaves did. Many state-owned slaves had escaped from the mines in the countryside during the war, but few privately owned domestic slaves tried to run away. All but the poorest families continued to have at

least one or two slaves to do household chores and look after the children. If a mother did not have a slave to serve as a wet nurse to suckle her infants, she would hire a poor free woman for the job if her family could afford the expense.

Socratic Knowledge

The conviction and execution of Socrates (469–399 B.C.), the most famous philosopher of the late fifth century B.C., was the most infamous event in the history of Athens after the Peloponnesian War. Socrates' life had been devoted to combating the idea that justice should be equated with the power to work one's will. His death, coming as it did during a time of social and political turmoil, indicated the tenuousness of Athenian justice in practice. His mission to find valid guidelines for leading a just life and to prove that justice is better than injustice under all circumstances gave Greek philosophy a new direction: an emphasis on ethics. Although thinkers before him, especially poets and dramatists, had wrestled with moral issues, Socrates was the first philosopher to make ethics and morality his primary concern.

Compared to most sophists, Socrates lived in poverty, for he disdained material possessions. Still he served as a hoplite in the army and supported his wife and several children. He may have inherited some money, and he also received gifts from wealthy admirers. He paid so little attention to his physical appearance and clothes that many Athenians regarded him as eccentric. Sporting, in his words, a stomach "somewhat too large to be convenient," he wore the same nondescript cloak summer and winter and scorned shoes no matter how cold the weather. His physical stamina was legendary, both from his tirelessness as a soldier and from his ability to outdrink anyone at a symposium.

Whether participating at a symposium, strolling in the agora, or watching young men exercise in a gymnasium, Socrates spent his time in conversation. He and his fellow Athenians valued and took great pleasure in speaking with each other at length. He wrote nothing; our knowledge of his ideas comes from others' writings, especially those of his pupil Plato. Plato's dialogues, so called because they present Socrates and others in extended conversation about philosophy, portray Socrates as a relentless questioner of his fellow citizens, foreign friends, and various sophists. Socrates' questions aimed at unsettling his interlocutors (his partners in the conversation), forcing them to examine the basic assumptions of their way of life. Employing what has come to be called the Socratic method, Socrates never directly instructed his conversational partners; instead he led them to answers to his probing questions that refuted their presumptions.

This indirect method of searching for the truth often left Socrates' interlocutors puzzled because they found themselves forced to conclude that they were ignorant: ideas they had believed inviolate had been proven false. Socrates insisted that he too was ignorant of the best definition of virtue, but that his wisdom consisted of knowing that he did not know. He was trying to improve rather than undermine his interlocutors' beliefs, even though, as one put it, a conversation with Socrates made a man feel as numb as if he had just been stung by a stingray (a sea creature whose venom paralyzes its victims). Through reasoning, Socrates wanted to discover universal standards for morality. He especially attacked the sophists' view that conventional morality served as the "fetters that bind nature." They proclaimed that only the weak and foolish believed in accepted standards of right and wrong; for such sophists, it was natural and fitting for the strong to take whatever they could. This declaration, Socrates asserted, equated human happiness with power and "getting more."

Socrates believed passionately that justice was better for humans than injustice and that morality was justified because it created happiness. He argued that just behavior, or virtue, was identical to self-knowledge and that true knowledge of justice would inevitably lead people to choose good over evil and therefore to have truly happy lives, regardless of their material wealth, because they would then be true to their nature. Because Socrates believed self-knowledge alone was sufficient for happiness, he claimed that no one knowingly behaved unjustly and that behaving justly was always in the individual's self-interest. It might seem, he maintained, that individuals could promote their interests by cheating or using force on those weaker than themselves, but this appearance was deceptive. It was in fact ignorance to believe that the best life was the life of unlimited power to pursue whatever one desired. Instead the most desirable human life was concerned with virtue and guided by rational reflection. Moral knowledge was all one needed for the good life, as Socrates defined it.

The Condemnation of Socrates

Unlike the sophists, Socrates offered no courses and took no fees. But his effect on many people was as unsettling as the relativistic doctrines of the sophists had been. Indeed Socrates' rebuttal of his fellow conversationalists' most cherished certainties, though expressed indirectly through his method of questioning, made some of his interlocutors decidedly uncomfortable. Unhappiest of all were fathers whose sons, after listening to Socrates reduce someone to utter bewilderment, tried the same technique at home on their parents. Men who experienced this reversal of the traditional hierarchy of education between parent and child—the father was supposed to educate the son—felt that Socrates, however unintentionally, was undermining the stability of society by questioning Athenian traditions. We do not know what Athenian women thought of Socrates. The realities of Athenian society meant that Socrates circulated primarily among men and addressed his ideas to them and their situations. Reportedly he had numerous conversations with Aspasia, the courtesan who lived with Pericles for many years. Plato, in one of his dialogues, depicts Socrates attributing his ideas on love to a woman, the otherwise unknown priestess Diotima of Mantinea.

The public perception that Socrates could be a danger to conventional society gave Aristophanes the inspiration for his comedy *Clouds* of 423 B.C. In the play, Socrates is presented as a cynical sophist who, for a fee, offers instruction in the Protagorean technique of making the weaker argument the stronger. When Socrates' instruction transforms the protagonist's son into a rhetorician able to argue that a son has the right to beat his parents, the protagonist ends the comedy by burning down Socrates' Thinking Shop, as it is called in the play.

Athenians who felt that Socrates posed a danger to conventional society had their fears confirmed in the careers of Alcibiades and, especially, Critias, one of the Thirty Tyrants. Socrates' critics blamed him for Alcibiades' contempt for social conventions, because Alcibiades had been one of Socrates' most devoted supporters. Critias,

Socrates
This statuette depicts the homely face and awkward figure that the philosopher Socrates joked about in describing himself.

prosecutors, as also required by Athenian law, the accusers argued their case against Socrates before a jury of 501 that had been assembled by lot from that year's pool of eligible jurors (male citizens over thirty years old). The prosecutors' case featured both a religious and a moral component. They accused Socrates of not believing in the gods of the city-state and of introducing new divinities, actions they labeled as impiety. They also charged that he had lured the young men of Athens away from Athenian moral conventions and ideals. After the prosecutors concluded their remarks, Socrates spoke in his own defense, per Athenian law. Plato writes that Socrates used this occasion not to rebut all the charges or beg for sympathy, as jurors expected in serious cases, but to reiterate his unyielding dedication to goading his fellow citizens into examining their preconceptions. This irritating process of constant questioning, he maintained, would help them learn to live virtuous lives. Furthermore, they should care not about their material possessions but about making their true selves—their souls—as good as possible. He vowed to remain their stinging gadfly no matter what the consequences.

After the jury narrowly voted to convict, standard Athenian legal procedure required the jurors to decide between alternative penalties proposed by the prosecutors and the defendant. Anytus and his associates proposed death. In such instances the defendant was then expected to offer exile as an alternative, which the jury usually accepted. Socrates, however, replied that he deserved a reward rather than a punishment, until his friends at the trial prevailed upon him to propose a fine as his penalty. The jury chose death. Socrates accepted his sentence with equanimity because, as he put it in a famous paradox, "no evil can befall a good man either in life or in death." In other words, nothing can take away the knowledge that is virtue, and only the loss of that wisdom could ever count as a true evil. He was executed in the customary way, by being given a poisonous drink concocted from powdered hemlock. The silencing of Socrates did nothing to restore Athenian confidence or the feelings of invincibility that had characterized their Golden Age. Ancient sources report that the Athenians soon came to regret the condemnation and execution of Socrates as a tragic mistake that left a blot on their reputation.

another prominent follower, played a leading role in the murder and plunder perpetrated by the Thirty Tyrants in 404–403 B.C. In blaming Socrates for the crimes of Critias, Socrates' detractors chose to overlook his defiance of the Thirty Tyrants when they had tried to involve him in their violent schemes and his utter rejection of the immorality Critias had displayed.

The hostility some Athenians felt toward Socrates after the horrors of the Thirty Tyrants encouraged the distinguished Athenian Anytus, who had suffered personally under this regime, to join with two other, less notable men in prosecuting Socrates in 399 B.C. Because the amnesty precluded bringing any charges directly related to the period of tyranny, they accused Socrates of impiety. Athenian law did not specify precisely what offenses constituted impiety, so the accusers had to convince the jurors that Socrates had committed a crime. As usual in Athenian trials, no judge presided to rule on what evidence was admissible or how the law should be applied. Speaking for themselves as the

The International Struggle for Power

In the fifty years after the Peloponnesian War, Sparta, Thebes, and Athens struggled for international power in the Greek world. Athens never regained the economic and military strength it had wielded in the fifth century B.C., perhaps because its silver mines no longer produced at the same level. Nevertheless, after the reestablishment of democracy in 403 B.C., Athens again became a major force in international politics. Sparta's widespread attempts to extend its power after the Peloponnesian War gave Athens and the other Greek city-states ample opportunity for diplomatic and military action. In 401 B.C. the Persian satrap (provincial governor) Cyrus, son of a previous king, hired a mercenary army to try to unseat Artaxerxes II, who had ascended to the Persian throne in 404 B.C. Xenophon, who joined Cyrus's army, wrote *Anabasis,* which included a stirring account of the expedition's disastrous defeat at Cunaxa near Babylon and the arduous journey home made by the terrified Greek mercenaries from Cyrus's routed army. Sparta had supported Cyrus's rebellion, thereby arousing the hostility of Artaxerxes. The Spartan general Lysander, the victor over Athens in the last years of the Peloponnesian War, pursued an aggressive policy in Anatolia and northern Greece in the 390s B.C., and other Spartan commanders meddled in Sicily. Thebes, Athens, Corinth, and Argos thereupon formed an anti-Spartan coalition because they felt this Spartan activity threatened their interests at home and abroad.

In a reversal of the alliances at the end of the Peloponnesian War, the Persian king initially supported Athens and the other Greek city-states against Sparta in the so-called Corinthian War, which lasted from 395 to 386 B.C. This alliance ultimately failed because both the king and the Greek allies pursued their own self-interests rather than peaceful accommodation. The war ended with Sparta once again cutting a deal with Persia. In a blatant renunciation of its claim to defend Greek freedom, Sparta acknowledged the Persian king's right to control the Greek city-states of Anatolia in return for permission to secure Spartan interests in Greece without Persian interference. Their agreement, called the King's Peace, of 386 B.C., effectively returned the Greeks of Anatolia to their dependent status of a century past, before the Greek victory in the Persian Wars of 490–479 B.C.

Spartan forces attacked city-states all over Greece in the years after the peace. In Athens the rebuilt walls restored its invulnerability to invasion. A new kind of foot-soldier, called a peltast (armed now with a light leather shield, instead of a heavier bronze one, javelins, and sword) made Athenian ground forces more mobile and fleet, a development attributed to the Athenian general Iphicrates. Athens's reconstructed navy built up its offensive strength. By 377 B.C., Athens had again become the leader of a naval alliance of Greek city-states, called the Second Athenian League. But this time the league members insisted their rights be specified in writing to prevent a recurrence of high-handed Athenian behavior. Sparta's hopes for lasting power were dashed in 371 B.C. when a resurgent Thebes defeated the Spartan army at Leuctra in Boeotia and then invaded the Spartan homeland in the Peloponnese. At this point the Thebans seemed likely to challenge Jason, tyrant of Pherae in Thessaly, for the position of the dominant military power in Greece.

The alliances of the various city-states shifted often in the many conflicts during the early decades of the fourth century B.C. The threat from Thessaly faded with Jason's murder in 370 B.C., and the former enemies Sparta and Athens temporarily allied against the Thebans in the battle of Mantinea in the Peloponnese in 362 B.C. Thebes won the battle but lost the war when its great leader Epaminondas was killed at Mantinea and no credible replacement for him could be found. The Theban quest for dominance in Greece had failed. Xenophon succinctly summed up the situation after 362 B.C. with these closing remarks from the history he wrote of the Greeks in his time: "Everyone had supposed that the winners of this battle would be Greece's rulers and its losers their subjects; but there was only more confusion and disturbance in Greece after it than before." The truth of his analysis was confirmed when the Second Athenian League fell apart in a war between Athens and its allies over the close ties some allies were developing with Persia and Macedonia.

All the efforts of the various major Greek city-states to extend their hegemony over mainland Greece in this period failed. By the mid 350s B.C. no Greek city-state had the power to rule more than itself. The struggle for supremacy in Greece that had begun eighty years earlier with the outbreak of the Peloponnesian War had finally ended in a stalemate of exhaustion that opened the way for a new power—the kingdom of Macedonia.

New Directions in Philosophy and Education

One reason the sophists who flocked to Athens in the fifth century B.C. stirred up controversy was that many people felt their teachings undermined time-honored moral traditions. Their relativistic doctrines implied that justice in reality meant, to paraphrase Thucydides describing Athenian wartime behavior, the strong seizing all that their power permits and the weak enduring what they are forced to accept. The fourth-century B.C. philosopher Plato attacked this doctrine in the course of his many intellectual pursuits. Plato's famous pupil, Aristotle, combined his teacher's passion for theoretical philosophy with a scientific curiosity about the phenomena of the natural world. Their work helped create a new foundation for ethical and scientific inquiry. But many believed the ideas of Plato and Aristotle were too theoretical, too far removed from the realities of everyday life to have much relevance to the concrete concerns of a public career. Men like the orator Isocrates insisted that a proper education centered on rhetoric and practical wisdom.

The Writings of Plato

Socrates' fate profoundly affected his most brilliant follower, Plato (c. 428–348 B.C.), who even though an aristocrat nevertheless withdrew from political life after 399 B.C. The condemnation of Socrates apparently convinced him that citizens in a democracy were incapable of rising above narrow self-interest to knowledge of any universal truth. In his works dealing with the organization of society, Plato bitterly rejected democracy as a justifiable system of government. Instead he sketched what he saw as the philosophical basis for ideal political

and social structures among humans. His utopian vision had virtually no effect on the actual politics of his time, and his attempts to advise Dionysius II (*367–344 B.C.), tyrant of Syracuse in Sicily, on how to rule as a true philosopher ended in utter failure. But political philosophy was only one of Plato's interests, which ranged from astronomy and mathematics to metaphysics (theoretical explanations for phenomena that cannot be understood through direct experience or scientific experiment). After Plato's death his ideas attracted relatively little attention among philosophers for the next two centuries; but they were revived and debated vigorously in the Roman era. The sheer intellectual power of Plato's thought, and the controversy his ideas have engendered throughout the years have established him as one of the great philosophers.

Plato intended his dialogues to provoke readers into thoughtful reflection rather than to spoon-feed them a predetermined set of beliefs. His views apparently changed over time—nowhere did he present one cohesive set of doctrines. He seems to have disagreed with Socrates' insistence that fundamental knowledge meant moral knowledge based on inner reflection. Plato concluded that knowledge meant truths that are independent of the observer and can be taught to others. He acted on this latter belief by founding the Academy, a shady gathering spot just outside the walls of Athens, which he named after a local hero whose shrine was nearby. The Academy was not a school or college in the modern sense but rather an informal association of people who studied philosophy, mathematics, and theoretical astronomy under Plato's guidance. Intellectuals gathered at the Academy for nine hundred years after Plato died; in some periods distinguished philosophers directed it, but at other times mediocre thinkers held court there.

Plato taught that we cannot define and understand absolute virtues such as goodness, justice, beauty, or equality by the concrete evidence of these qualities in our lives. Any earthly examples will in some other context display the opposite quality. For example, always returning what one has borrowed might seem just. But what if a person who has borrowed a friend's weapon is confronted by that friend, who wants the weapon back to commit murder? In this case returning the borrowed item would be unjust. Examples of equality are also only relative. The equality of a stick two feet long, for example, is evident when it is compared with another two-foot stick. Paired with a three-foot stick, however, it is unequal. In sum, in the world that humans experience with their senses, every virtue and every quality is relative to some extent.

Plato refused to accept the relativity of virtues as reality. He developed the theory that virtues cannot be discovered through experience; rather they are absolutes that can be comprehended only by thought and that somehow exist independently of human existence. In some of his works, Plato referred to the separate realities of the pure virtues as Forms; among the Forms were Goodness, Justice, Beauty, and Equality. He argued that the Forms were invisible, invariable, and eternal entities located in a higher realm beyond the empirical world of humans. According to Plato, the Forms are the only true reality; what humans experience through their senses are the impure shadows of this reality. Plato's views on the nature and significance of Forms altered throughout his career, and his later works seem quite divorced from this theory. Nevertheless, Forms exemplify both the complexity and the wide range of Plato's thought. His theory of Forms elevated metaphysics, the consideration of the ultimate nature of reality beyond the reach of the human senses, to a central and enduring issue for philosophers.

Plato's idea that humans possessed immortal souls distinct from their bodies established the concept of *dualism,* a separation between spiritual and physical being. This notion influenced much of later philosophical and religious thought. In a dialogue Plato wrote late in his life, he said the pre-existing knowledge possessed by the immortal human soul is in truth the knowledge known to the supreme deity. Plato called this god the Demiurge ("craftsman") because the deity used knowledge of the Forms to craft the world of living beings from raw matter. According to Plato, because a knowing, rational god created the world, the world has order. Furthermore, the world's beings have goals, as evidenced by animals adapting to their environments in order to thrive. The Demiurge wanted to reproduce the perfect order of the Forms in the material world, but the world turned out imperfect because matter is imperfect. Plato believed the

proper goal for humans is to seek perfect order and purity in their own souls by making rational thoughts control their irrational desires, which are harmful. The desire to drink wine to excess, for example, is irrational because the drinker fails to consider the hangover to come the next day. Those who give-in to irrational desires fail to consider the future of both their body and soul. Finally, because the soul is immortal and the body is not, our present, impure existence is only one passing phase in our cosmic existence.

One version of Plato's utopian vision is found in his most famous dialogue, the *Republic.* This work, whose title would be more accurate as *System of Government,* primarily concerns the nature of justice and the reasons people should be just instead of unjust. Like a just soul, a just society would have its parts in proper hierarchy. Plato presents these parts as three classes of people, distinguished by their ability to grasp the truth of Forms. The highest class constitutes the rulers, or "guardians," as Plato calls them, who are educated in mathematics, astronomy, and metaphysics. Next come the "auxiliaries," whose function is to defend the polis. The lowest class comprises the "producers," who grow the food and make the objects the whole population requires. Each part contributes to society by fulfilling its proper function.

According to Plato's *Republic,* women as well as men can be guardians because they possess the same virtues and abilities as men, except for a disparity in physical strength between the average woman and the average man. The axiom justifying the inclusion of women—namely, that virtue is the same in women as in men—is a notion Plato may have derived from Socrates. The inclusion of women in the ruling class of Plato's utopian city-state represented a startling departure from the actual practice of his times. Indeed never before in Western history had anyone proposed that work be allocated in human society without regard to gender. Moreover, to minimize distraction, guardians are to have neither private property nor nuclear families. Male and female guardians are to live in houses shared in common, to eat in the same mess halls, and to exercise in the same gymnasiums. They are to have sexual relations with various partners so that the best women can mate with the best men to produce the best children. The children are to be raised together in a common environment by special caretakers. Although this scheme would supposedly free women guardians from child-care responsibilities and enable them to rule equally with men, Plato fails to mention that women guardians would in reality have a much tougher life than men because they would be pregnant frequently and undergo the strain and danger of giving birth. But he evidently does not disqualify women from ruling on this account. The guardians who achieve the highest level of knowledge in Plato's ideal society would qualify to rule over the ideally just state as philosopher-kings.

The severe regulation of life Plato proposed for his ideally just state in the *Republic* was an outgrowth of his tight focus on the question of a rational person's true interest. Furthermore, he insisted that objective truths can be found in the fields of politics and ethics by using reason. Despite his harsh criticism of existing governments, such as Athenian democracy, Plato recognized the practical difficulties in implementing radical changes in the way people actually lived. Indeed his late dialogue *The Laws* shows him wrestling with the question of improving the real world in a less radical, though still authoritarian, way than in the *Republic*. Plato hoped that instead of ordinary politicians, whether democrats or oligarchs, the people who know truth and can promote the common good would rule because their rule would be in everyone's real interest. For this reason above all, he passionately believed the study of philosophy mattered to human life.

Aristotle, Scientist and Philosopher

Plato's most brilliant follower was Aristotle (384–322 B.C.). Aristotle's great reputation as a thinker in science and philosophy rests on his influence in promoting scientific investigation of the natural world and in developing rigorous systems of logical argument. The enormous influence of Aristotle's works on later scholars, especially those of the Middle Ages, has made him a monumental figure in the history of Western science and philosophy.

The son of a wealthy doctor from Stagira in northern Greece, Aristotle came to Athens at the age of seventeen to study in Plato's Academy. In 335 B.C., Aristotle founded his own informal philo-

STA·JĪ·RAH

sophical school in Athens, named the Lyceum, later called the Peripatetic School after the covered walkway *(peripatos)* in which its students carried on conversations while strolling out of the glare of the Mediterranean sun. Aristotle lectured with dazzling intelligence and energy on nearly every branch of learning: biology, medicine, anatomy, psychology, meteorology, physics, chemistry, mathematics, music, metaphysics, rhetoric, political science, ethics, and literary criticism. He also worked out a sophisticated system of logic for precise argumentation. Creating a careful system to identify the forms of valid arguments, Aristotle established grounds for distinguishing a logically sound case from a merely persuasive one. He first named contrasts such as "premise versus conclusion" and "the universal versus the particular," concepts featured in thought and speech ever since. He also studied the process of explanation itself, formulating the influential *doctrine of four causes.* According to Aristotle, four different categories of explanation exist that are not reducible to a single, unified whole: form (defining characteristics), matter (constituent elements), origin of movement (similar to what we commonly mean by "cause"), and *telos* (aim or goal). This doctrine exemplifies Aristotle's care never to oversimplify the complexity of reality.

Apparently an inspiring teacher, Aristotle encouraged his followers to conduct research in numerous fields of specialized knowledge. For example, he had student researchers compile reports on the systems of government of 158 Greek city-states. Much of Aristotle's philosophical thought reflected the influence of Plato, but he also refined and even rejected ideas his teacher had advocated. He denied the validity of Plato's theory of Forms, for example, on the grounds that the separate existence Plato postulated for them did not make sense. This position typified Aristotle's general preference for explanations based on common sense rather than metaphysics. By modern standards his scientific thought relied little on mathematical models of explanation and quantitative reasoning; but mathematics in his time had not yet become sophisticated enough for such work. His method also differed from that of modern scientists because it did not include controlled experiments. Aristotle believed that investigators had a better chance of understanding objects and beings by observing them in their natural setting than under the artificial conditions of a laboratory. His coupling of detailed investigation with perceptive reasoning worked especially well in such physical sciences as biology, botany, and zoology. For example, as the first scientist to try to collect and classify all the available information on the animal species, Aristotle recorded the facts about more than five hundred different kinds of animals, including insects. Many of his findings represented significant advances in learning. His recognition that whales and dolphins were mammals, for example, which later writers on animals overlooked, was not rediscovered for another two thousand years.

Some of Aristotle's most influential discussions concentrated on understanding qualitative concepts that humans tend to take for granted, such as time, space, motion, and change. Through careful argumentation he probed the philosophical difficulties that lie beneath the surface of these familiar notions, and his views on the nature of such things powerfully affected later thinkers. Aristotle was conventional for his times in regarding slavery as natural, based on the argument that some people were by nature bound to be slaves because their souls lacked the rational part that should rule in a human. Individuals propounding the contrary view were rare, although one fourth-century B.C. orator, Alcidamas,* asserted that "God has set all men free; nature has made no one a slave." Also in tune with his times was Aristotle's conclusion that women were by nature inferior to men. His view of women's inferiority was based on faulty notions of biology. He wrongly believed, for example, that in procreation the male's semen actively gave the fetus its form, whereas the female passively provided its matter. He justified his assertion that females were less courageous than males by dubious evidence about animals, such as the report that a male squid would stay-by as if to help when its mate was speared but that a female squid would swim away when the male was impaled. Although erroneous information led Aristotle to evaluate females as incomplete males, he believed human communities could be successful and happy only if both women and men contributed. Aristotle argued that marriage was meant to provide mutual help and comfort but that the husband should rule.

Aristotle departed sharply from the Socratic idea that knowledge of justice and goodness was all a person needed to behave justly. He argued that people's souls often possess knowledge of what is right but that their irrational desires overrule this knowledge and lead them to do wrong. People who know the misery of gluttony still stuff themselves, for example. Recognizing a conflict of desires in the human soul, Aristotle advocated achieving self-control by training the mind to win out over instincts and passions. Self-control did not mean denying human desires and appetites; rather it meant striking a balance between suppressing and heedlessly indulging physical yearnings, of finding "the mean." Aristotle claimed that the mind should rule in finding this balance because the intellect is the finest human quality and the mind is the true self, indeed the godlike part of a person.

Aristotle regarded science and philosophy not as abstract subjects isolated from the concerns of ordinary existence but as the disciplined search for knowledge in every aspect of life. That search epitomized the kind of rational human activity that alone could bring the good life and genuine happiness. Some modern critics have pointed out that Aristotle's work lacks a clear moral code. Even so, he did the study of ethics a great service by insisting that standards of right and wrong have merit only if they are grounded in character and aligned with the good in human nature and do not simply consist of lists of abstract reasons for behaving in one way rather than another; that is, an ethical system must be relevant to the actual moral situations humans experience. In ethics, as in all his scholarship, Aristotle distinguished himself by insisting that the life of the mind and experience of the real world are inseparable components in the quest to define a worthwhile existence for humans.

Practical Education and Rhetoric

Despite his interest in subjects such as the history of the constitutions of states and the theory and practice of rhetoric, Aristotle remained a theoretician in the mold of Plato. This characteristic set him apart from the major educational trend of the fourth century B.C., which emphasized practical wisdom and training that applied directly to the public lives of upper-class male citizens in a swiftly

+ AL·KÍ·DA·MAS

changing world. The most important component of this education was rhetoric, the skill of persuasive public speaking, which itself depended not only on oratorical techniques but also on the knowledge of the world and of human psychology that speakers required to be effective. The ideas about education and rhetoric that emerged in this period had a tremendous impact on later Greeks and Romans and on others long after.

Even many who had admired Socrates, who had dismissed such matters, believed in the general value of practical knowledge and rhetoric. Xenophon, for example, knew Socrates well enough to write extensive memoirs re-creating many conversations with the great philosopher. But he also wrote a wide range of works in history, biography, estate management, horsemanship, and the public revenues of Athens. The subjects of these treatises reveal the manifold topics Xenophon considered essential to the proper education of men.

The ideas of the famous Athenian orator Isocrates (436–338 B.C.) exemplified the dedication to rhetoric as a practical skill that Plato rejected as utterly wrong. Isocrates was born to a rich family and studied with sophists and thinkers, including Socrates. Because he lacked the voice to address large gatherings, Isocrates composed speeches for other men to deliver and endeavored to influence public opinion and political leaders at Athens and abroad by publishing his own speeches. He regarded education as the preparation for a useful life doing good in matters of public importance. He sought to develop an educational middle ground between the theoretical study of abstract ideas and purely crass training in rhetorical techniques for influencing others to one's personal advantage. In this way he stood between the ideals of Plato and the promises of unscrupulous sophists.

Isocrates believed that rhetoric was the skill men who aspired to public office must master. Becoming a good rhetorician, he insisted, required natural talent and practical experience in worldly affairs, which trained orators to understand public issues and the psychology of the people whom they had to persuade for the common good. Isocrates saw rhetoric not as a device for cynical self-aggrandizement but as a powerful tool for human betterment, if wielded by properly gifted and trained men with developed consciences. (Women could not become orators because they were excluded from politics.) Isocrates' emphasis on rhetoric and its application in real-world politics won many more adherents among men in Greek and, later, Roman culture than did Plato's vision of the philosophical life, and it came to exert great influence when revived in Renaissance Europe, two thousand years later.

Throughout his life, Isocrates tried to put his doctrines to use by addressing works to powerful leaders whose policies he wanted to influence. In his later years he believed Greece had become so unstable that he promoted the cause of pan-Hellenism—political harmony among all the Greek city-states—by urging Philip II, king of Macedonia, to unite the Greeks under his leadership in a crusade against Persia. This radical recommendation was Isocrates' practical solution to the persistent conflicts among Greek city-states and to the social unrest created by friction between the richer communities and the many poor areas in Greece. Isocrates believed that if the fractious city-states accepted Philip as their leader in a common alliance, they could avoid wars among themselves and relieve the impoverished population among them by establishing Greek colonies on land to be carved out of Persian-held territory in Anatolia. That a prominent Athenian would openly appeal for a Macedonian king to save the Greeks from themselves reflected the startling new political and military reality that had emerged in the Greek world by the mid-fourth century B.C.

The Restructuring of Power in Greece and the Near East

The kingdom of Macedonia soon filled the power vacuum that had been created by the futile wars the Greek city-states waged against one another in the early fourth century B.C. Macedonia was a rough land of mountains and lowland valleys just north of Greece. Life there was harder than in Greece because the climate was colder and more dangerous and because the Macedonians' western and northern neighbors periodically launched devastating raids into Macedonian territory. The Macedonians were especially vulnerable to these raids because

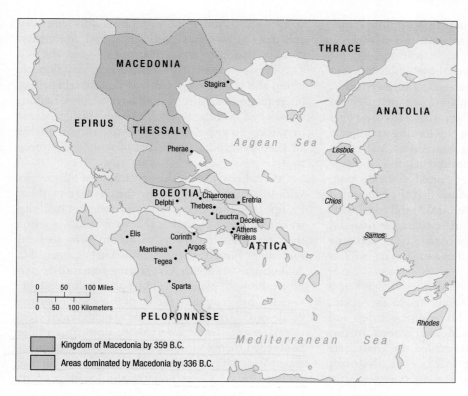

The Expansion of Macedonia

they generally lived in small villages and towns without protective walls. That this formerly minor kingdom became the greatest power in Greece and conquered the Persian Empire ranks as one of the major surprises in ancient military and political history.

The Creation of Macedonian Power

Macedonian tradition dictated that the king listen to his people, who were used to addressing their monarch with considerable freedom of speech. This custom constrained the king's power; he could govern effectively only as long as he maintained the support of the most powerful aristocrats, who counted as the king's social equals and controlled large bands of followers. Fighting, hunting, and heavy drinking were the favorite pastimes of these men. The king was expected to demonstrate his prowess in these activities to show he was a Macedonian "man's man" capable of heading the state. Macedonian queens and royal mothers received respect in this male-dominated society because they

came from powerful families in the Macedonian nobility or the ruling houses of lands bordering Macedonia. In the king's absence these royal women often vied with the king's designated representative for power at court.

Macedonians had their own language, related to Greek but not comprehensible to Greeks. The aristocrats who dominated Macedonian society routinely learned to speak Greek because they thought of themselves and indeed all Macedonians as Greek by blood. At the same time, Macedonians looked down on the Greeks to the south as a soft lot unequal to the adversities of life in Macedonia. The Greeks reciprocated this scorn. The famed Athenian orator Demosthenes (384–322 B.C.) lambasted the Macedonian king Philip II (✶359–336 B.C.) as "not only not a Greek nor related to the Greeks, but not even a barbarian from a land worth mentioning; no, he's a pestilence from Macedonia, a region where you can't even buy a slave worth his salt." Barbed verbal attacks like this characterized Demosthenes' speeches on foreign and domestic policy to the Athenian assembly, where he consistently tried to convince his fellow Athenians to oppose Macedonian expansion in Greece.

Demosthenes spoke so forcefully against Philip because he recognized how ambitious and potentially dangerous he was—against heavy odds, Philip had forged Macedonia into an international power. Before Philip's reign, strife in the royal family and disputes among the leading aristocrats had been so common that Macedonia had never united sufficiently to mobilize its full military strength. Macedonian kings feared violence from their own countrymen so much that they stationed bodyguards both outside and inside the royal bedroom. Macedonian princes married earlier than did most men, soon after the age of twenty, because the instability of the kingship demanded male heirs as soon as possible.

The situation was grave in 359 B.C., when a force of Illyrians, hostile neighbors to the north, slaughtered the current Macedonian king and around four thousand Macedonian troops. In this moment of crisis, Philip persuaded the aristocrats to recognize him as king in place of his infant nephew, for whom he was serving as regent after the king's death in battle. Philip then rallied the army by teaching the infantrymen an unstoppable new tactic. Macedonian troops carried thrusting spears fourteen to sixteen feet long, which they had to hold with two hands. Philip drilled his men in handling these heavy weapons in a phalanx formation, whose front line bristled with outstretched spears like a lethal porcupine. With the cavalry of aristocrats deployed as a strike force to soften up the enemy and protect the infantry's flanks, Philip's reorganized army promptly routed Macedonia's attackers and defeated his local rivals to the kingship.

Philip then embarked on a whirlwind of diplomacy, bribery, and military action to force the Greek city-states to acknowledge his superiority. He financed his ambition by prodigiously spending the gold and silver coins he had minted from the ore of Macedonia mines and those captured in Thrace. A Greek contemporary, the historian Theopompus of Chios, labeled Philip "insatiable and extravagant; he did everything in a hurry . . . he never spared the time to reckon up his income and expenditure." By the late 340s B.C., Philip had cajoled or coerced most of northern Greece to follow his lead in foreign policy. His goal then became to lead a united Macedonian and Greek

army against the Persian Empire. He shrewdly culled a thorn from Greece's past and announced it as the reason to attack Persia: to avenge the 480 B.C. Persian invasion of Macedonia and Greece. Philip also feared the potentially destabilizing effect his reinvigorated army would have on his kingdom if they had nothing to do. To launch his grandiose invasion, however, he needed to strengthen his alliance by adding the forces of southern Greece to it.

At Athens, Demosthenes castigated the Greeks with his stirring rhetoric for their failure to resist Philip: they stood by, he thundered, "as if Philip were a hailstorm, praying that he would not come their way, but not trying to do anything to head him off." Finally, Athens and Thebes headed a coalition of southern Greek city-states to try to block Philip's plans. In 338 B.C., Philip and his Greek allies trounced the coalition's forces at the battle of Chaeronea in Boeotia. The defeated city-states retained their internal freedom, but Philip compelled them to join an alliance under his undisputed leadership. (Modern scholars call this alliance the League of Corinth, after the location of its headquarters.) The course of later history proved the battle of Chaeronea a decisive turning point in Greek history: never again would the city-states of Greece make foreign policy for themselves without considering, and usually following, the wishes of outside powers. This change marked the end of the Greek city-states as independent actors in international politics, though they did remain the basic economic and social units of Greece. Macedonia's King Philip and his son Alexander now stepped onto center stage. The people of the Greek city-states became subjects or allies of the new kingdoms these two rulers and their successors carved out. The Hellenistic kingdoms, as these new monarchies are called, like the Roman provinces that eventually replaced them as political masters of the Greeks, depended on the local leaders of the Greek city-states to collect taxes for the imperial treasuries and to ensure the loyalty and order of the citizens.

Alexander's Conquest of Persia

A Macedonian assassinated Philip in 336 B.C. Unconfirmed rumors speculated that the murder had been instigated by one of his several wives, Olympias, a princess from Epirus to the west

Alexander Winning the Battle of Issus
This wall-sized, Roman-era mosaic shows Alexander attacking the Persian king at Issus
in 333 B.C. Based on a famous painting, it shows dramatic foreshortening—a technique
that added a three-dimensional feeling to the work—as in the horse's hindquarters.

of Macedonia. Philip's son by her, Alexander (356–323 B.C.), promptly murdered potential rivals for the throne and won recognition as king. In several lightning-fast campaigns, he subdued Macedonia's traditional enemies to the west and north. Next he forced the southern Greeks, who had defected from the Macedonian-led League of Corinth at the news of Philip's death, to rejoin the alliance. To demonstrate the price of disloyalty, Alexander destroyed Thebes in 335 B.C. as punishment.

With Greece begrudgingly quiescent, Alexander in 334 B.C. led a Macedonian and Greek army into Anatolia to fulfill his father's plan to avenge Greece by attacking Persia. Alexander's astounding success in conquering the entire Persian Empire while in his twenties earned him the sobriquet "the Great" in later ages. In his own time his greatness consisted of his ability to motivate his men, however reluctantly, to follow him into hostile, unknown regions. Alexander inspired his troops with his reckless disregard for his own safety. He often plunged into

the enemy's front line at the head of his men, sharing the danger of the common soldier. No one could miss him in his plumed helmet, vividly colored cloak, and armor polished to reflect the sun. So intent on conquering distant lands was Alexander that he rejected advice to delay his departure from Macedonia until he had married and fathered an heir, to forestall instability in case of his death. He further alarmed his principal adviser by giving away virtually all his land and property in order to strengthen the army, thereby creating new land-owners who would furnish troops. "What," he was asked, "do you have left for yourself?" "My hopes," he replied. Those hopes centered on constructing a heroic image of himself as a warrior as splendid as the incomparable Achilles of Homer's *Iliad.* Alexander always kept a copy of the *Iliad* under his pillow, along with a dagger. Alexander's aspirations and his behavior represented the ultimate expression of the Homeric vision of the glorious conquering warrior, still the prevailing ideal of male Greek culture.

Alexander cast a spear into the earth of Anatolia when he crossed the Hellespont strait from Europe to Asia, thereby claiming the Asian continent for himself in Homeric fashion as "territory won by the spear." The first battle of the campaign, in 334 B.C. at the River Granicus in western Anatolia, proved the worth of Alexander's Macedonian and Greek cavalry, which charged across the river and up the bank to rout the opposing Persians and their Greek mercenaries. Alexander visited Midas's old capital of Gordion in Phrygia, where an oracle had promised the lordship of Asia to whoever could loose a seemingly impenetrable knot of rope tying the yoke of an ancient chariot preserved in the city. The young Macedonian, so the story goes, cut the Gordian knot with his sword. In 333 B.C. the Persian king, Darius, finally faced Alexander in battle at Issus, near the southeastern corner of Anatolia. Alexander's army defeated its more numerous opponents with a characteristically bold strike of cavalry through the left side of the Persian lines followed by a flanking maneuver against the king's position in the center. Darius had to flee from the field to avoid capture, abandoning his wives and daughters, who had accompanied his campaign in keeping with royal Persian tradition. Alexander's scrupulously chivalrous treatment of the Persian royal women after their capture at Issus reportedly boosted his reputation among the peoples of the Persian Empire.

When Tyre, a heavily fortified city on the coast of what is now Lebanon, refused to surrender to him in 332 B.C., Alexander employed the artillery towers, armored battering rams, and catapults flinging boulders developed by his father to breach its walls. The capture of Tyre rang the death knell of supposedly impregnable walled city-states. Although effective attacks on cities with defensive walls remained rare even after Alexander, because well-constructed city walls still presented formidable barriers, Alexander's success at Tyre increased the terror of a siege for a city's general population. No longer could a city-state's citizens confidently assume their defensive system could withstand the technology of their enemy's offensive weapons indefinitely. The now present fear that armed warriors might actually penetrate into the city made it much harder psychologically for city-states to remain united in the face of threats from aggressive enemies.

Alexander next conquered Egypt, which had fallen to Persian conquest in 525 B.C., regained its independence later for a time, and then once again been taken over by the Persian Empire. Hieroglyphic inscriptions show that he probably presented himself as the successor to the Persian king as the land's ruler rather than as an Egyptian pharaoh. On the coast, to the west of the Nile River, he founded a new city in 331 B.C. and named it Alexandria after himself. Alexandria was the first of many cities he founded, as far east as Afghanistan. During his time in Egypt, Alexander also paid a mysterious visit to the oracle of the god Ammon, whom the Greeks regarded as identical to Zeus, at the oasis of Siwah far out in the western Egyptian desert. Alexander told no one the details of his consultation with the oracle, but the news leaked that he had been informed he was the son of Ammon and that he joyfully accepted the designation as true.

In 331 B.C., Alexander crushed the Persian king's main army at the battle of Gaugamela in northern Mesopotamia (near the border of modern Iraq and Iran). He subsequently proclaimed himself king of Asia in place of the Persian king. For the heterogeneous populations of the Persian Empire, the succession of a Macedonian to the Persian throne changed their lives very little. They continued to send the same taxes to a remote master, whom they rarely if ever saw. As in Egypt, Alexander left the local administrative system in place, even retaining some Persian governors. His long-term aim seems to have been to forge an administrative corps composed of Macedonians, Greeks, and Persians working together to rule the territory he and his army conquered.

The Expedition to India

So fierce was Alexander's love of conquest and adventure that he next led his army farther east into territory hardly known to the Greeks. He pared his force to reduce the need for supplies, which were hard to acquire in the arid country through which they were marching. Each hoplite in Greek armies customarily brought a personal servant to carry his armor and pack. Alexander, imitating Philip, trained his men to carry their own equipment, thereby creating a leaner force by cutting the number of army servants significantly. As with all

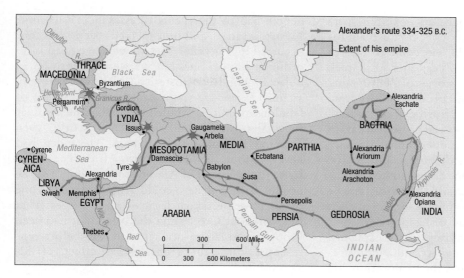

Alexander's Route to India and Back

ancient armies, however, many noncombatants trailed after the fighting force: merchants who set up little markets at every stop, prostitutes, women whom soldiers had taken as mates along the way, and their children. Although supplying these hangers-on was not Alexander's problem, their foraging for themselves made it harder for Alexander's quartermasters to find what they needed to supply the army proper.

From the heartland of Persia, Alexander in 329 B.C. marched northeast into the trackless steppes of Bactria (modern Afghanistan). When he proved unable to subdue completely the highly mobile locals, who avoided pitched battles in favor of the guerrilla tactics of attack and retreat, Alexander settled for an alliance that he sealed by marrying the Bactrian princess Roxanne in 327 B.C. From Bactria, Alexander headed east into India. He probably intended to push all the way through to China in search of the edge of the farthest land on the earth, which Aristotle, who had once tutored the young Alexander, had taught was a sphere. Seventy days of marching through monsoon rains, however, shattered the nerves of the soldiers. In the spring of 326 B.C. they mutinied on the banks of the Hyphasis River (the modern Beas) in western India. Alexander was forced to agree to lead them in the direction of home. Their return cost many casualties as they proceeded first southward along the Indus River and then westward, with some troops sailing along the coast, some taking a north-

ern route, and Alexander leading a contingent through the harsh Gedrosian desert. They finally reached safety in the heartland of Persia in 324 B.C. Alexander promptly began planning an invasion of the Arabian peninsula and, after that, of all North Africa west of Egypt.

By the time Alexander had returned to Persia he had dropped all pretense of ruling over the Greeks as anything other than an absolute monarch. Despite his earlier promise to respect the internal freedom of the Greek city-states, he impinged on their autonomy by issuing a peremptory decree ordering them to restore citizenship to the many exiles who had been created over the previous decades of war in Greece and whose status as wandering, stateless persons was creating unrest. Even more striking was his announcement that he wished to receive the honors due a god. Initially dumbfounded by this request, the leaders of most Greek city-states soon complied by sending honorary delegations to him as if he were a god. The Spartan Damis pithily expressed the only prudent position on Alexander's deification open to the cowed Greeks: "If Alexander wishes to be a god, we agree that he be called a god." Scholars continue to debate Alexander's motive for wanting the Greeks to acknowledge him as a god, but few now accept a formerly popular theory that he sought divinity because he believed the city-states would then have to obey his orders as originating from a divinity, whose authority would supersede that of all earthly regimes. Scholars now think personal rather than political motives best explain his request. He almost certainly had come to believe he was actually the son of Zeus; after all, Greek mythology contained many stories of Zeus mating with a human female and producing children. Most of those legendary offspring were mortal, but Alexander's conquests proved he had surpassed them. His feats must be superhuman because they exceeded the bounds of human possibility. Alexander's accomplishments demonstrated that he had achieved godlike power and therefore must be a god himself. Alexander's divinity was, in ancient terms, a natural consequence of his power.

Alexander's overall aims can best be explained as interlinked goals: the conquest and administration of the known world and the exploration and possible colonization of new territory beyond. Conquest through military action was a time-honored pursuit for Macedonian aristocrats like Alexander. He included non-Macedonians in his administration and army because he needed their expertise, not because he wished to promote an abstract notion of what has been called "the brotherhood of man." Alexander's explorations benefited numerous scientific fields from geography to botany because he took along scientifically minded writers to collect and catalog the new knowledge they acquired. The far-flung cities that he founded served as loyal outposts for keeping the peace in conquered territory and providing warnings to headquarters in case of local uprisings. They also created new opportunities for trade in valuable goods such as spices that were not produced in the Mediterranean region.

Alexander's plans to conquer Arabia and North Africa were extinguished by his premature death from a fever and heavy drinking on June 10, 323 B.C. He had been suffering for months from depression brought on by the death of his best friend, Hephaistion.* Close since their boyhoods, Alexander and Hephaistion were probably lovers. Like Pericles, Alexander had made no plans about what should happen if he died unexpectedly. His Bactrian wife, Roxanne, gave birth to their first child a few months after Alexander's death. When at Alexander's deathbed his commanders asked him to whom he bequeathed his kingdom, he replied, "To the most powerful."

The Athenian orator Aeschines (c. 397–322 B.C.) well expressed the bewildered reaction many people had to the events of Alexander's lifetime: "What strange and unexpected event has not occurred in our time? The life we have lived is no ordinary human one, but we were born to be an object of wonder to posterity." Alexander certainly attained legendary status in later times. Stories of fabulous exploits attributed to him became popular folk tales throughout the ancient world, even reaching distant regions where Alexander had never set foot, such as deep into Africa. The popularity of the legend of Alexander as a symbol of the heights a warrior-hero could achieve served as one of his most persistent legacies to later ages. That the worlds of Greece and the Near East had been brought into closer contact than ever before represented the other long-lasting effect of his astonishing career.

The Development of a Hellenistic Culture

The word *Hellenistic* was coined in the nineteenth century to designate the period of Greek and Near Eastern history from the death of Alexander the Great in 323 B.C. to the death of Cleopatra VII, the last Macedonian queen of Egypt, in 30 B.C. (By 30 B.C. the Romans had become the dominant power in the eastern Mediterranean.) The term *Hellenistic* conveys the idea that a mixed, cosmopolitan form of social and cultural life combining Hellenic (that is, Greek) traditions with indigenous traditions emerged in the eastern Mediterranean region in the aftermath of Alexander's career. Greek ideas and practices had their greatest impact on the urban populations of Egypt and southwestern Asia. The many people who farmed in the Near Eastern countryside and rarely visited the cities had much less contact with Greek ways of life.

Significant social and cultural changes of the Hellenistic period occurred against the backdrop of a new form of kingship, compounded of Macedonian and Near Eastern traditions, which became the predominant political structure in the eastern Mediterranean after Alexander's premature death. The kings who founded the Hellenistic kingdoms were self-proclaimed monarchs with neither a blood relationship to any traditional royal family

*HEF·IST·EE·ON

line nor any special claim to a particular territory. (For this reason historians often describe such a kingdom as a "personal monarchy.") They transformed themselves into kings using their military might, their prestige, and their ambition.

The Creation of Successor Kingdoms

After Alexander's death his mother, Olympias, tried for several years to establish her infant grandson, Alexander's son by Roxanne, as the Macedonian king under her protection. Her plan foundered because Alexander's former army commanders wanted to rule instead, and within twenty years, three of his most powerful generals had established new kingdoms in place of the old. Antigonus (c. 382–301 B.C.) took over in Anatolia, the Near East, Macedonia, and Greece; Seleucus (c. 358–281 B.C.) in Babylonia and the East as far as India; and Ptolemy (c. 367–282 B.C.) in Egypt. Because these men became the de facto heirs to the largest parts of Alexander's conquests, they were referred to as the "successor kings."

Antigonus tried to conquer the other kingdoms to reunite Alexander's domain, but the other

successor kings temporarily banded together and defeated his forces and killed him at the battle of Ipsus in Anatolia in 301 B.C. Seleucus then added Syria to his kingdom. Antigonus's son, Demetrius (c. 336–283 B.C.), regained the Macedonian throne from about 294 to 288 B.C., but further defeats forced him to spend his last years in benign captivity as a helpless guest under the thumb of Seleucus. Demetrius's son, Antigonus Gonatas (c. 320–239 B.C.), reestablished his family's kingdom in Macedonia around 276 B.C., but the city-states of southern Greece remained nominally independent. The Seleucid kingdom had to cede its easternmost territory early in its history to the Indian king Chandragupta (*323–299 B.C.), founder of the Mauryan dynasty, and later lost most of Persia to the Parthians, a north Iranian people. The Ptolemaic kingdom retained its control of the rich land of Egypt. By the middle of the third century B.C., the three kingdoms had reached a balance of power that precluded their expanding much beyond their core territories. Even so, the Hellenistic monarchs remained competitive, especially in conflicts over contested border areas. The armies of the Ptolemaic and Seleucid kingdoms, for

Principal Hellenistic Kingdoms and Locations

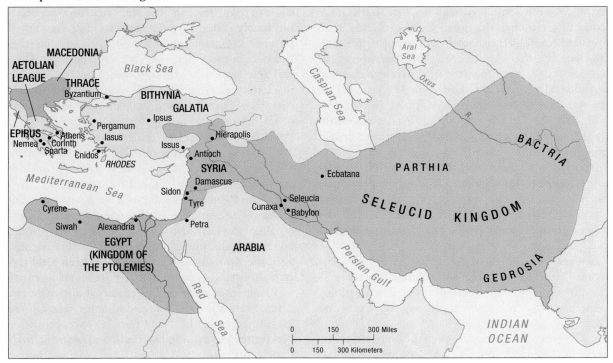

Theater at Hellenistic Pergamum
Prosperous cities like Pergamum in western Anatolia (Asia Minor) built steeply pitched theaters that seated thousands of spectators for dramas and festivals.

example, periodically engaged in a violent tug-of-war over Palestine and Syria.

Some smaller, regional kingdoms also developed in the Hellenistic period. Most famous was the kingdom of the Attalids in Anatolia, with the wealthy city of Pergamum as its capital. The Attalids were strong enough to defeat the large band of Celtic people, called Celts or Gauls, who invaded Anatolia from northern Europe in 278 B.C., and confine them to an area thereafter known as Galatia, after their name. (A separate band had invaded Macedonia and Greece in 279 B.C.) As far away as central Asia, in modern Afghanistan, a new kingdom formed when Diodotus I led a successful rebellion of Bactrian Greeks from the Seleucid kingdom in the mid-third century B.C. These Greeks, whose ancestors had been settled in Bactria by Alexander the Great, had flourished because their land was the crossroads for overland trade in luxury goods between India and China and the Mediterranean world. By the end of the first century B.C. the Bactrian kingdom had fallen to Asian invaders from north of the Oxus River (now the Amu Daria), but the region continued to serve as a cauldron for the interaction of the artistic, philosophical, and religious traditions of East and West.

The successor kings adopted different strategies to meet the goal shared by all new political regimes: to establish a tradition of legitimacy for their rule. Legitimacy was essential if they were to found a royal line that had a chance of enduring beyond their deaths. As a result, Hellenistic queens enjoyed a high social status as the representatives of distinguished families, who then became the mothers of a line of royal descendants. The successors' positions ultimately rested on their personal ability and their power. Lysimachus (c. 360–281 B.C.), another Macedonian who temporarily carved out a kingdom in Thrace and Asia Minor, summed up the situation in a letter to a Greek city: "My rule depends mostly on my own excellence (*arete*), and on the good will of my friends and on my forces."

All the Hellenistic kingdoms in the eastern Mediterranean region eventually fell to the Romans. Diplomatic and military blunders by the Macedonian kings beginning in the third century B.C. first drew the Romans into Greece, which they dominated by the middle of the second century B.C. Smaller powers, such as the city-state of Rhodes and the Attalid kings in Pergamum, further encouraged the Romans to intervene in eastern Mediterranean affairs. Despite its early losses of territory and later troubles from both internal uprisings and external enemies, the Seleucid kingdom remained a major power in the Near East for two centuries. Nevertheless, it too fell to the Romans in the mid-first century B.C. As for Egypt, even though

Ptolemy II (*282–246 B.C.) created difficulties for his successors by imposing disastrous financial measures to pay for a war in Syria, the Ptolemaic kingdom survived the longest. Eventually, however, its growing weakness forced the Egyptian kings to summon intermittent Roman support. When Queen Cleopatra chose the losing side in the Roman civil war of the late first century B.C., a Roman invasion in 30 B.C. ended her reign and the long succession of Ptolemaic rulers.

The Organization of Hellenistic Kingdoms

The armies and navies of Hellenistic kingdoms provided security against internal unrest as well as external enemies. Unlike the citizen militias of the classical period's city-states, professional soldiers made up Hellenistic royal forces. The Greek city-states of the Hellenistic period also hired mercenaries increasingly, as had the Persian kings, instead of mustering citizens. To develop their military might, the Seleucid and Ptolemaic kings vigorously promoted immigration by Greeks and Macedonians, who received land grants in return for military service. When this source later dwindled, the kings had to rely more on the local populations, often employing indigenous troops. Military expenditures rose because the kings faced ongoing pressure to pay their mercenaries regularly and because technology had developed more expensive artillery, such as catapults capable of flinging a projectile weighing one hundred seventy pounds a distance of nearly two hundred yards. Hellenistic navies were expensive because warships were larger, with some dreadnoughts requiring hundreds of men as crews. War elephants, popular in Hellenistic arsenals for their shock effect on enemy troops, were also extremely costly to maintain.

Hellenistic kings initially depended mostly on Greek and Macedonian immigrants to administer their kingdoms. The title "king's friends" identified the inner circle of advisers and courtiers. Like Alexander before them, however, the Seleucids and the Ptolemies also employed indigenous men in the middle and lower levels of their administrations. Even if local men had successful careers in government, however, only rarely were they admitted to the highest ranks of royal society, such as the king's friends. Greeks and non-Greeks tended to live in separate communities. Greeks and Macedonians generally saw themselves as too superior to mix with locals.

Local men who aspired to a government career bettered their chances of succeeding if they learned to read and write Greek in addition to their native languages. This bilingualism qualified them to fill positions communicating the orders of the highest ranking officials, all Greeks and Macedonians, to the local farmers, builders, and crafts producers. The Greek these administrators learned was *koine* ("common Greek"), a standardized form of Greek based on the Athenian dialect. For centuries koine was the common language of commerce and culture from Sicily to the border of India. The New Testament was written in koine during the early Roman Empire, and it was the parent language of Byzantine and modern Greek.

Administrators' principal jobs were to maintain order and to direct the kingdom's tax systems. In many ways the goals and structures of Hellenistic royal administrations recalled those of the earlier Assyrian, Babylonian, and Persian empires. They kept order among the kingdom's subjects by mediating between disputing parties whenever possible, but they could call on troops serving as police if necessary. Overseeing tax collection could be complicated. For example, in Ptolemaic Egypt, the most tightly organized Hellenistic kingdom, royal officials collected customs duties of 50 percent, $33\frac{1}{3}$ percent, 25 percent, or 20 percent depending on the type of goods imported. The renowned Ptolemaic organization was based on methods of central planning and control inherited from much earlier periods of Egyptian history. Officials continued to administer royal monopolies, such as that on vegetable oil, to maximize the king's revenue. Ptolemaic administrators, in a system much like modern schemes of centralized agriculture, decided how much land farmers should sow in oil-bearing plants, supervised production and distribution of the oil, and set all prices for every stage of the oil business. The king, through his officials, also often entered into part-

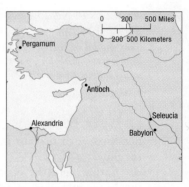

Principal Hellenistic Cities of the Eastern Mediterranean

Model of Priene
This model of the city of Priene in Anatolia shows the rectilinear layout of buildings and streets, with an agora at the center, that characterized Greek cities in the classical and Hellenistic periods.

nerships with private investors to produce more revenue.

Cities were the economic and social hubs of the Hellenistic kingdoms. In Greece some cities outside the Macedonian kingdom tried to increase their strength (to counterbalance that of the monarchies) by banding together into new federal alliances, such as the Achaean League in the Peloponnese and the Aetolian League in northwestern Greece. Making decisions for the league in a common assembly, these cities agreed to use, for example, the same coinage and weights and measures, and to offer equal legal protection for their citizens. Many Greeks and Macedonians now lived in new cities founded by Alexander and the successor kings in the Near East. Hellenistic kings also reestablished existing cities to bring honor to themselves and to introduce new immigrants and social patterns supportive of their policies. The new

settlements had the traditional features of classical Greek city-states, such as gymnasiums and theaters. Although these cities often also possessed such traditional political institutions of the city-state as councils and assemblies for citizen men, the limits of their independence depended strictly on the king's will. When writing to the city's council, the king might express himself in the form of a polite request, but he expected his wishes to be fulfilled as if they were commands. These cities often had to pay taxes directly to the king.

The kings needed the goodwill of the wealthiest and most influential city-dwellers—the Greek and Macedonian urban elites—to keep order in the cities and ensure a steady flow of tax revenues. These wealthy people had the crucial responsibility of collecting taxes from the surrounding countryside as well as from their cities and sending them on to the royal treasury. The kings honored and flat-

tered these members of the cities' upper class to secure their favor and cooperation. Accommodating
cities would receive benefactions from the king to
pay for expensive public works like theaters and
temples or restorations after such natural disasters
as earthquakes. The wealthy men and women of the
urban upper classes in turn helped keep the general
population tractable by providing donations and
loans that secured a reliable supply of grain to feed
the city's residents, subsidize teachers and doctors,
and construct public works. The Greek tradition
of the wealthy and the aristocrats of a city-state
making contributions for the common good was
therefore continued in a new way, through the social
interaction of the kings and the urban upper classes.

The kings also needed to court the good graces
of well-to-do members of the local populations.
Because indigenous cities had long been powerful
in Syria and Palestine, for example, the kings had
to develop cordial relations with their leading citizens. Non-Greeks and non-Macedonians from
eastern regions also moved westward to Hellenistic
Greek cities in increasing numbers. Jews in particular moved from Palestine to Asia Minor, Greece,
and Egypt. The Jewish community eventually
became an influential minority in Alexandria, the
most important Hellenistic city. In Egypt the king
also had to come to terms with the priests who controlled the temples of the traditional Egyptian gods,
because the temples owned large tracts of arable
land worked by tenant farmers. The linchpin in the
organization of the Hellenistic kingdoms was the
system of mutual rewards by which the kings and
their leading subjects—Greeks, Macedonians, and
indigenous elites—became partners in government
and public finance.

The successor kingdoms nevertheless amounted
to foreign rule over local populations by kings and
queens of Macedonian descent. Although monarchs had to maintain harmony with the urban elites
and the favored immigrants in their kingdoms,
royal power pervaded the lives of the kingdoms'
subjects, above all in meting out justice. Seleucus,
for one, claimed this right as a universal truth: "It
is not the customs of the Persians and other peoples that I impose upon you, but the law which is
common to everyone, that what is decreed by the
king is always just." Even Antigonus's successors,
who claimed to lead the Greeks in a voluntary alliance that allegedly reestablished Philip's League

of Corinth, frequently interfered in the internal
affairs of the Greek city-states. Like the other
kings, they regularly installed their own governors
and garrisons in cities where loyalty was suspect.

The Layers of Hellenistic Society

Hellenistic society in the eastern Mediterranean
world was clearly divided into separate layers. The
royal family and the king's friends topped the hierarchy. The Greek and Macedonian elites of the
major cities ranked next. Just under them came the
wealthy and aristocratic upper classes of the indigenous cities, the leaders of large minority urban
populations, and the traditional lords and princes
of local groups maintaining their ancestral domains
in more rural regions. Lowest of the free population were the masses of small merchants, crafts producers, and laborers. Slaves remained where they
had always been, outside the bounds of society,
although those who worked at court could live
physically comfortable lives.

Poor people performed the overwhelming bulk
of the labor required to support the economies of
the Hellenistic kingdoms. Agriculture remained the
economic base, and conditions for farmers and field
workers changed little over time. Many worked on
the royal family's huge agricultural estates, but in
city-states that retained their countrysides, free
peasants still worked small plots as well as on the
larger farms of wealthy landowners. Rural people
rose with the sun and began working before the
heat became unbearable, raising the same kinds of
crops and animals as their ancestors had with the
same simple hand tools and beasts of burden.
Perhaps as many as 80 percent of all adult men and
women, free as well as slave, had to work the land
to produce enough food to sustain the population.
Along certain international routes, however, trade
by sea thrived. More than eighty thousand amphoras
(large ceramic jars used to transport commodities
such as olive oil and wine) made on the Greek island
of Rhodes, for example, have been found in
Ptolemaic Egypt. Consortiums of foreign merchants
turned the Aegean island of Delos into a busy
transportation hub for the cross-shipping of goods,
such as the ten thousand slaves a day the port could
handle. In the cities, poor women and men could
work as small merchants, peddlers, and artisans,
producing and selling goods such as tools, pottery,

clothing, and furniture. Men could sign on as deck hands on the merchant ships that sailed the Mediterranean and Indian oceans.

In the Seleucid and Ptolemaic kingdoms a large portion of the rural population existed in a state of dependency somewhere between free and slave. The "peoples," as they were called, farmed the estates belonging to the king, who owned the most land in the kingdom. Theoretically, the king owned all his kingdom's land because Alexander had claimed it as "won by the spear." In practice, however, the king ceded much territory to cities and favored individuals. The peoples were not landowners but compulsory tenants. Although they could not be sold like chattel slaves, they were not allowed to move away or abandon their tenancies. They owed a certain quota of produce per area of land to the king as if rent to a landlord. The rent was sufficiently heavy that the peoples had virtually no chance of improving their economic lot in life.

The social and political status of women in the Hellenistic world depended on the social layer to which they belonged. Hellenistic queens, like their Macedonian predecessors, commanded enormous riches and received honors commensurate with their elevated status. They usually exercised power only to the extent that they could influence their husbands' decisions, but in some cases they ruled on their own when no male heir existed. Because the Ptolemaic royal family observed the pharaonic tradition of brother-sister marriage, royal daughters as well as sons could rule. Arsinoë II (c. 316–270 B.C.), the daughter of Ptolemy I, first married the Macedonian successor King Lysimachus, who gave her four towns as her personal domain. After Lysimachus's death she married her brother, Ptolemy II of Egypt, and exerted at least as much influence on policy as he did. The virtues publicly praised in a queen reflected traditional Greek values for women. When the city of Hierapolis around 165 B.C. passed a decree in honor of Queen Apollonis of Pergamum, for example, it praised her piety toward the gods, her reverence toward her parents, her distinguished conduct toward her husband, and her harmonious relations with her "beautiful children born in wedlock."

Some queens evidently paid special attention to the condition of women. About 195 B.C., for example, the Seleucid queen Laodice gave a ten-year endowment to the city of Iasus in southwestern Asia Minor to provide dowries for needy girls. Her endowment reflected the wealthy's increasing concern for the welfare of the less fortunate during the Hellenistic period. The royal families led the way in this tendency toward philanthropy as part of their cultivation of an image of generosity befitting kings and queens, in the best tradition of Greek aristocratic benefaction. That Laodice funded dowries shows that she recognized the importance to women of owning property, the surest guarantee of a certain respect and a measure of power in their households.

Most women still remained under the control of men. "Who can judge better than a father what is to his daughter's interest?" remained the dominant creed of fathers with daughters. Once a woman married, "husband" and "wife's" replaced "father" and "daughter's" in the creed. Upper-class women continued to live separated, most of the time, from men not members of their families; poor women still worked in public. Greeks continued to abandon infants they could not, or would not raise—girls were abandoned more often than boys. Other peoples, such as the Egyptians and the Jews, did not practice abandonment, or exposure, as it is often called. Exposure differed from infanticide because the parents expected someone else to find the child and rear it, albeit usually as a slave. The third-century B.C. comic poet Posidippus overstated the case by saying, "A son, one always raises even if one is poor; a daughter, one exposes, even if one is rich." Daughters of wealthy parents were not usually abandoned, but up to 10 percent of other infant girls were. In some limited ways, however, women achieved greater control over their own lives in the Hellenistic period. The rare woman of exceptional wealth could enter public life, for example, by making donations or loans to her city and being rewarded with an official post in her community's government. Of course, such posts were less prestigious and important than in the days of the independent city-states, because the king and his top administrators now controlled the real power. In Egypt, women acquired greater say in the conditions of marriage because contracts, a standard procedure, gradually evolved from an agreement between the groom and the bride's parents to one made by the bride and groom themselves.

Even with power based in the cities, most of the population continued to live where people always had—in small villages in the countryside. There different groups of people lived side by side but nevertheless separately. In one region of Anatolia, for example, twenty-two different languages were spoken. Life in the new and refounded Hellenistic cities developed independently of indigenous rural society. Urban life acquired special vitality because the Greek and Macedonian residents of these cities, surrounded by the non-Greek countryside, tended to stay in them more than had their predecessors in the classical city-states, who had usually gone back and forth frequently between city and countryside to attend to their rural property, participate in local festivals, and worship in local shrines. Now the city-dwellers' activities centered more and more on the city. Urban existence also offered new advantages over country life because of the endowments the wealthy bestowed on their cities. On the island of Samos, for example, wealthy contributors endowed a foundation to finance the distribution of free grain to all the citizens every month so that food shortages would no longer trouble their city. State-sponsored schools for educating children, often funded by wealthy donors, also sprang up in various Hellenistic cities. In some places girls as well as boys could attend school. Many cities also began ensuring the availability of doctors by sponsoring their practices. Patients still had to pay for medical attention, but at least they could count on finding a doctor when they needed one. The wealthy whose donations and loans made many of the cities' new services possible were paid back by the respect and honor they earned from their fellow citizens. Philanthropy even touched international relations occasionally. When an earthquake devastated Rhodes, many cities joined kings and queens in sending donations to help the Rhodians recover. In return, the Rhodians showered honors on their benefactors by appointing them to prestigious municipal office and erecting highly visible inscriptions expressing the city's gratitude.

Wealthy non-Greeks adopted Greek habits more and more in the process of adapting to the new social hierarchy. Diotimus of Sidon (in Lebanon), for example, although not Greek by birth, had a Greek name and pursued the premier Greek sport, chariot racing. He traveled to Nemea

* DEE·AWT·EE·MUHS

NE·MAY·AH

Woman with a Fan *Inexpensive terracotta figurines like this one imitated the poses and elaborate drapery of bronze and marble sculpture.*

in the Peloponnese to enter his chariot in the race at the prestigious festival of Zeus there. When he won he put up an inscription in Greek to announce that he was the first Sidonian to do so. He announced his victory in Greek because koine Greek had become the international language of the eastern Mediterranean coastal lands. The explosion in the use of Greek by non-Greeks certainly indicates the emergence of an international culture based on Greek models, which rulers and their courts, the urban upper classes, and intellectuals all adopted during the Hellenistic period. The most striking evidence of the spread of Greeks, and Greek, throughout the Hellenistic world comes from Afghanistan. There, Asoka (*c. 268–232 B.C.), third king of the

AH·SOK·AH

Mauryan dynasty and a convert to Buddhism, used Greek as one of the languages in his public inscriptions that announced his efforts to introduce his subjects to Buddhist traditions of self-control such as abstinence from eating meat. Even in far-off Afghanistan, non-Greeks communicated with the Greeks they encountered in Greek.

Literature and Art
Under New Conditions

As the use of the Greek language spread throughout the Hellenistic world, Greek literature began to reflect the new conditions of life. The burlesquing of contemporary people and politics characteristic of comedy in fifth-century B.C. Athens, for example, disappeared along with the city-state's autonomy. Comic dramatists like Menander (c. 342–289 B.C.) and Philemon (c. 360–263 B.C.) now presented plays with timeless plots concerning the trials and tribulations of fictional lovers, in works not unlike modern soap operas. These comedies of manners, as the genre is called, proved so popular that later Roman comedy writers imitated their style.

Poets such as Theocritus (c. 300–260 B.C.) from Syracuse in Sicily and Callimachus (c. 305–240 B.C.) from Cyrene in North Africa, both of whom came to Alexandria under the patronage of the Ptolemies, made individual emotions a central theme in their work. Their poetry broke new ground in demanding great intellectual effort as well as emotional engagement from the audience. Only the erudite could fully appreciate the allusions and complex references to mythology that these poets employed in their elegant poems, which were mostly much shorter than Homeric epics. Theocritus was the first Greek poet to express the splitting between the town and the countryside, a poetic stance corresponding to a growing reality. His pastoral poems, the *Idylls,* emphasized the discontinuity between the environment of the city and the bucolic life of the country-dweller, although the rural people depicted in Theocritus's poetry appeared in idealized landscapes rather than the actual Egyptian fields. Nevertheless, his *Idylls* reflected the fundamental social division of the Ptolemaic kingdom between the food consumers of the town and the food producers of the countryside.

The themes of Callimachus's prolific output underscored the division between the intellectual elite and the uneducated masses in contemporary society. "I hate the crowd" describes Callimachus's authorial stance toward poetry and its audience. A comparison between Callimachus's work and that of his literary rival, Apollonius of Rhodes, emphasizes the Hellenistic preference for intellectually demanding poetry. Even though Apollonius wrote long epics (including one about Jason and the Argonauts) instead of short poems, Apollonius's verses also displayed an erudition only readers with a literary education could understand. Like the earlier lyric poets, who in the sixth and fifth centuries B.C. often wrote to please rich patrons, these Hellenistic authors necessarily had to consider the tastes of royal patrons, who were paying the bills. In one poem expressly praising his patron, Ptolemy II, Theocritus spelled out the quid pro quo of Hellenistic literary patronage: "the spokesmen of the Muses [that is, poets] celebrate Ptolemy in return for his benefactions."

The Hellenistic kings promoted intellectual life principally by offering to support scholars financially if they relocated to the royal capitals, proving royal magnanimity and grandeur. The Ptolemies won this particular competition by making Alexandria the leading intellectual center of the Hellenistic world. There they established the world's first scholarly research institute. Its massive library had the impossible goal of trying to collect all the books (that is, manuscripts) in the world; it grew to hold a half million scrolls, an enormous number for the time. Linked to it was a building in which the hired scholars dined together and produced encyclopedias of knowledge such as *The Wonders of the World* and *On the Rivers of Europe* by Callimachus (he was a learned prose writer as well as a poet). The name of this building, the Museum (meaning "place of the Muses," the Greek goddesses of learning and the arts), is still used to designate institutions that preserve and promote knowledge. The output of the Alexandrian scholars was prodigious. Their champion was Didymus (c. 80–10 B.C.), nicknamed "Brass Guts" for his indefatigable writing of nearly four thousand books.

None of the women poets known from the Hellenistic period seem to have enjoyed royal

The Masks of Comedy
This sculpted panel shows the kinds of masks with exaggerated expressions worn by comic actors on stage.

patronage. But women excelled in writing epigrams, a style of short poems originally used for funeral epitaphs (for which Callimachus was famed). In this era the epigram expressed a wide variety of personal feelings, love above all. Elegantly worded epigrams written by women from diverse regions of the Hellenistic world—Anyte of Tegea in the Peloponnese, Nossis of Locri in southern Italy, Moero of Byzantium—still survive. Women, from courtesans to respectable matrons, figured as frequent subjects in their poems. No Hellenistic literature better conveyed the depth of human emotion that their epigrams, such as Nossis' poem on the power of Eros (Love, regarded as a divinity): "Nothing is sweeter than Eros. All other delights are second to it—from my mouth I spit out even honey. And this Nossis says: whoever Aphrodite has not kissed knows not what sort of flowers are her roses."

Like their literary contemporaries, Hellenistic sculptors and painters featured human emotions prominently in their works. Classical artists had consistently imbued their subjects' faces with a serenity that represented an ideal rather than reality. Numerous examples, usually surviving only in later copies, show that Hellenistic artists tried to depict emotions more naturally in a variety of genres. In portrait sculpture, Lysippus's famous bust of Alexander the Great captured the young commander's passionate dreaminess. A sculpture from Pergamum by an unknown artist commemorates the third-century B.C. Attalid victory over the plundering Gauls by showing a defeated Gallic warrior stabbing himself after having killed his wife to prevent her enslavement by the victors. A large-scale painting of Alexander battling with the Persian king Darius portrayed Alexander's intense concentration and Darius's horrified expression (page 125). The artist, who was probably either Philoxenus of Eretria or a Greek woman from Egypt named Helena (one of the first female artists known), used foreshortening and strong contrasts between shadows and highlights to accentuate the emotional impact of the picture.

To appreciate fully the appeal of Hellenistic sculpture, we must remember that, like earlier Greek sculpture, it was painted in bright colors. The fourth-century B.C. sculptor Praxiteles reportedly remarked that his best statues were "the ones colored by Nicias" (a leading painter of the time). But Hellenistic art differed from classical art in its social context. Works of classical art had been commissioned by the city-states for public display or by wealthy individuals to donate to their city-state as a work of public art. Now sculptors and painters created their works more and more as commissions

(right) **Dying Gauls** *This sculpture shows a Gaul stabbing himself after killing his wife to prevent their capture by the enemy. Hellenistic artists excelled in the depiction of deeply emotional scenes such as this one.*

(far right) **Realism in Hellenistic Sculpture** *Sculptors during the Hellenistic period often depicted subjects that reflected the harsh reality of everyday life, such as this woman bowed by age and the burden she carries.*

from royalty and from the urban elites who wanted to show they had artistic taste like their social superiors in the royal family. To be successful, artists had to please their rich patrons, and so the increasing diversity of subjects that emerged in Hellenistic art presumably represented a trend approved by kings, queens, and the elites. Sculpture best reveals this new preference for depictions of humans in a wide variety of poses, many from private life (again in contrast with classical art). Hellenistic sculptors portrayed subjects never before shown: foreigners (such as the dying Gaul), drunkards, battered athletes, wrinkled old people. The female nude became a particular favorite, presumably for male owners. A naked Aphrodite, which Praxiteles sculpted for the city of Cnidos, became so renowned that Nicomedes, king of Bithynia in Asia Minor, later offered to pay off Cnidos's entire public debt if he could have the statue. The Cnidians refused.

A lasting innovation of Hellenistic art was the depiction of abstract ideas as sculptural types. Such statues were made to represent ideas as diverse as Peace and Insanity. Modern statues such as the Statue of Liberty belong in this artistic tradition. Modern neoclassical architecture also imitates the imaginative public architecture of the Hellenistic period, whose architects often boldly combined the Doric and Ionic style of architectural decoration on the same building and energized the Corinthian order with florid decoration.

Innovation in Philosophy, Science, and Medicine

Greek philosophy in the Hellenistic period reached a wider audience than ever before. Although the masses of working poor as usual had neither the leisure nor the resources to attend philosophers' lectures, the more affluent members of society studied philosophy in growing numbers. Theophrastus (c. 370–285 B.C.), Aristotle's most brilliant pupil, lectured to crowds of up to two thousand in Athens. Most philosophy students continued to be men, but women could now join the groups attached to certain philosophers. Kings competed to attract famous thinkers to their courts, and Greek settlers took their interest in philosophy with them, even to the most remote Hellenistic cities. Archaeological excavation of a city located thousands of miles from Greece on the Oxus River in Afghanistan, for example, turned up a Greek philosophical text as well as inscriptions of moral advice imputed to Apollo's oracle at Delphi.

Fewer Hellenistic thinkers concentrated on metaphysics. Instead they focused on philosophical materialism, a doctrine asserting that only things made of matter truly existed. It therefore denied the concept of soul Plato described, and ignored any suggestion that such nonmaterial phenomena could exist. The goal of much philosophical inquiry now centered on securing human independence from the effects of chance or worldly events by withdrawing from as much of the business of daily life as possible and cultivating calmness in the face of all troubles. Scientific investigation of the physical world became a specialty separate from philosophy. Hellenistic philosophy was regularly divided into three related areas: logic (the process for discovering truth), physics (the fundamental truth about the nature of existence), and ethics (the way humans should achieve happiness and well-being as a consequence of logic and physics). The most significant new philosophical schools of thought were Epicureanism and Stoicism. (Epicurean and Stoic doctrines became exceptionally popular among upper-class Romans.) The various philosophies of the Hellenistic period in many ways asked the same question: what is the best way for humans to live? Different philosophies recommended different paths to the same answer: individual humans must attain personal tranquility to achieve freedom from the turbulence of outside forces. For Greeks the changes in political and social life accompanying the rise to dominance of the Macedonian and later Hellenistic kings make this focus understandable. Outside forces in the persons of aggressive kings had robbed the city-states of their freedom of action internationally, and the fates of city-states as well as individuals now rested in the hands of dis-

tant, often fickle monarchs. More than ever before, human life and opportunities for free choice seemed poised to career out of the control of individuals. It therefore made sense, at least for those wealthy enough to spend time philosophizing, to look for personal, private solutions to the unsettling new conditions of life in the Hellenistic era.

Epicureanism took its name from its founder, Epicurus (341–271 B.C.), who settled his followers in Athens in a house amidst a verdant garden (hence The Garden as the name of his informal school). Under Epicurus the study of philosophy assumed a social form that broke with tradition, because he admitted women and slaves as regular members of his group. His lover, Leontion, became notorious for her treatise criticizing the views of Theophrastus. Epicurus believed humans should pursue pleasure, but his notion of pleasure had a unique definition. He insisted that true pleasure consisted of an "absence of disturbance" from pain and the everyday turbulence, passions, and desires of ordinary human existence. A sober life lived in the society of friends apart from the cares of the common world could best provide this essential peace of mind. This teaching represented a serious challenge to the ideal of Greek citizenship, which required men of means to participate in city-state politics and for citizen women to engage in public religious cults.

Humans should above all be free of worry about death, Epicurus taught. Because all matter consisted of microscopic atoms in random movement, as Democritus and Leucippus had earlier theorized, death was nothing more than the painless disassociation of the body's atoms. Moreover, all human knowledge must be empirical, that is, derived from experience and perception. Phenomena that most people perceive as the work of the gods, such as thunder, do not result from divine intervention in the world. The gods live far away in perfect tranquility, paying no attention to human affairs. Humans therefore have nothing to fear from the gods, in life or in death.

The Stoics recommended a different, less isolationist path for individuals. Their name derived from the Painted Stoa in Athens, where they discussed their doctrines. Zeno (c. 333–262 B.C.) from Citium on Cyprus founded Stoicism, but Chrysippus (c. 280–206 B.C.) from Cilicia in Asia Minor did the most to make it a comprehensive guide to life. Stoics believed humans should make the pursuit of

The Stoa of Attalus in the Athenian Agora
This long building with columns, a gift to Athenians from King Attalus II of Pergamum in the second century B.C., offered a shady place for conversation and meetings. The stone building in the foreground is a church from a later period.

virtue their goal. Virtue, they said, consisted of putting oneself in harmony with universal Nature, the rational force of divine providence that directed all existence under the guise of Fate. Reason as well as experience should be used to discover the way to that harmony, which required the "perfect" virtues of good sense, justice, courage, and temperance. According to the Stoics the doctrines of Zeno and Chrysippus applied to women as well as men. In fact, the Stoics advocated equal citizenship for women and doing away with the conventions of marriage and families as the Greeks knew them. Zeno even proposed unisex clothing as a way to obliterate unnecessary distinctions between women and men.

The Stoic belief that everything that happened was fated created for them the question of whether humans truly have free will. Employing some of the subtlest reasoning ever applied to this fundamental issue, Stoic philosophers concluded that purposeful human actions did have significance. A Stoic should therefore take action against evil, for example, by participating in politics. Nature, itself good, did not prevent vice from occurring, because virtue would otherwise have no meaning. What mattered in life was the striving for good, not the result. To be a Stoic also meant to shun desire and anger while enduring pain and sorrow calmly, an attitude that informs the current meaning of the word *stoic*. Through endurance and self-control, a Stoic attained tranquility. Stoics did not fear death because they believed people lived over and over again infinitely in identical fashion to their present lives. This repetition would occur as the world would be destroyed by fire periodically and then reformed after the conflagration. *cf THE CYLICAL KALPAS OF HINDUISM*

Other schools of thought carried on the work of earlier philosophical leaders such as Plato and Pythagoras. Still others, like the Sceptics and the Cynics, struck out in idiosyncratic directions. Sceptics aimed at the same state of personal imperturbability as did Epicureans, but from a completely different premise. Following the doctrines of Pyrrho (c. 360–270 B.C.) from Elis in the Peloponnese, they believed that secure knowledge about anything was impossible because the human senses yield contradictory information about the world. All people can do, they insisted, is to depend on appearances of things while suspending judgment about their reality. Pyrrho's thought had been influenced by the Indian ascetic wise men (the magi) he met while a member of Alexander the Great's entourage. The basic premise of scepticism inevitably precluded any unity of doctrine.

Cynics ostentatiously rejected every convention of ordinary life, especially wealth and material comfort. They believed humans should aim for complete self-sufficiency. Whatever was natural was good and could be done without shame before anyone; according to this idea, even public defecation and fornication were acceptable. Women and men alike should be free to follow their sexual inclinations. Above all, Cynics should disdain the comforts and luxuries of a comfortable life. The name *Cynic*, which meant "like a dog," reflected the common evaluation of this ascetic and unconventional way of life. The most famous early Cynic, Diogenes (died 323 B.C.) from Sinope on the Black

SI·NO·PEE

Sea, was reputed to wear borrowed clothing and sleep in a big storage jar. Almost as notorious was Hipparchia, a female Cynic of the late fourth century B.C. She once bested an obnoxious philosophical opponent named Theodorus the Atheist with the following argument, which recalled the climactic episode between father and son in Aristophanes' *Clouds:* "That which would not be considered wrong if done by Theodorus would also not be considered wrong if done by Hipparchia. Now if Theodorus strikes himself, he does no wrong. Therefore, if Hipparchia strikes Theodorus, she does no wrong."

Science benefited from its widening divorce from philosophy during the Hellenistic period. Historians have called this era the Golden Age of ancient science. Various factors contributed to this flourishing of thought and discovery: the expeditions of Alexander had encouraged curiosity and increased knowledge about the extent and differing features of the world; royal patronage supported scientists financially; and the concentration of scientists in Alexandria promoted a fertile exchange of ideas that could not otherwise take place because of the difficulty of travel and communication. The greatest advances came in geometry and mathematics. Euclid, who taught at Alexandria around 300 B.C., made revolutionary progress in the analysis of two- and three-dimensional space. The utility of Euclidean geometry still endures. Archimedes of Syracuse (287–212 B.C.) was an arithmetical polymath who calculated the approximate value of pi and devised a way to manipulate very large numbers. He also invented hydrostatics (the science of the equilibrium of a fluid system) and mechanical devices such as a screw for lifting water to a higher elevation. Archimedes' shout of delight, "I have found it" (*heureka* in Greek), when he solved a problem while soaking in his bathtub has been immortalized in the modern expression "Eureka!"

The sophistication of Hellenistic mathematics affected other fields that also required complex computations. Aristarchus of Samos early in the third century B.C. first proposed the correct model of the solar system by theorizing that the earth revolved around the sun, which he also identified as being far larger and far more distant than it appeared. Later astronomers rejected Aristarchus's heliocentric model in favor of the traditional geocentric one because calculations based on the orbit he postulated for the earth failed to

correspond to the observed positions of celestial objects. Aristarchus had made a simple mistake: he had postulated a circular orbit instead of an elliptical one. (It would be another eighteen hundred years before the heliocentric system would be recognized by the Polish astronomer Copernicus [A.D. 1473–1543] as the correct one.) Eratosthenes of Cyrene (c. 275–194 B.C.) pioneered mathematical geography. He calculated the circumference of the earth with astonishing accuracy by simultaneously measuring the length of the shadows of widely separated but identically tall structures. Ancient scientists in later periods, especially the astronomer and geographer Ptolemy, who worked in Alexandria in the second century A.D., would improve and refine the image of the natural world elaborated by Hellenistic researchers. But the basic ideas of these Hellenistic scientists dominated Western scientific thought until the advent of modern science.

Greek science was as quantitative as it could be, given the limitations of ancient technology. Precise scientific experimentation was not possible because no technology existed for the precise measurement of very short intervals of time. Measuring tiny quantities of matter was also next to impossible. But the spirit of invention prevailed in spite of these difficulties. Ctesibius of Alexandria (born c. 310 B.C.), a contemporary of Aristarchus, devised machines operated by air pressure. In addition to this

---

INTELLECTUALS IN THIRD-CENTURY ALEXANDRIA

Euclid from Alexandria(?) (born c. 340 B.C.)
mathematician

Ctesibius of Alexandria (born c. 310 B.C.)
mechanical engineer

Callimachus from Cyrene (c. 305–240 B.C.)
poet, encyclopedist

Theocritus from Syracuse (c. 300–260 B.C.)
poet

Herophilus of Chalcedon (born c. 300 B.C.)
physician and anatomist

Eratosthenes of Cyrene (c. 275–194 B.C.)
polymath

Aristophanes from Byzantium (c. 257–180 B.C.)
literary scholar

invention of pneumatics, he built a working water pump, an organ powered by water, and the first accurate water clock. His fellow Alexandrian of the first century A.D., Hero, continued the Hellenistic tradition of mechanical ingenuity by building a rotating sphere powered by steam. This invention did not lead to viable steam engines, perhaps because the metallurgical technology to produce metal pipes, fittings, and screws was not yet developed. As in the modern world, much of the engineering prowess of the Hellenistic period was applied to military technology. The kings hired engineers to design powerful catapults and wheeled siege towers many stories high, which were capable of battering down the defenses of walled cities. The most famous large-scale application of technology for nonmilitary purposes was the construction of a lighthouse three hundred feet tall (the Pharos) for the harbor at Alexandria. Using polished metal mirrors to reflect the light from a large fire fueled by wood, it shone many miles out over the sea. Awestruck sailors regarded it as one of the wonders of the world.

Medicine also shared the progressive mood exemplified by Hellenistic science. The increased contact between Greeks and people of the Near East in this period made the medical knowledge of the ancient civilizations of Mesopotamia and Egypt better known in the West and gave an impetus to the study of human health and illness. Around 325 B.C., Praxagoras of Cos discovered the value of measuring the human pulse in diagnosing illness. A bit later, Herophilus of Chalcedon (born c. 300 B.C.), working in Alexandria, became the first scientist in the West to study anatomy by dissecting human cadavers. Anatomical terms Herophilus coined are still used (such as *duodenum,* a section of the small intestine). Other Hellenistic advances in understanding anatomy included the discovery of the nerves and nervous system. Anatomical knowledge, however, outstripped knowledge of human physiology. The earlier idea that human health depended on the balance of four humors remained the dominant theory in physiology. A person was healthy—in "good humor"—so long as the correct proportions of the four humors were maintained. Because illness was thought to result from an imbalance of the humors, doctors prescribed various regimens of drugs, diet, and exercise to restore balance. Doctors also believed that drawing blood from patients

could help rebalance the humors. (This practice of "bleeding" was used into the 1800s.) Doctors thought many illnesses in women were caused by displacements of the womb, which they wrongly believed could move around in the body.

Transformation in Hellenistic Religion

The expansion and diversification of knowledge that characterized Hellenistic intellectual life was matched by the growing diversity of religious practice. The traditional cults of Greek religion remained very popular, but new cults, such as those that deified ruling kings, responded to changing political and social conditions. Preexisting cults that previously had only local significance, such as that of the Greek healing deity Asclepius or the mystery cult of the Egyptian goddess Isis, grew prominent all over the Hellenistic world. In many cases, Greek cults and indigenous cults from the eastern Mediterranean meshed and shared practices, each influencing the other. Their traditions blended well because their cults were found to share many assumptions about how to remedy the troubles of human life. In other instances, local cults and Greek cults existed side by side, with some overlap. The inhabitants of villages in the Fayum district of Egypt, for example, continued worshiping their traditional crocodile god and mummifying their dead according to the old ways but also paid homage to Greek deities. In the tradition of polytheistic religion, people could worship in both old and new cults.

New Hellenistic cults picked up a prominent theme of Hellenistic philosophy: a concern for the relationship between the individual and what seemed the controlling, unpredictable power of the divinities Luck and Chance. Greek religion had always addressed randomness at some level, but the chaotic course of Greek history since the Peloponnesian War had made human existence appear more unpredictable than ever. Yet advances in astronomy revealed the mathematical precision of the celestial sphere of the universe. Religious experience now had to address the apparent disconnection between that heavenly uniformity and the shapeless chaos of life on earth. One increasingly popular approach to bridging that gap was to rely on astrology for advice deduced from the movement of the stars and planets, thought of as divinities.

In another approach offering devotees protection from the capricious tricks of Chance or Luck, the gods of popular Hellenistic cults promised salvation of various kinds. One form of salvation could come from powerful rulers, who enjoyed divine status in what are known as ruler cults. These cults were established in recognition of great benefactions. The Athenians, for example, deified the Macedonians Antigonus and his son Demetrius as savior gods in 307 B.C., when they bestowed magnificent gifts on the city and restored democracy (which had been abolished in 321 B.C. by another Macedonian). Like most ruler cults, this one expressed both spontaneous gratitude and a desire to flatter the rulers in the hope of obtaining additional favors. As a rule, the Antigonid kings had no divine cult in their honor in Macedonia, but many cities in the Ptolemic and Seleucid kingdoms instituted ruler cults for their kings and queens. An inscription put up by Egyptian priests in 238 B.C. concretely described the qualities appropriate for a divine king and queen:

> *King Ptolemy III and Queen Berenice, his sister and wife, the Benefactor Gods, . . . have provided good government . . . and [after a drought] sacrificed a large amount of their revenues for the salvation of the population, and by importing grain . . . they saved the inhabitants of Egypt.*

Healing divinities offered another form of protection to anxious individuals. Scientific Greek medicine had rejected the notion of supernatural causes and cures for disease ever since Hippocrates had established his medical school on the Aegean island of Cos in the late fifth century B.C. Nevertheless, the cult of Asclepius, son of Apollo, who offered cures for illness and injury at his many shrines, grew popular during the Hellenistic period. Suppliants seeking Asclepius's help would sleep in special dormitories at his shrines to await dreams in which he prescribed healing treatments. These prescriptions emphasized diet and exercise, but numerous inscriptions set up by grateful patients also testified to miraculous cures and surgery performed while the sufferer slept. The following example is typical:

> *Ambrosia of Athens was blind in one eye. . . . She . . . ridiculed some of the cures [described in inscriptions in the sanctuary] as being*

> *incredible and impossible. . . . But when she went to sleep, she saw a vision; she thought the god was standing next to her . . . he split open the diseased eye and poured in a medicine. When day came she left cured.*

Other cults proffered secret knowledge as a key to worldly and physical salvation. They believed protection from physical danger was more urgent than the care of the soul or the afterlife. The Mysteries of Demeter at Eleusis, however, continued to address a person's soul and the afterlife. The mystery cults of the Greek god Dionysus and, in particular, the Egyptian goddess Isis gained followers in this period. The popularity of Isis, whose powers extended over every area of human life, received a boost from King Ptolemy I, who established an official seat for her cult in Alexandria. He also refashioned the Egyptian deity Osiris in a Greek mold as the new god Sarapis, whose job was to serve as Isis' consort. Sarapis reportedly performed miracles of rescue from shipwreck and illness. The cult of Isis, who became the most popular female divinity in the Mediterranean, involved extensive rituals and festivals incorporating features of Egyptian religion mixed with Greek elements. Disciples of Isis apparently hoped to achieve personal purification as well as the aid of the goddess in overcoming the sometimes demonic influence of Chance and Luck on human life.

That an Egyptian deity like Isis could achieve enormous popularity among Greeks (and Romans in later times) alongside the traditional gods of Greek religion, who also remained popular, is the best evidence of the cultural cross-fertilization of the Hellenistic world. Equally striking on this score was that many Jews, especially those living in the large Jewish communities that had grown up in Hellenistic cities outside Palestine, such as Alexandria, adopted the Greek language and many aspects of Greek culture. The Hebrew Bible was even translated into Greek in Alexandria in the early third century B.C., reportedly at the request of King Ptolemy II. Hellenized Jews largely retained the ritual practices and habits of life that defined traditional Judaism, and they refused to worship Greek gods. Hellenistic politics and culture also affected the Jewish community in Palestine. The region, caught between the great kingdoms of the Ptolemies in Egypt and the Seleucids in Syria, was controlled militarily and politically by the

Ptolemies in the third century B.C. and by the Seleucids in the second century B.C. Both the Ptolemies and the Seleucids allowed the Jews to live according to their ancestral tradition under the political leadership of a high priest in Jerusalem. Internal dissension among Jews erupted in second-century B.C. Palestine over the amount of Greek influence that was compatible with traditional Judaism. The Seleucid king Antiochus IV (*175–163 B.C.) intervened in the conflict in support of an extreme Hellenizing faction of Jews in Jerusalem, who had taken over the high priesthood. In 167 B.C., Antiochus converted the main Jewish sanctuary there into a Greek temple and outlawed the practice of Jewish religious rites such as observing the Sabbath and circumcision. A revolt led by Judah the Maccabee eventually won Jewish independence from the Seleucids after twenty-five years of war. The most famous episode of the Maccabean Revolt was the retaking of the temple in Jerusalem and its rededication to the worship of the Jewish god, Yahweh, a triumphant moment commemorated by Jews ever since on the holiday of Hanukkah. That Greek culture attracted Jews, whose strong traditions reached far into antiquity, provides a striking example of the transformations that affected many—though far from all—people of the Hellenistic world.

CONCLUSION

After Athens recovered its prosperity following the Peloponnesian War, the city-state was again strong enough to participate in the struggles among Sparta, Corinth, and Thebes over political and military dominance in Greece in the first half of the fourth century B.C. When the wars and shifting alliances of the city-states in this period led to weakness and instability after the battle of Mantinea in 362 B.C., a power vacuum resulted, which the kingdom of Macedonia promptly filled through the actions of its aggressive king, Philip II. The conquests of Philip and his son, Alexander the Great, eventually led to the restructuring of the political landscape of the eastern Mediterranean world. The philosophers Socrates, Plato, and Aristotle, whose careers together spanned the period from before the Peloponnesian War through the life of Alexander the Great, gave new directions to Greek thought in ethics, metaphysics, logic, and scientific investigation of the natural world.

The personal monarchies of the Hellenistic kings both exploited the long-term structures of government already established in their conquered territories and built up an administrative system staffed by Greeks and Macedonians. Indigenous elites as well as Greeks and Macedonians cooperated with the Hellenistic monarchs in governing their society, which was divided along hierarchical ethnic lines. To enhance their image of magnificence, the kings and queens of the Hellenistic world supported writers, artists, scholars, philosophers, and scientists, thereby encouraging the distinctive energy of Hellenistic intellectual life. The traditional city-states continued to exist in Hellenistic Greece, but their external freedom was constrained by the need to stay on good terms with powerful monarchs. With the ultimate control of political power removed from their hands, citizen men tended less and less to constitute militias to defend the city-state, a task increasingly performed by hired mercenaries.

The diversity of the Hellenistic world encompassed much that was new. Its queens commanded greater wealth and status than any women since the queens of the New Kingdom of Egypt. Its philosophers, such as Epicurean and Stoic scholars, defined different paths humans could take to achieve personal tranquility in a tumultuous world. Its scientists and doctors expanded the range of human knowledge enormously. Its new cults expressed a yearning for protection from the perils of life shared by worshipers from varied backgrounds. At the same time, its most fundamental elements remained unchanged—the labor, the poverty, and the necessarily limited horizons of the mass of ordinary people working in its fields, vineyards, and pastures.

Suggestions for Further Reading

Source Materials

Aristotle. *The Complete Works.* 2 vols. Edited by Jonathan Barnes. 1984. Translations of the writings of Aristotle, including the *Constitution of Athens.*

Arrian. *The Campaigns of Alexander.* Translated by Aubrey de Sélincourt. 1971. The best ancient account of Alexander's exploits, by a historian of the early Roman Empire. Also available in the Loeb Classical Library series.

Austin, M. M. *The Hellenistic World from Alexander to the Roman Conquest: A Selection of Ancient Sources in Translation.* 1981. Excerpts of sources from political, social, and economic history, with useful introductions to each selection.

Plato. *The Collected Dialogues.* Edited by Edith Hamilton and Huntington Cairns. 1961. Contains the translated writings of Plato.

Plutarch. *The Age of Alexander: Nine Greek Lives.* Translated by Ian Scott-Kilvert. 1973. A selection of biographies of famous Greek men of the fourth and third centuries B.C., including Alexander, Demosthenes, and Demetrius. All Plutarch's biographies are available in the Loeb Classical Library series.

Xenophon. *A History of My Times.* Translated by Rex Warner. 1979. A translation of the *Hellenica,* which continues *The Peloponnesian War* by Thucydides and covers events in Greek history until 362 B.C. The Loeb Classical Library series publishes all of Xenophon's works in seven volumes, including *The Oeconomicus,* on household management.

Interpretive Studies

Adcock, F. E. *The Greek and Macedonian Art of War.* 1957. The classic introduction to the strategy and technology of the subject.

Barnes, Jonathan. *Aristotle.* 1982. A succinct yet comprehensive introduction to the thought of Aristotle.

Bowman, Alan K. *Egypt After the Pharaohs, 332 B.C.–A.D. 642.* 1986. A topically arranged and well-illustrated survey.

The Cambridge Ancient History. Vol. VII, pt. 1, *The Hellenistic World.* 2d ed. 1984. Surveys Hellenistic history from the death of Alexander to 217 B.C., with an emphasis on political history but including sections on culture, economy, science, agriculture, and building and town planning.

Gosling, J. C. B. *Plato.* 1973. A critical discussion of some of the central ideas of Plato.

Grant, Michael. *From Alexander to Cleopatra: The Hellenistic World.* 1982. A readable survey of political and intellectual history.

Green, Peter. *Alexander to Actium: The Historical Evolution of the Hellenistic Age.* 1990. A massive, vividly written volume with many provocative interpretations.

Hamilton, J. R. *Alexander the Great.* 1973. A reliable introduction to the Macedonian background and career of Alexander.

Hornblower, Simon. *The Greek World, 479–323 B.C.* 1983. An interpretative survey of Greek history in the Golden Age and the fourth century B.C.

Lewis, Naphtali. *Greeks in Ptolemaic Egypt.* 1986. Case studies in the social history of Greek immigrants to Egypt.

Long, A. A. *Hellenistic Philosophy: Stoics, Epicureans, Sceptics.* 2d ed. 1986. A scholarly yet readable introduction to the main developments in Greek philosophy during the Hellenistic period.

Martin, Luther. *Hellenistic Religions: An Introduction.* 1987. An intriguing analysis of the social and intellectual changes in Greek religion after the Classical Age.

Phillips, E. D. *Greek Medicine.* 1973. An introduction to the subject, presented chronologically.

Pollitt, J. J. *Art in the Hellenistic Age.* 1986. A comprehensive treatment of the various genres of Hellenistic art.

Pomeroy, Sarah B. *Women in Hellenistic Egypt: From Alexander to Cleopatra.* 1984. Includes histories of women from slaves to queens.

Richter, G. M. A. *Portraits of the Greeks.* Rev. ed. 1984. Includes illustrations of Aristophanes, Socrates, Plato, Aristotle, Alexander, Hellenistic kings and queens, and many others.

Snyder, Jane M. *The Woman and the Lyre: Women Writers in Classical Greece and Rome.* 1989. Includes women poets and philosophers of the Hellenistic period.

Tarn, W. W. *Hellenistic Civilization.* 3d ed. Revised by G. T. Griffith. 1961. A still valuable survey with a broad range.

Tcherikover, Victor. *Hellenistic Civilization and the Jews.* Translated by S. Applebaum. A classic study of the contacts between Jews and Greeks in the Hellenistic period.

White, K. D. *Greek and Roman Technology.* 1984. A splendidly illustrated survey including Hellenistic inventions.

Witt, R. E. *Isis in the Greco-Roman World.* 1971. Surveys the cult of Isis from its Egyptian roots to the worlds of Greece and Rome.

The Rise and Fall of the Roman Republic, c. 800–44 B.C.

Romulus, the legendary first king of Rome, reputedly vanished forever during a windstorm. The legend goes on to say that his people felt distressed about the mysterious loss of their king and suspected his aristocratic advisers had murdered him. To calm the crowd, Julius Proculus, a prominent citizen, explained the king's disappearance:

Romulus, the father of our city, descended from the sky at dawn this morning and appeared to me. In awe and reverence I stood before him, praying that it would be right to look upon his face. "Go," Romulus said to me, "and tell the Romans that by the will of the gods my Rome shall be capital of the world. Let them learn to be soldiers. Let them know, and teach their children, that no power on earth can stand against Roman arms." Having spoken these words, he returned to the sky.

According to legend, this speech placated the people of early Rome by assuring them of their king's immortality.

This story about Romulus's mandate to Rome, though certainly fictional, summed up the way the Romans eventually came to view their destiny: the gods willed that Rome should rule the world by military might. But simultaneously the legend highlights the tensions between Roman aristocrats and the mass of Roman citizens. This tale shows a member of the upper class manipulating the ordinary people of Rome by deceiving them. Most significant, the story implies that the aristocrats hated the monarchy whereas the common people were content to be ruled by a king. This part of the legend foreshadowed a fundamental discord that periodically plagued the Roman state as it developed over the centuries from a monarchy to a republic to an empire: all

Julius Caesar the Dictator
When Julius Caesar placed his portrait and the inscription "Caesar, perpetual dictator" on coins, he flaunted his breaking of the prohibition against a dictator serving indefinitely. This sort of self-aggrandizing led to civil war and the destruction of the Roman Republic.

Romans gradually came to believe it their fate to rule others by conquest, but at crucial moments in Roman history the upper and lower classes clashed over the way power should be shared.

According to tradition, seven kings ruled Rome in succession after its legendary foundation by Romulus and his brother Remus in 753 B.C., in the same period the city-states emerged in Greece. (Like all dates for events in early Roman history, we cannot be certain this one is absolutely accurate.) The Roman Republic was created around 509 B.C. when some disgruntled aristocrats expelled the last recorded king of Rome. The word *republic,* which the Romans used to describe the new political system these aristocrats established, comes from the Latin phrase *res publica* ("public property" or "commonwealth") and distinguishes this period (509–27 B.C.) from the era of the seven kings (753–509 B.C.).

Roman history is the story of the expansion of Rome's power far beyond its origins as a tiny settlement in central Italy. Starting as villagers with only a patch of territory to their name, the Romans eventually dominated Europe, North Africa, and the ancient Near East. From the sixth century B.C., Roman republican government distributed social, economic, and political power among the Roman people. By the late second century B.C., however, internal strife had weakened the republic, which began to disintegrate early in the first century B.C. as political violence escalated. During the middle of the first century B.C., ferocious conflicts brought anarchy to the streets of Rome and nearly paralyzed its government. The assassination of Julius Caesar in 44 B.C. ushered in a decade and a half of climactic political conflict and civil war that finally destroyed the republic. Augustus (63 B.C.–A.D. 14) eventually quelled the violence and by 27 B.C. had transformed Rome's republican government into what we call the Roman Empire.

IMPORTANT DATES

753 B.C. Rome founded under a monarchy

509 B.C. Roman Republic established

451–449 B.C. Formulation of the Twelve Tables, Rome's first written law code

264–241 B.C. First Punic War between Rome and Carthage

Late third century B.C. Appearance of Roman literature

218–201 B.C. Second Punic War between Rome and Carthage

149–146 B.C. Third Punic War between Rome and Carthage

91–87 B.C. Social War between Rome and its Italian allies

60 B.C. First Triumvirate of Julius Caesar, Pompey the Great, and Marcus Crassus

49–45 B.C. Civil war, with Caesar emerging the victor

44 B.C. Caesar appointed as dictator for life, assassinated in same year

beginning in 30 B.C., wrote the most extensive accounts of early Roman history. But these authors compiled their histories of Rome more than seven hundred years after Rome was founded. Inevitably, their interpretations of events that happened so long ago were colored by the concerns of their own time, the period during which the Romans were transforming their republic into an empire. Archaeological evidence adds only a limited amount of information to the conclusions of Livy and Dionysius. For these reasons, any reconstruction of early Roman and Italian history necessarily contains some unexplainable gaps, uncertainties, and educated guesses. Exactly how this tiny settlement grew into the greatest power in the Mediterranean region remains one of history's mysteries.

The Development of Early Rome

Trying to understand the history, chronology of events, and politics of early Rome is especially challenging because no contemporary written sources for this period exist. The Roman Livy (59 B.C.–A.D. 17) and his Greek contemporary, Dionysius of Halicarnassus, who lived in Rome for many years

The Geography of Early Rome

Geography certainly played a part in Rome's rise to greatness. Rome's location in central Italy gave the settlement access to fertile farmland and a nearby harbor on the Mediterranean Sea. The terrain of Italy is a jumble of plains, river valleys, hills, and mountains crowded into a narrow, boot-shaped

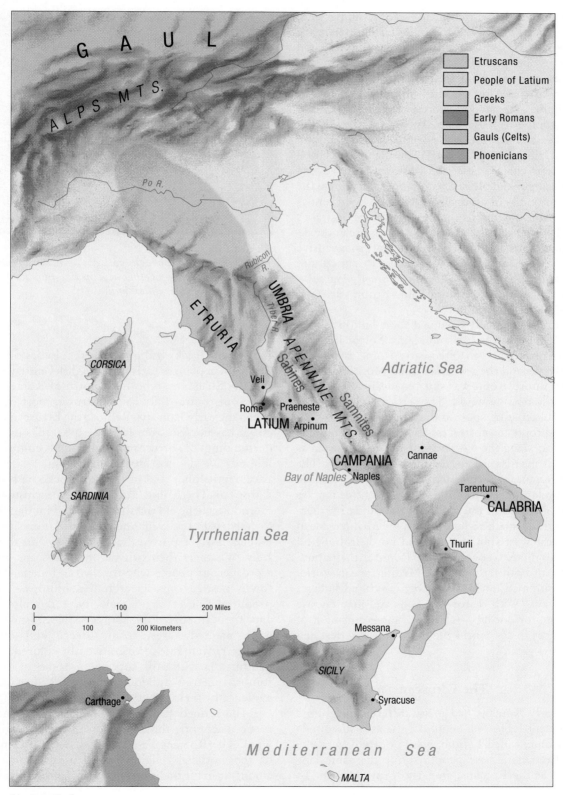

Ancient Italy

peninsula. A large, rich plain lies at its upper end, north of the Po River. Mountains farther north, the towering Alps, divide this plain from continental Europe and provide Italy a natural barrier that makes invasion from the north difficult. To the south of the Alps, another mountain range, the Apennines, separates the northern plain from central and southern Italy. The Apennines then snake southeastward through the peninsula like a knobby spine. Hills and small coastal plains flank this central mountain chain on east and west, with the western plains larger and blessed with more rainfall than the eastern ones. An especially fertile area, the Campanian plain, surrounds the Bay of Naples on Italy's southwestern coast. Compared to the relentlessly mountainous terrain of Greece, Italy's expansive plains were much more conducive to agriculture and animal husbandry. The more open geography of Italy also made political unification easier, at least on the physical level.

Rome originally occupied some hilltops above one of the western lowland plains. Fortunately for the farmers who inhabited early Rome, their land was fertile and their weather mild. Most important for its future, Rome was situated ideally for contact with the outside world. The settlement controlled a useful crossing spot on the Tiber River, astride a natural route for northwest-southeast land communication along the western side of the peninsula as well as northward along the river's valley. The Mediterranean Sea, offering numerous opportunities for trade and exploration, lay only fifteen miles west of Rome, at the mouth of the Tiber. Furthermore, Italy stuck so far out into the Mediterranean that east-west ship traffic could not help but find its way there. Geography put Rome at the natural center of both Italy and the Mediterranean world. Livy summed up Rome's geographical advantages this way: "With reason did gods and men choose this site for our city—all its advantages make it of all places in the world the best for a city destined to grow great."

The Etruscans

The early Romans had many different neighbors in ancient Italy. The people of the area surrounding Rome, called Latium, were poor villagers like the Romans. These people spoke the same language as the Romans, an early form of Latin. To

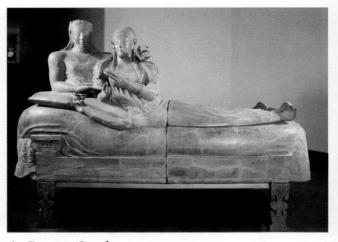

An Etruscan Couple
This terra-cotta sarcophagus portrays an Etruscan married couple reclining together at a meal, symbolizing the harmony of their union in life.

the south, Greeks had established colonies on the Campanian plain as early as the eighth century B.C. But the Etruscans, who lived north of Rome in a region of central Italy called Etruria, most influenced the early Romans. Because the Etruscan language has not yet been fully deciphered, our understanding of Etruscan origins and culture is limited. We do not know what language group Etruscan belongs to, but it seems not to be Indo-European. The fifth-century B.C. Greek historian Herodotus believed the Etruscans had immigrated to Italy from Lydia in Anatolia, but Dionysius of Halicarnassus reported they had always inhabited Italy. Whatever their origins, the Etruscans were a prosperous people who dwelled in independent towns nestled on central Italian hilltops. They produced fine art work, jewelry, and sculpture, and they imported luxurious objects, such as large painted vases, from Greece and other Mediterranean lands. Magnificently colored wall paintings, which still survive in some of their tombs, portray funeral banquets and games, evidence of their society's sophistication.

The refined Etruscans influenced their more rustic neighbors, the early Romans, in numerous ways. The Romans based many essential features of their official religion on Etruscan practices, among them the tradition of erecting temples divided

Etruscan-style Banqueting
This painting in an Etruscan tomb depicts couples reclining as they drink wine and converse. Pictures of musicians playing for the party decorated the adjoining wall.

into three sections for worshiping a triad of main gods: for the Romans, they were Jupiter, the king of the gods; Juno, the queen of the gods; and Minerva, the goddess of wisdom. The Romans also learned from the Etruscans the practice of divining the gods' will by looking for clues in the shapes of slaughtered animals' entrails (a process called haruspicy). Official divinations regularly preceded significant Roman public actions to ensure that the gods did not oppose the intended plan. Roman society even derived its fundamental social hierarchy—the patron-client system—from the Etruscan tradition by which people were obligated to each other as patrons (social superiors) and clients (social inferiors). The Roman convention of allowing women to join men for social gatherings probably also originated in Etruscan society. Tomb paintings confirm what Aristotle reported: respectable Etruscan women participated in banquets, apparently in an equal position with the men who attended, not in some subservient role. (In Greek society the only women who ever attended dinner parties with men were courtesans, hired musicians, and slaves.)

Rome's first political system, a monarchy, was also rooted in Etruscan precedents; Etruscan kings even ruled Rome for a time. And the Romans modeled their army, a citizen militia of heavily armed hoplites who fought in formation, on the Etruscan military. When Rome began to emerge from its early poverty and obscurity, many developments that fed its growth were grounded in Etruscan culture: the Greek alphabet (which the Romans learned from the Etruscans and used to write their own language); trade with other areas of the Mediterranean, which promoted economic growth; and sound civil engineering, which helped transform early Rome from a village to a complex, urban society.

The Political Background of the Republic

The distant ancestors of the Romans were Indo-European-speaking peoples who had migrated to Italy from the interior of Europe at an unknown date, certainly many centuries before Rome was founded. By the eighth century B.C., Romans lived in a small village of huts on Palatine Hill, one of the seven hills that eventually formed the heart of the city of Rome. The culture of the neighboring people of Latium so resembled that of Rome's early inhabitants that some Latin people had merged with the Romans in a loose political alliance. This first stage of Rome's growth foreshadowed the basic principle of its later expansion: incorporate certain outsiders into the Roman state by giving them political rights, and in some cases by making them Roman citizens. This process of integration contrasted with the exclusionist policies of the Greek city-states and resulted in some ethnic diversity in early Rome.

Slaves in Rome had an opportunity for upward social mobility, a condition unusual in the ancient world. Although Roman slaves were chattel slaves, like those in Greece, slaves freed by Roman citizens received Roman citizenship if they could acquire enough money to buy their freedom or if they were manumitted in their owner's will. Freed slaves still owed special obligations to their former owners, and they were barred from holding Roman elective office or serving in Rome's legions. Otherwise these freedmen and freedwomen, as they were officially designated, had full civic rights, such as legal marriage. Children born to freedmen and freedwomen were granted citizenship without any limitations.

Rome's practice of expanding its territory by appropriation sometimes led to violence. The legend of the kidnapping of the Sabine women during the rule of Rome's first king illustrates that those who would not join Rome peaceably were often forced. As Livy tells the tale, when Romulus feared Rome would wither because it lacked enough women to marry the village's men and bear children to increase the population, he sent envoys to all the surrounding peoples to ask for the right of intermarriage. The ambassadors were instructed to say that although Rome was only a tiny hamlet, the gods had granted it a brilliant future and Rome's more prosperous neighbors should not disdain an alliance with this people of destiny. Everyone refused the Roman request. Romulus therefore invited Rome's neighbors to a religious festival, to which the Sabine men and their wives and children came from their villages just northeast of Rome. By prearrangement, Rome's men kidnapped the unmarried Sabine women and fought off attacks launched to rescue them. Romulus told the women they would be cherished as beloved wives, and the men of Rome married the captives, who became citizens. A massive Sabine counterattack on Rome resulted in a bloody battle that halted only when the Sabine women rushed between the warring men. They implored their new husbands, the Romans, and their parents and brothers, the Sabines, either to

cease the slaughter or kill them on the spot to end the war. The men thereupon made peace and agreed to merge their populations under Roman rule. Besides showing the potential for violence inherent in Rome's policy of expansion through assimilation, this legendary story exemplifies Rome's self-image as a military power destined to rule.

Tensions could arise even when immigrants joined the Roman state peacefully. Another legend of early Rome recounts that the fifth king of Rome, named Tarquin the Elder, was an Etruscan whose wife, Tanaquil, prodded him to emigrate from Etruria to make their fortune in the new city. There he became an adviser to the king and then his successor, reaching the throne peacefully. But Tarquin was murdered in a political power struggle. Tanaquil acted boldly, however, and secured the crown for her son-in-law. This story symbolized the opportunities for immigrants to early Rome and perhaps prompted many to move there. Where else in the ancient world could a foreigner resettle and become king of his new community? Tarquin's unfortunate demise, however, suggested that some Romans strongly disapproved of having an Etruscan rule them.

In the period of the kings (753–509 B.C.), Rome became a large settlement for its time, but hardly glorious. People lived in thatched-roof huts on the hills of Rome surrounding an open area at the foot of the hills called the forum. Using Etruscan engineering techniques, the Romans in the sixth century B.C. drained this formerly marshy section so the land could be used as the public center of their emerging city. Coincidentally, the Romans created the forum at about the same time the Athenians fashioned the agora, the open, public center of their growing city. By this time the Romans controlled some three hundred square miles of Latium, enough agricultural land to support a population of thirty thousand to forty thousand people.

The later kings of Rome clashed with the city's upper class. These rich aristocratic families resented the monarchy's power and authority. The kings, in turn, feared that a powerful aristocrat might try to overthrow them. The aristocrats were especially disturbed by the monarchy's general popularity. To secure allies against their upper-class rivals, the kings had cultivated support from citizens possessing enough wealth to furnish their own weapons

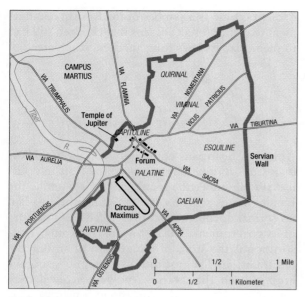

Early Rome

king on the Romans after Tarquin the Proud had been deposed. As Livy told the story, Horatius, while blocking the enemy's access to Rome over the bridge crossing the Tiber River, berated the Etruscans as slaves who had lost their freedom because they were ruled by haughty kings. For upper-class Romans, a compelling reason to install a new system of government—the republic—was to make one-man rule impossible.

The Struggle of the Orders

The republic as a system of government evolved slowly. After expelling Tarquin the Proud, the Romans took more than two hundred years to work out a stable arrangement for society and politics. Turmoil between the elite (called the patricians) and the rest of Rome's citizen population (the plebeians), the republic's two "orders" in Roman parlance, marked these centuries. Historians refer to this period as "the struggle of the orders."

A clear picture of this conflict eludes us, as it did the Roman historians we depend on for our information about early Rome. We do know that patricians were privileged citizens and that the only way to become a patrician was to be born to the right family: certain families were patrician, and no others could achieve this status. Patricians constituted only a tiny percentage of the population but nearly monopolized the secular and religious offices of early republican government; they were usually extremely wealthy as well. Patrician men were early Rome's social and political leaders, and they often controlled large bands of followers. A recently discovered inscription to the war god Mars, for example, says that "the comrades of Publius Valerius" erected the monument. These men designated themselves followers of the patrician Valerius rather than Roman citizens, even in a dedication to a national deity. Another patrician family, the Fabians, was able to raise a private army from among its many followers to fight against the neighboring town of Veii in 479 B.C. when no general militia force could be assembled. Patricians proudly advertised their status. In the early republic they wore red shoes to set themselves apart. Later they changed to the black shoes worn by all senators but adorned them with a small metal crescent to mark their special station.

but not enough money or social standing to count as members of the upper class. However, public support did not save King Tarquin the Proud, the seventh and last king of Rome. In 509 B.C. aristocrats deposed him, ostensibly for a vicious crime his son committed: the rape at knifepoint of Lucretia, a virtuous Roman woman. Despite pleas from her husband and father not to blame herself, Lucretia committed suicide after denouncing her attacker. Lucretia subsequently became a kind of martyr, an example of the ideal Roman woman: chaste, courageous, and honorable, preferring death to any possible sullying of her moral reputation. This story also illustrates the double standard Roman men held regarding women: foreign women, such as the Sabines, could be kidnapped and coerced into forced marriages, but the rape of a woman of their own class was cause for moral outrage.

Labeling themselves liberators, the aristocrats who ousted Tarquin the Proud abolished the monarchy on the grounds that crimes such as the rape of Lucretia sprang from rule by one man, which they equated with tyranny. The distrust of monarchy became a central feature of the aristocratic republic and was enshrined in the famous legend of the Roman warrior Horatius, who single-handedly held off an Etruscan bid to reimpose a

Economic and social issues fueled the struggle between the patricians and the plebeians. Most plebeians wanted more land for farming and relief from the crushing debts that the poor among them incurred just to survive. The patricians, on the other hand, tried to protect their privileges by walling themselves off socially from the plebeians. No matter how rich a plebeian family was (and some were), it could not rival a patrician family in prestige. The patricians even banned intermarriage between the orders as a tactic for sustaining their social exclusion.

To force change in such matters as intermarriage, the plebeians periodically resorted to drastic measures. More than once, disputes became so bitter that they physically withdrew from the city to a temporary settlement on a neighboring hill, and the men refused to serve in the army. This tactic of secession worked because it depleted the city's military strength. The patricians, numbering only some one hundred thirty families in the early republic, could not defend Rome by themselves and were obliged to compromise with the plebeians. Over time the two orders hammered out a series of written laws to guarantee the plebeians more political clout and upward social mobility. The earliest code of Roman law, called the Twelve Tables, was enacted between 451 and 449 B.C. in response to a plebeian secession. The Twelve Tables encapsulated the prevailing legal customs of early Rome's agricultural society in simply worded provisions such as, "If plaintiff calls defendant to court, he shall go," and "If a wind causes a tree from a neighbor's farm to be bent and lean over your farm, action may be taken to have that tree removed." Although these laws did not make plebeians the social equals of patricians, they marked a turning point in the plebeians' struggle to obtain legal recognition and equality. In Livy's words, these laws prevented the patrician public officials who judged most legal cases from "arbitrarily giving the force of law to their own preferences." Emphasizing matters such as disputes over property, the Twelve Tables demonstrated the Romans' overriding interest in civil law. Roman criminal law never became extensive, so courts never had a full set of rules to guide their verdicts in all cases. Magistrates decided most cases without juries. Trials before juries became common only in the late republic of the second and first centuries B.C. So important did the Twelve

Tables become as a symbol of the Roman commitment to justice for all citizens that children still had to memorize its laws four hundred years later.

The Roman Constitution

Although historians commonly use the term *Roman Constitution* in referring to the Roman political system under the republic, Rome—unlike the United States with its written constitution—had no formal document that prescribed the structure of its government. The history of the Roman constitution is the story of the growth of an unwritten tradition. The institutions of republican government and their various powers evolved over time through trial and error, and in some cases duties and responsibilities overlapped among institutions or were divvied up piecemeal among them. Different assemblies having a variety of structures elected magistrates and made policy decisions according to their own rules, contributing to the complex messiness of Roman republican government. One feature was clearcut, however: as in Greece, the Roman tradition of public life excluded women from formal participation. Only men could vote or hold political office.

The Consuls and the Senate

From the beginning of the republic, two elected magistrates, later called consuls, shared the highest state office. Consuls held office for only a year and were not supposed to serve consecutive terms. Having two magistrates serve annual terms prevented what Roman aristocrats detested in monarchies: the continued concentration of political authority in the hands of one person. The kings of Rome, in truth, had not customarily made important decisions by themselves but had acted only after consulting with a body of advisers. The tradition that government officials should seek advice continued under the republic. The highest magistrates consulted a body called the Senate, which had 300 members during most of the republic. (The general and politician Sulla increased the membership to 600 as part of his reforms in 81 B.C., Julius Caesar raised it to 900 in the mid-40s B.C., and

Augustus brought it back to 600 by 13 B.C.) Originally, the kings had chosen senators from among Rome's most distinguished men. Under the republic, the highest magistrates at first selected senators from the pool of patricians and plebeians who had previously served as lesser magistrates. Two magistrates of high prestige, called censors, later chose senators from the same group. The censors could also expel men from the senate for alleged immoral conduct; all they needed to do to remove a senator was to place a black dot opposite his name on the roll. In time the Senate exerted tremendous influence over republican domestic and foreign policy, state finance, official religion, and all types of legislation. Senators were especially involved in decisions about declaring and conducting wars. Because republican Rome fought wars almost continually, this Senate function was critical.

The Senate's influence stemmed not from any constitutional right to legislate, but solely from its members' social status. The senators could not enact laws, only advise the republic's magistrates, signaling either their consent to or disapproval of various courses of action. No official power compelled the magistrates to heed the senators' wishes. But the unwritten yet understood code that governed the relationship between the senators and the magistrates, which also reflected the essence of Roman politics and society, demanded that the magistrates comply with the senators' recommendations. The senators' high social status gave their opinions the force—even if not the form—of law. Any magistrate who refused the Senate's "advice" found his political career in severe jeopardy. And since magistrates aspired to become members of the Senate, they could ill afford to offend that body. Senators were not shy about advertising their social status: their black, high-top shoes and tunics embroidered with a broad, purple stripe made them highly visible.

The Senate decided what advice to offer in an ostensibly democratic procedure—majority vote of the members. Even in senatorial democracy, however, status counted. Before a vote the most distinguished senator had the right to express his opinion first. The other senators then followed in descending order of prestige. The opinions of the most eminent, usually older senators carried great weight. Only a junior senator who did not aspire to being a senior senator would dare give an opinion that differed from theirs.

The Course of Offices

Republican Rome had a roster of annually elective offices. These offices were ranked according to their prestige in what is called the *cursus honorum* ("course of offices"). After 337 B.C. all offices were open equally to patricians and wealthy plebeians. Various assemblies elected men to these posts. An ambitious and successful Roman man would climb this ladder by winning election to one post after another, each more important than the preceding one. After up to ten years of service on military campaigns as a young man, he would begin by seeking the lowest of the chief annual offices, that of *quaestor.** This post in financial administration was usually filled by a man in his late twenties or early thirties; his duties involved overseeing revenues and payments for the treasury in the capital, for commanders on campaign, and in the overseas provinces Rome established beginning in the third century B.C. Eventually, laws set minimum age requirements for the various offices. After Sulla in 81 B.C. prescribed strict regulations for progress through the *cursus honorum,* a man who had been a quaestor was automatically eligible to be chosen as a senator when a place opened up in the Senate.

A Roman man aspiring to higher office would often seek election as an *aedile* after serving as a quaestor. Aediles had the irksome duty of looking after Rome's streets, sewers, temples, markets, and the like. After either his quaestorship or his aedileship, if he served one, a man sought election as a *praetor,* a prestigious magistracy whose responsibilities included the administration of justice. With fewer praetorships than quaestorships (the number of both changed over time), competition for them was fierce, and only men of wealth and high social status could proceed directly from quaestor to praetor. The praetorship's distinction came mainly from the praetors' role as commanders of military forces when needed. Military success, like high birth and wealth, won a man status in Roman society. Only those who achieved the highest status could hope to become a *consul,* the epitome of social and political success under the republic. Consuls were older men; according to Sulla's regulations they were supposed to be at least forty-two years old. The two consuls had a voice in every important matter of state and served as the supreme commanders of Roman armies in the field. Like praetors,

* <u>KWĔS̬TOR</u>

their military power could extend beyond their one-year term of office if they were needed to command abroad. Ex-magistrates on these tours of duty were called *propraetors* and *proconsuls.* Their special grant of power ended when they returned to Rome.

During their term of office, consuls and praetors were endowed with a power called *imperium* (from which comes our word *empire*). It was imperium that gave them the right to demand Roman citizens to obey their orders and to command an army on military expeditions. It also bestowed the official right to perform the rites of divination called *auspicia* (auspices), another Etruscan legacy to Rome. Roman tradition required consuls and praetors to use the auspices to discern the gods' will concerning significant public events such as elections, inaugurations, a magistrate's entrance into a province, and military operations.

Finally, the Roman government included two special, nonannual magistrates, *censors* and *dictators.* Every five years, two censors were elected to serve

for eighteen months. Censors were ex-consuls, elder statesmen with the exceptional prestige and wisdom necessary to carry out their crucial duties. They conducted a census of all male Roman citizens and the amount of their property, so male citizens could be classified for conscription and taxes levied. The censors decided who would fill openings in the Senate, and they would strike from its rolls any man they believed to have behaved immorally. They also supervised state contracts and oversaw the renewal of official prayers to ensure the gods' goodwill toward the Roman people.

The office of dictator was the sole instance of one-man rule sanctioned by Roman tradition. Chosen by the Senate on rare occasions to lead the republic at times of extreme crisis, such as a military emergency, a dictator had absolute power to make decisions. His term of office, however, was six months at the most. The most famous dictator was Cincinnatus. His conduct as dictator in 458 B.C. epitomized the Roman ideal of selfless public service: in only sixteen days he defeated an enemy threat-

Roman Expansion, 500–44 B.C.

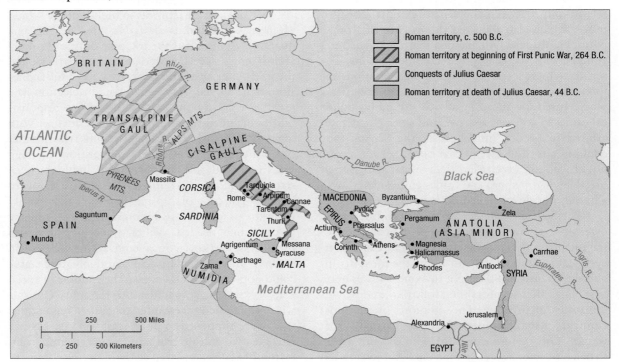

ening Rome and then immediately laid down his supreme power to return to his former existence as a farmer working a modest plot with his own hands.

In republican Rome, as in ancient Greece, the only honorable and desirable career for a man of high social standing was holding public office, or as we might label it, a career in government. Public office added to a successful man's social status. Following Etruscan tradition, Roman men displayed their status obviously. For example, twelve attendants preceded a consul wherever he went. Each attendant, called a *lictor,* carried the *fasces,* the symbol of the consul's imperium. Inside the city limits the fasces consisted of a bundle of sticks to symbolize the consul's right to beat citizens who disobeyed his orders; outside the city an ax was added to the sticks to signify his right to execute disobedient soldiers in the field. Lictors also accompanied praetors, who also had imperium; but praetors had only six lictors instead of twelve, indicating that they had less status than the consuls.

The value of a public career had nothing to do with earning money, at least not in the early republic. In fact, Roman officials earned no salaries. On the contrary, they were expected to spend their own money, supplemented by that of family and friends, on their careers. Roman political expenses could be crushing. Candidates spent large sums, their own or borrowed, to win popular support by entertaining the electorate, for example, with lavish shows that featured gladiators (trained fighters) and wild beasts, such as lions and tigers imported from Africa. Financing such exhibitions could put a candidate deeply in debt. Once in office a magistrate had to pay for public works such as roads, aqueducts, and temples that benefited the whole populace, fulfilling the expectation that a public officeholder would serve the common good. Their rewards were originally only the status their positions carried and the esteem they could win by meritorious service to the republic. But as the Romans gradually came to control more and more overseas territory through warfare, the opportunity to make money became an increasingly important component of a public career. Magistrates could enrich themselves legitimately with booty gained while commanding in successful foreign wars. While administering the Roman provinces created from conquered territory,

less scrupulous magistrates extorted money and other valuables from the local people and financed their political careers with these profits of war.

The Assemblies

The free, adult male citizens of Rome met in outdoor gatherings called assemblies to pass laws, hold certain trials, and elect magistrates. Roman tradition required assemblies to be summoned by a magistrate, held only on days proper under religious law, and sanctioned by favorable auspices. Assembly members voted only on matters presented by the magistrates, whose proposals could not be amended. Women were barred from the assemblies, where voting took place, but like noncitizens they could attend (but not speak at) the public discussion meeting, called a *contio,* that preceded assemblies. All official policy debates were supposed to occur at the *contio.* The presiding magistrate decided which assembly members could speak at a *contio* and thus could guide the course of the debate. Nevertheless, the *contio* provided an opportunity for those excluded from voting to express their approval or disapproval of issues by their reactions to the speakers' remarks.

The organizational complexity of the major republican assemblies almost defies description. The most significant point about the assemblies is that the members voted in groups; that is, the men in the various assemblies were divided into groups according to criteria particular to each assembly and voted within these groups. The members of a group cast their individual votes to determine their group's single vote. Each group's single vote, regardless of the number of members in the group, counted the same in determining the assembly's decision by simple majority vote. In other words, the one-man, one-vote principle applied only within groups.

Group voting severely limited the democracy of the assemblies. The Centuriate Assembly offers the clearest example of the effects of this procedure. This important assembly elected censors, consuls, and praetors; enacted laws; declared war and peace; and could inflict the death penalty. The groups in this assembly, called *centuries* (hence the assembly's name), were meant to correspond to the divisions of the male citizens when they were drawn up as an army. As in the city-states of archaic and classical Greece, early Rome relied not on a standing army financed by taxes but on a citizen militia, in which every male citizen armed himself at his own expense as best he could. This principle of national defense through individual contributions meant that the richer citizens had more and better weapons than did the poorer, more numerous citizens. Consequently, the rich were seen as deserving more power in the assembly, to reflect their greater military expenses. In line with this principle, cavalrymen, who incurred the highest military costs, made up the first 18 groups of the assembly. The following 170 groups consisted of foot soldiers ranked in property classes from highest to lowest according to the amount of their expenditure. The next 5 groups comprised noncombatants. Some of these were military engineers of higher status, but the last group, the proletarians, was composed of those too poor to afford military arms and thus barred from serving as soldiers. All they contributed to the state were their offspring (their *proles,* hence the word *proletarian*).

In essence, the groups of the Centuriate Assembly corresponded to the distribution of wealth in Roman society. Far more men belonged to the groups at the bottom of the social hierarchy than to those at the top. The proletarians, for example, formed the largest group. But their group still had only one vote. The groups voted in order from richest to poorest, and the polling ended as soon as a majority had been reached. The voting procedure in the Centuriate Assembly allowed the rich to vote as a block and thus muster a majority of group votes well before the voting reached the groups of the poor. When the elite voted together, the Centuriate Assembly could make a decision without the wishes of the lower classes ever being heard.

The Tribal Assembly also voted by groups. Roman men were divided into groups, called tribes, according to where they lived. The structuring of the tribes gave wealthy rural landowners disproportionate influence. In its original form the Tribal Assembly excluded patricians. Meeting as the Tribal Assembly of the Plebeians, the assembly conducted nearly every form of public business, including holding trials. In 287 B.C. its resolutions, called *plebiscites,* were officially recognized as laws, making it a principal source of Roman legislation.

The recognition of these "resolutions of the plebs" as legally binding ended the struggle of the orders because it formalized the power of the people in helping set policy and define Roman justice. Later, the Tribal Assembly could also meet in a second form that included patricians as well as plebeians. When convened in this form it was called the Tribal Assembly of the People and elected the quaestors, the two curule aediles (the aedileships of the highest prestige, originally open only to patricians), and the six senior officers of each army legion (called military tribunes). The Tribal Assembly of the People also enacted laws and held minor trials.

The Tribal Assembly of the Plebeians elected the plebeian aediles and, most important, the ten *tribunes,* special and powerful magistrates devoted to protecting the plebeians' interests. As plebeians themselves, tribunes derived their power not from official statutes but from the sworn oath of the plebeians to protect them against all attacks. This inviolability of the tribunes, called sacrosanctity, allowed them the right to *veto* (a Latin word meaning "forbid") other tribunes and to intercede in other government bodies and with other officials on behalf of the plebeians. Tribunes could use their power to block the actions of magistrates, prevent the passage of laws, suspend elections, and counter the advice of the Senate. Their clout, derived from the threat of a plebeian secession, gave tribunes an extraordinary potential to influence Roman government. Tribunes who tried to exercise their full powers could become the catalysts for bitter political disputes, and the office itself became controversial because tribunes sometimes seemed to operate with scant regard for the Senate's wishes.

The republic's political system, with its jumbled network of offices and assemblies, lacked an overall structure to consolidate it. Many different political bodies enacted laws, or in the Senate's case, opinions that amounted to laws. Yet Rome had no judicial body, such as the U.S. Supreme Court, that could resolve disputes about the validity of conflicting laws. The republic's political well-being and stability did not depend on clearly defined institutions of government but rather on a reverence for tradition, the "way of the elders [or ancestors]." This reliance on tradition ensured that the most socially prominent and the richest Romans dominated government—because the "way of the elders" was their way.

Roman Social Institutions

Social institutions that reflected the Roman tradition of deriving power from social status supported Rome's developing political system. A complex social hierarchy that subordinated clients to patrons but also obligated the patron to the client bolstered political relationships. Roman family life was legally based on the father's overwhelming authority, but in practice his power was limited by the expectation that he would consult others before making important decisions. Education was intended primarily for males and designed to make them good citizens. Similarly, the public cults of Roman religion supported the goals of the republic.

The Client-Patron System

The client-patron system institutionalized the differences in status so key in Roman society. A patron was a man of superior status who could provide *kindnesses,* as they were officially called, to those people of lower status who paid him special attention. These were his clients, who in return for his kindnesses owed him *duties.* Patrons could also be the clients of still more distinguished men, just as clients could be the patrons of those below them in the social hierarchy. Under this pervasive system, Roman society developed an interlocking network of personal relationships that obligated people to each other. These obligations were binding. The Twelve Tables, for example, declared any patron who defrauded his client an outlaw. The Romans regarded the client-patron relationship as one of friendship with clearly defined roles for each party. A sensitive patron would greet a client as "my friend," not as "my client." A client, on the other hand, would honor his patron by addressing him as "my patron."

The client's duties included supporting his patron financially and politically. In early Rome tradition dictated that a client had to help fund dowries for his patron's daughters. A client could also be called upon to lend money to his patron when the latter was a magistrate and incurred large expenses in providing the public works expected of him in office. In political life a client was expected to aid in the election campaign when his patron or one of his patron's friends sought a magistracy. Clients could be especially helpful in swinging votes to their patrons' side in the elections that took place in the two forms of the Tribal Assembly. Furthermore, because it was a mark of great status for a patron to have numerous clients surrounding him like a swarm of bees, the patron expected his clients to gather at his house early in the morning and accompany him to the forum. A Roman aristocrat needed a large, fine house to hold his throng of clients and to entertain his social equals, and a crowded house signified social success.

Patrons' kindnesses to their clients took various forms. By the time of the empire, the patron was supposed to provide a picnic basket of food for the breakfast of his clients who clustered on his doorstep at daybreak. Under the republic, a patron might help a client get started in a political career by supporting his candidacy or might provide financial support from time to time. A patron's most important kindness was the obligation to support a client and his family if they got into legal difficulties, such as in lawsuits involving property, which were common. People of lower social status had a distinct disadvantage in the Roman judicial system if they lacked influential friends to help protect their interests. The aid of a patron well versed in public speaking was particularly needed, because in court both accusers and accused either had to speak for themselves or have friends speak for them. Rome had no state-sponsored prosecutors or defenders, nor any lawyers to hire. Priests monopolized knowledge of the law and customary procedures until the third century B.C. By that time, however, prominent men known to be experts on law, called jurists, had begun to play a central role in the Roman judicial system. Although jurists frequently developed their expertise by serving in Roman elective office, they operated as private citizens, not officials, in their role of giving legal advice to other citizens and magistrates. The reliance on jurists, a distinctive feature of Roman republican justice, endured under the empire.

The mutual obligations that constituted a client-patron relationship were supposed to be stable and long lasting. In many cases client-patron ties would endure over generations. Ex-slaves, who automatically became the clients for life of the masters who had manumitted them, often passed on to their children their relationship with the patron's family. Romans with contacts abroad could acquire clients among foreigners; particularly distinguished and wealthy Romans sometimes had entire foreign communities as their clients. With its emphasis on duty and permanence, the client-patron system epitomized the Roman view that social stability and well-being were achieved by faithfully maintaining the ties that linked people to one another. This view reflected a central concept in Roman morality, that of *fides* (from which our word *fidelity* derives), the trustworthy honoring of the web of various obligations among people that defined so much of Roman public and private life.

Power in Roman Families

Republican Rome was a patriarchal society, and under Roman law the father of the family possessed the *patria potestas* ("power of a father") over his children, no matter how old, and his slaves. *Patria potestas* made the father the sole owner of all the property acquired by anyone in the household. As long as their father was alive, no son or daughter could own anything, accumulate money, or possess any independent legal standing—in theory at least. In practice, however, adult children could acquire personal property and money, much as favored slaves might build up some savings. By law the father also held power of life and death over these members of the household. However, fathers rarely exercised this power on anyone except infants. Exposing unwanted babies, so that they would die, be adopted, or be raised as slaves by strangers, was an accepted practice to control the size of families and dispose of physically imperfect infants. Statistics on exposure of infants are lacking, but baby girls suffered this fate more often than boys—a family enhanced its power more by investing its resources in its sons.

Few fathers contemplating the drastic decision to execute an adult member of their household would have made the decision completely on their own. As in government, where senators advised the magistrates, or in legal matters, where jurists shared their expertise, Romans in private life regularly conferred with others on important family issues to seek a consensus. Each Roman man had his own circle of friends and relatives, his "council," whom he consulted before making significant decisions. In this way decision making in the Roman family resembled the process in the Roman republic. A father's council of friends would certainly have advised him to think again if he proposed killing his adult son except for an extremely compelling reason. For example, one outraged father had his son put to death in 63 B.C. because his son had committed treason by joining a conspiracy to overthrow the government. Such violent exercises of a father's power happened rarely.

A wife also lived under her husband's power unless her marriage agreement specifically prohibited it. By the late republic "free" marriages were by far the most common. In free marriages the wife remained in her father's power as long as he lived. But probably few aged fathers actually controlled the lives of their mature, married daughters: because so many people died young in the ancient world, few fathers survived long enough to oversee the lives of their adult daughters. By the time most Roman women married, in their late teens, half of them had already lost their fathers. Because males generally did not marry until their late twenties, by the time they married and formed their own household, only one man in five still had a living father. Like a son whose father had died, an adult woman without a living father was relatively independent. Legally she needed a male guardian to conduct business for her, but the guardianship of adult women was primarily an empty formality by the first century B.C. A later jurist commented on women's freedom of action even under a guardian: "the common belief, that because of their instability of judgment women are often deceived and that it is only fair to have them controlled by the authority of guardians, seems more specious than true. For women of full age manage their affairs themselves."

Women grew up fast in Roman society. Tullia (c. 79–45 B.C.), the daughter of the famous politician and orator Cicero (106–43 B.C.), was engaged at twelve, married at sixteen, and widowed by twenty-two. Women of wealth often led busy lives. They oversaw the household slaves, monitored the nurturing of their young children by wet nurses, accompanied their husbands to dinner parties, and often kept account books to track the property they personally owned. Wealthy men spent much of their time outside the house visiting friends or pursuing public careers, but they used their homes extensively to meet with and entertain their circle of clients and friends.

Children played at home or in the streets, and their education, if their family could afford formal schooling, was provided by tutors at home or in the quarters of private teachers. A mother's power in shaping the moral outlook of her children was especially valued in Roman society and constituted a major component of female virtue. Women like Cornelia, an aristocrat of the second century B.C. and mother of two famous tribunes, the Gracchus brothers, won enormous respect for their accomplishments both in raising outstanding citizens and managing property. When her distinguished husband died, Cornelia refused an offer of marriage from the Ptolemaic king of Egypt so she could oversee the family estate and educate her daughter and two sons. Her other nine children had died. The number of children she bore exemplifies the fertility and stamina required of a Roman wife to ensure the survival of her husband's family line. Cornelia was renowned for entertaining important people and for her stylish letters, which were still being read a century later. Her sons, Tiberius and Gaius Gracchus, grew up to be among the most influential—and controversial—politicians of the late republic.

Recent archaeological discoveries suggest that by the end of the republic some women owned large businesses, such as brick-making companies. Because both women and men could control property, prenuptial agreements to outline the rights of both partners in the marriage were common. Legally, divorce was a simple matter, with fathers

A Mother's Gift
This bronze urn for holding toilet articles dates from the end of the fourth century B.C. and bears two inscriptions: "Dindia Malconia gave this to her daughter" and "Novios Plautios made me in Rome." Its engraving shows scenes from the story of the Argonauts.

A Roman Food Store
This sculpture shows a woman selling food in a store. Roman women could own property, and this woman may have been the shop's owner.

usually keeping the children after the dissolution of a marriage. Most poor women, like poor men, had to toil for a living, but few occupations allowed women. Usually they had to settle for jobs selling things in small shops or from stands. Even if their families produced crafts, the predominant form of producing goods in the Roman economy, women normally sold rather than made the goods the family manufactured. The men in these families usually worked the raw materials and finished the goods. Those women with the worst luck or from the poorest families often ended up as prostitutes. Prostitution was legal, but prostitutes were regarded with contempt. Roman law forbade female prostitutes to wear a *stola,* the long robe reserved for married women, to signal their lack of chastity: they therefore wore the outer garment of men, the toga.

Women in the mainstream of Roman society could wield political influence. Nevertheless, the impact even wealthy Roman women had on politics was almost exclusively indirect, through their influence on their husbands and male children and relatives outside the household. Women seem to have participated in very few public demonstrations in the course of republican history, and they apparently were well-off women protesting limits imposed on their riches and display of status. For example, in 215 B.C., at the height of a wartime financial crisis, the tribune Oppius had a law passed forbidding women from possessing more than a half ounce of gold, wearing multicolored clothing in public, or riding in horse-drawn carriages within a mile of Rome or other Roman towns except for public religious events. His measure presumably was intended to quiet public discontent over resources controlled by wealthy women at a time when the republic faced an acute need for funds, even though the Senate had required women to contribute to the war's expenses two years earlier. In 195 B.C., after the war, the women affected by Oppius's law successfully rallied to have the restrictions lifted. They forced the political men of Rome to rescind the law by pouring out into the streets of Rome to express their demands to the magistrates and besiege the houses of the two tribunes who had been using their veto power to block repeal. Even this dramatic exception to the ordinary public behavior of Roman women shows that they could exercise political power only through their effect on the male citizens who controlled politics. Cato (234–149 B.C.), a

famous senator and author who had bitterly opposed the repeal of Oppius's law, hinted at the limited reality of women's power in public life with a biting comment directed at his fellow politicians: "All mankind rule their wives, we rule all mankind, and our wives rule us."

The Goals of Roman Education for Public Life

As in Greece, only well-to-do families could afford formal education for their children. If parents in the many crafts-producing families knew how to read, write, and do simple calculations, then they could pass that knowledge on to their children, who labored alongside them. Roman children of wealthier families customarily received their basic education at home. In the early republic, parents did the educating, at least until the children reached the age of seven, when they might be sent to classes offered by independent schoolmasters in their lodgings. Fathers carefully instructed their sons in the rudiments of masculine virtue, especially physical training, fighting with weapons, and courage. If the slaves purchased to tend children were literate, they helped educate them (a practice derived from Greece). Girls usually received less training than boys, but in upper-class households both girls and boys learned to read. Repetition was the usual teaching technique, with corporal punishment frequently used to keep pupils attentive. Aristocratic girls would be taught literature, perhaps some music, and the basics of making conversation (for dinner parties). A principal aim of the education of women was to prepare them for the important role Roman mothers were expected to play in instilling respect for Roman social and moral traditions in their children.

Rhetoric—the skill of persuasive public speaking—dominated an upper-class Roman boy's curriculum because it was crucial to a successful public career. To win elections, a man had to persuade men to vote for him; to win legal cases, he had to speak effectively in the courts, where lawsuits were the vehicle for building political coalitions and fighting personal feuds. A boy would hear rhetorical techniques in action by accompanying his father, a male relative, or a family friend to public meetings, assemblies, and court sessions. By listening to the speeches he would learn to imitate winning techniques. Wealthy parents would also hire special teachers to instruct their sons in the skills and general knowledge an effective speaker requires. Roman rhetoric owed much to Greek rhetorical techniques, and many Roman orators studied with Greek teachers of rhetoric. When Roman textbooks on rhetoric began to be written in the second century B.C., they reflected material derived from Greek works.

Cicero was the republic's finest example of how far rhetorical skill could carry a man. His father paid for Cicero to leave home and study rhetoric in both Rome and Greece. There he developed the brilliant style of public speaking that allowed him to overcome his lack of prestige (his family came from a small Italian town rather than Rome). Cicero began his rhetorical career by defending men accused of crimes, a relatively safe debut for an unknown orator because defendants were grateful for such help and prosecutors usually did not retaliate against the defendants' supporters. Prosecution was far riskier because a man who lodged an accusation against a powerful pub-

lic figure could expect his target to seek revenge by bringing a countercharge. Cicero therefore electrified the Roman political community in 70 B.C. when his speech accusing Gaius Verres of flagrant corruption in office drove the ex-provincial governor into exile. In 63 B.C., Cicero achieved the pinnacle of success by being elected consul, the first man in decades from a family without consuls in its history to reach that office. Throughout his career, Cicero used his rhetorical skills to attempt to reconcile warring factions of aristocrats, and he became the speaker feared by more politicians than any other. Later orators studied his speeches, many of which he published after he had delivered them, to absorb the techniques of their carefully structured arguments, clarity of expression, and powerful imagery. Cicero also wrote influential treatises in which he explained his rhetorical doctrines and his belief that to be a good speaker a man had to develop moral excellence. Cicero heeded the advice he once received on the importance of rhetoric: "excel in public speaking. It is the tool for controlling men at Rome, winning them over to your side, and keeping them from harming you. You fully realize your own power when you are a man who can cause your rivals the greatest fears of meeting you in a trial."

Religion in the Interests of the State and Family

In the early republic the patricians who dominated political offices also controlled the public cults of Roman religion. But by 300 B.C. aristocratic plebeians began to serve as religious officials. Men and women from the top of the social hierarchy filled the priesthoods that directed official worship of the many Roman gods. The people who acted as priests and priestesses were not usually professionals who devoted their lives solely to religious activity; rather, they were fulfilling one aspect of a successful Roman's public life. As in Greek public religion, the duty of these directors of religion was to ensure the gods' goodwill toward the state, a crucial relationship the Romans called the *pax deorum* ("peace of/with the gods"). To maintain the gods' favor toward Rome, priests and priestesses conducted frequent festivals, sacrifices, and other rituals that conformed strictly with ancestral tradition. Because Rome came to house hundreds of shrines

Marcus Tullius Cicero
This bust of the famous orator Cicero portrays him as concerned but resolute.

and temples, these sacred activities required much time, energy, and expense. The most important board of priests, which had fifteen members for most of the republic's history, advised magistrates on their religious responsibilities as agents of the Roman state. The leader of this group, the *pontifex maximus* ("highest priest"), served as the head of state religion and the ultimate authority on religious matters affecting government. The political power of the *pontifex maximus* motivated Rome's most prominent men to seek the post, which by the third century B.C. was filled by a special election in the Tribal Assembly. Roman government and Roman public religion were inextricably intertwined. No official occasion could proceed without a preparatory religious ritual; the agenda of every Senate meeting began with any religious business; and commanders with imperium regularly sought to discern the will of the gods through various forms of divination.

Many religious festivals reflected the concerns of an agricultural community with an unstable future, the circumstances of early Rome. Roman religion traditionally sought to protect farming, the basis of the community's life. Prayers therefore commonly requested the gods' aid in ensuring good crops, warding off disease, and promoting healthy reproduction among domestic animals and people. In urgent times the Romans even sought foreign gods to protect them, such as when the government imported the cult of the healing god Asclepius from Greece in 293 B.C. hoping he would save Rome from a plague. Private individuals worshiped other foreign gods, such as the Greek god Dionysus, called Bacchus by the Romans. The worship of Bacchus stirred controversy because the cult's secret meetings aroused fears of potential political conspiracies. As long as foreign or new religious cults did not appear to threaten the stability of the state, however, they were permitted to exist and the government took no interest in their doctrines.

Official Roman religious rituals did not vary significantly over time because Romans felt that changing the customary honors paid to the gods was potentially offensive to them and thus hazardous to the community. The religion of the late republic preserved many ancient rituals, such as the Lupercalia festival. During its celebration, naked young men streaked around Palatine Hill, lashing any women they met with strips of goatskin. Women who had not yet borne children would run out to

be struck, believing this would help them become fertile. At the Saturnalia festival at the winter solstice, a time Christians much later in the Roman Empire adopted for Christmas, the social order temporarily turned topsy-turvy. As the playwright and scholar Accius (c. 170–80 B.C.) described the Saturnalia, "people joyfully hold feasts all through the country and the towns, each owner acting as a waiter to his slaves." The social inversion of masters and servants both released tensions caused by the inequalities of ordinary life and reinforced the slaves' ties to their owners by symbolizing kindness from the latter, which the former had to repay with faithful service.

Romans viewed their chief deity, Jupiter, who corresponded to the Greek god Zeus, as a powerful, stern father. Juno, queen of the gods, and Minerva, goddess of wisdom, joined Jupiter to form the central triad of the state cults, in imitation of Etruscan practice. These three deities shared Rome's most revered temple on Capitoline Hill. Worshipers offered them regular sacrifices as the protectors of the city—guarding Rome's physical safety and prosperity was their major function in Roman religion. These and the numerous other major gods of Roman public religion had only limited connections with human morality, with certain exceptions, such as Jupiter's responsibility to punish those who broke oaths. Roman tradition did not acknowledge the anthropomorphic gods as the primary originators of the society's moral code, in contrast, for example, to the Hebrew belief that Yahweh handed down the Ten Commandments and other laws governing human life. In the first century B.C., Cicero explained the general nature of Rome's official religion with this description of Jupiter's official titles: "We call Jupiter the Best (*Optimus*) and Greatest (*Maximus*) not because he makes us just or sober or wise but, rather, healthy and rich and prosperous."

Romans nevertheless incorporated a strict morality in their religious consciousness by regarding abstract moral qualities such as *fides* as special divine beings or forces. Also regarded as divine was *pietas* (a Latin word that provides the root of the English word *piety*). *Pietas* connoted a sense of devotion and duty—to family, to friends, to the republic, to keeping one's word. A temple to *pietas* dedicated in Rome in 181 B.C. housed a statue of this moral quality represented as a female divinity in anthropomorphic form. This personification of abstract moral qualities provided a focus for the rituals associated with their cults. Another revered quality was *virtus* (derived from the Latin word for *man—vir*; the root of the English word *virtue*), a primarily masculine value stressing courage, strength, and loyalty. But *virtus* also included wisdom and moral purity, qualities that aristocrats were expected to display in their public and private lives. In this broader sense *virtus* applied to women as well as men. The religious aura surrounding moral qualities emphasized that they were ideals to which every Roman should aspire.

The republic also supported the worship of many other special deities. The shrine of Vesta, the goddess of the hearth and therefore a protector of the family, housed the official eternal flame of Rome. The Vestal Virgins, six unmarried women sworn to chastity for terms of thirty years, tended Vesta's shrine. Their most important duty was to protect the flame, because as the historian Dionysius of Halicarnassus reported, "the Romans dread the extinction of the fire above all misfortunes, looking upon it as an omen which portends the destruction of the city." If a Vestal Virgin was convicted of a minor offense, the *pontifex maximus* publicly flogged her. Should the flame happen to go out, the Romans assumed one of the Vestal Virgins had broken her vow of chastity; a Vestal Virgin convicted of breaking that vow was carried on a funeral bier, as if a living corpse, to be entombed in an underground chamber, where she was walled up to die. Female chastity symbolized the safety and protection of the Roman family structure and thus the preservation of the republic itself.

Reverence for the cult of Vesta was only one way in which Roman religion was associated with the family as well as the state. As part of private religion, each Roman family maintained a sacred space in its home for small shrines housing its Penates (spirits of the pantry) and Lares (spirits of the ancestors), who were connected with keeping the family well and its moral traditions alive. The statuettes representing these family spirits signified the family's respect for its heritage, a commitment made explicit by the habit of hanging death masks of distinguished ancestors on the walls of the home's main room as reminders of the virtuous ideals of the family and the responsibility of the current generation to live up to ancestral standards. The strong sense of family tradition instilled by these practices and by instruction from parents (especially mothers) represented the principal

A Roman Household Shrine
This wooden cabinet, carved to resemble a temple, held statuettes of the gods worshiped in a Roman home, the Lares and Penates. Its lower section held glassware and ornaments.

source of Roman morality. The shame of losing public esteem by tarnishing this tradition, not the fear of divine punishment, was the strongest deterrent to immoral behavior.

Many other divine spirits were believed to participate in crucial moments in life, such as birth, marriage, and death. So pervasive was religious activity in Roman existence that special rituals accompanied activities as diverse and commonplace as breast-feeding babies and spreading manure to fertilize crops. People performed these rituals in search of protection from harm in a world fraught with dangers and uncertainties.

The Foreign Wars of the Republic

War and expansion propelled republican domestic and foreign policy and made conquest and military service central to the lives of Romans. During the fifth and fourth centuries B.C. the Romans fought war after war in Italy until Rome became the most powerful state on the peninsula. In the third and second centuries B.C. they fought wars far from home in the West, the North, and the East, but above all they battled Carthage, a powerful state in Africa (modern Tunisia). Their success in these campaigns made Rome the premier power in the Mediterranean.

Expansion in Italy

The Romans believed they were militarily successful because they respected the will of the gods. Reflecting on the earlier history of the republic, Cicero claimed, "we have overcome all the nations of the world, because we have realized that the world is directed and governed by the gods." Believing that the gods supported defensive wars as just, the Romans always insisted they fought only in self-defense. The most debated question about Roman expansion under the republic is the extent to which this claim was valid.

Rome and Central Italy After a victory over their Latin neighbors in 499 B.C., the Romans spent the next hundred years warring with the Etruscan town of Veii, a few miles north of the Tiber River. Their eventual victory in 396 B.C. doubled Roman territory. By the fourth century B.C. the Roman infantry legion had surpassed the Greek and

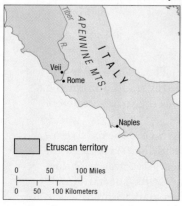

Etruscan territory

0   50   100 Miles
0   50   100 Kilometers

Macedonian phalanx as an effective fighting force. Its internal division into squads gave it greater mobility on the battlefield, and the open space left between soldiers gave them enough room to throw their spears and hack with their cut-and-thrust swords, specially designed for this formation. Even a devastating sack of Rome in 387 B.C. by marauding Gauls (Celts) from the distant north proved only a temporary check. By around 220 B.C. Rome controlled all of Italy south of the Po River.

The conduct of the wars of conquest in Italy was brutal. When the Romans won, they sometimes enslaved many of the defeated or forced them to give up large parcels of their land. Yet the Romans also regularly struck generous peace terms with former enemies. Some defeated Italians immediately became Roman citizens; others gained limited citizenship without the right to vote; still other communities received treaties of alliance. No conquered Italian peoples had to pay taxes to Rome. All, however, had to render military aid to the Romans in future wars. These new allies then received a share of the booty, chiefly slaves and land, that Rome and its allied armies seized on victorious campaigns against a new crop of enemies. In this way the Romans adroitly co-opted their former opponents by making them partners in the spoils of conquest, an arrangement that in turn enhanced Rome's wealth and authority.

To ensure the security of Italy, the Romans planted colonies of citizens throughout the country and constructed a network of roads up and down the peninsula. These roads connected the diverse peoples of Italy, hastening the creation of a more unified culture dominated by Rome. Latin, for example, came to be the common language. But Rome too was influenced by the new contacts. In southern Italy the Romans found sophisticated cities like Naples, which had been founded hundreds of years before by Greek colonists. Greek communities like Naples, too weak to resist Roman armies, were overpowered. But though Rome dominated them militarily, they never surrendered their artistic traditions. In fact the Greek traditions in art, music, and literature provided models for Roman developments in the arts. When in the late third century B.C., Roman authors began to record history for the first time, they imitated Greek forms and aimed at Greek readers, even to the point of writing in Greek.

VEII → VAY·ee

Rome's urban population grew tremendously during this period. By around 300 B.C. perhaps one hundred fifty thousand people lived within its walls. Newly built aqueducts funneled fresh water to this burgeoning population, and the plunder from successful wars financed a massive building program inside the city. Outside the city about seven hundred fifty thousand free Roman citizens inhabited various parts of Italy on land taken from the local peoples. Much conquered territory was declared public land, supposedly open to any Roman to use for grazing flocks. Many rich landowners, however, ended up controlling huge parcels of this land for their private benefit. This illegal monopolization of public land later created enormous strife between rich and poor.

The ranks of the rich included both patricians and plebeians, an alliance of the wealthy and politically successful that amounted to a new kind of upper class, a new kind of "order," exploiting the expanding Roman territories. They derived their wealth mainly from agricultural land and booty gained as officers in military expeditions. Rome levied no regular income or inheritance taxes, so financially prudent families could pass down this wealth from generation to generation. Families in the top social stratum in this new upper class consisted of those who at some point had a consul in the family. They called themselves "the nobles" in honor of this illustrious achievement. (Some historians think a praetor in the family also earned this status.) Rich Roman men with no consul on their family tree tried fervently to win election as consul to bestow nobility on themselves and their descendants.

The First and Second Punic Wars

The nobles, the elite of Roman society, dominated republican politics during the third and second centuries B.C. War preoccupied Roman government in this period. From 280 to 275 B.C. the Romans battled the forces of Pyrrhus (319–272 B.C.), the king of Epirus in northwest Greece, who had brought an army to southern Italy to aid the Greek city of Tarentum against Rome. Rome's alliance with another Greek city in southern Italy, Thurii, had drawn Roman forces into conflict with Tarentum, which feared the growing Roman involvement in its region. But the enemy Rome soon fo-

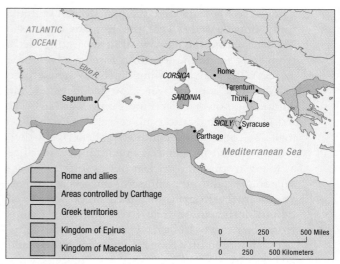

First Punic War

cused on was Carthage, a prosperous and sophisticated state located across the Mediterranean Sea in North Africa. Phoenicians had colonized Carthage (near modern Tunis) in the late ninth century B.C. The Romans therefore called the Carthaginians the *Punici*, their word for Phoenicians (hence the adjective *Punic*). Punic riches stemmed from large, well-managed agricultural estates and a thriving maritime commerce. Long experience at sea meant that the Carthaginians completely outstripped the Romans in naval capability. Rome and Carthage were both oligarchic republics, and for centuries they had maintained peaceful relations because their economic interests and political domains had not yet overlapped. But by the mid-third century B.C. the Romans, who had expanded their power to the southern tip of Italy's boot, came face to face with the power of Carthage, which had settlements on the islands of Sicily and Sardinia.

Hostilities between Rome and Carthage erupted in 264 B.C. over a petty local affair in the region where their respective spheres of power met. A beleaguered band of mercenaries in Messana at Sicily's northeastern tip appealed to both cities for help in settling a violent dispute there. The Roman senators disagreed about what to do, but a patrician consul, Appius Claudius, persuaded the people to demand a Sicilian expedition by raising hopes of lucrative conquest. The troops dispatched to Messana were the first Roman military foray outside Italy. That the Romans could see Messana across the narrow strait separating Sicily from Italy made the leap into foreign adventures easier. When Carthage simultaneously sent a force to Messana, a fierce war exploded between the competing powers. The First Punic War (264–241 B.C.) lasted a generation and revealed why the Romans so consistently conquered their rivals: they were prepared to spend as much money, sacrifice as many troops, and stick it out as long as necessary to prevail. In the course of this twenty-three-year war, the Romans and their allies persevered despite losing more than five hundred warships from their newly built navy and perhaps as many as two hundred fifty thousand men from their land and sea forces. The Greek historian Polybius, writing a century later, regarded the First Punic War as "the greatest war in history in its duration, intensity, and scale of operations."

At the end of the First Punic War the Romans were the masters of Sicily, a large island made prosperous by its fertile soil. Their domination of Sicily proved so profitable that in 238 B.C. the Romans seized the nearby islands of Sardinia and Corsica from the Carthaginians. In 227 B.C. the Romans turned Sicily into one overseas province and Sardinia and Corsica into another. Thus began the Roman provincial system. New praetors were created to serve as governors; their job was to keep the provinces peaceful and out of enemy hands. Roman provincial governors used local administrative arrangements. For example, in Sicily they collected the same taxes that the earlier Greek kingdom there had levied. The province's indigenous people did not become Roman citizens. Eventually, taxes the noncitizens of the provinces paid provided great wealth to the Roman state, as well as opportunities for personal enrichment to the upper-class Romans who served in high offices in the republic's provincial administrations.

The Romans also made alliances in Spain, where the Carthaginians had long had important interests. When Saguntum, a city located in the Carthaginian-dominated part of Spain, appealed to Rome for help against Carthage, the Senate responded favorably despite an apparent pledge in 226 B.C. not to interfere in Spain south of the Ebro River. When Saguntum fell to a Carthaginian siege,

Roman fear of a revived and powerful Carthage led to the Second Punic War (218–201 B.C.).

The Second Punic War became a vicious life-and-death struggle for both sides. First, the Carthaginian general Hannibal (247–182 B.C.) shocked the Romans by marching troops and war elephants over the Alps into Italy. With their treacherous, snowy passes, these high mountains had seemed a secure barrier against human invasion, to say nothing of warm-climate behemoths like elephants. Then, after Hannibal had followed up some early victories by killing more than thirty thousand Romans at the battle of Cannae in 216 B.C., he hoped to provoke widespread revolts among the numerous Italian cities allied to Rome. But disastrously for him, most Italians remained loyal to Rome. His alliance with King Philip V of Macedonia (238–179 B.C.) in 215 B.C. forced the Romans to fight in Greece as well, but they refused to crack. Hannibal made Romans' lives miserable by marching up and down Italy, ravaging Roman territory for fifteen years. The best the Romans could do militarily was to engage in stalling tactics, made famous by Fabius, called "the Delayer."

War Elephant

The Carthaginian commander Hannibal astonished the Romans in the Second Punic War by marching over the Alps into Italy with elephants. The huge animals were trained to charge the enemy on the battlefield.

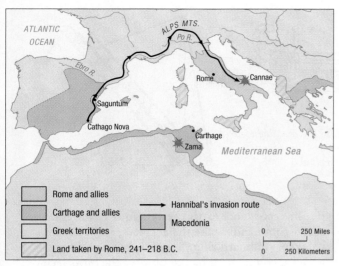

Second Punic War

Eventually Hannibal had to abandon his rampages in Italy to rush his army back to North Africa in 203 B.C., when the Romans, led by their general Scipio, daringly attacked Carthage itself. After battling in the field in Spain and Italy for thirty-four years, Hannibal was defeated in his home territory in North Africa at the battle of Zama in 202 B.C. by Scipio, who was dubbed "Africanus" to commemorate his triumph. The victorious Romans imposed a punishing peace settlement on the Carthaginians in 201 B.C., forcing them to scuttle their navy, pay huge war indemnities scheduled to last for fifty years, and relinquish their territories in Spain. The Romans subsequently had to fight a long series of wars with the indigenous Spanish peoples for control of the area, but the enormous profits reaped from Spain's mineral resources made the effort worthwhile. The revenues from Spain's silver mines, for example, financed expensive building projects in Rome.

The end of the Second Punic War allowed the Romans to resume their efforts to subjugate the Gauls (Celts) in northern Italy, who inhabited the rich plain of the Po River. By about 220 B.C., Rome controlled the Po valley. The Romans felt no qualms about their aggressive and bloody campaigns against these northern peoples, whom they lumped together as barbarians along with the Carthaginians and others to the west and north of Italy. Because the Romans respected the military prowess of the Gauls and, remembering their sack of Rome in 387 B.C., feared invasion from them, Romans considered their attacks on these peoples defensive and just, on the theory that the best defense is a good offense. Most important for their self-justification was that the Romans regarded themselves morally superior to all "barbarians." For example, they condemned the Carthaginians for their practice of occasionally sacrificing children to try to secure divine favor in times of great trouble for Carthage.

New Consequences of War

Before the First Punic War, Roman warfare had followed the normal Mediterranean pattern of short campaigns timed not to interfere with the fluctuating labor needs of agriculture. This seasonal warfare allowed men to remain home during the times of the year they needed to sow and harvest their crops and oversee the mating and culling of their flocks of animals. The campaigns of the First Punic War, prolonged year after year, disrupted this pattern. The women in farming families, like those in urban families, normally worked in and around the house, not in the fields. A farmer absent on military campaigns therefore had two choices: rely on a hired hand or slave to manage his crops and animals, or have his wife try to take on what was traditionally man's work in addition to her usual tasks of bringing water, weaving cloth, storing and preparing food, caring for the family's children, and managing the slaves.

The story of the consul Regulus, who led a Roman army to victory in Africa in 256 B.C., reveals the severe problems a man's absence could cause. When the man who managed Regulus's four-and-one-third acre farm died while the consul was away fighting Carthage, a hired hand absconded with all the farm's tools and livestock. Regulus implored the Senate to send a general to replace him so he could return home to prevent his wife and children from starving on his derelict farm. The senators took measures to save Regulus's family and property from ruin because they wanted to keep Regulus as a commander in the field, but ordinary soldiers could expect no such special aid. Women and children in the same plight as Regulus's family faced disaster because they had no marketable skills even if they moved to a city in search of work. Even unskilled jobs were scarce, because slaves

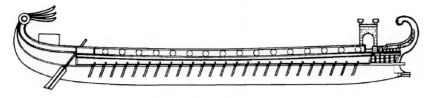
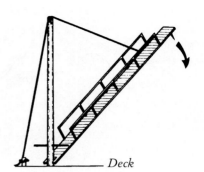

Roman Warship and "Raven"
The Romans mounted spiked boarding ramps ("ravens"), like the one depicted here, on the bows of warships. Roman soldiers could then cross onto enemy ships and turn sea battles into land battles, at which they excelled.

worked in domestic service and family members labored in small-scale manufacturing businesses run by families. Many rural women, reduced to destitution by their husbands' absence or death in war, could survive only by becoming urban prostitutes. The new style of warfare thus had the unintended consequence of disrupting the traditional forms of life in the Roman countryside, the base of Rome's agricultural economy. At the same time, women in the propertied classes amassed even more wealth through dowry and inheritance as the men in their families, who filled the elite positions in the army, brought home the greater share of booty to which their high rank entitled them under the Roman system of distributing the spoils of war.

The need to fight at sea in the Punic Wars forced Rome to develop new military technology, but these innovations applied only to weaponry. Agricultural and manufacturing technology did not benefit from the inventions that supplemented Rome's military power. Most remarkably, the Romans built a navy from scratch during the First Punic War and then overcame their inferiority to the Carthaginians in naval warfare with an ingenious technical innovation, a beam fitted with a long spike at its outer end positioned on the prows of their warships. In battle they snared enemy ships by dropping these spiked beams, called ravens because of their resemblance to the sharp-beaked bird, onto the enemy ship's deck. Roman troops then boarded the captive ship to fight hand to hand, their specialty. So successfully did the Romans learn and apply naval technology that they lost very few major sea battles in the First Punic War. One famous loss in 249 B.C. they characteristically explained as divine punishment for the consul Claudius Pulcher's sacrilege before the bat-

tle. In accordance with the religious requirement that a commander take the auspices, he had sacred chickens on board ship. Before battle could be engaged, a commander had to observe the birds feeding energetically as a sign of good fortune. When his chickens, no doubt seasick, refused to eat, Claudius hurled them overboard in a rage, sputtering, "Well, then, let them drink!" He thereupon lost 93 of his 123 ships in a spectacular naval defeat. As a result, Claudius had to stand trial at Rome and was condemned to pay a very heavy fine.

The Roman Problem in Greece

The Romans felt less confident when confronting the Greeks, as they did on a large scale in the second century B.C., than when coercing people they regarded as barbarians. They found it harder to claim the preeminence of their own customs—a typical ethnocentric chauvinism—when faced with the illustrious culture of the cities and kingdoms of Greece and Asia Minor. In 200 B.C. the Senate again sent Roman forces abroad eastward to fight Philip V of Macedonia (who had been allied with Hannibal from 215 B.C. until he made peace with Rome on favorable terms in 205 B.C.). In 200 B.C. the senators were responding to a plea from Pergamum and Rhodes to prevent an alliance between the Macedonian and Seleucid kingdoms, which these smaller powers feared would overcome them. After thrashing Philip in the Second Macedonian War (200–197 B.C.), the Roman commander Flamininus in 196 B.C. proclaimed the "freedom of the Greeks." The cities and federal leagues of Greece naturally thought the proclamation meant they could behave as they liked. They misunderstood.

The Romans rationalized that they had become the Greeks' patron through the kindness of proclaiming their freedom. The idea that this act of friendship (as the Romans defined friendship) created strong ties of obligation between the superior Roman patron and the inferior (yet liberated) Greek clients understandably eluded the Greeks. The Greek system of personal and political obligations differed vastly from the Roman client-patron system; Greeks based their foreign allegiances on the idea of contracts between independent and equal partners. As so often in history, trouble developed because two parties failed to realize that common and familiar words like *freedom* and *friendship* could carry very different implications in different societies. The Greeks, taking the Roman proclamation of freedom literally, resisted Roman efforts to intervene in the local disputes that continued to disrupt Greece and Macedonia after 196 B.C. The Romans regarded Greek intransigence as a betrayal of the client's duty to acquiesce to the patron's wishes. They were especially upset by the military support that certain Greeks solicited from King Antiochus III (c. 242–187 B.C.), the Seleucid monarch who invaded Greece after the Romans had withdrawn in 194 B.C. The Romans therefore crushed Antiochus and his allies in what is called the Syrian War (192–188 B.C.), parceled out his territories to friendlier states in the region, and again withdrew to Italy. When the energetic policy of the Macedonian king Perseus (∗179–168 B.C.) led King Eumenes of Pergamum to ask Rome to return to Greece, a Roman army fought Perseus's forces in the Third Macedonian War (171–168 B.C.) and won a decisive victory at the battle of Pydna. It took yet another twenty years before Rome decisively restored peace for the benefit of its friends and supporters in Greece and Macedonia. Rome formally incorporated Macedonia and Greece into the Roman provincial system after the so-called Fourth Macedonian War (148–146 B.C.). In 146 B.C. the Roman commander Mummius destroyed the famous and wealthy city of Corinth as a calculated act of terror to show what continued resistance to Roman domination would mean.

The year 146 B.C. also saw the annihilation of Carthage at the end of the Third Punic War (149–146 B.C.). The war had begun when the Carthaginians, who had once again revived economically after paying the indemnities imposed by Rome after the Second Punic War, retaliated against their neighbor, the Numidian king Masinissa, a Roman ally who had been aggressively provoking them for some time. Carthage finally fell before the blockade of Scipio Aemilianus (185–129 B.C.), the adopted grandson of Scipio Africanus. Romans razed Carthage and converted Carthaginian territory into a Roman province. This disaster did not obliterate Punic social and cultural ways, however, and under the Roman Empire this part of North Africa became distinguished for its economic and intellectual vitality, which emerged from a synthesis of Roman and Punic traditions.

The Reasons for Roman Imperialism

The destruction of Carthage as an independent state was a response, posthumously as it happened, to the oft-expressed wish of the crusty and influential Roman senator Cato. For several years before 146 B.C., Cato had taken every opportunity in senatorial debate to intone, "Carthage must be destroyed!" Cato presumably had two reasons for his insistence. One was fear that a resurgent Carthage would again threaten Rome. Another was a desire to eliminate Carthage as a rival for the riches and glory Roman aristocrats could accumulate through expansion in the Mediterranean area. Historians seem to agree with Cato's reasoning at least, advancing two main reasons to explain Roman imperialism under the republic: fear for Roman security that induced the Senate to advise preemptive strikes against those perceived as enemies, and Roman aristocrats' eagerness for the fabulous wealth that could be gained by capturing booty as commanders in foreign military campaigns. Along with wealth came the especially valued prestige and glory of having been a successful military leader and the chance to serve as a provincial governor.

In the third and second centuries B.C., the process of Roman imperial conquest and administration beyond the shores of Italy was neither simple nor uniform. No single principle determined its course. The Romans used various methods depending on the subject peoples and their locations. In the western Mediterranean the Romans followed their conquests by immediately imposing direct rule and maintaining a permanent military presence. In Greece and Macedonia they preferred to rule indirectly, through compliant local governments. Roman aristocrats befriended their Greek counterparts to promote their common interests in keeping the peace. By 146 B.C., Rome's power extended across two-thirds the length of the Mediterranean, from Spain to Greece. In 133 B.C. the king of Pergamum, Attalus III, increased Roman power with an astonishing bequest: he left his kingdom to Rome in his will. The Romans could not have achieved so much had they not been both tenacious in fighting and adaptable in governing what they conquered.

The Consequences of Roman Expansion

Although Romans greatly expanded their power, territory, and wealth and came into contact with new peoples and cultures during their conquests, these gains came at a price. The city of Rome was no longer a close-knit and insular community. Centuries of war had also widened the gap between the social classes. Military victory brought an influx of riches to some, mostly the nobles and others at the top of the social hierarchy, enhancing their already prominent economic and social status; but the demands of military expeditions created hardships for many more men, whose service to their republic brought them increased burdens rather than rewards. The exposure to foreign peoples and their different traditions during campaigns waged far from home influenced Rome's society and culture, effecting some changes that were largely unanticipated and often controversial.

The Beginnings of Literature in Latin

Roman activity in the East greatly intensified their contact with the Greeks, which had begun when Rome expanded its power into southern Italy and Sicily. The first Roman history was written about 200 B.C.—in Greek. The earliest literature in Latin, which was exclusively poetry, also owed a debt to Greek models. By the time Romans came into frequent contact with Greek literature in the third century B.C., it had already been shaped by the Hellenistic trend toward exotic erudition. The

great classics of Greek literature nevertheless still retained their appeal, such as Homer's *Iliad,* with its concentration on the pain of war, and *Odyssey,* with its tales of fabulous adventure and travel. The first work of literary Latin, in fact, was an adaptation of the *Odyssey* written sometime after the First Punic War (264–241 B.C.). Remarkably, the author was not a Roman but a Greek from Tarentum in southern Italy, Livius Andronicus. A former prisoner of war, he lived in Rome after being freed, taking his master's name. Many of the most famous early Latin authors were not native Romans. They came from all over: the poet Naevius (died 201 B.C.) from Campania, south of Rome; the poet Ennius (died 169 B.C.) from even farther south, in Calabria; the comic playwright Plautus (died c. 184 B.C.) from north of Rome, in Umbria; his fellow comedy writer Terence (c. 190–159 B.C.) from North Africa. These writers gave Latin literature an eclectic pedigree and testified to the intermingling of cultures in the Roman world—a process well under way by this time.

Literature shows clearly that Rome found strength and vitality by combining the foreign and the familiar. Plautus and Terence, for example, wrote their famous comedies in Latin for Roman audiences, but they adapted their plots from Greek comedies. They displayed their genius by keeping the settings of their comedies Greek while creating sprightly characters who were unmistakenly Roman in outlook and behavior. The comic figure of Plautus's *The Braggart Warrior,* for one, mocked the pretensions of Romans who claimed elevated social status on the basis of the number of enemies they had slaughtered.

Not all Romans applauded Greek influence. Cato, although he studied Greek himself, repeatedly thundered against the deleterious effect the "effete" Greeks had on the "sturdy" Romans. He established Latin as an appropriate language for prose with the publication of his history of Rome, *The Origins* (written between 168 and 149 B.C.), and of his treatise on running a large farm, *On Agriculture* (published about 160 B.C.). He glumly predicted that if the Romans ever became infected with Greek literature, they would lose their dominions. In fact, despite its debt to Greek literature, early Latin literature reflected traditional Roman values. Ennius, for example, was inspired by Greek epic poetry to compose his path-breaking Latin epic, *Annals,* a

Greek Style in Rome
Built in the late second century B.C., this building is the earliest surviving marble temple in Rome. Its purely Greek style reveals how heavily Greece had influenced Rome by this date.

poetic version of Roman history. But its contents were anything but subversive of ancestral tradition, as a famous line demonstrates: "On the ways and the men of old rests the Roman commonwealth." As it turned out, the unanticipated social and economic changes brought on by Roman imperialism were far more troubling than Greek influence on Roman culture.

The Rewards of Conquest

Rome's aristocrats reaped rich political and material rewards from Roman imperialism in the third and second centuries B.C. The increased need for commanders to lead military campaigns abroad meant more opportunities for successful men to enrich themselves from booty. By using their gains to finance public buildings, they could enhance their reputations while benefiting the general population. Building new temples, for example, was thought to increase everyone's security because the Romans believed it pleased their gods to have more shrines

in their honor. In 146 B.C. a victorious general, Caecilius Metellus, paid for the first Roman temple built of marble. This temple to Jupiter started a trend toward magnificence in the architecture of Roman public buildings.

Eventually, territorial expansion created a need for military and political leadership that the usual number of magistrates could no longer handle. More and more magistrates therefore had their powers prolonged to command armies and administer the provinces. Because a provincial governor ruled by martial law, no one in the province could curb a greedy governor's appetite for graft, extortion, and plunder. Not all Roman magistrates were corrupt, of course, but some did use their unsupervised power to squeeze all they could from the provincials. Normally such offenders faced no punishment because their colleagues in the Senate preferred to excuse each other's depredations; the notorious Verres prosecuted by Cicero in 70 B.C. was a rare exception. Ostentatious, large country villas became a favorite symbol of wealth. The new taste for luxurious living became a matter of controversy because it contradicted Roman aristocratic ideals, which emphasized private moderation and frugality. Cato, for example, made his ideal Roman the military hero Manius Curius (died 270 B.C.), legendary for his meals of turnips boiled in his humble hut. The new opportunities for extravagance financed by the fruits of expansion abroad strained this tradition of austerity.

The Plight of Small Farmers in Italy

The economic basis of the republic was agriculture. For centuries, farmers working little plots had been the backbone of Roman agricultural production. These small property owners also constituted the principal source of soldiers for the Roman army (men were required to own a certain amount of property before they could enlist). The republic faced grave economic, social, and military difficulties when the successful wars of the third and second centuries B.C. ironically turned out to be disastrous for many small farmers and their families throughout Italy.

The farmers' troubles started with Hannibal's years of ravaging Italy at the end of the third century B.C., during the Second Punic War. The presence of a Carthaginian army had made it hard for farmers to keep up a regular schedule of planting and harvesting in the regions Hannibal terrorized, and Fabius's defensive tactics of delay and attrition had exacerbated their losses. Their problems multiplied in the second century B.C., when many farmers had to spend years away from their fields fighting in Rome's nearly constant military expeditions abroad. More than 50 percent of Roman adult males spent at least seven years in military service during this period, leaving their wives and children to cope as best they could. Because women were not trained to do agricultural labor, their family farms often failed unless their slaves and hired laborers (assuming they could afford such help) were diligent, honest, and lucky enough to keep production going. Many farmers and their families fell into debt and were forced to sell their land. Rich landowners then bought many small plots and created large estates. Landowners further increased their holdings by illegally occupying the public land Rome had confiscated from defeated peoples in Italy. The rich gained vast estates, called *latifundia*, worked by slaves as well as free laborers. They had a ready supply of slaves because of the many captives taken in the same wars that displaced Italy's small farmers. In the words of one modern scholar, "Roman peasant soldiers were fighting for their own displacement."

Not all regions of Italy suffered as severely as others, and some impoverished farmers and their families in the badly affected areas managed to remain in the countryside by working as day laborers for others. Many displaced people, however, emigrated to Rome, where the men looked for work as menial laborers and women might hope for some piecework making cloth—but often were forced into prostitution. This influx of desperate people swelled the poverty-level population in the city, and the difficulty these landless, urban poor had supporting themselves made them a potentially explosive element in Roman politics. They were willing to support any politician who promised to address their needs. They also represented a problem for Rome because they had to be fed to avert food riots. Like Athens in the fifth century B.C., Rome by the late second century B.C. needed to import grain to feed its huge urban population. The Senate supervised the market in grain to prevent speculation and to ensure wide distribution in times of shortage. Supplying low-priced (and eventually free) grain to Rome's poor at the state's expense became one of the most contentious issues in late republican politics.

The Splintering of Aristocratic Politics

The plight of those who had lost their land attracted the attention of the brothers Tiberius Gracchus (died 133 B.C.) and Gaius Gracchus (died 121 B.C.), aristocrats of distinguished lineage. (Their mother Cornelia was the daughter of Scipio Africanus.) Their actions in favor of dispossessed farmers were probably not altogether altruistic—they had scores to settle with their political rivals and could gain popular support by championing these farmers. But we would be overly cynical to deny their apparent sympathy with the displaced families. Tiberius, the older brother, eloquently dramatized the tragic dimensions of the situation.

> The wild beasts that roam over Italy have their dens. . . . But the men who fight and die for Italy enjoy nothing but the air and light; without house or home they wander about with their wives and children. . . . They fight and die to protect the wealth and luxury of others; they are styled masters of the world, and have not a clod of earth they can call their own.

As tribune in 133 B.C., Tiberius outraged the Senate by having the Tribal Assembly of the Plebeians adopt reform laws designed to redistribute public land to landless Romans without the senators' approval, a formally legal but extremely nontraditional maneuver. Also unprecedented was his convincing the assembly to depose a fellow tribune, who had been vetoing Tiberius's legislation. Tiberius further broke with tradition by circumventing the will of the Senate on the question of financing this agrarian reform. Before the Senate could render an opinion on whether to accept the bequest of all his property the recently deceased king of Pergamum, Attalus III, made to Rome, Tiberius moved that the gift be used to equip the new farms that were to be established on the redistributed land.

When Tiberius announced his intention to stand for reelection as tribune for the following year, he violated the republican constitution. Even some of his supporters abandoned him, because the "way of the elders" forbade serving consecutive terms. What happened next signaled the beginning of the end of the republic's political health. An ex-consul, Scipio Nasica, instigated a surprise attack on his cousin, Tiberius, by a group of senators and their clients. This aristocratic mob clubbed Tiberius and some of his adherents to death on Capitoline Hill in late 133 B.C.. Thus began the sorry history of murder as a political tactic in the republic.

Gaius Gracchus, tribune in 123 B.C. and again in 122 B.C., despite tradition, also initiated reforms that threatened the Roman elite, including keeping alive the agrarian reforms initiated by his brother. He also introduced laws to assure grain to Rome's citizens at subsidized prices, to mandate public works projects throughout Italy to provide employment for the poor, and to found colonies abroad. Most revolutionary of all were his proposals to give Roman citizenship to some Italians and to establish jury trials for senators accused of corruption as provincial governors. The citizenship proposal failed. The creation of a system to prosecute corrupt senators became an intensely controversial issue because it threatened the power of the ruling oligarchy in the Senate to protect its own members and their families. The new juries were to be manned not by senators but by members of the social class called *equites* (meaning "equestrians" or "knights"). These were wealthy men without public careers, who came mostly from the local landed aristocracy with family origins outside Rome proper. In the earliest republic the equestrians had been what the word suggests—men rich enough to own horses for cavalry service. But by this time equestrians had become a kind of second-class aristocrats, whose political ambitions were often thwarted by the dominant aristocrats in the Senate. Senators drew a distinction between themselves and equestrians by maintaining that it was unseemly for a senator to soil his hands in commerce, an activity some equestrians embraced rather than pursue their limited opportunities for a public career. A law passed by the tribune Claudius in 218 B.C. made it illegal for senators and their sons to own large-capacity cargo ships, but senators nevertheless sometimes did have commercial interests. They masked their income from this source by clandestinely employing intermediaries or favored slaves to do the work and then return the profits to their senatorial backers. The legislation authorizing equestrians to compose juries to try senators accused of malfeasance in the provinces marked the emergence of the equestrians as a political force in Roman politics, to the dismay of the Senate.

Gaius acquired a bodyguard to try to protect himself against violence from senatorial enemies bent on blocking his program. The senators in 121 B.C. used the violence they had themselves initiated as an excuse to issue the "ultimate decree" for the first time, a vote of the Senate advising the consuls to take whatever measures were necessary to defend the republic. The consul Opimius was therefore granted implicit permission to use military force inside the city of Rome, where magistrates ordinarily had no such power. To escape arrest, Gaius had one of his slaves cut his throat. The deaths of Tiberius and Gaius Gracchus prompted the disintegration of the cohesive oligarchy that had dominated Roman government. Both the reforming brothers and their murderers came from the upper class, which could no longer govern through a consensus that protected its interests. From now on, Roman aristocrats increasingly saw themselves either as supporters of the *populares,* who sought power by promoting the interests of the common people (*populus*), or as members of the *optimates,* who supported the "best people" (the *optimi,* meaning the nobles) and relied on aristocratic political sentiment. Some identified with one faction or the other out of genuine allegiance to its policies. Others picked a group to support based simply on political expediency; depending on which side promoted their own political advancement, they would pretend to be sincere proponents of either the people or the upper class. In any case this division of the Roman upper class into political factions persisted as a source of friction and violence until Augustus finally imposed peace and the unity of one-man rule at the end of the first century B.C.

The Rise of the "New Man"

Even as Rome's traditional ruling elite was losing its cohesiveness, the republic continued to need effective military leaders. Seventy thousand slaves from the *latifundia* in Sicily revolted from 134 to 131 B.C. A war with an ungrateful client king in North Africa, Jugurtha, began in 112 B.C. Not long after, formidable bands of Celtic tribesmen began to menace the northern border of Italy. In response to the disarray of the upper class and these threats, a new force arose in Roman politics—the man not born into the charmed circle of the highest nobility at Rome but nevertheless able to force his way to fame, fortune, influence, and the consulship by sheer ability as a military leader. This "new man" challenged the traditional political dominance of the Roman aristocracy.

The Origin of Client Armies

The man who set this new political force in motion, Gaius Marius (c. 157–86 B.C.) came not from Rome but from the wealthy aristocracy of Arpinum, a town in central Italy. Ordinarily, an equestrian like Marius had little chance of cracking the ranks of Rome's ruling oligarchy of noble families, who virtually monopolized the office of consul. The best an equestrian could usually hope for in a public career was to advance to the junior ranks of the Senate as the dutiful client of a powerful noble. Fortunately for Marius, however, Rome at the end of the second century B.C. had a pressing need for men who could lead an army to victory. Marius made his reputation by running for office in the interests of noble patrons, marrying above his social rank into a famous patrician family (from whose line Julius Caesar would be born in 100 B.C.), and serving with distinction in the North African war. Capitalizing on his military record and popular dissatisfaction with the nobles' conduct of the war against Jugurtha, Marius won election as one of the consuls for 107 B.C. In Roman terms this election made him a "new man"—that is, the first man in the history of his family to become consul. "New men" were rare in the republic. Marius had gained distinction because of his military prowess. His success, first as a general in the African war and then against the invasions of Italy by the "barbarian" Teutones and Cimbri, led to his election as consul for an unprecedented six terms by 100 B.C., including consecutive terms, a practice previously illegal.

So celebrated was Marius that the Senate voted him a triumph, Rome's ultimate military honor. On the day of a triumph the general who had earned this award rode through the streets of Rome in a military chariot. His face was painted red for reasons the Romans could no longer remember. Huge crowds cheered him. His army traditionally lambasted him with off-color jokes, perhaps to ward off the evil eye at this moment of supreme glory. For a similar reason a slave rode behind him in the chariot and kept whispering in his ear, "Look behind you, and remember that you are a mortal." For a former equestrian like Marius to be granted a triumph was a mammoth social coup.

Despite his triumph, the "best people" never fully accepted Marius. They saw him as an upstart and a threat to their preeminence. Marius's mainstay of support came from the common people and wealthy equestrians, who favored his attempt to break into the nobility or were concerned that the incompetence of senatorial leaders would ruin their economic interests abroad. His dramatic reform of entrance requirements for the army made him particularly popular with poor men. Previously, only men with property could enroll as soldiers. Marius opened the ranks even to proletarians. For these men who had virtually nothing, serving in the army meant an opportunity to better their lot by acquiring booty under a successful general. They willingly traded the risk of getting killed in combat for a chance to seize some property for themselves while on military campaigns. The republic at this time made no provisions for regular rewards to ex-soldiers; their fortunes depended on the success and generosity of their general, who could keep the lion's share of booty for himself and his high-ranking officers. Proletarian troops naturally felt grateful to a commander who led them to victory and then generously divided the spoils with them. Troop loyalty became more and more directed at their commander, not to the republic, and poor Roman soldiers began to behave as an army of clients following their patron, the general. Marius, who created this potential source of power, was only the first to use it to promote his own career. He lost his political importance soon after 100 B.C., when he no longer commanded armies and had alienated his own supporters. His enemies among the *optimates* succeeded in keeping him from power. When others who came after Marius proved even more successful in employing client armies as tools in political struggles, the fall of the republic could no longer be avoided.

Uprisings and the War with the Allies

Rome's Italian allies shared in the bounty of military victory, but because most of them lacked Roman citizenship, they had no voice in decisions concerning Roman domestic or foreign policy, even when their interests were directly involved. This political disability made them increasingly unhappy as wealth from conquest piled up in Italy in the late republic. The allies wanted a share in the growing prosperity of the upper class. Gaius Gracchus had seen the wisdom of including the allies and tried to extend Roman citizenship to the loyal allies of Rome in Italy, who would have increased his own power by becoming his clients. His enemies, however, had convinced the Roman people that they would lessen their own political and economic power by granting these people citizenship.

The allies' discontent finally erupted in the Social War of 91–87 B.C. (so called because the Latin word for "ally" is *socius*). The Italians formed a confederacy to fight Rome, minted their own coins to finance their operations, and died valiantly in the field. One ancient source claims the war took three hundred thousand casualties. In the end the Roman army proved victorious in battle, but the allies won the political war. The Romans granted the Italians the citizenship for which they had begun their rebellion. From this time on the freeborn peoples of Italy south of the Po River enjoyed the privileges of Roman citizenship. Most important, if their men made their way to Rome, they could vote in the assemblies. The bloodshed of the Social War was the unfortunate price paid to reestablish Rome's early principle of seeking strength through including people in the political process through citizenship.

Farther from Rome, the conquered peoples of Asia Minor chafed under Roman rule. King Mithridates VI of Pontus (120–63 B.C.) won the support of these populations for a rebellion because they so bitterly resented the notorious Roman tax collectors. Groups of Romans from the class of the *equites* formed private companies that bid for provincial tax contracts. Such a group would agree to deliver a set amount of revenue to the Roman republic in return for the right to collect taxes in a certain province. These "tax farmers," as they are called, could keep as profit any additional amount their collectors, called publicans, managed to obtain,

an arrangement that gave them great incentive to exploit the provincials. It is no wonder that Mithridates found a sympathetic ear in Asia Minor for his charge that the Romans were "the common enemies of all mankind." He reportedly capitalized on these hostile feelings to engineer the slaughter of thousands of Roman residents in Asia Minor and create a crisis for Roman authority there in the First Mithridatic War (88–85 B.C.).

The Demise of Roman Republic Tradition

The Social War and the threat from Mithridates brought a ruthless Roman noble named Lucius Cornelius Sulla (c. 138–78 B.C.) to power. He came from a patrician family that had lost much of its status. Anxious to restore his line's prestige, Sulla had first schemed to advance his career while serving under Marius against Jugurtha. His subsequent military success against the allies in the Social War propelled him to the prominence he coveted: he won election as consul for 88 B.C. The Senate promptly rewarded him with the mission of fighting Mithridates.

Marius, now the jealous enemy of his former subordinate Sulla, connived to have the command against Mithridates transferred to himself just as Sulla was marshaling an army. Sulla's reaction to this setback showed that he understood the source of power that Marius had gained by creating a client army. Instead of accepting the loss of the command, Sulla led his Roman army against Rome itself. All his officers except one deserted him in horror at

MITH·RI·DAY·TEEZ

The Kingdom of Mithridates VI of Pontus

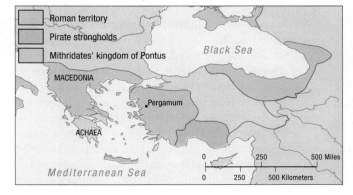

Roman territory
Pirate strongholds
Mithridates' kingdom of Pontus

MACEDONIA

Black Sea

Pergamum

ACHAEA

0   250   500 Miles

0   250   500 Kilometers

Mediterranean Sea

this unthinkable outrage. His common soldiers, by contrast, followed him to a man. Neither they nor their commander shrank from starting a bloody civil war. When Sulla took Rome, he killed or exiled his opponents. His men went on a rampage in the capital city. He then led them off to campaign in Asia Minor despite a summons to stand trial.

When Sulla marched against Mithridates, Marius and his friends regained power in Rome and embarked on their own reign of terror. Murderous violence had become frighteningly routine in Roman politics. Marius soon died of natural causes, but his friends held undisputed power until 83 B.C., when Sulla returned to Italy after forcing Mithridates to make peace and provide funds for Sulla's army. Another civil war ensued. Sulla's enemies joined some of the Italians, especially the Samnites from central and southern Italy, to hold him off for nearly two years. The climactic battle of the war took place in late 82 B.C. at the Colline Gate of Rome. The Samnite general whipped his troops into a frenzy against Sulla by shouting, "The last day is at hand for the Romans! These wolves that have made such ravages upon Italian liberty will never vanish until we have cut down the forest that harbors them."

Unfortunately for the Samnites, they lost the battle and the war. Sulla proceeded to exterminate them and distribute their territory to his supporters. He also brutally massacred his opponents at Rome by means of proscription. This practice, which became a frequent weapon in Roman civil war, meant posting a list of those supposedly guilty of treasonable crimes so that anyone could hunt them down and execute them. Because the property of those proscribed was confiscated, Sulla's supporters fraudulently added to the list the name of anyone whose wealth they desired. The Senate in terror appointed Sulla dictator without any limitation of term. He used the office to legitimize his reorganization of the government, under which the Senate became the supreme power in the state. He reversed Gracchan jury reforms so that equestrians no longer judged senators. He tried to disable the tribunate by forbidding the tribunes from offering legislation without the prior approval of the Senate and barring any man who

became a tribune from holding any other magistracy thereafter. Minimum age limits were imposed for holding the various posts in the sequence of the course of offices. In short, Sulla's vision was that of a state completely dominated by the "best people"—a repudiation of the idea of the "new man."

Convinced by an old prophecy that he had only a short time to live, Sulla retired to private life in 79 B.C. and indeed died the next year. His remarkable career had starkly revealed the strengths and the weaknesses of the social and political traditions of the later republic. First, success in war had come to mean profits for common soldiers and commanders alike, primarily from selling prisoners of war into slavery and seizing booty. This incentive to war made it all the harder to resolve problems peaceably. Many Romans were so poor that they preferred war to a life without prospects. Sulla's troops in 88 B.C., for example, did not want to disband because they had their eyes on the riches they hoped to win in a war against Mithridates. Second, the pervasiveness of the client-patron system meant that poor soldiers felt stronger ties of obligation to their general, who acted as their patron, than to their republic. Sulla's men obeyed his order to attack Rome because they owed obedience to him as their patron and could expect benefits in return. Sulla obliged them by permitting the plundering of Rome and of the vast riches of Asia Minor.

Finally, the concern of aristocrats with public status worked both for and against the republic's stability. When the desire for status motivated important men to seek office to promote the welfare of the population as a whole—the traditional ideal of an aristocratic public career—it was a powerful force for social peace and general prosperity. But pushed to its extreme, as in the case of Sulla, the concern for personal standing based on personal prestige and individual wealth could overshadow all considerations of public service. Sulla in 88 B.C. simply could not bear to lose the glory and status that a victory over Mithridates would bring. He preferred to initiate a civil war rather than to see his cherished status diminished.

The republic was doomed once its leaders and its followers forsook the "way of the elders" that valued respect for the peace and prosperity of the republic and its constitution above personal gain. Sulla's career helps to reveal how the social and political structure of the republic contained the seeds of its own destruction.

The End of the Republic

The great generals whose names dominate the history of the republic after Sulla all took him as their model: while professing allegiance to the state, they relentlessly pursued their own advancement. The motivation—that a Roman aristocrat could never have too much glory or too much wealth—was a corruption of the finest ideals of the republic. In their fevered pursuit of self-aggrandizement they ignored the honored tradition of public service to the commonwealth. Pompey and Caesar gained glory and prodigious amounts of money for themselves, but the brutal civil war they eventually fought against each other's armies ruined the republic and opened the way for the return of monarchy to Rome after an absence of nearly five hundred years.

The Irregular Career of Pompey

Gnaeus Pompey (106–48 B.C.) had forced his way onto the scene in 83 B.C. when Sulla first returned to Italy after defeating Mithridates. Only twenty-three years old at the time, he gathered a private army from his father's clients in Italy and joined Sulla, for whom he won victories in Italy and, soon thereafter, in Sicily and North Africa, where Sulla's rivals had fled. These successes meant that Sulla could not refuse Pompey's bold demand for a triumph. A triumph honoring such a young man, who had never held a formal magistracy, shattered another ancient tradition of the republic. Pompey did not have to wait his turn for acclaim or earn his accolades only after years of service. Because he was so powerful, he could demand his stamp of glory from Sulla on the spot. As Pompey said to Sulla, "People worship the rising, not the setting, sun." Pompey's "triumph" betrayed the hollowness of Sulla's vision of the Roman republic. Sulla had proclaimed a return to the rule of the "best people"

and, according to him, Rome's finest political traditions. Instead he fashioned a regime controlled by violence and power politics. His government reforms disintegrated in the decade after his death. A modern historian offers a blunt assessment: "The Sullan oligarchy had a fatal flaw: it governed with a guilty conscience."

The course of Pompey's subsequent career shows how the traditional checks and balances of republican government failed to operate in the late republic. After helping suppress a rebellion in Spain and a massive slave revolt in Italy led by the escaped gladiator Spartacus, Pompey demanded and won election to the consulship in 70 B.C., well before he had reached the legal age of forty-two or even held any elective office. Three years later he received a command with unprecedented powers to exterminate the pirates currently infesting the Mediterranean. He smashed them in a matter of months. This success in 67 B.C. made him wildly popular with the urban poor at Rome, who depended on a steady flow of imported grain subsidized by the state; with the wealthy commercial and shipping interests, which depended on safe sea lanes; and with coastal communities everywhere, which had suffered from the pirates' raids. The next year the command against Mithridates, who was still stirring up trouble in Asia Minor, was taken away from the general Lucullus so it could be given to Pompey. Lucullus had made himself unpopular with his troops by curbing their looting of the province, and with the publicans by regulating their extortion of the defenseless provincials. Pompey conquered Asia Minor and the ancient Near East in a series of bold campaigns. He marched as far south as Jerusalem, which he captured in 63 B.C. When he then annexed Syria as a province, he initiated Rome's formal presence in that part of the world and created a client kingdom.

Pompey's success in the East was spectacular. People compared him to Alexander the Great and referred to him as *Magnus* ("Great"). Not one for self-effacement, he boasted that he had increased Rome's provincial revenues by 70 percent. He distributed money equal to twelve and a half years' pay each to his soldiers. Moreover, during his time in the East he operated largely on his own initiative. He never consulted the Senate when he set up new political arrangements for the territories he conquered. For all practical purposes he behaved more like an independent king than a Roman magistrate. He had pithily expressed his attitude early in his career when replying to some foreigners after they had objected to his treatment as unjust. "Stop quoting the laws to us," he told them. "We carry swords."

Pompey's enemies at Rome feared him and tried to strengthen their own positions while he was abroad. His principal foes among them were two unscrupulous aristocrats, the fabulously wealthy Marcus Licinius Crassus (died 53 B.C.), who had defeated Spartacus, and the young Julius Caesar (100–44 B.C.). They promoted themselves as *populares,* concerned with the plight of the common people. And there was much cause for concern. The population of Rome had soared to perhaps a million people. Hundreds of thousands of them lived crowded together in shabby apartment buildings no better than slums. Work was hard to find. Many people subsisted on the dole of grain the government distributed at a subsidized low price. The streets of Rome were dangerous because the city had no police force. To make matters worse, Rome was grappling with special economic problems in the 60s B.C., perhaps a result of the falling value of land that Sulla's confiscations had created by flooding the market with properties for sale. Credit seems to have been in short supply at the very time those in financial difficulties were trying to borrow their way back to respectability.

The conspiracy of Lucius Sergius Catilina in 63 B.C. reveals to what lengths debt and poverty could drive people. Catiline, as he is known in English, was a debt-ridden aristocrat who rallied a band of fellow upper-class debtors and victims of Sulla's confiscations to his cause. Frustrated in his attempts to win the consulship, he planned to use violence to seize tyrannical power, with the aim of redistributing wealth and property to his supporters after their victory. The consul Cicero, however, discovered the plot before the conspirators could murder him and the other consul and forced them to flee to northern Italy, where a Roman army killed them in battle. Even if their misguided plot had brought them power, Catiline and his co-conspirators never had a realistic chance of redressing their grievances. They would have had to kill all the currently successful property owners! Nevertheless, their futile effort demonstrates the desperation of many people at Rome, even aristocrats, during this period.

When Pompey returned from the East in 62 B.C., the "best people" shortsightedly refused to support his settlement of the ancient Near East or the reward of land to the veterans of his army. This setback forced Pompey to negotiate with Caesar and Crassus. In 60 B.C. these three formed an informal troika, commonly called the First Triumvirate (that is, "coalition of three men"), to advance their own interests. They succeeded. Pompey got laws to confirm his eastern arrangements and give land to his veterans; Caesar got the consulship for 59 B.C. along with a special command in Gaul for five years; Crassus got financial breaks for the Roman tax collectors in Asia Minor, whose support helped make him powerful and in whose business he had a stake. This astounding coalition of former political enemies provided each triumvir (member of the triumvirate) a means for achieving his personal ambitions: Pompey wanted status as patron to his troops and to the territories he had conquered; Caesar wanted the consulship and the chance to win glory and booty from fighting "barbarians"; and Crassus wanted increased financial profits for himself and his clients so he could remain politically competitive with Pompey and Caesar, whose military and political reputations far exceeded his. The First Triumvirate was an association formed only for the advantage of the moment. Because its three members shared no common philosophy of governing, their cooperation lasted only as long as they continued to profit from it personally.

The first triumvirs recognized the potentially transitory nature of their coalition, and they used a popular form of political alliance to try to give their arrangement some permanence: they contracted marriages among one another. Women were the pawns traded back and forth in these alliances. In 59 B.C., for example, Caesar married his daughter Julia to Pompey. She had been engaged to another man, but this political marriage now took precedence to create a bond between Caesar and Pompey. Pompey simultaneously soothed Julia's jilted fiance by having him marry Pompey's daughter, who had been engaged to yet somebody else. Through these marital machinations, the two powerful antagonists now had a common interest: the fate of Julia, Caesar's only daughter and Pompey's new wife. (He had divorced his second wife after Caesar

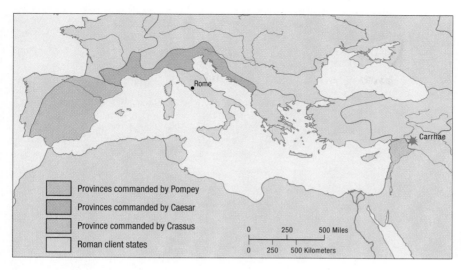

Provinces commanded by Pompey
Provinces commanded by Caesar
Province commanded by Crassus
Roman client states

0   250   500 Miles
0   250   500 Kilometers

**Provincial Commands of
the "First Triumvirate"**

allegedly had seduced her.) Pompey and Julia apparently fell deeply in love in their arranged marriage. As long as Julia lived, Pompey's affection for her helped restrain him from an outright break with her father, Caesar. But when she died in childbirth in 54 B.C., the bond linking Pompey and Caesar was severed.

The Victory of Caesar

Caesar had left Rome to take up a command in Gaul (modern France) in 58 B.C. For the next nine years he attacked one "barbarian" people after another throughout what is now France, the western part of Germany, and even the southern end of Britain. The slaves and booty his army seized not only paid off the enormous debts he had incurred in his political career but also enriched him and his soldiers. For this reason above all, his troops loved him. His political enemies at Rome dreaded him even more as his military successes mounted; his supporters meanwhile tried to prepare the ground for his eventual return to Rome. The two sides' rivalry soon exploded into violence. By the mid-50s B.C., political gangs of young men regularly roamed the streets of Rome in search of opponents to beat up or murder. Street fighting reached such a pitch in 53 B.C. that it was impossible to hold elections, and no consuls were chosen that year. The triumvirate completely dissolved that same year with the death of Crassus in battle at Carrhae in northern Mesopotamia; in an attempt to win the

military glory his career so conspicuously lacked, he had led a Roman army across the Euphrates River to fight the Parthians, an Iranian people whose military aristocracy, headed by a king, ruled a vast territory stretching from the Euphrates to the Indus River. In 52 B.C. the most extreme *optimates*—Caesar's most determined enemies—took the extraordinary step of having Pompey appointed as sole consul for the year. The traditions of republic government had plainly fallen into the dust. When Caesar prepared to return to Rome in 49 B.C., he too wanted a special arrangement to protect himself. He demanded the consulship for 48 B.C.

When the Senate responded by ordering him to surrender his command, Caesar, like Sulla before him, led his army against Rome. As he crossed the Rubicon River in northern Italy in early 49 B.C., he uttered the famous words signaling the start of a bitter civil war: "The die is cast." His troops followed him without hesitation, and the people of the towns and countryside of Italy cheered him on enthusiastically. He had many backers in Rome, too, among the many to whom he had lent money or political support. Some of those glad to hear of his coming were ruined aristocrats, who hoped to recoup their once-great fortunes by backing Caesar against the rich. These were in fact the people whom Caesar had always refused to help politically or financially, saying to them, "What you need is a civil war."

The enthusiastic response of the masses to Caesar's advance induced Pompey and Caesar's enemies in the Senate to transport their forces to

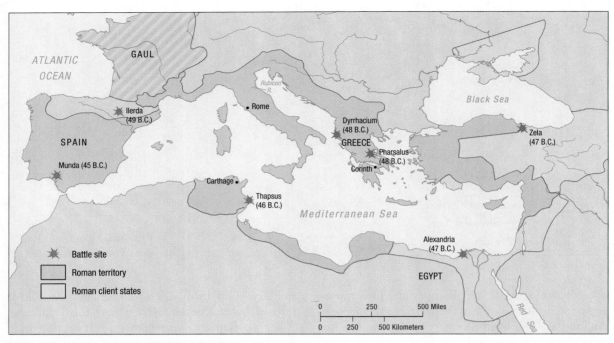

Julius Caesar's Battles During the Civil War (49–45 B.C.)

Greece for training before facing Caesar's experienced troops. Caesar entered Rome peacefully, soon departed to defeat the army his enemies had raised in Spain, and then followed Pompey to Greece in 48 B.C. There he nearly lost the war when Pompey cut off his supplies with a blockade. But his loyal soldiers stuck with him even when they were reduced to eating bread made from roots. When Pompey saw what Caesar's troops were willing to subsist on he lamented, "I am fighting wild beasts." The high morale of Caesar's army and Pompey's weak generalship eventually combined to bring Caesar a stunning victory at the battle of Pharsalus in 48 B.C. Pompey fled to Egypt, where he was treacherously murdered by the ministers of the boy-king Ptolemy XIII (63–47 B.C.), who had earlier exiled his sister and co-ruler, Queen Cleopatra VII (69–30 B.C.), and supported Pompey in the war. Caesar followed Pompey to Egypt and won a difficult campaign against Ptolemy's army that ended with the drowning of the pharaoh in the Nile and the return to the Egyptian throne of Cleopatra, who had begun a love affair with Caesar. He next had to spend three years battling his remaining Roman enemies in North Africa and Spain. But by 45 B.C. he had won the

civil war. Now he faced the intractable problem of ruling Rome.

Caesar's predicament had deep roots. Experience had shown that only a sole ruler could end the chaotic violence of factional politics in the first century B.C., but the oldest tradition of the republic was its abhorrence of monarchy. Cato had best expressed the Roman aristocrats' feelings about monarchy: "A king," he quipped, "is an animal that feeds on human flesh." Caesar's solution was to rule as king in everything but name. He first had himself appointed dictator in 48 B.C., with his term in this traditionally temporary office eventually extended to a lifetime tenure around 44 B.C. "I am not a king," he insisted. But the distinction was meaningless. As dictator he controlled the government despite the appearance of normal procedures. Elections for offices continued, for example, but Caesar manipulated the results by recommending candidates to the assemblies, which his supporters dominated. Naturally his recommendations were followed. His policies as Rome's ruler were ambitious and broad. He reduced debt moderately; limited the number of people eligible for subsidized grain; initiated a large program of public works, including the construction of public libraries; established colonies for his veterans in Italy and abroad; reestablished Corinth and Carthage as commercial centers; proclaimed standard constitutions for Italian towns; and extended citizenship to such non-Romans as the Cisalpine Gauls (those on the Italian side of the Alps). He also admitted non-Italians to the Senate when he expanded its membership from 600 to 900. Unlike Sulla, he did not proscribe his enemies. Instead he prided himself on his clemency, whose recipients were, by Roman custom, bound to be his grateful clients. In return, he received unprecedented honors, such as a special golden seat in the Senate house and the renaming of the seventh month of the year after him (*Julius,* hence our *July*). He also regularized the Roman calendar by initiating a year of 365 days, which was based on an ancient Egyptian calendar and roughly forms the basis for our modern calendar.*

His office and his honors pleased most Romans but outraged the narrow circle of the "best people." These men resented their exclusion from power and their domination by one of their own, a "traitor" who had deserted to the other side in the perpetual conflict between the republic's rich and poor. A band of senators consequently stabbed Julius Caesar to death on March 15 (the Ides of March), 44 B.C. in the Senate house at the foot of a statue of Pompey. The liberators, as they called themselves, had no concrete plans for governing Rome. They apparently believed the traditional political system of the republic would somehow reconstitute itself without any action on their part and without further violence; in their profound naiveté they ignored the bloody reality of the previous forty years, starting with Sulla. In fact, rioting broke out at Caesar's funeral as the common people vented their anger against the upper class that had robbed them of their hero. Far from presenting a united front, the aristocrats resumed their squabbles with one another to secure political power. By 44 B.C. the republic was damaged beyond repair.

---

*This so-called Julian calendar introduced an extra day every four years (the idea of a "leap year"), but this modification still left a discrepancy between the calendar and the solar year. In 1582 the Roman Catholic church under Pope Gregory XIII introduced the modern (Gregorian) calendar, which eliminated leap years in century years not evenly divisible by 400, such as 1800 and 1900. Protestant European countries adopted the Gregorian calendar only much later—Great Britain, for example, in 1752. In Russia the Julian calendar remained in effect until 1918, after the Bolshevik Revolution.

Commemorating the Murder of Caesar
Julius Caesar's assassins minted this coin in 43 B.C. The inscription says, "Ides of March," the date of the murder. The cap between the daggers symbolized liberty; the conspirator Brutus had his own portrait stamped on the other side of the coin.

Realism in Late Republican Literature and Portraiture

Because the sources of creativity are so diverse, historians necessarily must be cautious about postulating overly specific relationships between authors' and artists' works and the events of their times. The events of the late republic, however, were directly reflected in some of the contemporary literature. In the work of other authors, as in sculptural portraiture, we can suspect, although not prove, a connection to the conditions of the times.

Contemporary references to Roman affairs provided directly relevant material for some of the poems of Catullus (c. 84–54 B.C.). He moved to Rome from the province of Cisalpine Gaul in northern Italy, where his family had been sufficiently prominent to entertain Julius Caesar when he had been governor of that area. That connection did not prevent Catullus from including Caesar among the politicians of the era whose sexual behavior he savaged with his witty and explicit poetry. Catullus also wrote poems on more timeless themes, love above all. He employed a literary style popular among a circle of poets who modeled their Latin poems on the elegant Greek poetry of Hellenistic authors such as Callimachus. Catullus's most famous series of love poems concerned his passion for a married woman named Lesbia, whom he entreated to think only of the pleasures of the present: "Let us live, my Lesbia, and love, and value at one penny all the talk of stern old men. Suns can set and rise again: we, when once our brief light has set, must sleep one never-ending night. Give me a thousand kisses, then a hundred, then a thousand more. . . . "

Sculpture for a Roman Couple's Grave
Wealthy Romans frequently commissioned sculptures of themselves for their tombs, such as this one showing a couple standing together to signify their marriage bond.

clarity established the style that later European prose authors tried to match when writing polished Latin—the common language of government, theology, literature, and science throughout Europe for the next fifteen hundred years and more. Cicero also wrote many letters to his family and friends in which he commented frankly on political infighting and his motives in pursuing his own self-interest. The over 900 surviving letters offer a vivid portrait of Cicero's joys, sorrow, worries, pride, and love for his daughter. For no other figure from the ancient world do we have such copious and revealing personal material.

During periods when he temporarily withdrew from public affairs because his political opponents held the upper hand, Cicero wrote numerous works on political science, philosophy, ethics, and theology. He was not an original thinker in philosophy and ethics, taking his inspiration mainly from Greek philosophers, but he adapted their ideas to Roman life and infused his writings on these topics with a deep understanding of the need to appreciate the uniqueness of each human personality. His doctrine of *humanitas* ("humanness, the quality of humanity") combined various strands of Greek philosophy, especially Stoicism, to express an ideal for human life based on generous and honest treatment of others and an abiding commitment to morality derived from natural law (the right that exists for all people by nature, independent of the differing laws and customs of different societies). This ideal would exercise a powerful and enduring influence on later Western ethical philosophy. Cicero's legacy comes from his philosophical works and the style of his Latin prose, not from his distinguished political career. What he passed on to later ages was perhaps the most attractive ideal to come from ancient Greece and Rome: the spirit of *humanitas*.

The poet Lucretius (c. 94–55 B.C.) indirectly reflected the uncertainty and violence of his times. By explaining the nature of matter as composed of tiny, invisible particles called atoms, his long poem called *On the Nature of Things* sought to dispel the fear of death, which in his words, served only to feed "the running sores of life." Dying, his poem taught, simply meant the dissolution of the union of atoms, which had come together temporarily to make up a person's body. There could be no eternal punishment or pain after death, indeed no existence

Catullus's call to live for the moment, heedless of convention, well suited a time when the turmoil of Rome could make the concerns of tradition seem irrelevant.

The many prose works of Cicero, the master of rhetoric, also directly concerned events of his time. Fifty-eight of his speeches survive in the revised versions he published, and their eloquence and

at all, because a person's soul, itself made up of atoms, perished along with the body. Lucretius took this "atomic theory" of the nature of existence from the work of the Greek philosopher Epicurus (341–270 B.C.), whose views on the atomic character of matter were in turn derived from the work of the fifth-century B.C. thinkers Leucippus and Democritus. Although we do not know when he began to compose his poem, Lucretius was still working on it at Rome during the 50s B.C. when politically motivated violence added a powerful new danger to life in Rome. Romans in Lucretius's time had ample reasons to need reassurance that death had no sting.

We might also surmise that the starkly realistic style of Roman portraiture of men in the first century B.C. reflected a recognition of life's harshness in this turbulent period, even for those wealthy enough to have likenesses of themselves sculpted in marble. The Roman upper-class tradition of making death masks of ancestors and displaying them in their homes presumably contributed to the artistic style of realistic portraiture. Another influence on this veristic, or "truthful," style may have been the taste in Hellenistic Greek sculpture for unflattering representations of human stereotypes, such as drunkards or elderly people. In any case the many portraits of specific individuals that survive from this era did not try to hide unflattering features. Long noses, receding chins, deep wrinkles, bald heads, careworn looks—all these were sculpted. Portraits of women from the period, by contrast, were generally more idealized, and children were not portrayed until the early empire. Because either the men depicted by the portraits or their families paid for the busts, they presumably wanted the subject's experience of life to show. Perhaps this insistence on realism mirrored the toll exacted on men who participated in the brutal arena of late republican politics.

CONCLUSION

The greatest challenge in studying the Roman Republic is to understand how such a powerful and militarily successful state lost its political stability. From its beginnings the republic flourished because the small farmers of Italy produced agricultural surpluses. These surpluses supported a growth in population that supplied the soldiers for a strong army of citizens and allies. The Roman willingness to endure great losses of life and property helped make this army invincible in prolonged conflicts. Rome might lose battles, but never wars. Because Rome's wars initially brought profits, peace seemed a wasted opportunity. Aristocratic commanders especially liked war because they could win glory and riches to enhance their status in Rome's social hierarchy.

But the continued wars of the republic had unexpected consequences that spelled disaster. Many of the small landowners on whom Italy's prosperity depended were ruined. When the dispossessed flocked to Rome, which had a temporarily booming economy because of the influx of booty from overseas, they created a new, unstable political force: the urban mob subject to the violent swings of the urban economy. The upper class escalated their competition with each other for the increased career opportunities constant war presented. These rivalries became unmanageable when successful generals began to extort advantages for themselves instead of the republic by acting as patrons to their client armies of poor troops. In this dog-eat-dog atmosphere, violence and murder became the preferred means for settling political disputes. But violent actions provoked violent responses. The powerful ideas of Cicero's ethical philosophy, which greatly influenced later thinkers, went ignored in the murderous conflicts of the civil wars that wracked Rome. No reasonable Roman could have been optimistic about the chances for an enduring peace in the aftermath of Caesar's assassination. That Augustus would forge such a peace less than fifteen years later would have seemed an impossible dream in 44 B.C. But history is full of surprises.

SUGGESTIONS FOR FURTHER READING

Source Materials

Lefkowitz, Mary R., and Maureen B. Fant. *Women's Life in Greece and Rome.* 1982. A collection of primary sources arranged by topics.

Lewis, Naphtali, and Meyer Reinhold. *Roman Civilization: Sourcebook I: The Republic.* 1990. An indispensable collection of annotated primary sources on a wide variety of subjects.

Livy. *The Early History of Rome; Rome and Italy; The War with Hannibal; Rome and the Mediterranean.* 1971, 1982, 1965, and 1976, respectively. Detailed narratives full of lively stories, written at the time of Augustus.

Plutarch. *Makers of Rome; Fall of the Roman Republic.* 1965 and 1972 (rev. ed.), respectively. Sprightly biographies of prominent figures from the republic, written by this prolific Greek author about A.D. 100.

Polybius. *The Rise of the Roman Empire.* 1979. A history of how Rome came to dominate the Mediterranean world written by a Greek of the second century B.C.

Interpretive Studies

Astin, Alan E. *Cato the Censor.* 1978. A scholarly account of the political and literary career of Cato.

Badian, E. *Publicans and Sinners: Private Enterprise in the Service of the Roman Republic.* 1972. A study of the economic and political role of Rome's primary big-business interests, its tax farmers.

————. *Roman Imperialism in the Late Republic.* 2d ed. 1968. Explains Roman expansion as a response to a perceived need for military defense.

Beard, Mary, and Michael Crawford. *Rome in the Late Republic.* 1985. A provocative interpretation of later republican history, especially on the relationship between religion and politics.

Boardman, John, Jasper Griffin, and Oswyn Murray, eds. *The Oxford History of the Classical World.* 1986. Brief, interpretive chapters covering the political, economic, social, and literary history of the republic.

Boëthius, Axel. *Etruscan and Early Roman Architecture.* 2d ed. 1978. Copiously illustrated discussion of republican architecture.

Bonfante, Larissa, ed. *Etruscan Life and Afterlife: A Handbook of Etruscan Studies.* 1986. Articles on the main aspects of Etruscan civilization in the light of recent research.

Brunt, P. A. *Social Conflicts in the Roman Republic.* 1971. A brief, authoritative account of the struggle of the orders and the social problems of the later republic.

Christ, Karl. *The Romans.* 1984. A topically arranged introduction to Roman civilization.

Cornell, Tim, and John Matthews. *Atlas of the Roman World.* 1982. A concise historical summary linked to excellent and colorful maps.

Crawford, Michael. *The Roman Republic.* 1978. A survey that emphasizes primary sources in its narrative.

Earl, Donald. *The Moral and Political Tradition of Rome.* 1967. A standard work on the ethical conceptions of the Roman aristocracy.

Errington, R. M. *The Dawn of Empire: Rome's Rise to World Power.* 1972. A detailed textbook on Roman wars and expansion in the third and second centuries B.C.

Gardner, Jane. *Women in Roman Law and Society.* 1986. Especially thorough treatment of the legal status of women in Roman history.

Gelzer, Matthias. *Caesar: Politician and Statesman.* 6th ed. Translated by Peter Needham. 1968. A classic work by a great German scholar of the earlier twentieth century.

Harris, William V. *War and Imperialism in Republican Rome, 327–70 B.C.* Corrected ed. 1985. A detailed discussion arguing that the desire for profits and social prestige motivated Roman expansion.

Henig, Martin, ed. *A Handbook of Roman Art.* 1983. An illustrated survey.

Hopkins, Keith. *Conquerors and Slaves: Sociological Studies in Roman History.* Vol. I. 1978. A controversial treatment of the effect increasing wealth had on Roman institutions, especially slavery.

Keaveney, Arthur. *Sulla: The Last Republican.* 1982. A biography that takes a sympathetic approach to Sulla's career.

Leach, John. *Pompey the Great.* 1978. A biography that emphasizes political history.

Nicolet, Claude. *The World of the Citizen in Republican Rome.* Translated by P. S. Falla. 1980. A scholarly treatment of a citizen's responsibilities and privileges under the republic.

Ogilvie, R. M. *Early Rome and the Etruscans.* 1976. A readable analysis of the murky history of early Rome.

————. *Roman Literature and Society.* 1980. A discussion of the history of Roman literature in its social context.

Potter, T. W. *Roman Italy.* 1987. An innovative survey of the history of the Italian countryside in Roman antiquity.

Rawson, Beryl, ed. *The Family in Ancient Rome.* 1986. A collection of essays by different authors.

Scullard, H. H. *From the Gracchi to Nero: A History of Rome, 133 B.C. to A.D. 68.* 5th ed. 1982. The classic introduction to this period.

Warmington, B. H. *Carthage.* 1964. A comprehensive but concise survey of Carthaginian history.

In A.D. 69 a general named Vespasian (A.D. 9–79, *69–79) became the ninth Roman emperor. One day his son, Titus, complained about the fee the imperial government charged for entering public latrines. Most people in Rome had to use these facilities because they had no bathroom where they lived. But Vespasian's son protested that it was unworthy of the emperor of the Roman world to derive revenue from such an undignified source. The emperor thereupon pulled out a small coin and held it to his son's nose, asking, "Does it stink?" With this demonstration, Vespasian made the point that the government could not afford to be too particular about the sources of its income.

Because the Roman Empire, like the republic before it, had few direct taxes, finding enough money to pay government expenses posed problems. Although certain taxes were collected, no personal income tax was levied. The empire's tax system was just one of the economic, social, and political traditions handed down from republican times that affected the imperial government's freedom of action. In fact, Roman attachment to "the ways of the elders" created a dangerous situation after Caesar's murder in 44 B.C. The old style of politics—competition among aristocratic men for status and power—had failed to bring peace and social stability, because personal success had become more important than the tradition of service to the commonwealth. The republic's collapse meant that Roman government needed a major overhaul to function effectively again. But abandoning the republican model of governing was too great a departure from ancestral tradition for the Romans. In response to this predicament, Augustus (63 B.C.–A.D. 14, *27 B.C.–14 A.D.), the man who

CHAPTER

6

The Roman Empire, 44 B.C.–A.D. 284

Building the Roman Empire
This concrete and stone bridge, financed by eleven local communities in Roman Spain in A.D. 106, soared one-hundred fifty feet over a river below. Construction on this massive scale testified to the early Roman Empire's prosperity and shared culture.

eventually succeeded Caesar as the most powerful Roman leader, consciously erected a new political system upon what had come before. He appealed to Roman reverence for tradition by keeping old institutions—the Senate, the magistrates, the client-patron system, for example—while fundamentally reshaping the distribution of power by creating a sole ruler. Augustus's justification for this new system, which we call the Roman Empire, was that it reestablished the old system the way it should have been. He deftly masked the reality of sweeping change, however, by propaganda in which innovation was called restoration, and the powerful new emperor was called merely the "first man" of the state. In this way tradition appeared to have been preserved when in fact it had been reinvented. The system Augustus created restored peace to the Roman world and endured until a prolonged political and economic crisis fatally weakened it in the third century A.D. By then, Christianity had emerged as a growing new religion, setting the stage for the religious and cultural transformation of the Roman Empire in the following centuries.

The Pax Romana: Unity After Civil War

The process of developing a new Roman political system headed by a sole ruler was accomplished neither quickly nor peacefully. In the long run, however, the new arrangement brought an extended period of peace for most people who lived inside the boundaries of Rome's empire. This tranquil time, sometimes called the *pax Romana* ("Roman peace"), was particularly welcome after the horrors of the civil wars between Caesar and his opponents and among the potential heirs to Caesar's power after his assassination. The story of the transformation of the republic into the empire begins with this gruesome struggle of Roman against Roman after the death of the dictator Caesar.

Caesar's Heir

When Julius Caesar was murdered, his grand-nephew Gaius Octavius, as Augustus was then named, was eighteen years old. The reading of Caesar's will revealed that he had adopted Octavius

---

IMPORTANT DATES

43 B.C. Octavian, Antony, and Lepidus form the Second Triumvirate

31 B.C. Octavian defeats Antony and Cleopatra at Actium in western Greece

27 B.C. Octavian announces the restoration of the republic and takes the title Augustus, thus beginning the principate

c. A.D. 5 Election of magistrates begins to be removed from the assemblies and placed under the control of the Senate and the emperor (process completed under Tiberius)

A.D. 41 Senate fails to restore the republic after Emperor Gaius's murder

A.D. 68–69 Civil war during the Year of the Four Emperors

A.D. 98 Last recorded instance of the passage of a law by a Roman assembly

A.D. 193 Praetorian guards auction off the rule of Rome after Emperor Commodus's murder

A.D. 212 Emperor Caracalla confers Roman citizenship on almost all free inhabitants of the empire (*Constitutio Antoniniana*)

A.D. 251–253 Serious epidemic spreads across the Roman world

A.D. 258–275 Prices rise by almost 1000 percent in many regions in an economic crisis

---

as his son and made him heir to a considerable fortune. (Roman families without sons often adopted an adult man, who then took over a son's responsibilities: continuing the family name and keeping the property in the male line.) Octavius, as Caesar's adopted son, took the name Gaius Julius Caesar Octavianus (known today as Octavian). He immediately thrust himself into the middle of the hornet's nest of Roman politics. The political infighting at Rome was ferocious, as politicians competed to fill the vacuum of power created by Caesar's sudden death. The most prominent competitor was Mark Antony (83–30 B.C.), who had served as a military commander under Caesar and had been his colleague as consul at the time of the murder. Antony patched together a temporary peace in Rome by convincing the Senate that it must carry out Caesar's various reforms to placate Caesar's veterans and secure the goodwill of the ordinary people of Rome, who had loved Caesar. Caesar's assassins were sent to posts in the provinces so their

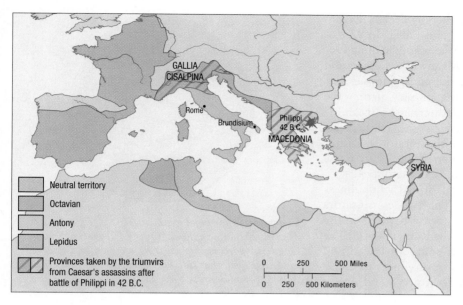

Neutral territory

Octavian

Antony

Lepidus

Provinces taken by the triumvirs
from Caesar's assassins after
battle of Philippi in 42 B.C.

0   250   500 Miles

0   250   500 Kilometers

**Territorial Division of
the Second Triumvirate
by 40 B.C.**

presence in Rome would not further provoke the people. Antony gained the support of Lepidus, who commanded Caesar's veterans, by promising him the post of *pontifex maximus* (which Caesar had held). Antony's ascent to dominant leadership seemed a sure thing until Octavian's new status as Caesar's adopted son was revealed and his evident ambitions made him an unwelcome obstacle to Antony's dream.

Because the veterans of Caesar's army now supported Octavian out of loyalty to their murdered commander, the Roman senators tried to use him as a political counterweight to Antony, even after Octavian demonstrated his disdain for regular procedure by illegally assembling an army on his own. Many senators thought they could control the inexperienced young man more easily than they could Antony, who they feared was aiming for dictatorial power. Cicero baldly asserted, "We will praise and honor the youngster and then get rid of him." The Senate directed the consuls of 43 B.C. to help Octavian against Antony, who was besieging Decimus Brutus, one of Caesar's assassins and now a provincial governor in Cisalpine Gaul (northern Italy). Octavian's troops headed north and forced Antony to retreat across the Alps. Meanwhile, the two consuls of 43 B.C. apparently died of battle wounds, although rumor said that Octavian had poisoned one of them. Octavian proved that discarding him was not going to be an easy task: he marched his

army back to Rome and demanded that he and an obscure relative be appointed consuls for the rest of 43 B.C. The Senators yielded and gave Octavian and his relative the consulships for the remainder of the year, once again disregarding the tradition that required a man to progress gradually through the course of offices to reach the pinnacle of power. This acquiescence to the demands of powerful military men, as in Pompey's irregular career, seemed more and more to be standard practice rather than a rare exception to tradition.

From Second Triumvirate to Civil War

Because the Roman armies, led by Octavian, Antony, and Lepidus (now a provincial governor in Narbonese Gaul, today southern France), balked at fighting each other, their commanders decided to reconcile and join forces to compel the Senate to recognize their supremacy. The three leaders met in the presence of their armies in November 43 B.C. to form the so-called Second Triumvirate. Unlike the First Triumvirate (60 B.C.), this alliance received official sanction when the triumvirs compelled the Senate to pass a law bestowing on them responsibility for reconstituting the state. Their power was now unrivaled, and the republic was in truth, if not in law, defunct. Octavian and Antony, who overshadowed the more lethargic Lepidus, ruthlessly proscribed the real and imagined enemies of Caesar, thereby declaring them outlaws to be hunted down and killed. In 42 B.C. the Senate recognized Caesar as a god, making Octavian the son of a divinity. Meanwhile, Cassius and Marcus Brutus, leaders in the conspiracy against Caesar, had been extorting money from the provinces of the eastern Mediterranean in an attempt to mount resistance to the triumvirate. (Antony had executed the conspirator Decimus Brutus, whose army had deserted him.) But at the battles of Philippi in Macedonia, in October 42 B.C., Antony defeated Cassius and Brutus while illness kept Octavian in his tent. The two conspirators committed suicide, and the uneasy partners in the triumvirate agreed to divide the Roman world. The pact made at Brundisium in southern Italy in 40 B.C. gave Italy and the western provinces to Octavian, the eastern provinces to Antony, and Africa to Lepidus.

Octavian secured Italy as his power base by settling veterans from his army on land confiscated from Italians who had supported Cassius and Brutus, causing great hardship and discontent for many. Those who lost their land had few options besides emigrating to Rome to join the poor masses there. From 39 to 36 B.C. Octavian fought a bitter war against the republican general Sextus Pompey in the western Mediterranean, who threatened to cut off grain shipments to Rome from that region and thus foment unrest among the urban poor, the recipients of subsidized grain. The brilliant naval operations of Octavian's general Agrippa finally vanquished Sextus. When Lepidus challenged Octavian's right to control Sicily after Sextus's defeat, Octavian trounced Lepidus's army and forced him out of the triumvirate into private life. The stage was now set for a confrontation between Octavian and Antony, men whose individual ambitions were too great to share Rome's rule. While Octavian had been fighting Sextus, Antony had been conducting military campaigns to increase his power in the ancient Near East. In the course of diplomatic negotiations over the reorganization of Roman-controlled territory in the eastern Mediterranean, he met and fell in love with Cleopatra VII (69–30 B.C.), the remarkable queen who had earlier entranced Caesar. Through her wit and intelligence, Cleopatra had made Caesar and then Antony her political supporters and her lovers.

Cleopatra, Queen of Egypt
This silver coin, inscribed "Queen Cleopatra, Younger Goddess," portrays her wearing a crown and swathed in pearls. The other side bore a portrait of Mark Antony to commemorate their partnership in ruling the Eastern Mediterranean.

Because Cleopatra commanded a sizable fleet and a rich country, her alliance with Antony strengthened his position in his rivalry with Octavian. Playing on the Roman fear of foreigners, Antony's enemies in Rome launched a propaganda campaign claiming that he planned to take over the Roman world and share it with Cleopatra. Octavian promptly moved to crush the pair. He shrewdly required the residents of Italy and the western provinces to swear a personal oath of allegiance to him, effectively making them all his clients in the traditional Roman system of patronage. The civil war ended in Antony's ignominious defeat in 31 B.C., at the naval battle of Actium in northwest Greece. Cleopatra fled with her ships to Egypt, and Antony followed. There she committed suicide in 30 B.C. as Octavian's armies advanced. To rob Octavian of the chance to parade her as a captive in his triumph in Rome, Cleopatra ended her life by allowing a poisonous snake, a symbol of royal authority, to bite her.

The capture of Egypt in 30 B.C. left Octavian without a viable military rival in the Roman world. It also made him fabulously rich because Egypt essentially became his private property, to be inherited by future Roman emperors. Egypt also exported much grain to Rome, providing a third of the city's annual needs. Rome's emperors needed Egyptian grain to feed the urban poor, who might riot if

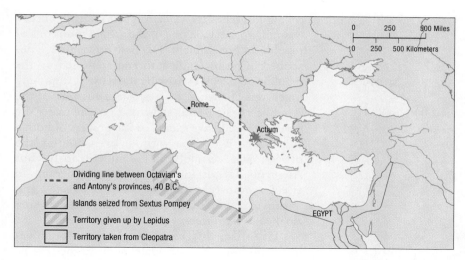

Territories Gained by Octavian, 40–30 B.C.

shortages occurred. Preserving the revenues and exports from Egypt always remained a priority for Rome's emperors. About ten years later, for example, Rome went to great lengths to head off a threat to the region's security by making concessions to Candace, the queen of Nubia, whose army had fought the Roman defenders of southern Egypt to a standstill.

The Creation of the Principate

After again distributing land to veterans of his army to create more settlements loyal to him, Octavian formally announced in 27 B.C. that he was restoring the republic. It was up to the Senate and the Roman people, he proclaimed, to decide how to preserve it thereafter. Recognizing that Octavian possessed real power in this unprecedented situation, the Senate promptly asked him to safeguard the restored republic and gave him the honorary name "Augustus." Octavian had wanted to change his name to Romulus, after Rome's legendary first king, but as an ancient observer reports, "when he realized the people thought this preference meant he longed to be their king, he accepted the title of Augustus instead, as if he were more than human; for everything that is most treasured and sacred is called *augustus.*"

The system of government Augustus created to replace the republican system is called the *principate,* from the Latin word *princeps* (meaning "first man," the root of the English word *prince*). Augustus used this term to describe his position as ruler, but modern historians usually refer to the *princeps* as the emperor, from the title *imperator.* This was a republican honorary designation meaning "military commander" that troops bestowed on their general after a great victory, and it became customary to give this title to every *princeps* to signify his control over the army.

In the years after 27 B.C. the annual election of consuls and other officials, the continuation of the Senate, and the passing of legislation in the assemblies of the people maintained the facade of republican normality. In truth, Augustus exercised power because he controlled the army. To preserve appearances, however, Augustus made sure the Senate periodically renewed its formal approval of his powers. An arrangement decreed in 23 B.C. promoted stability after Augustus had nearly died from two severe illnesses—with no successor ready—and opposition had arisen from disgruntled aristocrats. Augustus resigned his consulship and ceased to hold it in later years, making room for other upper-class men to gain this coveted post. The Senate in turn granted Augustus the power of a consul without him needing to hold the office, declaring that his imperium was greater than that of any actual consul. He also received a lifetime grant of the power of a tribune, giving him the authority to halt the action of all magistrates, the assemblies, and the Senate. Finally, he controlled the state treasury. The

Roman Family Pride
This Roman senator holds busts of his ancestors. Prominent Romans kept such items in their homes to display their lineage.

senators granted supreme power—the power of a king—to Augustus but camouflaged it in these republican trappings so they and he could claim they had restored the republic and its traditions.

Augustus's choice of *princeps* as his title instead of "king" or "dictator" was a cleverly calculated move. In the republic, *princeps* had designated the most prestigious man in the Roman Senate, the leader other senators looked to for guidance. By calling himself a *princeps,* Augustus was implicitly claiming to carry on one of the valued traditions of republican government. His new powers were described in terms familiar to and respected by the republic's citizens, conveying the sense that nothing much was changing. In fact, Augustus revised the republic's basic power structure: no one under the republic could have exercised the powers of both a consul and a tribune without even holding the offices, and certainly not simultaneously. But Augustus did just that: the principate became in effect a monarchy disguised as a corrected and improved republic, headed by Augustus, a king cloaked as a *princeps.*

Historians disagree about Augustus's motives in establishing the principate: some argue that he was a cynical despot bent on suppressing the traditional freedoms of the republic; others insist that he had little choice but to impose an autocratic system to stabilize a world jolted by the violence of aristocratic rivals for power. To evaluate the principate, we must recognize the demands on Augustus to balance his society's need for peace, Rome's traditional commitment to its citizens' freedom of action, and his own political ambitions.

Augustus's constitutional position has been aptly described by the wonderfully paradoxical phrase "first among equals." In his own account of his career, the *Res gestae* ("Things Accomplished"), he wrote that he ruled not by power but through his moral authority (*auctoritas*)—that is, people would regard his advice as the equivalent of commands. In this way the traditional Roman paternalism in social relations, represented by the client-patron system, was officially transferred to politics. It was not a hollow gesture when Augustus was named "father of his country" in 2 B.C., in Roman eyes the greatest honor he could receive. With the emergence of the principate, Rome had a sole ruler who presided over the people like a Roman father: stern but caring, expecting obedience and loyalty from his children, and obligated to nurture them in return. The goal of such an arrangement was stability and order, not political freedom.

Augustus's loyal troops backed up his moral authority. Like the generals of the late republic, he had given his veterans land to sustain their loyalty in the years of civil war, and he continued to pay attention to their needs. He institutionalized the strategy of using military strength to secure political rule by constituting the army as a permanent,

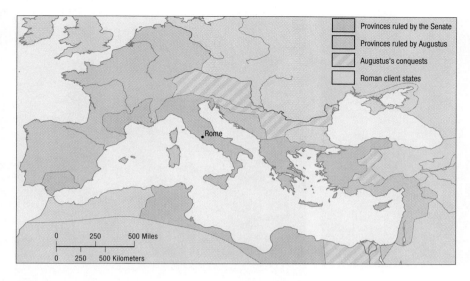

Provinces ruled by the Senate
Provinces ruled by Augustus
Augustus's conquests
Roman client states

Rome

0   250   500 Miles
0 250   500 Kilometers

**The Roman Empire
Under Augustus**

standing force with defined responsibilities and benefits. As *princeps* he established regular terms of service and for the first time guaranteed soldiers that they would receive substantial benefits after their retirement. To pay the costs of maintaining this permanent army, Augustus imposed an inheritance tax; this direct tax mainly affected the rich and thus was unpopular with the upper classes. The soldiers, in return for the *princeps'* patronage, obeyed and protected him. For the first time in Roman history, troops, called praetorians, were stationed in Rome itself. These soldiers were Augustus's bodyguards, a visible reminder that the superiority of the Roman emperor, as we will call him for convenience, was in reality guaranteed by the threat of force as well as the weight of his moral authority.

The Precariousness of City Life in Augustan Rome

Augustus remained Roman emperor until his death in A.D. 14. The greatest benefit of his rule was peace within the empire after the nearly constant civil war that had plagued Roman Italy for more than fifty years. At last the government could attend to economic and social problems, a response that the Roman tradition of paternalism demanded. The most pressing problems were in Rome itself, a teeming city of more than a million inhabitants, many of whom had too little to eat and not enough jobs. A variety of archaeological and literary

sources allow us to sketch a composite picture of life in Augustan Rome. Although some of the sources refer to times after Augustus and to cities other than Rome, they nevertheless help us understand this period; economic and social conditions were essentially the same in all Roman cities throughout the early centuries of the empire.

Rome's inhabitants, except for the rich, had hard lives. The population of Augustan Rome was vast for the ancient world; no European city would have nearly this many people again until London in the 1700s. Such a huge population meant overcrowding. The streets were packed: "One man jabs me with his elbow, another whacks me with a pole; my legs are smeared with mud, and from all sides big feet step on me" is one resident's description of walking in Rome. To ease congestion in the narrow streets, the city banned carts and wagons in the daytime. This regulation made Rome's nights noisy with the creaking of axles and the shouting of drivers caught in traffic jams.

Most people lived in small apartments in multi-storied buildings called *insulae* ("islands"). These dwellings outnumbered private houses by twenty-six to one. The first floor of the building usually housed shops, bars, and simple restaurants. Graffiti of all kinds—political endorsements for municipal elections, the posting of rewards for the return of stolen property, personal insults, and what we would call advertising—frequently decorated the exterior walls. Well-off tenants occupied the lower stories. The higher the floor in the building, the

(above) **Roman Snack Bar**
This establishment on the first floor of an apartment building at Ostia, the port of Rome, was typical of the small restaurants of Roman cities. Customers could take out food and drink or sit for a more leisurely meal.
(right) **Roman Public Bath**
This "warm room" (tepidarium) *from a luxuriously decorated Roman bath included couches on which clients could rest.*

cheaper the apartment. The poorest people lived in single rooms rented by the day. Because they had no running water, apartment dwellers had to lug buckets of water from one of Rome's hundreds of public fountains up the stairs. A wealthy few had piped-in water (though researchers now surmise they ran some risk of slow poisoning from the lead used to make the pipes). But most people lacked plumbing and had to use the public latrines or buckets for toilets at home. People either haphazardly flung the noisome contents of these containers out the window or carried the buckets down to the streets to be emptied by people who made their living collecting excrement. Because the population of Rome generated about sixty tons of human waste every day, sanitation was an enormous problem. For example, archaeologists have found seventy-five large pits that had been filled with a nauseating mixture of dead bodies, animal carcasses, and sewage of all sorts not far from the center of Rome. They also found signs reading, "No dumping of corpses or garbage allowed here."

To keep clean, people used public baths. Because admission fees were low, almost everyone could afford to go to the baths daily. Imperial Rome had scores of these establishments, which like modern health clubs served as centers for exercising and socializing as well as washing. Bath patrons progressed through a series of increasingly warm, humid areas until they reached a saunalike room. Bathers swam naked in their choice of hot or cold pools. The sexes bathed apart, either in separate rooms or at different times of the day, and women had full access to the public baths.

In Rome, as in all ancient cities, unsanitary conditions prevailed despite the many baths, fountains with running water, and the ongoing efforts of officials (the aediles) to keep the streets clean. Bathing was thought to be particularly valuable for sick people, for example, and the baths contributed to the spread of communicable diseases. Furthermore, although the Roman government in its concern for public sanitation built a sewer system, its contents emptied untreated into the city's Tiber

River. The technology for sanitary disposal of waste simply did not exist. People regularly left human and animal corpses in the streets, to be gnawed by vultures and dogs. The poor were not the only people affected by such conditions: a stray mutt once brought a human hand to Vespasian's table while he was eating lunch. Flies buzzing everywhere and a lack of mechanical refrigeration contributed to frequent gastrointestinal ailments; the most popular amulet of the time was supposed to ward off stomach trouble. Although the wealthy could not eliminate such discomforts, they made their lives more pleasant with amenities such as having snow brought from the mountains to ice their drinks and having their slaves clean their airy houses, which were built around courtyards and gardens.

City residents faced other hazards besides infectious disease. Broken crockery and other debris were routinely hurled out of the upper stories of apartment buildings and rained down like missiles on unwary pedestrians below. "If you are walking to a dinner party in Rome," one poet remarked, "you would be foolish not to make out your will first. For every open window is a source of potential disaster." The *insulae* could be dangerous to their inhabitants as well as to passersby because they were in constant danger of collapsing. Roman engineers, despite their expertise in using concrete, brick, and stone as durable building materials, lacked the technology to calculate precisely how much stress their constructions could stand. Builders trying to cut costs paid little attention to engineering safeguards in any case, which led Augustus to impose a height limit of seventy feet on new apartment buildings, a regulation that unscrupulous operators largely ignored. Often built in valleys because the sunny hilltops were occupied by the homes of the rich, these apartment buildings were also susceptible to floods. Fire presented an even greater risk; one of Augustus's many services to the urban masses was to provide Rome with the first public fire department in Western history. He also established Rome's first police force, despite his reported fondness for stopping to watch the frequent brawls that the crowding in Rome's streets encouraged. The squalid conditions and commonplace violence that characterized Augustan Rome were in fact a normal part of city life in antiquity.

Roman Street in Herculaneum
Multi-storied houses abutting directly onto streets paved with flat stones characterized prosperous Roman towns. This street in Herculaneum was preserved by the volcanic eruption of Mt. Vesuvius in A.D. *79.*

Augustus also tried to improve the condition of the urban masses by assuring an adequate food supply for Rome's poor, many of whom could find only sporadic employment. He viewed this as part of his responsibility as the patron of all the people, and he freely drew upon his own vast fortune to help pay for imported grain. Distributing free grain to Rome's poor had been a tradition for decades, but the scale of Augustus's dole system was immense: two hundred fifty thousand recipients were entitled to the distributions. Because many of these poor people had families, this statistic suggests that perhaps seven hundred thousand people in Rome depended on the government for their grain, the basic food staple of most Romans. Poor people usually made this grain, a form of wheat not well suited for baking bread, into a watery porridge, which they washed down with cheap wine. If they were lucky, they might have some beans, leeks, or sheep lips on the side. The rich, as we learn from a surviving Roman cookbook, ate more delectable dishes, such as spiced roast pork or lobster, often flavored with a sweet-and-sour sauce concocted from honey and vinegar.

Slaves and Spectacles

To produce the agricultural products Rome's consumers required, both free laborers and slaves toiled on farms throughout Italy. The conditions of slavery under the empire remained much as they had been under the late republic, when Rome's foreign wars resulted in a great influx of foreign slaves to Italy. Slaves working in agriculture or manufacturing that required a lot of physical strength often endured grueling existences. Most such slaves were men, although slave women might be assistants to the foremen who managed gangs of rural slave laborers. An ancient author offers this grim description of slave men at work in a flourmill in the eastern part of the empire: "Through the holes in their ragged clothes you could see all over their bodies the scars from whippings. Some had on only loincloths. Letters had been branded on their foreheads and irons manacled their ankles." Worse than the mills were the mines, where the foremen constantly flogged the slave miners to keep them working in such a dangerous environment.

Slaves who worked as household servants had an easier physical existence. Although Roman households employed more male than female slaves, many domestic slaves were women, who worked as nurses, maids, kitchen help, and clothesmakers. Some male slaves ran businesses for their masters, and they were often allowed to keep part of the profits as an incentive. Female household slaves had less opportunity to earn money. Masters sometimes granted tips for sexual favors. Female prostitutes, who were mostly slaves owned by men, had more chances to make money for themselves. Slaves who somehow acquired funds would sometimes buy slaves themselves, thereby creating a kind of slave hierarchy. A male slave, for example, might buy a female slave for a mate. Slaves could thus sometimes have a semblance of a family life, though a formal, legal marriage was impossible because the man and woman remained their master's property, as did their children. If truly fortunate, slaves could save enough to buy themselves from their masters or could be manumitted by their masters' wills. They then became free Roman citizens. Some tomb epitaphs testify to affectionate feelings certain masters had for their slaves, but even household slaves could suffer miserable lives if their masters were cruel. Slaves had no recourse; if they retaliated against their owners because of inhumane treatment, their punishment was death.

The most visible slaves were the men and women who fought as gladiators for public entertainment. Women, perhaps daughters trained by their gladiator fathers, first appeared in the arena during the republic and continued to fight in public until the emperor Septimius Severus (*A.D. 193–211) banned their appearance. Not all gladiators were slaves; prisoners of war and condemned criminals could also be forced to fight. Gladiatorial combat was often to the death, but the crowd could shout for a defeated fighter to be spared if he or she had shown special courage. Free men and women also voluntarily enrolled themselves as gladiators in return for a fee. Early in the first century A.D., the Senate apparently became alarmed at the number of citizens entering this disreputable occupation. It forbade men and women of senatorial or equestrian rank and all freeborn women under the age of twenty from fighting as gladiators or appearing on stage as entertainers, another unsavory profession by upper-class standards.

Under the republic, private individuals had financed gladiatorial combats as part of a distinguished man's funeral. Gladiatorial shows became the rage under the empire in cities across the Roman world. Augustus himself paid for more than five thousand pairs of gladiators to fight it out in spectacular festivals staged at Rome. Gladiatorial shows and chariot races were staged as the main attractions at celebrations of great occasions, such as a victory in war. These shows provided a main source of a city's public entertainment. Theatrical productions also flourished. Mimes were the most popular form of theater; these dramas of everyday life and explicit sexual farces were unique in employing female actresses to play female roles.

Enormous crowds of men and women attended shows in Rome and in cities across the empire to watch chariot races, bouts between gladiators, mock naval battles on artificial lakes, fights between humans and savage beasts, and displays of exotic African animals that sometimes mangled condemned criminals as a form of capital punishment. Tens of thousands of spectators would crowd into amphitheaters to see the gladiatorial combats, with women segregated in the uppermost tiers of seats. To make the fights more unpredictable, Romans matched gladiators with different kinds of weapons. One favorite kind of bout pitted a lightly armored fighter, called a "net-man" because he used a net and a trident, against a more heavily armored "fish-man," so named from the design of his helmet crest. Chariot racing held in the Circus Maximus stadium at Rome drew gigantic crowds of perhaps two hundred thousand people. Women could sit next to men at chariot races, at which betting was a great attraction. Crowds at these events could be rowdy. One contemporary source described his fellow Roman sports fans: "Look at the mob coming to the show—already they're out of their minds! Aggressive, heedless, already in an uproar about their bets! They all share the same suspense, the same madness, the same voice." As the Roman Empire gradually became more autocratic, mass gatherings such as sports events or theater productions became a medium for ordinary people to communicate with the emperors, who were expected to attend. On more than one occasion, for example, the poor rioted in the amphitheaters or the Circus Maximus to confront the emperor and express their concern about a shortfall in the free grain supply.

Communicating the Emperor's Image

The emperor sent messages to the populace through media both small and large. In the ancient world, coins were the only mass-produced source of official messages and therefore could function something like modern political advertising. Coins produced in the imperial mints carried propaganda messages such as Augustus's title "father of his country" to remind people of their emperor's moral authority over them, or "the roads have been rebuilt" to emphasize the emperor's personal generosity in paying for highway construction. Augustus had to do something about Italy's roads and bridges because Rome's wealthy men had failed to fulfill their traditional duty of funding such public works projects. The rich now preferred to show their public-spirited munificence by paying for el-

egant buildings such as temples or halls for law courts instead of low-visibility projects such as fixing the roads, which did not garner them as much publicity and prestige.

Augustus outmaneuvered the aristocracy by turning the construction of public buildings into a virtual monopoly of the emperor. Dipping into his overwhelmingly vast fortune, he paid to erect grand buildings in Rome, winning glory for his generosity. These projects served utilitarian purposes but also communicated a particular image of the emperor to the Roman people. The vast imperial forum (public square) Augustus built illustrates how his image was conveyed. To commemorate the victory over Caesar's assassins at Philippi in 42 B.C., Augustus had vowed to build a temple to Mars, the Roman god of war, and Venus, the Roman goddess of love, whom Julius Caesar had claimed as his divine ancestor and thus made Augustus's relative, too. In 2 B.C. the massive temple, constructed on a lofty podium, was completed. Out from the temple, the forum's centerpiece, stretched two-story colonnades and curved statue galleries displaying famous heroes from Roman history. The forum served various practical purposes, such as providing space for religious services and the formal ceremonies marking the passage into adulthood of upper-class Roman boys. It also communicated an image of the emperor who had paid for it: the imposing size and the elevation of the temple communicated the benefactor's grandeur; the statues indicated his respect for the lessons of history about the proper goals for a Roman man; and the fulfillment of the promise to build the forum testified to his loyalty to the gods, the valued quality of *pietas*. These messages constituted Augustus's ideology of empire, which he wished his subjects to accept. As with his patronage of the urban poor through the distribution of free food, he was trying to promote political and social stability while at the same time win glory and status for himself in traditional Roman fashion. With his many prestigious achievements, Augustus overshadowed his rich and aristocratic contemporaries. His successors in ruling Rome imitated his methods of reinforcing the emperor's image as the Roman world's preeminent figure.

Under the empire the upper class of Rome never regained the political dominance it had enjoyed during the republic. Even the wealthiest of the elite could not compete with the emperor because of the power he derived from his command of a standing army and from his control of the treasury. Moreover, as patron of upper-class Romans, the emperor was often bequeathed wealth in the wills of his clients and became even richer. Finally, the upper class failed to reproduce itself sufficiently, perhaps because its members felt that the expense and trouble of raising children threatened their high standard of living. Children became so rare among this class that Augustus passed a law designed to encourage more births by granting special legal privileges to the parents of three or more children. In the same spirit he also promulgated new laws intended to strengthen marriage ties and made adultery a criminal offense. Ironically, he had to exile his own daughter—his only child—and a granddaughter after adultery scandals. He also banished Ovid (43 B.C.–A.D. 17), ostensibly for writing poems like *The Art of Love* and *Love Affairs,* in which the poet as part of his complex reflection on Roman society playfully described how to flirt at the races or deceive a spouse. Augustus's legislation had little effect, however, and the prestigious old families withered away under the empire, aided by banishment and execution if they ran seriously afoul of the emperors. Recent demographic research suggests that three-quarters of the families of senatorial status died out in every generation. New people from below the senatorial class who won the emperors' favor continuously took their places in the social hierarchy.

Despite often poor health, Augustus ruled as emperor until his death at age seventy-five in A.D. 14. The length of his reign (forty-one years) helped institutionalize the changes in Roman government he brought about with the principate. As the Roman historian Tacitus later remarked, by the time Augustus died, "almost no one was still alive who had seen the republic." The gradual dying out of the important families of the republic over the following decades eliminated a major source of potential opposition to the new system. And Augustus could destroy those who got in his way. Rome's urban masses favored the empire because their rich patron, the emperor, looked out for their needs. Through his longevity, his rapport with the army, and his crafty manipulation of the traditional vocabulary of Roman politics to disguise his power, Augustus ensured the transformation of the republic into the empire. His position as a sole ruler also effectively redefined the Roman constitution, which under the republic had been incompatible with monarchy.

New and Old Education in Imperial Rome

Although some traditional educational practices remained unchanged in the transformation of the republic into an empire, Roman education's primary subject, rhetoric, underwent important changes. Since the republic, mastering rhetoric had been a major goal in the education of young Roman men because persuasive speaking skills had traditionally been the key to success for men in politics and the courts. The ability to make stirring speeches had been such a powerful weapon in the late republic that it had catapulted a man like Cicero, who lacked distinction as a military leader, to the political forefront. Cicero's stinging attacks on Antony, in fact, so enraged him that he ordered Cicero murdered during the proscriptions of 43 B.C. In a grisly display of his hatred of Cicero's words, Antony had the orator's severed head and hands nailed up for display at Rome's center, where Cicero had so often spoken.

Under the empire the study of rhetoric changed. The supremacy of the emperor ruled out the kind of freewheeling political debate and decision making in which rhetoric had been so important in the late republic. The subject matter of rhetorical training now, one orator complained, "is far removed from reality." Instead of matters concerning government, he went on, students debated topics such as "a rape victim's alternatives,"or "cures for the plague" in stilted, grandiloquent style. Despite this shying away from current politics, rhetorical studies continued to dominate Roman education under the empire. Ambitious men now needed rhetorical skills to praise the current emperor on the numerous public occasions that promoted his image as a competent and compassionate ruler as well as for legal matters and the trials of government officials. The power of rhetoric was thus redirected from its republican aim of influencing votes to a new imperial goal: legitimizing and strengthening the new Roman system of government.

Rome had no free public schools, so the poor were lucky to pick up even rudimentary knowledge from their harried parents; even wealthier people rarely pursued their education further than acquiring practical skills. A character in the *Satyricon,* a satirical literary work of the first century A.D., expressed this utilitarian attitude toward education succinctly: "I didn't study geometry and literary criticism and worthless junk like that. I just learned how to read the letters on signs and how to work out percentages, and I learned weights, measures, and the values of the different kinds of coins."

As the historian Tacitus described, the Roman ideal called for mothers to teach their children right and wrong:

> *Once upon a time children were reared not by a hired nurse in her den but at their mother's breast and on her lap. For her the highest merit was to keep house and raise the children. An older female relative of high character was chosen to look after the family's children, and in her presence nobody dared to say anything rude or do anything wrong. She governed not only the children's lessons and tasks but also recreation and play.*

Under the empire servants or hired teachers usually looked after the children of families with some means. They would send their sons and daughters to private elementary schools from the ages of seven to eleven to learn reading, writing, and basic arithmetic. Teachers used rote methods in the classroom, with frequent corporal punishment for mistakes. Some children went on to the next three years of school, in which they were introduced to literature, history, and grammar. Only a few boys thereafter advanced to the study of rhetoric.

For the Romans, advanced study principally concerned literature, history, ethical philosophy, law, and dialectic (determining the truth by identifying contradictions in arguments). Mathematics and science were little studied for themselves, but Roman engineers and architects necessarily became extremely proficient at calculation. Rich men and women would pursue their interest in books by having slaves read aloud to them. Reading required manual dexterity as well as literacy because books, instead of being bound page by page, consisted of continuous scrolls made from the papyrus reed or animal skin. A reader had to unroll the scroll with one hand and simultaneously roll it up with the other.

Celebrated Ideals in Literature and Portraiture

New literature blossomed in the time of Augustus. Modern critics call the period from about 100 B.C. through Augustus's reign the Golden Age of Latin literature. Although writers like the historian Livy (54 B.C.–A.D. 17) and the encyclopedist Varro (116 B.C.–27 B.C.) produced volume after volume in prose, the most glamorous literature of Augustus's age was poetry. Augustus himself tried to write poetry, and he served as the patron of a circle of writers and artists. The emperor did not approve of an irreverent wit like Ovid. His favorites, Horace (65–8 B.C.) and Virgil (70–19 B.C.), were more amenable to the establishment. Horace, for example, celebrated Augustus's victory over Antony and Cleopatra at Actium in a poem opening with the line, "Now is the time for a toast." Virgil's most famous work was *The Aeneid,* an epic poem inspired by Homeric poetry, which told the legend of the Trojan Aeneas, the most distant ancestor of the Romans and therefore a predecessor of Romulus, Rome's first king. In this poem, Virgil tempered his praise of the Roman state and Aeneas's great virtues, especially *pietas,* with a dramatic recognition of the price he paid for success. According to Virgil, Aeneas's flight from the ruins of Troy displayed his piety in obeying the gods' command to found a new city in Italy as the base for future Roman expansion and glory. In the course of doing his duty, however, Aeneas paid a heavy personal price. He had to desert the woman he loved, Dido, queen of Carthage, thereby establishing the background for the hostility between Romans and Carthaginians, which erupted into the bloody Punic Wars. To found a new state in Italy, Aeneas also had to fight fierce wars against indigenous peoples. In *The Aeneid,* Virgil explored with deep emotion the paradoxical pairing of human success and human suffering. On another level, *The Aeneid* also underscored the complex mix of gain and loss that followed the Augustan transformation of Roman politics and society. In the poem the gods teach the pious (in the Roman sense) Aeneas the moral code of ruling: be merciful to the conquered but lay low the haughty. Augustus followed this same code.

When Augustus was growing up, the complexity of human experience had characterized the style of sculptural portraits: busts sculpted in the late republic were starkly realistic. The sculptures Augustus ordered after he became emperor displayed a more idealized style, reminiscent of classical Greek sculpture and the portraits of Alexander the Great by Lysippus. In renowned works of art such as the First Gate statue of himself or the sculpted frieze on his Altar of Peace, Augustus was portrayed as serene and dignified, not careworn and sick, as he often was. As with his monumental architecture, Augustus used sculpture to project a calm and competent image of himself as, to use the vocabulary of his propaganda, the "restorer of the world."

Much of the poetry and portraiture of the new empire reflected Augustus's chosen vision of himself: the great father selflessly restoring peace to his war-torn people. This image lulled Romans into accepting a new way of life without realizing the hidden costs. Augustus was a generous patron to Rome's poor, and he did force reluctant aristocrats to contribute to maintaining the state's infrastructure and supporting the standing army. But underneath his benevolence lay a vein of ruthlessness. Many people were murdered under the proscriptions of 43 B.C. Many lost their homes in the confiscations that provided land for his army veterans. And perhaps most telling, the ironic guarantee of the *pax Romana* was the threat of Augustus's force as commander of the army. The free discussion and agreement among citizens that had been the most cherished ideal of the Roman Republic had been lost—they were the price of social and political order in the monarchy of the early Roman Empire.

The Political and Social Amalgam of the Early Empire

When Augustus died in A.D. 14, no procedure existed for selecting a new emperor because open concern with imperial succession would have been incompatible with Augustus's insistence that the republic had been restored. During his lifetime, Augustus had tried to ensure that a son would indeed succeed him. But he had no natural son, and the men he adopted as his heirs died prematurely. Finally he had settled on Tiberius (42 B.C.–A.D. 37,

*A.D. 14–37), a distinguished military commander who was the son of his wife Livia by a previous marriage. Tiberius paid a steep personal price for the emperor's favor: Augustus forced him to divorce his beloved wife, Vipsania, to marry Augustus's daughter, Julia, a marriage that proved disastrously unhappy. After Augustus's funeral and some awkward debate, the Senate formally asked Tiberius to take over the state. He accepted with apparently genuine reluctance. In this hesitant fashion, then, the imperial government set a precedent for the succession of a new emperor after the death of the preceding ruler. Nevertheless, the Roman Empire was not yet fully rooted as a political institution.

The Consolidation of Monarchy Through Politics and Religion

At first Tiberius tried to govern in cooperation with the Senate. He did, however, end the pretense that the republic still lived on by completing the transfer of the election of magistrates from the assemblies of the people to the Senate, a process Augustus had begun. Giving this power to the Senate provided the emperor with greater control over elections because he could direct the appointment of senators, and it pleased the senators because they no longer had to try to win public favor by campaigning. Furthermore, for some offices, Tiberius indicated his favorite candidates and thus ensured their election. The people, one Roman historian reported, "did not complain about the loss, except for some trivial grumbling." Another commentator applauded the change by asserting that the emperor's selection of winning candidates meant "genuine merit has replaced clever campaigning." Eventually, Tiberius decreased the importance of the Senate in Roman government, a trend that following emperors continued until the emperor's control over the election of magistrates and the passing of legislation became absolute.

Events after Tiberius's death demonstrated that most of the Roman upper class had no deep-seated desire for a genuine restoration of the republic. Tiberius had designated as the next emperor his young grandnephew Gaius (A.D. 12–41, *37–41), who was also the great grandson of Augustus's sister. Gaius has since become known as Caligula ("Baby Boots"), the nickname soldiers gave him as a child because he wore little leather shoes imitating theirs. He ruled through cruelty and violence, and his lack of any serious training in the skills of governing and his prodigal spending made his administration worse. He developed a hatred for the Senate and pushed the principate closer to open autocracy in the style of Hellenistic monarchy. He frequently outraged Roman social conventions by appearing on stage as a singer and actor, fighting mock gladiatorial combats, and appearing in public in women's clothing or costumes imitating statues of the gods. His demand for honors normally reserved for the gods earned him a reputation as a megalomaniac. His plan to have a statue of himself placed in the main Jewish temple in Jerusalem caused severe unrest among the Jews there. When two officers of the praetorian guard murdered Caligula in A.D. 41 to avenge personal insults, some senators debated the idea of truly restoring the republic by refusing to choose a new emperor. They soon capitulated, however, when Claudius (10 B.C.–A.D. 54, *A.D. 41–54), Augustus's grandnephew and Caligula's uncle, obtained the backing of the praetorian guard with promises of money. The praetorians forced the Senate to acknowledge Claudius as the new emperor; as he pointed out to the senators, without troops they had no other choice. The succession of Claudius under the threat of the use of force against the Senate made it abundantly clear that soldiers would always insist on having an emperor, a patron to look after their interests. It also revealed that any senatorial yearnings for the return of a republic would never be fulfilled.

From the reign of Claudius on, the emperors and the senatorial class developed a patron-client relationship; no longer could senators dream of reestablishing their former primacy in government, although they retained great status and expected the emperor to listen to their concerns respectfully. As patron the emperor chose the Senate members and then fostered their careers in public office. Claudius expanded the pool of imperial clients by enrolling men from a Roman province (Transalpine Gaul) in the Senate for the first time, an important change foreshadowing the crucial roles provincials would eventually play in the society and politics of the Roman Empire. As the emperor's clients, senators were supposed to remain loyal to him and support his programs. Tensions of course persisted. Many senators remained hostile toward Claudius because

they resented the power play he had used to become emperor and because he kept pushing them to be dutiful. They also objected to the broad administrative powers Claudius gave to some freedmen on his personal staff, a key step in developing an imperial administration. Finally, senators accused Claudius of being too influenced by his first wife, Messalina, and after her execution following a sexual scandal, his next wife, Agrippina.

At the age of sixteen, Nero (A.D. 37–68, *54–68) succeeded Claudius as emperor. Nero was Claudius's grandnephew and adopted son, whose mother, Agrippina, had married Claudius (her uncle) to ensure Nero's succession to the throne. The rumor that she hastened the event by feeding Claudius poisoned mushrooms cannot be confirmed. Nero's passion for singing and acting in public earned him the contempt of the upper class, who despised actors. The spectacular public festivals he put on and the cash he distributed to the masses in Rome kept him generally popular with the poorer people throughout his reign, although a giant fire in Rome in A.D. 64 aroused suspicions that he might have ordered the conflagration to clear the way for new building projects. As Nero grew older, he increasingly oppressed the upper class, and his strong preference for Greek culture offended traditional Romans. He even toured Greece in 67 and 68 A.D. to compete as a singer in the pan-Hellenic games; naturally, he won all the events he entered. While there, he announced "the freedom of Greece" in imitation of Flamininus's famous proclamation in 196 B.C. But for the Greeks this declaration rang as hollow as the previous one; Greece still remained part of the Roman Empire. To raise money for his profligate spending, Nero would trump up charges against wealthy men and women in order to seize their property. The revolts of three powerful provincial governors drove him to commit suicide in A.D. 68, when the praetorian guard was bribed to switch its loyalty to one of the governors. Assisted by one of his freedmen, Nero cut his own throat with the parting words, "To die! And such a great artist!"

Vespasian (A.D. 9–79, *69–79) became emperor after a year of civil war in which three others tried and failed to hold the throne (the Year of the Four Emperors, as it is called today). All the emperors from Augustus to Nero had come from one group of aristocratic families known as the Julio-Claudians.

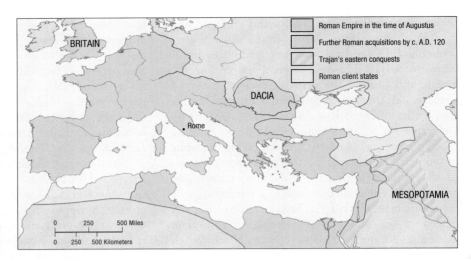

The Expansion of the Roman Empire

Vespasian, who was succeeded by his sons Titus (A.D. 39–81, *79–81) and Domitian (A.D. 51–96, *81–96), belonged to a different family, the Flavians. Their rule demonstrated that the Roman monarchy was not necessarily the inherited property of a single family group but rather a prize that could be won in competition and transferred to a new family dynasty. To legitimize his position, Vespasian had the Senate issue a law proclaiming his right to the powers exercised by previous emperors, probably in keeping with similar decrees passed for earlier emperors. Because respect for tradition was such a powerful force among the Romans, such proclamations in effect institutionalized the Roman Empire as a political system by acknowledging the precedents for the emperor's rule.

Vespasian also sought to secure his position by encouraging the spread of the imperial cult (worship of the emperor as a living god) in the provinces outside Italy, where most of the empire's population resided. With Julius Caesar as precedent, Augustus and Claudius had been declared gods after their deaths as a mark of great honor, and temples had been built for regular sacrifices to them. In the eastern provinces of the empire, however, people had spontaneously begun to worship the ruling emperor as a living god as early as the reign of Augustus. They had earlier expressed their respect for top officials and generals of the Roman Republic in this way. The deification of the current ruler seemed normal to them because they had honored their kings as divinities for centuries, even

before the Romans had conquered them. The imperial cult broadcast the same image of the emperor to the people of the provinces as the city's architecture and sculpture did to the people of Rome: he was larger than life, worthy of loyal respect, and a source of potential benefactions. Because emperor worship was already well established in Greece and the ancient Near East, Vespasian concentrated on spreading it in the provinces of Spain, southern France, and North Africa. Italy, however, had no temples to the living emperor. Traditional Romans scorned the imperial cult as a provincial aberration. Vespasian, known for his wit, revealed his personal attitude toward deification when, as he lay dying, he muttered, "Oh me! I'm afraid I'm becoming a god."

Although the emperor Trajan (*A.D. 98–117) fought extensive campaigns to try to expand the Roman Empire northward across the Danube River into Dacia (today Romania) and eastward into Mesopotamia, most emperors of the second century A.D. followed a less aggressive set of goals: to maintain law and order inside the vast empire's boundaries; to keep the army strong enough to defend the border regions; to provide free food and entertainment for the poor in Rome; to initiate public building projects both in the capital and the provinces; to furnish occasional relief to provincial communities after natural disasters, such as the devastating earthquakes common in the eastern empire; and, most important, to collect enough taxes to pay for all this. The imperial government was quite small compared to the size of the empire being administered. As under the republic, governors with small staffs were sent to the provinces, which eventually numbered about forty. In Rome the emperor employed a substantial palace staff, and several officials called *prefects,* who came from the equestrian ranks, oversaw the city itself. The Roman Empire had no swollen bureaucracy during this time: no more than several hundred top Roman officials governed a population of around 50 million.

The Roman Empire could operate with so few high officials because it fostered the traditional republican ideal of public service in the upper classes in the provinces outside Italy. A tax on provincial agricultural land (Italy was exempt) provided the principal source of the empire's revenue. The local officials of the provincial cities, which were self-governing, collected this tax. In this decentralized system the wealthy and public-spirited people who ran these cities were personally responsible for seeing that the appropriate amount of tax money was forwarded to the central Roman administration. The level of taxation varied from province to province, but taxes everywhere seem to have been particularly difficult for the poor to pay, perhaps more because they were so destitute than because taxes were especially high. Most emperors under the early empire attempted to keep taxes low. As Tiberius put it once when refusing a request from provincial governors for tax increases, "I want you to shear my sheep, not skin them alive."

Because rich and powerful men and women in the provincial cities had to make up from their own pockets any shortfall in tax revenues from their community, their responsibility could be expensive. The prestige of their position, however, made the risk worthwhile. The emperor rewarded some faithful public servants with priesthoods in the imperial cult, a local honor open to both men and women. Or they could petition the emperor for special help for their area after an earthquake or a flood. In other words, the members of the local social elite were the patrons of their communities and the clients of the emperor. The decentralized Roman tax system certainly made possible financial corruption and exploitation of the lower classes, but the more enlightened emperors tried to minimize such depredations. As long as there were enough rich people in the provinces satisfied with the characteristically Roman value system of financial

obligations and nonmaterial rewards, the empire could function effectively. It ran so smoothly by the second century A.D. that modern historians have labeled this period a Golden Age.

Social Distinctions in the Empire's Golden Age

In the second century A.D. more people in the Roman Empire experienced peace and relative prosperity than ever before. As always, the upper classes constituted a tiny portion of the population. Only about one in every fifty thousand had enough money to qualify for the highest-ranking class, the senatorial order (so named because men of this class could be appointed to the Senate). Men in the senatorial class sported a broad purple stripe on their tunics, an emblem of their status. Men of the second highest order, called equestrians even though they no longer had anything to do with horses, had to have a substantial amount of wealth and to come from a family that had been freeborn for two generations. About one in a thousand belonged to the equestrian class. Equestrians could display their status by wearing a gold ring and a narrow purple stripe on their outer garment. The third highest order consisted of the propertied and influential people who served as local council members in provincial towns. Members of this class were called *curiales* because their ownership of a legal minimum of property made them eligible to serve as magistrates (*decurions*) on their municipal city council (*curia*). To retain their special status, they also had to pay for festivals, sacrifices, and public works. Rich women as well as men could become *curiales.*

The requirement that equestrians come from freeborn families signifies a remarkable aspect of the demography of the Roman Empire: much of the population in many areas had slaves as ancestors. Moreover, many men and women in the empire had themselves once been slaves but had either bought their freedom or been manumitted in their masters' wills. These freedmen and freedwomen often worked as craftspeople or merchants in the cities and on farms in the countryside. During the first century A.D. some of them became prominent members of the emperor's personal staff and thus of the empire's central administration. Although ordinary freedmen and freedwomen formed the economic backbone of the empire, the rich scorned

A Roman Couple
This painting from a house in Pompeii probably portrays the wealthy baker P. Paquius Proclus and his wife. He holds a scroll and she holds a wax-covered writing tablet and stylus to proclaim their literacy.

them. Cicero had long before expressed a typical upper-class republican attitude that persisted under the empire: "The occupations of all workers, merchants, craftsmen, dancers, and actors are vulgar and unsuitable for gentlemen."

Those who were not members of the social elite faced even greater disadvantages than social snobbery. Even in a so-called Golden Age people at the bottom of the economic heap continued to endure a desperate existence. The republican distinction between the "better people" (*honestiores*) and "humbler people" (*humiliores*) became more pronounced throughout the principate, and by the third century A.D. it pervaded Roman legal affairs. No detailed description of the criteria for dividing people into "better" and "humbler" survives, but we do know the "better people" included senators, equestrians, *curiales,* and retired army veterans.

Everybody else (except for slaves, who counted as property, not people) made up the vastly larger group of "humbler people." These people faced their gravest disadvantage if they were brought to trial: the law imposed harsher penalties on *humiliores* than on *honestiores,* even for the same crimes. A person was probably classified as "better" or "humbler" at his or her trial. Humbler people convicted of capital crimes were regularly executed by being crucified or torn apart by wild animals before a crowd of spectators. Better people rarely suffered the death penalty, but if they were condemned, they received a quicker and more dignified execution by the sword. When being questioned in criminal investigations, humbler people could also be tortured, even if they were Roman citizens. Romans regarded this inequality under the law fair on the grounds that a person's higher status reflected a higher level of genuine merit. As one provincial governor expressed it, "nothing is more unequal than equality itself."

In Roman society one important function of law was to make discriminations among people. Romans prided themselves on their ability to order their society through law. As Virgil said, the Roman mission was "to establish law and order within a framework of peace." Perhaps the most distinctive characteristic of Roman law was its recognition of the principle of equity. Equity meant using law to bring about what was "good and fair" even if the letter of the law had to be ignored to do so. A concern for equity led Roman legal thinkers to insist, for example, that the intent of parties in a deal outweighed the words of their contract and that the burden of proof lay with the accuser rather than the accused. The emperor Trajan ruled that no one should be convicted on the grounds of suspicion alone because it was better for a guilty person to go unpunished than for an innocent person to be condemned. These principles of Roman law influenced most legal systems in modern Europe.

A concern for fairness and compassion also extended to other aspects of Roman life under the empire. Both public and private sources assisted the poor, especially if the aid might promote agriculture. The emperors initiated welfare assistance for needy children, although their aim was to encourage Romans to have more children. Wealthy people sometimes adopted children in their communities. One North African man gave enough money to support 300 boys and 300 girls each year until they grew up. The relative value of male and female children in Roman society is evident in these efforts: boys often received more aid than did girls under these assistance programs.

Marriage and Medicine

The status of some Roman women improved under the empire. Beginning in the late republic, Roman women had started to gain more power over property and divorce. Rich Roman women could operate almost as free agents by the time of the empire because marriage no longer gave the husband legal authority over whatever property the wife had received from her parents. A wife could instigate and obtain a divorce and still retain control over the property she had owned as a single woman, just as widows did. Most women continued to work at low-paying jobs, such as dressmakers or fish sellers, and had little property to control. For them an improved legal status had little or no effect on their economic status. As before, the poorest women often had to resort to prostitution to earn money.

Just as under the republic, girls in the Roman Empire often married in their early teens or even younger. Although marriages were usually arranged between spouses who hardly knew each other, husbands and wives could grow to admire and love each other. A butcher in Rome put up this memorial to his dead wife, who had the virtues Roman husbands deemed appropriate for a married woman: "She was my one and only wife, chaste in body and displaying a loving spirit. She remained faithful to her faithful husband. Always cheerful, even when times were tough, she never neglected her duties."

Complications during childbirth and after delivery could easily lead to the mother's death. Roman women often began bearing children in their early teens, when complications are more common, and Roman medicine could do little to cure any resulting illness or infection. Midwives and folk practitioners provided some information about sex and childbirth, but knowledge about such matters probably came mostly from family members. Young women who were not told about sex and pregnancy sometimes suffered dismal consequences. The upper-class government official Pliny, for example, once sent the following report to the grandfather of his third wife, Calpurnia: "You will be very sad to learn that your granddaughter has suffered a miscarriage. She is a young girl and did not realize she was pregnant. As a result she was more active than she should have been and paid a high price for her lack of knowledge by falling seriously ill." Male specialists were also ill informed about the process of reproduction; gynecologists erroneously recommended the days just before and after menstruation as the best time to become pregnant.

Concern about reproduction permeated marriage. Because so many children died young, families had to produce numerous children to keep from disappearing. The tombstone of Veturia, a soldier's wife married at eleven, tells a typical story: "Here I lie, having lived for twenty-seven years. I was married to the same man for sixteen years and bore six children, five of whom died before I did." Not all people wanted children, and some ways to prevent pregnancy were known and freely practiced. Women's contraceptive methods included using a tuft of wool as a diaphragm or drinking a potion prepared from the sap of the silphium plant, a now extinct species of giant fennel that grew near Cyrene in North Africa. Recent medical research seems to confirm that a drug made from silphium would have been an effective contraceptive or abortifacient and helps explain why the plant was worth more than its weight in silver as an export. Some women resorted to less expensive aids believed to deter conceiving, such as wearing a spider's head on a necklace as a magical charm. The available methods of abortion, which was a controversial practice, were extremely dangerous. The Roman emphasis on child bearing in marriage brought its own hazards to women, but to remain single represented social failure for a Roman girl.

Once children were born, they were cared for by both their mothers and any household help in all but the more affluent families. Women who could afford child care routinely had their babies attended to and breast-fed by wet nurses. Scholars disagree on whether this practice weakened the ties of affection between Roman mothers and their children. Inevitably, some babies were not wanted by their parents. The practice of exposure continued during the empire, more so for baby girls than baby boys.

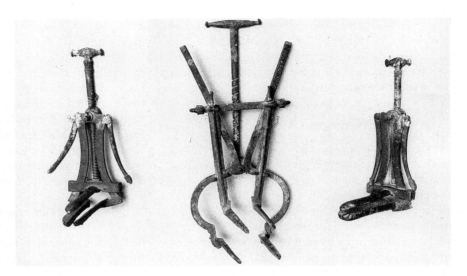

Roman Medical Instruments
Ancient medical practition-
ers used a variety of metal
tools for surgery and other
treatments. The most elab-
orate tools were obstetrical.

Most therapies of everyday Roman general medicine were comparable to those used in Hellenistic Greece. Treatments were mainly limited to potions, such as the drink of wild boar's manure boiled in vinegar customarily given to chariot drivers who had been injured in crashes. Roman technology did, however, provide carefully crafted instruments for surgery and for physical examinations of female and male patients. Many doctors were freedmen from Greece and other provinces, and they usually had only informal training. The public considered their occupation low status, unless the doctor served the emperor or other members of the upper class. The most famous court physician of the Roman Empire was Galen (c. A.D. 129–199), who began his career ministering to gladiators but eventually became the doctor of the emperor Marcus Aurelius (✳A.D. 161–180). Galen accepted the traditional theory of the four bodily humors, but he also increased medical knowledge. In anatomy, for example, he demonstrated by careful dissection that the blood circulates through the arteries as well as the veins. He also studied neurology, physiology, pharmacology, and diet, and the many books he wrote to explain his doctrines affected later medical thought tremendously. Particularly influential were his ideas that doctors should constitute an elite profession and that medical science required systematic, comprehensive knowledge of health and illness rather than the compartmentalized specialization frequent in his times.

The Merging of Cultures in the Roman Provinces

By the second century A.D. the provinces of the Roman Empire covered a vast territory stretching from Spain to Mesopotamia in one direction and from the British Isles to North Africa in the other. These provinces contained a wide diversity of peoples speaking different languages, observing different customs, dressing in distinctive styles, and worshiping various divinities. In the rural areas of the empire, Roman contact had virtually no effect on local customs. Where new towns were built, however, Roman influence was evident. Many towns in the western empire originated with the settlements peopled by army veterans the emperors had spread around the provinces, and others grew up around Roman forts. Some regions sprouted cities much earlier than others. Prominent men from Roman towns in Spain, for example, had successful public careers at Rome by the first century A.D. Eventually even emperors came from Roman families in the provinces; Trajan, whose family had settled in Spain, was the first.

The growth of Roman towns in regions the Romans had considered barbarian was most conspicuous in what is today Europe west of the Rhine River. Prominent modern cities such as Trier and Cologne near Germany's western border started as Roman towns. Even in this part of the empire, however, the countryside remained much less influenced

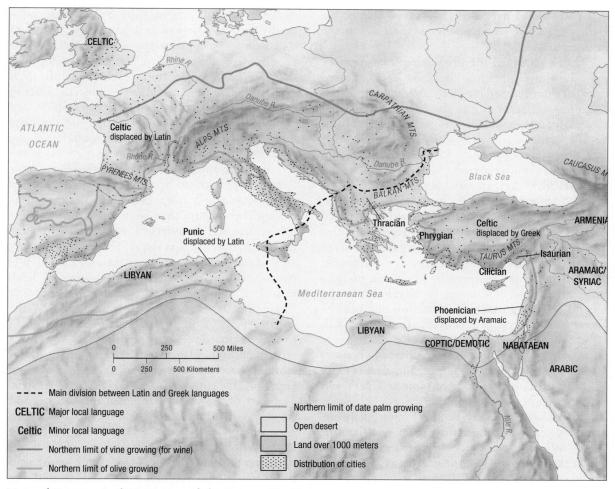

Natural Features and Languages of the Roman World

by the Roman presence. Moreover, the Romans and "Romanized" provincials in the towns were themselves affected by local traditions. In such provinces as Gaul, Britain, and North Africa, the interaction of Romans and provincials produced new, mixed cultural traditions. *Romanization* of the western provinces meant a gradual merging of Roman and local culture, not the unilateral imposition of Roman ways of life on provincials. Romanization also raised the standard of living for many people in the provinces as roads and bridges improved, trade increased, and agriculture flourished under the peaceful conditions secured by the Roman army. Where Roman troops were stationed in the provinces, their need for supplies meant new

business for farmers and merchants. Non-Romans who lived more prosperously under Roman rule than ever before found Romanization easy to take.

The Eastern provinces of the Roman world retained their Greek and Near Eastern character under the empire. Such great cities as Alexandria in Egypt and Antioch in Syria had been thriving for centuries. Compared to Rome, they had more individual houses for the well-to-do, fewer blocks of high-rise tenements, and equally magnificent temples. The local elites of the eastern cities easily fit into the Roman system of patronage as the clients of the emperor and the patrons of their communities. They had long ago become accustomed to the comparable paternalistic social relationships that had formed part of the system of rule of the Hellenistic kings, who had reigned there before the Romans arrived.

Greek remained the predominant language in these bustling centers in the East, and educated Romans there learned it as well. Already in the first century A.D., authors like the poets Lucan (A.D. 39–65), Statius (c. A.D. 45–96), and Martial (c. A.D. 40–104) and the philosophical essayist and tragedian Seneca (c. 4 B.C.–A.D. 65) had contributed to a revival in Latin literature, what literary scholars called its Silver Age. Its most famous authors, such as the historian Tacitus (c. A.D. 56–120) and the satiric poet Juvenal (c. A.D. 65–130), wrote with acid wit and verve. By the middle of the second century A.D., however, Greek literature experienced a renaissance that relegated Latin literature to second rank. New trends, often inspired by the work of Hellenistic authors, blossomed in Greek literature. Second-century authors like Chariton and Achilles Tatius penned romantic novels. Lucian (c. A.D. 117–180) composed satirical dialogues that fiercely mocked both people and gods. As part of his enormous and varied literary output, Plutarch (c. A.D. 50–120) wrote biographies of famous Greek and Roman men as character studies.

In much of the eastern Roman Empire, daily life, including education and artistic endeavors, continued to follow Greek models. The Roman emperors lacked any notion of themselves as missionaries who had to impose Roman civilization on foreigners. Rather, they saw themselves primarily as peacekeepers and preservers of law and social order. They allowed the traditional Greek forms of civic life and government to continue largely unchanged. The willing cooperation of the upper classes of the provinces in the task of governing the empire was crucial in making it possible for the emperors to provide these benefits.

The Army and the Limits of the Roman Empire

The strength of the Roman imperial army was also crucial in ensuring the empire's stability. Because Roman rule maintained the privileged position of local elites, stable and peaceful provinces had no need for garrisons of troops. Roman soldiers were a rare sight in many places. Even Gaul, which had originally resisted its Roman conquerors with an almost suicidal frenzy, was, according to a contemporary witness, "kept in order by 1,200 troops— hardly more soldiers than it has towns." Most of the Roman troops were concentrated in the provinces on the northern and eastern fringes of the empire. There the Romans feared that the local residents, less Romanized than provincials closer to the center of the empire, might cause trouble, and that hostile neighbors living just beyond the boundaries of imperial territory would raid the empire's outlying towns and farms.

The Roman army in the late republic and the Augustan period had been an engine of prosperity because its success in war brought in huge amounts of capital that more than compensated for its cost to the treasury. Prisoners of war, captured by the thousands, were sold as slaves. The victorious army also seized movable property of all kinds as war booty. And it conquered great expanses of land, providing new tax revenues. (Augustus's capture of Egypt was the most spectacular addition.) By the end of Augustus's reign, the territory of the Roman Empire encircled the Mediterranean Sea. Augustus's most ambitious plan was to extend the northern frontier eastward into what is today western Germany, the former Czechoslovakia, and Austria. The part of his scheme designed to push beyond the Rhine River failed disastrously in A.D. 9, when his general Varus was wiped out in the Teutoburg Forest with three legions (a legion was a unit of five thousand to six thousand troops). For months after this catastrophe, Augustus stormed around the palace with his hair and beard untrimmed, pounding his head on a door while shouting, "Varus, give me back my legions!" The Rhine River subsequently marked the easternmost extent of Roman territory in Europe.

The loss of Varus's troops left the Roman army with twenty-five legions, which nominally contained six thousand men each at full strength, but retirements and losses usually kept each legion at least several hundred men below full enrollment. Soldiers enlisted for terms of twenty to twenty-five years. The famous discipline and maneuverability in battle of the Roman legions stemmed from their organization into smaller units under a precise system of command. Each legion consisted of ten cohorts, each cohort of three maniples, and each maniple of two centuries. A century, named for its theoretical strength of 100 men, was commanded by a centurion. Drawn from the nonaristocratic ranks of society, centurions maintained

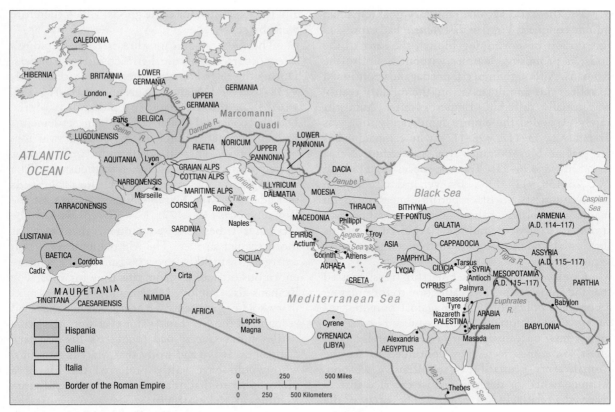

The Provinces of the Roman Empire at its Largest Extent (Second Century A.D.)

discipline and provided invaluable advice to the aristocratic officers, who normally lacked long experience in military service. The best centurions could reach the rank of *primus pilus* ("chief unit commander"), the leader of a legion's first century. These successful military men earned the social rank of equestrians and a retirement benefit of 600,000 sesterces (a basic unit in Roman coinage).* An ordinary legionary soldier earned 900 sesterces a year in the first century A.D., from which

expenses were deducted, and received 12,000 sesterces on retirement. Members of the emperor's praetorian guard earned far greater sums. Soldiers' regular pay was supplemented by the substantial bonuses (donatives) that emperors paid on their accession and other special occasions. The material rewards made an army career very desirable for many men, and enlistment counted as a privilege restricted to free male Roman citizens. The Roman army also included auxiliary units manned by noncitizens, often specialized troops such as cavalry, archers, and slingers. The auxiliaries, whose numbers probably approached that of the regular legionary soldiers, learned some Latin and were introduced to Roman customs by serving under Roman commanders. Little is recorded about the terms of their service, but upon discharge from the army they received Roman citizenship for themselves and their descendants. In this way the Roman army served as an indirect instrument in spreading the Roman way of life.

---

*Meaningful calculations of the value of ancient money are difficult because prices changed over time and varied from region to region. Some items, especially cloth, were proportionally more expensive in antiquity than today because the lack of mass production kept prices high. In the first century A.D., table wine in the taverns of Pompeii in southern Italy cost from one-quarter to one sesterce per pint, and a loaf of bread in the same period cost about three-quarters of a sesterce. The notoriously frugal Cato in the second century B.C. paid 400 sesterces for one outfit of clothing (toga, tunic, and shoes). The cost of a blanket in A.D. 202 is recorded as 100 sesterces.

The theoretical Roman military goal remained infinite conquest. Virgil in *The Aeneid* had expressed this notion by portraying Jupiter, the king of the gods, as promising "empire without limit" to the Romans. Although imperial propaganda continued to reflect this grandiose vision, the military reality was usually different. Emperors after Augustus rarely expanded the empire significantly; one was Trajan (A.D. 53–117, ✳98–117), who campaigned as far east as Mesopotamia after succeeding Nerva (A.D. 30–98 ✳96–98). Trajan's successor, Hadrian (A.D. 76–138, ✳117–138), however, had to relinquish these conquests. Most emperors concentrated on maintaining order within the empire rather than trying to extend it; but some acquired additions that lasted, and the dream of further conquest never vanished.

Controversial recent scholarship has suggested that the emperors paid less attention to formulating a coherent policy of defense against potential invaders than historians often assume, because no matter how unrealistic their hopes of foreign conquest sometimes were they continued to see the Roman army primarily as an offensive weapon. Arrangements for defense against external threats received a relatively low priority. The safety of the empire probably owed more to geography than to a preconceived defensive strategy. The great deserts stretching along its frontiers in North Africa and the ancient Near East provided natural obstacles to invasion. The troops positioned near the empire's frontiers did serve a defensive purpose besides squelching local disturbances. They alerted Rome if attacked and could mobilize to repel any invaders, such as the Germanic bands that often crossed the Danube and Rhine rivers (easier to cross than the great deserts) to raid Roman territory. But the defense of the empire against threats from outside was often more a matter of responding to attacks after the fact than of planning ahead to prevent them.

The army's mobility depended on a vast network of roads and bridges stretching across the empire all the way to its frontier zones. The Romans made these roads primarily for infantry on the march rather than for wheeled vehicles, and their surfaces could be bumpy and their grades steep: Roman engineers punched these rough, straight roads through otherwise nearly impassable terrain, such as marshes and dense forests. Civilians used the roads for travel, but land transportation was gener-

ally too expensive for trade goods, which therefore went by sea.

The most significant threats to the empire's safety occurred on its northern and eastern frontiers. During the reigns of Antoninus Pius (A.D. 86–161, ✳138–161) and Marcus Aurelius (A.D. 121–180, ✳161–180), the Germanic peoples north of the Danube constantly menaced Roman settlements. Roman prosperity lured their bands of warriors bent on booty. These bands lived in family groups loosely united by shared beliefs and customs. The men in these tribes usually fought in ragtag bands of raiders, but the Marcomannic wars against the Romans (A.D. 166–172, 177–180) provoked the Germanic tribes into reorganizing themselves as more regular armies. The Germanic armies that emerged from this process caused the empire enormous difficulties from this time forward. The Romans also employed Germanic warriors as auxiliary soldiers in their own army because they had recognized the Germans' valor ever since the fierce battles Julius Caesar had fought on his northern campaigns. It is a sad irony that Marcus Aurelius, who would have vastly preferred the life of a philosopher to that of a soldier, had to spend years fighting in the northern wilderness against the Germanic peoples the Quadi and the Marcomanni.

Roman Roads
Stone-paved roads like the Via Appia, which led south out of Rome, connected the empire's capital to other cities. These routes facilitated swift marches by Rome's armies.

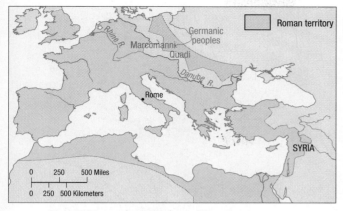

**Pressures on the Northern Frontier,
Second Century** A.D.

Remarkably, despite the rigors of war, he persisted in writing down his musings on life, in Greek. The resulting book, *The Meditations,* offers often gloomy but touching reflections on the human condition, such as his belief that people exist for each other. "Either make them better, or just put up with them," he advised.

The revolt of a Roman general in Syria who hoped to become emperor himself forced Aurelius to abandon any plan of establishing unchallenged Roman control in the eastern Danube region. The best he could do was to settle bands of rough-hewn, non-Roman locals south of the river and hope they would serve as a buffer against the hostile groups to the north. Aurelius therefore established a precedent for settling Germanic peoples, barbarians to the Romans, in Roman territory to try to secure peace. This policy, born of desperation, was an early hint that in the long run the only way to preserve the Roman Empire was to find ways to accommodate all those who wished to live within its territory.

The Economic Origins of the Crisis of the Third Century A.D.

The emperors from Nerva through Marcus Aurelius are known as "the five good emperors" because their relations with the Roman upper class were generally less hostile than those of infamous past tyrants like Caligula or Nero or those future rulers like Commodus (A.D. 161–192, *180–192). Commodus was Aurelius's son, whom he designated as his successor at the age of nineteen despite Com-

modus's obvious cruelty. Aurelius's choice of Commodus ended the custom followed by each of the previous four emperors, who designated the best available man as his successor by adopting him as his son. Commodus embarked on a reign marred by murdering his closest associates and scandalously appearing in the arena as a gladiator, dispatching wild beasts by the score and battling other fighters who did not try to lose just to make the emperor look good. When Commodus's advisers bribed an athlete to strangle him in a wrestling match, no one regretted the end of his reign, especially not the neglected military. The political chaos that ensued, however, could hardly have been worse. The praetorians murdered the first successor to Commodus and then demanded huge bribes to support further candidates for the throne. It had long been the custom for a new emperor to pay a donative to the troops in Rome, but this time the praetorians auctioned off the throne of the Roman Empire to the highest bidder. The winner lasted only a couple of months. A soldier, Septimius Severus (A.D. 145–211, *193–211), then took over.

Severus was a soldier's emperor who came from the great North African city of Lepcis Magna in what is today Libya. He vigorously pursued the imperial dream of foreign conquest with campaigns beyond the ends of the empire in Mesopotamia and Scotland. By his time the Roman army had expanded by a hundred thousand more troops than under Augustus, enrolling perhaps as many as three hundred fifty thousand to four hundred thousand regular and auxiliary troops (some historians believe the number to be substantially smaller). Army life was harsh because the troops trained constantly. Soldiers had to be fit enough to carry their forty-three pound packs up to twenty miles in five hours, swimming any rivers in their way. Because a Roman legion on the march built a fortified camp every night, the troops essentially carried all the makings of a wooden-walled city with them everywhere they went. As one ancient commentator noted, "Roman infantrymen were little different from loaded pack mules." Huge quantities of supplies were required to support the army. At one temporary fort in a frontier area, for example, archaeologists found a supply of a million iron nails—ten tons' worth. The same encampment required seventeen miles of timber for its barracks walls. To outfit a single Roman legion with tents took fifty-four thousand calf hides.

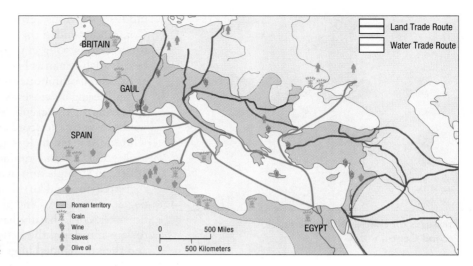

Trade Routes in the Roman Empire

Successful conquests had dwindled under the empire, and the army had become a source of negative instead of positive cash flow to the Roman treasury. The economy had not expanded sufficiently to compensate for the difference. Economic changes of the early empire had reestablished the traditional Mediterranean pattern of mainly intraregional commerce for bulk commodities. During the late republic and Augustan period, a nontraditional pattern had developed when central Italian producers established a flourishing export trade to the western provinces. For example, immense quantities of wine and olive oil were shipped to the markets of Gaul and Spain. Gangs of slaves working on Italian plantations produced these cash crops specifically for export. In the first centuries of the empire, however, the western regions developed their own local production by tenant farmers whose prices undercut those of the imports from Italy.

With the loss of these export markets, Italian producers in the second century A.D. increasingly rid themselves of their slave gangs and changed over to a more diverse mix of agriculture and stock raising by tenants, who were mostly free men and women. Their products met the increased demand from imperial Rome and other Italian markets, which the peaceful conditions of the early empire had encouraged. Even olive oil was now imported to Italy from Spain, to be replaced by A.D. 200 by oil from North Africa. These African imports took over because they could piggyback at little cost on the constant traffic of ships bringing African grain to Italy. These shipments constituted taxes levied

on the province of Africa and supplied the state-sponsored giveaway of grain to the urban masses in Rome. In other words, only the existence of this state-organized and financed transportation system allowed African producers to sell their products abroad at a profit. Otherwise, the high cost of transporting goods in antiquity made such trade often impractical. Transportation over land was so slow and difficult that the costs of shipments often doubled and tripled after even short trips. Shipments by sea moved slowly, too. A superfast ship could sail from Egypt to Rome's port in a week, but an ordinary voyage lasted fifty days. Under these conditions the only consistent long-range trade was in luxury items such as spices, ivory, or silk. Roman merchant ships in search of such exotic treasures for import at exorbitant prices regularly sailed as far east as India and Ceylon (today Sri Lanka).

The Roman government's need for revenue had grown faster than the empire's tax base. The state needed more income because the army had grown by a third and inflation had driven up prices. A principal cause of inflation under the early empire may have been, ironically, the long period of peace that promoted increased demand for the empire's relatively static production of goods and services. Over time, some emperors responded to inflated prices by debasing imperial coinage in a vain attempt to cut government costs for purchasing goods and services. By putting less silver in each coin without changing its face value, emperors hoped to create more cash with the same amount of precious metal. But merchants simply raised prices to make up

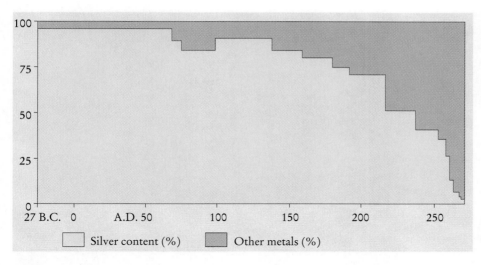

Roman Imperial Silver Coinage, 27 B.C.–A.D. 272

for the loss in value from the debased currency, increasing the momentum of the inflationary spiral.

The Political Catastrophe After Severus

By the time Severus became emperor in A.D. 193, inflation had diminished the value of the soldiers' wages to virtually nothing after the cost of basic supplies and clothing had been deducted from their pay. They routinely expected the emperors as their patrons to favor them with gifts of money, especially when a new emperor was first chosen. Severus set out to improve conditions for the soldiers more fundamentally. He ended the prohibition against troops' marrying while in service and raised their pay by a third. This pay raise for an army a third larger than in Augustus's time further strained the imperial budget and increased inflationary pressures. For Severus the financial consequences of his military policy were of no concern. His deathbed advice to his sons was to "stay on good terms with each other, be generous to the soldiers, and pay no attention to anyone else."

Severus's sons followed their father's advice only on the last two points. Caracalla (A.D. 188–217, *211–217) seized the throne by murdering his brother Geta. Caracalla's profligate reign signaled the end of the relative peace and prosperity of the early Roman Empire. He increased the soldiers' pay by another 40 percent to 50 percent and spent gigantic sums on building projects such as the largest public baths Rome had ever seen. Caracalla's extravagant spending put added pressure on the people responsible for collecting taxes and on those who had to pay them. Caracalla's most famous enactment, the granting in A.D. 212 of Roman citizenship to almost every man and woman in the empire except slaves (Constitutio Antoniniana), had a financial goal. Because only citizens paid inheritance taxes and fees for freeing slaves, an increase in citizens meant an increase in revenues, much of which was earmarked for the army. Despite this tactic, Caracalla wrecked the imperial budget and paved the way for the ruinous inflation to come in the third century A.D. He summed up his disastrous policy once when his mother upbraided him for his excess. "Never mind, mother," he said, drawing his sword, "we shall not run out of money as long as I have this."

Political instability accompanied the financial weakening of the empire. After Macrinus, the commander of the praetorians, murdered Caracalla to make himself emperor, Caracalla's female relatives convinced the army to overthrow Macrinus in favor of a young male relative. The restored dynasty did not last long, however, and by A.D. 235 the secret was out: bribing the soldiers was the way to become emperor. The following forty-nine years included numerous rebellions by pretenders to the throne and the reigns of over twenty separate emperors, sometimes more than one claiming rule at the same time. (The total number of emperors varies depending on how many men claiming rule in this tumultuous period are counted as genuine emperors.) Many of these emperors were members of local elites in the Balkan region of the empire

Palmyra in Syria
Located at an oasis on a caravan trade route between Syria and Mesopotamia,
Palmyra, the city of Queen Zenobia, flourished under the Roman Empire. Its
architecture combined Greek, Roman, and Near Eastern styles.

and had risen through the ranks because of their military prowess. Their skill was needed because the foreign enemies of Rome took advantage of this period of crisis to attack, especially along the eastern frontier. Roman fortunes hit bottom when Shapur I, king of the Sassanid Empire of Persia, rolled over a Roman army and captured the emperor Valerian (✳A.D. 253–260) during a Persian invasion of Syria in A.D. 260. Even the tough Aurelian (✳A.D. 270–275) could manage only defensive operations, such as recovering Egypt and Asia Minor from Zenobia, the warrior queen of Palmyra in Syria. He also had to encircle Rome with a massive wall to ward off surprise attacks from northern tribes who were already smashing their way into Italy.

Territory of Zenobia, Queen of Palmyra, A.D. 269–272

This period of political anarchy, hyperinflation, and military disaster in the middle of the third century A.D. had dire repercussions for people of every status in the empire. Natural disasters compounded the social crisis when devastating earthquakes and a virulent plague struck the Mediterranean region in the middle of the third century A.D. The population declined significantly as food supplies became less dependable, civil war killed soldiers and civilians alike, and epidemic diseases ravaged large regions of the empire. The loss of population meant fewer soldiers for the army, whose efficiency as a defense and police force deteriorated severely in any case under the pressures of political and financial chaos. More regions of the empire therefore became vulnerable to raids, and the attacks of invaders and the roving bands of robbers who became more and more common as economic conditions worsened scourged the countryside and its residents. Agricultural producers, the main support of the Roman economy, found it increasingly difficult to pay the higher

FATES OF ROMAN EMPERORS TO A.D. 235

Died of natural causes	*Assassinated, executed, or forced to commit suicide*
Augustus (*27 B.C.–A.D. 14)	Gaius, also known as Caligula (*A.D. 37–41)
Tiberius (*A.D. 14–37)	Claudius (*A.D. 41–54)
Vespasian (*A.D. 69–79)	Nero (*A.D. 54–68)
Titus (*A.D. 79–81)	Galba (*A.D. 68–69)
Nerva (*A.D. 96–98)	Otho (*A.D. 69)
Trajan (*A.D. 98–117)	Vitellius (*A.D. 69)
Hadrian (*A.D. 117–138)	Domitian (*A.D. 81–96)
Antoninus Pius (*A.D. 138–161)	Commodus (*A.D. 180–192)
Marcus Aurelius (*A.D. 161–180)	Pertinax (*A.D. 193)
Lucius Verus (*A.D. 161–169, co-emperor)	Didius Julianus (*A.D. 193)
Septimius Severus (*A.D. 193–211)	Caracalla (*A.D. 211–217)
	Geta (*A.D. 211–212, co-emperor)
	Macrinus (*A.D. 217–218)
	Elagabalus (*A.D. 218–222)
	Severus Alexander (*A.D.. 222–235)

extremely difficult to find people willing to serve as local officials. The old way of public service, in which rich and prominent members of society financed public works and acted as patrons to those lower on the social hierarchy, increasingly broke down. Some of the wealthy elite who were supposed to serve as local council members even moved away from their own towns to escape the demands of government service. Others joined the army or petitioned the emperor for a special exemption from public service and its financial obligations. In short, during this period the political and social structure on which the empire had depended for more than two hundred years was gutted, and the separation between rich and poor in Roman society became more marked than ever before.

The economic and political crisis of the Roman Empire was resolved at the end of the 200s, when new patterns of life and government began to emerge. The most significant changes in the later Roman Empire revolved around the importance of Christianity.

The Emergence of Early Christianity

Christianity began as a kind of splinter group within Judaism. The Jewish and Roman worlds did not readily embrace the new Christian movement, however, and virtually every book of the New Testament refers to the resistance the adherents of this new faith faced. As long as believers in Jesus remained members of Jewish synagogues, they found opponents in their fellow Jews. But the main opposition to the new movement came from the non-Jewish Roman world. The appeal and strength of Christianity flowed from its message of salvation, its early believers' sense of mission, and the strong bonds of community it inspired. The new religion's inclusion of women and slaves allowed it to draw members from the entire population. To understand early Christianity we must appreciate developments within Judaism in the Greek and Roman periods.

The Jews Under Greek and Roman Rule

After Alexander conquered the ancient Near East in the late fourth century B.C., the territory called Judaea, where many Jews lived, was controlled at

taxes the government demanded. Tenant farmers, called *coloni,* were legally compelled to stay on the land they rented until they paid their taxes, a restriction that applied to their children if any bills were left unpaid. Because revenues from the countryside could not meet the emperors' demands for money, the *curiales,* who were responsible for collecting a set amount of taxes, were often driven to bankruptcy as a result of making up the difference from their own pockets. Consequently, it became

different times by the Ptolemies, whose kingdom centered in Egypt, and by the Seleucids, who ruled Syria. These Hellenistic dynasties fought over Judaea because it occupied the land route between Egypt and Syria. Both the Ptolemaic and the Seleucid kings customarily allowed the Jews in Judaea to govern themselves according to Jewish law. After winning independence from the Seleucid kingdom in the Maccabean revolt that ended in 142 B.C., Judaea was ruled as an independent kingdom by the Hasmoneans, descendants of the Maccabees, until Pompey placed it under Roman control in 63 B.C.

The Romans allowed the Jews a certain measure of independence under local rulers, the most famous of whom was Herod the Great (＊37–4 B.C.). Herod's taste for a Greek style of life, which broke Jewish law, made him unpopular with his Jewish subjects despite his magnificent rebuilding of the temple in Jerusalem. In A.D. 6, after a decade of unrest following Herod's death, Augustus began the tradition of sending governors to Judaea directly from Rome. These officials, first known as prefects, then as procurators, imposed high taxes, but the Jews retained the right to practice their religion. The Roman policy of ruling primarily with an eye to increasing their own wealth and power provoked a Jewish uprising, which the Romans harshly repressed. A full-scale war broke out in A.D. 66 and did not end until 70, when the emperor Domitian's son, Titus, conquered Jerusalem. He ordered his troops to destroy the great temple and sell much of the city's population into slavery. Only a small band of guerrillas, known as "knife-men" from the short sword they used to kill their opponents, held out on the mountain fortress of Masada that Herod had built. After a long siege the Romans finally broke through the walls, only to find that the rebels, including almost all their families, had committed mass suicide the preceding night rather than allow themselves to be captured. The remnants of Jewish resistance to Roman rule flared up again sixty years later. Under the leadership of Simon Bar Kokhba, in the time of the Emperor Hadrian, the Jews fought a bloody war (A.D. 132–135) against the Romans, which once again ended in a crushing defeat. Jerusalem thereafter became a pagan city named Aelia Capitolina, which Jews were forbidden to enter.

Their harsh experiences of economic and political repression raised for many Jews the ques-

tion of divine justice: How could a just God allow the wicked to prosper and the righteous to suffer? At the time of the persecution under the Seleucid king Antiochus IV, which resulted in the Maccabean revolt, a complex of emerging ideas began to answer this question, not only for the Jews of that time

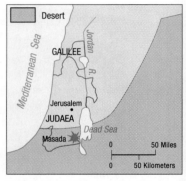

Judea in the First Centuries B.C. and A.D.

but for many Jews, Christians, and Muslims in later ages. According to this worldview, evil powers, divine and human, controlled the present world. This regime would soon end, however, when God and his agents would conquer the forces of evil. A final judgment would follow, after which the wicked would receive eternal punishment and the righteous eternal reward. Apocalypticism, as this worldview is usually designated today (from the Greek word for "uncovering" or "revelation"), proved immensely popular, especially among the Jews living in Judaea under Roman rule. Often associated with apocalypticism was the ancient belief that a divine agent, sometimes designated the "anointed one" (Hebrew, "Meshiah" or "Messiah"; Greek, "Christ") would initiate the final battle against the forces of evil. Several figures in the early Roman period claimed this title, including Simon Bar Kokhba, the leader of the second Judaean revolt against the Romans. The most important figure for world history, however, was Jesus of Nazareth.

Jesus of Nazareth and the Spread of His Teachings

Jesus of Nazareth (c. 4 B.C.–A.D. 30)* began his career as a teacher and healer in his native Galilee, the northern region of Palestine. The New Testament Gospels, written between about A.D. 70 and 90, offer the earliest accounts of Jesus' life. They begin the story of his public ministry with his baptism by John the Baptist, who preached a message of the need for repentance for sins in the face of the

---

*An explanation of the apparent anomaly of dating the birth of Jesus to 4 B.C. is in the section on dates before the Prologue.

coming final judgment. John was executed by Herod Antipas (*4 B.C.–A.D. 39), a son of Herod the Great, whom the Romans supported as ruler of Galilee; Herod feared John's apocalyptic preaching might provoke riots. After John's death, Jesus in some respects continued his mission by proclaiming the imminence of God's kingdom. He stressed that this kingdom was open to everyone, regardless of their social status or apparent sinfulness in the eyes of the world. The Gospels interpret Jesus' healings and exorcisms as signs of his conquering the power of Satan, whom those who believed the apocalyptic worldview regarded as the ruler of this world. The Roman prefect Pontius Pilate (*A.D. 26–36), who no doubt viewed Jesus' popularity with the crowds as a threat to public order in politically volatile Judaea, ordered Jesus' execution in Jerusalem in A.D. 30.

In contrast to the fate of many other charismatic leaders the Romans executed, Jesus' influence did not end with his death. His followers reported that he had been raised from the dead, and they set about convincing other Jews that he was the promised anointed one, the Messiah, who would soon return to judge the world and usher in God's kingdom. At this point those who believed that Jesus was the Messiah had no thought of starting a new religion. They considered themselves good Jews and continued to follow the commandments of the Sinai covenant.

A radical change took place with the conversion of Paul of Tarsus, a pious Jew with Roman citizenship who had formerly persecuted those who accepted Jesus as the Messiah. After a religious experience that he interpreted as a direct revelation from Jesus, Paul became a follower of Jesus, or a Christian (follower of Christ), as members of the new movement came to be known. Paul taught that accepting Jesus' death as the ultimate sacrifice for the sins of humanity was the only way of becoming regarded as righteous in the eyes of God. Those who accepted Jesus as divine and followed his teachings could expect to attain salvation in the world to come.

Although Paul stressed the necessity of ethical behavior, especially the rejection of sexual immorality and worship of pagan gods, he taught that there was no need to keep all the provisions of the Jewish law. His main mission was to the non-Jews of Syria, Asia Minor, and Greece, and he did not require the males who entered the movement to undergo the

Painting of the "Good Shepherd"
This third century A.D. fresco shows the Good Shepherd carrying the bowl of milk that Christians received on their baptism to symbolize their entry into the Promised Land.

Jewish initiation rite of circumcision. This tenet and his teachings that his congregations did not have to keep the Jewish dietary laws or celebrate the Jewish festivals led to tensions with the followers of Jesus who lived in Jerusalem, who believed Christians had to follow Jewish law. Roman authorities executed Paul around A.D. 64, labeling him a criminal troublemaker.

After the destruction of Jerusalem in A.D. 70, Paul's position on the proper relationship between Christians and Jewish law won out. His impact on the new movement can be gauged by his thirteen letters that appear in the New Testament, a collection of twenty-seven early Christian writings. Christians came to regard the New Testament as having equal authority with the Jewish Bible, which they now called the Old Testament. Christianity, whose adherents were now predominantly non-Jewish, became a separate religion. Its early congregations were composed mainly of what we might call urban middle-class men and women, with some richer and some poorer members. Women as well as men could hold offices in these congregations, and the first head of a congregation we hear of in the New Testament was a woman. Most early Christians were city-dwellers because teachers like Paul preached primarily in the cities, where contact with crowds of people was easier than in the smaller communities of the countryside.

Persecution and Martyrdom

Unlike Jews, Christians espoused a novel faith, not a traditional religion handed down from their ancestors, and so deserved no special treatment as far as Rome was concerned. Rome furthermore viewed Christians as potential political and social subversives because they proclaimed as king a man the Roman government had crucified as a criminal. Christian ritual also led to accusations of cannibalism in a setting of sexual promiscuity because Christians symbolically ate the body and drank the blood of Jesus during their central rite, which they called the Love Feast. In short, Romans saw Christians as a dangerous new threat to ordinary society.

The Roman historian Tacitus vividly describes the persecution of Christians in Rome in A.D. 64. In that year an inferno of fire destroyed block after block of the *insulae* of apartments in Rome. The urban masses blamed the emperor Nero for the destruction of their homes, believing the fire was his way of clearing the slums to make room for his own pet building program. To divert the mob's rage, Nero accused the Christians of Rome of being the arsonists. He chose them as scapegoats because he knew non-Christians would believe Christians committed criminal acts. As Tacitus reports, Nero had Christians "covered with the skins of wild animals and mauled to death by dogs, or fastened to crosses and set on fire to provide light at night." The harshness of their punishment ironically earned the Christians some sympathy from the general population of Rome.

After the persecution under Nero, the Roman government acted against Christians only intermittently. No law under the early empire specifically forbade Christianity, but Christians were easy prey for Roman officials, who could punish them or order their deaths in the name of maintaining public order. The action of Pliny as a provincial governor in Asia Minor illustrates the Christians' predicament. In about A.D. 112 he had to decide the fate of some Christians local people had brought to his notice. He asked those accused of practicing this new religion if they were indeed Christians, urging those who admitted it to reconsider. Those who denied they had ever been Christians, as well as those who stated they were former Christians who no longer believed, Pliny freed after they sacrificed to the spirit of the emperor and cursed Christ to prove the truth of their statements. He executed those who persisted in declaring themselves Christians.

Fortunately for historians, Pliny reported this incident in a letter to the emperor Trajan, which has survived, along with Trajan's reply. The Christians Pliny executed were killed not because he found them guilty of any crimes but because they refused to surrender their religion and therefore to pay the usual honor to recognized divinities and to the emperor. From the official Roman point of view, Christians had no right to retain their religion if it created disturbances. Trajan's letter to Pliny shows, however, that the government had no policy of tracking down Christians. They concerned the government only when their presence was so disruptive that non-Christians complained to the authorities or the authorities noticed their refusal to participate in official sacrifices. At those times, Roman officials were prepared to execute Christians who would not renounce their religion—just for being Christians—on the grounds that they would suppress anyone whose existence unsettled the peace and order of society.

Perhaps the Romans felt hostile toward Christians mostly because they feared that tolerating them would offend the gods of traditional Roman religion—that is, Romans believed their safety and welfare depended on preserving the *pax deorum* ("peace of/with the gods"). This "contract" between the state and the divine called for humans to pay due respect to the gods of the official cults. Otherwise the gods would retaliate by sending disasters into the world. The Christians' refusal to participate in the imperial cult particularly troubled Romans. Because the Christians denied the existence of the Roman gods and the divine associations of the emperor, they naturally seemed likely to provoke the anger of the gods and therefore deserved blame for natural catastrophes. Tertullian (c. A.D. 160–225), a North African Christian teacher trained in Latin rhetoric, summed up pagan feeling about the danger Christians represented to their safety: "If the Tiber River overflows, or if the Nile fails to flood; if a drought or an earthquake or a famine or a plague hits, then everyone immediately shouts, 'To the lions with the Christians.'"

In response to persecution, Christian intellectuals like Tertullian and Justin (c. A.D. 100–165), a Palestinian Christian who became a prominent Christian teacher in Rome, defended their cause by arguing that the Romans had nothing to fear from the Christians. Far from teaching immorality and subversion, these writers insisted, Christianity taught an elevated moral code and respect for authority. Christianity was not a foreign superstition but the true philosophy that combined the best features of Judaism and Greek philosophy and was thus a fitting religion for the Roman world. Tertullian pointed out that Christians actually prayed for the safety of the empire: "We invoke the true god for the safety of the emperors. We pray for a fortunate life for them, a secure rule, safety for their families, a courageous army, a loyal Senate, a virtuous people, a world of peace."

Persecution did not destroy Christianity, and there is much truth in Tertullian's assertion that "the blood of the martyrs is the seed of the Church." The Christians regarded public trials and executions as an opportunity to become witnesses ("martyrs" in Greek) to their faith. Their willingness to die for their religion, recorded by Christians in stirring accounts, must have impressed many nonbelievers and drawn them to the new faith. Christian martyrs' firm conviction that their deaths would lead directly to heavenly bliss allowed them to face excruciating tortures with courage. Some courted martyrdom. Ignatius (c. A.D. 35–107), the bishop of Antioch, begged the Roman church not to intervene on his behalf after his arrest: "Let me be food for the wild animals (in the arena) through whom I can reach God," he pleaded. "I am God's wheat, to be ground up by the teeth of beasts so that I may be found pure bread of Christ." Similarly, the martyr Perpetua, in writing about her experiences leading up to her execution in about A.D. 203, revealed the depth of emotion prospective martyrdom could elicit for martyrs and their families. She poignantly described her father's bitter grief at her determination to die for her religion. A mother

nursing a young infant, she gave up her child and went willingly to a painful death rather than save herself by denying her faith. Stories recounting the courage of martyrs like Perpetua inspired Christians facing hostility from non-Christians and helped shape the identity of this new religion as a faith that gave its adherents the spiritual power to endure great suffering.

The Development of Christian Institutions

The earliest Christians had expected Jesus to return to pass final judgment on the world during their lifetimes. When these expectations about the timing of the physical coming of the kingdom of God were not met, Christians transformed their religion from an apocalyptic Jewish sect into one that would survive over the long term. Over time they developed religious organizations and institutions that supported the survival of their religion. Paul's early congregations had no clear-cut hierarchy because the members thought none was needed, given that they believed the ordinary world would soon end. Each Christian was also seen as possessing different spiritual gifts, with none superior to the other. By the end of the first century A.D., however, Christian congregations began to organize themselves hierarchically. In the congregations of the cities and towns around the Roman Empire, officials called *bishops* gained the authority to define doctrine and conduct, with authority that superseded the *elders,* or leaders, of local churches. The development of the *episcopate* (leadership by bishops, from the Greek word *episkopos,* meaning "overseer, bishop") combatted the splintering effect of the differing interpretations of Christianity that emerged in the early church. Bishops had the power to define what was true doctrine (orthodoxy) and what was not (heresy), and they used their authority over congregations to try to maintain as much uniformity in belief as possible. Most important, bishops decided who could participate in Christian worship, especially the Eucharist, or Lord's Supper, which many regarded as necessary for achieving eternal life. Exclusion meant the loss of salvation. For all practical purposes the meetings of the bishops of different cities constituted the Christian church as a whole, though the church was by no means a unified organization in this early period.

Only men could be bishops, a rule reflecting the spirit of Paul's view that Christian women should be subordinate to Christian men, just as slaves should be subordinate to their masters. In the congregations of Paul's time, women had held positions of leadership unusual in the Jewish and Roman world, and their active participation in the early movement probably contributed to Roman suspicions of Christianity. By the time bishops began to be recognized, however, women were usually relegated to inferior positions in many churches. In the second and third centuries women still had positions of authority in some Christian groups. The late second-century prophetesses Prisca and Maximilla, for example, proclaimed the apocalyptic message of Montanus that the Heavenly Jerusalem would soon descend in Asia Minor. Second-century Christians could also find proof that women could preach and baptize in fictional literature such as *The Acts of Paul and Thecla.* In this story, Thecla calls off her engagement to a prominent noble in order to follow Paul and help him spread the Christian message and found churches. Her mother's words reflect her family's horror at her decision: "My daughter, like a spider bound at the window by that man's words, is controlled by a new desire and a terrible passion." Like the invented literary character Thecla, many Christian women chose a life of celibacy and service to their church. Their commitment to chastity as proof of their devotion to Christianity gave these women the power to control their own bodies by removing their sexuality from the control of men. It also bestowed social status upon them among other Christians, as women with a special closeness to God. By rejecting the traditional roles of wife and mother and by becoming leaders, at least among similarly minded women, celibate Christian women achieved a measure of independence and authority generally denied them in the non-Christian world.

Gnostics

Unlike Judaism and the traditional religions of Greece and Rome, Christianity placed belief ahead of practice as the primary criterion of who was a good and genuine member of the religion. Defining "right" belief, Christian orthodoxy, thus became a critical issue. From the first century A.D. to the present, disagreements about doctrine and accusations of heresy have separated one Christian group from another, sometimes with violent consequences.

One of the great battles over Christian doctrine in the second and third centuries A.D. was the struggle between Gnostics and other Christians. The Gnostics believed an inferior or evil god, in disobedience to the high god, from whom all spirit derives, created the material world. This creator god was the God of the Old Testament, who kept humans in ignorance by claiming he was the only god and by imposing laws on them to keep them enslaved. Salvation could be achieved only by rejecting the material world and recognizing that the soul's true origin and destiny were with the high god. He periodically sent various redeemers into the world to reveal the truth to humanity. According to some Gnostics, the first of these redeemers was the snake in the Garden of Eden, who tried to impart true knowledge to Adam and Eve. The final redeemer was Jesus, who handed down his secret spiritual message to his apostles after his resurrection. It was this saving knowledge (Greek *gnosis*) the Gnostics said they offered the world.

Christian opponents of Gnosticism fought what they saw as its heretical doctrines not only through sophisticated theological treatises refuting its tenets but also through accounts attacking Gnosticism's leaders and demonstrating the power of the orthodox faith. The *Acts of Peter,* for example, told how the apostle Peter fought a duel in Rome with Simon the Magician, the reputed founder of Gnosticism. When Simon demonstrated his power by flying around Rome, Peter used his own magic to cause Simon to crash. The Roman emperor, the story continued, later put Peter to death after the emperor's mistresses converted to Christianity and refused to have sex with him anymore.

Judging from the spirited attacks on it by Church authorities, we can surmise that Gnosticism presented a formidable challenge to what was to become orthodox Christianity. The Gnostic message of redemption through esoteric revelation and rejection of the material world, rather than through belief in the death and physical resurrection of Jesus, as well as its rejection of the Old Testament and its God, represented a radically different form of Christianity from the orthodoxy represented in the New Testament. Ultimately, Gnosticism faded out because most Christians, especially those in positions of power and prosperity, were not ready to turn away from this world and cut all ties to Judaism's Bible. Much of Christianity's appeal resided in Jesus' identity as a man who had been raised from the dead in the recent past; he was not a figure of ancient mythology or a spirit from an alien world. Early Christianity gave its believers the feeling that their God was close to them, loved them, and bound them together to love each other with tenderness and compassion, rich and poor alike, in a community in this world and the next.

Parallel Religious Experience in Paganism

The diverse nature of early Christianity was matched by the diversity of pagan religion under the early empire. In A.D. 200 the overwhelming majority of people in the Roman world were still polytheists. Their deities ranged from the stalwarts of the state cults, such as Jupiter and Minerva, to spirits traditionally thought to inhabit local groves and springs. Several popular new cults also emerged. The Iranian god Mithras developed a large following among merchants and soldiers as the god of the morning light, a superhuman hero requiring ethical conduct and truthful dealings from his followers. But tradition excluded women from Mithraism, and this restriction put the cult at a disadvantage in expanding its membership. In the third century A.D., the emperors enthusiastically introduced worship of the sun as the supreme deity of the empire as part of the official religion. The cult of the goddess Isis, however, best shows how paganism as well as Christianity could provide believers with a religious experience arousing strong personal emotions and demanding a moral way of life.

Isis was a deity of ancient Egyptian religion, and her cult had already attracted Romans by the time of Augustus. He tried to suppress it because it was Cleopatra's religion, but Isis' stature as a loving, compassionate goddess who cared for the suffering of each of her followers made her cult too popular to crush. The Egyptians said it was her tears for famished humans that caused the Nile to flood every year and bring them good harvests. Her image was that of a loving mother, and in art she was often shown nursing her son. A central doctrine of her cult concerned the death and resurrection of her husband, Osiris. Isis promised her followers hope for life after death for themselves, too. Her

Mithras and the Bull
The all-male cult of the god Mithras originated in Persia and became especially popular among soldiers. Here Mithras's role in creation is symbolized by his slaying a bull, from whose blood springs life and vegetation.

cult was open to both men and women, and a preserved wall painting shows people of both dark- and light-skinned races officiating at her rituals.

Like Christianity, the cult of Isis expected its adherents to behave morally. In inscriptions put up for all to read, Isis was portrayed as expressing her expectations for her followers by referring to her own civilizing accomplishments: "I broke down the rule of tyrants; I put an end to murders; I caused what is right to be mightier than gold and silver." A similar concern for upright conduct by Isis' devotees was described in the novel *The Golden Ass* by Apuleius (born A.D. 123), a wealthy and well-educated Roman from North Africa. The hero of his story, Lucius, had trouble obeying Isis' laws of chastity and obedience. At the end of the book, however, Isis' power purified Lucius in a miraculous transformation and prepared him for a new life. Lucius's prayer to her expressed his intense joy after having been spiritually reborn: "O

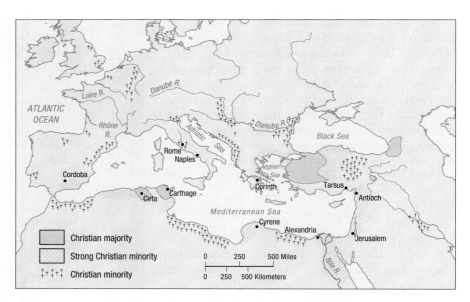

**Christian Populations,
c. A.D. 300**

holy and eternal guardian of the human race, who always cherishes mortals and blesses them, you care for the troubles of miserable humans with a sweet mother's love. Neither day nor night, nor any moment of time, ever passes by without your blessings."

Other pagan cults also required their adherents to lead morally upright lives. Numerous inscriptions from remote villages in Asia Minor, for example, record the confessions of pagan peasants to sins such as sexual transgressions for which their local god had imposed harsh penance on them. Mithraism required its followers to adhere to a strict moral code. For many upper-class Romans in the early empire, the tenets of Stoic philosophy, derived from the teachings of the Greek Zeno (335–263 B.C.), directed their personal lives. Stoics believed in self-discipline above all, and their code of personal ethics left no room for riotous conduct. As the Roman Stoic Seneca (died A.D. 65) put it, "It is easier to prevent harmful emotions from entering the soul than it is to control them once they have entered." For the Stoics the universe was guided by a single creative force that incorporated reason, nature, and divinity. Humans shared in the essence of this universal force and found happiness by living in accordance with it.

Other philosophical challenges caused Christian intellectuals to defend the new faith. Origen (c. A.D. 185–255), for example, argued that Christianity was

both true and superior to pagan philosophy as a guide to correct living. At about the same time, however, pagan belief achieved its most philosophical formulation in the works of Plotinus (c. A.D. 205–270). Plotinus's spiritual philosophy, called Neoplatonism (meaning "New Platonism") because it developed new doctrines based on Plato's philosophy, influenced many educated Christians as well as pagans. Plotinus's religious doctrines focused on a human longing to return to the universal Good from which human existence was derived. By turning away from the life of the body through the intellectual pursuit of philosophy, individual souls could ascend to the level of the universal soul, becoming the whole of which, as individuals, they formed a potential part. This mystical union with what the Christians would call God could be achieved only through strenuous self-discipline in personal morality as well as intellectual life. Neoplatonism's stress on spiritual purity gave it a powerful appeal to Christian intellectuals.

Pagan systems of belief, like those of the cult of Isis or the philosophy of the Stoics and Neoplatonists, paralleled those of Christianity in their ability to provide guidance, comfort, and hope to people through good times or bad. The bad times of the economic and political crisis of the third century A.D. gave particular relevance and appeal to the spiritual relief these creeds could offer. It was in this period of crisis that Christianity came under the most violent attack yet. The emperor Decius

(✱A.D. 249–251) instituted a systematic persecution of Christians, styling himself "Restorer of the Cults" while proclaiming, "I would rather see a rival to my throne than another bishop of Rome."

He ordered all inhabitants of the empire to prove their loyalty to the welfare of the state by participating in a sacrifice to its gods. Christians who refused were killed.

CONCLUSION

The Roman Empire began when Augustus created the principate, a new political system of disguised monarchy. The principate endured because it restored peace and stability while maintaining the political vocabulary of the republic and many of its offices. As the patron of all Romans, the emperor exercised paternalistic authority over them in the tradition of the client-patron system. Ultimately, however, his power rested on his control of the army. The succession of Claudius with the backing of the praetorian guard blatantly revealed that force made emperors and set a precedent that would be followed on later occasions when the succession was disputed.

Perhaps the most significant economic trend under the early empire was the shift in the impact of the Roman army. During the republic and the reign of Augustus, the army had been a successful offensive force whose conquests strengthened the empire's economy. Thereafter, only rarely did emperors use it to conquer territory and bring in capital in the form of booty and slaves. When the army spent most of its time maintaining internal security or repelling invaders, as it did for long stretches under the early empire, it severely drained the empire's resources, especially because it had grown by perhaps a third since Augustus's time.

The loss of conquest as a source of income helped precipitate a breakdown in the traditional Roman system of patronage, which had always provided a foundation for the financial and social health of the cities and towns of the empire.

Later emperors who lacked the full treasury Augustus enjoyed could no longer function as patrons of the population of the empire in the same generous way as he. The decline in imperial revenues increased the financial pressure on the wealthy elites of the provinces to support public services. When they could no longer meet the government's demand for revenue without ruining their fortunes, these people began to look for ways to escape their traditional duties as patrons.

Roman traditions faced further challenge with the emergence of Christianity. The separation of Christianity from its Jewish origins created a new religion that appealed to men and women across the empire, although its members were still a minority by A.D. 200. The emperor Decius's persecution of them shows the depth of the Roman Empire's troubles in the third century A.D. Authorities sought out Christians to punish because, as so often in history, it was more convenient to blame difficult problems on outsiders rather than those in the government's inner circle. The crisis of the third century A.D. in reality occurred as the culmination of long-term trends complicated by the coincidence of the natural disasters that devastated the Mediterranean world at this time. This combination of events had pushed the Roman Empire to the brink of near anarchy and economic collapse by the 280s A.D. The remarkable history of the changes that brought about a recovery and the equally remarkable transformation of the Roman Empire into a Christian Empire form the next part of the story.

SUGGESTIONS FOR FURTHER READING

Source Materials

Juvenal. *The Sixteen Satires.* 1967. Stinging satires on Roman urban life under the early empire. Also available in a bilingual Latin/English edition in the Loeb Classical Library series.

Kraemer, Ross E., ed. *Maenads, Martyrs, Matrons, Monastics: A Sourcebook on Women's Religions in the Greco-Roman World.* 1988. A topically arranged selection of sources on the religious experiences of women in Greco-Roman paganism, Judaism, and Christianity.

Lefkowitz, Mary R., and Maureen B. Fant. *Women's Life in Greece and Rome: A Source Book in Translation.* 1982. Contains selected sources on the occupations, daily life, and political and religious experiences of women.

Lewis, Naphtali, and Meyer Reinhold, eds. *Roman Civilization: Sourcebook II: The Empire.* 1990. Offers a wide selection of sources arranged chronologically and topically, with useful introductions to each excerpt; includes political and administrative history.

Suetonius. *The Twelve Caesars.* 1979. Biographies of the rulers of Rome from Caesar to Domitian by an insider with access to the imperial archives. Also available in a bilingual Latin/English edition in the Loeb Classical Library series.

Tacitus. *The Annals; The Histories.* 1978; 1975. A caustic narrative of the imperial reigns from A.D. 14 to 70 by a premier historical stylist. Also available in a bilingual Latin/English edition in the Loeb Classical Library series.

Interpretive Studies

Balsdon, J. P. V. D. *Romans and Aliens.* 1979. A fascinating account of Roman attitudes toward non-Romans in the empire, and vice versa.

Birley, Anthony. *Marcus Aurelius: A Biography.* Rev. ed. 1987. An engaging biography of the most philosophical Roman emperor, which uses Aurelius's own book, *The Meditations.*

Chadwick, Henry, and G. R. Evans. *Atlas of the Christian Church.* 1987. Includes a brief, masterful survey of the history of the early church, with an emphasis on theological and doctrinal history.

Christ, Karl. *The Romans.* 1984. A topically arranged introduction to Roman civilization.

Cornell, Tim, and John Matthews. *Atlas of the Roman World.* 1982. A concise historical survey linked to excellent and colorful maps.

Earl, Donald. *The Age of Augustus.* 1968. An accessible discussion of all aspects of the Augustan age, with many illustrations.

Frend, W. H. C. *The Rise of Christianity.* 1984. An exhaustive study including Jewish background and doctrinal history.

Garnsey, Peter, and Richard Saller. *The Roman Empire: Economy, Society, and Culture.* 1987. A detailed thematic treatment of the political, social, economic, religious, and cultural life of the principate (27 B.C.–A.D. 235).

Grant, Michael. *Cleopatra.* 1972. A readable biography of the last member of the royal line of the Ptolemies.

———. *The Roman Emperors: A Biographical Guide to the Rulers of Imperial Rome, 31 B.C.–A.D. 476.* 1985. Contains short biographies of the Roman emperors from Augustus to Romulus Augustulus.

Greene, Kevin. *The Archaeology of the Roman Economy.* 1986. Presents recent archaeological evidence for trade, transport, finances, and agriculture in the Roman Empire.

Henig, Martin, ed. *A Handbook of Roman Art: A Comprehensive Survey of All the Arts of the Roman World.* 1983. Features broad coverage, including architecture, with many illustrations.

Isaac, Benjamin. *The Limits of Empire: The Roman Army in the East.* 1989. A reassessment of the Roman army's role as more directed toward conquest and internal security than defense against foreign invasion.

Jackson, Ralph. *Doctors and Diseases in the Roman Empire.* 1988. A stimulating study of illness, medical treatment, and the interaction of doctors and healing divinities in the Roman imperial world.

MacMullen, Ramsay. *Paganism in the Roman Empire.* 1981. A comprehensive survey of the great variety of pagan religious beliefs and practices in the Roman Empire.

Meeks, Wayne A. *The First Urban Christians: The Social World of the Apostle Paul.* 1983. A study of what it was like to be an ordinary Christian in Paul's time.

Scarborough, John. *Roman Medicine.* 1969. A wide-ranging introduction for a nonspecialist audience.

Schürer, Emil. *The History of the Jewish People in the Age of Jesus Christ (175 B.C.–A.D. 135).* Rev. ed. 4 vols. 1973, 1979, 1986. An authoritative scholarly work on the history of the Jews in the late republic and early empire.

Sitwell, N. H. H. *Roman Roads of Europe.* 1981. Discusses the Roman road system province by province, and includes many color illustrations.

Stambaugh, John E. *The Ancient Roman City.* 1988. A synthesis of Roman social history in the context of urban architecture and the physical space of the city.

Stambaugh, John E., and David L. Balch. *The New Testament in Its Social Environment.* 1986. A clearly presented introduction to the social world of early Christianity, in the valuable series *The Library of Early Christianity.*

Thompson, Lloyd A. *Romans and Blacks.* 1989. A study of Roman attitudes toward blacks, arguing that skin color was an aesthetic rather than a social issue.

Webster, Graham. *The Roman Imperial Army of the First and Second Centuries A.D.* 3d ed. 1985. Discusses all aspects of the Roman military in this period.

Witt, R. E. *Isis in the Greco-Roman World.* 1971. An account for a general audience of the cult of Isis in ancient Egypt, Greece, and Rome.x

The dry sands of Egypt have preserved many ancient documents written on paper made from the reeds of the papyrus plant. One typical example from the third century, a personal letter from an Egyptian woman named Isis to her mother, was found among the remains of a village near the Nile River. The letter offers us a tantalizing glimpse of some of the unsettling changes that affected the lives of many people in the Roman Empire of the time.

> I make supplication for you every day
> before the lord Sarapis and his fellow gods.
> I want you to know that I have arrived
> in Alexandria safely after four days. I
> send fond greetings to my sister and the
> children and Elouath and his wife and
> Dioscorous and her husband and children
> and Tamalis and her husband and son and
> Heron and Ammonarion and . . . Sanpat
> and her children. And if Aion wants to be
> in the army, let him come. For everybody
> is in the army.

Unfortunately, we do not know the relations between Isis and each person she mentioned, with their mixture of Greek and Semitic names. Nor can we tell whether Isis knew how to write or, as was common, had hired a scribe.

Why did Isis go to Alexandria? Why did Aion want to become a soldier? Why was "everybody" in the army? The answers suggest the many dimensions of the third-century crisis in the Roman Empire. Perhaps economic troubles forced Isis to leave her home to look for work in the largest city in her area. Perhaps Aion wanted to join the army to better his condition. Perhaps it seemed that everybody was in the army because the political crisis of the empire

The Fragmentation and Transformation of the Late Roman Empire, 284–568

The Soaring Architecture of Santa Sophia
Golden mosaics originally shone from the high walls and domes of Santa Sophia ("Holy Wisdom"), Emperor Justinian's great church in Constantinople. Its magnificence reflected the scope of Justinian's dream to reunite the eastern and western parts of the Roman Empire.

frequently led to military conflicts. These possibilities seem plausible in the context of the primary challenge facing the Roman Empire by the second half of the third century: to restore the state's traditional function as the guarantor of peace and order through military force, government administration, and enough economic prosperity to prevent turmoil.

Rome's rulers also faced growing religious tensions between Christians and pagans like Isis (named after the Egyptian goddess). By the end of the fourth century this conflict had been formally resolved in favor of Christianity, which became the empire's official religion. Yet the social and cultural effects of this transformation took much longer to settle because pre-Christian Roman traditions persisted. Eventually, the western and eastern sections of the empire split into two systems. In the western portion, Germanic peoples organized their tribes into kingdoms whose authority eventually replaced centralized Roman rule. They and the inhabitants of the former Roman provinces there lived side by side, each keeping some customs of their heritage intact but merging other parts of their disparate cultures and developing a new sense of ethnic identity. These new kingdoms and the general decentralization of authority set the pattern for the later political divisions of medieval western Europe. Provinces in the eastern Roman Empire stayed under Roman rule for another thousand years, even though hostile neighbors frequently wrenched away some of the empire's territory in wars. This eastern part of the empire became the Byzantine Empire, a power that endured until the mid-1400s. Starting in the third century, the Roman world began to evolve into two distinct entities—the West and the East—whose fates would unfold along separate paths.

The Reorganization of the Roman Empire

The Roman Empire reemerged from the economic and political crisis in the mid-third century as a unified state ruled by a strong central authority. The penetration of the empire's borders by different invaders over several decades, however, had imposed

---

IMPORTANT DATES

c. 285 Anthony withdraws to the Egyptian desert to become the first known Christian monk

301 Emperor Diocletian issues the Edict on Maximum Prices

312 Constantine defeats Maxentius and converts to Christianity

313 Co-emperors Constantine and Licinius abolish official hindrances to Christianity and proclaim a policy of religious tolerance

361–363 Emperor Julian the Apostate tries to restore paganism as Rome's official religion, but fails

378 The Visigoths defeat the eastern emperor Valens at the battle of Adrianople

391 Emperor Theodosius bans pagan sacrifice and closes the temples

410 The army of Alaric, king of the Visigoths, sacks Rome

476 The German commander Odoacer deposes the final western emperor, Romulus Augustulus

529 The Byzantine emperor Justinian orders the closing of the Academy originally founded by Plato in Athens

538 Justinian dedicates the Church of the Holy Wisdom in Constantinople

c. 540 Benedict of Nursia draws up his regulations for monastic life (The Rule of St. Benedict)

---

a pressing need to reorganize its defenses and its system of collecting revenue. In the religious arena the pagan emperors confronted the thorny issue of a growing Christian church, whose presence was now felt throughout the Roman world. The definitive responses to these challenges came during the reign of the emperors Diocletian (✴284–305) and Constantine (✴306–337).

Administrative and Military Reforms

Diocletian was an uneducated military man from Dalmatia (a region in what used to be Yugoslavia). His courage and intelligence propelled his rise through the ranks to commander of the emperor

Numerian's personal bodyguard. When Numerian (✱283–284) was assassinated soon after taking the throne, the army made Diocletian emperor to avenge the crime. Diocletian swiftly executed the commander of the praetorian guard, Numerian's father-in-law, as the murderer and defeated other rivals for the throne. As emperor, Diocletian used his exceptional talent for administration and control to reorganize the structure of the Roman Empire, reasserting its tradition of centralized authority. The imperial administration needed revamping so the provinces could be governed more effectively; this meant restoring tax revenues and setting new limits on the provincial administrators' power, making it possible for Rome to keep them from rebelling. The third-century invasions had clearly demonstrated that military reforms were necessary; the empire had to have better defensive strategies. The imperial Roman army had two traditional purposes: fighting wars of conquest to satisfy the emperors' desires for glory, booty, and territory, and suppressing unrest in the outlying provinces. Defense, which had previously been considered secondary to offense, became crucial when a double threat arose along the empire's frontiers. The Sassanids, who had created a new Persian Empire, menaced Roman territory in the east, while bands of Germanic warriors raided the empire along its nearly three-thousand-mile-long northern frontier along the Rhine and Danube rivers.

Diocletian's administrative reforms divided the empire into four districts, each with its own ruler, capital city, and military forces. No longer did a single emperor rule the Roman Empire. Under the *tetrarchy* ("rule by four rulers"), as the new system was called, two of the rulers were the senior members (*augusti;* singular, *augustus*) and two the junior (*caesars*). The *augusti* adopted the caesars as their sons and made them heirs to their thrones to try to prevent the civil wars that had regularly erupted in the third century when a new emperor had to be chosen. When an *augustus* retired or died, his caesar took over as *augustus* and then selected and adopted a new caesar for the junior position. Diocletian himself became the *augustus* of the eastern half of the empire and lived there in Nicomedia, near the Bosphorus Strait in western Asia Minor; and he dominated the *augustus* in the western empire, Maximian. Under Diocletian's arrangement the city of Rome lost its special position as the capital; Diocletian did not even visit Rome

until 303, nearly twenty years after becoming emperor. The generals who now determined the empire's fate came from rough lands in the provinces, and the Senate of Rome had lost all power to control them. The northern city of Milan was better located to defend Italy and this became one of Diocletian's new capitals; the others were Nicomedia, Sirmium, near the Danube River border, and Trier, near the Rhine River border. Italy was henceforth just another section of the empire, on an equal footing with the other imperial provinces and subject to the same taxation system (except for the district of Rome itself).

To increase administrative efficiency and prevent provincial governors from becoming too powerful, Diocletian reduced the size of the old provinces, thereby creating new ones and doubling the total number of provinces. The now more than one hundred provinces were divided into twelve groups, called *dioceses,* each headed by a vicar who reported to one of the four praetorian prefects. At this time each emperor had as his principal assistant a prefect who traveled with him wherever he went. Later in the fourth century the prefects were permanently assigned to head the four territorial districts of the empire, which became known as prefectures. Naturally, the increased number of subdivisions required a larger imperial staff. Diocletian chose the administrators almost exclusively from the equestrian class, men who had risen through the military ranks from relatively humble beginnings; the traditional senatorial domination of the top offices in Roman provincial administration thus ceased. Diocletian also departed from tradition by beginning to separate military from civil authority, a development concluded by his successor, Constantine. Governing the provinces and commanding troops now became separate functions overseen by different men, reducing the possibilities of individual officials rebelling against the central government.

Diocletian revised Roman military strategy both by greatly increasing the size of the Roman army and by devising a new defense against invaders. He stationed troops on the frontiers (the *frontiersmen*) under regional commanders. The frontiersmen settled on the land with their families to farm the area they guarded. But they were not just a peasant militia called out only in times of trouble. They served as sentries, warning the empire of any threats along its borders, and as fighting troops, buffering the interior in case of attack. Constantine,

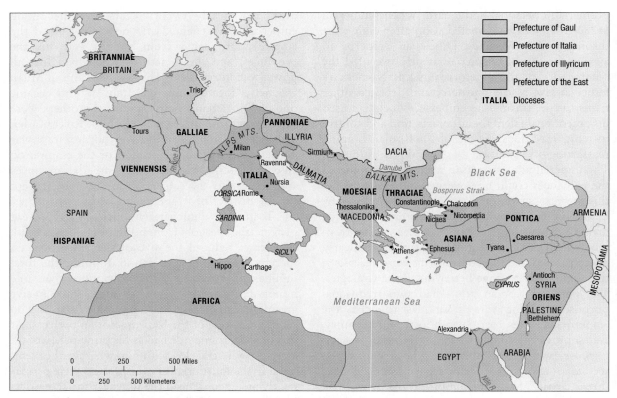

Dioceses of Diocletian, c. 300, and the Later Geographical Prefectures

who became sole emperor in 324 after nearly two decades of civil wars, dramatically modified Diocletian's strategy by reducing the emphasis on stationary defense in the frontier regions. He created a number of centrally located, mobile contingents (the *convoyers*) based in a zone of forts well to the rear, who would be dispatched by an area commander to meet any enemy force that had broken through the frontiersmen.

The military reforms of Diocletian and Constantine succeeded in temporarily ending the danger of invasions. Later emperors again tried to employ the army for conquest, especially against Persia, and thought little about defense. But any territory they acquired never stayed in the empire for long, and Rome's history as a relentless and seemingly invincible conqueror of foreign land ended.

The reforms Diocletian initiated made the empire more stable and therefore helped it emerge by about 300 from the worst crisis in its history.

But this reorganization was no cure-all. The tetrarchy introduced a significant weakness by increasing the number of rulers and thus the opportunities for conflict among them. Constantine sought to correct this flaw by eliminating joint rule, but in the long run it proved impossible for one emperor to govern the entire empire.

Tax Reform

The most urgent consequence of Diocletian's reforms was the need to raise more revenue to pay the increased costs of administration and defense, especially because the civil wars and unrest of the mid-third century had ruined the government financially. Simply paying the troops, for example, was considerably more expensive than before because the army had been expanded. Some scholars estimate Diocletian's army to have been as large as five hundred thousand men—an increase of more than one hundred thousand over the size of the third-century armies. By modern standards the Roman army was not extraordinarily big relative to the size of the empire's population, which totaled at least several tens of millions. Nevertheless, the cost of the army severely burdened the structurally weak imperial financial system. The system had been stressed almost to the breaking point by the devaluation of Roman currency in the third century and the accompanying hyperinflation. Prices soared to unheard-of levels. High prices caused people to hoard whatever they could buy, driving up prices even higher. "Hurry and spend all my money you have; buy me any kinds of goods at whatever prices they are available," wrote one official to his servant on hearing of another impending devaluation. In 301, Diocletian tried to curb inflation with an elaborate system of wage and price controls. His Edict on Maximum Prices, which blamed high prices on profiteers of "unlimited and frenzied avarice," forbade hoarding and set ceilings on the amounts that could legally be charged or paid for about a thousand goods and services. The edict, promulgated only in the eastern part of the empire, soon became ineffective because merchants refused to cooperate, and government officials proved unable to enforce it, despite the threat of death or exile as the penalty for violations.

Devaluation and inflation had destroyed the old revenue system, under which people paid taxes in money that the government then used to buy goods and services. Diocletian and Constantine revised the empire's revenue system so it relied mainly on taxation in kind: most citizens now had to pay tax assessments largely in goods and services rather than in coinage. Taxation in kind remained the empire's principal source of revenue until the end of the fourth century, when payments were more and more commuted into gold and silver. In earlier times the Roman government had occasionally requisitioned supplies for the army, sometimes even paying for them. But now the state regularly demanded goods in lieu of monetary taxes. These "taxes"—barley, wheat, meat, salt, wine, vegetable oil, horses, camels, mules, and so on—provided food and transport animals for the army.

The government used a complex formula to determine tax assessments. The major components of the system, which varied in different regions of the empire, were a tax on land, assessed according to its productivity, and a head tax on individuals.

In some areas, both men and women from the age of about twelve to sixty-five paid the full tax, but in others women paid only one-half the tax assessment or none at all. It is unclear how the head tax applied to people living in cities; they may have been liable only for a tax on their property, if they had any, and for periodic unpaid labor, especially on public works projects. By Constantine's reign every kind of urban business people, from shopkeepers to prostitutes, owed monetary taxes, and members of the senatorial class, who were exempt from the general tax system, were subject to various levies. The compulsory public services levied on the mutual support organizations (*collegia*) in which urban crafts producers and shopkeepers were traditionally organized, also constituted an important, often burdensome, form of taxation. These services ranged from cleaning the municipal drains to repairing dilapidated buildings. The *collegia* either had to do the work themselves or pay for others to do it. In another effort to guarantee essential materials at the lowest cost, the government established state factories to manufacture armaments and to weave and dye cloth to provide fine garments for imperial officials and uniforms for soldiers.

The new tax system could work only if agricultural production remained stable and the government could control the people liable for the head tax. Hence Diocletian further restricted the movement of the *coloni,* or tenant farmers, the empire's economic base. Tenant farmers had traditionally been free to move to different farms under different landlords as long as their debts were paid. Now, male tenant farmers, as well as their wives in those areas in which women were assessed for taxes, were increasingly tied to a particular plot. Their children also had to stay on and farm their allotted land throughout their lives, thereby making agriculture a hereditary occupation. Binding the rural population to the land simultaneously stabilized agricultural production and made it easier to assess and collect the head tax. Each year the government calculated its budget solely on the amount of revenue its plans required and then gathered that amount by dividing it by the number of assessments on people and land in the empire. Over time, more and more taxes were imposed without much regard for how much people could pay. The tax on land eventually reached one-third of its gross yield, and the increasing tax burden on the rural population led to revolts in some areas, especially fifth-century Spain.

The government also deemed some occupations outside agriculture essential and prohibited such workers from taking other jobs. Crucial in preventing riots, for example, was assuring a supply of free grain for Rome's poor, following a tradition begun in the Roman Republic. About one hundred twenty thousand people in Rome were now entitled to receive free bread produced in state bakeries. The state bakers could not leave their jobs, and anyone who acquired a baker's property had to assume that occupation. A man marrying the daughter of a baker in Rome had to take up his father-in-law's trade and keep it even in the event of a divorce. Shippers in the state-regulated system of seaborne transport, who brought grain to Rome, were also legally bound to their occupation. From Constantine's reign on, the sons of military veterans had to serve in the army, which was a lifetime career. Army recruits, like workers in the imperial armament factories, were branded on the arm so that runaways could be identified.

It had always been common in the ancient world for a son to take up his father's trade, but this custom increasingly became a legal obligation in the late Roman Empire, at least in the West. As the economy in the West deteriorated in later years, the western emperors prohibited a greater variety of crafts producers and shopkeepers from leaving their jobs. The government's goal was to keep up civic services by maintaining a supply of workers in essential occupations and regularly requiring them to donate labor. The more prosperous eastern empire never imposed a similar degree of regulation.

The Curial Class and Autocracy

In the long term the empire's increasing demand for revenue and compulsory services from citizens had a tremendous impact on the propertied class in the cities and towns, the *curiales.* In this period almost all men in the curial class were obliged sooner or later to serve as unsalaried council members, who had to use their own funds if necessary to provide costly municipal services. This arrangement stemmed from the Roman tradition that the wealthy should use their riches for the public benefit in return for honor and prestige. The *curiales* were responsible for services such as repairing aqueducts, supplying animals for the imperial

postal and land-transport system (an expensive service that carried official mail and valuables such as gold and silver), and feeding and lodging troops. For the central government the *curiales'* most important obligation was to collect taxes in their region. Although this responsibility provided them an opportunity to profit by raking off more taxes than were legally due, it also committed them to making up any shortfalls, which had become increasingly common because of the third-century economic crisis, from their own pockets.

Curiales varied in wealth, and in smaller towns the property qualification for this status could be relatively low. Many poorer *curiales* owned nothing more than a small farm, and the burden of having to make up tax deficits often crushed them. The regulations governing *curiales* usually referred to men, but women and orphans with property also had the same obligations to make up tax shortfalls and pay for public services. The financial responsibility of the curial class increased during the reigns of Constantine and his immediate successors. By then the imperial government demanded even the income that cities had traditionally received from their indirect taxes, such as sales taxes, customs fees, and rent on publicly owned lands. Now that the cities had lost their private tax revenues, the *curiales* struggled harder than ever to fulfill their official obligations to help pay for their city's waterworks and other communal needs.

Curiales essentially inherited their status, because property that passed from generation to generation in even a moderately wealthy family automatically made its possessors members of the curial class. For centuries, having civic-minded and propertied citizens in curial positions in the cities and towns had been critical to the empire's financial welfare. This system was now clearly breaking down, as more and more *curiales* could no longer afford their financial responsibilities. A telling indication of the dire change in the curial system was that compulsory service on a municipal council became one of the punishments for a minor crime. Eventually, to prevent *curiales* from escaping their obligations, imperial policy forbade them to move away from the town where they had been born. They even had to ask official permission to travel. *Curiales* had only two avenues of escape. They could obtain an exemption from service by using their connections to petition the emperor, by bribing the appropriate officials, or by taking up one of the occupations (such as service in the army, imperial administration, or the church) that relieved people of the financial burdens of the curial class. Or they could flee, abandoning home and property. Because the obligations of exempt or fugitive *curiales* were simply passed on to those unfortunates still around, the scramble to gain exemptions increased exponentially.

The tax reform of the later third century, however, improved Roman imperial finances compared to the disastrous conditions of mid-century, and this relative financial stability helped restore peace to the provinces in Diocletian's time. Still, the failure of the Edict on Maximum Prices foreshadowed the problems this rigid centralization of economic activity would cause later on, as the government's increased demand for revenue severely outpaced the population's ability to pay. Official attempts to direct the economy reflected the autocratic nature of imperial rule. Collaboration between emperor and Senate in ruling the empire, the hallmark of the principate and a tradition that rulers such as Marcus Aurelius had genuinely respected, became a thing of the past. Culminating a century-long trend, Diocletian was now formally recognized not as *princeps,* or "leader," but rather as *dominus,* or "Lord."

From the Latin word *dominus* comes the term historians use to designate Roman imperial rule from Diocletian onward—the *dominate.* The autocracy and theology of the dominate reflected traditions of rule in the ancient Near East and the Hellenistic kingdoms. To mark their supreme status as autocrats ruling without any peers other than each other, emperors as "Lords" dressed themselves in jeweled robes and surrounded themselves with courtiers and ceremony. A series of veils separated the palace's waiting rooms from the inner space where the emperor held audiences. Officials marked their rank in the strictly hierarchical imperial administration with grandiose titles such as "most perfect" and wore special shoes and belts with their costly clothing. In their style and propaganda the imperial courts of the late Roman Empire more closely resembled that of the Great King of Persia a thousand years earlier than that of the first Roman emperors. Continuing a trend already visible in the time of earlier emperors like Caracalla (＊211–217), the architecture of the dominate reflected the image of its rulers as all-powerful autocrats. When Diocletian built a public bath in Rome, its size rivaled that of the baths Rome's most

extravagant earlier emperors constructed. The soaring vaults and domes of the Baths of Diocletian covered a space over three thousand feet long on each side.

As in the past, religious language was used to mark the emperor's special status above mere humans. The title *et deus* ("and God") could be added to *dominus,* for example, as a mark of supreme honor. Diocletian also adopted the title *Jovius,* claiming himself descended from Jupiter (Jove), the chief Roman god. In so designating himself, Diocletian was following the lead of emperors from at least as early as the mid-third century. His fellow *augustus,* Maximian, boasted of his own descent from Hercules (the son of Jupiter, and thus subordinate to Diocletian). The emperors did not take these titles to present themselves as gods like the traditional deities of Roman religion. Rather their titles expressed the sense of complete respect and awe they expected from their subjects and also demonstrated that government on earth replicated divine organizations. Just as the deified hero Hercules had been his father's helper, so Maximian was Diocletian's loyal supporter, his "son." This theological framework for legitimating imperial rule had roots in Hellenistic kingship, and its linking of father and son as rulers and benefactors of humans found a parallel in Christian theology. After his conversion to Christianity, Constantine (like the Christian emperors following him) continued this tradition, by believing God had appointed him ruler.

The Christianizing of the Empire

By the end of the fourth century, imperial support for paganism, like that Diocletian provided, was abolished, and Christianity became the official religion of the Roman state. Many people remained pagans, but most of the empire's population had adopted the new faith. The sense of community Christianity brought to its believers, its openness to men and women of all classes, and the advantages of belonging to the sanctioned state religion gave it a social appeal to complement its theological promise of personal salvation. The startling transformation of the Roman Empire into a Christian state proved the most influential legacy from

TAPE
11
B

TAPE
12
A

Greco-Roman antiquity to the later history of the Western world.

Confrontation Between Pagans and Christians

Diocletian firmly believed in the traditional pagan divinities and the established religion of the Roman state. He made clear his attitude toward new religions in a letter to a provincial governor: "Through the providence of the immortal gods, eminent, wise, and upright men have in their wisdom established good and true principles. It is wrong to oppose these principles or to abandon the ancient religion for some new one. . . . " Diocletian obviously feared that any weakening of Roman polytheism would have dire consequences for the state.

Having survived periods of persecution and developed an institutional organization that extended all over the Roman world, Christianity had become prominent in the empire by Diocletian's time. Indeed a Christian church had been built in sight of Diocletian's imperial headquarters in Nicomedia. Every city of any size had a church. Large cities had a central church, presided over by a bishop, as well as smaller churches. Bishops appointed the priests, deacons, and deaconesses who ministered to their city's Christian congregations. Bishops also controlled the congregations' finances and admitted or expelled their members. This hierarchical system set Christianity apart from paganism, whose priests and priestesses had never presided over organizations like those bishops controlled. Some bishops commanded great wealth through their congregations, which increasingly received donations from rich Christians. Many donors were widows, who controlled the property of their households after the death of their husbands and could therefore decide on its disposal. Their generosity accorded them status and prominence in their congregations.

The bishops in the very largest cities, such as Rome, Alexandria, Antioch, and Carthage, became the most influential Christian leaders. The main bishop of Carthage, for example, oversaw at least one hundred local bishops in the surrounding area. Regional councils of bishops exercised supreme authority in appointing new bishops and deciding the doctrinal disputes that frequently polarized bishops and congregations. Christianity was still a religion of small, diverse, and separate groups spread throughout the empire, and they frequently clashed over theology and practice. The bishop of Rome later emerged as the supreme leader of the western church, but in the fourth century, when Christianity had no single center, he did not yet dominate. The preeminence the bishop of Rome eventually gained is recognized in his designation as *pope* (from *pappas*, a Greek word for "father"), the title still used for the head of the Roman Catholic church. Many bishops other than the bishop of Rome were called popes, however, especially in the western empire, and the title did not specifically denote the bishop of Rome for several hundred years. Although the bishop of Rome's rise to dominance in the western Christian church depended principally on the wealth and power he commanded, later popes found a scriptural basis for their position in the New Testament (Matt. 16:18–19). There Jesus speaks to the apostle Peter: "You are Peter, and upon this rock I will build my church. . . . I will entrust to you the keys of the kingdom of heaven. Whatever you bind on earth shall be bound in heaven. Whatever you loose on earth shall be loosed in heaven." Because Peter's name in Greek and Aramaic means "rock" and because Peter was believed to have been the first bishop of Rome, later bishops of Rome claimed that this passage recognized their superior position.

Christianity started as an urban religion and spread to the countryside only gradually. The continuing strength of traditional polytheism in the thousands of tiny villages of the empire is symbolized by the word *pagan,* which derives from a Latin word meaning "country person." Pagans still constituted most of the population around 300 in both city and country. At this time, Christians may have numbered as few as 5 percent of the empire's people, and certainly no more than 20 percent. By now, however, the government and the pagan majority no longer feared the Christians were political subversives bent on destroying public order and overthrowing Roman rule in a violent revolution. The empire had no official policy of toleration, but neither did it sponsor further violence against Christians after vicious but relatively short-lived persecutions under the emperors Decius and Valerian in the mid-third century—at least not until the so-called Great Persecution, which Diocletian launched in 303. He sought first to purge his administration of Christians and then issued edicts to destroy churches, seize Christians' property, and execute Christians who refused to participate in Roman religious rituals. He feared the Christians' refusal to worship the traditional gods would anger the state's deities and lead them to punish him and his empire. In the western part of the empire the violent persecution stopped after about a year; in the eastern portion it continued until early 313 in some areas. As a result, a number of Christians became martyrs, and their gruesome public executions aroused the sympathy of some of their pagan neighbors.

Christians and pagans debated passionately about whether there was one God or many and about what kind of interest the divinity (or divinities) took in the world of humans. But Christian and pagan beliefs sometimes resembled each other as well. The imperial theology of rule on earth by father and son paralleled the Christian doctrine of God the Father and Jesus the Son as rulers in heaven. The tendency of the emperors to choose a particular god as their protector faintly echoed Christian monotheism. Both pagans and Christians also assigned a potent role to spirits and demons as ever-present influences on human life. The two beliefs occasionally converged. For example, a silver spoon used in the worship of the pagan forest spirit Faunus has been found engraved with a fish, the common symbol whose Greek letters (ΙΧΘΥΣ) stood for "Jesus Christ the Son of God, the Savior."

The differences between pagans and Christians, however, far outweighed their similarities. Pagans from the emperor to the common people still participated in frequent festivals and sacrifices to many different gods. Why, pagans asked, did the many festivals and joyous occasions of polytheistic worship not satisfy the Christians' yearning for contact with divinity? Pagans also found it incomprehensible that Christians could believe in a savior who had not only failed to overthrow Roman rule but had even been executed as a common criminal. The Romans' gods, by contrast, had bestowed a world empire on their worshipers. Moreover, pagans pointed out, cults such as that of the goddess Isis and philosophies such as Stoicism insisted that only the pure of heart and mind could be admitted to their fellowship. Christians, on the other hand, sought out the impure. Why, asked perplexed pagans, would Christians want to associate with sinners?

An African Dedication to Saturn
This inscribed sculpture from North Africa depicts the solar god Saturn, who had been the chief god of Carthage under the name of Baal Hammon. The sculpture was dedicated in 323 and reflects the persistence of local pagan religion in the Roman Empire in the time of Constantine, the first Christian emperor.

By the fourth century, Christian intellectuals had been defending their faith against such accusations for more than one hundred years, with their pagan counterparts refuting these defenses as quickly as they appeared. For example, whereas some Neoplatonists tried to find points of correspondence between their doctrines and Christian theology, others mounted withering attacks, such as *Against the Christians* by Porphyry (c. 234–305), a Greek scholar who ironically was devoted to the doctrines of the Neoplatonist Plotinus that also appealed to some Christians. Porphyry presented a detailed critique of both the Old Testament and the New Testament and denigrated the prominence that women could achieve in Christian congregations. He also asserted that Jesus' contemporary, the magician Apollonius of Tyana, had been a greater wonder worker because he could criticize the authorities and then vanish after they arrested him. In short, argued Porphyry, Christians were unjustified in claiming they possessed the sole version of religious truth, for no doctrine that provided "a universal path to the liberation of the soul" had ever been devised.

Porphyry's most powerful accusation motivated Diocletian and another fiercely anti-Christian tetrarch named Galerius to launch the Great Persecution in 303. Porphyry charged that the Christians by their innovative worship of Jesus and their refusal to participate in acts of worship in the imperial cult were corroding the ability of the ancestral religion of the Roman state to maintain the goodwill of the gods toward the Roman people. The empire's recovery from the worst effects of the third-century crisis proved to its autocratic rulers that they had regained divine favor, and they were anxious not to lose it again. Therefore they ordered Christians to turn over their scriptures and sacred treasures to Roman officials and to participate in state-sponsored sacrifices; those who refused were tortured until they complied or executed if they remained obstinate. By escalating pagan fears about Christianity's effect on Rome's fate into the violence of persecution, however, Diocletian and Galerius only undermined the peace and order of society that their other reforms had been intended to restore.

Constantine's Conversion

Official persecution of Christians remained possible as long as the emperor adhered to the traditional Roman religion. Fortunately for Christians, Diocletian's successor, Constantine, converted to Christianity and soon ended further persecution. He also set in motion the process that eventually made Christianity the late Roman Empire's official religion. Constantine's conversion occurred when he

was a Roman general, one of several commanders who claimed to be the *augusti* and were vying with each other over who would rule the empire.

Protracted civil war had followed Diocletian's retirement because of ill health in 305. Constantine and another caesar, Maxentius, eventually faced off at Rome in 312, culminating their military struggle for control of the western empire. Constantine had previously received unfavorable omens from pagan gods during his campaign, but just before the crucial confrontation at Rome he experienced a dream-vision promising him the support of the Christian God. His Christian biographer, Eusebius (c. 260–340), later reported that Constantine had also seen a vision of Jesus' cross in the sky surrounded by the words, "In this sign you shall be the victor." Constantine ordered his soldiers to emblazon their shields with the Christogram or *labarum,* a monogram composed of the first two Greek letters of the word *Christ* (chi, X, and rho, P) superimposed on one another. These entwined letters later became the official symbol of the Christian emperors. When Constantine's army defeated and killed Maxentius at the Battle of the Milvian Bridge in 312, the emperor attested that the miraculous power of Christianity's God needed no further demonstration; he was now a Christian believer— and the new *augustus* of the western empire. Constantine renounced the pagan gods he had worshiped until this momentous turning point—in particular his chosen protecting divinity, the Unconquered Sun—and declared the Christian God his divine guardian.

Although Constantine's conversion did not immediately make the Roman Empire a Christian state, it did officially end the persecutions soon thereafter and led to a policy of religious toleration. One version of this new policy promulgated by Constantine and the eastern *augustus,* Licinius (who did not become a Christian), survives in the so-called Edict of Milan. This edict, which Licinius announced in 313, proclaimed free choice of religion for everyone and referred to the "highest divinity"—an imprecise term designed to satisfy both pagans and Christians. Despite this official policy for toleration of all religions, the edict clearly favored the Christians (proof of Constantine's patronage), repeatedly emphasizing that all official impediments to the practice of their religion were to be removed. Constantine matched his moral support of Christianity with practical backing. He returned all property seized from Christians during the Great Persecution to its previous owners, requiring the imperial treasury to compensate those who had bought the confiscated property at auction (to avoid resentment among non-Christians). Constantine also gave the Lateran basilica (meaning a long rectangular hall, derived from the Greek word for "belonging to the king") to the bishop of Rome for his headquarters.

Over time, Constantine provided Christianity with many advantages, such as exempting its clergy from taxation and from service as *curiales.* He gave bishops the authority to decide legal cases on appeal from the civil judiciary system. When bitter doctrinal disputes broke out among Christians, however, he personally presided over councils of bishops to try to settle them. In 321 the Lord's Day (Sunday) was made a holy day on which no official business or manufacturing work could be performed. It was a mark of Constantine's shrewdness in handling religious matters that he called this new Christian holiday Sunday. The name was suitably ambiguous; pagans could argue that the name equally honored an important ancient deity: the sun.

Constantine's declaration of Sunday as a holiday led to the gradual imposition of a calendar of seven-day weeks, replacing the old Roman system of nine-day cycles marked by market days. Christians had adopted the seven-day week from the Hebrews, who in turn had maintained an ancient Babylonian tradition. The popularity of astrology in the Mediterranean world had already given some momentum to the idea of reckoning time in units of seven days. Many Christians and pagans subscribed to astrological beliefs, such as that each day was guided by a particular celestial power: Sun, Moon, Mars, Mercury, Jupiter, Venus, and Saturn, respectively. This tradition is commemorated in the names for various days of the week in most modern Western languages.

Constantine increased imperial support for Christianity cautiously, recognizing that he had to move slowly in an empire still permeated by polytheism and populated by a majority of non-Christians. Christian symbols gradually appeared on the imperial coinage, but they were placed alongside the images of pagan gods. Moreover, Constantine maintained official ties with the ancient pagan imperial cults. For example, he respected tradition by continuing to hold the office of *pontifex maximus* ("chief priest"), which Roman emperors

Colossal Statue of Constantine
This gigantic head came from a statue of Emperor Constantine. The thirty-foot-high statue sat at the end of a towering basilica.

had filled ever since Augustus. Constantine's conversion did not cost him the support of the empire's pagan majority. After all, imperial tradition allowed him to choose a special deity as his protector, and his success in battle showed the wisdom of his choice. When the Senate of Rome voted Constantine a triumphal arch to commemorate his great victory in 312, its members officially recognized the divine favor demonstrated by his success. In the inscription on the arch, which still stands, the senators discreetly sidestepped the question of precisely which god had helped Constantine, referring only to "divinity."

Constantine chose the ancient city of Byzantium, near the mouth of the Black Sea, to serve as his capital—the "new Rome." Refounded as Constantinople ("the city of Constantine," today Istan-

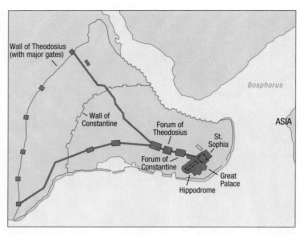

Constantinople

bul, in Turkey) in 324 and formally inaugurated six years later, the capital was centrally and strategically located on an easily fortified peninsula astride the principal land routes from the western to eastern Mediterranean region. To recall the glory of pagan Rome and thus claim for himself the political legitimacy carried by the memory of the old capital of the empire, Constantine graced his new capital with a forum, an imperial palace, a hippodrome for chariot races, and numerous statues of the traditional gods. But to mark his new religious allegiance, he started construction on the great Church of the Holy Wisdom (St. Sophia), which in its later form became one of the architectural marvels of late antiquity. Like the pagan Roman emperors before him, Constantine realized the value of mortar and stone for building his own immortal reputation.

Autocracy and the Growing Strength of Christianity

Because Constantine presented his support of Christianity as a continuation of the Roman tradition of securing divine goodwill for the empire, he was able to minimize opposition from pagans. In 324 he consolidated his power by ousting his pagan colleague Licinius in a bloody struggle more concerned with political domination than religion. Constantine thereafter ruled as sole emperor over a united empire, strongly reasserting the ancient tradition of centralized authority familiar from ancient Near Eastern history and Hellenistic king-

ship. He increased the blatantly autocratic image and reality of rule under the dominate that Diocletian had initiated. Ceremony to reinforce the emperor's status became even more elaborate as petitioners at the imperial court were expected to prostrate themselves and kiss the hem of his purple and gold robe adorned with precious stones. Upon his head rested a diadem (a headband of precious metal studded with jewels). His image was erected in every law court and church in which a bishop presided. Even though they ruled a more fragmented empire, the emperors who succeeded Constantine perpetuated this autocratic style, which they, too, justified as a manifestation of their especially close relationship with the supreme deity.

The structure of the new state-supported Christian church that emerged under Constantine paralleled the imperial autocracy. Early Christianity's relatively loose, democratic form had by now been replaced by a rigid hierarchy based on the authority of bishops. Since the second century, bishops had claimed they had special authority. Now, deriving from the New Testament the power that Jesus had bestowed on the apostles, bishops ruled their congregations almost as monarchs.

Beginning with Constantine, all power was openly vested in the Roman emperors. They commanded the army, issued laws, and exercised supreme judicial authority. The old aristocracy based on birth and inherited wealth, which had always participated in governing the empire, gradually gave way to a new aristocracy of salaried imperial administrators chosen and rewarded by the emperors. Constantine completed the separation of civil and military functions, begun by Diocletian, to prevent the same official from exercising both forms of power. Old symbols of prestige, such as membership in the Senate or the consulship, remained intact; but though these high-ranking officials retained significant financial and legal privileges, they no longer had any real political power. Both pagans and Christians could aspire to such status. Still, despite their desire to conciliate pagans, Constantine and his immediate successors used their autocratic rule to promote Christianity and gradually limit pagan worship. At some point before he died, Constantine may even have issued an edict forbidding pagans to sacrifice. His son Constans, ruling in the west, certainly forbade pagan sacrifice in 341, but the ban seems to have proved largely ineffectual. Throughout the empire, official support for Christianity increased the number of conversions. Soldiers, for example, now found it comfortable to be Christian and still serve in the army. Earlier, Christian soldiers had sometimes created disciplinary problems by renouncing their military oath. As one senior infantryman had said at his court martial in 298 for refusing to continue his duties, "A Christian serving the Lord Christ should not serve the affairs of this world." Once the emperors had become Christians, soldiers could justify military duty as serving the affairs of Christ.

Christianity's openness to women, who were barred from some pagan cults such as Mithraism, promoted the growth of the new religion—it could draw its strength and increase its membership from the entire population. Many men who wanted public careers were still reluctant to embrace Christianity fully, fearing that a public Christian affiliation would inhibit their participation in the oaths, sacrifices, and festivals that remained enormously important in the official ceremony of Roman life. Women's exclusion from public careers correspondingly freed them from this constraint. Augustine (354–430), the famous Christian theologian, eloquently recognized women's contribution to the strengthening of Christianity in a letter he wrote to the unbaptized husband of a baptized woman: "O you men, who fear all the burdens imposed by baptism. You are easily bested by your women. Chaste and devoted to the faith, it is their presence in large numbers that causes the Church to grow." Although women no longer held high offices in the church hierarchy as they had in the beginning of Christianity, they could earn renown and status not only by giving their property to their congregation but also by renouncing earthly marriage to dedicate themselves to Christ. Consecrated virgins and widows who chose not to remarry thus joined large donors as especially respected women.

Christianity grew because it offered believers a strong sense of community in this world as well as the promise of salvation in the next. Wherever Christians traveled or migrated, they could find a warm welcome in a new congregation. Christian congregations became even more popular by emphasizing such charitable works as caring for the poor, widows, and orphans. By the mid-third century, for example, the church in Rome was supporting 1,500 widows and other poor persons. The practice of hospitality, fellowship, and philanthropy, which pagans had always valued as well, was enormously important in the ancient world because people had to depend mostly on their relatives and friends for practical help and advice; state-sponsored social services were rare and limited.

Only one concerted attempt to restore the empire's pagan traditions was made. In 361, Julian (✳361–363) became emperor and tried to restore polytheism as the official religion. A relative of Constantine and a successful military commander, Julian gained the throne in a civil war against his Christian cousin, Constantius, the reigning emperor. Julian had been baptized, but he later rejected Christianity—hence he was known as Julian the Apostate—in favor of a strict Neoplatonism. Constantius's politically motivated murders of Julian's father in 337 and brother in 354 might have influenced Julian's rejection of Christianity. But he was in any case a well-read and deeply religious man who expressed his belief in a supreme deity corresponding to Greek philosophical traditions: "This divine and completely beautiful universe, from heaven's highest arch to earth's lowest limit, is tied together by the continuous providence of god, has existed ungenerated eternally, and is imperishable forever." Julian's attempt to suppress Christianity failed, however, perhaps in part because his religious vision seemed too abstract and his image too effete. When he lectured to a large audience in Antioch, for example, the crowd made fun of his philosopher's beard instead of listening to his message. Julian's early death in battle against the Sassanids in 363 ended this last-ditch effort to reinstate polytheism as the Roman state religion.

The emperors who followed Julian chipped away at paganism by slowly removing its official privileges, completing the process Constantine had initiated. During the overlapping reigns of Gratian (✳367–383), Valentinian II (✳375–392), and Theodosius I (✳379–395), all the cults of pagan polytheism were officially suppressed. In 382 came the highly symbolic gesture of removing the altar and statue of Victory, which had stood in the Senate house in Rome for centuries, along with a ban on government support for pagan cults. Symmachus (c. 340– 402), a pagan senator who held the prestigious post of prefect of Rome, objected to what he saw as an outrage to the Roman religious tradition of diversity. Symmachus spoke eloquently in this last protest of the old pagan aristocracy against the new religious order: "We all have our own way of life and our own way of worship. . . . So vast a mystery cannot be approached by only one path." But the emperors held firm at the direction of Ambrose (c. 339–397), the bishop of Milan. Ambrose insisted that in moral matters the emperors had to submit to the church. So unassailable was Ambrose's influence in the newly Christian empire that in 390 he compelled the emperor Theodosius to perform a humiliating public penance as atonement for a bloody massacre at Thessalonica. The emperor had ordered the killings after a crowd there had murdered a general, who had earlier arrested their favorite charioteer on a charge of pederasty. Ambrose cowed the emperor by refusing him Communion until Theodosius laid aside his crown and purple robe and tearfully stood among the ordinary members of Ambrose's congregation in Milan to beseech the bishop for absolution from his sin. Ambrose's assertion of spiritual authority over even an emperor foreshadowed the disputes between ecclesiastical and secular leaders over the boundaries of their respective authority that flared up repeatedly in later European history.

Official paganism in the Roman Empire ended in 391 when Theodosius again prohibited pagan sacrifices, which had evidently continued despite earlier bans. Cutting off public funding for sacrifices severed any connection between pagan religion and the Roman state. Following Gratian's lead, Theodosius rejected the title of *pontifex maximus*. Furthermore, Theodosius made divination by the inspection of entrails punishable as high treason and closed all the pagan temples, confiscating their sites. Many temples, among them the Parthenon in Athens, became Christian churches. Worship of Jesus or homage to a Christian saint, for example, replaced the cult of Asclepius in many of that god's healing sanctuaries. The ban on public support for pagan cults did not require individual pagans to convert to Christianity, nor did it forbid non-Christian schools. The Platonic Academy in Athens, for example, continued for another 140 years. Nor did capable non-Christians such as Symmachus find themselves denied successful careers in the imperial administration under the Christian emperors of the late fourth century and even later. But pagans were now the outsiders in a Roman Empire that had

officially been transformed into a monarchy devoted to the Christian God. The church thus became the focus for state-supported Christianity.

Unlike pagan religion, Judaism was not disestablished in the Christian Roman Empire, but the religion of the Jews faced increasing legal restrictions. For example, imperial decrees eventually banned Jews from holding government posts. But Jews frequently had to assume the financial burdens of *curiales* without receiving the honor of curial status. By the late sixth century, Jews were barred from making wills, receiving inheritances, or testifying in court. Although these developments began the long process that made Jews into second-class citizens in later European history, they did not disable Judaism. Magnificent synagogues existed in late Roman Palestine, where some Jews still lived, although most had been dispersed throughout the cities of the empire and the lands to the east. The study of Jewish law and lore flourished in this period, during which the massive compilations known as the Palestinian and the Babylonian Talmuds and the scriptural commentaries of the Midrash were produced. These works of religious scholarship laid the foundation for later Jewish life and practice.

Christian Disputes over Religious Truth

Serious controversies among Christians over what they should believe became more visible as Christianity was becoming official and no longer had to contend with pagan cults for recognition. Bitter disputes frequently arose over what views constituted orthodoxy (the official doctrines of the church as enforced by church councils) as opposed to heresy (from the Greek word meaning a "private choice"). Church authorities had always been concerned with defining orthodoxy. Now, with official support for Christianity, the state inevitably joined in these disputes. The emperor became ultimately responsible for enforcing orthodox creed (a summary of beliefs), although that creed could vary from emperor to emperor and from one council of bishops to another.

Theological questions about the nature of the Trinity of Father, Son, and Holy Spirit caused the deepest divisions. A severe argument ensued, for example, when a priest named Arius (c. 260–336) from Alexandria maintained that Jesus, as the son of God the Father, had not existed eternally; rather, God had created his son from nothing and bestowed on him his special status. Thus, Jesus was not coeternal with God and not divine by nature. This doctrine, known as Arianism, found widespread support among ordinary people, perhaps because it relieved the difficulty of understanding how a son could be as old as his father and because its subordination of son to father corresponded to the norms of family life. Arius used popular songs to make his views known, and people everywhere became engrossed in the controversy. "When you ask for your change from a shopkeeper," one observer remarked in describing Constantinople, "he harangues you about the Begotten and the Unbegotten. If you inquire how much bread costs, the reply is that 'the Father is superior and the Son inferior'; if in a public bath you ask 'Is the water ready for my bath?' the attendant answers that 'the Son is of nothing.' "

Many Christians became so incensed over Arianism's apparent denigration of Jesus that Emperor Constantine intervened to try to restore ecclesiastical peace and to find the answers to Arius's troubling questions. Despite his lack of any official position in the church hierarchy, Constantine convened the Council of Nicea in 325 with 220 bishops, who tried to settle the dispute over Arius's teachings. The bishops voted to banish Arius to Illyria, a rough region in the Balkan mountains, and issued a creed declaring that the Father and the Son were indeed "of one substance" and coeternal. Constantine's changing reactions to Arius reflected how perplexing he found Arius's issues: he recalled Arius from exile some years after the council, only to reproach him again not long after. Many of the Germanic peoples who later came to live in the empire were converted to Arian Christianity, and the dispute between Arian and non-Arian Christians raged for centuries.

Other persistent disputes about the nature of the incarnate Christ also set Christians at odds with one another, especially in the eastern empire. Nestorius, a Syrian who became bishop of Constantinople in 428, argued that Christ incarnated two separate persons, one divine and one human. (The orthodox position held that Christ was one person with a double nature, simultaneously God and man.) Nestorianism enraged orthodox Christians by rejecting the designation *theotokos* (Greek

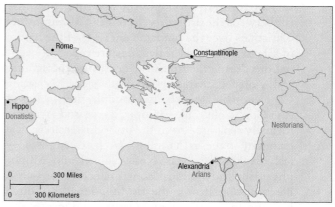

Original Areas of Christian Religious Disputes

for "bearer of God") as an appellation of Mary, the mother of Jesus. Orthodox Christians used the word as a theological expression of their growing devotion to the Virgin as the mother of God. The bishops of Alexandria and Rome had Nestorius deposed and his doctrines officially rejected at councils held in 430 and 431; they condemned his writings in 435. Nestorian bishops in the eastern empire refused to accept these decisions, however, and they formed a separate church centered in Persia. Nestorian Christians continued to flourish there for centuries, generally enjoying the support of Persia's non-Christian rulers. Eventually, Persia's Nestorian church established Christian communities that still endure in Arabia, India, and China.

Monophysites rivaled Nestorians in the fierceness of their convictions about the nature of Christ, but disagreed with them as ardently as they did with orthodox Christians. Monophysitism (from the Greek words meaning "of a single nature") maintained that Christ had a single—divine—nature. The emperor Marcian (✷450–457) convened five hundred to six hundred bishops in 451 at the Council of Chalcedon to deal with the Monophysitical views of the prominent monk Eutyches of Constantinople, a vehement opponent of Nestorianism. The council issued the Chalcedonian Definition to repudiate the theological views of both Eutyches and Nestorius. Adherents of Monophysitism thereupon organized themselves in a persistent opposition movement to the orthodox church, although internal disputes created many varying forms of Monophysite doctrine. The bitter rift between the orthodox church and Monophysite Christians over the fundamental issue of the nature of Christ was never healed, despite repeated negotiations during the following centuries. Intolerance and violence characterized both sides. Rejecting Chalcedonian orthodoxy, Monophysites in Egypt (the Coptic church), Ethiopia, Syria, and Armenia formally separated from the orthodox ecclesiastical hierarchy in the sixth century. Deep-seated theological divisions such as Nestorianism and Monophysitism had political consequences later, when heretical Christians in the east found that they often had greater freedom of worship and protection from violence under non-Christian rulers in Persia and Arabia.

Economic and social differences among Christians sometimes fueled the fire of theological disputes, as the clash between orthodoxy and Donatism in North Africa shows. A dispute arose there in the fourth century over whether to readmit to their old congregations those Christians who had escaped martyrdom during the Great Persecution by cooperating with imperial authorities. Some North African Christians felt these lapsed members should be forgiven, but the Donatists (followers of the North African priest Donatus) insisted that the church should not be polluted with such "traitors." Most important, Donatists insisted, unfaithful priests and bishops could not administer the sacraments. So bitter was the clash that it even sundered Christian families. A son threatened his mother thus: "I will pass over to the party of Donatus, and I will drink your blood." Augmenting the theological issues of the controversy were the economic differences between many Donatists, who tended to be poorer country people, and their opponents, largely Christian landowners and urban residents. Violence leading to bloodshed erupted between government forces and roving bands of Donatist rebels, whom the authorities called encirclers (*circumcelliones*) from their technique for attacking the buildings of country estates. The Donatist controversy persisted despite repeated efforts to settle it. Finally, a conference of more than five hundred bishops and an imperial representative met in Carthage in 411 to resolve the conflict, but their decision against the Donatists and the subsequent persecution of Donatists by the authorities only embittered the rebels. Donatist doctrines endured in North Africa for at least another century.

Augustine's Impact on Christianity

No one person had a stronger impact on the formation of what eventually came to be the orthodox doctrines of later Western Christianity than Augustine. Born to a Christian mother and pagan father in the hill country of North Africa west of Carthage, Augustine (354–430) was exceptionally well read in the Latin classics, although he knew little Greek. His reading of Cicero's now-lost work *Hortensius,* he later said, "converted him to philosophy." He absorbed the ideas of Plato through his study of Neoplatonism. Augustine began his career by teaching rhetoric at Carthage. He had a son by a mistress there and was befriended by the famous pagan aristocrat, Symmachus, after moving to Italy. In 386, however, he converted to Christianity under the influence of his mother and Ambrose, bishop of Milan. From 395 until his death, Augustine served as the bishop of Hippo, a small seaport in North Africa, where he had to balance his interest in study and writing with a bishop's busy schedule.

Augustine's reputation rests on his writings, not on his work as a bishop. For the next thousand years his works would be the most influential texts in Western Christianity, save for the Bible. He wrote so prolifically in Latin about religion and philosophy that a later scholar was moved to declare: "The man lies who says he has read all your works." Augustine deeply affected later thinkers with his views on the role of authority in human life. His most influential exposition of the proper role of secular authority came in his *City of God,* a "large and arduous work," as he called it. The book's immediate purpose was to refute those who expected that Christianity, like the pagan cults it had replaced, would automatically guarantee Christians earthly success and to counter those who rejected any place for the state in a Christian world. For example, some pagans asserted that the sack of Rome by Germanic marauders in 410 was divine retribution for the official abandonment of the pagan gods; Augustine sought to reassure Christians troubled by this calamity that their faith had not caused Rome's defeat. His larger aim, however, was to redefine the ideal state as a society of

Christians. Not even Plato's doctrines offered a true path to purification, Augustine asserted, because the real opposition for humans was not between emotion and reason. Emotion, especially love, was natural and desirable, but only when directed toward God. Humans were misguided to look for value in life on earth. Earthly life was transitory. Only life in God's heavenly city had meaning.

Nevertheless, Augustine said, secular law and government were required because humans are inherently imperfect. God's original creation in the Garden of Eden was full of goodness, but humans lost their initial perfection by inheriting a permanently flawed nature after Adam and Eve had disobeyed God. Their disobedience caused humans to fall from God's grace and permanently destroyed the harmony between the human will and human desires that had existed in the paradise of Eden. The doctrine of original sin—a subject of theological debate since at least the second century—purported that humans suffered from a hereditary moral disease that turned the human will into a disruptive force. Augustine insisted that only God's grace could bring salvation from this evil. The corruption of the human will meant that governments had to use coercion to try to suppress vice, even if they had little power to inculcate virtue. Although desperately inferior to the ideal that would exist if humans were not flawed, civil government was based on a moral order and should endeavor to imitate divine justice. In this way its actions could serve as an extension of divine providence, imposing order on the chaos of human life after the Fall from grace in the Garden of Eden. The state had a right to compel people to remain united to the church, by force if necessary.

Order in society, Augustine asserted, could turn to comparatively good purposes such inherently evil practices as slavery. Augustine detested slavery, but he acknowledged that well-treated slaves in rich homes were materially better off than destitute free laborers. Social institutions like slavery were lesser evils than the violent troubles that would follow if anarchy were to prevail. Christians therefore had a duty to obey the emperor and participate in political life. Soldiers, too, had to follow their orders. Torture and capital punishment as judicial procedures, on the other hand, had no place in a morally upright government. The purpose of secular author-

ity was to maintain a social order based on a moral order. Augustine was certainly no advocate of separation of church and state, but neither did he mean that bishops should rule over emperors, as some later thinkers interpreted his views.

In *City of God,* Augustine sought to show a divine purpose, not always evident to humans, in the events of history. He presented the destiny of the earthly city as hell and of the divine city as heaven but spelled out no specific theory of history and did not predict the future. All that Christians could know with certainty was that history progressed toward an ultimate goal. But only God could know the meaning of each day's events. What could not be doubted was God's guiding power.

> *To be truthful, I myself fail to understand why God created mice and frogs, flies and worms. Nevertheless, I recognize that each of these creatures is beautiful in its own way. For when I contemplate the body and limbs of any living creature, where do I not find proportion, number, and order exhibiting the unity of concord? Where one discovers proportion, number, and order, one should look for the craftsman.*

The repeated "I" in this example exemplified the intense personal engagement Augustine brought to matters of faith and doctrine. Many other Christians shared this intensity, a trait that energized their disagreements over orthodoxy and heresy.

New Patterns of Life

Striking changes in social and intellectual life occurred in the late Roman Empire and in the following centuries, when the Roman world was increasingly separating into eastern and western halves. Christian thinkers, principally Augustine, viewed human sexual desire as much more of a problem than pagan Roman tradition had considered it. Many devout Christians, unsatisfied with their lives in the ordinary world and no longer being martyred by a hostile state, looked for new ways to express their piety and emulate the suffering of Jesus. In increasing numbers, especially in the eastern empire, people disengaged from secular society and became monks, living lives of self-denial.

Christian Reevaluation of Sexual Desire

A fundamental issue Christians disagreed on was the proper attitude toward sexual desire. Augustine's views eventually became the orthodox position. Throughout his life Augustine had pondered how to define the proper relationship between the soul and the body in a life of virtue. Both Christian and pagan thinkers had struggled with this issue for centuries. Augustine's knowledge of Stoicism inclined him as a young man to reject all self-indulgence, but (he wrote) his sensual desires continued unabated. His ten-year adherence to the doctrines of Mani (c. 216–276) exacerbated this conflict. Mani, a sage from Mesopotamia, had cre-

Christian Art
Christians adapted Roman artistic style to portray Biblical scenes, like this one of Adam and Eve, which decorated the sarcophagus of a fourth-century Roman official.

ated a new religion that emphasized self-denial. Contrary to mainstream Christian doctrine, Mani had taught that the crucifixion of Jesus should be understood as a symbol of humanity's suffering, not as a historical event: no redeemer sprung from God could have been physically born or killed. Furthermore, the universe was split between good and evil, represented by the forces of light and dark, respectively. This dualism, Mani argued, better accounted for the origin of evil in the world than the Christian notion of a god who had permitted evil despite his omnipotence. Mani's code of extreme asceticism (the practice of strict self-denial; from the Greek *askesis,* meaning "training") not only forbade indulgence in food and drink, but also demanded celibacy from its most advanced devotees, a rank Augustine never achieved. Augustine later immersed himself in Neoplatonism, a philosophy that also denigrated the physical side of human existence. Augustine's autobiographical *Confessions,* written shortly before 400, revealed his deep conflict between his sexual desire and the philosophies he had studied. Only after a long period of reflection and doubt could he pledge his future chastity as part of his conversion to Christianity.

Augustine chose sexual abstinence because he believed Adam and Eve's disobedience in the Garden of Eden had forever ruined the original, perfect harmony God created between the human will and human passions. According to Augustine, God punished his disobedient children by imposing an eternal conflict on humans: sexual desire would forever become a disruptive force in human life because humans could never completely control it through their will. Not even conversion and the purifying effect of baptism could wash away this legacy of Original Sin. Augustine reaffirmed the value of marriage in God's plan, but sexual intercourse even between loving spouses carried the melancholy reminder of humanity's fall from grace. A married couple should "descend with a certain sadness" to the task of procreation, the only unblameworthy reason for sex. Sexual pleasure could not be a human good. The only completely virtuous course was to renounce sex, through the power of God's grace. But Augustine recognized that most Christians could not do this. Only God could put an end to this struggle through his mysterious grace of salvation: "You have made us for Yourself, and our hearts are restless till they find rest in You."

Augustine formed his doctrines on sexual desire against a long background of Christian thought. The apostle Paul in the first century had recommended sexual renunciation for Christians who could bear it. Christians of Paul's day expected the imminent end of the world and the coming of the kingdom of God on earth; thus, they were not concerned that celibacy for all would mean the end of society because no more children would be born. The theologian Origen (c. 185–254) had written that to maintain virginity was to assert one's freedom from the demands of ordinary society, which expected citizens to marry and bear children to perpetuate the state. So fervently did he reject sexuality that at about the age of twenty he had himself castrated. This operation, when performed on adult men, renders them infertile without removing sexual desire or ability and was far from unknown in the third and fourth centuries. By being castrated men sought not necessarily to end their sexual activity (although Origen certainly did) but to free themselves from obligations to head a household, raise children, and provide for a family.

Jerome (c. 348–420), one of Augustine's contemporaries, ennobled virginity and sexual renunciation as the highest Christian virtues, greater even than martyrdom. He greatly influenced Christian thought by his strong personality and energetic scholarship. The bishop of Rome entrusted Jerome with the crucial task of accurately translating the Bible into Latin. Jerome's translation, known as the Vulgate ("popular") edition, became the most widely used version of the Bible in the western church. Both Augustine and Jerome rejected one of the traditional assumptions underlying Roman family life: that sex between loving spouses was desirable as a personal pleasure and a civic responsibility to produce children. They would have approved of the sentiment expressed in the inscription on the tombstone of Simplicia, a Christian woman who rejected marriage: "she paid no heed to producing children, treading beneath her feet the snares of the body."

Like pagan and Jewish ascetics before them, Christian ascetics rejected the traditional idea that reproduction was a fundamental human responsibility. The powerfully argued theology of ascetics had an impact on Christianity despite their relatively few adherents. Virgin women, widows who did not remarry, and spouses who gave up conjugal sex had special status in the church. Their congregations honored these people because their renunciation of sex testified powerfully to their dedication to God. Their devoutness reflected the purity of angels and the sacrifice of earlier Christian martyrs. In Jerome's words, virginity was a "daily martyrdom." Because Constantine had earlier revoked Augustus's laws on marriage, people no longer felt any legal pressure to marry or bear children. Celibate men and women had equal legal standing to married people. Women could even refuse to marry, so better to worship God. The religious dedication of celibate women improved their educational opportunities because it justified their insistence that they be taught Greek and Hebrew to read the Bible. Rape, intended to force the victim to marry her assailant, apparently became more common as men feared a shortage of women would prevent them from forming households and continuing their lineages. By the end of the fourth century, pressure was growing to choose priests and bishops who had never had sexual relations rather than widowers or men who did not have sex with their spouses. This call for male virgins in ecclesiastical service represented a dramatic change in tradition, which had previously propounded virginity as a virtue exclusively for women.

Despite early Christianity's respect for those who forswore sex, Augustine's conception of Original Sin and his insistence that sexual desire was inescapably tainted with sin aroused vehement opposition from scholarly critics such as Pelagius, a monk from Britain (died after 419), and his follower Julian (c. 386–454), an Italian bishop. These critics of Augustine, called Pelagians, argued that humans can take the initial steps toward salvation by their own choice, independent of God's grace, and that the human will was not irretrievably deformed. They insisted that humans are free to choose good and shed their bad inclinations. As Pelagius put it, "If I ought, I can." The doctrine of Original Sin, Pelagians objected, deprived people of their choice to sin or not to sin by making sin inevitable. Moreover, as Julian asserted, sex was God's merciful gift to humanity as a defense against time and death, a guarantee of immortality through the bearing of children. In response to views like those of Ambrose that "a legal husband must not allow himself to be tempted, through love of sensuous delight, to play the adulterer to his own wife," Julian insisted that sexual pleasure was the "chosen instrument of any self-respecting marriage . . . acceptable in and of itself and blameworthy only in its excesses." These pointed objections to Augustine's interpretation of Original Sin, combined with the support Pelagians found among some bishops, led Augustine and Jerome to counterattack energetically and denounce the Pelagians as heretics. When most of the empire's bishops joined the bishop of Rome in condemning the Pelagian view in 418, the Augustinian view linking sexual desire and Original Sin was on its way to becoming the orthodox position of the western Christian church, a victory that profoundly influenced the subsequent development of official Christian attitudes toward human sexuality.

The First Christian Monks

The appearance of monks, both male and female, represented a new pattern of Christian life.* The word *monk* (from the Greek *monos,* meaning "single, solitary") described the essential experience of monasticism: these people withdrew from everyday society to live an ascetic life as a demonstration of their devotion to God. They wore the roughest clothes, ate barely enough food to survive, and renounced sex. This disengagement from the world corresponded to the notion of separateness and apartness that was theoretically fundamental to the Christian identity. Christians saw themselves as spiritually set apart from ordinary society by their bonds to Christ, which were supposed to take precedence over their ties to the community and even their own families. Monks gave Christian separateness a literal dimension by physically removing themselves not only from secular life but also from regular Christian congregations.

When Christian monasticism emerged in the latter half of the third century, choosing to live an ascetic life was not a revolutionary phenomenon. Self-styled followers of the sixth-century B.C. Greek philosopher Pythagoras and also Cynic philosophers had practiced certain forms of abstinence. Jewish monastic communities already existed. The missionaries spreading the doctrines of Mani in third-century Mesopotamia also practiced asceti-

cism. Non-Christian philosophers had long taught that humans should exercise sexual restraint because physical passion interfered with reason's rule in the human soul.

Christian monasticism was distinctive not in its practice of asceticism, but rather in the large number of people who over the following centuries abandoned their normal existence to become monks. The first Christian monks emerged in Egypt. These monks lived as solitary hermits in extremely ascetic conditions to seek a relationship with God unsullied by the demands of the body and material comforts. Although earlier Christian ascetics had certainly existed, the first known Christian monk was a prosperous Egyptian farmer named Anthony (c. 251–356). One day, Anthony abruptly abandoned all his property after hearing a sermon based on Jesus' admonition to a rich young man to sell his possessions and give the proceeds to the poor (Matt. 19:21). Placing his sister in a home for unmarried women, Anthony lived as an ascetic on the outskirts of his village at the edge of the desert for some fifteen years, rejecting family life and marriage. In about 285 he withdrew from even limited contact with the secular world by moving into an isolated region. He wanted to be a hero for God. About 305 he reemerged to inspire disciples and then, after 313, withdrew to the desolation of a barren mountain to live out his life in surroundings whose quiet emptiness echoed his spiritual serenity.

Christians chose to emulate Anthony's disengagement from society for a variety of reasons, social and economic as well as theological. Prosperous Christian villagers in Egypt (like Anthony), for example, from whose ranks many early monks came, lived under constant social tension because they had to negotiate continually with each other in managing the flooding of the Nile to control agriculture. Their obligation to be cooperative, combined with their religious beliefs, made anger socially unacceptable. This pressure to conform to social norms was accompanied by worry about the heavy taxes that successful producers always owed. Like the fourth-century *curiales* who deserted their posts and their possessions, these villagers often found ordinary life unbearable. Some early Egyptian monks also came from very poor backgrounds. For them, monastic asceticism seemed little different from everyday life, with its famine-level diet and malnutrition that suppressed sexual desire. Still

---

*Because monastic women were not called nuns until a later period, *monk* here will refer to women as well as men.

others believed that Christians should literally suffer for their sins, just as Jesus had suffered on the cross. By becoming monks, Christians hoped to achieve the inner peace promised by detachment from worldly concerns. But the reality of monastic life was constant struggle, not least against the dreams and visions of earthly pleasures (of food more than sex) that haunted those who had renounced their previous lives.

Christian monasticism spread from Egypt across the late Roman world. As in so many areas of ancient life, regional differences characterized its practice. In Syria, for example, "holy women" and "holy men" attracted great attention for their deeds of piety, such as Symeon's (390–459) living atop a tall pillar for thirty years; people gathered at the foot of his perch to hear him preach. With the emergence of this kind of highly visible public holiness, Christianity developed a new group of living heroes. Christians in Egypt came to believe that the piety of the land's male and female monks ensured the annual flooding of the Nile, the duty once associated with the magical power of the ancient pharaohs.

Because the empire was increasingly Christian, martyrdom was virtually impossible. Monasticism allowed people another way to follow Jesus' model. Their aura of holiness seemed to endow monastic people with special wisdom. They were often asked to arbitrate disputes in the villages of fourth- and fifth-century Syria, where the undoing of many large estates and their powerful landlords through economic crisis had left a vacuum of authority. Monks with reputations for exceptional holiness exercised even greater influence after death. The relics—body parts or clothing—of these saints (people venerated after their deaths for their special holiness) became treasured sources of protection and healing. Christian relics thus took over a function previously fulfilled by relics of heroes in pagan religion, like the bones of Theseus that the fifth-century B.C. general Cimon had returned to classical Athens to the delight of the people there.

The Development of Monastic Communities

The earliest monks usually lived alone. Organized communities of monks living together appeared around 320 in the Nile valley. Military-style discipline was the paramount vow, subjecting the monks to God's will and the monastery's rules. People in monasteries separated themselves from worldly concerns and possessions, but not from fellow ascetics. Men and women founded such coenobitic ("life in common") monasteries all over the Roman world. Male and female monastic communities were sometimes located side by side, although an individual monastery had only men or women. Coenobitic monks grew their own food, made their own clothes, and crafted what few tools and goods their sparse life required. Some monasteries strove for self-sufficiency to minimize transactions with the outside world. Basil ("the Great") of Caesarea (c. 330–379), however, put together different monastic requirements and created a model that became important in the eastern empire. For example, he required monks to perform charitable service outside the monastic community, such as ministering to the sick, which led to the foundation of the first hospitals, attached to monasteries.

Members of social elites joined monasteries for a variety of motives, but one common reason was the long-standing Roman tradition that sexual desire, although natural and not evil, had to be strictly controlled. Monasticism provided a way to achieve that control with the support of like-minded people. Because monks as individuals kept a vow of poverty, rich people entering monasteries donated their land, buildings, and wealth to the monastic community. Rich Christian women were prominent donors to and founders of monasteries. For example, Paula (347–404), a widow of distinguished Roman ancestry, donated her fortune to establish monasteries in Palestine. Christian women of means could attain a certain independence by traveling the world on their own to visit holy places and using their fortunes to set up monastic communities for women. These female communities, however, sometimes existed under the protection and moral supervision of the local bishop or of the male abbot (head of a monastery) from a neighboring monastery. (Physical protection was necessary because even in a monastery a woman from a propertied family might be kidnapped, raped, and thus forced to marry, allowing her husband to gain control of her inheritance.) Monasteries also acquired resources from those who were healed of illness or injury after praying to a saint whose relics had been housed in the monastery. Those who recovered from their afflictions, believing they had experienced a miracle through direct contact with God,

Monastery of St. Catherine in the Sinai
In 527 the Byzantine emperor Justinian built this stronghold in the desert of the Sinai peninsula as proof of his piety and as protection for the monks who were to live there.

often expressed gratitude by donating money or property. Some were so inspired that they devoted their lives to serving that monastic community.

The nature of the monasteries' relations with their secular neighbors and the degree of austerity imposed on the monks varied by region. The most isolationist and ascetic monasticism was practiced in the eastern empire. Some western monasteries, such as those established by the followers of Martin of Tours (c. 316–397), an ex-soldier famed for his pious deeds, and those filled by aristocrats in Gaul, were also known for their austerity. Benedict from Nursia in central Italy (c. 480–553) devised what became the most influential monastic code in the West, and its tenets established a western monasticism that was generally milder than the East's strict asceticism. His Rule, as such organizational codes came to be known, prescribed the monks' daily routine of prayer, Scriptural readings, and manual labor. Benedict's Rule divided the day into seven parts, each with a compulsory service of prayers

and lessons, but no Mass. The required worship for each part of the day was called the liturgy and became part of monastic practice. Unlike the harsh regulations of Egyptian and Syrian monasticism, Benedict's code did not isolate the monks from the outside world or deprive them of sleep, adequate food, or warm clothing. Benedict's monks lived very simply, however, all wearing standard garb and eating the same plain food. Although the abbot had full authority over the institution, Benedict's Rule instructed him to listen to what every member of the community, even the youngest monk, had to say before deciding important matters. The abbot disciplined the monks, but not so severely as to "sadden" or "overdrive" them. He was not allowed to beat them for lapses in discipline, as sometimes happened under other, stricter systems. The Benedictine Rule eventually became the standard for western monasteries.

Thousands of Christians became monks in the fourth century and thereafter. Some had been given as babies to a monastery by parents who could not raise them or were fulfilling pious vows. The practice of turning over children to monasteries, called oblation, helped replenish the monastic population. Jerome, himself a monk in a monastery for men that was located next to one for women, once gave this advice to a mother who decided to send her young daughter to a monastery:

> *Let her be brought up in a monastery, let her live among virgins, let her learn to avoid swearing, let her regard lying as an offense against God, let her be ignorant of the world, let her live the angelic life, while in the flesh let her be without the flesh, and let her suppose that all human beings are like herself.*

When she reaches adulthood as a virgin, he added, she should avoid the baths so she would not be seen naked or give her body pleasure by dipping in the warm pools. Jerome promised that in recompense for the dedication of her daughter, the child's mother would bear sons. Evidently even in Christian society, boys were more valued than girls.

By the early fifth century many adults were joining monasteries as a reaction against the worldliness and secularity of ordinary Christians. Some men fled from the army to enter monastic communities. For women, monasticism offered a rare opportunity to achieve status and recognition comparable to that of men; as Jerome explained: "We evaluate people's virtue not by their gender but by their character, and deem those to be worthy of the greatest glory who have renounced both status and riches." Monasticism endured because it attracted a steady stream of adherents who sought a way to serve God and be saved in the next world. Many also found the austerity of a community of like-minded members of the same sex more desirable than a civilian life of family, property, and secular responsibilities. Speaking of Italy, Jerome joyfully related that "monastic establishments for virgin women became numerous, and there were countless numbers of hermits. So numerous were God's servants that monasticism, which had previously been a term of reproach, became one of honor."

As Jerome implied, not all Christians approved of the shift in morals and manners of life that monasticism represented. The theologian Origen had argued against monastic withdrawal: renunciation of the world, he said, was not achieved by physically removing oneself to the desert. Bishops had little reason to rejoice when devoted members of their congregations became monks and thus ceased to serve as supporters or financial contributors benefiting their local churches. Monasticism also represented a possible threat to the bishops' authority, despite the fact that monasteries in the Benedictine Rule generally granted bishops the right to oversee them, and that bishops had to perform essential rituals such as consecrating abbots and altars. Both anchorite ("solitary") and coenobitic monks were less closely controlled and guided by the episcopal ("headed by bishops") hierarchy of the Christian church than were the members of ordinary congregations: monks earned their authority by their own action; that is, they acquired their special status of holiness not by having it bestowed by the church but by their own act of renunciation and their obedience to their monastery's rule. One of the few ways by which bishops could control charismatic monks who were attracting large followings was to reintegrate them into the church's hierarchy by compelling them to take positions ministering to congregations. Bishops and monks did share a spiritual goal—salvation and service to God. The distinctiveness of monasticism was that its members pursued this goal not by seeking to unite the physical, human side of their nature with the spiritual, divine side—the kind of union exemplified in Christian doctrine by Jesus as the incarnation of God—but rather by separating the two.

Transformations in a Divided Empire

In its new role as the official religion of the Roman Empire, Christianity was the primary unifying force in an otherwise divided state. The essentially independent emperors who ruled the East and the West cooperated in theory only. Constantine had abolished the tetrarchy but had designated his three surviving sons as heirs to his throne, hoping they would share power peaceably. Yet they fought one another after their father's death, so that divided responsibility among eastern and western emperors became the general practice. This division continued ever after because the empire had become too large for one ruler to govern efficiently and defend effectively against major military threats.

The eastern emperor continued Constantine's tradition of making Constantinople his capital. In 404 the emperor Honorius (✳395–423) selected Ravenna, on Italy's northeastern coast, as the western imperial headquarters because its walls and marshes protected it from attack by land, while its excellent port kept it from being starved out in a siege. The geographical division between the two realms of the empire roughly followed a northwest–southeast line between Italy and Greece. The eastern half was largely populated by Greeks and the indigenous peoples of the eastern Mediterranean. It was richer than the West, had more large cities, and was easier to defend. The western half encompassed the diverse peoples of Roman North Africa and western Europe. The western empire's northern border had little natural protection from the Germanic peoples across the Rhine and the Danube, who for centuries had traded with Romans and served as mercenaries in their army. These northern provinces found it difficult to defeat Germanic bands raiding for booty.

The empire's two halves eventually experienced markedly different fates. For example, the three-tiered administrative structure (prefectures/diocese/province) inaugurated by Diocletian lasted only until 476 in the West but until the seventh century in the East. The most important change, however, was in the demography of the western empire, where in the late fourth century, Germanic peoples started moving into its northern regions in unprecedented numbers. Their growing presence eventually transformed the military, political, and social structures of Roman Europe.

Germanic Society

The various peoples whom we call ancient Germans and whom the Romans regarded as barbarians had never been part of a unified nation or single political entity. Moreover, they probably had little sense of a common identity before they settled in Roman territory in large groups. The word *German* in this context therefore refers only to some common linguistic origins of these peoples, not to an ancient and strongly shared ethnicity.

In their original homelands in northern Europe, these Germanic peoples lived in small settlements whose economies depended on farming, herding, and iron working. One common form of German house was constructed of interwoven branches and reeds on a timber frame, built large enough to house the family's people and cattle; the animals' body heat helped warm the house during the region's cold winters. Cattle were also valued highly for food and as measures of prestige. German society consisted of a welter of diverse groups loosely led by men averse to strong central authority. Even groups with clearly defined leaders were constituted as chiefdoms, whose members could be only persuaded, not compelled, to follow the chief. The chiefs maintained their status by giving gifts to their followers and by leading warriors on frequent raids against their neighbors to seize cattle and slaves. German society was patriarchal: men headed German households and exercised authority over their women, children, and slaves. German women

Marks of Identity
This skull sports the kind of topknot in the hair that some Germanic peoples used to identity themselves as members of a particular group.

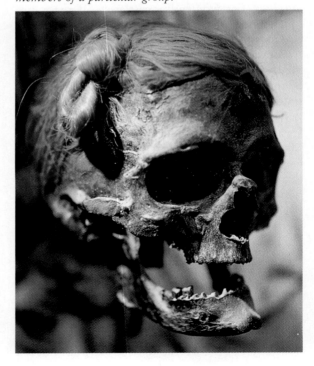

were valued above all for their ability to bear children, and rich men could have more than one wife and perhaps concubines as well. A clear division of labor made women responsible for agriculture, pottery making, and the production of textiles, while men worked iron and herded cattle. Men acquired prestige through their prowess as warriors and their possessions. Warfare and its accompaniments preoccupied German men, as their ritual sacrifices of weapons preserved in northern European bogs have shown. Women had certain rights of inheritance and could control property, and married women received a dowry of one-third of their husbands' property.

Households were organized into clans on kinship lines based on maternal as well as paternal descent. The members of a clan were supposed to keep peace among themselves, and violence against a fellow clan member was the worst possible offense. Clans in turn grouped themselves into very loose and fluctuating coalitions called tribes. People belonged to tribes by claiming a common, though distant, kinship or by being allowed to join the group regardless of their ethnic origin if they observed tribal tradition. Tribes and their armies seem to have been polyethnic, including even non-German people. Members of a particular tribe identified themselves primarily by their clothing, hair styles, jewelry, weapons, religious cults, and oral stories. These distinctions seem to have formed a stronger sense of tribal identity and rivalry than did the different, though related, languages the different tribes spoke. An assembly of the tribe's free male warriors provided the only form of tribal political organization. Some tribes had leaders, whom historians have called kings, but their functions were restricted mostly to religious and military matters. Tribes could be very unstable and prone to internal conflict. Clans frequently feuded, with bloody consequences, and tribal law tried to set boundaries to the violence acceptable in seeking revenge. Tribal stability was also threatened by bands of young warriors who collected around leaders known for their ability to organize raids and seize plunder. These warrior bands operated outside the political and social control of the larger tribal group, somewhat like modern urban gangs.

Germanic peoples along the frontiers of the Roman Empire came into frequent contact with Romans during the early empire, and they developed a taste for Roman goods as marks of prestige. This desire for the material fruits of Roman civilization led more and more Germans to enter Roman territory, where they could also hope to escape the frequent attacks from other groups. At the same time, German men regularly found employment as soldiers recruited by the Roman emperors. Both Germans and Romans, then, used and needed one another from early imperial times. Germanic families in small groups had begun to settle in the outer fringe of the northern frontier zones by the second century; others had raided in Roman territory. Among these families were a group, related to the peoples later known as Goths, who roamed and marauded in the eastern provinces for thirty years, beginning in 238, before they were finally defeated. After epidemic disease and civil war had decimated the empire's population during the third-century crisis, the emperors encouraged many more Germans to settle in Roman territory because they were eager to recruit German warriors. By Constantine's time, German settlers provided a significant proportion of the military forces of the western empire. The men in these groups usually farmed less than in their homelands and depended on Roman pay for their incomes; the government ensured their cooperation and obedience by paying their military wages. By the late fourth century many Roman provincials and Germans had lived side by side for a long time.

From the Visigoths to the Franks

The settled provincial life of Roman northern Europe was suddenly disturbed in the late fourth century when thousands of Germanic people started moving from central Europe into the northern Roman frontier areas. Although the experiences of these groups varied, many were fleeing in panic from the Huns, nomads from the steppes of central Asia, who had invaded German territory north of the Danube River in 376. The appearance alone of the Hunnic warriors terrified the Germans—the Huns' skulls were elongated from having been bound between boards in infancy and their arms were covered with fantastic tattoos. The Hunnic cavalry was particularly frightening because its horsemen could wield their powerful composite bows of wood and bone while riding full tilt.

The Germanic peoples who came to be known as Visigoths ("West Goths") composed the first groups in this period to escape from the Huns into Roman territory. Like other Germans, in their homelands the Visigoths seem to have been broadly polyethnic, with no overwhelming sense of a particular ethnic or political identity (although the extent to which they might have conceived of themselves as a particular ethnic group is debatable). Intense pressure from the Huns compelled them to request permission in 376 to move into the Balkans. The emperor granted the appeal on the condition that their warriors enlist in the Roman army to battle the Huns.

The movement of the Visigoths into the Roman Empire was not an invasion or a carefully planned migration but rather a flight to safety of people who had been forced out of their traditional homes and who were now a horde of squatters. Greedy and incompetent Roman officers charged with helping these refugees failed miserably to provide for even their basic needs. As the Visigoths approached starvation, Roman officials forced them to sell some of their own people into slavery in return for dogs to eat. In desperation, the Visigoths rebelled. In 378 they defeated and killed the eastern emperor Valens (*364–378) at Adrianople in Thrace. His successor, Theodosius I (*379–395), then had to allow them to settle permanently in Roman territory and pay them a large annual subsidy, which enabled them to survive. In contrast to earlier policy on Germanic settlements inside the empire, the Visigoths were subject to their own laws and government instead of Roman institutions, but they were designated as "federates" (allies) of the empire, obliged to support its safety and prosperity. After Theodosius's reign the Visigoths began to move westward when their subsidies were cut off and their future in the eastern empire seemed threatened. In 410, under their commander Alaric, who resented his failure to obtain an important command in the empire, they stunned the Roman world by briefly occupying and sacking Rome itself. For the first time since the Gauls eight hundred years before, a foreign force held the ancient capital. The Visigoths destroyed many areas around Rome and terrorized its people, as expressed in Alaric's comment to the Romans after he had demanded all their gold, silver, movable property, and foreign slaves: "What will be left to us?" they asked him. "Your lives," he replied. The Roman government finally agreed to settle the Visigoths in southwestern Gaul (present-day France) in 418, once again as federates of

the empire. Within a century they had expanded into Spain. Visigothic control of much of Spain would last until the Arab conquest in 711.

In their new territories the Visigoths gradually replaced the chiefdom structure of earlier Germanic society in favor of a kingdom with a strong central ruler. Their religion was Arian Christianity. New problems created by living close to Romans, especially disputes over property, led the Visigothic kings to develop the first-known written laws from Germanic society. Written in Latin and heavily influenced by Roman legal traditions, these laws used fines and compensation as the primary method for resolving disputes. Visgothic law applied to Visigoths, and perhaps also to Romans living in Visigothic territory. Official arrangements for subsidizing Visigothic settlement are also obscure; some large Roman landowners may have had to divide their estates with Visigothic nobles. Romans often retained full possession of their property, however, and paid the German leaders the taxes they had previously paid the Roman government, and many Romans worked as Visigothic advisers, lawyers, and tax collectors. As federates of the western empire, the Visigoths in 451 even helped the western emperor successfully defend Gaul against the onslaught of the Hunnic king Attila (*434–453), whose conquests extended from the Alps to the Caspian Sea.

Clovis (*485–511), the son of a federate of the Roman Empire and the king of another Germanic tribe called the Salian Franks, eventually overthrew Visigothic control of Gaul. Frankish men had regularly served in the Roman army ever since the imperial government had settled the tribe in a rough northern border area (now in the Netherlands) in the early fourth century and had allowed it gradually to move south into more civilized Roman territory. Clovis then extended his kingdom at the expense of surrounding Germanic groups in Gaul. His wife, Clotilda, was a Christian, and the bishop and historian Gregory of Tours (538–594) reports the famous story of her urging her husband to convert from the traditional paganism of the Germanic tribes. According to this tale, around 500, Clovis became an orthodox Christian (not an Arian like so many German converts to Christianity) to fulfill a vow he had made: when a battle had been going against him, he had sworn to be baptized if Clotilda's Christian God would grant him a victory. His army followed suit in adopting the new religion. Clovis's support of orthodoxy then won him the favor of orthodox Christians, who looked to him as a defender against such Arian Christian Germans as the Visigoths. Recent research, however, suggests that Clovis may have been an Arian all along. In any case, Clovis defeated the Visigothic king in 507 with support from the eastern Roman emperor. When that emperor named him an honorary consul, Clovis celebrated his new status by having himself crowned with a diadem.

Clovis's kingdom, called Merovingian after the legendary Frankish ancestor Merovech, foreshadowed the kingdom that would emerge much later as the forerunner of modern France. Clovis's ruthlessness—he murdered almost all his relatives to acquire their wealth and followers—contributed to the durability of his monarchy, as recognized by Gregory, who later praised Clovis's violent toughness in the history he wrote of the Franks. Clovis's ability to organize his society in the best Roman tradition also helped him provide stability. He insisted on written laws, for example—a Roman rather than a Germanic tradition. Preserved as the Code of Salic Law, his collection of laws promulgated in Latin had as a principal goal the promotion of social order through uniform sanctions for specific crimes. Clovis formalized a system of fines intended to regulate the divisive feuds and vendettas between individuals and clans that often broke out in Germanic society. The most prominent component of this system was *Wergild,* the payment a murderer had to make as compensation for his crime. Most of the *Wergild* was paid to the victim's kin, but the king received perhaps one-third of the amount. The differing amounts of *Wergild* imposed offer a glimpse of the relative values of different categories of people in Frankish society. The compensation for murdering a freeborn man, young girl, and a woman past childbearing age (specified as sixty years old) was 200 gold coins. This fine was large, sufficient to buy 200 cattle. The *Wergilds* for women of childbearing age, boys under twelve, and men in the king's retinue were 600 gold coins. The fine was tripled if the murder had occurred in the victim's home or at the hands of conspirators. The *Wergild* for ordinary slaves was 35 coins.

Above all, Clovis's kingdom derived its strength from his cultivation of good relations with his kingdom's Roman nobles, including the bishops of the towns. The bishops' support was key both because these men frequently came from the upper classes, at least in cities, and because they could be appointed to their post by popular acclaim, as happened with Martin (died 397), bishop of Tours. Bishops therefore represented a point of contact between the upper classes and the population at large. His support from ecclesiastical leaders and large landowners helped Clovis control the population of Gaul now that the Roman provincial administration in the western empire had largely disappeared, undermined by the diversion of taxes to German hands. Although the Merovingian dynasty was weakened when in 511 Clovis divided it among his four sons (recalling the Roman tetrarchy), it endured for another two hundred years, far longer than several other Germanic kingdoms in the West. The Merovingians survived because they had achieved a workable symbiosis between Germanic military prowess and Roman aristocratic social power.

Vandals, Anglo-Saxons, and Ostrogoths

Another major movement of Germanic peoples occurred when an enormous number of men, women, and children crossed the Rhine River into Roman territory in 406, perhaps also driven by the Huns. Known as the Vandals, these Germans had traditionally lived by agriculture and fought as infantry. They cut a swath of destruction through Gaul on their way to Spain (the modern word *vandal,* meaning "destroyer of property," perpetuates the memory of their destructiveness). In 429, eighty thousand Vandals ferried across the Mediterranean Sea to Roman North Africa. There they initially became federates of the western empire, but soon threw off their allegiance to Roman government. They took the region by force and ended its traditional tax shipments of grain and vegetable oil to Rome. The Vandals caused tremendous hardship for local inhabitants by systematically confiscating Roman property in the countryside rather than (like the Visigoths) allowing property owners to make periodic payments to "ransom" their land. In 455 they attacked and plundered Rome. Vandal naval expeditions in the Mediterranean further disrupted commerce and the transportation of food from North Africa to both the western and the eastern empires. The eastern empire nearly bankrupted itself to finance military expeditions to oust the Vandals from North Africa and to restore the transport of supplies. These efforts failed until 534, when the forces of the eastern emperor Justinian (*527–565) finally overthrew the Vandal kingdom.

Another movement of Germanic peoples, although involving fewer people than the others, occurred at the northwestern edge of the empire and affected Britain, from where Roman legions had been recalled by about 407 to defend Italy against the Visigoths. From the 440s onward, Angles from the area that is now Denmark and Saxons from the northwestern region of modern Germany invaded Britain. There they carved out a territory for themselves by wresting land from the native Celtic peoples, especially the Picts and Scots, as well as Britain's remaining Roman inhabitants. Gradually the eastern regions of Britain were transformed by the Germanic culture of the now-dominant Anglo-Saxons. The Celtic peoples of Britain lost most of their language and other cultural traditions, including those introduced by the Romans, and they lost contact with Christianity, which survived only in Wales and Ireland.

Elsewhere in the West, Roman customs had slowly merged with those of the Germanic peoples. Germans held administrative posts in the remnants of western imperial government and commonly served in the army, often as high officers. The German Ricimer, serving as commander in chief of the western empire's armed forces composed of various groups of non-Roman troops, was so powerful that he determined which Romans would serve as emperors in the West for nearly twenty years until his death in 472. Similarly, the commander Orestes made his young son, Romulus Augustulus, emperor in Ravenna in 475. But Odoacer, a non-Roman general from the Danube region, killed the father and overthrew the son in 476 after the troops turned against Orestes: he had unwisely refused their demands for more money. Odoacer, who like Orestes had earlier served the Hunnic king Attila, then proceeded to reign as an independent king, not as Romulus's successor.

Historians have traditionally fixed 476 as the date of the "fall" of the Roman Empire and the beginning of the European Middle Ages. But in fact the empire continued after that because Odoacer, in ruling Italy, acknowledged his subordinate status to the eastern emperor. Odoacer was himself deposed in 493 at the behest of the eastern emperor. Theodoric the Great, who overthrew Odoacer, was king of the Ostrogoths ("East Goths"), another mixed population group that included some Romans as well as Germans and had originally been allowed into Roman territory in the mid-fifth century. Until his death in 526, Theodoric administered his Ostrogothic kingdom from the traditional western imperial capital at Ravenna. Although the rank and file of Ostrogothic society often remained hostile to those Romans not in the tribe, Theodoric nevertheless saw an advantage in accommodating Roman aristocrats. He especially needed their support to maintain the novel arrangement under which a king ruled the fractious Ostrogoths, who as members of a Germanic tribe were accustomed to very loose authority. Moreover, Theodoric and his Ostrogothic nobles wanted to enjoy the luxurious life of the empire's aristocracy, not destroy it. As a young man, Theodoric had received a Roman upbringing in Constantinople while living there as a hostage (a kind of diplomatic exchange common to the times), and he appreciated Roman customs and institutions. He therefore allowed the Senate and the consulships to continue, while Goths dominated the leadership of the army. Himself an Arian Christian like the other Ostrogoths, he nevertheless announced a policy of religious toleration: "No one can be forced to believe against his will." In practice, he did sometimes take harsh measures against orthodox Christians, especially if their loyalty was suspect. The army of the eastern emperor Justinian destroyed Theodoric's Ostrogothic kingdom in Italy in the mid-sixth century. The eastern empire then ruled the former Ostrogothic territory in northern Italy until another Germanic people, the Lombards, settled there in 568 and established their own kingdom.

From Cities to Countryside in the West

While movements of Germanic peoples were transforming political and cultural life in the late Roman world, its landscape was also changing. Some cities, particularly those where the emperors made their capitals, rose to new prominence and prosperity; urban communities in other areas shriveled. Ravenna, the western imperial capital, with its glorious cathedral and churches embellished with colorful mosaics, prospered and grew at Rome's expense, as did Constantinople. The violence of some of the Germanic immigrations severely damaged many towns in the northern regions of the western empire; there the emphasis increasingly shifted to the countryside. Wealthy aristocrats built sprawling villas as their headquarters on extensive estates located at a distance from the dangerous frontier regions. Staffed by *coloni*, these estates became independent economic units capable of self-defense and self-sufficiency. Their owners consequently shunned participation in municipal administration, the traditional lifeblood of the empire. The nobles' riches and power further allowed them to avoid their obligations to the Roman government, taxes above all. One Roman aristocrat in Gaul described his life on a country estate as "close to the sources of delight and distant from ambition."

The contrasts between urban and rural life could be striking. Synesius (c. 370–413), a bishop in eastern North Africa, remarked that the emperor was such a remote figure to local people in his area that few knew his name; some people thought the legendary Greek king Agamemnon was still ruling, he joked. In Augustine's home region farther to the west, some peasants still spoke Punic, the ancient Carthaginian language, six hundred years after the Roman conquest. Carthage, on the other hand, was a vibrant Roman city with architecture rivaling the capitals' great buildings and all the refinements of Roman urban life, from baths to theaters. It became the Vandal capital after its capture in 439.

The eastern empire largely retained its economic vitality. Its many cities teemed with merchants from far and wide, and its wealthiest inhabitants spent freely on luxury goods imported from the east: silk, precious stones, and prized spices such as pepper. Rich and poor alike, urban people enjoyed the spirited religious festivals and spectacular games that frequently filled the public gathering places. Chariot racing was a special passion of the masses in cities big enough to support a racetrack. The situation in many parts of the western empire grew grimmer, however, as its economic infra-structure deteriorated. Roads and bridges fell into disrepair as the cities and the provincial adminis-trations ceased to maintain them. Self-sufficient Roman nobles on their estates had no interest in a restored central authority with the power to collect taxes. By avoiding taxes, the rich alienated the poor, financially strangled Roman provincial administra-tion, and effectively privatized most services, even justice and law and order. Nobles in the West could

Late Roman Country Estate
This mosaic depicts the kind of large country house and grounds that wealthy Romans made into self-sufficient, even fortified, retreats in the later empire.

be astonishingly rich compared to the anemic finances of the western empire. The pagan aristo-crat Symmachus, for example, owned three houses in Rome and fifteen villas scattered throughout Italy. The very wealthiest senators (the social and financial rank surviving from republican times) could have an annual income rivaling that of even an entire province. The Germanic kingdoms propped up the tottering structures of Roman provincial government only to support their local regimes, not to revitalize the empire.

Decreased population as a result of the third-century crisis meant a smaller-scale economy in many regions despite the great wealth of a few. Furthermore, inflation again mounted in the fourth century because Constantine had put an enormous quantity of gold confiscated from pagan temples into circulation. The most vivid demonstration of depopulation and economic failure in the late empire was the abandonment of farmlands. A veritable flight from the land ensued: first the *coloni* ran away; then their landlords followed because they remained responsible for the tax due from the land even though its workers were now gone. As much as 20 percent of arable Roman territory became deserted in the most seriously affected areas. The abandonment of taxable land increased the demands for revenues from those who remained and encour-aged the authorities to bring in still more German settlers. The desertion of the land further weakened the economy; the economic downturn then severely restricted the government's ability to finance imperial defense, especially in the West. The difficulty of the late Roman world in defending itself, which resulted from economic failure and depopulation, was its greatest administrative weakness.

Coloni had few incentives to endure the increasingly harsh conditions of their lives because their status had become virtually indistinguishable from that of slaves. They still retained more legal rights than slaves—for example, they could bring charges in court for criminal offenses committed against them—but the difference in power between landlords and tenants was so great that it resembled the relationship between masters and slaves. For example, *coloni* could not bring civil suits against their landlords except on a charge of exacting excessive rent. In justifying this restriction, the law indeed spoke of tenants who were tied to the land as the virtual equivalent of slaves: "They seem almost bound in a kind of servitude to those to whom they are subject by their annual payments of rent and by the obligation of their status. It is all the less to be tolerated that they should dare to bring (civil) charges against those by whom, as by owners, they can without doubt be sold together with their possessions." *Coloni*, like poor peasants who owned only tiny plots and like peddlers in the towns, always lived on the edge of disaster; bad harvests could leave them with no recourse except to flee to a large city to beg. The famous rhetoric teacher Libanius (c. 314–493) described such a scene in his hometown of Antioch in 384: "Famine had filled our city with beggars, some of whom had abandoned their fields because they lacked even grass to eat, since it was winter, and some had abandoned their native cities." Such destitution contrasted starkly with the enduring affluence of the wealthy urban classes of the empire and the general prosperity enjoyed by the proprietors of productive farms in areas that escaped raids by invaders and natural disasters. As always, the economic health of the empire varied from region to region over time.

The tying of tenants to the land and making selected occupations into hereditary obligations increased the categories of unfree people in the late Roman Empire. Slaves, of course, still constituted the least-free category. Few slaves now worked in agriculture, but they were common as household servants, assistants in the emperors' entourages, and workers in certain imperial enterprises such as the mint. Christians continued to buy and sell slaves, although Christian influence on law did lead to slaves being allowed to marry. Children born to married slaves, however, remained slaves. Gregory (c. 330–395), bishop of Nyssa, was the first Christian of stature to denounce slavery as an institution. More common was the view of Augustine, who sadly reported that he saw no way of abolishing slavery. He concluded it was an outcome of the fall of humans from God's grace.

Mixing of Roman and German Ways in the West

The western Roman Empire of the fifth and sixth centuries experienced a mixing of Roman and German customs that brought the styles of people's lives closer together in significant ways, although differences still persisted. In practice it mattered little to most people that a Roman emperor no longer ruled the western empire, and in many areas German settlement did not mean catastrophic disruption. Some land cultivated by previous inhabitants was confiscated and given to the new settlers, but sometimes the land the Germans farmed was uninhabited land that had fallen out of cultivation during the loss of population in the third century. Moreover, Germans often became in effect absentee landlords by being granted as rent the taxes due from lands on which the previous owners were allowed to remain, retaining their homes and property. Roman authorities had to forgo the tax revenue the old inhabitants of these lands now paid the Germans, but agricultural production continued, and as soldiers the Germans contributed to the region's defense.

Augustine had said that the city of God had as much room for Goths as for Romans. So did the western Roman Empire. As it developed inside Roman territory, German society transformed from its traditional tribal structure into monarchies, built upon landowning aristocracies, and developed new notions of ethnic identity. Moreover, the successful German kings cooperated with the Roman provincial nobility, despite their differences in Christian faith (many Germans were Arian Christians, while most ethnic Romans were orthodox). As their traditions came into contact with Roman traditions, the Germans were "Romanized." The other side of the historical coin, of course, was that the western Roman Empire was simultaneously changed by the effects of the move-

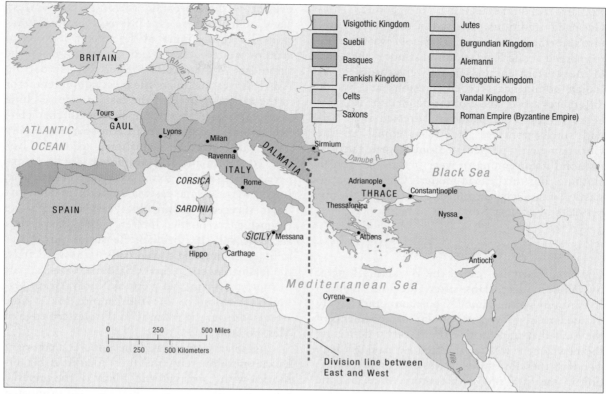

Peoples and Kingdoms of the Roman World, c. 526

ments of many Germanic peoples into Roman territory. This "barbarization," as it is sometimes called, has often been blamed for the West's weakening. But the German influence was more an effect than a cause. The western empire's weakness had its origins in the civil wars and epidemics of the third century, which decimated its population, precipitated its economic decline, and shattered its peace and order. The Germanic peoples' migrations to the West and the demographic and cultural transformations their presence brought had been made possible by these earlier blows to Roman military, political, and social well-being.

As the two societies began to co-exist, they found they shared assumptions about the fundamental relationship between men and women. The traditional patriarchy of the Germanic tribes continued in the new Gothic kingdoms established in Roman territory and corresponded to Roman customs. Both Romans and Germans also practiced some of the new Christian customs that affected traditionally devalued members of the community—

women and the poor. For example, Christians allowed poor women and men to be buried near the graves of saints, on equal terms with aristocrats; and rich women could become prominent in their congregations if they donated generously to Christian causes. Yet women in general remained largely under male control.

Shifts in political power also altered the ways in which Roman and German men interacted. Because Romans and Germans served together in the army, military service exposed ordinary men from both societies to one another. Roman noblemen in Gaul had to be clever in dealing with the now-dominant Gothic kings. Sidonius Apollinaris, a well-connected noble from Lyons (c. 430–479), for example, once purposely lost a backgammon game to the Visigothic king as a way of getting the king to approve a request for a favor. Sidonius's skill in delivering flattering orations allowed him to succeed under a series of rulers; he was appointed bishop of a region in south-central Gaul and tried to prevent the Goths from exploiting

Romans. An undercurrent of indigenous Celtic-Germanic traditions persisted in the western empire's northern provinces. These old ways simply reemerged as the Roman administration and elites of the western empire left or were absorbed. As Italian dominance receded, tensions and visible differences arose. The Goths offended the Romans because they wore pants and dressed their hair with smelly pomades made from animal fat. The Christian clergy perpetuated old Roman sartorial fashion by continuing to wear traditional Roman clothing. For this reason modern Christian ecclesiastical vestments resemble the clothing of the upper class of ancient Rome.

The Byzantine Empire

The eastern empire (called the Byzantine Empire by modern historians after the old name—Byzantium—of its capital, Constantinople) largely escaped massive German population movements of the kind that transformed the West by deflecting the newcomers westward, often by paying them. The East therefore suffered less economic dislocation in the fifth and sixth centuries than did the West. The inhabitants of the eastern empire regarded themselves as the heirs of ancient Roman culture: they referred to themselves as Romans. Although Latin remained the language of government and of command in the army until the seventh century, many people in the eastern empire spoke Greek as their native language (westerners referred generically to easterners as Greek). The eastern empire's population was quite heterogeneous, however, and a traveler in its provinces would have heard many different languages and seen many styles of dress.

Fearing that contact with Germans and other northern peoples would "barbarize" their empire just as it had the West, the eastern emperors did everything they could to preserve the "Romanness" of their world. As early as the end of the fourth century, for example, they had forbidden residents of Constantinople to dress in Germanic style—in pants, boots, and clothing made from animal furs—instead of traditional Roman garb. Unfortunately for such dreams of maintaining pure Roman cultural traditions, military needs compelled the Byzantine army to hire many Germans and Huns.

Ironically, the eastern emperors needed these "barbarian" mercenaries because through the reign of Justinian (527–565) they repeatedly tried to overthrow the Germanic kingdoms in the West. They launched these expeditions attempting to restore the former unity of the Roman Empire, to acquire western tax revenues, and to revive the shipments of foodstuffs formerly received from North Africa. Justinian, the most famous emperor in the early centuries of the eastern empire's long history, pursued these campaigns with characteristic enthusiasm. Born to a Latin-speaking family in a small Balkan town, Justinian acquired a Roman education and was promoted rapidly in imperial service thanks to the patronage of his uncle, Justin, who became eastern emperor in 518. Justinian succeeded Justin nine years later, and like Augustus, surrounded himself with skilled generals, especially the brilliant Belisarius. Justinian's military commanders eventually recaptured Italy, the Dalmatian coast, Sicily, Sardinia, Corsica, part of southern Spain, and western North Africa. Justinian's version of the old empire for a time stretched from the Atlantic to the western edge of Mesopotamia.

Justinian strengthened the autocratic nature of Byzantine monarchy and fully identified his authority with Christian rule. Many of the imperial political traditions and ceremonies had originated in the early and therefore pagan Roman Empire. Justinian managed to sustain the ancient tradition of the Roman emperor's visible supremacy while recasting the symbols of rule in a Christian context. A gleaming mosaic in his church at San Vitale in Ravenna, for example, displayed his vision of the emperor's role: Justinian stood at the center of the cosmos shoulder to shoulder with both the ancient Hebrew patriarch Abraham and Christ. No wonder Justinian proclaimed the emperor the "living law," an old idea made explicit for the first time. His autocracy also reduced the autonomy of the eastern empire's cities. City councils ceased to govern as more and more imperial officials were installed throughout the eastern provinces. *Curiales* were still responsible for assuring payment of the full amount of taxes from their area due the central government, but they no longer enjoyed the compensating reward of deciding local matters. Now the imperial government dominated all aspects of decision making and status. Men of property from the provinces who aspired to power and prestige knew they could best satisfy their ambitions by entering the imperial administration, whether in the capital or the provinces. They also

Justinian's Empire and the Spread of Christianity up to 600

realized the great financial advantage of an imperial post: it freed them from the financial burdens of the *curiales.*

Justinian's attempt to reunite the Roman Empire by crushing the German kingdoms came at enormous cost to the economic infrastructure of the West and the finances of the East. His extended military campaigns against the Goths in Italy caused death and destruction on a massive scale. To finance the expeditions, the emperor squeezed even more taxes out of his already overburdened population. Worsening his financial straits was the need to pay large amounts of money every year to hostile neighbors to keep them from attacking the eastern empire while he directed his attention westward. This protection money went to various peoples in the north and, most of all, to the Sassanids in Mesopotamia. Banditry increased in many areas as the economic situation deteriorated, and crowds poured into the capital from rural areas, seeking relief from poverty. In the 540s a horrific epidemic killed perhaps a third of the people in the eastern empire; a quarter of a million succumbed in Constantinople alone, half the capital's population. The loss of so many people meant vacant agricultural land, reduced tax revenues, and a shortage of army recruits. The epidemic devastated the cities and towns of the East, and their continuing weakness

made them ill-equipped to respond to the crises that would come in the seventh century, when the Byzantine Empire faced aggressive challenges from Persians and Arabs.

Justinian also strained imperial finances with his urban building program, which drained the West of many builders and craft specialists. Some of his projects were public works, like the huge cistern built in Constantinople, whose roof supported by a forest of columns still stands. Also surviving, although modified through the centuries, is his magnificent reconstruction of Constantine's Church of the Holy Wisdom (St. Sophia, in Istanbul). Facing the palace, the location of St. Sophia corresponded to Justinian's interlacing of imperial and Christian authority. Abandoning the conventional basilica-style architecture of Christian churches, Justinian's architects erected a huge building on a square plan capped by a dome 107 feet across and soaring 160 feet above the floor below. Its interior walls glowed like the sun from the light reflecting off their four acres of gold mosaics. Imported marble of every color added to the sparkling effect. When he first entered his just-completed masterpiece, dedicated in 538, Justinian exclaimed, "Solomon, I have outdone you." (He was referring to the Biblical story of the glorious temple King Solomon built for the ancient

Emperor Justinian and Empress Theodora
These sparkling mosaics from Ravenna, Italy, show Emperor Justinian and Empress Theodora leading court processions to make offerings at the altar. The circles (nimbi) around their heads signify holiness.

Hebrews.) Justinian's costly building projects did provide employment, but like his wars to reunite the Roman Empire, they were ultimately justified by the traditional ethos of Roman rulers: the pursuit of glory and a magnificent imperial image were the proper goals of an emperor.

Further reflecting his zeal for reform, Justinian had the laws of the empire codified to try to bring greater consistency and uniformity to the often confusing welter of rules that different emperors had revised and enacted over the centuries. A team of scholars condensed millions of words of regulations to produce the *Digest.* This collection of laws, which superseded the Theodosian Code of 438, influenced legal scholars for centuries. Justinian's experts also compiled a textbook for law students, the *Institutes,* which continued to appear in law-school reading lists until modern times.

The emperor's costly projects left his successors a legacy of bankruptcy and imposed a terrible burden on the general population. So heavy and so unpopular were his taxes and so notorious was his tax collector, the ruthless John of Cappadocia, that they provoked a major riot in 532. This so-called Nika Riot almost ended the emperor's reign. It epitomized the tumultuous life in the eastern capital. The residents of Constantinople had long divided themselves into factions called the Blues and the Greens, names derived from the racing colors of the teams of charioteers around whom the

groups had originally formed as ardent fans. By Justinian's time, the Blues and Greens had come to detest each other more out of religious hatred than sports rivalry. The Blues favored orthodox Christian doctrines, whereas the Greens supported Monophysitism. When the Blues and Greens met in Constantinople's hippodrome to watch races, for example, they often came to blows over their theological differences. In 532, however, they unexpectedly united against the emperor, shouting "Nika! Nika!" ("Win! Win!") as their battle cry. After nine days of violence in which much of Constantinople was burned, Justinian was ready to abandon his throne and flee in panic, but his wife, Theodora, sternly rebuked him: "Once born, no one can escape dying, but for one who has held imperial power it would be unbearable to be a fugitive. May I never take off my imperial robes of purple, nor live to see the day when those who meet me will not greet me as their sovereign." Justinian then sent in troops, who quelled the disturbance by slaughtering thirty thousand rioters trapped in the hippodrome.

Empress Theodora dramatically showed the influence women could achieve in the eastern imperial family. Uninhibited by her humble origins (she was the daughter of a bear trainer and had been an actress with a scandalous reputation), Theodora had married into royalty and, like those born into it, could rival anyone in influence and wealth. John

Lydus, a contemporary government official, judged her "superior in intelligence to any man." Some ancient reports suggest that she had a hand in every aspect of Justinian's rule until her death in 548. But Theodora was exceptional. The luxurious and powerful position of royal women bore no resemblance to the lives of most women in this part of the Roman world. For them the pattern of life reflected ancient tradition. For example, both Christian and non-Christian women were expected to minimize their contact with men outside their families. They could not fulfill various public functions, such as witnessing wills. Women and children were subject to the authority of their husbands and fathers, and women veiled their heads (though not their faces). Pagan and Christian sexual mores overlapped significantly, but Christian theologians generally went beyond Roman tradition in frowning on remarriage and supporting increased legal penalties for sexual offenses. Nevertheless, female prostitutes, often poor women desperate for income, continued to abound in the streets and inns of eastern cities, just as in earlier days.

Following the tradition of Roman imperial rule, Justinian considered it his sacred duty to ensure the well-being of the empire and its subjects. Their welfare, he believed, depended especially on the religious purity of the empire, which could not flourish if God became angered by the presence of those who offended him. As emperor, Justinian decided who the offenders were. He zealously enforced long-standing laws against pagans and heretics. For example, he compelled pagans, both in cities and the countryside, to be baptized or forfeit their lands and official positions. Three times he purged heretical Christians whom he could not reconcile to his version of orthodoxy. And his laws made male homosexual relations illegal for the first time in Roman history. Homosexual marriage, apparently not uncommon earlier, had been officially prohibited in 342, but civil sanctions had never before been imposed on men engaging in homosexual activity. All the previous emperors, for example, had taxed male prostitutes. The legal status of homosexual activity between women is less clear; it probably counted as adultery when married women were involved and was thus a crime. For Justinian the use of the force and sanctions of the law against pagans, heretics, and people convicted of homosexual relations expressed his devotion to God and his concern for his own reputation as a pious and successful ruler. In this sense, Justinian's compulsion to purify the empire was part of the same imperial program that promoted the building of magnificent Christian basilicas.

Transformation and Divisiveness

The social, cultural, and political changes in the late Roman Empire took place gradually in a process of transformation. The widespread idea that maintains the empire started on a decline in the third century and then in the fifth century fell, meaning disappeared, stems perhaps more than anything else from the great renown of the title of the English historian Edward Gibbon's multivolume work *The Decline and Fall of the Roman Empire* (published 1776–1788). Gibbon recognized that the Roman Empire did not disappear in 476 with the deposition of the western emperor Romulus Augustulus, because he continued his mammoth history until the Turks captured Constantinople in 1453, the final end of the eastern empire. Its so-called decline and fall therefore lasted more than a thousand years. Gibbon entitled his history when he published its first volume in 1776, twelve years before he finished the final volume that reached the events of 1453. (He might well have chosen a different title had he completed writing the long story of the eastern Roman Empire before he named his work, and the erroneous idea that the Roman Empire fell once and for all in 476 might not have gained such currency.) The end of the short reign of Romulus Augustulus in 476 undeniably marked a change, because he was the last Roman emperor in the West. No longer did one central authority head Roman government there; a welter of local administrations and Germanic kingdoms now governed. In this narrow sense the western empire did fall; but that distinction has little, if any, historical significance. The reality of political power in the West remained the same after 476 as it had been for generations before: German commanders and troops dominated the Roman army and therefore controlled the western empire's political fate.

The most remarkable aspect of the transformation of the late Roman Empire was the divergence of its western and eastern portions. For centuries to come, the East largely retained its centralized authority, complex financial administration, and sense of being the continuation of the ancient Roman Empire. The western empire changed far more profoundly, and the decentralization of authority there plus the impact of the influx of Germanic peoples turned it into something markedly different. The traditional practices of Roman administration faded away in the western provinces as the German kingdoms became more independent. By Romulus's reign in the late fifth century, the annual revenues at the western emperor's disposal had shrunk to a small fraction of the eastern emperor's. Tax revenues that previously would have supported the central government now enriched German potentates and Roman nobles. The violence that had sometimes accompanied the appearance of large groups of Germanic peoples in the West had also weakened the economy in some regions. The western empire found these losses especially difficult to overcome because its population had probably never recovered its former size after the disasters of the third century.

Both halves of the Roman world probably did share at least one experience in this period: an increasing lack of social cohesiveness and a sense of belonging among their populations. A tremendous gulf had always separated rich and poor Romans, and theological disputes had divided Christians from the earliest years of their new religion. Nevertheless, as these tendencies became more pronounced in the later Roman Empire, people grew more alienated from one another and thus less able to find cooperative solutions to their society's problems.

People of limited means and status found it increasingly difficult to get government officials to issue permits, redress grievances, and deal with the many other affairs of daily life requiring official intervention. Romans of all social ranks had always relied on personal connections when dealing with the government, sometimes seeking preferential treatment, sometimes simply trying to ensure that officials did what they were supposed to do. The administration of late Roman imperial government imposed special burdens on citizens, however, not only because its officials continued to expect generous tips routinely, but also because there were now considerably more officials to tip. Because interest rates were high, people could incur onerous debt trying to raise the cash to pay high officials to act on important matters. Many officials depended on this system to augment their generally paltry salaries. John Lydus, for example, who worked in

Justinian's administration, earned thirty times his annual salary in payments from petitioners during his first year in office. The emperors approved petitioners' payments to their officials as a way to keep salary costs down, and they published an official list of the maximum bribes officials could exact. The idea was to keep officials from crippling the administration by pricing their services too highly. The increased importance of paying extra in return for service obviously made it harder and harder for people without much money to obtain help from government officials.

Another source of divisiveness in the late Roman Empire was the increasing autocracy of the emperors and the severity of the legal penalties they imposed as lawmakers. Already in the second century the legal scholar Gaius had argued that the emperor's decrees had the full force of law without any need for Senate approval. In the late Roman world the emperors employed many legal scholars to tell them that their word alone was law. Indeed the emperors came to be above the law because they were not bound even by the decrees of their predecessors, and they thus had less interest than ever in consulting the aristocracy, ruling by consensus, and observing tradition. The emperors depended on their personal staff for advice and grew farther apart from the aristocrats. The emperors also used their greater legal powers to increase the severity of judicial penalties for crimes, continuing a trend already evident during the Great Persecution. For example, the law mandated that if, after due warnings, officials did not keep their "greedy hands" off bribes (presumably exorbitant ones), "they shall be cut off by the sword." Constantine revived the ancient punishment of tying certain malefactors in a leather sack with snakes and drowning them in a river. The guardians of a young girl who allowed a lover to seduce her were punished by having molten lead poured into their mouths. Fewer condemned criminals, however, were dispatched to the amphitheater to die as gladiators or by fighting animals. Nevertheless, punishments grew especially harsh for the large segment of the population legally designated as *humiliores* ("humbler people"). The upper ranks of the population (*honestiores*) could generally escape harsh treatment for crimes. Although the lack of direct evidence for what common people felt makes generalization uncertain, the increased severity with which the government punished the masses could hardly have strengthened their sense of attachment to the Roman state, whose privileges were more than ever before limited to the wealthy and socially well-connected.

The late Roman world was also split spiritually by frequent, bitter controversies over Christian doctrine and by the disengagement from everyday society epitomized by monasticism. These divisions in Christianity disrupted society much more than had the formation of new pagan cults in earlier times. Whereas paganism had incorporated new divinities and new practices without rejecting time-honored traditions, Christianity required its adherents to serve only one divinity in a prescribed fashion. But Christian orthodoxy required political enforcement, and not even the growing secular power of church officials sufficed either to persuade or to compel unwilling believers to accept orthodox views. In some cases, oppressed Christians fled the empire, as when the Nestorians moved to Persia. Emperors like Justinian tried to convince heretical Christians to return to orthodox theology and the hierarchy of the church, but they did not shrink from using force when persuasion failed. Rulers took these extreme measures believing that they were helping to save lost souls. But the persecution of Christian subjects by Christian emperors symbolized the dire consequences of divisiveness for the late Roman world.

The Survival of Roman Language and Education

Language and literature in the later Roman Empire represented a continuation of tradition because they clearly reflected their earlier Roman heritage; but they were also transformed through the demographic changes and conflicts among the inhabitants of the Roman world and the ever-increasing influence of Christianity. As Roman and Germanic traditions mingled, creating new ways of life in the western empire, "Romanness" there became something that one acquired more by education rather than by birth or ethnic origin. Upper-class Roman and German men of the late empire came to share a taste for education in traditional Roman subjects, rhetoric above all. German leaders who gained this learning became the intellectual peers of educated Roman men, while remaining their political supe-

riors in the new kingdoms. The German tribes originally had no written language, but a script for writing the Goths' spoken tongue was invented in the late fourth century so the Bible could be translated into Gothic. The Germans who forged successful careers in the western empire before the formation of the Germanic kingdoms, especially those who served in the Roman army, learned to write and speak Latin. (For more than a thousand years, in fact, Latin would remain the principal language of official communication in Europe.) Familiarity with classical texts, although limited, remained the distinguishing mark of an educated person. Augustine had a friend who knew Virgil so well that if someone quoted him a line of the poet's work, he could recite the preceding line.

Some Roman scholars and intellectuals viewed German influence as a threat because they feared Roman literary and cultural traditions would gradually be obliterated in the new Germanic kingdoms. Latin literature had experienced a renaissance at the end of the fourth century and the beginning of the fifth century with great prose works like those of Augustine and Jerome. Poetry had again flourished in Latin, too, as in the evocative poem by Ausonius of Bordeaux (c. 310–395) that describes the natural wonders of the Moselle River (which flows from what is now France into Germany). Christian poets, such as Paulinus of Nola (353–431) also began writing in Latin. Several generations later, Boethius and Cassiodorus, both of whom worked for Ostrogothic kings of Italy, became famous for their scholarly efforts to preserve the traditions of Roman literature and philosophy. Boethius (c. 480–524) rose to the consulship under Theodoric, but he was subsequently imprisoned on suspicion of treason and later executed. Boethius's scholarship was motivated by his "fear that many things which are now known soon will not be." This worry that classical learning might be forgotten led him to want to translate Plato and Aristotle into Latin and provide commentaries to explain the texts. He was killed, however, before he had progressed very far with this work. His *Consolation of Philosophy,* written in prison when he had no recourse to a library, nevertheless abounded in references to classical texts and was filled with Neoplatonic doctrines. Cassiodorus (c. 490–585) spent time in Constantinople but returned to Italy to live in a monastery he had founded. There he developed a new monastic goal,

Christ as the Sun God
This mosaic from a second-century Roman catacomb portrays Christ as the radiant Sun God driving his chariot, illustrating how Christian art made use of pagan traditions.

the copying of manuscripts to keep their contents alive as old ones disintegrated, which became a function for the monks in monasteries he founded. Cassiodorus wrote his book *Institutions* to prescribe the works a person of superior education should read. His ideal curriculum included secular texts as well as Scripture and Christian literature, encapsulating the cultural diversity of the late Roman Empire.

Pagan literature in Latin continued to be widely read because no other suitable texts existed for basic education. Educated Christians therefore received at least a rudimentary knowledge of some pre-Christian classics. And such an education was necessary for a distinguished career in government service. In the words of an imperial decree of 360, "No person shall obtain a post of the first rank unless it shall be shown that he excels in long practice of liberal studies, and that he is so polished in literary matters that words flow from his pen faultlessly." Christian literature, which flourished in the late empire, followed distinguished pagan models. Classical eloquence, for example, was used to disseminate Christian theology and guidance. When Ambrose composed the first systematic description of Christian ethics for young priests, he consciously imitated the great Roman writer Cicero. Writers employed the dialogue form pioneered by Plato to refute heretical Christian doctrines, and traditions

of laudatory biography survived in hagiography, or saints' lives. These works demonstrated how Christianity could use literature to promote religion. Moreover, Christians often communicated their beliefs and emotions in paintings, mosaics, and carved reliefs that combined pagan and Christian traditions of representation. A famous mosaic of Christ with a sunburst surrounding his head, for example, recalled pagan depictions of the radiant Sun as a god.

The development of specifically Christian literature was accompanied by a significant technological evolution in the production of manuscripts (books). Pagan literature had always been written mainly on sheets made of thin animal skin or paper made from the papyrus plant. This material was then attached to a rod at either end to make a scroll, which the reader unrolled to read. For ease of use, Christians preferred their literature in the form of the *codex*—a book with bound pages. During the fourth century the codex became the standard form of book production in the Roman world. Because it was less susceptible to damage and could contain text more efficiently than scrolls, which were cumbersome for long works, the codex aided the preservation of literature. This technological innovation helped keep the memory of ancient Greco-Roman culture as embodied in its literature from disappearing as it evolved into new forms during and after the late Roman Empire.

New literary developments also helped perpetuate the memory of classical learning. Around 470, for example, the pagan Martianus Capella in Vandal Carthage composed an allegory in Latin prose and verse to tell the story of Philology, the goddess of learning, accompanied by her handmaidens, the seven Liberal Arts (grammar, rhetoric, logic, arithmetic, geometry, astronomy, and music), ascending to the heavens where Philology was to marry the god of eloquence, Mercury. Such elaborate allegories later became a very popular literary form.

But despite such continuing importance of classical Greek and Latin literature, preserving pagan literature became increasingly problematic. By the fifth century, knowledge of Greek in the West had faded so drastically that very few could read Homer's *Iliad* and *Odyssey*—the traditional foundations of a pagan literary education—in the original. Classical Latin fared better, and well-read Christians like Augustine and Jerome knew ancient Latin literature extremely well. But they also saw

(far left) **The Old Form of the Book**
*This sculpture from a Roman sarco-
phagus shows a man reading a book
in the form of a scroll, which had to
be unrolled and then rolled up again
as its reader proceeded through the
text.*

(left) **The New Form of the Book**
*This mosaic from the church of
S. Vitale in Ravenna (completed in
546) shows the evangelist Mark holding a codex, a kind of book featuring
bound pages that Christians favored
for their scriptures over traditional
scrolls.*

the Latin classics as potentially too seductive for a
pious Christian. Jerome in fact once had a nightmare
of being condemned on Judgment Day because he
had been a Ciceronian instead of a Christian. Like
Greek, Latin survived in a form increasingly different from the classical language of an earlier time.
The Latin of literature became simpler in the late
empire. For example, Benedict's Rule used colloquial, nonclassical words to make the code intelligible to simply educated monks. Educated people, however, frequently preferred an ornate style
recalling Greek Hellenistic poetry and the Latin
prose of the second century. This preference reflected
the educational gap between the masses and the few
who could appreciate traditional literature.

In the eastern empire the region's original
Greek culture reemerged as the dominant influence. Men of affairs, such as the emperor Julian and
his fourth-century contemporary Libanius, the
influential pagan rhetorician from Antioch, produced copious works in Greek that dealt with
religion, politics, and intellectual issues. Novels
with plots of romance and adventure captured the
imagination of a wide public. Schoolboys memorized
passages from Homer, as they had in classical
Greece. The most famous Byzantine historian, Procopius, a high official under Justinian, wrote both
his conventional *History of the Wars of Justinian*
and his provocative *Secret History,* a scurrilous

attack on the policies and personal habits of
Justinian and Theodora, in a classical Greek style.
Educated members of the upper class tried to speak
in the Greek forms of ancient times. This tendency
sprang from the traditionally narrow notion of
education in Roman society: training in elite
knowledge whose purpose was to separate its
holders from the masses. Ordinary Greek speakers
used koine ("common" Greek) that kept evolving
away from classical models. Already in the fourth
century, for example, some people were ceasing to
use the classical Greek word *hydor* for "water" and
instead using *nero*—the word used in modern
Greek.

The administration of the eastern empire was
bilingual, with Latin remaining the language of law
and the army throughout this period. For example,
Justinian's code of laws, the *Digest,* was written in
Latin. But in court cases people routinely spoke
Greek, and Greek translations of the codified laws
soon became available. Latin scholarship in the
eastern empire received a boost when Justinian's
wars in Italy impelled Latin-speaking scholars to
flee for safety to Constantinople. Their labors there
helped to conserve many works of Latin literature
that might otherwise have disappeared, because
conditions in the West were hardly conducive to
safekeeping ancient learning, except in such rare instances as the monasteries founded by Cassiodorus.

The handing down of knowledge from classical antiquity suffered a great symbolic blow when Justinian in 529 closed the Academy in Athens, originally founded by Plato. The emperor shut down this famous pagan school after nine hundred years of operation because he was outraged by its virulently anti-Christian head, Damascius. But fortunately for the future of classical texts, Justinian did not attack non-Christian learning at large. The Neoplatonist school at Alexandria, for example, he simply ignored, perhaps because its leader, John Philoponus (c. 490–570), was a Christian. In addition to Christian theology, Philoponus wrote commentaries on the works of Aristotle; some of his ideas anticipated those of Galileo. Philoponus symbolizes the synthesis of old and new that was one of the fruitful outcomes of the transformation of the late Roman world—that is, he was a Christian in sixth-century Egypt, heading a school founded long before by pagans, studying the works of an ancient Greek philosopher as the inspiration for his forward-looking scholarship.

CONCLUSION

The most significant and enduring development in the history of the late Roman Empire was that masses of people converted to Christianity. Pagans continued their traditions long after Christianity had become the empire's official religion in the late fourth century, and Judaism maintained its vitality, but Christian doctrines and patterns of life were now assured a central role in Western civilization. The autocratic rule of the late Roman emperors and the development of a hierarchy of monarchical bishops helped secure Christianity's success.

Demographic changes also helped set the stage for the future, especially in the western region of the now-divided empire. The movements of polyethnic tribes—Visigoths, Vandals, Anglo-Saxons, Ostrogoths, and Lombards—into the western empire created a new culture that meshed Roman and German traditions and led to the formation of Germanic kingdoms in place of Roman provincial administration. The damage many European and North African cities and towns suffered in this period, combined with a loss of population in many places, weakened the economic and political infrastructure of the region for a long time to come, making the area difficult to defend. In the eastern empire, largely unchanged by the movements of Germanic peoples (except in the Balkans), urban life remained vital until the increasing autocracy of the Byzantine Empire and the ravages of the epidemic of the 540s severely weakened its cities. The administrative efficiency and financial health of the East deteriorated because, in the words of a recent scholar, the government and the cities directly competed for the same human and financial resources. The government attracted more and more of the urban elites into imperial administration, where their offices automatically entitled them to exemption from the financial responsibilities imposed on municipal *curiales*. The dwindling supply of *curiales* meant that the cities and towns experienced chronic difficulties in fulfilling their traditional role as the collectors of revenues for the imperial government.

Taxation became ever heavier as the emperors tried to raise money to pay the army, to bribe foreign enemies not to attack, and to erect glorious buildings to demonstrate their grandeur. People in cities benefited from the emperors' public works projects, but the urban poor, along with their compatriots in the countryside, found little comfort in a government that pinched them for taxes and served them only if they could pay its officials or otherwise obtain favors.

Monasticism represented the most visible manifestation of many people's longing for a dramatic change in their lives. Becoming a monk was a way to escape everyday cares and, through the continual worship of God, to attain a level of personal contentment many people felt secular life could not match. The problem presented by withdrawal from ordinary life was that it might satisfy an individual's needs but offered no resolution to the difficulties facing a society in crisis.

SUGGESTIONS FOR FURTHER READING

Source Materials

Augustine. *City of God.* Translated by Henry Bettenson. 1984. The major theological work of one of Christianity's most influential thinkers.

———. *Confessions.* Translated by Henry Chadwick. 1991. Augustine's spiritual autobiography.

Geanakoplos, D. J. *Byzantium: Church, Society, and Civilization Seen Through Contemporary Eyes.* 1984. A collection of excerpts from primary sources on many aspects of Byzantine life.

Hillgarth, J. L., ed. *Christianity and Paganism, 350–750: The Conversion of Western Europe.* Rev. ed. 1986. A selection of documents and literary texts concerning the spread of Christianity in western Europe.

Kraemer, Ross S., ed. *Maenads, Martyrs, Matrons, Monastics: A Sourcebook on Women's Religions in the Greco-Roman World.* 1988. Includes sources through the late Roman world, with extensive coverage of asceticism and monasticism.

Procopius. *History of the Wars; Secret History; Buildings.* Edited by Averil Cameron. 1967. An abridged edition of the diverse works of this sixth-century Byzantine official, including his scathingly gossipy *Secret History.*

Interpretive Studies

Bowersock, G. W. *Julian the Apostate.* 1978. An elegantly written study of the last pagan emperor of Rome.

Brown, Peter. *Augustine of Hippo.* 1967. The standard biography of this seminal figure in early Christianity.

———. *The Body and Society: Men, Women, and Sexual Renunciation in Early Christianity.* 1988. A masterful and provocative treatment of a fundamental episode in the shaping of Western attitudes toward sexuality.

———. *The World of Late Antiquity,* A.D. *150–750.* 1971. The most intriguing brief introduction to the transformation of the Roman world into the early medieval world.

Cochrane, Charles N. *Christianity and Classical Culture.* Rev. ed. 1944. An enduring analysis of the impact of Christianity on thought and action in the Roman world from the first to the fourth century.

Dodds, E. R. *Pagan and Christian in an Age of Anxiety.* 1965. A classic introduction to religious experience in the Roman world from the late second century to the time of Constantine.

Geary, Patrick J. *Before France and Germany: The Creation and Transformation of the Merovingian World.* 1988. A sprightly analysis of the diverse forces and traditions involved in the formation of the Germanic kingdoms in Roman Europe.

Gibbon, Edward. *The Decline and Fall of the Roman Empire.* Edited by J. B. Bury. 1946. An annotated edition of this still stimulating classic work, whose first volume was originally published in 1776.

Heather, P. J. *Goths and Romans, 322–448.* 1991. A study of the interaction of Goths with the Roman Empire, arguing that these Germans originally had a stronger sense of ethnic identity than is usually acknowledged.

Isaac, Benjamin. *The Limits of Empire: The Roman Army in the East.* 1989. A refreshingly revisionist argument that Roman military planning was often haphazard and not very geared toward defense.

James, Edward. *The Franks.* 1988. A readable treatment of the history and customs of this Germanic people.

Jones, A. H. M. *The Decline of the Ancient World.* 1966. An abbreviated version of his multivolume work combining chronological narrative and topical analysis.

———. *The Later Roman Empire.* 2 vols. 1964. Still the most complete account by an expert with profound knowledge of this vast subject.

MacMullen, Ramsay. *Christianizing the Roman Empire,* A.D. *100–400.* 1984. An interpretive survey of the process through which Christianity became the dominant religion in the Roman Empire.

———. *Constantine.* 1969. A clearly written introduction to the career of the first Christian emperor.

———. *Corruption and the Decline of Rome.* 1988. A controversial indictment of the role of official corruption in the weakening of the late Roman Empire.

Mango, Cyril. *Byzantium: The Empire of New Rome.* 1980. A wide-ranging study of Byzantine social, cultural, and intellectual history.

Murray, Alexander C. *Germanic Kinship Structure.* 1983. A tightly argued study of bilateral kinship relationships in the Germanic tribes.

Ostrogorsky, George. *History of the Byzantine State.* Rev. ed. 1969. The standard scholarly treatment of the subject, primarily concerned with political, diplomatic, and military history.

Pagels, Elaine. *Adam, Eve, and the Serpent.* 1988. A thought-provoking interpretation of the effect of Augustine's concept of the doctrine of original sin.

Rousselle, Aline. *Porneia: On Desire and the Body in Antiquity.* Translated by Felicia Pheasant. 1988. A compendium of fascinating evidence on attitudes toward the human body and sexuality.

Wolfram, Herwig. *History of the Goths.* Rev. ed. Translated by Thomas J. Dunlap. 1988. A comprehensive study of the ethnogenesis of the Goths and what it meant to be German in a Roman world.

Masons and Sculptors, Stained Glass in Chartes Cathedral, France

II

The Quickening of the West, 568–1560

With the end of imperial rule in the West, northern and central Europe became an important historical stage as new political, economic, and cultural communities competed and cooperated with one another as well as with the older communities of the Mediterranean and the Near East. New peoples, speaking new languages, came on the scene: joining those who spoke Latin, Greek, and Germanic and Celtic tongues were Slavic peoples and immigrants from the steppes of western Asia. Once Europe's dense forests were cut back and its thick grasslands tamed, the way was opened for population growth, the emergence of cities, and the development of centralized states.

Although these changes were under way, no one in the sixth century proclaimed the end of the ancient world or the beginning of the Middle Ages. Only much later, when some people self-consciously imitated the art and literature of classical antiquity, did the idea of a "middle age in between" the classical and modern period emerge. Thus the intellectual movement known as the Renaissance (meaning "rebirth") created the Middle Ages. Nevertheless, the Renaissance itself represented a period of retrenchment of medieval institutions and attitudes.

The Middle Ages called on the legacy of antiquity. Byzantine emperors, Muslim caliphs, and German kings followed Roman administrative and legal traditions; scholars revived interest in Greek and Roman philosophy and literature; and churchmen built on the theology and commentary of the great spokesmen for the early church. The very idea that the Roman Empire had ended seemed absurd, for emperors continued to rule in the East until 1453; and new-style Western emperors, the first of whom was crowned in the year 800, governed into the nineteenth century.

The Middle Ages also replaced some ancient practices with its own enduring traditions. In place of slavery, peasants settled on the land in households; wage labor began; and the use of water mills, heavy plows, and massive looms marked the beginning of industry. For the first time, cities were more hubs of commercial activity than centers of politics and religious ritual. Latin ceased to be spoken, while the ancestors of modern languages such as French, German, English, and Spanish became literary as well as oral languages. Medieval scholars crafted unique syntheses of divine revelation and human knowledge. Twelfth-century troubadour poets and religious mystics created a new literature of love, and a few centuries later Renaissance humanists spoke to the experiences and concerns of lay men and women in courts and cities.

National states ruled by kings overturned the ancient Roman model of empire. The contours of these states foreshadowed the current political map of Europe. Ever on the move, Western medieval kings, warriors, and churchmen pushed eastward along the Baltic coast, southward into the Holy Land, and westward to Ireland. So

although the Mediterranean was still the focus of Western culture at the beginning of the Middle Ages, by the end of the period a New World had been "discovered" and Westerners were transplanting their brand of civilization across the Atlantic.

The Middle Ages saw the rise and fall of a united Christendom. The hierarchical church, led by a pope and his bishops, asserted its authority and power in the twelfth and thirteenth centuries, when it clashed with the Western emperor. But even in the twelfth century, for many people this hierarchical conception of the church was partly overshadowed by other potent manifestations of divine power, from miracles at the shrines of saints to the monastic devotions of monks. The papal view conflicted as well with the growing power of monarchs and princes, with the rising prestige of pious lay groups, and with new visions of the world set out by scholars. In the sixteenth century, leaders of the religious movement known as the Reformation rebelled against the medieval papacy and forever split Christian Europe into rival sects.

In everyday parlance today, the term *Middle Ages* has two meanings. Sometimes it connotes the so-called Dark Ages, a period of ignorance, intolerance, and violence. At other times it suggests an age of chivalry and romance, of knights in shining armor and damsels in distress. Although each image contains a bit of truth, the whole truth is far more complex and specific. Seventh-century illiteracy must not obscure the twelfth century's surge of scholarship or the creation of a new institution, the university. Cruel intolerance of Jews and other groups in the twelfth century does not negate the acceptance of Jews in tenth-century society. Medieval life was marred by violence but also soothed and steadied by peace movements and other attempts to channel and control warfare. Knighthood and the romantic literature that portrayed it were products of the eleventh and twelfth centuries, a response to specific conditions of the era. As these conditions passed away, they brought in their wake a new world, constrained in its turn to build upon and change the legacy of the Middle Ages.

According to a writer who was not very sympathetic to the Byzantines, Emperor Heraclius (*610–641) had a dream: "Verily [he was told] there shall come against thee a circumcised nation, and they shall vanquish thee and take possession of the land." Heraclius thought the vision betokened a rising of the Jews, and he ordered mass baptisms in all his provinces. "But," continued the story,

> after a few days there appeared a man of the Arabs, from the southern districts, that is to say, from Mecca or its neighborhood, whose name was Muhammad; and he brought back the worshipers of idols to the knowledge of the One God. . . . And he took possession of Damascus and Syria, and crossed the Jordan and dammed it up. And the Lord abandoned the army of the Romans before him.

This tale, however fanciful, alerts us to the most astonishing development of the seventh century: the Arabs conquered much of the Roman Empire and became one of its heirs. The western and eastern parts of the empire, both diminished, were now joined by yet a third—Arab and Muslim—power. The resulting triad has endured in various guises to the present day: the western third of the old Roman Empire became western Europe; the eastern third, occupying what is now Turkey, Greece, and part of the Balkans, became part of eastern Europe and helped to create Russia; and North Africa, together with the area of the ancient Near East (now called the Middle East), remains the Arab world.

As diverse as these cultures are today, they share some of the same roots and

The Heirs of the Roman Empire, 568–756

Lindisfarne Gospels Evangelist Page
Far both in time and spirit from the classical Mediterranean world, the seventh-century English monks who drew this picture of St. Matthew transformed classical human and architectural representations into bold and decorative designs.

assumptions. All were heirs of Hellenistic and Roman traditions; most important, each believed in monotheism. The western and eastern halves of the empire had Christianity in common, although they differed at times in interpreting it. The Arab world's religion, Islam, accepted the same one God as Christianity but considered Jesus one of God's prophets rather than his son.

The history of the seventh and eighth centuries is a story of adaptation: in different ways, all three heirs combined elements of their Roman heritage with new values, interests, and conditions. The divergences among them resulted inevitably from disparities in geographical and climatic conditions, material and human resources, skills, and various local traditions. But these differences should not blind us to the fact that the Byzantine, Muslim, and western European worlds were sibling cultures.

Byzantium: A Christian Empire Under Siege

The Byzantine emperor Justinian had tried to re-create the old Roman Empire. On the surface he succeeded. The map of his empire once again included Italy, North Africa, and the Balkans. Vestiges of old Roman society persisted: an educated elite maintained its prestige, town governments continued to function, and old myths and legends were retold in poetry and depicted on silver plates and chests. By the beginning of the seventh century, however, the eastern empire began to undergo a transformation as striking as the one that had earlier remade the western half. From the last third of the sixth century, Byzantium was almost constantly at war, and its territory shrank drastically. Cultural and political change came as well. Cities—except for a few such as Constantinople—decayed, and the countryside became the focus of government and military administration. In the wake of these shifts the old elite largely disappeared, and classical learning gave way to new forms of education, mainly religious in content. The traditional styles of urban life, dependent on public gathering places and community spirit, faded away.

IMPORTANT DATES

c. 570–632 Life of Muhammad, prophet of Islam

590–604 Papacy of Gregory the Great

622 *Hijra* to Medina and beginning of Islamic calendar

657 Queen Balthild, wife of Clovis II, king of the Franks, becomes regent during her son's minority

664 Synod of Whitby; English king opts for Roman Christianity

687 Battle of Tertry; Pippin II becomes mayor of two Frankish kingdoms

726–843 Period of iconoclasm at Byzantium

751–768 Pippin III rules as king of the Franks

Byzantium at War

The state of nearly constant warfare against invaders of the Byzantine Empire persisted from the last third of the sixth century to the middle of the eighth century. To the west Byzantium faced the Lombards, a Germanic people from Pannonia (modern Hungary), some of whom had been used by Justinian's generals in their destructive war against the Ostrogoths in Italy. In 568, pursued by a Turkic people known as the Avars, the Lombards had invaded Italy and pushed back the Byzantines. Byzantium's western foothold shrank severely, although it retained nominal control over a swath of land through the middle of Italy called the Exarchate of Ravenna, of which Rome was a part. Byzantium also kept control of the toe and heel of the Italian boot, the island of Sicily, and Venice. But most of Italy was now out of the eastern emperor's grasp, and he would soon lose more land and power elsewhere.

To the north the Byzantines had to ward off tribal groups attacking from just beyond the Danube. First were the Slavs, who, much like the Germans of earlier centuries, combined sedentary agriculture with raiding expeditions. Lightly armed and fleet, Slavic raiding parties could not breach the Byzantine walled cities of the Balkans, but they easily devastated the countryside, looting and taking prisoners, then riding their swift horses to safety across the Danube River.

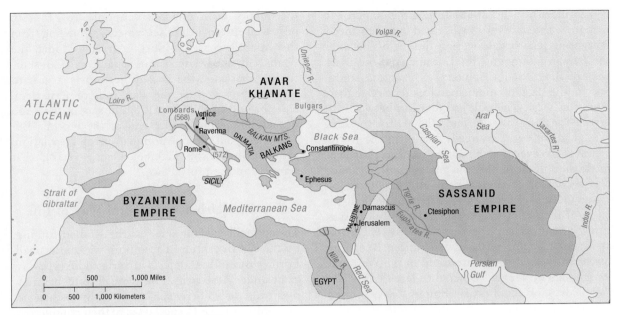

Byzantine and Sassanid Empires, c. 600

Soon, however, the Slavs were joined by the Avars. These nomadic pastoralists and warriors were driven into Europe from the east by rival tribes at their backs, as well as lured by visions of conquest and plunder. Under their ruler, called a *khagan,* the Avars forged a formidable military force. By the 560s they had settled in Pannonia, organizing a state with fixed borders and subjecting local Slavic and Hunnic tribes. From this base, Avar armies, bolstered by their more numerous (if less well organized) tribal allies, besieged the cities in the Balkans. Throughout the last third of the sixth century and into the seventh, they fought the Byzantine forces. They raided mostly on the Dalmatian coast, but sometimes struck down into Greece or marched (and sailed, in small boats) as far as the Bosphorus. In 626, for example, they attacked Constantinople. But here the Avars found a veritable fortress, surrounded by nearly impregnable walls and further defended by the formidable Byzantine fleet. The attack of 626, at least, was foiled.

Meanwhile, Slavs and Avars were penetrating more peacefully—through simple settlement—into the Balkans. Sometimes displacing, more often intermingling with the indigenous population, they absorbed local agricultural techniques and burial practices while imposing their language and religious cults. By 626 the Avars were waning as a fighting force, and their client tribes rebelled against them. Now a new people, the Croats, established themselves in the western Balkans, and another, related group called the Serbs moved a little to the south of what is now Serbia. Both new groups were successful conquerors because they boasted a well-disciplined cavalry, just as the Avars had. However, again like the Avars, they were not very numerous and depended on allied support. The population of the entire Balkan region by the end of the seventh century was mostly Slavic peasantry. The Croats and Serbs soon assimilated with these Slavs, adopting much of their language and culture. By the beginning of the eighth century, the ethnic mix that would eventually form the population of the present-day Balkans had largely been established.

From the Byzantines' point of view the arrival of the Croats and the Serbs and the weakening of Avar power hardly mattered, for Byzantium was attacked in turn by the Bulgars. These originally Turkic people came from the Black Sea region, where after forging a multiethnic federation led by a chief, they had been pushed out (in a familiar pattern) by yet another group. Entering what is now Bulgaria in the 670s, they defeated the

Byzantine army and in 681 forced the emperor to recognize the state they had carved out of formerly Byzantine territory. Covering the region between the Balkan mountains, the Danube, and the Black Sea, the Bulgar state crippled the Byzantines' influence in the Balkans and helped further isolate them from the West. The political division between the Greek-speaking world and the Latin-speaking West had, of course, already begun in the fourth century. The events of the seventh century, however, made the split both physical and cultural. Avar and Slavic control of the Balkans effectively cut off trade and travel between Constantinople and the cities of the Dalmatian coast, and the Bulgar state threw a political barrier across the Danube. Perhaps as a result of this physical separation, Byzantine historians ceased to be interested in the West, and its scholars no longer bothered to learn Latin. The two halves of the Roman Empire, once united, communicated very little in the seventh century.

Byzantium was unsuccessful in the Balkans mostly because it simultaneously had to fight the Persians on its eastern border. The Sassanid Empire was a superpower of the early seventh century (it included the regions known today as Iran and Iraq), and it fought with Byzantium off and on during the late sixth century. War broke out once again in 604, and from then until 620, Persian armies won resounding victories against Byzantines, taking, for example, Damascus in 613, Jerusalem the following year, and Egypt in 619. But Emperor Heraclius reorganized his army and inspired his troops to avenge the sack of Jerusalem, thus turning the tide and regaining all lost territory by 627.

The significance of this period of war lay not in the taking and retaking of territory but in the sapping of both Persian and Byzantine military strength. Exhausted, these empires were now vulnerable to attack by the Arabs, whose military prowess was to create a new empire and spread a new religion, Islam. In the 630s, Arab armies overran Palestine and Jerusalem. In 637 they defeated the Persians at the very gates of their capital, Ctesiphon. During the 640s they invaded North Africa, and by 651 all of Persia was in Muslim hands. Now the two superpowers that faced one another were Byzantine and Arab. For more than two hundred years, from the 640s to the 860s, they remained at war, not always locked in battle but nevertheless continually threatening one another. Each year between 673 and 678, Arab forces attacked the mighty walls of Constantinople. In 718–719, now well entrenched in settlements stretching from the Atlantic coast of North Africa to India, the Arabs launched a ferocious assault on Constantinople that took the Byzantines nearly a year to repulse. No wonder the Patriarch of Jerusalem, chief bishop of the entire Levant, saw in the Arab onslaught the impending end of the world: "Behold," he said, "the Abomination of Desolation, spoken of by the Prophet Daniel [9:27], that standeth in the Holy Place."

From an Urban to a Rural Way of Life

Though still viewing itself as the Roman Empire, by the eighth century, Byzantium was quite small. Former Byzantine subjects in Syria and Egypt now came under Arab sway. For them, despite their new overlords, daily life remained essentially unchanged. Non-Muslims paid a special tax to their conquerors, but they could practice their own religions. In the countryside they were permitted to keep and farm their lands, and their cities remained centers of government, scholarship, and business.

Ironically, the most radical transformations for seventh- and eighth-century Byzantines occurred not in the territories lost but in the shrunken empire itself. Under the ceaseless barrage of war, many towns, formerly bustling nodes of trade and centers of the imperial bureaucratic network, vanished or became unrecognizable in their changed way of life. The public activity of marketplaces, theaters, and town squares gave way to the family table and hearth. City baths, once places where people gossiped, made deals, and talked politics and philosophy, disappeared in most Byzantine towns—with the significant exception of Constantinople. Warfare reduced some cities to rubble, and when they were rebuilt, the limited resources available went to construct thick walls and solid churches instead of marketplaces and baths. Marketplaces moved to overcrowded streets that looked much like the souks of the modern Middle East. People under siege sought protection rather than community pastimes. In the Byzantine city of Ephesus, for example, the citizens who built the new walls in the seventh century did not enclose the old public edifices but rather their homes and churches.

Along with the decline of the cities came a further deterioration in the class of local town

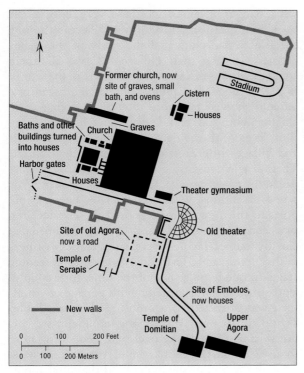

City of Ephesus
The center of classical Ephesus had been the Agora and the Embolos (a wide street, paved with marble and rimmed by shops and monuments). After the seventh century, the city was partially destroyed, its population declined, and the rebuilt city—without Agora or Embolos—was located to the north and protected by walls.

A New Rural Ideal
While incessant wars led to the depopulation of the Byzantine Empire and the decline of its cities, rural life gained importance both in reality and as a pastoral ideal. This mosaic on the floor of the imperial palace at Constantinople, probably made in the seventh century, shows an idyllic view of the farm.

councilors (the *curiales*), the elite that for centuries had mediated between the emperor and the people.* The pressures of war against the Arabs brought a change in Byzantine society parallel to the West a few centuries before, spelling the end of the curial class. But an upper class nevertheless remained: as in the West, bishops and their clergy continued to form a rich and powerful upper stratum even within declining cities.

Indeed, Constantinople and a few other urban centers retained much of their old vitality. Some industry and trade continued, particularly the manufacture of fine silk textiles. These were the prestige items of the time, coveted by enemies as well as friends, and their production and distribution was monitored by the government. In the mid-

sixth century, silkworms from China had been introduced into the empire, relieving Byzantium's dependence on imports of raw silk. State-controlled factories produced the very finest fabrics, which legally could be worn only by the emperor, his court, and his friends. In private factories, merchants, spinners, and weavers turned raw silk into slightly less luxurious cloth for both internal consumption and foreign trade. Even though Byzantium's economic life became rural and barter-based in the seventh and eighth centuries, the skills, knowledge, and institutions of urban workers made long-distance trade and the domestic manufacture of luxury goods possible. The full use of these resources, however, had to await the end of centuries of debilitating wars.

As urban life declined, agriculture, always the basis of the Byzantine economy, became the center of its social life as well. But unlike the West, where an extremely rich and powerful elite dominated the agricultural economy, the Byzantine Empire of the seventh century was predominantly a realm of free and semifree peasant farmers. On their small plots of land they grew food, herded cattle, and tended vineyards. In the shadow of decaying urban cen-

---

*See Chapter 7.

ters, the social world of the farmer was narrow. "If two farmers agree one with the other before two or three witnesses to exchange land," says the legal compilation called the Farmers' Law, "let their determination and their exchange remain firm and secure and unassailable." Two or three neighbors were enough to ratify a land transfer. Farmers interacted mostly with their families or with monasteries. The buffer once provided by the curial class was gone; these families now felt the impact of imperial rule directly. In turn, the emperors of the seventh and eighth centuries tried to give ordinary family life new institutional importance. Imperial legislation narrowed the grounds for divorce and set new punishments for marital infidelity. Husbands who committed adultery were whipped and fined, and their noses were slit. Female adulterers suffered a similar penalty. Abortion was prohibited, and new protections were set in place against incest with children. Mothers were given equal power with fathers over their offspring and, if widowed, became the legal guardians of their minor children and controlled the household property.

New Military and Cultural Forms

The transformations of the countryside went hand in hand with political, military, and cultural reforms. Determined to win wars on many fronts, the imperial government exercised greater autocratic control, abetting the decline of the curial class, wresting power from other elite families, and encouraging the formation of a middle class of farmer-soldiers. In the seventh century an emperor, possibly Heraclius, divided the empire into military districts called *themes* and put all civil matters there into the hands of generals, *strategoi* (singular, *strategos*). Landless men were lured to join the army with the promise of land and low taxes; they fought side by side with indigenous farmers, who provided their own weapons and horses. The *strategoi*, who received no land but rather a handsome salary and the promise of a hefty share of any booty, not only led the local troops into battle but also served as the emperor's regional tax collectors. The *strategoi* soon became the vanguard of a new elite and began to dominate the rural scene. Nevertheless, between about 650 and 800 the reorganization of the countryside worked to the peasants' advantage.

The military and social changes brought about by the new network of *themes* went hand in hand

with changes in values; and these were reflected, in turn, in education and culture. Whereas the old curial elite had cultivated the study of the pagan classics, sending their children (above all, their sons) to schools or tutors to learn to read the works of Greek poets and philosophers, eighth-century parents showed far more interest in giving their children, both sons and daughters, a religious education. Even with the decay of urban centers, cities and villages often retained an elementary school. There teachers used the *Psalter* (a book of poems, called the *Psalms*, in the Bible) as their primer. With a few exceptions, which would later become important, this new culture ignored the classics. For two centuries, secular, classical learning remained decidedly out of favor, whereas dogmatic writings, saints' lives, and devotional works took center stage. In one popular tale of the time, for example, a prostitute arriving at an inn with a group of young men was attracted to a monk reading the Bible. "Unfortunate one, you are very impudent; are you not ashamed of coming over here and sitting next to us?" asked the monk. "No, Father . . . I have hope in the Son of the living God that after today I shall not remain in sin," replied the penitent woman. Thereupon she followed the monk and entered a monastery for women.

Religion and Politics: The Clergy and Iconoclasm

The importance placed on religious learning and piety complemented both the autocratic imperial ideal and the powers of the bishops in the seventh century. While the bishops consolidated their positions as the elite of the cities, Byzantine emperors ruled as religious as well as political figures. In theory, imperial and church power were separate but interdependent. In fact, the emperor functioned as the head of the church hierarchy, appointing the chief prelate, the patriarch of Constantinople; formulating Christian doctrine; calling church councils to determine dogma; and setting out the criteria for bishops to be ordained. Beginning with Heraclius, the emperors considered it one of their duties to baptize Jews forcibly, persecuting those who would not convert. In the view of the imperial court, this was part of the ruler's role in upholding orthodoxy.

Bishops functioned as state administrators, not in spite of being churchmen but rather because the spiritual and secular realms were understood to be inseparable. Bishops acted as judges and tax collectors. They distributed food in times of famine or siege, provisioned troops, and set up military fortifications. As part of their charitable work, they cared for the sick and the needy. Byzantine bishops were part of a three-tier system: they were appointed by "metropolitans," bishops who headed up an entire province; and these metropolitans, in turn, were appointed by the patriarchs, bishops with authority over whole regions. Theoretically, monasteries were under limited control by the local bishop, but in fact they were enormously powerful institutions that often defied episcopal and even imperial authority. Because monks commanded immense prestige as the holiest of God's faithful, they could influence the many issues of church doctrine that wracked the Byzantine church.

The most important of these issues revolved around icons. Icons were images of holy people—Christ, the Virgin, saints—that were far more than mere representations to Byzantine Christians. Icons were believed to be infused with holy power that directly affected people's daily life as well as their chances for salvation.

Many seventh-century Byzantines made icons the focus of their religious devotion. To them, icons were like the incarnation of Christ; they turned spirit into material substance. Thus, the icon manifested in physical form the holy person whom it depicted. Some Byzantines actually worshiped icons; others, particularly monks, considered icons a necessary part of Christian piety. As the monk St. John of Damascus put it in a vigorous defense of holy images, "I do not worship matter, I worship the God of matter, who became matter for my sake, and deigned to inhabit matter, who worked out my salvation through matter."

But other Byzantines abhorred icons. Most numerous of these were the soldiers on the frontiers, who were shocked by Arab triumphs. They found the cause of their misfortunes in the Biblical injunction against graven images. When they compared their defeats to Muslim successes, they could not help but notice that Islam prohibited all representations of the divine. To these soldiers and others who shared their view, icons revived pagan idolatry and desecrated Christian divinity. As iconoclastic (anti-icon or, literally, icon-breaking) feeling grew, some churchmen became vociferous in their opposition to icons. As one church council

of 754 put the issue, "What avails, then, the folly of the painter who from sinful love of gain depicts that which should not be depicted—that is, with his polluted hands he tries to fashion that which should only be believed in the heart and confessed with the mouth."

Byzantine emperors shared these religious objections, but they also had important political reasons for distrusting icons. First, they were anxious to support their troops in every way. Second, icons diffused loyalties, setting up intermediaries between worshipers and God that undermined the emperor's exclusive place in the divine and temporal order. Third, the emphasis on icons in monastic communities made the monks potential threats to imperial power; the emperors hoped to use this issue to break the power of the monasteries. Fourth, some churchmen had begun to question the emperor's right to interfere in religious affairs. Thus the issue of icons became a test case of imperial authority.

The controversy climaxed in 726, after Emperor Leo III the Isaurian (*717–741) had defeated the Arabs besieging Constantinople in 717 and 718 and turned his attention to consolidating his political position. In the wake of the victory, officers of the imperial court tore down the great golden icon of Christ at the gateway of the palace and replaced it with a cross. In protest, a crowd of iconodule (literally, icon-worshipping) women went on a furious rampage. This event marked the beginning of the period of iconoclasm (icon-smashing); soon afterward, Leo ordered all icons destroyed, a ban that remained in effect, despite much opposition, until 787. A modified ban would be revived in 815 and last until 843.

Iconoclasm had an enormous impact on daily life. At home, where people had their own portable icons, it forced changes in private worship: the devout had to destroy their icons or worship them in secret. Iconoclasm meant ferocious attacks on the monasteries: splendid collections of holy images were destroyed; vast properties were confiscated; and monks were ordered to marry. In this way iconoclasm destroyed communities that might otherwise have served as centers of resistance to imperial power.

Wracked by wars, its cities devastated, its frontiers shrunk, its dominance over the Christian church challenged, Byzantium experienced hard times in the seventh and eighth centuries. But it proved resilient. Building on its inheritance of administrative skills, land resources, and control over religious symbols and the hierarchy of the Christian church, the Byzantine state adapted to changing circumstances. The new *theme* organization in the countryside effectively countered frontier attacks. The Byzantine cavalry, clad in heavy iron—the "boiler boys" (*cataphracts*)—were the human equivalent of modern tanks and could easily mow down less well-armed enemy soldiers. And "Greek fire," invented in the seventh century, proved an ingenious and deadly weapon. It was a combustible oil, shot through tubes or sprayed from a pump, that burst into flames upon hitting its target. Greek fire was especially effective against ships, since the burning oil floated on water. Its creation was part of the general reorganization and reorientation of Byzantine institutions that allowed the state to survive against the Arab onslaught under the banner of Islam.

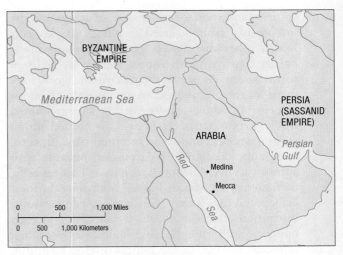

Arabia in Muhammad's Lifetime

Islam: A New Religion and a New Empire

Islam, meaning "submission" to the will of God, is the religion of people who call themselves Muslims. Its roots are in the same soil as Christianity and Judaism: the Fertile Crescent and the Iranian hinterland. Indeed the Muslims' God is the God of Abraham, Moses, and Jesus. Emerging in seventh-century western Arabia (today Saudi Arabia), in the shadow of Persian and Byzantine culture, Islam thrived initially among nomadic herding peoples. Their world contained few cities and placed little emphasis on the political and cultural institutions of a polis-centered life. Whereas Greco-Roman civilization rimmed the Mediterranean Sea, Arabian life was based inland, in the desert, where water was the very source of life: "The heavens and the earth were an integrated mass, then We split them and made every living thing from water," says God in the Qur'an,* the Holy Recitation that serves

---
*Older books use *Koran*, but the new standardized transliteration of Arabic worked out by Islamicists dictates a different spelling.

Muslims much as the Bible does Christians and Jews.

Yet much of the Greco-Roman heritage would become grafted irrevocably onto Islamic culture. First, and perhaps most important, was that the Muslim conquerors allowed older monotheistic religions to persist in their new empire. This was particularly important to groups espousing forms of Christianity not considered orthodox by Byzantine emperors. For example, Monophysite Christians, who believed Christ's nature wholly divine—not both divine and human—constituted a large part of the population of Syria, Egypt, and northern Iraq. Under Byzantine rule they had suffered forced conversions and savage persecutions. People such as these welcomed Muslim overlords. Second, the Arabs soon became used to a settled existence, initially in garrison towns separate from the cities of the ancient world but then gradually in urban centers resembling those that had flourished before their conquest. Finally, Muslims absorbed into their ranks members of the native population who converted to Islam, and at the same time they adopted many of the traditions of the ancient world, above all its literary, philosophical, and scientific heritage.

Bedouin Tribal Society

Pre-Islamic Arabia became aware of wider currents through contact with the Persians and Byzantines, who in their wars against one another employed Arab tribesmen as mercenaries and encouraged border tribes to organize buffer states. Elsewhere in Arabia, Romanized Jews and Monophysites, refugees from Byzantine persecution, settled in town-oases alongside native populations. But most Arabs did not have sustained, regular contact with these refugees. Most were Bedouins who lived in tribes—loose confederations of clans, or kin-groups—that herded flocks for meat and milk and traded (or raided) for grain, dates, and slaves. Poor Bedouin tribes herded sheep, whereas richer ones kept camels—extremely hardy animals, splendid beasts of burden, and good producers of milk and meat. (The word *Arab* was the name camel nomads called themselves.)

Tribal, nomadic existence produced its own culture, including a common language of extraordinary delicacy, precision, and beauty. In the absence of written language, the Bedouins used poetry and story-telling to transmit their traditions, simultaneously entertaining, reaffirming values, and teaching new generations.

Modern Bedouins

There are still Bedouins in the modern Middle East, as in Muhammad's time. They live as nomads, in small groups, with their belongings carried by camels.

Even in town-oases, where permanent settlements arose, the clan was the key social institution and focus of loyalties. Clans grouped together in tribes, their makeup shifting as kin-groups joined or left. These associations, however changing, nevertheless saw outsiders as rivals, and tribes constantly fought with one another. Yet clan rivalry was itself an outgrowth of the values the various tribes shared. Bedouin men prized "manliness," which meant far more than sexual prowess. They wanted to be brave in battle and feared being shamed. Manliness also entailed an obligation to be generous, to give away the booty that was the goal of intertribal warfare. Women were often part of this booty; a counterpart to Bedouin manliness was therefore the practice of polygyny (having more than one wife at the same time). Bedouin wars rarely involved much bloodshed; their main purpose was to capture and take belongings. It was not much of a step from this booty-gathering to trading and from there to the establishment of commercial centers.

Although historians once thought Mecca, the birthplace of Muhammad and therefore of Islam, served as a commercial center for the eastern luxury trade with the Byzantine Empire, recent reviews of the evidence cast doubt on this view. Nevertheless, Mecca did play a commercial role. Meccan caravans, for example, were organized to sell Bedouin products—mainly leather goods and raisins—to more urbanized areas in the north, at the border between Arabia and Syria. More important, Mecca had for centuries been one of the foci of Bedouin life because it contained a shrine, the Ka'ba. Long before Muhammad was born, the Ka'ba, hedged about with 360 idols, served as a sacred place within which war and violence were prohibited. The tribe that dominated Mecca, the Quraysh, controlled access to the shrine and was able to tax the pilgrims who flocked there as well as sell them food and drink. In turn, plunder was transformed into trade as the visitors bartered with one another on the sacred grounds, assured of their security.

The Prophet Muhammad and Islamic Society

Thus Muhammad was born (c. 570) in a center with two important achievements—one religious, the other commercial. His early years were inauspicious: orphaned by the age of six, he spent two years with his grandfather and then came under the care of his uncle, a leader of the Quraysh tribe. Eventually, Muhammad became a trader. At the age of twenty-five, he married Khadija, a rich widow much older than he. They had at least four daughters and lived (to all appearances) happily and comfortably. Yet Muhammad would sometimes leave home and spend a few days in a nearby cave in prayer and contemplation, reflecting a model of piety that had also inspired early Christians.

Then beginning in 610 and continuing until he died in 632, Muhammad heard a voice speaking what he came to identify as the words of God (Allah means "the God" in Arabic). "Recite!" began the voice, and to Muhammad it entrusted a special mission: to speak God's words, to live by them, eventually to preach them, and to convert others to follow them. The holy book of Islam, the Qur'an, means "recitation"; each of the verses, or *suras*, are understood to be God's revelation as told to Muhammad, then recited in turn by Muhammad to a scribe who wrote them down word for word. The first revelations emphasized the greatness, mercy, and goodness of God; the obligations of the rich to the poor; and the certainty of Judgment Day. In time they covered the gamut of human experience and the life to come; for the Muslim the Qur'an contained the sum total of history, prophecy, and the legal and moral code by which men and women should live: "Do not set up another god with God, ... Do not worship anyone but Him, and be good to your parents.... Give to your relatives what is their due, and to those who are needy, and the wayfarers."

The Qur'an emphasized the nuclear family— a man, his wife, and children—as the basic unit of Muslim society. It cut the tribespeople adrift from the protection and particularism of the tribe but gave them in return an identity as part of the *ummah*, the community of believers, who shared both a belief in one God and a set of religious practices. Islam depended entirely on individual belief and adherence to the Qur'an. Muslims had no priests, no mass, no intermediaries between the divine and the individual. Instead, Islam stressed the relationship between the individual and God, a relationship characterized by gratitude to and worship of God, by the promise of reward or punishment on Judgment Day "when the sky is cleft

The Image of Mecca
In this sixteenth-century depiction of Mecca, the Ka'ba is in the center. The lines, like spokes in a wheel, connect to the names of the Islamic countries.

asunder"; and by exhortations to human kindness: "Do not oppress the orphan,/And do not drive the beggar away." The Ka'ba, with its many idols, had gathered together tribes from the surrounding vicinity. Muhammad, with his one God, forged an even more ecumenical religion.

The first to convert was Muhammad's wife and then a few friends and members of his immediate family. Discontented young men, often eluded by commercial success, joined his converts, as did some wealthy merchants. Soon, however, the new faith polarized Meccan society. Muhammad's insistence that all other cults be abandoned brought him into conflict with leading clan members of the Quraysh tribe, who found their own positions of leadership and livelihood threatened. Lacking political means to expel him, they insulted Muhammad and harassed his adherents.

Disillusioned with his own tribe and with Mecca, where he had failed to make much of an impact, Muhammad tried to find a place and a population receptive to his message. Most important, he expected support from Jews, whose monotheism (he thought) prepared them for his own faith. When a few of Muhammad's converts

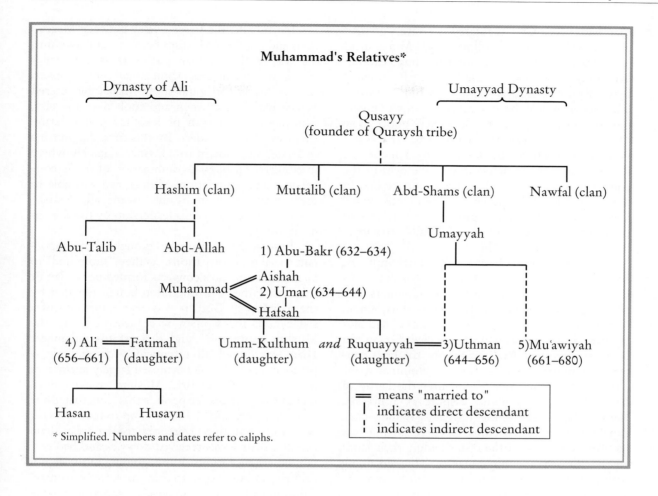

Muhammad's Relatives*

Dynasty of Ali

Umayyad Dynasty

Qusayy
(founder of Quraysh tribe)

Hashim (clan)   Muttalib (clan)   Abd-Shams (clan)   Nawfal (clan)

Umayyah

Abu-Talib   Abd-Allah   1) Abu-Bakr (632–634)

Muhammad ⟨ Aishah
2) Umar (634–644)
Hafsah

4) Ali ══ Fatimah   Umm-Kulthum   *and* Ruquayyah ══ 3)Uthman   5)Mu'awiyah
(656–661) (daughter)   (daughter)   (daughter)   (644–656)   (661–680)

Hasan   Husayn

═══ means "married to"
| indicates direct descendant
⋮ indicates indirect descendant

* Simplified. Numbers and dates refer to caliphs.

from Medina promised to protect him if he would join them, he eagerly accepted the invitation, largely because Medina had a significant Jewish population. In 622 Muhammad made the *Hijra*, or emigration, to Medina, an oasis about two hundred miles northeast of Mecca. This journey proved a crucial event for the fledgling movement. At Medina, Muhammad found followers ready not only to listen to his religious message but also to regard him as the leader of their community. They expected him, for example, to act as a neutral and impartial judge in their interclan disputes. Muhammad's political position in the community set the pattern by which Islamic society would be governed afterward; rather than add a church to political and cultural life, as the Romans had done with Christianity, the Muslims made their political and religious institutions inseparable. After Muham-

mad's death the *Hijra* was named the first year of the Islamic calendar; it marked the beginning of the new Islamic era.[†]

At Medina, Muhammad established the *ummah*, a single community distinct from other people. But the Muslims were not content to confine themselves to a minor outpost at Medina. Above all, it was essential for the success of the new religion to control Mecca, still a potent holy place. Muhammad's following was not large enough to launch a direct siege on the city, so he first attacked Meccan caravans that were going to and from Syria. The Muslims no longer felt bound by the etiquette

---

[†]Thus 1 A.H. (1 *Anno Hegirae*) on the Muslim calendar is equivalent to A.D. 622 (*Anno Domini* 622) on the Christian calendar.

that had previously regulated warfare and had emphasized raiding over killing. In 624 Muhammad led a small contingent to ambush a huge caravan brimming with goods; at the battle of Badr, aided by their position near an oasis, he and his followers killed forty-nine of the Meccan enemy, took numerous prisoners, and confiscated rich booty. The Qur'an commentary on the battle was, "It was not you who killed them, but God did so. You did not throw what you threw (sand into the eyes of the enemy at Badr), but God, to bring out the best in the faithful by doing them a favor of His own." Thus traditional Bedouin plundering was grafted on to the Muslim duty of *jihad* (literally "striving," but often translated as "holy war").

The battle of Badr was a great triumph for Muhammad, who was now able to consolidate his position at Medina, gaining new adherents and silencing all doubters. The Jews at Medina, whom Muhammad had at first seen as allies, had not converted to Islam as he had expected. Organized by clans, like their Arab neighbors, the Jews controlled important date groves and dominated the city's trades and crafts. Right after the battle of Badr, seizing on a minor dispute as a pretext, Muhammad attacked the Jewish Qaynuqa clan, expelling them from Medina. In the following year he drove out most of the rest, dividing their lands among himself and his converts. The remaining Jewish men were eventually executed, and the women and children sold into slavery.

At the same time Muhammad broke with the Jews, he distanced himself from Judaism and instituted new practices to define Islam as a unique religion. Among these were the *zakat*, a tax on possessions to be used for alms; the fast of Ramadan, which took place during the month in which the battle at Badr had been fought; the *hajj*, a yearly pilgrimage to Mecca; and the *salat*, formal worship at least three times a day (later increased to five), which could include the *shahadah*, or profession of faith: "there is no divinity but God, and Muhammad is the messenger of God." Emphasizing his repudiation of Jewish traditions, Muhammad now had the Muslims turn their prayers away from Jerusalem, home of the Jews, toward Mecca and the Ka'ba. Detailed regulations for these practices, sometimes called the "five pillars of Islam," were worked out in the eighth and early ninth centuries.

Meanwhile, the fierce rivalry between Mecca's clans and Medina's Muslims began to spill over into the rest of the Arabian peninsula as both sides strove to win converts. Muhammad sent troops to subdue Arabs north and south. In 630 he entered Mecca with 10,000 men and took over the city, assuring the Quraysh of leniency and offering alliances with its leaders. By this time the prestige of Islam was enough to convince clans elsewhere to convert. Through a combination of force, conversion, and negotiation, Muhammad was able to unite many, though by no means all, Arabic-speaking tribes under his leadership by the time of his death in 632.

In so doing, Muhammad brought about important social transformations. As they "submitted" to Islam, Muhammad's converts formed not a clan or tribe but rather a brotherhood bound together by the worship of God. It was also something of a sisterhood, for women were accepted into the Muslim community and their status enhanced. Islam prohibited all infanticide, for example, a practice that had long been used largely against female infants; and at first, Muslim women joined men during the prayer periods that punctuated the day. Men were allowed to have up to four wives at one time, but they were obliged to treat them equally; their wives received dowries and had certain inheritance rights. But beginning in the eighth century, women began to pray apart from the men. Adopting a symbol of upper-class superiority—the veil worn by noble Byzantine women to separate them symbolically from humbler folk—Muslim women veiled themselves as a symbol of their separation from the public, male world. Like Judaism and Christianity, Islam retained the practices of a patriarchal society in which women's participation in community life was circumscribed.

Even though Islamic society was a new sort of community, in many ways it functioned as a tribe or rather a "supertribe," obligated to fight common enemies, share plunder, and resolve peacefully any internal disputes. Muslims participated in group rituals, such as the *salat* and public recitation. The Qur'an was soon publicly sung by professional reciters, much as the old tribal poetry had been. Most significantly for the eventual spread of Islam, Muslim men continued to be warriors. They took up where Meccan traders had been forced to leave off; along the routes once taken by caravans to Syria, their armies reaped profits at the point of a sword. But this differed from intertribal fighting; it was the "striving" of people carrying out the injunction of God against unbelievers. "Strive, O Prophet," says the Qur'an, "against the unbelievers and the hypocrites, and deal with them firmly. Their final abode is Hell: And what a wretched destination!"

Muhammad's successors commanded a force to reckon with: fully armed, on horseback, and employing camels as convoys, they stormed the Near East, already weakened by war. In the 630s and 640s alone, they invaded the areas that today comprise Iran and Iraq (both part of the Sassanid Empire) and Syria and Egypt (held by the Byzantines). Where they conquered, the Muslims built garrison cities from which soldiers requisitioned taxes and goods. Sometimes whole Arab tribes, including women and children, were imported to settle conquered territory, as happened in parts of Syria. In other regions, such as Egypt, a small Muslim settlement at Fustat sufficed to gather the spoils of conquest.

Muhammad's Successors

In founding a new political community in Arabia, Muhammad reorganized traditional Arab society as he cut across clan allegiances and welcomed converts from every tribe. His political power in this community of believers was far greater than that of any former tribal chief, for Muslims believed Muhammad to be the chosen prophet of God, the source of law. Around him formed a new elite, based not so much on ties of kinship or the traditional virtues of manliness, but rather on closeness to Muhammad and participation in his movement's crucial events, above all the *Hijra*. His was a personal government, and it did not outlive him. His successors needed other models to rule the vast territories they conquered, and so they adapted the machinery of government of the Byzantines and, later, the Persians. In so doing, the Muslims further sank their roots into the soil of the Roman Empire and became one of its heirs.

The death of Muhammad marked a crisis in the government of the new state. The *caliphs* (literally "successors") who followed Muhammad did not

assume authority without dispute. The first four caliphs came from the new elite, the Muslims in the prophet's inner circle, but each of them had to face opposition from other would-be leaders and their supporters. Abu-Bakr (*632–634), the first caliph, was Muhammad's father-in-law, as was Umar (*634–644), who was largely responsible for the policies that encouraged Islamic expansion and its new administrative and political order.

The third caliph, Uthman (*644–656), was a member of the Umayyad family and son-in-law (by marriage with two daughters) of Muhammad; but his position aroused jealousy among other clan members of the "inner circle." Growing discontent—in part based on enmities dating back to the days at Mecca, partly on the new circumstances of conquest, and partly on different religious sensibilities—exploded in bloodshed and rioting. Uthman championed Meccan tradesmen; but Muslim soldiers were unhappy with his distribution of high offices and revenues, accusing him of favoritism and injustice. They looked to Ali—a member of the Hashim clan (to which Muhammad had belonged) and also (like Uthman) Muhammad's son-in-law—to put things right.

In 656 Uthman was murdered by a group of these discontented soldiers, and civil war broke out between the followers of Ali and the supporters of Mu'awiyah, leader of the Umayyad family. For a short time Ali was recognized as caliph in nearly all regions; but on the brink of defeat by Mu'awiyah, he was assassinated by one of his erstwhile supporters. Although some of Ali's followers elevated his son Hasan to the caliphate, Hasan negotiated with Mu'awiyah a graceful retirement for himself. The caliphate was now (661) in Umayyad hands.

Nevertheless, the *Shi'at Ali*, the followers of Ali, did not fade away. Ali's memory lived on among groups of Muslims (the *Shi'ites*) who saw in him a symbol of justice and righteousness. For them Ali's death was the martyrdom of the only true successor to Muhammad. They remained faithful to his dynasty, shunning the "mainstream" caliphs of the other Muslims (*Sunni* Muslims, as they were later called). The Shi'ites awaited the arrival of the true leader—the *imam*—who in their view could come only from the house of Ali and his wife (daughter of Muhammad) Fatimah. The enmity between Shi'ite and Sunni Muslims, based on this dispute over the legitimacy of Muhammad's successors, continues even today.

Under the Umayyads the Muslim world became a state with its capital at Damascus, today the capital of Syria. Borrowing from the institutions well known to the civilizations they had just conquered, the Arabs issued coins and hired former Byzantine and Persian officials. They made Arabic a tool of centralization, imposing it as the language of government on regions not previously united linguistically. Taxes poured into Damascus, and military expeditions continued. Muslim armies, still predominantly Arab, took all of North Africa between 643 and 711, and troops then crossed the Strait of Gibraltar northward into Spain, conquering most of the Visigothic Kingdom by 718. At the same time, other armies marched east, taking the Indus valley (today Pakistan) between 710 and 713. Their thrust eastward was stopped only in 751, in a defeat by Chinese forces, just beyond the Jaxartes River (today the Syr Darya River) southeast of the Aral Sea; in the west their farthest reach brought them almost to the banks of the Loire in France. Constantinople, almost alone among the cities under attack, held fast against its Arab besiegers. For Byzantium this period was one of unparalleled military crisis, the prelude to iconoclasm. For the Muslim world, now a multiethnic society of Muslim Arabs, Syrians, Egyptians, Iraqis, and so on, it was a period of settlement, new urbanism, and literary and artistic flowering.

Yet the question of Islamic government was not settled. In 750 a civil war brought a new dynasty—the Abbasids—to the caliphate. The Abbasids found support in an uneasy coalition of Shi'ites and non-Arabs who had been excluded from Umayyad government and now demanded a place in political life. The new regime signaled a revolution. The center of the Islamic state shifted

Arab Coin
The Arabs learned coinage and minting from those whom they conquered. This silver dirham *from the seventh century is based on a Byzantine model; the word* dirham *is derived from the Greek* drachma.

Expansion of Islam to 750

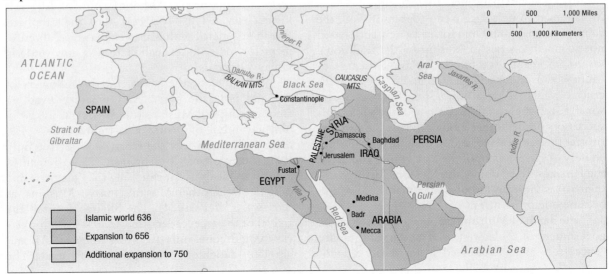

Umayyad Mosque
The mosaics in this mosque, built at Damascus in the eighth century, adopted classical motifs.

from Damascus, with its roots in the Roman tradition, to Baghdad, a new capital city built by the Abbasids in the heart of Persian culture. Here the Abbasid caliphs imitated the Persian King of Kings and adopted the court ceremony of oriental potentates. Administration grew increasingly centralized: the caliph controlled the appointment of regional governors; his staff grew, and their jobs became more complex. Although some Shi'ites were reconciled to this new regime, others, a minority, continued to tend the flame of Ali's memory—and the justice and purity it stood for.

Peace and Prosperity in Islamic Lands

Ironically, the Arab conquerors brought peace. While the conquerors stayed within their fortified cities or built magnificent hunting lodges in the deserts of Syria, the conquered went back to work, to study, to play, or (in the case of Christians and Jews, who were considered "protected subjects," *dhimmis*) to worship as they pleased. At Damascus, local artists and craftspeople worked on the lavish decorations for a mosque in a neoclassic style at the

very moment Muslim armies were storming the walls of Constantinople. Here too, St. John of Damascus inherited from his Christian father the job of financial officer for the new Arab government. Leaving the Byzantine institutions in place, the Muslim conquerors allowed Christians and Jews to retain their posts and even protected dissidents. In the 730s, for example, safe under Muslim rulers, John wrote treatises against the Byzantine imperial iconoclastic decrees. No one at Constantinople could have acted with such impunity. John later retired to a monastery near Jerusalem to live the quiet life of an ascetic and write poetry and prose.

During the seventh and eight centuries, Muslim scholars wrote down the hitherto largely oral Arabic literature. They determined the definitive form for the Qur'an and compiled pious "reports" about the Prophet (*hadith* literature). Scribes composed these works in exquisite handwriting; Arab calligraphy became an art form. A new literate class, composed mainly of the old Persian and Syrian elite now converted to Islam and schooled in Arabic, created new forms of prose writing, from official documents to essays on topics ranging from hunting to ruling. Umayyad poetry explored new worlds of thought and feeling. Patronized by the caliphs, who found in poetry an important source of propaganda and a buttress for their power, the poets also found a wider audience that delighted in their clever use of words, their satire, and their invocations of courage, piety, and sometimes erotic love:

I spent the night as her bed-companion,
    each enamoured of the other,
And I made her laugh and cry, and stripped
    her of her clothes.
I played with her and she vanquished me; I
    made her happy and I angered her.
That was a night we spent, in my sleep,
    playing and joyful,
But the caller to prayer woke me up. . . .

Such poetry scandalized conservative Muslims, brought up on the ascetic world-denying tenets of the Qur'an. But this love poetry was a product of the new urban civilization of the Umayyad period, where wealth, cultural mix, and the confidence born of conquest inspired diverse and experimental literary forms.

The Arabs, who at best had lived in the shadow of Roman civilization, exploded into Western civilization in the seventh century under the impetus of their inspired religious and military leader, Muhammad. Their armies conquered peoples and states from the Jaxartes River in the east to the Pyrenees in Spain. Although the Arabs were originally nomadic Bedouins, they quickly assimilated many aspects of the cultures they conquered. By the end of the Umayyad period, Islamic civilization was multiethnic, urban, and sophisticated, a true heir of Roman and Persian traditions.

The Western Kingdoms

With the demise of Roman imperial government in the West, the primary institutions providing power and stability in Europe were kinship networks, church patronage, royal courts, and wealth derived from land and plunder. In contrast to Byzantium, where an emperor still ruled as the successor to Augustus and Constantine, drawing upon an unbroken chain of Roman legal and administrative traditions, political power in the West was more

diffuse. Churchmen and rich magnates, sometimes one and the same men, held sway. Power derived as well from membership in royal dynasties, such as that of the Merovingian kings, who traced their ancestry back to a sea monster whose magic ensured the fertility and good fortune of the Franks. Finally, people believed power lodged in the tombs and relics of saints, who represented and wielded the divine forces of God. Although the patterns of daily life and the procedures of government in the West remained recognizably Roman, they were also in the process of change, borrowing from and adapting local traditions. In its merging of cultures, Europe resembled the Islamic world.

Frankish Kingdoms with Roman Roots

The Franks had established themselves as dominant in Gaul during the sixth century, and by the seventh century the limits of their Merovingian kingdoms roughly approximated the eastern borders of present-day France, Belgium, the Netherlands, and Luxembourg. Moreover, the Merovingian kings had subjugated many of the peoples beyond the Rhine, foreshadowing the contours of modern Germany. Although the little-Romanized northern and eastern regions were important to the Frankish kingdoms, the core of these kingdoms was Roman Gaul; and their inhabitants lived with the vestiges of Rome at their very door.

Travelers making a trip to Paris in the seventh century, perhaps on a pilgrimage to the tomb of St. Denis, for example, would probably rely on river travel, even though some Roman roads would still be in fair repair. (They would prefer water routes because land travel was very slow and because even large groups of travelers on the roads were vulnerable to attacks by robbers.) Like the roads, other structures in the landscape would seem familiarly Roman. Coming up the Rhône from the south, voyagers would pass Roman amphitheaters and farmlands neatly and squarely laid out as they had been by Roman land surveyors. The great stone palaces of villas would still dot the countryside.

What would be missing, if the travelers were very observant, would be thriving cities. Hulks of cities remained, of course, and they served as the centers of church administration; but gradually during the late Roman period, many urban centers had lost their commercial and cultural vitality. Depopulated, many survived as mere skeletons,

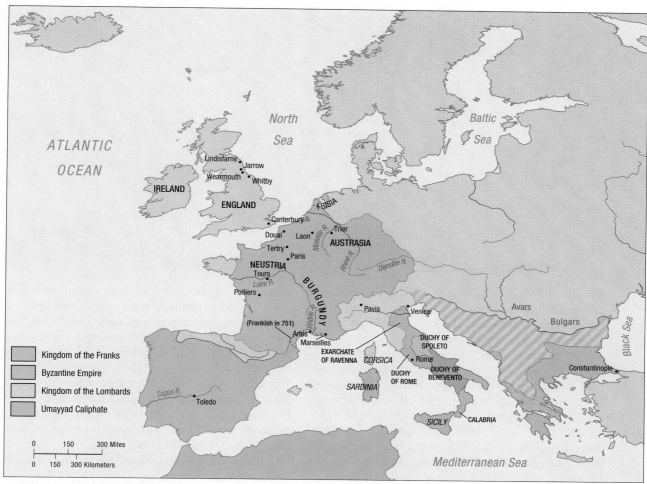

Europe in the Eighth Century

with the exception of such thriving commercial centers as Arles and Marseilles. Moreover, if the travelers were to approach Paris from the northeast, they would pass through dense, nearly untouched forests as well as land more often used as pasture for animals than for cereal cultivation. These areas would not have been much influenced by Romans, and they would represent far more the farming and village settlement patterns of the Franks. Yet even on the northern and eastern fringes of the Merovingian kingdoms some structures of the Roman Empire remained. Fortresses were still standing at Trier (near Bonn, Germany, today), and great stone villas, such as the one excavated by archaeologists near Douai (today in France, near the Belgian border), loomed over the more humble wooden dwellings of the countryside.

In the south, gangs of slaves still might occasionally be found cultivating the extensive lands of wealthy estate owners, as they had done since late Republican times. Scattered here and there, independent peasants worked their own small plots as they, too, had done for centuries. But for the most part, seventh-century travelers would find semifree peasant families settled on little holdings, their *manses*—including a house, a garden, and cultivable land—for which they paid dues and owed labor services to a landowner. Some of these peasants were descendants of the *coloni* (tenant farmers) of the late Roman Empire; others were the sons and daughters of slaves, now provided with a small plot of land; and a few were

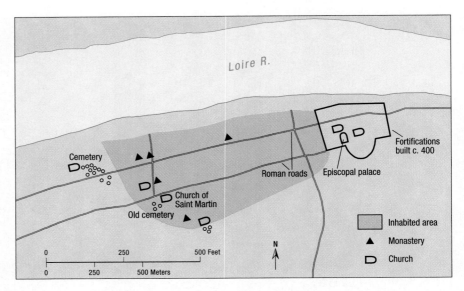

Tours, c. 600

people of free Frankish origin who for various reasons had come down in the world. At the lower end of the social scale, the status of Franks and Romans had become identical.

At the upper end of the social scale, Romans (or more precisely, Gallo-Romans) and Franks had also merged. Although people south of the Loire River continued to be called Romans and people to the north Franks, their cultures were strikingly similar: they shared language, settlement patterns, and religious sensibilities. There were many dialects in the Frankish kingdoms in the seventh century, but most were derived from Latin, though no longer the Latin of Cicero. "Though my speech is rude," Gregory, bishop of Tours (*c. 573–c. 594), wrote at the end of the sixth century,

> I have been unable to be silent as to the struggles between the wicked and the upright; and I have been especially encouraged because, to my surprise, it has often been said by men of our day, that few understand the learned words of the rhetorician but many the rude language of the common people.

Thus Gregory began his *Histories,* a precious source for the Merovingian period. He was trying to evoke the sympathies of his readers, a traditional Roman rhetorical device; but he also expected that his "rude" Latin—the plain Latin of everyday speech—would be understood and welcomed by the general public.

Whereas the Gallo-Roman aristocrat of the fourth and fifth centuries had lived with his *familia*—his wife, children, slaves, and servants—in isolated villas, aristocrats of the seventh century lived in more populous settlements: in small villages surrounded by the huts of peasants, shepherds, and artisans. The early medieval village, constructed mostly out of wood or baked clay, was generally built near a waterway or forest for protection, or around churches (for the same purpose). Intensely local in interests and outlook, the people in the Frankish kingdoms of the seventh and eighth centuries clustered in small groups next to protectors, whether rich men or saints.

Tours—the city in which Gregory, the historian of plain speech, was bishop—exemplified this new-style settlement. Once a Roman city, Tours's main focus was now outside the city walls, where a church had been built. The population of the surrounding countryside was pulled to this church as if to a magnet, for it housed the remains of the most important and venerated person in the locale: St. Martin. This saint, a fourth-century soldier-turned-monk, was long dead, but his relics—his bones, teeth, hair, and clothes—remained at Tours, where he had served as bishop. There, in the succeeding centuries, he remained a supernatural force: a protector, healer, and avenger through whom God manifested divine power. In Gregory of Tours's view, for example, Martin's relics (or rather God *through* Martin's relics) had prevented armies from plundering local peasants. Nor was Martin the only human to have great supernatural power; all of God's saints were miracle workers.

At the tomb of St. Illidius in Clermont (now Clermont-Ferrand), for example, it was reported that "the blind are given light, demons are chased away, the deaf receive hearing and the lame the use of their limbs." In the early Middle Ages the church had no formal procedures for proclaiming saints; rather, holiness was "recognized" by influential local people and the local bishop. Even a few women were so esteemed: "[Our Savior] gave us as models [of sanctity] not only men, who fight [against sinfulness] as they should, but also women, who exert themselves in the struggle with success," wrote Gregory as a preface to his story of the nun Monegundis, who lived with a few other ascetic women and whose miracles included curing tumors and prompting paralyzed limbs to work again. No one at Tours doubted that Martin had been a saint, and to tap into the power of his relics his church was constructed in the cemetery directly over his tomb. For a man like Gregory of Tours, the church was above all a home for the relics of the saints. Whereas in the classical world the dead had been banished from the presence of the living, in the medieval world the holy dead held the place of highest esteem.

Economic Hardship in a Peasant Society

Relics were important protectors for people who lived on the very edge of survival, as seventh- and eighth-century Europeans did. Studies of Alpine peat bogs show that from the fifth to the mid-eighth centuries glaciers advanced and the mean temperature in Europe dropped. This climatic change spelled shortages in crops, exacerbating the problems of primitive farming. The dry, light soil of the Mediterranean region had been easy to till, and wooden implements were no liability there. But the northern soils of most of the Merovingian world were heavy, wet, and difficult to turn and aerate. The primary fertilizer was animal dung. We know from chronicles, histories, and saints' lives that crop shortages, famines, and diseases were a normal part of life. For the year 591 alone, Gregory of Tours reported that

a terrible epidemic killed off the people in Tours and in Nantes. Each person who caught the disease was first troubled with a slight headache and then died. . . . In the town of Limoges a number of people were consumed by fire from heaven for having profaned the

Peasant Dues
This seventh-century ledger sheet from the church of St. Martin of Tours lists the dues owed by tenants on St. Martin's estates.

Lord's day by transacting business. . . . There was a terrible drought which destroyed all the green pasture. As a result there were great losses of flocks and herds. . . . [Elsewhere] the hay was destroyed by incessant rain and by the rivers which overflowed, there was a poor grain harvest, but the vines yielded abundantly.

The meager population of the Merovingian world was too large for its productive capacities. Technological limitations meant a limited food supply; and agricultural work was not equitably or efficiently allocated and managed. A leisure class of landowning warriors and churchmen lived off the work of peasant men, who tilled the fields, and peasant women, who gardened, brewed, baked, and wove cloth. Surpluses did occasionally develop, whether from peaceful agriculture or plunder in warfare, and these were traded, although not in an impersonal, commercial manner. Most economic transactions of the seventh and eighth centuries were part of a gift economy, a system of give and take: booty was taken, tribute demanded, harvests hoarded, and coins struck, all to be redistributed to friends, followers, and dependents. Those benefiting from this largess included religious people and institutions: monks, nuns, bishops; monasteries and churches. We still have a partial gift economy today. At holidays, for example, goods change hands for social purposes: to consecrate a holy event, to express love and friendship, to "show off" wealth and status. In the Merovingian world, the gift economy was the dynamic behind many other moments when goods and money changed hands. Kings and other rich and powerful men and women amassed gold, silver, ornaments, and jewelry in their treasuries and grain in their storehouses to mark their power, add to their prestige, and prove their generosity.

Some economic activity in the seventh century was purely commercial. Impersonal transactions took place especially in long-distance trade, in which the West supplied human and raw materials like slaves, furs, and honey and in return received luxuries and manufactured goods such as silks and papyrus from the East. Trade was a way in which the three descendants of the Roman Empire kept in tenuous contact with one another. Seventh- and eighth-century sources speak of Byzantines, Syrians, and Jews as the chief intermediaries. Some continued to live in the still thriving port cities of the Mediterranean. Gregory of Tours especially associated Jews with commerce, complaining that they sold things "at a higher price than they were worth."

Despite the hostility toward Jews that Gregory's words reveal, Jews in seventh- and eighth-century Europe were not usually persecuted. (The exception was Visigothic Spain, where both church and monarchy legislated with great thoroughness against the Jews.) In many regions—in Burgundy and along the Rhône River valley, for example— Jews were almost entirely integrated into every aspect of secular life. They used Hebrew in worship, but otherwise they spoke the same languages as Christians and used Latin in their legal documents. Their children were often given the same names as Christians (and, in turn, Christians often took Biblical names, such as Solomon); they dressed as everyone else dressed; and they engaged in the same

Silver, Gold, and Garnet Brooch
Precious ornaments such as this, which comes from a seventh-century aristocrat's tomb, were used to display status and might become part of a gift exchange.

occupations. Many Jews planted and tended vineyards, in part because of the importance of wine in synagogue services, in part because the surplus could easily be sold. Some Jews were rich landowners, with slaves and dependent peasants working for them; others were independent peasants of modest means. Whereas some Jews lived in towns with a small Jewish quarter where their homes and synagogues were located, most Jews, like their Christian neighbors, lived on the land. Only much later, in the tenth century, would their status change, setting them markedly apart from Christians.

Nor were women as noticeably set apart from men in the Merovingian period as they had been in Roman times. As in the Islamic world, Western women received dowries and could inherit property. In the West they could be entrepreneurs as well: we know of at least one enterprising peasant

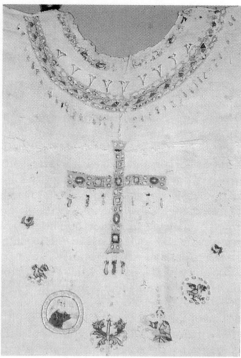

Symbolic Jewels
The embroidery on this blouse depicts the jewels worn by Merovingian aristocratic women. Tradition has it that this particular blouse belonged to Queen Balthild: rather than wear real jewels, she distributed them to the poor and contented herself with their memento in embroidery.

woman who sold wine at Tours to earn extra money. Along with their economic power, peasant women enjoyed a good deal of social independence; for example, they—rather than their parents or their lords—chose husbands from the men in the villages. This was a function of demographics—the fact that rich Merovingian men had several wives and mistresses meant that eligible women were in short supply for other men. A woman's legal status determined the social rank of her children: if a free-woman married a male slave, the children of the union were recognized as free. Such marriages contributed to the upward mobility of ambitious peasants; although, of course, the children of slave women would have the status of slaves, even if their father were free. Some women catapulted to even higher positions. Balthild (who died c. 680), a slave in the king's household but "beautiful, clever and

of strong character," as her biographer described her, attracted the attention of King Clovis II (*639–657). Their marriage produced three sons, all of whom became kings; and after Clovis's death in 657, during the minority of her oldest son, Queen Balthild served as regent for her son until he came of age. She staunchly opposed slavery and infanticide and lent equally strong support to monasteries and pious clerics. Male slaves could never rise to royal power; but some became royal favorites and achieved wealth and status that way. Andarchius, for example, born a slave, became a scholar and an ambassador for a Merovingian king.

The Powerful in Merovingian Society

Aristocratic men, who lived mostly in rural areas, controlled the activities of women more closely than did men of the lower classes. Merovingian aristocrats did not form a separate legal group, but they held hereditary wealth, status, and political influence. Noble parents determined whom their daughter was to marry, for such unions bound together whole kindreds rather than simply husbands and wives. As was true for brides of the lower classes, aristocratic wives received a dowry (usually land) over which they had some control; if they were widowed without children, they were allowed to sell, give away, exchange, or rent out those estates as they wished. Moreover, men could give women property outright in written testaments. Fathers so often wanted to share their property with their daughters that an enterprising compiler drew up a formula for scribes to follow when drawing up such wills. It began:

> For a long time an ungodly custom has been observed among us that forbids sisters to share with their brothers the paternal land. I reject this impious law: God gave all of you to me as my children and I have loved you all equally, therefore you will all equally rejoice in my goods after my death.... I make you, my beloved daughter, an equal and legitimate heir in all my patrimony.

Because of such bequests, dowries, and other gifts, many aristocratic women were very rich. Childless widows frequently gave grand and generous gifts to the church from their vast possessions. But a woman need not have been a widow to control enormous wealth: in 632, for example, the nun Burgundofara, who had never married, drew up a will giving her monastery the land, slaves, vineyards, pastures, and forests she had received from her two brothers and her father. In the same will she gave other property near Paris to her brothers and sister. Aristocratic women maintained close ties with their relatives. They did what they could to find powerful husbands for their sisters and prestigious careers for their brothers; in turn, they relied on their relatives for personal support.

Though legally under the authority of her husband, a Merovingian woman often found ways to take control of her life and of her husband's life as well. Queens like Fredegund, wife of Chilperic, plotted against her husband's brothers, bribed bishops to speak against her enemies, and poisoned her stepson. Tetradia, wife of Count Eulalius, left her husband, taking all his gold and silver, because

> *he was in the habit of sleeping with the women-servants in his household. As a result he neglected his wife. He used to knock her about when he came from these midnight exercises. As a result of his excesses, he ran into serious debt, and to meet this he stole his wife's jewellery and money.*

At a court of law Tetradia was sentenced to repay Eulalius four times the amount she had taken from him, but she was allowed to keep and live on her own property. Other women were able to exercise behind-the-scenes control through their sons. Artemia, for example, used the prophecy that her son, Nicetius, would become a bishop to prevent her husband from taking the bishopric himself. Although the prophecy eventually came to pass, well into his thirties, Nicetius remained at home with his mother, working alongside the servants and teaching the younger children of the household to read the Psalms.

Some women exercised direct power. As mentioned, Balthild, the mother of a king, acted as her son's regent before he came to power. Rich widows with fortunes to bestow wielded enormous influence. Some Merovingian women were abbesses, rulers in their own right over female monasteries and sometimes over "double monasteries," with separate facilities for men and women. These could be very substantial centers of population: the female monastery at Laon, for example, had 300 nuns in the seventh century.

Housed in populous convents or monopolized by rich men able to support several wives and mistresses at one time, women were scarce in society at large and therefore valuable. Marriage, especially the most formal kind, was expensive for an upper-class man. He had to pay a dowry to his bride; and after the marriage was consummated, he gave her a morning gift. A less formal marriage, and less expensive, was the *Friedelehe*, in which a man "abducted" his wife in a kind of elopement. These were not clandestine marriages, however, and they too involved payment of the morning gift. Churchmen had many ideas about the value of marriages, but in practice they had little to do with the matter. No one got married in a church. The purpose of marriage, as it was understood in the seventh and eighth centuries, was procreation. The marriage bed, not the altar, was its focus. For aristocrats marriage existed to maintain the family.

Aristocrats lived lives of leisurely abundance. At the end of the sixth century, for example, Bishop Nicetius inhabited a palace that commanded a view of his estates overlooking the Moselle River:

> *From the top you can see boats gliding by on the surface of the river in summertime; it has three stories and when you reach the top, the edifice seems to overshadow the fields lying at its feet. . . . On these slopes, formerly sterile, Nicetius has planted juicy vines, and green vineshoots clothe the high rock that used to bear nothing but scrub. Orchards with fruit-trees growing here and there fill the air with the perfume of their flowers.*

Sixth-century aristocrats with wealth and schooling like Nicetius still patterned their lives on those of Romans, teaching their children Latin poetry and writing to one another in phrases borrowed from Virgil.

Less than a century later, however, aristocrats no longer adhered to the traditions of the classical past. Most important, they spoke a language far removed from literary Latin. New-style aristocrats paid little attention to Latin poetry. Some still learned Latin, but they cultivated it mainly to read the Psalms. A religious culture emphasizing Christian piety over the classics was developing in the West at the same time as in Byzantium.

The new religious sensibility was given powerful impetus by the arrival (c. 591) on the Continent of the Irish monk St. Columbanus (c. 543–615).

The Merovingian aristocracy was much taken by Columbanus's brand of monasticism, which stressed exile, devotion, and discipline. The monasteries St. Columbanus established in both Gaul and Italy attracted local recruits, some of them grown men and women, from the aristocracy, but many were young children given to a monastery by their parents. This practice (called *oblation*) was not only accepted but also often considered essential for the spiritual well-being of both the children and their families. Irish monasticism introduced aristocrats on the Continent to a deepened religious devotion. Those aristocrats who did not actively join or patronize a monastery still often read (or listened to others read) books about penitence, and they chanted the Psalms.

Along with their religious activities, male aristocrats of the mid-seventh century spent their time honing their skills as warriors. To be a great warrior in Merovingian society, just as in the otherwise different world of the Bedouin, meant more than just fighting: it meant perfecting the virtues necessary for leading armed men. Aristocrats affirmed their skills and comradeship in the hunt; they proved their worth in the regular taking of booty; and they rewarded their followers afterward at generous banquets. At these feasts, following the dictates of the gift economy, fellowship was combined with the redistribution of wealth, as lords gave abundantly to the retainers who surrounded them.

Bishops were generally also aristocrats and ranked among the most powerful men in Merovingian society. Gregory of Tours, for example, considered himself the protector of "his citizens" at Tours. When representatives of the king came to collect taxes there, Gregory stopped them in their tracks, warning them that St. Martin would punish anyone who tried to tax his people. "That very day," Gregory reported, "the man who had produced the tax rolls caught a fever and died." Gregory then obtained a letter from the king, "confirming the immunity from taxation of the people of Tours, out of respect for Saint Martin."

Like other aristocrats, many bishops were married even though church councils demanded celibacy. For example, Bishop Priscus of Lyon had a wife, Susannah, and a son. As the overseers of priests, however, bishops were expected to be their moral superiors and refrain from sexual relations with their wives. Since bishops were ordinarily appointed late in life, long after they had raised a family, this did not threaten the ideal of a procreative marriage.

Atop the aristocracy were the Merovingian kings, rulers of the Frankish kingdoms from about 486 to 751. The dynasty owed its longevity to good political sense: it had allied itself with local lay aristocrats and ecclesiastical authorities. The kings relied on these men to bolster their power derived from other sources: their tribal war leadership and access to the lion's share of plunder; their quasi-magical power over crops and fertility; and their appropriation of the taxation system, the fisc (public lands), and the legal framework of Roman administration. The kings' courts functioned as schools for the sons of the aristocracy, tightening the bonds between royal and aristocratic families and loyalties. When kings sent officials—counts and dukes—to rule in their name in various regions of their kingdoms, these regional governors worked with and married into the aristocratic families that had long controlled local affairs, so that the kings' officials themselves merged with local aristocrats.

The king acted as arbitrator and intermediary for the competing interests of these aristocrats while taking advantage of local opportunities to appoint favorites and garner prestige by giving out land and privileges to supporters and religious institutions. Both kings and aristocrats, therefore, had good reason to want a powerful royal authority. Gregory of Tours's history of the sixth century is filled with stories of bitter battles between Merovingian kings, as royal brothers fought over territories, wives, and revenues in seemingly endless vendettas. Yet what seemed like royal weakness and violent chaos to the bishop was in fact one way in which the kings focused local aristocratic enmities, preventing them from spinning out of royal control. By the beginning of the seventh century, three relatively stable Frankish kingdoms had emerged: Austrasia to the northeast; Neustria, with its capital city at Paris; and

The Frankish Kingdoms

Burgundy, incorporating the southeast. These divisions were so useful to local aristocrats and the Merovingian dynasty alike that even when royal power was united in the hands of one king, Clothar II (✳613–623), he made his son the independent king of Austrasia.

The very power of the kings in the seventh century, however, gave greater might to their chief court official, the mayor of the palace. In the following century, allied with the Austrasian aristocracy, one mayoral family would displace the Merovingian dynasty and establish a new royal line, the Carolingians.

Christianity and Classical Culture in England and Ireland

The Merovingian kingdoms exemplify some of the ways in which Roman and non-Roman traditions combined. Anglo-Saxon England shows still another in its formation of a learned monastic culture. The impetus for this culture came not from native traditions but from Rome and Ireland. After the Anglo-Saxon conquest, England gradually emerged politically as a mosaic of about a dozen kingdoms ruled by separate kings, all of whom traced their ancestry to the god Woden. Like Clovis, the English kings carved out their territories and made good their authority by battling rival leaders and tribes; but unlike Clovis, the Anglo-Saxon kings did not find a strong Christian aristocracy with which to ally. No proud and dignified bishops met them at their cities' gates, for by the time of the Anglo-Saxon invasions the cities were mere shells and the Romans who built them had fled. The British Christians who remained were either absorbed into the pagan culture of the invaders or pushed west into Wales or north into Scotland, where Christianity survived.

Christianity was reintroduced in England from two directions. In the south of England, missionaries arrived from Rome, sent by Pope Gregory the Great. In the north of England, Irish monks came with a somewhat different brand of Christianity. Converted in the fifth century by St. Patrick and other missionaries, the Irish had rapidly evolved a church organization that corresponded to its rural clan organization. Abbots and abbesses, who generally came from powerful dynasties, headed monastic *familiae*, communities composed of blood relatives, servants, slaves, and, of course, monks or nuns. Bishops were often under the authority of abbots, and the monasteries rather than cities were the centers of population settlement in Ireland.

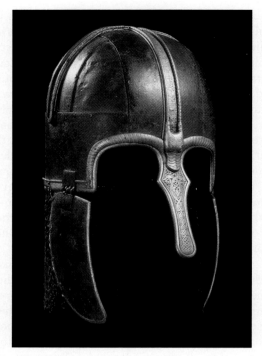

Warrior Helmet
The English aristocracy of the seventh and eighth centuries was largely a class of warriors. Finely wrought helmets like this one were made of iron and copper alloy and were worn only by the very richest warriors; the others had to be content with leather.

Because their families and communities were so important, pious Irishmen considered self-imposed exile to be one of the greatest sacrifices they could make for God. St. Columbanus, according to his seventh-century biographer,

> longed to go into strange lands, in obedience to the command which the Lord gave Abraham: "Get thee out of thy country, and from thy kindred, and from thy father's house, into a land that I will show thee."

In 635 another monk, Aidan, left Ireland to found a monastery, Lindisfarne, on the coast of northern England.

Thus Christianity had already arrived in England from one direction when, in 596, Pope Gregory the Great sent churchmen to Kent, England's southernmost kingdom. The missionaries, under the leadership of Augustine (not the same Augustine as the bishop of Hippo), intended to convert the king and through him his people. Arriving in 597, Augustine and his party brought with them Roman practices at odds with those of Irish Christianity, stressing ties to the pope and the organization of the church under bishops rather than abbots. Using the Roman model, they divided England into territorial units (*dioceses*) headed by an archbishop and bishops. Augustine, for example, became archbishop of Canterbury. A major bone of contention between the Roman and Irish churches was the calculation of the date of Easter. Both sides thought that Christians could not be saved unless they observed the day of the Resurrection properly and on the right date, but they argued on behalf of entirely different dates.

Aidan had close ties with the king of Northumbria (in the north of England), and he and his disciples were given royal support to preach Christianity and the Irish position on Easter. In the south of England the Roman view prevailed, and it eventually triumphed in the north as well when the Northumbrian king, Oswy, organized a synod at Whitby (664). There Wilfred, a churchman raised in the north but zealous on behalf of the Roman position, convinced Oswy that Rome spoke with the voice of St. Peter, the heavenly doorkeeper. Oswy opted for the Roman calculation of Easter and embraced the Roman church as a whole.

The path to the Roman triumph had been well prepared. To many English monks, Rome had great prestige; for them, it was a treasure trove of knowledge, piety, and holy objects. Benedict Biscop (c. 630–690), the founder of two important English monasteries, Wearmouth and Jarrow, made many arduous trips to Rome, bringing back relics, liturgical vestments, and even a cantor to teach his monks the proper melodies in a time before written musical notation. Above all, he went to Rome to get books. At his monasteries in the north of England, he built up a grand library. In Anglo-Saxon England as in Ireland, both of which lacked a strong classical tradition from Roman times, a book was considered a precious object, to be decorated as finely as a garnet-studded brooch.

The Anglo-Saxons and Irish Celts had a thriving oral culture but extremely limited uses for writing. Books became valuable only when these societies converted to Christianity. Just as Islamic reliance on the Qur'an made possible a literary culture under the Umayyads, so Christian dependence on the Bible, written liturgy, and patristic

Lindisfarne Gospels Text Page
To the monks who copied the Gospels in the north of England, the book was a precious object, to be decorated much as a brooch might be enhanced. Here the letters that begin a chapter are treated as part of a design.

thought helped make England and Ireland centers of literature and learning in the seventh and eighth centuries. Under Archbishop Theodore (*669–690), who had studied at Constantinople and was one of the most learned men of his day, a school at Canterbury was established where students mined Latin and even some Greek manuscripts to comment on Biblical texts. Men like Benedict Biscop soon sponsored other centers of learning, and here again the texts from the classical past were used. Although women did not found famous schools, many abbesses ruled over monasteries that stressed Christian learning. Here as elsewhere, Latin writings, even pagan texts, were studied diligently, in part because Latin was so foreign a language that mastering it required systematic and formal study. One of the Benedict Biscop's pupils was Bede (673–735), a monk and historian of extraordinary breadth. Bede in turn taught a new generation of monks who became a kind of brain trust for late eighth-century rulers.

The vigorous pagan Anglo-Saxon oral tradition was only partially suppressed; much of it was adapted to the new Christian culture. Bede told the story of Caedmon, a layman who had not wanted to sing and make up poems, as he was expected to do at the convivial feasts of warriors. One night, slipping out of the dinner hall to sleep with the animals in the barn, Caedmon had a dream: he was commanded by an unknown man to sing about Creation. In his sleep Caedmon dreamed an Anglo-Saxon poem that praised God as author of all things. He became a kind of celebrity, joined a monastery, and spent the rest of his days turning "whatever passages of Scripture were explained to him into delightful and moving poetry in his own English [that is, Anglo-Saxon] tongue." Although Bede himself translated Caedmon's poem into Latin when he wrote down the tale, he encouraged and supported the use of Anglo-Saxon, urging Christian priests, for example, to use it when they instructed their flocks. Sometimes Bede himself wrote in Anglo-Saxon: he was translating the Gospel of St. John into the vernacular at the time of his death. In contrast to other European regions, where the vernacular was rarely written, Anglo-Saxon came to be a written language used in every aspect of English life, from government to entertainment.

After the Synod of Whitby, the English church was tied by doctrine, friendship, and conviction to the church of Rome. An influential Anglo-Saxon monk and bishop, Wynfrith even changed his name to the Latin Boniface to symbolize his loyalty to the Roman church. Preaching on the Continent, Boniface (680–754) worked to set up churches in Germany and Gaul that, like the ones in England, looked to Rome for leadership and guidance. His zeal would give the papacy new importance in the West.

Visigothic Unity and Lombard Division

In contrast to England, southern Gaul, Spain, and Italy had long been part of the Roman Empire and preserved many of its traditions. Nevertheless, as they were settled and fought over by new peoples, their histories came to diverge dramatically. When Clovis defeated the Visigoths in 507, their vast kingdom, which had sprawled across southern Gaul into Spain, was dismembered, and the Franks and Ostrogoths vied for its control. By mid-century, however, the Ostrogoths were too busy struggling against Justinian's forces to be concerned with matters outside Italy, and the Franks came into possession of most of the Visigothic kingdom in southern Gaul, while in Spain the Visigothic king survived only to meet with fierce revolts by rebellious nobles and townsmen.

The Visigothic king Leovigild (*569–586) at last established territorial control over most of Spain by military might. But no ruler could hope to maintain his position there without the support of the Hispano-Roman population, which included the great landowners and leading bishops; and their backing was unattainable while the Visigoths remained Arian.* Leovigild's son, Reccared (*586–601), took the necessary step in 587. Two years later, at the Third Council of Toledo, most of the Arian bishops followed their king by announcing their conversion to Catholicism, and the assembled churchmen enacted decrees for a united church in Spain.

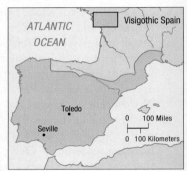

Visigothic Spain, c. 600

Thereafter the bishops and kings of Spain cooperated to a degree unprecedented in other regions. While the king gave the churchmen free reign to set up their own hierarchy (with the bishop of Toledo at the top) and to meet regularly at synods to regulate and reform the church, the bishops in turn supported their Visigothic ruler. A leading writer of the period, Bishop Isidore of Seville (*c. 600–636), argued that the king ruled as a minister of the Christian people. Rebellion against him was tantamount to rebellion against Christ. The Spanish bishops reinforced this idea by anointing the king, daubing him with holy oil in a ritual that paralleled the ordination of priests and demonstrated divine favor. Toledo became the city not only where the highest bishop presided but also where the kings were "made" through anointment.

---

*See Chapter 7.

While the bishops in this way made the king's cause their own, their lay counterparts, the great landowners, helped supply the king with troops, allowing him to maintain internal order and repel his external enemies.

Ironically, it was precisely the centralization and unification of the Visigothic kingdom that proved its undoing. When the Arabs arrived in 711, they needed only to kill the king, defeat his army, and capture Toledo to deal it a crushing blow.

By contrast, the Lombard king faced at all times a hostile papacy in the center of Italy and virtually independent dukes in the south of Italy who, although theoretically royal officers, in fact ruled Benevento and Spoleto on their own behalf. Although many Lombards were Catholics, others, including important kings and dukes, were Arian. The "official" religion varied with the ruler in power. Rather than signal a major political event, then, the conversion of the Lombards to Catholic Christianity occurred gradually, ending only around the mid-seventh century. Partly as a result of this slow development, the Lombard kings, unlike the Visigoths, Franks, or even the Anglo-Saxons, never enlisted the wholehearted support of any particular group of churchmen.

Lacking strong and united ecclesiastical favor, Lombard royal power still had strong bulwarks. Chief among these were the traditions of leadership associated with the royal dynasty, the kings' control over large estates in northern Italy and their military ability, and the Roman institutions that survived in Italy. Although the Italian peninsula had been devastated by the wars between the Ostrogoths and the Byzantine Empire, the Lombard kings took advantage of the still-urban organization of Italian society and economy, assigning dukes to city bases and setting up a royal capital at Pavia. Recalling emperors like Constantine and Justinian, the kings built churches, monasteries, and other places of worship in the royal capital, maintained the walls, and minted coins. Revenues from tolls, sales taxes, port duties and court fines filled their

Lombard Italy

coffers, although (and this was a major weakness) they could not revive the Roman land tax. Like other Germanic kings, the Lombards issued law codes that revealed a great debt to Roman legal collections such as those commissioned by Justinian. Although individual provisions of the law code promulgated by King Rothari (✳636–652), for example, reflected Lombard traditions, the code also suggested the Roman idea that the law should apply to all under his rule, not just Lombards: "We desire," Rothari wrote,

> *that these laws be brought together in one volume so that everyone may lead a secure life in accordance with the law and justice, and in confidence thereof will willingly set himself against his enemies and defend himself and his homeland.*

Unfortunately for the Lombard kings, the "homeland" they hoped to rule was not united under them. As soon as they began to make serious headway into southern Italy against the duchies of Spoleto and Benevento, the pope feared for his own position in the middle and called on the Franks for help.

Political Tensions and Reorganization at Rome

By the end of the sixth century the position of the pope was anomalous. On the one hand, believing himself the successor of St. Peter and head of the church, he buttressed this claim with real secular power. Pope Gregory the Great (✳590–604) in many ways laid the foundations for the papacy's later spiritual and temporal ascendancy during his tenure. He made the pope the greatest landowner in Italy; he organized the defense of Rome and paid for its army; he heard court cases, made treaties, and provided welfare services. The missionary expedition he sent to England was only a small part of his involvement in the rest of Europe. For example, Gregory maintained close ties with the churchmen in Spain who were working to convert the Visigoths from Arianism to Catholicism; and he wrote letters to the Merovingian queen Brunhilda, assuring her that faith in God would help solidify her rule. A prolific author of spiritual works and Biblical exegeses, Gregory digested and simplified the ideas of church fathers like St. Augustine, making them accessible to a wider audience. His prac-

Byzantium and Rome
*This mosaic, commissioned by Pope Theodore (*642–649), shows the strong influence of Byzantine styles on early seventh-century Roman art, attesting to the political, cultural, and theological links between Rome and Constantinople.*

tical handbook for the clergy, *Pastoral Rule*, was matched by practical reforms within the Church: he tried to impose in Italy regular episcopal elections and to enforce clerical celibacy.

But the pope was not independent: he was only one of many bishops in the Roman Empire, which was now ruled from Constantinople; and he was therefore juridically tied to the emperor and Byzantium. For a long time the emperor's view on dogma, discipline, and church administration prevailed at Rome. This authority began to unravel in the seventh century. In 691 Emperor Justinian II convened a council that determined 102 rules for the church, and he sent the rules to Rome for papal endorsement. Most of the rules were unobjectionable, but Pope Sergius I was unwilling to agree to the whole because it permitted priestly marriages (which the Roman church did not want to allow), and it prohibited fasting on Saturdays in Lent (which the Roman church required). Outraged by Sergius's refusal, Justinian tried to arrest the pope, but Italian armies (theoretically under the emperor) came to the pontiff's aid, while Justinian's arresting officer cowered under the pope's

bed. The incident reveals that some local forces were already willing to rally to the side of the pope against the emperor. By now Constantinople's influence and authority over Rome was tenuous at best. Sheer distance, as well as diminishing imperial power in Italy, meant the popes were in effect the leaders of the parts of Italy not controlled by the Lombards.

The gap between Byzantium and the papacy widened in the early eighth century as Emperor Leo III tried to increase the taxes on papal property to pay for his all-consuming war against the Arab invaders. The pope responded by leading a general tax revolt. Meanwhile, Leo's fierce policy of iconoclasm collided with the pope's tolerance of images. In the West, Christian piety focused not so much on icons as on relics, but the papacy was not about to allow sacred images to be destroyed. The pope argued that holy images could and should be venerated—but not worshiped. His support of images reflected popular opinion as well. A later commentator wrote that iconoclasm so infuriated the inhabitants of Ravenna and Venice that "if the pope had not prohibited the people, they would have attempted to set up a [different] emperor over themselves."

These difficulties with the emperor were matched by increasing friction between the pope and the Lombards. The Lombard kings had gradually managed to bring the duchies of Spoleto and Benevento under their control, as well as part of the Exarchate of Ravenna. By the mid-eighth century, the popes feared that Rome would fall to the Lombards, and Pope Zachary (*741–752) looked northward for friends. He created an ally by sanctioning the deposition of the last Merovingian king and his replacement by the first Carolingian king, Pippin III the Short (*751–768). In 753 a subsequent pope, Stephen II (*752–757), called on Pippin to march to Italy with an army to fight the Lombards. Thus events at Rome had a major impact on the history of not only Italy but the Frankish kingdom as well.

The Rise of the Carolingians

The popes were not dealing with naive upstarts; the Carolingians,* part of an aristocratic kin network accustomed to power and buttressed by vast estates in Austrasia, had long prepared to take over. The Carolingians were among many aristocratic families on the rise during the Merovingian period, a time of great competition and alliances among kindred groups. Consolidating power through marriages, royal grants, and probably also episcopal offices, the Carolingians also served as the mayor of the palace (chief minister) for the Merovingian kings in Austrasia. In 687 one Carolingian mayor, Pippin II (d. 714), made a bold move: at the battle of Tertry he defeated the mayor of the palace of Neustria. More important than this victory for his dynasty's success, Pippin allied himself with the aristocrats of Neustria through marriages and patronage. For example, he married his son Drogo to Anstrud, daughter of the most important Neustrian family. Because of these alliances, Pippin was able to assume the mayor's office in Neustria as well as in Austrasia.

---

*The name *Carolingian* derives from Carolus, the Latin name of several of the dynasty's most famous members, including Charles Martel and Charlemagne (or Charles the Great).

The son of Pippin II, Charles Martel (mayor, *714–741), was also a warrior and politician. Although he spent most of his time fighting vigorously against opposing aristocratic groups, later generations would recall with nostalgia his defeat of a contingent of Muslims between Poitiers and Tours in about 732. In contending against regional aristocrats who were carving out independent lordships for themselves, Charles and his family turned aristocratic factions against one another, rewarded supporters, crushed enemies, and dominated whole regions by controlling monasteries that served as focal points for both religious piety and land donations. Allying themselves with these influential religious and political institutions, the Carolingians took advantage of a fatal biological problem of the last Merovingian kings: few

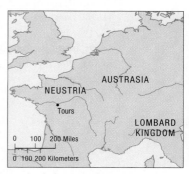

Rise of the Carolingians

of them survived to adulthood. The exalted place of the aristocracy in Merovingian society made it likely that a number of powerful groups would emerge as autonomous rulers. The Carolingians' astonishing feat was to counteract this disintegration.

The Carolingians chose their allies well. Anglo-Saxon missionaries like Boniface, who went to Frisia (today, the Netherlands) and Germany, helped them expand their control, converting the population as a prelude to conquest. Many of the areas Boniface reached had long been Christian, but the churches there had followed local or Irish models rather than Roman. Boniface, who came to Germany from England as the pope's ambassador, set up a hierarchical church organization and founded monasteries dedicated to the Rule of St. Benedict rather than to the Columbanian or other traditions. His newly appointed bishops were loyal to Rome and the Carolingians, not to regional aristocracies. They knew that their power came from papal and royal fiat rather than from local power centers. The Carolingians enhanced their own position by enforcing Boniface's reforms and allying themselves with the new episcopacy and with the pope at Rome.

Although at first men like Boniface worked indirectly to bring about the Carolingian alliance

HEIRS OF THE ROMAN EMPIRE

Byzantium

604–627 Persians and Byzantines at war

610–641 Reign of Emperor Heraclius

626 Avars defeated at the walls of Constantinople

717–741 Reign of Emperor Leo III the Isaurian

718–719 Major Arab attack on Constantinople repulsed

726–843 Period of iconoclasm

Islam

c. 570 Muhammad born at Mecca

610 Muhammad first hears the word of God

622 *Hijra*, the emigration to Medina and the beginning of the Islamic calendar

624 Battle of Badr, Islamic victory against the Meccans; expulsion of Jewish Qaynuqa clan from Medina

632 Arabs largely united under Muhammad; death of Muhammad

661–750 Umayyad caliphate

711–718 Muslim troops take North Africa and Spain

713 Muslim armies take the Indus valley

The West

590–604 Gregory the Great is pope at Rome

c. 591 Columbanus, an Irish monk, arrives on the Continent

596–597 Augustine of Canterbury sent to England by Pope Gregory the Great to convert the Anglo-Saxons

664 Synod of Whitby; Northumbrian King Oswy opts for Roman Christianity

680–754 Life of Boniface, an Anglo-Saxon missionary with strong ties to Rome

687 Battle of Tertry; Pippin II becomes mayor of both Austrasia and Neustria

714–741 Charles Martel is mayor of Neustria and Austrasia

751–768 Reign of Pippin III, king of the Franks (first of the Carolingian dynasty)

756 So-called Donation of Pippin

---

with the papacy, Pippin III and his supporters cemented the partnership when they decided that the time was ripe to depose the Merovingian king. Having petitioned Pope Zachary to legitimize their actions, the Carolingians readily returned the favor a few years later when the pope asked for their help in defense against hostile Lombards. The request signaled a major shift. Hitherto the papacy had been part of the Byzantine Empire; but in 754 it turned to the West. In that year the papacy and the Franks formed a close, tight alliance based, as their agreement put it, on *amicitia, pax et caritas* (mutual friendship, close relations, and Christian love). In 756 Pippin launched a successful campaign against the Lombard king that ended with the so-called Donation of Pippin, a peace accord between the Lombards and the pope. The treaty gave back to the pope cities that had been wrested from the Exarchate of Ravenna by the Lombard

king. The new arrangement recognized what the papacy had long ago created: a territorial "republic of St. Peter" ruled by the pope, not by the Byzantine emperor. Henceforth the fate of Italy would be tied largely to the policies of the pope and the Frankish kings to the north, not to the emperors of the East.

The Carolingian partnership with Roman-style churchmen gave the dynasty a new kind of Christian aura, expressed in symbolic form by anointment. Carolingian kings, as Visigothic kings had been, were rubbed with holy oil on their foreheads and on their shoulders in a ceremony that reminded contemporaries of the Old Testament kings, such as David, who had been anointed by God. The son of Pippin III, Charles the Great, would be known to history as Charlemagne; but his nickname, David—the Hebrews' heroic king— tells us better the image he cultivated of himself.

CONCLUSION

The three heirs of the Roman Empire—Byzantines, Muslims, and the peoples of the West—built upon three distinct legacies. Byzantium directly inherited the central political institutions of Rome; its people called themselves Romans; its emperor was the Roman emperor; and its capital, Constantinople, was the new Rome. Sixth-century Byzantium also inherited the cities, laws, and religion of Rome. Despite many changes in the seventh and eighth centuries—contraction of territory, urban decline, disappearance of the old elite, a ban on sacred images—the Byzantine Empire never entirely lost its Roman character. Byzantium itself remained an important and thriving city, with trade and manufacturing continuing even in the darkest hours of war and with administrative and fiscal institutions allowing the emperor to reorganize and adapt government to new demands. Education maintained vestiges of classical traditions even as it was reoriented to Christian texts. By 750, however, Byzantium was less Roman than it was a new resilient political and cultural entity, a Christian polity on the borders of the new Muslim empire.

The Muslims were the stepchildren of the Roman world, with Islam built on Jewish monotheism and only indirectly on Roman Christianity. Under the guidance of the Prophet Muhammad, Islam became both a coherent theology and a tightly structured way of life with customs defined in the Qur'an and based on Arabian tribal life. Once the Muslim Arabs embarked on military conquests, however, they too became heirs of Rome, preserving its cities, hiring its civil servants, and adopting its artistic styles. Drawing upon Roman traditions, the Muslims created a powerful Islamic state, with a capital city in Syria, regional urban centers elsewhere, and a culture that tolerated a wide variety of economic, religious, and social institutions so long as the conquered paid taxes to their Muslim overlords.

The West also inherited Roman institutions and transformed them with great diversity. In Italy and at Rome itself, the traditions of the classical past remained living parts of the fabric of life. The roads remained, the cities of Italy survived (although depopulated), and both the popes and the Lombard kings ruled in the traditions of Roman government; otherwise they would not have written out peace treaties. In Spain the Visigothic kings allied themselves with a Hispano-Roman elite that maintained elements of the organization and vigorous intellectual traditions of the late empire. In England, however, once the far-flung northern summit of the Roman Empire, the Roman legacy had to be reimported in the seventh century, as pagan Anglo-Saxon kings accepted Christianity from Roman missionaries and monks learned Latin as a new, exotic language. Frankish Gaul built on Roman traditions that had long been transformed by provincial and Germanic custom. There, for example, Roman-style coins became precious gifts, and such Roman government tasks as tax collecting were adopted to the interests of Frankish aristocratic factions.

All three heirs to Rome suffered the ravages of war. In all three societies the social hierarchy became simpler, with the loss of "middle" groups like the *curiales* at Byzantium and the near-suppression of tribal affiliations among those who professed Islam. As each of the three heirs shaped Roman institutions to its own uses and advantages, each also strove to create a religious polity. In Byzantium the emperor was a religious force, presiding over the destruction of images. In the Islamic world the caliph was the successor to Muhammad, a religious and political leader. In the West the Carolingians were anointed rulers of the Franks. Despite their many differences, all these leaders had a common understanding of their place in a divine scheme; they were God's agents on earth, ruling over God's people.

SUGGESTIONS FOR FURTHER READING

Source Materials

Bede, *A History of the English Church and People.* Translated by Leo Sherley-Price. 1991. The most important source for the history of the conversion of the English, written by an extraordinary eighth-century monk.

Geanakoplos, Deno John, ed. and trans. *Byzantium: Church, Society, and Civilization Seen Through Contemporary Eyes.* 1986. Contains translations of key primary source documents.

Gregory of Tours. *The History of the Franks.* Translated by Lewis Thorpe. 1976. Our major source for the history and the mentality of the Merovingian world. Gregory called this work his *Histories*, but Thorpe's translation refers to it by its later name.

Lewis, Bernard, ed. and trans. *Islam: From the Prophet Muhammad to the Capture of Constantinople.* 2 vols. 1987. A useful collection of documents concerned with the politics, war, religion, and economy of the Islamic world.

Interpretive Studies

Beeston, A. F. L. et al., eds. *Arabic Literature to the End of the Umayyad Period.* 1983. A collection of essays by specialists on every aspect of Umayyad literature.

Brown, Peter R. L. *The World of Late Antiquity, a.d. 150–750.* 1971. An exceptionally masterful but brief survey of the transition from the ancient to the medieval world, beautifully illustrated.

Browning, Robert. *The Byzantine Empire.* 1980. A thoughtful survey of change in Byzantium.

Chapelot, Jean, and Robert Fossier. *The Village and House in the Middle Ages.* Translated by Henry Cleere. 1985. Written jointly by a historian and an archaeologist. This text is a detailed study of the material remains of medieval settlements.

Collins, Roger. *Early Medieval Spain: Unity in Diversity, 400–1000.* 1983. Studies the Visigothic Kingdom and its transformation under the Muslims.

Crone, Patricia. *Meccan Trade and the Rise of Islam.* 1987. A controversial work that questions Mecca's place as a center of trade.

Donner, Fred McGraw. *The Early Islamic Conquests.* 1981. Concentrates on the tribal and religious forces behind the early Arab-Muslim expansion.

Dvornik, Francis. *Byzantium and the Roman Primacy.* Translated by Edwin A. Quain. 1966. A masterful study of the growth and development of the notion of papal primacy in the context of Byzantine political history.

Fine, John V. A., Jr. *The Early Medieval Balkans: A Critical Survey from the Sixth to the Late Twelfth Century.* 1991. A unique study that looks at the Balkans from the point of view of the people who settled there rather than from the Byzantines' perspective.

Geary, Patrick J. *Before France and Germany. The Creation and Transformation of the Merovingian World.* 1988. An insightful synthesis of the newest research on the period.

Goffart, Walter. *The Narrators of Barbarian History (a.d. 550–800): Jordanes, Gregory of Tours, Bede, and Paul the Deacon.* 1988. Examines early medieval histories as literary texts and as implicit statements about the task of the historian.

Grierson, Philip. "Commerce in the Dark Ages: A Critique of the Evidence." *Transactions of the Royal Historical Society* 5th ser. 9 (1959): 123–139. A pathbreaking study in which the notion of the gift economy is used to explain problematic aspects of the early medieval economy.

Haldon, J. F. *Byzantium in the Seventh Century: The Transformation of a Culture.* 1990. An important and comprehensive survey of continuity and change in Byzantine society, culture, and institutions.

Hallenbeck, Jan T. *Pavia and Rome: The Lombard Monarchy and the Papacy in the Eighth Century.* 1982. A clear and detailed account of the relationship between the Lombard kings and the popes in the eighth century.

Herlihy, David. *Medieval Households.* 1985. An important synthesis of historical knowledge about the varieties of and changes in medieval family units, written by an authority in the field.

Hodges, Richard, and David Whitehouse. *Mohammed, Charlemagne and the Origins of Europe. Archaeology and the Pirenne Thesis.* 1983. Two archaeologists discuss the evidence concerning trade and economic vitality in the early Middle Ages.

Hodgson, Marshall G. S. *The Venture of Islam: Conscience and History in a World Civilization.* Vol. 1, *The Classical Age of Islam.* 1974. An authoritative account of the early period of Islamic history.

Hussey, Joan M. *The Orthodox Church in the Byzantine Empire.* 1986. Covers the organization of the Greek Orthodox church and the controversies that beset it until the fall of Byzantium in 1453.

James, Edward. *The Origins of France. From Clovis to the Capetians, 500–1000.* 1982. A survey of the transformations that turned Gaul into France.

———. *The Franks.* 1988. Brings together written and archaeological materials in a careful and insightful appraisal of Frankish culture through the seventh century.

Kennedy, Hugh. *The Prophet and the Age of the Caliphates: The Islamic Near East from the Sixth to the Eleventh Century*. 1986. A detailed political history of early Islam.

Kitzinger, Ernst. *Early Medieval Art*. rev. ed. 1983. Treats art as a window onto changes in attitudes and ideas about this world and the hereafter.

Lapidus, Ira. *A History of Islamic Societies*. 1988. A panoramic overview of the history of Islamic civilization from its beginnings to the twentieth century.

Latouche, Robert. *The Birth of Western Economy: Economic Aspects of the Dark Ages*. Translated by E. M. Wilkinson. 1961. A careful look at trade, farming, and urban life in the early Middle Ages.

Lewis, Bernard. *Islam and the Arab World: Faith, People, Culture*. 1976. Various topics treated in short and richly illustrated articles by different experts.

Noble, Thomas F. X. *The Republic of St. Peter: The Birth of the Papal State, 680–825*. 1984. Discusses the papacy during a major period of transition.

Norwich, John Julius. *Byzantium: The Early Centuries*. 1989. A well-written introduction that concentrates on political figures.

Ostrogorsky, George. *History of the Byzantine State*. rev. ed. Translated by J. M. Hussey. 1969. The standard and essential one-volume account of Byzantine history.

Peters. F. E. "The Commerce of Mecca Before Islam." In *A Way Prepared: Essays on Islamic Culture in Honor of Richard Bayly Winder*, edited by Farhad Kazemi and R. D. McChesney. 1988. Presents a nuanced view of the economic role of Mecca in the period before Muhammad.

Riché, Pierre. *Education and Culture in the Barbarian West: Sixth Through Eighth Centuries*. Translated by John J. Contreni. 1975. A monumental study of the shift from lay classical culture to religious culture in early medieval Europe.

Ruthven, Malise. *Islam in the World*. 1984. An excellent introduction to the history of Islam and its importance in the modern world.

Van Dam, Raymond. *Leadership and Community in Late Antique Gaul*. 1985. Gaul before and during the time of Gregory of Tours.

Waddy, Charis. *Women in Muslim History*. 1980. Focuses on the part played by women at decisive moments in Islam's history.

Watt, William Montgomery. *Muhammad: Prophet and Statesman*. 1961. A scholarly and sympathetic biography of the Prophet.

Weitzmann, Kurt. *The Icon: Holy Images, Sixth to Fourteenth Century*. 1978. A beautifully illustrated guide to the topic by the dean of Byzantine art-historical studies.

Wemple, Suzanne Fonay. *Women in Frankish Society. Marriage and the Cloister, 500–900*. 1981. A pioneering study of women in the Merovingian and Carolingian periods.

Wickham, Chris. *Early Medieval Italy: Central Power and Local Society, 400–1000*. 1981. An important survey of complex transformations, based on primary sources and anthropological insights.

Wood, Ian. *The Merovingian Kingdoms, 450–751*. 1994. A comprehensive and penetrating study.

In 841 a fifteen-year-old boy named William went to serve at the court of King Charles the Bald. William's father was Bernard, an extremely powerful noble. His mother was Dhuoda, a well-educated, pious, and able woman; she administered the family's estates in the south of France while her husband occupied himself in court politics and royal administration. In 841, however, politics had become a dangerous business. King Charles, named after his grandfather Charlemagne, was fighting with his brothers over his portion of the Carolingian Empire, and Bernard (who had been a supporter of Charles's father, Louis the Pious) held only a precarious position at the young king's court. In fact, William was sent to Charles's court as a kind of hostage, to ensure Bernard's loyalty. Anxious about her son, Dhuoda wanted to educate and counsel him, so she wrote a *Handbook* of advice for William, outlining what he ought to believe about God, about politics and society, about his obligations to his family, and above all, about his duties to his father, which she emphasized even over loyalty to the king:

> *In the human understanding of things, royal and imperial appearance and power seem preeminent in the world, and the custom of men is to account those men's actions and their names ahead of all others. . . . But despite all this . . . I caution you to render first to him whose son you are special, faithful, steadfast loyalty as long as you shall live.*

William heeded his mother's words, with tragic results: when Bernard ran afoul of Charles and was executed, William died in a failed attempt to avenge his father.

CHAPTER
9

The Remaking of Three Societies, 756–1054

Learned Women
In the eighth through the eleventh century many noblewomen were well educated and important patrons of the arts. This illustration is from a book of the Gospels commissioned by a German noblewoman, Abbess Hitda, who is depicted offering the manuscript to St. Walburgis.

Dhuoda's *Handbook* reveals the volatile political atmosphere of the mid-ninth century, and her advice to her son points to one of its causes: a crisis of loyalty. Loyalty to emperors and kings competed with allegiances to local authorities; and those, in turn, vied with family ties. Between 756 and 1054, European political structures changed in fundamental ways, reflecting the pressures of these competing loyalties. At the beginning of this period, centralized rulers controlled huge realms; by its end, these realms had fragmented into smaller, more local units. Eventually in the West, as these units sometimes broke apart further, sometimes joined together, the modern map of western Europe began to take shape. The Islamic world also separated into regional states. Of the three heirs of the Roman Empire—Byzantium, the Islamic world, and western Europe—only Byzantium remained relatively unchanged politically, retaining its imperial monarchy. However, under its influence new political entities in the Balkans and Russia emerged.

Byzantium: Renewed Strength and Influence

By the middle of the ninth century, Byzantium was recovering well, both economically and militarily, from its debilitating wars. Beginning in the mid-ninth century and lasting until 1025, Byzantine forces advanced on all fronts, recapturing Crete (960) and Antioch (969) from the Muslims and consolidating control over southern Italy. In 1014 Emperor Basil II Bulgaroctonos (*976–1025)—his epithet meant "Slayer of the Bulgars"—ended two centuries of indecisive battles by destroying the fledgling Bulgar state and incorporating its territories into Byzantium. Victories such as these gave new prestige to the army and to the imperial court, contributing to important social and economic changes.

Most significant, a vital new elite emerged from the military reorganization of the seventh and eighth centuries. The heirs of some of the peasant-soldiers settled on virtually tax-free land, adding to their holdings and forming a new class of large

IMPORTANT DATES

768–814 Charlemagne rules as king of the Franks

786–809 Caliphate of Harun al-Rashid

843 End of iconoclasm at Byzantium; Treaty of Verdun: Frankish kingdom divided

c. 870–c. 1025 Macedonian renaissance at Byzantium

871–899 Reign of King Alfred the Great in England

969–1171 Fatimid Dynasty in Egypt

976–1025 Reign of Byzantine Emperor Basil II Bulgaroctonos

1054 Schism between Roman Catholic and Greek Orthodox churches

Basil II Bulgaroctonos
Despite the Bulgars' conversion to Byzantine Christianity, they were continually at war with the Byzantine state until 1014, when Emperor Basil II defeated them decisively. In this illustration, made just after his victory, Basil is shown in triumph, with the Bulgarians prostrate at his feet.

Kievan Russia and Byzantium, c. 1000

landowners. Many smaller peasants, unable or unwilling to pay their taxes,were compelled to give up their small freeholds to become dependents of these great landlords. They still tilled the soil, but they no longer owned it.

The most powerful of the large landowners were the generals, the *strategoi*, who had been set up as imperial appointees to rule the new districts, the *themes*, and who now found their prestige enhanced by victory. The *strategoi* took orders from the emperor or empress (during the period 756–1054 three powerful women ruled, generally as regents for their young sons), who told them

when to prepare for campaigns and summon troops. But the *strategos* also exercised considerable power on his own. One *strategos*, Michael Lachanodracon, disbanded the monasteries in his *theme* and sold off their property on his own initiative, sending the proceeds to the imperial treasury as a gesture of comradery with his war companion, Emperor Constantine V. Although individual *strategoi* could be demoted or dismissed by irate emperors, most *strategoi* formed a powerful hereditary class of landowners. In these ways, the social hierarchy of Byzantium began to resemble that of western Europe, where grand estates owned by aristocrats were farmed by peasants whose tax and service obligations bound them to the fields they cultivated.

Some Byzantine emperors tried to counteract this new development. Moved by the plight of peasants who had been forced to sell or give up their properties to powerful men, for example, Basil II guaranteed their right to bring suit no matter how much time had elapsed since their land had been appropriated. "We have been very disturbed on behalf of the poor," he wrote. "The poor man ought in no case to be prevented from seeking and gaining the return of his own property." Such legislation slowed, but did not stop, the subjugation of the peasantry in the Byzantine Empire.

The Macedonian Renaissance

The most vocal and visible members of the new elite resided not in the countryside, however, but in the imperial court at Constantinople. Flushed with victory, reminded of Byzantium's past glory, they now revived classical intellectual pursuits. Basil I (*867–886) from Macedonia founded the imperial dynasty that presided over the so-called Macedonian renaissance (c. 870–c. 1025). Those now in power in Byzantium came from families that had bided their time during the dark days of the seventh and eighth centuries, when the Byzantine Empire had been under siege and the Byzantine emperors had suppressed the use and production of icons. Even in those anxious times, however, some of the educated elite had persisted in studying the classics in spite of the trend toward a simple religious education.

Now, with the empire slowly regaining its military eminence and with icons permanently restored in 843 by Empress Theodora, this scholarly elite thrived again. Byzantine artists produced new works of art, and emperors and other members of the new court society, liberated from sober taboos, sponsored sumptuous artistic productions. Emperor Constantine VII Porphyrogenitos (*913–959) wrote books of geography and history and financed the work of other scholars and artists. He even supervised the details of his craftspeople's products, insisting on exacting standards: "Who could enumerate how many artisans the Porphyrogenitos corrected? He corrected the stonemasons, the carpenters, the goldsmiths, the silversmiths, and the blacksmiths," wrote a historian supported by the

Art Sponsored by Constantine Porphyrogenitos
In this relief, carved during the rule of Constantine Porphyrogenitos out of a piece of jasper, the artist rendered Christ in a gesture of blessing with body-clinging drapery that reflected pagan classical Greek styles.

same emperor's patronage. When a westerner, Liutprand, bishop of Cremona, visited Porphyrogenitos's court, he marveled at its luxury and called the emperor himself "a skillful artist." Unfortunately, none of Porphyrogenitos's own work survives; but some art produced under his patronage shows extraordinary mastery of classical techniques in the modeling of figures and suggestion of three-dimensional space and atmosphere.

Other members of the imperial court also supported writers, philosophers, and historians. Scholars wrote summaries of classical literature, encyclopedias of ancient knowledge, and commentaries on classical authors. Others copied manuscripts of religious and theological commentaries, such as the Homilies of St. Gregory Nazianzen, liturgical texts, Bibles, and Psalters. They hoped to revive the intellectual and artistic achievements of the heyday of imperial Roman rule. But the Macedonian renaissance could not possibly succeed in this endeavor: too much had changed since the time of

The Macedonian Renaissance
The figures in this Psalter illustration appear to live and move in a landscape and to have a relationship with one another, as in classical art. The figures, too, are modeled on classical prototypes: for example, King David, the supposed author of the Psalms, is patterned on Orpheus, the famous musician of pagan mythology.

Justinian. Nevertheless, the renaissance permanently integrated classical forms into Byzantine political and religious life. A jasper carving of Christ in a gesture of blessing illustrates this point: the theme is religious, but the figure of Christ, with his lively movement and naturally falling drapery, recalls classical models.

The merging of classical and Christian traditions is clearest in manuscript illuminations (painted illustrations). Both at Byzantium and in the West, artists chose their subjects by considering the texts they were to illustrate and the ways in which previous artists had handled particular themes. They drew upon traditional models to convey long-hallowed information. Artists thus worked within certain constraints in order to make their subjects identifiable. In much the same way that a modern illustrator of Santa Claus relies on a tradition dictating a plump man with a bushy white beard, medieval artists depended on particular visual cues. These characteristics constituted the iconography of their

subject. For example, the artist of one illuminated Psalter who wanted to illustrate King David, the supposed poet of the Psalms, turned to a model of Orpheus, the enchanting musician of Greek mythology. The style of this artist's painting—an atmospheric setting in which solid, weighty figures appear to act—was also based on classical models.

The Wealth and Power of Byzantium

New wealth matched Byzantium's revived power. The emperors drew revenues from vast and growing imperial estates. For example, when the usurper Emperor Romanos I Lacapenos (✳920–944) reconquered Mitelene on his eastern front, he incorporated it directly into imperial property. Emperors could levy revenues and services on the general population at will—requiring them to build bridges and roads, to offer lodging to the imperial retinue, and to pay taxes in cash. These taxes increased over time, partly because of fiscal reforms and partly because of population increases. The approximately 7 million people who lived in the empire in 780 had swelled to about 8 million less than a century later.

The emperor's or empress's power extended over both civil administration and military command. The only check on his or her authority was the possibility of an uprising, either at court or in the army. This is one reason that emperors surrounded themselves with eunuchs: castrated men were believed unfit for imperial office, and they could not have ambitions for their sons. Eunuchs were employed in the civil service; they held high positions in the army; and they were important palace officials. Eunuchs had a privileged place in Byzantine administrations because they were less liable than others to have an independent power base. Emperors, supported by their wealth and power, negotiated from a position of strength with other rulers. Embassies were exchanged, and the Byzantine court received and entertained diplomats with elaborate ceremonies. One such diplomat, Liutprand of Cremona, reported on his audience with Constantine Porphyrogenitos:

> *Leaning upon the shoulders of two eunuchs I was brought into the emperor's presence. At my approach [mechanical] lions began to roar and birds to cry out, each according to its kind.*
> *. . . After I had three times made obeisance to the emperor with my face upon the ground, I*

Muslim and Byzantine Interaction
This silk, which shows lions that symbolize the emperor's greatness, was produced at Constantinople between 976 and 1025. The style reflects silks produced in the Islamic world at about the same time and attests to the close relations between the two cultures.

lifted my head, and behold! the man whom just before I had seen sitting on a moderately elevated seat had now changed his raiment and was sitting on the level of the ceiling. How it was done I could not imagine, unless perhaps he was lifted up by some such sort of device as we use for raising the timbers of a wine press.

Although this elaborate court ceremonial clearly amused Liutprand, its real function was to express the serious, sacred, concentrated power of imperial majesty. Liutprand missed the point, because he was a westerner unaccustomed to such displays.

The emperor's wealth relied on the prosperity of an agricultural economy organized for trade.

State control and entrepreneurial enterprise were delicately balanced in Byzantine commerce. Although the emperor controlled craft and commercial guilds (such as those in the silk industry) to ensure imperial revenues and a stable supply of valuable and useful commodities, entrepreneurs organized most of the fairs held throughout the empire. Foreign merchants traded within the empire, either at Constantinople or in certain border cities. Because this international trade intertwined with foreign policy, the Byzantine government considered it a political as well as an economic matter. Emperors issued privileges to certain "nations" (as, for example, the Venetians, Russians, and Jews were called), regulating the fees they were obliged to pay and the services they were to render. At the end of the tenth century, for example, the Venetians bargained to reduce their customs' dues per ship from thirty *solidi* (coins) to two; in return they promised to transport Byzantine soldiers to Italy whenever the emperor wished. Merchants from each nation were lodged at state expense in certain areas of the city for about three months in order to transact their business. The Syrians, although Muslims, received special privileges: their merchants were allowed to stay at Constantinople for six months. In return, Byzantine traders were guaranteed protection in Syria, and the two governments split the income from the taxes on the sales Byzantine merchants made there. Thus Byzantine trade flourished in the Levant (the region bordering the southeastern part of the Mediterranean Sea) and, thanks to Venetian intermediaries, with the Latin West.

Equally significant was trade to the north. Byzantines may have mocked the "barbarians," dressed in animal skins, who lived beyond the Black Sea. Nevertheless, many Byzantines wore furs from Russia. Byzantines also imported Russian slaves, wax, and honey. Some Russians even served as mercenaries in the Byzantine army. The relationship between the two peoples became even closer at the end of the tenth century.

The Creation of Slavic States in the Balkans and Russia

The shape of modern Eastern Europe grew out of the Slavic kingdoms created during the period from the mid-eighth to the mid-tenth century. Byzantine influence predominated in some of these societies, notably Russia, Bulgaria, and Serbia.* Other new realms—the ancestors of the modern Polish, Czech, Slovak, and Croat states—eventually fell into the orbit of the Latin West.

By 800, Slavic settlements dotted the area from the Danube River down to Greece and from the Black Sea to Croatia. The Bulgar khagan ruled over the largest realm, populated mostly by Slavic peoples and situated northwest of Constantinople. Under Khagan Krum (*c. 803–814) and his son, Slavic rule stretched west all the way to the Tisza River in modern Hungary. At about the same time as Krum's triumphant expansion, however, the Byzantine Empire began its own campaigns to conquer, convert, and control these Slavic regions.

The Byzantine offensive began under Emperor Nicephorus I (*802–811), who waged war against the Slavs of Greece in the Peloponnesus, set up a new Christian diocese there, organized it as a new military *theme*, and forcibly resettled Christians in the area to counteract Slavic paganism. The Byzantines followed this pattern of conquest as they pushed northward. By the end of the ninth century Byzantium ruled all of Greece. Still under Nicephorus, the Byzantines launched a massive attack against the Bulgarians, took the chief city (Pliska), plundered it, burned it to the ground, and then marched against Krum's encampment in the Balkan Mountains. Krum took advantage of his position, however, attacked the imperial troops, killed Nicephorus, and brought home the emperor's skull in triumph. Cleaned out and lined with silver, the skull served as the victorious Krum's drinking goblet. In 816 peace was drawn up between the two sides that lasted for thirty years. But hostility remained latent, and wars between the Bulgarians and Byzantines broke out with increasing intensity. Skirmishes in 846, 852, and 863 gave way to longer wars in 894–897 and throughout the tenth century. The Byzantines slowly advanced, at first taking Bulgaria's eastern territory,

and then, in a slow and methodical conquest (1001–1018) led by Emperor Basil II, aptly called the "Bulgar-Slayer," subjecting the entire region to Byzantine rule.

Meanwhile, the Byzantines also embarked on a religious offensive. In 863 they sent two brothers, Cyril and Methodius, as missionaries to Old (or Great) Moravia, a Slavic domain probably centered along the Sava River. Cyril and Methodius, well-educated Greeks, spoke one dialect of Slavic fluently. They devised an alphabet for Slavic based on Greek forms (the ancestor of the modern Cyrillic alphabet used in Russia, Bulgaria, and Serbia, for example). They also created a written language, later called Old Church Slavonic, based on their dialect of Slavic mixed (when they found it necessary, especially for theological ideas) with Greek words. Armed with translations of the Gospel and other church writings, they began preaching in Moravia.

At about the same time, the Byzantines attacked Bulgaria and forced the khagan, Boris, to accept Christianity. Boris had already decided to convert to Christianity, but under Frankish rather than Byzantine auspices. He capitulated reluctantly and was forced to give up his Frankish alliance and accept Byzantine missionaries and churchmen, who used the methods and writings of Cyril and Methodius.

With the arrival around 899 of a new group of invaders, the Magyars, into the Danubian basin, the Slavic world was effectively divided. Those Slavs bordering on the Frankish kingdom, such as the Czechs and Poles, came under influences that tied them to the church at Rome rather than to the Byzantine church. But Bulgaria became a Byzantine province. The Serbs, encouraged by Byzantium to oppose the Bulgarians, began to form the state that would become Serbia,

The Balkans, c. 800–900

in the shadow of Byzantine interests and religion. Other small Slavic principalities, such as the future Montenegro, tried to maintain their independence by playing papal and Byzantine interests off against one another.

---

*Terms like these, which imply boundaries and national identities, are modern. Throughout the period discussed here, boundaries were vague, and although people had a sense of ethnic identity, the nature of this identity and even the name of the ethnic group was very fluid and changeable. Perhaps most important, such identity was not connected with a particular place. Thus a term like *Croatia* refers here to the region in which the Croats were settled rather than to a nation-state in the modern sense.

Ninth- and tenth-century Russia lay outside the sphere of direct Byzantine rule, but like Serbia and Bulgaria, it came under increasingly strong Byzantine cultural and religious influence. Vikings—Scandinavian adventurers who ranged over vast stretches of ninth-century Europe seeking trade, booty, and land—had penetrated Russia from the north and imposed their rule over the Slavs inhabiting the broad river valleys connecting the Baltic Sea with the Black Sea and thence with Constantinople. Like the Bulgars in Bulgaria, the Scandinavian Vikings gradually blended into the larger Slavic population. At the end of the ninth century, one Dnieper valley chief, Oleg, established control over most of the tribes in southwestern Russia and forced peoples farther away to pay tribute. The tribal association he created formed the nucleus of Kievan Russia, named for the city that had become the commercial center of the region and is today the capital of Ukraine.

Kievan Russia and Byzantium began their relationship with war, developed it through trade agreements, and finally sustained it by religion. Around 905, Oleg launched a military expedition to Constantinople, forcing the Byzantines to pay a large indemnity and open their doors to Russian traders in exchange for peace. Although a few Christians already lived in Russia—along with Jews and probably some Muslims—the Russians' conversion to Christianity was spearheaded by a Russian ruler later in the century. The grand prince of Kiev and all Russia, Vladimir (*c. 980–1015), and the Byzantine emperor, Basil II, agreed that Vladimir should adopt the Byzantine form of Christianity. He took the new name Basil in honor of the emperor and married the emperor's sister, Anne; then he reportedly had all the people of his state baptized in the Dnieper River.

Vladimir's conversion represented a wider pattern, not only of the Christianization of Slavic realms such as Old Moravia, Serbia, and Bulgaria but also (under the auspices of the Roman church rather than the Byzantine) of the rulers and peoples of Poland, Hungary, Denmark, and Norway. Russia's conversion to Christianity was especially significant, because Russia was geographically as close to the Islamic world as to the Christian and might conceivably have become an Islamic land. By converting to Christianity, Russians made themselves heirs to Byzantium, assuming its church, customs, art, and political ideology, although with

modifications. For example, their language of worship was not Greek but Old Church Slavonic, which they readily understood. Similarly, Russian builders modeled their new churches on Byzantine forms but adapted them to indigenous needs, such as pitching roofs steeply to prevent snow from accumulating during the harsh Russian winters. Russia's adoption of Christianity linked it to the Christian world. But choosing the Byzantine rather than the Roman form of Christianity later served to isolate Russia from western Europe, because in time the Greek and Roman churches became increasingly estranged over beliefs, practices, and administration.

Russian rulers at times sought to cement relations with central and western Europe, which in turn were tied to Rome. Prince Iaroslav the Wise (*1019–1054) forged such links through his own marriage and those of his sons and daughters to rulers and princely families in France, Hungary, Sweden, and Norway. Iaroslav encouraged intellectual and artistic developments that would connect Russian culture to the classical past. According to an account written about a half century after his death, Iaroslav

Rise of Kievan Russia at the Time of Iaroslav

applied himself to books and read them continually day and night. He assembled many scribes to translate from the Greek into Slavic. He caused many books to be written and collected, through which true believers are instructed and enjoy religious education.

At his own church of St. Sophia, at Kiev, which copied the one at Constantinople, Iaroslav created a major library.

When he died, Iaroslav divided his kingdom among his sons. Civil wars broke out between the brothers and eventually between cousins, shredding what unity Russia had known. Massive invasions by outsiders, particularly from the region of the steppes (grassy plains), further weakened Kievan rulers, who were eventually displaced by princes from northern Russia. At the crossroads of East and West, Russia could meet and adopt a great variety of traditions; but its situation also opened it to unremitting military pressures.

The Rise of Independent Islamic States

The Abbasids' overthrow of the Umayyads in 750 marked the end of exclusively Arab and Syrian control over the Islamic state. From their new capital in Baghdad (still the capital of present-day Iraq), the Abbasids built an empire based largely on Persia's political traditions and Iraq's prosperous commercial and agricultural economy. With a military force to bolster their claim to represent Islam as Muhammad's successors, the Abbasids dominated the Islamic world in the eight and ninth centuries, until regional and religious discontents and loyalties eventually undermined their hegemony and led to the formation of separate states.

Fragmentation and Diversity

The Abbasid caliph Harun al-Rashid (*786–809) presided over a flourishing empire from Baghdad. (He and his court are immortalized in *Thousand and One Nights*, a classic of world literature, which is a series of anonymous stories about Scheherezade's efforts to keep her husband from killing her by telling him a story each night for 1,001 nights.) Charlemagne, Harun's contemporary, was very impressed with the elephant Harun sent him as a gift, along with monkeys, spices, and medicines. But these items were mainstays of everyday commerce in Harun's Iraq. For example, a mid-ninth-century list of imports inventoried "tigers, panthers, elephants, panther skins, rubies, white sandal, ebony, and coconuts" from India; "silk, chinaware, paper, ink, peacocks, racing horses, saddles, felts, [and] cinnamon" from China.

The Abbasid dynasty began to decline after Harun's death, mostly because of economic problems. Obliged to support a huge army and increasingly complex civil service, the Abbasids found their tax base inadequate. They needed to collect revenues from their provinces, such as Syria and Egypt, but the most powerful people within those regions often refused to send the receipts. After Harun's caliphate, ex-soldiers, seeking better salaries, recognized different caliphs and fought for power in savage civil wars. The caliphs tried to bypass the regular army, made up largely of free Muslim foot soldiers, by turning to slaves, bought and armed to serve as mounted cavalry. This expedient failed, however, and in the tenth century the caliphs became increasingly powerless; independent rulers established themselves in the various regions of the Islamic world. To support themselves militarily, many of these new rulers themselves turned to independent military commanders who led armies of Mamluks—Turkish slaves or freedmen trained as professional mounted soldiers. Mamluks were well paid to maintain their mounts and arms, and many gained renown and high positions at the courts of regional rulers. Anushtakin al-Disbari, for example, a Turk from Transoxania who was captured and sold as a slave as a youth, proved himself an able soldier and administrator and garnered an appointment as governor of Palestine and Syria, a position he held until his death in 1041.

Thus in the Islamic world, as in the Byzantine Empire, a new military elite arose. But the Muslim and Byzantine elites differed in key ways. Whereas the Byzantine *strategoi* were rooted to particular regions, the Mamluks were highly mobile. They were organized into tightly knit companies bound together by devotion to a particular general and by a strong esprit de corps. They also easily changed employers, moving from ruler to ruler for pay.

Religion also contributed to political fragmentation. In the tenth century one group of Shi'ites, calling themselves the Fatimids (after Fatimah, Muhammad's daughter and wife of Ali), began a successful political movement. Allying with the Berbers in North Africa, the Fatimids established themselves in 909 as rulers in the region now called Tunisia. The Fatimid Ubayd Allah claimed to be not only the true *imam*,* descendant of Ali, but also the *mahdi*, the "divinely guided" messiah, come to bring justice on earth. In 969 the Fatimids declared

---

*By this time some Shi'ite groups believed that each *imam* after Ali had designated his successor, so that at any given time a single true *imam*, even if he had no political role, held power. This "line" of *imams* was called the *imamate*; Ubayd Allah claimed to belong to it.

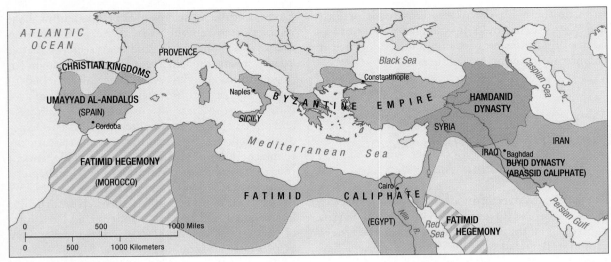

Islamic States, c. 1000

themselves rulers of Egypt. Their dynasty lasted for about two hundred years. Fatimid leaders also controlled North Africa, Arabia, and even Syria for a time. Under the Fatimids, Muslims followed Shi'ite customs and festivals, such as celebrating the day on which Muhammad was supposed to have recognized Ali as his successor. Shi'ism became predominant in much of the Islamic world until the arrival of the Sunni Seljuk Turks in the mid-eleventh century.

With the fragmentation of political and religious unity, each of the tenth- and early eleventh-century Islamic states built upon regional traditions under local rulers. Although western Europeans called all Muslims Saracens without distinction, Muslims in fact came from different regions, races, and traditions. Whereas the Shi'ites dominated Egypt, for example, Sunni Muslims ruled al-Andalus (Spain).

Unlike the other independent Islamic states, which were forged during the ninth and tenth centuries, the Spanish emirate of Cordoba (so called because its ruler took the secular title *emir*, commander, and fixed his capital at Cordoba) was created at the very start of the Abbasid caliphate. Abd al-Rahman, a member of the Umayyad family, founded the emirate. During the Abbasid revolution, he fled to Morocco, gathered an army, invaded Spain, and in 756, after only one battle, was declared emir. He and his successors ruled a broad range of peoples, including many Jews and Christians. After

the initial Arab conquest of Spain, the Christians had adopted so much of the new language and so many of the customs that they were called "Mozarabs," that is, "like Arabs." The Arabs allowed them freedom of worship and let them live according to their own laws. Some Mozarabs were content with their status; others converted to Islam; still others intermarried (most commonly, Christian women married Muslim men and raised their children as Muslims). A vocal and determined minority of Christians chafed under Muslim rule. At Cordoba in about 850, some of these malcontents openly declared Muhammad "the damned and filthy prophet," courting martyrdom. About fifty Christians were executed for blasphemy before the episode ended. Strict new measures against Christians resulted.

In the tenth century, however, tensions in al-Andalus eased enormously. Under Abd al-Rahman III (912–961) who took the title caliph in 929 (three caliphates now existed: Fatimid, Abbasid, and Umayyad), members of all religious groups were given absolute freedom of worship and equal opportunity to rise in the civil service. Concurrently, Abd al-Rahman initiated important diplomatic contracts with Byzantine and European rulers. He felt strong enough not to worry much about the weak and tiny Christian kingdoms squeezed into northern Spain, between the Duero River and the Atlantic Ocean. At about the same time as the

Macedonian renaissance at Byzantium, al-Rahman and his son, al-Hakam II (✳961–976), presided over a brilliant court culture, patronizing scholars, poets, and artists. The library at Cordoba contained the largest collection in Europe, and the traditions of philosophy and scholarship established there would survive many political changes and even the breakup of the Caliphate of Cordoba into *taifas* in 1031.

Commercial Unity

Although the regions of the Islamic world were diverse, they maintained a measure of unity. Their principal bond was the Arabic language. At once poetic and sacred (for it was the language of the Qur'an), Arabic was also the language of commerce and government from Baghdad to Cordoba. Moreover, despite political differences, borders were open: a craftsman could move from one place to another; a landowner in Morocco might very well own property in al-Andalus; a young man from North Africa would think nothing of going to Baghdad to find a wife; a young girl purchased as a slave in Mecca might become part of a prince's harem in Baghdad. With no national barriers to trade and few regulations (though every city and town had its own customs' dues), traders regularly dealt in far-flung, various, and often exotic goods.

Although we might expect that Islam itself was the primary reason for this internationalism, open borders extended to non-Muslims as well. For example, historians know a great deal about the Jewish community at a city near present-day Cairo, Egypt. The Jews who lived there left all their writings, including many notes and shopping lists, in a depository (*geniza*) of their synagogue. The *geniza* preserved these documents for burial. Originally only writings that contained the name of God were buried, but soon anything written in Hebrew was placed in the *geniza*. By chance, the materials in the Cairo *geniza* were preserved, and they show us the world of the Mediterranean between the tenth and the thirteenth centuries more vividly than any other single set of documents. Above all, they reveal a cosmopolitan middle-class society, occupied with trade, schooling, marriages, divorces, poetry, litigation—the issues and activities of everyday life. For example, some of these documents show us that middle-class Jewish women disposed of their own property and that widows often reared and educated their children on their own.

The Tustari brothers, Jewish merchants from southern Iran whose lives are illuminated by the *geniza* documents, typified the commercial activity in the Arabic-speaking world. By 1026 they had established a flourishing business in Egypt. Although the Tustaris did not have "branch offices," informal contacts allowed them many of the same advantages and much flexibility: friends and family in Iran shipped them fine textiles to sell in Egypt, and the Tustaris exported Egyptian fabrics to sell in Iran. Dealing in fabric could yield fabulous wealth, for

Jews Under Muslim Rule
This letter, written c. 1000 in Hebrew, ended up among the geniza *documents near Cairo. It illustrates the far-flung connections of Jewish merchants: the writer, who lived in Tunisia, writes to an acquaintance in Egypt about business matters in Spain.*

cloth was essential not only for clothing but also for home decoration: textiles covered walls; curtains separated rooms. The Tustari brothers held the very highest rank in Jewish society and had contacts with Muslim rulers. The son of one of the brothers converted to Islam and became *vizier* (chief minister) to the Fatimids in Egypt. But the sophisticated Islamic society of the tenth and eleventh centuries supported networks even more vast than those represented by the Tustari family. Muslim merchants brought tin from England; salt and gold from Timbuktu; amber, gold, and copper from Russia; and slaves from every region.

The Islamic Renaissance

Just as cosmopolitan as the merchants were the many scholars, both Jewish and Muslim, who traveled from Baghdad to Cordoba in search of learning or in hopes of teaching or other employment. Unlike the Macedonian renaissance of Byzantium, which was concentrated in Constantinople, a "Renaissance of Islam" occurred throughout the Islamic world. It was particularly dazzling in such urban court centers as Cordoba. Rather than hindering cultural activity, the dissolution of the caliphate into separate political entities multiplied the centers of learning and intellectual productivity.

Already in the eighth century, the Abbasid caliphs endowed research libraries and set up centers for translation where scholars culled the writings of the ancients, including the classics of Persia, India, and Greece. Scholars read, translated, and commented on the works of neo-Platonists and Aristotle. They imported texts from India, in which (around the mid-ninth century) an Arabic intellectual discovered Hindu numerical notation. Arab mathematicians realized the remarkable potential of these numbers: they added the zero and contributed significantly to algebraic theory (from the Arabic *al-jabr*, meaning "reunification"). Al-Khwarizmi wrote his famous book on equation theory in about 825. Other scholars, such as Alhazen (c. 1000), wrote further studies on cubic and quadratic equations. No wonder the numbers 1, 2, 3, and so on were known as "Arabic numerals" when they were introduced into western Europe in the twelfth century.

The newly independent Islamic rulers supported science as well as mathematics. Unusual because she was a woman was al-Asturlabi, who followed

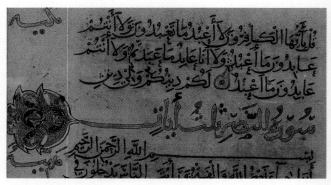

Arabic Calligraphy
This page from the Qur'an was copied by Ibn al-Bawwab, who helped develop a new form of Arabic cursive called naskhi *script around 1000.*

her father's profession as a maker of astrolabes (which measured the altitude of the sun and stars in order to calculate time and latitude) for the court at Syria. More typical were men like Ibn Sina (980–1037), known in the West as Avicenna, who wrote books on logic, the natural sciences, and physics. His *Canon of Medicine* systematized earlier treatises and reconciled them with his own experience as a physician. Active in the centers of power, he served as vizier to various rulers. In his autobiography he spoke with pleasure and pride about his intellectual development:

> One day I asked permission [of the ruler] to go into [his doctors'] library, look at their books, and read the medical ones. He gave me permission, and I went into a palace of many rooms, each with trunks full of books, back-to-back. In one room there were books on Arabic and poetry, in another books on jurisprudence, and similarly in each room books on a single subject. I read the catalogue of books of the ancients and asked for those I needed. . . . When I reached the age of eighteen, I had completed the study of all these sciences.

Ibn Sina's words reveal the importance of Arabic literature and Islamic law, even for a physician. Islamic governments put special emphasis on patronizing religious writings. *Hadith* or "tradition" literature, which recorded the sayings or actions of Muhammad as transmitted by a chain of informants, achieved its authoritative form in the ninth and tenth centuries.

In contrast to Byzantine scholars, whose work focused primarily on enhancing the prestige of the ruling classes, Islamic scholars had more pragmatic goals—to be physicians to the rich, teachers to the young, and contributors to passionate religious debates. They generally wrote "working manuscripts" rather than elegantly illuminated texts, and they used paper—relatively cheap sheets made of wood pulp and imported from China—rather than the expensive parchment that kept manuscripts in Byzantium and Europe out of the hands of all but the very rich.* Arabic manuscripts were made beautiful, however, by the further development of calligraphy in the so-called *naskhi* script.

The Creation and Division of a New Western Empire

Byzantium, the Islamic world, and Europe in the eighth and early ninth centuries all had monarchical governments, but this characteristic was one of the few they shared. In what is today western Europe, the Carolingians elaborated an exalted ideal of anointed kingship, but they exerted their power at the local level unevenly. They depended largely on the personal loyalties of their bishops, governors, and military men (counts, margraves, and—a title given out sparingly—dukes). These governors and other powerful men eventually began to go their own way, building castles, collecting public dues, hearing court cases without royal supervision; in effect, they carved out independent principalities. Like the king, these new rulers relied on personal loyalties, forming bonds of fealty (fidelity, trust, and service) with their vassals, who served them as armed and mounted warriors. The resulting system of decentralized loyalties is often called feudalism.

Public Power and Private Relationships

The Carolingian rulers maintained their political power in part through kin networks and personal alliances. Their sons served as semiautonomous rulers of subkingdoms, their daughters married

powerful nobles in the kingdom. Personal alliances were forged with vassals and *fideles* (literally, "faithful men"), with whom they had a relationship of mutual trust and interdependency. Their counts were *fideles* to whom the kings entrusted the public functions—holding courts, collecting dues, calling local freemen to arms—in the various regions of their realm. In addition to a share in the revenues of the county, the counts received benefices, later also called fiefs (pronounced "feefs"), which were temporary grants of land given in return for service. These short-term arrangements often became permanent, however, once a count's son inherited the job and the fiefs of his father. By the end of the ninth century, fiefs were often property that could be passed on to heirs.

From the middle Latin word for fief comes the word *feudal*, and historians often call the social and economic system created by the relationship between vassals, lords, and fiefs *feudalism*.* Medieval feudalism included the institutions created by the personal bonds between lords and vassals; the military style of life and values they shared; the small, local regions they dominated; and the economic system based on manors and dependent serfs that buttressed them. In the course of the ninth and tenth centuries, more and more members of the upper classes became part of feudalism, as vassals pledged themselves to a lord and lords tied themselves to vassals. By the eleventh century many members of the upper military classes considered these relationships ideal, and they were celebrated in poetry, defined in learned treatises, and described by observant chroniclers.

The chroniclers made clear that becoming the vassal of a lord often involved both ritual gestures and verbal promises. Witnessed by others, the vassal-to-be knelt and, placing his hands between

---

*Parchment is made from animal skin.

*The term *feudalism* has had (and continues to have) many different meanings. In France in the eighteenth century, it meant the system of privilege nobles enjoyed and the condition of unfree dependency serfs (peasants) suffered on the great estates they farmed for the nobility. In the nineteenth century, Karl Marx used *feudalism* to refer to a system dominated by a military ruling class of property owners. Many historians in England continue to use this definition. More recently, however, some historians have tried to differentiate between *manorialism*, involving serfs and landlords, and *feudalism*, involving only members of the upper classes. Still other historians find the term *feudalism* useless, precisely because it has so many different meanings.

the hands of his lord, said, "I promise to be your man." This act, known as homage, was followed by the promise of fealty, which the vassal swore with his hand on relics or a Bible. Then the vassal and the lord kissed. In an age in which many people could not read, a public ceremony like this represented a visual and verbal contract. Vassalage bound the lord and vassal to one another with reciprocal obligations: they would help, not harm, one another. The lord would provide food, clothing, and perhaps a fief for the vassal. The vassal would fight for his lord and counsel him.

Carolingian Warfare and Imperial Power, 750–850

This sort of feudalism was only just beginning in the time of the early Carolingian kings. The power of these kings rested on the prestige of their office, their inheritance of Merovingian administrative traditions, their alliance with the papacy and other churchmen, their ability to expand their kin networks through marriage, and their success at war, from which they gained land and plunder to distribute to their followers, whether vassals or not.

The most famous Carolingian king was Charles (*768–814). He was called "the Great" ("le Magne" in Old French) by his contemporaries, and epic poems portrayed Charlemagne as a just, brave, wise, and warlike king. In a biography written by Einhard, his friend and younger contemporary, and patterned closely upon Suetonius's *Lives of the Caesars*, Charlemagne was the very model of a Roman emperor. Other scholars at his court described him as another David, the anointed Old Testament king. Modern historians are less dazzled than his contemporaries were, knowing that even before Charlemagne's death Carolingian power had begun to wane. Nevertheless, Charlemagne's vision—an empire that would unite the martial and learned traditions of the Roman and Germanic worlds with the legacy of Christianity—remained a European goal long after Charlemagne and his dynasty had turned to dust. His vision lay at the core of his own political activity, his building programs, and his active support of scholarship and education.

Becoming sole ruler of the Franks after the death of his brother, Carloman, in 771, Charlemagne spent the early years of his reign conquering lands in all directions and subjugating the conquered peoples. In 773 he moved south and invaded Italy, seizing the crown of the Lombard kings and claiming northern Italy. Affirming the popes' rights to rule the region around Rome, Charlemagne nevertheless retained the title given to his father: *patrician* (a nebulous term at the time, meaning something like "protector") of the Romans. He then moved northward and began a long and difficult war against the Germanic Saxons, concluded only after over thirty years of fighting, during which he forcibly annexed Saxon territory and converted the Saxon people to Christianity. To the southeast Charlemagne waged a campaign against the Avars, the people who had fought the Byzantines almost two centuries before. His biographer Einhard exulted, "all the money and treasure that had been years amassing was seized, and no war in which the Franks have ever engaged within the memory of man brought them such riches and such booty." To the southwest Charlemagne led an expedition to Spain. Although suffering a notable but local defeat at Roncesvalles in 778, he did set up a *march*, or military buffer region, between al-Andalus and his own realm.

By the 790s Charlemagne's kingdom stretched eastward to the Saale River (today in eastern Germany), southeast to what is today Austria, and south to Spain and Italy. Such hegemony in the West was unheard of since the time of the Roman Empire. Flushed with success, Charlemagne began to act according to the old Roman model by sponsoring building programs to symbolize his authority, standardizing weights and measures, and acting as a patron of intellectual and artistic efforts. He built a capital city at Aachen, complete with a church patterned on one built by Justinian at Ravenna. He even dismantled the columns, mosaics, and marble from the church at Ravenna and carted them northward to use in constructing his new church. He initiated a revival of Christian and classical learning. To discourage corruption, Charlemagne appointed special officials, called *missi dominici* (meaning "those sent out by the lord king"), to oversee the counts on the king's behalf. These men, chosen from the same aristocratic class as bishops and counts, traveled in pairs to make a circuit of regions of the kingdom. As one of Charlemagne's capitularies (summaries of royal

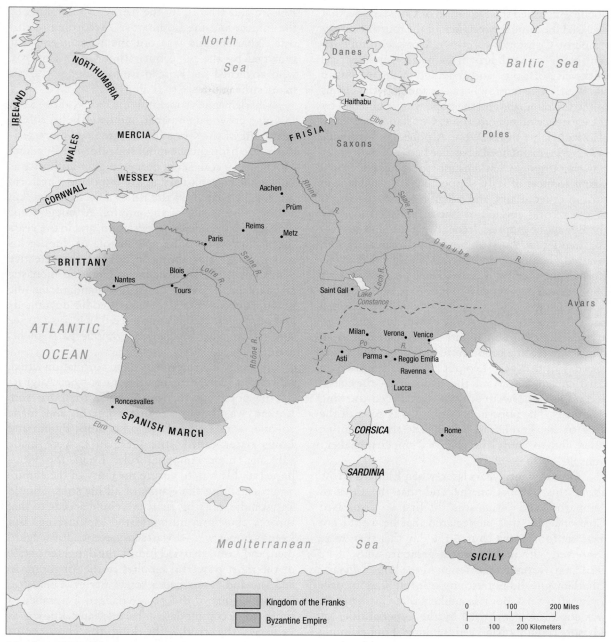

Charlemagne's Empire

decisions) put it, the *missi* "are to make diligent inquiry wherever people claim that someone has done them an injustice, so that the *missi* fully carry out the law and do justice for everyone everywhere, whether in the holy churches of God or among the poor, orphans, or widows."

While Charlemagne was busy imitating Roman emperors through his conquests, his building programs, his legislation, and his efforts at church reform, the papacy was beginning to claim imperial power for itself. At some point, perhaps in the mid-750s, members of the papal chancery forged a document, called the Donation of Constantine, that declared the pope the recipient of the fourth-century Emperor Constantine's crown, cloak, and military rank along with "all provinces, palaces, and districts of the city of Rome and Italy and of the regions of the West." The tension between the imperial claims of the Carolingians and the pope was heightened by the existence of an emperor at Constantinople who also had rights in the West. A pope like Hadrian I (✳772–795) maintained a balance between these three powers, urging Charlemagne to recognize papal claims to most of Italy, supporting Charlemagne in turn in other affairs, and assenting to the decisions of the second council of Nicea, presided over by the Byzantine empress Irene. But Hadrian's successor, Leo III (✳795–816), tipped the balance. In 799, accused of adultery and perjury by a faction of the Roman aristocracy, Leo narrowly escaped being blinded and having his tongue cut out. He fled northward to Charlemagne, who had him escorted back to Rome under royal protection and who arrived there himself in late November 800 to an imperial welcome orchestrated by Leo. On Christmas day of that year, Leo put an imperial crown on Charlemagne's head and the "Romans"—the clergy and nobles who were present—acclaimed the king Augustus. The pope hoped in this way to exalt the king of the Franks, to downgrade the Byzantine ruler, and to enjoy the role of "emperor maker" himself.

About twenty years later, when Einhard wrote about this coronation, he said that the titles of "emperor" and "Augustus" at first so displeased Charlemagne "that he declared that he would not have set foot in the church the day that they were conferred, although it was a great feastday, if he could have foreseen the design of the Pope." In fact, Charlemagne did not use any title but king for over a year afterward. But it is unlikely that Charlemagne was completely surprised by the imperial title; his advisors certainly had been thinking about claiming it. He might have hesitated because he feared the reaction of the Byzantine empress, as Einhard went on to suggest, or he might well have objected to the papal role in his crowning rather than to the crown itself. When he finally did call himself emperor, after establishing a peace with Empress Irene, he used a long and revealing title: "Charles, the most serene Augustus, crowned by God, great and peaceful Emperor who governs the Roman Empire and who is, by the mercy of God, king of the Franks and the Lombards." According to this title, Charlemagne was not the Roman emperor crowned by the pope but rather God's emperor, who governed the Roman Empire along with his many other duties.

Charlemagne's son, Louis the Pious (✳814–840), was also crowned emperor, and he took his role as guarantor of the Christian empire even more seriously. He brought the monastic reformer Benedict of Aniane to court and, harnessing his authority as king, issued a capitulary in 817 imposing a uniform way of life (based on the Rule of St. Benedict) on all the monasteries of the empire. Although some monasteries opposed this legislation, and in the years that followed the king was unable to impose his will directly, this moment marked the effective adoption of the Benedictine rule as the monastic standard in the West. Louis also standardized the practices of his notaries, who issued his documents and privileges, and he continued to use *missi* to see that justice was done in the various parts of his realm.

In a new development of the coronation ritual, Louis's first wife, Ermengard, was crowned Augusta by the pope in 816. In 817 their firstborn son, Lothar, was given the title emperor and made co-ruler with Louis. Their other sons, Pippin and Louis (later called "the German"), were made subkings under imperial rule. Louis the Pious hoped in this way to ensure the unity of the empire while satisfying the claims of all his sons. Should any son die, only his firstborn could accede to that throne, thus preventing further splintering. But Louis's hopes were thwarted by events. Ermengard died, and Louis married Judith, the daughter of one of the most powerful families in the kingdom. In 823 she and Louis had a son, Charles. Thereafter the provisions of 817 were changed a number of times to accommodate Charles (later known as "Charles the Bald," the king to whose court Dhuoda's son William was sent). The sons of Ermengard, bitterly discontented, rebelled against their father and fought one another. A chronicle written during the period suggests that nearly every year was filled with family tragedies:

[For 830] Pippin, who had with him a large proportion of the people, with Lothar's consent took away from the Emperor [Louis] his royal

Ancestry and Progeny of Louis the Pious

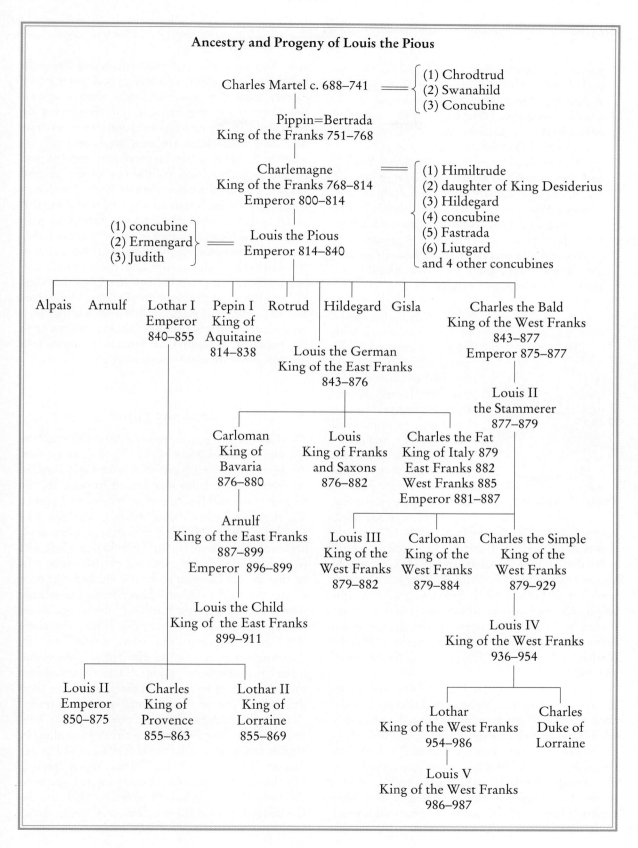

Charles Martel c. 688–741 ══ (1) Chrodtrud
(2) Swanahild
(3) Concubine

Pippin=Bertrada
King of the Franks 751–768

Charlemagne
King of the Franks 768–814
Emperor 800–814 ══ (1) Himiltrude
(2) daughter of King Desiderius
(3) Hildegard
(4) concubine
(5) Fastrada
(6) Liutgard
and 4 other concubines

(1) concubine
(2) Ermengard ══ Louis the Pious
(3) Judith Emperor 814–840

Alpais   Arnulf   Lothar I
Emperor
840–855   Pepin I
King of
Aquitaine
814–838   Rotrud   Hildegard   Gisla   Charles the Bald
King of the West Franks
843–877
Emperor 875–877

Louis the German
King of the East Franks
843–876

Louis II
the Stammerer
877–879

Carloman
King of
Bavaria
876–880   Louis
King of Franks
and Saxons
876–882   Charles the Fat
King of Italy 879
East Franks 882
West Franks 885
Emperor 881–887

Arnulf
King of the East Franks
887–899
Emperor 896–899

Louis III
King of the
West Franks
879–882   Carloman
King of the
West Franks
879–884   Charles the Simple
King of the
West Franks
879–929

Louis the Child
King of the East Franks
899–911

Louis IV
King of the West Franks
936–954

Louis II
Emperor
850–875   Charles
King of
Provence
855–863   Lothar II
King of
Lorraine
855–869

Lothar
King of the West Franks
954–986   Charles
Duke of
Lorraine

Louis V
King of the West Franks
986–987

power, and also his wife [Judith] whom they veiled and sent to the convent of St-Radegund at Poitiers. [Louis regained control of the situation, however.] [For 833] [Louis] had not been staying [at Aachen] for many days when news arrived that his sons had again got together in an alliance to revolt against him and were aiming to attack with a large force of his enemies. . . . Lothar came from Italy bringing Pope Gregory with him, Pippin from Aquitaine, and Louis from Bavaria with a very large number of men. [This time Louis was imprisoned. He was released by his sons Louis the German and Pippin, who now joined against their brother Lothar.]

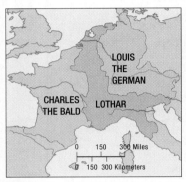

Treaty of Verdun

Family battles such as these continued, both during Louis's lifetime and, with great vigor, after his death. In 843, with the Treaty of Verdun, the three remaining brothers (Pippin had died in 838) finally arrived at an arrangement that would roughly describe the future political contours of western Europe. The western third, bequeathed to Charles the Bald (*843–877), would eventually become France; the eastern third, handed to Louis the German (*843–876), would become Germany. The "Middle Kingdom," which was given to Lothar (*840–855) along with the imperial title, had a different fate: parts of it were absorbed by France and Germany, and the rest eventually formed the modern states of the Netherlands, Belgium, Luxembourg, Switzerland, and Italy.

In 843 the European-wide empire of Charlemagne had dissolved. Forged by conquest, it had been supported by a small privileged aristocracy with lands and offices stretching across the whole of it. Their loyalty, based on shared values, real friendship, expectations of gain, and sometimes ties of vassalage and fealty, was crucial to the success of the Carolingians. The empire had also been supported by an ideal, shared by educated laymen and churchmen alike, of imperialism and Christian belief working together to bring good order to the earthly state. But powerful forces worked against the Carolingian empire. Once its borders were fixed and it could no longer expand, the aristocrats lost their expectation for new lands and offices. They put down roots in particular regions and began to gather local followings of *fideles* and vassals. Powerful local traditions such as different languages also undermined imperial unity. Finally, as Dhuoda revealed, some people disagreed with the imperial ideal. Asking her son to put his father before the emperor, she demonstrated her belief in the primacy of the family and the intimate and personal ties that bound it together. Dhuoda's ideal did not eliminate the emperor (European emperors would continue to reign until World War I), but it represented a new sensibility that saw real value in the breaking apart of Charlemagne's empire into smaller, more intimate, more local units.

Land and Power

The Carolingian economy contributed to both the rise and the dissolution of the Carolingian empire. At the onset its wealth came from land and plunder. After the booty from war ceased to pour in, the Carolingians still had access to money and goods. To the north, in Viking trading stations like Haithabu (today Hedeby, in northern Germany), archaeologists have found Carolingian glass and pots alongside Islamic coins and cloths, which tells us that the Carolingian economy meshed with that of the Abbasid caliphate. Silver from the Islamic world probably came north up the Volga River through Russia to the Baltic Sea. There the coins were melted down, the silver traded to the Carolingians in return for wine, jugs, glasses, and other manufactured goods. The Carolingians turned the silver into coins of their own, to be used throughout the empire for small-scale local trade.

Despite such far-flung networks of trade, land provided the most important source of Carolingian wealth and power. Like the landholders of the late Roman Empire and the Merovingian period, Carolingian aristocrats held many estates, scattered throughout the Frankish empire. But in the Carolingian period these estates were reorganized and their productivity carefully calculated. Modern historians often call these estates *manors*.

Typical was the manor called Villeneuve St. Georges, which belonged to the monastery of St.-Germain-des-Prés (today in Paris) in the ninth century. Villeneuve consisted of arable fields, vineyards, meadows where animals could roam, and woodland, all scattered about the countryside rather than connected in a compact unit. The land was not tilled by slave gangs, as had been the custom on great estates of the Roman Empire, but by peasant families, each one settled on its own manse, which consisted of a house, a garden, and small pieces of the arable land. They farmed the land that belonged to them and also worked the *demesne*, the very large manse of the lord (in this case the abbey of St.-Germain). These peasant farms marked a major social and economic development: the peasant household of the Carolingian period was the precursor of the modern nuclear family.

Peasants at Villeneuve practiced the most progressive sort of plowing, known as the three-field system, in which they farmed two-thirds of the arable land at one time. They planted one-third with winter wheat and one-third with summer crops, and left one-third fallow (to restore its fertility). The crops sown and the field of fallow land then rotated, so that land use was repeated only every three years. This method of organizing the land produced larger yields (because two-thirds of the land was cultivated each year) than the still prevalent two-field system, where only half of the arable land was cultivated one year, the other half the next.

All the peasants at Villeneuve were dependents of the monastery. Unlike slaves, they could not be separated from their families nor displaced from their manse; but they owed dues and services to St.-Germain. Their obligations varied enormously, depending on the status of the peasants and the manse they held. One family, for example, owed four silver coins, wine, wood, three hens, and fifteen eggs every year, and the men had to plow the fields of the demesne land. Another family owed the intensive labor of working the vineyards. One woman was required to weave cloth and feed the chickens. Peasant women spent much time at the lord's house in the *gynecaeum*—the women's workshop, where they made and dyed cloth and sewed garments—or in the kitchen, as cooks. Peasant men spent most of their time in the fields.

The Carolingian Renaissance

With the wealth coming in from trade and the profits of their estates, the Carolingians supported a revival of learning that began in the 790s and continued for about a century. Parallel in some ways to the renaissances of the Byzantine and Islamic worlds, the Carolingian renaissance revived the learning of the past. Scholars studied Roman imperial writers like Suetonius and Virgil; they read and

Adam and Eve as Carolingian Peasants
This full-page illumination from the Grandval Bible, dating from 834–843, depicts the story of Genesis. In the bottom tier, illustrating the expulsion from the Garden, Eve suckles her baby while Adam tills the soil. Like Adam, Carolingian peasants had primitive tools with which they eked out a precarious existence from the soil.

Freedom and Expressiveness in Carolingian Art
The Utrecht Psalter was made at Reims during the reign of Louis the Pious. Drawn in a sketchy, quick, lively style, each illustration corresponds to the verses of the psalms. For the thought in Vulgate Psalm 43 (in other editions 44) verse 7 depicted here, "For I will not trust in my bow; neither shall my sword save me," the artist drew a quiver filled with arrows and a sword discarded on the ground near the Psalmist, who leads a group of soldiers.

commented on the works of the church fathers; and they worked to establish complete and accurate texts. Their accomplishments helped to enhance royal glory, educate officials, reform the liturgy, and purify the faith.

The English scholar Alcuin (c. 732–804), a famous member of the circle of scholars whom Charlemagne recruited to form a center of study, brought with him the traditions of Anglo-Saxon scholarship that had been developed by men like Benedict Biscop and Bede. Invited to Aachen, Alcuin became Charlemagne's chief advisor, writing letters on the king's behalf, counseling him on royal policy, and tutoring the king's household, including the women. Charlemagne's sister and daughter, for example, often asked Alcuin to explain passages from the Gospel to them. Charlemagne entrusted Alcuin with the task of preparing an improved edition of the Vulgate (the Latin Bible).

Scholarship complemented the alliance between the church and the king symbolized by Charlemagne's anointment. In the Carolingian age, distinctions between politics and religion were meaningless: kings considered themselves appointed by the grace of God, often based their capitularies on Biblical passages, involved themselves in church reform, appointed churchmen on their own initiative, and believed their personal piety a source of power.

Just as in the Byzantine renaissance, artists often illuminated Carolingian texts using classical or patristic models. To these models Carolingian artists added exuberant decoration and design, often rendering architectural elements as bands of color and portraying human figures with great liveliness and verve. Greek pictorial models came from Byzantium, and perhaps some Carolingian artists themselves came originally from Greece, refugees from Byzantium during its iconoclastic period. Other pictorial models, from Italy, provided the kings' artists with examples of the sturdy style of the late Roman Empire. In turn, Carolingian art became a model for later illuminators. The Utrecht Psalter, for example, made at Reims in about 820, was copied by artists in eleventh-century England.

The Carolingian program was ambitious and lasting, even after the Carolingian dynasty had faded to a memory. The work of locating, under-standing, and transmitting models of the past continued in a number of monastic schools. In the materials they studied, the questions they asked, and the answers they suggested, the Carolingians offered a mode of inquiry fruitful for subsequent generations. In the twelfth century, scholars would build upon the foundations laid by the Carolingian renaissance. The very print of this textbook depends upon one achievement of the Carolingian period: modern letter fonts are based on the new letter forms, called Caroline minuscule, invented in the ninth century to standardize manuscript writing and make it more readable.

Muslim, Viking, and Magyar Invasions

Like the Roman emperors they emulated, Carolingian kings and magnates confronted new groups along their borders. The new peoples—Muslims to the south, Vikings to the north, and Magyars to the east—were feared and hated; but like the Germanic tribes that had entered the Roman Empire, they also served as military allies. As royal sons fought one another and as magnates sought to carve out their own principalities, their alliances with the newcomers helped integrate the outsiders swiftly into European politics. The impact of these foreign groups hastened, but did not cause, the dissolution of the empire.

Although Muslim armies had entered western Europe in the eighth century, the ninth-century Muslims were a different breed: they were freebooters, working independently of any caliph or other ruler. Taking advantage of Byzantium's initial weakness, in 827 they began the slow conquest of Sicily, which took nearly one hundred years. During the same century, Muslim pirates set up bases on Mediterranean islands and strongholds in Provence (today in southern France) and near Naples (today in southern Italy). Liutprand of Cremona reported on the activities of one such group:

> [Muslim pirates from al-Andalus], disembarking under cover of night, entered the manor house unobserved and murdered—O grievous tale!—the Christian inhabitants. They then took the place as their own ... [fortified it and] started stealthy raids on all the neighboring country.... Meanwhile the people of Provence close by, swayed by envy and mutual jealousy, began to cut one another's throats.... But inasmuch as one faction by itself was not able to satisfy upon the other the demands of jealous indignation, they called in the help of the aforesaid Saracens.

The Muslims at this base, set up in 891, robbed, took prisoners, and collected ransoms. But they were so useful to their feuding Christian neighbors that they were not ousted until 972, when they caused a scandal by capturing the holiest man of his era, Abbot Maieul of Cluny. Only then did the count of Provence launch a successful attack against their lair.

The Vikings came from the north, from Scandinavian lands that would eventually become Denmark, Norway, and Sweden. They shared the same language, and to their victims they were all one: the Franks called them Northmen; the English called them Danes. They were, in fact, much less united than their southern contemporaries thought. When they began voyages at the end of the eighth century, they did so in independent bands. Merchants and pirates at the same time, Vikings followed a chief, seeking profit, prestige, and land. Many traveled as families: husbands, wives, children, and slaves.

The Vikings perfected the art of navigation. In their longships they crossed the Atlantic, settling Iceland and Greenland and (about A.D. 1000) landing on the coast of North America. Eastward, they voyaged through watercourses and portaged to the Volga River or the Dnieper, eventually seizing Kiev and creating the first Russian state. Other Viking bands navigated the rivers of Europe. The Vikings were pagans, and to them monasteries and churches—with their reliquaries, chalices, and crosses—were storehouses of booty. "Never before," wrote Alcuin, who experienced one attack, "has such terror appeared in Britain as we have now suffered from a pagan race.... Behold the church of St. Cuthbert spattered with the blood of the priests of God, despoiled of all its ornaments."

England confronted sporadic attacks by the Vikings in the 830s and 840s. By mid-century, Viking adventurers regularly spent winters there. The Vikings did not just destroy. In 876 they settled in the northeast of England, plowing the land and preparing to live on it. The region where they settled and imposed their own laws was later called the *Danelaw*.

In Wessex, the southernmost kingdom of England, King Alfred the Great (*871–899) bought

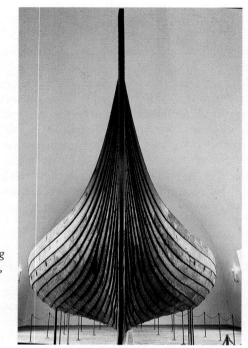

Viking Ship

Ships were the major technological reason for Viking success. A replica of the Gokstad Ship, pictured here, crossed the Atlantic in 1893 in less than a month.

Muslim, Viking, and Magyar Invasions

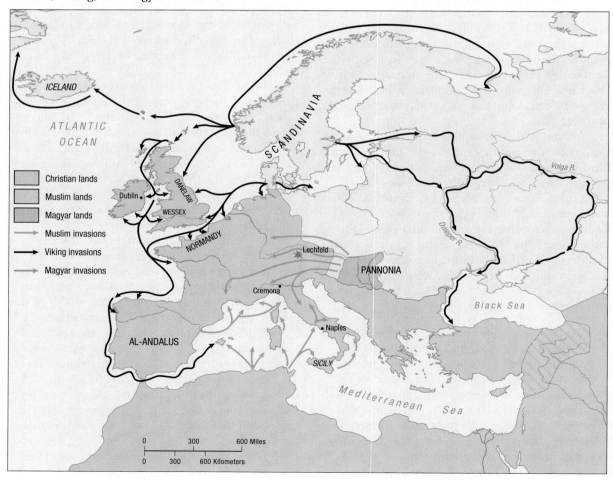

time and peace by paying tribute and giving hostages. Such tribute, later called *Danegeld*, was collected as a tax that eventually became the basis of a relatively lucrative taxation system in England. Then in 878, Alfred led an army that, as his biographer put it, "gained the victory through God's will. He destroyed the Vikings with great slaughter and pursued those who fled . . . hacking them down." Thereafter the pressures of invasion eased as Alfred reorganized his army, set up strongholds, and deployed new warships.

Vikings also attacked Ireland, setting up fortified bases along the coast from which they attacked and plundered churches and monasteries. But they also established Dublin as a commercial center and, in the tenth century, began to intermarry with the Irish and convert to Christianity.

On the Continent, too, the invaders set up trading emporia and settled where originally they had raided. Beginning about 850, their attacks became well-organized expeditions for regional control. At the end of the ninth century, one contingent settled in the region of France that soon took their name: Normandy, the land of the Northmen. The new inhabitants converted to Christianity during the tenth century. Rollo, the Viking leader in Normandy, accepted Christianity in 911, at the same time Normandy was formally ceded to him by the Frankish king Charles the Simple (or Straightforward).

Although most Vikings adopted the sedentary ways of much of the rest of Europe, some of their descendants continued their voyages and raids. In southern Italy the popes first fought against and then made peace with the Normans, who in the early eleventh century traveled southward from Normandy to hire themselves out as warriors. They fought for the Byzantines or the Muslims, siding with whoever paid them best.

The Magyars (or Hungarians) were latecomers to the West. Originally a nomadic people from the Asian steppes, they were pushed westward by the pressures of other steppes people. Moving into the middle Danubian plains, they helped the Franks destroy Old Moravia (c. 899) and from their bases in present-day Hungary raided far to the west. They attacked Germany, Italy, and even northern Gaul frequently between 899 and 955. Then in the summer of 955, one marauding party of Magyars was met at the Lech River by the German king Otto I, whose army decimated them. Otto's victory, his subsequent military reorganization of his eastern frontiers, and the cessation of Magyar raids around this time made Otto a great hero to his contemporaries. However, historians today think the containment of the Magyars had more to do with their internal transformation from nomads to farmers than with their military defeat.

The Emergence of Local Rule

The invasions shocked the inhabitants of western Europe, and they demonstrated the structural weaknesses of the Carolingian empire. Charlemagne's conquests had removed buffer groups, such as the Saxons and the Avars, bringing the Franks face to face with peoples used to living in mobile communities, quick to seize the opportunity to raid. As the Carolingian empire ceased to expand, the counts and other magnates stopped looking to the king for new lands and offices and began to develop and exploit what they already had. They built castles, set up markets, collected revenues, kept the peace, and began to see themselves as independent regional rulers.

The myth of the Carolingian kingdom—that it was united by one man crowned by God—never quite died. Yet by the end of the tenth century, Charlemagne's empire lay in fragments. In the region that would become France, local magnates exercised most powers of government and commerce. In Italy, bishops in the cities took over most government functions. They built fortifications around their churches and sometimes extended their power to the surrounding countryside, as happened at Asti, Parma, and Reggio Emilia by the 960s. In Germany and England, kings continued to wield power, but there, too, local lords challenged royal authority. The new rulers increased their wealth and power through improved agricultural productivity and direct control of the land and its inhabitants.

Agricultural Growth in the Post-Carolingian Age

New methods of cultivation and a growing population helped transform the rural landscape. With a growing number of men and women to work the land, the lower classes now had more mouths to feed and faced the hardship of food shortage. Landlords began reorganizing their estates to run more profitably. In the tenth century the three-field system became more prevalent; heavy plows came into wider use; and horses (more efficient than oxen) were harnessed to pull the plows. The result was surplus food and a better standard of living for nearly everyone.

In search of greater profits, some lords lightened the dues and services of peasants temporarily to allow them to open up new lands by draining marshes and cutting down forests. Some landlords converted dues and labor services into money payments, a boon for both lords and peasants. Lords gained liquidity: they now had money to spend on what they wanted rather than hens and eggs they might not need or want. Peasants benefited because their tax was fixed despite inflation. Thus, as the prices of their hens and eggs went up, they could sell them on the market, reaping a profit in spite of the dues they owed their lords.

By the tenth century many peasants lived in populous rural settlements, true villages. In the midst of a sea of arable land, meadow, wood, and wasteland, these villages developed a sense of community. Boundaries—sometimes real fortifications, sometimes simple markers—told nonresidents to keep out and to find shelter in huts located outside the village limits. The church often formed the focal point of local activity: there people met, received the sacraments, drew up contracts, buried their parents and children. Religious feasts and festivals joined the rituals of farming to mark the seasons. The church dominated the village in another way: men and women owed it a tax called a *tithe* (equivalent to a tenth of their crops or income, whether paid in money or in kind), which was first instituted on a regular basis by the Carolingians. Village peasants developed a sense of common purpose based on their practical interdependence, as they shared oxen or horses for the teams that pulled the plow or turned to village craftsmen to fix their wheels or shoe their horses. A sense of solidarity sometimes fostered banding together to ask for privileges as a group. Near Verona, Italy, for example, twenty-five men living around the castle of Nogara in 920 joined together to ask their lord, the monastery of Nonantola, to allow them to lease plots of land, houses, and pasturage there in return

for a small yearly rent and the promise to defend the castle. The abbot of Nonantola granted their request.

Village solidarity could be compromised, however, by varied and conflicting loyalties and obligations. A peasant in one village might very well have one piece of land connected with a certain manor and another bit of arable field on a different estate; and he or she might owe several lords different kinds of dues. Even peasants of one village working for one lord might owe him varied services and taxes. At a manor belonging to Autun Cathedral in France, for example, Rictred and Gautier held one manse and owed two shillings in March and twelve pennies (equal to one shilling) in May, or else a pig worth the same amount; they also owed labor, which they could redeem for twelve more pennies. On the same manor, however, a church endowed with three manses owed ten shillings but no labor services; presumably the priest living there paid the dues.

Various obligations such as these were even more striking across the regions of Europe. The principal distinction was between free peasants, such as small landowners in Saxony and other parts of Germany, and unfree peasants, who were especially common in France and England. In Italy peasants ranged from small independent landowners to leaseholders (like the tenants at Nogara); most were both, owning a parcel in one place and leasing another nearby.

Post-Carolingian Territorial Lordships

As the power of kings weakened, the system of peasant obligations became part of a larger system of local rule. When landlords consolidated their power over their manors, they collected not only dues and services but also fees for the use of their flourmills, bakehouses, and breweries. Some built castles, fortified strongholds, and imposed the even wider powers of the *ban*: the rights of public power to collect taxes, hear cases, levy fines, and muster men for defense.

In France, for example, as the king's power waned, political control fell into the hands of counts and other princes. By 1000, castles had become the key to their power. In the south of France, power was so fragmented that each man who controlled a castle—a castellan—was a virtual ruler, although often with a very limited reach. In north-western France territorial princes, basing their rule on the control of *many* castles, controlled much broader regions. For example, Fulk Nerra, Count of Anjou (987–1040), built more than thirteen castles and captured others from rival counts. By the end of his life, he controlled a region extending from Blois to Nantes along the Loire valley.

Castellans extended their authority by subjecting everyone near their castle to their ban. Peasants, whether or not they worked on a castellan's estates, had to pay him a variety of dues. Castellans also established links with the more well-off landholders in the region, tempting or coercing them to become vassals. Lay castellans often supported local monasteries and controlled the appointment of local priests. But churchmen themselves sometimes held the position of territorial lords, as, for example, the archbishop of Milan in the eleventh century.

The development of virtually independent local political units, dominated by a castle and controlled by a military elite, marks an important turning point in western Europe. Although this development did not occur everywhere simultaneously (and in some places it hardly occurred at all), the social, political, and cultural life of the West was now dominated by landowners who saw themselves as both military men and regional leaders. This phenomenon paralleled certain changes in the Byzantine and Islamic worlds; at just about the same time, the Byzantine *strategoi* were becoming a landowning elite and Muslim provincial rulers were employing Mamluk warriors. But crucial differences existed. The *strategoi* were still largely under the emperor's command, whereas Muslim dynasties were dependent on mercenaries. In contrast, castellans acted as quasi-kings; they were the lords of their vassals, whom they had kissed in token of their sworn bond of mutual service.

Warfare and a New Warrior Class

The castellans were part of a social transformation in post-Carolingian France (and elsewhere to a lesser extent) in which two classes emerged: an unfree laboring class of peasants and a free class of fighters. Naturally, many gradations existed within the warrior group. Kings still had great prestige and in some places, such as Germany, considerable

power; counts and castellans had local influence, though their authority varied from place to place. Other nobles included local magnates, who might be both vassals of more powerful lords and lords of less powerful vassals. Knights were considered members of the nobility in some regions and warriors of lower status in others.

Warfare was the occupation of most noblemen and knights, who fought one another for honor, power, land, and the profits of control. But battles affected more than the elite fighting forces, as Raoul Glaber, an eleventh-century monk, observed in his account of the battle of Nouy (1044). The battle pitted the son of Fulk of Anjou, Geoffrey Martel, against the sons of Count Odo II of Blois over control of the city of Tours, which had been part of Odo's territory:

> [Geoffrey] had gathered a great army and had been besieging the city for more than a year when the two sons of Odo came against him in force, meaning to fight in order to aid the beleaguered and starving city. When Geoffrey realized this, he prayed for the aid of St. Martin, promising to restore to this holy martyr, and indeed all other saints, any property of theirs which he had stolen. Then he took his standard, attached it to his lance, and marched out against his enemies with a great force of cavalry and infantry. When the two armies came close fear so struck the troops of the two brothers that they were all unable to fight. There is no doubt at all that victory over his enemies went to the man who had piously invoked the aid of St. Martin. . . . It is true that the sons of Odo had robbed the poor of St. Martin in order to supplement the pay of their troops.

At Nouy the elite fighters, armed and mounted on horses, composed the cavalry. Subordinate to them were the foot soldiers, neither nobles nor knights but rather men compelled to go to war under Geoffrey's ban. The unhappy citizens of Tours were harassed by both sides, subjected to Geoffrey's siege and Odo's sons' robbery. Still another group suffered from these warriors: the peasants and clergy concerned with the "property of St. Martin" and other saints, which Geoffrey had plundered.

Most knights lived in the households of their lord, unmarried, hoping eventually to earn a fief

Patrilineal "Family Portrait"
In the twelfth century, Siboto, count of Falkenstein (in southern Germany), drew up a "family portrait" reflecting the new patrilineal mode: his daughters were literally "not in the picture." But Siboto's wife was included, and their first-born son was named after Siboto's maternal grandfather. Thus the transition to the patrilineal model did not deny a place to women altogether.

from their lord, then find a wife, father a family, and become lords themselves. No matter how old they might be, these unmarried men were called "youths" by their contemporaries. Such perpetual bachelors were something new, the result of a profound transformation in the organization of families and inheritance. Before about 1000, noble families had recognized all their children as heirs and had divided their estates accordingly. In the mid-ninth century, Count Everard and his wife, for example, willed their large estates, scattered from Belgium to Italy, to their four sons and three daughters (although they gave the boys far more than the girls, and the oldest boy far more than the others). By the end of the tenth century, however, adapting to diminished opportunities for land and office and wary of fragmenting the estates they had, French nobles changed both their conception of their family and the way its property passed to the next generation. Recognizing the overriding claims of one son, often the eldest, they handed down their entire inheritance to him. The heir, in turn, traced his lineage only through the male line, backward through his father

and forward through his own eldest son. Such patrilineal families (tracing their bloodline only through the father and one of his sons) left many younger sons without an inheritance and therefore without the prospect of marrying and founding a family; instead they lived at the courts of the great as "youths," or they join the church as clerics or monks. The development of territorial rule and patrilineal families went hand in hand, as fathers passed down to one son undiminished not only manors but titles, castles, and the authority of the ban.

Patrilineal inheritance tended to bypass daughters and so worked against aristocratic women, who lost the power that came with inherited wealth. In families without sons, however, widows and daughters did inherit property; but land given out as a fief, normally for military service, was not usually given to a woman. Thus a major source of control over land, people, and revenues was denied to them. Yet women played an important role in this warrior society. A woman who survived childbirth and the death of her husband could marry again and again, becoming a peace broker as she forged alliances between great families and powerful "lords" on behalf of her younger sons. In the early eleventh century, for example, Agnes, the daughter of a count, first married the duke of Aquitaine, and after his death married Geoffrey Martel, count of Anjou. When her first husband died, her sons were still young, and she wielded ducal powers in Aquitaine and disposed of property there in her own name. In some areas women could carry out military service by using a male proxy. And wives often acted as lords of estates when their husbands were at war.

The Containment of Violence

Constant warfare benefited territorial rulers in the short term, but in the long run their revenues suffered as armies plundered the countryside and sacked the walled cities. Bishops, who were themselves from the class of lords and warriors, worried about the dangers to church property. Peasants cried out against wars that destroyed their crops or forced them to join regional infantries. Monks and religious thinkers were appalled at violence that was not in the service of an anointed king. By the end of the tenth century, all classes clamored for peace.

Beginning in the south of France, sentiment against local violence was harnessed in a movement called the Peace of God. At meetings of bishops, counts, and lords, and often crowds of lower-class men and women, proclamations setting forth the provisions of this Peace were issued: "No man in the counties or bishoprics shall seize a horse, colt, ox, cow, ass, or the burdens which it carries. . . . No one shall seize a peasant, man or woman," ran the decree of one council held in 990. Anyone who violated this peace was to be excommunicated: cut off from the community of the faithful, denied the services of the church and the hope of salvation.

The peace proclaimed at local councils like this limited some violence but did not address the problem of conflict between armed men. A second set of agreements, the Truce of God, soon supplemented the Peace of God. The truce prohibited fighting between warriors at certain times: on Sunday because it was the Lord's day; on Saturday because it was a reminder of Holy Saturday; on Friday because it symbolized Good Friday; and, finally, on Thursday because it stood for Holy Thursday. Enforcement of the truce fell to the local knights and nobles, who swore over saints' relics to uphold it and to fight anyone who broke it.

The Peace of God and Truce of God were only two of the mechanisms by which violent confrontations were contained or defused in the tenth and eleventh centuries. At times, lords and their vassals mediated wars and feuds in assemblies sometimes called feudal courts. In other instances, monks or laymen tried to find solutions to disputes that would leave the honor of both parties intact. Rather than try to establish guilt or innocence, winners or losers, these methods of adjudication often resulted in compromises on both sides. When a woman named Eve and the monastery of Cluny contested the ownership of a piece of property, both sides won: Cluny got the property; but Eve received money, a special place in the monks' prayers, and a burial plot in Cluny's cemetery.

Life in the early Middle Ages did not become less contentious because of these expedients, but the attempts to contain violence did affect society. Some aggressiveness was channeled into the church-sanctioned militias mandated by the Truce of God. At other times, disputes prodded neighbors to readjust their relationships and become friends. Churchmen made the rituals of swearing to uphold the peace part of church ceremony, the oaths backed by the power of the saints. In this way any bloodshed involved in apprehending those who violated the peace was made holy. Geoffrey Martel sought to sanctify his own violence by placating St. Martin when he battled for Tours; Raoul Glaber, who reported the incident, thought Geoffrey had succeeded and his victory was the manifestation of St. Martin's power.

The Cities of Italy: An Urban Localism

Northern Italy had also been part of the Carolingian empire, and local rule was as much a feature there as in post-Carolingian France. But in Italy, power was exercised from the cities. The urban centers of the Roman Empire had never quite disappeared, and in the tenth century many great landlords who in France would have built their castles in the countryside instead constructed their family seats within the walls of cities like Milan and Lucca. Churches, as many as fifty or sixty, were built within the city walls, the proud work of rich laymen and women or of bishops. From their perch within the cities, the great landholders, both lay and clerical, denominated the countryside.

Italian cities also functioned as important marketplaces. Peasants sold their surplus goods there; artisans and merchants lived within the walls; foreign traders offered their wares. These members of the lower classes were supported by the noble rich, who depended, even more than elsewhere, on cash to satisfy their desires. In the course of the ninth and tenth centuries, both servile and free tenants became renters who paid in currency.

The social and political life in Italy was conducive to a familial organization somewhat different from the patrilineal families of France. To stave off the partitioning of their properties among heirs, families organized themselves by formal contract into *consorteria*, in which all male members shared the profits of the family's inheritance and all women were excluded. The consorterial family became a kind of blood-related corporation, a social unit upon which early Italian businesses and banks would later be modeled.

In some ways Rome in the tenth century closely resembled other central Italian cities. Large and powerful families who built their castles within its walls and controlled the churches and monasteries in the vicinity dominated and fought over it.

The urban area of Rome had shrunk dramatically in the early Middle Ages, and it no longer commanded an international market: the population depended on local producers for their food, and merchants brought their wares to sell under its walls. Yet the mystique of Rome remained. Although it was no longer the hub of a great empire, it was still the *see*, the center of church authority, of the bishop of Rome. The pope (his special name since the ninth century) claimed the highest position in the church on the basis of "Petrine theory": citing a passage in Matthew's Gospel, the pope argued that he was the successor of St. Peter, the "rock" upon whom Christ had founded his church, the superior of all bishops, the holder of the keys of the kingdom of heaven.

Although this Petrine theory had relatively little practical impact during the ninth and tenth centuries, the papacy did command great prestige. Rome was the goal of pilgrims; and the papacy was the prize of powerful families, like that of Alberic, prince of Rome, whose son became John XII (*955–963). In the second half of the tenth century the king of Germany, Otto I (*936–973), considered Rome so essential to his imperial ambitions that he invaded it, put his own appointee on the papal throne, and had himself crowned emperor there. Rome's myth made it an international jewel.

Regional Kingship in the West

As a consequence of the splintering of the Carolingian empire, the western king of the Franks—who would only later receive the territorial title of king of France—was a relatively weak figure in the tenth and eleventh centuries. The German and English kings had more power, controlling much land and wealth and appointing their followers to both secular and ecclesiastical offices.

In France[*] during most of the tenth century, Carolingian kings alternated on the throne with kings from a family that would later be called the Capetian. As the Carolingian dynasty waned, the most powerful men of the kingdom—dukes, counts, and important bishops—prevented serious

---

[*]Terms such as "France," "Germany," and "Italy" are used here for the sake of convenience; they do not imply that these regions had the characteristics of modern nation-states.

civil war by electing Hugh Capet (*987–996). This event marked the end of Carolingian rule and the beginning of the new dynasty that would last, handing down the royal title from father to son, until the fourteenth century. In the eleventh century the reach of the Capetian kings was limited by territorial lordships in the vicinity. The king's scattered but substantial estates lay in the north of France, in the region around Paris—the Ile-de-France (literally "the island of France"). His castles and his vassals were

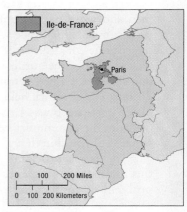

The Kingdom of the Franks Under Hugh Capet

there. Independent castellans, however, controlled areas nearby, such as Montmorency, less than ten miles from Paris. In the sense that he was a neighbor of castellans and not much more powerful militarily than they, the king of France was just another local magnate. Yet the Capetian kings had considerable prestige. They were anointed with holy oil, and they represented the idea of unity inherited from Charlemagne. Most of the counts, at least in the north of France, became their vassals, swearing fealty and paying homage to the kings as feudal lords. As vassals they did not promise to obey the king, but they did vow not to try to kill or depose him.

In contrast with the development of territorial lordships in France, Germany's fragmentation hardly began before it was reversed. Five duchies (regions dominated by dukes) emerged in Germany in the late Carolingian period, each much larger than the counties and castellanies of France. With the death of the last Carolingian king in Germany, Louis the Child, in 911, the dukes elected one of themselves king. Then, as the Magyar invasions increased, the dukes gave the royal title to the duke of Saxony, Henry I (*919–936), who proceeded to set up fortifications and reorganize his army, crowning his efforts with a major defeat of a Magyar army in 933.

Otto I, the son of Henry I, was an even greater military hero. In 951 he marched into Italy and

The Empire of Otto I

took the Lombard crown. At the battle at the Lech River (the Battle of Lechfeld) in 955 he and his troops beat back the Magyars decisively. Against the Slavs, with whom the Germans shared a border, Otto set up marches from which he could make expeditions and stave off counterraids. After the pope crowned him emperor in 962, he claimed the Middle Kingdom carved out by the Treaty of Verdun and cast himself as the agent of Roman imperial renewal.

Otto's victories brought tribute and plunder, ensuring a following but also raising the German nobles' expectations for enrichment. He and his successors, Otto II (*973–983), Otto III (*983–1002)—not surprisingly, the dynasty is called the Ottonian—and Henry II (*1002-1024), were not always able or willing to provide the gifts and inheritances their family members and followers expected. To maintain centralized rule, for example, the Ottonians did not divide their kingdom among their sons: like castellans in France, they created a patrilineal pattern of inheritance. But the consequence was that younger sons and other potential heirs felt cheated out of their inheritance, and disgruntled royal kin led revolt after revolt against the Ottonian kings. The rebels found followers among the aristocracy, where the trend toward the patrilineal family prompted similar feuds and thwarted expectations.

Relations between the Ottonians and the German clergy were less rancorous. With a ribbon of new bishoprics along his eastern border, Otto I appointed bishops, gave them extensive lands, and subjected the local peasantry to their overlordship. Like Charlemagne, Otto believed that the well-being of the church in his kingdom depended on him. The Ottonians placed the churches and many monasteries of Germany under their special protection. Bishops were given the powers of the ban, allowing them to collect revenues and call men to arms. Answering to the king and furnishing him with troops, they became royal officials, while also carrying out their pastoral and religious duties. German kings claimed the right to select bishops, even the pope at Rome, and to "invest" them by participating in the ceremony that installed the bishop in his office. The higher clergy joined royal court society; most first came to the court to be schooled; then, in turn, they taught the kings, princes, and noblewomen there.

Like all the strong rulers of the day, whether in the West or in the Byzantine and Islamic worlds, the Ottonians presided over a renaissance of learning. For example, the tutor of Otto III was Gerbert (c. 945–1003), the best-educated man of his time. Placed on the papal throne as Sylvester II, Gerbert knew how to use the abacus and to calculate with Arabic numerals. He "used large sums of money to pay copyists and to acquire copies of authors," as he put it. He studied the classics as models of rhetoric and argument, and he loved logic and debate. Not only did churchmen and kings support Ottonian scholarship, but to an unprecedented extent noblewomen in Germany also

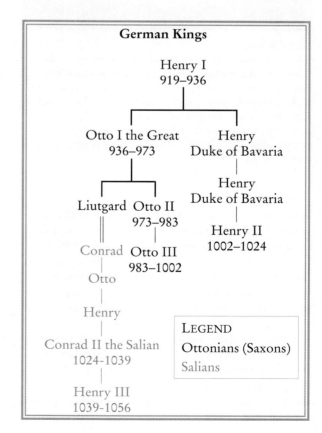

German Kings

Henry I
919–936

Otto I the Great
936–973

Henry
Duke of Bavaria

Henry
Duke of Bavaria

Liutgard   Otto II
973–983

Conrad   Otto III
983–1002

Henry II
1002–1024

Otto

Henry

Conrad II the Salian
1024-1039

Henry III
1039-1056

LEGEND
Ottonians (Saxons)
Salians

Sacral Kingship
The Ottonian kings were sacral, that is, anointed by God. This illumination from 1002-1014 shows Christ placing a crown on the heads of King Henry II and his wife, Queen Kunigunde, flanked by Saints Peter and Paul. Below are the symbols of empire. The artistic style reflects Byzantine influence, but the exaggerated gesture and simplicity of the background is unique to Ottonian art.

acquired an education and participated in the intellectual revival. Aristocratic women spent much of their wealth on learning. Living at home with their kinsfolk and servants or in convents that provided them with comfortable private apartments, noblewomen wrote books and occasionally even Roman-style plays. They also supported other artists and scholars.

Despite their military and political strength, the kings of Germany faced resistance from dukes and other powerful princes, who hoped to become petty rulers themselves. The Salians, who succeeded the Ottonians, tried to balance the power among the German dukes but could not meld them into a corps of vassals the way the Capetian kings tamed

their counts. In Germany vassalage was considered beneath the dignity of free men. Instead of relying on vassals, the Salian kings and their episcopal supporters used ministerials, men who were legally serfs, to collect taxes, administer justice, and fight on horseback. Ministerials retained their servile status even though they often accumulated wealth and rose to high position. Under the Salian kings, ministerials became the mainstay of the royal army and administration.

In late ninth-century England, King Alfred also developed new mechanisms of royal government, instituting reforms that his successors continued. He fortified settlements throughout Wessex and divided the army into two parts, one with the duty of defending these fortifications (or *burhs*), the other with the job of operating as a mobile unit. Alfred also started a navy. These military innovations cost money, and the assessments fell on peasants' holdings.

Burhs might afford regional protection, but in Alfred's view they would be effective only if religion were strengthened as well. In the ninth century, people interpreted invasions as God's punishment for a sinful people; sin, then, was the real culprit. Hence Alfred began a program of religious reform by bringing scholars to his court to write and to educate others. Above all, Alfred wanted to translate key religious works from Latin into Anglo-Saxon (or Old English). He was determined to "turn into the language that we can all understand certain books which are the most necessary for all men to know." Alfred and scholars under his guidance translated works by Gregory the Great, Boethius, and St. Augustine. Even the Psalms were rendered into Anglo-Saxon. Whereas in the rest of ninth- and tenth-century Europe Latin remained the language of scholarship and writing, separate from the language people spoke, in England the vernacular was a literary language. With Alfred's work giving it greater legitimacy, Anglo-Saxon came to be used alongside Latin for both literature and administration. It was the language of royal *writs*, which began as terse directives from the king or queen to their officials.

Alfred's reforms strengthened not only military defense, education, and religion but also royal power. He consolidated his control over Wessex and fought the Danish kings, who by the mid-870s had taken Northumbria, northeastern Mercia, and East Anglia. Eventually, as he harried the Danes who were pushing south and westward, he was recognized as king of all the English not under Danish rule. He issued a law code, the first by an English king for a century. Unlike earlier codes, drawn up for each separate kingdom of England, Alfred drew his laws from all of the English kingdoms. In this way Alfred became the first king of all the English.

Alfred's successors rolled back the Danish hegemony in England. "Then the Norsemen departed in their nailed ships, bloodstained survivors of spears," wrote one poet about a battle the Vikings lost in 937. But many Vikings remained. Converted to Christianity, their great men joined Anglo-Saxons in attending the English king at court. As peace returned, new administrative subdivisions were established throughout England: shires and hundreds, districts used for judicial and taxation purposes. The powerful men of the kingdom swore fealty to the king, promising to be enemies of his enemies, friends of his friends. England was united and organized to support a strong ruler.

England in the Era of Alfred the Great

An English king like Edgar (∗957–975), Alfred's grandson, commanded all the possibilities early medieval kingship offered. He was the sworn lord of all the great men of the kingdom. He controlled appointments to the English church and sponsored monastic reform. In 973, following the continental fashion, he was anointed. The fortifications of the kingdom were in his hands, as was the army, and he took responsibility for keeping the peace by proclaiming certain crimes—arson and theft—to be under his special jurisdiction and mobilizing the machinery of the shire and hundred to find and punish thieves.

Despite its apparent centralization, England was not a unified state in the modern sense, and the king's control over it was often tenuous. Many royal officials were great landowners who (as on the Continent) worked for the king because it was

King Alfred's Jewel
This jewel bears an Anglo-Saxon inscription that says, "Alfred ordered me to be made." It may have been used as a "pointer" (to point to a passage in a manuscript) or as a book mark. It demonstrates the relationship between fine craftsmanship and manuscript production, both of which flourished in the age of King Alfred.

in their best interest. When it was not, they allied with different claimants to the throne. The kingdom built by Alfred and his successors could fragment easily, and it was easily conquered. At the beginning of the eleventh century the Danes invaded England, and Cnut (Canute), who would soon be king of Denmark, became king of England (∗1017–1035); in 1030 he became ruler of Norway as well. Yet under Cnut, English kingship did not change much. By the mid-tenth century the kings of Denmark and their people had become Christian, and Cnut's conquest of England, bitterly opposed though it was, kept intact much of the administrative, ecclesiastical, and military apparatus already established. In any event, by Cnut's time Scandinavian traditions had largely merged with those of the rest of Europe, and the Vikings were no longer an alien culture.

The Emergence of Central Europe

Cnut's expansion was nearly matched by that of the German kings, for whom the region from the Elbe to Russia formed a vast frontier both tempting and threatening. The Slavs who lived in present-day eastern Germany and Poland offered opportunities for plunder, and the Germans waged wars against them with zeal. Otto I indicated his plans to expand by establishing the archbishopric of Magdeburg without any eastern boundary so that it could increase as far as future conquests and conversions to Christianity would allow.

Whereas Byzantine influence predominated in Russia and the Balkans, German military pressure and papal interests fostered the emergence of Christian monarchies in what are today Croatia, Hungary, the Czech and Slovak Republics, and Poland. The Magyars precipitated the decisive break between the Byzantine and western zones of influence. They settled in the region known as Hungary today, setting themselves up as landowners, using the native Slavs to till the soil, and imposing their language. At the end of the tenth century the Magyar ruler, Stephen I (✳997–1038), decided to accept Christianity and used German knights and monks to help him consolidate his power and convert his people. According to legend, the crown placed on Stephen's head in 1001 was sent to him by the pope. To this day it remains the most hallowed symbol of Hungarian nationhood.

By the time St. Stephen had gained his crown, the Czechs and Poles were also well on the way toward accepting Latin Christianity. The Czechs, who lived in the region of Bohemia, converted under the rule of Václav (✳920–929), who gained recognition in Germany as the duke of Bohemia. Yet he and his successors did not become kings, remaining politically within the German sphere. Václav's murder by his younger brother made him a martyr and the patron saint of Bohemia, a symbol around which later movements for independence rallied.

The Poles gained a greater measure of independence than the Czechs, but they still faced severe German pressure, especially after 955. In 966, Mieszko I (c. 922–992), the leader of the Slavic tribe known as the Polanians, accepted baptism in order to forestall the attack the Germans were already mounting against pagan Slavic peoples along the Baltic coast and east of the Elbe River. Busily engaged in bringing the other Slavic tribes of Poland under his control, Mieszko adroitly shifted his alliances with various German princes as suited his needs. In 991, he placed his realm under the protection of the pope at Rome, establishing a tradition of Polish loyalty to the see of St. Peter.

Mieszko's son Bolesław the Brave (✳992–1025) greatly extended Poland's boundaries, at one time or another holding sway from the Bohemian border to Kiev. In 1000 he, like Stephen the next year, gained a royal crown with papal blessing, a symbol of his independence from the German emperor. These symbols of rulership, consecrated by Chris-

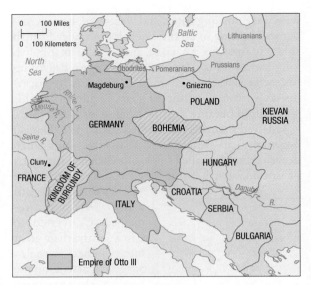

The Empire of Otto III

tian priests and accorded a prestige almost akin to saints' relics, were among the most vital institutions of kingly rule in central Europe. Profits from slave raids provided the initial economic basis for much of the power of central European rulers. But as organized states emerged in Europe to ward them off, such forays became more difficult. Landownership and the revenues from agriculture displaced the slave trade as the chief source of profit; but this change encouraged a proliferation of regional centers of power that challenged monarchical rule. From the eleventh century onward, all the medieval Slavic states contended constantly with problems of internal division.

Monastic Piety and the Secular Clergy

The breakup of the Carolingian empire meant that local kings and magnates came to dominate local churches, a relationship between religious and political power that later generations would deem scandalous. Yet before about 1000, western Europeans believed that all power—worldly and spiritual—derived from God. In the age of Charlemagne, observers of political power like Alcuin argued that God had given the king his realm precisely so that through him, "God's holy Church might be ruled, exalted, and preserved for the Christian people." When Charlemagne's kingdom split up—some territories controlled by kings;

others by dukes, counts, castellans, local lords, and bishops—these rulers began to control local churches as well. Most contemporaries saw nothing wrong with this development; the political order still seemed God given.

The focal point of regional piety, however, was more often the local monastery than the local church. People in the neighborhood, both men and women, supported these monasteries by giving them land. The little monastery of Prataglia was founded in 1001 in Tuscany, Italy, by the local bishop of Arezzo, who endowed it with bits and pieces from the larger estates belonging to his cathedral. Soon other landowners in the vicinity, many of them peasants with only small holdings to their name, gave small plots and sold other land to the monastery. As Prataglia gained prestige, it attracted more and larger gifts and purchased less. But even at the height of its celebrity, Prataglia's landholdings did not lie much more than twenty-five kilometers away from the monastery and were concentrated particularly in one river valley. Prataglia was a purely local monastery.

Some monasteries, such as Cluny in France, achieved more than regional fame. Cluny was founded in 910 by a wealthy and powerful magnate, William the Pious, duke of Aquitaine, and his wife, Ingelberga. They gave the monastery to Saints Peter and Paul at Rome, renouncing their own rights over it, to protect it from potential oppressors and to guarantee the monks the independence they needed to follow the Rule of St. Benedict and spend their lives in prayer. During the tenth and eleventh centuries, donations of land poured into Cluny on an unprecedented scale. In a period of local loyalties, Cluny became an exception, a truly international institution whose monks were called upon to reform monasteries in Italy, many parts of France, Germany, the small Christian kingdoms of Spain, and England. Despite their regional loyalties and interests, eleventh-century Europeans maintained an ideal of a united Christendom that transcended boundaries and linked all Christians together into a single community.

At the beginning of the eleventh century, the secular clergy (that is, the bishops, archbishops, and priests, as distinct from the "regular clergy," the monks) were typically allied with the local nobility and, in Germany, Italy, and England, with kings who made high churchmen their agents. In Germany bishops administered lands, enforced the ban, collected tithes, and supported knights on behalf of the monarchy. Rich families enhanced their repute, power, and chances for salvation by placing their sons in bishoprics, in the process giving gifts to whoever controlled the episcopal office. Episcopal duties were relatively worldly, and in daily life the secular clergy were almost indistinguishable from the laity. Wearing the finest clothes, riding on horses, surrounded by an entourage of armed men, bishops were great lords. Parish priests also blended with their lay peers, in this case members of the lower classes. Typically married and fathers of children, parish priests were special in that they alone could perform the sacraments, most important the saying of Mass. Yet in an age when most people did not regularly take Communion, the importance of this distinction was minimal. Reacting to the worldliness of the secular church in their day, a small group of influential churchmen claimed that the priesthood should be a clearly separate order within the church and called for radical reform.

Church Reform, Papal Control, and East-West Schism

A small group of clerics and monks spearheaded the movement for church reform. Buttressing their arguments for change with their interpretation of canon law (the laws decreed over the centuries at church councils and by bishops and popes), they concentrated on two breaches of those laws: nicolaitism (clerical marriage) and simony (buying church offices). Their larger goal was expressed by their motto: free the church. They intended to free priests from the coils of mundane cares by requiring celibacy; and they meant to free church offices from the domination of the laity by ending the payments that made episcopacies lucrative sources of revenue for aristocratic families. Most of the men who promoted these ideas lived in the Rhineland (the region along the northern half of the Rhine River) or Italy, the most commercialized regions of Europe. Their familiarity with the impersonal practices of a profit economy led the reformers to interpret as crass purchases the gifts that

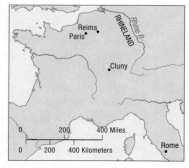

Beginnings of Church Reform

REMAKING THREE SOCIETIES

Byzantium	Islamic World	The West
843 Icons restored; end of iconoclasm	**756–929** Emirate of Cordoba	**768–814** Reign of Charlemagne (sole ruler 771–814; crowned emperor in 800)
802–811 Reign of Emperor Nicephorus I; reconquest of Peloponnesus; attacks on Bulgaria begin	**786–809** Caliphate of Harun al-Rashid	**843** Treaty of Verdun; division of Carolingian empire
863 Cyril and Methodius sent to convert Old Moravia	**825** Al-Khwarizmi's book on algebra published	**871–899** Reign of King Alfred the Great in England
c. 870–c. 1025 Macedonian renaissance	**929** Caliphate of Cordoba begins under Abd al-Rahman II	**936–973** Otto I, king in Germany and (from 962) emperor
c. 899 Magyars arrive in Pannonia	**969–1171** Fatimid Dynasty in Egypt	**955** Battle of Lechfeld; end of Magyar invasions
913–959 Reign of Emperor Constantine VII Porphyrogenitos	**1037** Death of Ibn Sina (Avicenna), important figure in the Islamic renaissance	**966** Mieszko I of Poland converts to Christianity
976–1025 Reign of Emperor Basil II Bulgaroctonos; annexation of Bulgaria		**987–996** Reign of Hugh Capet; end of Carolingian rule in France
c. 980–1015 Reign of Vladimir, prince of Russia; Russians convert to Christianity		**1001** Coronation of King Stephen of Hungary
		1017–1035 Reign of Cnut, king of England
		1049–1054 Papacy of Leo IX
		1054 Schism between Roman Catholic and Greek Orthodox churches

churchmen gave in return for their offices—a practice not only acceptable but necessary in a gift economy.

In Germany Emperor Henry III (*1039–1056) supported the reformers. Taking seriously his position as the anointed of God, Henry felt responsible for the well-being of the church. He denounced simony and refused to accept money in return for church offices. When in 1046 three men, each representing a different faction of the Roman aristocracy, claimed to be pope, Henry traveled to Italy to settle the matter. The Synod of Sutri (1046), over which he presided, deposed all three popes and elected another. In 1049, Henry appointed Leo IX (*1049–1054), a bishop from the Rhineland, to the papacy. But this appointment marked an unanticipated turning point for the emperor when Leo set out to reform the church under papal control. The Catholic church changed irrevocably during his tenure.

Leo knew canon law. He insisted, for example, that he be elected by the clergy and people of Rome before assuming the papal office. During his five years as pope, he traveled to Germany and France and held church councils. Before this time, popes had made the arduous journey across the Alps from Italy to the rest of Europe only rarely. They were, after all, mainly the bishops of Rome. But under Leo, the pope's role expanded. He sponsored the creation of a canon lawbook—the "Collection in 74 Titles"—which emphasized the pope's power. To the papal court Leo brought the most zealous reformers of his day: Humbert of Silva Candida, Peter Damian, and Hildebrand (later Gregory VII). These men played vital parts in the next episodes of the reform.

When Humbert went to Constantinople in 1054 on a diplomatic mission, he argued against the patriarch of Constantinople on behalf of the new, lofty claims of the pope. Furious at the contemptuous way he was treated, Humbert ended his mission by excommunicating the patriarch. In retaliation the emperor and his bishops excommunicated Humbert and his party, threatening them with eternal damnation. Clashes between the two churches had occurred before and had been patched up, but this one, called the Great Schism, proved insurmountable.*

---

*Despite occasional thaws and liftings of the sentences, the excommunications largely remained in effect until 1965, when Pope Paul VI and the Greek Orthodox patriarch, Anthenagoras I, publicly deplored them.

In the West, Leo's claims to new power over the church hierarchy were complacently ignored at first. The Council of Reims (in France), which he called in 1049, for example, was attended by only a few bishops and boycotted by the king of France. Nevertheless, Leo made it into a forum for exercising his authority. Placing the relics of St. Remegius (the patron saint of Reims) on the altar of the church, he demanded that the attending bishops and abbots say whether or not they had purchased their offices. A few confessed guilt; some did not respond; others gave excuses. The new and extraordinary development was that all felt accountable to the pope and accepted his verdicts. One bishop was stripped of his episcopal office; another was summoned to Rome to explain himself. The power of St. Peter had come to match the force of a king's, but with a scope that encompassed the western half of Europe.

CONCLUSION

In the early ninth century the three heirs of the Roman Empire all appeared to be organized like their "parent": centralized, monarchical, imperial. Byzantine emperors writing their learned books, Abbasid caliphs holding court in their resplendent palace at Baghdad, and Carolingian emperors issuing their directives for reform to the *missi dominici* all mimicked the Roman emperors. Yet they confronted tensions and regional pressures that tended to decentralize political power. Byzantium felt this fragmentation least, yet even there a new elite, the *strategoi*, led to decentralization and the emperor's loss of control over the countryside. In the Islamic world economic crisis, religious tension, and the ambitions of powerful dynasts decisively weakened the caliphate and opened the way to separate successor states. In the West powerful independent landowners strove with greater or lesser success (depending on the region) to establish themselves as effective rulers, and the states that would become those of modern Europe began to form.

In western Europe local conditions determined political and economic organizations. In the tenth and eleventh centuries, for example, French society was transformed by the development of territorial lordships, patrilineal families, and feudal ties. These factors figured less prominently in Germany, where a central monarchy remained, buttressed by churchmen, ministerials, and victories to the east.

The tendency toward local rule affected the church as well: monks were supported largely by local patrons, and bishoprics were filled by the sons of neighboring aristocrats, causing outraged reformers to call for drastic changes in the church. In the next century their movement would redefine the relationship between the laity and the clergy.

Suggestions for Further Reading

Source Materials

Einhard and Notker the Stammerer. *Two Lives of Charlemagne*. Translated by Lewis Thorpe. 1969. One of many translations of Einhard's important biography of Charlemagne, here paired with another biography dating from the late ninth century.

Nelson, Janet, trans. *The Annals of St.-Bertin*. 1991. Covering the period 830–882, a chronicle of the problems and resources of ninth-century kings.

Psellus, Michael. *Fourteen Byzantine Rulers: The Chronographia*. Translated by E. R. A. Sewter. 1966. A work of history written in the eleventh century by a member of the Byzantine scholarly elite.

Whitelock, Dorothy, ed. *English Historical Documents*. Vol. 1, *c. 500–1042*. 2d ed. 1979. Contains the essential primary source materials for Anglo-Saxon England.

Interpretive Studies

Ashtor, E. *A Social and Economic History of the Near East in the Middle Ages*. 1976. Stresses change in the Islamic world from the point of view of the lower classes.

Bachrach, Bernard S. *Fulk Nerra, the Neo-Roman Consul, 987–1040: A Political Biography of the Angevin Count*. 1993. The thoughts and activities of a count who created a major principality for himself and his successors.

Bloch, Marc. *Feudal Society*. Translated by L. A. Manyon. 1961. The classic synthesis of social, cultural, and economic history.

Boussard, Jacques. *The Civilisation of Charlemagne*. Translated by Frances Partridge. 1968. Surveys the Carolingian period topically, with useful maps and illustrations.

Davies, Norman. *God's Playground: A History of Poland*. Vol. 1, *The Origins to 1745*. 1982. Emphasizes the way in which Poland's history paralleled that of other European states.

Duby, Georges. *The Chivalrous Society*. Translated by Cynthia Postan. 1977. Fifteen essays by a master of social history.

———. *The Early Growth of the European Economy. Warriors and Peasants from the Seventh to the Twelfth Century*. Translated by Howard B. Clark. 1974. Explores the relationship between economy, society, and mentality.

———. *Rural Economy and Country Life in the Medieval West*. Translated by Cynthia Postan. 1968. A thorough survey that also includes primary sources, covering the subject from c. 800 to c. 1400.

Fell, Christine E., Cecily Clark, and Elizabeth Williams. *Women in Anglo-Saxon England, and the Impact of 1066*. 1984. Covers such topics as daily life, sex and marriage, family and kinship.

Fichtenau, Heinrich. *Living in the Tenth Century*. Translated by Patrick J. Geary. 1991. A discussion of important and ordinarily neglected topics, such as ideas about order and disorder, table manners, and gestures.

Frantzen, Allen J. *King Alfred*. 1986. A thoughtful analysis of Alfred's writings by a literary scholar.

Ganshof, F. L. *Feudalism*. Rev. ed. Translated by Philip Grierson. 1964. A concise discussion of the institution and its evolution.

Glick, Thomas. *Islamic and Christian Spain in the Early Middle Ages: Comparative Perspectives on Social and Cultural Formation*. 1979. Views the history of Spain as a totality rather than as the story of separate Christian and Islamic spheres.

Goitein, S. D. *A Mediterranean Society. The Jewish Communities of the Arab World as Portrayed in the Documents of the Cairo Geniza*. 4 vols. 1967–1983. Uses the *geniza* documents to explore the economy (vol. 1), the community (vol. 2), the family (vol. 3), and daily life (vol. 4) of the medieval Mediterranean.

Head, Constance. *Imperial Byzantine Portraits: A Verbal and Graphic Gallery*. 1982. Presents short biographies of each emperor along with contemporary portraits, in this way linking political authority with iconography.

Head, Thomas, and Richard Landes, eds. *The Peace of God: Social Violence and Religious Response in France around the Year 1000*. 1992. A series of essays on an important medieval social movement to contain and channel violence.

Jenkins, Romilly. *Byzantium: The Imperial Centuries. a.d. 610–1071*. 1966. A general survey.

Jones, Gwyn. *A History of the Vikings*. Rev. ed. 1984. A detailed and well-written account of the Vikings at home and abroad.

Kennedy, Hugh. *The Prophet and the Age of the Caliphates: The Islamic Near East from the Sixth to the Eleventh Century*. 1986. A solid overview of the period, concentrating on political history.

Lewis, Archibald R., and Timothy J. Runyan. *European Naval and Maritime History, 300–1500*. 1985. A revealing look at the medieval period through the prism of its naval history.

Leyser, Karl J. *Rule and Conflict in an Early Medieval Society: Ottonian Saxony*. 1979. An anthropologically informed look at one tenth-century society.

Little, Lester K. *Benedictine Maledictions: Liturgical Cursing in Romanesque France*. 1993. Discusses ritual cursing in monastic communities as a way for monks to counter their enemies.

Manteuffel, Tadeusz. *The Formation of the Polish State. The Period of Ducal Rule, 963–1194*. Translated by Andrew Gorski. 1982. A political history from the Polish point of view.

Marenbon, John. *From the Circle of Alcuin to the School of Auxerre: Logic, Theology, and Philosophy in the Early Middle Ages*. 1981. Demonstrates the continuity between Carolingian and later medieval philosophical inquiry.

McKitterick, Rosamond. *The Carolingians and the Written Word*. 1989. Discusses literacy in the Carolingian empire.

———. *The Frankish Kingdoms Under the Carolingians, 751–987*. 1983. A detailed and learned overview of the period.

Nelson, Janet. *Charles the Bald*. 1987. Shows how Charlemagne's grandson was a strong and canny ruler in a difficult period.

Ostrogorsky, George. *History of the Byzantine State*. Rev. ed. 1969. Remains the basic one-volume account of the Byzantine Empire.

Reuter, Timothy. *Germany in the Early Middle Ages, c. 800–1056*. 1991. An astute and up-to-date survey of the period.

Riché, Pierre. *Daily Life in the World of Charlemagne*. Translated by JoAnn McNamara. 1978. Takes up topics usually neglected: diet, language, travel, birth control.

Rosenwein, Barbara H. *To Be the Neighbor of Saint Peter: The Social Meaning of Cluny's Property, 909–1049*. 1989. Discusses the relationships between the monastery and its donors.

Runciman, Steven. *Byzantine Style and Civilization*. 1971. A survey of Byzantine art.

Searle, Eleanor. *Predatory Kinship and the Creation of Norman Power, 840–1066*. 1988. A fresh interpretation of the development of Normandy as a Viking creation.

Treadgold, Warren. *The Byzantine Revival, 780–842*. 1988. An integrated account of the economic, military, political, and cultural revival of the period.

Waddy, Charis. *Women in Muslim History*. 1980. A general history, covering the time of Muhammad to modern times, that looks at the changing role of women in the Islamic world.

White, Lynn, Jr. *Medieval Technology and Social Change*. 1962. Three classic essays on the relationship between medieval technology and society.

Wilson, David. *The Vikings and Their Origins. Scandinavia in the First Millennium*. 1970. Discusses the Vikings from an archaeological perspective, with many fine illustrations.

Wilson, N. G. *Scholars of Byzantium*. 1983. The history of Byzantine scholarship from the late Roman period to the fourteenth century.

Around 1115, Guibert, the abbot of a monastery at Nogent (in France), wrote his memoirs. A remarkably intelligent and opinionated man, Guibert used his autobiography as a pulpit from which he could criticize and praise the people, movements, and ideas of his time. One man he esteemed highly was Bruno of Cologne (c. 1030–1101) who was "learned in the liberal arts and the director of higher studies" at the prominent cathedral school of Reims. Highly respected by both his many students and his peers, Bruno might have been expected to rise to the position of bishop or archbishop over a major see, the pinnacle of a career to many churchmen. But Bruno repudiated the city and his leading position there, leaving Reims because its new archbishop, Manasses, had purchased his office, or as Guibert put it, had "thrust himself by simony into the rule of that city." Guibert reported that Manasses was so worldly that he once reportedly said, "The archbishopric of Reims would be a good thing if one did not have to sing Mass for it."

In 1084, rejecting both the worldly goals of the secular clergy and the communal goals of Benedictine monks, Bruno set up a hermitage at Chartreuse, high in the Alps, on the top of "a high and dreadful cliff," in Guibert's words. The monks who gathered there lived in isolation and poverty. "They do not take gold, silver, or ornaments for their church from anyone," Guibert marveled. Yet "although they subject themselves to complete poverty, they are accumulating a very rich library." Thus began La Chartreuse, the chief house of the Carthusian order, an order still in existence. The Carthusian monks lived as hermits, eschewed

Vitality and Reform, 1054–1144

Church over State
Gratian wrote a concordance of canon laws illustrated here by a late twelfth-century artist. Its design emphasized the primacy of the Church over the State: the churchman, a saint, is on top; the king, below him, holds a sword as the symbol of his office and a scroll telling him his duties.

material wealth, and emphasized learning. In some ways their style of life was a reaction against the monumental changes rumbling through their age: their heremetic solitude ran counter to the burgeoning cities, and their austerity contrasted sharply with the opulence and power of princely courts. On the other hand, their reverence for the written word reflected the growing interest in scholarship and learning. The growth of cities and the concurrent desire of their citizens to exert more political power; church reform, including experimental forms of religious life; the revival of monarchies; and the new popularity of learning were issues that Carthusian monks and everyone else grappled with during this period.

Between 1054 and 1144, western European communities were transformed; many villages and fortifications turned into cities where traders, merchants, and artisans conducted business. Although most people still lived in less populated, rural areas, their lives were touched in many ways by a developing profit economy. Economic concerns also continued to drive changes within the church, where by the second half of the eleventh century the leadership in church reform came from the papacy. One extremely influential pope, Gregory VII, gave his name to a phase of this movement, the Gregorian Reform, a series of fundamental changes in the church that were often passionately supported by common people, both clerical and lay. In a short time the powerful forces unleashed by this reform led to the First Crusade and an important European presence in the Levant that lasted until 1144.

Redefining the role of the clergy and elaborating new political ideas, popes, kings, and princes came to exercise power in a society with a commercial economy. At the same time, city-dwellers began to demand their own governments. Monks and clerics reformulated the nature of their own communities and, like Bruno of Cologne, sought intense spiritual lives. All of these developments inspired (and in turn were inspired by) new ideas, forms of scholarship, and methods of inquiry. The rapid pace of religious, political, and economic change was matched by new developments in thought and learning.

IMPORTANT DATES

1066 Norman conquest of England; Battle of Hastings

1077 Canossa: Henry IV does penance before Gregory VII

1086 Domesday Book commissioned by William I of England

c. 1090–1153 Life of St. Bernard

1095 Preaching of the First Crusade at Clermont

1097 Commune of Milan established

1122 Concordat of Worms: end of the Investiture Conflict

c. 1122 Abelard writes *Sic et Non*

1130 Norman Kingdom of Sicily established

1140 Gratian's *Decretum* published

1144 Consecration of Suger's new choir at St. Denis; beginning of Gothic architecture

The Commercial Revolution

As the population of Europe continued to expand in the eleventh century, cities, long-distance trade networks, and local markets meshed to create a profit-based economy. With improvements in agriculture and more land in cultivation, the great estates of the eleventh century produced surpluses that helped feed the new urban population and at the same time enrich the great lords, both in the cities and in the countryside. The system of territorial lordships created a class of rich and powerful men and women eager to use markets to sell their surpluses and spend their money on luxuries to enhance their style of life and their prestige. Many members of the old elite became rich from commerce, while a new urban elite arose, enriched from the same source. Wealth was power: it allowed city dwellers to become employers, princes to hire officials to do their bidding, and courtly aristocrats to become patrons.

Commerce was not new to the history of the West, of course, but the commercial economy of

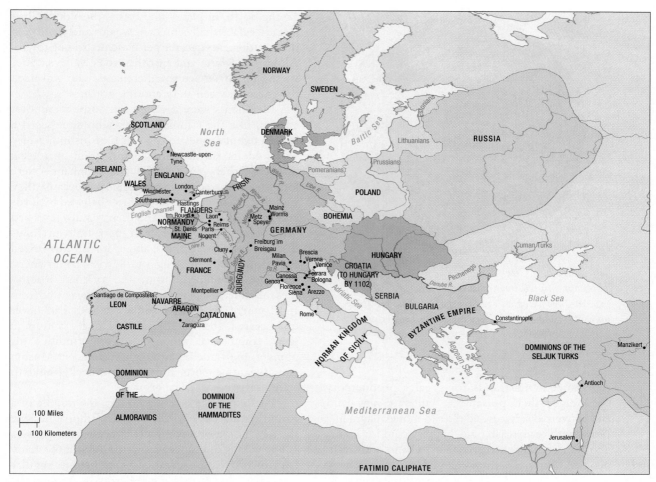

Europe and the Mediterranean, c. 1097

the Middle Ages produced the institutions that would be the direct ancestors of western businesses: corporations, banks, accounting systems, and above all, urban centers that thrived on economic vitality. Whereas ancient cities had primarily religious, social, and political functions, medieval cities were above all centers of production and economic activities.

Commercial Centers

Commercial centers developed around castles, monasteries, and within the walls of ancient towns. At Bruges (today in Belgium), for example, the castle became the magnet around which a city formed. As a medieval chronicler observed:

> *To satisfy the needs of the people in the castle at Bruges, first merchants with luxury articles began to surge around the gate; then the wine-sellers came; finally the innkeepers arrived to feed and lodge the people who had business with the prince. . . . So many houses were built that soon a great city was created.*

Thus the needs and desires of territorial lords and their families, vassals, and servants for food and luxuries drew people from the surrounding countryside and sometimes from far away. Lords had

Self-image of a City
This coin, minted by Archbishop Anno of Cologne (*1056–1075), depicts the "image" of Cologne (Germany), a symbol of the city including towers, walls, and a grand edifice.

reorganized their lands for greater productivity, encouraged their peasants to cultivate new land, and converted services and dues to money payments. Now, with ready cash, they happily paid for luxury goods offered by enterprising merchants and craftspeople. Moreover, they charged these merchants tolls and sales taxes, in this way profiting even more from trade. Local peasants and servants, who benefited from commerce, devoted some of their own time to reap profits as traders or craftsmen. Former servants of the bishop of Mâcon, for example, set up a bakery near the bridge of the city and sold bread to travelers. They soon grew rich.

Castles were not the only nuclei of revitalized trade. Some commercial centers clustered around Benedictine monasteries, which by the eleventh century had become large communities of several hundred monks with many needs to supply. Still other markets formed just outside the walls of older cities; these gradually merged into new and enlarged urban communities as town walls were built around them to protect their inhabitants. Sometimes peasants had surpluses and sold them at an informal market, set up in the middle of the countryside. If the surpluses continued from year to year, the market might eventually gain permanent structures.

To the north, in places like Frisia, the Vikings had already established centers of wealth and trade, and these settlements became permanent, thriving towns. Along the Rhine and in other river valleys, cities sprang up to service the merchants who traversed the route between Italy and the north.

Merchants were a varied lot. Some were local traders, like the Cluniac monk who supervised a manor twenty miles to the south of his monastery and sold its surplus horses and grain at a local market. Others—mainly Jews and Italians—were long-distance traders, in great demand because they supplied the fine wines and fabrics beloved by lords and ladies, their families, and their vassals. Jews had often been involved at least part time in long-distance trade as vintners; and as lords reorganized the countryside, driving out Jewish landowners, most Jews were forced to turn to commercial activities full time. Other long-distance traders came from Italy, where urban mercantile activities had never quite ceased, and where contact with Byzantium (a great commercial center) and opportunities for plunder and trade on the high seas and in Muslim and Byzantine ports provided the background to Italy's early commercial growth.

At Reims, the city Bruno left, the middle of a forum dating back to the Roman Empire became the new home of a commercial center. As early as 1067 the king of France was writing about the many fairs in his realm—great markets held at regular intervals—that attracted large crowds. Around the marketplace at Reims grew a network of streets whose names revealed their essentially commercial functions: Street of the Butchers; Street of the Wool Market; Street of the Wheat Market.

The look and feel of such developing cities varied enormously. Nearly all included at least a marketplace, a castle, and several churches. And most had to adapt to increasingly crowded conditions. At the end of the eleventh century in Winchester, England, city plots were still large enough to accommodate houses parallel to the street; but the swelling population soon necessitated destroying these houses and building instead long, narrow, hall-like tenement houses, constructed at right angles to the thoroughfare. These were built on a frame made from strips of wood filled with wattle and daub—twigs woven together and covered with clay. If they were like the stone houses built in the late twelfth century (about which we know a good deal) they

Building and Construction
In this early twelfth-century fresco on a wall of the Romanesque church St.-Savin-sur-Gartempe in France, workers are depicted building the Tower of Babel. The commercial revolution was accompanied by a great building boom in the cities of western Europe.

had two stories: a shop or warehouse on the lower floor and living quarters above. Behind was the kitchen and perhaps also enclosures for livestock, as archaeologists have found at Southampton. In the early twelfth century even city-dwellers clung to rural pursuits, living largely off the food they raised themselves.

The construction of wattle and daub houses, churches, castles, and markets was part of a building boom that began in the tenth century and continued at an accelerated pace through the thirteenth. Specialized buildings for trade and city government were put up—charitable houses for the sick and indigent, community houses, and warehouses. In addition to individual buildings the new construction involved erecting masses of walls. Medieval cities were ringed by walls. By 1100 Speyer had three: one around its cathedral, the next just beyond the parish church of St. Moritz, the third still farther out to protect the marketplace. Within the walls lay a network of streets, often narrow, dirty, dark, and winding, made of packed clay or gravel. In English towns the main street broadened as it approached a rectangular or V-shaped marketplace. Bridges spanned the rivers; on the Meuse, for example, six new bridges were built during the eleventh century.

Before the eleventh century, Europeans had depended on boats and waterways for bulky long-distance transport; now carts could haul items overland because new roads through the countryside linked the urban markets.

Although commercial centers developed throughout western Europe, they grew fastest and became most dense in regions along key waterways: the Mediterranean coasts of Italy, France, and Spain; Northern Italy along the Po River; the river system of the Rhône-Saône-Meuse; the Rhineland; the English Channel; the shores of the Baltic Sea. During the eleventh century these waterways became part of a single interdependent economy.

Tools of the Trade

The development of commercial centers betokened a new attitude toward money. Although the gift economy did not disappear, a market economy arose alongside it. The new mode of commerce marked a change in the social relations involved in economic transactions. In the gift economy, exchanges of coins, gold, and silver were components of ongoing relationships. Kings offered treasures to their followers, peasants gave dues to their lords, and pious donors presented land to the saintly patrons of churches, all in the expectation of long-term relationships. In the market economy, which thrived on the profit motive, transactions had no personal component: the obligations of the seller to the buyer and vice versa ended once a purchase was made. The value of a coin in the gift economy was determined by the friendships it made or the obligations it incurred. In the money economy, value was carefully calculated, and profit was determined by monetary gain.

As significant for the commercial revolution as this new attitude toward money was the creation of new kinds of business partnerships. Although they took many forms, all new business agreements had the common purpose of bringing people together to pool their resources and finance larger enterprises. The *commenda*, for example, an Italian invention, was a partnership established for commerce by sea. In one common arrangement, one or more investors furnished the money, and the other partners under took the risks of the actual voyage. If a trip proved successful, the investors received three-quarters of the profit and the travelers the rest. But if the voyage failed, the investors lost their outlay, and the travelers expended their time and labor to no profit. This sort of agreement had many variations. In 1073, for example, Giovanni Lissado put up 100 Venetian pounds and Sevasto Orefice put up twice as much to buy shares in a commercial voyage to Thebes. Giovanni himself was to go on the journey. He drew up a contract promising to "put to work this entire [capital] and to strive the best way I can" and if successful to divide the profits equally with Sevasto. But "if all these goods are lost because of the sea or of [hostile] people" then Sevasto would have to accept the loss of his capital. The impermanence of such partnerships (they lasted for only one voyage) meant that capital could be shifted easily from one venture to another and could therefore be used to support a variety of enterprises.

Land trade often involved a more enduring partnership. In Italy this took the form of a *compagnia*, based on the consorterial family (which pooled its resources and shared its profits among male members) and formed when family property was invested in trade. Unlike the *commenda*, in which the partners could lose no more than they had put into the enterprise, the *compagnia* left its members with joint and unlimited liability for all losses and debts. This provision enhanced family solidarity, because each member was responsible for the debts of all the others; but it also risked bankrupting entire households.

Besides partnerships, the chief tools of the commercial revolution were contracts for sales, exchanges, and loans. In a society with widely varying coinage standards, bills of exchange were crucial to international trade because they established equivalencies among different coinage systems while avoiding the need to ship actual coins from one place to another. Moreover, the terms of these bills could be used to mask loans. The church prohibited usury (profiting from loans) but loans were essential for business ventures. In the Middle Ages, as now, interest payments were the chief inducement for an investor to supply money. To circumvent the church's ban on usury, interest was often disguised as a penalty for "late payment" under the rules of the contract. This new willingness to finance business enterprises with loans signaled a changed attitude toward credit: risk was acceptable if it brought profit. Italian merchants and bankers were the pioneers in experimenting with credit institutions. Italian city governments also later invented bonds—credit investments issued to finance projects on the basis of promised returns from future revenues. Modern governments still finance public enterprises this way, though few realize we are using a medieval invention.

New forms of production matched these new methods of finance. Light industry spread in the eleventh century. Water mills, for example, not only ground grain but also powered other machines, such as flails to clean and thicken cloth and presses to extract oil. New technology to exploit deep mines provided Europeans with hitherto untapped sources of metals. Forging techniques improved, and iron was shaped into weapons as well as the tools and ploughs, that helped intensify agricultural productivity. Precious metals were fashioned into ornaments or coins, which fueled commercial activity. Such production relied on the expertise of artisans who could dye the woolens, work the metals, and mint the coins.

In part to regulate and protect these emerging industries, artisans formed guilds: local social, religious, and economic associations whose members plied the same trade. The shoemakers' guild at Ferrara began as a prayer confraternity, an association whose members gathered and prayed for one another. If a member or his wife died, the others would bear the body to the church, bury it with honors, and offer money for masses to be said for the salvation of the dead person's soul. In time this guild's membership came to be limited to shoemakers. Although mothers, wives, daughters, and female apprentices often knew how to make shoes, weave cloth, or sell goods, women did not ordinarily join guilds. Largely social and convivial fraternities, guilds undertook to regulate their members' hours, materials, and prices and to set quality standards. Although not eliminating all competition among craftsmen in the same field, the guild prevented any one artisan from gaining unfair advantages over another. Most important, the guild guaranteed each member a place in the market by controlling the production of shoes, fabrics, candles, and other items in each city.

Clearly the legitimacy and enforceability of the regulations of guilds and other trade and crafts organizations depended upon recognition by the political powers that ruled each city. Guild rules could not supersede city and church laws. But in most cities guilds and the city rulers had comfortable relationships based on mutual benefit. For example, when in 1106, twenty-three fishermen at Worms wanted exclusive rights to the wholesale fish market there, they petitioned the local bishop to give them the privilege and impose penalties on anyone who violated it. In return, they promised to give him two salmon every year and the local count one salmon a year.

Self-Government for the Cities

Townspeople seemed odd to tradition-bound commentators, accustomed to old categories of society that recognized only three classes: those who prayed (the monks and clerics), those who fought (the knights, castellans, and lords), and those who worked (the peasants). Tradesmen, artisans, ship captains, innkeepers, and money changers fit none of these categories. Townspeople themselves shared the sense that they were outsiders, and this bond often gave them a sense of solidarity with one another. But practical reasons also contributed to their feeling of common purpose: they lived in close quarters with one another; and they shared a mutual interest in sound coinage, laws that would facilitate commerce, freedom from servile dues and services, and independence to buy and sell as the market dictated. Already in the early twelfth century the

king of England granted to the citizens of Newcastle-upon-Tyne the privilege that any unfree peasant who lived there unclaimed by his lord for a year and a day would be thereafter a free person. The guilds were one way townspeople expressed their mutual concerns and harnessed their collective energies. Movements for self-government were another. The general desire for personal liberty and economic freedom led many townspeople to collective action. They petitioned the political powers who ruled them—bishops, kings, counts, castellans—to allow them their own officials and law courts. Often they formed communes, sworn associations of townspeople that generally cut across the boundaries of rich and poor, merchants and craftspeople, clergy and laity.

Sometimes communes gained their independence peacefully. William Clito, who claimed the county of Flanders (today in Belgium), willingly granted the citizens of St. Omer the rights they asked for in 1127 in return for their support of his claims: he recognized them as legally free, gave them the right to mint coins, allowed them their own laws and courts, and lifted certain tolls and taxes. Although all the citizens of St. Omer benefited from these privileges, the merchant guild there profited the most, as it alone gained freedom from all tolls in the entire county of Flanders.

Those in power did not always respond favorably to townspeoples' demands for self-government, and violence sometimes ensued. Guibert of Nogent described a revolt at Laon (in northern France), where the community had chafed under the rule of the bishop. Even Guibert, who opposed communal revolt, pointed out that "the public authority" at Laon—the bishop and the nobles who followed him—"was involved in rapine and murder." Unable to gain redress peacefully, on the day before Good Friday, 1112, "a great crowd of burghers attacked the episcopal palace, armed with rapiers, double-edged swords, bows and axes, and carrying clubs and lances," killing the bishop and his men. Although the king of France, Louis VI, squelched the revolt, he finally recognized the commune of Laon in 1128.

Such collective movements for urban self-government were not confined to France, but also emerged in Italy and Germany. Except in Italy, the newly independent cities usually took their place within the framework of larger kingdoms or principalities. They sometimes retained their independence by playing off overlapping authorities in their region. In other instances lords realized they could profit economically from these self-governing cities. The town of Freiburg im Breisgau in Germany was created by a prince who wanted the benefits of a nearby market. He invited people to come to his town and live by their own laws, and he ensured their prosperity by guaranteeing safe passage for merchants going through his territory. Such resourceful lords gained from the taxes they levied on their towns more than enough to make up for what they lost in the direct exercise of power.

Unlike the towns of northern Europe, Italian cities were centers of regional political power even before the commercial revolution. Castellans constructed their fortifications and bishops ruled the countryside from such cities. The commercial revolution swelled the Italian cities with tradesmen, whose interest in self-government was often fueled by religious as well as economic concerns. At Milan in the second half of the eleventh century, popular support for ecclesiastical reform fed local discontent with the archbishop's power there. In 1097, after many clashes, the townspeople succeeded in transferring political power over Milan from the archbishop and his clergy to a government of consuls. These consuls were the leading men of the city, soldiers (*milites*) who, though neither merchants nor artisans, nevertheless claimed to speak for all the townsmen. Subsequent archbishops of Milan generally came from the same military class; they dominated the church while the consuls took charge of the laws and revenues. The title *consul* that these new governors took recalled the government of the ancient Roman Republic, affirming their status as representatives of the people. The consuls' power, like the archbishop's before them, extended beyond the town walls into the *contado*, the outlying countryside.

Milan's experience was more representative of northern Italian cities than the experience of Venice, which did not struggle for self-government

Land trade routes
Water trade routes

London
Bruges
St. Omer
Ghent
Laon
Paris
Cologne
Prague
Magdeburg
GERMANY
Weser R.
Elbe R.
Rhine R.
Seine R.
Freiburg
FRANCE
Milan
Venice
Po R.
Rhône R.
Marseilles
Pisa
Rome
Adriatic Sea
Mediterranean Sea

0   100 Miles
0   100 Kilometers

Urban Revival

because it was already virtually independent. Nominally under the control of Byzantium until the eleventh century, it was in fact ruled by a *doge*. The doge relied on the support of Venice's great aristocratic families, whose power and wealth came from commerce in the Adriatic Sea. These aristocratic Venetian men, whose ships linked the Muslim world with Byzantium and the West, continued to dominate the city, both politically and economically, until the middle of the twelfth century, when newly successful families took on a consultative role as members of a Council of the Wise. The citizens of Venice had no interest in dominating their *contado*; they had all of the Adriatic to ply.

Papal Reform and Ensuing Struggles

The link between the development of the commune at Milan and the movement for religious reform there illustrates the interrelationship of the commercial revolution and ecclesiastical reform. Reformers who abhorred simony joined with members of the new commercial classes to replace churchmen whose worldliness distracted them from their religious mission. But economic and religious issues only partially defined the forces for change: the reform movement encompassed a new theory about how power ought to be exercised. After Leo IX (*1049–1054) had asserted his authority over local bishops in all parts of Europe, his successors immersed the papacy even more in issues outside Italy. Popes sought to extend their control and to mold the church and the world to fit an ideal vision in which their spiritual authority took precedence over secular power, so that kings were subordinate to popes. In the process of implementing this, as they supported some rulers and clashed with others, the popes too became monarchs with armies, officials, ambassadors (called legates), and elaborate revenue-raising systems.

The Papacy as a European Power

The papacy intervened in the politics of many regions of Europe. For example, in southern Italy the popes first fought against and then made peace with the Normans, the descendants of the Vikings who had settled in Normandy (in northwestern France) a century before. In the early eleventh century, Norman adventurers had come to southern Italy, hiring themselves out as warriors and fighting for the Byzantines or the Muslims, depending on who paid them best. Around the middle of the century, the Normans began to carve out territories for themselves in southern Italy. Leo IX led an army against them in 1053, delaying their settlement; but by 1059 they were there to stay. Pope Nicholas II (✶1058–1061) decided to make the best of the situation: he gave the Normans, as a fief, the "toe," "heel," and "ankle" of Italy—Calabria, Apulia, and Capua, respectively—as well as Sicily, where the

The Rise of the Papacy

Normans had begun a slow conquest that eventually led to the creation of a new Kingdom of Sicily in 1130. Most of these territories had been part of the Byzantine Empire, though Sicily had been taken by the Muslims in the ninth century. The pope's "gift" therefore was not really the territories, which were not his to give, but instead the promise of St. Peter's support, something the Normans needed in order to legitimize their power. From this investment the popes gained new and powerful vassals—a Norman army.

The popes also interceded in northern Italy. In Milan they allied themselves with some members of the emerging commune, the Patarines. This group, composed of clerics and laypeople, the well-to-do and the poor, was united by the conviction that a powerful and wealthy clergy was immoral and intolerable. Like Bruno of Cologne two decades later, they considered gold and silver morally compromising. The Patarines demanded of their clergy the poverty and chastity they believed the Apostles had practiced. They dreamed of a church pure in all its members: monks, clerics, and laity. This vision fueled their opposition to the archbishop and contributed to the successful political revolt of 1097. To a papacy determined to establish the superiority of spiritual power, the Patarines were sometimes useful because they openly—and sometimes violently—opposed the churchmen the

emperor had appointed. Pope Alexander II (✶1061–1073) demonstrated his solidarity with the Patarines by allowing one of their leaders to fight under his flag, the so-called banner of St. Peter.

Seizing another opportunity to assert a papal role in secular affairs, Alexander II chose sides in the question of succession to the English throne in 1066, when William, duke of Normandy, challenged the other claimant, Harold, earl of Wessex. William sought papal approval for his expedition to cross the English Channel and capture the throne. By giving William the banner of St. Peter, Alexander both legitimized the duke's claims and made the papacy a participant in the Norman conquest. "Wherever he could throughout all the world, Alexander corrected evil without compromise," wrote a contemporary, "and William gladly received from him the gift of another banner as a pledge of the support of St. Peter."

Similarly, the pope participated in wars in Spain, where he supported Christians against the dominant Muslims. With al-Andalus (Islamic Spain) extending over most of the Iberian Peninsula, independent Christian communities remained only in the far north. Political fragmentation after 1031, however, turned al-Andalus into a mosaic of small, weak lordships, or *taifas*, making the Muslims fair game for the Christians. At first the Christian kings mainly demanded tribute from the Muslims, but slowly the idea of the *reconquista*, the Christian "reconquest" of Spain, took shape. In 1064 an army composed of men from northern Spain, France, and Normandy attacked and temporarily seized the fortress of Barbastro (at Zaragoza), deep in Muslim territory. The churchmen and princes of Spain proclaimed the Peace of God just before the battle, linking the idea of Christian solidarity with hostility against non-Christians. Just before this attack on Barbastro (or possibly in connection with an expedition about ten years later), Alexander II granted an indulgence to the Christians on their way to battle: "By the authority of the holy apostles, Peter and Paul, we relieve them of penance and grant them remission [forgiveness] of sins." For Christians the

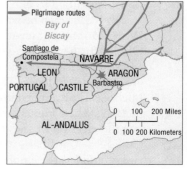

Spain in the Eleventh Century

campaign of Barbastro was a holy war, and they battled zealously. The conquerors killed the Muslim defenders, raped the women, sold the children into slavery, and loaded up on plunder. Christian victories like these forced the Islamic leaders of the *taifas* to call for help from the Almoravids in North Africa. In 1086 the Almoravids entered al-Andalus and drove back the Christians, but they then turned upon their hosts and took control of the *taifas*.

Although suffering military reverses at the hands of the Muslims after 1086, the Spanish Christians had great success in attracting western Europeans to their shrines. Pilgrims made their way across France and northern Spain to Santiago de Compostela, where St. James was said to be buried. The faithful believed that his relics worked miracles, especially for warriors. Although few women were reportedly helped by his cures, many stories were circulated of soldiers freed from their captors and of warriors victorious in battle through his intercession. St. James became the patron saint of victory against the Muslims in Spain, linking pilgrimage with military success. The popes became part of St. James's holy circle by giving special privileges to his see, eventually elevating it to an archbishopric.

Gregory VII Versus Henry IV: The Investiture Conflict

The papacy had its greatest political impact in Germany and Italy, where the emperor had checked the growth of local territorial lords by using bishops and archbishops as his trusted agents. In the hands of an anointed and pious king like Henry III (*1039–1056), nothing seemed more natural than the union of political and religious authority. Yet contrary forces began to grow inadvertently when Leo IX, the ally of Henry III, began to use his office to enhance papal power.

In 1056, when he was just five years old, Henry IV (*1056–1106) ascended to the German throne. Obviously, he was too young to be a strong ally of a reforming papacy or an obstacle to a pope seeking greater independence. Thus it was no accident that Nicholas II promulgated the Papal Election Decree in 1059, when Henry was only eight. The decree put the election of the pope into the hands of the College of Cardinals, which was a select group of clergy, and left the emperor's role in papal elections

extremely ambiguous. The decree said simply that "in the papal election . . . due honor and reverence shall be shown our beloved son, Henry, king and emperor elect." The situation had changed radically since the days of Henry III, when Leo IX had been handpicked by the emperor.

Henry IV reached legal adulthood in 1066 and soon had to deal with Gregory VII, who became pope in 1073. Gregory (*1073–1085) was (and remains) a controversial figure. Describing himself, he declared, "I have labored with all my power that Holy Church, the bride of god, our Lady Mother, might come again to her own splendor and might remain free, pure, and Catholic." But Henry viewed Gregory as an ambitious and evil man, who "seduced the world far and wide and stained the Church with the blood of her sons." With both king and pope competing for loyalty from the same

Emperor Henry IV
This "portrait" of Henry was made in the early twelfth century. He holds the orb and scepter of his imperial rule.

people and control over the same officials, the stage was set for a confrontation.

The clash between Henry IV and Gregory VII (and their successors) is called the Investiture Conflict. It began in 1075, when Gregory prohibited lay investiture. Specifically, investiture was the ritual by which a priest or bishop received his church and the land that went with it; more generally, it was the act that created a churchman and put him into office. Gregory's ban on lay investiture was intended as much more than a ceremonial change. He meant to revamp the very structure of the church. Gregory believed only a churchman could choose another churchman, and only a churchman could invest another. But more important, he did not consider rulers churchmen in his scheme; Gregory asserted that every temporal (that is, worldly) ruler was a layman and *only* a layman, despite the religious and spiritual roles associated with anointed kings that had developed over many centuries in the West.

The ensuing struggle was about whether the king or the pope would head the church and indeed all Christian society. The first confrontation came over the archbishopric of Milan. After Gregory forbade lay investiture, Henry decided to ignore the candidate for archbishop who had been selected and consecrated (by laying on of hands and anointment) by the Patarines but not invested by the pope. Instead Henry sent his delegates to invest a different man. Fast and furious denunciations and counterdenunciations by pope and emperor followed. In 1076, Henry called a council of German bishops who demanded that Gregory, that "false monk," resign. In reply Gregory called a synod that both excommunicated and suspended Henry from office:

> *I deprive King Henry, son of the emperor Henry, who has rebelled against [God's] Church with unheard-of audacity, of the government over the whole kingdom of Germany and Italy, and I release all Christian men from the allegiance which they have sworn or may swear to him, and I forbid anyone to serve him as king.*

The last part of this decree gave it a secular punch because it authorized anyone in Henry's kingdom to rebel against him. Henry's enemies, mostly German princes (that is, German aristocrats),

now threatened to elect another king. They were motivated partly by religious sentiments, as many had established links with the papacy through their support of reformed monasteries, and partly by political opportunism, as they had chafed under the strong German king, who had tried to keep their power in check. Some bishops, such as Hermann of Metz, also joined forces with Gregory's reform party, a great blow to royal power because Henry desperately needed the troops supplied by his churchmen.

The Investiture Conflict

Attacked from all sides, Henry traveled to Gregory, who in turn was journeying northward to visit the rebellious princes. In early 1077 king and pope met at Canossa, high in central Italy's snowy Apennine Mountains. Gregory was inside a fortress there; Henry stood outside as a penitent. This posture was an astute move by Henry because no priest could refuse absolution to a penitent; Gregory had to receive Henry back into the church. But Gregory now had the advantage of the king's humiliation before the majesty of the pope. Gregory's description of Henry suggests that the pope believed himself to have triumphed:

> *There, on three successive days, standing before the castle gate, laying aside all royal insignia, barefooted and in coarse attire, he did not cease, with many tears, to beseech the apostolic help and comfort.*

Although Henry was technically back in the fold, nothing of substance had been resolved and war began. The princes elected an antiking, and Henry and his supporters elected an antipope. From 1077 until 1122 Germany was ravaged by civil war.

The Investiture Conflict was finally resolved long after Henry IV and Gregory VII had died. In 1122 the Concordat of Worms ended the fighting with a compromise that relied on a conceptual distinction between two parts of investiture—the spiritual (in which a man received the symbols of his clerical office) and the secular (in which he received the symbols of the material goods that would allow him to function). Under the terms of the concordat, the ring and staff, the symbols of pastoral office, would be given by a churchman in the first part of the ceremony. The emperor or his representative would touch the bishop with a scepter, a symbolic gesture that stood for the land and other possessions that went with his office, in the second part of the ceremony. Elections of bishops in Germany would take place "in the presence" of the emperor—that is, under his influence. In Italy the pope would have a comparable role.

Thus in the end secular rulers continued to have a part in choosing and investing churchmen, but few people any longer claimed the king was the "head of the church." Just as the new investiture ceremony broke the ritual into spiritual and secular parts, so too it implied a new notion of kingship that separated it from priesthood. The Investiture Conflict did not produce the modern distinction between church and state—that would develop only very slowly—but it set the wheels in motion.

Winners of the Investiture Conflict: German Princes and Italian Communes

The Investiture Conflict and the civil war it generated shattered the delicate balance among political and ecclesiastical powers in Germany and Italy. The German princes consolidated their lands and their positions at the expense of royal power, and the Italian communes flexed their political muscles and defied the authority of the emperor.

The disintegration of strong central authority allowed regional powers to assert themselves, much as the fragmentation of the Carolingian empire had done in France two centuries before. In Germany many nobles, including bishops, built castles and began to impose the powers of the ban over the residents of the countryside. Free peasants became serfs bound to local lords. Finding mounted warriors far superior to foot soldiers, the princes soon surrounded themselves with knights. Some of these new warriors were free men now bound to the princes as vassals; others advanced from the ranks of the ministerials, losing their servile status. In some parts of Germany the twelfth century marked the beginning of the fusing of the ranks of free knights and ministerials, and the servile origins of the ministerials were forgotten. The ministerials of the archbishop of Cologne, for example, pledged

their fealty to him as their lord and received fiefs in return. Expected to go off to battle and other expeditions with him, they profited from his largess on these occasions. When they accompanied the archbishop to Rome, he gave them provisions for themselves and their servants:

> *The archbishop shall give each one of them ten marks and forty yards of cloth which is called "scarlet," and to every two knights [ministerials] he shall give a packhorse and a saddle with all that belongs to it, and two bags with a cover for them . . . and four horseshoes and twenty-four nails. After they reach the Alps the archbishop shall give each knight a mark a month for his expenses.*

These ministerials had achieved the status of the lower nobility. However, in Germany knighthood never achieved as high a status as it did in France. German members of the upper nobility scorned the titles of knight or vassal and never referred to themselves in those terms. Their conviction that vassalage was demeaning added to the German princes' resistance to becoming vassals of the king. Yet after 1122 the German king considered their homage and fealty to him a necessity. The king's power had been based on his land, his episcopacy, his ministerials, and his troops of free men. With these resources diminished, he needed to control the princes in a new way. The bonds of vassalage, the castles that dotted the countryside, the new monasteries that were founded in Germany, and the ministerial troops commanded by bishops enhanced the powers of the princes but (too often) not of the king. If he could make the princes his vassals, he could use their troops and demand their loyalty. Throughout the twelfth century the German king struggled to become the feudal lord of the princes of Germany. In the end he succeeded, but at a very high price. The princes became virtual monarchs within their own principalities, whereas the emperor, though retaining his title, became a figurehead.

As overlord of northern Italy the emperor also lost power to the communes and other movements for local self-government, which developed in the late eleventh and early twelfth century. People in cities like Pavia, Genoa, Brescia, Bologna, Siena, Arezzo, and Florence followed the lead of communes like Milan, forming town councils and governing themselves. Although many of these governments began, as in Milan, with uprisings against the city's bishop, most bishops soon learned to adapt to the new conditions. Before 1122 the bishops of Verona had been imperial appointees, foreigners who came from Germany and often the imperial court. After the Investiture Conflict, local leading families supplied the candidates from which Verona's bishops were chosen. These local men involved themselves vigorously in local affairs. For example, Bishop Tebaldus of Verona (*1135–1157) asserted his rights over the parish churches in his diocese, energetically pursued litigation on behalf of his own church's patrimony, and rebuilt his cathedral on a grand scale. His activities showed the new way in which local religious and political life would mesh in the urban centers of Italy.

The rise of the Italian communes in a time of war between the emperor and the pope left an indelible mark on these new political entities. Every commune, in Italy and elsewhere, had rival factions: conflicts between poor and rich or between competing aristocratic families raged from time to time. But in Italy a third conflict, between the supporters of the emperor and those of the pope, caused friction throughout the twelfth century. The ongoing hostilities of popes and emperors mirrored fierce communal struggles in which factions, motivated in part by local grievances, claimed to fight on behalf of the papal or imperial cause.

Religious Sanctions for Marriage

The Gregorian reform affected not only politics but also married life. When in 1125 a German bishop undertook (with the connivance of the king of Poland) a mission to convert the pagan Pomeranians (who lived along the Baltic Sea coast, now mostly in Poland), he did not simply require them to believe in Christ and be baptized. He demanded, above all, that they observe the church's laws concerning marriage, by now well established: "He forbade them to marry their godmothers or their own cousins up to the sixth and seventh generation and told them that each man should be content with only one wife."

Today we take it for granted that religious authorities exercise control over marriages and require monogamy, but in the Middle Ages the effective involvement of the church in these matters came only after the Gregorian reform. Only in the twelfth century did people regularly come to be married by a priest in church, and only then did

churchmen assume jurisdiction over marital disputes, not simply in cases involving royalty but also in those of lesser aristocrats. The clergy's prohibition of marriage partners as distant as seventh cousins (marriage between such cousins was considered incest) had the potential to control dynastic alliances. Because many noble families kept their inheritance intact through a single male heir, those heirs' marriages took on great significance. The church's incest prohibitions gave the clergy a measure of power over all European states. For example, when the king of England, Henry I (*1100–1135), wanted to marry one of his daughters to William of Warenne, early of Surrey (his good friend, advisor, and important political ally), he asked Anselm, the archbishop of Canterbury, for his advice. Anselm warned against the union on the grounds that William and his prospective bride shared two ancestors several generations back. The match was broken off.

Intense ecclesiastical interest in marriage accompanied the church's increased accentuation of the sacraments and the special nature of the priest, whose chief role was to perform them. Christians believed the sacraments were the regular means by which God's heavenly grace infused mundane existence. Sacraments marked the path of life from birth to death, the route of the sinner to salvation. The priest's control over these vehicles of grace exalted his position and set him apart from everyone else. Gregory VII claimed the sacrament of the Mass was "the greatest thing in the Christian religion." No layman could perform anything equal to it. This new emphasis on the sacraments, which were now more clearly and carefully defined, along with the desire to set priests clearly apart from the laity, led to vigorous enforcement of an old element of church discipline: the celibacy of priests.

The demand for a celibate clergy had far-reaching significance for the history of the church. It distanced western clerics even further from their eastern Orthodox counterparts (who did not practice celibacy), exacerbating the schism of 1054. It also broke with traditional local practices, as clerical marriage was in some places the norm. In Normandy even the highest clergymen had wives: in the eleventh century one archbishop of Rouen was married and had three sons; a bishop of Sées was the father of an archbishop. Gregorian reformers exhorted every cleric in higher orders, from the humble parish priest to the exalted bishop, not to marry or to abandon his wife. Naturally many churchmen resisted. The historian Orderic Vitalis (1075–c.1142) reported that John, the archbishop of Rouen,

> fulfilled his duties as metropolitan with courage and thoroughness, continually striving to separate immoral priests from their mistresses [wives]: on one occasion when he forbade them to keep concubines he was stoned out of the synod.

Undaunted, the reformers persisted, and in 1123 the pope proclaimed all clerical marriages invalid. No wonder a poem of the twelfth century had a lady repulse a cleric's officer of love with the reply: "I refuse to commit adultery; I want to get married." Clearly clerics were no longer suitable candidates for matrimony.

The same reformers who preached against clerical marriage, however, attributed new sanctity to lay marriages. A twelfth-century thinker like Hugh of St. Victor dwelled on the sacramental meaning of marriage:

> Can you find anything else in marriage except conjugal society which makes it sacred and by which you can assert that it is holy? . . . See now the nature of the contract by which they bind themselves in consented marriage. Henceforth and forever, each shall be to the other as a same self in all sincere love, all careful solicitude, every kindness of affection, in constant compassion, unflagging consolation, and faithful devotedness.

Hugh saw marriage as a matter of love. The topic of love—married and unmarried, human and divine—dominated twelfth-century thought.

The "Papal Monarchy"

The newly reformed and strengthened papacy enhanced its position by consolidating and imposing canon (church) law. The prohibition against clerical marriage, for example, was a law derived from decrees promulgated by meetings of churchmen at church councils and synods since the fourth century. Although canon law originated at such meetings, not until the Gregorian reform were these decrees— until now scattered here and there—compiled in a great push for systematization. This movement to organize canon law was part of a wider legal devel-

---

IMPORTANT POPES

1058–1061 Nicholas II. In 1059 he proclaimed the Papal Election Decree and gave southern Italy to the Normans.

1073–1085 Gregory VII. In 1075 he forbade lay investiture; in 1076 he excommunicated Henry IV; in 1077 he was briefly reconciled with Henry at Canossa.

1088–1099 Urban II. In 1095 he preached the First Crusade (1096–1099) at the Council of Clermont.

---

opment: reformers began to study church canons in the same formal and orderly manner that legal scholars were beginning to use for Roman and other secular laws. A landmark in canon law jurisprudence was the *Concordance of Discordant Canons*, also known as the *Decretum*, compiled in about 1140 by Gratian, a monk who taught law at Bologna in northern Italy. Gratian gathered thousands of passages from the decrees of popes and councils with the intention of showing their harmony. To make conflicting canons conform to one another, he adopted the principle that papal pronouncements superseded the laws of church councils and all secular laws.

At the time Gratian was writing, the papal *curia*, or government, resembled a court of law with its own collection agency. The papacy had developed a bureaucracy to hear cases and rule on petitions. Disputed episcopal elections, for example, flooded into Rome in the wake of the Investiture Conflict. Hearing cases cost money: lawyers, judges, and courtroom clerks had to be paid. Churchmen not involved in litigation went to Rome for other sorts of benefits: to petition for privileges for their monasteries or to be consecrated by the pope, vicar of St. Peter. These services were also expensive, requiring hearing officers, notaries, and collectors. The lands owned by the papacy were not sufficient to support the growing administrative apparatus these services required, and therefore the petitioners and litigants themselves had to pay, a practice they resented. A satire written about 1100, in the style of the Gospels, made bitter fun of papal greed:

> There came to the court a certain wealthy clerk, fat and thick, and gross, who in the

*sedition had committed murder. He first gave
to the dispenser, second to the treasurer, third
to the cardinals. But they thought among
themselves that they should receive more. The
Lord Pope, hearing that his cardinals had received many gifts, was sick, nigh unto death.
But the rich man sent to him a couch of gold
and silver and immediately he was made
whole. Then the Lord Pope called his cardinals
and ministers to him and said to them:
"Brethren, look, lest anyone deceive you with
vain words. For I have given you an example:
as I have grasped, so you grasp also."*

The First Crusade

Like other medieval rulers, the pope supported and
proclaimed wars. The Crusades were a series of
wars authorized by the papacy in which armies of
European Christians set forth to battle non-
Christians, especially Muslims in the Holy Land.
In 1095 on the last day of a church council devoted
to the Peace and Truce of God, Pope Urban II
preached the First Crusade. Urban's sermon, occurring at a time of affirmed peace among Christians
and solidarity against all violators of the Truce of
God, galvanized a popular response similar to the
militant fervor before the battle of Barbastro, but
on a scale unprecedented in the medieval world.
Armies of crusaders trekked from all parts of Europe
to the Holy Land, their leaders eventually setting
up fragile states in what is today the Middle East.
Crusades continued throughout the following
centuries to bolster or try to reconquer the lands
wrested from the Muslims. Although the Crusades
ultimately failed in the sense that the crusaders did
not succeed in permanently retaining the Holy
Land for Christendom, they were a pivotal episode
in Western civilization. They marked the first stage
of European overseas expansion, of what later
would become imperialism.

The events that led to the First Crusade began
in Asia Minor. The Muslim world had splintered
into numerous small states in the tenth century; by
the 1050s the fierce, nomadic, and Sunni Muslim
Seljuk Turks had captured Baghdad, subjugated the
caliphate, and begun to threaten Byzantium. The
difficulties Emperor Romanus IV had in pulling
together an army to attack the Turks in 1071 revealed
how weak his position had become. Unable to
muster Byzantine troops—the *strategoi* were busy

defending their own districts, and provincial nobles
were wary of sending support to the emperor—
Romanus had to rely on a mercenary army made
up of Normans, Franks, Slavs, and even Turks. This
motley force met the Seljuks under Sultan Alp
Arslan at Manzikert in what is today eastern
Turkey. The battle was a disaster for Romanus: the
Seljuks routed his army and captured him.
Manzikert marked the end of Byzantine domination
in the region.

The Turks, gradually settling in Asia Minor,
extended their control across the empire and beyond, all the way to Jerusalem, which had been
under Muslim control since the seventh century. In
1095 the Byzantine emperor Alexius I appealed to
Pope Urban II (∗1088–1099) for help, hoping to
get new mercenary troops for a fresh offensive.

Urban II chose to interpret the request differ-
ently. At the Council of Clermont (in France) in
1095, after finishing the usual business of proclaiming the Truce of God and condemning simo-
niac clergy, Urban moved outside the church and
addressed an already excited throng:

> *Oh, race of Franks, race from across the
> mountains, race beloved and chosen by
> God. . . . Let hatred depart from among you,
> let your quarrels end, let wars cease, and let all
> dissensions and controversies slumber. Enter
> upon the road to the Holy Sepulcher; wrest
> that land from the wicked race, and subject it
> to yourselves.*

The crowd reportedly responded spontaneously in
one voice: "God wills it." Historians remain divided
over Urban's motives for his massive call to arms.
Certainly he hoped to return the Holy Land to
Christian control. He was also anxious to fulfill the
goals of the Truce of God by turning the entire "race
of Franks" into a peace militia dedicated to holy
purposes, an army of God. Just as the Truce of God
mobilized whole communities to fight against anyone who broke it, so the First Crusade impelled
armed groups sworn to free the Holy Land of its
enemies to form. Finally, Urban's call placed the
papacy in a new position of leadership, one that
complemented in a military arena the position the
popes had gained in the church hierarchy.

The early Crusades involved many people.
Both men and women, rich and poor, young and
old participated. They abandoned their homes and
braved the rough journey to the Holy Land to fight

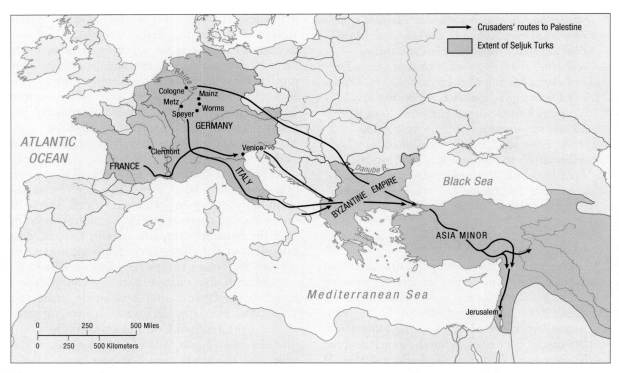

The First Crusade

for their God. They also went—especially younger sons of aristocrats, who could not expect an inheritance in Europe because of the practice of primogeniture—because they wanted land. Some knights took the cross because in addition to their pious duty they were obligated to follow their lord. Others hoped for plunder. Some crusaders were accompanied by their wives, who went partly to be with their husbands and partly to express their own militant piety. Other women went as servants; a few may have been fighters. Children and old men and women, not able to fight, sewed the hides used on siege engines—giant machines used to hurl stones at enemy fortifications. As more Crusades were undertaken during the twelfth century, the transport and supply of these armies became a lucrative business for the commercial classes of maritime Italian cities such as Venice.

The armies of the First Crusade were not organized as one military force but rather as separate militias, each commanded by a different individual. Fulcher of Chartres, an eyewitness, reported:

So with such a great band proceeding from western parts, gradually from day to day on

the way there grew armies of innumerable people coming together from everywhere. Thus a countless multitude speaking many languages and coming from many regions was to be seen. However, all were not assembled into one army until we arrived at the city of Nicaea.

Fulcher was speaking of the armies led by nobles and authorized by the pope. One band, not authorized by the pope, consisted of commoners. This Peasant's Crusade, which started out before the others under the leadership of an eloquent but militarily unprepared preacher, Peter the Hermit, was butchered as soon as it reached Asia Minor.

In some crusaders' minds the "wicked races" were much closer to home: some armies stopped along their way to the Holy Land to kill Jews. By this time most Jews lived in cities, many in the flourishing commercial region of the Rhineland. Under Henry IV the Jews in Speyer and elsewhere in the empire had gained a place within the government system by receiving protection from the local bishop (an imperial appointee) in return for paying a tax. Within these cities the Jews lived in their own neighborhoods—Bishop Rüdiger even built walls around the one at Speyer—and their tightly knit communities focused around the synagogue, which was a school and community center as well as a place of worship. Nevertheless, Jews also participated in the life of the larger Christian community. Archbishop Anno of Cologne dealt with Jewish moneylenders, and other Jews in Cologne were allowed to trade their wares at the fairs there. Although officials pronounced against the Jews from time to time and Jews were occasionally expelled from cities like Mainz, they were not persecuted systematically until the First Crusade. Then, as Guibert of Nogent put it, the crusaders considered it ridiculous to attack Muslims when other infidels lived in their own backyard: "That's doing our work backward." A number of Crusade leaders threatened Jews with forced conversion or death but relented when the Jews paid them money. Others, however, attacked. Jews sometimes found refuge with bishops or in the houses of Christian friends, but in many cities—Metz, Speyer, Worms, Mainz, and Cologne—they were massacred. Laden with booty from the Jewish quarters, the crusaders continued on their way to Jerusalem.

The main objective of the First Crusade—to wrest the Holy Land from the Muslims and subject it to Christian rule—was accomplished largely because of Muslim disunity. After nearly a year of ineffectual attacks, the crusaders took Antioch on June 3, 1098, killing every Turk in the city; on July 15, 1099, they seized Jerusalem. The leaders of the First Crusade set up four states—called *Outremer*, the lands "beyond the sea"—on the coastal fringe of the Muslim west. They held on to them until 1144.

The Revival of Monarchies

The establishment of states was characteristic of twelfth-century political life. Everywhere, princes and kings consolidated their rule. They found new and old ideologies to justify their hegemony; they hired officials to work for them; and they found vassals and churchmen to support them. Money gave them increased effectiveness, and the new commercial economy supplied them with increased revenues.

Louis the Fat: A Model King of France

During the Investiture Conflict the papacy had been preoccupied with the emperor, who controlled many church officials and whose title implied authority over Rome. Although the emperor's dominion was weakened after 1122, the French king, whose role had been slight in the tenth and eleventh centuries, escaped the conflict untouched. In the twelfth century he used the many institutions of French society to bolster his rule: money, money makers, vassals, castles, churchmen, lawyers, intellectuals, and artists.

Louis VI, known as Louis the Fat (*1108–1137) because by the end of his life he had become so heavy that he had to be hoisted onto his horse by a crane, was a tireless defender of royal prerogatives. We know a good deal about him and his reputation because a contemporary, Suger (1081–1152) the abbot of St. Denis, wrote Louis's biography. Suger and Louis had attended school together as boys and remained close associates until Louis's death. In fact, Suger tutored Louis's son, Louis VII (*1137–1180), and acted as regent of France when Louis VII left to lead the Second Crusade in 1147.

Suger was a chronicler and propagandist for Louis the Fat. In the area around Paris, the Ile-de-France, Louis set himself the task of consolidating territory and subduing opponents. In Suger's view these were righteous undertakings. He thought of the king as the head of a political hierarchy in which Louis had rights over the French nobles because they were his vassals or because they broke the peace. Sugar also believed Louis had a religious role: to protect the church and the poor. He viewed Louis as another Charlemagne, a ruler for all society, not merely an overlord of the nobility. Louis waged war to keep God's peace. Of course, the Gregorian reform had made its mark: Suger did not claim Louis was the head of the church, but he emphasized the royal dignity and its importance to the papacy. When Pope Paschal II arrived in France

for the love of God [Louis and his father] humbled their royal majesty before his feet, in the way that kings bow down with lowered diadem before the tomb of the fisherman Peter. The lord pope lifted them up and made them sit before him like devout sons of the apostles. In the manner of a wise man acting wisely, he conferred with them privately on the present condition of the church. Softening them with compliments, he petitioned them to bring aid to the blessed Peter and to himself, his vicar, and to lend support to the church.

Here the pope was shown needing the king's advice. Meanwhile, Suger stressed Louis's independent religious role:

Accompanied by the clergy, to whom he was always humbly attached, he turned off the road toward the well-fortified castle of Crécy. Helped by his powerful band of armed men, or rather by the hand of God, he abruptly seized the castle and captured its very strong tower as if it were simply the hut of a peasant. Having startled those criminals, he piously slaughtered the impious.

Stained Glass: Illuminating the Spirit
In this detail from a stained-glass window made for Suger's chapel of the Virgin Mary at St. Denis, Suger himself appears as the small, bowing figure. In Suger's view, the windows of the choir, glowing in rich and splendid colors, led viewers to spiritual illumination.

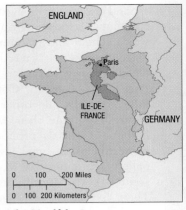

The Twelfth-Century French Monarchy

When Louis VI died in 1137, Suger's notion of the might and right of the king of France reflected reality in an extremely small area. The king controlled only the territory around Paris and extending southward toward the Loire valley; here he was recognized as the lord of other territorial lords. Elsewhere he was, at best, the nominal lord of powerful vassals. Nevertheless, Louis laid the groundwork for the gradual extension of royal power in France. As a lord the king could call upon his vassals to aid him in time of war (though the great ones sometimes disregarded his wishes and chose not to help). From the ban and his rights as a landlord, the king obtained many dues and taxes. He also drew revenues from Paris, a thriving city not only of commerce but also of scholarship. Officials, called provosts, enforced royal laws and collected taxes. The offices were auctioned off to the highest bidder, so in effect the provosts acted as tax-farmers for the king. With money and land, Louis could dispense the favors and give the gifts that added to his prestige and his power. Louis VI and Suger together created the territorial core and the royal ideal of the future French monarchy.

Norman England

Unlike the kings of France, who consolidated their hold gradually, the twelfth-century kings of England ruled the whole kingdom by right of conquest. When Edward the Confessor died childless in 1066, three main contenders desired the English throne: Harold, earl of Wessex, an Englishman close to the king but not of royal blood; Harald Hardrada, the king of Norway, who had unsuccessfully attempted to conquer the Danes and now turned hopefully to England; and William (1027–1087), the duke of Normandy, who claimed that Edward had promised him the throne fifteen years earlier. On his deathbed, Edward had named

Earl Harold to succeed him, and the *witan*, a royal advisory committee that had the right to choose the king, had confirmed the nomination.

When he learned that Harold had been anointed and crowned, William prepared for battle. Appealing to the pope, he received the banner of St. Peter, and with this symbol of God's approval William launched the invasion of England, filling his ships with warriors recruited from many parts of France. As a Norman writer put it:

> *He retained them all, giving them much and promising more. Many came by agreement made by them beforehand; many bargained for lands, if they should win England; some required pay, allowances and gifts.*

About a week before William's invasion force landed, Harold defeated Harald Hardrada. When he heard of William's arrival, Harold wheeled his forces south, marching them 250 miles and picking up new soldiers along the way to meet the Normans. The two armies clashed at Hastings on October 14, 1066, in one of history's rare decisive battles. Both armies had about seven or eight thousand men, Harold's in defensive position on a slope, William's attacking from below. All the men were crammed into a very small space as they began the fight. Most of the English were on foot, armed with battle-axes and stones tied to sticks, which could be thrown with great force. William's army consisted of perhaps three thousand mounted knights, a thousand archers, and the rest infantry. At first William's knights broke ranks, frightened by the fiercely thrown battle-axes of the English; but then some of the English also broke rank as they pursued the knights. William removed his helmet so his men would know him, rallying them to surround and cut down the English who had broken away. Similar skirmishes lasted the entire afternoon, and gradually Harold's troops were worn down, particularly by William's archers, whose arrows flew a hundred yards, much farther than an English battle-ax could be thrown. By dusk, King Harold was dead and his army utterly defeated. No other army gathered to oppose the successful claimant.

Some people in England supported William willingly; in fact, the first to come forward was a most illustrious woman, Queen Edith, Harold's sister and the widow of Edward the Confessor. Those English who backed William considered his victory a verdict from God, and they hoped to be granted a place in the new order themselves. But William and his men wanted to replace, not assimilate, the Anglo-Saxons. In the course of William's reign, families from the Continent almost totally supplanted the English aristocracy.

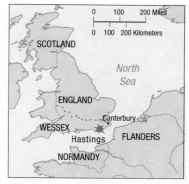

Norman Conquest of England

And although the English peasantry remained—now with new lords—they were severely shaken. A twelfth-century historian "recorded" William's deathbed confession:

> *I have persecuted [England's] native inhabitants beyond all reason. Whether gentle or simple, I have cruelly oppressed them; many I unjustly disinherited; innumerable multitudes, especially in the county of York, perished through me by famine or the sword.*

Modern historians estimate that one out of five people in England died as a result of the Norman conquest.

Although the Normans destroyed a generation of English men and women, they did preserve and extend many Anglo-Saxon institutions. For example, the Norman kings used the writ to communicate orders, and they retained the old administrative divisions of shires (counties) and hundreds. But William and his successors also drew from continental institutions. Norman England became a graded political hierarchy, culminating with the king and buttressed by his castles. The land was treated as the monarch's booty; William kept about 20 percent of it for himself and divided the rest, distributing it in large but scattered fiefs to a relatively small number of his greatest vassals (his barons) and family members, lay and ecclesiastical, as well as to some lesser men, such as personal servants and soldiers. In turn these men maintained their own vassals; they owed the king military service (and the service of a fixed number of their vassals) along with certain dues and rights, such as reliefs (money paid upon

William the Conqueror
The battle of Hastings and the events leading up to it were chronicled in an extraordinary embroidery measuring about 230 feet long and 20 inches high called the Bayeaux Tapestry. The portion shown here depicts Duke Harold swearing an oath to William the Conqueror, seated on a throne.

inheriting a fief) and aids (payments made on important occasions).

These revenues and rights came from the nobles, but the king of England commanded the peasantry as well. Twenty years after his conquest, William ordered a survey and census of England, the so-called Domesday Book. It was the most extensive inventory of land, agricultural produce, taxes, and population that had ever been compiled anywhere in Europe. William

> sent his men over all England into every shire and had them find out how many hundred hides [a measure of land] there were in the shire, or what land and cattle the king himself had in the country, or what dues he ought to receive every year from the shire. . . . So very narrowly did he have the survey to be made that there was not a single hide or yard of land, nor indeed . . . an ox or a cow or a pig left out.

Local surveys were carried out by consulting Anglo-Saxon tax lists and by taking testimony from local jurors, men sworn to answer a series of formal questions truthfully. From these inquests scribes wrote voluminous reports filled with facts and statements from villagers, sheriffs, priests, and barons. These reports were then summarized in the Domesday Book, a concise record of England's resources that supplied the king and his officials with information such as how much and what sort of land England had, who held it, and what revenues —including the lucrative Danegeld, which was now in effect a royal tax—could be expected from it.

The Norman kings retained the Anglo-Saxon legal system, based on the shire and hundred courts. Although great lords in England set up law courts (just as on the Continent), the peculiarly English system of royal district courts continued to flourish. A sheriff appointed by the king to police the shire and muster military levies also acted as judge. If he took advantage of his position, a strong king like William could call him to account: "Summon my sheriffs by my order," began a writ from William to his magnates,

> and tell them that they must return to my bishoprics and abbacies all the demesne, and all the demesne-land which . . . they have consented to hold or which they have seized by violence.

William and his successors intended to control conflicts. If the disagreement involved their barons, they expected the litigants to come to "their own" court, the court of the king. "But if the dispute is between the vassals of two different lords let the plea be held in the shire court." The "men of the shire" had attended the meetings of these courts during the Anglo-Saxon period, and the practice continued under the Normans. These courts had been the sites of the regional inquests for the Domesday Book. Hence the courts had a popular as well as a royal component. Eventually the county courts would encroach on the courts of the great lords and extend the king's law across all of England to create English "common law."

The Norman conquest tied England to the languages, politics, institutions, and culture of the Continent. Modern English is an amalgam of Anglo-Saxon and Norman French, the language the Normans spoke. English commerce was linked to the wool industry in Flanders. The continental

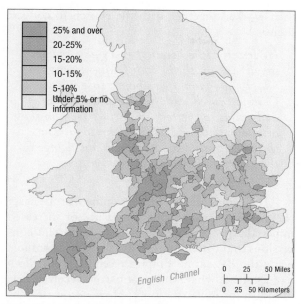

25% and over
20-25%
15-20%
10-15%
5-10%
Under 5% or no
information

English Channel

0   25   50 Miles
0   25   50 Kilometers

Distribution of Slaves in England in 1086 as Reported in Domesday
The Domesday Survey has been used by historians to understand issues such as the distribution of slaves in eleventh-century England. Domesday is only a partial guide to the full reality, however, because its coverage of the English shires was somewhat uneven.

movement for church reform had its counterpart in England, with a controversy similar to the Investiture Conflict: in 1097 and again from 1103 to 1107, the archbishop of Canterbury, St. Anselm (1033–1109) and the sons of William clashed over the king's prerogatives over churchmen and church offices, the same issues that had engaged Henry IV and the pope. The English compromise of 1107 anticipated the provisions of the Concordat of Worms of 1122 by rescinding the king's right to bestow the staff and ring but leaving him the right to receive the homage of churchmen before their consecration. The English Channel served as a bridge rather than a barrier to the interchange of culture. St. Anselm, the most brilliant intellect of his day, for example, was born in Italy and became abbot of the Norman monastery of Bec before his appointment as archbishop in England. Finally, the barons of England retained their estates in Normandy and elsewhere, and the kings of England often spent more time on the Continent than they

did on the island. The story of England after 1066 is, in miniature, the story of Europe.

A Byzantine Revival

At the very end of the eleventh century the Byzantine Empire began to recover from the disastrous battle at Manzikert. In 1081, ten years after that debacle, the energetic soldier Alexius Comnenus seized the throne. He faced considerable unrest in Constantinople, whose populace suffered from a combination of high taxes and rising living costs; and on every side the empire was under attack—from Normans in southern Italy, Seljuk Turks in Asia Minor, and new groups in the Balkans. But Alexius I (✴1081–1118) managed to turn actual and potential enemies against one another, staving off immediate defeat. For example, he called upon the Cuman Turks to help him beat back the Pecheneg Turks, who in 1091 marched toward Constantinople. The battle was a great success for Alexius; the Pechenegs were annihilated. (Although the Cumans assisted the Byzantines in this instance, in the 1120s they attacked the empire in turn.) Similarly, Alexius asked Urban II to supply him with some western troops to fight his enemies. When he learned that crusaders rather than mercenaries were on the way, he closed the gates of Constantinople to the troops, who were eager to plunder, and negotiated their transport to Asia Minor. He also extracted an oath from their leaders (which was later broken, however) that formerly Byzantine cities captured by the crusaders be returned to him. His daughter, Anna Comnena (1083–c. 1148), later wrote an account of the Crusades from the Byzantine perspective in a book about her father, the *Alexiad*: to her the crusaders were barbarians and her father the consummate statesman and diplomat:

> *[A large contingent of crusaders arrived], a numberless heterogeneous host gathered together from almost all the Keltic lands [lands of the Franks] with their leaders (kings and dukes and counts and even bishops). The emperor sent envoys to greet them as a mark of friendship and forwarded politic letters. It was typical of Alexius: he had an uncanny prevision and knew how to seize a point of vantage before his rivals. Officers appointed for this particular task were ordered to provide*

victuals on the journey—the pilgrims must have no excuse for complaint for any reason whatever. Meanwhile they were eagerly pressing on to the capital. . . . With the idea of enforcing the same oath that Godfrey [a Crusade leader who had arrived earlier] had taken, Alexius . . . refuted their objections with no difficulty at all and harried them in a hundred ways until they were driven to take the oath.

To wage all the wars he had to fight, Alexius relied less on the peasant-farmers and the *theme* system than on mercenaries and great magnates armed and mounted like western knights and accompanied by their own troops. In return for their services he gave these nobles *pronoia*, lifetime possession of large imperial estates and their dependent peasants. The *theme* system, under which peasant-soldiers in earlier centuries had been settled on imperial lands, gradually disappeared. Alexius conciliated the great families by giving the provincial nobility *pronoia* and satisfied the urban elite by granting them new offices. Although the emperor sometimes used church property to generate revenue, he normally got on well with the patriarch and Byzantine clergy, for emperor and church depended on one another to suppress heresy and foster orthodoxy. Anna Comnena wrote that her father imprisoned some heretics and then worked together with the church to convert them:

He sent for [the heretics] every day and personally taught them, with frequent exhortations, to abandon their abominable cult. Certain church leaders were told to make daily visits to the rest, to instruct them in the orthodox faith and advise them to give up their heretical ideas. And some did change for the better and were freed from prison, but others died in their heresy.

The emperors of the Comnenian dynasty (1081–1185) thus bought a measure of increased imperial power, but at the price of important concessions to the nobility. The distribution of *pronoia* made the Byzantine Empire resemble a kingdom like England, where the great barons received fiefs in return for military service. However, at first the *pronoia* could not be inherited, nor could their holders subdivide them to give to their own warriors. In this way the emperor retained more direct authority over every level of the Byzantine populace than did the rulers of Europe.

Alexius's son, John II (✳1118–1143), regained Byzantine control of much of Asia Minor, decimated the tribes that had invaded the Balkans, firmly reestablished Byzantine dominion over the Slavic groups of Serbia and Bulgaria, and held off Hungarian incursions from the north. When John died in a hunting accident in 1143, Byzantium again occupied a formidable position in Europe and Asia Minor.

Despite Byzantium's unsettled political affairs, Constantinople in the eleventh and early twelfth centuries remained a rich, sophisticated, and highly cultured city. Sculptors strove to depict ideals of human beauty and elegance; mosaicists recognized body weight and physical presence over pattern and design. Churches built during the period were decorated with a scheme of mosaics meant to show the hierarchy of the cosmos and the calendar of the church. Significant innovations occurred in the realm of scholarship and literature. The neo-Platonic tradition of late antiquity had always permeated all aspects of Byzantine religious and philosophical thought, but now scholars renewed their interest in the wellsprings of classical Greek philosophy, particularly Plato and Aristotle. Some

Byzantine Revival Under the Comnenians

scholars sought so enthusiastically to reconcile ancient Greek philosophy with Christianity that they found themselves accused of abandoning essential Christian beliefs. The rediscovery of ancient culture inspired Byzantine writers to reintroduce old forms into the grammar, vocabulary, and rhetorical style of Greek literature. Anna Comnena wrote her *Alexiad* in this newly learned Greek:

> I, Anna, daughter of the Emperor Alexius and the Empress Irene, born and bred in the Purple, not without some acquaintance with literature—having devoted the most earnest study to the Greek language, in fact, and being not unpracticed in rhetoric and having read thoroughly the treatises of Aristotle and the dialogues of Plato. . . . I, having realized the effects wrought by time, desire now by means of my writings to give an account of my father's deeds.

The revival of ancient Greek writings, especially Plato's, in eleventh- and twelfth-century Byzantium had profound consequences for both eastern and western European civilization in centuries to come as these ideas slowly penetrated European culture.

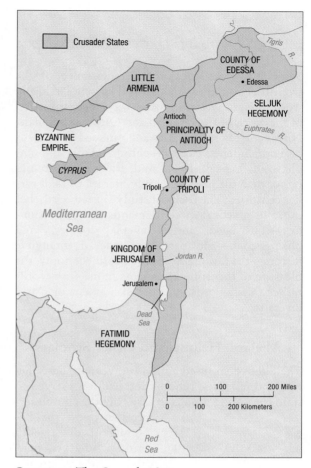

Outremer: The Crusader States

A West European Outpost: Outremer

Like Norman England, the states of Outremer were created by conquest. The crusaders carved out four tiny regions around Edessa, Antioch, Jerusalem, and (after a major battle in 1109) Tripoli. Like England, these states were feudal lordships, with a ruler at the apex of a triangular scheme of vassals. The ruler granted fiefs to his own vassals, and some of these men in turn gave portions of their holdings as fiefs to some of their own vassals. Many other vassals simply lived in the households of their lords.

Thus foreign knights, who imposed their rule on indigenous populations with vastly different customs and religions, ruled Outremer. Although European peasants clearly differed from knights and nobles by occupation, dress, and style of life, they often lived near the upper class on the same estates, and they shared the same religion. In Outremer, by contrast, the Europeans lived in towns and had little

in common with the Muslims, Jews, and even native Arab-speaking Christians who tilled the soil.

The ruling classes of the Latin (or western) states of Outremer held on to their positions precariously. They were constantly on the alert against wars with their Muslim neighbors and occasionally with the Byzantines and with one another. When a new Seljuk chieftain, Zengi, succeeded in uniting Muslim forces behind him, the Latin rulers could not hold out against him. Edessa fell in 1144, and the slow but steady shrinking of Outremer began. Despite numerous new crusades, most Europeans were simply not willing to commit the vast resources and personnel that would have been necessary to maintain outposts in the Levant. Outremer fell to the Muslims permanently in 1291.

New Forms of Western Scholarship

Some historians speak of a renaissance of the twelfth century, but this revival of scholarship in western Europe was in many ways a continuation of the work of Carolingian and Ottonian scholars. Now centered in the cities and pursued by crowds of avid students, twelfth-century scholarship emphasized logical, legal, and theoretical studies rather than the predominantly literary ones of earlier centuries. The focus of study shifted partly because of practical career demands and opportunities—the need for lawyers, doctors, and businessmen—and partly because of intangible factors—the rationality of the profit economy, the pleasure of thrusting arguments home with words rather than swords, and the excitement of urban diversity.

Abelard, Heloise, and Other Scholars

The old system of education had centered in cathedral and monastic schools and had long served to train clerics and monks to carry out the church services. Around the beginning of the twelfth century, however, hundreds and eventually thousands of students sought teachers at the cathedral schools in urban centers like Reims, Paris, Bologna, and Montpellier. One contemporary described a typical student in this way:

The Intellectual Revival

Instilled with an insatiable thirst for learning, whenever [the young monk Gilbert of Liège] heard of somebody excelling in the arts, he rushed immediately to that place and drank whatever delightful potion he could draw from the master there. . . . Later, after having filled himself with the sweet honey of knowledge like a bee flying across bloomy fields he returned to the sanctuary of his monastery.

For Gilbert and other students a good lecture had the excitement of theater. Teachers at cathedral schools found themselves forced to find larger halls to accommodate the crush of students. Other teachers simply declared themselves "masters" and set up shop by renting a room. If they could prove their mettle in the classroom, they had no trouble finding paying students.

Many young men in the early twelfth century were "wandering scholars" like Gilbert of Liège. As far as we know, these scholars were all male; and because schools had hitherto been the training ground for clergymen, all were considered clerics, whether or not they had been ordained. Wandering became a way of life as the consolidation of castellanies, counties, and kingdoms made violence against travelers less frequent. Urban centers soon responded to the needs of transients with markets, taverns, and lodgings. Using Latin, Europe's common language, students could drift from, say, Italy to Germany, England, and France, wherever a noted master had settled. Along with crusaders, pilgrims, and merchants, students made the roads of Europe very crowded indeed.

We know a good deal about one of these early students, who later became a master: Peter Abelard (1079–1142). Born into a family of the petty nobility, destined for a career as a warrior and lord, Abelard instead became a pioneering thinker. He wrote a virtual autobiography in his *Historia calamitatum* (*Story of My Calamities*). There Abelard described his shift from the life of the warrior to the no less glorious life of the scholar:

I was so carried away by my love of learning, that I renounced the glory of a soldier's life, made over my inheritance and rights of the eldest son to my brothers, and withdrew from the court of Mars [war] in order to kneel at the feet of Minerva [learning].

Arriving eventually at Paris, Abelard studied with William of Champeaux and then challenged his teacher's scholarship. Later Abelard began to lecture and to gather students of his own.

His fame as a teacher was such that a cleric named Fulbert gave Abelard room and board and engaged him as tutor for Heloise (c. 1100–c. 1163/1164), Fulbert's niece. Heloise was one of the few learned women of the period to leave any traces.

Brought up under Fulbert's guardianship, she had been sent as a young girl to a convent school, where she received a thorough grounding in literary skills. Her uncle had hoped to continue her education at home. Abelard, however, became her lover as well as her tutor. "Our desires left no stage of love-making untried," wrote Abelard in his *Historia*. At first their love affair was kept secret. But Heloise became pregnant, and Abelard insisted they marry. They did so clandestinely to prevent damaging Abelard's career, for the new emphasis on clerical celibacy meant that Abelard's professional success and prestige would have been compromised if news of his marriage were made public. Thus after they were married, Heloise and Abelard rarely saw one another. Fulbert, suspecting foul play with regard to his niece, decided to punish Abelard. He paid a servant to castrate Abelard, and soon after, both husband and wife entered separate monasteries.

For Heloise, separation from Abelard was a lasting blow. Although she became a successful abbess, carefully tending to the physical and spiritual needs of her nuns, she continued to call on Abelard for "renewal of strength." In a series of letters addressed to him, she poured out her feelings as "his handmaid, or rather his daughter, wife, or rather sister":

> *You know, beloved, as the whole world knows, how much I have lost in you, how at one wretched stroke of fortune that supreme act of flagrant treachery robbed me of my very self in robbing me of you. . . . You alone have the power to make me sad, to bring me happiness or comfort.*

For Abelard, however, the loss of Heloise and even his castration were not the worst disasters of his life: the cruelest blow came later, and it was directed at his intellect. Having applied "human and logical reasons" (as he put it) to the Trinity, he saw his book on the subject condemned at the Council of Soissons in 1121 and was forced to throw it into the flames. Bitterly weeping at the injustice, Abelard lamented, "this open violence had come upon me only because of the purity of my intentions and love of our Faith which had compelled me to write."

Abelard had written the treatise on the Trinity for his students, maintaining that "words were use-less if the intelligence could not follow them, [and] that nothing could be believed unless it was first understood." The demand that logic—not just reason, but the application of technical rules—illuminate a matter of faith was something relatively new. It typifies the shift in the emphasis of intellectual life from literary studies to logic and to the second part of the "liberal arts," the *quadrivium*.

The Liberal Arts and Other Subjects

In the Middle Ages, as in ancient Rome, students still had to learn grammar, the first step of the seven liberal arts. Grammar was part of the *trivium*, which consisted of three areas of study—grammar, rhetoric, and logic (or dialectic)—that were considered the foundation of education. Logic, involving the technical analysis of texts as well as the application and manipulation of mental constructs, was a transitional subject leading to the second, higher part of the liberal arts, the *quadrivium*. This comprised four areas of study in what we might call theoretical math and science: arithmetic, geometry, music (theory rather than practice), and astronomy. Above all, logic delighted Abelard, who originally came to Paris to hear William of Champeaux (c. 1070–c. 1120) speak about the existence of universals, ideas such as "man," "truth," and "goodness." But Abelard soon engaged in hot debate with William. Logic excited enormous interest at the time because people wanted to be sure that what they were trying to prove with words was in fact true. They saw logic as the tool that could reveal and clarify each issue.

At the heart of the debate over universals was the nature of the individual. The *nominalist* position held that each individual was unique. For example, Tom and Harry (and Carol, for that matter) may be called "man" (a word that includes both males and females), but that label (to the nominalist) is merely a convenience, a manner of speaking. In reality (in the nominalist view) Tom and Harry and Carol are so unlike that each can be truly comprehended only as separate and irreducible entities. Only very few people in Abelard's time argued this position, in part because it led to clearly heretical results: applied to the Trinity, it shattered the unity of the Father, Son, and Holy Ghost, leaving the idea of the Trinity an empty name. (The word *name* in Latin is *nomen*, from which *nominalist* was derived.)

The *realist* position, argued by William of Champeaux, was more acceptable in the twelfth century. Realists argued that the "real," the essential, aspect of the individual was the universal qualities of its group. Thus Tom and Harry and Carol were certainly different, but their differences were inessential "accidents." In truth (argued the realists) all three people must be properly comprehended as "man." This view also raised theological problems—if taken to an extreme, the Trinity would melt into one. And it certainly did not satisfy a man like Abelard, who was adamant about his own individuality.

Abelard created his own position, called modified realism, by focusing on the observer, who sees "real" individuals and who abstracts "real" universals from them. The key for Abelard was the nature of the knower: the concept of "man" was formed by the knower observing the similarities between Tom, Harry, and Carol and deriving a universal concept that allowed him (or her) to view individuals properly in its light. Abelard's treatise on ethics was entitled *Know Thyself*, after the motto of the Delphic oracle and Socrates' philosophy of virtue through self-knowledge. Interested above all in the knower, Abelard went on to discuss interior motivation:

> *When the same thing is done by the same man at different times, by the diversity of his intention . . . his action is now said to be good, now bad.*

This is why Abelard so mourned the burning of his book on the Trinity, for in his view it had sprung from the purest intentions and was burned out of the basest motives.

Later in the twelfth century, scholars discovered that Aristotle had once elaborated a view parallel to Abelard's, but until the middle of the twelfth century very little of Aristotle's work was available in Europe because it had not been translated from Greek into Latin. Most of the Church Fathers had considered Aristotle's philosophy irrelevant and had not incorporated it into the Christian worldview. The only works of Aristotle available in Latin were his basic treatises on logic, which Abelard relied upon when launching his own system. However nearly the full corpus of Aristotle's philosophy

had been translated into Arabic by the eleventh and twelfth centuries. Ibn Sina (Avicenna), the great Muslim scientist and doctor, also commented on Aristotle, showing how Aristotle's philosophy fit into neo-Platonism. By the mid-twelfth century, Christian and Jewish European scholars were translating Aristotle's works, along with Muslim scholars' commentaries on them, from Arabic into Latin (and Hebrew). (Later scholars translated Aristotle from the original Greek.) In a sense, early twelfth-century scholars like Abelard, with their pioneering efforts in logic, opened the way for Christian Europe to welcome Aristotle. By the thirteenth century, Aristotle had become the primary philosopher for *scholastics* (the scholars of the European medieval universities).

Around 1122–1123, shortly after writing his book on the Trinity, Abelard prepared an unusual textbook, the *Sic et Non* (*Yes and No*). It covered 156 questions, among them issues such as: "That God is one and the contrary"; "That all are permitted to marry and the contrary"; "That it is permitted to kill men and the contrary." Arrayed on both sides of each question were the words of authorities: the Bible, the church fathers, the letters of popes. Abelard argued that his method "excites young readers to the maximum of effort in inquiring into the truth." In fact, in Abelard's view the inquiring student followed the model of Christ himself, who as a boy sat among the rabbis, questioning them. The juxtaposition of authoritative sentences was nothing new; what was new was calling attention to their contradictions. The formula of *Sic et Non* was characteristic of the work of scholars in the urban schools, though those who came after Abelard were careful to reconcile the contradictions. Gratian used a similar method in his study of canon law, juxtaposing variant canons and then suggesting how to resolve their contradictions. The same development was occurring even before the time of Abelard and Gratian in the area of secular—particularly Roman—law.

Roman law had been passed down, at least in manuscripts in northern Italy, but regional laws and customs were the principal basis of legal practice until the eleventh century, which saw a renewed interest in codes of law. At Pavia in the mid-eleventh century, law teachers might be found surrounded by clutches of students, much as the masters at Paris attracted followings several decades later. Here the laws, mainly Lombard laws but also Roman laws, were subject to systematic exposition and to disputes over interpretations.

By the end of the eleventh century, Italian jurists were applying these analytical methods to Roman law alone. Justinian's law books attracted readers in the West, and within a few decades each study became institutionalized. At Bologna, Irnerius (died c. 1129) was the guiding light of a law school where students studied Lombard, Roman, or canon law. Men skilled in canon law served popes and bishops; and popes, kings, princes, and communes all found that Roman law, which claimed the emperor as its fount, justified their claims to power.

Religious Life in the Age of Reform and Commerce

Monks continued to repudiate the world in this age of reform, but as the nature of the world changed, so did the character of their repudiation. By the end of the eleventh century, the so-called black monks, the "old-fashioned" Benedictine monks and nuns, spent nearly the entire day in a gigantic and splendidly outfitted church singing an expanded and complex liturgy. Rejecting the extravagance of this life, the so-called white monks and the nuns who followed them promoted a life of pared-down liturgy within the plainest of churches. Numerous forms of monastic life flourished. Many of these new religious foundations enjoyed enormous popularity and attracted the most able men and women of the period.

Black Monks and Artistic Splendor

The monks and nuns who dyed their habits black and followed the Rule of St. Benedict reached the height of their popularity in the eleventh century. Monasteries often housed hundreds of monks; convents for nuns were usually less populated. Cluny was one of the largest monasteries, with some four hundred brothers in the mid-eleventh century.

The chief occupation of the monks, as befitted (in their view) citizens of the *City of God*, was prayer. The black monks and nuns devoted them-

Gregorian Chant
This side of a capital atop a column in the choir at Cluny shows a musician personifying the first tone of the Gregorian chant. Notice how the shape of the sculpture echoes the shape of the architectural element—the capital—that it decorates. This subordination to architectural form was characteristic of Romanesque sculpture.

selves to singing the Psalms and other prayers specified in the Rule of St. Benedict, adding to them still more Psalms. The rule called for chanting the entire psalter—150 psalms—over the course of a week, but some monks, like those at Cluny, chanted that number in a day.

Their devotions were neither private nor silent. Black monks had to know not only the words but also the music that went with the divine office; they had to be musicians. The music of the Benedictine monastery was plainchant (also known as Gregorian chant), which consisted of melodies, each sung in unison, without accompaniment. Although chant was rhythmically free, lacking a regular beat, its melodies ranged from extremely simple to highly

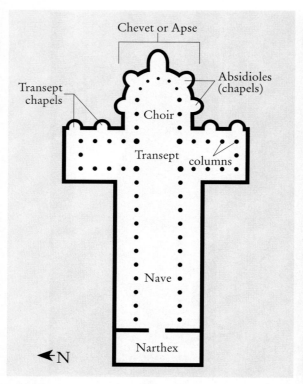

Schematic Romanesque Church

Romanesque Tunnel Vault
Santiago de Compostela, which boasts the relics of St. James, was a major pilgrimage shrine. The church, built in 1078–1124, is a good example of the Romanesque style, which frequently used round arches as in the "tunnel vault" shown here.

ornate and embellished. By the twelfth century a large repertoire of melodies had grown up, at first through oral composition and transmission, then in written notation, which first appeared in manuscripts of the ninth century.

The melodies preserved by this early notation probably originated in Rome and had been introduced into northern Europe at the behest of Charlemagne, who wanted to unify the liturgical practices of his empire. Musical notation was developed to help monks remember unfamiliar melodies and to ensure that they were sung in approximately the same way in all parts of the Carolingian realm. The melodies were further mastered and organized at this time by fitting them into the Byzantine system of eight modes, or scales. This music survived

the dissolution of the Carolingian empire and remained the core music of the Catholic Church into the twentieth century.

At Cluny, where singing the liturgy occupied nearly the entire day and part of the night, the importance of music was made visible—the modes were personified and depicted in sculpture on some of the columns circling the choir of the church. The church of Cluny, rebuilt around 1100, was enormous. Constructed of stone, it must have reverberated with the voices of the hundreds of monks who sang in it.

Cluny was part of the building boom that saw the construction or repair of town walls, dwellings, mills, castles, monasteries, and churches. The style of many of these buildings, like the church of

These three images come from the Romanesque church of St. Lazarus at Autun, France. They were sculpted c. 1120–1135 by the master craftsman Gislebertus, one of a handful of medieval artists we know by name, or by one of the stone carvers under his tutelage.

(left) **The Fall of Simon Magus**
The legend of Simon's plunge and the devil who waits for him (on the right) was already popular in the early Christian period.

(below left) **Suicide of Judas**
Devils leer on each side in this depiction of the suicide of Judas.

(above) **Eve**
Eve is shown as beautiful but serpentine.

Cluny, was Romanesque. Although they varied greatly, most Romanesque churches had massive stone and masonry walls decorated on the interior with paintings in bright colors. The various parts of the church—the chapels in the *chevet* (the east end), for example—were handled as discrete units, retaining the forms of cubes, cones, and cylinders. Inventive sculptural reliefs, both inside and outside the church, enlivened these pristine geometrical forms. Emotional and sometimes frenzied, Romanesque sculpture depicted themes ranging from the horrors of the Last Judgment to the beauty of Eve.

In such a setting, gilded reliquaries and altars made of silver, precious gems, and pearls were the fitting accoutrements of worship. Prayer, liturgy, and music in this way complemented the gift economy: richly clad in vestments of the finest materials, intoning the liturgy in the most splendid of churches, monks and priests offered up the gift of prayer to God; in return they begged for the gift of salvation of their souls and the souls of all the faithful.

New Monastic Orders of Poverty

Not all agreed that such opulence pleased or praised God. At the end of the eleventh century the new commercial economy and the profit motive that fueled it led many to reject wealth and to embrace poverty as a key element of religious life. The Carthusian order, founded by Bruno of Cologne, was one such group. Each monk took a vow of silence and lived as a hermit in his own small hut. Monks occasionally joined others for prayer in a common prayer room, or oratory. When not engaged in prayer or meditation, the Carthusians copied manuscripts. They considered this task part of their religious vocation, a way to preach God's word with their hands rather than their mouths. The Carthusian order grew slowly. Each monastery was limited to only twelve monks, the number of the Apostles.

The Cistercians, on the other hand, expanded rapidly. Rejecting even the conceit of blackening their cowls, they left their habits the original color of wool (hence their nickname, the white monks). The Cistercian order began as a single monastery, Cîteaux (in Latin, *Cistercium*), founded in 1098. It grew to include more than three hundred monasteries spread throughout Europe by the middle of the twelfth century. Despite the Cistercian order's official repudiation of female Cistercian houses, many nunneries followed its lead and adopted its customs. Women were as anxious as men to live the life of simplicity and poverty that they believed the Apostles had enjoyed and endured.

The guiding spirit and preeminent Cistercian abbot was St. Bernard (c. 1090–1153), who arrived at Cîteaux in 1112 along with about thirty friends and relatives. But even before Bernard's arrival, the program of the new order had been set. A chronicle of the order reports that

> They rejected anything opposed to the [Benedictine] Rule: frocks, fur tunics, linsey-woolsey shirts and cowls, straw for beds and various dishes of food in the refectory, as well as lard and all other things which ran counter to the letter of the Rule.

Although they held up the Rule of St. Benedict as the foundation of their customs, the Cistercians elaborated a style of life all their own. Largely supported, as the black monks were, by land donations from pious nobles and knights, the Cistercians created a class of lay monks called *conversi* to till the soil and reap the harvest. Drawn from the peasantry, the *conversi* were clearly a second-class group living separately from the monks. Although they could enter the monastic church, they were confined to the back. The *conversi* and the "real" monks hardly ever saw one another.

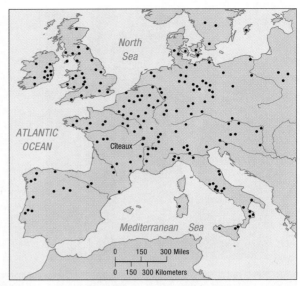

The Spread of Cistercian Monasticism in the Twelfth Century

Cistercian churches, though built of stone, were initially unlike the great Romanesque churches of the black monks. They were remarkably standardized; the church and the rest of the buildings of any Cistercian monastery were almost exactly like those of any other. The churches were small, made of smoothly hewn, undecorated stone. Wall paintings and sculpture were prohibited. St. Bernard wrote a scathing attack on Romanesque sculpture in which he acknowledged, in spite of himself, its exceptional allure:

> What is the point of ridiculous monstrosities in the cloister where there are brethren reading— I mean those extraordinary deformed beauties and beautiful deformities? What are those lascivious apes doing, those fierce lions, monstrous centaurs, half-men and spotted leopards? . . . It is more diverting to decipher marble than the text before you, and to spend the whole day in gazing at such singularities in preference to meditating upon God's laws.

The Cistercians had no such diversions, but the simplicity of their buildings and of their clothing also had its beauty. Illuminated by the pure white light that came through clear glass windows, Cistercian houses were luminous, cool, and serene.

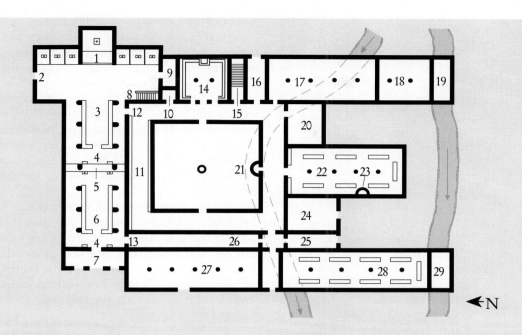

1 Sanctuary
2 Lych gate, the door through which bodies were carried from the funeral service to the graveyard
3 Monks' choir
4 Benches for the sick
5 Rood screen, separating the monks' choir from that of the conversi
6 Choir of the conversi, or lay brothers
7 Narthex
8 Night stairs from the church to the dormitory
9 Sacristy
10 'Armarium', where books were kept
11 Benches for reading, and for the 'maundy' ceremony of foot-washing
12 Monks' entry
13 Lay brothers' entry
14 Chapter house
15 Stairs from the cloister to the dormitory, which extended over the whole range 14–19

16 Parlor
17 Monks' common room
18 Room for novices
19 Latrine (used from the upper storey)
20 Calefactorium, or warming room
21 Fountain, for washing
22 Refectory (Dining room)
23 Pulpit, for reading during the meal
24 Kitchen
25 Cellarer's parlor
26 'Lane' or 'alley' of the lay brothers
27 Cellar, or storeroom
28 Lay brothers' refectory. The dormitory of the conversi, or lay brothers, extended over the whole range 27–28
29 Latrines for the lay brothers

Schematic Cistercian Monastery

All Cistercian monasteries were built on a similar plan, illustrated here. The church was integrated with the other monastic buildings, half of which were used by the monks and half by the "lay brothers." Because of their emphasis on purity, the monks built their monastery near a stream.

True to this emphasis on purity, the communal liturgy of the Cistercians was simplified and shorn of the many additions that had been tacked on in the houses of black monks. Only the *opus Dei* (the liturgy) as prescribed in the Rule of St. Benedict— plus one daily mass—was allowed. Even the music for the chant was changed; the Cistercians rigorously suppressed the B flat, even though doing so made the melody discordant, because of their insistence on strict simplicity.

Cistercian Architecture
The whiteness and simplicity of Cistercian churches may be seen in this view of the south transept of the church at Pontigny, France.

With their time partly freed from the choir, the white monks dedicated themselves to private prayer and contemplation and to monastic administration. In some ways these activities were antithetical—one internal and the other external. The Cistercian *Charter of Charity*, in effect a constitution of the order, provided for a closely monitored network of houses, and each year the Cistercian abbots met to hammer out legislation for all the monasteries. The

abbot of the mother (or founding) house visited the daughter houses annually to make sure the legislation was being followed. Each house, whether mother or daughter, had large and highly organized farms and grazing lands called granges. Cistercian monks spent much of their time managing their estates and flocks of sheep, both of which yielded handsome profits by the end of the twelfth century. Clearly part of the agricultural and commercial revolutions of the Middle Ages, the Cistercian order made managerial expertise a part of the monastic life.

At the same time, the Cistercians elaborated a spirituality of intense personal emotion. Although St. Bernard and Abelard clashed—Bernard argued that Abelard was "presumptuously prepared to give a reason for everything, even of those things which are above reason"—they both valued inward and emotional awareness. As Bernard said,

> *often enough when we approach the altar to pray our hearts are dry and lukewarm. But if we persevere, there comes an unexpected infusion of grace, our breast expands as it were, and our interior is filled with an overflowing love; and if somebody should press upon it then, this milk of sweet fecundity would gush forth in streaming richness.*

The Cistercians emphasized not only human emotion but also Christ's and Mary's humanity. While pilgrims continued to stream to the tombs and reliquaries of saints, the Cistercians dedicated all their churches to the Virgin Mary, for whom they had no relics, because for them she signified the model of a loving mother. Indeed the Cistercians regularly used maternal imagery (as Bernard's description invoking the metaphor of a flowing breast illustrates) to describe the nurturing care provided to humankind by Jesus himself. The Cistercian God was approachable, human, protective, and even mothering.

Similar views of God were held by many who were not members of the Cistercian orders; their spirituality signaled wider changes. For example, around 1099, St. Anselm wrote a theological treatise entitled *Why God Became Man* in which he argued that since Man had sinned, Man had to redeem himself. St. Anselm's work represented a new theological emphasis on the redemptive power of human charity, including that of Jesus as a human being. The crusaders had trodden the very place of Christ's crucifixion, making his humanity both more real and more problematic to people who walked in the holy "place of God's humiliation and our redemption," as one chronicler put it. Yet this new stress on the loving bonds that tied Christians together also led to the persecution of others, like Jews and Muslims, who lived outside the Christian community.

St. Denis and the Beginning of Gothic

About ten years after Bernard had written about approaching the altar "dry and lukewarm," Suger, the abbot of St. Denis and biographer of Louis the Fat, wrote about the new altar at St. Denis that he had encased in gold and studded with precious gems:

> *When—out of my delight in the beauty of the house of God—the loveliness of the many-colored gems has called me away from external cares, and worthy meditation has induced me to reflect on the diversity of the sacred virtues . . . then it seems to me . . . that I can be transported from this inferior [world on earth] to that higher world [in Heaven].*

For Suger, color and light had a mystical effect, transporting the worshipper from the "slime of earth" to the "purity of Heaven," an idea Suger had read in the writings of a neo-Platonist Syrian theologian who lived about 500. Suger and most of his contemporaries mistakenly believed this theologian to be Dionysius the Areopagite, a disciple of St. Paul, whom they further misidentified as St. Denis (Dionysius in Latin), Apostle to the Gauls. Since Suger's monastery was dedicated to St. Denis, he and his monks read the Syrian thinker's mystical theology of light with the reverence due a patron saint. In this theology, God was the Father of lights, and the emanations of his light flowed through a hierarchy of beings, from angels down to the vilest matter. For Suger, precisely because people were trapped in material and mortal bodies, they could rise to God through their senses:

> *Every creature, visible or invisible, is a light brought into being by the Father of the*

> *lights. . . . This stone or that piece of wood is a light to me. . . . For I perceive that it is good and beautiful. . . . As I perceive such and similar things in this stone they become lights to me, that is to say, they enlighten me.*

When Suger embarked on a program to rebuild St. Denis, in about 1135, he turned this theology of light into an architectural style, later called Gothic. The term *Gothic* was not Suger's. It was coined centuries later by people who criticized medieval architecture as ungainly and barbaric, like the Visigoths who had sacked Rome. Although distinctions between Romanesque and Gothic are artificial since both evolved alongside one another and often shared many elements, certain characteristic features of each style can be isolated. Gothic churches were, by Romanesque standards, compact in length and unified in structure, without clear geometrical building blocks. For example, the chapels of Suger's rebuilt chevet, completed in 1144, were not separated from one another like cylinders but rather flowed together. The walls, so important in the Romanesque church, were largely replaced by stained glass in the Gothic. As the sun shone into the church, the glass glowed. As Suger put it in a poem, "And bright is the noble edifice which is pervaded by the new light." By "new light" Suger meant not just the sun but also the "clarity" of the Father of lights, God himself, who "brightens" the minds of men. Being in the church was a glance at heaven.

The Capetian monarchs associated themselves with St. Denis as they sought to extend their power. Already in 1124, for example, before riding out to a particularly important battle, Louis VI went to the church of St. Denis to obtain its banner and proclaimed the saint "the special patron and, after God, special protector of the realm." At the same time, Louis confirmed the church's right to hold a lucrative fair. About fifteen years later, when Suger rebuilt the portals (doorway areas) at the west end of St. Denis, he had them decorated with the figures of Old Testament kings, queens, and patriarchs. Their presence signified the interdependence between the monarchy and the church. Gothic architecture was the creation of a fruitful melding of royal and ecclesiastical interests and ideals in the north of France.

CONCLUSION

The commercial revolution and the building boom it spurred profoundly changed the look of Europe. Thriving cities of merchants and artisans brought trade, new wealth, and new institutions to the West. Mutual and fraternal organizations like the commune, the *compagnia*, and the guilds expressed and reinforced the solidarity and economic interest of city-dwellers. But many rural people were wary of urban life and its cash economy; church reformers warned against the buying and selling of church offices; and monastic reformers sought to escape money by stressing austerity and poverty.

Political consolidation accompanied economic growth, as kings and popes exerted their authority and tested its limits. The Gregorian reform pitted the emperor against the pope and in the end two separate political hierarchies emerged, the secular and the ecclesiastical. The two might cooperate, as Suger and Louis VI showed in their mutual respect, admiration, and dependence; but they might also clash, as Anselm did with the sons of William the Conqueror. Secular and religious leaders developed new and largely separate systems of administration, reflecting in political life the new distinctions, such as clerical celibacy and allegiance to the pope, that differentiated clergy and laity. Although in some ways growing apart, the two groups never worked so closely as in the Crusades, military pilgrimages inspired by the pope and led by lay lords.

The commercial economy, political stability, and ecclesiastical needs fostered the growth of schools and the achievements of new scholarship. Young men like Abelard, who a generation before would have become knights, now sought learning to enhance their careers and bring personal fulfillment. Women like Heloise could gain an excellent basic education in a convent and then go on to higher studies, as she did, with a tutor. Logic fascinated students because it seemed to clarify what was real about themselves, the world, and God. Churchmen like St. Bernard, who felt that faith could not be analyzed, rejected scholarship based on logic.

While black monks added to their hours of worship, built lavish churches, and devoted themselves to the music of the plainchant, a reformer like St. Bernard insisted on an intense, interior spiritual life in a monastery austerely and directly based on the Rule of St. Benedict. Other reformers, like Bruno of Cologne, sought the high mountaintop for its isolation and hardship. These reformers repudiated urban society, yet unintentionally reflected it: the Cistercians were as interested as any student in their interior state of mind and as anxious as any tradesman in the success of their granges, and the Carthusians were dedicated to their books.

The early twelfth century saw a period of renaissance and reform in the church, monarchies, and scholarship. The later twelfth century would be an age when people experimented with and rebelled against various forms of authority.

SUGGESTIONS FOR FURTHER READING

Source Materials

Benton, John F., ed. *Self and Society in Medieval France: The Memoirs of Abbot Guibert of Nogent (1064?– c. 1125)*. 1970. An autobiography by an outspoken and opinionated critic of his age.

Peters, Edward, ed. *The First Crusade. The Chronicle of Fulcher of Chartres and Other Source Materials*. 1971. Various sources brought together to chronicle the First Crusade.

Radice, Betty, trans. *The Letters of Abelard and Heloise*. 1974. Includes Abelard's famous *Historia calamitatum*, which is essentially his autobiography, along with other letters.

Suger. *The Deeds of Louis the Fat*. Translated by Richard C. Cusimano and John Moorhead. 1992. A biography of Louis written by his friend, Abbot Suger of St. Denis.

Tierney, Brian, ed. *The Crisis of Church and State, 1050–1300*. 1964. A collection of documents illustrating papal and royal clashes, with useful introductions by the editor.

Interpretive Studies

Barraclough, Geoffrey. *The Origins of Modern Germany*. 1963. Although written at the end of World War II, remains a useful and passionate account of medieval German political history.

Benson, Robert L., and Giles Constable, eds. with the assistance of Carol Lanham. *Renaissance and Renewal in the Twelfth Century*. 1982. Contains articles by experts on key aspects of the intellectual and religious life of the twelfth century.

Berman, Constance Hoffman. *Medieval Agriculture, the Southern French Countryside and the Early Cistercians. A Study of Forty-Three Monasteries*. 1986. Details the nature of Cistercian economic activities.

Bouchard, Constance B. *Holy Entrepreneurs: Cistercians, Knights, and Economic Exchange in Twelfth-Century Burgundy*. 1991. An important book on Cistercian economic activities.

———. *Sword, Miter, and Cloister: Nobility and the Church in Burgundy, 980–1198*. 1987. Shows the role of nobles in the movement for church and monastic reform.

Braunfels, Wolfgang. *Monasteries of Western Europe. The Architecture of the Orders*. 1972. An excellent survey of monastic architecture.

Bynum, Caroline Walker. *Jesus as Mother: Studies in the Spirituality of the High Middle Ages*. 1982. Discusses the imagery of twelfth- and thirteenth-century religious writing.

Cattin, Giulio. *Music of the Middle Ages*. 2 vols. Translated by Steven Botterill. 1984. An excellent survey that includes some primary source readings.

Chibnall, Marjorie. *Anglo-Norman England 1066–1166*. 1986. A discussion of the impact of the Norman conquest that stresses the way both Anglo-Saxon and Norman institutions were adapted and shaped after 1066.

Dillard, Heath. *Daughters of the Reconquest: Women in Castilian Town Society, 1100–1300*. 1984. Examines the roles of women in Christian Spain.

Douglas, David C. *William the Conqueror: The Norman Impact Upon England*. 1967. A very readable account of political events by an eminent scholar.

Duby, Georges. *Medieval Marriage: Two Models from Twelfth-Century France*. Translated by Elborg Forster. 1978. Studies clerical and lay notions of marriage.

Dunbabin, Jean. *France in the Making, 843–1180*. 1985. Explores the ways in which a sense of community emerged in France.

Erdmann, Carl. *The Origin of the Idea of Crusade*. Translated by Marshall W. Baldwin and Walter Goffart. 1977. A translation from German of one of the most important studies of the crusading idea.

Finucane, Ronald C. *Soldiers of the Faith: Crusaders and Moslems at War*. 1983. Views the Crusades as an interaction between Muslims and Christians.

Fletcher, R. A. *St. James' Catapult: The Life and Times of Diego Gelmírez of Santiago de Compostela*. 1984. Biography of Diego Gelmírez, a bishop of the pilgrimage center of Santiago de Compostela, illuminating the politics, religion, and mentality of the eleventh century.

Fuhrmann, Horst. *Germany in the High Middle Ages c. 1050–1200*. Translated by Timothy Reuter. 1986. An excellent survey that emphasizes social as well as political issues.

Geary, Patrick J. *"Furta Sacra": Thefts of Relics in the Central Middle Ages*. 1978. Discusses a little-known aspect of medieval economic and religious life—the "pious theft" of relics.

Green, Judith A. *The Government of England Under Henry I*. 1986. Examines the extraordinary growth of institutions of government during the early twelfth century.

Hallam, Elizabeth M. *Capetian France, 987–1328*. 1980. A good survey, with many helpful maps and tables.

———. *Domesday Book Through Nine Centuries*. 1986. A beautifully illustrated and comprehensive account of the origins and uses of the Domesday Book.

Haskins, Charles Homer. *The Renaissance of the Twelfth Century*. 1927. A classic exposition of the intellectual developments of the twelfth century.

Hyde, J. K. *Society and Politics in Medieval Italy: The Evolution of Civil Life, 1000–1350*. 1973. Surveys the emergence and history of the Italian communes.

Kapelle, William E. *The Norman Conquest of the North. The Region and Its Transformation, 1000–1135*. 1979. A new perspective on the Norman Conquest of England, stressing northern England's continuity with its Anglo-Saxon past and its staunch opposition to Norman encroachments.

Lewis, Andrew W. *Royal Succession in Capetian France*. 1981. Explores the royal notion of kin within the context of the French nobility's dynastic sensibilities.

Little, Lester K. *Religious Poverty and the Profit Economy in Medieval Europe*. 1978. Discusses the relationship between the commercial economy and new religious sensibilities in the twelfth and thirteenth centuries.

Lopez, Robert S. *The Commercial Revolution of the Middle Ages, 950–1350*. 1976. A survey of the medieval commercial economy by a first-rate historian.

Murray, Alexander. *Reason and Society in the Middle*

Ages. 1978. A fresh view of the renaissance of the twelfth century.

Newman, Charlotte A. *The Anglo-Norman Nobility in the Reign of Henry I: The Second Generation.* 1988. Looks at noble families in the generation following the Norman conquest, emphasizing the position of women, children, and bastards in noble society.

Nichols, John A., and Lillian Thomas Shank, eds. *Distant Echoes: Medieval Religious Women.* Vol. I. 1984. A collection of essays on women's monastic experience, concentrating on the tenth through the thirteenth centuries.

O'Callaghan, Joseph F. *A History of Medieval Spain.* 1975. A useful survey of medieval Spanish history that covers both Islamic and Christian societies.

Riley-Smith, Jonathan. *The First Crusade and the Idea of Crusading.* 1986. Traces the ways in which the idea of the First Crusade preached by Urban II was reinterpreted by the crusaders themselves and by writers of the next generation.

Spiegel, Gabrielle M. "The Cult of Saint Denis and Capetian Kingship." *Journal of Medieval History* 1 (1975): 43–69. Shows the relationship between the French monarchy and the monastery of St. Denis.

Tabacco, Giovanni. *The Struggle for Power in Medieval Italy.* 1989. A history of Italy focusing on its changing power structures.

Treadgold, Warren, ed. *Renaissances Before the Renaissance. Cultural Revivals of Late Antiquity and the Middle Ages.* 1984. Articles by experts on such cultural revivals as the Macedonian (at Byzantium), Carolingian, and twelfth-century renaissances.

In 1155, King Frederick Barbarossa of Germany (*1152–1190) met representatives of the fledgling Roman commune on his way to Rome, where he intended to be crowned emperor. Recalling the glory of the Roman Empire, these ambassadors of the "senate and people of Rome" claimed that they alone could make Frederick emperor. To deliver the imperial title, they demanded five thousand pounds of gold "as expense money." Frederick, "inflamed with righteous anger," according to his uncle and biographer, Otto of Freising, interrupted them. Rome was not theirs to give, he retorted. The spotlight of history that Rome had once basked in had shifted onto him: "Do you wish to know the ancient glory of your Rome? The worth of senatorial dignity? The impregnable disposition of the army camp? . . . Behold our state. All these things are to be found with us. All these have descended to us, together with the empire."

Frederick's self-assertion and confidence characterized an age in which participants in emerging institutions of government, commerce, and religion commanded enhanced authority. He shared with the ambassadors of the Roman commune, with whom he was for the moment at odds, a newly precise and proud notion of his rights and goals. Kings, princes, popes, city-dwellers, and even heretics in the second half of the twelfth century were acutely conscious of themselves as individuals and as members of like-minded groups with identifiable objectives and plans to promote and perpetuate their aims. For example, by about 1200 many schools, which in the early twelfth century had crystallized around charismatic

An Age of Confidence, 1144–1215

Frederick Barbarossa
This twelfth-century bronze head of Frederick Barbarossa is not so much a portrait as the embodiment of the "firmness" that so impressed contemporaries.

teachers like Peter Abelard, became permanent institutions called universities. Staffs of literate government officials now preserved both official documents and important papers; lords reckoned their profits with the help of accountants; craft guilds and religious associations defined and regulated their membership.

The new institutions of the late twelfth century reflected the post-Gregorian division between religious and secular authority. Asserting a new, confident secularism, Frederick called his empire "holy" (*sacrum*, sacred). In his view, the newly named Holy Roman Empire, although a secular state, was nevertheless so precious, worthwhile, and God-given that it, like the church, was sacred. Rather than place king above priest or priest above king, Frederick asserted a new autonomy for secular power and authority.

IMPORTANT DATES

1135–1154 Reign of King Stephen and civil war in England

1147–1149 Second Crusade

1152–1190 Reign of Emperor Frederick Barbarossa

1166 Assize of Clarendon; extension of common law in England

1176 Battle of Legnano; Frederick Barbarossa defeated in northern Italy

1180–1223 Philip II Augustus rules as king of France

1182–1226 Life of St. Francis

1198–1216 Papacy of Innocent III

c. 1200 Incorporation of University of Paris

Governments as Institutions

By the end of the twelfth century, Europeans for the first time began to speak of their rulers not as kings of a people (for example, king of the Franks) but as kings of territories (for example, king of France). This new designation reflected an important change in medieval rulership. However strong rulers had been, their political power had been personal (depending on ties of kinship, friendship, and vassalage) rather than territorial (touching all who lived within the borders of their state). Because new patrilineal families now provided clearly defined lines of inheritance and because a renewed interest in Roman legal concepts supplied models for strong, central rule, the process of state building began to encompass clearly delineated regions, most strikingly in western Europe but in central and eastern Europe as well.

Western European rulers now began to employ professional administrators, sometimes, as in England, through a system so institutionalized that government did not require the king's presence to function. In other regions, such as Germany, bureaucratic administration did not develop very far. In eastern Europe it hardly began at all.

Consolidated and Fragmented Realms in Eastern Europe and Byzantium

Although local rulers in central and eastern Europe controlled certain regions for a time, few of them consolidated their hold for long periods. An exception was Leopold VI, duke of Austria (*1194–1230), who owned most of the land in his duchy, promoted trade and the growth of towns like Vienna, and patronized poets who sang of aristocratic virtues. Because most of the noble families who might have challenged him had either died out or been eliminated by his predecessors, his power was nearly unopposed.

A more characteristic pattern, especially in eastern Europe, alternated building and fragmenting states. Just before Leopold began to rule Austria, for example, his neighbor to the east, King Béla III of Hungary (*1172–1196), was emulating rulers in the West. With his marriage to a French princess and employment of at least one scholar from Paris, he allowed French cultural influences to flourish. In his palace, built in Romanesque style, he enjoyed an annual income from his estates, tolls, dues, and taxes equal to that of the richest western monarchs. But the wars between Béla's sons in the decades that followed his death splintered the monarchical holdings, and in a sequence familiar earlier in western Europe, aristocratic supporters divided royal wealth.

Russia underwent a similar process. Although twelfth-century Kiev was politically fragmented, autocratic princes to the north constructed Suzdal', the nucleus of the later Muscovite state. The borders of Suzdal' were definite; well-to-do towns like Moscow prospered; monasteries and churches dotted its countryside; the other princes of Russia recognized its ruler as the "grand prince." Yet in 1212 this nascent state began to crumble as the sons of the grand prince fought one another for territory, much as Béla's sons had done in Hungary.

Twelfth-Century Russia

Although the Byzantine Empire was already a consolidated, bureaucratic state, after the death of John II (*1118–1143) it gradually ruptured. Thus while the West developed administrative institutions, the Comnenian emperors who ruled during the twelfth century downgraded the old civil servants, elevated their relatives to high offices, and favored the military elite. Byzantine rule grew more personal and western rule became more bureaucratic, the two gradually becoming more like one another.

The Rise and Fall of the German Monarchy

In electing Frederick I Barbarossa king, the princes of Germany acted with rare unanimity. For decades they had enjoyed their independence, building castles on their properties and establishing control over whole territories. Ensuring that the emperors who succeeded Henry V (1081–1125) would be weak, the princes supported only rulers who agreed to give them new lands and powers. The ruler's success depended on balancing the many conflicting interests of his own royal and imperial offices, his family, and the German princes. He also had to contend with the increasing influence of the papacy and the Italian communes, which forged alliances with one another and with the German princes, preventing the consolidation of power under a strong German ruler during the first half of the twelfth century.

The tensions between the imperial and prince-papal positions had led to civil wars in Germany before Frederick's accession. The sides were represented by two families: the Staufer, often called the Hohenstaufen in German or Ghibellines in Italian,* fought for the imperial party; their opponents, the prince-papal party, were the Welfs,† or Guelphs in Italian. (The enmity between these families became so legendary that their names remained attached to the two sides, imperial and papal, even after the families themselves had receded in importance.) Warfare between these groups raged almost continually during the first half of the twelfth century. In Franconia, for example, in one typical year the Staufer dukes first fought King Lothar III at Nuremberg, then wheeled around to face down the Welf duke of Bavaria. Exhausted from constant battles, by 1152 all parties longed for peace, and in Frederick they seemed to have a candidate who could end the strife: his mother was a Welf, his father a Staufer. Otto of Freising, whose contemporary accounts of the king's career provide most of our information about the period, saw in Frederick the image of Christ as the "cornerstone" that joined two houses and reconciled enemies.

Frederick's appearance impressed his contemporaries—the name *Barbarossa* refers to his red-blond hair and beard. But even more, Otto explained, he inspired those around him by his "firmness." He affirmed royal rights, even when he handed out duchies and allowed others to name bishops, because in return for these political powers Frederick required the princes to concede that they held their rights and territories from him as their feudal lord. By making them his vassals, although with near royal rights within their principalities, Frederick defined the princes' relationship to the German king: they were powerful yet personally subordinate to him. In this way Frederick hoped to save the

---

*These names derived from their properties: *Hohenstaufen* came from the castle and estates at Staufen, and *Ghibellines* came from the Italian name for their nearby estates at Waiblingen.

†*Welf* means "whelp" or "cub."

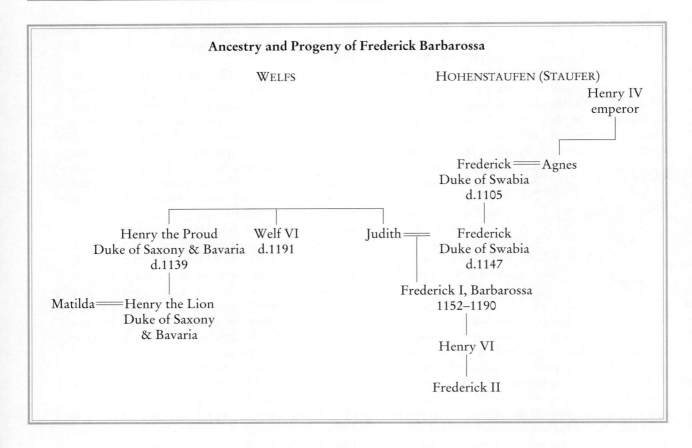

Ancestry and Progeny of Frederick Barbarossa

monarchy and to coordinate royal and princely rule, thus ending Germany's chronic civil wars.

Frederick also declared royal prerogatives outside Germany, as his comments to the "ambassadors" of Rome illustrated; but his words antagonized Pope Hadrian IV (✱1154–1159), who thought the papacy, not Frederick, represented the glory of Rome. Frederick further angered the pope when he married Beatrice, heiress to vast estates in Burgundy and Provence. Her inheritance enabled Frederick to establish a powerful political and territorial base centering in what is now Switzerland. From there he moved into Italy, threatening the pope's sphere of influence.

Since the Investiture Conflict, the emperor had ruled Italy in name only. The communes of the northern cities guarded their liberties jealously. The pope claimed jurisdiction over Rome and, since the time of Charlemagne, the right to anoint the emperor. In Frederick's day a fresco on one wall of the Lateran palace (the pope's residence) went further: it showed the German king Lothar III receiving the imperial crown from the pope as if the empire were a papal fief, as the papacy would have liked the world to believe. Soon after Frederick's imperial coronation, Hadrian's envoys arrived at a meeting called by the emperor at Besançon in 1157 with a letter detailing the dignities, honors, and other *beneficia* the pope had showered on Frederick. The word *beneficia* incensed the assembled company of Frederick's supporters because it meant not only "benefits" but also "fiefs," as if Frederick were the pope's vassal. The incident opened old wounds from the Gregorian period, revealing the gulf between papal and imperial conceptions of worldly authority.

Although papal claims meant that conquering Italy would be especially problematic, northern

Central Europe in the Age of Frederick Barbarossa, 1152–1190

The Self-Image of the Papacy
In this sixteenth-century sketch of a lost twelfth-century fresco on a wall of the Lateran palace, Lothar III (on the far right) receives the imperial crown from the pope. A verse below the painting reads: "After he becomes the vassal of the pope, he receives the crown from the pope," implying that the empire was a papal fief.

Italy enticed Frederick. Control there would make his base in Swabia (in southwest Germany) a central rather than a peripheral part of his empire, and the flourishing commercial cities of Italy would make him rich. Taxes on agricultural production there alone would yield 30,000 silver talents annually, an incredible sum, equal to the annual income of the richest ruler of the day, the king of England.

Alternately negotiating with and fighting against the great Lombard cities, especially Milan, Frederick achieved military control in Italy in 1158. No longer able to use Italian bishops as royal governors as German kings had done earlier—the Investiture Conflict had effectively ended that practice—Frederick insisted that the communes be governed by podestas, magistrates from outside the commune appointed (or at least authorized) by the king, who would collect revenues on his behalf. The heavy hand of these officials, many of them ministerials from Germany, created enormous resentment. Markward von Brumbach, for example, podesta at Milan, immediately ordered an inventory of all taxes due the emperor, and he levied new and demeaning labor duties, even demanding the citizens to carry the wood and stones of their plundered city to Pavia, twenty-five miles away, for use in constructing new houses there. By 1167 most of the cities of northern Italy had joined with Pope Alexander III (*1159–1181) to form the Lombard League against Frederick. With his defeat at the Battle of Legnano in 1176, Frederick sued for peace. The battle marked the triumph of the city over the crown in Italy, which would not have a centralized government until the nineteenth century; its political history would instead be that of its various regions and their dominant cities.

Thus the development of government institutions in the later twelfth century did not always benefit kings. Despite Frederick I Barbarossa's creative use of the podestas and of the feudal institutions of vassalage and fief, the truly lasting governments of Italy and Germany were the communes, the principalities, and the papal states. A German monarch would have one more chance to rule effectively in Italy and Germany, when Frederick's grandson, Frederick II, would become king; but the opportunity would be lost.

Henry the Lion: A New Style of Princely Rulership

During Frederick I Barbarossa's reign many princes of Germany enjoyed near royal status, acting as independent rulers of their principalities, though acknowledging Frederick as their feudal lord. One of the most powerful was a Welf who took the family name as his symbol and called himself Henry the Lion. Married to Matilda, daughter of the English King Henry II and Queen Eleanor of Aquitaine, Henry was duke of Saxony and Bavaria, a territory stretching across Germany from north to south. A self-confident and aggressive ruler, Henry not only dominated his territory by investing bishops, collecting dues from his demesnes, and exercising judicial rights and duties but also actively extended his rule, especially in Slavic regions, pushing northeast past the Elbe River to reestablish episcopal sees and to build the commercial emporium of Lübeck.

Lord of many vassals, commander of a large army composed chiefly of ministerials and some Slavic reinforcements, Henry, like Frederick, realized that government institutions could enforce his authority and help him maintain control of his territories. Ministerials acted not only as his soldiers but as his officials as well; they collected his taxes

Monument of Henry the Lion
Henry the Lion had this monumental lion cast from iron in 1166. It had a double meaning, signifying both his family name and his power.

and his share of profits from tolls, mints (like kings, Henry took a percentage of the silver to be minted into coins), and markets. Because they were unfree, Henry could shuffle them about or remove them at will. At court his steward, treasurer, and stable marshal were all ministerials. Other officials were notaries, normally clerics, who wrote and preserved some of his legal acts. Thus Henry the Lion created a small staff to carry on the day-to-day administration of his principality without him. Here, as elsewhere, administration no longer depended entirely on the personal involvement of the ruler.

Yet like kings, princes could fall. Henry's growing power so threatened other princes, and even Frederick, that in 1179, Frederick called Henry to the king's court for violating the peace. When Henry chose not to appear, Frederick exercised his authority as Henry's feudal lord and charged him with violating his duty as a vassal. Because Henry refused the summons to court and avoided serving his lord in Italy, Frederick condemned him, confiscated his holdings, and drove him out of Germany in 1180. Although he wished to retain Henry's duchy for himself, Frederick had to divide and distribute it to supporters whose aid he needed to enforce his decrees against Henry.

Late twelfth-century kings and emperors often found themselves engaged in this balancing act of ruling yet placating their powerful lords. The process almost always involved a gamble. Successfully challenging one recalcitrant prince-vassal meant negotiating costly deals with the others, since their support was vital. Rulers like Frederick often lost as much as they gained in such actions, usually defeating the targeted truant but ending up with little to show for it after paying off all the favors required to win. Not until the early thirteenth century would a ruler emerge with enough power, skill, and sheer luck to control what he confiscated: about a quarter-century later, King Philip II (Augustus) of France denounced King John of England and duke of Normandy and expropriated the duchy of Normandy. This effort consolidated rather than sapped Philip's power.

England: Unity Through Law

By the mid-twelfth century the English kings had established the most well-developed system of administration and record keeping in Europe.

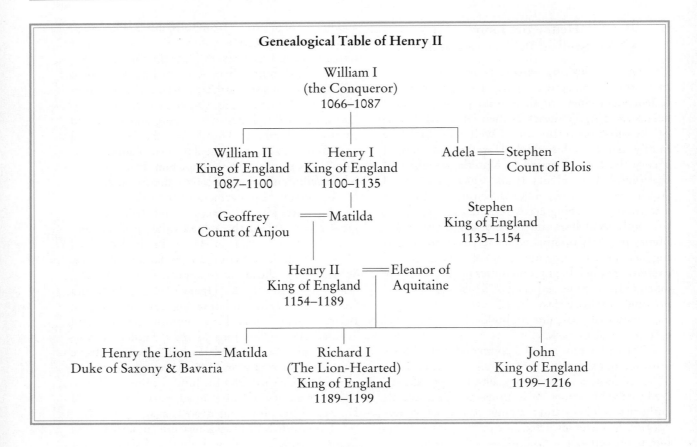

Genealogical Table of Henry II

William I
(the Conqueror)
1066–1087

William II
King of England
1087–1100

Henry I
King of England
1100–1135

Adela ══ Stephen
Count of Blois

Stephen
King of England
1135–1154

Geoffrey
Count of Anjou ══ Matilda

Henry II ══ Eleanor of
King of England   Aquitaine
1154–1189

Henry the Lion ══ Matilda
Duke of Saxony & Bavaria

Richard I
(The Lion-Hearted)
King of England
1189–1199

John
King of England
1199–1216

English institutions reflected both the Anglo-Saxon tradition of conveying the king's orders via writs and the Norman tradition of retaining the ruler's control over his officials, over taxes (paid in cash), and over court cases involving all capital crimes. In addition, the very circumstances of the English king favored the growth of an administrative staff: his frequent travels to and from the Continent meant that officials needed to work in his absence, and his enormous wealth meant that he could afford them. King Henry II (*1154–1189) was the driving force in extending and strengthening the institutions of English government.

Henry II became king in the wake of a civil war that threatened the new Norman dynasty in England. Henry I (*1100–1135) had died without a male heir and had unsuccessfully called the great barons to swear that his daughter Matilda would rule after him. The Norman barons could not imagine a woman ruling them, and they feared her husband, Geoffrey of Anjou, their perennial enemy. The man who succeeded to the throne, Stephen of Blois, was the son of Henry's sister, Adela. With Matilda's son, the future Henry II, only two years old, the struggle for the control of England during Stephen's reign (*1135–1154) became part of a larger territorial contest between the house of Anjou and the house of Blois. Continual civil war in England, as in Germany, benefited the lay magnates and high churchmen, who gained new privileges and powers as the monarch's authority waned. Newly built private castles, already familiar on the Continent, now appeared in England. But Stephen's coalition of barons, high clergymen, and townsmen eventually fell apart, causing him to agree to the accession of Matilda's son, Henry of Anjou. Thus Henry II became the first Angevin king of England.* His marriage to Eleanor of

---

*Henry's father was Geoffrey of Anjou, nicknamed Plantagenet from the *genêt*, a shrub he liked. Historians sometimes use the sobriquet to refer to the entire dynasty, so Henry II was the first *Plantagenet* as well as the first *Angevin* king of England.

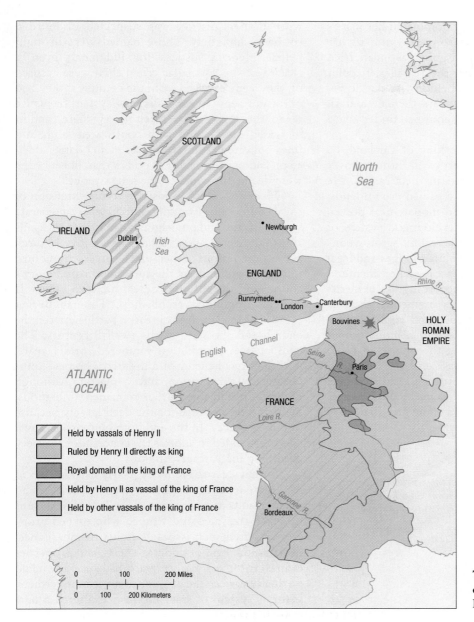

**The Monarchy
of Henry II:
England and France**

Legend:
- Held by vassals of Henry II
- Ruled by Henry II directly as king
- Royal domain of the king of France
- Held by Henry II as vassal of the king of France
- Held by other vassals of the king of France

Aquitaine brought the enormous inheritance of the duchy of Aquitaine to the English crown. Although he remained the vassal of the king of France for his continental lands, Henry in effect ruled a territory that stretched from England to southern France.

Henry valued Eleanor because she was duchess of Aquitaine and because she bore him sons to maintain his dynasty. Before her marriage to Henry in 1152, Eleanor had been married to King Louis VII of France; he had the marriage annulled because she had borne him only daughters. Nevertheless, as queen of France, Eleanor had enjoyed an important position: she disputed with St. Bernard, the most renowned churchman of the day; she accompanied her husband on the Second Crusade, bringing more troops than he did; and she determined to separate from her husband even before he considered leaving her. But she lost much of her power under her

English husband, for Henry dominated her just as he would dominate his barons. Turning to her offspring in 1173, Eleanor, disguised as a man, tried to join her eldest son, Henry the Younger, in a plot against his father. But the rebellion was put down, and she spent most of the years thereafter, until King Henry's death in 1189, confined under guard at Winchester Castle.

When Henry II became king of England, he immediately sought to reassert royal authority over the barons newly ensconced in their castles. He razed new strongholds and regained crown lands. Then he proceeded to extend monarchical power, imposing royal justice by developing a system of royal courts. "Throughout the realm," wrote a contemporary admirer, "he appointed judges and legal officials to curb the audacity of wicked men and dispense justice to litigants according to the merits of their case." Henry's courts augmented the role of the crown in both criminal and civil cases by claiming jurisdiction over certain heinous crimes such as murder and offering the option of royal justice for others. At the Assize of Clarendon in 1166, for example, Henry ordered local free men across the entire kingdom to meet under oath, constituting themselves into a grand jury to declare who in their district was suspected of murder, robbery, and theft. Those named were brought before Henry's justices for judgment; even if cleared of the particular crime they were accused of, they were expelled from the country if they had notorious reputations. This new system of justice made the king's power felt everywhere, and it increased his income with confiscated lands and fines collected from criminals. Henry later added arson and rape to the list of crimes that, like murder, were deemed to violate "the king's peace."

Henry's stiffest opposition to the extension of royal courts came from the church, where a separate system of trial and punishment had long been available to the clergy and to others who enjoyed church protection. Jealous of their prerogatives, churchmen refused to submit to the jurisdiction of Henry's courts, and the ensuing contest between Henry II and his appointed archbishop, Thomas Becket (1118–1170), became the greatest battle between the church and the state in the twelfth century. The conflict over jurisdiction simmered for six years, until Henry's henchmen murdered Thomas, unintentionally turning him into a martyr. Although Henry's role in the murder remained ambiguous, he had to do penance for the deed largely because of public outcry. In the end both church and royal courts expanded to address the concerns of a society becoming increasingly litigious.

For civil cases, Henry regularly used *justices in eyre* (*eyre* from the Latin *iter*, or "journey"), who made circuits throughout the kingdom to hear cases in which free men and women who owned property disputed such issues as rights to inheritance, dowries, the land of underage heirs, and properties claimed by others. Earlier courts had generally relied on duels between the litigants to determine verdicts. Henry's system of traveling justice offered a new option, an inquest under royal supervision. It also gave the king a new source of revenue. For example, a widow named Mabel might dispute the possession of a parcel of land at Stoke with a man named Ralph. By purchasing a royal writ she could set the wheels of the king's new justice in motion. The writ would order the sheriff to summon a jury of twelve free men from Stoke to declare in front of the justices whether Ralph or Mabel had the better right to possess the land. The power of the king would then back the verdict. Thus English kings used the law to enhance their power and income.

Castle of Henry II

Henry II rebuilt or took over many castles in order to counter the power of English barons who held private castles. This castle in Suffolk is the only one that Henry built from scratch.

The Martyrdom of Thomas Becket
*After years of quarreling with Becket, Henry utter-
ed the words that sent some of his men to Becket's
cathedral to kill him. In this miniature, Henry's
knights murder Becket before the altar. Becket's
martyrdom gave the clerical cause a strength it had
lacked in his lifetime.*

A contemporary legal treatise known as
Glanvill, after its presumed author, applauded the
new system for its efficiency, speed, and conclu-
siveness: "This legal institution emanates from
perfect equity. For justice, which after many and
long delays is scarcely ever demonstrated by the
duel, is advantageously and speedily attained
through this institution." *Glanvill* might have
added that the king also speedily gained a large
treasury; the Exchequer, as the financial bureau of
England came to be called, recorded all the fines
paid for judgments and the sums collected for writs.
The amounts, entered on parchment sewn together

and stored in rolls, became the Receipt Rolls and
Pipe Rolls, the first of many such records of the
English monarchy and an indication that writing
had become a mechanism for institutionalizing
royal power in England.

The English monarchy was rich; it received
revenues from its courts, income from its demesne
lands in England and on the Continent, taxes from
its cities, and customary feudal dues (aids) from
its barons and knights for such occasions as the
knighting of the king's eldest son and the marriage
of the king's eldest daughter. Dependent on the
increasingly commercial society of the late twelfth
century, the English kings encouraged their knights
and barons not to serve them personally in battle
but instead to pay the king a tax called *scutage* in
lieu of service. The monarchs preferred to hire
mercenaries both as troops to fight external enemies
and as police to enforce the king's will at home.

In 1214, however, the English army was defeated
on the Continent. In 1204 the king of France, Philip
II (*1180–1223), had confiscated the northern
French territories of King John (*1199–1216), the
son and heir of Henry II. Between 1204 and 1214,
John added to the crown revenues and forged an
army to fight Philip. To finance his plans, he repeatedly forced his vassals to pay ever-increasing scutages
and extorted money in the form of new feudal aids.
He compelled the widows of his vassals to marry
men of his choosing or pay him a hefty fee if they
refused. In 1214 the defeat of his forces at the Battle
of Bouvines caused discontented English barons to
rebel openly against the king. At Runnymede in
June 1215, John agreed to the charter of baronial
liberties that has come to be called the Magna Carta,
or "Great Charter."

The Magna Carta was essentially a conservative
document defining the "customary" obligations
and rights of the nobility and forbidding the king
to break from these customs without consulting his
barons. For example, one provision specified that:

> *No scutage or aid shall be imposed in our
> kingdom unless by common counsel of our
> kingdom [i.e., in consultation with the barons],
> except for ransoming our person, for making
> our eldest son a knight, and for once marrying
> our eldest daughter [all of these being
> customary]; and for these only a reasonable aid
> shall be levied . . .*

The Magna Carta also maintained that all free men in the land had certain customs and rights in common, and that the king must uphold these customs and rights:

> *No free man shall be arrested or imprisoned or disseised [dispossessed] or outlawed or exiled or in any way victimized, neither will we attack him or send anyone to attack him, except by the lawful judgment of his peers or by the law of the land.*

In this way, the Magna Carta documented the subordination of the king to custom; it implied that the king was not above the law. The growing royal power of the king was matched by the self-confidence of the English barons, certain of their rights and eager to articulate them.

France: From Acorn to Oak

Whereas the power of the English throne led to a baronial movement to curb it, the weakness of the French monarchy ironically led to its expansion. Unencumbered by Italian territorial claims like those of Frederick I and enriched by revenues from new communes like Laon, by the mid-twelfth century the king of France had carved out a compact kingdom in the middle of equally compact principalities. When Philip II, who eventually bested the English King John, became king, the Ile-de-France was sandwiched between territory controlled by the counts of Flanders, Champagne, and Anjou. By far the most powerful ruler on the Continent, King Henry II of England was both the count of Anjou and the duke of Normandy; he also held the duchy of Aquitaine through his wife and exercised hegemony over Poitou and Brittany.

The Consolidation of France

Henry and the counts of Flanders and Champagne vied to control the newly crowned, fourteen-year-old king of France. Philip, however, quickly learned to play them off against one another, in particular by setting the sons of Henry II against their father. For example, Philip helped Henry the Younger rebel against his father in 1183 by sending the young man a contingent of mercenary troops. Despite his apparent political competence, contemporaries were astounded when Philip successfully gained territory: he wrested Vermandois and Artois from Flanders in the 1190s and Normandy, Anjou, Maine, Touraine, and Poitou from King John of England in 1204. A contemporary chronicler dubbed him Philip Augustus, the augmenter.

Modern historians are less impressed with Philip's conquests than with his ability to keep and administer his new territories.[*] Philip instituted a new kind of French administration run, as in England, by officials who kept accounts and files of outgoing and incoming documents. Before Philip's day the decrees of the French king, like those of Frederick I and Henry the Lion, had been written down and saved by the recipient—if they were recorded at all. For example, when a monastery wanted a confirmation of its privileges from the king, its own scribes wrote the document for its archives to preserve it against possible future challenges. Those documents the king did keep generally followed him in his travels like personal possessions; but most royal arrangements were committed to memory rather than written down. In 1194, Philip Augustus lost his meager cache of documents, along with much treasure, when he had to leave his baggage train behind in a battle with the king of England. After 1194, written decrees replaced this essentially oral tradition.

Whereas German rulers employed ministerials to do the daily work of government, Philip, like the English king, relied largely on members of the lesser nobility—knights and clerics, many of whom were "masters" educated in the city schools of France. They served as officers of his court; as *prévôts*, who oversaw the king's demesne and collected his taxes; and as *baillis* (or *sénéchaux* in the south), who not only supervised the *prévôts* but also functioned as regional judges, presiding over courts (called *assizes*, from the Old French word for "seatings") that met monthly, making the king's power felt locally as never before.

Nevertheless, before 1204 the French king's territory was minuscule compared to the vast regions

---

[*]Philip was particularly successful in imposing royal control in Normandy; later French kings gave most of the other territories to collateral members of the royal family.

Ribbed Gothic Vault
This Gothic cathedral at Mantes (France) was begun during the lifetime of Philip Augustus. During the century following 1140, architectural features such as the pointed arch and the ribbed vault were adopted in much of northern France, and their aesthetic and structural possibilities were explored.

held by the English king. Although it seems logical to us today that the French king would inevitably rule all of France, twelfth-century observers would not have been surprised if France had become the cornerstone of the English king's power, with England functioning merely as his "offshore outpost." True, some pivotal forces led to the extension of the French king's power and the territorial integrity of France. The Second Crusade brought together many French lords as vassals of the king and united them against a common foe. The language they spoke was becoming increasingly uniform and "French." Nevertheless, royal personalities and strategies that worked accidentally rather than by plan largely determined that Philip would conquer

Normandy and thereby gain a commanding position in France. In 1204, having declared his vassal, the duke of Normandy (who was, of course, also the English king, John), disobedient for not coming to court when summoned, Philip confiscated most of John's continental territories. He confirmed this triumph decisively at the Battle of Bouvines ten years later, in which, mainly by luck, Philip's armies routed the major opponents and took others prisoner. With the English threat safely across the channel, the French monarch could boast being the richest and most powerful ruler in France. Unlike Frederick I Barbarossa, who was compelled to divide the territory he had seized from Henry the Lion among the German princes, Philip had sufficient support and resources to keep tight hold on Normandy. He received homage and fealty from most of the Norman aristocracy; his *baillis* carefully carried out their work there in accordance with Norman customs. For ordinary Normans the change from duke to king brought few changes.

The Growth of a Vernacular High Culture

In consolidating their power, kings, barons, and princes supported new kinds of literature and music. The second half of the twelfth century saw a flood of literature often meant to be read aloud or sung, sometimes with accompanying musical instruments, to a large audience of clerics, knights, castellans, and counts, and their mothers, wives, daughters, and sons. Although not overtly political, these new works, written in the vernacular (that is, the spoken language rather than Latin), celebrated and extolled the lives of the nobility. They provided a common experience in a common language under the aegis of the court. Whether in the cities of Italy or the more isolated courts of northern Europe, patrons and patronesses, enriched by their seigneuries and by the commercial growth of the twelfth century, now spent their profits on the arts.

Vernacular literature thrived at the court of Henry the Lion and Matilda, whose wealth and power allowed them to support writers and artists, some of whom reworked French and English narra-

Princely Patronage of Churches
Henry the Lion and his wife Matilda commissioned many church ornaments. This detail from an iron candlestick that they commissioned depicts a winged dragon.

tive poetry into German. Poetry in the language of everyday life appealed to a wide audience, revealing the new self-confidence of German culture in the age of Frederick. Henry even had his clerics compile a brief encyclopedia of knowledge about the world and God, the *Lucidarius*, one of the earliest prose pieces in Germany. Henry and Matilda also contributed handsomely to building new churches in cities such as Lübeck and Brunswick, commissioned illuminated manuscripts, and ordered the production of fine gold reliquaries and church furnishings. Their patronage not only helped develop the German language but also heightened their prestige as aristocrats.

Poets of Love and Play: The Troubadours

Already at the beginning of the twelfth century the grandfather of Eleanor of Aquitaine, Duke William of Poitiers (1071–1127), had written lyric poems in Occitan, the vernacular of southern France. Perhaps influenced by love poetry in Arabic and Hebrew from al-Andalus, his own poetry in turn provided a model for poetic forms that gained popularity through repeated performances. The final four-line

stanza of one such poem demonstrates the composer's skill with words:

Per aquesta fri e tremble,	For this one I shiver and tremble,
quar de tan bon' amor l'am;	I love her with such a good love;
qu'anc no cug qu'en nasques semble	I do not think the like of her was ever born
en semblan de gran linh n'Adam.	in the long line of Lord Adam

The rhyme scheme of this poem appears to be simple—*tremble* goes with *semble*, *l'am* with *n'Adam*—but the entire poem has five earlier verses, all six lines long and all containing the -*am*, -*am* rhyme in the fourth and sixth lines, while every other line within each verse rhymes as well.

Troubadours, lyric poets who wrote in Occitan, varied their rhymes and meters endlessly to dazzle their audience with brilliant originality. Most of their rhymes and meters resemble Latin religious poetry of the same time, indicating that the vernacular and Latin religious cultures shared the same milieu. Such similarity is also evident in the troubadour's choice of subjects. The most common topic, love, echoed the twelfth-century emphasis on the emotional relationship between God and humankind. The Cistercians expressed this new emotional connection when they dedicated their churches to the Virgin Mary, thinking of her role less as Queen of Heaven and more as mother, with the monks "curled up against her breast." The troubadours also sang about feelings while inventing new variations of nuance and imagery. When William of Poitiers sang of his "good love" for a woman unlike any other born in the line of Adam, the words could be interpreted in two ways. They reminded listeners of the Virgin, a woman unlike any other, but they also referred to William's

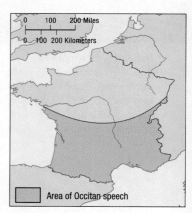

Areas of Occitan Speech

lover, recalled in another part of the poem, where he had complained

> *If I do not get help soon*
> *and my lady does not give me love,*
> *by Saint Gregory's holy head I'll die*
> *if she doesn't kiss me in a chamber or under*
> *   a tree.*

His lady's character is ambiguous here: she is like Mary, but she is also his mistress.

Later troubadours, both male and female, expressed prevalent views of love much as popular singers do today. The Contessa de Dia (c. 1060–1140; probably the wife of the lord of Die, in France) wrote about her unrequited love for a man:

> *Of things I'd rather keep in silence I must*
> *   sing:*
> *so bitter do I feel toward him*
> *whom I love more than anything.*
> *With him my mercy and fine manners*
> *   [cortesia] are in vain,*
> *my beauty, virtue and intelligence.*
> *For I've been tricked and cheated*
> *as if I were completely loathesome.*

The idea of *cortesia* is key to troubadour verse: it refers to courtesy, the refinement of people living at court, and the struggle to achieve an ideal of beauty, virtue, and intelligence. The Contessa's fine manners proved that her love was courteous. Historians and literary critics sometimes use the term *courtly love* to refer to one particular mix of eroticism, ritual, and rules in the new courtly ideal: the poet expresses overwhelming love for a beautiful married noblewoman far above him in status and therefore unattainable. The theme of courtly love created a fantasy world in which women controlled the happiness and even the lives of men and were valued for their youth, beauty, and status, not their reproductive capabilities. Little wonder that Eleanor of Aquitaine and other aristocratic women paid and protected troubadours to sustain these illusions. Yet powerful men at princely courts enjoyed troubadour music as well; it did not threaten the reality of power relations between men and women or change the view that aristocratic women were valuable mainly as heiresses and mothers of sons.

Music was part of the charm of troubadour poetry, which was always sung, typically by a *jongleur* (musician). Unfortunately, we have no record of troubadour music before the thirteenth century, and even then for only a fraction of the poems. By this time music was written on four- and five-line staves, so we can at least determine relative pitches, and modern musicians can sing some troubadour songs with the hope of sounding reasonably like the original. This is the earliest popular music that can be re-created authentically. For example, the beginning of a song by the troubadour Bernart de Ventadorn, transcribed in the modern G-clef and key of C, goes as shown below. Each syllable normally corresponds to one note, except for the notes tied together with a slur, which were sung more quickly so as not to drag out the syllable's length too much.

From southern France the lyric love song spread to Italy, northern France, England, and Germany—regions in which Occitan was a foreign language and instruments probably accompanied performances that would otherwise bore audiences who did not understand the words. Similar poetry appeared in other vernacular languages: the minnesingers (literally "love singers") sang in

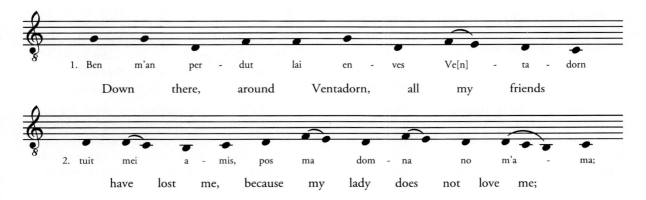

Troubadour Song
The songs of Raimon de Miraval, like those of other troubadours, were not written down until the thirteenth century. Here the song that begins A penas *is set to music with a five-line staff.*

German; the trouvères sang in the Old French of northern France. One trouvère was the English King Richard I (*Coeur de Lion*, or "the Lion-Hearted"), son of Henry II and Eleanor of Aquitaine. Taken prisoner in 1192 by Duke Leopold VI of Austria, Richard wrote a poem expressing his longing not for a lady but for the good companions of war, the knightly "youths" he had joined in battle:

> *They know well, the men of Anjou and
>   Touraine,*
> *those bachelors, now so magnificent and
>   safe,*
> *that I am arrested, far from them, in
>   another's hands.*
> *They used to love me much, now they love
>   me not at all.*
> *There's no lordly fighting now on the barren
>   plains,*
> *because I am a prisoner.*

The Literature of Epic and Romance

The yearning for the battlefield was not as common a topic in lyric poetry as love, but long narrative poems about heroic deeds (chansons de geste) appeared frequently in vernacular writing, after a long oral tradition, at about the same time as

William of Poitiers began to write about his shivering and trembling love. Like the songs of the troubadours, these poems implied a code of behavior for aristocrats, this time on the battlefield. By the end of the twelfth century, warriors wanted a guide for conduct and a common class identity. Nobles and knights had begun merging into one class because they felt threatened from below by newly rich merchants and from above by newly powerful kings. Their ascendancy on the battlefield, where they were used to unhorsing one another with lances and long swords and taking prisoners rather than killing their opponents, was also beginning to wane in the face of mercenary infantrymen who wielded long hooks and knives that ripped easily through chain mail. A knightly ethos and sense of group solidarity emerged in the face of these social, political, and military changes.

Thus the protagonists of heroic poems yearned not for love but for battle, as in Raoul de Cambrai:

> *The armies are in sight of one another. They go
> forward cautiously and reconnoitre as they go.
> The cowards tremble as they march, but the
> brave hearts rejoice for the battle.*

Examining the moral issues that made war both tragic and inevitable, the poet plays on the often contradictory values of his society, in *Raoul* a vassal's right to a fief versus a son's right to his father's land. *Raoul* tells of an emperor who made the grievous error of granting Raoul a fief claimed by the sons of the vassal who first held it. Complicating matters further is Raoul's squire and friend, Bernier, a member of the family against whom Raoul must fight to win his fief. Thus filial duties clash with principles of friendship and vassalage. Raoul attacks the land that he claims, killing Bernier's mother in the process and forcing Bernier to replace his oath of vassalage with one of vengeance: "Noble vassals," he cries to his men, "can you give me good advice? My lord Raoul hates me, for he has burnt my mother in the chapel yonder. God grant I may live long enough to avenge her." The poet matches delight in the sheer physicality of battle with the agony of loss:

> *Young Bernier was resolute and bold. He
> pulled forth his sharp sword and struck the son
> of Guerri such a blow on his pointed helmet
> that the flowers and stones were scattered, the
> headpiece of his hauberk was pierced and he*

was cloven to the teeth. . . . Guerri rode away, for he hardly knew what he was doing. As he rode back over the upland his grief for his sons [he lost his other son in the same battle] became even greater, and it was a pitiful sight to see him tearing his hair with his hands.

Whereas these vernacular narrative poems, later called epics, focused on war, other poems, later called romances, explored the relationships between men and women. These romances reached their zenith of popularity during the late twelfth and early thirteenth centuries. The legend of King Arthur inspired a romance by Chrétien de Troyes (c. 1150–1190) in which a heroic knight, Lancelot, in love with the wife of his lord, comes across a comb bearing some strands of Queen Guinevere's radiant hair:

Never will the eye of man see anything receive such honour as when [Lancelot] begins to adore these tresses. A hundred thousand times he raises them to his eyes and mouth, to his forehead and face. . . . He would not exchange them for a cartload of emeralds and carbuncles, nor does he think that any sore or illness can afflict him now; he holds in contempt essence of pearl, treacle, and the cure for pleurisy; even for St. Martin and St. James he has no need.

At one level this is a commentary on the meaning of relics. Chrétien evokes the familiar imagery of relics as items of devotion. Making Guinevere's hair an object of adoration not only conveys the depth of Lancelot's feeling but also pokes a bit of fun at him. Like the troubadours, the romantic poets delighted in the interplay between religious and amorous feelings. Just as the ideal monk merges his will in God's will, Chrétien's Lancelot's loses his will to the queen. For example, when she sees Lancelot—the greatest knight in Christendom—fighting in a tournament, she tests him by sending him a message to do his "worst":

When he heard this, he replied: "Very willingly," like one who is altogether hers. Then he rides at another knight as hard as his horse can carry him, and misses his thrust which should have struck him. From that time till evening he continued to do as badly as possible in accordance with the Queen's desire.

The Romance of King Arthur
The story of King Arthur gained currency in the twelfth century, inspiring numerous romances and artistic representations.

Such an odd, funny, and pitiful moment, when the greatest of all knights subjects his pride to the whim of a lady, presents one aspect of a new kind of hero, a chivalric knight. The word *chivalry* comes from the French word *cheval*, meaning "horse"; the chivalric hero is a warrior constrained by a code of refinement, fair play, and devotion to an ideal.

New Lay and Religious Associations

Codes of behavior, not only for knights but for all groups, became increasingly important as society grew more complex. Commercial growth in the twelfth century gradually created a new social hierarchy. In the cities and in other areas touched by the commercial revolution, new groups, new identities, and new values both challenged and transformed the knightly ethos. Whereas in the early twelfth century, communes provided their leading citizens with self-government, the second half of the century saw new forms of association delineate commercial society more precisely. As towns grew and their social structures became more varied, guilds, universities, and religious movements offered men and women new affiliations and allegiances.

The new money economy now extended to the countryside, blurring the distinction between rural districts and towns in many parts of northern Europe as it had already done in the tenth-century Italy. In the late twelfth century new lay and religious associations arose principally in regions with the greatest commercial development: northern Italy, the Rhineland, and southern France. We can trace these groups best in the cities, where the documents are more plentiful, but they had their counterparts in the countryside as well.

The Penetration of the Commercial Revolution

By the middle of the twelfth century the commercial revolution had altered rural as well as urban life. On the great estates of the rich, farms were now organized to make money rather than merely sustain the estates' inhabitants. Great lords hired trained, literate agents to administer their estates, calculate profits and losses, and make marketing decisions. Aristocrats needed money not only because they relished luxuries but also because their honor and authority continued to depend on their personal generosity, patronage, and displays of wealth. In the late twelfth century, when some townsmen could boast fortunes that rivaled the riches of the landed aristocracy, the economic pressures on the nobles increased as their extravagance exceeded their incomes. Most went into debt.

The lord's need for money changed peasant life, so that peasants too became integrated into the developing commercial economy. As the population increased, the demand for food required more farmland. By the middle of the twelfth century the isolated and sporadic attempts to cultivate new land had become a regular and coordinated activity. Great lords offered special privileges to peasants who would do the backbreaking work of plowing marginal land. In 1154 the bishop of Neissen (eastern Germany) announced that

I have brought together and established in an uncultivated and almost uninhabited place

energetic men coming from the province of Flanders, and . . . I have given in stable, eternal and hereditary possession to them and to all their descendants, the village called Kühren.

Experts in drainage, these Flemish settlers had rights to the land they reclaimed and owed only light monetary obligations to the bishop, who nevertheless expected to reap a profit from their tolls and tithes. In effect the bishop and the settlers together created the new village of Kühren. Similar encouragement came from lords throughout Europe, especially in northern Italy, England, Flanders and the other Low Countries, and Germany. In Flanders the great monasteries sponsored drainage projects; and canals linking the cities to the agricultural regions let ships ply the waters to virtually every nook and cranny of the region. With its dense population, Flanders provided not only a natural meeting ground for long-distance traders from England and France but also numerous markets for local traders.

Sometimes free peasants acted on their own initiative to clear land and relieve the pressure of overpopulation, as when the small freeholders in England's Fenland region cooperated to build banks and dikes to claim the land that led out to the North Sea. Villages were founded on the drained land, and villagers shared responsibility for repairing and maintaining the dikes even as each peasant family farmed its new holding individually.

On old estates the rise in population strained to the breaking point the manse organization, in which each household was settled on the land that supported it. Twenty peasant families might live on what had been—in the tenth century—the manse of one family. Labor services and dues had to be recalculated with the manse supporting so many more people, and peasants and their lords often commuted services and dues into money rents, payable once a year. Although peasant men gained more control over their plots—they could sell them, will them to their sons, or even designate a small portion for their daughters—they had either to pay extra taxes for these privileges or, like communes, join together to buy their collective liberty for a high price, paid out over many years to their lord. Peasants, like town citizens, gained a new sense of identity and solidarity as they bargained with a lord keen to increase his income at their expense.

Peasants now owed more taxes to support the new administrative apparatuses of monarchs and princes. Kings' demands for money from their subjects filtered , either directly or indirectly, to the lowest classes. In Italy the cities themselves often imposed and enforced dues on the peasants, normally tenant farmers who leased their plots in the *contado*, the countryside surrounding each city. In the mid-twelfth century at Florence the urban officials, working closely with the bishop, dominated the roads and river valleys of the *contado*, collecting taxes from its cultivators, calling up its men to fight, and importing its food into the city. Therefore peasants' gains from rising prices, access to markets, greater productivity, and increased personal freedom were partially canceled out by their cash burdens. Peasants of the late twelfth century ate better than their forebears, but they also had more burdens.

Urban Corporations: The Craft Guilds and Universities

As the guilds in the towns and cities developed from confraternities for religious devotion, convivial feasting, charitable activities, and craft regulation, these organizations became interested in drawing up increasingly detailed statutes and rules to protect themselves and control the activities of their members. Guild regulations determined working hours, fixed wages, and set standards for materials and products.

Guilds naturally wanted to protect themselves and expand their influence, but communal governments did not always consider these goals to be in the city's best interest. Bread was too important a commodity in Italian towns, for example, for the communes to allow bakers to form a guild. And communes sometimes fixed prices to ensure that the guilds would not drive prices higher than town consumers could bear. But communes also supported guild efforts to control wages, reinforcing guild regulations with statutes of their own.

When great lords rather than communes governed a city, they too tried to control and protect the guilds. King Henry II of England, for example, eagerly gave some guilds in his Norman duchy special privileges so that they would depend on him:

> *Know that I have conceded and, by this my charter, have confirmed to my tanners of Rouen their guild, dyeing and greasing processes, and all customs and laws of their guild . . . and [I have confirmed] that no one [else] may perform their craft in Rouen.*

The tanners of Rouen sold raw materials to the shoemakers, who had their own guild. The manufacture of finished products often required the cooperation of several guilds. Producing wool cloth involved numerous guilds—shearers, weavers, fullers, dyers—generally working under the supervision of the merchant guild that imported the raw wool. Some guilds were more prestigious than others: in Florence, for example, professional guilds of notaries and judges ranked above craft guilds.

Within each guild existed another kind of hierarchy among the artisans or merchants themselves, with apprentices at the bottom, journeymen and -women in the middle, and masters at the top. Apprentices were boys and occasionally girls placed under the tutelage of a master for a number of years to learn a trade. Normally the child's parents made the formal contract; but sometimes the children themselves took the initiative, as did a young man named John at Genoa in 1180 when he apprenticed himself to a turner, an expert in the use of the lathe. John promised to serve his master faithfully for five years, do whatever was expected of him, and not run away. In turn, his master promised to give him food, clothing, shelter, and a small salary; to teach him the turner's art; and to give him a set of tools after the five years were up.

It would take many more years for a young person like John to become a master, however. First he would likely spend many years as a day laborer, a journeyman, hired by a master who needed extra help. Journeymen and -women did not live with their masters; they worked for them for a wage. This marked an important stage in the economic history of the West. For the first time, workers were neither slaves nor dependents but free and independent wage earners. Although we know more about journeymen than journeywomen, we know that at least a few day workers were female; invariably they received wages far lower than their male counterparts. Sometimes a married couple worked at the same trade and hired themselves out as a team. Often journeymen and -women had to be guild members—for their dues and so their masters could keep tabs on them.

Masters occupied the top of the guild hierarchy. Almost exclusively men, they dominated the offices and policies of the guild, hired journeymen, and recruited and educated apprentices. They drew up the guild regulations and served as chief overseers, inspectors, and treasurers. Because the number of masters was few and the turnover of official posts frequent, most masters eventually had a chance to serve as guild officers. Occasionally they were elected, but more often they were appointed from among the masters of the craft by the governor—whether a prince or a commune—of the city.

During the late twelfth century, women's labor in some trades gradually declined in importance. In Flanders, for example, as the manufacture of woolen cloth shifted from rural areas to cities, women participated less in the process. Only isolated manors still needed a *gynaeceum*, where female dependents spun, wove, and sewed garments. Instead new-style large looms in cities like Ypres and Ghent were run by men working in pairs. They produced a heavy-weight cloth superior to the fabric made on the lighter looms that women had worked. Similarly, women once ground grain tediously into flour by hand; but water mills and animal-powered mills gradually took the place of female labor, and most millers who ran the new machinery were male. Some women were certainly artisans and traders, and their names occasionally appeared in guild memberships. But they did not become guild officers, and they played no official role in town government. Their families were dominated by men. Bernarda Cordonaria (Shoemaker) was not the only woman in Toulouse at the beginning of the thirteenth century who took her last name not from her own trade but from her husband's craft.

Another nearly exclusively male group that developed by the end of the twelfth century was the university, an institution formed by students and masters from the spontaneous growth of schools around particular teachers in the early part of the century. Students and masters together formed a guild (*universitas*), and with special privileges from

popes or kings, who valued the services of scholars, they formed small, virtually independent jurisdictions within the town. Historians sometimes speak of the hostility between "town" and "gown." Yet university towns often depended on scholars to patronize local restaurants, shops, and hostels.

Oxford, once a sleepy town where a group of students clustered around one or two masters, became in the twelfth century a center of royal administration, church courts, the study of canon law, and the teaching of Roman law, theology, and the liberal arts. It had about three hundred students by 1209, and masters gradually came to regulate student discipline, proficiency, and housing. Because all scholars were considered clerics, they had special privileges from civil law. When a student at Oxford was suspected of killing his mistress, however, the townspeople took his punishment into their own hands, sparking a revolt by the masters, who refused to teach and left town; some of them went to Cambridge to found a university there. The papacy defended the masters' strike, whereas King John supported the town. In 1214, when John was politically weak and forced to seek the pope's aid, he had to allow a papal legate to patch up a peace at Oxford that favored the university. According to the agreement, the townspeople had to rent lodgings and sell food to the students at reasonable prices, and they had to pay a yearly stipend for poor students. The local bishop appointed a chancellor to receive the money and to hear, every year, town representatives swear to uphold the agreement. Soon the masters themselves named the chancellor.

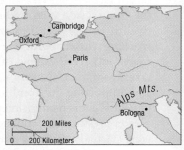

University Cities

At the University of Paris the students and masters also sought autonomy, but here the king guaranteed their rights. When in 1200 a clash between students and Parisians, led by the royal provost, left several students dead, the masters appealed to the king. Philip Augustus issued a charter that promised the students that his officials at Paris would not "lay hands on a student for any offense whatever." A few years later the masters formed a formal guild in which they swore an oath of fraternity, determined proper dress, agreed to follow a certain "order in lectures and disputations," and committed themselves to attend one another's funerals. They already had the right to determine which students were proficient enough to become masters themselves.

Bologna, long a center of legal studies, had two guilds: one of students and one of professors. Unlike young men interested in the liberal arts, Bologna's growing crowds of students were mostly men in their thirties or forties seeking career advancement through expertise in Roman and canon law. As at universities in other cities, the Bolognese students incorporated themselves by "nationality." Two "nations" coexisted at Bologna: Italian (the Cismontanes) and non-Italian (the Ultramontanes).* Each nation protected its members. The nations wrote statutes, elected rectors, and attempted to exact concessions and privileges from the citizens of Bologna and the masters of law. The students participated in the appointment of masters and the payment of their salaries, even though by 1215 the professors at Bologna had organized a guild of their own. Hostility between students and masters sometimes led to the students' boycotting classes, leaving the city, and canceling their teachers' payments. These actions brought the professors to heel. At Bologna the students dominated the university.

Religious Fervor and Dissent

Conflict over authority in the new universities was mirrored in the religious fervor that developed about 1200, when individual piety and new religious movements involved ever greater numbers of lay women and men. For women in particular, mass involvement in new sorts of piety was unprecedented, even in the monasteries of the past. Now beckoning to women of every age and every walk of life, the new piety spread beyond the convent, punctuating the routines of daily life with Scriptural reading, fasting, and charity. Some of this intense religious response developed into official, orthodox movements within the church; other religious movements so threatened established doctrine that church leaders declared them heretical.

St. Francis (c. 1182–1226) founded the most famous orthodox religious movement—the Franciscans. Francis was a child of the commercial revolution. Although expected to follow his well-to-do father in the cloth trade at Assisi, Francis began to experience doubts, dreams, and illnesses, which spurred him to religious self-examination. Eventually he renounced his family's wealth, dramatically marking the decision by casting off all his clothes and standing naked before his father, a crowd of spectators, and the bishop of Assisi. Francis then went about preaching penance to anyone who would listen. Clinging to poverty as if, in his words, "she" was his "lady," he accepted no money, walked without shoes, wore only one coarse tunic, and refused to be cloistered. Intending to follow the model of Christ, he received, as his biographers put it, a miraculous gift of grace: the stigmata, the five wounds of the crucified Christ.

By all accounts Francis was a spellbinding speaker, and he attracted many followers. Recognized as a religious order by the pope, the Brothers of St. Francis (or friars, from the Latin meaning "little brothers") spent their time preaching, ministering to lepers, and doing manual labor. Eventually they dispersed, setting up fraternal groups throughout Italy and then in France, Spain, the Holy Land, and eventually Germany and England. Unlike Bruno of Cologne and the Cistercians, who had rejected cities, the friars sought town life, sleeping in dormitories on the outskirts and becoming part of urban community life, preaching to crowds and begging for their daily bread. St. Francis converted women, too. In 1212 an eighteen-year-old noblewoman named Clare formed the nucleus of a community of pious women, the future Order of the Sisters of St. Francis. At first the women worked alongside the friars; but the church disapproved of their activities in the world, and soon Franciscan sisters were confined to cloisters under the Rule of St. Benedict.

Clare was one of many women who experimented with different styles of religious expression. Some women joined convents; others became recluses or sought membership in new lay sisterhoods. In northern Europe at the end of the twelfth century, lay women who lived together in informal pious communities were called Beguines. Without permanent vows or an established rule, the Beguines chose to be celibate (though they were free to leave the beguinage to marry) and often made their living

---

Cismontane means "from this side of the mountains," that is, the Alps, whereas *Ultramontane* means "from the other side of the mountains."

by weaving cloth or working with the sick and old. Although their daily occupations were ordinary, the Beguines' private, internal lives were often emotional and ecstatic, infused with the combined imagery of love and religion so pervasive in both monasteries and courts. One renowned Beguine, Mary of Oignies, who like St. Francis was said to have received the stigmata, felt herself to be a pious mother entrusted with the Christ child:

Sometimes it seemed to her that for three or more days she held [Christ] close to her so that He nestled between her breasts like a baby, and she hid Him there lest He be seen by others. Sometimes she kissed him as though He were a little child and sometimes she held Him on her lap as if He were a gentle lamb.

Intensely focused on the life of Christ, men and women in the late twelfth century made his childhood, agony, death, and presence in the Eucharist the most important experiences of their own lives.

According to the established church, the Eucharist required an ordained priest to consecrate the wine and bread. In the late twelfth century, however, some reformers opened the consecration to the laity, a practice the church condemned as heretical. This was just one of a veritable explosion of heretical ideas and doctrines contradicting those officially accepted by church authorities. The idea of heresy was of course not new in the twelfth century. But the Gregorian reform had created for the first time in the West a clear church hierarchy headed by a pope who could enforce a single doctrine, discipline, and dogma. Such clearly defined orthodoxy meant that people would, for the first time in western Europe, perceive heresy as a serious problem. The growth of cities, commerce, and intellectual life fostered a new sense of community for many Europeans. But when intense religious feeling led to the fervent espousal of new religious ideas, established authorities often felt threatened and took steps to preserve their power.

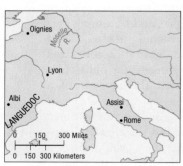

Franciscans, Heretics, and Reformers

Frederick Barbarossa's outraged reply to the representatives of the Roman commune, for example, was in part a rejection of a heretical cleric named Arnold of Brescia, leader of the commune. As Otto of Freising described him, Arnold was "a disparager of the clergy and of bishops, a persecutor of monks, a flatterer only of the laity." His heresy was both social and religious: "He used to say that neither clerics that owned property . . . nor monks with possessions could in any wise be saved. . . . Besides this, he is said to have held unreasonable views with regard to the sacrament of the altar and infant baptism." We do not know precisely what Arnold taught because we have only the reports of his orthodox critics. We do know that his radical critique of clerical riches and his questioning the meaning of the Eucharist and the efficacy of infant baptism were prevalent heretical ideas.

Among the most visible heretics were dualists, who saw the world torn between good and evil. Already important in Bulgaria and Asia Minor, dualism became a prominent ingredient in the religious life in Italy, Languedoc (a part of southern France), and the Rhineland by the end of the twelfth century. Described collectively as Cathars, or "Pure Ones," these groups believed the Devil had created the material world. Therefore they renounced the world, abjuring wealth, sex, and meat. Their repudiation of sex reflected some of the attitudes of eleventh-century church reformers (whose orthodoxy, however, was never in doubt), while their rejection of wealth echoed the same concerns that moved Bruno of Cologne to forswear city life and led St. Francis to embrace poverty. In many ways the heretics simply took these attitudes to an extreme; but unlike orthodox reformers, they also challenged the efficacy and value of the church hierarchy.

Attracting both men and women, and giving women access to the highest positions in the Cathar hierarchy, Cathars young and old, literate and unlettered saw themselves as followers of Christ's original message; as members of one condemned group protested, "the bishop who had given sentence was a heretic and not they." At Lombers in Languedoc, where they were called Albigensians,[*]

---

[*]The name was derived from the town of Albi, near Lombers.

they explained their ideas concerning the Eucharist with complete assurance:

> *They answered that those who received worthily were saved; and those who received unworthily, procured to themselves damnation; and they said that [the Eucharist] was consecrated by every good man, whether an ecclesiastic or a layman; and they answered nothing else, because they would not be compelled to answer concerning their faith.*

The church condemned other, nondualist, groups as heretical not on doctrinal grounds but because these groups allowed their lay members to preach, challenging the authority of the church hierarchy. In Lyon (in southeastern France) in the 1170s, for example, a rich merchant named Waldo decided to take literally the Gospel message "If you wish to be perfect, then go and sell everything you have, and give to the poor" (Matt. 19:21, Latin Vulgate Bible). The same message had inspired countless monks and would worry the church far less several decades later, when St. Francis established his new order. But when Waldo went into the street and gave away his belongings, announcing "I am really not insane, as you think," he scandalized not only the bystanders but the church as well. Refusing to retire to a monastery, Waldo and his followers, men and women called Waldensians, lived in poverty and went about preaching, quoting the Gospel in the vernacular so that everyone could understand. But the papacy rebuffed Waldo's bid to preach freely; and the Waldensians—denounced, excommunicated, and expelled from Lyon—wandered to Languedoc, Italy, northern Spain, and the Moselle valley.

European Aggression Within and Without

Classifying a particular group as a threat to society was a common method of asserting political and religious control in the second half of the twelfth century. Segregated from Christian society, vilified, and persecuted, those who were singled out, principally Jews and heretics, provided a rallying point for popes, princes, and Christian armies. Taking the offensive against those defined as different also meant launching campaigns to defeat peoples on Christendom's borders, a trend begun earlier with the First Crusade and the *reconquista* of Spain. In the early thirteenth century, war against the Muslims to the south, the unbelievers to the north, and the Byzantine Empire to the east made crusading a permanent feature of medieval life. Even the West did not escape: the crusade waged against the Albigensians starting in 1208 in southern France replaced the ruling class and eclipsed the court culture of the troubadours there.

Jews as Strangers, Heretics as Threats

Socially isolated and branded as outcasts, Jews and heretics helped define the larger society as orthodox. Like lepers, whose disease cut them off from ordinary communities, Jews were believed to threaten the health of those around them. Lepers had to wear a special costume, were forbidden to touch children, could not eat with those not afflicted, and were housed in leprosaria; Jews were similarly segregated from emerging Christian institutions, though they were not confined to hospices. Forced off their lands during the eleventh century, most ended up in the cities as craftsmen, merchants, or moneylenders, providing capital for the developing commercial society, whose Christian members

Jewish Communities

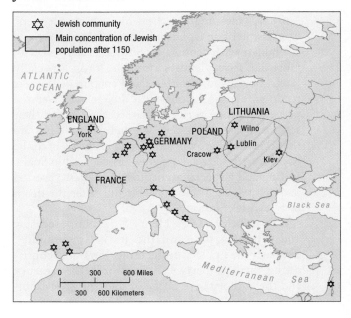

The Jew as the Other
Beginning in the second half of the twelfth century, Jews were increasingly portrayed as different from Christians, with beady eyes, hooked noses, and tall pointed hats. In this illustration clerics are borrowing money from a Jew in a conical hat.

were prohibited from charging interest as usury forbidden by Christ. The growing monopoly of the guilds forced Jews out of the crafts: in effect Jews were compelled to become "usurers" because other fields were closed to them. The slang and derogatory "to Jew," meaning "to cheat like a moneylender," was first used, in its Latin form (*judaizare*), around the mid-twelfth century by St. Bernard. Even with Christian moneylenders available, lords, especially kings, borrowed from Jews and encouraged others to do so because, along with their newly asserted powers, European rulers claimed the Jews as their serfs and Jewish property as their own. "Jews are the serfs of the crown and belong exclusively to the royal treasury," was one view proclaimed in Spain. In England a special exchequer of the Jews created in 1194 collected unpaid debts due after the death of a Jewish creditor.

Even before 1194, Henry II had imposed new and arbitrary taxes on the Jewish community. Similarly in France, persecuting Jews and confiscating their property benefited both the treasury and the authoritative image of the king. For exam-

ple, early in his reign Philip Augustus's agents surprised Jews at sabbath worship in their synagogues and seized their goods, demanding that they redeem their own property for a large sum of money. Shortly thereafter, Philip declared forfeit 80 percent of all debts owed to Jews; the remaining 20 percent was to be paid directly to the king. About a year later, in 1182, Philip expelled the Jews from the Ile-de-France:

> The king gave them leave to sell each his movable goods. . . . But their real estate, that is, houses, fields, vineyards, barns, winepresses, and such like, he reserved for himself and his successors, the kings of the French.

When Philip allowed the Jews to return, in 1198, he intended for them to be moneylenders or money changers exclusively, whose activities would be taxed and monitored by his officials.

Limiting Jews to moneylending in an increasingly commercial economy also served the interests of lords in debt to Jewish creditors. For example, in 1190, local nobles orchestrated a brutal attack on the Jews of York (in England) to rid themselves of their debts and of the Jews to whom they owed money. Churchmen too used credit in a money economy but resented the fiscal obligations it imposed. One of the most virulent attacks against the Jews came from Peter the Venerable, a twelfth-century abbot of Cluny, who wrote an entire book about the "obstinacy" of the Jews, including a chapter on their "absurd and utterly stupid tales." But Peter's mockery was hardly disinterested; Cluny was deeply in debt—in part to the Jews in its neighborhood—when he became its abbot. The papacy, with agents and bureaucrats to support, also depended on credit granted by professional moneylenders. With their drive to create centralized territorial states and their desire to make their power known and felt, powerful rulers of Europe—churchmen and laity alike—exploited and coerced the Jews while drawing upon and encouraging a wellspring of elite and popular anti-Jewish feeling.

The sentiment against Jews grew over time. Ever since the Roman Empire had become Christian, Jews had been seen as different from Christians, and imperial law had prohibited them from, for example, owning Christian slaves or marrying Christian women. Canon laws had added to these restrictions, and in the twelfth century intellectuals elaborated objections against Jewish doctrine. These official views now merged with sensational popular stories. For example, after a little boy was murdered at Norwich, in England, Thomas of Monmouth, a local monk, charged that the child was the victim of a Jewish conspiracy. Each year, Thomas imagined, a conclave of rabbis met to decide on a place to sacrifice a Christian child. The story became commonplace, told with local variations, and typically caused the lynching of local Jews. Although Jews must have looked exactly like Christians—contemporaries complained that no one could tell the two apart—Jews now became clearly identified in sculpture and in drawings by conical hats and, increasingly, by demeaning features.

Attacks against Jews coincided with campaigns against heretics, whose beliefs spread in regions where political control was less centralized, as, for example, in southern France. By the end of the twelfth century, however, church and secular powers combined to stamp out heresies. These efforts were not always violent. Papal legates preached to heretics to convert them. The Dominican order, for example, developed after about 1205 from papal missions to Languedoc to address heretical groups. Its founder, St. Dominic (1170–1221), recognized that preachers of Christ's word who came on horseback, followed by a crowd of servants, and wearing fine clothes had no moral leverage with their audience. Therefore, like their adversaries the Cathars, the Dominicans rejected material riches and instead went about on foot, preaching and begging. Like the Franciscans, whom they resembled both organizationally and spiritually, the Dominicans were called friars.

However, the church sometimes resorted to armed force in its campaign against heretics. In 1208 the murder of a papal legate in southern France prompted Pope Innocent III (✳1198–1216) to demand that northern princes take up the sword, invade Languedoc, wrest the land from the heretics, and populate it with orthodox Christians. This Albigensian Crusade marked the first time the pope offered warriors fighting an enemy in Christian Europe all the spiritual and temporal benefits of a crusade to the Holy Land: he suspended their monetary debts and promised their sins would be forgiven after forty days' service. Like all crusades, the Albigensian Crusade had political as well as religious dimensions. It pitted southern French princes, like Raymond VI, count of Toulouse (1194–1222), against northern leaders like Simon IV de Montfort l'Amaury (c. 1160–1218), a castellan from the Ile-de-France eager to demonstrate his piety and win new possessions. After twenty years of fighting, from 1209 to 1229, leadership would be taken over by the Capetian kings of France, southern resistance broken, and Languedoc brought under the control of the French crown.

More Crusades to the Holy Land

The second half of the twelfth century saw new crusades outside western Europe. When in 1144 the Muslim ruler of Syria captured the Christian city of Edessa, at the northernmost edge of Outremer, the news fired churchmen, particularly the pope and St. Bernard, to preach a new crusade, the Second Crusade (1147–1149), undertaken to resecure Edessa and to attack Damascus, a Muslim stronghold. The crusaders' crushing defeat helped create a Muslim hero, Nur al-Din, who united Syria under his command and presided over a renewal of Sunni Islam. His successor, Saladin, became all too well known to Europeans at the time of the Third Crusade.

Saladin and the Christian king of Jerusalem fought over Egypt, which Saladin ruled by 1186 together with Syria. Effectively squeezed between two Islamic pincers, Outremer lost Jerusalem to Saladin's armies in 1187. The Third Crusade (1189–1192), called to retake Jerusalem, marked a military and political watershed for Outremer. The European outpost survived, but it was reduced to a narrow strip of land. Christians could continue to enter Jerusalem as pilgrims, but Islamic hegemony over the Holy Land would remain a fact of life for centuries.

Led by the greatest rulers of Europe—Frederick I Barbarossa, Philip II Augustus, Leopold of Austria, and Richard I the Lion-Hearted—the Third Crusade refracted the political tensions among the European ruling class as the leaders quarreled among themselves. Richard, in particular, seemed to cultivate enmities: he argued with Philip about dividing the spoils of war; he fought with the king of Sicily and then patched up a peace by promising to support him against Frederick's son, Henry VI (1165–1197); he seized Cyprus from a

Battle of Hattin

In 1187 the Christian forces from Outremer were utterly defeated by Saladin's army. The Third Crusade was organized by the princes of Europe in response to calls for *help from the few survivors. In this thirteenth-century depiction of the battle, the Muslims, led by Saladin, are on the left.*

relative of the Byzantine emperor (thereby destroying the possibility of good relations with Constantinople); and he offended Leopold at the siege of Acre. These seemingly personal tensions reflected the hostility between the kings of England and France. Leopold, for example, was Philip's ally. Captured by Leopold and held for a huge ransom by Henry VI on his return home, Richard had good reason to write his plaintive poem bemoaning his captivity and the lost "love" of former friends.

Frederick I went overland on the Third Crusade, passing through Hungary and Bulgaria* and descending into the Byzantine Empire. "But the Greeks were worse than the Bulgarians," wrote a contemporary chronicler:

> At the command of the Greek emperor they showed the army no kindness and even refused to sell them anything to eat. . . . It made Frederick angry to receive such treatment from Christians, and so he permitted his army to plunder the country.

*Bulgaria regained its independence in 1185 after a successful rebellion against Byzantine rule.

Such hostilities made the Third Crusade a dress rehearsal for the Fourth Crusade (1202–1204), called by Pope Innocent III as part of his more general plan to define, invigorate, and impose his brand of Christianity on both believers and nonbelievers. From the first, Innocent intended to direct a new crusade that would reverse the failures of the past. The pope, in Innocent's view, was "less than God but greater than man, judge of all men and judged by none." Forces beyond Innocent's control, however, took over the Fourth Crusade, whose warriors sacked Constantinople in 1204. Prejudices, religious zeal, and self-confidence had become characteristic of western European attitudes toward the Greeks. The mutual mistrust between Byzantium and the West dated from eighth-century theological differences that stoked the flames of envy and disdain: "In every respect," wrote a Frenchman about Constantinople at the time of the Second Crusade, "she exceeds moderation; for, just as she surpasses other cities in wealth, so, too, does she surpass them in vice."

Such attitudes help explain the course of events from 1202 to 1204. The crusading army turned out to be far smaller than had been expected. Its leaders

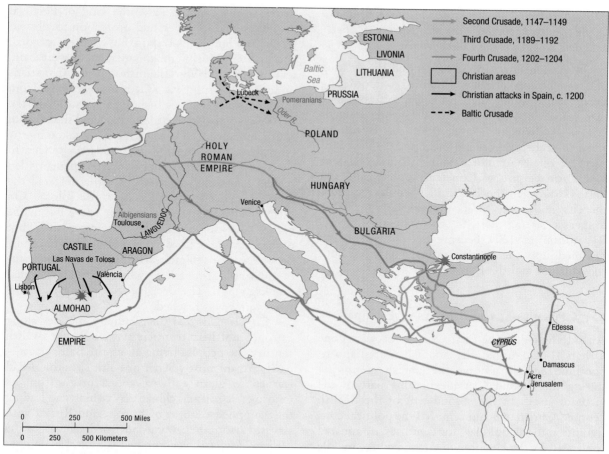

Crusades and Anti-Heretic Campaigns, 1144–1261

could not pay the Venetians, who had fitted out a large fleet of ships in anticipation of carrying multitudes of warriors across the water to Jerusalem. Seizing the opportunity to enhance its commercial hegemony, the Venetians convinced the Crusade's leaders to pay their way by attacking Zara, a Christian city but Venice's competitor in the Adriatic. The Venetians then turned their sights toward Constantinople, hoping to control it and gain a commercial monopoly there. They persuaded the crusaders to join them on behalf of a member of the ousted imperial family, Alexius, who claimed the Byzantine throne and promised the crusaders that he would reunite the eastern with the western church and fund the expedition to the Holy Land. Most of the crusaders convinced themselves that the cause was noble. "Never," wrote a contemporary, "was so great an enterprise undertaken by any

people since the creation of the world." The siege took nearly a year, but on April 12, 1204, the crusaders sacked Constantinople, killing, plundering, and ransacking the city for treasure and relics. When one crusader discovered a cache of relics, a chronicler recalled, "he plunged both hands in and, girding up his loins, he filled the folds of his gown with the holy booty of the Church." But, of course, the Byzantines saw the same events as a great tragedy. The bishop of Ephesus wrote:

And so the streets, squares, houses of two and three stories, sacred places, nunneries, houses for nuns and monks, sacred churches, even the Great Church of God and the imperial palace, were filled with men of the enemy, all of them maddened by war and murderous in spirit. . . . [T]hey tore children from their mothers and mothers from their children, and they defiled the virgins in the holy chapels, fearing neither God's anger nor man's vengeance.

Although Pope Innocent decried the sacking of Constantinople, he also consented to it, ordering the crusaders to stay there for a year to consolidate their gains. The Crusade leaders chose one of themselves—Baldwin of Flanders—to be Byzantine emperor, and he, the other princes, and the Venetians parceled out the empire among themselves. This new Latin empire of Constantinople would last until 1261, when the Byzantines would recapture the city and some of its outlying territory. No longer a strong heir to the Roman Empire, Byzantium in 1204 became overshadowed and hemmed in by the stronger military might of both the Muslims and the Europeans.

Crusades at the Borders of Europe

Already linked to the First Crusade because Pope Urban II had urged the Spanish Christians to continue the fight at home, the Spanish *reconquista* during the Second Crusade became part of the Crusade itself. In the second half of the twelfth century, Christian Spain achieved the political configuration that would last for centuries, dominated to the east by the kingdom of Aragon; in the middle by Castile, whose ruler styled himself emperor; and in the southwest by Portugal, whose ruler similarly transformed his title, from prince to king. The three leaders competed for territory and power, but above all they sought an advantage against the Muslims to the south.

Muslim disunity aided the Christian conquest of Spain. The Muslims of al-Andalus were themselves beset, from the south, by a new group of Muslims from North Africa, the Almohades. Claiming religious purity, the Almohades declared their own holy war against the Andalusians. These simultaneous threats caused alliances in Spain to be based on political as well as religious considerations. The Muslim ruler of Valencia, for example, declared himself a vassal of the king of Castile and bitterly opposed the Almohades' expansion.

But the crusading ideal held no room for such subtleties. During the 1140s, armies under the command of the kings of Portugal, Castile, and Aragon scored resounding victories against Muslim cities. Enlisting the aid of crusaders on their way to the Holy Land in 1147, the king of Portugal promised land, plunder, and protection to all who would help him attack Lisbon. His efforts succeeded, and Lisbon's Muslim inhabitants fled or were slain, its Mozarabic bishop (the bishop of the Christians under Muslim rule) was killed, and a crusader from England was set up as bishop in his stead. In the 1170s, when the Almohades conquered the Muslim south and advanced toward the cities taken by the Christians, their exertions had no lasting effect. In 1212 a Christian crusading army of Spaniards led by the kings of Aragon and Castile defeated the Almohades decisively at Las Navas de Tolosa. "On their side 100,000 armed men or more fell in the battle," the king of Castile wrote afterward, "but of the army of the Lord . . . incredible though it may be, unless it be a miracle, hardly 25 or 30 Christians of our whole army fell. O what happiness! O what thanksgiving!" The decisive turning point in the *reconquista* was reached.

Christians flexed their military muscles along Europe's northern frontiers as well. By the twelfth century the peoples living along the Baltic coast—partly pagan; mostly Slavic or Baltic speaking—had learned to glean a living and a profit from its inhospitable soil and climate. By fishing and trading they supplied the rest of Europe and Russia with slaves, furs, amber, wax, and dried fish. Like the earlier Vikings, they combined commercial competition with outright raiding, so that the Danes and the Saxons (that is, the Germans in Saxony) both benefited and suffered from their presence. When St. Bernard began to preach the Second Crusade in Germany, he discovered that the Germans were indeed itching to attack the infidels—those across the Elbe! St. Bernard pressed the pope to add these northern heathens to the list of those against whom holy war should be launched and urged their conversion or extermination. Thus began the Northern Crusades, whose start paralleled the Second Crusade in 1147. These Crusades continued intermittently until the early fifteenth century.

The King of Denmark, Valdemar I (∗1157–1182), and the Saxon duke Henry the Lion led the first phase of the Northern Crusades. Their initial attacks on the Slavs were uncoordinated—in some instances they even fought each other. But in key raids in the 1160s and 1170s the two leaders worked together briefly to bring much of the region west of the Oder River under their control. They took some land outright—Henry the Lion

Valdemar I, Crusader of the North
King Valdemar I of Denmark had his image cast on this penny, along with a palm leaf (a symbol of pilgrimage) and, on the reverse, a flag with a cross (a symbol of crusade).

apportioned conquered territory to his followers, for example—but more often the Slavic princes surrendered and had their territories reinstated once they became vassals of the Christian rulers. Meanwhile, churchmen arrived: the Cistercians, for example, came long before the first phase of fighting had ended, confidently building their monasteries to the very shores of the Oder River. Slavic peasants surely suffered from the conquerors' fire and pillage, but the Northern Crusades ultimately benefited all the ruling classes—Danish, German, and Slavic. The newly converted peoples paid abundant tithes to their bishops, and once converted, Slavic princes found it advantageous for both their eternal salvation and their worldly profit to join new crusades to areas still farther to the east.

Although less well known than the Crusades to the Holy Land, the Northern Crusades had far more lasting effects: they settled the Baltic region with German-speaking lords and peasants and forged a permanent relationship between the very north of Europe and its neighbors to the south and west. With the Baltic dotted with churches and monasteries and its peoples dipped into baptismal waters, the region would gradually adopt the institutions of western medieval society—cities, guilds, universities, castles, and manors. The Livs (whose region was eventually known as Livonia) were conquered by 1208, and their bishop sent knights northward to conquer the Estonians. The Prussians would be conquered with the cooperation between the Polish and German aristocracy; German peasants eventually settled Prussia. Only the Lithuanians successfully resisted western conquest, settlement, and conversion.

RELIGION AND POLITICS IN AN AGE OF AMBITION

1144 Fall of Edessa to the Turks; in response, the Second Crusade and the Northern Crusades launched

1152–1190 Reign of Frederick Barbarossa
- 1157 Tension with Pope Hadrian IV at the Diet of Besançon
- 1167 Italian policy provokes the formation of the Lombard League
- 1176 Lombard League defeats Frederick at the Battle of Legnano
- 1180 Engineers the fall of Henry the Lion
- 1190 Dies on the Third Crusade (1189–1192)

1154–1189 Reign of Henry II, king of England (on the Continent he was duke of Anjou, Normandy, and Maine, and his wife, Eleanor, was duchess of Aquitaine)
- 1166 Extends the scope of common law in England with the Assize of Clarendon

1180–1223 Reign of Philip II Augustus, king of France
- 1182 Expels the Jews from the royal demesne
- 1204 Conquers Normandy and other territory
- 1214 Makes good his claim on Normandy at the Battle of Bouvines

1182–1226 Life of St. Francis; the mendicant order he founded was recognized by Pope Innocent III

1199–1216 Reign of John, king of England
- 1215 Assents to the Magna Carta under great pressure from barons

1204–1205 Fourth Crusade; Constantinople sacked (1204)

1209–1229 Albigensian Crusade

1212 Battle of Las Navas de Tolosa; most of Spain in Christian hands

CONCLUSION

The second half of the twelfth century saw the consolidation of Europe's new political configuration, reaching the limits of a continental expansion that stretched from the Baltic to the Strait of Gibraltar. European settlements along the coast of the Levant, on the other hand, were nearly obliterated. When western Europeans sacked Constantinople, Europe and the Islamic world became the dominant political forces in the West.

Powerful territorial kings and princes now began to establish the institutions of bureaucratic authority. They hired staffs to handle their accounts, write down acts, collect taxes, issue writs, and preside over courts. Flourishing cities, a growing money economy, and trade and manufacturing provided the finances necessary to support the personnel and offices now used by medieval governments. Clerical schools and, by the end of the twelfth century, universities, became the training grounds for the new administrators.

Rulers were not alone in their quest to document, define, and institutionalize their power. The second half of the twelfth century was a great age of organization. Associations, which had earlier been fluid, now solidified into well-defined corporations—craft guilds and universities, for example—with statutes providing clearly articulated rights, obligations, and privileges to their members. Developing out of the commercial revolution, such organizations in turn made commercial activities a permanent part of medieval life.

Religious associations also formed. The Franciscans, Dominicans, Waldensians, and Albigensians—however dissimilar their beliefs—all articulated specific creeds and claimed distinctiveness. In rejecting wealth and material possessions, they revealed how deeply the commercial revolution had affected the moral life of some Europeans, who could not accept the profit motive inherent in a money economy. In emphasizing preaching they showed that a lay population, already Christian, now yearned for a more intense and personal spirituality.

New piety, new exclusivity, and new power arose in a society both more confident and less tolerant. After about 1147, crusaders fought more often and against an increasing variety of foes. With heretics setting forth their beliefs, the church, led by the papacy, now defined orthodoxy and declared dissenters its enemies. The Jews, who had once been fairly well integrated into the Christian community, were treated ambivalently, alternately used and abused. The Slavs and Balts became targets for new evangelical zeal; the Greeks became the butt of envy, hostility, and finally enmity. European Christians still considered Muslims arrogant heathens, and the deflection of the Fourth Crusade did not stem the zeal of popes to call for new crusades to the Holy Land.

Confident and aggressive, the men leading Christian Europe in the following decades of the thirteenth century would attempt to impose their rule, legislate morality, and create a unified worldview impregnable to attack. But this drive for order would be countered by unexpected varieties of thought and action, by political and social tensions, and by intensely personal religious quests.

SUGGESTIONS FOR FURTHER READING

Source Materials

Chrétien de Troyes. *Yvain: The Knight of the Lion.* Translated by Burton Raffel. 1987. One of the most famous medieval romances.

Goldin, Frederick. *Lyrics of the Troubadours and Trouvères: Original Texts, with Translations.* 1973. Contains some of the major troubadour poems, with the original and English versions on facing pages.

The Little Flowers of Saint Francis. Translated by L. Sherley-Price. 1959. Stories about the deeds of St. Francis, told by his disciples.

Otto of Freising. *The Deeds of Frederick Barbarossa.* Translated by Charles C. Mierow. 1953. The chief source for the reign of Frederick I by an important historian who was also Frederick's uncle.

Peters, Edward, ed. and trans. *Heresy and Authority in Medieval Europe*. 1980. Contains important source readings for medieval heresies and the responses to them.

The Song of Roland. Translated by Patricia Terry. 1965. The most famous Old French epic.

Interpretive Studies

Baldwin, John W. *The Government of Philip Augustus. Foundations of French Royal Power in the Middle Ages*. 1986. Details the transition to bureaucratic kingship.

Bartlett, Robert. *The Making of Europe: Conquest, Colonization, and Cultural Change, 950–1350*. 1993. Looks at both external and internal effects of European expansion and expansionism.

Boswell, John. *Christianity, Social Tolerance, and Homosexuality: Gay People in Western Europe from the Beginning of the Christian Era to the Fourteenth Century*. 1980. Studies shifting attitudes toward homosexuals, who, like lepers and Jews, were vilified in the twelfth century.

Christiansen, Eric. *The Northern Crusades: The Baltic and the Catholic Frontier, 1100–1525*. 1980. A well-written account of these less well-known crusades, which had more lasting consequences than those to the Holy Land.

Clanchy, Michael T. *From Memory to Written Record, 1066–1307*. 1979. Traces the development of an oral to a written culture in England.

Duby, Georges. *William Marshall*. 1985. Uses the life of one knight to illuminate the world of an entire class.

Fuhrmann, Horst. *Germany in the High Middle Ages, c. 1050–1200*. Translated by Timothy Reuter. 1986. Especially useful for tracing shifting notions of German kingship.

Gold, Penny Shine. *The Lady and the Virgin: Image, Attitude, and Experience in Twelfth-Century France*. 1985. Examines the image of women in art, literature, and life.

Hallam, Elizabeth M. *Capetian France, 987–1328*. 1980. A good overview of the period, with excellent bibliographies, maps, and figures.

Jordan, Karl. *Henry the Lion: A Biography*. Translated by P. S. Falla. 1986. A useful study of the great Welf prince of Germany.

Kazhdan, A. P., and Ann Wharton Epstein. *Change in Byzantine Culture in the Eleventh and Twelfth Centuries*. 1985. Considers the many ways in which Byzantine culture was transformed before the Fourth Crusade.

Kendrick, Laura. *The Game of Love: Troubadour Wordplay*. 1988. Discusses troubadour songs from the point of view of literary criticism.

Lewis, Andrew W. *Royal Succession in Capetian France: Studies on Familial Order and the State*. 1981. Studies the relationship between ideas about the family and the development of the French monarchy.

Little, Lester K. *Religious Poverty and the Profit Economy in Medieval Europe*. 1978. Places the heretics and friars in the historical context of a newly commercial society.

Moore, R. I. *The Formation of a Persecuting Society: Power and Deviance in Western Europe, 950–1250*. 1987. Explores the nature and causes of persecution of heretics, Jews, lepers, and homosexuals in the Middle Ages.

Newman, Barbara. *Sister of Wisdom: St. Hildegard's Theology of the Feminine*. 1987. An illuminating study of Hildegard of Bingen, who had a theology that relied predominantly on feminine imagery.

Nicholas, David. *Medieval Flanders*. 1992. An excellent survey of this socially turbulent and commercially flourishing region.

O'Callaghan, Joseph F. *A History of Medieval Spain*. 1975. A general survey of the period.

Page, Christopher. *Voices and Instruments of the Middle Ages: Instrumental Practice and Songs in France, 1100–1300*. 1986. Explores the relationship between songs and the use of musical instruments.

Queller, Donald E. *The Fourth Crusade: The Conquest of Constantinople, 1201–1204*. 1977. A well-written narrative of the events.

Reynolds, Susan. *Kingdoms and Communities in Western Europe, 900–1300*. 1984. Sheds light on the importance and prevalence of communities such as villages, guilds, and kingdoms.

Wakefield, Walter L. *Heresy, Crusade, and Inquisition in Southern France, 1100–1250*. 1974. An analytical narrative of events related to the Albigensian Crusade.

Warren, William L. *Henry II*. 1973. A massive and authoritative biography.

———. *King John*. 1978. A judicious assessment of the king and his times.

In the summertime, King Louis IX of France (*1226–1270) would go to the woods near his castle of Vincennes on the outskirts of Paris. "Then," his biographer, Joinville, recounted, "he would sit down with his back against an oak, and make us all sit round him. Those who had any suit to present could come to speak to him without hindrance. The king would address them directly and ask, 'Is there anyone here who has a case to be settled?' Those who had one would stand up. Then he would say, 'Keep silent all of you, and you shall be heard in turn, one after the other.'" Thus the king dispensed justice.

The image of the good king, out in the warm air, lounging under a shady tree, accessible to all his people, righting wrongs, and giving wise counsel conveyed order, peace, harmony, and control. The king could not personally hear all the grievances of his people, of course; yet the fair and wise king who maintained harmonious relations in his realm was an ideal of the thirteenth century. Kings settling disputes, church councils striving to define and organize a diverse European population, scholastics working to reconcile conflicting theological ideas, poets contemplating the design of a teeming universe—all participated in the quest for order and control. Reminding his subjects of the wise King Solomon uniting his people in a godly society, Louis IX symbolized the proper relationship between ruler and subject; not long after his death, the church declared him a saint. The quest for control, however, contained a paradox: as different factions imposed the various brands of order they favored on society, clashes over power, ideology, and territory that jeopardized the very possibility of peace ensued.

The Quest for Order and Control, 1215–1320

Vault of Amiens Cathedral
The Gothic church was made of stone, but it created an illusion of lightness. The glass formed a band of light just below the vault, and the vault seemed to perch above it without weight. In fact the great thrust of the vault was carried down to earth by the piers, the walls of the aisles, and the flying buttresses.

The Royal Dignity
The young St. Louis sits at the top right; his mother, who acted as his regent during his minority, sits opposite him. Below is a scribe taking down dictation from a monk.

While the Fourth Lateran Council sought to define the nature of the Eucharist and control its use within the church, female mystics in the intimacy of their homes denied themselves all food except the consecrated Host, giving it a meaning in their lives never dreamt of by priests. On the international stage of high politics, Pope Innocent IV declared a crusade against the Christian emperor, Frederick II, and launched a war that ended only when the last male in the Staufer dynasty had been killed. Thus behind the supposed harmony in the thirteenth century lurked wildly diverse ideas and ideals.

The Church's Mission

Ever since the Gregorian reform of the eleventh century the papacy had conceived of salvation as implying a mission that included reforming the secular world. In the Gregorian period this task had focused on the king, because in Gregory's view a godless king threatened the redemption of all his subjects. Later, in the twelfth century, the church sought to purify social institutions, extending its influence over courts, government administrations, and new urban corporations. Now in the thirteenth century, churchmen elaborated coherent intellectual bases for their actions. Above all, they applied logic to theological questions, creating a rigorously argued understanding of God and an intellectual system embracing all aspects of life and the afterlife.

The Fourth Lateran Council

With his call in 1213 for a great new council to prepare for a new crusade and to reform the church, Pope Innocent III (*1198–1216) asserted the grand plan of the papacy: to order the world in the image of heaven. Claiming spiritual rather than temporal grounds for his actions, Innocent saw himself as an intermediary between earth and heaven: "[The pope is] set between God and man, lower than God but higher than man, who judges all and is judged by no one." Such a view justified political and military intervention, including the expansion of the papal states. Previously a student of theology at Paris and of law at Bologna, Innocent had learned at school the traditions that informed his view of the papacy.

The Fourth Lateran Council, over which Innocent presided in 1215, produced comprehensive legislation in just three days, mainly because the pope and his committees had prepared it beforehand. They envisioned a thorough regulation of Christian life, with canons (provisions) aimed at reforming not only the clergy but also the laity. One canon declared as dogma the meaning of the Eucharist, a matter of debate in centuries past: "[Christ's] body and blood are truly contained in the sacrament of the altar under the species of bread and wine, the bread being transubstantiated into the body and the wine into the blood by the divine power." *Transubstantiation,* a word coined by twelfth-century scholars, was a technical term to explain the belief that though the Eucharist continued to *look* like bread and wine, after consecration the wafer became the actual flesh and the wine the real blood of Christ. The Fourth Lateran Council's emphasis on transubstantiation reinforced the gulf between the clergy and the laity. Only the clergy could celebrate this mystery (that is, transform the bread and wine into Christ's body and blood), through which God's grace was transmitted to the faithful.

Some canons affected laypeople's lives even more directly, regardless of social status, by defining the relationship of the laity to the sacraments. One required Christians to attend Mass and to confess their sins to a priest at least once a year. Others codified the traditions of marriage, in which the church had involved itself more and more since the twelfth century. Now besides declaring marriage a sacrament and claiming jurisdiction over marital disputes, the Fourth Lateran Council decreed that marriage bans (announcements) had to be made publicly by local priests to ensure that people from the community could voice any objections to the marriage. For example, the intended spouses might be related within degrees prohibited by the church.

Innocent III
This fresco of Innocent III shows him as a young man of aristocratic bearing. He was indeed a member of a very powerful noble family.

Priests now became responsible for ferreting out this information and identifying any other impediments to the union. The canons further insisted that children conceived within clandestine or forbidden marriages were illegitimate; they could not inherit from their parents or become priests.

The council also made the status of Jews obvious and public: "We decree that [Jews] of either sex in every Christian province and at all times shall be distinguished from other people by the character of their dress in public." Like all the council's legislation, this decree took effect only when secular authorities enforced it. But sooner or later Jews almost everywhere had to wear a badge as a sign of their second-class status.

The council's longest decree blasted heretics: "Those condemned as heretics shall be handed over to the secular authorities for punishment." If the secular authority did not "purge his land of heretical filth," he was to be excommunicated, his vassals released from their oaths of fealty, and his land taken over by orthodox Christians. Such actions rarely occurred in practice; but they reveal the council's intense hostility against "any whose life and habits differ from the normal way of living of Christians."

Scholasticism

Just as the members of the Fourth Lateran Council considered all aspects of worldly life crucial to salvation, so contemporary thinkers linked human and divine activities. Called scholastics, these men taught in the universities, modeling their thought on Aristotle's comprehensive and logical philosophical scheme, which embraced physical, moral, psychological, and aesthetic phenomena. The scholastics believed the whole world, created by God, revealed the divine plan. They built on the methods of twelfth-century scholars—on Peter Abelard's *Sic et Non*, for example, and on Muslim commentators of Aristotle such as Ibn Rushd (1126–1193), a Cordoban legal scholar and physician known in the Latin West as Averoës. The scholastics pondered questions about human morality as well as issues more narrowly theological; they sought nothing less than to reconcile reason and revelation, earth and heaven.

Some scholastics considered scientific questions, observing the natural world to develop their ideas. Albertus Magnus (c. 1200–1280), for example, was a major theologian, but he also contributed to the fields of biology, botany, astronomy, and physics. His treatise *On Animals* shows he was a perceptive naturalist: "The swan," he noted, "belongs to the class of geese and, like a goose, has a serrated beak whose dentate edge resembles the saw-toothed blade of a sickle; it uses this beak to strain the mud in search of food and then chews what it finds with the serrated edges." In physics he discussed the commentaries of Averoës and Avicenna on Aristotle's view of motion. He advocated considering motion as inhering in the moving object itself rather than dependent upon an outside mover. Later scholastics separated the idea of motion (for example, of a ball rolling across a field) from other sorts of fluctuations (for example, of a knife rusting). These distinctions helped scientists in the sixteenth and seventeenth centuries arrive at the modern notion of inertia.

One of Albertus's students was St. Thomas Aquinas (c. 1225–1274), perhaps the most famous

scholastic. Huge of build, renowned for his composure in debate, Thomas came from a noble Neapolitan family that had hoped to see him become a powerful bishop rather than a poor university professor. When he was about eighteen years old he thwarted his family's wishes and joined the Dominicans. Soon he was studying at Cologne with Albertus. At thirty-two he became a master at the University of Paris, traveling often to Rome and Naples.

Thomas, like other scholastics, considered Aristotle "the Philosopher," the authoritative voice of human reason, which he sought to pair with divine revelation in a universal and harmonious scheme. In 1273 he published his monumental *Summa Theologiae*, which covered all important human and divine topics. After dividing each topic into questions and building upon methods such as Abelard's to discuss each one thoroughly and systematically, Thomas concluded each question with a decisive position and a refutation of opposing views.

For example, Thomas analyzed each sin individually; for the sin of cheating, he isolated four questions, called articles. The first article asked, "Is it lawful to sell a thing for more than its worth?" Following the article, Thomas introduced the point with which he disagreed, the objection, by citing an authority—in this case civil law:

Objection I: *It seems that it is lawful to sell a thing for more than its worth. For in human transactions, civil laws determine what is just. According to these laws it is just for buyer and seller to deceive one another. Therefore it is lawful to sell a thing for more than its worth.*

For this particular article, Thomas had two further objections, one a quote taken out of context from St. Augustine and the other a point by Aristotle.

After the objections came the "On the contrary" section, the position with which Thomas agreed, the *non* to the *sic* posed by the objections:

On the contrary, *It is written [Matt. 7:12]: "Do unto others what you would have them do unto you." Now no man wants to buy something for more than its worth. Therefore no one should sell a thing to anyone else for more than its worth.*

Thomas then began an extended discussion of the question, prefaced by the words *I answer that.* Unlike Abelard, whose method left differences unresolved, Thomas wanted to reconcile the two points of view, and so he pointed out that price and worth depended on the particular circumstances of the buyer and seller and concluded that charging more than a seller had originally paid could be legitimate at times.

For townspeople engaged in commerce and worried about Biblical prohibitions on money-making, Thomas's ideas about cheating addressed burning questions. Hoping to go to heaven as well as reap the profits of their business ventures, laypeople listened eagerly to preachers who delivered their sermons in the vernacular but who based their ideas on the Latin *summae* (treatises) of St. Thomas and other scholastics. Thomas's conclusions aided townspeople in justifying their worldly activities.

Thomas's article ended with a "Reply" to each of the objections:

> Reply Objection I: *As stated above, human law is given to the people, many of whom lack virtue; it is not given to the virtuous alone. Therefore human law cannot forbid all that is contrary to virtue.*

Thus Thomas did not declare civil law, the authority of the first objection, invalid but rather incorporated it into a moral universe in which it had clear limitations. He rated human law low in the hierarchy of divine and human inventions. Such ranking characterized the way in which Thomas and other scholastics attuned ideas and institutions. They did not deny differences and contradictions; rather they defined and distinguished among them, constructing a conceptual hierarchy.

In his own day, St. Thomas was a controversial figure, and his ideas, emphasizing reason, were by no means universally accepted. Yet even Thomas departed from Aristotle, who had explained the universe through human reason alone. In Thomas's view, God, nature, and reason were in harmony, so that Aristotle's arguments could be used to explore both the human and the divine order, but with some exceptions. "Certain things that are true about God wholly surpass the capability of human reason, for instance that God is three and one," Thomas wrote. But he thought these exceptions rarely occurred.

Other scholastics emphasized God's role in human knowledge. St. Bonaventure (1221–1274), for example, argued that we know something truly because our minds are illuminated by divine light, a light that can come only from God because He alone is unchangeable, eternal, and creative. Bonaventure used St. Augustine, rather than Aristotle, as his key authority and based his philosophical position on Augustine's neo-Platonism.

The synthetic work of the mid-thirteenth-century scholastics continued for another generation. Yet at the beginning of the fourteenth century, cracks began to appear. In the *summae* of John Duns Scotus (c. 1266–1308), for example, the world and God were less compatible. For John, as for Bonaventure, human reason could know truth only through the "special illumination of the uncreated light," that is, by divine illumination. But for Scotus this illumination came not as a matter of course but only when God chose to intervene. People experienced God as willful rather than reasonable. John thus separated the divine and secular realms; reason could not soar to God.

Religious Institutions and Town Life

Many scholastics were friars. Albertus Magnus and Thomas Aquinas, for example, belonged to the Dominican order; St. Bonaventure was a Franciscan. Both orders insisted on travel, preaching, and poverty, vocations that pulled the friars into cities and towns, where laypeople eagerly listened to their words and supported them with food and shelter. Although St. Francis had wanted his followers to sleep wherever they found themselves, most Franciscans and Dominicans lived in convents just outside cities by the second quarter of the thirteenth century. As their numbers grew, nearly every moderately sized city had such houses outside its walls—414 Dominican houses for men by 1277 and more than 1,400 Franciscan houses by the early fourteenth century. About a fifth of these Franciscan convents housed nuns, who, entirely unlike their male counterparts, lived in strict seclusion. Yet they too ministered to the world by taking in the sick. The mendicant orders further tied their members to the lay community through tertiaries, a Third Order of affiliated men and women who adopted many Franciscan practices—prayer and works of charity, for example—while continuing to live in the world, raise families, and tend to the normal tasks of daily life, whatever their occupation. Even St. Louis, king of France, was a tertiary.

Thirteenth-century scholastics taught at universities. At the University of Paris, for example, Thomas Aquinas debated with other masters, lectured to students, and wrote his great *summae* linking the doctrinal concerns of the friars, the economic concerns of the townspeople, and the scholarly concerns of the university. In turn, his students preached the results of Thomas's scholarship to the lay community: as one scholastic explained, "First the bow is bent in study, then the arrow is released in preaching."

The thirteenth century was a great age of preaching, as large numbers of learned friars and other scholars took to the road to speak to throngs of townsfolk. For example, when Berthold, a Franciscan who traveled the length and breadth of

Friars and Usurers
Friars ministered to city dwellers and commented on their activities. In this illumination from c. 1250, a Franciscan and Dominican refuse offerings from two usurers, whose profession they are thus shown to condemn.

Germany giving sermons, came to a town, a high tower was set up for him outside the city walls. A pennant advertised his presence and let people know which way the wind would blow his voice. St. Anthony of Padua

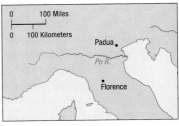

Florence and Padua

preached in Italian to huge audiences lined up hours in advance to be sure they would have a place to hear him.

New Syntheses in Writing and Music

Thirteenth-century literary writers, like preachers, often expressed complicated ideas and feelings in the vernacular. Like the scholastics, Dante Alighieri (1265–1321) harmonized disparate traditions, but in his case these included the scholastic vision of the universe, romantic poetry, and monastic spirituality. He combined these in the dramatic and expressive Italian poem *Commedia,* later known as the *Divine Comedy.*

The *Divine Comedy* is the story of Dante's (and allegorically of all people's) journey through Hell, Purgatory, and Paradise. Dante describes his passage from Hell to Paradise so precisely that the reader can map and time his movements. Influenced by the scientific work of scholastics like Albertus Magnus, Dante's trip explores matter and motion at the same time it details Dante's approach to God.

Three major characters guide Dante: first Virgil, second a young woman named Beatrice, and finally St. Bernard. Dante regarded Virgil, who leads him through Hell and most of Purgatory, as the supreme pagan poet, representing the best of the classical literary tradition, much as Aristotle embodied philosophy for the scholastics. Beatrice (a character based on Beatrice Portinari, a woman Dante had loved and idealized) guided him through the last part of Purgatory and most of Paradise. Dante had met the real Beatrice in their native Florence, where she had died in her twenties; in his poem she symbolized the connection between human and divine love and the temporal and spiritual world. At the very end of the trip through Paradise, St. Bernard, the Cistercian abbot, leads Dante to God. Bernard's devotion to the Virgin

The Last Judgment
In Italy the artistic style of the mid-thirteenth century borrowed much from Byzantine models. This mosaic of the damned at the Last Judgment decorates the vault of the baptistery at Florence.

Mary and in turn her solicitude for Bernard epitomized for Dante the highest form of love. Such love merited the poet the most precious gift—the vision of God:

> *What I then saw is more than tongue can*
> *   say.*
> *Our human speech is dark before the vision.*
> *The ravished memory swoons and falls*
> *   away.*

Reflecting his own social and political concerns, Dante delighted in putting his enemies into Hell and his protectors into Paradise. Exiled from Florence by an opposing political faction, the bitter Dante prophesied:

> *Their bestiality will be made known*
> *   by what they do; while your fame shines*
> *   the brighter*
> *for having become a party of your own.*

Here the "you" refers to Dante, who thought of himself as a one-man party for unity and peace.

Like Dante, other writers of the period tried to harmonize the Aristotelian universe with the mysteries of faith. But they did not always follow the scholastic model in doing so. The anonymous author of the *Quest of the Holy Grail* (c. 1225), for example, used an Arthurian romance (a tale involving the knights of King Arthur's Round Table),

onto which he grafted theological and ecclesiastical teachings. His Lancelot is a sinner, spiritually blinded by his adultery with Guinevere. Galahad—whose virginity symbolizes both spiritual purity and chivalric gallantry—is the hero of the tale; he alone experiences the bliss of seeing fully the splendor of the grail:

> *a man [Josephus] came down from heaven*
> *garbed in a bishop's robes, and with a crozier*
> *in his hand and mitre on his head; four angels*
> *bore him on a glorious throne, which they set*
> *down next to the table supporting the Holy*
> *Grail . . . [On the table was a Holy Vessel.*
> *Josephus] took from the Vessel a host made in*
> *the likeness of bread. As he raised it aloft there*
> *descended from above a figure like to a child,*
> *whose countenance glowed and blazed as*
> *bright as fire; and he entered into the bread,*
> *which quite distinctly took on human form.*

Familiar characters were thus used to teach a lesson about the Eucharist, human morality, and the well-ordered universe.

Musicians, like poets, developed new forms that bridged sacred and secular subjects in the thirteenth and early fourteenth centuries. This connection appears in the most distinctive musical form of the thirteenth century, the *motet* (from the French *mot*, meaning "word"). The motet is an example of polyphony, music that consists of two or more melodies performed simultaneously. Before about 1215 almost all polyphony was sacred; purely secular polyphony was not common before the fourteenth century. The motet, a unique combination of the sacred and the secular, evidently originated in Paris, the center of scholastic culture as well.

The typical thirteenth-century motet has three melody lines (or "voices"). The lowest, usually from a liturgical chant melody, typically has no words and may have been played on an instrument rather than sung. The remaining melodies have different texts, either Latin or French (or one of each), which are sung simultaneously. Latin texts were usually sacred, whereas French ones were secular, dealing with themes such as love and springtime. In one example the top voice chirps in quick rhythm about a lady's charms ("Fair maiden, lovely and comely; pretty maiden, courteous and pleasing, delicious one . . . "); the middle voice slowly and lugubriously laments the "malady" of love; and the lowest voice sings a liturgical melody. The motet thus wove the sacred (the chant melody in the lowest voice) and the secular (the French texts in the upper voices) into a sophisticated tapestry of music. Johannes de Grocheo, writing in Paris around 1300, pronounced the motet far too subtle for ignorant people to appreciate. Like the scholastic *summae*, the motets were written by and for a clerical elite. Yet they also touched the lives of ordinary people. At least one motet included the calls of street vendors, and others reflected student life in the Paris cafes.

Complementing the motet's complexity was the development of a new notation for rhythm. By the eleventh century, musical notation could indicate pitch but had no way to denote the duration of the notes. Music theorists of the thirteenth century, however, developed increasingly precise methods to indicate rhythm. Franco of Cologne, for example, in his *Art of Measurable Song,* used different shapes to mark the number of beats each note should be held. His system became the basis of modern musical notation. Because each note could be allotted whatever duration the composer specified, notation with fixed beats allowed written music to express new and complicated rhythms. Thus music also reflected both the melding of the secular and the sacred and the possibilities of greater order and control.

The Order of High Gothic Art and Architecture

The drive for order and harmony also inspired developments in Gothic architecture. Gothic was largely an urban style popular across France, England, Spain, Germany, and the Low Countries. The construction of a Gothic church created jobs and promoted commerce, as new cathedrals required a small army of quarrymen, builders, carpenters, and glass cutters. Bishops, papal legates, and clerics planned and helped pay for these grand cathedrals, but townspeople generously financed and filled them. At Chartres (in France), for example, guilds raised money to pay for stained-glass windows, which depicted their patron saint; the shoemakers built their window to the Virgin Mary. The towns- people had good reason to support the church. Not only was the cathedral at Chartres a major shrine of the Virgin—it housed her blouse—but it was

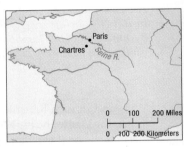

Chartres and Paris

Chartres Cathedral
The exterior of a Gothic church had an opaque and bristling look due to the patina of its stained glass and to its flying buttresses. Here Chartres cathedral towers above the other buildings. Little wonder that civic pride as well as religious piety focused on cathedrals.

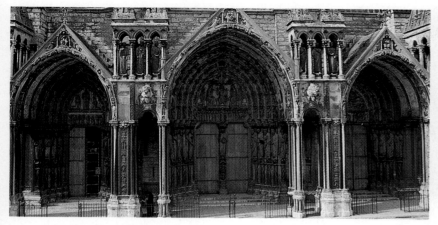

Chartres's Portal Program
At Chartres three flanking portals were used to present a complex and unified message in stone sculpture, as in this south portal complex. The left portal depicts the Martyrs, the right the Confessors, and the center the Last Judgment.

Christ Showing His Wounds
On the tympanum of the central door of the south portal, a wounded Christ sits between two intercessors, revealing both his human suffering and his divine power in one image.

also the town's center of commercial activity. In its crypt, wine merchants plied their trade, while just outside vendors sold every sort of goods. During great fairs honoring important holy days in Mary's life, pilgrims thronged the streets, the poor buying small lead figures of the Virgin, the rich purchasing wearable replicas of her blouse.

Workers began rebuilding the cathedral at Chartres after a fire in 1194 had burned all but the west facade. Learned masters, architects, and sculptors together created, in stone and glass, an image of heaven that made the cathedral a physical parallel to the scholastic *summae.* Just as St. Thomas Aquinas had presented the design of his arguments with utter clarity, so the Gothic church revealed its structure without disguise; and just as Thomas had bridged the earthly and celestial realms, so the cathedral elicited a response beyond reason, evoking a sense of awe.

Even today the church's exterior bristles with flying buttresses; these along with thick interior piers (pillars) and side aisles support the thrust of the vault, relieving the walls of the roof's heavy downward weight. Windows of stunning stained glass are set in the walls. The ribs of the vault start from the top of each regularly spaced pier, tying the building together formally, much like the repetition of the articles and objections in a Thomistic argument. Yet like the scholastic tension between reason and faith, the strain between what

is visible and rational and what defies reason is evident at Chartres cathedral. One knows the vault is heavy and pushes down on the piers, yet one "sees" the ribbed arches springing upward from the piers and the vault floating above on a band of light.

Gothic sculpture also reflected the triumphs and limits of knowledge, with each sculptural element part of a larger whole. On the south portal of Chartres cathedral, for example, stone figures and scenes surround three doors. The central pillar depicts Christ the teacher flanked by his Apostles. Over the central door, on the tympanum (the semicircular area above the doorway), two scenes illustrate the relationship between this world and the next. Below, Christ appears as judge in the Last Judgment while gleeful devils on his left "welcome" souls to hell; above this scene, Christ as the Son of Man shows his wounds. Christ the teacher thus establishes the church that leads to salvation because of his suffering on the cross. The two side portals address the same themes: the left tympanum shows the martyrdom of St. Stephen, who followed Christ in suffering; the right portrays several scenes of the good works necessary for redemption. Like Dante's *Divine Comedy*, these images represent a pilgrimage from this world to eternal life, with each element leading toward heaven. Working within a tradition of Gothic style, yet also experimenting with new combinations, the builders of Chartres

Orvieto Cathedral
In Italy Gothic elements were used only selectively. The cathedral of Orvieto shown here was begun c. 1290. Its builders chose to use round arches and abundant wall space decorated with patterns of light and dark.

Baptistery Pulpit by Nicola Pisano
The Italian sculptor Nicola Pisano drew upon many traditions, including those of the classical world. Here the panel of the Magi adoring the Christ child is part of a complex program of sculpture on a pulpit at Pisa.

cathedral used elements from earlier Gothic churches, such as the cathedral at Laon, where one tympanum had also placed the Last Judgment below the sculpture of Christ as Son of Man. At Chartres, however, the scene became part of a coherent scheme that could be read across three doors.

The Gothic style varied by region, no more so than in Italy, where local traditions prevailed. The outer walls of the cathedral at Orvieto, for example, alternate bricks of light and dark color, providing texture instead of glass and light; and the vault over the large nave is round rather than pointed, recalling the Roman aqueducts that could still be seen in Italy when the builders were designing the cathedral. With no flying buttresses and relatively few portals surrounded by sculpture, Italian churches conveyed a spirit of austerity and spareness, even though they incorporated other characteristically "Gothic" features. San Andrea, in Vercelli, for example, had pointed arches and a rose window in the apse. The importance of walls and the interplay between light- and dark-colored elements in the interior made Italian churches very different from French Gothic cathedrals.

The Italian sculptor Nicola Pisano (c. 1220–1278?) fused Gothic sculptural forms with classical Roman styles. Nicola's baptistery pulpit at Pisa shows drapery much like that in contemporary French figural sculpture, and the themes depicted (scenes from Christ's life) stretch across several panels, as at Chartres cathedral; but the heads of the figures are clearly based on ancient reliefs. Nicola's work thus synthesized several traditions.

By the early fourteenth century the expansive sculptures so prominent in architecture were reflected in painting as well. This new style is evident in the paintings of Giotto (1266–1337), a Florentine artist. For example he filled the walls of a private chapel at Padua with frescoes depicting scenes from Christ's life. In these frescoes he experimented with the illusion of depth. Giotto's figures, appearing weighty and voluminous, expressed a range of emotions as they seemed to move across interior and exterior spaces. In bringing sculptural realism to a flat surface, Giotto changed the emphasis of painting, which had been predominantly symbolic, decorative, and intellectual. His works instead stressed three-dimensionality, illusional space, and human emotion. By melding earthy sensibilities with religious themes, Giotto found yet another way to bring together the natural and divine realms.

Giotto's Pietà
The grieving Mary of Giotto's pietà is an example of the artist's ability to depict deeply personal human feeling. This scene is part of a large cycle of frescos that Giotto painted on the walls of a private chapel at Padua. Private patronage of such art went hand-in-hand with interest in celebrating individuality.

The Politics of Control

The quest for order, control, and harmony also became part of the political agendas of princes, popes, and cities. These rulers and institutions imposed—or tried to—their authority more fully and systematically through taxes, courts, and sometimes representative institutions. The roots of modern European parliaments and of the U.S. Congress can be traced to this era. In the thirteenth century both secular and church rulers endeavored to expand their spheres of power and eliminate opposition. This process forced them to increase their sources of revenues to pay for new militias and officials in an era of economic contraction.

Limits of Economic Growth

Economic expansion in the early thirteenth century had benefited from the demographic growth and land reclamation that had begun in the tenth century.

But by 1300 the only land left uncleared in France and England was marginal or unworkable with the tools of the day. People produced more than ever before, but families also had more hungry mouths to feed: by the end of the thirteenth century, a single plot in England, for example, was divided into twenty tiny parcels for the progeny of the original peasant holder. In the region around Paris, one small farm had fragmented into seventy-eight pieces. The last known French *villeneuve* ("new town") was founded in 1246; after that new settlements ceased. Population growth seems to have leveled off by then, but the static supply of farmland meant that France and England from the mid-thirteenth century onward faced sudden and severe grain shortages. Climatic changes compounded the demographic situation. In 1309 an extremely wet growing season ruined the grain harvest in southern and western Germany; the towns, where food had to be imported, were especially hard hit. When heavy and persistent rains inundated Flanders in 1315, grain prices soared. A chronicler lamented,

The people were in such great need that it cannot be expressed. For the cries that were heard from the poor would move a stone, as they lay in the streets with woe and great complaint, swollen with hunger and remaining dead of poverty, so that many were thrown by set numbers, sixty and even more, into a pit.

Warfare also took its toll on economic life. In attempts to consolidate their rule, princes hired mercenary troops but paid them such poor wages that they plundered the countryside even when they were not fighting. Warring armies had always disrupted farms, ruining the fields as they passed; but in the thirteenth century, burning became a battle tactic, used both to devastate the enemy's territory and to teach a lesson. Here too the cities felt the repercussions. A city's own army could defend its walls against roving troops, but it could not stop the flow of refugees who streamed in seeking safety. Lille's population, for example, nearly doubled as a result of the wars between Flanders and France during the first two decades of the thirteenth century. Meanwhile, like other Flemish cities, Lille had to impose new taxes on its population to pay for its huge war debts.

Pressed by war debts, the need for food, and the desire for gain, landlords and town officials alike strove to get more money. Everywhere, customary and other dues were deemed inadequate. In 1315 the king of France offered liberty to all his serfs, but mainly to assess a new war tax on all free men. In other parts of France, lords imposed a *taille*, an annual money payment; many peasants went into debt to pay it. Professional moneylenders set up loan offices in the countryside; or wealthy neighbors served as unofficial creditors. Although richer peasants might prosper as creditors, the cycle of loan, debt, and payment left poorer peasants even more impoverished.

In other areas, such as Italy, England, and southern Germany, lords found it useful to give their peasants short-term leases. Bypassing the fixed and customary dues whose value decreased as prices rose, these lords simply charged a rent that changed with the market. In Bavaria, for example, the abbot of Baumburg met with his peasants each year to announce new leases and negotiate new rents. In Italy, where peasants had long labored under twenty-five-year leases, landlords and cities introduced a short-term lease. This new lease enabled one monastery in Milan to double its rental income.

To enforce their new taxes and lease arrangements, great lords, both lay and ecclesiastical, installed local agents eager to collect taxes and to draft young village men into military service. These officials lived near the villages in fortified houses and maintained a watchful eye on local conditions. They kept account books and computed their profits and costs. One calculated, for example, that

You can well have three acres weeded for a penny, and an acre of meadow for fourpence, and an acre of waste meadow for threepence-halfpenny. . . . And know that five men can well reap and bind two acres a day of each kind of [grain], more or less. And where each takes twopence a day then you must give five-pence an acre.

Although the cities were affected by the crises in the countryside during the thirteenth century, they were cushioned from their most devastating effects. In many instances the cities acted as lords over local cultivators, with rights to tax and requisition food as needed. Wars brought grief to some cities, but others profited from weapons trade. The textile industry in the older cities of Flanders declined after 1270 because a political dispute cut off supplies of wool from England; but new textile centers arose to replace them. Throughout the thirteenth century the "busts" of the business cycle were followed by "booms," so that despite hints of serious decline, such as the cessation of population growth in Florence, major decreases in business activity in the urban sector would become clear only later in the fourteenth century.

The Clash of Imperial and Papal Aims

Thirteenth-century kings and princes everywhere worked to expand and consolidate their territories as well as their taxes. With the aid of salaried agents and the backing of lawyers schooled in Roman and canon law, this impulse for growth proceeded with thoroughness even when the enlarged territory ultimately split apart, as happened when Frederick II (1194–1250) attempted to unite the kingdom of Sicily with the empire of his father, Henry VI, and his grandfather, Frederick I Barbarossa. Frederick II, called in his own day the *stupor mundi*, or "won-

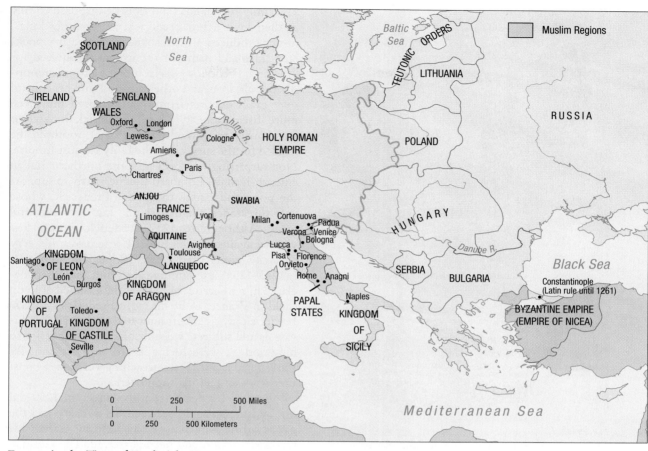

Europe in the Time of Frederick II, 1212–1250

der of the world," spanned two cultures, as heir to Sicily on his mother's side and to Germany through his father. In Sicily he dealt with a diverse and cosmopolitan population of Jews, Muslims, and Christians; employed Muslim servants and concubines at court; and drew upon Byzantine and Norman traditions to rule his kingdom. From Byzantium he had the model of the late Roman emperor, fount of law and head of the church; from the Normans he acquired his position as feudal monarch holding sway over his barons. The Norman conquerors of Sicily had become vassals of the pope, so the king also had (at least theoretically) both the obligation of defending the pope and the honor of representing him. In Germany, however, Frederick found a different set of traditions; there Christian princes, often churchmen with ministerial retinues, were

acutely aware of their constitutive role in kingship and their government rights and privileges.

Frederick wanted to retain both his kingdoms, but the popes feared the papal states would be encircled and strangled; and the popes themselves were interested in territorial expansion. Already, Innocent III had raised money and troops to make good his claim to "all the land from Radicofani [in the north] to Ceprano [in the south], the exarchate of Ravenna, Pentapolis, the march, the duchy of Spoleto [and so on]." From these regions the pope expected dues and taxes, military service, and the profits of justice.

Almost as soon as he was crowned emperor, in 1220, Frederick's policies alienated the papacy, and he and his successors struggled against the popes, often in outright warfare, through almost

Frederick II
Emperor Frederick II was interested not only in politics but also in the natural world. On the margins of a treatise on falconry that he wrote, Frederick is depicted as both ruler and teacher.

the entire thirteenth century. Frederick had a three-pronged strategy. First, he left Germany to the princes, granting them concessions that allowed them to turn their principalities into virtually independent states in exchange for their support or neutrality. Second, Frederick revamped the government of Sicily to give him more control and yield greater profits. The *Constitutions of Melfi*, a collection of old and new laws issued by Frederick in 1231, touched upon every important aspect of his kingdom. Anxious that official documents be legible, for example, he declared that notaries must use a simple style of handwriting; concerned that Jews and Muslims were unfairly persecuted, he allowed them to initiate court cases. The *Constitutions* exhorted agents of the government to be just, specifying that no justiciar could hold court where

his family held lands (and thus be disposed to rule in their favor). For Frederick, as for other kings, justice produced profits, as the royal treasury pocketed fines and many of the expenses required for litigation. Frederick's declaration of a royal monopoly on salt, iron, and other minerals and his control over grain exports from Sicily assured him even more fiscal bounty. Third, Frederick looked to Lombardy to provide the crucial foothold he needed for the survival of the Holy Roman Empire. Not surprisingly, however, some northern Italian cities revived the Lombard League, partly to support the pope and partly to oppose Frederick, whose rule threatened them with the loss of rights and taxes. Although in 1237 Frederick won a key victory against the league at Cortenuova, his very success jeopardized him: Pope Innocent IV (*1243–1254) excommunicated him and then declared him a heretic. In 1245, at the Council of Lyon (held in France, to be far from Frederick's forces) Frederick was excommunicated and deposed; his vassals and subjects were absolved of their fealty to him; and all were forbidden to support him. By 1248, papal legates were preaching a crusade against Frederick and all his supporters.

Frederick's death from dysentery in 1250 did not end the struggle between his dynasty and the papacy. But long before the fighting ended, his territorial vision had been shattered. The German princes won their independence, so that between 1254 and 1273, a period called the Great Interregnum, Germany had virtually no king. Finally in 1273 the princes elected Rudolf (*1273–1291), whose family, the Habsburgs, was new to imperial power. Rudolf used the imperial title to consolidate his own principality in Swabia (southwestern Germany), but he did not try to maintain traditional imperial prerogatives. Although emperors continued to be crowned for centuries thereafter, they wielded power based on their estates and principalities rather than on a tradition of imperial rights. A fragmented Germany would endure until the nineteenth century.

Sicily was also severed from imperial rule. In 1254, Pope Innocent IV asked Henry III of England to accept the crown of Sicily on behalf of the king's second son, Edmund. When Henry could not rally the support the papacy required, however, the offer was rescinded. In 1262, Pope Urban IV (*1261–1264) called upon Charles, the count of Anjou and brother of France's king Louis IX, to lead a crusade against Sicily and its ruler, Frederick's son Manfred. Promised troops, ships, and the proceeds from a crusading tax levied on French churchmen, Charles marched into Sicily in 1266, killed Manfred, and took the title of king. As a result, France was tied to southern Italy. Rebellion soon followed, however, beginning in 1282 during the so-called Sicilian Vespers, and forces loyal to Manfred's daughter called in her husband, the king of Aragon (in Spain), to take Sicily's throne and oust the Angevins. The move left two enduring claimants to Sicily's crown: the kings of Aragon and the house of Anjou. And it spawned a long war that impoverished the region.

Sicily and Italy at the End of the Thirteenth Century

In the struggle between pope and emperor, the pope had clearly won, at a moment that marked a high point in the political power of the medieval papacy. Innocent's attack on Frederick's orthodoxy had been so convincing that even Dante—no friend of the papacy—placed Frederick in the circle of Hell reserved for heretics. Nevertheless, others agreed with Frederick II's view that the popes' tampering with secular matters had demeaned and sullied their office: "these men who feign holiness," Frederick sneered, referring to the popes, are "drunk with the pleasures of the world." Scattered throughout Germany were groups of devout (but heretical) Christians who believed Frederick was a divine scourge sent to overpower a materialistic papacy. The papacy won the war against the Staufer, but at a cost. Even St. Louis criticized the popes for doing "new and unheard of things."

The Separation of Royal and Ecclesiastical Power

The power and prestige of the king of France increased greatly under St. Louis, who vigorously imposed his laws and justice over much of France while maintaining generally excellent relations with the pope. The influence of the *Parlement** of Paris, the royal court of justice, increased significantly during his reign. Originally a changeable and moveable body, part of the king's personal entourage when he dealt with litigation, it was now permanently housed in Paris and staffed by professional judges who heard cases and recorded their decisions. Louis also thoroughly restructured the administration of Paris by appointing a salaried official there. The interests of good government and fiscal well-being went hand-in-hand. As Joinville pointed out:

> People came to [Louis's kingdom] for the good justice to be obtained. Population and prosperity so increased that the revenue from sales of land, death duties, commerce and other sources was double what the king received before.

Louis's subjects began to develop a new ideal of kingship, that of a ruler who was less concerned with military matters than with staying home to administer justice and maintain civil peace. Although Louis remained in France for long periods, he left home more often than his subjects would have liked, twice leading unsuccessful crusades to the Holy Land. When Louis took his second crusading vow, Joinville complained:

> I considered that all those who had advised the king to go on this expedition committed mortal sin. For at that time [before the king left] the state of the country was such that there was perfect peace throughout the kingdom . . . while ever since King Louis went away the state of the kingdom has done nothing but go from bad to worse.

Because Louis had died on this crusade, Joinville's words here implicitly criticized the government of Louis' successor, Philip III (*1270–1285). However, he was also making a point about good

---

*Although *Parlement* and *Parliament* are very similar words, both deriving from the French word *parler*, meaning "to speak," the institutions they named were very different. The Parlement of France was a law court, whereas the English Parliament, although beginning as a court to redress grievances, had by 1327 become above all a representative institution. The major French representative assembly, the Estates General, first convened at the beginning of the fourteenth century.

rulership, praising the steady administrator above the heroic crusader.

Accepting limits on his power in relation to the church, Louis did not demand greater jurisdiction over churchmen; but he deftly maintained the royal dignity while recognizing church authority. Joinville liked to tell of a confrontation between the king and a French bishop:

Your Majesty [said the bishop], the archbishops and bishops here present have charged me to tell you that the honor of Christendom is declining in your hands. It will decline still further unless you give some thought to it, because no man stands in fear of excommunication at this present time. We therefore require your Majesty to command your bailiffs and your other officers of the law to compel all persons who have been under sentence of excommunication for a year and a day to make their peace with the Church.

Louis responded by saying that he would be happy to intervene if he were allowed to judge each case himself. The bishop refused, denying the king jurisdiction in spiritual matters. Then, concluded Joinville,

The King replied that he in his turn would not give them knowledge of such matters as fell within his jurisdiction, nor order his officers to compel all excommunicated persons to obtain absolution, irrespective of whether sentence of excommunication had been rightly or wrongly pronounced. "For if I did so," he added, "I should be acting contrary to God's laws and the principles of justice."

Thus without questioning the church's power in spiritual matters such as excommunication, Louis asserted the independence of his own temporal authority.

The Birth of Representative Institutions

As thirteenth-century monarchs and princes expanded their powers, they devised formal institutions to enlist more broadly based support: all across Europe, from Spain to Poland, from England to Hungary, rulers summoned parliaments. These grew out of the ad hoc advisory sessions kings had held with their nobles and clergy, men who informally represented the two most powerful classes, or orders, of medieval society. In the thirteenth century the advisory sessions turned into solemn, formal meetings of representatives of the orders to the king's Great Council, the origin of parliamentary sessions. Although these bodies differed from place to place, the impulse behind their creation was similar. Beginning as assemblies where kings celebrated their own royal power and prestige and where the orders simply assented to royal policy, they eventually became organs through which people not ordinarily at court could articulate their wishes.

The orders, which evolved from the idealized functional categories of the tenth century (those who pray, those who fight, and those who work), consisted of the clergy, nobles, and commoners of the realm. Unlike modern "classes," which are defined largely by economic status, medieval orders cut across economic boundaries. The "order of clerics," for example, embraced the clergy from the most humble parish priest to the most exalted archbishop and pope. The "order of commoners" theoretically included both rich merchants and poor peasants. But the notion of orders was an idealized abstraction; in practice thirteenth-century kings did not so much command representatives of the orders to come to court as they simply summoned the most powerful members of their realm, whether clerics, nobles, or important townsmen, to support their policies. In thirteenth-century León (present-day Spain), for example, the king sometimes called only the clergy and nobles; sometimes, especially when he wanted the help of their militias, he sent for representatives of the towns. As townsmen gradually began to participate regularly in advisory sessions, kings came to depend upon them and their support. In turn commoners became more fully integrated into the work of royal government.

The *cortes* of Castile-León were among the earliest representative assemblies called to the king's court and the first to include townsmen. As the *reconquista* pushed southward across the Iberian Peninsula, Christian kings called for settlers to occupy new frontiers. Enriched by plunder, fledgling villages soon burgeoned into major commercial centers. Like the cities of Italy, Spanish towns dominated the countryside. Their leaders—called *caballeros villanos,* or "city horsemen," because they were rich enough to fight on horseback—monopolized the municipal offices. In 1188, when King

Spain in the Thirteenth Century

Alfonso IX (*1188–1230) had summoned townsmen to the *cortes,* the city caballeros served as their representatives, agreeing to Alfonso's plea for military and financial support and for help in consolidating his rule. Once convened at court (Toledo, Burgos, and Seville were favorite places) these wealthy townsmen joined bishops and noblemen in formally counseling the king and assenting to royal decisions. They played a role, for example, in recognizing Berenguela, the daughter of King Alfonso X (*1252–1284), as his heir in 1254. They were also present in 1277 when the *cortes* granted the same king a special tax to defend his king-dom, and two years later reluctantly agreed to still another levy. Thus beginning with Alfonso X, Castilian monarchs regularly called on the *cortes* to participate in major political and military issues and to assent to new taxes to finance them.

The English Parliament also developed at a time of royal strength, when the twelfth-century King Henry II had consulted prelates and barons at Great Councils. Henry II had used these parliaments as his tool, but the government of Henry III (*1216–1272) marked a change. Crowned at the age of nine, Henry III was king in name only during the first sixteen years of his reign, when England was governed by a council consisting of a few barons, professional administrators, and a papal legate. Although not quite "government by Parliament," this council set a precedent for baronial self-rule later, when Henry's popularity plummeted.

Periodically during the first half of Henry's reign the barons would make sure that he reaffirmed the provisions of the Magna Carta, which (in their view at least) gave them an important and permanent role in royal government as the king's advisors and a solid guarantee of their customary rights and privileges. As late as 1237, when Henry needed money to pay for military campaigns against Louis IX (whom he was fighting for the lands lost by John), the barons insisted that he reissue the Magna Carta in return for their agreement to pay an extra-

ordinary feudal aid. But Henry had no intention of consistently soliciting or heeding the barons' advice, preferring instead to listen to a group of nobles from Poitiers, his half-brothers by his mother's second marriage, and favoring another faction of notables from Savoy (today in southeastern France), his wife's relatives. He further alienated the barons because all his military objectives ultimately failed. At the same time, he estranged the English clergy by allowing the pope to appoint "foreigners" (mostly Italians) to well-endowed church positions. Many nobles and commoners alike complained that Henry was acting arbitrarily and unjustly.

When in 1254, Henry agreed to accept the Sicilian crown from the pope on behalf of his son Edmund, he also promised to pay the papacy's enormous war debt, incurred in its ongoing battle against the Staufer kings. Henry tried to raise the money, but the barons thwarted his attempts. The pope, angry that payments were not forthcoming, threatened to excommunicate Henry. In 1258, matters came to a head when a parliament of great magnates, lay and clerical, met at Oxford to discuss the papal demands. The barons, enraged and determined not to be deluded again by a temporary reissue of the Magna Carta, threatened to rebel; they forced Henry to dismiss his foreign advisors; to rule with the advice of a Council of Fifteen chosen jointly by the barons and the king; and to make his chief officers, such as the treasurer and chancellor, more professional by limiting their terms and making them accountable to the council.

The new government, controlled by the barons, swiftly repudiated the Sicilian crown and the financial commitments that went with it and made peace with Louis IX. But when it appointed new judges to consider local grievances, some barons defected, for the reforms struck at their own local authority. Torn by factions, the baronial party grew weaker, whereas Henry rallied new support. The pope even absolved him from his promise at Oxford. Both sides—the baronial reformers and the monarchists—were armed and intransigent, and in 1264 civil war erupted. At the battle of Lewes in the same year, the leader of the baronial opposition, Simon de Montfort (c. 1208–1265), routed the king's forces, captured the king, and became England's de facto ruler. Because only a minority of the barons followed Simon, he sought new support by convening a parliament in 1265, to which he summoned not only the earls, barons, and churchmen who backed him but also representatives from the towns, the "commons"—and he appealed for their help. Thus for the first time the commons were given a voice in government. Even though Simon's brief rule ended that very year and Henry's son Edward I (*1272–1307) became a rallying point for royalists, the idea of representative government in England had emerged, born out of the interplay between royal initiatives and baronial revolts.

The Collision of Pope and King

In France, too, the king sometimes called local assemblies representing the orders; but a French national representative body—the Estates General—originated in the conflict between Pope Boniface VIII and King Philip IV (Philip the Fair) (*1285–1314). This confrontation seemed at the time simply one more episode in the ongoing struggle between medieval popes and rulers for power and authority. On both sides arguments about jurisdictions and rights echoed themes raised in the eleventh century during the Gregorian reform movement and in the twelfth and early thirteenth centuries during the clashes between popes and emperors. But western European kings now, at the end of the thirteenth century, had more power, making the standoff between Boniface and Philip a turning point that weakened the papacy and strengthened the monarchy.

The Reign of Philip the Fair

When Boniface VIII (*1294–1303) became pope, France's Philip the Fair and England's Edward I had just begun a war, which the kings financed by taxing their prelates along with everyone else, as if they were preparing for a crusade and could expect church support. Without even pretending any concern for clerical autonomy, Edward's men, for example, forced open church vaults to confiscate money for the royal coffers.

For the kings of both England and France the principle of national sovereignty now allowed them to claim jurisdiction over all people, even churchmen, who lived within their borders. For the pope, however, the principle at stake was his role as head of the clergy. Boniface asserted that only the pope could authorize the taxation of clerics, and in 1296 he issued the bull* *Clericis Laicos,* which conveyed in sharp language his anger over royal taxation of the clergy:

> *That laymen have been very hostile to the clergy antiquity relates; and it is clearly proved by the experiences of the present time. For not content with what is their own the laity strive for what is forbidden and loose the reins for things unlawful.*

Boniface threatened to excommunicate kings who taxed prelates without papal permission, and he called upon clerics to disobey any such royal orders.

Edward and Philip reacted swiftly to *Clericis Laicos.* Taking advantage of the important role English courts played in protecting the peace, Edward declared that all clerics who refused to pay his taxes would be considered outlaws—literally "outside the law." Clergymen who were robbed, for example, would have no recourse against their attackers; if accused of crimes, they would have no defense in court. Relying on a different strategy, Philip forbade the exportation of precious metals, money, or jewels, effectively sealing French borders. Immediately the English clergy cried out for legal protection, while the papacy itself cried out for the revenues it had long enjoyed from France. Just one year after issuing *Clericis Laicos,* Boniface backed down, conceding that kings had the right to tax their clergy in emergencies.

In 1301, Philip the Fair tested his jurisdiction in southern France by arresting Bernard Saisset, the bishop of Pamiers, on a charge of treason for slandering the king by comparing him to an owl, "the handsomest of birds which is worth absolutely nothing." Saisset's imprisonment violated the principle, maintained both by the pope and by French law, that a clergyman was not subject to lay justice. Boniface's angry reaction declared that the pope "holds the place on earth of Him who is alone lord and master," and that Philip should never imagine "that you have no superior or that you are

---

*An official papal document was called a bull from the *bulla*, or seal, that was used to authenticate it.

Philip the Fair and Edward I
*Philip the Fair on the right and Edward I on the left
confront each other in this contemporary sketch, written on a copy of the truce that the two kings declared
in 1298. The impassive look on Philip's face is consistent with Bernard Saisset's wry comparison of Philip
and an owl.*

not subject to the head of the ecclesiastical hierarchy," suggesting that the pope was the king's
superior in matters both temporal and spiritual.
Philip quickly seized the opportunity to deride and
humiliate Boniface, directing his agents to forge
and broadly circulate a new papal letter, a parody
of the original, which read, "We want you to know
that you are subject to us in spiritualities and
temporalities." At the same time, he convened
representatives of the clergy, nobles, and townspeople to explain, justify, and propagandize his
position. This new assembly, which met at Paris in
1302, was the ancestor of the Estates General,[*]
which would meet sporadically for centuries thereafter—for the last time in 1789, at the beginning of

the French Revolution. Most of those present at the
assembly of 1302 supported Philip, wrote letters of
protest to the cardinals, and referred to Boniface
not as pope but as "he who now presides over the
government of the Church."

Boniface's reply, the bull *Unam Sanctam*, intensified the situation to fever pitch with the words:
"Therefore we declare, state, define and pronounce
that it is altogether necessary to salvation for every
human creature to be subject to the Roman Pontiff."
At meetings of the king's inner circle, Philip's
agents declared Boniface a false pope and accused
him of sexual perversion, various crimes, and
heresy: "He has a private demon whose advice he
follows in all things. . . . He is a Sodomite and keeps
concubines. . . . He has had many clerics killed in
his presence, rejoicing in their deaths . . . ," and so
on. The king sent his commissioners to the various
provinces of France to convene local meetings to
popularize his charges against Boniface and gain
support. These meetings, which included clergy,
local nobles, townspeople, and even villagers, almost
unanimously denounced the pope, although a few
nobles, such as the officials of Montpellier, demurred.
Perhaps the most striking support came from the
clergy, who were beginning to view themselves as
members of a free Gallican church largely independent of the papacy. Finally in 1303, royal agents,
acting under Philip's orders, invaded Boniface's
palace at Anagni (southeast of Rome) to capture
the pope, bring him to France, and try him. Fearing
for the pope's life, however, the people of Anagni
joined forces and drove the French agents out of
town. Yet even after such public support for the
pope, the king had won. Boniface died very shortly
thereafter, and the next two popes quickly pardoned
Philip and his agents for their actions.

Significantly, the second of those popes,
Clement V (*1305–1314) was a Frenchman.
Though he sought a path of compromise with the
cardinals faithful to the memory of Boniface VIII,
civil strife prevented him from entering Italy. After moving about in France for several years,
Clement finally in 1309 set up his headquarters at
Avignon, a central location for Germany, France,
and Italy. Here the popes remained until 1378. The
period from 1309 to 1378 came to be called the
Babylonian Captivity by Europeans sensitive to
having the popes live far from Rome, on the Rhône
River. Fourteenth-century popes continued to
preside over a wealthy and busy ecclesiastical

---

[*]In France the various orders—clergy, nobles, and commoners—
were called "estates."

enterprise, but the pope's prestige and authority had diminished. The delicate balance between church and state, a hallmark of the years of St. Louis, reflecting as much a search for harmony as a quest for power, broke down by the end of the thirteenth century. The quest for control led not to harmony but to confrontation and extremism. Recognizing new limits, the Avignon popes established a sober and efficient organization that took in regular revenues and gave the popes more say than ever before in the appointment of churchmen. They would, however, slowly abandon the idea of leading all of Christendom and tacitly recognize the growing power of the secular states to regulate their own internal affairs.

The Fate of the Communes

Like kings, the cities of northern and central Italy asserted their power, but on a lesser scale. Florence, for example, imposed its rule still more firmly on its *contado,* where serfdom had long ago given way to the system of short-term land leasing and sharecropping. Statutes drawn up by the Italian city governments supported the interests of landowners in the city rather than the cultivators. At Bologna, for example, the laws demanded tenant farmers plow the land fully four times before sowing seed; this measure was meant to ensure greater yield, but it greatly burdened the country folk.

Major Cities of Northern and Central Italy

With such statutes, Italian cities regulated, ordered, and controlled the countryside. Control over the communal government meant power to tax and distribute the revenues, make appointments to both clerical and government positions, and market the food produced by the *contado.* Dominated by rival noble families, the cities were arenas of strife during the wars between the popes and the Staufer, with the Guelph nobles and their allies taking up the papal cause and the Ghibellines championing the emperor. Hiding behind these labels, however, were often self-interested communal factions who struggled to undermine one another and appropriate their opponents' power and property.

In the course of the thirteenth century still newer groups, generally from the nonnoble classes, also attempted to take over the reins of power in the commune. The *popolo,* as such groups were called, incorporated members of other city associations—craft and merchant guilds, parishes, and the commune itself. In fact, the *popolo* was itself a kind of alternative commune, a sworn association in each city, dedicated to upholding the interests of its members. Generally the wealthier craftsmen rather than the poor joined the *popolo:* at Padua, for example, the right to elect *popolo* officers was denied to "sailors, gardeners, agricultural labourers, landless men and herdsmen." Despite the exclusivity of its membership, the *popolo* welcomed the military aid of the lower classes. Armed and militant, the *popolo* demanded a share in city government, particularly to gain a voice in matters of taxation. In 1222 at Piacenza, for example, the *popolo's* members won half the government offices; a year later they and the nobles worked out a plan to share the

Siena Communal Palace
This communal palace, built at Siena between 1297 and 1310, expresses the enormous power Italian city governments wanted to hold over both the citizens within the walls and the peasants who lived in the outlying contado.

election of their city's podesta. Such power sharing often resulted from the *popolo's* struggle. In some cities nobles overcame and dissolved the *popolo;* but others virtually excluded the nobles from government. Constantly confronting one another, quarreling, feuding, and compromising, such factions as the Guelphs, Ghibellines, nobles, and *popolo* turned Italian cities into centers of civil discord.

Weakened by this constant friction, the communes were tempting prey for great regional nobles who, allying with one or another faction, tried to establish themselves as *signori* (singular, *signore,* meaning "lord") of the cities, keeping the peace at the price of repression. Ezzelino da Romano, for example, whose family commanded knightly vassals and great swaths of land in the countryside around Venice, seized control over most of the cities surrounding Verona by allying himself with Frederick II and his supporters. Here, as in other cities, the commune gave way to the *signoria* (a state ruled by a signore), with one family dominating the government. Based in one city, the signore extended his authority to neighboring cities as well. Oberto Pallavicini, with a following of German mercenaries, for example, first gained Cremona and then had himself declared "perpetual podesta" at Pavia, Vercelli, and Piacenza. The fate of Piacenza over the course of the thirteenth century was typical: first dominated by nobles, its commune eventually granted the *popolo* a voice by the first quarter of the thirteenth century; but then by the middle of the century the signore's power eclipsed both the nobles and the *popolo.*

The Mongol Invasions in a Fragmented East

Outside western Europe the fragmentation of political power left the East vulnerable to invasions from Asia in the thirteenth century. Byzantium had a tradition of central authority and administration, but military and economic factors weakened its government. With Constantinople seized by western Europeans in the Fourth Crusade, a Byzantine "government in exile" moved to parts of Greece and Asia Minor. In 1261, Michael VIII Palaeologus (*1261–1282) recaptured Constantinople and reestablished the Byzantine Empire. But Byzantium's position was precarious. It had to combat renewed invasions by western princes and protect its eastern flank, where the Ottoman Turks had

seized territories. These military emergencies prevented the Byzantine emperors from restoring central government with the old *theme* system. Instead the empire's lands were divvied up among members of the imperial family and other aristocrats, and what taxes were collected more often ended up in the pockets of local magnates than the coffers of the emperor.

Nevertheless, Byzantium remained strong enough to deter an attack from the Mongols, whose invasions elsewhere across Russia, eastern Europe, and Asia constituted one of the most astonishing movements of the Middle Ages. On the northern border of China in present-day Mongolia, various tribes of mixed ethnic origins and traditions fused into an aggressive army under the leadership of Chingiz (or Genghis) Khan (c. 1162–1227) at the beginning of the thirteenth century. In part, economic necessity impelled them, because climatic changes had reduced the grasslands that sustained their animals and their nomadic way of life. But their advance out of Mongolia also represented the political strategy of Chingiz, who reckoned that military offensives would keep the tribes united under him. By 1215 the Mongols (also called the Tatars or Tartars) held Beijing and most of northern China. Some years later they moved through central Asia and skirted the Caspian Sea. In the 1230s they began concerted attacks in Europe—in Russia, Poland, and Hungary, where their formidable armies and tactics were no match for weak native princes. Only the death of their Great Khan, Chingiz's son Ögödei (1186–1241), and disputes over his succession prevented a concentrated assault on Germany. In the course of the 1250s the Mongols took Iran, Baghdad, and Damascus, stopped in their conquest of the Muslim world only by the Egyptian armies.

The Mongols' sophisticated and devastating military tactics led to their overwhelming success. Organizing their campaigns at meetings held far in advance of their planned attack, they devised two- and three-flank operations. The invasion of Hungary, for example, was two-pronged: one division of their army arrived from Russia while the other moved through Poland and Germany. Perhaps half the population of Hungary perished in the assault as the Mongols, fighting mainly on horseback, with heavy lances and powerful bows and arrows whose shots traveled far and penetrated deeply, crushed the Hungarian army of mixed infantry and cavalry.

The attack on the West began with Russia, where the Mongols had the most lasting impact. At Vladimir in Suzdal', the strongest Russian principality, they broke through the defensive walls of the cities and burned the populace huddled for protection in the cathedral. Their most important victory in Russia was the capture of Kiev in 1240. Making the mouth of the Volga River the center of their power in Russia, the Mongols dominated all of Russia's principalities for about two hundred years.

The Mongol empire in Russia, later called the Golden Horde ("golden" probably from the color of their leader's tent; "horde" from a Turkish word meaning "camp"), adopted much of the local government apparatus. The Mongols standardized the collection of taxes and the recruitment of troops by basing them on a population census, and they allowed Russian princes to continue ruling as long as they paid homage and tribute to the khan. The Mongol overlords even exempted the Russian church from their taxes. At Ryazan (southeast of Moscow), for example, the traditional princely dynasty continued to sit upon the throne, and there (in the words of a later writer), "The pious Grand Prince Ingvar . . . renewed the land of Ryazan and built churches and monasteries, he consoled new-comers and gathered together the people." Alexander Nevsky, grand prince of Novgorod (*1252–1263), came from an old ruling family, but he personally owed his accession to the throne to Mongol support, and he continued to rely on their help as he skirmished with the Swedes, Germans, and Lithuanians who raided his principality; feuded with other claimants to his throne; and put down rebels who opposed his submission to the Mongols.

The Mongol invasions changed the political configuration of Europe and Asia. Because the Mongols were willing to deal with westerners, one consequence of their conquests was to open China to Europeans for the first time. Some missionaries, diplomats, and merchants traveled overland to China; others set sail from the Persian Gulf (where, in Iran, the Mongols had set up a khanate) and rounded India before arriving in China. Some hoped to enlist the aid of the Mongols against the Muslims; others expected to make new converts to Christianity; still others dreamed of lucrative trade routes. The most famous of these travelers was Marco Polo (1254–1324), son of a merchant family from Venice. Marco's father and uncle had already been to China and met Khubilai, the Great Khan,

The Mongol Empire After 1259

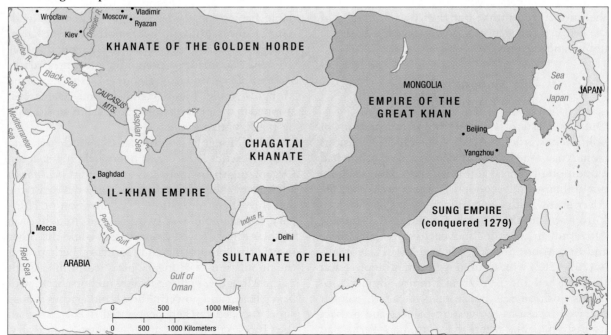

Mongols
In 1258, under the leadership of Hülegü, the Mongols captured Baghdad and brought the Abbasid Caliphate to an end. This Persian manuscript shows the Mongol army besieging a citadel.

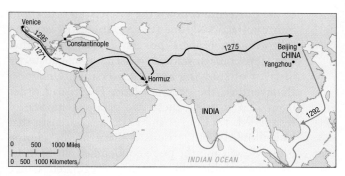

Marco Polo's Travels to and from China

conquerors in China, they trusted foreigners more than native Chinese and willingly received Europeans. In fact, evidence suggests that an entire community of Venetian traders lived in the city of Yangzhou in the mid-thirteenth century. Both women and men dwelled in this community; Catherine Vilioni, an unmarried girl from a prosperous family of traders, died there in 1342.

Merchants paved the way for missionaries. Friars, preachers to the cities of Europe, became missionaries to new continents as well. In 1289 the pope made the Franciscan John of Monte Corvino his envoy to China. Preaching in India along the way, John arrived in China four or five years after setting out, converted one local ruler, and built a church. A few years later, now at Beijing, he boasted that he had converted six thousand people, constructed two churches, translated the New Testament and Psalms into the native language, and met with the Great Khan.

who reportedly used them as envoys to ask the pope to send "men able to show by clear reasoning that the Christian religion is better than [that of the Mongols]." The delegation sent back to China, however, consisted not of missionaries but of the Polos—father, uncle, and now son—who traveled through lands where, as Marco later described, the water was "so bitter that no one could bear to drink it. Drink one drop of it and you void your bowels ten times over." After three or four years of travel, mostly on foot, the Polos' party arrived at the court of Khubilai, north of Beijing.

Marco Polo stayed in China for about seventeen years. The Mongols welcomed him: ruling as

The Limits of Control

Regulation and control characterized much of the thirteenth century, from the Mongols' insistence on counting the Russian population in order to tax and recruit it, to the Fourth Lateran Council's desire to direct Christian worship and behavior, to St. Louis' attempts to legislate a moral community: "I would willingly," Louis said, "be branded with a hot iron if all filthy oaths could be abolished in my Kingdom." Uniformity and conformity were sometimes achieved; even when they were not, variations could often be tolerated. For example, in the middle of the thirteenth century the Franciscan order split into two factions. One (the Spirituals) insisted on following St. Francis' poverty literally; the other (the Conventuals) wanted to deemphasize austerity in favor of studying at the universities. Under St. Bonaventure, the general of the Franciscan order from 1257 to 1274, these two groups temporarily reconciled. Yet in 1317 and 1318 the consensus that had allowed both groups a place in the church broke down, and the pope condemned the Spirituals. Many joined illegal and unregulated fringe groups whose existence revealed a paradox: the quest for control created whole classes of people apparently out of control. Religious and political institutions found that their coercive power had limits.

The Food of Piety

The Fourth Lateran Council's promulgation of the doctrine of transubstantiation and the requirement that the laity receive Holy Communion at least once a year placed new emphasis on the holiness of the Eucharist, and the wine and wafer became objects of adoration. Now regularly denied to the laity, the cup became a privilege for priests, and the Mass became a priestly ritual of consecration rather than of communion by the congregation. Priests elevated the Host so all could see it, while bells rang and incense burned. In the *Quest of the Holy Grail,* the Eucharist was the Christ child himself. No wonder this "food" held extraordinary meaning for many. Yet the church's attempt to define and control the Eucharist produced unintended results.

From the thirteenth to the sixteenth centuries, some pious women throughout western Europe ate nothing but the Eucharist. Some women would eat spoiled foods so that their eating might become a sacrifice and a kind of martyrdom, but others refused all other foods. Angela of Foligno (1248–1309), for example, reported that the consecrated wafer swelled in her mouth and tasted sweeter than any other food. She wanted to relish it on her tongue but knew it should be swallowed right away; it went down "with that savor of unknown meat," and Angela was so moved that her hands trembled. For women like Angela, eating the Host was literally eating God, for this is how they understood the church's teaching that the consecrated wafer was actually Christ's body. In the minds of these holy

women the Crucifixion thus became a kind of sacrificial feast. Angela had a vision in which the friars at Foligno suckled from the wound in Christ's side, participating fully and truly in his death. Eating Christ became a way to imitate him, and renouncing other food could become part of service to others, for many of these pious women gave the poor the food they refused to eat. These women lived in every sort of urban setting. They might be lay women—daughters, wives, and mothers living at home—or they might be Beguines or nuns living in cloistered or semi-cloistered communities. Angela of Foligno fed and ministered to the sick as a member of the tertiaries. Even if not engaged in community service, holy women felt their suffering itself was a work of charity, helping to release souls from purgatory.

Although men dominated the institutions that governed political, religious, and economic affairs, women found ways to control their own lives and to some extent the lives of those around them. Typically involved with meal preparation and feeding, these holy women found a way to use their monopoly over ordinary food to gain new kinds of social and religious power that could force the clergy to confront female piety. Insisting on distancing themselves from "normal" food, these pious women became "holy vessels" into which only the Eucharist could enter, and they often gained exceptional prestige. Some became seers and prophetesses. If a pious woman doubted the morality of her priest, for example, she might vomit out the Host, mortifying the priest publicly; or she might even bypass her priest altogether and receive the Eucharist directly from Christ in the form of a vision.

The Suppression of Heretics

Most holy women of the late Middle Ages were not considered heretics, and they did not openly defy clerical authority. Dissenters who refused to accept church doctrine, such as the Cathars of southern France, however, had been condemned as heretics at the time of the Albigensian Crusade (1209–1229). After the crusade the region came under royal control, but the continuing presence of heretics led church authorities to set up inquisitorial tribunals. An inquisition was simply an inquiry, a method long used by secular rulers to summon people together, either to discover facts or to uncover and punish crimes. The church in its zeal to end heresy and save souls used it to ferret out "heretical depravity." Calling suspects to testify in the 1230s and 1240s, inquisitors, aided by secular authorities, would round up virtually entire villages and interrogate everyone. By the mid-fourteenth century, Catharism had been eradicated.

First the inquisitors typically called the people of a district to a "preaching," where they gave a sermon and promised clemency to those who confessed their heresy promptly. Then at a general inquest they questioned each man and woman who seemed to know something about heresy: "Have you ever seen any heretics or Waldenses? Have you heard them preach? Attended any of their ceremonies? Adored heretics?" The judges assigned relatively lenient penalties to those who were not aware that they held heretical beliefs and to heretics who quickly recanted. But unrepentant heretics were burned at the stake, because the church believed such people threatened the salvation of all. Their ashes were sometimes tossed into the water so they could not serve as diabolical relics. Anyone who died while still a heretic could not be buried in consecrated ground. Raymond VII, the count of Toulouse, saw the body of his father—who died excommunicate—rot in its coffin as the pope denied all requests for its burial. Houses where heretics had resided or even simply entered were burned and the sites turned into garbage dumps. Children of heretics could not inherit any property nor become priests, even if they adopted orthodox views.

In the thirteenth century, for the first time, long-term imprisonment became a tool to repress heresy, even if the heretic had confessed: "It is our will," wrote one tribunal, "that [Raymond Maurin and Arnalda, his wife,] because they have rashly transgressed against God and holy church . . . be thrust into perpetual prison to do condign penance, and we command them to remain there in perpetuity." The inquisitors also used imprisonment to force someone to recant, to give the names of other heretics, or to admit a plot. Guillaume Agasse, for example, confessed to participating in a wicked (and imagined) meeting of leprosaria directors who planned to poison all the wells. As the quest for religious control spawned

---

THE QUEST FOR CONTROL

c. 1162–1227 Chingiz Khan, Mongol leader, dominates northern China and Central Asia to the Caspian Sea

1240 Mongols capture Kiev, beginning the Golden Horde

1216–1272 Reign of Henry III, king of England

1258–1265 The barons, led by Simon de Montfort, revolt

1265 Simon convenes the first Parliament including commons

1220–1250 Reign of Emperor Frederick II, ruler of Germany and Sicily

1245 Deposed by the pope at Council of Lyon

1248 Crusade launched against him

1226–1270 Reign of St. Louis (Louis IX), king of France; increased the functions of Parlement and reformed royal administration

1273–1291 Reign of Rudolf I of Hapsburg, emperor after the Great Interregnum in Germany (1254–1273)

1285–1314 Reign of Philip the Fair (Philip IV), king of France

1294–1303 Embroiled in disputes with Boniface VIII

1302 Calls first meeting of the Estates at Paris

1309–1378 Avignon Papacy

---

wild fantasies of conspiracy, the inquisition pinned its paranoia on real people.

The inquisition also created a new group—penitent heretics—who lived on as marginal people. Like Jews, now forced to wear yellow badges as a mark of disgrace, penitent heretics were stigmatized by huge yellow fabric crosses sewn on the front and back of their shirts. To ensure that the crosses would be visible, the penitent was forbidden to wear yellow clothing. Moreover, every Sunday and every feast day repentant heretics had to attend church twice; and during religious processions these men and women were required to join with the clergy and the faithful, carrying large branches in their hands as a sign of their penance.

CONCLUSION

In different ways the conflict between Boniface VIII and Philip the Fair of France, the mystical visions of pious women, and the creation of a class of permanent penitents all showed the limits of medieval control. Although Boniface saw himself as a supreme power to whom everyone was subject, he failed to impose his will on Philip, who was equally certain of his own exalted position. Philip, though undermining much of the papacy's power, ultimately failed to control the popes, now staying in nearby Avignon. Similarly, priests who claimed a monopoly on the mysteries of the Eucharist encountered pious women who influenced its meaning and its use. The inquisition too could not control subversive fantasies, even those of its own making, although it effectively quelled overt heresy.

The quest to dominate through new institutions was matched by new achievements in scholarship and the arts. Thirteenth-century scholastics sought philosophical control by harmonizing the thinking of the pagan Aristotle with a sophisticated Christian theology. Preachers communicated to ordinary people ideas expounded in the learned halls of the universities. Artists and architects integrated sculpture, stone, and glass to depict religious themes and fill the light-infused space of Gothic churches. Musicians wove together disparate melodic and poetic lines into motets. Writers melded heroic and romantic themes with theological truths and mystical visions.

Political leaders also aimed at order and control: to increase their revenues, expand their territories, and enhance their prestige. The kings of England and France and the governments of northern and central Italian cities partially succeeded in achieving these goals. The king of Germany failed bitterly, and Germany remained fragmented until the nineteenth century.

But the harmonies became discordant at the end of the thirteenth century. The balance between church and state achieved under St. Louis, for example, disintegrated into irreconcilable claims to power in the time of Boniface and Philip. The carefully constructed tapestry of St. Thomas' *summae*, which wove together Aristotle's secular philosophy and divine scripture, began to unravel in the teachings of John Duns Scotus. The eclectic Italian Gothic style, which gathered together indigenous as well as northern elements, gave way to a new artistic style, that of Giotto, whose work would be the foundation of Renaissance art in the fourteenth century.

SUGGESTIONS FOR FURTHER READING

Source Materials

Dante. *The Divine Comedy*. A classic with many translations. Two highly recommended versions are by Mark Musa and John Ciardi.

Joinville, Jean de, and Geoffroy de Villehardouin. *Chronicles of the Crusades*. Translated by M. R. B. Shaw. 1963. Contains Joinville's *Life of St. Louis* and an account of the Fourth Crusade.

Pegis, Anton C., ed. *Introduction to St. Thomas Aquinas*. 1945. Contains excerpts from the *Summa Theologiae* (here entitled *Summa Theologica*) and the *Summa Contra Gentiles*.

Quest of the Holy Grail. Translated by P. M. Matarasso. 1969. Written as a kind of pious answer to Arthurian romance literature. Introduces Sir Galahad to the Round Table.

Interpretive Studies

Abulafia, David. *Frederick II: A Medieval Emperor*. 1988. Stresses the continuity between Frederick's political vision and the outlooks of his forebears and contemporaries.

Bynum, Caroline Walker. *Holy Feast and Holy Fast: The Religious Significance of Food to Medieval Women*. 1987. A sensitive and insightful discussion of late medieval women mystics.

Campbell, Mary B. *The Witness and the Other World: Exotic European Travel Writing, 400–1600*. 1989.

Places the writings of Marco Polo, Columbus, and others into the wider arena of the development of travel literature.

Duby, Georges. *The Age of the Cathedrals: Art and Society, 980–1420.* 1981. An overview of the high and late Middle Ages with special emphasis on the significance of artistic expression.

Erler, Mary, and Maryanne Kowaleski. *Women and Power in the Middle Ages.* 1988. A collection of essays that explores the various ways and the different times in which women exercised power.

Fennell, John. *The Crisis of Medieval Russia, 1200–1304.* 1983. Discusses Russia under the Mongols.

Fernández-Armesto, Felipe. *Before Columbus: Exploration and Colonization from the Mediterranean to the Atlantic, 1229–1492.* 1987. Makes the important point that the exploration of the New World was not the sudden invention of Columbus but rather grew out of long-time activities along the Atlantic seaboard.

Katzenellenbogen, Adolf. *The Sculptural Programs of Chartres Cathedral.* 1959. The classic analysis of the meaning of the west, south, and north portal complexes of Chartres cathedral.

Klapisch-Zuber, Christiane, ed. *A History of Women in the West.* Vol. 2, *Silences of the Middle Ages.* 1992. A series of essays focusing on such issues as medieval medical views of women, medieval preaching directed at women, and ideal images of women.

Larner, John. *Italy in the Age of Dante and Petrarch, 1216–1380.* 1980. A thoughtful synthesis of economic, political, and social changes in a crucial period of Italian history.

McCall, Andrew. *The Medieval Underworld.* 1979. Discusses the people on the fringes of medieval society: criminals, prostitutes, and heretics.

Morgan, David. *The Mongols.* 1986. A look at the Mongols and their history in all parts of their empire.

Nicholas, David. *Medieval Flanders.* 1992. Discusses the social, economic, and political development of a key region in the Middle Ages.

O'Callaghan, Joseph F. *The Cortes of Castille-León, 1188–1350.* 1989. A study of one of the earliest representative assemblies. Also notes comparable events elsewhere in Europe.

Panofsky, Erwin. *Gothic Architecture and Scholasticism.* 1951. A brilliant discussion of the affinities between Gothic architecture and medieval *summae* as well as between Gothic architects and scholastics.

Partner, Peter. *The Lands of St. Peter: The Papal State in the Middle Ages and the Early Renaissance.* 1972. Looks at the papal monarchy from the point of view of the lands it ruled or claimed to rule directly.

Phillips, J. R. S. *The Medieval Expansion of Europe.* 1988. Emphasizes the importance of European contact with other continents and cultures before the age of Columbus.

Powers, James F. *A Society Organized for War: The Iberian Municipal Militias in the Central Middle Ages, 1000–1284.* 1988. Discusses the rise and character of "frontier towns" in the age of the *reconquista.*

Sargent, Steven D., ed. and trans. *On the Threshold of Exact Science: Selected Writings of Anneliese Maier on Late Medieval Natural Philosophy.* 1982. Translations of important articles that show the originality and integrity of medieval scientific thought.

Smart, Alastair. *The Dawn of Italian Painting, 1250–1400.* 1978. An introduction to an era of transition in Italian art, written by an art historian.

Southern, R. W. *Robert Grosseteste: The Growth of an English Mind in Medieval Europe.* 1986. Discusses an important English scholastic and political figure.

Stacey, Robert. *Politics, Policy, and Finance Under Henry III, 1216–1245.* 1987. Covers the early, often overlooked years of Henry's reign.

Strayer, Joseph R. *The Reign of Philip the Fair.* 1980. The definitive biography of this king.

Wood, Charles T. *Philip the Fair and Boniface VIII: State vs. Papacy.* 2d ed. 1971. Presents the different ways historians have viewed the personalities, issues, and events involved in the confrontation between Philip and Boniface.

A chronicle written in the first years of the fifteenth century contains a terse entry for 1349: "In the year of Our Lord 1349," noted an anonymous cleric of Mainz (in Germany), "both the mighty and the powerless, the rich and the poor, the old and the young traveled around all lands, beating themselves cruelly with whips, doing penance with prayers and hymns, and reading fictive and false writings against the Christian faith. At that time also, the Jews were almost everywhere in the world slaughtered by Christians." The chronicler certainly exaggerates the numbers of people involved, but the events he describes accurately depict the fourteenth century. After decades of increasing control through religious and political institutions, order now gave way to chaos and violence. Groups of flagellants, who performed self-inflicted acts of violence as a form of penance, roamed the empire. Jews were persecuted on a scale not surpassed until the twentieth century. Christians massacred Jews throughout the Holy Roman Empire, southern France, Aragon, and Castile, ravaging the once-flourishing Jewish culture of the Middle Ages.

Both the flagellant movement and the antisemitic violence were manifestations of a more general crisis. In the mid-fourteenth century a series of disasters scourged a society already weakened by overpopulation, economic stagnation, social conflicts, and war. These disasters—famine, climatic changes, and disease—brought European civilization to its knees in 1348 through 1350. The plague (also called the Black Death) wiped out at least a third of Europe's population. With recurring plagues and continuous warfare through the second half of the fourteenth century, population density

The Collapse of Medieval Order, 1320–1430

The Dance of Death
Sudden death was an ever-present reality in premodern European life. One of the most widespread popular religious images was that of the Dance of Death, showing a grim skeletal figure leading young and old, rich and poor, relentlessly to the grave. In this example, a powerful clergyman vainly resists his fate.

would not reach thirteenth-century levels again until the sixteenth, and in many areas not until the eighteenth, century.

Dynastic conflicts, popular uprisings, and an external menace to the Christian nobility as the Muslim Ottoman Turks advanced steadily into southeastern Europe all undermined political authority and threatened the social order. During the later Middle Ages, the idea of universal Christendom that had sustained the Crusades receded, while loyalties to state, community, and social group deepened. The papacy, the very symbol of Christian unity and authority, remained divided by the claims of rival popes and challenged by heretical movements.

Early fifteenth century Europe stood at a turning point. Crises of confidence and control that had led to retrenchment and depressed economic growth brought about challenges to established power by the lower social classes. The cultural and religious ferment of the Late Middle Ages, however, produced an atmosphere of anxiety.

Origins and Results of the Demographic Collapse

At least a generation before the Black Death, at the end of the thirteenth century, European economic growth had slowed and then stopped. By 1300 the economy could no longer support Europe's swollen population. Having cleared forests and drained swamps, the peasant masses now divided their plots into ever smaller parcels and farmed marginal lands; their income and the quality of their diet eroded. In the great urban centers, where thousands depended on steady employment and cheap bread, a bad harvest, always followed by sharply rising food prices, meant hunger and eventual famine. A cooling of the European climate contributed to the crisis in the food supply. Modern studies of tree rings indicate that fourteenth-century Europe entered a colder period, with a succession of severe winters beginning in 1315. The extreme cold upset an ecological system already overtaxed by human cultivation. Crop failures were widespread. In many cities of northwestern Europe the price of bread tripled in a month, and thousands

IMPORTANT DATES
1315–1317 Famine in Europe
1337 Beginning of the Hundred Years' War
1346 Battle of Crécy
1348–1350 The Black Death
1349–1351 Anti-Jewish massacres in the Empire
1358 Jacquerie uprising in France
1378 Beginning of the Great Schism in the papacy
1381 English peasant uprising
1389 Ottomans defeat Serbs at Kossovo
1414–1417 Council of Constance
1415 Execution of Jan Hus; Hussite Revolution in Bohemia begins
1430 Joan of Arc saves French monarchy

starved to death. Some Flemish cities, for example, lost 10 percent of their population. But the Great Famine of 1315 to 1317 was only the first in a series of catastrophes the overpopulated and undernourished society of fourteenth-century Europe faced. Death, in the form of an epidemic, mowed down masses of weakened bodies in mid-century.

The Spread of the Plague

Brought to Russia and western Asia via caravans and ships from central, east, and southeast Asia, the bubonic plague spread rapidly along the trade routes that linked all parts of Europe. From its breeding ground in central Asia, the plague passed eastward into China, where it decimated the population and wiped out the remnants of the tiny Italian merchant community in Yangzhou. Bacteria-carrying fleas, living on black rats, transmitted the disease. They traveled back to Europe alongside valuable cargoes of silk, porcelain, and spices. In 1347 the Genoese colony in Caffa in the Crimea contracted the plague from the Tatars. Fleeing by ship in a desperate but futile attempt to escape the disease, the Genoese in turn communicated the plague to the seaports of the Mediterranean; by January 1348 the Black Death had infected Sicily, Sardinia, Corsica, and Marseilles. Six months later the plague had spread to Aragon, all of Italy, the Balkans, and most of France. The disease then crept

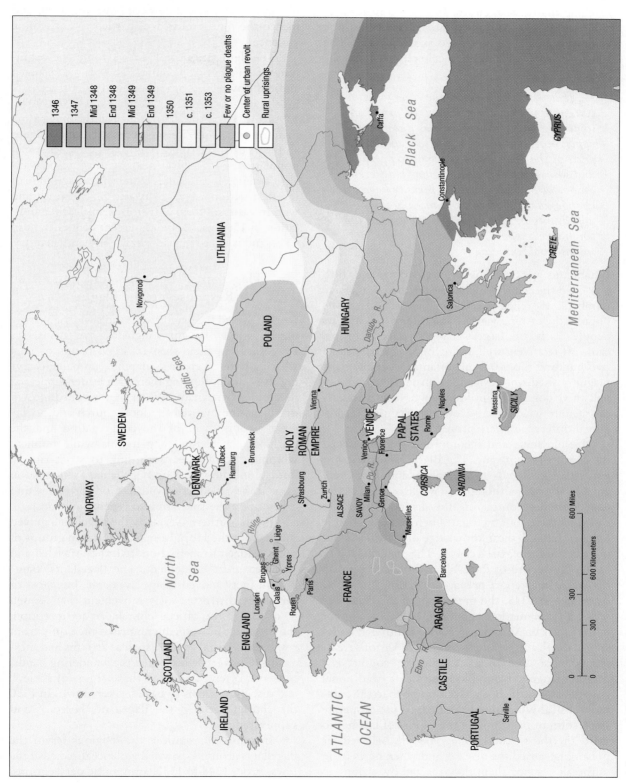

Advance of the Black Death

Legend:
1346
1347
Mid 1348
End 1348
Mid 1349
End 1349
1350
c. 1351
c. 1353
Few or no plague deaths
Center of urban revolt
Rural uprisings

northward to Germany, England, and Scandinavia, reaching the Russian city of Novgorod in 1350.

Nothing like the Black Death had struck Europe since the great plague in the sixth century. The Italian writer Giovanni Boccaccio reported that the plague

> . . . *first betrayed itself by the emergence of certain tumors in the groin or the armpits, some of which grew as large as a common apple, others as an egg. . . . From the two said parts of the body this . . . began to propagate and spread itself in all directions indifferently; after which the form of the malady began to change, black spots or livid making their appearance in many cases on the arm or the thigh or elsewhere, now few and large, now minute and numerous.*

Inhabitants of cities, where crowding and filth increased the chances of contagion, died in massive numbers. Florence lost almost two-thirds of its population of ninety thousand; Siena lost half its people; Paris, the largest city of western Europe, came off relatively well, losing only a quarter of its two hundred thousand inhabitants. Most cities the plague visited on its deadly journey lost roughly half their population in less than a year. Rural areas seem to have suffered fewer mortalities, but regional differences were pronounced.

Helplessness and incomprehension worsened the terror of the plague. The Black Death was not particular: old and young, poor and rich were equally affected, although the wealthy had a better chance of not contracting the disease if they escaped to their country estates before the epidemic hit their city. Medical knowledge of the time could not explain the plague's causes. The medical faculty of the University of Paris blamed the calamity on the stars. In a report prepared for King Philip VI of France in 1348, the professors of medicine described a conjunction of Saturn, Mars, and Jupiter in the house of Aquarius in 1345, resulting in widespread death and pestilence on Earth. Various treatments were used in an attempt to combat the plague, ranging from bloodletting, a traditional cure to balance the body's four humors; to the commonsensical lying quietly in bed; to the desperate suggestion of breathing in the vapors of latrines to ward off the sickness. Many people believed air poisoning caused the disease, and when news of an outbreak reached them they reacted by walling in

their neighbors. In the search for someone to blame, others accused Jews of poisoning wells and loosed the murderous rage that led to antisemitic violence.

The devastation of 1348 was only the beginning of an age of epidemics. The plague recurred and cut down Europeans repeatedly. Further outbreaks occurred in 1361, 1368–1369, 1371, 1375, 1390, and 1405; they continued, with longer dormant intervals, into the eighteenth century. Plagues and wars caused a significant long-term decrease in population. Although general figures are unavailable, detailed local studies convey the magnitude of the destruction wreaked by the Black Death and war. In eastern Normandy, for example, the population in 1368 was only 42 percent of its height in 1314, and it fell to its nadir in the fifteenth century.

Flagellants, Preachers, and Jews: Responses to the Plague

Some believed the plague was God's way of chastising a sinful world and sought to save themselves by confessing their sins. In 1349, bands of men wearing tattered clothes, marching in pairs, carrying flags, and following their own leaders appeared in southern Germany. When they reached a town or village they visited the local church and, to the great astonishment of the congregation and the alarm of the clergy, sang hymns while publicly whipping themselves, according to strict rituals, until blood flowed. The flagellants, as they soon came to be called, cried out to God for mercy and called upon the spectators to repent their sins.

From southern Germany the flagellants moved throughout the Holy Roman Empire. In groups of several dozen to many hundred, they traveled and attracted great excitement. The flagellants' flamboyant piety moved many laypeople, but most of the clergy distrusted a lay movement that seemed to challenge the official church. At its inception, the flagellant movement comprised men only from respectable social groups, such as artisans and merchants. Converts who joined the wandering bands, however, often came from the margins of society, and discipline seems to have broken down. In 1350 the church declared the flagellants heretical and suppressed them.

In some communities the religious fervor the flagellants aroused spawned violence directed at the Jews. From 1348 to 1350, antisemitic persecutions, beginning in southern France and spreading through Savoy to the Holy Roman Empire, destroyed many Jewish communities in central and western Europe. Between November 1348 and February 1351 violence against Jews erupted in at least one hundred German cities. Sometimes the clergy incited the attacks against the Jews, calling them Christ-killers, accusing them of poisoning wells and kidnapping and ritually slaughtering Christian children, and charging them with stealing and desecrating the Host (the communion wafer that Christians believed became the body of Christ during Mass). Economic resentment fueled antisemitism in some areas, as those in debt turned on creditors, often Jews, in towns throughout Europe. Perhaps most cynical were the nobility of Alsace, heavily indebted to Jewish bankers, who sanctioned the murder of Jews to avoid repaying money they had borrowed.

Many antisemitic incidents were spontaneous, with mobs plundering Jewish quarters and killing those who refused baptism. Authorities orchestrated some of the violence, however, seeking a focus for the widespread anger and fear the plague caused. Relying on contemporary chronicles, historians have long linked the arrival of the Black Death with anti-Jewish violence. More recent historical research shows that in some cities the antisemitic violence actually preceded the epidemic. This revised chronology of events demonstrates official complicity and even careful premeditation in the destruction of Jewish communities. For example, in 1349 the magistrates of Nuremberg obtained approval from Emperor Charles IV before organizing a persecution directed by the city government. Thousands of German Jews were slaughtered. Many fled to Poland, where the incidence of plague was low and where the authorities welcomed Jews as productive taxpayers. In western and central Europe, however, the persecutions of 1348 to 1350 destroyed the financial power of the Jews, who had benefited from the commercial revolution of the thirteenth century, and culminated in waves of expulsions in the fifteenth century.

Social, Economic, and Cultural Consequences of the Plague

Although the Black Death took a horrible human toll, the disaster actually profited some people. In an overpopulated society with limited resources,

massive death opened the ranks for advancement. For example, after 1350, landlords had difficulty acquiring new tenant farmers without making concessions in land contracts; the vast army of priests found more benefices* to support them; and workers received much higher wages because the supply of laborers had dwindled. The Black Death and the resulting decline in urban population meant a lower demand for grain relative to the supply and thus a drop in cereal prices. Noble landlords all across Europe had to adjust to these new circumstances. Some revived seigneurial demands for labor services; others looked to their central government for legislation to regulate wages; and still others granted favorable terms to peasant proprietors, often after bloody peasant revolts. Many noblemen lost a portion of their wealth and a measure of their autonomy and political influence. Consequently, European nobles became more dependent on war and on their monarchs to supplement their incomes and enhance their power.

For the peasantry and the urban working population the higher wages generally meant an improvement in living standards. To compensate for the lower demand and price for grain, many peasants and landlords turned to stock breeding and grape and barley cultivation. As European agriculture diversified, peasants and artisans consumed more beer, wine, meat, cheese, and vegetables, a better and more varied diet than their forebears in the thirteenth century had eaten. The reduced cereal prices also stimulated sheep raising in place of farming, so that a portion of the settled population, especially in the English midlands and in Castile, became migratory.

Because of the shrinking population and thus less of a demand for food, cultivating marginal fields was no longer profitable, and in areas settled during the previous centuries of demographic and geographic expansion, many settlements were simply abandoned. In the hundred years following the Black Death, for example, some four hundred fifty large English villages and many smaller hamlets disappeared. In central Europe east of the Elbe River, where German peasants had migrated, large tracts of cultivated land reverted to forest. Estimates suggest that some 80 percent of all villages in parts of Thuringia vanished.

---

*A *benefice* is an ecclesiastical office that is funded by an endowment; priests collected the revenues from the endowment.

Also as a result of the plague, urban resources shifted from manufacturing for a mass market to producing for a highly lucrative, if small, luxury market. The drastic loss in urban populations had reduced the demand for such mass-manufactured goods as cloth. Fewer people now possessed proportionately greater concentrations of wealth. Per capita income increased at every social level because of inheritance. In the southern French city of Albi the proportion of citizens possessing more than 100 livres doubled between 1343 and 1357, while the number of poor people, those with less than 10 livres, declined by half.

Faced with the possibility of imminent and untimely death, the urban populace sought immediate gratification. The Florentine Matteo Villani described the newfound desire for luxury in his native city in 1351: "the common people . . . wanted the dearest and most delicate foods . . . while children and common women clad themselves in all the fair and costly garments of the illustrious who had died." Those with means increased their consumption of luxuries: silk clothing, hats, doublets (snug fitting men's jackets), and boots from Italy; expensive jewelry; and spices from Asia became fashionable in northwestern Europe. Whereas agricultural prices continued to decline, prices of manufactured goods, particularly luxury items, remained constant and even rose as demand for them outstripped supply.

The long-term consequences of this new consumption pattern spelled the end for the traditional woolen industry that had produced for a mass market. Diminishing demand for wool caused hardships for woolworkers, and social and political unrest shook many older industrial centers dependent on the cloth industry. In the Flemish clothing center of Ypres, production figures fell from a high of ninety thousand pieces of cloth in 1320 to fewer than twenty-five thousand by 1390. In Ghent, where 44 percent of all households earned their livelihood as weavers and fullers (a person who shrinks and thickens wool) and where some 60 percent of the working population depended on the textile industry, the woolen market's slump meant constant labor unrest.

Hard Times for Business

Compared to the commercial prosperity of the twelfth and thirteenth centuries, the Late Middle Ages was an age of retrenchment for those in business. During the commercial revolution, merchants had invented many techniques of the modern capitalist economy, such as banking, credit, and currencies with established rates of exchange. International bankers, all Italians, had become financiers to kings and popes. As the fourteenth-century crises afflicted the business community, a climate of pessimism and caution permeated commerce, especially during the second half of the century.

The first major crisis that undermined Italian banks was the financing of a war between France and England in which English king, Edward III, borrowed heavily from the largest Italian banking houses, the Bardi and Peruzzi of Florence. Edward was resorting to a traditional financial arrangement, dating back to the 1280s, between the English crown and Italian financiers. With many of their assets tied up in loans to the English monarchy, the Italian bankers had no choice but to extend new credits, hoping vainly to recover their initial investments. In the early 1340s, however, Edward defaulted on his loans. Adding to their problems, the Florentine bankers were forced to make war loans at home. These once-illustrious and powerful banks could not rebound from the losses they incurred because of these strains. In 1343 the banking house of the Peruzzi fell, followed by the Bardi in 1346. This international financial crisis also bankrupted the Acciaiuoli, the third-largest Florentine banking house. Other Florentine bankers, notably the Medici, founded in 1397, eventually replaced these international giants, though on a smaller scale.

This breakdown in the most advanced economic sector reflected the general recession. Merchants were less likely to take risks and more willing to invest their money in local government bonds than in venture capital. Fewer merchants traveled to Asia, partly because of the danger of being attacked by the Ottoman Turks on the overland routes that had once been protected by the Mongols. Late fourteenth-century Italian merchants no longer hazarded long overland journeys to eastern Asia, as Marco Polo and his father had done a hundred years earlier. The Medici of Florence, who would dominate Florentine politics during the Renaissance, stuck close to home, investing part of their banking profits in art and politics and relying mostly on business agents (factors) to conduct their affairs in other European cities.

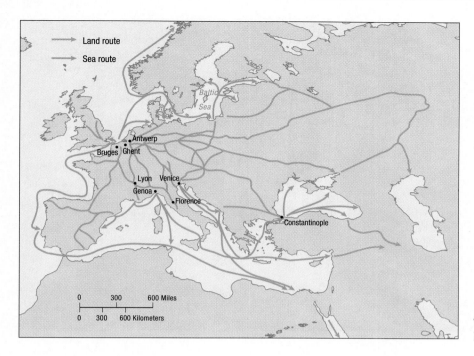

Land route

Sea route

Baltic Sea

Antwerp

Bruges Ghent

Lyon Venice

Genoa

Florence

Constantinople

| 0 | 300 | 600 Miles |

| 0 | 300 | 600 Kilometers |

Trade in the Late Fourteenth Century

Historians have argued that this fourteenth-century economic depression diverted capital away from manufacturing and to investments in the arts and luxuries for immediate consumption. Instead of plowing their profits back into their businesses, merchants acquired land, built sumptuous town-houses, purchased luxury items, and invested in bonds. During the last decades of the fourteenth century, the maritime insurance in the great merchant republics of Venice and Genoa rose, also reflecting the pessimism of the times. The grim reality of the plague motivated many merchants to forgo long-term investments, such as in manufacturing, and instead to seek short-term profits, such as in trading luxury foods.

The most important trade axis continued to link Italy with the Low Countries. Italian cities produced silk, wool, jewelry, and other luxury goods northern Europeans desired, and they also imported spices, gold, and other coveted products from Asia and Africa. Traveling either by land through Lyons or by sea around Gibraltar, these products reached Bruges, Ghent, and Antwerp, where they were transshipped to England, northern Germany, Poland, and Scandinavia. The reverse flow carried raw materials and silver, the latter to

help balance the trade between northern Europe and the Mediterranean. Diminished production and trade eventually caused turmoil in northern Europe and a crisis for financiers in the Low Countries. Bruges, the financial center for northwestern Europe, saw its power fade during the fifteenth century when a succession of its money changers went bankrupt. The Burgundian dukes eventually enacted a series of monetary laws that undermined Bruges's financial and banking community and, by extension, the city's political autonomy as well.

Challenges to Spiritual Authority

After Philip the Fair of France humiliated Pope Boniface VIII, the papacy's prestige had suffered a heavy blow when the papal seat was transferred from Rome to Avignon (bordering the French kingdom) in 1309. Until 1378 the Avignon popes were all Frenchmen. Many now called for church reform. Some clerics supported establishing a church council to limit papal power; others argued against the papacy's secular powers; some dissenters even

The Palace of the Popes at Avignon *For over a century the papacy resided not at Rome but in the small southern French city of Avignon. The massive papal palace attests to the size and complexity of the bureaucracy that grew up to serve the church's needs.*

rejected the very legitimacy of the Roman church. But the most serious challenge to the late medieval church was the coalescence of social, economic, and religious discontent expressed in new movements offering alternative visions and institutions for the faithful's spiritual guidance and salvation.

Papal Authority and Dissent

Papal government continued to grow even after Avignon became the papal residence. In the fourteenth century the papacy's institutions were more sophisticated than those of secular states. A succession of popes, all lawyers by training, concentrated on consolidating the financial and legal powers of the church, mainly through appointments and taxes. Claiming the right to assign all benefices, the popes gradually secured authority over the clergy throughout western and central Europe. Under the skillful guidance of John XXII (∗1316–1334), papal rights increased incrementally without causing much protest. By the second half of the century the popes had secured the right to appoint all major benefices and many minor ones. To gain these lucrative positions, potential candidates often made gifts to the papal court to win favor. The imposi-

tion of papal taxes on all benefice holders developed from taxation to finance the Crusades. Out of these precedents the papacy instituted a regular system of papal taxation that produced the money to consolidate papal government.

Papal government, the *curia*, consisted of the pope's personal household, the Sacred College of Cardinals, and the church's financial and judicial apparatus. Combining elements of monarchy and oligarchy, the *curia* developed a bureaucracy that paralleled the organization of secular government. The pope's relatives often played a major role in his household; many popes came from extended noble lineages, and they often gave their family members preferential treatment (hence the term *nepotism*, from the Latin *nepos*, meaning "nephew"—but often a euphemism for the pope's illegitimate children—which denotes showing favoritism to one's kin). The papal household expanded rapidly in Avignon. As patrons of the arts the popes brought writers and artists into their households. Francesco Petrarch, the most famous poet of the age, worked in Avignon as a young man, before achieving his success.

After the pope, the cardinals, as a collective body, were the most elevated entity in the church.

Like great nobles in royal courts, the cardinals, many of them nobles, advised and aided the pope. They maintained their own households, employing scores of scribes, servants, and retainers. Together, the cardinals were strong enough to challenge papal authority; indeed factions of cardinals played an instrumental role in the fourteenth-century crisis of the church.

Papal bureaucracy consisted of the apostolic chamber (to manage finances), the chancery (to deal with a mountain of correspondence with all corners of Christendom), and the papal tribunal (to adjudicate ecclesiastical disputes). Most posts went to clerics with legal training, thus accentuating the juristic and administrative character of the highest spiritual authority in Christendom. During the fourteenth and fifteenth centuries, the papal army also grew, as the popes sought to restore and control the Papal States in Italy.

William of Ockham (c. 1285–1349) and Marsilius of Padua (c. 1290–1343) sharply criticized the papal monarchy, which had been developing since the twelfth century. Asserting the poverty of Christ, Ockham, an English Franciscan, denounced the papal pretension to worldly power and wealth. Rejecting further the confident synthesis of Christian doctrine and Aristotelian philosophy by Thomas Aquinas, Ockham denied that universal concepts had any reality in nature. Instead, Okham asserted, such concepts as "man" or "papal infallability" were mere representations, words in the mind. Perceiving and analyzing these ideals offered no assurance that they expressed truth. Observation and human reason were limited as means to understand the universe and to know God. Consequently, God might be capricious, contradictory, or many rather than one. Denying the possibility of an evil or erratic God, Ockham emphasized the covenant between God and his faithful. God promises to act consistently—for example, to reward virtue and punish vice. Ockham stressed simplicity in his explanations of universal concepts. His insistence that shorter explanations were superior to wordy ones became known as "Ockham's razor." Yet Ockham's so-called nominalism threatened the established order in which the church was the supreme theological authority. Ockham believed church power derived from the congregation of the faithful, both laity and clergy, not from the pope or the church council. Imprisoned by Pope John XXII for heresy, Ockham escaped in 1328 and found refuge with Emperor Louis of Bavaria.

Another antipapal refugee at the imperial court was Marsilius of Padua, a citizen of an Italian commune, a physician and lawyer by training, and the rector of the University of Paris. Marsilius attacked the very basis of papal power in *The Defender of the Peace* (1324). The true church, Marsilius argued, was constituted by the people, who had the right to select the head of the church, either through the body of the faithful or through a "human legislator." Papal power, Marsilius asserted, was the result of historical usurpation, and its exercise represented tyranny. In 1327, Pope John XXII, the living target of the treatise, decreed the work heretical. *The Defender of the Peace* would become an important intellectual justification for the Protestant reformers of the sixteenth century.

The Great Schism

While papal authority resided in Avignon, many voices urged the popes to return to Rome, the see of St. Peter. For three years (1367–1370), Urban V did return to Rome, where he received the Holy Roman emperor Charles IV in 1368 and the Byzantine emperor John V Palaeologus in 1369. The Byzantine ruler had come to seek western help to fight off the Ottoman Turks. In exchange for John's agreement to submit to Rome's spiritual authority and his promise to end the schism between the Catholic and Greek Orthodox churches, Urban called for a crusade to the East. But war broke out again between England and France, and Urban needed peace in the West as a prerequisite for the crusade. To conduct his diplomacy, Urban returned to Avignon, but he died before achieving anything.

By the second half of the fourteenth century the Avignon papacy had taken on a definitive French character. All five popes elected between 1305 and 1378 were natives of southern France, as were many of the cardinals and most of the *curia*. Moreover, French parishes provided half of the papacy's income. Nonetheless, Gregory XI, elected to the pontificate in 1371, was determined to return to Rome, where he expected to exert greater moral force to organize a crusade against the Muslim Ottomans. Before he could carry out his plans, however, Florence declared war against the Papal

States in 1375, and Gregory hastened to Rome to prevent the collapse of his territorial power in Italy.

Gregory died in 1378. Sixteen cardinals—one Spanish, four Italian, and eleven French—met in Rome to elect the new pope. Although many in the *curia* were homesick for Avignon, the Roman people, determined to keep the papacy and its revenues in Rome, clamored for the election of a Roman. An unruly crowd rioted outside the conclave, drowning out the cardinals' discussions. Fearing for their lives, the cardinals hurriedly elected the archbishop of Bari, an Italian, who took the title of Urban VI. If the cardinals thought they had elected a weak man who would both do their bidding and satisfy the Romans, Urban's immediate attempt to curb the cardinals' power dispelled any such illusions. Thirteen cardinals retired to Anagni, elected Clement VII, and returned to Avignon.

Thus began the Great Schism that political divisions in Europe perpetuated. Charles V of France, who did not want the papacy to return to Rome, immediately recognized Clement, his cousin, as did the rulers of Sicily, Scotland, Castile, Aragon, Navarre, Portugal, Ireland, and Savoy. One of the enemies of Charles V, Richard II of England, professed allegiance to Urban and was followed by the rulers of Flanders, Poland, Hungary, most of Germany, and central and northern Italy. Faithful Christians were equally divided in their loyalties. Catherine of Siena (1347–1380), a famous religious woman, and Vincent Ferrer (1350–1419), a popular Dominican preacher, supported Urban and Clement, respectively. All Christians theoretically found themselves deprived of the means of salvation, as bans from Rome and Avignon each placed a part of Christian Europe under interdict forbidding the performance of sacraments. Because neither pope would step down willingly, the leading intellectuals in the church tried to end the schism.

Religious Schism

The Conciliar Movement

According to canon law, only a pope could summon a general council of the church. But given the state of confusion in Christendom, many intellectuals argued that the crisis justified calling a general council to represent the body of the faithful, over and against the head of the church. Jean Gerson, chancellor of the University of Paris, spoke for all the conciliarists when he asserted that "the pope can be removed by a general council celebrated without his consent and against his will." He justified his claim by reasoning that "normally a council is not legally . . . celebrated without papal calling. . . . But, as in grammar and in morals, general rules have exceptions. . . . Because of these exceptions a superior law has been ordained to interpret the law."

The first attempt to resolve the question of church authority came in 1409, at the Council of Pisa, attended by cardinals who had defected from the two popes. The council asserted its supremacy by declaring both popes deposed and electing a new pontiff. When the popes at Rome and Avignon refused to yield, Christian Europe found itself in the embarrassing position of choosing among three popes. Pressure to hold another council then came from central Europe, where a new heretical movement, ultimately known as Hussitism, undermined orthodoxy from Bohemia to central Germany. Threatened politically by challenges to church authority, Emperor Sigismund pressed the Pisan pope John XXIII to convene a church council at Constance in 1414.

The cardinals, bishops, and theologians assembled in Constance felt compelled to combat heresy, heal the schism, and reform the church. They ordered Jan Hus, the Prague professor and inspiration behind the Bohemian movement, burned at the stake in spite of an imperial safe conduct he had been promised, but this act failed to suppress dissent. They deposed John XXIII because of tyrannical behavior, condemning him as an antipope. The Roman pope, Gregory, accepted the council's authority and resigned in 1415. At its closing in 1417 the council also deposed Benedict XIII, the "Spanish mule," who refused to abdicate the Avignon papacy and lived out his life in a fortress in Spain, still regarding himself as pope and surrounded by his own *curia*. The rest of Christendom, however, hailed Martin V as the new pope. The council had taken a stand against heresy and had achieved unity under one pope.

Church reform, however, would have to wait. The council could not agree on a system under which the pope would share power with a church council, and the Council of Constance was too large and cumbersome to facilitate reform, even though delegates from various states convened and voted together. The delegates did declare the supremacy of general councils and attempted to ensure continuity in conciliar government by directing the church to call new councils periodically. But the powerful prelates who dominated the three years of meetings at Constance were unwilling to limit their own privileges or to accept the laity as equals in matters of salvation.

Dissenters and Heretics

Religious conflict in the later Middle Ages took a variety of forms. The dissatisfaction manifested as squabbling within the papacy, but perhaps more significantly as opposition to the papacy and religious expression outside the official church and even political dissent and social unrest.

After the great struggle in 1317 and 1318 between the papacy and the Franciscan Spirituals, who advocated apostolic poverty and rejected the wealth of the church, their remnants sought protection in central and southern Italy, where they came to be called the Fraticelli. Many civic and village authorities tolerated the Fraticelli because the lower classes sympathized with them, admiring their vows of evangelical poverty, and because they opposed the pope, whom they identified as the Antichrist, echoing the views of many poorer Italians. The cloth workers residing in the poorer districts of Florence supported them. During the crisis of the 1370s the Fraticelli were among the voices preaching antipapal rhetoric. Because the Italian city-states curbed the Inquisition's power, few Fraticelli were tried for heresy. The movement's gradual decline after 1400 removed the threat of their contributing to any further social unrest.

Unlike the Fraticelli, the Free Spirits did not oppose the pope, yet the church still labeled them heretics. The Free Spirits practiced an extreme form of mysticism. They asserted that humans and God

CRITICS OF PAPAL POWER

1320 Dissidents from the Franciscan Order, known in Italy as the Fraticelli, attack papal wealth

1324 Marsilius of Padua, a legal scholar, denies the legitimacy of papal supremacy in *Defender of the Peace*

1328 Pope John XXII imprisons the English Franciscan and philosopher William of Ockham for criticizing papal power

1378 John Wycliffe advances the view that the true church is a community of believers rather than a clerical hierarchy in *On the Church*

1414 Wycliffe's followers, called Lollards, rebel in England

1415 The Council of Constance condemns two Prague professors, Jan Hus and Jerome of Prague, for criticizing papal and clerical privileges

1436 Radical followers of Hus, known as Taborites, suffer defeat in their attempt to create a Christian community in Bohemia free from papal authority

were of the same essence and that individual believers could attain salvation, even sanctity, without the church and its sacraments. In the fourteenth century the Free Spirits found supporters among the Beguines, pious lay women who lived together, and the Beghards, men who did not belong to a particular religious order but who led pious lives by begging for their sustenance. Living in community houses (beguinages), the Beguines imitated the convent lives of nuns but did not submit to clerical control. First prevalent in northern Europe, beguinages sprang up rapidly in the Low Countries and the Rhineland, regions of heavy urbanization. This essentially urban development represented the desire by large segments of society to achieve salvation through piety and good works, as many began to feel that the clergy did not adequately address their spiritual needs.

For the church the discovery of Free Spirits among the Beghards and Beguines raised the larger question of ecclesiastical control, for this development threatened to eliminate the boundary between the laity and the clergy. In the 1360s, Emperor

Charles IV and Pope Urban V extended the Inquisition to Germany in a move to crush this heresy. In the cities of the Rhineland, fifteen mass trials took place between 1320 and 1430, most around the turn of the century. Through condemnations and the subjection of beguinages under the mendicant orders, the church contained potential dissent. Throughout the fifteenth century the number of beguinages continued to drop.

Intellectual dissent, social unrest, and nationalist sentiment combined to create a powerful anticlerical movement in England that became known as Lollardy. John Wycliffe (c. 1330–1384), who inspired the movement, was an Oxford professor. Initially employed as a royal apologist in the struggle between state and church, Wycliffe gradually developed ideas that challenged the very foundations of the Roman church. His treatise *On the Church,* composed in 1378, advanced the view that the true church was a community of believers rather than a clerical hierarchy. In other writings, Wycliffe repudiated monasticism, excommunication, the Mass, and the priesthood, substituting reliance on Bible reading and individual conscience in place of the official church as the path to salvation. Responsibility for church reform, Wycliffe believed, rested with the king, whose authority exceeded that of the pope.

Not only did Wycliffe gather around him likeminded intellectuals at Oxford, but he also influenced and reflected a widespread anticlericalism in late medieval England. Wycliffe actively promoted the use of English in religious writing. He and his disciples attempted to translate the Bible into English and to popularize its reading throughout all ranks of society, although he died before completing the project. His supporters included members of the gentry, but most were artisans and other humbler urban people who had some literacy. The church hierarchy called them Lollards (from *lollar,* meaning "idler"). Religious dissent was key in motivating the 1381 peasant uprising, and the radical preacher John Ball was only one of many common priests who supported the revolt. Real income for parish priests had fallen steadily after the Black Death. The sympathy of these impoverished clergy lay with the common folk against the great bishops, abbots, and lords of the realm.

Wycliffe had powerful protectors, foremost among them John of Gaunt, duke of Lancaster and brother of King Edward III. After Wycliffe's death,

however, the English bishops quickly suppressed intellectual dissent at Oxford. In 1401, Parliament passed a statute to prosecute heretics. The only Lollard revolt occurred when John Oldcastle, a knight inspired by Wycliffe's ideas, plotted an assault on London. It was suppressed in 1414. But in spite of persistent persecutions, Lollardy survived underground during the fifteenth century and resurfaced during the Reformation.

The Hussite Revolution

In Bohemia religious dissent became a vehicle for social and political revolutions and the most fundamental manifestation of the crisis of the Later Middle Ages. In the Hussite revolt, nationalist, religious, and social dissenters challenged the very legitimacy of the Christian order in Europe.

Under Emperor Charles IV the pace of economic development and social change in the Holy Roman Empire quickened. Prague, the capital, became one of Europe's great cities: the new silver mine at Kutná Hora boosted its economic growth, and the first university in the empire was founded there in 1348. Many German merchants and artisans migrated to Bohemian cities, and many Czech peasants, uprooted from the land, flocked to the cities in search of employment. The hard times of the later fourteenth century turned this diverse society into a potentially explosive mass when heightened expectations of commercial and intellectual growth collided with the grim realities of plague and economic problems. Tax protests, urban riots, and ethnic conflicts signaled growing unrest, but it was religious discontent that became the focus for popular revolt.

Critics of the clergy, often clergy themselves, decried the moral conduct of priests and prelates who held multiple benefices, led dissolute lives, and ignored their pastoral duties. Living in a state of mortal sin, many argued, how could the clergy legitimately perform the sacraments? Advocating greater lay participation in the Mass and in the reading of Scripture, religious dissenters drew some of their ideas from the writings of Wycliffe, whose work was introduced following the marriage of the Bohemian princess Anna to Richard II of England in 1383. Among those influenced by Wycliffe's ideas were Jan Hus and his follower, Jerome of Prague, both Prague professors, ethnic Czechs, and leaders of a reform party in Bohemia. Although

Jan Hus at the Stake
Wearing the humiliating garb traditional on such occasions (including a cap with dancing devils), Hus is about to be burned. News of his execution touched off a religious and nationalist uprising in Bohemia. To this day Jan Hus is revered by the Czech people as a national hero.

the reform party attracted adherents from all social groups among Czech speakers, the German minority, who dominated the university and urban elites in Prague, opposed it because of ethnic rivalry. The Bohemian nobility protected Hus; the common clergy were rebelling against the bishops; and the artisans and workers in Prague were ready to back the reform party by force. Their disparate social interests all focused on one symbolic but passionately felt demand: communion in both bread and wine (*utraque* in Latin, meaning "both") at Mass. In traditional Roman liturgy the chalice was reserved for the clergy; the Utraquists, as their opponents called them, also wanted to drink from the chalice, showing a measure of equality between laity and clergy.

Despite a guarantee of safety from Emperor Sigismund of the Holy Roman Empire, Hus was burned at the stake while attending the Council of Constance. Jerome of Prague also died at the stake. Hus's death caused a national uproar, and the reform movement, focusing thus far on religious issues, burst forth as the Hussite revolution with two main streams: the radical Taborites and the more moderate Prague Hussites. In Prague the moderate faction triumphed over the radicals. With the nobility

and the merchant community as its backbone, the Prague Hussites became the party of tradition and order. They wanted to reform the church but not to subvert the secular social hierarchy. Many nobles supported the Hussite cause as an excuse to seize church properties and had no intention of yielding to the radicals' egalitarian demands. Prepared for a dialogue with Sigismund and the papacy, the Prague Hussites instead faced an escalating conflict between the Taborites and the emperor in the provinces.

Sigismund's initial repression in the provinces was brutal, and many dissenters were massacred. To organize their defense, Hussites gathered at a mountain in southern Bohemia, which they called Mt. Tabor after the mountain in the New Testament where the transfiguration of Christ took place. These Taborites began to restructure their community according to the Bible. Like the first Christian church, they initially

The Hussite Revolution

practiced communal ownership of goods and thought of themselves as the only true Christians awaiting the return of Christ and the end of the world. As their influence spread the Taborites compromised with the surrounding social order, collecting tithes from peasants and retaining magistrates in towns under their control. The leaders among the Taborites were radical priests, who ministered to the godly community in Czech, exercised moral and judicial leadership, and even led the people into battle. One famous Taborite was the general Procop the Shaven (so named because he was clean shaven even though most Taborite priests usually wore beards.).

Modeling themselves after the Israelites of the Old Testament and the first Christians of the New Testament, the Taborites impressed even their enemies. Aeneas Sylvius Piccolomini, the future Pope Pius II (*1458–1464), observed that "among the Taborites you will hardly find a woman who cannot demonstrate familiarity with the Old and New Testaments." The Taborite army, drawn from many social classes and led by priests, repelled five attacks by the "crusader" armies from neighboring

Germany, triumphing over their enemies using a mixture of religious fervor and military technology, such as a wagon train to protect the infantry from cavalry charges. They would not be defeated until 1436, and then only by the combined forces of the Hussites and royalists, who were eager for a compromise with Rome. By suppressing the more radical revolution of the Taborites, the Bohemians in turn retained the right to receive communion in both bread and wine until the sixteenth century.

Disintegration of the Political Order

The crises of the fourteenth century affected political allegiances as well as social and religious tensions. Just as many people no longer blindly accepted the church's dictates, so did citizens refuse to trust the politicians in power to serve the ordinary person's best interests. The ideology of Christian solidarity, always stronger in theory than in practice, dissolved in the face of national rivalries, urban and rural revolts, and the military resurgence of the Muslims. The conflict between the English and the French that came to be called the Hundred Years' War destroyed the lives of countless thousands of noncombatants as well as soldiers. Commoners—town residents and peasants—challenged the political status quo, wanting a share of the power their rulers wielded over them or at least a say in how they were governed. The Ottoman Turks battled Christian Europe in a bloody jihad (Holy War), reclaiming the land westerners had conquered in the Crusades in West Asia (now the Middle East). The political crises of the Late Middle Ages shaped the pattern of conflicts for the next two hundred years.

From Knights to Mercenaries

Although the nobility continued to dominate European society in the Late Middle Ages, their social and political roles gradually but fundamentally transformed. Even though the nobility encompassed a wide range of people, from great magnates whose power and wealth rivaled kings to humble knights who lived much like peasants, two developments in the later Middle Ages affected all of them: the agrarian crisis and the changing nature of warfare.

The nobles had traditionally been defined as the warrior class and supported by the profits from the land they owned. In the wake of the Black Death, their income from their land dwindled as food prices declined. Forced to seek additional revenues, knights turned enthusiastically to war. The extended Anglo-French conflict of this time largely reflected an English nobility addicted to the glory and profit of war. Noblemen from many nations served willingly in foreign campaigns, forming units at their own expense, motivated solely by material gain. The English knight John Hawkwood put it best: "Do you not know that I live by war and peace would be my undoing?" Captain of an army that sold its services to various Italian states vying for power, Hawkwood represented the new soldier: the mercenary who lived a life of violence and whose loyalty was given to the side that paid the most. Led by noble captains, these mercenary bands terrorized France for most of the Hundred Years' War, which devastated France from 1337 to 1453. During interludes of peace, they earned money fighting in Castile.

As if to compensate for the cynical reality of mercenary warfare, the European nobility emphasized the traditional knightly ethos in an effort to rationalize their authority by appealing to moral and aesthetic values. Arthurian romances became a vogue, not only in reading but also in life. Edward III of England, for example, created the Order of the Garter in 1344 to revive the ideal of chivalry. During truces, English and French knights jousted, glorifying mock combat according to the rules of chivalry. According to the chronicler Jean Froissart, English and French knights scorned their German counterparts for failing to follow the rules of war and observe the rituals that masked the exercise of violence and power.

Yet chivalric combat waged by knights on horseback was quickly yielding to new military realities. By the last decades of the fourteenth century, cannons were common in European warfare. New military technologies—firearms, siege equipment, and fortifications, for example—undermined the nobility's preeminence as a fighting force. A full war chest, which meant a well-equipped fighting force, counted more than valor and often determined the outcome of battles. The nobles were forced to become entrepreneurs to maintain their social eminence, be it as military captains or

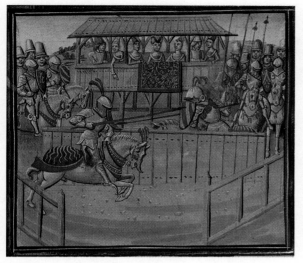

A joust
Evolving out of the practice bouts that knights used to keep in fighting trim, by the late Middle Ages the joust had become a stylized show mounted before courtiers and townspeople on special occasions. Many knights were virtual professional athletes, working a regular circuit of jousts at which they competed for rich purses.

estate managers. Many turned to state service to reinforce their social stations. By appointing nobles to the royal household, as military commanders and councilors, kings and princes could further consolidate the power of emerging states.

The Hundred Years' War

The Hundred Years' War had no single political or diplomatic cause, although warring monarchs claiming preeminence for their dynasties provided a justification. A protracted struggle in western Europe that involved the nobility of almost every nation, the war was sparked by conflicting French and English interests in Aquitaine in southwestern France. As part of the French royal policy of centralizing jurisdiction, in 1337, Philip VI of France confiscated Aquitaine, which had been held by the English monarchs as a fief of the French crown. To recover his lands, Edward III of England, the only surviving male heir of Philip the Fair, laid claim to the French throne.

Elaborate chivalric behavior, savage brutality, and unabashed profiteering permeated the Hundred Years' War. One episode at the battle of Crécy (1346), recounted by the chronicler Froissart, illustrates both the grandeur and the futility of chivalric combat. John of Luxembourg, the king of Bohemia, took the French side, and although he was old and blind he insisted that his vassals guide him into battle "so that he could strike one blow with his sword"; he and his attendants were all killed, falling side by side on the battlefield. Warfare in this era involved defined rules whose application depended on social status. English and French knights took one another prisoner and showed all the formal courtesy required by chivalry—but they slaughtered captured common soldiers like cattle. Overall the pattern of war was not pitched battles but a series of raids in which English fighters plundered cities and villages, causing terrible destruction. English knights financed their own campaigns, and war was expected to turn a profit, either in captured booty or in ransom paid to free noble prisoners of war. As the conflict dragged on, English and Gascon (Gascony, a province in southwestern France controlled by the English crown) warriors formed their own armies that plundered and terrorized the countryside or sold their services to some faction of the French nobility.

Historians divide the Hundred Years' War into three periods: the first marked by English triumphs, the second in which France slowly gained the upper hand, and the third ending in the English expulsion from France.

In the first period, from 1338 to 1360, the English won several famous victories such as Crécy, in which the vastly outnumbered English knights and longbowmen routed the French cavalry. In another victory at Poitiers (1356), Edward the Black Prince (heir to the English throne, named for his black armor) defeated a superior French army and captured the French king John and a host of important noblemen, whom they ransomed for hefty sums. Divided and demoralized, the French signed the peace treaty of Brétigny in 1360, ceding vast territories in the southwest to England.

The second phase of the war lasted from 1361 to 1413. Taking advantage of the Black Prince's death and Edward III's failing health, the French, commanded by Bertrand du Guesclin, the constable of France, chipped away at the English conquests. In Charles V (∗1364–1380) and his brother, Philip the Bold (the duke of Burgundy, ∗1364–1404), the French finally found energetic leaders who could

The Hundred Years' War   The English in France, 1338–1360   The English in France, 1413–1453

resist the English. In 1372, aided by a Castilian fleet, a French force took La Rochelle, long an English stronghold in Gascony. In 1386, in the aftermath of a peasant revolt in England, the French even assembled a fleet to conquer England. Although unsuccessful in landing an army, the French raided English ports into the early fifteenth century.

At the turn of the century a new set of players entered the political stage. In 1399 the English noble Henry Bolingbroke forced Richard II (grandson of Edward III) to abdicate. The coup made Bolingbroke Henry IV of England (*1399–1413), whose story was later made famous (and much distorted) by Shakespeare's plays. Factional strife poisoned French political unity. The struggle for power began in 1392 after Charles VI (*1380–1422), called the Mad King of France, suffered his first bout of insanity. Two factions then began to coalesce—one around John of Burgundy (the son of Philip the Bold) and the other around the duke of Orléans. In 1407, Burgundian agents assassinated the duke, whose followers, called the Armagnacs, sought vengeance and plunged France into civil war. When both parties appealed for English support in 1413, the young King Henry V (*1413–1422), who had just succeeded his father Henry IV, launched a full-scale invasion of France.

The third phase of the war (1413–1453) began when Henry V crushed the French at Agincourt (1415). Unlike the earlier battles of Crécy and Poitiers, however, this isolated victory achieved

little in the long run. Three parties now struggled for domination. Henry occupied Normandy and claimed the French throne; the dauphin (heir apparent to the French throne), son of Charles VI and later Charles VII of France (*1422–1461), ruled central France with the support of the Armagnacs; and the duke of Burgundy held a vast territory in the northeast that included the Low Countries. Burgundy was thus able to broker war or peace by shifting support first to the English and then to the French. English power reached its height under Henry VI (*1422–1461) during the 1420s, when combined English and Burgundian rule extended over all of France north of the Loire. But the English could not establish firm control. In Normandy a savage guerrilla war harassed the English army. Driven from their villages by pillaging and murdering soldiers, the Norman peasants retreated into forests, formed armed bands, and attacked the English. The miseries of war inspired prophecies of miraculous salvation; among the predictions was the belief that a virgin would deliver France from the English invaders.

At the court of the dauphin, in 1429, a sixteen-year-old peasant girl presented herself and her vision to save France. Born in a village in Lorraine, Joan of Arc, *la Pucelle* (The Maid), as she always referred to herself, grew up in a war-ravaged country longing for divine deliverance. The young maid, guided by an inner voice, presented herself as God's messenger to the local noble, who was sufficiently

Joan of Arc at Orléans
Joan of Arc's career as a charismatic military leader was an extraordinary occurrence in fifteenth-century France. In this manuscript illumination Joan, in full armor, directs French soldiers as they besiege the English at Orléans. The victory she gained here stunned the French people.

impressed to equip Joan with horse, armor, and a retinue and to send her to the dauphin's court. (According to her later testimony, Joan ran away from home when her father threatened to drown her because she refused an arranged marriage.) Her hair cut short, dressed in armor and holding a sword, Joan of Arc's extraordinary appearance inspired the French to trust in divine providence and turn the tide. In 1430 she accompanied the French army that raised the siege of Orléans, was wounded, and showed great courage in battle. Upon her urging, the dauphin traveled deep into hostile Burgundian territory to be anointed King Charles VII of France at Reims cathedral, thus strengthening his legitimacy by the traditional ritual of coronation.

Yet as captain of her own company of troops, Joan's fortunes declined after Reims. She promised to capture Paris and attacked the city on the Feast of the Virgin Mary, thus violating one of the holiest religious feast days. After the Anglo-Burgundian defenders drove her back, the French began to lose faith in The Maid. When the Burgundians captured her in 1431 during a minor skirmish, Charles and his forces did little to save her. Still, Joan was a powerful heroic and divine symbol, and the English were determined to undermine her legitimacy. In a

trial conducted by French theologians in Anglo-Burgundian service, Joan was accused of false prophecy, suspected of witchcraft because she wore male clothes and led armies, and tricked into recanting her prophetic mission. Almost immediately, however, she retracted her confessions, returned the female attire given her after an English soldier had raped her in prison, and reaffirmed her divine mission. The English then burned her at the stake as a relapsed heretic.

After Joan's death the English position crumbled when their alliance with the Burgundians fell apart in 1435. The duke of Burgundy recognized Charles VII as king of France, and Charles entered Paris in 1437. Skirmish by skirmish, the English were driven off French soil, retaining only the port of Calais when hostilities ceased in 1453. Two years later the French church rescinded the 1431 verdict that had condemned Joan of Arc as a heretic.

Popular Uprisings

English and French knights triumphed at the expense of the common people. French peasants and townsfolk were taxed, robbed, raped, and murdered by marauding bands. Their English counterparts had to pay ever higher taxes to support their kings'

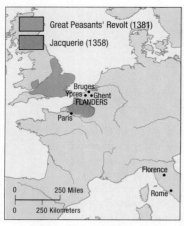

Popular Uprisings of the Late 1300s

wars. Popular uprisings, fueled by widespread resentment, now contributed to the general disintegration of political and social order. In 1358 a short but savage rebellion erupted in the area around Paris, shocking the nobility. And in 1381 a more widespread and broadly based revolt broke out in England. Although both rebellions were suppressed, rural and urban uprisings continued through the later Middle Ages, indicating the deep social conflicts that would reshape society.

Historians have traditionally described the 1358 Jacquerie, named after the jacket (*jacque*) worn by serfs, as a "peasant fury," implying that it represented simply a spontaneous outburst of aim-

The English Peasant Uprising, 1381

In this manuscript illumination, depicting a much more orderly scene than must have been the reality, a host of rebellious peasants led by John Ball (on horseback) confronts troops gathered under the royal banners of England and St. George. Such confrontations, all too frequent in late-medieval and early modern Europe, always ended with the same result, as well-armed soldiers mowed down desperate village folk.

less violence. More recent research, however, reveals the complex social origins of the movement. The revolt broke out after the capture of King John at the battle of Poitiers, when the Estates of France met to discuss monarchical reform and national defense. Unhappy with the heavy war taxes and the incompetence of the warrior nobility, the townspeople sought greater political influence under Étienne Marcel, the provost of the merchants of Paris. Through its merchants' and artisans' guilds, the Parisian commune (the citizens and government of Paris) now assumed a new political importance. In the absence of royal authority the common people vied with the nobles for control of government, and a clash between peasants and nobles near Paris lead to a massive uprising.

Long prey to arrogant and powerful noble lords, and lacking the protection of city walls, rural artisans, wealthy peasants, minor royal functionaries, and even a few rural priests joined the rebellion of townspeople, who began to destroy manor houses and castles near Paris, massacring entire noble families in a savage class war. Contemporaries were astonished at the intensity and violence of the Jacquerie. The chronicler Froissart, sympathetic to the nobility, reflected the views of the ruling class in describing the rebels as "small, dark, and very poorly armed." As for the violence, Froissart continues, "They thought that by such means they could destroy all the nobles and gentry in the world. . . ." Noble repression was even more savage, as thousands of rebels died in battles and were executed. In Paris the rebel leader Marcel was killed in factional strife, but urban rebellions continued into the fifteenth century.

In 1381 in England rural and urban discontent intensified as landlords, peasants, and workers pursued increasingly opposing interests. For the landowning class, composed of both ecclesiastical and secular lords, the Black Death and recurring plagues meant a steady erosion of income, as noble lords, forced to pay higher wages because of the labor shortage, also paid higher prices for goods. Most resorted to seigneurial rights and coercion to make up for the loss of income, either by restraining the free movement of labor or by levying fines on free tenants and serfs alike. For the lowest echelons in rural society, the serfs and agricultural workers, these new restrictions on their recently improved economic opportunities only deepened resentment. For the peasant elite, the free proprietors who managed to acquire more land and increase their income, the new economic conditions gave them more confidence in challenging the lord's power. The renewed exercise of seigneurial authority combined with a novel sense of peasant power created the conditions for a general rural uprising.

The trigger for the English peasant revolt was the imposition of a poll tax passed by Parliament in 1377 to raise money for the war against France. Unlike traditional subsidies to the king, the poll tax was levied on everyone. In May 1381 a revolt broke out to protest these taxes to finance a war that benefited only the king and the nobility. Rebels in Essex and Kent joined bands in London who confronted the king. The famous couplet of the radical preacher John Ball, who was executed after the revolt, expressed the rebels' egalitarian, antinoble sentiment:

> *When Adam delved [dug] and Eve span*
> *Who was then a gentleman?*

Forced to confront the rebels, the young king Richard II agreed to abolish serfdom and impose a ceiling on land rent, concessions immediately rescinded after the rebels' defeat. The revolt spread to many parts of England before it was suppressed. Although a current of discontent survived in the religious dissent and egalitarian views of the Lollards, market forces quickly began to dominate the manorial economy, and villeinage effectively disappeared as landlords came to accept the forces of supply and demand. Free labor, land rents, and a market for goods would eventually be accepted ways of life in fifteenth-century England.

Urban Life and Insurrections

The German saying "City air makes you free" referred to serfs who fled bondage and gained their freedom after residing for a year and a day in towns that had their own charters of rights. For some, medieval cities were places of heady excitement and possibilities in the Later Middle Ages. But as the great social melting pots of the fourteenth century, cities experienced much turmoil, as war, plague, and related economic crises led to challenges to political authority. Ghent, Rome, and Florence reveal the different patterns of social conflicts.

In the middle of Flanders, the most densely populated and urbanized region of Europe, stood the great industrial city of Ghent. In 1350, after the plague, the population was sixty thousand, smaller only than Paris and London in Europe north of the Alps. For over a century, Flanders had been Europe's industrial and financial heartland, importing raw wool from England, manufacturing fine cloth in the Flemish cities, and exporting woolen goods to all parts of Europe. Bankers, money changers, and merchants from all nations congregated in Bruges, second in size and importance only to Ghent.

Because the region depended on trade for food and goods, Flanders was especially sensitive to the larger political and economic changes. Between 1323 and 1328, unrest spread from rural Flanders to Bruges and Ypres, as citizens refused to pay the tithe to the church and taxes to the count of Flanders. Later the Hundred Years' War undermined the woolen industry as Edward III of England declared a trade embargo, thus halting shipments of raw materials to Flemish industries. Although Flanders was a French fief, weavers and other artisans opposed their count's pro-French policy. From 1338 to 1345, under the leadership of Jacques van Arteveld, the burghers (citizens) of Ghent rebelled against their prince. In the revolutionary years of 1377 through 1383, the townspeople of Ghent sought an alliance with the commune of Paris, fielded an army to battle the count, and held out into the fifteenth century despite their disastrous defeat by the French army at Roosebeke in 1382. Thus the urban insurrections in Flanders became part of the economic and political struggles of the Hundred Years' War. The English Channel became a pirate's lair, as English and French sailors plundered merchant ships and raided coastal ports.

In Italy revolts in Rome and Florence resulted in part from the long absence of the popes during the Avignon papacy. Factional violence between powerful noble clans in Rome fueled popular hatred of local magnates and provided the background for the dramatic episode of the Roman commune. The Florentine chronicler Giovanni Villani narrates that "on May 20, 1347 . . . a certain Cola di Rienzo had just returned to Rome from a mission on behalf of the Roman people to the court of the Pope, to beg him to come and live, with his court, in the see of St. Peter, as he should do." Although unsuccessful in his mission to Avignon, Rienzo so impressed the Romans with his speech that they proclaimed him "tribune of the people," a title harking back to the plebians' representatives in the ancient

The Money Exchange and Bankers' Houses in Bruges *Fourteenth-century Bruges was one of Europe's great industrial and financial centers. Many Italian merchants and bankers made the city their headquarters in northern Europe; in the building on the left the Genoese businessmen lived and worked, while their Florentine rivals did the same in the one on the right.*

Roman Republic. "Certain of the Orsini and the Colonna," continues Villani, "as well as other nobles, fled from the city to their lands and castles to escape the fury of the tribune and the people."

Son of an innkeeper and orphaned early in life, Rienzo (1313–1354) became a notary. Inspired by his reading of ancient Roman history, Rienzo and his followers took advantage of the nobles' flight and tried to remake their city in the image of classical Roman republicanism. In their efforts to achieve social equality they pursued an antinoble campaign. Rienzo also invented elaborate civic rituals to honor the commune, thereby elevating the body of citizens, with himself as their leader, to equal status with the emperor and the pope. Noble plottings and Rienzo's own extravagant schemes eventually caused his downfall, and although he briefly returned to power in 1354, he was soon assassinated. The Roman commune, however, represented more than a passing episode; its historical models and inspirations were the ancient Roman Republic and contemporary Franciscan ideas of divine justice and social equality. These twin themes of classical antiquity and religious devotion would represent European ideals during the next two centuries.

Economic and political dissatisfaction also spurred revolt in Florence, the center of banking and the woolen industry in southern Europe and one of the largest European cities in the fourteenth century. There the large population of woolworkers depended on the wool merchants, who controlled both the supply of raw material and the marketing of finished cloth. Unlike artisans in other trades, woolworkers were prohibited from forming their own guild and thus constituted a politically unrepresented wage-earning working class. As the wool industry declined in the wake of the plague and falling demand, unemployment became an explosive social problem. During the summer of 1378, the lower classes, many of them woolworkers, rose against the regime, demanding a more egalitarian social order. The immediate cause of the uprising was the war against the papacy, called the War of the Eight Saints (1375–1378) after the eight magistrates who directed Florentine foreign policy, and popular dissatisfaction with their performance galvanized broad opposition to the government. A coalition of artisans and merchants, supported by woolworkers, demanded more equitable power sharing with the bankers and wealthy merchants who controlled city government. By midsummer, crowds thronged the streets; citizens paralyzed the government; and woolworkers set fire to the palaces of the rich and demanded the right to form their own guild. The insurrection was subsequently called the Ciompi rebellion, meaning the uprising by the "little people." Alarmed by the radical turn of events, the guild artisans turned against their worker allies and defeated them in fierce street battles. The revolt ended with a restoration of the patrician regime, although Ciompi exiles continued to plot worker revolts into the 1380s.

The Ciompi rebellion, like the uprisings in Rome and Flanders, signaled a pattern of change in late medieval Europe. Although they represented a continuation of the communal uprisings of the eleventh and twelfth centuries, which helped establish town governments in some parts of Europe, the primary causes were the disruptions of the Black Death and the subsequent economic depression. Seeking to establish a more egalitarian regime, the Ciompi espoused some of the antipapal notions of the Fraticelli. But as significant as their motivations was their failure. Urban revolts did not redraw the political map of Europe, nor did they significantly alter the distribution of power. Instead they were subsumed by larger political transformations from which the territorial states would emerge as the major political forces.

Fragmentation and Power Amid Changing Forces

During the fourteenth century, central Europe established institutional forms that lasted, with minor variations, until the Holy Roman Empire dissolved in the early nineteenth century. The four most significant developments were the shift of political focus from the South and West to the East, the changing balance of power between the emperor and the princes, the development of cities, and the rise of self-governing communes in the Alps.

Three of the five German kings in this period belonged to the House of Luxembourg: Charles IV (∗1347–1378), Wenceslas (∗1378–1400), and Sigismund (∗1410–1437). Having obtained Bohemia by marriage, the Luxembourg dynasty based its power in the East, and Prague became the imperial capital. This change accelerated social and religious ferment within Bohemia, leading to the Hussite revolution in the early fifteenth century. From the standpoint of the Holy Roman Empire, the Luxembourgs' basing themselves in Bohemia initiated a shift of power within the empire, away from the Rhineland

and Swabia toward east central Europe. This trend would be consolidated when an unbroken series of Austrian Habsburgs were elected emperor after 1440. Except for a continuous involvement with northern Italy, theoretically a part of the Holy Roman Empire, German institutions became more closely allied with eastern rather than western Europe. For example, the Holy Roman Empire's first university, named the Charles University after its royal founder, Charles IV, was at Prague. Bohemians and Hungarians also began to exert more influence in imperial politics.

Another development that separated Germany from western Europe was the fragmentation of political authority at a time when French, English, and Castilian monarchs were consolidating their power. For Charles IV, even his coronation as emperor in 1355 did not translate into more power at home. The Bohemian nobility still refused to recognize his supreme authority, and the German princes secured from him a constitutional guarantee for their own sovereignty. In 1356, Charles had to agree to the Golden Bull, which required the German king to be chosen by seven electors: the archbishops of Mainz, Cologne, and Trier; and four princes, including the king of Bohemia, the elector of Saxony, the count of the Palatinate, and the margrave of Brandenburg. The imperial electoral college also guaranteed the existence of numerous local and regional power centers, a distinctive feature in German history into the modern age.

Although no single German city rivaled Paris, London, Florence, or Ghent in population, urban communes made Germany the economic equal of northern Italy and the Low Countries. But powerful princes prevented the urban communes from evolving into city republics like those in Italy. In 1388, for example, the count of Württemberg defeated the Swabian League of cities, formed in 1376. Nevertheless, the cities were at the forefront of economic growth. In the great imperial cities of southern Germany, subject only to the emperor and represented at the Imperial Diet (a periodic meeting of the leading princes, nobles, and city representatives of the Holy Roman Empire), the leading patrician mercantile families had a voice in imperial politics. Nuremberg and Augsburg became centers of the north-south trade, linking Poland, Bohemia, and the German lands with the Mediterranean. During the fifteenth century, German

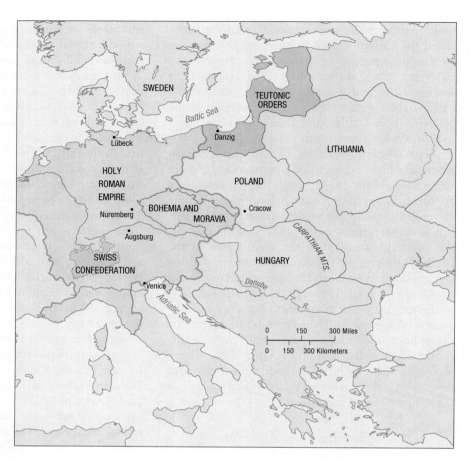

Central and Eastern Europe in the Thirteenth and Fourteenth Centuries

burghers would overtake their Italian counterparts in finance and the production of handicraft. In northern Germany the Hanseatic League, under the leadership of Lübeck, united the many towns trading between the Baltic and the North Sea. At its zenith in the fifteenth century, the Hanseatic fleet controlled the Baltic, and the league was a power to be reckoned with by kings and princes.

Another sign of political fragmentation was the growth of self-governing peasant and town communes in the high Alpine valleys that became the Swiss Confederation. In 1291 the peasants of Uri, Schwyz, and Unterwalden had sworn a perpetual alliance against their Habsburg overlord. After defeating a Habsburg army in 1315, these free peasants took the name of "Confederates" and developed a new alliance that would become Switzerland. By 1353, Luzerne, Zurich, Glarus, Zug, and

Bern had joined the confederation. Its recognition in 1415 by Emperor Sigismund established the new entity as a polity, unique in its rejection of noble lordship. The Swiss Confederation grew into the sixteenth century, defeating armies sent by different princes to undermine its liberties.

Two large monarchies took shape in northeastern Europe. In the early twelfth century, Poland had splintered into petty duchies, and the Mongol invasion of the 1240s caused frightful devastation. But recovery was under way by 1300, and unlike almost every other part of Europe, Poland experienced an era of demographic and economic expansion in the fourteenth century. Both Jewish and German settlers, for example, helped build thriving towns like Cracow. Monarchical consolidation followed. King Casimir III (*1333–1370) won recognition in most of the country's regions for his royal authority, embodied in comprehensive law codes. A problem that persisted throughout his reign, however, was conflict with the neighboring princes of Lithuania—Europe's last pagan rulers, who for centuries fiercely resisted Christianization by the German crusading order, the Teutonic Knights, based in Prussia and Livonia (modern Latvia). After the Mongols overran Russia, Lithuania extended its rule southward, offering west Russian princes protection against Mongol and Muscovite rule. By the late fourteenth century a vast Lithuanian principality had arisen, embracing modern Lithuania, Belarus, and Ukraine. Casimir III's death in 1370 without a son and the failure of a new dynasty to take hold opened the way for the joining of Poland and Lithuania. In 1386 the Lithuanian prince Jogailo accepted Roman Catholic baptism, married the young queen of Poland, and later assumed the Polish crown. Under the Jagiellonian dynasty, Poland and Lithuania kept separate legal systems. Catholicism and Polish culture prevailed among the principality's upper class, although most native Lithuanian village folk remained pagan for several centuries. With only a few interruptions, the Polish-Lithuanian federation would last for five centuries. In 1410 it won a resounding victory over the Teutonic Knights, and by 1454 it regained from the crusaders direct access to the Baltic Sea at Danzig (today Gdansk).

Between Islam and Christianity

Two regions at opposite ends of the Mediterranean—Spain and Byzantium—were unusual in medieval Europe for their religious and ethnic diversity. As a result of the Spanish Reconquista of the twelfth and thirteenth centuries, the Iberian Christian kingdoms contained large religious and ethnic minorities. In Castile, where historians estimate the population before the plague at between 4 million and 5 million, some three hundred thousand inhabitants were Muslims and Jews. In Aragon, of the 1 million people in 1359, perhaps 3 percent to 4 percent belonged to these two religious minorities. In the Iberian peninsula the Christian kingdoms continued to consolidate their gains against Muslim Granada through internal colonization, bringing sizable minority populations into newly Christian

regions. At the same time, the orthodox Byzantine Empire, hardly recovered from the Fourth Crusade, fought for its survival against the Ottoman Turks. In the Balkans and Anatolia, the Ottomans created a multiethnic state, but one different from the model of the Hispanic kingdoms.

In the mid-fourteenth century, the Iberian peninsula encompassed six areas: Portugal, Castile, Navarre, Aragon, and Catalonia—all Christian—and Muslim Granada. Among these territories, Castile and Aragon were the most important, both politically and economically. For example, the monarchy of Aragon, which included the prosperous seaport of Barcelona, enhanced its commercial domination of the western Mediterranean by expanding into Sicily and Sardinia. The Muslim population concentrated in the south: from the Algarve in Portugal, eastward across Andalusia and Murcia, to Valencia. As Christian conquerors and settlers advanced, most Muslims (called Moors) were driven out of the cities or if allowed to stay were confined to specific quarters. Initially, Muslims could

Christian Expansion in Iberia

own property, practice their religion, and elect their own judges, but conditions worsened for them in the fifteenth century as fears of rebellions and religious prejudices intensified among Christians. Many Muslims were captured by Christian armies and became slaves who worked in Christian households or on the large estates, the *latifundia,* granted by the Castilian kings to the crusading orders, the church, and powerful noble families. Slavery existed on a fairly large scale at both ends of the Mediterranean, where Christian and Muslim civilizations confronted one another: in Iberia, North Africa, Asia Minor, and the Balkans.

Unlike the Muslims, Jews congregated exclusively in cities, where they practiced many urban professions. Prior to 1391 they encountered few social obstacles to advancement. Jewish physicians and tax collectors made up part of the administration of Castile, but the Christian populace resented their social prominence and wealth. Moreover, the religious fervor and sense of crisis in the later fourteenth century intensified the ever-present intolerance toward Jews. In June 1391, incited by the sermons of the priest Fernando Martínez, a mob attacked the Jewish community in Seville, plundering, burning, and killing all who refused baptism. The antisemitic violence spread to other cities in Andalusia, Castile, Valencia, Aragon, and Catalonia. Sometimes the authorities tried to protect the Jews, who were legally the king's property. In Barcelona the city government tried to suppress the mob until the riot became a popular revolt that threatened the rich and the clergy. About half of the two hundred thousand Castilian Jews converted to Christianity to save themselves; another twenty-five thousand were murdered or fled to Portugal and Granada. The survivors were to face even more discrimination and violence in the fifteenth century.

The fourteenth century also saw a great power rise at the other end of the Mediterranean. Under Osman I (1280–1324) and his son Orhan Gazi (1324–1359), the Ottoman dynasty became a formidable force in Anatolia and the Balkans, where political disunity opened the door for Ottoman advances. The Ottomans were one of several Turkish tribal confederations in central Asia. As converts to Sunni Islam and as warriors, the Ottoman cavalry raided Byzantine territory. In 1326, Orhan captured

Ottoman Expansion in the Balkans

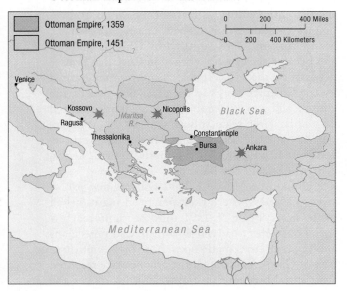

Bursa on the Marmara Sea, across from Constantinople, and two years later defeated a Byzantine army led by Emperor Andronicus III (*1328–1341). In 1341 both contenders for the Byzantine imperial throne hoped to defeat the other with Ottoman aid; as payment they invited the swift Turkish cavalry to plunder Byzantine territory, thus opening Europe to Ottoman conquest.

Under Murat I (*1360–1389), the Ottomans reduced the Byzantine Empire to the city of Constantinople and the status of a vassal state. In 1364, Murat defeated a joint Hungarian-Serbian army at the Maritsa River, alerting Europe for the first time to the threat of an Islamic invasion. In 1366, Pope Urban V called for a crusade, but the Christian kingdoms in the West were already warring. In the Balkans the Ottomans skillfully exploited the political fragmentation to maintain their influence. Fortunately for the Ottomans, Serbian, Albanian, Wallachian, Bulgarian, and Byzantine interests rarely coincided. Moreover, Venice, Genoa, and Ragusa (today Dubrovnik in Croatia) each pursued separate commercial interests. The Latin principalities in Greece established after the Fourth Crusade were also disunified. Thus an Ottoman army allied with the Bulgarians and even some Serbian princes won the battle of Kossovo (1389), destroying the last organized Christian resistance south of the Danube. The Ottomans secured control of southeastern Europe after 1396, when they crushed a crusading army summoned by Pope Boniface IX and consisting of knights from many countries at Nicopolis.

It would be misleading to interpret the Ottoman invasion only as a continuation of the struggle between Christendom and Islam. The battle for territory transcended the boundaries of faith. Christian princes as vassals and Christian slave soldiers, the *Yeni Çeri*, or Janissaries (meaning the New Force, the Ottoman infantry), fought for the sultan against other Turkish princes in Anatolia. The Janissaries, Christian children the sultan raised as Muslims, constituted the fundamental support of the Ottomans. They formed a service class, the *devshirme*, which was both dependent on and loyal to the ruler.

At the sultan's court, Christian women were prominent in the harem; thus many Ottoman princes had Greek or Serbian mothers. In addition to the Janissaries, Christian princes and converts to Islam served in the emerging Ottoman administration. In areas conquered by the Ottomans, existing religious and social structures remained intact when local people accepted Ottoman suzerainty (overlordship) and paid taxes. Only in areas of persistent resistance did the Ottomans drive out or massacre the inhabitants, settling Turkish tribes in their place. A distinctive pattern of Balkan history was thus established at the beginning of the Ottoman conquest: the extreme diversity of ethnic and religious communities woven together in the fabric of an efficient central state.

By the mid-fourteenth century the territory of the Byzantine Empire consisted of only Constantinople, Thessalonika, and a narrow strip of land in modern-day Greece. Byzantium never recovered from the Fourth Crusade. During the fourteenth century, three civil wars (1321–1328, 1341–1347, 1376–1379) between rivals to the throne, the Black Death, and numerous Ottoman incursions devastated the land and the population. Constantinople was saved in 1402 from a five-year siege by the Ottomans when Mongol invaders crushed another Ottoman army near Ankara in Asia Minor. Although the empire's fortunes declined, Byzantium experienced a religious and cultural ferment, as the elites compensated for their loss of power in a search for past glory and asserted their cultural superiority as Greeks over the militarily stronger but to them culturally inferior Ottomans and Latins. The majority asserted the superiority of the Greek orthodox faith and opposed the reunion of the Roman and Greek churches, a political price for western European military aid. Still others adhered to tradition, attacking any departures from ancient literary models and Byzantine institutions. A handful, such as the scholar George Gemistos (1353–1452), abandoned Christianity and embraced Platonic philosophy. Gemistos even changed his name (meaning "full" in Greek) to Plethon, its classical equivalent, which sounds like the name of Plato (Platon in Greek). Only a minority, such as Demetrius Kydones (c. 1376), an imperial minister, urged people to learn from the strengths of the Latin West. The scholar Manuel Chrysoloras became professor of Greek in Florence in 1397, thus establishing the study of ancient Greece in western Europe.

Toward the Renaissance: The Social Order and Cultural Change

An abundance of written and visual records documenting the lives of all social groups has survived from the fourteenth century. Much of our knowledge of the period comes from the vernacular literature that transcended traditional linguistic and thematic boundaries. Sources ranging from chronicles of dynastic conflicts and noble chivalry to police records of criminality paint a vivid picture of late medieval society, showing the changed relations between town and country, noble and commoner, and men and women. These sources reveal the impact the crisis had on their lives, as Europeans struggled to adjust to uncertainties and changes related to the plague, war, and religious dissent. New material wealth allowed some to enjoy more prosperous lives, but the disruptions and dislocations caused by various crises forced many on the margins of society—the poor, beggars, and prostitutes—into a violent underworld of criminality.

As the Byzantines recovered their appreciation of Greek antiquity, so did Italians revive ancient Roman culture. This cultural movement focused initially on imitating classical Latin rhetoric, but it later extended to the other disciplines of the humanities, such as the study of history, and finally blossomed into a broad cultural movement. This movement, which inspired brilliant achievements in the visual arts and vernacular literature, came to be called the Renaissance (meaning "rebirth").

The Household

Family life and the household economy formed the fabric of late medieval society. In contrast to the nobility and great merchants, whose power rested on their lineages, most Europeans lived in a more confined social world, surrounded by kin and neighbors. The focus of their lives was the house, where parents and children, and occasionally a grandparent or other relative, lived together. This pattern generally characterized both urban and rural society. In some peasant societies, such as in

Languedoc (southern France), brothers and their families shared the same roof; but the nuclear family was by far the dominant social model.

Compared to the nobility, residing in castles, artisans and peasants lived modestly. For those of medium wealth the family dwelling usually consisted of a two- to three-story building in the city and a single farmhouse in the countryside. For these social groups the household usually served as both work and private space; shopkeepers and craftspeople used their ground floors as workshops and storefronts, reserving the upper stories for family life. By our standards late medieval urban life was intolerably crowded, with little privacy. Neighbors could easily spy on each other from adjoining windows or even come to blows, as did two Florentine neighbors who argued over the installation of a second-story latrine that emptied out on a neighbor's property. In rural areas the family house served a variety of productive purposes, not least to shelter the farm animals during the winter.

In a society with an unequal distribution of power between women and men, the worlds of commerce and agriculture were those in which women came closest to partnership with their husbands. As a consequence of the plague and labor shortages, women found themselves in relatively favorable working positions. In cities all over Europe, women worked in retail trade. They sold dairy products, foods, meat, cloth, salt, flour, and fish; brewed beer; spun and wove cloth; and often acted as their husband's informal business partner. Although excluded from many handicrafts and professions and barred from all but a few guilds, fourteenth-century women played a crucial role in the urban economy, especially when widowed. Experienced in their late husband's business, owners of valuable assets, they represented attractive marriage candidates for ambitious men. Daughters of guild artisans similarly influenced their husband's economic advancement. The degree to which women participated in public life, however, varied with class and region. Women in Mediterranean Europe, especially in upper-class families, lived more circumscribed lives than their counterparts in northern Europe. The former, for example, could not dispose of personal property without the consent of males, be they fathers, husbands, or grown sons, whereas the latter regularly represented them-

June
Real farmwork in fourteenth-century France was never as genteel as in this miniature painting, part of a series illustrating the months of the year in a beautiful devotional book created for the duke of Berry. Nevertheless, the scene does faithfully represent the haying and suggests the gendered division of village labor, as the men swing their scythes and the women wield rakes.

selves in legal transactions and testified in court. Partnership in marriage characterized the peasant household. True, men and women performed different tasks, such as plowing and spinning, but many chores required cooperation. During harvests, all hands were mobilized. The men usually reaped with sickles, while the women gleaned the fields. Viticulture (cultivating grapes for wine making) called for full cooperation between the sexes: both men and women worked equally in picking grapes and trampling them to make wine. Because the

The improved material life of the middle classes was represented in many visual images of the Late Middle Ages. Italian and Flemish paintings of the late fourteenth and early fifteenth centuries depicted the new comforts of urban life such as fireplaces and private latrines. Painters developed an interest in material objects: beds, chests, rooms, curtains, and buildings provided the ubiquitous background of Italian paintings of the period. In rural areas the new prosperity could be seen in more elaborate farmhouses with greater differentiation between private and work space for the peasant elite. An illustration in *The Book of Hours* (1416), commissioned by the duke of Berry, brother of the French king, depicts a romanticized view of country life that might have characterized the peasant elite. Surrounded by a low fence, the compound includes the family house, a granary, and a shed. Animals and humans no longer intermingled, as they had in the thirteenth century and still did in poorer peasant households. The picture shows peasants warming themselves and drying their laundry in front of the fire, while the sheep are safe and warm in the shed.

February
As in all the miniatures in the duke of Berry's prayer-book, this cozy scene shows how the late-medieval nobility liked to imagine their peasants and livestock lived—both securely housed in warm and separate shelters, while the customary work of rural society goes on peacefully.

The Underclasses

If family life and the household economy formed the fabric of late medieval society, the world of poverty and criminality represented its torn fringes. Indeed the boundary between poor and criminal was very thin. Fourteenth-century society resembled a pyramid, with a broad base of underclasses—poor peasants and laborers in the countryside, workers and servants in the cities. Still one level lower were the marginal elements of society, straddling the line between legality and criminality.

Women featured prominently in the underclasses, reflecting the unequal distribution of power between the sexes. In Mediterranean Europe some 90 percent of slaves were women in domestic servitude. Their actual numbers were small—several hundred in fourteenth-century Florence, for example—because only rich households could afford slaves. They came from Muslim or Greek Orthodox countries and usually served in upper-class households in the great commercial city republics of Venice, Florence, and Ragusa. Urban domestic service was also the major employment for girls from the countryside, who worked to save money

household constituted the basic unit of agricultural production, most partners remarried quickly after a spouse died. The incidence of households headed by a single person, usually a poor widow, was much lower in villages than in cities. Studies of court records for fourteenth-century English villages show relatively few reports of domestic violence, perhaps reflecting the economic dependency between the sexes. Violence against women was more visible in urban societies where many women worked as servants and prostitutes.

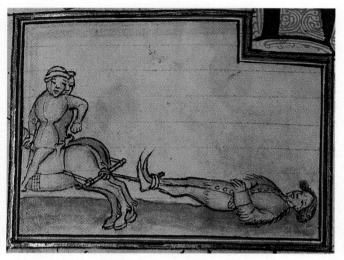

A Baron Tortured
This illumination, from a French chronicle, shows the torture meted out to a Gascon baron, Jordan de Lille, to punish his rebelliousness. Such degrading penalties (normal for ordinary transgressors) were occasionally inflicted on nobles to emphasize the gravity of their offenses.

for their dowries. In addition to the usual household chores, women also worked as wet nurses.

Given their exclusion from many professions and their powerlessness, many poor women found prostitution the only available means of living. Male violence forced many women into prostitution: rape stripped away their social respectability and any prospects for marriage. Condemned by the church, prostitutes were tolerated throughout the Middle Ages, but in the fourteenth and fifteenth centuries, the government intensified its attempts to control sexuality by institutionalizing prostitution. Restricted to particular quarters in cities, supervised by officials, sometimes under direct government management, prostitutes found themselves confined to brothels, increasingly controlled by males. In legalizing and controlling prostitution, officials aimed to maintain the public order. In Florence such state sponsorship provided a means to check homosexuality and concubinage. Female sexuality directed by the state in this way also helped define and limit the role of women in society at large. Although their legal status improved in the Late Middle Ages, prostitutes had only partial legal

rights, similar to those of Jews, and were constantly subject to violence.

Men populated the violent criminal underworld. Organized gangs prowled the larger cities. In Paris, a city teeming with thieves, thugs, beggars, prostitutes, and vagabonds, the Hundred Years' War led to a sharp rise in crime. In 1389, for example, police officials tracked down a criminal ring, arresting many for highway robbery and murder. Gang members were mostly artisans who vacillated between work and crime. Sometimes disguised as clerics, they robbed, murdered, and extorted from prostitutes. Often they served as soldiers. War was no longer an occupation reserved for knights but had become a vocation that absorbed young men from poor backgrounds. Initiated into a life of plunder and killing, discharged soldiers adjusted poorly to civilian life; between wars, these men turned to crime.

A central feature of social marginality was mobility. Mostly young, lacking stable families, those on society's fringes wandered extensively, begging and stealing. Criminals were also found among the clergy. While some were lay men who assumed clerical disguises to escape the rigors of secular courts, others were bona fide clerics who turned to crime to make ends meet during an age of steadily declining clerical income. "Decent society" treated these marginal elements with suspicion and hatred. Townspeople and peasants distrusted travelers and vagabonds. During the later Middle Ages, attitudes against poverty hardened. New laws restricted vagabonds and begging clerics, although cities and guilds began building hospitals and almshouses to deal with these social problems.

Middle-Class Writers and the Birth of Humanism

From the epics and romances of the twelfth and thirteenth centuries, vernacular literature blossomed in the fourteenth. Poetry, stories, and chronicles composed in Italian, French, English, and other national languages helped articulate a new sense of aesthetics. No longer did Latin and the church culture dominate the intellectual life of Europe, and no longer were writers principally clerics or aristocrats.

The great writers of late medieval Europe were of bourgeois (urban middle-class) origins, from families that had done well in government or church service or in commercial enterprises. Unlike the troubadours, with their aristocratic backgrounds, the men and women who wrote vernacular literature in this age typically came from the cities, and their audience was the literate laity. Francesco Petrarch (1304–1374), "crowned" as the poet laureate of his age in Rome, was born in Arezzo, where his father, a notary, lived in political exile from Florence. His younger contemporary and friend, Giovanni Boccaccio (1313–1375), was also Florentine. Boccaccio's father worked for the Florentine banking firm of Bardi in Paris, where Boccaccio was born; for generations the family had been small landowners outside Florence. Geoffrey Chaucer (1340–1400?) was the first great vernacular poet of medieval England. His father was a wealthy wine merchant; Chaucer worked as a servant to the king and controller of customs in London. Even writers who celebrated the life of the nobility were children of commoners. Although born in Valenciennes to a family of moneylenders and merchants, Jean Froissart (1337–1410), whose chronicle vividly describes the events of the Hundred Years' War, was an ardent admirer of chivalry. Christine de Pizan (1365–1429), whose numerous works defended feminine honor against misogyny, was the daughter of a Venetian municipal counselor.

Life in all its facets found expression in the new vernacular literature, as writers told of love, greed, and salvation. In *Songs* (*Canzoniere*), Petrarch juxtaposes divine and carnal desires to create beautiful short poems, praising the beauty of his idealized love for Laura, a young Florentine woman he admired from afar, and the Virgin Mary; after Petrarch the sonnet became the standard form for love poetry. Boccaccio's *Decameron* popularized the short story, as the characters in this novella told sensual and bizarre tales in the shadow of the Black Death. These stories reflect the world of the Italian merchant, drawing on Boccaccio's own experiences in banking and commerce. Members of different social orders parade themselves in Chaucer's *Canterbury Tales,* journeying together on a pilgrimage. In colorful verse written in Middle English, Chaucer makes his world come alive.

He describes a merchant on horseback: "A marchant was ther with a forked berd/ In mottelee, and hye on horse he sat/ up-on his heed a Flaundrish bever hat/ his botes clasped faire and fetisly. . . . For sothe he was a worthy man with-alle/ but sooth to seyn, I noot how men him calle." Chaucer also vividly portrayed other social classes—yeomen, London guildsmen, and minor officials. Whereas Chaucer created his characters from a middle-class urban society, Froissart, in *Chronicles,* idealized the world of knightly exploits and the castle, a world of glory and riches, where people are only vaguely aware of the misery of the poor.

Noble patronage was crucial to the growth of vernacular literature, a fact reflected in the careers of the most famous writers. Perhaps closest to the model of an independent man of letters, Petrarch nonetheless relied on powerful patrons at various times: his early career began at the papal court in Avignon, where his father worked as a notary; during the 1350s, he enjoyed the protection and patronage of the Visconti duke of Milan. For Boccaccio, who started out in the Neapolitan world of

Christine de Pizan Presents Her Book to Queen Isabella
Illustrations depicting an author ceremoniously kneeling to present a book to a patron were commonplace in the Late Middle Ages and Renaissance. Notice that this stylized scene depicts the exclusively female sphere of the queen of France and her ladies-in-waiting.

commerce, the court of King Robert of Naples initiated him into the world of letters. Chaucer served in administrative posts and on many diplomatic missions, during which he met Petrarch and Boccaccio. Noble patronage shaped the literary creations of Froissart and Christine de Pizan. Froissart owed his early career to Count John of Hainault and later enjoyed the favors of the English and French royal houses, respectively, a shift discernible in the changed sympathies of his chronicle of the Hundred Years' War. Christine grew up in the French royal household, where her father served as court astrologer. Commissioned to write the official biography of King Charles V, Christine would have been unable to produce most of her writings without the patronage of women in the royal household. She presented her most famous work, *The Book of the City of Ladies* (1405), a defense of women's reputation and virtue, to Isabella of Bavaria, the queen of France and wife of Charles VI. Christine's last composition was a poem praising Joan of Arc, restorer of French royal fortunes, and like Christine herself, a distinguished woman in a world otherwise dominated by men.

Vernacular literature blossomed not at the expense of Latin but alongside a classical revival. In spite of the renown of their Italian writings, Petrarch and Boccaccio, for example, took great pride in their Latin works. Latin represented the language of salvation and was also the international language of learning. The Vulgate Bible was the only sanctioned version, although the Lollard Bible, intended for the laity, was the first English translation of Latin Scripture. Professors taught and wrote in Latin; students spoke it as best as they could; priests celebrated Mass and dispensed sacraments in Latin; and theologians composed learned treatises in Latin. Church Latin was very different from the Latin of the ancient Romans, both in syntax and in vocabulary. In the second half of the fourteenth century, writers began to imitate the rather antiquated "classical" Latin of Roman literature. In the forefront of this literary and intellectual movement, Petrarch traveled to many monasteries in search of long-ignored Latin manuscripts. For writers like Petrarch, medieval church Latin was an artificial, awkward language, whereas classical Latin, and after its revival, Greek too, was the mother tongue of the ancients. Thus the classical writings of Greece and Rome represented true vernacular literature, only more authentic, vivid, and glorious than the poetry and prose written in Italian and other contemporary European languages. Classical allusions and literary influences abound in the works of Boccaccio, Chaucer, Christine de Pizan, and others. The new intellectual fascination with the ancient past also stimulated translations of these works into the vernacular.

Italy led this new intellectual movement that came to be called humanism. In its original sense, humanism was simply the study of the seven liberal arts that constituted the introductory curriculum at universities before students moved on to the professional fields of theology, medicine, and law. Italian lawyers and notaries had a long-standing interest in classical rhetoric because eloquence was an essential skill of their profession. Gradually the imitation of ancient Roman rhetoric led to the absorption of ancient ideas. In the writings of Roman historians such as Livy and Tacitus, fifteenth-century Italian civic elites (many of them lawyers) found echoes of their own devout patriotism. Between 1400 and 1430 in Florence, which at the time was at war with the duchy of Milan, the study of the humanities evolved into a republican ideology that historians call civic humanism. Under the

Italy at the Dawn of the Renaissance

leadership of three chancellors—Coluccio Salutati (1331–1406), Leonardo Bruni (1374–1444), and Poggio Bracciolini (1380–1459)—the Florentines waged a highly successful propaganda war on behalf of virtuous republican Florence against tyrannical Milan, invoking the memory of the overthrow of Etruscan tyrants by the first Romans. Thus the study of ancient civilization was not only an antiquarian quest but a call to public service and political action.

CONCLUSION

The word *crisis* implies a turning point, a decisive moment, and during the hundred-plus years between 1320 and 1430, European civilization faced such a time. Departing from the path of expansion, it instead entered a period of uncertainty, disunity, and contraction. The traditional order, achieved during the optimism and growth of the High Middle Ages, was undermined in the mid-fourteenth century, most obviously by the Black Death and the Hundred Years' War, both of which decimated the population and altered agricultural production and seigneurial relations between lords and peasants. Empire and papacy, long symbols of unity, crumbled into political disintegration and spiritual malaise in the later Middle Ages.

In the eastern Mediterranean, European civilization retreated in the face of Ottoman Turk advances. Christian Europe continued to grow, however, in the Iberian Peninsula; for the next three centuries the Mediterranean would become the arena for struggles between Christian and Islamic empires. The papacy would clamor for new crusades.

Although instrumental in ending the Great Schism, the conciliar movement failed to limit supreme papal power, identified by its critics as the source of spiritual discontent. Traumatized, perhaps by the crisis of authority, the next generations of popes would concentrate on consolidating their worldly power and wealth. Successful in repressing or compromising with the Lollard, Hussite, and other heretical movements, the church would focus its attention on control and would neglect, to their future regret, the spiritual needs of a laity increasingly estranged from domination by a clerical elite.

The disintegration of universal order hastened the consolidation of some states, as countries such as England and France developed political, linguistic, and cultural boundaries that largely coincided. Other areas, such as Castile, Portugal, and the Ottoman Empire, included different linguistic and religious groups under one political authority. Still other regions, principally central Europe and Italy, remained divided into competing city-states characterized more by the sense of local differences than by their linguistic similarity.

The artistic productions of the age best reflect the new aesthetic sensibilities. Conscious of their departure from the past, writers and artists—principally in Italy—invented new forms to express their ideas. In the process, they created an elegant and sophisticated vernacular Italian literature that was much admired and imitated in other countries. Those devoted to Latin literature turned not to the language of the church but to the classical models of ancient Rome, harking back to the splendor of Roman civilization and institutions. The ancient past also inspired a creative revolution in the visual arts. In the 1420s and 1430s, a new generation in Florence discovered the beauty of the human form and classical space. They created a new style, more individualistic and innovative, that would characterize a cultural blooming in the fifteenth century.

SUGGESTIONS FOR FURTHER READING

Source Materials

Froissart, Jean. *Chronicles.* Translated by Geoffrey Brereton. 1968. A judicious selection of the highlights of Froissart's massive chronicle of the Hundred Years' War, particularly informative on the feudal nobility's ethos.

Joan of Arc: By Herself and Her Witnesses. Edited by Régine Pernoud. 1966. Contains documents on the life of Joan of Arc arranged chronologically, including important transcripts of her trial.

Pizan, Christine de. *The Book of the City of Ladies.* Translated by Earl Jeffrey Richards. 1982. Written by the celebrated author of the French court, a book defending the honor and virtues of women.

Interpretive Studies

Allmand, Christopher. *The Hundred Years' War: England and France at War, c. 1300–1450.* 1988. A readable survey of the recent literature.

Bois, Guy. *The Crisis of Feudalism: Economy and Society in Eastern Normandy, c. 1300–1550.* 1984. A stimulating, difficult book that analyzes the relationship between socioeconomic changes and warfare using a Marxist perspective.

Branca, Vittore. *Boccaccio: The Man and His Works.* 1976. A masterly synthesis by one of the leading Boccaccio scholars.

Duby, Georges. *A History of Private Life: II. Revelations of the Medieval World.* 1988. A collection of fascinating essays that portray social history; profusely illustrated.

Geremek, Bronisław. *The Margins of Society in Late Medieval Paris.* 1987. An intriguing and scholarly portrait of the Parisian underworld by a leading Polish historian and leader in the Solidarity movement.

Hanawalt, Barbara A., ed. *Women and Work in Preindustrial Europe.* 1986. Ten essays on the history of working women between the thirteenth and sixteenth centuries in western and central Europe.

Hilton, R. H., and T. H. Aston, eds. *The English Rising of 1381.* 1984. The most recent research on the English uprising, as well as on the Jacquerie and the Ciompi revolts.

Kaminsky, Howard. *A History of the Hussite Revolution.* 1967. A detailed narrative based on extensive primary research.

Leff, Gordon. *Heresy in the Later Middle Ages: The Relation of Heterodoxy to Dissent, c. 1250–1450.* 1967. Stresses the fluid landscape of theological and religious dissent; includes the Fraticelli, Free Spirits, Lollards, and Hussites.

Leuschner, Joachim. *Germany in the Late Middle Ages.* 1980. The best survey in English: balanced, readable, and particularly good on political and urban history.

Miskimin, Harry A. *The Economy of Early Renaissance Europe, 1300–1460.* 1975. A succinct and authoritative synthesis.

Mollat, Michel, and Philippe Wolff. *The Popular Revolutions of the Late Middle Ages.* 1973. A wide-ranging narrative and analysis of the many urban revolts and peasant uprisings from 1280 to 1435 by two prominent French medievalists.

Nichols, David. *The van Arteveldes of Ghent: The Varieties of Vendetta and the Hero in History.* 1988. Two generations of this leading merchant family set against the political and social background of Ghent.

Oakley, Francis. *Council Over Pope? Towards a Provisional Ecclesiology.* 1969. A succinct introduction to the history and doctrines of conciliarism and their implications for church history.

O'Callaghan, Joseph F. *A History of Medieval Spain.* 1975. A massive survey of Spanish history; a good reference book.

Ozment, Steven. *The Age of Reform, 1250–1550: An Intellectual and Religious History of Late Medieval and Reformation Europe.* 1980. A particularly lucid exposition of intellectual history of the Late Middle Ages.

Renouard, Yves. *The Avignon Papacy, 1305–1403.* 1970. A lively, comprehensive account of the Great Schism and the growth of papal government.

Rörig, Fritz. *The Medieval Town.* 1967. A succinct analysis of late medieval German cities by a leading social and economic historian.

Shaw, Stanford J. *History of the Ottoman Empire and Modern Turkey.* Vol. I. *Empire of the Gazia: The Rise and Decline of the Ottoman Empire, 1280–1808.* 1976. A detailed narrative, particularly good on political and institutional history.

Warner, Marina. *Joan of Arc: The Image of Female Heroism.* 1981. A careful and brilliant analysis of Joan's life and her legend after death.

Ziegler, Philip. *The Black Death.* 1970. The best synthesis of the vast literature on the plague.

Reflecting on the history of the Italian states between 1434 and 1494, the Florentine historian Niccolò Machiavelli (1469–1527) commented on the relationship between war and peace, culture and chaos:

> Usually provinces go most of the time, in the changes they make, from order to disorder and then pass again from disorder to order, for worldly things are not allowed by nature to stand still. . . . For virtue gives birth to quiet, quiet to leisure, leisure to disorder, disorder to ruin; and similarly, from ruin, order is born; from order, virtue; and from virtue, glory and good fortune. Whence it has been observed by the prudent that letters come after arms and that . . . captains [of war] arise before philosophers. For, as good and ordered armies give birth to victories and victories to quiet, the strength of well-armed spirits cannot be corrupted by a more honorable leisure than that of letters, nor can leisure enter into well-instituted cities with a greater and more dangerous deceit.

Machiavelli brilliantly described the paradox of the Renaissance—a time of intense political and social conflicts, and simultaneously a period of immense cultural creativity. In painting, literature, architecture, philosophy, and history and political thought, new ideas and forms gave identity and meaning to an unstable, changeable world. For Europeans of the fifteenth century, that unstable world was defined by an incessant quest for glory on the part of ruling elites of the Renaissance states and by the disruption of that order at the turn of the century.

Renaissance Europe, 1430–1493

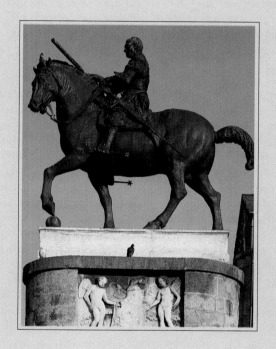

Donatello, Gattamelata
Consciously based on Roman statues of mounted emperors, this depiction of a relatively minor professional soldier (ironically nicknamed "Honey Cat") in the Venetian service at Padua attests to the power of classical models in fifteenth-century Italian public art.

Fifteenth-Century Economy and the Renaissance State

By the fifteenth century a handful of Italian states had swallowed up the many city-republics that had dotted Italy during the Middle Ages. Locked in an intense competition between powerful republics (Florence and Venice), principalities (Naples and Milan), and the papacy, the Italian states developed an elaborate system of warfare and diplomacy that, by mid-century, served to create a balance of power. Having withstood heretical attacks and the challenge of the conciliar movement, the popes saw the consolidation of their monarchical power as a church priority, leading most of them to participate eagerly in the rivalry among the states.

Outside Italy the process of state building intensified during the fifteenth century, and rulers used diplomacy, military might, and symbols of power and authority (for example, court ceremonies, linguistic unity, and the reduction of urban autonomy) to bring autonomous regions under central control. The most instructive example in western Europe was Burgundy (part of today's France and Low Countries), whose spectacular rise and fall demonstrated the fragility of a political construction that cut across three linguistic regions and followed no natural geographic boundary. In eastern Europe thousand-year-old Byzantium fell victim to the expanding Ottoman Empire, which was to remain a European presence until the early twentieth century. Some European states also achieved permanent successes, such as the further consolidation of the monarchy and the central government in Spain, Muscovy-Russia, France, and England.

The Italian States: Republics and Principalities

With the exception of the Papal States, the Italian states of the Renaissance can be divided into two broad categories: republics that preserved the traditional institutions of the medieval commune by allowing a civic elite to control political and economic life, and principalities ruled by one dynasty. The most powerful and influential states were the republics Venice and Florence and the principalities

IMPORTANT DATES
1440s Gutenberg introduces the printing press
1453 Fall of Constantinople; end of Byzantium
1454 Treaty of Lodi; power balance in Italy
1460–85 War of the Roses; Tudor dynasty ascendant
1462–1505 Reign of Ivan III of Muscovy
1467–92 Height of Florentine Renaissance
1471–84 Reign of Pope Sixtus IV; Renaissance in Rome
1474–1516 Spain unified under Isabella of Castile and Ferdinand of Aragon
1477 Death of Charles the Bold; end of Burgundy
1478 Inquisition established in Spain
1492 Columbus's first voyage; Christians conquer Muslim Granada and expel Jews from Spain

the duchy of Milan and the kingdom of Naples. In addition to these "Big Four," a handful of smaller states, such as Siena, Ferrara, and Mantua (Siena a republic and the other two principalities), stood out as important cultural centers during the Renaissance.

The picturesque gondolas beloved by contemporary tourists symbolize Venice's long history as a powerful maritime republic. During the fifteenth and sixteenth centuries, Venice, a city built on a lagoon, ruled an extensive colonial empire that extended from the Adriatic to the Aegean Sea. Venetian merchantmen sailed the Mediterranean, the Atlantic coast, and the Black Sea; Christian pilgrims to Palestine booked passage on Venetian ships; in 1430 the Venetian navy numbered some forty-five galleys (large warships propelled by sails and oars), three hundred sailing ships, and three thousand smaller vessels, mustering a total of over thirty thousand sailors in a population of only one hundred fifty thousand. Symbolizing their intimacy with and dominion of the sea, the Venetians celebrated an annual "Wedding of the Sea" on Ascension Day. Amid throngs of spectators and foreign dignitaries, the Venetian doge (the elected duke) sailed out to the Adriatic, threw a golden ring into its waters to renew the union, and intoned, "Hear us with favor, O Lord. We worthily entreat Thee to grant that this sea be tranquil and quiet for our men and all others who sail upon it." This prayer epitomized the importance of maritime power in the Venetian economy, for the city and its ruling class depended on long-distance trade for their prosperity. Control of the seas was vital, and Venetian noblemen were both sailors and warriors.

In the early fifteenth century, however, Venetians faced threats from the mainland. From 1425 to 1454, Venice fought the expanding duchy of Milan and brought its growth to a standstill, defending Venice's substantial territorial dominion on the Italian mainland. The second and greater danger came from the eastern Mediterranean, where the Ottoman Turks finally captured Byzantine Constantinople in 1453. Although a long campaign against the Turks (1463–1479) ended in defeat for Venice, this rivalry would be subsumed in a larger conflict between Christian Europe and Muslim Ottoman that would continue to the end of the seventeenth century.

By the Renaissance an oligarchy of aristocratic merchants ruled Venice and controlled all government functions. The Venetian constitution stated that only hereditary noblemen could serve in the Great Council. Their number in the fifteenth century fluctuated between two thousand and twenty-five hundred, although only between one thousand and fifteen hundred ever showed up for the Great Council meetings. Through a complicated electoral process (eleven steps were involved), the nobility elected a doge for life. Sometimes glory in war elevated a man to this highest office, as it did Pietro Mocenigo, a victorious admiral in the Turkish war. Other doges had extensive political and diplomatic experience. Limited in authority, the doge was the first among equals of the greatest Venetian nobles, who exercised power collectively via the Senate and the Council of Ten, institutions less unwieldy than the Great Council. Through military service, public office, financial sacrifices, and charity to the poor, the Venetian nobility dominated a republic remarkable for its political consensus and internal peace. Overseas trade and colonial territories benefited most social classes in Venice, who shared in the maritime profits as sailors, soldiers, and workers. A society with a strict hierarchy of classes and a tradition of conserving this social order, the Venetian Republic was widely admired for its political stability. The epithet *Serenissima Repubblica* (Most Serene Republic) pointed to the sharp contrast

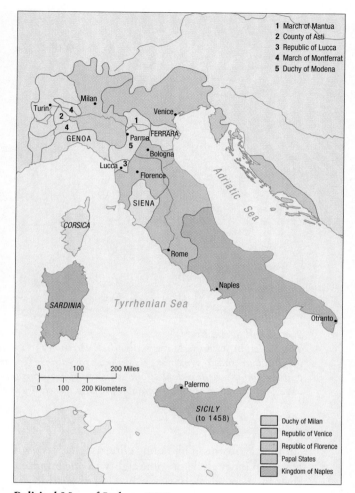

1 March of Mantua
2 County of Asti
3 Republic of Lucca
4 March of Montferrat
5 Duchy of Modena

Duchy of Milan
Republic of Venice
Republic of Florence
Papal States
Kingdom of Naples

Political Map of Italy, c. 1450

between Venice's stability and the political turmoil of the other Italian states.

Unlike serene Venice, Florence was in constant agitation: responsive to political conflicts, new ideas, and artistic styles. Like Venice, Florence described its government in the language of ancient Roman republicanism. Florentine liberty, however, rested on the subjugation of other city-republics, and Florentine armies systematically imposed their rule on the rest of Tuscany. Within Florence, despite the rhetoric of civic humanism, the social base of republican government continued to narrow in the early fifteenth century. Before 1434 a small oligarchy of four hundred thirty to five hundred seventy men ruled the quarter-million people of Florence and its

Sacred and Social Body
The Venetian state used lavish, dignified ceremony to impress citizens and visitors with its grandeur and to symbolize its divine protection. Here the great Venetian Renaissance painter Gentile Bellini depicts one such scene, a procession of the Eucharist across the Piazza San Marco uniting in common purpose the clergy and the Venetian governing elite.

subject territories. This ruling elite, too, had its own elite—an inner circle of some eighty to one hundred twenty men who consistently held the principal offices and three hundred fifty to four hundred fifty men of lesser prestige who served as the clients of the inner circle and occupied the minor offices.

Despite a system of rotation and short office terms designed to encourage political participation and prevent the entrenchment of power, the Medici family emerged victorious in 1434 in a factional struggle. Cosimo de' Medici (1388–1464), leader of the strongest faction, exiled scores of rivals and inaugurated a new era during which power increasingly became concentrated in his household. Although they maintained the traditional republican institutions and symbols, the Medici and their supporters controlled access to public office by manipulating the elaborate electoral process with screening, nominations, eligibility lists, and ad hoc committees. Pope Pius II, a native of Siena, traditionally a city in bitter rivalry with Florence, did not mince words when he described Medici

power: "Cosimo, having thus disposed of his rivals, proceeded to administer the state at his pleasure and amassed wealth. . . . In Florence he built a palace fit for a king." As head of one of the largest banks of Europe, Cosimo de' Medici used his immense wealth to influence politics. Even though he did not hold any formal political office, Cosimo wielded influence in government through business associates and clients who were indebted to him for loans, political appointments, and other favors.

As the largest bank in Europe, the Medici Bank handled papal finances, and branch offices were also established in many Italian cities and the major northern European financial centers. With a total of 90,000 florins of original capital (72,000 from the Medici family), the Medici Bank (including its subsidiary wool and silk manufacturing interests) gained a profit of 290,000 florins between 1435 and 1450. (By comparison, the total public debt of the Florentine government in 1428 to 1429 amounted to 2.78 million florins.) Assiduously avoiding the trappings of princely power and scrupulously up-

Lorenzo de' Medici, "the Magnificent"
Grandson of Cosimo and ruler of Florence from 1467 to his death in 1492, Lorenzo epitomized the Renaissance prince, although he paid lip-service to republican institutions. He was equally skilled as a statesman, a patron of art and learning, a poet of haunting love- and drinking-songs, and—as his broken nose testifies— an athlete.

holding the republican facade, Cosimo de' Medici was nonetheless not above cheating the republic. In his 1459 tax return, for example, he declared only 3,000 florins for the capital of the Milanese branch of the bank; the actual investment totaled 13,500 florins. Backed by this immense private wealth, Cosimo became the arbiter of war and peace, the regulator of law, more master than citizen. Yet the prosperity and security that Florence enjoyed made him popular as well. At his death, Cosimo was lauded as the "father of his country" (*pater patriae*)— much to the irritation of his opponents.

Cosimo's death encouraged these opponents. In 1466 several patricians raised the banner of ancient republican liberty by opposing Piero de' Medici, Cosimo's son. But the opposition, lacking unity and fearful of arousing another popular revolt that might engulf the entire ruling class, was crushed by Piero. Piero's son, Lorenzo (called "the Magnificent"), who assumed power in 1467, bolstered the regime's legitimacy with his lavish patronage of the arts. In 1478 Lorenzo narrowly escaped an assassination attempt while attending Mass in the so-called Pazzi conspiracy, named after its principal instigators. Two years after Lorenzo's death in 1494, the Medici were driven from Florence. They returned in 1512, only to be driven out again in 1527. In 1530 the republic was finally defeated, and Florence became a duchy under the Medici family.

Unlike Florence, with its republican aspirations, the duchy of Milan had been ruled by one dynasty since the fourteenth century. The most powerful Italian principality, Milan was known as a military state relatively uninterested in the support of the arts but with a first-class armaments and textile industry in the capital city and rich farmlands in Lombardy. Until 1447 the duchy was ruled by the Visconti dynasty, a group of powerful lords whose plans to unify all of northern and central Italy failed due to the combined opposition of Venice, Florence, and other Italian powers. In 1447 the last Visconti duke died without a male heir, and the nobility then proclaimed Milan to be the Ambrosian republic (named after the city's patron saint, Saint Ambrose), thus bringing the Visconti rule to a close.

For three years the new republic struggled to maintain Milan's political and military strength. Cities that the Visconti family had subdued rebelled against Milan, and the two great republics of Venice and Florence plotted its downfall. Milan's ruling nobility, seeking further defense, appointed Francesco Sforza, who had married the illegitimate daughter of the last Visconti duke, to the post of general. Sforza promptly turned against his employers, claiming the duchy as his own. A bitter struggle between the nobility and the bourgeoisie in Milan further undermined the republican cause, and in 1450, Sforza entered Milan in triumph.

To consolidate his rule, Francesco constructed an imposing moated fortress in the middle of Milan, a structure that dominates the heart of the city to this day. Equipped with sixty-two drawbridges, the fortress housed twelve hundred soldiers ready to crush any civic rebellion. Military strength coupled with economic growth won over erstwhile supporters of the republic. Francesco promoted manufacturing and commerce and curbed the privileges of the nobility in an attempt to broaden his government's social base.

The Sforzas never felt completely secure in their rule. Francesco's successors used both violent as well as artistic means to establish order and legitimacy. This dichotomy was epitomized by Francesco's son, Galeazzo Maria. A cruel and brutal man, he was devoted to music, paying thirty-three singers from northern Europe extravagant stipends to satisfy his musical tastes. Yet life in this sumptuous court could turn brutal at a moment's notice. In 1475, Galeazzo casually ordered a tailor thrown into prison because he had spoiled a courtier's doublet of crimson silk. A year later, while attending Mass, the tyrant himself was assassinated by three noblemen avenging their honor.

The power of the Sforza dynasty reached its height during the 1490s. In 1493, Duke Ludovico married his niece Bianca Maria to Maximilian, the newly elected Holy Roman emperor, promising an immense dowry in exchange for the emperor's legitimation of his rule. But the newfound Milanese glory was soon swept aside by France's invasion of Italy in 1494, and the duchy itself eventually came under Spanish rule.

After a struggle for succession between Alfonso of Aragon and René d'Anjou, a cousin of the king of France, the kingdoms of Naples and Sicily came under Aragonese rule between 1435 and 1494. Unlike the northern Italian states, Naples was dominated by powerful feudal barons who retained jurisdiction and taxation over their own vast estates. Alfonso I (*1435–1458), called "the Magnanimous" for his generous patronage of the arts, promoted the urban middle class to counter baronial rule, using as his base the city of Naples, the only large urban center in a relatively rural kingdom. Alfonso's son, Ferante I (*1458–1494), continued his father's policies: two of his chief ministers—Francesco Coppola and Antonello Petrucci—hailed from humble backgrounds (mercantile and farming families, respectively), and Petrucci was himself a notary. With their private armies and estates intact, however, the barons constantly threatened royal power, and in 1462 many rebelled against Ferante, supporting instead the Anjou claim. More ruthless than his father, Ferante readily crushed the opposition. He kept rebellious barons in the dungeons of his Neapolitan castle and confiscated their properties. When his own ministers Coppola and Petrucci plotted against him in 1486, siding with yet another baronial rebellion, Ferante feigned reconciliation, then arrested them at a banquet and executed the two men and their families.

Embroiled in Italian politics, Alfonso and Ferante shifted their alliances among the papacy, Milan, and Florence. But the greater threat to Neapolitan security came from external forces. In 1480, Ottoman forces captured the Adriatic port of Otranto, where they massacred the entire male population. And in 1494 a French invasion ended the Aragonese dynasty in Naples, although, as in Milan, France's claim would eventually be superseded by that of Spain.

The Burgundian State

Locked in a fierce competition in the peninsula, the Italian states paid little attention to large territorial states emerging in the rest of Europe that would soon overshadow Italy with their military power and economic resources. Burgundy, whose rise during the fifteenth century was a result of military might and careful statecraft, is just such an example. The spectacular success of the Burgundian dukes—and the equally dramatic demise of Burgundian power—bears testimony to the artful creation of the Renaissance state, paving the way for the development of the European nation-state.

Part of the French royal house, the Burgundian dynasty expanded its power rapidly by acquiring territory, primarily in the Netherlands. Between 1384 and 1476 the Burgundian state filled the territorial gap between France and Germany, extending from the Swiss border in the south to Friesland, Germany, in the north. Through purchases, inheritance, and conquests, the dukes ruled over French-, Dutch-, and German-speaking subjects, creating a state that resembled a patchwork of provinces and regions, each jealously guarding its laws and traditions. The Low Countries with their flourishing cities constituted the state's economic heartland, and the region of Burgundy

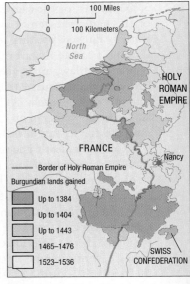

The Expansion of Burgundy

itself, which gave the state its name, offered rich farmlands and vineyards. Unlike England, whose insular character made it a natural geographical unit; or France, whose geography was forged in the national experience of repelling English invaders; or Castile, whose national identity came from centuries of warfare against Islam, Burgundy was an artificial creation whose coherence depended entirely on the skillful exercise of statecraft.

At the heart of Burgundian politics was the personal cult of its dukes. Philip the Good (*1418–1467) and his son, Charles the Bold (*1467–1477), were very different kinds of rulers, but both were devoted to enhancing the prestige of their dynasty and the security of their dominion. A bon vivant who fathered many illegitimate children, Philip was a lavish patron of the arts who commissioned numerous illuminated manuscripts, chronicles, tapestries, paintings, and music in his efforts to glorify Burgundy. Charles, on the other hand, was addicted to hunting and war and spent more time on war campaigns than at court, preferring to drill his troops rather than seduce noblewomen. Personally courageous (hence his nickname), he died in 1477 when his army was routed by the Swiss at Nancy.

The Burgundians' success depended in large part on their personal relationship with their subjects. Not only did the dukes travel constantly from one part of their dominion to another, as did the Italian rulers, they also staged elaborate ceremonies to enhance their power and promote their legitimacy. Princely entries into cities and at ducal weddings, births, and funerals became the centerpieces of a "theater" state in which the dynasty provided the only link among very diverse territories. New rituals became propaganda tools. In 1430, for example, Philip the Good created the Order of the Golden Fleece, inviting the greatest noblemen of his lands to join this latter-day Jason as his Argonauts. Philip's revival of chivalry in the ducal court transformed the semi-independent nobility into courtiers more closely tied to the prince.

In addition to sponsoring political propaganda, the Burgundian rulers created institutions to administer their geographically dispersed state by developing a financial bureaucracy and a standing army. But maintaining the army, one of the largest in Europe, left the dukes chronically short of money. They were forced to sell political offices to

The Marriage of Philip the Good and Isabella of Portugal in 1430
The Burgundian court embodied to the highest degree the ideals of late medieval courtly style. This painting, executed in the workshop of the Flemish master Jan van Eyck, conveys the atmosphere of chivalric fantasy in which the Burgundian court enveloped itself.

raise funds, which led to an inefficient and corrupt bureaucracy. The final demise of the Burgundian state had two sources: the loss of its duke, Charles the Bold, who died without a male heir; and an alliance between France and the Holy Roman Empire. When Charles fell in battle in 1477, France seized the duchy of Burgundy. The Netherlands remained loyal to Mary, Charles's daughter, and through her husband, the future Holy Roman Emperor Maximilian, some of the Burgundian lands and the dynasty's political and artistic legacy passed on to the Habsburgs.

New Monarchies and Empires

Other rulers had more success than the Burgundian dukes in preserving their states. After the mutually ruinous Hundred Years' War, both France and England turned inward. The Iberian Peninsula saw the long war against the Muslims come to an end and the unification of Castile and Aragon. Central Europe's Holy Roman emperors nominally ruled over a bewildering mass of virtually independent principalities and cities. On Christian Europe's eastern fringe, Muscovy emerged as a new power when it threw off Mongol rule and started on a long path of expansion. And in the Balkans the Ottoman Turks completed their conquest of the Byzantine Empire.

Except for the Italian states, the Swiss Confederation, and some semiautonomous German urban leagues, monarchy was the prevalent form of government in the Renaissance. A mid-century period of turmoil gave way to the restructuring of central monarchical power in the last decades of the fifteenth century. Notably, the rulers Henry VII (*1485–1509) of England, Louis XI (*1461–1483) of France, and joint monarchs Isabella (*1474–1504) of Castile and Ferdinand (*1479–1516) of Aragon all developed stronger, institutionally more complex central governments in which middle-class lawyers played an increasingly prominent role.

In England civil war at home followed defeat in the Hundred Years' War. Henry VI (*1422–1461), ascended to the throne as a child, proved in maturity to be a weak and, on occasion, mentally unstable monarch. He was unable to control the great lords of the realm, who sowed the seeds of anarchy with their numerous private feuds; between 1450 and 1455 six of the thirty-six peers in the House of Lords were imprisoned at some time for violence. Henry was held in contempt by many, particularly his cousin Richard, the duke of York (d. 1460), who resented bitterly that the House of Lancaster had usurped the throne in 1399, depriving the House of York of its legitimate claim. In 1460, York rebelled; although he was killed in battle, his son, later crowned Edward IV (*1461–1483), defeated and deposed Henry. England's intermittent civil wars, later called the War of the Roses (after the white and red roses worn by the Yorkists and Lancastrians, respectively), continued until 1485, fueled at home by factions among nobles and regional discontent and abroad by Franco-Burgundian intervention. Edward IV crushed the Lancastrian claim in 1470 at the battle of Tewesbury, and the Yorkist succession died in 1485 when Richard III (*1483–1485), Edward's younger brother, died at the battle of Bosworth. The ultimate victor was Henry Tudor, who married Elizabeth of York, the daughter of Edward IV, and became Henry VII (*1485–1509). The Tudor claim benefited from Richard's notoriety: Richard was widely suspected of obtaining the throne by murdering his young nephews, two of Edward IV's sons—a sinister legend that Shakespeare gave even more fantastic proportions one century later in his famous play *Richard III*.

Unlike the Hundred Years' War, which had devastated large areas of France, the War of the Roses did relatively little damage to England's soil. Except for the campaign of 1460 to 1461, the battles were short, and, in the words of the French chronicler Philippe de Commynes (c. 1447–1511), " . . . England enjoyed this peculiar mercy above all other kingdoms, that neither the country, nor the people nor the houses, were wasted, destroyed or demolished, but the calamities and misfortunes of the war fell only upon the soldiers, and especially on the nobility." As a result, the English economy continued to grow during the fifteenth century. Its cloth industry expanded considerably, and the English now used much of the raw wool that they had been exporting to the Low Countries to manufacture goods at home. London merchants, taking a more vigorous role in trade, also assumed greater political prominence not only in the governance of London but as bankers to kings and members of Parliament; they constituted a small minority in the House of Commons, which was dominated by the country gentry. In the countryside the landed classes—the nobility, the gentry, and the yeomanry (free farmers)—benefited from rising farm and land-rent income as the population increased slowly but steadily. Some peasants lost their farms when landlords enclosed large tracts of arable land to convert into sheep pastures.

A similar postwar development took place in the Iberian monarchies. Decades of civil war over the royal successions began to wane only in 1469, when Isabella of Castile and Ferdinand of Aragon married. Retaining their separate titles, the two monarchs ruled jointly over their domains, which retained traditional laws and privileges. Their union represented the first step toward the creation of a unified Spain out of two medieval kingdoms. Isabella and Ferdinand limited the privileges of the nobility and allied themselves with the cities, relying on the *Hermandad* (civic militia) to enforce justice and on lawyers to staff the royal council. Like Henry VII of England, Isabella and Ferdinand seldom summoned the representative assemblies (respectively, Parliament and the *Cortes*) because these institutions represented the interests of the nobility, not of the people.

The united strength of Castile and Aragon brought the *reconquista* to a close with the final crusade against the

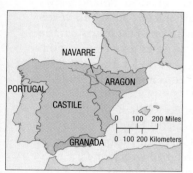

The Unification of Spain

Muslims. After more than a century of peace, war broke out in 1478 between Granada, the last Iberian Muslim state, and the Catholic royal forces. Weakened by internal strife, Granada finally fell in 1492. Two years later, in recognition of the crusade, Pope Alexander VI bestowed the title "Catholic monarchs" on Isabella and Ferdinand, ringing in an era in which militant Catholicism shaped Spanish national consciousness itself.

The relative religious tolerance of the Middle Ages, in which Iberian Muslims, Jews, and Christians had lived side by side, now yielded to the demand for religious conformity. Catholicism became both a test of one's loyalty and an instrument of state authority. In 1478 royal jurisdiction introduced the Inquisition to Spain primarily as a means to control the *conversos* (Jewish converts to Christianity), whose elevated positions in the economy and the government aroused widespread resentment from the so-called Old Christians. *Conversos* often were suspected of practicing their ancestral religion in secret while pretending to adhere to their new Christian faith. Some Old Christians saw a person's refusal to eat pork, for example, as a sign of covert apostasy (betrayal of one's faith). Appointed by the monarchs, the clergy (the "inquisitors") presided over tribunals set up to investigate those suspected of religious deviancy. The accused, who were arrested on charges based on anonymous denunciations and information gathered by the inquisitors, could defend themselves but not confront their accusers. The wide spectrum of punishments ranged from monetary fines, to the *auto de fé* (a sort of public confession), to burning at the stake. After the fall of Granada many Moors were forced to convert or resettle in Castile, and in 1492 the Jewish communities had to choose between exile and conversion.

France, too, was recovering from its war years. Although France won the Hundred Years' War, it emerged in the shadow of the brilliant Burgundian court. Under Charles VII (*1422–1461) and Louis XI (*1461–1483), the French monarchy embarked upon a slow process of expansion and recovery. Abroad, Louis fomented rebellion in England, his traditional enemy, first by helping the Lancastrians and later by aiding Henry Tudor. At home, however, lay the more dangerous enemy, Burgundy. In 1477, with the death of Charles the Bold, Louis dealt a death blow to the duchy by seizing large tracts of Burgundian territory. France's horizons expanded even more when Louis inherited most of southern France after the royal collateral line of Anjou died out. By the end of the century, France had doubled its territory, almost assuming its modern-day boundary. To strengthen royal power at home, Louis promoted industry and commerce, imposed permanent salt and land taxes (called the *gabelle* and the *taille*) on his subjects, maintained the first standing army in western Europe, and dispensed with the Estates of France. The French kings further increased their power with important concessions from the papacy. With the 1438 Pragmatic Sanction of Bourges, Charles asserted the superiority of a general church council over the pope. Harking back to a long tradition of the High Middle Ages, the Sanction of Bourges established what would come to be known as Gallicanism (after Gaul, the ancient Roman name for France), in which the French king would effectively control ecclesiastical revenues and the appointment of French bishops.

Royal power was not absolute, however, because Louis XI failed to curb the power of the great magnate families. Unlike the English nobility, whose strength had been decimated by the War of the Roses, the French nobility remained eager for military adventure. Partly to divert the attention of the warlike nobility and also motivated by dynastic claims on Naples, the French monarchy would invade Italy in 1494, a new adventure abroad that would have disastrous consequences for French royal authority in the sixteenth century.

The rise of strong, new monarchies in western Europe contrasted sharply with the weakness of centralized state authority in central and eastern Europe, where developments in Hungary, Bohemia, and Poland resembled the Burgundian model of personal dynastic authority. Under Matthias Corvinus (*1456–1490), the Hungarian king who briefly united the Bohemian and Hungarian crowns, an eastern European empire seemed to be emerging. A patron of the arts and a humanist, Matthias created a great library in Hungary that, unfortunately, was dispersed after his death. He repeatedly defeated the encroaching Austrian Habsburgs and even occupied Vienna in 1485. His empire did not outlast his death in 1490, however. The powerful Hungarian magnates, who enjoyed the constitutional right to elect the king, refused to acknowledge his son's claim to the throne.

Poland's nobility, who followed the eastern European model of succession (the nobility elected the monarch), always chose from the Jagiellonian dynasty, which by hereditary right ruled Lithuania as well. The Jagiellonians stepped into the power vacuum created by the death of Corvinus. Casimir IV, king of Poland and grand prince of Lithuania after 1444, succeeded in having his son, Władysław, elected king of Bohemia in 1471 and king of Hungary in 1490. The Jagiellonians owed their success in Bohemia and Hungary to the nobility's fear that a native prince, once enthroned, might curb their own power—power entrenched in Poland's laws and in its emerging parliament, or *Sejm*. When Casimir died in 1492, the union of these aristocratic realms dissolved amid disputes over succession. Only in 1506 would Poland and Lithuania again form a loosely united "commonwealth" under a single Jagiellonian ruler.

In the Balkans, under Sultan Mehmed II (*1451–1481), the Ottoman Empire became a serious threat to all of Christian Europe. After he ascended the throne, Mehmed proclaimed a holy war and laid siege to Constantinople in 1453. A city of one hundred thousand, the Byzantine capital could muster only six thousand defenders (including a small contingent of Genoese) against an Ottoman force estimated at between two hundred thousand and four hundred thousand men. The city's fortifications, many of which dated from the time of Emperor Justinian, were no match for fifteenth-century canons. The defenders held out for fifty-three days: while the Christian defenders confessed their sins and prayed for divine deliverance, in desperate anticipation of the Second Coming, the Muslim besiegers pressed forward, urged on by the certainty of rich spoils and Allah's promise of a final victory over the infidel Rome. Finally the defenders were overwhelmed, and the last Byzantine emperor, Constantine Palaeologus, died in battle. Some sixty thousand residents were carried off in slavery, and the city was sacked. Mehmed entered Constantinople in triumph, rendered thanks to Allah in Church of St. Sophia, which had been turned into a mosque, and was remembered as "the Conqueror." Greek Constantinople became Turkish Istanbul, but Byzantine culture managed to survive in the Greek Orthodox church, thanks to the religious toleration in the Ottoman Empire.

Eastern Europe in the Fifteenth Century

Ivan III
Taking the imperial title of tsar, Ivan pushed the boundaries of Muscovy in all directions. Here he is depicted with a saintly visage in the tradition of Russian Orthodox icon painting.

North of the Black Sea and east of Poland-Lithuania, a very different polity was taking shape. In the second half of the fifteenth century the princes of Muscovy embarked on a spectacular path of success that would make their state the largest on earth. Subservient to the Mongols in the fourteenth century, the Muscovite princes began to assert their independence with the collapse of Mongol power. Ivan III (*1462–1505) was the first Muscovite prince to claim an imperial title, referring to himself as the tsar (from the name *Caesar*) of all the lands of Rus. In 1471, Ivan defeated the city-state of Novgorod, whose territories encompassed a vast region in northern Russia. Six years later he abolished the local civic government of this proud city, which had enjoyed independent trade with economically thriving cities of central Europe. To consolidate his autocratic rule and wipe out memories of past freedoms, in 1484 and 1489, Ivan forcibly relocated thousands of leading Novgorodian families to lands around Moscow. He also expanded his territory to the south and east when his forces pushed back the Mongols, now fragmented into different khanates along the Volga River.

Unlike monarchies in western and eastern Europe, whose powers were bound by corporate rights and laws, Ivan's Russian monarchy claimed absolute property rights over all lands and subjects. The expansionist Muscovite state was shaped by two traditions: religion and service. After the fall of the Byzantine Empire, the tsar was the Russian Orthodox church's only defender of the faith against Islam and Catholicism. Orthodox propaganda thus gave imperial legitimation by proclaiming Moscow the "Third Rome," (the first two being Rome and Constantinople) and praising the tsar's autocratic power as the best protector of the faith. The Mongol system of service to rulers also deeply informed Muscovite statecraft. Ivan III and his descendants considered themselves heirs to the steppe empire of the Mongols. In their conception of the state as private dominion, their emphasis on autocratic power, and the division of the populace into a landholding service elite and a vast majority of taxpaying subjects, the Muscovite princes created a state more in the political tradition of the central Asian steppes and the Ottoman Empire than of western Europe.

Renaissance Diplomacy

Many features of diplomacy among today's nation-states first appeared in fifteenth-century Europe. By mid-century, competition between states and the extension of warfare served to make diplomatic conventions into institutions in Italy and western Europe. The first diplomatic handbook, composed in 1436 by Frenchman Bernard du Rosier, later archbishop of Toulouse, declared that the business of the diplomat was "to pay honor to religion . . . and the Imperial crown, to protect the rights of kingdoms, to offer obedience . . . to confirm friendships . . . make peace . . . to arrange past disputes and remove the cause for future unpleasantness."

The emphasis on ceremonies, elegance, and eloquence (Italians referred to ambassadors as "orators") masked the complex game of diplomatic intrigue and spying. In the fifteenth century a resident ambassador was to keep a continuous stream of foreign political news flowing to the home government, not just conduct the traditional temporary diplomatic missions. In some cases the presence of semiofficial agents developed into full-fledged ambassadorships: the Venetian em-

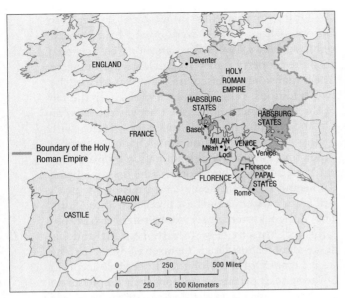

Renaissance Diplomacy and the Church

bassy to the sultan's court in Istanbul developed out of the merchant-consulate that had represented the body of all Venetian merchants, and Medici Bank branch managers eventually acted as political agents to the Florentine republic.

One mid-century episode illustrates the role of diplomatic ceremony as ritualized aggression. A Sienese ambassador at Naples, comporting himself in the grandiose style of his city, regularly appeared before King Alfonso of Naples dressed in gold brocade. The king's custom, in contrast, was to dress in black, with just a gold chain around his neck. Annoyed by the ostentation of the ambassador—who, after all, represented a minor city-state in comparison to the kingdom of Naples—Alfonso arranged to give audience in a tiny room occupied by all the ambassadors. He ordered that everyone in the crowd jostle and bump up against the Sienese ambassador. In the words of a Florentine bookseller, Vespasiano da Bisticci, who related this anecdote, " . . . when they came out of the room no-one could help laughing when they saw the brocade, because it was crimson now, with the pile all crushed and the gold fallen off it . . . it looked the ugliest rag in the world. When he saw him go out of the room with his brocade all ruined and messed up, the King could not stop laughing."

Foremost in the development of diplomacy was Milan, a state with political ambition and military might. Under the Visconti dukes, Milan sent ambassadors to Aragon, Burgundy, the Holy Roman Empire, and the Ottoman Empire. For seven years, from 1425 to 1432, an imperial diplomat resided in Milan while the Visconti's interests were likewise represented in Vienna. Under the Sforza dynasty Milanese diplomacy continued to function as a cherished form of statecraft. For generations Milanese diplomats at the French court sent home an incessant flow of information on the rivalry between France and Burgundy. Francesco Sforza, founder of the dynasty, also used his diplomatic corps to extend his political patronage. In letters of recommendation to the papacy, Francesco would comment on the political desirability of potential ecclesiastical candidates by using code words, sometimes supplemented with instructions to his ambassador to the papacy to indicate his true intent regardless of the "coded" letter of recommendation. In more sensitive diplomatic reports ciphers were routinely used in order to prevent them from being intercepted by hostile powers.

As the center of Christendom, Rome became the diplomatic hub of Europe. During the 1490s well over 243 diplomats were stationed in Rome, whereas 161 were represented at the court of Emperor Maximilian, 135 at the French court, and 100 in Milan. The papacy sent out far fewer envoys, and only at the end of the fifteenth century were papal nuncios, or envoys, permanently represented in the European states. In the 1490s there were 60 papal nuncios, whereas 138 imperial, 159 French, and 165 Milanese ambassadors appeared in European courts. The primary diplomatic effort of fifteenth-century popes—calling a crusade against the Ottomans—met with little practical success; the Christian princes were too embroiled in their own quarrels to march against Istanbul.

Italy's Renaissance diplomacy achieved its most outstanding achievement with the negotiation of a general peace treaty that settled the decades of warfare engendered by Milanese expansion and civil war. The Treaty of Lodi (1454) established a complex balance of power among the major Italian states and maintained relative stability in the peninsula for half a century. Renaissance diplomacy eventually failed, however, when more powerful northern European neighbors invaded in 1494, leading to the collapse of the whole Italian state system.

The Renaissance Church

Although the church council had restored the papacy in 1417, after the Great Schism the popes found their authority unduly restricted. In 1432, Pope Eugenius IV (✳1431–1449) unsuccessfully tried to claim the sole right to convene church councils. Instead he was forced to abide by the reform decrees passed by the Council of Basel in 1433, which included restrictions on papal income and limitations on the number of cardinals. Between 1427 and 1436, papal revenues declined by almost two-thirds. In 1438, Eugenius ordered the Council of Basel to reconvene in a papal city in order to facilitate discussions that would lead to the short-lived union between the Roman and Greek Orthodox churches. Many church fathers in Basel refused to dissolve their council, and instead elected an antipope, Felix V (✳1439–1449). Eventually papal authority triumphed over conciliarism, reflecting a trend that was taking place in the west European Renaissance states: the ascendancy of kingship over parliamentary government. The defection of several prominent conciliarists, such as Nicholas of Cusa (1401–1464), had turned the tide, and by 1447 most conciliarists were supporting Eugenius's successor, Nicholas V (✳1447–1458), and urging the antipope Felix V to abdicate. In 1460 the humanist pope Pius II (✳1458–1464) established papal supremacy in the church when he forbade appeals to councils beyond papal authority.

From the second half of the fifteenth century on, the Italian aristocracy began to dominate the papacy: Pius II came from the Piccolomini family, part of Siena's urban aristocracy; Sixtus IV (✳1471–1484) hailed from the della Rovere, a noble family living near Savona in Liguria; and Innocent VIII (✳1484–1492) from the Cibo family in Genoa, who had spent his youth in the Neapolitan court, where he had fathered three illegitimate children. With its character shaped by noble lineage and family loyalties, the papal court became a resource for family patronage, a trend initiated by Sixtus's appointment as cardinals of his nephews, who also became his close policy advisors. The popes' aristocratic tastes also transformed medieval Rome, with its desolate ruins and delapidated churches, into one of Europe's major cultural centers. Pius II, who had written erotic Latin poetry in his youth, sponsored a circle of humanists at court, and Sixtus established the Vatican Library, built the first bridge across the

Tiber, and commissioned the Sistine Chapel, the papal chapel that, although not completed until long after his death, would glorify his name.

While the Renaissance papacy immersed itself in Italian politics and culture, a new style of religious devotion was evolving in northern Europe's heavily urbanized Low Countries and the Rhineland. Emphasizing inner spirituality and practical charity, this "modern devotion," as contemporaries called it, helped to bridge the gap between the clergy and the laity. By emphasizing inner spirituality, Christian morality, and works of charity, the modern devotion called into question the official church's emphasis on external ceremony and theological doctrine. Representative of this synthesis between official and popular religion was the Brethren of Common Life, a religious organization founded in the late fourteenth century by Gert Groote (1340–1384) in Deventer in the Netherlands that was flourishing rapidly in northern Europe.

Private Life and the State

Just as lineage and descent shaped political power in dynastic states in the fourteenth century, the state itself, through its institutions and laws, now attempted to shape families and households. Florence introduced a census, established a dowry fund and a hospital for abandoned children, and tried to regulate the sexual behavior of its citizens. Considerations of state power intruded into the most intimate personal concerns: sexual intimacy, marriage, and childbirth could not be separated from the values of the ruling classes. With a society dominated by upper-class, patriarchal households, Renaissance Italy specified rigid roles for men and women, making marriage a vehicle for consolidating a hierarchy of classes that was further reinforced by the subordination of women.

The Florentine Social Hierarchy

To deal with a mounting fiscal crisis, in 1427 the government of Florence ordered that a comprehensive tax record of households in the city and territory be compiled. Completed in 1430, this survey represented the most detailed population

Florence, c. 1490
Astride the Arno River, Florence was a typically crowded medieval Italian city.
What made Florence unusual was its relatively large population, its wealth, and
the splendid flowering of art and literature that this wealth supported.

census then taken in European history. From the census's mass of fiscal and demographic data, historians have been able to reconstruct a detailed picture of Florence—the most important city of the Renaissance and a city whose historical records are unparalleled in their detail.

The state of Florence, roughly the size of Massachusetts, had a population of more than two hundred sixty thousand. Tuscany, the area in which the Florentine state is located, was one of the most urbanized regions of Europe (together with Lombardy and Flanders), where 27 percent of the people lived in the largest ten cities. With thirty-eight thousand inhabitants, the capital city of Florence (as distinguished from the state of Florence) claimed 14 percent of the total population; the next largest city, Pisa, numbered only seventy-three hundred. The wealth of the city of Florence made its dominance even more striking: it possessed 67 percent of the state's declared wealth. As the center of its universe, the city's brilliance outshone that of the state's other cities and towns, and cast a long shadow over a countryside whose predominant form of agriculture was practiced by sharecroppers working for urban landlords. Florence

illustrates the intensely urban character of Italian Renaissance civilization.

Straddling the Arno River, Florence was a beautiful, thriving city with a defined social hierarchy. In describing class divisions the Florentines themselves referred to the "little people" and the "fat people." Some 60 percent of all households belonged to the "little people"— workers, artisans, petty merchants—whose household possessions did not exceed 200 florins in value. In 1430 an unskilled worker could expect to make 23 florins annually, while a skilled worker earned almost double that wage. The "fat people," roughly our middle class, comprised 30 percent of the urban population. At the very bottom of the hierarchy were slaves and servants, largely women employed in domestic service. Whereas the small number of slaves were of Balkan origin, the much larger population of domestic servants came to the city from the surrounding countryside as contracted wage earners. At the top a tiny elite of patricians, bankers, and wool merchants controlled the state with their enormous wealth. In fact, the richest 1 percent of the urban households (approximately one hundred families) owned more than one-quarter of the city's wealth and one-sixth of Tuscany's total wealth. The patricians in particular owned almost all government bonds, a lucrative investment with interest rates frequently over 15 percent and guaranteed by a state they dominated.

Surprisingly, men seem to have outnumbered women in the 1427 survey. For every one hundred women there were one hundred ten men, unlike most populations, which have women as the majority. In addition to female infanticide, which was occasionally practiced, the survey itself reflected the society's bias against women: persistent underreporting of women probably explained the statistical abnormality; and married daughters, young girls, and elderly widows frequently disappeared from the memories of householders just as they often escape the attention of historians. Most people, men and women alike, lived in households with at least six inhabitants, although the greatest number of households consisted of variants on the basic conjugal family. Among the urban patriciate and the landowning peasantry, the extended family held sway. Households of more than ten members, with married brothers living under one roof, were common both in Florence and in the countryside. The number of children in a family, it seems, reflected class differences as well. Wealthier families had more children; childless couples existed almost exclusively among the poor, who were also more likely to abandon the infants they could not feed.

The Strozzi Palace, Florence
The Strozzi, a powerful and wealthy family of medieval Florence, surrendered most of its political influence to the Medici. Behind the walls of their imposing palace, the Strozzi flourished as patrons of art and learning. The interior courtyard was rebuilt in the classical style of the fifteenth century.

Family Alliances

Wealth and class also clearly determined family structure and the pattern of marriage and childbearing. In a letter to her eldest son, dated 1447, Alessandra Strozzi announced the marriage of her daughter, Caterina, to the son of Parente Parenti. She described the young groom, Marco Parenti, as "a worthy and virtuous young man, and . . . the only son, and rich, 25 years old, and keeps a silk workshop; and they have a little political standing." The dowry was set at 1,000 florins, a substantial sum—but for 400 to 500 florins more, Alessandra admitted, Caterina would have fetched a husband from a more prominent family.

The Strozzi belonged to one of Florence's most distinguished traditional families, but at the time of Caterina's betrothal the family had fallen into political disgrace. Alessandra's husband, an enemy of the Medici, was exiled in 1434; her son, Filippo, a rich merchant in Naples, lived under the same political ban. Although Caterina was clearly marrying beneath her social station, the marriage represented an alliance in which money, political status, and family standing all balanced out in the end. More an alliance between families than the consummation of love, a marriage was usually orchestrated by the male head of a household. In this case, Alessandra, as a widow, shared the matchmaking responsibility with her eldest son and other male relatives. Eighteen years later, when it came time to find a wife for Filippo, Marco Parenti, the brother-in-law, would also serve as matchmaker.

The upper-class Florentine family was patrilineal in structure; it traced descent and determined inheritance through the male line. Because the distribution of wealth depended on this patriarchal system, women occupied an ambivalent position in the household. A widow found herself torn between loyalty to her children and to her own paternal family, who pressured her to remarry and form a new family alliance. A daughter could claim inheritance only through her dowry, and she often disappeared from family records after her marriage. A wife seldom emerged from the shadow of her husband, and consequently the lives of many women have been lost to history.

In the course of a woman's life, her family often pressured her to conform to conventional expectations. At the birth of a daughter, most wealthy Florentine fathers would open an account at the Dowry Fund, a public fund established in 1425 to raise state revenues and a major investment instrument for the Florentine upper classes. In 1433 the fund paid annual interest of between 15 percent and 21 percent, and fathers could hope to raise handsome dowries by the time their daughters became marriagable in their late teens. The Dowry Fund supported the structure of the marriage market, in which the circulation of wealth and women consolidated the social coherence of the ruling classes.

Women's subordination in marriages often reflected the age differences between spouses. In Renaissance Italy most women married, before age twenty, husbands ten years older who were financially and socially established. The Italian marriage pattern contrasted sharply with the northern European model, in which partners were much closer in age. Significant age disparity also left many women widowed in their twenties and thirties, and remarriage was difficult for many. A widow's father and brothers often would want her to remarry to keep the patrimony (in the form of a dowry) circulating through a new family alliance. A widow, however, could not bring her children into her new marriage because they belonged to her first husband's family. Faced with the choice between her children and her paternal family, not to mention her own happiness, a widow could only hope to gain greater autonomy in her old age, when she could advance the fortunes of her adult sons.

The fictional Griselda from the last tale of Boccaccio's *Decameron* (1353) was the archetype of the meek and submissive wife. Completely dependent on her husband, Griselda did not even own her wedding ring and clothes. After her husband orders her to return his gifts to her after the wedding, he sends her away naked to test her loyalty. Only when Griselda proves her sexual fidelity does her husband receive her back with gifts and affection. The Griselda story, immensely popular in the Renaissance, illustrates the utter powerlessness of the married woman who had no dowry.

In northern Europe, however, women enjoyed a relatively more secure position. In England, the Low Countries, and Germany, for example, women played a significant role in the economy—not only in the peasant household, in which everyone worked, but especially in the town, serving as peddlers, weavers, seamstresses, shopkeepers, midwives, and brewers. In Cologne, for example, women could join one of several artisans' guilds, and in Munich they ranked among some of the richest brewers. Women in northern Europe shared inheritances alongside their brothers, retained control of their dowries, and had the right to represent themselves before the law. Italian men who traveled to the north marveled at the differences in gender relations, denigrating English women as violent and brazen and disapproving of the mixing of genders in German public baths.

The Regulation of Sexuality

Child care also reflected the class differences in Renaissance life. Florentine middle- and upper-class fathers arranged business contracts for most infants to go to wet nurses for breast-feeding; the baby often spent a prolonged period of time away from the family. Such elaborate child care was beyond the reach of the poor, who often abandoned their children to strangers or to public charity.

By the beginning of the fifteenth century, Florence's two hospitals were accepting large numbers of abandoned children, in addition to the sick and infirm. In 1445 the government opened a foundling hospital, the *Ospitale degl' Innocenti*, to deal with the large number of abandoned children. These unfortunate children came from two sources: poor families who were unable to feed another mouth, especially in times of famine, war, and economic depression; and women who had given birth out of wedlock. A large number of the latter were domestic slaves or servants who had been impregnated by their masters; in 1445 one-third of the first hundred foundlings at the newly opened hospital were children of the unequal liaisons between masters and

Griselda
The tale of Griselda was retold by many late medieval and Renaissance writers. In this illustration of the bestowal of a wedding ring, Griselda symbolizes the fidelity and dependence expected of a bride.

women slaves. For some women the foundling hospital provided an alternative to infanticide. Over two-thirds of abandoned infants were girls, a clear indicator of the inequality between the sexes. Although Florence's government employed wet nurses to care for the foundlings, the large number of abandoned infants overtaxed the hospital's limited resources. The hospital's death rate among infants was much higher than the already high infant mortality rate of the time.

Illegitimacy in itself did not necessarily carry a social stigma in fifteenth-century Europe. Most upper-class men acknowledged and supported their illegitimate children as a sign of virility, and illegitimate children of noble lineage often rose to social and political prominence. Any social stigma was borne primarily by the woman, whose ability to marry usually became compromised. Shame and guilt sometimes drove some poor single mothers to kill their infants, a crime for which they paid with their own lives.

In addition to prosecuting infanticide, the public regulation of sexuality focused on prostitution and homosexuality. While prescribing marital fidelity and chastity as feminine virtues, Renaissance society allowed greater freedoms when it came to male heterosexuality. As the 1415 statute that established government brothels in Florence declared, state-sponsored prostitution was intended "to eliminate a worse evil by a lesser one." Concurrent with its higher tolerance of prostitution, the Renaissance state had a low tolerance of homosexuality. In 1432, the Florentine state appointed magistrates "to discover—whether by means of secret denunciation, accusations, notifications, or any other method—those who commit the vice of sodomy, whether actively or passively. . . . " The government set fines for homosexual acts and carried out death sentences against pederasts.

Fifteenth-century European magistrates took violence against women less seriously than the sanctions against illegal male sexual behavior, as the different punishments indicate. In Renaissance Venice, for example, the typical jail sentence for rape and attempted rape was only six months. Magistrates often treated noblemen with great leniency, and handled rape cases according to class distinctions. For example, Agneta, a young girl living with a government official, was abducted and raped by two millers, who were sentenced to five years in prison; several servants who abducted and raped a slave woman were sentenced to three to four months in jail; and a nobleman who abducted and raped Anna, a slave woman, was freed. The gender and social class of both victim and rapist clearly were major factors in determining the sentence. Social inequalities placed noblemen at the top of the hierarchy and slave women at the bottom.

The Sanctification of Kinship

Throughout Europe, in keeping with the emphasis on family relationships, expressions of piety used the Holy Family as a symbol of everyday life. The Holy Family, an ordinary working family, gave the common people a religious identification: Jesus' family life became the model and reflection of their own kin. Numerous images of Jesus depicted him surrounded by his relatives—his parents, Joseph and Mary; his grandparents, Joachim and Anne; his uncles, aunts, and cousins. The world of the extended family was, of course, the reality of daily life. Popular woodcuts from Alsace showed the child Jesus riding on his hobbyhorse or helping with the wine harvest. A woodcut from the Netherlands represented the Holy Family as the ideal household; Joseph, the carpenter, a hard-working father; Mary, the loving mother; and Jesus, the sweet, well-behaved child. By adopting the Holy Family as their own, ordinary people were also sanctifying their own lives.

The cult of the Virgin Mary and her mother, St. Anne, was particularly popular. These two women symbolized maternal care and mercy in a religion anchored in the harsh judgment of sins and the horrible postmortem tortures of purgatory and hell. St. Anne became the patron saint of miners and pregnant women; a popular concoction, St. Anne's water, promised a childbirth free from fevers and pains. As the mother of God, Mary personified the ideal of maternal love. Representations of the Madonna and child were the single most frequent motif in paintings, wood sculpture, and woodcuts.

The sanctification of family and daily life presented a more accessible piety than that which the church had traditionally provided through clerical chastity, cloisters, and religious orders. The common aspects of the Holy Family now suggested that keeping the traditions of household and marriage could lead one to eternal salvation. In addition to church sacraments and doctrines, neighborly charity and love of kin assumed importance. And the virtues of charity and mercy that guided Christ's life inspired laypeople to show the same qualities in their own actions.

Widening Mental Horizons

Recovering from the devastating plagues and wars that had ravaged fourteenth-century Europe, fifteenth-century society could lend support to the arts. In addition to their traditional ecclesiastical

and noble patronage, the urban elites, facing a less favorable climate for business investment due to lower rates of return and greater insecurity, sought to enhance their prestige by investing more heavily in culture. The consumers, producers, and content of these new artistic achievements offer a new view of the world and humankind's place in it.

The consumers of Renaissance art—the people who commissioned paintings, buildings, and musical and literary works—belonged in overwhelming numbers to the upper classes. The Catholic church was the single largest patron of the arts, followed by princes, bankers, rich merchants, and corporate sponsors (craft guilds and confraternities, or voluntary associations for religious laypeople). Religious themes featured prominently in the works, especially in music and the visual arts. Italy, the Low Countries, and Germany were particularly rich in artistic talent. In representing their world, Renaissance artists fulfilled both the taste of their patrons and their own artistic ideals and assumptions. Their created world of religious devotion was also one of natural beauty, human achievement, and secular glory.

Recovery of the Past

A new activism that focused on the human achievements of this world rather than on other-worldly salvation intensified Europeans' interest in Greek and Roman civilizations. The focus of this new movement, or *studia humanitatis*, which spread from Italy to northern Europe, was rhetoric; beautiful orations and writings became a mark of the elite and a claim to fame.

By the early fifteenth century the study of classical Latin (which had begun in the late fourteenth century) as well as classical and biblical Greek had become fashionable among a small intellectual elite, first in Italy and, gradually, throughout Europe. The fall of Constantinople in 1453 sent Greek scholars to Italy for refuge, giving extra impetus to the revival of Greek learning in the West. Venice and Florence assumed leadership in this new field—the former by virtue of its commercial and political ties to the eastern Mediterranean, the latter thanks to the patronage of Cosimo de' Medici, who sponsored the Byzantine refugee Gemistos Pletho, the Italian Marsilio Ficino, (1433–1499), and other Florentines, all of whom were part of the

Leonardo da Vinci, **The Last Supper** *(1495–1497)*
Adorning the dining hall of a Milan monastery, Leonardo's mural painting is one of the artist's masterpieces—but also a technical failure. He used a novel technique that would permit him to follow his accustomed slow, *painstaking pace. Sadly, the result was rapid deterioration. But enough of the work survives to reveal the Apostles' individual features and Leonardo's dramatic psychological insights.*

discussion group called the Platonic Academy. Thinkers of the second half of the fifteenth century had more curiosity about Platonic and various mystical neo-Platonic ideas—particularly alchemy, numerology, and natural magic—than about the serious study of natural phenomena and universal principles.

In Latin learning the fifteenth century continued in the tradition of Petrarch. Reacting against the painstaking logic and abstract language of scholastic philosophy, the humanists of the Renaissance advocated eloquence and style in their discourse, imitating the writings of Cicero and other great Roman authors. The Roman influence manifested itself especially in the transformation of historians' writings. Roman historians served as models for Italian humanists, who used the classical genre to explore the role of human agency in political affairs. Through their activities as educators and civil servants, professional humanists gave new vigor to the humanist curriculum of grammar, rhetoric, poetry, history, and moral philosophy. By the end of the fifteenth century European intellec-

tuals considered a good command of classical Latin, with perhaps some knowledge of Greek, as one of the requirements of an educated man. This humanist revolution would weigh heavily in determining school curricula up to the middle of the nineteenth century and even beyond.

Most humanists did not consider the study of ancient cultures as a conflict with their Christian faith. In "returning to the sources"—a famous slogan of the time—philosophers attempted to harmonize the disciplines of Christian faith and ancient learning. The foremost Platonic scholar of the Renaissance, Ficino, a man deeply attracted to natural magic, was a priest. He argued that the immortality of the soul, a Platonic idea, was perfectly compatible with Christian doctrine, and that much of ancient wisdom actually foreshadowed later Christian teachings.

As a group the humanists were far from homogeneous, although they were overwhelmingly wellborn. Some were professional scholars, others high-ranking civil servants, still others rich patricians who had acquired a taste for learning. Many were notaries or government officials. In early fifteenth-century Florence, the humanists' active involvement in civic life shaped the general tone of their writings. Salutati, Bruni, and Poggio, who questioned the medieval ideal of contemplative learning, embodied the humanists' efforts to use ancient knowledge of humanity and nature in active participation in political and social life.

The social diversity of the humanists was matched by the wide spectrum of their political philosophy. Humanists in Florence and Venice lauded the virtues of the republican city-states of Athens and Rome; in contrast, humanists in Milan, who enjoyed the patronage of princes, applied their literary talent in praise of strong, often autocratic rulers. Whereas Florentine humanists modeled their praise of republicanism after the Romans Livy and Cicero, humanists serving the duke of Milan drew their inspiration from the writings of Suetonius's biographies of Roman emperors.

The Advent of Printing

The invention of mechanical printing aided greatly in making the Latin classics and other texts widely available. Printing with moveable type—a radical departure from the old practice of copying by hand—was invented in the 1440s by a German goldsmith in Mainz, Germany, by the name of Johannes Gutenberg (c. 1400–1470). Mass production of identical books and pamphlets made the world of print more accessible to a literate audience. Two preconditions proved essential for the advent of printing: the existence of commercial production of manuscripts and the industrial production of paper.

Paper making came to Europe from China via Arab intermediaries. By the fourteenth century paper mills were operating in Italy, producing paper that was more fragile but much cheaper than parchment or vellum—the animal skins that Europeans had hitherto used for writing. To produce paper, old rags were soaked in a chemical solution, beaten by mallets into a pulp, washed with water, treated, and dried in sheets—a method that produces good-quality paper even today. The commercial production of paper in the fourteenth and fifteenth centuries was the first stage in the rapid growth of manuscript books, leading to the invention of mechanical printing.

By the fifteenth century a brisk industry in manuscript books flourished in Europe's university towns and major cities. The production was in the hands of stationers, who organized workshops, known as *scriptoria*, for producing manuscripts, and acted as retail booksellers. The largest stationers, in Paris or Florence, were extensive operations. The Florentine Vespasiano da Bisticci, for example, created a library for Cosimo de' Medici by employing forty-five copyists to complete two hundred volumes in twenty-two months. Nonetheless, bookmaking in *scriptoria* was slow and expensive.

Printing—or "mechanically writing," as contemporaries called it—was not unknown: the Chinese had been printing by woodblocks since the tenth century, and woodcut pictures made their appearance in Europe in the early fifteenth century. The real technological breakthrough, however, came with the invention of the printing press. The process involved casting different durable metal molds to represent the alphabet. The letters, cast in relief at the end of the mold, were set to represent the text on a page. Pressed in ink against a sheet of paper, the imprint could be repeated numerous times with only a small amount of human labor. In 1467 two German printers established the first press in Rome and produced twelve thousand volumes in five years, a feat that in the past would have required one thousand scribes working full time for the same number of years.

After the 1440s printing spread rapidly from Germany to other European countries. Mainz, Cologne, Strasbourg, Nuremberg, Basel, and Augsburg had major presses; many Italian cities had established their own by 1480. In the 1490s the German city of Frankfurt-am-Main became an international meeting place for printers and booksellers. The Frankfurt Book Fair, where printers from different nations exhibited their

The Origins and Diffusion of Printing

newest titles, represented a major international cultural event and remains an unbroken tradition to this day.

Early books from the presses were still rather exclusive and inaccessible, especially to a still largely illiterate population. Perhaps the most famous early book, Gutenberg's two-volume edition of the Latin Bible, was an unmistakable luxury item. Altogether 185 copies were printed—35 in vellum (requiring 5,000 calfskins) and 150 in paper (50,000 sheets in all). First priced at well over what a fifteenth-century professor could earn in a year, the Gutenberg Bible has always been one of the most expensive books in history, both for its rarity and exquisite crafting. (In 1987 Volume One of the Gutenberg Bible—a vellum copy—sold in the United States for $4.9 million.) Like many inventors throughout history, Gutenberg did not reap the material benefits of his invention, and he died impoverished.

Assessing the long-term impact of printing is more difficult than telling the story of its invention. Some historians argue that the advent of the printed word gave rise to a "communications revolution" more significant than, for example, the widespread use of the personal computer today. The multiplication of standardized texts could have altered the thinking habits of Europeans by freeing individuals from the necessity to memorize everything they had learned; it certainly made possible the relatively speedy and inexpensive dissemination of knowledge, and it facilitated intellectual exchange and created a more effective community of scholars. The creation of the book market transformed the structure of intellectual life. The audience for texts was now larger, impersonal, no longer dependent on personal patronage or church sponsorship. Printing facilitated the free expression and exchange of ideas, and its disruptive potential did not go unnoticed by political and ecclesiastical authorities. Emperors and bishops in Germany, the homeland of the printing industry, moved quickly to issue censorship regulations.

From Artisan to Artist

Like the copyists before them, the printers who ran the new presses saw themselves as artisans practicing a craft. The result might be genuinely artistic, but the producer did not think of himself as an artist, uniquely gifted. The artist, as opposed to the artisan, was a new animal to the Renaissance. In exalting the status of the artist, Leonardo da Vinci (1452–1519), painter, architect, and inventor who was himself trained in the artisan tradition, described his freedom to create, as a gentleman of leisure: "The painter sits at his ease in front of his work, dressed as he pleases, and moves his light brush with the beautiful colors . . . often accompanied by musicians or readers of various beautiful works." If this picture fits in with today's image of the creative genius, so do the stories about Renaissance painters and their eccentricities: some were violent, others absentminded; some worked as hermits, others cared little for money. Leonardo himself was described by his contemporaries as "capricious," and his work habits (or lack of them) irritated at least one employer.

The point of these stories about "genius," often told by Renaissance artists themselves, was to convince society that the artists' works were unique and their talents priceless. During the fifteenth century the artist's status in society underwent a gradual transformation. Instead of being an artisan laboring by hand to produce a given object, the artist claimed respect and recognition for his unique genius. Although artists wished to create as their genius dictated, the reality was that most relied on wealthy patrons for their support. And not all patrons of the arts allowed artists to work without restrictions. While Ludovico Sforza, the duke of Milan (*1452–1508), appreciated Leonardo's genius, a man like Borso d'Este, the duke of Ferrara (*1450–1471), paid for his art by the square foot. For every successful artist—such as the painter Andrea Mantegna (1431–1506), who was ennobled by Pope Innocent VIII—there were many others who painted marriage chests and look-alike madonnas for middle-class homes.

For painters the conditions of work fell into three categories: long-term service in princely courts, commissioned piecework, and production for the market. Mantegna, for example, worked from 1460 until his death in 1506 for the Gonzaga princes of Mantua. In return for a monthly salary and other gifts, he promised to paint panels and frescoes (paintings on a wet plaster surface). His masterpieces—fresco scenes of courtly life with vivid and accurate portraits of members of the princely family—decorated the walls of the ducal palace. In practice, however, Mantegna sometimes was treated more as a skilled worker in service to the prince than as an independent artist: he was once asked to adorn the ducal tapestry with life sketches of farm animals.

The workshop—the norm of production in Florence and in northern European cities such as Nuremberg and Antwerp—afforded the artist greater autonomy. As heads of workshops, artists

Fresco of the Camera degli Sposi
In 1474 Andrea Mantegna completed a cycle of frescos for the Gonzaga family, who ruled the duchy of Mantua in northern Italy. Mantegna's work, a masterpiece of perspective technique, creates a stunning illusion of greatly extended space.

trained apprentices and negotiated contracts with clients, with the most famous artists fetching good prices for their work. Studies of art contracts have shown that in the course of the fifteenth century artists gained greater control over their work. Early on in the century clients routinely stipulated detailed conditions to works of art. Gold paint or "ultramarine blue" were among the most expensive pigments, and consumers clearly wanted to ensure

that painters did not skimp on material. Clients might also determine the arrangement of figures in a picture, leaving little more than the execution to the artist. After mid-century, however, such specific directions became less common. In 1487, for example, Filippino Lippi (1457–1504), in his contract to paint frescoes in the Strozzi chapel, specified that the work should be " . . . all from his own hand and particularly the figures." The shift underscores the increasing recognition of the unique skills of individual artists. Famous artists developed a following, and wealthy consumers came to pay a premium for work done by a master instead of apprentices.

A market system for the visual arts emerged in the Renaissance, initially in the Low Countries. Limited at first to smaller altarpieces, woodcuts, engravings, sculpture, and pottery paintings, the art market began to extend to larger panel paintings. In the fifteenth century most large-scale art was commissioned by specific patrons, but the art market, for which artists produced works without prior arrangement for sale, was to develop into the major force for artistic creativity, a force that still prevails in contemporary society. A vigorous trade in religious art sprang up in Antwerp, which was becoming the major market and financial center in Europe. Ready-made altarpieces were sold to churches and consumers from as far away as Scandinavia, and merchants could buy small portable religious statues to take along on their travels. The commercialization of art celebrated the new context of artistic creation itself: artists working in an open, competitive, urban civilization.

Representation in Perspective

An inventory of over two thousand paintings executed in Italy between 1420 and 1539 shows that about 87 percent dealt with religious subjects, more than half representations of the Virgin Mary and the rest portraits of Christ or the saints. Of those paintings with secular subjects, some two-thirds were portraits.

The predominance of religious themes in art reflected the continuing significance of church patronage and the importance of religion and the social uses of religious art in Renaissance society. The papal court in Rome was the greatest patron of the fifteenth-century arts. Beginning with Six-

Botticelli,
Adoration of the Magi
In this painting, commissioned by the Medici in the 1470s, the Holy Family appears surrounded by Florentine notables, including (many art historians believe) Cosimo de' Medici, his son, and his grandson as the Three Kings. Besides exalting the Medici, the painting also symbolizes the union between Christ and humanity.

tus IV, the Roman pontiffs embarked upon an ambitious plan that was to transform entirely the physical appearance of the Eternal City. Lay patrons commissioned religious art for two purposes: as a work of charity and piety and as a demonstration of personal power and wealth. For example, Sandro Botticelli's (1447–1510) *Adoration of the Magi* honors the Medici family of Florence along with the Holy Family: at the painting's extreme left is the young Lorenzo (later called "the Magnificent" because he patronized the arts), and touching the feet of the infant Jesus is Piero, the Medici patriarch.

Beyond the predominance of religious themes and homage to the powerful, certain stylistic innovations, through ways of depicting the world as the eye perceives it, distinguished Renaissance art from its predecessors. The Italian painters were keenly aware of their new techniques, and criticized the Byzantine and the northern Gothic stylists for their "flat" depictions of the human body and the natural world. The highest accolade for a Renaissance artist was to be described as an "imitator of nature"; nature, not design books or master painters, was the teacher of artists. Leonardo described how "paint-

ing . . . compels the mind of the painter to transform itself into the mind of nature itself and to translate between nature and art, setting out, with nature, the causes of nature's phenomena regulated by nature's laws. . . ." To imitate nature, Leonardo continued, required the technique of visual perspective, which helped to render three dimensions on a flat surface. A contemporary biography of Filippo Brunelleschi (1377–1446), the sculptor and architect, provided perhaps its earliest definition: "what the painters nowadays call perspective . . . is in practice the good and systematic diminution or enlargement, as it appears to men's eyes, of objects that are respectively remote or close at hand—of buildings, plains, mountains and landscapes of every kind. . . ."

The use of visual perspective—an illusory three-dimensional space on a two-dimensional surface and the ordered arrangement of painted objects from one single viewpoint—became one of the distinctive features of Western art. Neither Persian, Chinese, Byzantine, nor medieval Western art—all of which has been more concerned with conveying symbolism than reality—expressed this aesthetic for order through perspectival composition. Un-

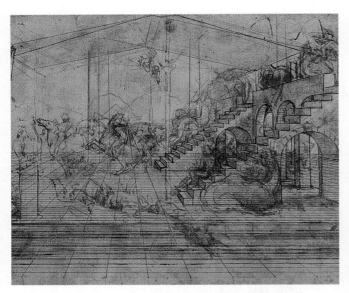

Leonardo da Vinci, Perspective Drawing (detail)
Leonardo was a master of the technique of having all planes recede to a vanishing point. Architectural settings lent themselves readily to perspectival draftsmanship. This drawing illustrates the means by which Renaissance artists achieved their three-dimensional effect.

derlying the idea of perspective was a new Renaissance worldview: humans asserting themselves over nature in painting and design by controlling space. The eye of the beholder became the organizing principle of the natural world in that it detected the "objective" order in nature.

Human perception now dominated artistry, a tenet illustrated so aptly by Mantegna's frescoes for the Gonzaga Palace and the paintings of Piero della Francesca (1420–1492). Completed between 1465 and 1474, Mantegna's frescoes in the palace's bridal chamber (*Camera degli sposi*), his most brilliant achievement, create an illusory extension of reality, a three-dimensional representation of life, as the actual living space in the chamber "opens out" to the painted landscape on the walls. Piero della Francesca, who apprenticed in Florence, was so fascinated by perspective that he wrote a book about it. In the fresco *The Flagellation of Christ*, della Francesca sets his detached and expressionless figures in a geometrical world of columns and tiles, framed by intersecting lines and angles. Human existence, if della Francesca's painting can be taken as a reflection of his times, was shaped by human design, in accordance with the human faculties of

Piero della Francesca, The Flagellation of Christ
Active in Urbino in the mid-fifteenth century, the Tuscan artist Piero della Francesca was a master of dramatic perspective design, as exemplified in this small panel painting. His use of cool colors and his imaginative manipulation of geometrical space has spurred a favorable reevaluation of his art by twentieth-century critics.

reason and observation. Thus the artificially constructed urban society of the Renaissance was the ideal context in which to understand the ordered universe.

The Idea of Human Dignity

In practicing perspective a painter needed some knowledge of mathematics and optics, in addition to the usual mastery of color and line. Thus the Renaissance sought to unite artistic creativity and scientific knowledge. Architecture, which required an artist's eye as well as a scientist's knowledge, attracted some of the greatest minds of the age. Brunelleschi was a great Florentine architect whose designs included the dome of the city's cathedral, modeled after ancient Roman ruins; the *Ospitale degl' Innocenti* for abandoned children; and the interiors of several Florentine churches. Son of a lawyer and a goldsmith by training, Brunelleschi also invented machines to help with architectural engineering.

Another Florentine architect, Leon Battista Alberti (1404–1472), came from a wealthy merchant family. A lawyer and papal official, Alberti's theoretical interest in the arts led him to become an architect. One of his first buildings, the Rucellai Palace in Florence (1446), shows a strong classical influence and inaugurated a trend in the construction of urban palaces for the Florentine ruling elite. Although Alberti undertook architectural designs for many princes, his significance lies more in his theoretical works, which influenced his contemporaries. In a book on painting dedicated to Brunelleschi, Alberti analyzed the technique of perspective as the method of imitating nature. In *On Architecture*, modeled after the ancient Roman book by Vitruvius, Alberti argued for large-scale urban planning, with monumental buildings set on open squares, harmonious and beautiful in their proportions. His ideals were put into action by successive popes in the urban renewal of Rome, and they served to transform that unruly medieval town into a geometrically constructed monument to architectural brilliance by recalling the grandeur of its ancient origins.

Ancient history also supplied Renaissance Europe with symbolic heroes and great men. The political propaganda of the Burgundian court, for example, regularly praised the dukes as contemporary Caesars and Alexanders or compared them to the mythological hero Hercules. This marriage between classical antiquity and Renaissance propaganda graced the lesser courts of Europe, too, from Milan to Ferrara. For the most famous *condottieri* (military captains) of the time, bronze statues were cast, in the manner of those cast in ancient Rome—such as Donatello's (c. 1386–1466) *Gattamelata* (meaning "honey cat"), the nickname of a successful Venetian mercenary who actually had not won many battles. The increasing number of portraits in Renaissance painting also illustrates this new, elevated view of human existence. Initially limited to representations of pontiffs, monarchs, princes, and patricians, portraiture of the middle classes became more widespread toward the end of the fifteenth century. Painters from the Low Countries such as Jan van Eyck distinguished themselves in this genre; their portraitures achieved a sense of detail and reality unsurpassed until the advent of photography.

The ideal of a universal man, as exemplified by Alberti and other artists, was elaborated by Giovanni Pico della Mirandola (1463–1494). Born to a noble family, Pico avidly studied Latin and Greek philosophy. He befriended Ficino, Florence's leading Platonic philosopher, and enjoyed the patronage of Lorenzo de' Medici (1449–1492), who provided him with a villa after the papacy condemned some of his writings. Pico's oration, *On the Dignity of Man*, embodied the optimism of Renaissance philosophy. To express his marvel at the human species, Pico imagined God's words at his creation of Adam: "In conformity with your free judgment, in whose hands I have placed them, you are confined by no bounds, and you will fix limits of nature for yourself." Pico's construct placed humankind at the center of the universe as the measure of all things, and "the molder and maker of himself." In his efforts to reconcile Platonic and Christian philosophy, Pico stressed both the classical emphasis on human responsibility in shaping society and the religious trust in God's divine plan.

Renaissance Europe's glorification of males transformed religious culture at a fundamental level: it gave the traditional doctrine of the humanity of Christ a new emphasis, one supported both by popular preachers and in sermons at the papal court. The visual arts used representations of the Virgin and child as their central image. These paintings emphasized the human emotions of the Holy Mother and child. They expressed the humanistic beliefs of the times by depicting divinity's participation in human nature: Christ as a suckling infant, his genitals signifying both the sexuality and innocence of the divine child.

New Musical Harmonies

If Italy set the standards for the visual arts in Europe, it was more open to musical styles from the northern countries. At around 1430, simultaneous with the revival of painting in the Low Countries, a new style of music appeared that would dominate composition for the next two centuries. Instead of writing pieces with one major melodic line, composers were writing for three to four instrumental or human voices, each equally important in expressing a melodic line in harmony with the others. This new style, known as polyphonic (many sounds) music, found its greatest expression in the Burgundian Netherlands, although many musicians sought employment in Italy and in France.

The leader of this new musical movement was Guillaume Dufay (1400–1474), a native of Cambrai, whose musical training began in the cathedral choir of his hometown. His successful career took him to all the cultural centers of the Renaissance, where nobles sponsored new compositions and maintained a corps of musicians for court and religious functions. In 1438, Dufay composed festive music to celebrate the completion of the cathedral dome in Florence designed by Brunelleschi. Dufay expressed the harmonic relationship among the four voices in ratios that matched the mathematically precise dimensions of Brunelleschi's architecture. After a period of employment at the papal court, Dufay returned to his native north and composed music for the Burgundian and French courts.

Dufay's career was typical. His younger counterpart, Johannes Ockeghem (c. 1420–1495), whose influence rivaled Dufay's, worked almost exclusively at the French court. Other composers were more mobile: Josquin des Prés (1440–1521), another Netherlander, wrote music in Milan, Ferrara, Florence, Paris, and at the papal court. The new style of music was beloved by the elites: Lorenzo

de' Medici sent Dufay a love poem to set to music, and the great composer maintained a lifelong relationship with the family.

Within Renaissance polyphony were three main musical genres: the canon (central texts) of the Catholic Mass; the motet, which used both sacred and secular texts; and the secular *chanson*, often using the tunes of folk dances. Composers often adapted folk melodies for sacred music, expressing religious feeling primarily through human voices, and not using instruments such as the tambourine and the lute, which were indispensible for dances. Small ensembles of wind and string instruments with contrasting sounds performed with singers in the fashionable courts of Europe. Also in use in the fifteenth century were the new keyboard instruments—the harpsichord and clavichord—which could play several harmonic lines at once.

The Renaissance and the Jews

Although a few Christian intellectuals were willing to explore Jewish learning, the larger Christian world in the fifteenth century remained intolerant of religious differences. Already devastated by the persecutions of the fourteenth century, many Jewish communities, especially those in the Holy Roman Empire and Spain, faced expulsion or exile during the Renaissance. Jews in Christian Europe were divided into two main groups—the German-speaking Ashkenazim and the Spanish-speaking Sephardim, each with its own cultural and liturgi-

Jewish Centers in Fifteenth-Century Europe

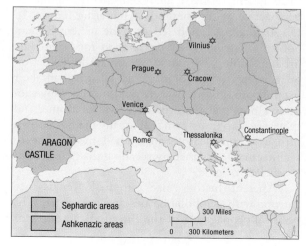

cal tradition. Additional Jewish communities, including many in Palestine and Egypt, existed under Ottoman protection. Multicultural by definition, the Jews of the Renaissance adhered to their ancestral religion and language, Hebrew, while participating in the culture of their surrounding Gentile societies, speaking Castilian, Portuguese, Italian, German, Turkish, or Arabic in daily life. In addition to the male-dominated religious culture of rabbinic learning, a secular culture flourished in the Jewish communities in which both men and women read vernacular literature (including translations from Christian authors) and took part in festivals such as carnival. Excluded from most trades by Christian authorities, Jews took on specific professions: the wealthier practiced medicine and moneylending, the middle classes peddled small wares and slaughtered animals for their communities, and the lower classes became servants in rich households or subsisted on community charity.

The single most dramatic event for the Jews of Renaissance Europe was their 1492 expulsion from Spain, the country with the largest and most vibrant Jewish communities. On the eve of the expulsion, approximately two hundred thousand Jews were living in Castile and Aragon. To that must be added roughly three hundred thousand *conversos* (Jewish converts to Christianity), many of whom maintained clandestine ties to Judaism and had relatives who had resisted the pressure to convert. Fearful that real or imagined Judaizers would corrupt the purity of Christianity, the Spanish Inquisition maintained close surveillance of the *conversos*, feeding popular resentment toward all Jews for their perceived economic privileges and religious differences. In 1492, Ferdinand and Isabella ordered all Jews in their kingdoms to convert to Christianity or leave. Well over one hundred thousand Jews chose exile. The priest Andrés Bernáldez described the expulsion with these sympathetic words: "Just as with a strong hand and outstretched arm, and much honor and riches, God through Moses had miraculously taken the other people of Israel from Egypt, so in these parts of Spain they had . . . to go out with much honor and riches, without losing any of their goods, to possess the holy promised land, which they confessed to have lost through their great and abominable sins which their ancestors had committed against God." The exiles departed for Portugal, North Africa, Italy, and the Ottoman Empire, settling in Thessalonika, Istanbul, and Palestine, thus extending the Sephardic diaspora (*diaspora* is Greek for "dispersion") to the entire Mediterranean.

On the Threshold of World History

The fifteenth century represented the first era of world history. The significance of the century lies not so much in the European "discovery" of Africa and the Americas, but in the breakdown of cultural frontiers that European colonial expansion inaugurated. Before the maritime expansion of Portugal and Spain, Europe had remained at the periphery of world history. Thirteenth-century Mongols were more interested in conquering China and Persia—lands with sophisticated cultures—than in invading Europe; Persian historians of the early fifteenth century dismissed Europeans as "barbaric Franks"; and China's Ming dynasty rulers, who sent maritime expeditions to Southeast Asia and East Africa around 1400, seemed unaware of the Europeans, even though Marco Polo and other Italian merchants had appeared at the court of the preceding Mongol Yuan dynasty. In the fifteenth century the ingenuity, endurance, and greed of the Portuguese and Castilians were motivation enough for them to seek direct and permanent contact with non-European peoples. For the first time Native American peoples were brought into a larger historical force that threatened to destroy not only their culture but their very existence. European exploitation, conquest, and racism helped to define this historical era, in which, in the transition from the medieval to the modern world, Europeans left the Baltic and the Mediterranean for wider oceans.

The Hanseatic "Lake"

Long before the voyages of exploration, European ships were roaming in waters closer to home. In the thirteenth century, on northern Europe's Baltic coast, a merchant league emerged that came to be called the Hanseatic League (*Hansa* means a band of merchants). By the fifteenth century it had expanded into an international association of merchants with extensive diplomatic and military power.

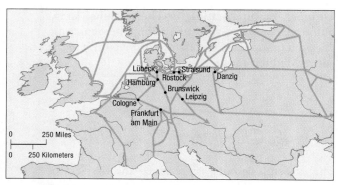

Hanseatic Towns

At the league's height, merchants from Bruges, Flanders, to Reval (today Tallin, Estonia) claimed Hanseatic privileges; about eight towns were full members and a further one hundred enjoyed associate status as Hanseatic towns. The Hanseatic League came to dominate maritime trade in the North Sea and the Baltic.

Several German-speaking seaports made up the core of the Hanseatic League. Lübeck, Hamburg, Rostock, Stralsund, and Danzig (today Gdansk, Poland)—all governed by merchant elites linked by marriage and business interests—provided most of the league's finances, personnel, and political direction. Annual Hanseatic conventions, usually held in Lübeck, decided on common policies and arbitrated disputes between members. The league set up a trade structure between eastern and western Europe: Hanseatic merchants and ships carried timber, fur, and honey from Russia, iron ore from Sweden, herring from Norway, and grain from Poland to the German, English, and Flemish cities of the West. In turn, western Europe's financial and manufacturing centers sent capital and manufactured goods back in the other direction.

By the end of the fifteenth century, however, the Hanseatic League faced serious competition. In a series of wars, the Danish monarchy tried to seize the league's Baltic trade. In the West, England and the Low Countries adopted policies that favored local merchants over the Hansa. Worst of all, intense competition among leading Hanseatic cities destroyed the league's cohesion. Antwerp, Amsterdam, and Hamburg, all league members, would replace the league as individual entrepôts (intermediary trade centers) in the next century. The decline of the Hanseatic League underlines the changing importance of trade in Europe after the Atlantic

voyages: the Baltic Sea became a backwater as Europeans discovered new avenues for trade. The northern Hanseatic League remained a mere lake in comparison to the ocean of trade that was developing to the south and west.

The Divided Mediterranean

The Mediterranean Sea, which had dominated medieval maritime trade, lost its preeminence to the Atlantic Ocean in the second half of the fifteenth century. The Atlantic became Europe's door to the world, whereas the Mediterranean was divided into Christian and Muslim halves. Unlike the Arabs, who had never developed a strong navy, the Ottomans embarked upon an ambitious naval program to transform their empire into a major maritime power. The Mediterranean was to remain divided until the demise of the Turkish navy in the seventeenth century. War and piracy disrupted its flow of trade: the Venetians mobilized all their resources to fight off Turkish advances, and the Genoese largely abandoned the eastern Mediterranean, turning instead to the trade opportunities presented by the Atlantic voyages sponsored by the Castilian and Portuguese crowns.

The Mediterranean states used ships made with comparatively backward naval technology. The most common ship, the galley—a flat-bottomed vessel propelled by sails and oars—dated from the time of ancient Rome. Most galleys could not withstand open-ocean voyages, although Florentine and Genoese galleys still made long journeys to Flanders and England, hugging the coast for protection. The galley's dependence on manpower was a more serious handicap. Because prisoners of war and convicted criminals toiled as oarsmen in both Christian and Muslim ships, victory in war or the enforcement of criminal penalties were crucial to a state's ability to float large numbers of galleys. Slavery, too, a traditional Mediterranean institution, sometimes provided the necessary labor.

Although it was divided into Muslim and Christian zones, the Mediterranean still provided a significant opportunity for cultural exchange. Sugar cane came to the western Mediterranean from western Asia. From the Balearic Islands off Spain (under Aragonese rule), the crop then traveled to the Canary Islands in the Atlantic, where the native population was enslaved by Spain to work the new sugar plantations. In this way, slavery was exported from the western Mediterranean to the Atlantic, and then on to the New World.

Different ethnic groups also moved across this maritime cultural frontier. After Granada fell in 1492, many Muslims fled to North Africa and continued to raid the Spanish coast. When Castile expelled its Jews, some of them settled in North Africa, more in Italy, and many in the Ottoman Empire, Greek-speaking Thessalonika, the Jewish quarter of Istanbul, and Palestine. Conversant in two or three languages, Spanish Jews often served as intermediaries between the Christian West and Muslim East. Greeks occupied a similar position. Most Greeks in the homeland adhered to the Greek Orthodox church under Ottoman protection, but some converted to Islam and entered imperial service, making up a large part of the Ottoman navy. The Greeks on Crete, Chios, and other Aegean islands, however, lived under Italian rule, some of them converting to Roman Catholicism and entering Venetian, Genoese, and Spanish service.

New Geographical Horizons

Looking back, the sixteenth-century Spanish historian Francisco López de Gómara described Spain's maritime voyages to the East and West Indies as "the greatest event since the creation of the world, apart from the incarnation and death of him who created it." This first phase of European overseas expansion, which began in 1433 with Portugal's systematic exploration of the West African coast, culminated in 1519 to 1522 with Spain's circumnavigation of the globe.

In many ways a continuation of the struggle against Muslims in the Iberian Peninsula, Portugal's maritime voyages displayed that country's mixed motives of piety, glory, and greed. The Atlantic explorations depended for their success on several technological breakthroughs, such as the lateen sail adapted from the Arabs (it permitted a ship to tack against headwinds), new types of sailing vessels, and better charts and instruments. But the sailors themselves were barely touched by the expanding mental universe of the Renaissance; what motivated these explorers was a combination of crusading zeal and medieval adventure stories, such as the tales of Marco Polo and John Mandeville. Behind the spirit of the crusade lurked stories of vast gold mines in West Africa (the trade across the Sahara was controlled by Arabs) and the mysterious Christian kingdom established by Prester John (actually the Coptic Christian kingdom of Abyssinia, or Ethiopia, in East Africa). Moreover the Portuguese hoped to reach the spice-producing lands of South and Southeast Asia in order to circumvent the Ottoman Turks, who controlled the lands between Europe and Asia.

By 1415 the Portuguese had captured Ceuta on the Moroccan coast, thus establishing a foothold in Africa. Thereafter Portuguese voyages sailed farther and farther down the West African coast. By mid-century the Portuguese chain of forts had reached Guinea and could protect the gold and slave trades. By 1478 to 1488, Bartholomeu Dias could take advantage of the prevailing winds in the South Atlantic to reach the Cape of Good Hope. A mere ten years later (1497–1499), under the captainship of Vasco da Gama, a Portuguese fleet rounded the cape and reached Calicut, India, the center of the spice trade.

In 1455, Pope Nicholas V sanctioned Portuguese overseas expansion, commending King John II's crusading spirit and granting him and his successors the monopoly on trade with inhabitants of the newly "discovered" regions. At home the royal house of Portugal financed the fleets, with crucial roles played by Prince Peter, regent of the throne between 1440 and 1448; his more famous younger brother, Prince Henry the Navigator; and King John II. As governor of the Order of Christ, a noble crusading order, Henry financed many voyages out of the order's revenues; Peter and John used the state's income to support the enterprise. Private monies also helped, as leading Lisbon merchants participated in financing the gold and slave trades off the Guinea coast.

After the voyages of Christopher Columbus, Portugal's interests clashed with the Crown of Castile's new maritime activities. Papal diplomacy resulted eventually in the Treaty of Tordesillas (1494), by which the two royal houses divided the maritime world between them. A demarcation 370 leagues west of the Cape Verdes Islands divided the Atlantic Ocean, reserving for Portugal the African coast and the route to India and giving Castile the oceans and lands to the west.

The Voyages of Columbus

Historians agree that Christopher Columbus (1451–1506) was born of Genoese parents; beyond that, we have little accurate information about this man who conjoined the history of Europe and the Americas. As a young man, Columbus sailed and traveled in the Mediterranean, living for a time on the Greek island of Chios, then a Genoese colony. In 1476 he arrived in Portugal, apparently a survivor in a naval battle between a Franco-Portuguese and a Genoese fleet; in 1479 he married a Portuguese noblewoman. He spent the next few years mostly in Portuguese service, gaining valuable experience in regular voyages down the west coast of Africa. In 1485, after the death of his wife, Columbus settled in Spain.

Fifteenth-century Europeans already knew that Asia lay beyond the vast Atlantic Ocean, and *The Travels of Marco Polo*, written more than a century earlier, still exerted a powerful hold on European images of the East. Columbus read it many times, along with other travel books, and proposed to sail westward across the Atlantic to reach the lands of the Khan, unaware that the Mongol Empire had already collapsed in East Asia. Vastly underestimating the distances, he dreamed of finding a new route to the East's gold, spices, and lost Christians, and partook of the larger European vision that had inspired the Portuguese voyages. (His critics had a much more accurate idea of the globe's size and of the difficulty of the venture.) But after the Portuguese and French monarchs rejected his proposal, Columbus found royal patronage with the recently proclaimed Catholic monarchs Isabella of Castile and Ferdinand of Aragon.

In August 1492, equipped with a modest fleet of three ships and about ninety men, Columbus set sail for the Atlantic. The contract stipulated that Columbus would claim Castilian sovereignty over any new land and inhabitants and share any profits with the crown. Reaching what is today the Bahamas on October 12, Columbus mistook the islands to be part of the East Indies, not far from Japan and "the lands of the Great Khan." Exploring the Caribbean islands, the Castilian crew encountered communities of peaceful Indians, the Arawaks, who were awed by the Europeans' military technology, not to mention their appearance. Exchanging gifts of beads and broken glass for Arawak gold—an exchange that evoked Columbus's admiration for the trusting nature of the Indians—the crew established peaceful relationships with many communities. Yet in spite of many positive entries in the ship's log referring to Columbus's personal goodwill toward the Indians, the Europeans' objectives were clear: search for gold, subjugate the Indians, and propagate Christianity.

Leaving behind a small garrison on the West Indian island of Hispaniola, Columbus returned to Spain, parading the gold and Indians he had brought from the New World. Religion and greed were the twin motives of European contact with Native American civilization. In his log entry dated December 26, 1492, Columbus expressed his dreams for the future: by the time of his return, he hoped that the small garrison would have accumulated such quantities of gold and spices "that within three years the Sovereigns will prepare for and undertake the conquest of the Holy Land."

Excited by the prospect of easy riches, many flocked to join the second voyage. When Columbus departed Cadiz in September 1493, he commanded seventeen ships that carried between twelve hundred and fifteen hundred men, many believing all they had to do was "to load the gold into the ships." Failing to find the imaginary gold mines and spices, however, the colonial enterprise quickly switched its focus to finding contenders for the slave trade. Columbus and his crew first enslaved the Caribs, enemies of the Arawaks; in 1494, Columbus proposed a regular slave trade based in Hispaniola. They exported enslaved Indians to Spain, and slave traders sold them in Seville. Soon the Spaniards began importing sugar cane from Madeira, forcing

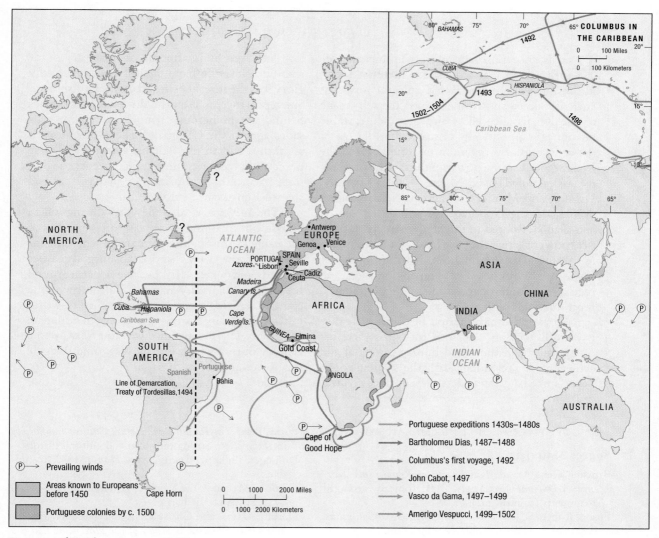

Voyages of Exploration to c. 1500

large numbers of Indians to work on plantations to produce enough sugar for export to Europe.

Columbus himself was edged out of this new enterprise. When the Spanish monarchs realized the vast potential for material gain that lay in their new dominions, they asserted direct royal authority by sending officials and priests to the Americas. Columbus's place in history embodied the fundamental transformations of his age. A Genoese in the service of Portuguese and Spanish employers, Columbus had a career that illustrated the changing balance between the Mediterranean and the Atlantic waters. As the fifteenth-century Ottomans

drove Genoese merchants out of the eastern Mediterranean, they turned to the Iberian Peninsula. Columbus was one of many Genoese adventurers who served the Spanish and Portuguese crowns. The Portuguese and Spanish search for gold, spices, and slaves in the New World mirrored the well-established pattern of Portuguese colonialism in Africa, a ruthless enterprise that Europeans justified in the name of religion. The voyages of 1492–1493 would eventually draw the triangle of exchange among Europe, the Americas, and Africa, an exchange gigantic in its historical significance and brutal in its human cost.

CONCLUSION

Renaissance Europe's interest in ancient culture was in fact a quest for identity. Ideas, idioms, and the political and cultural forms of ancient Greece and Rome shaped the self-image of the Renaissance elites and provided a stable medium for a politically unstable world. One of the central idioms common to antiquity and the Renaissance was the power of the family: princely dynasties ruled over Milan, Naples, Ferrara, Urbino, and Monferrato, and patrician families dominated the city-states of Florence, Venice, and Genoa. Rooted in the family structure, political power shaped the very nature of households, informing marriage alliances, distributing power (most unevenly) between women and men, and regulating domestic production and biological reproduction.

An extraordinary period of cultural creativity, the Renaissance seemed to express a spirit of optimism, of unlimited human potential and achievement. Yet underneath the secular confidence stirred a great anxiety. Renaissance civilization had been built, after all, on a century of instability. Never far from the brilliance of worldly glory was the threat of sin and divine punishment. Sin, repentance, and reform: these were the themes behind the numerous sermons calling for crusades against the Ottomans. The 1490s brought an abrupt end to the Italian Peninsula's relative peace and prosperity, destroying forever the delicate balance of optimism and anxiety that had shaped Renaissance culture.

The 1490s were also the years during which Christopher Columbus set sail for the Indies in the name of the Spanish monarchs, when the interests of the Valois and Habsburg dynasties clashed, and when Italy became a battleground for soldiers of many nations. The turn of the century signaled the dawn of a new era of world history shaped by European attempts to dominate the globe. The Renaissance was to give way to a century during which Europeans would struggle for power and for faith.

SUGGESTIONS FOR FURTHER READING

Source Materials

Brucker, Gene A., ed. *The Society of Renaissance Florence: A Documentary Study.* 1971. Topically arranged documents from the archive.

Fuson, Robert H., ed. *The Log of Christopher Columbus.* 1987. An accessible, scholarly translation.

Molho, Anthony, ed. *Social and Economic Foundations of the Italian Renaissance.* 1969. Includes primary and secondary sources.

Gragg, Florence A., trans., Leona C. Gabel, ed. *Memoirs of a Renaissance Pope: The Commentaries of Pius II.* 1962. An abridged version of insights from a leading Renaissance personality.

Interpretive Studies

Baxandall, Michael. *Painting and Experience in Fifteenth Century Italy: A Primer in the Social History of Pictorial Style.* 1972. A brilliant synthesis of art history and social history.

Boxer, C. R. *Four Centuries of Portuguese Expansion, 1415–1825.* 1969. A succinct survey.

Brucker, Gene A. *Giovanni and Lusanna: Love and Marriage in Renaissance Florence.* 1986. A good story, expertly told.

Burke, Peter. *The Italian Renaissance: Culture and Society in Italy.* 1986. Strong on social and cultural history.

Dollinger, Philippe. *The German Hansa.* 1970. Definitive.

Gilmore, Myron P. *The World of Humanism, 1453–1517.* 1952. Still a classic narrative.

Herlihy, David, and Christiane Klapisch-Zuber. *Tuscans and Their Families: A Study of the Florentine Catasto of 1427.* 1978. An English abridgement of the original French work.

Klapisch-Zuber, Christiane. *Women, Family, and Ritual in Renaissance Italy.* 1985. A collection of original essays on women's history.

Martin, Henri-Jean, and Lucien Febvre. *The Coming of the Book: The Impact of Printing 1450–1800.* 1976. The best comprehensive survey.

Martines, Lauro. *Power and Imagination: City-States in Renaissance Italy.* 1979. A tour de force.

Mattingly, Garrett. *Renaissance Diplomacy.* 1954. Still unsurpassed.

Murray, Peter, and Linda Murray. *The Art of the Renaissance.* 1963. Balanced discussion of Italian and northern European achievements.

Prevenier, Walter, and Wim Blockmans. *The Burgundian Netherlands.* 1986. Richly illustrated text by the two leading scholars on the subject.

Hille Feiken left the city of Münster, Germany, on June 16, 1534, elegantly dressed, bedecked with jewels, and determined to kill. Münster, which religious radicals had declared a holy city, lay under siege by armies loyal to its bishop, Franz von Waldeck. After reading the Book of Judith in the Apocrypha, Hille decided to deliver her city by imitating an ancient Israelite heroine named Judith. According to the Book of Ruth, Judith had approached the Assyrian general Holofernes, whose army was attacking Jerusalem. Charmed by Judith's beauty, Holofernes tried to seduce her; but after he had fallen into a drunken sleep, Judith cut off his head. Terrified, the Assyrian forces fled Jerusalem. Obsessed with this story, Hille crossed enemy lines and tried to persuade the commander of the besieging troops to take her to the bishop, promising to reveal a secret means of capturing the city without further fighting. Unfortunately, a defector recognized Hille and betrayed her. She was beheaded, in her own words, "for going out as Judith and trying to make the Bishop of Münster into a Holofernes."

Hille Feiken and the other besieged radicals in Münster were Anabaptists, part of a sect whose members believed themselves to be a community of saints amid a hopelessly sinful world. To prove their faith, adult Anabaptists received a second baptism in anticipation of the imminent Second Coming of Christ and the Last Judgment. The Anabaptists' determination to form a holy community tore at the foundations of the medieval European social and political order, and they met merciless persecution from the authorities. The Münster uprising represented an extreme (and uncharacteristically

The Struggle for Faith and Power, 1494–1560

Martin Luther
This painting by the German artist Lucas Cranach, one of the best-known likenesses of the reformer, captures Luther's firm faith in God and in his mission, an image that supporters of the Lutheran Reformation were at great pains to project.

violent) outburst of Anabaptist fervor—destined, as we shall see, to be brutally crushed.

Anabaptism was only one dimension of the Reformation, which had been set in motion by the German friar Martin Luther in 1517 and had become a sweeping movement to uproot church abuses and restore early Christian teachings. Hille Feiken's story was a sign of the times. Inspired by Luther—but often going far beyond what he would condone—ordinary men and women attempted to remake their heaven and earth. For more than two generations, such people's demands for freedom of worship and conscience occasionally were expressed in violent uprisings. Their story intertwined with bloody struggles among princes for domination in Europe, an age-old conflict now complicated by the clash of rival faiths. In the end the princes would prevail over both a divided Christendom and a restless people. Protestant or Catholic, European monarchs expanded their power at the expense of the church and disciplined their subjects in the name of piety and order.

IMPORTANT DATES

1494 French invade Italy; beginning of Valois-Habsburg struggles

1517 Martin Luther criticizes sale of indulgences; beginning of Reformation

1519 Spanish conquest of Mexico

1520 Reformer Huldrych Zwingli breaks with Rome

1525 Revolution in central Europe

1529 Formation of a "Protestant" party

1529–1558 Reign of Charles V

1529–1536 Henry VIII is head of the Anglican church

1532–1536 Spanish conquest of Peru

1534–1535 Anabaptist Kingdom of Münster

1541 John Calvin established permanently in Geneva

1545–1563 Council of Trent

1546–1547 War of Schmalkaldic League

1555 Religious Peace of Augsburg

1559 Treaty of Cateau-Cambrésis

A New Heaven and a New Earth

In the last book of the Bible, Revelation (also known as the Apocalypse), the prophet St. John the Evangelist foretells the passing of the old world and the coming of a new heaven and earth presided over by Christ. At the beginning of the sixteenth century, Europeans expected the Last Judgment to arrive soon. Indeed, the times seemed desperate. The Turks were advancing on Christian Europe while Christian princes fought among themselves. Some critics of the church labeled the pope as none other than the terrifying figure of the Antichrist, whose evil reign (according to Revelation) would end with Christ's return to earth.

It was in this frightening atmosphere that Martin Luther questioned the fundamental principles behind the church's teachings and practices. From its origins as a theological dispute in 1517, Luther's reform movement sparked explosive protests. By the time of his death in 1546, half of western Europe had renounced allegiance to Rome. Denying the Roman church's claim to absolute truth, a variety of Protestant churches asserted that they embodied the "simple and pure" Christianity of earliest apostolic times. In turn, ordinary people sometimes defied the new Protestant clergy and took religious reform into their own hands.

The Crisis of Faith

It was the established church, not Christian religion, that proved deficient to believers in Europe. Numerous signs before the Reformation pointed to an intense spiritual anxiety among the laity. People went on pilgrimages; new shrines sprang up, especially ones dedicated to the Virgin Mary and Christ; prayer books printed in various vernacular languages as well as Latin sold briskly. Alongside the sacraments and rituals of the official church, laypeople practiced their own rituals for healing and salvation.

Only a thin line separated miracles, which the church could accept, and magic, which it rejected. Clerics who wanted to reform the church denounced superstitions and the insatiable popular appetite for the sacred, but others readily exploited gullible laypeople. Perhaps the most notorious scandal prior to the Reformation occurred in the Swiss city of Basel. There in 1510 several Dominicans claimed that the Virgin Mary had worked "miracles" that they themselves had concocted. For a while their plot brought in crowds of pilgrims, but when the deception was uncovered, the perpetrators were burned at the stake.

The worst excesses in popular piety conjured up the religious and racial intolerance that had plagued Christian Europe throughout the Middle Ages. In the generation before the Reformation, Jews were frequently accused of ritually slaughtering Christian children and torturing the consecrated Eucharist, or Host, the consecrated bread that Christians believed was the body of Christ. Thus in 1510 a priest in Brandenburg accused local Jews of stealing and torturing the Eucharist. When, according to legend, the consecrated bread bled, the Jews were imprisoned and killed. A shrine dedicated to the bleeding Host attracted thousands of pilgrims seeking fortune and health.

Often the church gave external behavior more weight than spiritual intentions. For example, the number of prayers recited seemed to count for more than the believer's spiritual attitude. A case in point was the sacrament of penance—the confessing of sins and receiving of forgiveness, one of the central pillars of Christian morality and of the Roman church. On the eve of the Reformation, a mass of regulations defined the gradations of human sinfulness. For example, even married couples could sin if they had intercourse on one of the church's many holy days or made love "in lust" instead of for procreation. The church similarly regulated other kinds of behavior by, for example, prohibiting the eating of meat during feast days and censoring blasphemous language.

In receiving the sacrament of penance, sinners were expected to examine their conscience and sincerely confess their sins to a priest; in practice, however, confession proved highly unsatisfactory to many Christians. First, for those with religious scruples the demands of confession intensified their anxiety about salvation. Some could not get peace of mind because they were unsure if they had remembered to confess all their sins; others trembled before God's anger and doubted his mercy. Second,

some priests abused their authority by demanding sexual or monetary favors in return for penance. They seduced or blackmailed female parishioners and excommunicated debtors who failed to pay church taxes or loans from the clergy. Such reported incidents, although by no means widespread, seriously compromised the sanctity of the priestly office and sacrament. Finally, the practice of substituting monetary fines for religious tasks (such as pilgrimage or prayer) in penance suggested that the church was more interested in making money than saving souls—the charge, we shall see, that ignited Luther's reform movement.

To its critics, the Roman church was burdened by a vast, unresponsive, and sometimes corrupt clerical bureaucracy. Scandals involving church officialdom multiplied. In 1498 the archbishop of Cosenza, Bartolomeo Flores, the former private secretary to Pope Alexander VI, was sentenced to life imprisonment for having forged, with accomplices, more than three thousand papal bulls (documents that exempted holders from the church's many rules). For example, a Portuguese woman of royal blood had received permission to leave her nunnery and marry the late king's illegitimate son; a priest was allowed to marry without losing his position; and many clerics had bought the right to hold multiple benefices (ecclesiastical positions), a widespread abuse of canon law.

If papal dispensation could be bought, parishioners could also invest in the afterlife. Although a sincere confession saved a sinner from hell, he or she still faced doing penance, either in this life or the next. To alleviate suffering after death in purgatory, a pious person could go on pilgrimage, attend mass, do holy works, contribute to the church, and buy indulgences. A German prince, Frederick the Wise of Saxony (who later became Luther's protector), amassed the largest collection of relics outside of Italy. By 1518 his castle church contained 17,443 holy relics, including a piece of Moses' burning bush, parts of the holy cradle and swaddling clothes, thirty-five fragments of the true cross, and the Virgin Mary's milk. A diligent and pious person who rendered appropriate devotion to each of these relics could earn exactly 127,799 years and 116 days of remission from purgatory.

Dissatisfaction with the official church and its inflexible rules prompted several reform efforts prior to the Reformation; these were, however, limited to certain monastic houses and dioceses. More important, the church was losing touch with the religious sensibilities of the laypeople, who often resented clerical privileges. Urban merchants and artisans yearned for a religion more meaningful to their daily life and for a clergy more responsive to their needs. They wanted priests to preach edifying sermons, to administer the sacraments conscientiously, and to lead moral lives. They criticized the church's rich endowments that provided income for children of the nobility, who cared little about the salvation of townspeople. And they generously donated money to establish new preacherships for university-trained clerics, overwhelmingly from urban backgrounds and often from the same social classes as the donors. These young clerics, most of them schooled in humanism, often criticized the established church and hoped for reform.

A Christian Commonwealth?

Sickened by the endless warfare among Christian princes and outraged by the abuse of power, a generation of Christian humanists dreamed of ideal societies based on peace and morality. Within their own Christian society, these intellectuals sought to realize the ethical ideals of the classical world. Scholarship and social reform became inseparable goals. Two men, the Dutch scholar Desiderius Erasmus (c. 1466–1536) and the English lawyer Thomas More (1478–1535), stood out as outstanding representatives of these "Christian humanists," who, unlike Italian humanists, placed their primary emphasis on Christian piety.

Erasmus dominated the humanist world of early sixteenth-century Europe just as Cicero had dominated the glory of ancient Roman letters. He was on intimate terms with kings and popes, and his reputation extended across Europe. Following a brief stay in a monastery as a young man, Erasmus dedicated his life to scholarship. After studying in Paris, Erasmus traveled to Venice and served as an editor with Aldus Manutius, the leading printer of Latin and Greek books.

Through his books and letters, both disseminated by Manutius's printing press, Erasmus's fame spread. In the *Adages* (1500), a collection of quotations from ancient literature offering his witty and wise commentaries on the human experience,

Erasmus of Rotterdam
The great Dutch humanist was famous for his edition of the original Greek text of the New Testament, depicted here in the open book. Many contemporary portraits of Erasmus exist, attesting to his renown.

Erasmus established a reputation as a superb humanist dedicated to educational reform. Themes explored in the *Adages* continued in the *Colloquies* (1523), a compilation of Latin dialogues intended as language-learning exercises, in which Erasmus exerted his sharp wit to criticize the morals of his time. Lamenting poor table manners, Erasmus advised his cultivated readers not to pick their noses at meals, not to share half-eaten chicken legs, and not to speak while stuffing their mouths. Turning to political matters, he mocked the corruption of the clergy and the bloody ambitions of Christian princes.

Only through education, Erasmus believed, could individuals reform themselves and society. His goal was a unified, peaceful Christendom in which charity and good works, not empty ceremonies, would mark true religion; in which learning and piety would dispel the darkness of ignorance. Many of these ideas were elaborated in *Handbook of the Militant Christian* (1503), an eloquent plea for a simple religion devoid of greed and the lust for power. In *The Praise of Folly* (1509), Erasmus satirized values held dear by his contemporaries. Ignorance, humility, and poverty represented the true Christian virtues in a world that worshiped pomposity, power, and wealth, he said. The wise appeared foolish, he concluded, for their wisdom and values were not of this world.

Inspired by the Gospel ideal of Christianity, Erasmus devoted years to preparing a new Latin edition of the New Testament from the original Greek; it was published in 1516 by the Froben Press in Basel. Moved by the pacifism of the apostolic church, Erasmus admonished the young future emperor Charles V to rule as a just Christian prince. Erasmus vented his anger by ridiculing the warrior-pope Julius II and expressed deep sorrow for the brutal warfare that had been ravaging Europe for decades.

A man of peace and moderation, Erasmus found himself challenged by angry younger men and radical ideas once the Reformation took hold. Erasmus eventually decided in favor of Christian unity over reform and schism. His dream of Christian pacifism shattered, he lived to see dissenters executed—by Catholics and Protestants alike—for speaking their conscience. Erasmus spent his last years in Freiburg and died in Basel, isolated from the Protestant community, his writings condemned in Rome and ignored by many leaders of the Catholic church, which was divided over the intellectual legacy of its famous son.

If Erasmus found himself abandoned by his times, his good friend Thomas More, to whom *The Praise of Folly* was dedicated,* met a genuinely tragic fate. Having attended Oxford and the Inns of Court, where English lawyers were trained, More had legal talents that served him well in government. Variously a member of Parliament and a royal ambassador, he proved a competent and loyal servant to Henry VIII. In 1529 this ideal servant to the king became lord chancellor, but, tired of court intrigue and in protest against Henry's divorce, More resigned his position in 1532. As we shall

***Albrecht Dürer,* The Knight, Death, and the Devil**
An illustration for Erasmus's The Handbook of the Militant Christian, *this great engraving is often interpreted as depicting a Christian clad in the armor of righteousness on a path through life beset by death and demonic temptations. It aptly symbolizes the European mentality during the Reformation.*

see, he would later pay with his life for upholding conscience over political expediency.

More's best-known work, *Utopia* (1516), which describes an imaginary land inspired by the recent voyages of discovery, was intended as a critique of his own society. A just, equitable, and hardworking community, Utopia (meaning both "no place" and "best place" in Greek) was the opposite of England. In Utopia everyone worked on the land for two years; no private property meant there was no greed; and since they were served by public schools, communal kitchens, hospitals, and nurseries, Utopians had no need for money. Ded-

---

*The Latin title, *Encomium Moriae* ("The Praise of More"), was a pun on More's name.

icated to the pursuit of knowledge and natural religion, with equal distribution of goods and few
laws, Utopia knew neither crime nor war. But unlike More's "Nowhereland," in the real world social injustice bred crime and warfare. Deprived of
their livelihood, desperate men became thieves, and
"thieves do make quite efficient soldiers, and soldiers make quite enterprising thieves." More believed that politics, property, and war fueled human misery, whereas for his Utopians, "fighting
was a thing they absolutely loathe. They say it's a
quite subhuman form of activity, although human
beings are more addicted to it than any of the lower
animals."

More's tolerant and rational society did have a
few oddities—voluntary slavery, for instance, and
strictly controlled travel. Although premarital sex
brought severe punishment, prospective marriage
partners could examine one another naked before
making their final decisions. Men headed Utopia's
households and exercised authority over women
and children. And Utopians did not shy away from
declaring war on their neighbors to protect their
way of life. Nevertheless, this imaginary society
was paradise compared to a Christian Europe battered and devastated by the French invasion of Italy
in 1494.

The Struggle for Domination

A prosperous, fragmented land, Italy in 1494 to
1559 was the battlefield for the great powers of
western Europe. The struggle began when Charles
VIII of France (*1483–1498) laid claim to the
Neapolitan crown. Welcomed into Italy by the
Milanese and Florentines, who were playing political games of their own, the French army easily
conquered Naples. French successes soon gave way
to defeat as the political winds shifted and the Italian states scrambled to remake alliances in order to
preserve the balance of power. A second invasion,
under Louis XII (*1498–1515), only sucked France
deeper into a quagmire that yielded no permanent
conquests.

The first phase of the Italian Wars, as these general European conflicts came to be called, lasted
until 1520. On one side stood France and its Italian allies, usually Florence and Venice; on the other
were shifting anti-French alliances that included
the papacy, Spain, the Holy Roman Empire, and

various Italian states, each pursuing its own gain.
In the battlefields of northern Italy, French cavalry
and artillery challenged fierce Swiss fighters, who
served as papal and imperial mercenaries. At the
battle of Marignano (1515), the young French king
Francis I (*1515–1547) conquered Milan, dealing a
crushing blow to the Swiss.

The French king soon encountered a formidable opponent, Charles V (*1520–1558). Thanks to
a series of dynastic unions, Charles had inherited
the largest empire Europe had ever known. At the
age of nineteen he became the ruler of the Low
Countries, Spain and Spain's Italian and New
World dominions, and the Austrian Habsburg
lands. The next year, in 1520, Charles was elected
Holy Roman emperor.

The church offered paltry moral guidance in
this conflict among Christian princes; indeed, the
Vicar of Christ, as the pope was known, was simply one more participant in the power struggle.
During the fifty years before the Reformation,
popes had tried to subjugate the lands over which
they had long been nominal rulers. The names they
chose signified the style of the vainglorious papacy:* Rodrigo Borgia took the name of the ancient
Macedonian conqueror by naming himself Pope
Alexander VI (*1492–1503); his successor, Giuliano della Rovere, called himself Julius II (*1503–
1513) after another strongman from ancient history, Julius Caesar. Adopting the names of ancient
conquerors reflected the papal self-image; the pope
was not only the supreme spiritual head of Christendom but also a mighty prince who ruled over
an extensive territory.

Alexander VI and Julius II both came from
powerful noble blood-
lines. The Borgias of
Aragon ranked among
the twenty most pres-
tigious noble lineages
in Valencia. The della
Roveres, from Liguria
in northern Italy, mar-
ried into French roy-
alty. Both Alexander
and Julius owed their
ecclesiastical careers to

**Central Italy in the Beginning
of the Sixteenth Century**

---

*For centuries each newly elected pope had followed the custom
of choosing a new name. The custom continues to this day.

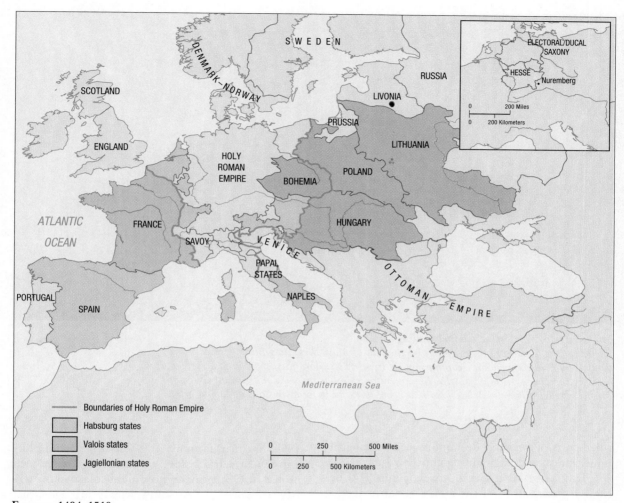

Europe, 1494–1519

family connections: their respective uncles were two popes, Calixtus III (✱1455–1458) and Sixtus IV (✱1471–1484). This practice of promoting nephews and sons to positions of power within the papal state led to the coining of the term *nepotism* (*nepos* in Latin means "nephew"). Family connections proved equally important in the sixteenth century, when two members of the Medici family ascended the papal throne as Leo X (✱1513–1521) and Clement VII (✱1523–1534).

In their private lives these princes of the church often behaved as their secular relatives did. Both before and after his election, Alexander VI fathered children—a practice generally tolerated in Rome. For Alexander, winning back the papal state was crucial for the papacy's survival. Competing as one of the Italian powers, the papacy was drawn into the dangers and allures of secular power politics. In a papal court torn by factional struggles, the appointment of nephews as cardinals was the only reliable means to preserve papal power. Cesare Borgia, Alexander's son, served as his father's trusted advisor when he was a cardinal. After the death of his brother (rumors circulated that Cesare murdered him), Cesare renounced his cardinalate to carve a principality out of the papal lands—an effort that collapsed when Julius II succeeded Alexander. But in spite of his bitter hatred for the Borgias, Julius continued their policies. Leading a papal army, Julius crushed the petty lords who

Michelangelo, *The Sistine Chapel Ceiling*
Depicting the Creation of the world and the Fall of Man, these magnificent frescos were painted by Michelangelo on a commission by Julius II to adorn the chapel in St. Peter's Basilica built by the pope's uncle, Sixtus IV. Recent restoration has revealed the vibrant colors of Michelangelo's original work, which had been obscured by centuries of smoke and grime.

ruled parts of the papal dominions, centralizing administration and augmenting church revenues.

To glorify his imperial image, Julius also became a great patron of the arts. His patronage led to the completion of the Sistine Chapel, begun under his uncle, Sixtus IV. The chapel's ceilings were graced by the brush of the Florentine artist Michelangelo, who also designed a grandiose but never-completed tomb for Julius based on the model of tombs for Roman emperors. Julius hoped to undertake a crusade against the Turks, a project proclaimed but unfulfilled by other popes since the mid-fifteenth century. Such a crusade, however, remained only a dream as long as Italy was threatened by foreign arms.

A Failed Reform: Savonarola, Machiavelli, and Florence

Nowhere amid this power struggle was the papacy's moral bankruptcy more apparent than in its treatment of Girolamo Savonarola (1452–1498), a Dominican friar in Florence. On November 1,

1494, Savonarola mounted the pulpit in the Florentine Cathedral before a swollen and frightened crowd of Florentines who sought solace in his terrifying words. "You know that years ago great tribulations were announced before there was any noise or smell of these wars launched by the men from over the mountains which we are now witnessing," roared the preacher. "You also know that not two full years have passed since I said to you: Behold the terrible swift sword of the Lord! Not I but God was responsible for this prediction to you, and behold, it has come and it is coming."

This "terrible swift sword" was the French army under King Charles VIII, on its way across the border to claim the Neapolitan throne. The Florentines, having just overthrown the Medici regime that had dominated their city since 1434, awaited the French king with trepidation. On November 5 they delegated Savonarola to head an embassy to Charles. During Charles's subsequent stay in Florence, Savonarola persuaded the king to depart in peace and proceed on to Naples as the instrument of God's wrath, sparing Florence.

Delivered from the French army, the Florentines hailed Savonarola as a great prophet.

For the next three and a half years, Savonarola held sway in Florence. He admonished the citizens to repent, proclaimed Florence a New Jerusalem, and denounced Alexander VI for corruption. His followers burned games, profane images, erotic books, playing cards, and all sorts of worldly "vanities." But gradually the Florentines tired of Savonarola's prophetic wrath, and when Alexander excommunicated him they turned him over to the church. On May 23, 1498, on the pope's explicit orders, Savonarola was hanged and burned for heresy.

In the crowd of spectators at Savonarola's execution was Niccolò Machiavelli (1469–1527), a Florentine civil servant. Machiavelli felt that Savonarola's rise and fall taught a valuable lesson in power. "It was the purity of his life, the doctrines he preached, and the subjects for his discourses that sufficed to make the people have faith in him," Machiavelli would write years later. But the people are fickle, he would note, and persuasion alone cannot maintain power: "Thus it comes about that all armed prophets have conquered, and unarmed ones failed." Savonarola was an example of an unarmed prophet "who failed entirely in his new rules when the multitude began to disbelieve in him, and he had no means of holding fast those who had believed or of compelling the unbelievers to believe." In short, Machiavelli would assert, the exercise of political power owed little to ethics.

Years later, after he lost office, Machiavelli set his political observations down on paper. In 1513 he dedicated a short political treatise, *The Prince*, to Giuliano de' Medici, whom papal troops had just restored to power in Florence. In this treatise (not published until 1531), Machiavelli pondered the laws of power as manifested by the political events of his day. Stripping politics of its ethical and religious veneer, Machiavelli held up Cesare Borgia, Alexander's son, as the model of a ruthless and successful prince. The aim of politics, according to Machiavelli, was to conquer fortune with human will and power.

In his admiration of power and in separating politics from morality, Machiavelli used the language of male domination to articulate power politics. Fortune, a feminine noun in Italian, is opposed by *virtù*, or manly strength (from the Latin *vir*, meaning "man"); princes must use violence to subject fortune to their will in order to prosper. Fortune, personified as feminine power, resembles the force of nature—ever-changing and fickle. A prince would soon come to grief, Machiavelli argued, if he were to depend entirely on fortune: "But I do feel this: that it is better to be rash than timid, for Fortune is a woman, and the man who wants to hold her down must beat and bully her. . . . Like a woman, too, she is always a friend of the young, because they are less timid, more brutal, and take charge of her more recklessly."

As satire and as objective political analysis, *The Prince* offered remarkable insights into the relationship between power and faith. To the strongman, or prince, Machiavelli conceded the possibility to control chaos by understanding the principles of politics. The exercise of power, according to Machiavelli, justified the use of religion as an instrument of rule, a view that scandalized his contemporaries. In spite of his perhaps despairing cynicism, Machiavelli was a republican, a patriot who wanted to restore the glory of Florence and expel the invaders from Italy. Although *The Discourses*, his extended commentary on the ancient Roman historian Livy, echoed Machiavelli's republicanism and patriotism, it was *The Prince* that made him notorious. The term *Machiavellian* quickly took on the negative meaning it still has today, and the machinations of Italian princes, these descendants of the ancient Romans, would horrify many pilgrims from the Holy Roman Empire.

The Reformation Begins

Since the mid-fifteenth century many clerics had tried to reform the church, criticizing clerical abuses and calling for moral rejuvenation, but their efforts came up against the church's inertia and resistance. Outside the clergy, many laypeople had become alienated from the church, feeling that its personnel and doctrines were indifferent to their spiritual needs. At the beginning of the sixteenth century widespread popular piety and anticlericalism existed side by side, fomenting an explosive mixture of need and resentment. A young German friar, tormented by his own religious doubts, was to become the spokesman for a generation.

THE PROGRESS OF THE REFORMATION

1517 Martin Luther publicizes the Ninety-five Theses attacking the sale of indulgences

1525 Death of Thomas Müntzer, a radical reformer who had urged revolution and extermination of the ungodly

1529 German princes who support Luther protest the condemnation of religious reform by Charles V at the Imperial Diet of Speyer, hence the sobriquet "Protestants"

1529–1536 The English Parliament establishes King Henry VIII as head of the Anglican church, severing ties to Rome

1531 Death of Huldrych Zwingli at the Battle of Kappel

1534–1535 A group of Anabaptists control the city of Münster, Germany, in a failed experiment to create a holy community

1541 John Calvin establishes himself permanently in Geneva, making that city a model of Christian reform and discipline

Martin Luther and the German Nation

Son of a miner and entrepreneur, Martin Luther (1483–1546) studied law, pursuing a career open to ambitious young men from middle-class families, which had been urged on him by his father. His true vocation, however, lay with the church. Caught in a storm on a lonely road one midsummer's night, the young student grew terrified by the thunder and lightning. Martin implored the help of St. Anne, the mother of the Virgin Mary, and promised he would enter a monastery if she protected him. Thus, to the chagrin of his father, Luther abandoned law for theology and entered the Augustinian order.

In the monastery the young Luther, finding no spiritual consolation in the sacraments of the church, experienced a religious crisis. Appalled at his own sense of sinfulness and the weakness of human nature, he lived in terror of God's justice in spite of frequent confessions and penance. A pilgrimage to Rome only deepened Luther's unease with the institutional church. Coming to his aid, a sympathetic superior sent Luther to study theology, a course of study that gradually led him to experience grace and insight into salvation. Luther recalled his monastic days in these words shortly before his death:

Though I lived as a monk without reproach, I felt that I was a sinner before God with an extremely disturbed conscience. I could not believe that he was placated by my satisfaction [in penance]. I did not love, yes, I hated the righteous God who punishes sinners, and secretly . . . I was angry with God. . . . Nevertheless, I beat importunately upon Paul [in Romans 1:17]. . . . At last, by the mercy of God, meditating day and night, I gave heed to the context of the words, namely, "In [the gospel] the righteousness of God is revealed, as it is written, 'He who through faith is righteous shall live.'" There I began to understand that the righteousness of God is that by which the righteous live by a gift of God, namely by faith. And this is the meaning: the righteousness of God is revealed by the gospel, namely, the passive righteousness with which merciful God justifies us by faith. . . . Here I felt that I was altogether born again and had entered paradise itself.

Luther followed this tortuous spiritual journey while serving as a professor of theology at the University of Wittenberg, recently founded by Frederick the Wise, Elector of Saxony. But events conspired to make Luther a public figure. In 1516 the new archbishop of Mainz, Albrecht of Brandenburg, commissioned a Dominican friar to sell indulgences in his archdiocese (which included Saxony); the proceeds would help cover the cost of constructing St. Peter's Basilica in Rome and also partly defray Archbishop Albrecht's expenses in pursuing his election. Such blatant profiteering outraged many, including Luther. In 1517, Luther composed ninety-five theses—propositions for an academic debate—that questioned indulgence peddling and the purchase of church offices. Once they became

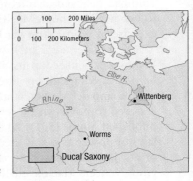

Luther's World

public, the theses unleashed a torrent of pent-up resentment and frustration in the laypeople.

What began as a theological debate in a provincial university soon engulfed the Holy Roman Empire. Two groups predominated among Luther's earliest supporters: younger humanists and those clerics who shared Luther's critical attitude toward the church establishment. It is difficult to generalize about these early clerical rebels, or "evangelicals," as they would call themselves, after the Gospels.* None of the evangelicals came from the upper echelons of the church; many were from urban middle-class backgrounds, and most were university-trained and well educated. As a group their profile differed from that of the poorly educated rural clergy, or from their noble clerical superiors, who often owed their ecclesiastical dignities to family influence rather than theological learning. The evangelicals also stood apart in that they represented those social groups most ready to challenge clerical authority—merchants, artisans, and literate urban laypeople.

Initially, Luther presented himself as the pope's "loyal opposition." In 1520 he composed three treatises. In *Freedom of a Christian*, which he wrote in Latin for the learned and addressed to Pope Leo X, Luther argued that the Roman church's numerous rules and its stress on "good works" were useless. He insisted that faith, not good works, would save sinners from damnation, and he sharply distinguished between true Gospel teachings and invented church doctrines. Basing himself on St. Paul and St. Augustine, Luther argued that by his suffering on the cross Christ had freed humanity from the guilt of sin, and that only through faith in God's justice and mercy could believers be saved. Thus the church's laws of behavior had no place in the search for salvation. Luther suggested instead "the priesthood of all believers," arguing that the Bible provided all the teachings necessary for Christian living, and that a professional caste of clerics should not hold sway over laypeople. *Freedom of a Christian* was immediately translated into German and was published widely. Its slogans "by faith alone," "by Scripture alone," and "the priesthood of all believers" came to encapsulate the reform movement.

In his second treatise, *To the Nobility of the German Nation*, which he wrote in German, Luther appealed to German nationalism. He denounced the corrupt Italians in Rome who were cheating and exploiting his compatriots and called upon the German princes to defend their nation and reform the church. This appeal to secular rulers to become church reformers had a long tradition dating back to the Investiture Conflict of the eleventh century. Luther's third major treatise, *On the Babylonian Captivity of the Church*, which he composed in Latin mainly for a clerical audience, condemned the papacy as the embodiment of the Antichrist.

From Rome's perspective, the "Luther Affair," as church officials called it, was essentially a matter of clerical discipline. Rome ordered Luther to obey his superiors and keep quiet. But the church establishment had seriously misjudged the gravity of the situation. Luther's ideas, published in numerous German and Latin editions, spread rapidly throughout the Holy Roman Empire, unleashing forces that Luther could not control. Social, nationalist, and religious protests fused into an explosive mass, one very similar to the Czech revolution that Jan Hus had inspired a century earlier. Like Hus, Luther appeared before an emperor: in 1521 he defended his faith before Charles V at the Imperial Diet of Worms, where he shocked Germans by declaring his admiration for the Czech heretic. But unlike Hus, Luther did not suffer martyrdom because he enjoyed the protection of Frederick the Wise.

During the 1520s the anti-Roman evangelicals included many German princes, city officials, professors, priests, and ordinary men and women, particularly in the cities; essentially, the early Reformation was an urban movement. As centers of publishing and commerce, German towns became natural distribution points for Lutheran propaganda. Moreover, urban people proved particularly receptive to Luther's message: many were literate and were eager to read the Scriptures, and merchants and artisans resented the clergy's tax-exempt status and the competition from monasteries and nunneries that produced their own goods. Magistrates began to curtail clerical privileges and subordinate the clergy to municipal authority. Luther's message—that clerical intercession was not necessary for a Christian's salvation—spoke to

---

*The word *Gospel*, meaning "good tidings," comes from the Old English translation of the Greek word *evangelion*.

the townspeople's spiritual needs and social vision. Inspired by Luther's message, many reform priests led their urban parishioners away from Roman liturgy, and from Wittenberg the reform movement quickly fanned out into a torrent of many streams.

Zwingli and the Swiss Confederation

While Luther provided the religious leadership for Protestant northern Germany, Germany's south came under the strong influence of the Reformation movement that had emerged in the poor, mountainous country of Switzerland. The Swiss Confederation (made up of thirteen cantons) had declared its independence from the Holy Roman Empire in 1291, although it would not be internationally recognized until 1648. In the late fifteenth and early sixteenth centuries, Switzerland's chief source of income was the export of soldiers: hardy Swiss peasants fought as mercenaries in papal, French, and imperial armies, earning respect as fierce pikemen. Military captains recruited and organized young men from village communes; the women stayed behind to farm and tend animals. Many young Swiss men died on the battlefields of Italy, and many others returned maimed for life. In 1520 the chief preacher of the Swiss city of Zurich, Huldrych Zwingli (1484–1531), criticized his superior, Cardinal Matthew Schinner, for sending the country's young men off to serve as cannon fodder in papal armies.

The son of a Swiss village leader, Zwingli became a reformer independently of Martin Luther. After completing his university studies, Zwingli was ordained as a priest and served as an army chaplain for several years, during which he witnessed the bloody battles of Novara and Marignano. Deeply influenced by Erasmus, whom he met in 1515, Zwingli adopted the Dutch humanist's vision of social renewal through education. In 1520, Zwingli openly declared himself a reformist and attacked the church rituals of fasting and clerical celibacy, and corruption among the ecclesiastical hierarchy.

Under Zwingli's leadership, the city and canton of Zurich served as the center for the Swiss reform movement. Guided by his vision of a theocratic (church-directed) society that would unite religion, politics, and morality, Zwingli refused to draw any distinction between the ideal citizen and the perfect Christian—an idea radically different from Luther's. While defending the reform movement in Zurich against the Catholic cantons, Zwingli also rooted out internal dissent.

Luther and Zwingli also differed in their view of the role of the Eucharist, or Holy Communion. Luther insisted that Christ was truly present in this central Christian rite, although not in the strict Catholic sense. Zwingli, influenced by Erasmus, viewed the Eucharist as simply a ceremony symbolizing Christ's union with believers.

In 1529, troubled by these differences and other disagreements, evangelical princes and magistrates assembled the major reformers at Marburg, in central Germany. After several days of intense discussions, the north German and Swiss reformers managed to resolve many doctrinal differences, but Luther and Zwingli failed to agree on the meaning of the Eucharist. Thus the German and Swiss reform movements continued on separate paths. The issue of Holy Communion would later divide Lutherans and Calvinists as well.

Although the Reformation spread from Zurich to other cities in Switzerland, five rural cantons in the heartland of the Swiss mercenary trade remained Catholic. Failing to settle their differences through political negotiations and theological debates, the Swiss plunged into civil war in 1531, with the five Catholic cantons fielding an army against Zurich. Marching as a chaplain with the citizen army from his hometown, Zwingli was killed in the battle of Kappel that same year. His enemies quartered and burned his body. The leadership of the Swiss reform movement was taken up by Zwingli's son-in-law, Heinrich Bullinger.

The Gospel of the Common People

While Zwingli was challenging the Roman church, some laypeople in Zurich secretly pursued their own path to reform. Taking their cue from the New Testament's descriptions of the first Christian com-

Zwingli's World

munity, these men and women believed that true faith was based on reason and free will. They found the baptism of infants invalid—how could a baby knowingly choose Christ?, they asked—and instead baptized one another as thinking adults. They came to be called Anabaptists—those who were rebaptized. Because the early church councils had explicitly condemned rebaptism, the Zurich Anabaptists challenged the new evangelical church, which saw itself as the source of the early Christian revival. The practice of rebaptism symbolized the Anabaptists' determination to withdraw from a social order corrupted (as they saw it) by power and evil; as pacifists who were rejecting the authority of courts and magistrates, they considered themselves a community of true Christians unblemished by sin.

Zwingli immediately attacked the Anabaptists for their refusal to bear arms and swear oaths of allegiance, sensing quite accurately that they were repudiating his theocratic order. When persuasion failed to convince the Anabaptists of their errors, Zwingli urged Zurich magistrates to carry out the death sentence against them. Thus the Reformation's first martyrs of conscience were victims of its evangelical reformers. Nevertheless, Anabaptism spread quickly from Zurich to many cities in southern Germany, despite the Holy Roman Empire's general condemnation of the movement in 1529. Vehemently antiestablishment, the Anabaptist movement, which included some ex-priests, drew its leadership primarily from the artisan class and its members from the middle and lower classes—men and women attracted by a simple message of peace and salvation.

Meanwhile, Luther found that he could no longer control the religious protests that were springing up throughout the Holy Roman Empire. Between 1520 and 1525 many city governments, often under intense popular pressure and sometimes in sympathy with the evangelicals, allowed the reform movement to sweep away church authority. Local officials appointed new clerics who were committed to reforming Christian doctrine and ritual. The turning point came in 1525, when the crisis of church authority exploded in a massive rural uprising that threatened the entire social order.

The church was the largest landowner in the Holy Roman Empire: about one-seventh of the empire's territory consisted of ecclesiastical principalities in which bishops and abbots exercised both secular and churchly power. Luther's anticlerical message struck home with peasants who were paying taxes to both their lord and the church. In the spring of 1525 many peasants in south and central Germany rose in rebellion, sometimes inspired by wandering preachers. The princes of the church, the rebels charged, were wolves in sheep's clothing, fleecing Christ's flock to satisfy their sanctimonious greed. Some urban workers and artisans joined the peasant bands, plundering monasteries, refusing to pay church taxes, and demanding village autonomy, the abolition of serfdom, and the right to appoint their own pastors. The more radical rebels called for the destruction of the entire ruling class. In Thuringia the rebels were led by an ex-priest, Thomas Müntzer, who promised to chastise the wicked and thus clear the way for the Last Judgment.

Müntzer (c. 1489–1525) was a volatile young man who led an unsettled life. Visiting Prague, he came under the influence of the Hussites (followers of Jan Hus). Unlike Luther, who had close ties to Frederick the Wise, Müntzer was a simple pastor in the small Saxon town of Allstedt. Convinced that the Last Judgment was at hand and that he himself was a latter-day prophet and an instrument of God, Müntzer tried to convince the Saxon princes to take up God's sword to destroy the ungodly. Frederick was not persuaded, and Luther took great alarm at Müntzer's radicalism. Anticipating repression, Müntzer fled Allstedt, only to return to Thuringia when the commoners rose in rebellion.

The revolution of 1525, known as the Peasants War, split the reform movement. Fearing a social revolution, princes and city authorities turned against the rebels. In Thuringia Catholic and evangelical princes joined hands to crush Müntzer and his supporters. All over the empire princes defeated peasant armies, hunted down their leaders, and uprooted all opposition. By the end of the year more than one hundred thousand had been killed and others maimed, imprisoned, or exiled. Luther had tried to mediate the conflict, chastising the princes for their brutality toward the peasants but also warning the rebels against mixing religion and social protest. Luther believed that rulers were ordained by God and thus must be obeyed even if they were tyrants. The Kingdom of God belonged not to this world but to the next, he insisted, and the body of true Christians (as opposed to the in-

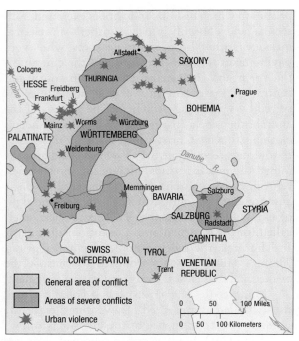

The Revolution of 1525 in Germany

stitutional church, in which sinners and Christians mingled) remained known only to God. Luther considered Müntzer's mixing of religion and politics the greatest danger to the Reformation, nothing less than "the Devil's work." When the rebels ignored Luther's appeal and followed more radical preachers, Luther called on the princes to restore the divinely ordained social order. Fundamentally conservative in its political philosophy, the new evangelical church would henceforth depend for its sustenance on established political authority.

Emerging as the champions of an orderly religious reform, many German princes eventually confronted Emperor Charles V, who supported Rome. In 1529, Charles declared the Roman faith the empire's only legitimate religion. The German princes protested, proclaiming their allegiance to the reform cause, and their party came to be called the Protestants. During the 1530s religious schism assumed political forms. In 1531 Protestant princes and imperial cities formed the Schmalkaldic League, a mutual defense alliance against the Catholic emperor.

The common people, however, did not disappear from the Reformation movement. Disillu-

sioned by the new alliance between religion and politics, some Anabaptists turned to violence. In 1534 one incendiary group, believing that the end of the world was imminent, gained control of the northwest German city of Münster. Proclaiming themselves a community of saints, this group of Anabaptists, imitating the ancient Israelites, were initially governed by twelve elders. Later, Jan of Leiden, a Dutch tailor who claimed to be the prophesied leader—a second "King David"—defeated an attack by the bishop of Münster, who had besieged the city. During this short-lived social experiment the Münster Anabaptists abolished private property in imitation of the early Christian church and dissolved traditional marriages, allowing men to have multiple wives like Old Testament patriarchs. As the siege tightened, messengers left Münster in search of relief while the leaders exhorted the faithful to remain steadfast in the hope of the Second Coming of Christ. Hille Feiken, as we have seen, tried to assassinate the bishop himself. But with food and hope exhausted, a soldier betrayed the city to the besiegers in June 1535. The leaders of the Münster Anabaptists died in battle or were horribly executed. Nevertheless, the Anabaptist movement in northwestern Europe would survive as the determined pacifist Mennonite congregation until this day, eventually spreading its membership from Russia to the United States.

A Contest for Mastery and a Continuing Reformation

In the sixteenth century new patterns of conflicts, generated by the Reformation, superimposed themselves on traditional dynastic strife. In every land rulers faced new and complex questions of power and faith: Are religious dissenters rebels by definition? Should dissenters be tolerated? Is peace preferable to religious unity? Can subjects assassinate or rebel against a ruler with different religious beliefs, and can the church sanction these acts? Who would succeed to the throne—is bloodline more important than religion? The conflicts that these questions raised would shape European history for more than a century beyond the Reformation.

The Giants Clash

While the Reformation was taking hold in Germany and common people were beginning to assert themselves, the great powers fought it out. The second phase of the Italian Wars was not confined to Italian battlefields; the Habsburg-Valois dynastic conflict escalated instead into a larger conflagration. A succession of battles, treaties, and alliances revealed the combatants' basic motives. Francis I was obsessed with conquering Milan, an ambition that a warlike French nobility, in search of booty and glory, supported. Defeated at Pavia (1525), Francis was captured, sent to Spain, and forced to sign a peace treaty. Upon his release the French king repudiated the treaty and even sought Turkish aid in defeating the Habsburg army.

All this prevented Charles V from dealing with the religious schism in his own empire. A devout monarch who dreamed of leading a crusade, Charles found himself embroiled in Italian and German politics. The Italian states were suspicious of joint imperial-Spanish domination, and German Protestant princes were hostile to an overmighty Catholic overlord such as Charles. Caught between Francis and Charles—the two most powerful Christian princes—the popes tried to promote a peace settlement, to be followed by a crusade against the Turks, while constantly shifting allegiances to prevent Italy's domination by either power. Not wanting to be left out, Henry VIII of England jumped into the fray, switching back and forth between sides to maximize his gains. The smaller Italian powers struggled for survival, acting as client states of one or the other protagonist.

In this arena of power politics, Christian and Muslim arms clashed in Hungary and the Mediterranean. The Ottoman Empire reached its apogee under Sultan Suleiman I "the Magnificent" (✻1520–1566). In 1526 a Turkish expedition destroyed the Hungarian army at Mohács. Three years later the Ottoman army unsuccessfully laid siege to Vienna. In 1535, Charles V led a campaign to capture Tunis, the lair of North African pirates under Ottoman suzerainty. Desperate to overcome superior imperialist forces, Francis I eagerly forged an alliance with the Turkish sultan. Coming to the aid of the French, the Turkish fleet be-

The Battle of Pavia (1525)
This crushing defeat of the French forces (including many Swiss mercenaries) by the Habsburg armies, shown here in a Flemish tapestry, by no means ended the bloody rivalry of Francis I and Charles V.

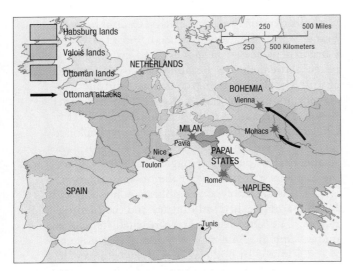

Habsburg-Valois-Ottoman Wars

sieged imperial-occupied Nice. Francis even ordered all inhabitants of nearby Toulon to vacate their town so that he could turn it into a Muslim colony for eight months, complete with a mosque and slave market.

With the deaths of Francis I and Henry VIII in 1547, the Italian Wars entered a new phase, and for the next twelve years the Habsburg-Valois struggle dominated central Europe. The new French king, Henry II (*1547–1559), the son of Francis, supported the German Protestants, while the papacy, terrorized by the imperial sacking of Rome in 1527, was torn by fear and hatred of the Catholic emperor Charles.

The sixteenth century marked the beginning of superior Western military technology. When Charles VIII of France invaded Italy in 1494, the size of his army and its artillery had awed the Italians. Over the next generations, all armies grew in size, and their firepower became ever more deadly. With new weapons and larger armies, the costs of war soared. For example, heavier artillery pieces meant that the rectangular walls of medieval cities had to be transformed into fortresses with jutting forts and gun emplacements. In 1542 to 1550—its years of conflict with Scotland and France—England spent about £450,000 per year on its armies; total royal revenues for the same period amounted to only £200,000 per year. To pay these bills, England devalued its coinage (the sixteenth-century equivalent

of printing more paper money), causing prices to rise rapidly during those years.

Other European powers fell into similar predicaments. Charles V boasted the largest army in Europe—one hundred forty-eight thousand men stationed in central Europe, the Netherlands, Italy, Spain, and North Africa during 1552—but he also sank ever deeper into debt. Between 1520 and 1532, Charles borrowed 5.4 million ducats (gold coins), primarily to pay his troops; from 1552 to 1556 his war loans soared to 9.6 million ducats. Francis I, his opponent, similarly overspent. During three years of truce (1535–1537), Francis saved 1.5 million French pounds for his war chest; when war broke out again, he spent more than 4.5 million in a single season. On his death in 1547, Francis owed the bankers of Lyon almost 7 million French pounds—approximately the entire royal income for that year.

The European powers literally fought themselves into bankruptcy. In the 1520s, Francis and Charles had to pay 14 to 18 percent interest on their loans. Taxation, the sale of offices, and outright confiscations failed to bring in enough money to satisfy the war machine. Both the Habsburg and the Valois kings looked to their leading bankers to finance their costly wars. The Italian, German, and Swiss banking houses in Lyon provided a steady stream of loans to the French monarchy. The Lyon bankers financed Charles VIII's Italian campaign in 1494 and supplied Francis with annual loans after 1542. The Habsburg Spanish monarchy relied on a consortium of Genoese, Florentine, and German banks.

Foremost among the financiers of the warring princes was the Fugger bank, the largest such international enterprise in sixteenth-century Europe. Based in the south German imperial city of Augsburg, the Fugger family and their associates built an international financial empire that helped to make kings. The enterprise began with Jakob Fugger (1459–1525), nicknamed "the Rich," who became the personal banker to Charles V's grandfather, Emperor Maximilian I. Constantly short of cash, Maximilian had granted the Fugger family numerous mining and minting concessions. The Fugger empire reaped handsome profits from its Habsburg connections: in addition to collecting interest and collaterals, the Fugger banking house, with branches in the Netherlands, Italy, and Spain, transferred funds for the emperor across the scattered Habsburg domains. To pay for the service of providing and accepting bills of exchange, the Fuggers charged substantial fees. By the end of his life, Maximilian was so deeply in debt to Jakob Fugger that he had to pawn the royal jewels.

In 1519, Jakob Fugger assembled a consortium of German and Italian bankers to secure the imperial election of Maximilian's grandson, Charles of Ghent. The consortium raised a huge sum, which went toward gifts for the electors. To block Francis I, Charles's only serious rival, the bankers refused to accept Francis's bills of exchange. The French king had to pay the German electors in sacks of gold, but it was too little too late, and Charles V became emperor. For the next three decades the alliance between Europe's largest international bank and its largest empire tightened. Between 1527 and 1547 the Fugger bank's assets grew from 3 million guldens (Germany's currency) to over 7 million; roughly 55 percent of the assets were from loans to the Habsburgs, with the Spanish dynasty taking the lion's share. Nothing revealed the power of international banking more than a letter Jakob Fugger wrote to Charles V in 1523 to recoup his investment in the 1519 imperial election, asking the emperor "[to] graciously recognize my faithful, humble service, dedicated to the greater well-being of Your Imperial Majesty, and that you will order that the money which I have paid out, together with the interest upon it, shall be reckoned up and paid, without further delay."

Charles barely stayed one step ahead of his creditors, and his successors gradually lost control of the Spanish state finances. To service debts, European monarchs sought revenues in war and tax increases. But paying for troops and crushing rebellions took more money and more loans. The cycle of financial crises and warfare persisted until the late eighteenth century.

The Reformation Continues: Calvin, France, and Geneva

Under the leadership of John Calvin (1509–1564), another wave of reform pounded at the gates of Rome. Born in Picardy, in northern France, to the secretary of the bishop of Noyon, Calvin benefited from his family connections and received a scholarship to study in Paris and Orléans, where he took

a law degree. A gifted intellectual who was attracted to humanism, Calvin could have enjoyed a brilliant career in government or church service. Instead, experiencing a crisis of faith, he sought eternal salvation through intense theological study.

Influenced by the leading French humanist Lefèvre d'Étaples and Bishop Briçonnet of Meaux, who sought to reform the church from within, Calvin gradually crossed the line from loyal opposition to questioning fundamental Catholic teachings. His conversion came about after a lengthy and anxious intellectual battle. Unlike Luther, who described his life in vivid detail, Calvin generally revealed nothing about personal matters.

During Calvin's youth the Reformation gained partisans in France. On Sunday, October 18, 1534, Parisians found ribald broadsheets denouncing the Catholic Mass posted on church doors. Smuggled into France from the Protestant and French-

John Calvin
This woodcut of Calvin in Geneva praises him for completing the work of Jan Hus and Martin Luther in overthrowing the Antichrist. Such linking of the reformers in a common tradition was a frequently evoked image in the visual propaganda of the Protestant Reformation.

speaking parts of Switzerland, the broadsheets unleashed a wave of repression in the capital. Rumors of a Protestant conspiracy and massacre circulated, and magistrates swiftly promoted a general persecution of reformist groups throughout France, including the hitherto unmolested religious dissidents. This so-called Affair of the Placards signaled a national crackdown on church dissenters. Hundreds of French Protestants were arrested, scores were executed, and many more, including Calvin, fled abroad.

On his way to Strasbourg, Germany, a haven for religious dissidents, Calvin stopped in Geneva—the city where he would find his life's work. This French-speaking city-republic had renounced allegiance to its bishop in anticipation of religious reform. The local reformer Guillaume Farel threatened Calvin with God's curse if he did not stay and labor in Geneva. This frightening appeal succeeded. Under Calvin and Farel the reform party became embroiled in a political struggle between two civic factions: their supporters, many of whom were French refugees, and the opposition, represented by the leading Old Genevan families, who resented the moralistic regulations of the new, foreigner-run clerical regime. A political setback in 1538 drove Calvin and Farel from Geneva, but Calvin returned in 1541 after his supporters triumphed and remained until his death in 1564.

Calvin's World

Under Calvin's inspiration and moral authority, Geneva became a disciplined Christian republic, modeled after the ideas in Calvin's *The Institutes of the Christian Religion*. The first edition of this book—Calvin's masterpiece and a brilliant intellectual accomplishment—appeared in 1536, but because Calvin continued to revise his ideas, the final Latin and French editions were not published until 1559 and 1561, respectively. No reformer prior to Calvin had expounded on the doctrines, organization, history, and practices of Christianity in such a systematic, logical, and coherent manner.

Calvin followed Luther's doctrine of salvation to its ultimate logical conclusion: if God is almighty and humans cannot earn their salvation, then no Christian can be certain of salvation. Developing the doctrine of "predestination," Calvin agreed that God had ordained every man, woman, and child to salvation or damnation—even before the creation of the world. Although God's intention was hidden from human intellect, the knowledge that a small group of "elect" would be saved illuminated the purposes of history and morality.

The elect, in Calvinist theology, were known only to God; in practice, however, Calvinist congregations often functioned as moral communities whose members voluntarily subjected themselves to religious and social discipline. A fourfold office made up of pastors, elders, deacons, and teachers defined the Calvinist church. Fusing church and society, Geneva became a single moral community, a development strongly demonstrated by the insignificant rate of extramarital births in the sixteenth century. Praised by supporters as a community less troubled by crime and sin and attacked by critics as a coercive despotism, Geneva under Calvin exerted a powerful influence on the course of the Reformation. Like Zwingli, Calvin did not tolerate dissenters. While passing through Geneva the Spanish physician Michael Servetus was arrested because he had published books attacking Calvin and questioning the doctrine of the Trinity. Upon Calvin's advice, Servetus was executed by the authorities. (Calvin did not, however, approve of the method of execution: burning at the stake.) Although Calvin came under criticism for Servetus's death, Geneva became the new center of the Reformation, the place from which pastors trained for mission work and books propagating Calvinist doctrines were exported. The Calvinist movement spread to France, the Netherlands, England, Scotland, Germany, Poland, Hungary, and eventually New England, becoming the established form of the Reformation in many of these countries.

The Divided Realm

The monarchs of Europe viewed religious divisions as a dangerous challenge to the unity of their realms and the stability of their rule. If they were to tolerate religious dissent, Protestantism might become a banner of the opposition. In addition, religious differences intensified the formation of noble factions, which exploited the situation when weak monarchs or children ruled. These themes are essential to any understanding of the Reformation in France, Scotland, and England.

As we have seen, the French king Francis I tolerated Protestants up until the Affair of the Placards in 1534. However, persecutions of Huguenots—as Calvinists were called in France—were sporadic, and the Reformed church grew steadily in strength. During the 1540s and 1550s many French noble families converted to Calvinism. Under noble protection, the Reformed church was able to organize quite openly and hold synods (church meetings), especially in southern and western France. Some of the most powerful noble families, such as the Montmorency and the Bourbon, openly professed Protestantism. The French monarchy tried to maintain a balance of power between Catholic and Huguenot and between hostile noble factions. Francis and his successor, Henry II, both succeeded to a degree. But after Henry's death in a jousting accident the weakened monarchy could no longer hold together the fragile realm. After 1560 France plunged into decades of religious wars.

The English monarchy played the central role in shaping that country's religious reform. Until 1527, Henry VIII (*1509–1547) firmly opposed the Reformation, even receiving the title "Defender of the Faith" from Pope Leo X for his treatise against Luther. Under his chancellors, Cardinal Thomas Wolsey (1475–1530) and Thomas More, Henry vigorously suppressed Protestantism and executed its leaders.

The challenge to Rome in England came from two sources: the native roots of Lollardy, whose adherents could still be found among urban artisans in the early sixteenth century; and the German reformers, whose works were smuggled into the country by English merchants abroad, especially by the Company of Merchant Adventurers, which had close ties to the Hanseatic League. During the 1520s English Protestants were few in number—a few clerical dissenters (particularly at Cambridge University) and, more significantly, a small but influential noble faction at court and a mercantile elite in London.

King Henry VIII changed all that. By 1527 the king wanted to divorce his wife, Katharine of Aragon (d. 1536), the daughter of Ferdinand and Isabella of Spain. The eighteen-year marriage had produced a daughter, Princess Mary. Henry desperately needed a male heir. Moreover, he was in love with Anne Boleyn, a lady-in-waiting at court and a strong supporter of the Reformation. Henry claimed that his marriage to Katharine had never been valid because she was the widow of his older brother, Arthur. This first marriage, which apparently was never consummated, had been annulled by Pope Julius II in 1509 so that a second marriage, between Henry and Katharine, could cement the dynastic alliance between England and Spain. Now, in 1527, Henry asked the reigning pope, Clement VII, to annul his predecessor's annulment.

Around "the king's great matter" unfolded a struggle for political and religious domination. The Catholic cause lost out when Henry failed to secure a papal dispensation from Clement VII, who, in addition to the dictates of his conscience, was also a virtual pawn of Emperor Charles V, Katharine's nephew, who had occupied Rome in 1527. Disappointed, Henry turned to the Protestant faction. He dismissed Wolsey and More and chose two Protestants as his new loyal servants: Thomas Cromwell (1485–1540) as chancellor and Thomas Cranmer (1489–1556) as archbishop of Canterbury. Under their leadership the English Parliament passed a number of acts between 1529 and 1536 that severed ties between the English church and Rome, established Henry as the head of the so-called Anglican church, invalidated the claims of Katharine and Princess Mary to the throne, recognized Henry's marriage to Anne Boleyn, and allowed the English crown to confiscate the properties of the monasteries.

By 1536, Henry had grown tired of Anne Boleyn, who had given birth to the future Queen Elizabeth I but had produced no sons. The king had her beheaded on the charge of adultery, an act that he defined as treason. Thereafter Henry married four other wives. The third, Jane Seymour, bore him a son, Edward, and the fifth, Katharine Howard, he had beheaded. Thomas More went to the block in 1535 for treason—that is, for refusing to recognize Henry as "the only supreme head on earth of the Church of England"—and Thomas Cromwell suffered the same fate in 1540 when he lost favor. When Henry died in 1547, the Anglican church, nominally Protestant, still retained much traditional Catholic doctrine and ritual. But the principle of royal supremacy in religious matters would remain a lasting feature of Henry's reforms.

Under Edward VI (*1547–1553) and Mary Tudor (*1553–1558), official religious policies oscillated between Protestant reforms and Catholic restoration. In spite of regional revolts, royal power remained firm. The boy king Edward furthered the Reformation by welcoming prominent religious refugees from the continent. With Mary Tudor's accession, however, everything was reversed, and English Protestants suffered a baptism of blood. Close to three hundred Protestants perished at the stake, and more than eight hundred fled to Germany and Switzerland. Finally, after Anne Boleyn's daughter Elizabeth succeeded her half-sister to the throne in 1558, the Protestant cause again gained momentum; it eventually defined the character of the English nation.

Still another pattern of religious politics unfolded in Scotland, where powerful noble clans directly challenged royal power. Up until the 1550s Protestants had been a small minority in Scotland, who were easy to suppress if they did not enjoy the protection of sympathetic local lords. The most prominent Scottish reformer, John Knox (1514–1572), spent many of his early years in exile in England and on the Continent. But when Scotland's powerful noble clans, caught in the conflict between crown and nobility, turned to Calvinism, the Protestant cause finally triumphed.

The queen regent, Mary of Guise (d. 1560), stood at the center of Scotland's conflict. After the death of her husband, James V (d. 1542), Mary of Guise cultivated the support of her native France. Her daughter and heir to the throne, Mary Stuart, had been educated in France and was married to the dauphin Francis, son of Henry II. The queen regent also surrounded herself with French advisors and soldiers. Alienated by this pro-French policy, by 1558 to 1559 many Scottish noblemen had joined the pro-English and anti-French Protestant party. Misogyny also played a part in Protestant propaganda, skillfully exploiting the era's suspicion of female rulers and regents. In 1558, John Knox published *The First Blast of the Trumpet Against the Monstrous Regiment [Rule] of Women*, a diatribe against both Mary Tudor and Mary of Guise. Knox declared that "to promote a woman to bear rule, superiority, dominion, or empire above any realm, nation, or city is repugnant to nature, contumely to God, a thing most contrarious to his revealed will and approved ordinance and, finally, it is the subversion of good order, of all equity and justice." In 1560, the Protestant party won, and the Scottish Parliament adopted a reformed confession of faith (a document setting out doctrines).

The Catholic Renewal

Many voices for reform had echoed within the Catholic church long before Luther, but the papacy had failed to sponsor any significant change. In response to events in the empire, however, a Catholic reform movement gathered momentum in Italy during the 1530s and 1540s. Drawn from the elite, especially the Venetian upper class, the Catholic evangelicals stressed biblical ethics and moral discipline. Gian Matteo Giberti, bishop of Verona from 1524 to 1543, resigned his position in the Roman *curia* to concentrate on his pastoral duties. Another cardinal, Gasparo Contarini (1483–1542), who was descended from a Venetian noble family and had served the republic as ambassador to Charles V, was elevated to cardinal, where he labored to heal the schism within the church.

A new mood of austerity descended on Rome. In 1527, to punish Pope Clement VII for his part in the anti-imperial coalition, Charles V sent his army into Rome. His unpaid and undisciplined German troops, many of them Lutheran, pillaged and terrorized the city. The Florentine historian Francesco Guicciardini described the humiliation suffered by the great princes of the church: "[M]any prelates were captured by soldiers, especially by the German mercenaries, who because of their hatred for the Roman Church, were cruel and insolent, contemptuously leading priests throughout Rome mounted on asses and mules. . . . Many were most cruelly tormented and died during the torture. . . ." This "second invasion of barbarians" shocked the Italians, who saw it as punishment for their sins.

Under Pope Paul III (*1534–1549) and his successors, the papacy finally took the lead in church reform. The Italian nobility played a leading role, and Spaniards and Italians of all classes provided the backbone for this movement, sometimes called the Counter-Reformation. The Counter-Reformation's crowning achievements were the calling of a general church council and the founding of new religious orders.

In 1545, Pope Paul III and Charles V convened a general church counsel at Trent, a town on the border between the Holy Roman Empire and Italy. The Council of Trent, which met sporadically over the next seventeen years and finally completed its work in 1562, shaped the essential character of Catholicism, as it would remain until the 1960s. It reasserted the supremacy of clerical authority over laypeople, stipulating that bishops reside in their dioceses (instead of absenting themselves and living off church revenues) and that seminaries be established

Catholic Reform

in each diocese to train priests. The council also confirmed and clarified church doctrine and sacraments. For the sacrament of the Eucharist, the counsel asserted that the bread actually *became* Christ's body—a rejection of all Protestant positions on this issue so emphatic as to preclude compromise. For the sacrament of marriage, the counsel stipulated that all unions must henceforth take place in churches and be registered by the parish clergy.

The energy of the Counter-Reformation expressed itself most vigorously in the founding of new religious orders. The most important of these, the Society of Jesus, was established by a Spanish nobleman, Ignatius of Loyola (1491–1556). Imbued with tales of chivalric romances and the national glory of the *reconquista,* Ignatius eagerly sought to prove his mettle as a soldier. In 1521, while defending the Spanish border fortress of Pamplona against a French attack, he sustained a severe leg injury. During his convalescence Ignatius read lives of the saints; once he recovered, he abandoned his

quest for military glory in order to serve the church.

After diligent university studies (Latin did not come easily to a man of thirty-one) in Spain and Paris, Ignatius went on a pilgrimage to the Holy Land. Attracted by his austerity and piety, young men gravitated to this charismatic figure. Thanks to Ignatius's noble birth and Cardinal Contarini's intercession, Ignatius gained a hearing before the pope, and in 1540 the church recognized his little band, known as the Jesuits. Organized on military principles, with Ignatius as its first general, the

Ignatius Loyola

The founder of the Society of Jesus, as imagined by the early seventeenth century artist Peter Paul Rubens, is depicted exorcising a demon from a possessed woman. Such imagery was not typical of contemporary representations of the first Jesuits, though they (like virtually all Christians of the age) believed in the reality of witchcraft and the devil.

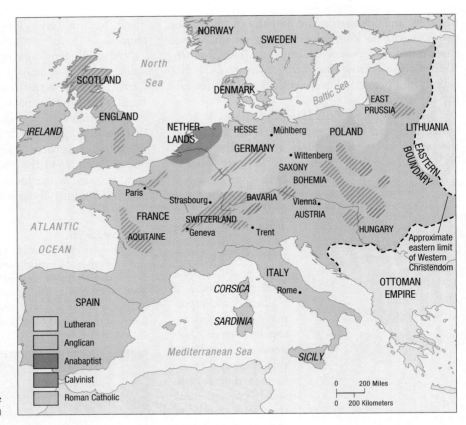

The Religious Balance in Europe, c. 1560

Jesuits became the most vigorous defenders of papal authority. Europe had one thousand Jesuits by the time of Ignatius's death in 1556. The society continued to expand, reclaiming souls who had been lost to the Reformation. Jesuit missionaries played a key role in the global Portuguese maritime empire and brought Roman Catholicism to Africans, Asians, and Native Americans.

The Religious Peace of Augsburg, 1555

While Catholic forces were gathering strength in Italy and Spain, confessional confrontation in the Holy Roman Empire led to military alliances. The Protestant Schmalkaldic League, headed by the Elector of Saxony and Philip of Hesse (the two leading Protestant princes), included most of the imperial cities, the chief source of the empire's wealth. On the other side, allied with Emperor Charles V, were the bishops and the few remaining Catholic princes. During the 1530s, Charles had to concentrate on fighting the French and the Turks. But now, having temporarily secured the western Mediterranean, he turned to central Europe to try to resolve the growing religious differences there.

In 1541, Charles convened an Imperial Diet at Regensburg, only to see negotiations between Protestant and Catholic theologians break down rapidly. The schism within the church seemed permanent. Vowing to crush the Schmalkaldic League, the emperor secured French neutrality in 1544 and papal support in 1545. Luther died in 1546. In the following year, war broke out. Using seasoned Spanish veterans and German allies, Charles occupied the German imperial cities in the south, restoring Catholic patricians and suppressing the Reformation. In 1547, he defeated the Schmalkaldic League armies at Mühlberg and captured the leading Protestant princes. Jubilant, Charles proclaimed a decree, the "Interim," which restored Catholics' right to worship in Protestant lands while permitting Lutherans to observe Holy Communion with both bread and wine. The final religious settlement would depend on the decision of the Council of Trent. Protestant resistance to the Interim was deep and widespread: many pastors went into exile, and riots broke out in many cities.

For Charles V, the reaction of his former allies proved far more alarming than Protestant resistance. His success had upset the balance of power. With Spanish troops controlling Milan and Naples and Spanish bishops vocal in the Council of Trent, Pope Julius III (∗1550–1552) feared that papal authority would be subjugated by imperial might. In the Holy Roman Empire Protestant princes spoke out against "imperial tyranny," referring to Charles's imprisonment of the Elector of Saxony and Philip of Hesse. Jealously defending their traditional liberties against an overmighty emperor, the Protestant princes, led by Duke Maurice of Saxony, a Protestant and former imperial ally, raised arms against Charles. The princes declared war in 1552, chasing a surprised, armyless, and practically bankrupt emperor back to Italy.

Forced to construct an accord, Charles V agreed to the Peace of Augsburg in 1555. The settlement recognized the Evangelical (Lutheran) church in the empire, accepted the secularization of church lands but "reserved" the still-existing ecclesiastical territories (mainly the bishoprics) for Catholics, and, most important, established the principle that all princes, whether Catholic or Lutheran, enjoyed the sole right to determine the religion of their lands and subjects. Significantly, Calvinist, Anabaptist, and other dissenting groups were excluded from the settlement. The religious revolt had culminated in a princes' Reformation. As the constitutional framework for the Holy Roman Empire, the Augsburg settlement preserved a fragile peace in central Europe until 1618, but the exclusion of Calvinists would plant the seed for future conflict.

Exhausted by decades of war and disappointed by the disunity in Christian Europe, Emperor Charles V resigned his many thrones in 1555 and 1556, leaving his Netherlandish-Burgundian and Spanish dominions to his son, Philip, and his Austrian lands to his brother, Ferdinand. Retiring to a monastery in southern Spain, the most powerful of the Christian monarchs spent his last years quietly seeking salvation. His son and successor as king of Spain, Philip II (∗1556–1598), found nothing but trouble. By the 1550s the Spanish monarchy could contract a loan only by paying 49 percent interest.

Charles V at Mühlberg
The great Venetian artist Titian painted a series of portraits of Charles V at stages of his career and showing various degrees of the emperor's success or failure (see also page 529). Titian here captures the emperor's sense of triumph at having finally crushed the German Protestant princes in battle in 1547. Charles's triumph was to be short-lived.

In 1557, Philip's financial crises came to a head, and he was forced to default on his loans.

Unending wars had left France even more exhausted than Spain. Henry II declared bankruptcy in 1557. In 1559 he agreed to the Treaty of Cateau-Cambrésis, in which France agreed to give up its conquests in Italy in exchange for peace and a marriage alliance with the Habsburg dynasty, leaving Spain as the western world's unchallenged leader for the rest of the century.

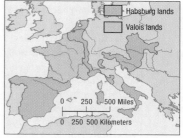

Habsburg and Valois Lands in 1559

For the Glory of God and the Prince

In northern Europe noble patrons and the royal court provided the institutional context behind the brilliant scientific, artistic, and literary achievements of the early sixteenth century, all of which adopted styles from the Italian Renaissance. While painters and poets glorified emperors and popes, the common people sought enjoyment from popular festivals such as the carnival. Highly sophisticated artists often looked to popular themes for inspiration, thus keeping the elite and popular cultures closely connected.

The Court

European princes used the institution of the royal court to bind their nobility and impress their subjects. Briefly defined, the court was the prince's household. Around the ruling family, however, a small community coalesced, made up of household servants, noble attendants, councilors, officials, artists, and soldiers. During the sixteenth century this political elite developed a sophisticated culture.

The French court of Francis I became the largest in Europe after the demise of the Burgundian dukes. In addition to the prince's household, the royal family also set up households for other members: the queen and the queen mother each had her own staff of maids and chefs, as did each of the royal children. The royal household employed officials to handle finances, guard duty, clothing, and food; in addition, physicians, librarians, musicians, dwarfs, animal trainers, and a multitude of hangers-on bloated its size. By 1535 the French court numbered 1,622 members, excluding the nonofficial courtiers.

Although Francis built many palaces (the most magnificent at Fontainbleu), the French court was often on the move. It took no fewer than eighteen thousand horses to transport the people, furniture, and documents—not to mention the dogs and falcons for the royal hunt. Hunting, in fact, was a passion for the men at court; it represented a form of mock combat, essential in the training of a military elite. Francis himself loved war games: in 1518 he staged a mock battle at court involving twelve hundred "warriors" and he himself led a party to lay siege to a model town during which several players were accidentally killed. Three years later, Francis almost lost his own life when, while

Carnival
Traditionally the day of merrymaking before the onset of the rigors of Lent (a tradition that survives in twentieth-century Mardi Gras festivities), carnival was one occasion on which the rules of social hierarchy and Christian morality were temporarily relaxed. Both Catholic and Protestant reformers considered carnival an occasion for sin and tried to rein it in.

storming a house during another mock battle, he was hit on the head by a burning log.

Italy gave Europe the ideological justification for the court culture. Two writers in particular were the most eloquent spokesmen for the culture of "courtesy": Ludovico Ariosto (1474–1533), in service at the Este court in Ferrara, and Baldassare Castiglione (1478–1529), a servant of the duke of Urbino and the pope. Considered one of the greatest Renaissance poets, Ariosto composed a long epic poem, *Orlando Furioso* ("The Mad Roland"), that represented court culture as the highest synthesis of Christian and classical values. Set against the historic struggle between Charlemagne and the Arabs, the poem tells the love story of Bradamente and Ruggiero. But before the separated lovers are reunited, the reader meets scores of characters and hundreds of adventures. The poem tells of imprisonments, betrayals, sieges, combats, jousts, and rescues, and takes the reader to caverns and far-off islands, Europe, Africa, and Asia. Modeled after Greek and Roman poetry, especially after the works of Virgil and Ovid, *Orlando Furioso* also

Francis I of France
Athlete, *bon vivant,* lover, *and Renaissance king, Francis I is depicted here as a self-satisfied young man in full splendor. The artist, Jean Clouet, was one of the finest French painters of the early sixteenth century, deeply influenced by the Italian style that Francis also loved.*

Fontainbleu
A French royal residence near Paris, this palatial complex represented the shifting of court life from urban centers to self-contained rural spaces, away from the turmoil and dangers of city life.

followed the tradition of the medieval chivalric romance. The tales of combat, valor, love, and magic captivated the court's noble readers, who, through this highly idealized fantasy, enjoyed a glimpse of their own world. In addition, the poem's characters represent the struggle between good and evil, and between Christianity and Islam, that was so much a part of the crusading spirit of the early sixteenth century.

Equally popular was *The Courtier* by the suave diplomat Castiglione. Like Ariosto, Castiglione tried to represent court culture as a synthesis of military virtues and literary and artistic cultivation. Speaking in eloquent dialogues, Castiglione's characters debate the qualities of an ideal courtier. The true courtier, Castiglione asserted, was a gentleman who spoke in a refined language and carried himself with nobility and dignity in the service of his prince and his lady. Clothing assumed a significant symbolism in *The Courtier*; in the words of one character, "I am not saying that clothes provide the basis for making hard and fast judgments about a man's character. . . . But I do maintain that a man's attire is also no small evidence for what kind of personality he has. . . ." The significance of outward appearance in court culture reflected the rigid distinctions between the classes and the sexes in sixteenth-century Europe. In Castiglione's words, the men at court had to display "valor," and the women "feminine sweetness."

The Sacred and Secular Patronage of Music

In musical composition, polyphony continued as the dominant style throughout the sixteenth century. But the Reformation strongly influenced musical life in other ways. In Catholic Europe the church and to a lesser extent the princely courts still employed and commissioned the leading musicians. The two leading composers of the sixteenth century, Orlando de Lassus (1532–1594) and Giovanni Pierluigi da Palestrina (1525–1594), were both in papal service as choirmasters. Lassus, a Fleming by birth, went to Munich in 1556 to enter the service of the Bavarian court, the most important German Catholic principality in the Holy Roman Empire. A prolific composer, Lassus left some three hundred ninety secular songs in Italian, French, and German, as well as approximately five hundred motets and other substantial sacred vocal works. Palestrina is remembered for his sacred music, especially for his polyphonies that accompanied the Liturgy of the Mass, in which he reaffirmed Catholic tradition by using themes from Gregorian chants.

In Protestant Europe the chorale emerged as a new musical form. In an attempt to engage the congregation in active worship, Martin Luther, an accomplished lutenist himself, composed many hymns in German. Unlike Catholic services, for which professional musicians sang in Latin, Protestant services enjoined the congregation to sing in unison. Drawing from Catholic sacred music as well as secular folk tunes, Luther and his collaborators wrote words to accompany familiar melodies. The best known of Luther's hymns, "Ein' feste Burg," became the beloved English Protestant hymn "A Mighty Fortress" and inspired many subsequent variations.

Protestants sang hymns to signify their new faith. During the Peasants War of 1525, Thomas Müntzer and the peasant rebels implored God's intercession by singing the hymn "Oh Come, Thou Holy Spirit" before they were mowed down by the knights and mercenaries in a one-sided slaughter. Eyewitnesses also reported Protestant martyrs singing hymns before their executions. In Lutheran Germany hymnals and prayer books adorned many urban households; the intimate relationship among religious devotion, bourgeois culture, and musical literacy would become a characteristic of Germany in later centuries.

The Beginning of the New Science

The first half of the sixteenth century laid the foundations for the scientific revolution that would take place one century later. The most important changes in sixteenth-century scientific thought were brought about by humanism and a new emphasis on observation. By reexamining the Greco-Roman past, the new humanist education encouraged scholars to view the traditional Greek scientific texts with a critical eye. The advent of printing, another prerequisite to the new science, meant that new scientific ideas and more accurate, stunningly illustrated texts could be circulated. The encounter with the New World—and with its fauna and flora, previously unknown to Europeans—also stimulated scientific advances. This expansion of the European global perspective seemed to inspire new questions about the cosmos, too. Amid all these changes, the university remained the most important institution for scientific work, seconded by the patronage of the church and secular rulers.

Among the many early sixteenth-century scientists whose work formed a bridge between medieval and modern science, three stood above the rest: Andreas Vesalius (1514–1564), who prepared the way for modern anatomy; Theophrastus Bombastus von Hohenheim, better known as Paracelsus (1493–1541), who laid the path for modern pharmacology and chemistry; and Nicolaus Copernicus (1473–1543), who fundamentally revised the human picture of the cosmos.

Educated in Paris and in Padua, Italy, Vesalius achieved distinction in 1543 for his *De Fabrica* ("On the Construction of the Human Body"). Until the early sixteenth century, medical knowledge in Christian Europe had been based on the writings of the second-century Greek physician Galen. Deriving his anatomical knowledge of the human body from partial dissections, Galen had made numerous inaccurate assertions about the body's composition and functioning. For more than a century before Vesalius, medical faculties in European universities revived the public dissection of cadavers. Drawing upon this accumulated knowledge, and sensing the need for accurate, graphic drawings of human anatomy such as those drafted by Leonardo da Vinci, Vesalius prepared his illustrated anatomical text as a revision of Galen's work. Reluctant at first to refute him, Vesalius eventually rejected Galen's authority in the 1555 second edition of *De Fabrica*, which was becoming the most influential anatomy textbook.

If Vesalius's original intent was merely to revise Galen, Paracelsus, a man given to forceful statements, had Galen's text burned at the University of Basel, where he was a professor of medicine. Paracelsus experimented with new drugs, performed operations (unlike most academic physicians of his day, who never went beyond medical theory), and developed a synthesis of religious, medical, and philosophical ideas. Through his deep interest in magic, alchemy, and astrology, Paracelsus became the forerunner of chemical and pharmaceutical progress. Also unorthodox in his other

views, he strongly condemned the persecution of religious dissenters.

Although Paracelsus might have been sympathetic to Protestantism, science did not recognize religious boundaries. A clergyman in the Polish church, Nicolaus Copernicus never would have dreamed that his ideas would give rise to a confrontation between religion and science. A protégé of a Polish archbishop, Copernicus studied medicine and canon law first in Cracow and then in the Italian cities of Bologna, Padua, and Ferrara. He returned to Poland in 1506 and entered ecclesiastical service. Developing his ideas over two decades, in 1543 Copernicus on his death bed published *On the Revolution of the Celestial Spheres* through the efforts of a Protestant German admirer and with the cooperation of Catholic prelates, but with a preface (not by Copernicus) that presented the work only as a curious paradox and not as a hypothesis to be taken seriously.

Nevertheless, Copernicus's work threw down a revolutionary challenge to authority. Hitherto, Europeans had derived their view of the universe from the second-century Greek astronomer Ptolemy. Fully compatible with the Judeo-Christian and Greco-Roman traditions and approved by the Catholic church, Ptolemaic astronomy put the earth at the center of the cosmos. Above earth were fixed the moon, the stars, and the planets in concentric crystalline spheres; beyond these fixed spheres dwelt God and the angels. The planets revolved around earth at the command of God, the *primum mobile* ("prime mover"). According to this scheme, the planets would revolve in perfectly circular obits, a theory belied by the actual elliptical paths that could be observed and calculated. To explain these inconsistencies, Ptolemy postulated orbits within orbits, which he called epicycles. His mathematical proofs were extremely cumbersome, to say the least. Copernicus discovered that by placing the sun instead of the earth at the center of this system of spheres, he could eliminate many epicycles from the calculations. Inspired only by the elegance of his simpler mathematics but unable to resolve many difficulties in his theory, Copernicus nevertheless forthrightly questioned traditional astronomy and set the agenda for future generations of scientists. The clash between astronomy and religion would come later, when confessional struggles permeated all aspects of European life.

The Artists and the Christian Knight

In the early years of the sixteenth century, before the Reformation, the Holy Roman emperor and the pope still represented the hope of Christian regeneration. Europe stood under the threat of the Turks, the church badly needed reform, and Christendom longed for justice and peace. Through their patronage of artists, the Habsburg emperors, the French kings, and the Catholic popes created glorified self-images, representations of their era's hopes.

The use of art for political glorification was nothing new, but below the glorified surface of sixteenth-century art flowed an undercurrent of idealism. For all his political limitations, Emperor Maximilian I was a visionary who dreamed of restoring Christian chivalry and even toyed with the idea of ruling as pope and emperor. He appointed the Nuremberg artist Albrecht Dürer (1471–1528) as court painter, to represent the Habsburg vision of universal Christian emperorship. Dürer's design for Maximilian's triumphal carriage in 1518 positioned the figures of Justice, Temperance, Prudence, and Fortitude at a level above the seated emperor, with other allegorical figures—Reason, Nobility, and Power—also in attendance.

For many artists, Emperor Charles V embodied the ideal Christian knight. The Venetian painter Titian (1477–1576) captured the emperor's life on canvas four times between 1532 and 1550. His 1532 portrait depicts a grand prince in his early thirties. Two portraits from 1548 and 1550, which Titian completed after Charles's victory over the Schmalkaldic League, present a man of deep ambiguity. Titian's equestrian portrait of Charles after his victory at Mühlberg (page 523) shows a Christian knight, somber and pious. In the later painting (page 529), the seated emperor, at the height of his success, seems burdened by his office. Charles's favorite was the *Gloria*, one of the two Titians he took with him to his monastic retirement: it shows the kneeling emperor wrapped in a white death shroud joining the throng of the saved to worship the Trinity.

The Habsburg dynasty did not monopolize artistic self-glorification, however. The Florentine Michelangelo Buonarroti (1475–1564) matured his multiple talents in the service of the Medici family, although his artistry served many masters. After

the overthrow of the Medici he was commissioned to sculpt an eighteen-foot statue of David, an Old Testament symbol of the restored Florentine republic. He became Pope Julius II's favorite artist, painting with furious energy the Sistine Chapel (including the ceiling) and working on a never-finished tomb and sculpture for that same warrior-pope. Later, Michelangelo was commissioned by Paul III, the first pope of the Counter-Reformation, to design palaces in Rome; in 1547, he became the chief architect of St. Peter's Basilica. Since Michelangelo's art commemorated both the famous and infamous of sixteenth-century Italy, his works

The Triumph of Maximilian I
A failure in virtually all his political schemes, the emperor Maximilian brilliantly succeeded in propagandizing his image as a triumphant Caesar. He commissioned the foremost German artist of the day, Albrecht Dürer, to execute a series of woodcuts depicting the German nobility and imperial court celebrating his grandeur in a seemingly endless procession.

The Burden of Rulership: Charles V
Not long after his victory at Mühlberg, Titian depicted Charles in a very different mood: worn down by a lifetime of striving without lasting success to unite Christendom under Habsburg rule, to purify the church, and to crush heresy and rebellion.

sometimes shared the fates of his patrons. In 1511, the people of Bologna rose in rebellion against Pope Julius II and tore down Michelangelo's fourteen-foot statue of the pope, melting it to cast a cannon. Most of Michelangelo's art has survived, however—a testimony both to his genius and to the grandiose self-image of the papacy and its remarkable self-confidence in the age of the Reformation.

New Worlds

The sixteenth century inaugurated a new era of world history. Portuguese and Spanish vessels, followed later by English, French, and Dutch ships, sailed across the Atlantic, Indian, and Pacific oceans, bringing with them people, merchandise, crops, and disease in a global exchange that would shape the modern world. In these encounters—at times peaceful but often brutal—Europeans imposed their culture on others through conquest, colonial settlement, and religious missions, all the while debating and marveling at the strange new worlds they had entered.

The Voyage to the East

Lured by the gold mines of West Africa, the Portuguese gradually extended their explorations down Africa's Atlantic coast, establishing garrisons at the Cape Verde Islands, Guinea, São Tomé, and Luanda (in present-day Angola). In 1499, Vasco da Gama reached India, and twenty-three years later Ferdinand Magellan, a Portuguese sailor in Spanish service, led the first expedition to circumnavigate the globe. By 1517 a chain of Portuguese forts dotted the Indian Ocean: at Mozambique, Hormuz (at the mouth of the Persian Gulf), Goa (in India), Colombo (in modern-day Sri Lanka), and Malacca (modern-day Malaysia). By 1557 the Portuguese had taken up residence in East Asia: in Macao on the south China coast and in Nagasaki, Japan.

Adapting to local conditions, the Portuguese employed a combination of force and diplomacy, their primary object being to control trade rather than territory. Exploiting and perpetuating tribal warfare in West Africa, the Portuguese traded in gold and "pieces," as African slaves were called, a practice condemned at home by some conscientious clergymen. A canon at Evora cathedral, Manoel Severim de Faria, observed that "one cannot yet see any good effect resulting from so much butchery; for this is not the way in which commerce can flourish and the preaching of the gospel progress. . . ." Critical voices, however, could not deny the enormous profits that the slave trade

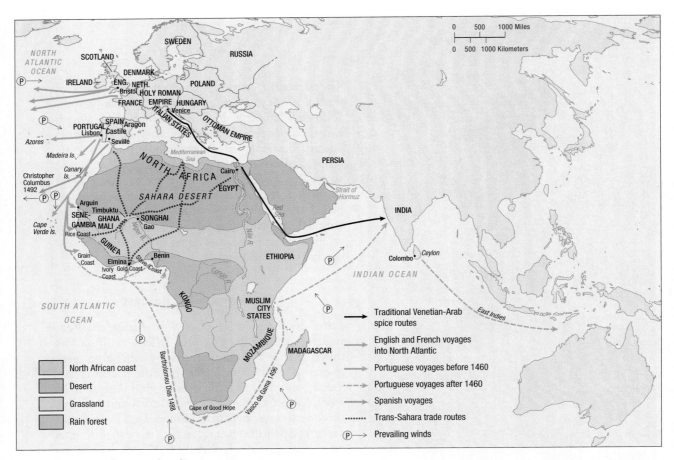

Europe, Africa, and India, c. 1500

brought to Portugal. Most slaves toiled in the sugar plantations of Brazil and the Atlantic islands; a fortunate few labored as domestic servants in Portugal, where freedmen and slaves constituted a distinct African minority in Lisbon.

America: Paradise or Hell?

On the eve of the European invasion, the native peoples of the Americas were divided into many sedentary and nomadic societies. Among the settled peoples, the largest political and social organizations centered in the Mexican and Peruvian highlands. The Aztecs and the Incas ruled over subjugated Indian populations in their respective empires. With an elaborate religious culture and a rigid social and political hierarchy, the Aztecs and Incas based their civilizations in large, urban capitals.

The Spanish explorers organized their expeditions to the mainland from a base in the Caribbean. Two prominent leaders, Hernando Cortés (1485–1547) and Francisco Pizarro (1470–1541), gathered men and arms and set off in search of gold. Catholic priests accompanied the fortune hunters to bring Christianity to allegedly uncivilized peoples and thus to justify brutal conquests. His small band swelled by peoples who had been subjugated by the Aztecs, Cortés captured the Aztec capital, Tenochtitlán, in 1519. Two years later Mexico, then named New Spain, was added to Charles V's empire. To the south, Pizarro conquered the Andean highlands, exploiting a civil war between rival Incan kings. After 1536, Lima became the administrative capital of the lands of the Spanish empire in the Andean region.

By the mid-sixteenth century the Spanish empire, built on greed and justified by its self-

The Spanish Conquest of Mexico and Peru

proclaimed Catholic mission, stretched unbroken from Mexico to Chile. In addition to the Aztecs and Incas, the Spaniards also subdued the Mayans on the Yucatán peninsula, a people with a sophisticated knowledge of cosmology and arithmetic. The gold and silver mines in Mexico proved a treasure trove for the Spanish crown, but the real prize was the discovery of vast silver deposits in Potosí (today in Bolivia). Precious metals from Spanish America would supply the major revenues for the Spanish monarchy during the second half of the sixteenth century—in insufficient quantity to save the crown from bankruptcies, but enough to fuel seemingly endless inflation.

Not to be outdone by the Spaniards, other European powers joined the scramble for gold in the New World. In 1500 a Portuguese fleet landed at Brazil, but Portugal did not begin colonizing until 1532, when it established a permanent fort on the coast. In North America the French went in search of a "northwest passage" to China. By 1504 French fishermen had appeared in Newfoundland. Thirty years later Jacques Cartier led three voyages that explored the St. Lawrence River as far as Montreal. An early attempt in 1541 to settle Canada failed due to the harsh winter and Indian hostility. More permanent settlements in Canada and the present-day United States would have to wait until the seventeenth century.

North America in the Sixteenth Century

Although the Indian populations were devastated by European diseases, the encounter in the Americas opened a new chapter in global ecological history. New World crops were introduced to the Old: maize, beans, and potatoes to enrich the European diet and tobacco to stimulate the senses. The exchange was by no means one-way. Nostalgic for home, Europeans imported familiar animals and crops: they introduced horses and sheep to the Americas and planted wheat in place of maize. Convinced of their technological and cultural superiority, European settlers attempted to remake the Americas in their own image, imposing their language and spreading their religion among the continents' first inhabitants.

"Preaching with the Sword and Rod of Iron"

Frustrated in his efforts to convert the Brazilian Indians, a Jesuit missionary wrote to his superior in Rome in 1563 that "for this kind of people it is better to be preaching with the sword and rod of iron." This attitude was common among Christian missionaries in the Americas and Africa, despite the isolated voices that condemned Europeans' abuse of native populations. The Dominican Bartolomé de Las Casas (1474–1566), an Erasmian idealist, was perhaps the most severe critic of colonial brutality in Spanish America, yet even he argued that Africans, constitutionally more suitable for labor, should be imported to the plantations in the Americas to relieve the Indians, who were being worked to death. Under the influence of Las Casas and his followers, the Spanish crown tried to curb the excesses of European settlers by placing the Indians under its protection, a policy whose success was determined by the struggle among missionaries, *conquistadores*, and royal officials for the bodies and souls of native populations.

To ensure rapid Christianization, European missionaries focused initially on winning over local elites. The recommendation of a Spanish royal official in Mexico City was typical: he wrote to the crown in 1525,

> In order that the sons of caciques [chiefs] and native lords may be instructed in the faith, Your Majesty must command that a college be founded wherein there may be taught . . . to the end that they may be ordained priests. For he who shall become such among them, will be of greater profit in attracting others to the faith than will fifty [European] Christians.

The Portuguese followed a similar policy in Africa and Asia. A number of young African nobles went to Portugal to be trained in theology, among them Dom Henry, a son of King Afonso I of Kongo, a Portuguese ally. In East Asia Christian missionaries under Portuguese protection again concentrated their efforts on the elites, preaching the gospel to Confucian scholar-officials in China and to the samurai (the warrior aristocracy) in Japan. Measured in numbers alone, the missionary enterprise seemed highly successful: by the second half of the sixteenth century vast multitudes of Native Americans had become nominal Christians, and thirty years after Francis Xavier's 1549 landing in Japan the Jesuits could claim over one hundred thousand Japanese converts.

After an initial period of relatively little racial discrimination, the Catholic church in the Americas and Africa adopted strict rules based on color. For example, the first Mexican Ecclesiastical Provincial Council in 1555 declared that holy orders were not to be conferred on Indians, *mestizos* (people of mixed European-Indian parentage), and mulattos (people of mixed European-African heritage); along with descendants of Moors, Jews, and persons who had been sentenced by the Spanish Inquisition, these groups were deemed "inherently unworthy of the sacerdotal office." Europeans reinforced their sense of racial superiority with their perception of the "treachery" that Native Americans and Africans exhibited whenever they resisted domination.

A different conversion tactic applied to Asia. There, European missionaries, who admired Chinese and Japanese civilization and were not backed by military power, used the sermon rather than the sword to win converts. But they too resisted ordaining indigenous priests because they implicitly connected European ethnicity with Christianity.

Discipline and Property

The emergence of a new urban, middle-class culture accompanied the sixteenth-century religious changes. More visible in Protestant Europe, marriage reforms, an emphasis on literacy, a new educational agenda, and the Protestant work ethic came together to represent a watershed in European civilization. Other changes transcended the Protestant-Catholic divide and represented the culmination of developments that stretched back to the Middle Ages: the advent of public relief for the poor, the condemnation of vagrancy, and a general disciplining of society. Many modern ideas and institutions had their origins in the sixteenth century.

The Bible

Prior to the Reformation the Latin Vulgate was the only Bible authorized by the church, although many vernacular translations circulated. The Vulgate contains errors of translation from the Greek and Hebrew, as humanists such as Erasmus pointed out. Nevertheless, textual authority was predicated upon church authority, and textual revisions touched a raw nerve in the church. The challenges to the Roman church from the Hussite and Lollard movements drew their legitimacy from the Scriptures; one of their chief aims was to translate the Bible into vernacular. Although most sixteenth-century Europeans were illiterate, the Bible assumed for them a new importance because biblical stories were transmitted by pictures and the spoken word as well as through print. As an independent source of Christian beliefs and customs, the Bible had the potential to subvert the established order.

In 1522, Martin Luther translated Erasmus's Greek New Testament into German, the first vernacular translation based on the original language of the Gospels. Illustrated with woodcuts, more than two hundred thousand copies of Luther's New Testament were printed over twelve years, an immense number for the time. In 1534, Luther completed a translation of the Old Testament. Peppered with witty phrases and colloquial expressions, Luther's Bible was a treasure chest of the German language, and it remains to this day the standard version. The popular reception of Luther's Bible was primed by a huge appetite for the story of salvation: between 1466 and 1522 more than twenty translations of the Bible had appeared in the various German dialects. Widespread among urban households, the German Bible—or, more commonly, the Gospels—occupied a central place in a family's history. Generations passed on valuable editions; pious citizens often bound the Scriptures with family papers or other reading material. To counter Protestant success, Catholic German

Bibles appeared—the first was Johann Eck's 1537 translation from the Vulgate—thus authorizing and encouraging Bible reading by the Catholic laity, a sharp departure from medieval church practice.

The relationship between Scripture reading and religious reform also highlighted the history of early French and English Bibles. In the same year that Luther's German New Testament appeared in print, the French humanist Jacques Lefèvre d'Étaples (1455–1530) translated the Vulgate New Testament into French. Sponsored by Guillaume Briçonnet, the bishop from Meaux, who wanted to distribute free copies of the New Testament to the poor, the enterprise represented an early attempt to reform the French church without breaking with Rome. The Meaux reformers had been protected expressly by royal authority. With King Francis I captive in Madrid after the battle of Pavia (1525), the Parlement of Paris (the kingdom's leading law court) and the queen regent dispersed the reformers on suspicion of heresy.

Although individual books of the Bible circulated among the Lollards, a complete edition of the English Bible was not readily available in the fifteenth century. Sensing the dangerous association that could be made between the vernacular Bible and heresy, England's church hierarchy reacted swiftly. In a country with few printing presses, the first English Protestants could not publish their writings at home. Inspired by Luther's Bible during a visit to Wittenberg, the Englishman William Tyndale (1495–1536) translated the Bible into English. After he had his translation printed in Germany and the Low Countries, Tyndale smuggled copies into England with the help of the Merchant Adventurers, a sympathetic English merchant group based in Antwerp and Brussels. After Henry VIII's break with Rome and adoption of the Reformation, the new Protestant archbishop of Canterbury, Thomas Cranmer, promoted an English Bible based on Tyndale's translation.

Although the vernacular Bible occupied a central role in Protestantism, Bible reading did not become widespread until the early seventeenth century. Educational reform and the founding of new schools proceeded slowly throughout the sixteenth century, thus limiting the number of literate people. Furthermore, the complete Bible was a relatively expensive book inaccessible to poorer households. But, perhaps most important of all, the Protestant clergy, like their Catholic counterparts, grew suspicious of unsupervised Bible reading. Just as the first reformers cited Scripture against Rome, ordinary men and women drew their own lessons from the vernacular Bible, questioning and challenging the authority of the new Protestant establishment.

Indoctrinating the Young

To implant Christ's kingdom, one must change hearts and minds, argued Luther in a plea to the princes and magistrates of the Holy Roman Empire. He urged them to establish schools, supported by confiscated church property, in order to educate boys and girls in the knowledge and fear of God. The ordinance for a girls' school in Göttingen spelled out that the school's purpose was "to initiate and hold girls in propriety and the fear of God. To fear God, they must learn their catechism, beautiful psalms, sayings, and other fine Christian and holy songs and little prayers. . . ."

The Reformation replaced late medieval church schools with a state school system. Controlled by state officials who examined, appointed, and paid teachers, the new educational system aimed to train obedient, pious, and hardworking Christian citizens. Discipline, not new ideas, informed sixteenth-century pedagogy. Teachers frequently used the rod to inculcate discipline while students memorized their catechisms, prayers, and other tidbits of Christian texts. In addition to reading and writing, girls' schools included domestic skills in their curriculum.

A two-tier system existed in Protestant education. Ideally, every parish had its German school for children between six and twelve; in practice, not surprisingly, educational reform was much more successful in cities than in the countryside. To train future pastors, scholars, and officials, the Protestant church developed a secondary system of humanist schools. As the fruition of pre-Reformation ideals, these higher schools for boys, called the *gymnasia,* were intended to prepare students for university study. Greek and Latin classics constituted the core of the curriculum, to which was added religious instruction.

In Catholic Europe educational reforms at the primary level proceeded unevenly. In northern and central Italian cities, most girls and boys received some education; this strong pedagogic tradition dated back to at least the thirteenth century. Concerning other Catholic territories, such as Spain, France, and south Germany, our knowledge is fragmentary. But if Catholics lagged behind Protestants in promoting primary education, they did succeed in establishing an excellent system of secondary education through the Jesuit colleges. Established to compete as university preparatory schools with the Protestant *gymnasia,* hundreds of Jesuit colleges dotted the landscape of Spain, Portugal, France, Italy, Catholic Germany, Hungary, Bohemia, and Poland by the late sixteenth century. Among their alumni would be princes (Duke Maximilian I of Bavaria, Emperor Ferdinand II of Austria), philosophers (the seventeenth-century French philosopher René Descartes), lawyers, churchmen, and officials—the elite of Catholic Europe.

God's Poor and Vagabonds

In the early sixteenth century secular governments began to take over the institutions of public charity from the church. This broad development, which took place in both Catholic and Protestant Europe, marked two trends that had become apparent during the late Middle Ages: the rise of a work ethic simultaneously with a growing hostility toward the poor, and the massive poverty brought about by population growth.

Based on an agrarian economy that had severe technological limitations, European society again felt the pressure of population growth on its food resources. By 1490 the cycle of demographic collapse and economic depression triggered by the Black Death of 1348 had passed. Between 1490 and 1560 a new cycle of rapid economic and population growth created prosperity and stress. Yet a series of bad harvests or pillaging troops could drive thousands from the countryside. Wandering and begging in cities was by no means novel. But the reaction to poverty was new.

Sixteenth-century moralists decried the crime and sloth of vagabonds. Rejecting the notion that the poor played a central role in the Christian moral economy, and that charity and prayers united rich and poor, these moralists cautioned against charlatans and criminals who brought disease in their wake. Instead, they said, one should distinguish between the genuine poor, or "God's Poor," and vagabonds; the latter, who were able-bodied, should be forced to work. This critique of poverty implicitly repudiated monasticism; it labeled monks and friars as social parasites who lived off the labor of others.

The Reformation provided an opportunity to reform poor relief. In Nuremberg (1522) and Strasbourg (1523) magistrates centralized poor relief with church funds. Instead of using decentralized, private initiative, magistrates appointed officials to head urban agencies that would certify the "genuine poor" and distribute welfare funds to them. This initiative progressed rapidly in urban areas, where poverty was most visible, transcending religious divides. During the 1520s cities in the Low Countries and Spain passed ordinances that prohibited begging and instituted public charity. In 1526 the Spanish humanist Juan Luis Vives wrote a Latin treatise, *On the Support of the Poor*, that was soon translated into French, Italian, German, and English. National measures followed urban initiatives: in 1531, Henry VIII asked justices of the peace (unpaid local magistrates) to license the poor in England and to differentiate between those who were capable of working and those who could not; in 1540, Charles V imposed a welfare tax in Spain to augment that country's inadequate system of private charity.

More prevalent in Protestant areas, public relief for the poor became a permanent feature of government once private charity ceased to be considered a "good work" necessary to earn salvation. In fact, the number of voluntary donations took a significant drop once poor relief was introduced. The new work ethic acquired a distinctly Protestant aura in that it equated laziness with a lack of moral worth (and frequently associated laziness with Catholics) and linked hard work and prosperity with piety and divine providence. In Catholic lands, in contrast, collective charity persisted, supported as it was by a theology of good works, by societies (in Italy and Spain, for example) more sharply divided between the noble rich and the poor, and by the elites' sense of social responsibility.

"What God Joined Together"

The Protestant reformers' fundamental goal was to establish order and discipline in worship and in society—one of the aims of the Catholic Counter-Reformation as well—by decrying sexual immor-

ality and praising the family unit. The idealized patriarchal family provided a bulwark against the forces of disorder. Protestant magistrates who established marital courts and promulgated new marriage laws also closed brothels and inflicted harsher punishments for sexual deviancy.

The new marriage laws aimed to reform the traditional sexual regime. Prior to the Reformation marriages had been private affairs between families; some couples never even registered their marriages with the church, despite the Fourth Lateran Council's clear stipulation in 1215 that marriage was a sacrament. Under canon law the Catholic church recognized any promise made between two consenting adults (age twelve for females, fourteen for males) as a marriage. In rural areas and among the urban poor, most couples simply lived together as common-law husband and wife. The problem with the old marriage laws had been their complexity and the difficulties of enforcement. Often young men readily promised marriage in a passionate moment only to renege later. The overwhelming number of cases in Catholic church courts involved young women seeking to enforce marriage promises after they had exchanged their personal honor (that is, their virginity) for the greater honor of marriage.

The Reformation proved more effective in suppressing these so-called "clandestine marriages" than the late medieval church. Protestant governments asserted greater official control over marriages, and governments in the Counter-Reformation followed suit. A marriage was legitimate only if it had been registered by an official and a pastor. In many Protestant countries, the new marriage ordinances also required parental consent, thus giving the householders immense power in regulating marriage and the transmission of family property.

Enjoined to become obedient spouses and affectionate companions in Christ, women approached this new sexual regime with ambivalence. The new marriage laws stipulated that women could seek divorce on account of desertion, impotence, and flagrant abuse, although in practice the marriage courts encouraged reconciliation. These changes from earlier marriage laws came with a price, however: a woman's role took on the more limited definition of obedient wife, helpful companion, and loving mother. Now the path to religious power was closed to women. Unlike Catherine of Siena, Teresa of Avila, or other female Catholic saints, Protestant women could not renounce family, marriage, and sexuality to attain recognition and power in the church.

In the fervor of the early Reformation years, the first generation of Protestant women attained greater equality than subsequent generations. Katherina Zell, who had married the reformer Matthew Zell, defended her equality by citing Scripture to a critic. The critic had invoked St. Paul to support his argument that women should remain silent in church; Katherina retorted, "I would remind you of the word of this same apostle that in Christ there is no male nor female." Further quoting the Book of Joel, she recited the prophecy that "[God] will pour forth [his] spirit upon all flesh and your sons and your daughters will prophesy."

Katherina was much more than the ideal pastor's wife, however. In 1525 she helped to feed and clothe the thousands of refugees who flooded Strasbourg after their defeat in the Peasants War. In 1534 she published a collection of hymns. She encouraged her husband to oppose Protestant persecution of dissenters. After Matthew's death in 1548, Katherina continued to feed the sick, the poor, and the imprisoned. Outraged by the intolerance of a new breed of Protestant clergy, she reprimanded the prominent Lutheran pastor Ludwig Rabus for his persecution of dissenters: "You behave as if you had been brought up by savages in a jungle." Comparing the Anabaptists to beasts pursued by hunters and wild animals, she praised them for bearing witness to their faith "in misery, prison, fire, and water." Rebuking Rabus, she wrote: "You young fellows tread on the graves of the first fathers of this church in Strasbourg and punish all who disagree with you, but faith cannot be forced."

A more typical role model for the average Protestant woman was Katherina von Bora (1499–1550), who married Martin Luther in 1525. Sent to a nunnery at the age of ten, Katherina, along with other nuns in her convent, responded to the reformers' calls attacking monasticism. With the help of Luther, she and other nuns escaped by hiding in empty barrels that had contained smoked herring. After their marriage, the couple lived in the former Augustinian cloister in Wittenberg, which the Elector of Saxony had given to Luther. Katie, as Luther affectionately called her, ran the establishment, feeding their children, relatives, and student boarders. Although she deferred to Luther—she addressed him as "Herr Doktor"—Katherina defended a woman's right as an equal in marriage. When Luther teased her about Old Testament examples of polygyny, Katherina retorted, "Well, if it comes to that, I'll leave you and the children and go back to the cloister." Accepting her prescribed role in a patriarchal household—one of the three estates in the new Christian society of politics, household, and church—Katherina von Bora represented the ideal Protestant woman.

CONCLUSION

Mocking the warlike popes, the Dutch humanist Erasmus compared his times to those of the early Christian Church. In *The Praise of Folly* he satirized Christian prelates and princes, who "continued to shed Christian blood," the same blood as that of the martyrs who had built the foundations of Christianity. Turning from the papacy to the empire, Erasmus and many intellectuals of his generation saw in Emperor Charles V the model Christian prince. As the most powerful ruler in all Europe, Charles was hailed as the harbinger of peace, the protector of justice, and the foe of the infidel Turks. For the generation that came of age before the Reformation, Christian humanism—and its imperial embodiment—represented an ideal for political and moral reform that would save Christendom from corruption and strife.

The Reformation changed this dream of peace and unity. Instead of leading a crusade against Islam—a guiding vision of his life—Charles V wore himself out in the ceaseless struggle against King Francis I of France and the German Protestants. Instead of the Christian faith of charity and learning that Erasmus had envisioned, Christianity split into a number of hostile camps that battled one another with words and swords. Instead of the intellectual unity of the generation of Erasmus, More, and Dürer, the mid-sixteenth-century cultural landscape erupted in a burst of confessional statements and left in its wake a climate of censorship, repression, and inflexibility.

Christians continued to shed Christian blood. After the brutal suppression of popular revolts in the 1520s and 1530s, religious persecution became a Christian institution: Luther called on the princes to kill rebellious peasants in 1525, Zwingli advocated the drowning of Anabaptists, and Calvin supported the death sentence for Michael Servetus. Meanwhile, in Catholic lands persecutions and executions provided Protestants with a steady stream of martyrs. The two peace settlements in the 1550s failed to provide long-term solutions: the Peace of Augsburg (1555) gradually disintegrated as the religious struggles in the empire intensified, and the Treaty of Cateau-Cambrésis (1559) was but a brief respite in a century of crisis.

SUGGESTIONS FOR FURTHER READING

Source Materials

Essential Works of Erasmus. Edited by W. T. H. Jackson. 1965.

Guicciardini, Francesco. *The History of Italy*. Translated by Sidney Alexander. 1969. The events from 1490 to 1534, written by a participant.

Hillerbrand, Hans J., ed. *The Protestant Reformation*. 1969. Strong on religious documents.

The Prince and Selected Discourses: Machiavelli. Translated by Daniel Donno. 1966.

Interpretive Studies

Bainton, Roland. *Women of the Reformation in Germany and Italy*. 1971. Fifteen portraits; lively.

Blickle, Peter. *The Revolution of 1525*. 1981. Stresses the role of the common people in the early Reformation movement.

Bouwsma, William J. *John Calvin: A Sixteenth Century Portrait*. 1988. Intellectual biography at its best.

Brady, Thomas A. *Turning Swiss: Cities and Empire, 1450–1550*. 1985. A grand synthesis of social and political history of central Europe.

Crosby, Alfred W. *The Colombian Exchange: Biological and Cultural Consequences of 1492*. 1972.

Elliott, J. H. *The Old World and the New, 1492–1650*. 1970. A thought-provoking essay.

Elton, G. R. *Reformation Europe, 1517–1559*. 1963. Clear political history is its strong point.

Evennet, Henry Outram. *The Spirit of the Counter-Reformation*. 1968. Short and stimulating.

Febvre, Lucien. *Life in Renaissance France*. 1977. An old classic, strong on cultural history.

Hsia, R. Po-chia. *The Myth of Ritual Murder: Jews and Magic in the Reformation*. 1988. Analyzes the impact of the Reformation on antisemitism.

Knecht, R. J. *Francis I*. 1982. The standard biography.

Oberman, Heiko A. *Luther: Man Between God and Devil*. 1990. A forceful biography.

Ozment, Steven E. *The Reformation in the Cities*. 1975. Successfully re-creates the religious and psychological appeal of the Reformation movement.

Parker, Geoffrey. *The Military Revolution: Military Innovation and the Rise of the West, 1500–1800*. 1988. A good synthesis.

Partridge, Loren, and Randolph Starn. *A Renaissance Likeness: Art and Culture in Raphael's Julius II*. 1980. Collaborative interpretation by a historian and an art historian.

Pitkin, Hanna F. *Fortune Is a Woman: Gender and Politics in the Thought of Niccolò Machiavelli*. 1984. Original and brilliant interpretation based on psychoanalysis, gender theories, and political history.

Prodi, Paolo. *The Papal Prince. One Body and Two Souls: The Papal Monarchy in Early Modern Europe*. 1982. An extremely informative interpretation.

Scribner, R. W. *For the Sake of Simple Folk: Popular Propaganda for the German Reformation*. 1981. Pioneering study of woodcuts and visual propaganda in the Reformation.

Strauss, Gerald. *Luther's House of Learning: Indoctrination of the Young in the German Reformation*. 1978. Stresses the failure of the Reformation to change social habits.

Trevor-Roper, Hugh. *Princes and Artists: Patronage and Ideology at Four Habsburg Courts, 1517–1633*. 1976.

Joachim Beuckelaer, Market in the Country

PART

III

The Take-off of the West, 1560–1894

After various peoples had settled the European continent and the British Isles and started forming centralized states with distinctive national identities, their dreams and ambitions ranged far beyond Europe. The voyages of "discovery" and conquest launched at the end of the 1400s gave rise to new forms of colonial rule. Settlers moved permanently from their home countries in Europe to found new colonies in the Americas—and later, in the 1800s, in Africa and Asia. Although relatively small, European countries thus assumed domination over much of the world, either directly, through colonization, or indirectly, through control of world trade.

European dynastic competition reflected these changes. Increasingly, European countries fought wars on a global scale. After

1650 the center of economic, political, and cultural power within Europe shifted from the Mediterranean to the northwestern Atlantic corner as the Dutch, English, and French wrested control of the seas from the Portuguese, Spanish, and Italians. In the next century, new forms of industrial growth radiated slowly eastward and southward from northwest Europe as new coal and iron deposits—now crucial to economic development—were discovered.

A constellation of factors catalyzed Europe's transformation from a backwater of the Roman Empire into the center of world power and wealth. The sixteenth-century religious movement known as the Reformation simultaneously shattered Catholicism's unity in western Europe and sapped the might of the one remaining imperial structure, the Holy Roman Empire. The disputes and conflicts spawned by the Reformation opened the door to new intellectual and political developments, including the idea of toleration of religious differences and of the separation of church and state. The collapse of Catholic uniformity also sparked scientific breakthroughs. Inspired by Greek ideas transmitted through Arab sources, Europeans strove not only to understand nature but to harness its energies. The scientific revolution of the 1600s provided scholars with the intellectual tools needed to understand every form of motion, from the movement of the planets in the heavens to the trajectory of cannonballs on the earth. Every great civilization had pursued scientific discoveries, but unlike others European societies relentlessly applied scientific principles to everyday life. Leading figures in the philosophic movement known as the Enlightenment held science up as the standard for *all* forms of truth, subjecting economic techniques, social relations, even religious beliefs to scientific scrutiny.

As scientific learning spread broadly through popular lectures and demonstrations, the work of academies and clubs, and university teaching, applied science reshaped the European economies and, gradually, the world landscape. The perfection of the steam engine in particular made possible not only deeper mines and the advent of factories organized around power looms but also the birth of the railroad. Travel and trade boomed, and every detail of daily life was soon affected. With the comforts and conveniences of life steadily increasing, "improvement" became a motto for the age. But industrialization had its costs. As little children toiled in dank and dangerous mines, and as working-class families crowded in sooty, polluted, urban slums, reformers and writers rallied to publicize—and to ease—their plight. And although the new technologies afforded Europeans an indisputable military edge over the rest of the world, they also fueled dangerous conflicts among the European powers at home.

The political organization of Europe also seemed to confer comparative advantages over the rest of the world. Larger than tribal organizations or city-states but smaller than the mighty empires of the ancient world, European states coalesced around national groupings. The variety of nation-states that emerged appeared best able to profit from the innovations of science, industry, and colonial exploitation. To maximize their advantages, rulers developed ever-larger bureaucracies and armies. Faced with the obvious success of such coherent nation-states as France and Great Britain, previously disunited national groups—most notably the Germans and the Italians—created their own distinctive national states. As soon as they became nations, they joined the scramble for colonial position, which in turn provoked new jealousies and rivalries. In the twentieth century, it would become apparent just how deadly national rivalries could turn.

By the late 1500s and 1600s, Europeans considered themselves "modern," that is, distinct from the peoples who lived in traditional societies. Europeans believed that as moderns, they had surpassed the achievements of the ancients. One measure of their modernity was the role of women as arbiters of manners and taste. Most European men rejected the idea of women's participation in political life, but they expected women to rule over the home and to assume responsibility for the moral improvement of society. The revolutions in science and industry confirmed and even reinforced Europeans' feelings of superiority not only to peoples of the past—especially those of the Dark, or Middle, Ages—but also to peoples living elsewhere in their world. This sense of superiority prompted them eagerly to pursue the colonization of "backward" native peoples in Asia and Africa and to condone, and even actively to support, the revived, expanding institution of human slavery.

Paradoxically, Europeans also came to associate their modernity with "freedom" and "democracy," words that gained currency in the 1700s at the very time of the greatest expansion of the slave system in the colonies. In the 1600s and 1700s, beginning in that same northwestern corner of Europe and its offshoots in the British North American colonies, people of the "middling sort"— merchants, lawyers, and landowners—agitated for an active role in politics. Rather than accept the traditional leadership of aristocratic elites, who in most countries dominated the armed forces and the state bureaucracy, they insisted on votes and offices for themselves as responsible male propertyowners. In this way began bitter struggles (which continue to this day) over the definition of democratic citizenship. The English Revolution of the 1640s and the American and French revolutions of the 1770s and 1780s demonstrated the explosive power of this issue. The French Revolutionary and Napoleonic wars revealed the advantages of mass armies commanded by men of talent who ascended the ranks, over traditional armies made up of unwilling conscripts or mercenaries and led by aristocrats with no connection to their men.

During the 1800s every European country faced the same question: whether to modernize and democratize (meaning to include all men as voters and potential officeholders) or to modernize and avoid democratization. By the end of the 1800s, much of western Europe had moved halfway toward democratization while still excluding women from politics. In eastern Europe, however, the question remained more unresolved. The twentieth century would show both the promise and perils of democracy.

One of the earliest German novels, *The Adventures of a Simpleton* by Grimmelshausen, tells an awful story from the early seventeenth-century religious wars. Looking up from playing his bagpipe, the boy Simplicius finds himself surrounded by enemy cavalrymen who drag him back to his father's farm; ransack the house; rape the maid, his mother, and his sister; force water mixed with dung down the farmhand's throat; and hold Simplicius's father's feet to the fire until he tells them where he hid his gold and jewels. The invaders then torture nearby peasants with thumbscrews, throw one alive into an oven, and strangle another with a crude noose. Simplicius hides in the woods but can still hear the cries of the suffering peasants and see his family's house burn down.

Grimmelshausen's story came out of his personal experience of the Thirty Years' War, as the wars of 1618 to 1648 came to be known. These wars grew out of an international crisis in the relationship between religious and political authority. In the wake of the Reformation, the dream of universal Christendom lay shattered. Although Catholics and Protestants continued to believe that state power and religious authority should be linked, the violence of religious conflicts began to undermine traditional connections between religion and politics. The devastations wrought by religious warfare convinced rulers and their advisers to strengthen state power. The Thirty Years' War would show that the interests of states had begun to outweigh those of religion. Bureaucracies, armies, and the powers of rulers all expanded, making wars more dangerous to and state power more intrusive in the lives of ordinary

Religious Warfare and Crises of Authority, *1560–1640*

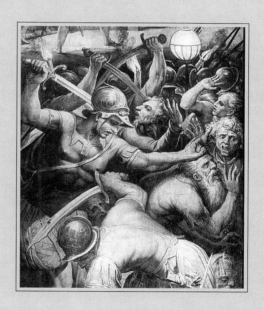

Massacre Motivated by Religion
The Italian artist Vasari painted the St. Bartholomew's Day Massacre (1572) for one of the public rooms in the pope's residence. Despite the scene's gruesomeness, both the pope and the artist intended to celebrate a Catholic victory over Protestant "heresy."

people. In a precarious world, religion gave many, whether Protestant or Catholic, the strength to accept hardship and turmoil as God's testing of their souls. In the realm of public policy, however, religious motivations eventually had to bend as state power increasingly diverged from religious sanctions.

Although particularly dramatic and deadly, the church-state crisis was only one of a series of economic, political, and cultural upheavals. In the early seventeenth century a major economic downturn resulted in food shortages, famine, and disease, creating greater burdens for states. Simultaneously, a secular (nonreligious) world view developed as the scientific revolution challenged age-old assumptions about heaven and earth. Scientists, writers, military men, and politicians all helped foster a belief in science and reason. Their emerging view of a world ruled by mechanical principles included a new vision of the social order governed by scientific laws and state powers. The scientific revolution did not prevent the persecution of witches, refute the persistent belief in magic, or alleviate the turbulence stirred by religious and dynastic conflicts. But it did set in motion forces that would ultimately help make western Europe the world's dominant power.

IMPORTANT DATES

1562 French Wars of Religion begin

1566 Revolt of Calvinists in the Netherlands against Spain begins

1569 Formation of Commonwealth of Poland-Lithuania

1571 Battle of Lepanto marks victory of West over Ottomans at sea

1587 Mary Queen of Scots executed

1588 Defeat of the Spanish Armada against England

1598 French Wars of Religion end with Edict of Nantes

1618 Thirty Years' War begins

1620 Defeat of the Czechs by Imperial armies at the Battle of White Mountain

1628 Charles I grants Petition of Right in England

1629 Emperor Ferdinand issues Edict of Restitution taking back Catholic lands confiscated by Lutherans

1635 France joins the Thirty Years' War by declaring war on Spain

1648 Peace of Westphalia ends the Thirty Years' War

State Power and Religious Conflict

The Peace of Augsburg (1555) had produced relative calm in central Europe by confirming the uneasy balance between Catholic and Lutheran German princes. John Calvin and his successors, however, made Geneva the headquarters for a religious revolution that threatened to shift the balance of power between Protestants and Catholics and within Protestantism itself. Calvinists challenged Catholic dominance in France, Scotland, Poland-Lithuania, and the Spanish-ruled Netherlands. They continued to attract adherents in the German states as well, and in England they sought to influence the new Protestant monarch, Elizabeth I. In 1558 one of the Catholic bishops under Elizabeth's predecessor, Mary Tudor, warned: "The wolves be coming out of Geneva and other places of Germany and have sent their books before, full of pestilent doctrines, blasphemy and heresy to infect the people." Calvinist preachers from Geneva converted thousands and organized new communities of men and women willing to oppose even monarchs who resisted their message. Their successes upset the international equilibrium.

French Religious Wars

Calvinist inroads in France had begun in 1555, when the Genevan Company of Pastors took charge of missionary work. Supplied with false passports and often disguised as merchants, the pastors moved rapidly among clandestine congregations, mostly in towns near Paris or in the south. Some ministers were former Catholic priests; most were laymen from middle-class or noble French families. Nobles provided military protection to local congregations and helped set up a national synod to organize the secret French Calvinist—or Huguenot—church.

Conversion to Calvinism in French noble families often began with the noblewomen, some

Peter Brueghel the Elder's, **The Triumph of Death,** *c. 1562*
Neither riches nor power can hold back the hand of death, represented in this work by a variety of terrifying skeletal figures. The painting seems to predict the death and destruction that would soon ravage much of Europe.

of whom sought intellectual independence as well as spiritual renewal in the new faith. Charlotte de Bourbon, for example, escaped from a Catholic convent, fled to Heidelberg, and eventually married William of Orange, leader of the anti-Spanish resistance in the Netherlands. Jeanne d'Albret, wife of Antoine de Bourbon and mother of the future French king Henry IV, became a Calvinist and convinced many of her clan to convert to Calvinism, though her husband died fighting for the Catholic side. Calvinist noblewomen protected pastors, provided money and advice, and helped found schools and establish relief for the poor. Calvinism also appealed to the wives of urban craftsmen, merchants, and professionals.

Religious divisions in France often reflected political disputes among noble families. About one-third of the nobles joined the Huguenots—a much larger proportion than in the general population. The Huguenots usually followed the lead of the Bourbon family. The most uncompromisingly anti-Protestant Catholic nobles took their cues from the Guise family. The Catholic royal family was caught between these two powerful factions, each with its own military organization. The situation grew even more volatile when Henry II (✴1547–1559) died unexpectedly in a tournament and his young son Francis II (✴1559–1560) succumbed soon after, leaving the ten-year-old Charles IX (✴1560–1574) king, with the Italian queen mother, Catherine de Medicis, as regent. France thus had no ruler who could command respect and obedience in difficult times. Catherine, a Roman Catholic, urged limited toleration for the Huguenots in an attempt to maintain political stability, but her influence was severely limited. As one ambassador commented, "It is sufficient to say that she is a woman, a foreigner, and a Florentine to boot, born of a simple house, altogether beneath the dignity of the Kingdom of France." Unwilling to obey a foreign woman of less-than-royal birth, the factions consolidated their forces, making general warfare inevitable.

For more than thirty years, French Catholics and Huguenots battled sporadically but fiercely. Both sides committed terrible atrocities. Priests and pastors were murdered, and massacres became frighteningly commonplace. Denouncing their enemies as idol worshipers, Huguenots destroyed altars and statues in Catholic churches. Catholics considered the Huguenots corrupt and polluted, deserving of the most horrible death. At Auxerre, for example, a Catholic mob slaughtered one hundred fifty Huguenots, dragged their naked bodies through the streets, and threw them into the river. Huguenots took their revenge on monasteries and abbeys, sometimes killing monks and nuns. Peasants, both Catholic and Protestant, suffered enormously from the ravages of hostile armies.

The most notorious atrocities occurred in the St. Bartholomew's Day Massacre, so-called because it began on the eve of St. Bartholomew's Day, the night of August 23, 1572. On August 22, assassins failed in their attempt to kill the Huguenot leader, Gaspard de Coligny. Panicking at the thought of Huguenot revenge and perhaps herself implicated in the botched plot, Catherine de Medicis convinced Charles IX to order the killing of the major Calvinist leaders, including Coligny. A bloodbath resulted. Catholic mobs murdered three thousand Huguenots in Paris, ten thousand in the provinces. Joyfully, the pope ordered the church bells rung throughout Catholic Europe; Spain's Philip II wrote Catherine that it was "the best and most cheerful news which at present could come to me." Protestants everywhere were horrified.

French Wars of Religion

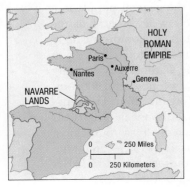

Repression did not solve the monarchy's problems, and the religious division was further complicated when a Protestant became heir to the crown. Two years after the massacre, Charles IX died, and his brother Henry III (✶1574–1589) became king. Henry III, like his brother before him, failed to produce an heir; he would be the last of the Valois monarchs. Next in line for the throne was none other than the Protestant Bourbon leader, Henry of Navarre. Yet for the moment, Henry III and Catherine de Medicis perceived an even greater threat in the Guises and their newly formed Catholic League, which had requested Spanish support in rooting out Protestantism in France. Henry and Catherine felt compelled to cooperate with Henry of Navarre because the league, believing the king was not taking a strong enough stand against the Protestants, began to encourage disobedience. Henry III responded with a fatal trick. In 1588 he summoned the two Guise leaders to a meeting outside Paris and had his men kill them. A few months later a fanatical monk stabbed Henry

III to death, and Henry of Navarre became Henry IV (＊1589–1610).

The new king soon realized that to establish control over the war-weary country he had to place the interests of the French state ahead of his Protestant faith. In 1593, therefore, Henry IV publicly embraced Catholicism (for the third time!) reputedly explaining his conversion with the phrase, "Paris is worth a Mass." Within a few years he defeated the last Catholics who refused to believe him sincere and drove out the Spanish, who had intervened militarily to block his accession. In 1598 he made peace with Spain, and in the Edict of Nantes he granted the Huguenots a large measure of religious toleration. The approximately 1.25 million Calvinists became a legally protected minority within an officially Catholic kingdom of some 18 million to 20 million people. Protestants were free to worship in specified towns and were allowed their own troops, fortresses, and even courts. The religious wars in France were over.

A New Relationship Between State and Religion: The *Politiques*

The Edict of Nantes would have been inconceivable earlier, when religious minorities seemed inherently treasonous. It represented a new arrangement prompted by the very practical need to pacify a religious minority too large to ignore and impossible to eradicate. Religious divisions proved especially threatening in the late sixteenth century because religious doctrines were now used to justify political resistance. Both Luther and Calvin had worried about this issue, and they had not advocated outright rebellion. After the St. Bartholomew's Day Massacre, however, Huguenot pamphleteers developed a constitutional theory of the right of resistance. Civil society, they held, rested on an implicit contract between the ruler and his magistrates, who represented the people; if a ruler broke that contract by tyranny or idol worship (which for the Calvinists meant Catholicism), the magistrates could justly depose him or her. The Protestant William of Orange used this argument to justify the Netherlands' struggles with Catholic Spain, and after Henry IV became king, Catholic writers took the same line, arguing that a heretical monarch such as Henry IV had no right to the throne.

In response to this growing challenge to established authority, some writers and statesmen began to insist that the need for political order and social stability superseded the importance of religious conformity. Called the *politiques* because of their emphasis on political concerns, they argued that a strong state must establish its independence from religious conflicts. One *politique* writer, Michel de Montaigne (1533–1592), explained the necessity of restraint in religious matters: "We see many whom passion drives outside the bounds of reason and makes them sometimes adopt unjust, violent, and even reckless courses." Montaigne advocated skepticism toward traditional beliefs; the words "all that is certain is that nothing is certain" were painted on the beams of his study. The *politiques'* most influential political analyst was Jean Bodin (1530–1596), who wrote *The Six Books of the Republic* (1576). Examining the different forms of government, Bodin concluded that only virtually unlimited monarchical power, under which subjects have no rights of resistance, offered hope for order. Bodin's ideas laid the foundation for absolutism (the idea that the monarch should be the sole and uncontested source of power) in the seventeenth century.

Henry IV's decision to compromise on religion in order to strengthen state power gave the *politiques* great hopes for a reign of toleration and stability. But the new king needed more than a good theory. To ensure his own safety and the succession of his heirs, he had to reestablish monarchical authority. Shrewdly mixing personal charm and effective bureaucratic development, Henry created a new splendid image of monarchy and extended his government's control. Like England's Elizabeth I, he cultivated rituals that glorified the monarch as a symbol of state power. Both rulers managed to control potentially fatal religious divisions, in part by rallying their subjects and officials around their own persons. Paintings, songs, court festivities, and royal processions all celebrated the ruler as a kind of mythological figure. Henry was depicted as an expert hunter, rider, fencer, dancer, and patron of the arts and learning.

Henry also fortified the monarchy by tapping new sources of revenue and by developing a new class of officials to counterbalance the fractious nobility. In 1604 his chief minister, the duke of Sully (1560–1641), introduced a new fee known as the *paulette*, which made administrative and judicial offices much easier to inherit. For some time the French crown had earned considerable revenue by selling offices to qualified bidders. Now, in exchange

Elizabeth I of England
Portraits of the monarch,
whether in full-scale paint-
ings or miniatures given as
gifts, reminded subjects
of the queen's glory,
power, and authority.

for the new annual payment, officeholders could not only own their offices but also pass them on to heirs or sell them to someone else. Because these offices carried prestige and often ennobled their holders, rich middle-class merchants and lawyers with aspirations to higher social status found them attractive. By buying offices they could become part of a new social elite known as the "nobility of the robe" (named after the robes that magistrates wore, much like those judges wear today). The nobility of the robe owed its status to the king, and the monarchy acquired a growing bureaucracy, though at the cost of granting broad autonomy to new officials who could not be dismissed. New income raised by the increased sale of offices reduced the state debt and eventually allowed Sully to balance the budget. Henry left the kingdom in good enough working order to ensure his son's succession, deter the renewal of religious warfare, and build the base for a strong monarchy. His efforts did not, however, prevent his own assassination in 1610 after nineteen unsuccessful attempts.

English Protestantism

Like Henry IV of France, Elizabeth I of England (*1558–1603) aimed to reestablish a strong monarchy, and against great obstacles she achieved her goal. England remained politically stable during her reign despite persistent troubles over reli-

gion. Having succeeded her half-sister, Mary Tudor, after five years of weak government and nearly constant religious unrest, Elizabeth returned England to Protestantism. Replacing the pope as the ultimate religious authority, Elizabeth assumed control as "supreme governor" of the Church of England. She insisted on retaining some Catholic ritual and an "episcopal" system in which the monarch appointed all bishops. Issued in 1563, the Church of England's Thirty-Nine Articles of Religion incorporated these elements of Catholicism along with such Calvinist doctrines as predestination.

England's political stability depended not only on preventing civil strife but also on ensuring a Protestant succession, situations that required Elizabeth's continual maneuvering over many years. She adroitly manipulated the prejudices of the age: "I know that I have the body of a weak and feeble woman," she once told Parliament, all the while insisting on her prerogatives as ruler. In the early years of her reign, the unmarried Elizabeth considered several possible dynastic alliances. She held out the prospect of marriage as long as her Catholic cousin, Mary, Queen of Scots, stood next in line to inherit the English throne. Scottish Calvinist nobles, however, forced Mary to abdicate in 1568 in favor of her year-old son, James, who was then raised as a Protestant. By the time of Elizabeth's death in 1603, her advisers had arranged

Mary, Queen of Scots
Even in prison, Mary served as a rallying point for
Catholics who resented Elizabeth's reinstatement of
Anglicanism. Elizabeth ordered her execution in 1587.

for James to become king of both England and Scotland, ensuring a Protestant succession.

Elizabeth had to parry challenges not only from Catholics but also from Puritans, strict Calvinists who opposed the vestiges of Catholic ritual in the Church of England. After Elizabeth became queen many English Protestants returned from exile. They soon became highly influential in English Protestant circles, but Elizabeth resisted their demands for drastic changes in church ritual and governance. Tacitly permitting English Catholics to worship in private, she allowed Catholicism to be kept alive by aristocrats who could afford to maintain their own chapels. Of those who considered themselves Catholic in the 1550s and 1560s, only a few were prepared to resist the new religious settlement violently. When they did rise up in support of Mary, Queen of Scots, in the Northern Rebellion of 1568–1569, they were immediately defeated. The Puritans, for their part, saw no need for armed rebellion, working instead from within to influence the Church of England.

During Elizabeth's reign the Puritans established a reputation for strict moral lives and for "plainness" in religion, characteristics that would grow more important in the seventeenth century. Puritan ministers constantly preached against the Church of England's "popish attire and foolish disguising . . . tithings, holy days, and a thousand more abominations." Puritan efforts focused largely on church

administration, attempting to place control in the hands of a local presbytery made up of the minister and the elders of the congregation. They had in mind something like the Presbyterian Church of Scotland, which was reorganized by the Scottish Calvinist nobility after Mary's expulsion. Elizabeth rejected any attempt to undercut bishops' authority or to substitute a presbyterian church government.

Elizabeth and her successor, James I (*1603–1625), regarded any attack on the church administration as an attack on the government as well. James echoed Elizabeth's thoughts when in response to Puritan critics of the church hierarchy he snapped, "No bishop, no king." Yet both Elizabeth and James relied on Puritan councilors and supported Puritans in high positions in the Church of England. At Puritan urging, in 1604 a new translation of the Bible—the Authorized Version, or King James Bible—was initiated; published in 1611, it encouraged laypeople to read the Scriptures. Meanwhile, the Church of England's authority reached into many aspects of life. Education was an ecclesiastical monopoly; bishops supervised the censorship of books; and local parish officials oversaw such matters as poor relief and the control of vagrants. An example of religious intervention in daily life can be seen in the Oxfordshire market town of Banbury, where in 1589, Puritan officials ordered maypoles taken down and suppressed traditional merrymaking such as morris dances and Sunday fairs. The sheriff and ultimately the highest royal officials overruled them. But even games and dances had become religious and therefore political issues, and Puritan attacks on the Church of England threatened government authority in daily life.

By the early seventeenth century the chief characteristics of Puritan teaching included a deep hatred of "popery" (the ceremonial trappings of Catholicism); a dedication to preaching, the instructional element of religion; an emphasis on keeping the Sabbath without such distractions as games and dancing; and an abhorrence of "licentious" behavior, such as theatrical productions that lacked a moral message. Puritan moral reform took place at every level, from the highest reaches of state power to the family. The family was the "Seminary of the Church and Common-wealth," and the master of the family should "make his house a little church." By stressing religious instruction within the family, Puritans inevitably focused much attention on the roles of wives and mothers. Puritan writers insisted that marriage existed for mutual spiritual comfort and companionship as well as for procreation, and mothers were expected to be counselors and religious mentors for their children. Although this emphasis on mothers' responsibilities accorded women a special importance, most Puritans continued to insist that fathers be the unquestioned heads of families. Children were supposed to stand or kneel in their parents' presence and generally to respect authority. Still, Puritan families also spawned religious and political resistance with their emphasis on Bible reading, studying catechism at home, and questioning the authority of those who did not agree with the Puritan program.

Believing themselves God's elect, English Puritans developed a fervent sense of mission about their predestined role—and England's, as an "elect nation," in international politics. In Elizabethan and particularly Puritan eyes, Catholic Spain became a diabolical force. Conversely, to pious Spanish Catholics, heretical England increasingly seemed not only a political rival but also a sinkhole of sin and error. Spanish Catholicism strove, as sternly as did Elizabethan Puritanism, to render the state a fit instrument of God's purpose. Yet the Spanish monarch, like his English and French counterparts, had to cope with a turbulent nobility and an inefficient bureaucracy at home. Against this backdrop of monarchies struggling to master chaos and earn divine favor, England and Spain headed toward a confrontation that would, before the end of the sixteenth century, engage them in hostilities on three continents.

Spanish Imperial and Religious Power

A deeply religious Catholic who was equally committed to his royal duties, Philip II (*1556–1598) came to the Spanish throne at age twenty-eight. Spanish Catholics joined their monarch in passionately rejecting the "heresy" of Protestantism and in vigorously opposing Muslim or Jewish influence; the Spanish Inquisition, which remained in force throughout Philip's reign, enforced religious conformity. Like Elizabeth and Henry IV, Philip cultivated an image of power and authority. He built a great gray granite palace, the Escorial, but had it constructed in the mountains, half-palace, half-monastery. There he lived in a small room and dressed in somber black. Most of all, observed the

Venetian ambassador, he liked "being by himself." Philip nonetheless relished the prerogatives of ruling; he personally supervised his gardens and building projects and oversaw the acquisition of paintings and books for his collections.

Philip faced enormous responsibilities because his empire was rich and far-flung. The Spanish colonies in the New World (called "the Indies") were just beginning to be settled, and their systematic exploitation commenced when silver mines opened in the 1540s. As the colonies funneled many of their profits into the Spanish economy, Spain prospered—for a while. Philip meanwhile contracted four successive marriages with the Portuguese, English, French, and Austrian royal families. His brief marriage to Mary Tudor (Mary I of England) did not produce an heir, but it and his subsequent marriage to the daughter of Henry II of France gave him reason enough for involvement in English and French affairs. In 1580, when the king of Portugal died without a direct heir, Philip took over this neighboring realm with its rich empire in Africa, India, and the Americas. The combined empires gave Spain an advantage at sea.

Religious conflict in Spain had an inevitable international dimension. Between 1568 and 1571 the Moriscos—Muslim converts to Christianity who secretly remained faithful to Islam—revolted in the south. Only distance and lack of resources prevented the Ottoman Turks from coming to their aid. As the Turks pushed into Hungary, the Spanish joined the pope and the Venetians in 1571 to defeat them in a great sea battle off the Greek coast at Lepanto. Although both sides suffered heavy losses—more than half the combatants were killed or wounded—the Christian allies drove the Turkish fleet out of the western Mediterranean. At home the Spanish forcibly resettled ninety thousand Morisco rebels in small groups in Castile.* When even this failed to squelch Muslim practices, two hundred seventy-five thousand Moriscos were expelled from Spain, most of them sent to France or North Africa.

Whereas in Spain the Inquisition successfully rooted out any sign of Protestant heresy, the Calvinists of Philip's northern possession, the Netherlands, were less easily intimidated: they

---

*Castile was one of the kingdoms united by the monarchy to form the Spanish state.

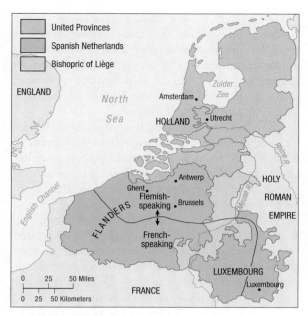

The Netherlands During the Revolt, c. 1580

Map legend:
- United Provinces
- Spanish Netherlands
- Bishopric of Liège

were far away and accustomed to being left alone. In 1566, Calvinists attacked Catholic churches, smashing objects of devotion. To punish his unruly subjects, Philip sent an army commanded by the duke of Alba (1507–1582). Philip's emissaries executed over eleven hundred people during the next six years, alienating much of the local population. Prince William of Orange (1533–1584) emerged as the leader of the anti-Spanish resistance in the Netherlands. He encouraged exiles and pirates known as the Sea Beggars to invade the northern ports, and their success sparked urban revolts. The Spanish responded with even more force, culminating in 1576 when Philip's long-unpaid mercenary armies mutinied and sacked Antwerp, then Europe's wealthiest commercial city. In eleven days of horror known as the Spanish Fury, seven thousand people perished. Out of this bloody confrontation emerged an alliance, the Pacification of Ghent (1576), between the ten southern provinces, largely Catholic, and the seven northern provinces, which had more Protestants. Under William of Orange local forces expelled the Spaniards in 1577.

Important religious, ethnic, and linguistic differences prevented enduring unity. The southern provinces remained Catholic (although, ironically, Calvinism got its start there), in parts French-speaking, and suspicious of the increasingly strict Calvinism in the north. William himself—once a Catholic, then a Lutheran, and only belatedly a Calvinist—did not always steer a steady course. In 1579 the southern provinces broke with William and returned to the Spanish fold. In the north the United Provinces (as they were then known), deposed Philip. Despite the 1584 assassination of William of Orange, outlawed by Philip II as "an enemy of the human race," Spanish troops never regained control in the north. Spain would not formally recognize the United Provinces (called more commonly the Dutch Republic) as independent until 1648, but by the end of the sixteenth century the Dutch Republic was a self-governing state sheltering a variety of religious groups.

Oligarchy and Religious Toleration in the Dutch Republic

The princes of Orange resembled a ruling family in the Dutch Republic (sometimes incorrectly called "Holland" after the most populous of the seven provinces), but their powers were limited and largely unofficial. Europeans living under monarchy wondered how the Dutch could live without a central authority figure or even a strong central administration, but the Dutch Republic developed instead an oligarchy (government by a few members of the elite class). Urban merchant and professional families (the "regents") controlled the towns and provinces. This was no democracy: governing explicitly included "the handling and keeping quiet of the multitude." In the absence of a national bureaucracy, a single legal system, and a central court, each province governed itself and sent delegates to the one common institution, the haphazardly organized States-General, largely run by the strongest individual provinces and their ruling families.

Well situated for maritime commerce, the Dutch Republic developed a thriving economy based on shipping and shipbuilding. Whereas aristocrats elsewhere focused on their landholdings, the Dutch looked for investments in trade. Amsterdam was the main European money market for two centuries after the municipally backed Bank of Amsterdam was established in 1609. The city was also a primary commodities market and a chief supplier of arms—to allies, neutrals, and even enemies. Dutch entrepreneurs produced goods at lower prices than anyone else, and they marketed them more efficiently. Dutch traders favored free trade in Europe because they could compete at an advantage. They controlled many overseas markets thanks to their preeminence in seaborne commerce; by 1670 the Dutch commercial fleet was larger than those of England, France, Spain, Portugal, and the Austrian Empire combined. Expanding opportunities for making money attracted immigrants from all over Europe, especially from the southern Netherlands, which remained under Spanish rule.

Because commercial capitalism—making money from investments in money or trade in commodities—fostered an openness to trading with anyone anywhere, it is perhaps not surprising that Dutch society appeared generally more tolerant of religious pluralism than the other European states. One-third of the Dutch population remained Catholic, and the secular authorities interfered little with it, although they did ban public worship. Because Protestant sects could generally count on toleration from the regents, they remained peaceful. The Netherlands had a relatively large Jewish population (many Jews had settled there after being driven out of Spain and Portugal), and from 1597, Jews could worship openly in their synagogues. Its relative openness to various religions helped make the Dutch Republic one of Europe's chief intellectual and scientific centers in the seventeenth and eighteenth centuries.

Religious Conflict and the International Balance of Power

Religion had long fueled conflict between Christian powers and the Muslim warrior states, and in the late sixteenth and early seventeenth centuries the Catholic Habsburgs continued the wars against Turkish Islam in eastern Europe. Since the Reformation, however, religious division increasingly divided Europe into internally battling factions. Western European religious conflicts threatened to become international when dissidents appealed to their sympathizers abroad for help. William of Orange, for example, sought help from the German Lutherans and from Protestants in France and England; English and Irish Catholics looked to the Catholic powers for assistance. These religious struggles inevitably exacerbated long-standing dynastic competition between the chief western European powers. In eastern Europe messianic Orthodoxy pitted Muscovite Russia against religiously mixed Poland-Lithuania.

By the early seventeenth century, nonetheless, state interests began to eclipse religious concerns as states looked for new alliances. Happening neither all at once nor very smoothly, this process of change failed to prevent the outbreak of the Thirty Years' War in 1618, with the devastating effects so vividly told in Grimmelshausen's tale of Simplicius. Beginning as yet another religiously motivated conflict within the Holy Roman Empire, the wars ended in a major realignment of the European balance of power, with some Catholic and Protestant states becoming allies for the first time.

Conflict Between England and Spain

Although, as one Englishman admitted, Philip II of Spain was "the most potent Monarch of Christendome," even he could not curb the Dutch rebels or stop the English from sending their fellow Protestants military aid and political advisers. Mary, Queen of Scots, brought the conflict between Elizabeth I and Philip to a head. The French-raised and Catholic queen had been under house arrest in England since fleeing her rebellious Calvinist subjects in 1568. As the great granddaughter of Henry VII, she had valid claims to the English throne, and her very presence rallied English Catholics who resented Elizabeth's church settlement. For the nearly twenty years of her imprisonment, she joined every Catholic plot against the English queen. In 1586 still more evidence of her intrigues came to light: a letter in which she offered her succession rights to Philip II, England's archenemy. Despite her reluctance to agree to the execution of another monarch, Elizabeth had Mary beheaded in 1587. In response, Pope Sixtus V decided to subsidize a Catholic crusade under Philip's leadership against the heretical queen, "the English Jezebel."

At the end of May 1588, Philip II sent his armada of one hundred thirty ships from Lisbon toward the English Channel. The Spanish king's motives were at least as political and economic as they were religious; he now had an excuse to strike

Anglo-Spanish War, 1580s

at the country whose pirates raided his shipping and encouraged Dutch resistance, and he hoped to use his fleet to ferry thousands of troops from the Netherlands across the channel to invade England itself. After several inconclusive engagements, the English scattered the Spanish Armada close to the French coast by sending blazing fireships into their midst. A gale then forced the Spanish to flee around Scotland. When the armada limped home in September, half the ships had been lost and thousands of sailors were dead or starving. Protestants everywhere rejoiced; Elizabeth struck a medal with the words, "God blew, and they were scattered." In his play *King John* a few years later (1596), Shakespeare wrote, "This England never did, nor never shall, Lie at the proud foot of a conqueror." A Spanish monk lamented, "Almost the whole of Spain went into mourning."

When Philip II died in 1598, his great empire had begun to lose its luster. The Dutch revolt ground on, and Henry IV seemed firmly established in France. The costs of fighting the Dutch, the English, and the French mounted up, and in the 1590s pervasive crop failures and the plague made hard times even worse. In his novel *Don Quixote* (1605, 1616) the Spanish novelist and playwright Miguel de Cervantes (1547–1616) captured the sadness of Spain's loss of grandeur. Cervantes's hero, a minor nobleman, reads so many romances and books of chivalry that he loses his wits and wanders the countryside hoping to recreate the heroic deeds of times past. His "tilting at windmills" provides an apt metaphor for a declining military aristocracy and a sense of thwarted ambition.

Eastern Europe: The Clash of Faiths and Empires

After the Christian naval triumph at Lepanto in 1571, the Austrian Habsburgs continued to battle the Ottoman armies in the Danube basin. The Habsburgs worked to consolidate the resources of their Bohemian and Austrian lands, of the slender strip of western Hungary they controlled, and of the Holy Roman Empire. But they had to make numerous concessions to the nobility of these lands in order to keep raising the money to hire mercenary armies capable of fighting the Turks in the series of inconclusive engagements that dragged on until the early seventeenth century.

Religious Divisions in Europe, c. 1600

Ottoman power had reached its zenith during the reign of Suleiman the Magnificent (✱1520–1566) and gradually declined thereafter. Defeat at Lepanto did not end Ottoman attacks in the western Mediterranean and did not hold off Turkish fleets, which subsequently seized Venetian-held Cyprus in 1573. Meanwhile Ottoman rule went unchallenged in the Balkans, where the Turks allowed their Christian subjects to cling to the Orthodox faith (and be taxed) rather than forcibly converting them to Islam. Orthodox Christians thus enjoyed relative toleration and were unlikely to look to the West for aid. Even less inclined to turn westward were the numerous and prosperous Sephardic Jewish communities of the Ottoman Empire, now joined by Jews expelled from Spain. Islam itself provided a powerful unifying force for the Turks and those conquered peoples or western "renegades" who embraced it, enabling the Ottoman Empire to withstand the sapping of the sultans' authority after Suleiman's death. The late sixteenth-century Ottoman monarchs became mere puppets of palace intrigues led by their elite troops, the Janissaries. However, the Habsburgs lacked the strength to drive the Ottomans back, and the Ottoman Empire still remained strong enough to avoid crumbling from within.

Whereas in the Balkans Orthodox Christians were obliged to collaborate with Ottoman power, in the Russian lands they found a champion in the Muscovite tsars. Building upon the base laid by his grandfather Ivan III, Tsar Ivan IV (✱1533–1584) fought to make Muscovy the center of a mighty Russian empire. Ivan brought the entire Volga valley under Muscovite control and initiated Russian expansion eastward into Siberia. In 1558 he struck out to the west, vainly attempting to seize the decaying state of the German-crusader knights in present-day Estonia and Latvia to provide Russia direct access to the Baltic Sea. Given to unpredictable fits of rage, Ivan killed numerous *boyars* (nobles), tortured priests, sacked the city of Novgorod on hearing rumors that it was siding with Lithuania, and killed his own son with an iron rod during a quarrel. His epithet "the Terrible" reflects not only the terror he unleashed but also the awesome impression he evoked. Cunning, intelligent, morbidly suspicious, and cruel, Ivan came to embody barbarism in the eyes of westerners. An English visitor wrote that Ivan's actions had bred "a general

hatred, distreccion [distraction], fear and discontentment throw his kyngdom. . . . God has a great plague in store for this people." Such warnings did not keep away the many westerners drawn to Moscow by opportunities to buy furs and sell western cloth and military hardware.

Two formidable foes blocked Ivan's way: Sweden (which then ruled Finland as well) and Poland-Lithuania. Both hoped to annex the eastern Baltic provinces, and both feared Russian expansionism. Poland and the Grand Duchy of Lithuania, united into a single commonwealth in 1569, controlled territory stretching from the Baltic Sea to deep within present-day Ukraine and Belarus. It was the largest state lying wholly within the boundaries of Europe. Poland-Lithuania, like the Dutch Republic, constituted one of the great exceptions to the general European trend toward greater monarchical authority. The Polish and Lithuanian nobles elected their

Russia, Poland-Lithuania, and Sweden in the Late 1500s

king, who tried to mediate between the great magnates soon dominant in the legislature (*Sejm*) and the gentry or lesser nobility.

The Protestant Reformation made inroads in Poland-Lithuania in the sixteenth century when many nobles converted to Lutheranism or Calvinism. The Protestants soon split into antagonistic camps, however: antitrinitarians, Anabaptists, and religious pacifists all found adherents among the Poles, Lithuanians, and many Italian religious refugees in the commonwealth. Fearful of religious persecution by the Catholic majority, the nobility insisted that their kings accept the principle of religious toleration as a prerequisite for election. The nobles' successful demand for limited monarchy and religious toleration greatly impressed the beleaguered French Huguenots in the 1570s and was closely studied (and sharply criticized) by Jean Bodin in his *Six Books of the Republic*. Ultimately, the French *politiques* embraced the idea of a stronger rather than a weaker monarchy as the best guarantee of civil peace and religious liberty. In Poland-Lithuania the nobles' insistence on maintaining their "golden liberty" ensured the survival of pockets of Protestantism until the mid-seventeenth century. Protected by the kings and magnates, the numerous Jewish communities remained prosperous during the late sixteenth and early seventeenth centuries.

Ivan's successors in Russia soon faced a serious threat from Poland-Lithuania. Boris Godunov (*1598–1605) became tsar when the last of Ivan's heirs perished, but he too died before his reform plans could take shape. Before Boris's death a usurper claiming to be Ivan IV's dead son Dmitri had appeared with Polish-Lithuanian backing, and in the turmoil this "false Dmitri" won the Russian crown—only to be quickly overthrown. A terrible period of chaos known as the Time of Troubles ensued, during which the king of Poland-Lithuania tried to put his son on the Russian throne. In 1613 an army of nobles, townspeople, and peasants finally drove out the westerners and installed a nobleman who established an enduring new dynasty: Michael Romanov (*1613–1645). With the return of peace, Muscovite Russia resumed the process of state building. Reorganizing tax gathering and military recruitment and continuing to create a service nobility to whom the peasantry was increasingly subject, the first Romanovs laid the foundations of the powerful Russian empire that would emerge late in the seventeenth century under Peter the Great.

The Thirty Years' War, 1618–1648

East-West contrasts sharpened during the long series of wars fought in central Europe in the first half of the seventeenth century. The lengthy campaigns that devastated much of Europe's heartland had their origins in the ethnic and religious differences that divided the huge Holy Roman Empire. The empire embraced some eight major ethnic groups, and its people were Catholic and Protestant (Lutheran, Calvinist, and Anabaptist). Catholics held the preponderance of power because the imperial Habsburg dynasty and four of the seven electors who chose the emperor were of that faith. The balance of religious and political power never stabilized because control of some territories within the empire shifted from one religious group

to another. Moreover, the Peace of Augsburg (1555) did not recognize Calvinism. Yet after 1555, Calvinism made inroads in Lutheran areas, and by 1613 two of the three Protestant imperial electors had become Calvinists. In addition, the Counter-Reformation—especially the zealous campaigns of the Jesuits—had won many Protestant cities back to Catholicism. The already fragile Augsburg settlement had no mechanism for resolving conflicts among the many minor princes and the emperor, and the disputing parties thus turned to war.

Fighting first broke out in Bohemia, whose relationship to the Holy Roman Empire resembled that of the Netherlands under Spanish rule. The Habsburgs held not only the imperial crown but also a collection of royal crowns (Bohemia was one) administered separately. When the devoutly Catholic Habsburg heir Archduke Ferdinand was crowned king of Bohemia in 1617, he began to curtail the religious freedom previously granted to Protestants. A resistance movement led by the largest ethnic group, the Czechs, quickly formed. In 1618 a group of Czech Protestant noblemen cornered two of the king's Catholic advisers and in the "defenestration of Prague" threw them out a window in the royal castle onto a dung heap far below. A Protestant assembly then formed a provisional government and appealed to other Protestants in the empire for help. A year later, when Ferdinand was elected emperor (as Ferdinand II, *1619–1637), the rebellious Bohemians deposed him and chose the young Calvinist Frederick V of the Palatinate (*1616–1623) to replace him. A quick series of clashes ended in 1620 when the imperial armies defeated the Czechs and their allies at the Battle of White Mountain, outside Prague. For the Czechs, White Mountain joined the martyrdom of Jan Hus in 1415 as symbols of the cruel squashing of their budding tradition of self-determination.

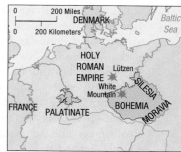

The Thirty Years' War

White Mountain did not end the war. Private mercenary armies commanded by soldiers of fortune began to form during the fighting, and the emperor had virtually no control over them. The amazing

---

THE THIRTY YEARS' WAR

1618 "Defenestration of Prague" opens the Thirty Years' War when Czech Protestants resist Austrian Catholic rule

1620 Austrians defeat Czechs and their allies at the Battle of White Mountain

1629 In the Edict of Restitution, Emperor Ferdinand II outlaws Calvinism and takes back Catholic properties previously confiscated by Lutherans

1632 Gustavus Adolphus of Sweden, a Lutheran, invades German lands with the aid of subsidies from the Catholic French government

1635 France openly joins the hostilities by declaring war on Spain and allying with the Dutch

1644 Opening of peace negotiations

1648 Peace of Westphalia ends the Thirty Years' War

---

career of the century's best-known soldier of fortune, Albrecht von Wallenstein (1583–1634), showed how political advantage and personal gain could confuse the expected division along religious lines. A Czech-speaking noble Bohemian Protestant by birth, Wallenstein took the Habsburg side during the Bohemian phase of the war and amassed a fortune in the process. In 1625 he offered to raise an army for Ferdinand, and within three years he had one hundred twenty-five thousand soldiers, who occupied and plundered much of northern Germany with the emperor's approval. The Lutheran king of Denmark, Christian IV (∗1596–1648), invaded to protect the north German Protestants and to extend his influence. Despite Dutch and English encouragement, Christian lacked adequate military support and Wallenstein's forces soon defeated him.

Emboldened by his general's victories, Ferdinand issued the Edict of Restitution in 1629, outlawing Calvinism and reclaiming Catholic church properties confiscated by the Lutherans. With Protestant interests in jeopardy, Gustavus Adolphus (∗1611–1632) of Sweden invaded Germany in 1630. Declaring his support for the Protestant cause, he clearly intended to gain control over trade in northern Europe as well (he had already ejected the Poles from present-day Latvia and Estonia in 1619). Now the primacy of political motives became obvious, for the Catholic French government, which hoped to block Spanish intervention in the war and to win influence and perhaps territory in the empire, subsidized Gustavus. The publication of the treaty between the Lutheran and Catholic powers to fight the Catholic Habsburgs showed that state interests now outweighed all other considerations. According to the treaty, France paid Sweden 1 million livres annually for five years for "the safeguarding of the Baltic and Oceanic Seas, the liberty of commerce, and the relief of the oppressed states of the Holy Roman Empire."

The Swedish king promptly defeated the imperial army and occupied the Catholic parts of southern Germany before he was killed at the battle of Lützen against Wallenstein in 1632. After eliminating Gustavus Adolphus, Wallenstein tried to parlay his military success into even greater personal influence and was rumored to be negotiating with Protestant powers. Ferdinand dismissed his general and had his henchmen assassinate him. The war dragged on. France openly joined the fray in 1635 by declaring war on Spain and soon after forged an alliance with the Calvinist Dutch in their struggle for independence. The conflict now effectively pitted France against the Spanish and Austrian Habsburgs. Not until 1644 did peace negotiations open, and only four years later, with the Peace of Westphalia, did they finally come to a close. France and Spain nonetheless continued fighting until 1659.

The Consequences of Constant Warfare

The central European wars accelerated changes in military armaments and tactics that had been evolving since the early sixteenth century. Improvements in artillery led states to build large defensive fortifications, and the increasing use of gunpowder weapons resulted in tactics that maximized opportunities to give fire. Soon the infantry, consisting of long, narrow lines of troops firing muskets joined by tightly packed formations of pike-carrying foot soldiers, overshadowed the cavalry. Everywhere, the size of armies increased dramatically. Most armies in the 1550s had fewer than fifty thousand men, but Gustavus Adolphus led one hundred thousand in 1631, and by the end of the seventeenth century, Louis XIV of France would have four hundred thousand soldiers. The cost of larger armies and new weapons such as cannon and warships strained the resources of every state.

Maintaining discipline in these huge armies required new, harsher methods. Drill, combat training, and a clear chain of command became essential. Newly introduced uniforms created—as their name suggests—a new standardization, but these outfits soon lost their distinctiveness in the conditions of early modern warfare. An Englishman who fought for the Dutch army in 1633 described how he slept on the wet ground, got his boots full of water, and "at peep of day looked like a drowned ratt."

Innovations came from many quarters. The Italians developed stronger fortifications to withstand shelling and assault. The Spanish became known for their military administration and medical facilities on the battlefield; they set up the first permanent military hospital. The Dutch introduced identical-caliber weapons and illustrated military textbooks. Gustavus Adolphus's Swedes used small, mobile units of thirty men each who could fire in lines rather than from squares.

To field larger armies, governments needed offices for supply and administration, new sources of funds, and more soldiers, often from social classes that had not usually served before. Although mercenaries still predominated in many armies, rulers began to recruit more of their own subjects. Volunteers proved easiest to find in dire economic times, when the threat of starvation induced men to accept the bonus offered for signing up. A Venetian general explained the motives for enlisting: "To escape from being craftsmen [or] working in a shop; to avoid a criminal sentence; to see new things; to pursue honour (though these are very few) . . . all in the hope of having enough to live on and a bit over for shoes, or some other trifle that will make life supportable." The men all had to be paid, however, and governments often fell short, leading to frequent mutinies, looting, and pillaging.

Not only were the larger armies more difficult to supply, but they also attracted all sorts of displaced people desperately in need of provisions. In the last year of the Thirty Years' War, for example, the Imperial-Bavarian Army had forty thousand men entitled to draw rations—and more

Jacob Duck, **Soldiers' Quarters,** *c. 1635*
Wherever they went, armies attracted all kinds of followers.

than one hundred thousand wives, prostitutes, servants, children, maids, and camp followers who had to scrounge for their own food. The bureaucracies of early seventeenth-century Europe simply could not cope with such demands. Consequently, armies and their hangers-on had to live off the countryside. If an army could not successfully occupy a territory, then it plundered the land so its goods would not fall into enemy hands. The horrific results were scenes like that witnessed by Simplicius.

Some towns were battered by up to ten or eleven sieges during the Thirty Years' War, and the invaders slaughtered many urban citizens when the cities fell. But on the whole the worst suffering took place in the countryside. Peasants fled their villages, which their attackers often burned down. At times, desperate peasants revolted and looted nearby castles and monasteries. War and intermittent outbreaks of plague cost some German towns one-third of their population; in certain locales two-fifths of the rural population perished. Bohemia lost more than a third of its population. As a poet of the time asked, "But we human beings, what are we? A house of grim pain . . . A scene of rude fear and adversity."

Economic Crisis and Realignment

The Thirty Years' War was waged against a backdrop of fundamental economic change. After a century of rising prices, caused partly by huge inflows of gold and silver from the New World and partly by population growth, prices began to level off and even to drop, and in most places the rate of population growth slowed. With fewer goods being produced, international trade fell into recession. Agricultural yields also declined. Just when states attempted to field ever-expanding standing armies, peasants and townspeople alike were less able to pay the escalating taxes needed to finance the wars. Famine and disease trailed grimly behind economic crisis and war, in some areas causing large-scale uprisings and revolts, already foreshadowed in Russia's Time of Troubles. Behind the scenes of rebellion, the economic balance of power began to shift as northwestern Europe, especially England and the Dutch Republic, rose to dominate international markets.

The Causes of Economic Crisis

The seventeenth-century economic crisis came as a shock after nearly one hundred fifty years of growth. The religious and dynastic wars of the late sixteenth century occurred during a time of population increase and general inflation. Even though religious and political turbulence led to population decline in some cities, such as Antwerp, overall rates of growth remained impressive: in the sixteenth century, parts of Spain doubled in population, and England's population grew by 70 percent. The supply of precious metals swelled too: improvements in mining techniques in central Europe raised the output of silver and copper mines, and in the 1540s new silver mines were discovered in Mexico and Peru. Spanish gold imports peaked in the 1550s, silver in the 1590s. This flood of precious metals combined with population growth to fuel an astounding increase in food prices (400 percent in the sixteenth century) and a more moderate rise in the cost of manufactured goods. Real wages rose much more slowly, at about half the rate of increase in food prices. Governments always overspent revenues, and by the end of the century, most of Europe's rulers faced deep deficits.

Economic crisis did not strike everywhere at the same time, but the warning signs were unmistakable. From the Baltic to the East Indies, foreign trade slumped as war and an uncertain money supply made business riskier. After 1625, silver imports to Spain declined, partly because so many of the Indians who worked in Spanish colonial mines died from disease. Textile production fell in many countries, and in some places it nearly collapsed, largely because of decreased demand and a shrinking labor force. Even the slave trade stagnated, though its growth would resume after 1650.

Demographic slowdown also signaled economic trouble. Overall, Europe's population may have actually declined, from 85 million in 1550 to 80 million in 1650. In the Mediterranean growth had stopped in the 1570s. The most sudden reversal occurred in central Europe as a result of the Thirty Years' War: the Holy Roman Empire lost about one-fourth of its population in the 1630s and 1640s. Population continued to grow only in England and Wales, the Netherlands (both the Dutch Republic and the Spanish Netherlands), and Scandinavia.

Agricultural production reflected differences in population growth. Where population stagnated or declined, agricultural prices dropped because of less demand, and farmers who produced for the market suffered as the prices they received declined. Many reacted by converting grain-growing land to pasture or vineyards, because the prices of other foods fell less than the price of grain. Interest in agricultural innovations diminished. In some places peasants abandoned their villages and left land to waste, as had happened in the late fourteenth century. The only country that emerged unscathed from the economic crisis was the Dutch Republic, principally because it had long excelled in agricultural innovation. Inhabiting Europe's most densely populated area, the Dutch developed systems of field drainage, crop rotation, and animal husbandry that provided high yields of grain for both people and animals. Their foreign trade, textile industry, agricultural production, and population all grew. After the Dutch, the English fared best.

Historians have long disagreed about the causes of the early seventeenth-century economic downturn. Some cite the inability of agriculture to support a rising population by the end of the sixteenth century; others the extensive mid-century wars, the states' demands for more taxes, the irreg-

Louis Le Nain,
Peasant's Repast, *1642*
*This painting depicts the
simplicity and poverty of
peasant life, but also its
dignity. Notice the darkness
of the men's clothing and
the lack of shoes for some.
Bread appears clearly as the
center of the meal.*

ularities in money supply due to primitive banking practices, or the waste caused by middle-class expenditures in the desire to emulate the nobility. To this list of causes, recent researchers have added climatic changes. Studies of tree rings, glacier movements, and dates of grape harvests have led experts to call the seventeenth century a "little ice age": glaciers advanced, average temperatures fell, and winters were often exceptionally severe. Cold winters and wet summers meant bad harvests, and these natural disasters ushered in a host of social disasters. When the harvest was bad, prices shot back up, and many could not afford to feed themselves.

Grain had become the essential staple of most Europeans' diets. Since the late Middle Ages, most of Europe's citizens (outside the Netherlands and England) ate little meat; only the wealthy could afford it. Most people consumed less butter, eggs, poultry, and wine and more grain products, ranging from bread to beer. The average adult European now ate more than four hundred pounds of grain per year. Peasants lived on bread, soup with a little fat or oil, peas or lentils, garden vegetables in season, and only occasionally a piece of meat or fish. In most places the poor existed on the verge of starvation; one contemporary observed that "the fourth part of the inhabitants of the parishes of England are miserable people and (harvest time excepted) without any subsistence."

Famine and Disease

The threat of food shortages haunted Europe whenever harsh weather destroyed crops, and local markets were vulnerable to problems of food distribution. Customs barriers inhibited local trade, overland transport moved at a snail's pace, bandits disrupted traffic, and the state or private contractors commandeered available food for the perpetually warring armies. Usually the adverse years differed from place to place, but from 1594 to 1597 most of Europe suffered from shortages, and the resulting famine led to revolts from Ireland to Muscovy. To head off social disorder, the English government drew up a new Poor Law in 1597 that required each community to support its poor, and many other governments also increased relief efforts.

Most people did not respond to their dismal circumstances by rebelling or mounting insurrections. They simply left their huts and hovels and took to the road in search of food and charity. Overwhelmed officials recorded pitiful tales of suffering. Women and children died while waiting in line for food at convents or churches. Husbands left their wives and families to search for better conditions in other parishes or even other countries. Those left behind might be reduced to eating chestnuts, roots, bark, and grass. In eastern France in 1637, a witness reported that "The roads were paved with people. . . . Finally it came to cannibalism." Eventually compassion gave way to fear, as these hungry vagabonds, who sometimes banded together to beg for bread, became more aggressive, occasionally threatening to burn a barn if they were not given food.

Successive bad harvests led to malnutrition, which weakened people, making them more susceptible to such epidemic diseases as the plague, typhoid fever, typhus, dysentery, smallpox, and influenza. Disease did not spare the rich, though many epidemics hit the poor hardest. The plague was feared most, because in one year it could cause the death of up to one-half of a town's or village's population and because it struck with no discernible pattern. Nearly 5 percent of France's population died in the plague of 1628 to 1632.

Patterns of Landholding and Family Life

Other effects of economic crisis were less visible than famine and disease, but no less momentous. The most important was the peasantry's changing status. Peasants had many obligations, including rent and—if the land had been subject to a lord's control in the past—various dues such as fees for inheriting or selling land and tolls for using mills, wine presses, or ovens. States collected an overwhelming array of taxes, ranging from direct taxes on land to taxes on such consumer goods as salt, an essential preservative. Protestant and Catholic churches alike exacted a 10 percent tax, or tithe, which they often collected in the field during harvest time. Millions of peasants lived on an economic margin that made these burdens nearly intolerable; any reversal of fortune could force them into the homeless world of vagrants and beggars, who (in France, for example) numbered in the hundreds of thousands.

In the seventeenth century the mass of peasants became more sharply divided into rich and poor. In England, the Dutch Republic, northern France, and northwestern Germany, the peasantry was disappearing: agricultural innovation gave some peasants the means to become farmers who rented substantial holdings, produced for the market, and in good times enjoyed relative comfort and higher status. Those who could not afford to plant new crops such as maize (American corn), buckwheat, and potatoes, or use techniques that ensured higher yields, became simple laborers, with little or no land of their own. The minimum plot of land needed to feed a family varied depending on the richness of the soil, available improvements in agriculture, and distance from markets. For example, only two acres could support a family in Flanders, as opposed to ten acres in Muscovy. One-half to four-fifths of the peasants did not have even this much land. They descended deeper into debt during difficult times and often lost their land to wealthier farmers or city officials intent on developing rural estates. In eastern Europe the situation was radically different because the noble landlords tied their peasants to the land, making them serfs.

The economic crisis directly affected family life. One-fifth to one-quarter of all children died in their first year; half, before age twenty. In 1636 an Englishman described his grief when his twenty-one-month-old son died, revealing the anguish the loss of so many babies brought: "We both found the sorrow for the loss of this child, on whom we had bestowed so much care and affection . . . far to surpass our grief for the decease of his three elder brothers, who dying almost as soon as they were born, were not so endeared to us as this [one] was." Demographic historians have shown that European families reacted almost immediately to economic crisis. During bad harvests they postponed marriages and had fewer children. When hard times passed, more of them married and they had more children.

We might assume that families would have more children to compensate for high death rates, but beginning in the early seventeenth century and continuing until the end of the eighteenth, families in all ranks of society started to limit the number of children. Because methods of contraception were not widely known, they did this by marrying later; the average age at marriage rose from the early

Philippe de Champaigne, The Children of Habert de Montmor, *1649*
Pictures of children separate from their parents became more common in the 1600s. These are the children of an ennobled judge; their clothing reflects the family's wealth. Even among the rich, three of the seven children in the family died before reaching adulthood. Here, as was the custom, the youngest boys wear clothes like those of girls.

twenties to the late twenties during the seventeenth century. The later a couple married, the fewer children they would have. The average family had about four children. Poorer families seem to have had fewer children (two or three for the poorer people in the cities) and wealthier ones more (an average of five, for example, in the English aristocracy). Peasant couples, especially in eastern and southeastern Europe, had more children than urban couples because cultivation still required intensive manual labor.

Why was postponing marriage—and smaller family size—seen as a response to economic crisis? If couples had many children, they would have to divide the family fortune to pay dowries for the girls and give the boys something to live on. With the family farm or shop already hard-pressed, families could not afford these expenses, so limits on the number of children were essential. The trend toward family limitation was more general, however, for it affected all social groups and continued even after the crisis had passed. Evidently, people came to see smaller families as a means to increase their standard of living; even English aristocrats had fewer children by the end of the century.

The consequences for individuals must have been profound. Young men and women were expected to put off marriage (*and* sexual intercourse)

until their mid- to late twenties—if they were among the lucky 50 percent who lived that long and not among the 10 percent who never married. Because both the Reformation and Counter-Reformation had stressed sexual fidelity and abstinence before marriage, the number of births out of wedlock was relatively small (2–5 percent of births); premarital intercourse was generally tolerated only after a couple had announced their engagement. Although abstinence before one's late twenties must have posed many a moral dilemma, women particularly benefited directly from family limitation; fewer than 10 percent now died in childbirth, an experience all women feared because of the great risks. Even in the richest and most enlightened homes, childbirth sometimes occasioned an atmosphere of panic. To allay their fears, women sometimes depended upon magic stones and special pilgrimages and prayers. Midwives delivered most babies; physicians were scarce, and even if they did attend a birth they were generally less helpful. The English woman Alice Thornton described in her diary how her doctor bled her to prevent a miscarriage after a fall; her son died anyway in a breech birth that almost killed her too.

Women also felt the effects of economic change. As hard times limited demand in some areas and urban commerce began to move beyond the guild system into national and international trade networks in others, opportunities within guilds were restricted to men. Widows who had been able to take over their late husband's trade now found themselves excluded or limited to short tenures. Because people assumed that almost all women would marry and that women's work was secondary to men's or a form of temporary support for the family, women always earned lower wages. Many went into domestic service until they married, some for their entire lives. As town governments began to fear the effects of "masterless" people, they carefully regulated women's work as servants, requiring them to stay in their positions unless they could prove mistreatment by a master.

The Changing Economic Balance in Europe

The long-term consequences of the economic crisis varied from region to region. The economies of southern and eastern Europe declined, whereas those of the northwest emerged stronger. Northern Italian industries were eclipsed, and Spanish commerce with the New World dropped. With growing populations and geographical positions that promoted overseas trade, England and the Dutch Republic became the leading mercantile powers. Amsterdam replaced Seville, Venice, Genoa, and Antwerp as the center of European trade and commerce. The plague also had differing effects. Whereas central Europe and the Mediterranean countries took generations to recover from its ravages, northwestern Europe quickly replaced its lost population, no doubt because this area's people had suffered less from the malnutrition related to the economic crisis and from the plague itself.

East-West differences overshadowed those between northern and southern regions. Because labor shortages coincided with economic recovery, peasants in western Europe gained more independence. In most places they became free to buy and sell property and to pass it on through inheritance. All but remnants of serfdom disappeared from western Europe. By contrast, from the Elbe River east to Muscovy, nobles reinforced their dominance over peasants, thanks to cooperation from rulers and lack of resistance from villagers, whose community traditions—particularly in Poland, Bohemia,

and the eastern German states—had always acknowledged nobles' rights of lordship.

The price rise of the sixteenth century prompted the eastern European nobles, especially in Polish and eastern German lands, to increase their holdings and step up their production of grain for western markets. To raise production, they demanded more rent and heavier dues from their peasants, whom the government decreed must stay in their villages. Although noble landlords lost income in the economic downturn of the first half of the seventeenth century, the peasants gained nothing. They became further indebted to their landlords; those who were still free became less so, and those who were already dependent became serfs—completely tied to the land. A city official from Pomerania might complain of "this barbaric and as it were Egyptian servitude," but townspeople had no power to fight the nobles. Most places still supported a social system ranging from freedom to serfdom, but in Muscovy the complete enserfment of the peasantry would eventually be recognized in the Code of Laws in 1649. Although enserfment produced short-term profits for landlords, in the long run it retarded economic development in eastern Europe and kept most of the population in a stranglehold of illiteracy and hardship.

The Scramble for Political Authority

As rulers expanded their bureaucracies, extended their powers of taxation, and boosted the size of their armies, they inevitably encountered resistance, especially because ordinary people, already strained economically and emotionally, found it difficult to meet government's increasing demands. The most sustained struggle for political authority took place in England between the crown and Parliament. Yet despite many setbacks, most states emerged by 1640 with more authority over their subjects' resources than ever before. The number of state-salaried employees multiplied, paperwork proliferated, and appointment to office depended more and more on university education in the law. Rulers themselves also had to change. Military prowess, once almost a prerequisite for a monarch, became less important than a knowledge of accounting and an ability to shrewdly navigate the maze of international issues. Although court pageantry still demanded constant attention, rulers had to learn to rely on bureaucrats. A few became bureaucrats themselves: Philip II, for example, insisted on seeing much of the government's incoming paperwork, and he took state papers with him wherever he went. Once when the royal family went sailing, he sat at his desk signing papers while others in the court danced.

Monarchical Authority

To make their power obvious, many rulers carefully nurtured the theatricality of court life that had developed in the fifteenth and sixteenth centuries. In addition to the pageants and plays put on for the court, even the rulers' meals became state occasions governed by precise ritual. In Spain regulations that set the wages, duties, and ceremonial functions of every official prescribed court etiquette. Hundreds, even thousands, of people made up such a court. The court of Philip IV (*1621–1665), for example, numbered seventeen hundred. In the 1630s he built a second palace outside Madrid, the Buen Retiro. There the courtiers lived amid parks and formal gardens, artificial ponds, grottoes, an iron aviary (which led some critics to call the whole thing a "chicken coop"), a wild animal cage, a courtyard for bullfights, and rooms filled with sculptures and paintings. At the Buen Retiro and elsewhere, rulers began collections that would become some of Europe's great museums.

Rising taxes and increasing demands for military supplies also reflected the growth of state power. Supporting armies and monarchical trappings required more money and more people to staff the armies, supervise tax collection, and oversee the extension of royal power. The great nobles often resisted being molded into docile officials or courtiers, so to enforce their will monarchs turned to personal favorites, often chosen from the lesser nobility, who created new client networks. For example, Axel Oxenstierna (1583–1654) directed the Swedish government during the reign of Gustavus Adolphus and also handled the transition to the regency when the king died in battle.

One of the most powerful royal favorites was Cardinal Richelieu (1585–1642), chief minister in France between 1625 and 1642. Richelieu directed the monarchy of Henry IV's son, Louis XIII (*1610–1643), and his name became synonymous with the phrase *reason of state*. The contrast between

Jusepe Leonardo, **Palace of the Buen Retiro in 1636–1637**
This painting depicts Philip IV's imposing new palace as it appeared in the 1630s.

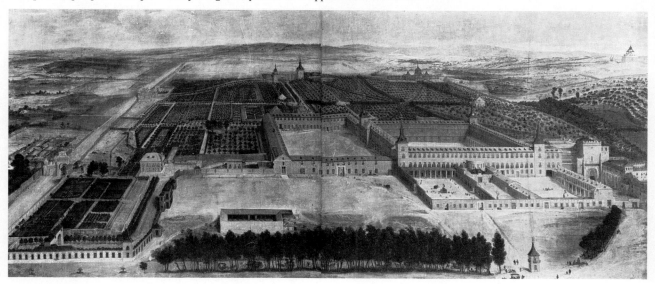

Richelieu's foreign and domestic policies indicates that by the seventeenth century even the rhetoric of religious difference did not interfere with political interests. While supporting Protestant states abroad, Richelieu silenced Protestants within France by banning their political organizations and separate law courts. He also crushed noble resistance to his rule and extended the use of intendants—delegates from the king's council dispatched to the provinces to oversee police, army, and financial affairs. This expansion of state authority allowed Richelieu to double the rate of land tax in just eight years, between 1635 and 1643.

Even before the Peace of Westphalia ended the Thirty Years' War, Spain already suffered from the

Diego Rodríguez de Silva Velázquez, The Count-Duke of Olivares

Velázquez painted Philip IV and many members of his court, including his chief minister Olivares, shown here as an energetic and powerful man of action, wearing the armor and sword of a military noble.

effects of its participation in the conflicts, as calls for more men and taxes provoked revolts in several provinces. Philip IV faced an inescapable financial problem: while silver shipments from America declined, his armies needed ever more money to fight the Dutch and French. After a twelve-year truce between Spain and the Dutch Republic expired in 1621, the two states struggled for another twenty-seven years. At issue was not only control over the Dutch homeland but also dominance in the colonies, for the Dutch carried the war to Brazil, which newly independent Portugal recovered only in 1654. Much to Philip's chagrin, his brother-in-law, Louis XIII of France, allied himself to the Dutch Protestant rebels in 1635 and began a war with Spain that lasted until 1659. "The king of France," wrote Philip, "defying God, law, and nature, . . . has gone to war with me . . . in support of heresy."

Raising money for these wars meant more taxes. Philip's mentor and chief minister, Gaspar de Guzmán, count-duke of Olivares (1587–1645), undertook a wide-ranging program to increase revenues by establishing new taxes, such as a state monopoly on salt (so effective in France), and by standardizing tax collection throughout the land. Spain was actually a union of several kingdoms, including Aragon, Valencia, and Portugal, each with their own representative institutions (*cortes*). Many provinces retained the constitutional right to approve new taxation, and they resisted the innovations. Olivares aimed to install a system in which all provinces paid relatively equal amounts so that most of the burden would not continue to fall on the central province of Castile; he described his program as "one king, one law, one coinage," a policy that actually meant an attack on the special privileges of many provinces. In almost every state of Europe, these regional privileges hindered the growth of central state power. In 1640 the northeastern province of Catalonia resisted Olivares's demands for more money and supplies for the war with France. This spark produced a revolutionary explosion throughout the Spanish monarchy.

All European states searched frantically for more revenues. In addition to raising taxes, governments frequently resorted to currency depreciations, the sale of newly created offices, forced loans, and manipulation of the embryonic stock and bond markets. When all else failed, they declared bankruptcy. The Spanish government, for example, did so three times in the first half of the seventeenth century. In these times of plague, famine, and stagnating growth, poor peasants and city workers could hardly bear new demands for money. The governments' creditors and the highest-ranking nobles also had grievances. Rebellion often resulted.

In the late sixteenth century most popular rebellions had originated in religious quarrels. Pockets of religious revolt still remained in the early seventeenth century, even outside the area of the Thirty Years' War, but in many places opposition to royal taxation set off new uprisings. From Portugal to Muscovy, peasants and city-dwellers resisted new impositions by forming makeshift armies and battling royal forces. With their colorful banners, unlikely leaders, unusual names (the *Nu-Pieds,* or "Bare-Footed," in France, for example), and crude weapons, the rebels were no match for state armies, but they did keep officials worried and troops occupied. These "days of shaking" also contributed to the massive constitutional and political revolts of the 1640s.

Constitutional Resistance in England

Although they lacked her political shrewdness, Elizabeth's Stuart successors were far from incompetent, and they faced less overwhelming problems than rulers of the continental states, partly because England stayed out of the Thirty Years' War. England's population was relatively small (one-fourth the size of France's) and homogeneous, but ethnic differences troubled relations among Scotland, Ireland, and England, all now ruled separately by the king of England. The crown had originally needed less money for armies because the surrounding seas offered these island states natural protection. Yet though the continental empires survived the seventeenth-century crisis, the Stuarts did not. The English crown was relatively poor—English per capita taxes were only a quarter of those in France—but when it needed more money, taxpayers were reluctant to pay. Subjects used Parliament, dominated by men from the gentry, or landowning, classes, to organize opposition. The very cohesion of the English state made possible the first successful national revolution, which would break out in 1640.

From the first, the Stuarts seemed destined to antagonize their parliaments. James I insisted on repeatedly making an issue of what Elizabeth had always left implicit: that he ruled by divine right and was accountable only to God. In his view, "The state of monarchy is the supremest thing on earth; for kings are not only God's lieutenants on earth, but even by God himself they are called gods." Like continental rulers, James needed more revenue; Elizabeth had left many debts, and inflation eroded the crown's income from its own properties. James tried every expedient to avoid asking Parliament for more money: he raised customs duties and sold noble titles and commercial monopolies. In the process he alienated the old nobility as well as ordinary people. Puritans found him unreceptive to their demands to reform the Church of England and criticized his court as too lavish. Many people were troubled by his obvious infatuation with George Villiers (1592–1628), the duke of Buckingham, who on the king's behalf pursued an unpopular Spanish marriage for Prince Charles and, when that failed, precipitated a disastrous and inconclusive war with Spain. None of these actions endeared the king to Parliament.

When Charles I (*1625–1649) succeeded his father, the antagonism between Parliament and king increased, even though Charles eventually stopped selling titles and cut back on court expenses. Supporting the court was still very expensive, however, because Charles not only entertained thousands of courtiers with masques (court dramas based on mythology or allegory) and plays but also continued to add to the impressive royal collection of Italian and Dutch paintings. The leaders of the House of Commons wanted to reassert Parliament's constitutional claims, and in 1628 they forced Charles to agree to a Petition of Right that outlined the rights of his subjects: the king promised not to levy taxes without parliamentary consent or to imprison critics without good cause. Later that year the duke of Buckingham was assassinated. He had used his position as a favorite of James and then of Charles to add to his relatives' fortunes, and he had encouraged the sale of offices and honors. The assassination devastated Charles. He blamed the leaders of Parliament for it and tried to halt continuing parliamentary agitation about royal policy by refusing to call Parliament between 1629 and 1640. Now the king's ministers had to find every loophole possible to raise revenues without parliamentary action. They tried to turn "ship money," a levy on seaports in times of emergency, into an annual tax collected everywhere in the country. The crown won the ensuing court case, but many subjects still refused to pay what they considered an illegal tax.

Attempting to clamp down, the king's minister Thomas Wentworth, earl of Strafford (1593–1641), and the archbishop of Canterbury, William Laud (1573–1645), initiated a policy called "thorough"—essentially a ruthless effort to use the royal and ecclesiastical courts to reestablish crown control over local affairs. As Wentworth wrote to Laud, "a little violence and extraordinary means" were needed. The religious part of the policy outraged many, especially among the Puritans, who hated Laud for emphasizing the ceremonies and liturgies of the Church of England and making it seem more like Catholicism. Charles married a French Catholic and seemed receptive to a Catholic-Anglican rapprochement. Laud used all available courts, especially the king's personally controlled High Court of Star Chamber, to persecute his Puritan critics—whipping, pillorying, branding them, sometimes even cutting off their ears or splitting their noses. But when Laud tried to apply his policies to Scotland, they backfired completely; the stubborn Presbyterian Scots rioted against the imposition of the Anglican prayer book—the Book of Common Prayer—and in 1640 they invaded northern England. To raise money to fight the war, Charles called Parliament into session. This was a fateful step.

Settlements in the New World

Across the seas in the New World colonies, Europeans experimented with new forms of political and economic authority that would eventually tran.form the populations and even the landscapes of the Americas. The English established precedents for North American colonization when in the 1580s they founded settlements in Ireland by driving the Irish clans from their strongholds and claiming the land for English and Scottish Protestants. When the Irish resisted with guerrilla warfare, English generals waged total war, destroying harvests and burning villages; one lined the path to his headquarters with Irish heads. Declaring the Irish "savages," the English forced them to submit. A few decades later, they would use the same tactics against the "savage" North American natives.

In settling the New World, Europeans acted on political and religious as well as economic motives. At the beginning of the seventeenth century, the English, Dutch, and French began competing with the Spanish and Portuguese in establishing both trading outposts and permanent settlements. Because Spain and Portugal (annexed to Spain between 1580 and 1640) were still the major powers in the New World, other prospective colonizers had to carve niches in seemingly less hospitable places, especially North America, considered inferior to South and Central America.

Governments chartered private joint-stock companies to enrich investors by importing fish, furs, tobacco, and precious metals, if they could be found, and to develop new markets for European products. These efforts were pure mercantilism (government-sponsored policies to increase national wealth). But in New England, religion motivated the Puritan colonists, who sought refuge from religious persecution. Some colonists justified their mission by promising to convert the native population to Christianity. As John Smith told his followers in Virginia, "The gaining provinces addeth to the King's Crown; but the reducing heathen people to civility and true religion bringeth honour to the King of Heaven." The native North Americans, however, resisted conversion to Protestantism much more resolutely than did the Indians of Mexico, Peru, and Canada to Catholicism. Protestantism did not mesh at all with native culture because it demanded a conversion experience based on a Christian notion of sin. Catholicism, in contrast, stressed rituals that were more accessible to the native populations. As a result, France and Spain were more successful in their colonial efforts to convert American natives.

In establishing permanent colonies, the Europeans created whole new communities across the Atlantic. Originally, the warm climate of Virginia made it an attractive spot, but the *Mayflower*, which had sailed for Virginia with its sectarian emigrants,* landed far to the north, near Cape Cod, Massachusetts, where in 1620 the settlers founded New Plymouth Colony. As the religious situation

---

*The "Pilgrim" settlers of Plymouth belonged to a tiny English sect that, unlike the Puritans, attempted to separate from the Church of England.

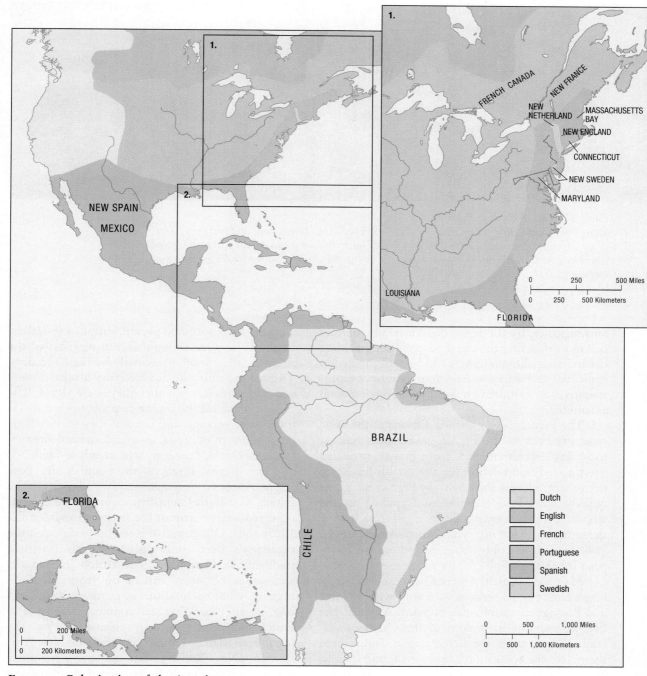

European Colonization of the Americas

for English Puritans worsened, wealthier people became willing to emigrate, and in 1629 a prominent group of Puritans incorporated themselves as the Massachusetts Bay Company. They founded a virtually self-governing colony headquarted in Boston. Migrating settlers, including dissident Puritans, soon founded new settlements in Connecticut and Rhode Island. Catholic refugees from England established a much smaller colony in Maryland, although the colony soon had a Protes-

Paolo Farinati, America, *1595*
Europeans found the "savages" of newly discovered lands fascinating and terrifying and
often described them as cannibals. Here a half-nude Indian seems to have been successfully
converted to Christianity (he holds a crucifix in one hand), but his comrades are roasting
human flesh.

tant majority. By the 1640s the American colonies had more than fifty thousand people—not including the Indians, whose numbers had been decimated in epidemics and wars—and the foundations of representative government in locally chosen colonial assemblies.

The French began settling Canada at the same time, but because the French government refused to let Protestants emigrate from France, it denied itself a ready population for the establishment of permanent colonies abroad. Many French emigrants quickly turned to trapping and trading in the woods, and they were not discouraged from leaving the settlements and marrying Native Americans. In 1640, Canada had only about three thousand European inhabitants.

Mainland North America was not the only target for colonial settlement. Faced with Spanish and Portuguese dominance in South America, the French and English turned to the Caribbean islands. For a while the fierce native Caribs kept them, like the Spanish, off the most fertile islands, but in the 1620s and 1630s they finally occupied St. Kitts (English and French), Barbados (English), Martinique (French), and Guadeloupe (French). The West Indies, as they were called, proved ideal for a plantation economy of tobacco and sugar cane. At first, white indentured servants, bound to

a master for a specified period, supplied the labor; black slaves were brought in during most of the seventeenth century, principally by Dutch traders. Virginia had only one hundred fifty blacks in 1640, and it is not clear whether they were slaves. The earliest black inhabitants were probably treated as indentured servants and freed, if they survived, after a number of years. A trend toward lifelong black servitude, however, was already evident.

The biggest threat to the Spanish and Portuguese came from Dutch traders and pirates. The Dutch West India Company, incorporated in 1621, captured a large strip of the Brazilian coast in the 1620s and 1630s (but lost it in the 1650s), and the company's fleets interrupted Spanish maritime trade in the Caribbean. The Dutch learned the techniques of sugar cultivation from the Portuguese, whose plantations in northern Brazil had become the world's chief source of sugar. The Dutch introduced sugar cultivation to the Caribbean islands. Dutch colonies from New Amsterdam (New York) to Curaçao provided ports for trade, and Dutch fleets carried much of the trade of the English and French colonies, too (including slaves). By the 1650s the English would become so obsessed with Dutch commercial success that they would be willing to go to war to break its hold.

All Coherence Gone: A Clash of World Views

Just as state interests became separated from religious motives and often came to supersede religious alliances, so too did a new secular and scientific attitude challenge religion and the orthodox view of a Judeo-Christian universe. During the late sixteenth and early seventeenth centuries, both art and science began to break some of their bonds with religion. The visual arts, for example, more frequently depicted secular subjects. Gradually, many came to doubt old certainties of an ordered universe, with the earth fixed between heaven and hell. The English poet John Donne (1572–1631) captured the new sense of doubts when he lamented,

> 'Tis all in pieces, all coherence gone,
> All just supply, and all Relation.

Yet traditional attitudes did not wither away. Belief in magic and witches pervaded all levels of society. People of all classes accepted supernatural explanations for natural phenomena and for the ordered universe, now threatened by new scientific and political ideas.

New Relations Expressed in the Arts

Writers, artists, and composers created works that reflected new secular attitudes and contemporary uncertainties about the proper sources of authority. Some of these works appeared in the new permanent professional theater companies of the last quarter of the sixteenth century. In previous centuries, traveling companies made their living by playing at urban religious festivals and by repeating their performances in small towns and villages along the way. In London, Seville, and Madrid, the first professional acting companies performed before paying audiences in the 1570s. A huge outpouring of play writing followed. The Spanish playwright Lope de Vega (1562–1635) alone wrote more than fifteen hundred plays. Between 1580 and 1640, three hundred English playwrights produced works for a hundred different companies of actors. Theaters did a banner business despite Puritan opposition in England and Catholic clerical objections in Spain to performances lacking a clear moral lesson. Puritan denunciations of the theater's "hideous obscenities" and "detestable matchless iniquities" did not stop countless shopkeepers, apprentices, lawyers, and court nobles from crowding into open-air theaters to see everything from bawdy farces to profound tragedies.

The most enduring and influential playwright of the time was the Englishman William Shakespeare (1564–1616), son of a glovemaker, who wrote three dozen plays and acted in one of the chief troupes. Although Shakespeare's plays were not set in contemporary England, they reflected the concerns of his age: the nature of power and the crisis of authority. His greatest tragedies—*Hamlet* (1601), *King Lear* (1605), and *Macbeth* (1606)—show the uncertainty and even chaos that result when power is misappropriated or misused. In each play, family relationships are linked to questions about the legitimacy of government, just as they were for Elizabeth herself. Hamlet's mother marries the man who murdered his royal father and usurped the crown; two of Lear's daughters betray him when he tries to divide his kingdom; Macbeth's wife persuades him to murder the king and seize the throne. Some of Shakespeare's female characters, like Lady Macbeth, are as driven, ambitious, powerful, and tortured as the male protagonists; others, like Queen Gertrude in *Hamlet*, reflect the ambiguity of women in public life—they were not expected to act with authority, and their lives were subject to men's control.

Shakespeare's stories of revenge, exile, political instability, broken families, betrayal, witchcraft, madness, suicide, and murder clearly mirrored the anxieties of the period. One character in the final act describes the tragic story of Hamlet as one "Of carnal, bloody, and unnatural acts; Of accidental judgments, casual slaughters; Of deaths put on by cunning and forced cause." Like many real-life people, Shakespeare's tragic characters found little peace in the turmoil of their times.

New styles of painting reflected such concerns less directly, but they too showed the desire for changed standards. In the late sixteenth century a new artistic style known as Mannerism developed in the Italian states and soon spread across Europe. Mannerism was an almost theatrical style that

Mannerist Painting
El Greco considered The Burial of Count Orgaz *his greatest work. Painted in 1588 for a Spanish Catholic church, it commemorates a local miracle, in which St. Stephen and St. Augustine descended from heaven to lay the Count of Orgaz in his tomb.*

allowed painters to distort perspective to convey a message or emphasize a theme. The great Mannerist painter, a Greek called El Greco, was trained in Venice and Rome before he moved to Spain in the 1570s. His paintings encapsulated the Mannerist style: he crowded figures or objects into every available space, used larger-than-life or elongated figures, and created new and often bizarre visual effects. This style departed abruptly from precise Renaissance perspective. The religious intensity of El Greco's pictures shows that faith still motivated many artists, as it did much political conflict.

The most important new style in seventeenth-century high art was the baroque, which, like Mannerism, originated in the Italian states. As is

the case with many such terms, *baroque* was not used as a label by people living in the seventeenth century; in the eighteenth century, art critics coined the word to mean shockingly bizarre, confused, and extravagant, and until a hundred years ago, art historians and collectors largely disdained the baroque. Stylistically, the baroque rejected Renaissance classicism: in place of the classical emphasis on line, harmonious design, unity, and clarity, the baroque featured curves, exaggerated lighting, intense emotions, release from restraint, and even a kind of artistic sensationalism.

In church architecture and painting the baroque melodramatically reaffirmed the emotional depths of the Catholic faith and glorified both church and monarchy. The Catholic church encouraged the expression of religious feeling through art because its emotional impact helped strengthen the ties between the faithful and the Counter-Reform church. As an urban and spectacular style, the baroque was well suited to public festivities and display. Along with religious festivals, civic processions, and state funerals that served the interests of the church and state, baroque portraits, such as the many portraits of Philip IV by Diego Velázquez, celebrated authority.

Closely tied to the Counter-Reformation, the baroque style spread from Rome to other Italian states and then into central Europe. The Catholic Habsburg territories, including Spain and the Spanish Netherlands, embraced the style. The Spanish built baroque churches in their American colonies as part of a massive conversion campaign. Within Europe, Protestant countries largely resisted the baroque, as we can see by comparing Dutch artists with Flemish painters from the Spanish Netherlands. The first great baroque painter was an Italian-trained Fleming, Peter Paul Rubens (1577–1640). A devout Catholic, Rubens painted vivid, exuberant pictures on religious themes, packed with figures. His was an extension of the theatrical baroque style, conveying ideas through broad gestures and dramatic poses. The great Dutch Protestant painters of the next generation, such as Rembrandt van Rijn (1606–1669), sometimes used Biblical subjects, but their pictures were more realistic and focused on everyday scenes. Many of them suggested the Protestant concern for an inner life and personal faith rather than the public expression of religiosity.

Baroque Painting
With his 2,000 paintings, Rubens defined the new baroque style, which emphasized monumentality, vastness of space, animation, almost violent movement, striking colors, luxury, and spiritual exaltation. As shown in this 1616 painting, The Fall of the Damned, *the baroque was never bland!*

As in the visual arts, differences in musical style during the late sixteenth and early seventeenth centuries reflected religious divisions. The new Protestant churches developed their own distinct music, which differentiated their worship from the Catholic Mass and also marked them as Lutheran or Calvinist. Lutheran composers developed a new form, the strophic hymn, or chorale, a religious text set to a tune that is then enriched through harmony. Calvinist congregations, in keeping with their emphasis on simplicity and austerity, avoided harmony and more often sang in unison, thereby encouraging participation.

A new secular musical form, the opera, grew up parallel to the baroque style in the visual arts.

First influential in the Italian states, opera combined music, drama, dance, and scenery in a grand sensual display, often with themes chosen to please the monarchy and the aristocracy. Operas could be based on typically baroque sacred subjects or on traditional stories. Like Shakespeare, opera composers often turned to familiar stories their audiences would recognize and readily follow. One of the dominant composers of opera—and perhaps the most innovative—was Claudio Monteverdi, whose work contributed to the development of both opera and the orchestra. His first operatic production, *Orfeo* (1607), was the first to require an orchestra of about forty instruments and to include instrumental as well as vocal sections.

The Mechanical Universe

During a time of upheaval and war, a quiet revolution in scientific ideas gathered momentum among Europe's intellectual elite. It would have far-reaching implications. The revolution began with astronomy, in debates over the motion of the heavens. In 1543, Nicolaus Copernicus had argued that the earth and planets revolved around the sun and could be analyzed mathematically. Most important was the Copernican notion that the sun, not the earth, was the center of the universe, an assertion that challenged long-established ancient and religious claims.

Motion provided the key to this new science. Since Aristotle, scientists had upheld the ancient view that objects in their natural state were at rest; now it appeared that motion, not rest, was the natural order of the universe. If so, then the same principles of mechanical movement might be common not only in everyday events like the fall of an object but also to such less-evident phenomena as the movement of the planets or the collisions of the tiniest particles of matter. The idea that the whole universe operated mechanically and predictably profoundly threatened established Christian beliefs, especially because Catholic doctrine held that the heavens were perfect and unchanging while the earth was "corrupted." The new science of motion erased this distinction, making all motion the same. If all nature partook of the motion of particles, then science might explain the movement of objects and inner workings of animals and humans—perhaps even the actions of states.

Despite their implications, Copernicus's views aroused little opposition during the latter half of the sixteenth century. A notable exception was the Italian monk Giordano Bruno (1548–1600), who taught Copernican theory all over Europe and extended its logic by arguing for an infinite universe; the Inquisition arrested him and burned him at the stake. As time passed, astronomers gathering new data on celestial motion became increasingly uncertain about the virtues of the Ptolemaic theory that the sun revolved around the earth. At the beginning of the seventeenth century, the Ptolemaic system began to crumble beneath the work of the German Johannes Kepler (1571–1630) and the Italian Galileo Galilei (1564–1642). Kepler followed Copernicus in asserting that mathematics could describe the movements of the heavens, and between 1609 and 1619 he published his three laws of planetary motion. Kepler's laws provided mathematical backing for the Copernican view—the heliocentric, or sun-centered, system—and directly challenged the claim long held, even by Copernicus, that planetary motion is circular. Kepler's first law stated that the orbits of the planets are ellipses, with the sun always at one focus of the ellipse.

Galileo provided the critical evidence to support the Copernican view. This Italian scholar had already designed a military compass when he heard in 1609 that two Dutch astronomers had built a telescope. He quickly made an even better one and published his findings for all the world to read. Using the telescope, he observed the moon, Jupiter's four satellites, the phases of Venus, and sunspots; his findings led him to dismiss the Ptolemaic system. The planets and the sun were no more perfect than the earth, he realized, and other planets also had moons. Galileo described the earth as a moving part of a larger system, which the Copernican view described more accurately.

Galileo then tried to make a connection between planetary motion and motion on earth. The Aristotelian view that a body's natural state is at rest meant that it must constantly be pushed to keep moving. Galileo insisted that a body would keep moving as long as nothing stopped its motion. Galileo's new way of thinking about bodies in motion would be crucial for the later theories of Sir Isaac Newton. He imagined geometrical bodies moving in absolutely empty space. This leap required abstract reasoning beyond the observation of natural phenomena and made mathematics the vehicle for scientific explanation. As Galileo wrote:

Philosophy is written in this grand book, the universe, which stands continually open to our gaze. But the book cannot be understood unless one first learns to comprehend the language and read the letters in which it is composed. It is written in the language of mathematics, and its characters are triangles, circles, and other geometric figures without which it is humanly impossible to understand a single word of it; without these, one wanders about in a dark labyrinth.

With this new mathematical language—and by implication, without the aid of the Bible or the church—people could understand God's creation.

To reach a lay audience, Galileo published his views in Italian rather than Latin. He appealed to the merchants and aristocrats of Florence by arguing that the new science was useful for everyday projects and by using comparisons to accounting and commercial exchanges. The new science, he insisted, suited "the minds of the wise" (whether lay or clerical) but not "the shallow minds of the common people." If the Bible were wrong about motion in the universe, the error was that the Scriptures used common language to appeal to the lower orders. The Catholic church responded quickly to Galileo's challenge. In 1616 the church forbade him to teach that the earth moves and in 1633 accused him of not obeying the earlier order. Forced to appear before the Inquisition, he agreed to publicly recant his assertion that the earth moved to save himself from torture and death. Afterward he lived under house arrest and could publish his work only in the Dutch Republic, which had become a haven for scientists and thinkers. Scientific research, like economic growth, would come to be centered in the northern, Protestant countries, where it was less constrained by church control.

Scientific Method

Despite the opposition of the Catholic church and of clergy of various faiths, the intellectual elite in the 1630s began to accept the Copernican view. Ancient learning, the churches and their theologians, and even cherished popular beliefs seemed to be undermined by a new standard of truth based on systematic observation, experiments, and rational deduction. Two men were chiefly responsible for spreading the prestige of the scientific method beyond the realm of science into the intellectual mainstream: the English writer and politician Sir Francis Bacon (1561–1626) and the French mathematician and philosopher René Descartes (1596–1650). Respectively, they represented the two essential halves of scientific method: inductive reasoning through observation and experimental research, and deductive reasoning from self-evident principles.

In *The Advancement of Learning* (1605), Bacon attacked reliance on ancient writers. The minds of the medieval scholars, he said, had been "shut up in the cells of a few authors (chiefly Aristotle, their dictator) as their persons were shut up in the cells of monasteries and colleges," and they could therefore produce only "cobwebs of learning" that were "of no substance or profit." Advancement would take place only through the collection, comparison, and analysis of information. Knowledge, in Bacon's view, must be empirically based (that is, gained by observation). Although not a scientist, Bacon supported the scientific method over popular beliefs, which he rejected as "fables and popular errors." Claiming that God had called the Catholic church "to account for their degenerate manners and ceremonies," Bacon looked to the English state, which he served as lord chancellor, and to the Protestant Reformation for evidence of rational principles in action.

Descartes, a French Catholic who served in the Thirty Years' War, also espoused rationality, but, unlike Bacon, he sought to test accepted doctrine with mathematical principles. Descartes agreed with Bacon's denunciation of traditional learning, but he argued for reliance on mathematics and logic (deductive method) rather than experiments (inductive method). His major contribution to mathematics was the invention of analytic geometry. Descartes aimed to establish science on philosophical foundations that would secure the authority of both church and state, yet he was so worried about the consequences of his work that he chose to move to the more hospitable atmosphere of the Dutch Republic.

In his *Discourse on Method* (1637), which became the most important piece of propaganda for the new methods of learning, Descartes argued—in French, not Latin—for a rational, deductive model of scientific knowledge, in which mathematical and mechanical principles would provide the way to understand all of nature, including the actions of people and states. Prior assumptions and ancient writings must be repudiated in favor of "the human will operating according to reason." Begin with the simple and go on to the complex, he asserted, and believe only those ideas that present themselves "clearly and distinctly." Descartes believed that rational individuals would see the necessity of strong state power and that only "meddling and restless spirits" would plot against it. Descartes insisted that human reason could not only unravel the secrets of nature but also prove the existence of God. Nevertheless, his books were banned in many places.

Ultimately, scientific method combined both experiment and deductive reason. The new understanding of motion, both in the heavens and on earth, soon had important applications in such fields as navigation, cartography, mechanics, ballistics, fortification, surveying, and even astrology. Startling discoveries took place in medicine, too, especially Englishman William Harvey's demonstration of the circulation of blood (1628). The heart, according to Harvey, was "a piece of machinery." The body too was part of the mechanical universe.

Magic and Witchcraft

Despite the new emphasis on clear reasoning, observation, and independence from past authorities, science had not yet become as separate from magic as might be expected. Many scholars studied alchemy along with physics. Elizabeth I maintained a court astrologer who was also a serious mathematician, and many writers distinguished between "natural magic," which was close to experimental science, and evil "black magic." One of the leading astronomers of the time, Tycho Brahe (1546–1601), defended his studies of alchemy and astrology as part of natural magic. For many of the greatest minds, magic and science were still closely linked.

In a world in which most people believed in astrology, magical healing, divination, prophecy, and ghosts, we should not be surprised that many of Europe's learned people also firmly believed in witchcraft. The same Jean Bodin who argued against religious fanaticism insisted on death for

**David Teniers the Younger,
Witches' Sabbath, c. 1650**
*This painting captures
many of the popular
views about female
witches, including their
alliance with the devil
and with the devil's
strange, monstrous
troupe of followers.*

witches—and even for those who did not believe in the dangers of witches. In France alone, 345 books and pamphlets on witchcraft appeared between 1550 and 1650. Witchcraft trials peaked in Europe between 1560 and 1640, the very time of the celebrated breakthroughs of the new science. Many people, including state officials, lawyers, and judges, believed that scientific reasoning confirmed the existence and danger of witches. Montaigne was one of the few notable people to speak out against executing accused witches: "It is taking one's conjectures rather seriously to roast someone alive for them," he wrote in 1580.

Belief in witches was not new in the sixteenth century. Witches had long been thought capable of almost anything: passing through walls, traveling through the air, destroying crops, and causing personal catastrophes from miscarriages to demonic possession. What was new was the official persecution of witches, justified by the notion that witches were agents of Satan whom the righteous must oppose. In a time of economic crisis, plague, warfare, and the clash of religious differences, witchcraft trials provided an outlet for social stress and anxiety, legitimated by state power. At the same time, the trials seem to have been part of the religious reform movement itself. In much of Europe the

spread of the trials coincided with the arrival of reform-minded clergy, whether Protestant or Catholic.

The victims of the persecution were overwhelmingly female; 80 percent of the accused witches in about one hundred thousand trials in Europe and North America during the sixteenth and seventeenth centuries were women. About a third were sentenced to death. Before 1400 (when witchcraft trials were rare), nearly half of those accused had been men. Some historians argue that this gender difference indicates that the trials expressed a hatred of women that came to a head during conflicts over the Reformation. Official descriptions of witchcraft oozed lurid details of sexual orgies, incest, homosexuality, and cannibalism, in which women acted as the devil's sexual slaves. Catholic and Protestant reforming clergy attacked the presumably wild and undisciplined sexuality of women as the most obvious manifestation of popular unruliness, peasant superstitiousness, and heretical tendencies. Lawyers and judges followed their lead.

Although people of any social station might be accused of witchcraft, those of certain social groups repeatedly found themselves on trial. Among the most commonly accused were beggar women. The accusers were almost always better off than those they accused, and they seem to have reacted out of a sense of guilt for having been slow to respond to pleas for charity. Because elderly spinsters and widows were often poor, perceived as socially marginal, and thus thought likely to hanker after revenge on those more fortunate, they were far more likely to be accused. Another com-

monly accused woman was the midwife, who was a prime target for suspicion in a time when childbirth was dangerous and frightening and medical care rudimentary at best. Although sometimes venerated for their special skill, midwives also numbered among the thousands of largely powerless women persecuted for their imagined consorting with the devil.

CONCLUSION

The witchcraft persecutions underscore the trauma that characterized these times. The trials took place all over Europe (and later in parts of North America), but they concentrated especially in the German lands of the Holy Roman Empire, an area of great religious division and the cockpit of the Thirty Years' War. Constant religious conflicts, marauding armies, escalating demands for new taxes, economic decline, disease, and sometimes starvation shattered the lives of many ordinary Europeans. In response to the uncertainties of the age, some people blamed the poor widow or the upstart midwife for their problems; others joined desperate revolts; still others left for more fortunate spots or emigrated overseas. A few among the literate elite began to look to the new science for a sense of certainty and order in a time of turmoil.

Out of the chaos and sense of crisis emerged several new patterns that had important long-term effects. The balance of political and economic power shifted from the Mediterranean world to the north—primarily to France and the Dutch Republic. Many Europeans now wanted governments that would maintain internal peace, even if it meant losing absolute religious uniformity. The growing disengagement of political motives from religious ones did not mean that violence or conflict had ended, but it did strengthen the rulers' power. An expanded scale of warfare required more state involvement. The growth of state power directly changed the lives of ordinary people; more men went into the armies and most families paid more taxes. This extension of state power was only just beginning; it would be one of the chief factors that defined the modern world, even into the twentieth century.

SUGGESTIONS FOR FURTHER READING

Source Materials

Drake, Stillman, ed. *Discoveries and Opinions of Galileo.* 1957. Translations with excellent introductions to some of Galileo's most important works on the new science.

Kors, Alan C., and Edward Peters. *Witchcraft in Europe, 1100–1700: A Documentary History.* 1972. Original documents from all over Europe including selections from trial transcripts.

Rabb, Theodore K. *The Thirty Years' War.* 2d ed. 1972. A useful collection of differing views of historians and participants.

Interpretive Studies

Ashton, Trevor H., ed. *Crisis in Europe.* 1965. Still the best collection of essays on the interrelated aspects of the seventeenth-century crises.

Bonney, Richard. *The European Dynastic States, 1494–1660.* 1991. Provides a good overview of social and economic developments as well.

Braudel, Fernand. *The Mediterranean and the Mediterranean World in the Age of Philip the Second.* 2 vols. Translated by Siân Reynolds. 1972–1973. A very influential view of the long-term development of the Mediterranean region.

Buisseret, David. *Henry IV.* 1984. A readable biography of the French king.

Davis, Natalie Zemon. *Society and Culture in Early Modern France.* 1975. An anthropologically informed set of essays on social and cultural life that includes pathbreaking work on women's participation in French Protestantism.

De Vries, Jan. *The Economy of Europe in an Age of Crisis, 1600–1750.* 1976. An excellent and thorough overview of the economic crisis.

Elliot, J. H. *Richelieu and Olivares.* 1984. A brief, readable comparative study of two great statesmen from France and Spain.

Hall, A. Rupert. *From Galileo to Newton.* Rev. ed. 1981. A clearly written history of the major scientific break-throughs and their significance.

Jacob, Margaret C. *The Cultural Meaning of the Scientific Revolution.* 1988. Includes excellent chapters on the social context of the scientific revolution.

Levack, Brian P. *The Witch-hunt in Early Modern Europe.* 1987. Synthesizes research on the witchcraft persecutions.

Limm, Peter. *The Thirty Years' War.* 1984. Includes documents as well as reviews of controversies about the war.

Lynch, John. *Spain Under the Habsburgs.* Vol. 1, *Empire and Absolutism: 1516–1598.* 1964. A solid, thorough account of Spain under Philip II.

Mattingly, Garrett. *The Armada.* 1959. Describes the decisive sea battle between the English and the Spanish with grace and verve.

Mitterauer, Michael, and Reinhard Sieder. *The European Family: Patriarchy to Partnership from the Middle Ages to the Present.* Translated by Karla Oosterveen and Manfred Hörzinger. 1982. A summary of modern research in family history, especially in eastern Europe.

Morse, David. *England's Time of Crisis: From Shakespeare to Milton.* 1989. A cultural history of England that links the most important writings of the time to polit-ical events.

Parker, David. *The Making of French Absolutism.* 1983. An excellent introduction to the origins of the French absolutist state; concentrates on the period from the religious wars to Louis XIV.

Parker, Geoffrey. *Europe in Crisis, 1598–1648.* 1979. The best one-volume textbook on the first half of the seventeenth century.

———. *The Military Revolution: Military Innovation and the Rise of the West, 1500–1800.* 1988. A cogent overview of the military revolution with an interesting emphasis on its effects on the colonies.

Parker, Geoffrey, and Lesley M. Smith. eds. *The General Crisis of the Seventeenth Century.* 1978. A collection of essays by specialists who critically examine the idea of a "general crisis" in the seventeenth century.

Parry, J. H. *The Age of Reconnaissance.* 1981. A useful and concise overview of the early colonies in the New World.

Redondi, Pietro. *Galileo, Heretic.* Translated by Raymond Rosenthal. 1987. A fascinating and controversial piece of detective work that uncovers the Catholic church's reasons for condemning Galileo.

Skinner, Quentin. *The Foundations of Modern Political Thought.* Vol. 2, *The Age of Reformation.* 1978. A new interpretation of the origins of constitutionalism in Reformation writings about the right of resistance.

Strong, Roy. *The Cult of Elizabeth: Elizabethan Portraiture and Pageantry.* 1977. A copiously illustrated analysis of the use of court ritual to emphasize royal power.

Thomas, Keith. *Religion and the Decline of Magic.* 1971. A fascinating and rich description of beliefs in magic and witchcraft in England.

Thornton, John. *Africa and Africans in the Making of the Atlantic World, 1400–1680.* 1992. The early history of relations between Africans and Europeans.

In August 1641 an anonymous tract denouncing women preachers appeared in England. It ridiculed them as "bibbing Gossips" and a "brazen-faced, strange, new Feminine Brood." The very idea of women preaching in their own homes, in barns, or in churches disturbed the person who wrote the tract; but what dismayed the author even more was that the women's sermons took a determined Puritan stance. Susan May, for example, preached "that the Devill was the father of the Pope, the Pope the father of those which did weare Surplices [a flowing gown clergymen wore, typical of the "frills" the Puritans wanted to eliminate in worship], wherefore consequently the Devill was the Father of all those which did not love Puritans."

Female preachers emerged in 1641 as part of the mid-seventeenth-century revolution in England. The revolution challenged a political and social order that had been largely unaffected by the Thirty Years' War, which dragged on in continental Europe until 1648. Popular uprisings confronted many European governments, but only England executed a king. The turmoil in England proved to be the most striking instance of a broad challenge to traditional authorities. State and religious institutions found their legitimacy disputed, as Europeans questioned traditional relations between women and men, church and community, and ruler and subjects.

Eventually the European states reasserted their power, and by the end of the seventeenth century almost all had some form of strong central government. Church and state now cooperated in the attempt to instill social and political discipline, and rulers devised ways to accommodate social elites, who had

Rebellion and State Building, 1640–1690

Judith and Her Maidservant, 1613–1614
This painting by Artemisia Gentileschi tells the legend of Judith, who stole into the enemy's camp and decapitated the Assyrian general Holofernes. Despite the obstacles facing women who would be artists, Gentileschi gained entrance to the Academy of Design in Florence and later painted for King Charles I.

stirred up so much trouble during the mid-century revolts. Kings and clergy worked together to control those whom they saw as backward and barbarous; they expected the lower classes to remain docile and to defer to their "betters." States demonstrated their authority through military drills and court manners and by regulating public behavior and maintaining a social hierarchy.

The English Revolution and Its Legacy

In England, aristocrats and commoners alike resisted the growth of monarchical power. Insisting that he ruled by divine right, Charles I (✳1625–1649) had refused to convene Parliament since 1629 and tried to collect revenues by other means. When he finally did summon Parliament in 1640 in order to raise money, he opened the door to a constitutional and religious crisis. Within two years, Charles was at war with Parliament, and all relations of authority came into question. Out of that struggle emerged striking new doctrines about the constitutional rights of citizens and the foundations of state power.

Civil War as Impetus for Change

The Parliament of 1640 did not intend revolution, but parliamentary reformers in the House of Commons wanted to undo what they saw as the royal tyranny of the 1630s. The architects of Charles's most unpopular policies were imprisoned or executed, and Parliament abolished the Court of Star Chamber, repealed recently levied taxes, and provided for a parliamentary assembly at least once every three years, thus establishing a check on royal authority. Moderate reformers expected to stop there and resisted Puritan pressure to abolish bishops and eliminate the Anglican prayer book.

The Puritans themselves were divided between the Presbyterians, who wanted a Calvinist church with some central authority, and the Independents, who favored entirely autonomous congregations free from other church government. The questions of religious and parliamentary authority came to a head in January 1642, when Charles and his soldiers

> ## IMPORTANT DATES
>
> **1640** Revolts against the Spanish crown in Catalonia and Portugal
>
> **1642** Beginning of civil war between King Charles I and Parliament in England
>
> **1648** Peace of Westphalia ends the Thirty Years' War (1618–1648); coalition of opponents makes war on French minister Mazarin in revolt called the Fronde; Ukrainian Cossack warriors revolt against the king of Poland-Lithuania, opening "the Deluge"
>
> **1649** Execution of Charles I of England by order of Parliament; new Russian legal code establishes a fixed social hierarchy assigning all subjects to a hereditary class
>
> **1660** Charles II restored to the English crown
>
> **1672** French begin war against the Dutch
>
> **1682** Louis XIV of France moves into Versailles
>
> **1683** The Austrian Habsburgs break the Turkish siege of Vienna
>
> **1685** Louis XIV revokes the Edict of Nantes and forces French Protestants to convert to Catholicism
>
> **1688** Parliament deposes James II and invites William of Orange and his English wife Mary to take the English throne
>
> **1689** William and Mary agree to a Bill of Rights and to toleration of all Protestant sects

invaded Parliament and tried unsuccessfully to arrest those leaders in the House of Commons who wished to curb his power. Faced with mounting opposition within London, Charles quickly withdrew from the city and organized an army.

For two years the king's army of royalists (known as Cavaliers) gathered supporters and maintained control in northern and western England. The parliamentary forces (called Roundheads because they cut their hair short) built up strength in the southeast. Putting aside their differences, the Puritans united under an obscure member of the House of Commons, the country gentleman Oliver Cromwell (1599–1658), who sympathized with the Independents. After Cromwell skillfully reorganized the parliamentary troops, his New Model Army defeated the Cavaliers at the battle of Naseby in 1645. Charles surrendered in 1646.

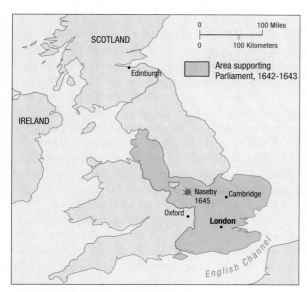

England During the Civil War

Oliver Cromwell
This contemporary engraving is filled with the religious and political allegories favored by the Puritans. Cromwell tramples the monstrous figures of Faction and Religious Error. On the right, the three kingdoms of England, Scotland, and Ireland offer him wreaths.

As in all subsequent revolutions, uncertainty about power at the top of society opened the way to political movements from below. Charles's capture settled nothing at first because the parliamentary side remained divided: the Presbyterians dominated Parliament, and the Independents controlled the army. Both factions' leaders belonged to the social and political elite, but the Independents were more tolerant of religious diversity. Advocating decentralized religious authority in the congregation (hence the term *congregationalism,* often associated with the Independents), they were also willing to consider more far-reaching political and social changes than the Presbyterians, who were nervous about radical ideas, especially notions of social equality that developed during the civil war.

Other groups drawn especially from the lower classes questioned the leadership of both Presbyterians and Independents. The most influential such group, the Levellers, emerged among disgruntled soldiers when Parliament tried to disband the New Model Army. Many soldiers refused to go home; some officers joined them; and a portion of the New Model Army soon challenged its Independent leaders. In 1647 the Levellers honed their ideas in a series of debates between soldiers and officers at an army camp near London. Here the Levellers insisted that Parliament should meet annually, that its members be paid so as to allow common people to participate, and that all male heads of households

be allowed to vote. At issue was a rudimentary democracy that excluded servants, the propertyless, and women but nonetheless "leveled" social differences.

Many artisans, shopkeepers, and modest farmers from the army's rank and file supported the Levellers, as did some of London's poor. Cromwell and the other army leaders rejected the Levellers' demands as threatening to property owners. Cromwell insisted, "You have no other way to deal with these men but to break them in pieces. . . . If you do not break them they will break you."

New religious sects grew out of the debate over church organization. These sects had in common only their emphasis on the "inner light" of individual religious inspiration and a disdain for hier-

A Quaker Meeting in England
Like other Christian sects of the period, the Quakers emphasized a less hierarchical organization than that of the Church of England. In this satirical print from the seventeenth century, a woman is shown preaching at a Quaker meeting.

archical authority. They appealed to the middle and lower classes because they stressed equality before God and democracy within the church. The Baptists, for example, insisted on adult baptism because they believed that Christians should choose their own church and that every child should not automatically become a member of the Church of England. The Quakers demonstrated their beliefs in equality and the inner light by refusing to doff their hats to men in authority or to swear oaths. They also undermined ministers' authority by asserting that the only justification for preaching was a direct experience of God's voice. Manifesting their religious experience by trembling, or "quaking," the Quakers believed that anyone so inspired could preach.

Other sects advocated even more sweeping political change. The Diggers promoted rural com-

munal living and collective ownership of all property. The Fifth Monarchists revolted because they thought the reign of Christ was imminent. Seekers and Ranters questioned just about everything. One notorious Ranter, John Robins, claimed to be God.

In keeping with their notions of equality and individual inspiration, the sects provided opportunities for women to become preachers and prophets. Of more than three hundred women prophets in the 1640s, two hundred twenty were Quakers. The Quakers thought women especially capable of prophecy. One prophet, Anna Trapnel, explained her vocation: "For in all that was said by me, I was nothing, the Lord put all in my mouth, and told me what I should say." When local officials accused her of being a witch, the ordinary people, whom she called "the rude multitude," defended her.

Parliamentary and army leaders feared the prospect of political and social anarchy that the new sects seemed to present; the outspoken women among them underscored the threat of a world turning upside down. Rumors abounded, for example, of naked Quakers running through the streets waiting "for a sign." A few men advocated free love. The Duchess of Newcastle complained in 1650 that women were "affecting a Masculinacy . . . practicing the behaviour . . . of men." Women presented petitions, participated prominently in street demonstrations, distributed tracts, and occasionally even dressed as men, wearing swords and joining armies. These developments convinced the political elite that tolerating the sects would lead to skepticism, atheism, anarchism, and debauchery.

From Cromwell's Rule to the Restoration

At the heart of the continuing political struggle was the question of the king, who tried to negotiate with the Presbyterians in Parliament. In late 1648, troops commanded by Colonel Thomas Pride excluded the Presbyterians from Parliament, leaving a "rump" of about seventy members, most of them Independents who supported the army. After Pride's Purge, the Rump Parliament created a high court to try Charles. The court found the king guilty of attempting to establish "an unlimited and tyrannical power" and pronounced a death sentence. On January 30, 1649, Charles was beheaded before an enormous crowd, which reportedly groaned as one when the axe fell. Although many English had objected to Charles's autocratic rule, few had contemplated executing a king. For royalists, Charles immediately became a martyr, and reports of miracles, such as the curing of blindness by the touch of a handkerchief soaked in his blood, soon circulated.

The Rump Parliament abolished the monarchy and the House of Lords and set up a Council of State with Oliver Cromwell as its first chairman. Although the commonwealth government was technically a republic in that it had no monarch, it was really a military regime. The army had purged Parliament, and Parliament's future depended on the army and its leader, Cromwell, a Puritan, who saw the hand of God in events and himself as God's agent.

Cromwell tolerated no opposition. When his agents discovered plans for mutinies within the army, they executed the perpetrators; and new decrees silenced the Levellers. Although Cromwell allowed the sects to worship rather freely and permitted Jews with needed skills to return to England for the first time since the thirteenth century, Catholics could not worship publicly, nor could Anglicans use the *Book of Common Prayer*. The elites—many of them still Anglican—were troubled by Cromwell's toleration of the sects but pleased to see some social order reestablished.

The new regime waged war even more vigorously than had the Stuart kings. The bloodiest conflict broke out in Ireland, where anti-English rebels had been in revolt since 1641, emboldened by the troubles between king and Parliament. As Irish Catholics continually attacked Scottish and English Protestant settlers, who retaliated when they could, thousands died. Finally, in 1649, Cromwell went to Ireland with a large force and easily defeated the rebels, massacring whole garrisons and their priests. Ten years of fighting, crop burning, famine, and plague reduced the Irish population of about 1.4 million by tens, perhaps hundreds, of thousands. Cromwell encouraged expropriating the lands of the Irish "barbarous wretches," and Scottish immigrants resettled the northern county of Ulster. English conquest left a legacy of bitterness that the Irish even today call "the curse of Cromwell."

Despite the civil strife, England steadily improved its international position. Cromwell conquered Scotland in 1650–1651, hoping to capture Prince Charles, son of the dead king. Pursuing the mercantilist policy that was increasingly dominant in Europe, by which the state regulated and supervised its businesses to protect the nation's commercial interests, Parliament passed the first Navigation Act in 1651. It forbade importing goods from Asia, Africa, or the Americas on ships not owned by the English or by the people sending or producing the cargo. The Navigation Act was aimed at the Dutch, against whom the English waged a naval war from 1652 to 1654.

At home, however, Cromwell faced growing resistance. His aggressive foreign policy required a budget twice the size of Charles I's, and he regularly quarreled with Parliament. The increase in property taxes and customs duties alienated landowners and merchants. The conflict reached a crisis in 1653; Parliament considered disbanding the army, whereupon Cromwell abolished the Rump Parliament in a military coup and made himself Lord Protector. During the final session, Cromwell attacked various members as corrupt men, drunkards, and whoremasters and insisted, "It's you that have forced me to do this."

Cromwell silenced his critics by banning newspapers and using networks of spies and mail readers to keep tabs on his enemies, but he did not institute a realistic alternative to monarchical rule. Although he assumed some trappings of royalty, he refused the crown. When he died in 1658, he intended that his son should succeed him, but his passing only revived the prospect of civil war and political chaos. A Scottish general marched his army south to restore order, and a newly elected Parliament invited Charles II (∗1660–1685) to return from exile. Most English welcomed him back. According to one royalist, "The ways were strewed with flowers, the bells ringing, the streets hung with tapestry, fountains running with wine."

The new regime whisked away the Puritan culture of introspective austerity. The restoration of old traditions of celebration—drinking, merrymaking, processions of young maidens in royalist colors—made one Puritan complain, "May-poles and players, and jugglers . . . now pass current." The traditional monarchical form of government was reinstated as well, but without the Court of Star Chamber so hated by critics of Charles I. Charles II also promised "a liberty to tender consciences" in an attempt to extend religious toleration, especially to Catholics, with whom he sympathized. Yet more than a thousand Puritan ministers lost their positions, and after 1664 attending a service other than one conforming with the Anglican prayer book was illegal.

The restored monarchy brought back order through central authority but could not prevent natural disasters like the plague, which appeared in London's rat-infested streets in May 1665 and claimed more than thirty thousand victims by September. Then in 1666 the Great Fire swept the city. Diarist Samuel Pepys described its terrifying progress: "It made me weep to see it. The churches, houses, and all on fire and flaming at once, and a horrid noise the flames made, and the cracking of houses at their ruine." The crown now had a city as well as a monarchy to rebuild.

Critical Responses to Revolution and Restoration

The English revolution prompted a major rethinking of the foundations of all authority. One of the greatest English men of letters was John Milton (1608–1674), a Puritan who defended personal liberty and individual conscience against state limitations. Because he denied that human goodness could be legislated, he opposed government limits on the free expression of ideas. In 1643 his writings in favor of divorce offended many in Parliament. When Parliament enacted a censorship law aimed at such literature, Milton responded in 1644 with the powerful defense of liberty of the press, *Areopagitica.* As secretary to the Council of State during Cromwell's rule, Milton had ample opportunity to witness the difficulties of basing a government on civil and religious liberty.

After 1660, Milton (now suffering total blindness) became a protesting voice in the wilderness against the restored monarchy. He had earned Charles II's enmity by writing a justification for the killing of his father, Charles I, based on Biblical precedents. In forced retirement, Milton published his epic poem *Paradise Lost* (1667), in which he used Adam and Eve's Fall to meditate on human freedom and the tragedies of rebellion and to "justify the ways of God to man." He personified evil in the compelling—almost heroic—figure of Satan, the proud angel who challenges God. In the end, Adam and Eve learn to accept moral responsibility and face the world "all before them."

The royalist Thomas Hobbes (1588–1679) responded less optimistically to the revolution. His masterpiece, *Leviathan* (1651), argued for unlimited authority in a ruler—either a king or a parliament. Yet neither side in the civil war welcomed his views. Hobbes enraged royalists by arguing that the basis of rule was not divine right but society's surrendering of rights to an all-controlling power, the Leviathan. Parliamentarians were alarmed by Hobbes's insistence that rulers must possess complete authority to prevent the greater evil of anarchy.

Hobbes sat out the English civil war in France, where he tutored the future king Charles II. Returning to England in 1651, he faced continued attacks for what many considered his cynical view of human nature. To Hobbes, human life in a state of nature—that is, any situation without firm authority—was "solitary, poor, nasty, brutish, and short." Desire for power and natural greed lead to unfettered competition. Only the assurance of social order makes people secure enough to act according to law, and consequently, giving up personal liberty is the price of collective security. Rulers thus derive their power from a contract in which absolute authority protects people's rights.

Hobbes's notion of rule by an absolute authority left no room for the political dissent or nonconformity Milton so prized. Believing that people are essentially self-centered and driven by the "right to self-preservation," Hobbes argued his case referring not to religion but to science. Like Francis Bacon, he insisted on careful observation and logical inquiry, and his work illustrates the importance of science in providing a new coherence for the social and political order.

Revolt as the Cost of War and Peace

Unlike England, where long-standing religious and political differences exploded in civil war only in the 1640s, continental Europe had been fighting over religion since the sixteenth century. Now exhausted by the death and destruction of the Thirty Years' War, the people of central and western Europe hungered for peace and stability. Yet international peace settlements did not bring automatic tranquility to the home front.

Of the principal contestants in the Thirty Years' War, debt-shackled Spain cracked first.

Revolts shook the Spanish monarchy's grip on Portugal and Catalonia in 1640. In 1643, Spanish troops suffered their first major defeat at French hands. Five years later, in 1648, the Thirty Years' War ended with the Peace of Westphalia, which acknowledged a shifting balance of power. Spain finally recognized Dutch independence. The states that had sponsored the war, however, teetered on the edge of bankruptcy and social chaos. Revolt spread to France in 1648. Even so, war between France and Spain dragged on until 1659, with neither willing to concede international dominance.

Revolts Against the Spanish Crown

Insisting that Catalonia (the far northeastern province) provide more men and supplies to Spain's war effort against France than it had in the past, Count-Duke Olivares (1587–1645) ignited a Catalan revolt. Catalonia was essential to Olivares's strategy because it lay on the border with hostile France. In 1640 the Catalan peasants rebelled, chasing the royal army to the coast and overrunning Barcelona, where they sacked the homes of royal officials and killed the viceroy. Olivares himself called the uprising "as complete a rebellion as Holland."

Iberia

The Catalan peasants resented government confiscation of their crops and animals and refused to billet the Italian mercenaries and Castilian soldiers forced upon them. Seeing their chance in the breakdown of central authority, the Portuguese, too, revolted in 1640, and rebels assassinated Olivares's principal agent in Portugal and proclaimed independence under the duke of Braganza (King John IV, *1640–1656). Of the year 1640, Olivares wrote that "in many centuries there cannot have been a more unlucky year than the present one." Faced with these policy failures and with resistance even in the king's court, Olivares resigned in 1643. The Spanish monarchy's troubles continued, however, when in 1647, Sicily and Naples revolted against the government of their Spanish viceroys to protest tax increases.

Despite its weaknesses, the Spanish crown maintained its position because none of the rebelling provinces was willing to cooperate with the others; each wanted its own autonomy. Conceding Portugal (a province only since 1580) its independence and quickly suppressing the revolts in the Italian states, the government again turned its attention to Catalonia. Here the rebels fell to feuding with each other, and the nobles, fearing the consequences of peasant revolts, sought Spanish royal protection. In 1652, Barcelona surrendered. The kingdom of Spain survived, though it lost extensive territory. In the Treaty of the Pyrenees (1659), which ended the war between Spain and France, Spain gave up lands north and east of the Pyrenees and much of Flanders in the Spanish Netherlands. In 1660, Philip IV had his daughter Maria Theresa married to Louis XIV of France, thus forging a new dynastic alliance between the two states.

The Peace of Westphalia and a New Balance of Power

In the 1640s peace negotiations eventually brought together all of the participants in the Thirty Years' War: Bavaria, Brandenburg, Denmark, the Dutch Republic, France, the Holy Roman Empire, Saxony, Spain, Sweden, and Switzerland. The comprehensive settlement provided by the Peace of Westphalia—named after the German province where negotiations took place—would long serve as a model for resolving conflict among warring European states. For the first time, a diplomatic congress addressed international disputes, and the signatories to the treaties guaranteed the resulting settlement. A method still in use, the congress was the first to bring *all* parties together, rather than two or three at a time.

The peace acknowledged the winners and losers in the Thirty Years' War. France and Sweden gained the most. France acquired Alsace, and Sweden took several northern territories from the Holy Roman Empire. The Habsburgs lost the most. The Spanish Habsburgs recognized Dutch independence after eighty years of war. Sensing the precarious position of the Austrian Habsburg emperor, the Swiss Confederation and the German princes demanded autonomy from the Holy Roman Empire. Each German prince gained the right to permit Lutheranism, Catholicism, or Calvinism in his state, a right denied to Calvinists in 1555 by the

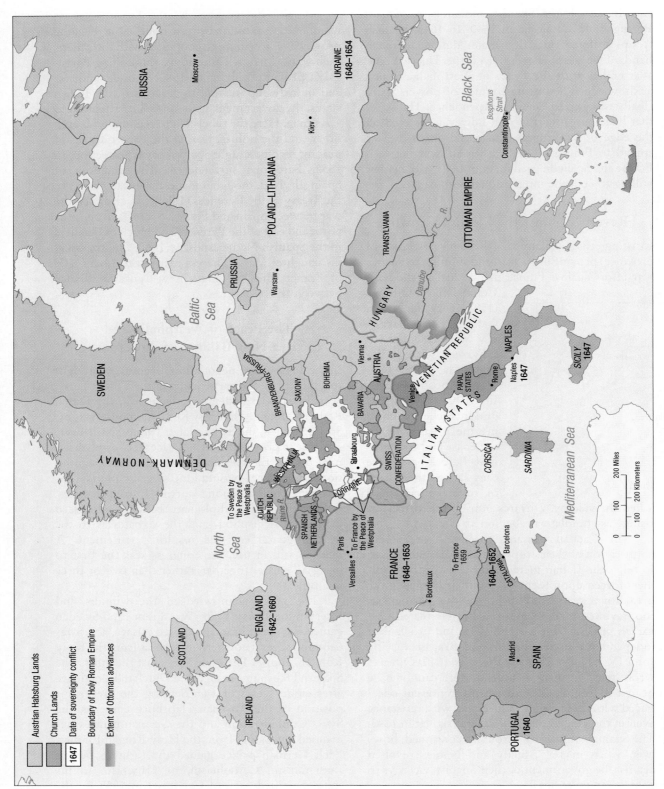

Europe in 1648

RUSSIA

Moscow

UKRAINE
1648–1654

Black Sea

Kiev

Bosphorus
Strait

POLAND–LITHUANIA

Constantinople

PRUSSIA

Warsaw

TRANSYLVANIA

OTTOMAN EMPIRE

Baltic Sea

HUNGARY

Danube R.

SWEDEN

BRANDENBURG–PRUSSIA

SAXONY

BOHEMIA

AUSTRIA

Vienna

VENETIAN REPUBLIC

NAPLES

SICILY
1647

DENMARK–NORWAY

BAVARIA

Venice

PAPAL STATES

Rome

Naples
1647

SWISS CONFEDERATION

ITALIAN STATES

WESTPHALIA

Strasbourg

LORRAINE

CORSICA

SARDINIA

North Sea

To Sweden by
the Peace of
Westphalia

DUTCH REPUBLIC

Rhine R.

SPANISH NETHERLANDS

Paris

Versailles

To France by
the Peace of
Westphalia

FRANCE
1648–1653

Mediterranean Sea

Bordeaux

To France
1659

Barcelona

1640–1652

CATALONIA

ENGLAND
1642–1660

SCOTLAND

Madrid

SPAIN

IRELAND

PORTUGAL
1640

200 Miles

100

200 Kilometers

0   100

0   100

Austrian Habsburg Lands

Church Lands

1647 Date of sovereignty conflict

Boundary of Holy Roman Empire

Extent of Ottoman advances

Peace of Augsburg. The independence ceded to German princes sustained political divisions that would endure until the nineteenth century.

The Peace of Westphalia ended the age of European religious wars. It permanently settled the distributions of the main religions in the Holy Roman Empire: Lutheranism would dominate in the north, Calvinism in the area of the Rhine River, and Catholicism in the south. Most of the territorial changes in Europe would remain intact until the nineteenth century. Religion had less influence on international relations after 1648; international warfare would be undertaken for reasons of national security, commercial ambition, or dynastic pride rather than to enforce religious uniformity. As the *politiques* of the late sixteenth century had come to believe, concerns of state now outweighed motivations of faith in political affairs.

Although France and Spain fought on until 1659 and Baltic conflicts were not resolved until 1661, the Peace of Westphalia signaled major shifts in the balance of European power, changes that French military intervention on the Protestants' side had foreshadowed. With France increasingly replacing Spain as the prevailing power on the Continent and after losing considerable territory in the West, the Austrian Habsburgs turned eastward and devoted their efforts to restoring Catholicism to Bohemia and wresting Hungary from the Turks. Free of Spanish rule, the Dutch focused on their commercial rivalry with the English. The German princes could now officially express their autonomy, as they did in 1657 when they elected Leopold I emperor in return for his promise not to assist Spain and not to interfere in the German states' affairs. This agreement helped pave the way for the growth of a new power, Frederick William of Hohenzollern, the Great Elector of Brandenburg, who increased his territories and developed a small but effective standing army. Brandenburg-Prussia would become a military and political force in the late seventeenth and early eighteenth centuries.

The Fronde in France

Although France became an important model for exercising state power in the seventeenth century, the French monarchy's road to mid-century dominance was rocky. Louis XIII (*1610–1643) and his chief minister, Cardinal Richelieu (1585–1642), had steered France through increasing involve-

ment in the Thirty Years' War, rapidly mounting taxes, and innumerable tax revolts. When Richelieu and Louis XIII died within a year of each other, France was left with a five-year-old king, Louis XIV (*1643–1715). His mother, Anne of Austria, who was named regent, and her Italian-born adviser and rumored lover, Cardinal Mazarin (1602–1661), Richelieu's protégé, ruled in the young monarch's name. French nobles and magistrates suspected the motives of the foreign-born Anne and Mazarin. Some of them hoped to use the crisis created by Louis XIII's death to move France toward a parliamentary government along English lines.

Like Spain, France labored under enormous financial pressure in the 1640s, and Mazarin sold new offices, raised taxes, and registered forced loans to make ends meet. In 1648 a coalition of Mazarin's opponents, led by the Parlement of Paris, presented Mazarin with a charter of demands that, if granted, would have given the parlements (high courts) a form of constitutional power with the right to approve new taxes. Mazarin responded by arresting the parlementary leaders. He soon faced a series of revolts collectively called the Fronde (1648–1653), which at one time or another involved nearly every social group in France. The word *Fronde* came from a slingshot children used in a Parisian street game; according to the monarchy's supporters, the *frondeurs* were merely childish troublemakers.

The Fronde posed an immediate menace to the young king. Fearing for their safety, Louis and members of his court fled Paris. With civil war threatening, Mazarin and Anne agreed to compromise with the parlements. Now the nobles saw an opportunity to reassert their claims to power against the weakened monarchy, and conflict resumed between the crown and the noble families, who renewed their demands for greater local control, which they had lost at the end of the religious wars a half-century earlier. Leading noblewomen often played key roles in the opposition, especially when male family members were in prison.

While the nobles sought to regain power and local influence, the middle and lower classes chafed at the constant tax increases. In Bordeaux in 1649, angry residents took over the municipal government and held out against royal forces until 1653. Conflicts erupted throughout the kingdom as nobles, parlements, and city councils all raised their own armies, to fight either the crown or each other. In some places the urban poor revolted as well. Rampaging soldiers devastated rural areas and disrupted commerce.

Despite the glaring weakness of central power, the monarchy survived. Neither the nobles nor the court magistrates really wanted to overthrow the king, and as in Spain, the various opposing forces failed to unite. But Louis XIV never forgot the humiliation and uncertainty that marred his childhood. Years later he recalled an incident in which a band of Parisians invaded his bedchamber to determine whether he had fled the city, and he declared the event an affront not only to himself but also to the state. His own policies as ruler would be designed to prevent the repetition of any such revolts; he created an "absolute" monarchy.

Versailles:
Model for Absolute Monarchy

France's Louis XIV personified the absolutist king, a ruler who shared power with no one. In an absolutist government, the king ruled by divine right and, either by himself or through agents, made all important policy decisions. No parliament stood in his way. When English kings tried to rule absolutely, however, they lost their crowns, if not their heads. Louis's long reign made absolutism seem distinctly French, and historians have typically viewed Louis's palace at Versailles as the embodiment of absolute monarchy.

The absolute rule of Louis XIV built upon a long French tradition of increasingly centralized government and state efforts to control aristocrats, parlements, and commerce, trends dating back to the Middle Ages. In the sixteenth century, the *politiques* had promoted the primacy of state over religious interests in government policy. Now in the mid-seventeenth century, the religious, political, and economic crises that sparked revolt also helped justify increased state authority. Bureaucrats, churchmen, and political thinkers who provided the apparatus and rationale for absolutism saw the state as an administrative, cultural, and religious force for restoring and maintaining order.

Austria, Brandenburg-Prussia, Spain, Sweden, and Russia also adopted versions of absolute authority. But in France more than elsewhere, state power became inextricably linked to the person of the monarch. The king himself was essential to all aspects of state, and Louis left no room for dissent or government by consensus. In 1651 he reputedly told the Parlement of Paris, *"l'état, c'est moi"* ("I am the state"), emphasizing that state authority rested in him personally.

Court Culture as a
Form of State Power

When Cardinal Mazarin died in 1661, Louis XIV decided to rule without a first minister. He described the dangers of his situation in his memoirs, for his son's instruction: "Everywhere was disorder. My Court as a whole was still very far removed from the sentiments in which I trust you will find it." Louis listed many other problems in the kingdom, but none occupied him more than his attempts to control France's leading nobles, some of whom came from families that had opposed him militarily during the Fronde.

Typically quarrelsome, the French nobles had long exercised local authority by maintaining their own fighting forces, meting out justice on their estates, arranging jobs for their clients, and resolving their own conflicts through dueling. Louis used pensions, offices, honors, gifts, and the threat of disfavor or punishment to induce the nobles to cooperate with him. Using a systematic policy, he made himself the center of French power and culture. At Louis's court the great nobles vied for his favor, attended the ballets and spectacles he put on, and learned the rules of etiquette he supervised—in short, became his clients. Insisting on more "gentlemanly" behavior, Louis set out to domesticate the warrior nobles by replacing violence with court ritual as a means to achieve political and social prestige.

Participation at court required constant study. The preferred styles changed without notice, and the tiniest lapse in attention to etiquette could lead to ruin. The Countess de Lafayette described the court in her novel *The Princess of Clèves* (1678): "The Court gravitated around ambition. Nobody

*Madame de Maintenon
with Her Niece*
Louis Elle the Younger,
who painted this portrait
c. 1686, was expelled from
the Academy because he
was Protestant and was
only readmitted when he
converted to Catholicism.

was tranquil or indifferent—everybody was busily trying to better their position by pleasing, by helping, or by hindering somebody else." Occasionally the results were tragic or absurd, yet those who surrounded Louis were too caught up in the mystique of court life to notice. A leading noblewoman and famous letter writer of the time, Marie de Sévigné (1626–1696), described the reaction of a well-known cook when the fish he had ordered for the king's supper did not arrive on time: feeling dishonored, the man went to his room, put his sword against the door, and ran it through his heart on the third try. After a moment of general sadness, she reported, "there was a very good dinner, light refreshments later, and then supper, a walk, cards, hunting, everything scented with daffodils, everything magical."

Mock battles, extravaganzas, ballets, theatrical performances, even the king's dinner—Louis's daily life was a public performance designed to enhance his prestige. Access to the king was the most valued commodity at court. Nobles vied for the honor of holding his shirt when he dressed; foreign ambassadors squabbled for places near him; and royal mistresses basked in the glow of his personal favor. Calling himself the Sun King, Louis adorned his court with statues of Apollo, Greek god of the sun. He also emulated the style and methods of ancient Roman emperors. At a celebration for the birth of his son in 1662, Louis dressed in similar attire, and many engravings and paintings showed him as a Roman emperor.

Likewise in the style of a Roman emperor, Louis glorified his image with the common people through massive public works projects. Military facilities, such as veterans' hospitals, fortifications, and new fortified towns on the frontier, represented his military might. Urban improvements, among them the building of the Place Vendôme and of the Place des Victoires in Paris, along with the reconstruction of the Louvre palace in Paris, proved his wealth. But his most remarkable project was a new palace at Versailles, twelve miles from the turbulent capital.

Fabulous material and human resources went into the construction, which began in the 1660s. By 1685 the effort engaged thirty-six thousand workers, not including the troops who diverted a local river to supply water for pools and fountains. Royal workshops produced tapestries, carpets, mirrors, and porcelains. The gardens designed by Le Nôtre captured the spirit of Louis XIV's rule: their geometrical arrangements and clear lines showed that art and design could tame nature and that order and control defined the exercise of power. Le Nôtre's geometrical arrangements were imitated in Spain,

Versailles
A bird's-eye view of Louis XIV's palace at Versailles. Notice the emphasis on geometric order in the layout of the buildings and gardens.

the Italian states, Austria, the German states, and later in faraway St. Petersburg, Annapolis, Maryland, and Washington, D.C.

Yet for all its apparent luxury and frivolity, life at Versailles was often cramped and cold. The thousands of people in residence made for serious overcrowding. Refuse collected in the corridors during the incessant building, and thieves and prostitutes overran the grounds. By the time Louis actually moved to Versailles in 1682, he was middle-aged and increasingly devout. After his wife's death in 1683, he secretly married his mistress, Françoise d'Aubigné, Marquise de Maintenon, and conducted most state affairs from her apartments at the palace. Her opponents at court complained that she controlled all the appointments, but her efforts focused on her own projects, favorite among them the founding in 1686 at Saint-Cyr of a royal school for girls from impoverished noble families. The school emphasized the value of work and duty for noblewomen, who would otherwise have remained uneducated.

As nearly constant wars drained royal resources, Louis withdrew inside his palace and avoided participating in the gaieties of Parisian life. Versailles symbolized his success in reining in the nobility and dominating Europe, and other monarchs eagerly mimicked French fashion and often conducted business in French. But by the time the palace was finished, the Sun King was losing his luster.

Bureaucracy and Mercantilism

Louis XIV loved administrative duties and never stopped working. In his memoirs he stressed the importance of work and the need to keep one's ear to the ground:

> *to learn each hour the news concerning every province and every nation, the secrets of every court, the mood and weaknesses of each Prince and of every foreign minister; to be well-informed on an infinite number of matters about which we are supposed to know nothing; to elicit from our subjects what they hide from us with the greatest care; to discover the most remote opinions of our courtiers and the most hidden interests of those who come to us with quite contrary professions.*

To gather all this information, Louis relied on a series of talented ministers, usually of modest origins, whose fame, fortune, and even noble status came through state service. Most important among them was Jean-Baptiste Colbert (1619–1683), the son of a wool merchant turned royal official. Colbert had managed Mazarin's personal finances and worked his way up under Louis XIV to become head of royal finances, public works, and the navy. Like many of Louis's other ministers, he founded a family dynasty of bureaucrats that included five ministers of state, an archbishop, two bishops, and three generals.

Louis's power was only theoretically absolute, for it depended in practice on an intricate network of patrons and clients that included both nobles and commoners. For example, Louis supported writers whose messages favored his aims. He protected the playwright Molière from clerical critics who objected to his satire of religious hypocrisy but reserved the right to censor anything he did not like. Writers who depended on the state for patronage thus could not risk royal displeasure.

As a good patron, Louis offered his clients something in return for service. For Colbert and many others, the king's patronage provided a chance for upward social mobility in an increasingly centralized government that, shorn of the monarchy and aristocracy, would eventually give rise to the modern state. Louis extended the bureaucratic forms his predecessors had developed, especially the use of intendants. About thirty intendants, one for each region, held their positions directly from the king rather than owning their offices, as crown officials had traditionally done. Rejecting the *frondeur* criticism of the intendants as petty tyrants, Louis handpicked them to represent his will against entrenched local interests such as the parlements, provincial estates, and noble governors. The intendants reduced local powers over finances and insisted on more efficient tax collection. Despite the doubling of taxes in Louis's reign, the local rebellions that had so beset the crown in the 1620s, 1630s, and 1640s subsided in the face of these better-organized state forces.

State bureaucracy extended into new areas under Colbert. To maintain its national wealth, as measured by the gold supply, and to make French industry and agriculture self-sufficient, the government established overseas trading companies, granted manufacturing monopolies, and standardized production methods for textiles, paper, and soap. Such mercantilist policies aimed to ensure France's ability to compete in world markets and sustain a favorable balance of trade. Although later economists questioned the value of this state intervention, virtually every government in Europe embraced mercantilism. Colbert installed an inspection system that regulated the quality of finished goods and compelled all craftsmen to organize into guilds, in which masters could supervise the work of their journeymen and apprentices. To protect French production, Colbert rescinded many internal customs fees but enacted high foreign tariffs, which cut imports of competing goods. To compete more effectively with England and the Dutch Republic, Colbert also subsidized shipbuilding, a policy that dramatically expanded the number of seaworthy vessels.

Colbert's plans extended to Canada, where in 1663 he took control of the trading company that had founded New France. He transplanted several thousand peasants from western France to the present-day province of Quebec, which France had claimed since 1608. To guard his investment, Colbert sent fifteen hundred soldiers to join the settlers. Of particular concern to the French government were the Iroquois, who regularly interrupted French fur-trading convoys. Shows of French military force, including the burning of Indian villages and winter food supplies, forced the Iroquois to make peace with New France, and from 1666 to 1680, French traders moved westward with minimal interference. In 1672 fur trader Louis Jolliet and Jesuit missionary Jacques Marquette reached the upper Mississippi River and traveled downstream as far as Arkansas. In 1684 French explorer Sieur de La Salle went all the way down to the Gulf of Mexico, claiming a vast territory for Louis XIV and calling it Louisiana.

The Army and War

Louis XIV's powerful ministry of war established increasingly firm state control over the armies. Barracks built in major towns received supplies from a central distribution system. The state began to provide uniforms for the soldiers and to offer veterans some care. A militia draft instituted in 1688 supplemented the army in times of war and enrolled one hundred thousand men. Louis's wartime army could field a force as large as that of all his enemies combined.

Louis's foreign policy had two aims: to consolidate French power in Europe against the threat of Habsburg (Spanish and Austrian) encirclement and to compete against the English and Dutch overseas. In the first of his major wars after assuming control of French affairs, Louis defeated the Spanish in an invasion of the Spanish Netherlands (1667–1668), where Spanish troops were garrisoned only three days' march from Paris. Beginning in 1672 he fought his former allies, the Dutch, in a long war of attrition that ended only when the Dutch opened the dikes and flooded the countryside. In the Treaty of Nijmegen of 1678, Louis gained Franche-Comté, linking Alsace to the rest of France, and several Flemish towns. Heartened by the Habsburgs' seeming weakness, Louis pushed eastward, seizing the city of Strasbourg in 1681 and invading the province of Lorraine in 1684. In 1688 he attacked some of the small German cities of the Holy Roman Empire and was soon involved in a long war against a European-wide coalition.

War required money and men, which Louis obtained by expanding state control over finances, conscription, and military supply. Thus absolutism and warfare fed each other, as the bureaucracy created new ways to raise and maintain an army. But constant warfare also eroded the state's resources. Further administrative and legal reform, the elimination of the buying and selling of offices, the lowering of taxes—all were made impossible by the need for more money.

Louis was the last French ruler until Napoleon to accompany his troops to the battlefield. In later generations, as the military became more professional, French rulers left the fighting to their generals. Although Louis had eliminated the private armies of his noble courtiers, he constantly promoted his own military prowess in order to keep his noble officers under his sway. He had miniature battle scenes painted on his high heels and commissioned tapestries showing military entries into cities, even those he did not take by force. He seized every occasion to assert his supremacy, insisting that other fleets salute his ships first.

Pierre Corneille (1606–1684), a leading French playwright of the time, wrote, no doubt optimistically, "The people are very happy when they die for their kings." What is certain is that the wars touched many peasant and urban families. The people who lived on the routes leading to the battle-fields had to house and feed soldiers (nobles were exempt from this requirement). Everyone, moreover, paid the higher taxes that were necessary to support the army. By the end of Louis's reign, one in six Frenchmen had served in the military.

Religious Challenges to Absolutism

Distrustful of religious diversity, Louis XIV hoped to convert the Protestant Huguenots, a minority that had enjoyed religious freedom and civil rights since the Edict of Nantes in 1598. Louis's campaign for religious conformity also extended to the Jansenists, Catholics whose doctrines resembled some aspects of Protestantism. Bishop Jacques-Benigne Bossuet (1627–1704), one of the king's advisers, explained the principle of divine right that justified the king's actions: "We have seen that kings take the place of God, who is the true father of the human species. We have also seen that the first idea of power which exists among men is that of the paternal power; and that kings are modeled on fathers." Absolutism, in this view, was natural, patriarchal, and based on Scriptural tradition. Such a picture offered little room for dissent.

Jansenism appealed to those who opposed the Jesuits for making the demands of religion too "easy." Following the posthumous publication of the book *Augustinus* (1640) by the Flemish theologian Cornelius Jansen (1585–1638), the Jansenists stressed the need for God's grace in achieving salvation. They accepted predestination; emphasized St. Augustine's teachings on original sin; and, in their austere religious practice, resembled the English Puritans. Prominent among the Jansenists was Blaise Pascal (1623–1662), a mathematician of genius, who wrote his *Provincial Letters* (1656–1657) to defend Jansenism against charges of heresy and to attack Jesuit ethics as ridiculously lax.

Louis feared any doctrine that encouraged the considerations of individual conscience, especially one that was gaining support among magistrates, who registered royal edicts. He preferred teachings that stressed obedience to authority. Therefore in 1660 he began enforcing various papal bulls against Jansenism and closed their theological centers. Jansenists were forced underground for the rest of his reign.

After many years of escalating pressure on the Protestants, Louis revoked the Edict of Nantes in

1685 and eliminated all of the Protestants' rights. He shut down their churches and schools, banned all their public activities, and exiled those who refused to convert to Catholicism. Thousands of French Protestants emigrated, most to the Dutch Republic or to England, where their printing presses poured out anti-French publications. Protestant Europe was shocked by this draconian enforcement of Catholic conformity.

Poverty, Charity, and the State

Beneath the glittering surface of French absolutism, profound changes transformed the experience of the poor. As hard times continued past the middle of the seventeenth century, growing worse as the state demanded more and more money, the numbers of poor wandering the roads swelled. Crime increased and became more violent. Quarrels ended more often in bloodshed and murder. Yet more important than the sheer rise in numbers was a new attitude toward the poor that originated in the religious changes of the sixteenth century and reached fruition in the seventeenth century.

In the Middle Ages poverty had been considered a fact of life and carried no social stigma. The poor, after all, were like Jesus; they suffered humiliation and hunger and were thought to be deserving of aid and comfort. But increasingly in the seventeenth century, the upper classes, the church, and the state came to regard the poor as dangerous, deceitful, and lacking in character. "Criminal laziness is the source of all their vices," wrote a Jesuit expert on poverty. The courts had previously ordered the arrest, whipping, and branding of beggars or their expulsion from the cities. Now, inspired by Counter-Reformation Catholicism, municipal magistrates collected poor taxes, and local notables organized charities; together they transformed hospitals into houses of confinement for beggars. Upper-class women's religious associations, known as confraternities, set up asylums that confined prostitutes (by arrest if necessary) and rehabilitated them. Confraternities also founded hospices where orphans learned order and respect. Other associations collected money to distribute to potential converts among the Protestants. They all advocated harsh discipline as the cure for poverty. Confinement and forced labor were the seventeenth-century answers to economic crisis.

Hospitals became holding pens for society's unwanted; the poor joined the disabled, the incurably diseased, and the insane in hospitals staffed by religious orders. It is hard to imagine that such an environment could ever succeed in creating order and discipline. Doctors believed most madness was caused by "melancholia," a condition they attributed to disorders in the system of body "humors." Their prescribed treatments included blood transfusions; ingestion of bitter substances such as coffee, quinine, tartar, and even soap; immersion in water; various forms of exercise; and burning or cauterizing the body to allow black vapors to escape. For their part, wealthy sick people avoided hospitals because contagious diseases ran rampant in them. Antiseptics were virtually unknown.

Abraham Bosse,
A Charity Hospital in Paris, *17th century*
This engraving, with its emphasis on austere geometrical design, probably exaggerates the degree of order established in seventeenth-century hospitals.

The monarchy gradually exerted control over these institutions. In 1676, Louis XIV ordered every city to establish a general hospital, and intendants took charge of their administration and finances. Yet hospitals did not become medical centers; they combined charity, welfare, public order, and punishment. And in the eighteenth century the hospitals made agreements with local businessmen to set up workshops for manufacturing. Other western European countries founded similar institutions at the same time.

Absolutism Versus Aristocratic Constitutionalism in Central and Eastern Europe

Louis XIV and other western rulers were not alone in clashing with turbulent aristocracies, rebellious common people, and religious dissidents. Similar conflicts played out in central and eastern Europe. The Thirty Years' War had little impact east of Bohemia and Brandenburg; but as the cycle of war temporarily abated in the West, turmoil struck the East. In 1648, tax increases sparked bloody riots in Moscow. Meanwhile, a Venetian fleet penetrated the Bosphorus and threatened Constantinople, provoking the Janissaries to revolt and murder the sultan. In Poland-Lithuania, 1648 marked the onset of the longest crisis of all, an explosion that sucked in the rest of eastern Europe.

Until the mid-seventeenth century, government in the German states, Sweden, and Poland-Lithuania had been shared between the monarchy and the privileged classes. But for one hundred fifty years the growth of princely bureaucracies, especially in the German states, had challenged this balance of power. The Thirty Years' War and east European conflicts after 1648 helped tilt the advantage toward monarchs everywhere except in Poland-Lithuania, where bureaucracy had always been weak.

The Russian and Ottoman (Turkish) empires had never fit the western model of shared power between rulers and privileged estates. But even in Russia the tsars had occasionally convoked a *Zemskii Sobor* ("assembly of the land") for consultation and to issue major legislation. The Ottoman Empire remained in theory a centralized autocracy, but in

the seventeenth century the sultan's regime degenerated, and Ottoman vassal states such as Transylvania and Moldavia (in modern Romania) seized freedom.

Although eastern Europeans saw in Louis XIV a powerful example of royalist state building, their rulers did not blindly emulate the Sun King. Their drive for enhanced power had deep historical roots, as did nobles' determination to preserve prerogatives. Whether the state or local elites won, however, the peasants lost. Poverty and (except in Sweden) tighter bonds of serfdom lay ahead for them.

Poland-Lithuania Overwhelmed

In 1648, Ukrainian Cossack warriors revolted against the king of Poland-Lithuania, inaugurating two decades of tumult known as the Deluge. Tough fighters, free from serfdom, self-governing, and Orthodox in religion, Cossack bands had formed from runaway peasants and poor nobles in the no-man's-land of southern Russia and Ukraine (the name *Ukraine* means "land at the border"). The Polish nobles who claimed this potentially rich land scorned the Cossacks as troublemakers; but to the Ukrainian peasant population they were liberators. The Cossacks defeated almost every cavalry force of Polish-Lithuanian nobles they fought. In 1654 the Cossacks submitted

Poland-Lithuania in the Seventeenth Century

Ukraine to Russian rule, provoking a Russo-Polish war that ended in 1667 when the tsar annexed eastern Ukraine and Kiev.

Invasion and civil war added to the horrors of the Deluge. Sweden, Brandenburg-Prussia, and Transylvania intervened, and various Polish-Lithuanian magnates bid to become virtually independent princes. The Deluge ruined the commonwealth and aggravated problems that would continue to plague Poland for centuries. Perhaps a third of the population perished or was carried off by Tatar slave-raiders. Most towns were destroyed, and the artisans and merchants devastated. The once-prosperous Jewish population suffered terribly. Some fifty-six thousand Jews were killed by the Cossacks, Polish peasants, or Russian troops, and thousands more had to flee or convert to Christianity. One rabbi wrote, "We were slaughtered each day, in a more agonizing way than cattle: they are butchered quickly, while we were being executed slowly." Surviving Jews moved from towns to *shtetls* (Jewish villages), where they took up petty trading, money lending, tax gathering, and tavern leasing—activities that fanned peasant antisemitism. Even the nobles suffered from the postwar loss of foreign grain markets, although they managed to shift the heaviest burdens onto their peasants: four, five, or even more days weekly of unpaid labor on nobles' estates became normal.

Poland-Lithuania's Protestant minority sustained almost mortal damage. Desperate for protection amid the war, most Protestant dissidents backed the violently anti-Catholic Swedes, leading the victorious Catholic majority to brand them as traitors. Some Protestant refugees fled to the Dutch Republic and England. In Poland-Lithuania (where the Virgin Mary was proclaimed "perpetual queen") it came to be assumed that a good Pole was a Catholic. The commonwealth had ceased to be an outpost of toleration.

Elsewhere the ravages of war had created opportunities for kings to increase their power; not so in Poland-Lithuania. Here the winners were the great nobles, who had emerged as semi-independent warlords. The great nobles dominated the *Sejm* (parliament), and to maintain an equilibrium among themselves, they gave each deputy absolute veto power. This system of "free veto" (*liberum veto*) soon deadlocked parliamentary government. The monarchy lost its room to maneuver, and with it much of its remaining power. An appalled Croat visitor in 1658 commented on the situation:

> Among the Poles there is no order in the state, and the subjects are not afraid either of the king or the judge. Everybody who is stronger thinks to have the right to oppress the weaker, just as the wolves and bears are free to capture and kill cattle. . . . Such abominable depravity is called by the Poles "aristocratic freedom."

The commonwealth revived briefly when a man of ability and ambition, Jan Sobieski (*1674–1696), was elected king. A southeastern noble famed as a cavalry commander and an admirer of Louis XIV's France (partly because of his marriage

Jan Sobieski, King of Poland
In 1683 the Polish king helped the Austrians turn back the Ottoman Turks besieging Vienna, but he failed in his efforts to install a strong monarchy at home.

to a politically shrewd French princess), Sobieski joined the Habsburgs against the Ottoman Turks. In 1683 when the Turks launched their greatest attack of the century against the Habsburgs and besieged Vienna, Sobieski led twenty-five thousand Polish cavalrymen into battle and helped rout the Turks. Despite his efforts to rebuild the monarchy and to emulate Louis XIV's patronage of the arts, he could not halt Poland-Lithuania's slide into political disarray and weakness.

An Uneasy Balance: Habsburgs and Ottoman Turks

As Holy Roman emperors, the Habsburgs theoretically controlled an enormous territory in central Europe; but the Peace of Westphalia had drastically limited imperial authority. The Habsburgs exerted real power only in Austria and Bohemia, although they hoped to do the same in Hungary. Because

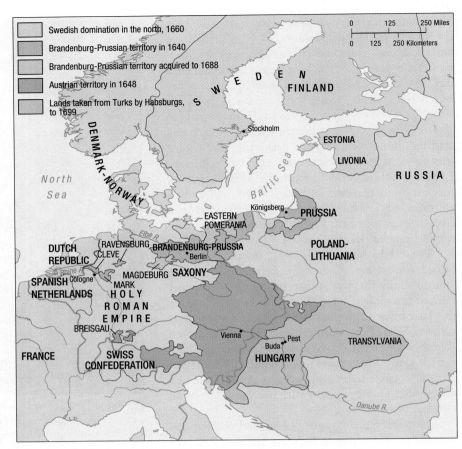

Swedish domination in the north, 1660

Brandenburg-Prussian territory in 1640

Brandenburg-Prussian territory acquired to 1688

Austrian territory in 1648

Lands taken from Turks by Habsburgs, to 1699

State-Building in Northern and Central Europe, 1648–1690

each land had its own institutions, however, the Austrian Habsburgs faced even greater regional problems than did Spain in Portugal and Catalonia or England in Ireland. Like Poland-Lithuania, the Habsburg lands were ethnically and religiously diverse, dominated by aristocrats, and ravaged by war; and they bordered on the alien, menacing Ottoman Empire, which Christians dreaded. Yet unlike Poland-Lithuania, the Habsburg monarchy gradually consolidated its central power. By 1690 it was pushing back the Turks deep into the Balkans.

Although Emperor Leopold I (∗1658–1705) considered his arch-rival Louis XIV arrogant and hypocritical, he yielded nothing to the Sun King in his determination to forge a powerful state. To do so, Leopold had to bring potentially disruptive nobles to heel and to modernize his army. Recruiting, provisioning, and strategic planning became direct responsibilities of the emperor and his

court war council. A permanent standing army with professional standards for officers and a centralized supply system replaced the chaotic arrangements of the Thirty Years' War era, during which privately hired mercenaries did most of the fighting. When the Habsburgs' centuries-long duel with the French resumed in 1672, Leopold's new imperial troops fought well; and thanks to the emperor's astute coalition building, the Habsburgs played a critical role in keeping Louis XIV's ambitions in check.

To pay for its army and wars and to staff its new imperial bureaucracy, the dynasty had to gain the support of local aristocrats and chip away at provincial institutions' powers. It had won its first major success in Bohemia, where after the failed revolt of 1618–1621, the Habsburgs substituted hereditary for elective kingship. In the place of Czech-speaking nobles who had supported the 1618 revolt, the Habsburgs advanced a new nobility made up of Czechs, Germans, Italians, Spaniards, and even Irish who used German as their common tongue, professed Catholicism, and loyally served the dynasty. Slow to recover from the Thirty Years' War, Bohemia was a virtual colony. "You have utterly destroyed our home, our ancient kingdom, and have built us no new one in its place," lamented a Czech Jesuit in 1670, addressing the Habsburgs. "Woe to you! . . . The nobles you have oppressed, great cities made small. Of smiling towns you have made straggling villages." Not for a century did Austrian censors allow this protest to be published.

The Habsburgs did not yet firmly control Hungary. They were elective kings of a strip in the north and west (including modern Slovakia and western Croatia); the Turks occupied the center; and to the east, Hungarian princes paying tribute to the Turks ruled Transylvania. The brunt of war with the Turks fell on the Hungarian nobles, and to maintain their support Leopold revived the moribund Hungarian Diet in 1681. The Habsburg-Ottoman struggle resumed in 1682, and in 1683 the Habsburgs broke the Turkish siege of Vienna—with the help of Polish cavalry—and mounted a sustained offensive. Eventually, in the Treaty of Karlowitz (1699), the Ottoman Turks surrendered almost all of Hungary to the Habsburgs.

"Liberation" came at a high price. The fighting, which had continued over one hundred fifty years, laid waste vast stretches of Hungary's central plain. Population had sunk from 8 million in 1526 to 2.5 million. To repopulate the land, the Habsburgs settled large communities of foreigners: Romanians in Transylvania, Catholic Croats and Orthodox Serbs in the lower Danube valley, and Germans everywhere. Magyar speakers became a minority in Hungary, and the seeds were sown for the poisonous nationality conflicts of nineteenth- and twentieth-century Hungary, Romania, and Yugoslavia.

Once the Turks had been beaten back, Habsburg rule over Hungary tightened. In 1687 the dynasty's hereditary right to the crown was acknowledged by the Diet, now dominated by nobles who had amassed huge holdings in the liberated territories. They formed the core of a pro-Habsburg aristocracy that would buttress the dynasty until the Habsburg empire fell in 1918. As the Turks retreated, Leopold systematically rebuilt

churches, monasteries, roadside shrines, and monuments in the florid Austrian baroque style, meant to serve Counter-Reformation Catholicism. Gothic altars disappeared from parish churches, replaced by highly decorated altars. Nobles vied in building or renovating town palaces and in donating elaborate altars to their favorite churches and chapels. Leopold enlarged his residence in Vienna and began building a vast summer palace, the Schönbrunn, which rivaled Versailles. These baroque monuments impart a unifying cultural style to central Europe even today.

Brandenburg-Prussia and Sweden: Militaristic Absolutism

The most impressive of all central European state builders was Frederick William of Hohenzollern, the Great Elector of Brandenburg-Prussia (✱1640–1688). Since the fifteenth century, the Hohenzollerns had been electors of Brandenburg (the seven German princes entitled to vote for the Holy Roman emperor took the title *elector*), a landlocked, impoverished state on the Elbe River. From the sixteenth century they ruled the duchy of East Prussia (hence the name, after 1618, of Brandenburg-Prussia). Through marriages and alliances, including French support in the Thirty Years' War, Brandenburg-Prussia slowly added lands on the Rhine and the Baltic coast. As in the Habsburg states, each Hohenzollern land had its own laws and representative institutions, called *estates.* It was the Great Elector's formidable accomplishment to weld these scattered territories into an autocratic state. His was the most clear-cut case in seventeenth-century Europe of a monarch's breaking down the old model of a realm based on ruler-estates cooperation.

Despite meager resources, Frederick William succeeded. He came to power while Brandenburg was still being torn by the Thirty Years' War; East Prussia suffered similar disasters during the Polish Deluge of 1650. Pressured by the necessities of warfare and later of reconstruction, he set for himself four main tasks: establishing autocratic government at the expense of the estates, founding a strong standing army, creating an efficient bureaucracy, and extending his territory.

The Great Elector's first crucial step was to force his territories' estates to grant him a permanent income. To this end, he struck a deal with the nobles (Junkers) of each land: in exchange for allowing him to collect permanent taxes, he gave them complete control over their enserfed peasants and exempted them from taxation. The tactic worked. By the end of his reign the estates met only on ceremonial occasions.

Supplied with a steady income, Frederick William could devote his attention to military and bureaucratic consolidation. Over forty years he expanded his army from eight thousand to thirty thousand men. The army reproduced the rigid domination of nobles over peasants characteristic of Brandenburg-Prussian society: peasants filled the ranks, and Junkers became officers. Both learned discipline and obedience to their increasingly powerful ruler—peasants served the nobles; the nobles served the elector. The bureaucracy followed the same model. Special war commissars took charge not only of military affairs but of tax collection. To hasten military dispatches, the Great Elector also established one of Europe's first state postal systems. For three centuries, Prussia would bear the Great Elector's militaristic stamp.

In such a militarized and Protestant state, it is not surprising that Frederick William avoided the ostentation of the French court, even while following the absolutist model of centralizing state power. As a Calvinist he boldly rebuffed Louis XIV by welcoming twenty thousand French Huguenot refugees after the revocation of the Edict of Nantes. The Great Elector spent some funds on public works, though hardly on the scale of his French counterpart. Berlin's population grew from six thousand to thirty thousand (though it remained tiny compared with Paris, London, or Moscow).

Frederick William followed Louis XIV in pursuing foreign and domestic policies that promoted state power and prestige. To further his own aims, he adroitly switched sides in the Polish Deluge and later in Louis's wars and would stop at almost nothing to crush resistance at home. The success of his state-building policies became strikingly apparent under his frivolous son Frederick I (*1688–1713). More determined to imitate Louis's personal habits than his absolutist policies, Frederick maintained an official mistress at court and sported wigs in Louis's style. Nevertheless, in 1701, Frederick would persuade Leopold I to allow him to take the royal title "king in Prussia." Prussia had arrived as an important power.

Across the Baltic, Sweden also stood out as an example of absolutist consolidation. In the Thirty Years' War, King Gustavus Adolphus's superb generalship and highly trained army had made Sweden the supreme power of northern Europe. The huge but sparsely populated state included not only most of present-day Sweden but also Finland, Estonia, half of Latvia, and much of the Baltic coastline of modern Poland and Germany. The Baltic, in short, was a Swedish lake. After Gustavus Adolphus died, his daughter Queen Christina (*1632–1654) conceded much authority to the estates. Absorbed by religion and philosophy, Christina eventually abdicated and converted to Catholicism. Her successors temporarily made Sweden an absolute monarchy.

In Sweden (as in neighboring Denmark-Norway), absolutism meant simply the estates' standing aside while the king led the army in lucrative foreign campaigns. The aristocracy went along because it staffed the bureaucracy and reaped war profits. Generally an ally of Louis XIV and intrigued by French culture, Sweden also gleamed with national pride. In 1668 the nobility demanded the introduction of a distinctive national costume: should Swedes, they asked, "who are so glorious and renowned a nation . . . let ourselves be led by the nose by a parcel of French dancing-masters?" Sweden spent the forty years after 1654 continuously warring with its neighbors. By the 1690s war expenses began to outrun the small Swedish population's ability to pay, threatening the continuation of absolutism.

Russia:
Foundations of Bureaucratic Absolutism

Superficially, seventeenth-century Russia seemed a world apart from the Europe of Louis XIV and the Great Elector. It stretched across Siberia to the Pacific Ocean. Western visitors either sneered or shuddered at the "barbarism" of Russian life, and Russians reciprocated by nursing deep suspicions of everything foreign. But under the surface, Russia was evolving along paths much like Europe's.

Up to mid-century, Russia's overwhelming need was to recover from the chaos of the Time of Troubles. Under the first Romanov tsars, Michael (*1613–1645) and Alexei (*1645–1676), a yearning to restore the old order permeated Russian society. To finance renewed government authority, however, new administrative structures and taxes were imposed, measures that set off protests such as the Moscow riots of 1648.

In 1649 the tsar convoked the *Zemskii Sobor* to enact a sweeping law code. The Code of 1649 prescribed a social hierarchy topped by the autocratic monarchy; it stayed in force for almost two centuries. The code assigned all subjects to a hereditary class according to their current occupation or state needs. Slaves and free peasants were merged into a serf class tied to the soil and to noble masters. To prevent tax evasion, the code forbade townspeople to move from the community where they resided. Nobles owed absolute obedience to the tsar and were required to serve in the army, but in return no other group could own estates worked by serfs. Serfs became the chattel of their lord, who could sell them like horses or land. Although the serfs' lot would worsen in the eighteenth century, Russian serfdom already differed little from slavery. The legal tradition behind the code was Byzantine, but the results suggested a more drastic version of the Great Elector's regime in Brandenburg-Prussia—all the more so because the *Zemskii Sobor* neither challenged the autocracy nor ever again met after 1653.

Likewise in the Byzantine spirit, yet unconsciously echoing Louis XIV, Tsar Alexei imposed firm control over the Russian Orthodox church. In 1666 a church council reaffirmed the tsar's role as God's direct representative on earth. The state-dominated church took action against a religious group called the Old Believers, who rejected church efforts to bring Russian worship in line with Byzantine tradition. At issue were such seemingly minor matters as making the sign of the cross with three fingers rather than two. Old Believer leaders, including the noblewoman Fedosia Morozova, endured exile, prison, and torture; whole communities of Old Believers starved or burned themselves to death rather than submit. Religious schism opened a gulf between the Russian people and the crown, nobility, bureaucracy, and established church.

Nevertheless, modernizing trends prevailed. The army swelled from thirty-five thousand men in the 1630s to nearly two hundred thousand men fifty years later. The government crushed a popular rebellion led in 1667 by Stenka Razin, a Cossack from the Don region in south Russia. Razin vaguely promised liberation from "the traitors and bloodsuckers of the peasant communes"—the great noble landowners, local governors, and Moscow courtiers. Captured four years later by the tsar's army, Razin's head and limbs were chopped off and publicly displayed, and his body thrown to the dogs. Thousands of his followers also suffered grisly deaths. His memory lived on in folk songs and legends, but like the Old Believers, his movement had succumbed to the autocratic state. Western influence kept seeping in, not only in military and administrative matters but also in literature and the arts. Under the next strong tsar, Peter the Great (*1682–1725), western currents would become a torrent.

West European and North American Constitutional Models

As authoritarian government spread in central and eastern Europe, some states in western Europe and their North American colonies took a different tack, developing new models of constitutional government that would eventually supplant autocracy. A constitutional system limited rulers' arbitrary power and guaranteed some rights for subjects, as well as representative institutions. Constitutional guarantees did not always extend to the common people; often they developed as part of accommodations between rulers and elites that explicitly excluded the lower classes.

The Merchant Republics

In the seventeenth century, three western states had republican governments: Venice, Switzerland, and the Dutch Republic. (In the East, Poland-Lithuania, with its weak elective monarchy, also called itself a commonwealth, or republic.) All three western republics were oligarchic—small groups of merchants dominated political life—and all pursued mercantilist policies designed to accumulate wealth and promote self-sufficiency.

The Dutch Domestic View
This domestic scene, Girl Reading a Letter at an Open Window, *is infused with a religious glow, but the artist, Jan Vermeer, did not neglect the rich draperies, cloths, and clothing that signaled Dutch prosperity.*

Contemporaries admired Venice as Europe's most stable state and the last survivor of the ancient and Renaissance city-state tradition. The republic's ships carried goods all over the world and made Venice a major market for Asian imports. No comparable wealth flowed into landlocked, mountainous Switzerland, whose main export was mercenary soldiers. Merchant oligarchies led most Swiss cantons (regions), which in turn maintained a federal system and cooperated in foreign policy. Despite speaking different languages (German, French, Italian) and adhering to different faiths, Switzerland too remained remarkably stable.

The Dutch Republic, like Switzerland, gained formal independence in 1648 and functioned as a federation. The Estates General set foreign policy but depended on the provincial estates, dominated by oligarchies of local regents, to handle each province's internal affairs. The princes of Orange, who frequently served as *stadholders,* acted more as presidents than as kings. One foreigner observed that the Dutch "behave as if all men were created equal," but in fact real power remained in the hands of the regents, not the common people.

The decentralized state encouraged and protected trade, and the Dutch Republic became Europe's financial capital. The Bank of Amsterdam offered interest rates as low as 3 percent, less than half the rates in England and France. The federation of provinces held off the English navies and French armies, developed the most prosperous economy in Europe, and became a center of European culture, all without forming a strong state structure.

Praised for industriousness, thrift, and cleanliness—and maligned as greedy, dull "butterboxes"—the Dutch dominated overseas commerce with their shipping industry. They imported products from all over the world: spices, tea, and silk from India and Asia; sugar from South America; wool from England and Spain; timber and furs from Scandinavia; grain from eastern Europe. One English traveler in 1660 described the riches of Amsterdam as superior to Venice and called the Hague "the most pleasant place in the world." A widely reprinted history of Amsterdam that appeared in 1662 described the city as "risen through the hand of God to the peak of prosperity and greatness. . . . The whole world stands amazed at its riches and from east and west, north and south they come to behold it."

The growing urban Dutch middle class supported the visual arts, especially painting, to an unprecedented degree. Artists and engravers produced thousands of works. Even the best known among them, Rembrandt van Rijn (1606–1669), did not often command high prices, but Dutch artists were nonetheless among the first to sell to a mass market. Whereas in other countries kings, nobles, and churches bought art, Dutch buyers were merchants, artisans, and shopkeepers. One foreigner commented that "pictures are very common here, there being scarce an ordinary tradesman whose house is not decorated with them." Engravings and illustrated histories were all relatively inexpensive, and even people of modest means could afford oil paintings. The pictures reflected the Dutch interest in the Bible and in familiar daily details: children at play, winter landscapes, and ships in port.

The family household, not the royal court, determined the moral character of this intensely commercial society. Dutch society fostered public enterprise in men and work in the home for women, who were expected to filter out the greed and materialism of commercial society by maintaining domestic harmony and virtue. Relative prosperity decreased the need for married women to work, so that Dutch society developed the clear contrast between male and female roles that would become prevalent elsewhere in Europe and in America more than a century later. As one contemporary Dutch writer explained, "The husband must be on the street to practice his trade; the wife must stay at home to be in the kitchen."

Extraordinarily high levels of urbanization and literacy created a large public for reading matter. Dutch presses printed books censored elsewhere, and the University of Leiden attracted students and professors from all over Europe. Dutch tolerance extended to the works of Benedict Spinoza (1633–1677), a Jewish philosopher and Biblical scholar who was expelled by his synagogue for alleged atheism but left alone by the Dutch authorities. Spinoza strove to reconcile religion with science and mathematics. But his work scandalized many Christians and Jews because he seemed to equate God and nature. Like nature, Spinoza's God followed unchangeable laws and could not be influenced by human actions, prayers, or faith.

The Dutch lived in a world of international rivalries. The English and French constantly threatened the security essential to Dutch trade. Anglo-Dutch naval wars (1652–1654, 1665–1667, 1672–1674) proved inconclusive but costly. Even more dangerous were the Dutch Republic's land wars with France, which continued into the eighteenth century. The Dutch survived but began to depend on alliances with other powers. At the end of the seventeenth century the regent class of merchants became more exclusive, more preoccupied with ostentation, less tolerant of deviations from strict Calvinism, and more concerned with imitating French styles. Increasingly, Dutch architecture, painting, and intellectual life came under French influence.

England's Glorious Revolution of 1688

In England the restoration of monarchy made some in Parliament fear that the English government would come to resemble French absolutism. This fear was not unfounded. In 1670, Charles II made a secret agreement, soon leaked, with Louis XIV in which he promised to announce his conversion to Catholicism in exchange for money for his war against the Dutch. Charles never proclaimed himself a Catholic, but in his Declaration of Indulgence he did suspend all laws against Catholics and Protestant dissenters in 1673. Since Tudor times, wealthy English landowners had become accustomed to participating in government through Parliament, and unlike the French nobility, they expected to be consulted on royal policy, especially in the matter of religion. The staunchly Anglican Parliament consequently refused to continue the Dutch war unless Charles rescinded his Declaration of Indulgence. Asserting its authority further, Parliament passed the Test Act, requiring all government officials to take the Church of England's sacrament and in effect disavow Catholic doctrine. Then in 1678, Parliament precipitated the so-called Exclusion Crisis by explicitly denying the throne to a Roman Catholic. This action was aimed at the king's brother and heir, James, an open convert to Catholicism. Charles refused to allow it to become law.

The dynastic crisis over the succession of a Catholic gave rise to two distinct factions in Parliament: the Tories, who supported a strong, hereditary monarchy and the restored ceremony of the Anglican church, and the Whigs, who advocated parliamentary supremacy and toleration for Protestant dissenters. Both labels were originally pejorative: *Tory* meant an Irish Catholic bandit; *Whig* was the Irish Catholic designation for the Presbyterian Scots. The Tories favored James's succession despite his Catholicism, whereas the Whigs opposed a Catholic monarch. The loose moral atmosphere of Charles's court offended some Whigs, who complained tongue in cheek that Charles was father of his country in much too literal a fashion (he had fathered more than one child by his mistresses but produced no legitimate heir).

On Charles's death, his brother James succeeded to the throne as James II (✶1685–1688). James pursued pro-Catholic and authoritarian policies even more aggressively. When a male heir was born who would take precedence over James's two adult Protestant daughters and be reared a Catholic, Tories and Whigs banded together. They invited the Dutch *stadholder,* William, Prince of Orange and the husband of James's older daughter, Mary, to invade England. Panicking, James fled to France, and hardly any blood was shed. Parliament offered the throne jointly to William (✳1689–1702) and Mary (✳1689–1694) on the condition that they accept a bill of rights that ensured constitutional government.

In the Bill of Rights, William and Mary agreed not to raise a standing army or to levy taxes without Parliament's consent, to call meetings of Parliament at least every three years and to guarantee free elections to parliamentary seats, and to abide by Parliament's decisions without the right to suspend duly passed laws. The agreement formally recognized Parliament as a self-contained, independent body that shared power with the rulers. Victorious supporters of the coup declared it the Glorious Revolution.

The propertied classes who controlled Parliament eagerly consolidated their power and prevented any resurgence of the popular turmoil of the 1640s. The Toleration Act of 1689 granted all Protestants freedom of worship, however non-Anglicans were still excluded from the universities; Catholics got no rights but were more often left alone to worship privately. In Ireland the Catholics rose to defend the Catholic king, but William and Mary's troops brutally suppressed them. An oligarchy of landowners, with the Whigs in power and the Tories in opposition, now controlled political life throughout the realm. The factions' differences, however, were minor; essentially, the Tories had less access to the king's patronage. A contemporary reported that King William had said "that if he had good places [honors and land] enough to bestow, he should soon unite the two parties."

The Glorious Revolution found its premier philosopher in John Locke (1632–1704), who had firsthand experience with political life as physician, secretary, and intellectual companion to the earl of Shaftesbury, a leading English Whig. In 1683, during the Exclusion Crisis, Locke had fled with Shaftesbury to the Dutch Republic. There he had continued work on his *Two Treatises of Government,* which, when published in 1690, seemed to justify the Glorious Revolution and the Bill of Rights and to refute Hobbes's gloomy view of human nature. Locke's position was thoroughly antiabsolutist. Denying the divine right of kings, he ridiculed the idea that political power in the state mirrored the father's authority in the family. Like Hobbes, he posited a state of nature that applied to all people. Unlike Hobbes, however, he thought people were reasonable and the state of nature was peaceful.

Locke insisted that government's only purpose was to protect life, liberty, and property, a notion that linked economic and political freedom. Ultimate authority rested in the will of a majority of men who owned property, and government should be limited to its basic purpose of protection. A ruler who failed to uphold his part of the contract between the ruler and the populace could be justifiably resisted, an idea that would become crucial for the framers of the United States Constitution a century later. For England's landowners, however, Locke helped justify a revolution that consolidated their interests and ensured their privileges in the social hierarchy.

New World Echoes

The English constitutional model profoundly influenced the English colonies of North America, although there the pervasiveness of slavery and the slave trade starkly contrasted those who had rights with those who had none. For most whites who were not indentured servants, the colonies provided greater political and religious freedom than Europe. For the steadily growing black African population, however, America offered only a degrading form of despotism. Slavery became associated with race, and in the English colonies it developed strict legal sanctions just as the colonies were establishing representative governments. For Native Americans, meanwhile, the expanding European presence brought death through disease and warfare and an accelerating loss of land.

Native Americans, unlike white settlers, believed that land was supernaturally provided for their use and not subject to individual ownership. Europeans' claims that they owned exclusive land rights triggered frequent skirmishes. In 1675–1676, for example, three tribes allied under Metacomet

(King Philip to the English) threatened the survival of New England settlers, who savagely repulsed the attacks and sold the Indian captives as slaves. Whites portrayed Indians as conspiring villains and sneaky heathens, akin to Africans in their savagery.

The decentralized government that had spurred the economic surge of the Dutch Republic in the seventeenth century also shaped the economies and politics of the Dutch and English colonies. Dutch expansion in North America proved short-lived, however; in 1664, New Netherland fell to the English, who renamed it New York. Virtually left to themselves during the turmoil in England, the fledgling English colonies in North America developed representative government on their own. Almost every colony had a governor and a two-house legislature. The colonial legislatures, or assemblies, constantly sought to increase their power and resisted the efforts of Charles II and James II to reaffirm royal control. Then William and Mary reluctantly allowed emerging colonial elites more control over local affairs. The social and political elites among the settlers hoped to impose an English social hierarchy dominated by rich landowners. Ordinary immigrants to the North American colonies, however, took advantage of plentiful land to carve out their own farms and to employ indentured servants and, later, in some colonies, African slaves.

As the colonies grew, slavery became more prevalent. Black slavery first became firmly established in the Caribbean island colonies, where the English, Spanish, French, and Dutch competed economically and militarily. Island slaves worked fields of sugar cane, a crop much more profitable than tobacco, and displaced most of the original white settlers, who moved to mainland colonies. After 1661, when Barbados instituted a slave code that stripped all Africans of rights under English law, slavery became codified as an inherited status that applied only to blacks. The result was a society of extremes: the very wealthy, about 7 percent of the population; and the enslaved, the powerless majority. The English brought little of their religious or constitutional development to the Caribbean.

The first slaves imported directly from Africa did not arrive on the North American continent until 1674. In the northern colonies of North America, Africans worked as domestic servants,

The Slave Trade in the 1600s
As European colonial enterprises grew, so too did the slave trade. This French engraving shows the sale of slaves in one of the Caribbean islands.

but in the Chesapeake and the South, they toiled in large numbers on tobacco and rice plantations. By the end of the seventeenth century, the English colonies' settler population of about two hundred fifty thousand was 10 percent black, and almost all blacks were slaves. The highest church and government authorities in Catholic and Protestant countries alike condoned the expanding slave trade; the governments of England, France, Spain, Portugal, the Dutch Republic, and Denmark all encouraged private companies to compete for the African trade. The Dutch West India Company was the most successful of these enterprises. And despite John Locke's emphasis on liberty and constitutionalism, he owned shares in the Royal African Company and justified slavery in his writings.

Coherence Regained: Elite and Popular Culture

"When I consider the short duration of my life . . . engulfed in the infinite immensity of spaces of which I am ignorant, and which know me not, I am frightened. . . . The eternal silence of these infinite spaces frightens me." Thus in his *Pensées* (Thoughts), notes on religion written around 1660, near the end of his brief life, the great mathematician Blaise Pascal vividly captured the bewilderment of early seventeenth-century thinkers. The intellectual revolution Copernicus, Kepler, and Galileo had begun was sweeping away the "commonsense" universe of the Bible, Aristotle, and Ptolemy, a universe crowned by God. "This is what I see and what troubles me," Pascal confessed. "I look on all sides, and I see only darkness everywhere. Nature presents to me nothing which is not a matter of doubt and concern. . . . It is incomprehensible that God should exist, and incomprehensible that He should not exist." Pascal, who discovered probability theory, literally wagered on God's existence. If God did not exist, nothing would be lost by believing in him, and salvation was sure if he did.

Yet by 1700 there would have seemed less reason for Pascal's desperate bet. Another mathematician of genius, Isaac Newton, supplied proofs that could explain how a wise, benevolent deity sustained the Copernican universe. In other respects, too, the intellectual and social elite found life more predictable and "reasonable." State power was reducing disorder. Gracious manners that had evolved at royal courts now filtered down into the middle class. Governments ended the terrifying witch hunts. Rulers financed academies of artists and writers, and scientific experimentation received official encouragement. Classical artistic style conveyed a message of ordered regularity. Tension remained, but the new, scientific coherence would provide the intellectual foundation for the eighteenth century's critical, "enlightened" spirit.

The Scientific Revolution Consolidated

Isaac Newton (1642–1727), a Cambridge University student at the time of Charles II's Restoration and a thinker who read Descartes and Hobbes when both were under attack, took the lead in reconciling science and faith. A pious Anglican, he sought to refute atheism while showing that the human mind could understand God's creation. By proving that the physical universe followed rational principles, Newton argued, scientists could prove the existence of God and so liberate humans from doubt and the fear of chaos. Building on the work of Copernicus, Kepler, and Galileo, whose refutation of traditional cosmology had threatened the established order, Newton applied mathematical principles to formulate three physical laws: (1) in the absence of force, motion continues in a straight line; (2) the rate of change in the motion of an object is a result of the forces acting on it; and (3) the action and reaction between two objects are equal and opposite. The basis of Newtonian physics thus required understanding mass, inertia, force, velocity, and acceleration—key concepts in modern natural sciences.

By extending these principles to the entire universe in his masterwork, *Principia Mathematica* (1687), Newton united celestial and terrestrial mechanics—astronomy and physics—with his law of gravitation. This law held that every body in the universe exerts over every other body an attractive force proportional to the product of their masses and inversely proportional to the square of the distance between them. Thus the elliptical orbits Kepler had discovered had a rational basis. Gravity, although a mysterious force, could be expressed mathematically. In Newton's words, "From the same principles [of motion] I now demonstrate the frame of the System of the World." No small ambition! The English poet Alexander Pope later captured the intellectual world's appreciation of Newton's accomplishment:

Nature and Nature's laws lay hid in night:
God said, Let Newton be! and all was light.

In fact, not all scientists accepted Newton's theories immediately; but within a couple of generations his work was preeminent, partly because of experimental verification. His "frame of the System of the World" remained the basis of all physics until the advent of relativity theory and quantum mechanics in the early twentieth century.

Newton's science was not just mathematical and deductive; he experimented with light and helped establish the science of optics. Scientific

Isaac Newton
The great English mathematician and natural philosopher labored to reconcile scientific understanding with religious faith. In this contemporary painting, he is portrayed as a man of penetrating intelligence.

method relied increasingly on experiments to verify hypotheses, and these required better instruments and laboratories. In the seventeenth century new scientific laboratories replaced the informal workshops of alchemists and apothecaries—though it should be remembered that Newton himself carried out alchemical experiments in his rooms at Cambridge University. Modern observatories, botanical gardens, and dissection rooms required a new organization of science, whether in new international journals, scientific societies, or direct government involvement.

Rulers in many countries encouraged scientific development. The Great Elector, for example, set up agricultural experiments in front of his Berlin palace, and various German princes supported the work of Gottfried Wilhelm Leibniz (1646–1716), the inventor of differential calculus. A lawyer, diplomat, and scholar who wrote about metaphysics and cosmology as well as history, Leibniz helped establish scientific societies in the German states.

In England the state supported science less directly. The English Royal Society was born out of informal meetings of scientists at London and Oxford. It received a royal charter in 1662 but maintained complete independence as a clearinghouse for information published in its *Philosophical Transactions* and presented at weekly meetings by leading scientists. The society's secretary described its business to be "in the first place, to scrutinize the whole of Nature and to investigate its activity and powers by means of observations and experiments; and then in course of time to hammer out a more solid philosophy and more ample amenities of civilization." Thinkers of the day now tied science explicitly to social progress.

John Locke, the most influential pioneer of social science, argued during the crisis years of the 1680s for educational reform and religious toleration (although he excluded English Catholics or atheists). Attacking practices of the time, he maintained that exercise was essential for children and that corporal punishment not only humiliated but harmed them. In his far-reaching *Essay Concerning Human Understanding* (1690), Locke denied the existence of any innate ideas and asserted instead that each human is born a *tabula rasa* (blank slate). Everything we know, he claimed, comes from sensory experience, a view that for many undermined the doctrine of Original Sin because it indicated that human personality is not shaped by inherent factors. Locke's views promoted the belief that "all men are created equal"—with some notable exceptions.

Government involvement in science and philosophy was greatest in absolutist France, where Louis XIV's support extended to manufacturing and the arts. In 1666, Colbert founded the Royal Academy of Sciences, which supplied fifteen fellows with government pensions. At about the same time, the government set up royal academies of dance, painting, architecture, and music and took control of the French Academy (*Académie française*), which decided on correct language usage. A royal furniture workshop at the Gobelins tapestry works turned out the delicate and ornate pieces whose style bore the king's name. Louis's government also regulated the number and location of theaters and censored all forms of publication. Colbert directed these activities with clear national purposes: the arts, manufacturing, and science were to enhance state prestige by enabling the French to produce their own commodities rather than to rely on foreigners.

Order and Power in the Arts

In an age of assertive authority the state and established churches used the arts to demonstrate their power and ambitions. The era's two dominant artistic styles, baroque and early classicism, both lent themselves to public display. Flamboyant, emotional, and dynamic, baroque style developed first in southern and western Europe. It became international by the mid-seventeenth century and dominated until the mid-eighteenth. First associated with Counter-Reformation Catholicism, the baroque now appeared in various Protestant countries and assumed particular prominence in the German states. In architecture the baroque style created tension between the strict geometric rationality of a carefully laid-out palace and grounds and an impression of the infinite, devised through views, perspectives, light, and color. Baroque palaces, gardens, and theaters provided spaces for the processions and receptions of aristocratic society. At the same time, they displayed sovereign authority through the arrangement of symbols and decorations.

The combination of religious and political purposes in baroque art is best exemplified in the architecture and sculpture of Gian Lorenzo Bernini (1598–1680), the papacy's official artist. His architectural masterpiece was the gigantic square facing St. Peter's basilica in Rome, his contributions to it dating from 1656 to 1671. His use of freestanding open colonnades and a huge open space impresses the beholder with the power of the popes and the Catholic religion. Bernini also sculpted tombs for the popes and a large statue of Constantine, the first Christian emperor of Rome—perfect examples of the marriage of power and religion. In 1665, Louis XIV hired Bernini to plan the rebuilding of the Louvre palace in Paris but then rejected his ideas as incompatible with French tastes. The one tangible result of his visit to Paris, a marble bust of Louis XIV, captured the king's strength and dynamism.

Although France was a Catholic country deeply influenced by the Counter-Reformation and the baroque style, French painters, sculptors, and architects, like their patron Louis XIV, preferred the standards of classicism, which French artists developed as a French national style, distinct from the baroque so closely associated with France's enemies, the Austrian and Spanish Habsburgs. As its name suggests, classicism reflected the ideals of the art of antiquity; geometric shapes, order, and harmony of lines took precedence over the sensuous, exuberant, and emotional forms of the baroque. It also reflected the symmetrical logic of Cartesian (Descartes's) principles. The influence of antiquity in French classicism was apparent in the work of the leading French painters of the period, Nicolas Poussin (1594–1665) and Claude Lorrain (1600–1682), both of whom worked in Rome and tried to re-create classical Roman values in their mythological scenes and Roman landscapes.

Not all the art of the age exalted rulers. Dutch painters found the baroque style less suited to their private market, where buyers sought smaller-scale works with ordinary subjects. Dutch artists came from common stock themselves—Rembrandt's father was a miller, and the father of Jan Vermeer (1632–1675) was a silkworker. And their clients were people like themselves who purchased paintings much as they bought chairs and tables. Rembrandt occasionally worked on commission for the *stadholder,* but even he painted ordinary people, suffusing his canvases with a radiant, otherworldly light that made the plainest people and objects appear deeply spiritual. Vermeer's best-known paintings show women working at home, and like Rembrandt he made ordinary activities seem precious and beautiful.

Musical performances could also express the state's growing authority. Louis XIV and other rulers commissioned operas to celebrate royal marriages, baptisms, and military victories. Louis XIV's favorite composer, Jean-Baptiste Lully (1632–1687), an Italian who began as a cook's assistant and rose to be virtual dictator of French musical taste, wrote sixteen operas for court performances, as well as many ballets. Lully's operas can be termed baroque because they had grandiose overtures and elaborate choral and instrumental effects. Opera was not limited to the aristocratic

Saint Peter's Church in Rome
Gian Bernini planned the gigantic square in front of the church using colonnades and a huge open space to reinforce the image of power of the papacy and of the Catholic religion.

French Classicism
In this 1638 painting, Moses Saved from the Floods of the Nile, *Nicolas Poussin sets a Biblical story in an antique Roman landscape (a pyramid is included to make it seem Egyptian). The effect is much more symmetrical, severe, and melancholy than the more exuberant baroque style.*

courts. From the 1670s, Italian cities built public opera houses, thereby opening performances to a wide section of the urban population.

Playwrights often presented their new plays directly to the court, and Louis XIV gave pensions to those who wrote for him. The French playwrights Pierre Corneille (1606–1684) and Jean-Baptiste Racine (1639–1699) wrote tragedies in the classical mode, often setting them in Greece or Rome. Their plays exhibited the same concern for order that the formal gardens and statuary of Versailles displayed. The action of each play unfolds in a single place in the confines of a single day, and every play is in verse, with a vocabulary specified by the French Academy. Classical dramas included no Shakespearean comic interludes; all the characters are regal or noble, all the language lofty, all the behavior aristocratic. Court society, both men and women, could find in them an example of their own ideals of disciplined behavior. Yet the plays incorporate fundamental human themes, often the individual's tragic struggle with fate.

The Cultivation of Manners

The greatest French playwright of the seventeenth century, Molière (the pen name of Jean-Baptiste Poquelin, 1622–1673), wrote sparkling comedies of manners that revealed much about French cultural norms. Son of a tradesman, Molière left law school to form a theater company, which eventually gained the support of Louis XIV. His play *The Middle-Class Gentleman,* first performed at the royal court in 1670, revolves around the yearning of a rich, middle-class Frenchman, Monsieur Jourdain, to learn to act like a *gentilhomme* (meaning both "gentleman" and "nobleman" in French). Monsieur Jourdain buys fancy clothes; hires private instructors in dancing, music, fencing, and philosophy; and lends money to a debt-ridden noble in hopes of marrying off his daughter to him. Only his sensible wife and his daughter's love for a worthier commoner impede his "transformation." The women in the family, including the servant girl Nicole, are reasonable, sincere, and keenly aware of what behavior is appropriate to their social station, whereas Monsieur Jourdain represents social ambition gone wild. The message for the court seemed to be a reassuring one: only nobles by blood can truly act like nobles. But the play also showed how the middle classes were emulating the nobility; if one could learn to *act* nobly through self-discipline, could not anyone with some education and money pass himself off as noble?

Molière's play exemplifies the trend toward discipline that characterized this period of growing state power, and it spotlights women's importance in maintaining the social system. Church and state alike expected everyone to learn new ways to control their behavior, whether in the form of re-

ligious decorum, military drill, or aristocratic manners. The upper classes began to reject popular festivals and fairs in favor of private theaters, where seats were relatively expensive and behavior was much more formal. Clowns and buffoons now seemed vulgar; the last king of England to keep a court fool was Charles I. Chivalric romances that had entranced the nobility down to the time of *Don Quixote* now passed into popular literature. The new aristocratic hero or heroine practiced self-control; he or she—and women were vital to the new manners—carefully fashioned personal behavior to accord with the tastes of the time, which were invariably French and courtly. In a sense, aristocratic men were expected to act more like women; their goal was to "please" their monarch or patron by displaying proper manners and conversing with elegance and wit. Men as well as women had to master the "arts of pleasing"—foreign languages (especially French), dancing, a taste for fine music, and attention to dress.

The court had long been the central arena for the development of self-discipline. Here one learned to hide all that was crass and to maintain a fine sense of social distinction. Watchfulness was essential; a courtier carefully had to observe everyone's behavior, including his or her own. New attention to manners trickled down from the court to the middle class. A French treatise on manners from 1672 explained,

> If everyone is eating from the same dish, you should take care not to put your hand into it before those of higher rank have done so. . . . Formerly one was permitted . . . to dip one's bread into the sauce, provided only that one had not already bitten it. Nowadays that would be a kind of rusticity. Formerly one was allowed to take from one's mouth what one could not eat and drop it on the floor, provided it was done skillfully. Now that would be very disgusting.

The key words *rusticity* and *disgusting* reveal the association of unacceptable social behavior with the peasantry, dirt, and repulsion. Similar rules now governed spitting and blowing one's nose in public. Ironically, however, once the elite had successfully distinguished itself from the lower classes through manners, scholars became more interested in studying popular expressions. They avidly collected proverbs, folktales, and songs—all of these now curiosities. In fact, many nobles at Louis XIV's court read fairy tales.

Courtly manners permeated the upper reaches of society via the salon, an informal gathering held regularly in private homes and presided over by a socially eminent woman. As in other questions of manners, the French led the way. In 1661 one French author claimed to have identified 251 Parisian women as hostesses of salons. Most were nobles, but their salons encouraged social interaction between nobles and high-ranking non-noble professionals. Although the government occasionally worried that these gatherings might be seditious, the three main topics of conversation were love, literature, and philosophy. Hostesses often worked hard to encourage the careers of budding authors. Before publishing a manuscript, many authors would read their compositions to a salon gathering. Corneille, Racine, and even Bishop Bossuet sought female approval for their writings.

Some women went beyond encouraging male authors and began to write on their own, but they faced many obstacles because of their sex. Marie-Madeleine de La Vergne, known as Madame de Lafayette, wrote several short novels that were published anonymously or after her death. Following the publication of *The Princess of Clèves* in 1678, she denied having written it. Hannah Wooley, the English author of many books on domestic conduct, published under the name of her first husband. Women were known for writing wonderful letters, many of which circulated in handwritten form; hardly any appeared in print during their authors' lifetimes. In the 1650s, in France, women began to turn out best-selling novels, in particular romances set in bygone days. Their success prompted Pierre Bayle to remark in 1697 that "our best French novels for a long time have been written by women."

The new importance of women in the world of manners and of letters did not sit well with everyone. Clergymen, lawyers, scholars, and playwrights attacked women's growing public influence. Women, they complained, were corrupting forces and needed restraint. Only marriage, "this salutary yoke," could control their passions and weaknesses.

IMPORTANT BOOKS

1651 Thomas Hobbes, *Leviathan*

1656 Blaise Pascal, *Provincial Letters*

1667 John Milton, *Paradise Lost*

1670 Molière, *The Middle-Class Gentleman*

1678 Countess de Lafayette, *The Princess of Clèves*

1687 Isaac Newton, *Principia Mathematica*

1690 John Locke, *Two Treatises of Government*

Salons drew fire as promoting unrestrained social ambition; women were accused of raising "the banner of prostitution in the salons, in the promenades, and in the streets." From the court the new manners had penetrated to the city, and the provinces would soon follow: "Thus, the entire nation, formerly full of courage, grows soft and becomes effeminate, and the love of pleasure and money succeeds that of virtue." Molière wrote plays denouncing women's pretention to judge literary merit. English versions of these plays inspired English playwrights to deride learned women with such names named Lady Knowall, Lady Meanwell, and Mrs. Lovewit. A real-life target of the English playwrights was Aphra Behn (1640–1689), the first professional woman author, who supported herself by journalism and wrote plays and poetry. She responded by demanding that "the privilege for my masculine part, the poet in me" be heard and by arguing that there was "no reason why women should not write as well as men."

Piety and Witchcraft

The illiterate peasants who made up most of Europe's population had little or no knowledge of the law of gravity, conventions of the theater, or upper-class manners. Their lives continued much as in centuries past. What changed most noticeably was the social elites' attitude toward the lower classes. In the seventeenth century the division between elite and popular culture widened. Clergymen became better educated, better behaved, and more removed from their parishioners, a development fostered by both Puritanism and Counter-Reform Catholicism.

In most of Catholic Europe as well as in northern and eastern Europe, the reform movements affected popular religion only after 1650. Before 1650, for example, "superstition" had meant false religion. Afterward it came to mean irrational fears, beliefs, and practices, something that anyone educated or refined would avoid. While Louis XIV was reforming his nobility at court through etiquette and manners, Catholic bishops in the French provinces were training parish priests to reform their flocks using catechisms in local dialects and insisting that they attend Mass. The problem was serious. As one bishop in France complained in 1671, "Can you believe that there are in this diocese entire villages where no one has even heard of Jesus Christ?" In some places believers sacrificed animals to the Virgin, prayed to the new moon, and worshiped at the sources of streams.

The Counter-Reform campaign against ignorance and immorality helped extend state power. Clergymen, officials, and local police worked together to limit carnival celebrations, to regulate pilgrimages to shrines, and to replace "indecent" images of saints with more restrained and decorous ones. The cult of the Virgin Mary and devotions closely connected with Christ, such as the Holy Sacrament and the Sacred Heart, took precedence over the celebration of more popular saints who seemed to have pagan origins or were credited with unverified miracles. Parallel reforming efforts appeared in Protestant countries. Norwegian pastors denounced a widespread belief in the miracle-working powers of St. Olaf. In England in the 1690s, lay societies carried forward the Puritan effort to combat fairs, gambling, masquerades, plays, taverns, prostitution and "obscene ballads" because they encouraged the licentiousness of the "mobs and rabble." Reformers everywhere tried to limit the number of feast days on the grounds that they encouraged lewd behavior.

Popular religion did not become arid or lifeless, however. An illiterate slave girl, Catarina de San Juan, known as *La China poblana,* exemplified religion's continuing power to move popular classes and elites alike. Born around 1600–1610 in what is now Bangladesh, Catarina was kidnapped by Portuguese pirates, baptized a Catholic, and sold into slavery in Manila. She was purchased by a Mexican couple and freed on their deaths. After the death of her husband, a Chinese slave whose freedom she had bought, she lived a holy life in poverty and had a series of visions and dreams in which she claimed to have visited the courts of Europe, China, and Japan. Her prayers were thought to have saved the Spanish fleet at crucial moments in the 1670s, and her visions became widely known.

Like many other unusual women, Catarina was accused of witchcraft—by none other than her own husband. He was incensed when she refused sexual relations with him, and he found himself mysteriously impotent whenever he got into her bed. No other trend reveals more clearly the steadily growing division between popular and elite culture than the decline of witchcraft trials in Europe and North America after 1650. People still believed in witches, and accusations and persecutions continued; in one of the most notorious cases, twenty supposed witches were executed in Salem, Massachusetts, in 1692. By this time, however, such executions were isolated instances, and the witch craze had passed. The tide turned everywhere at about the same time, as physicians, lawyers, judges, and even clergy came to suspect that accusations were based on popular superstition and peasant untrustworthiness—on "the stupid credulity of the people."

As early as the 1640s, French courts were ordering the arrest of witch *hunters* and releasing suspected witches. In 1682 a royal decree from Louis XIV treated witchcraft as fraud and imposture, meaning that the law did not recognize anyone as a witch. In 1693 the jurors who had convicted the Salem witches recanted, claiming: "We confess that we ourselves were not capable to understand . . . we justly fear that we were sadly deluded and mistaken." The Salem jurors had not stopped believing in witches; they had simply lost confidence in their ability to identify them. This was a general pattern. Popular attitudes had not changed; what had changed was elites' attitudes. When physicians and judges had believed in witches and persecuted them officially, with torture, witches had gone to their deaths in record numbers. But when the same groups distanced themselves from popular beliefs, the trials and the executions stopped.

CONCLUSION

The end of the witchcraft trials demonstrates the connection between the growth of state power and social and cultural developments. The rising influence of scientific methods and the new suspicion of popular ways prompted state officials to distance themselves from witchcraft accusations. Armed with new views, they extended state power by intervening to stop the persecutions. This was just one example of the many means by which states overcame the crises of the first half of the seventeenth century. Rulers everywhere forged some kind of agreement with the great nobles, who were now tied more closely than ever to state service. State navies protected their international traders, and rulers promoted culture to enhance their own prestige. Nothing, not even the way a noble knocked on a door, was beneath interest. In the eighteenth century, however, economic growth and the appearance of new social groups would create new problems for the European state system.

SUGGESTIONS FOR FURTHER READING

Source Materials

Graham, Elspeth, et al., eds. *Her Own Life: Autobiographical Writings by Seventeenth-Century English Women*. 1989. Includes writings by women prophets as well as diaries about daily life.

Haller, William, and Godfrey Davies, eds. *The Leveller Tracts, 1647–1653*. 1944. Still a useful collection of documents from the English revolution.

Sévigné, Madame de. *Selected Letters*. Translated by Leonard Tancock. 1982. An interesting and many-sided view of aristocratic life at the time of Louis XIV by the most famous letter writer of the seventeenth century.

Interpretive Studies

Beik, William. *Absolutism and Society in Seventeenth-Century France: State Power and Provincial Aristocracy in Languedoc*. 1985. An analysis of the meaning of absolutism from the viewpoint of one important province.

Briggs, Robin. *Early Modern France, 1560–1715*. 1977. A useful survey of France's rise to power on the Continent, including excellent sections on social and cultural history.

Burke, Peter. *The Fabrication of Louis XIV*. 1992. Generously illustrated analysis of Louis's construction of his self-image.

———. *Popular Culture in Early Modern Europe*. 1978. An encyclopedic history that shows a growing separation of elite and popular culture across Europe.

Carsten, F. L. *The Origins of Prussia*. 1954. The classic account of Prussia's rise and the Great Elector's achievements.

Davies, Norman. *God's Playground: A History of Poland*. Vol. 1, *The Origins to 1795*. 1981. The most current and comprehensive general history of Poland available, despite its confusing organization.

Davis, David Brion. *The Problem of Slavery in Western Culture*. 1966. Wide-ranging examination of European attitudes toward slavery.

Dukes, Paul. *The Making of Russian Absolutism, 1613–1801*. 1982. Overview that focuses on problems of state development.

Elias, Norbert. *The Civilizing Process: The Development of Manners*. Translated by Edmund Jephcott. 1978. The best introduction to the history of manners.

Elliot, J. H. *The Count-Duke of Olivares: The Statesman in an Age of Decline*. 1986. The definitive and very readable biography of Spain's leading statesman.

Fraser, Antonia. *The Weaker Vessel*. 1984. A useful overview of the lives of English women, including a good section on their participation in the civil wars and revolution.

Gibson, Wendy. *Women in Seventeenth-Century France*. 1989. Comprehensive treatment of all aspects of women's lives from birth and childhood to death.

Held, Julius S., and Donald Posner. *Seventeenth and Eighteenth Century Art: Baroque Painting, Sculpture, Architecture*. 1971. Includes extensive discussions of baroque art organized by country.

Hill, Christopher. *The World Turned Upside Down: Radical Ideas During the English Revolution*. 1972.

Lively, engaging study of the effects of the English revolution.

Ingrao, Charles. *The Habsburg Monarchy, 1618–1815.* 1994. Comprehensive history that argues against the idea that the Habsburgs were "backward."

Israel, Jonathan, ed. *The Anglo-Dutch Moment: Essays on the Glorious Revolution and Its World Impact.* 1991. An unusual comparative view of the Glorious Revolution.

———. *Dutch Primacy in World Trade, 1585–1740.* 1989. Excellent in-depth analysis of the factors that made Dutch trade dominant until the eighteenth century.

Mack, Phyllis. *Visionary Women: Ecstatic Prophecy in Seventeenth-Century England.* 1992. A sympathetic attempt to understand women prophet's beliefs and ordinary people's experience of religion.

Macpherson, C. B. *The Political Theory of Possessive Individualism: Hobbes to Locke.* 1962. Suggestive Marxist analysis of the great English political theorists, as well as of the Levellers and other radical political writers.

Mettam, Roger. *Power and Faction in Louis XIV's France.* 1988. An intelligent challenge to the idea that Louis XIV was an "absolute" ruler.

Roberts, Michael. *The Swedish Imperial Experience, 1560–1718.* 1979. Contrasts Sweden with the other great empires of the time.

Sabean, David Warren. *Power in the Blood: Popular Culture and Village Discourse in Early Modern Germany.* 1984. Includes a fascinating chapter on a late seventeenth-century German witch.

Schama, Simon. *The Embarrassment of Riches: An Interpretation of Dutch Culture in the Golden Age.* 1988. Lively and richly textured description of the Dutch attitudes toward their history, culture, and daily life.

Underdown, David. *Revel, Riot, and Rebellion: Popular Politics and Culture in England.* 1985. Study of the effects of the civil war and revolution on popular culture.

Vierhaus, Rudolf. *Germany in the Age of Absolutism.* Translated by Jonathan B. Knudsen. 1988. Synthesis of recent research on the German states, including both Brandenburg-Prussia and Austria.

Westfall, Richard S. *Never at Rest: A Biography of Isaac Newton.* 1980. The definitive intellectual biography of the great mathematician.

Johann Sebastian Bach (1685–1750), composer of mighty organ fugues and church cantatas, was not above amusing his Leipzig audiences, many of them university students. In 1732 he produced a cantata about a young woman in love—with coffee. Her old-fashioned father rages that he won't find her a husband unless she gives up the fad. She agrees, secretly vowing to admit no suitor who will not promise in the marriage contract to let her brew coffee whenever she wants. Bach himself supplied the concluding doggerel:

The cat won't give up its mouse,
Girls stay faithful coffee-sisters
Mother loves her coffee habit,
Grandma sips it gladly too—
Why then shout at the daughters?

Bach's era might well be called the age of coffee. European travelers at the end of the sixteenth century had noticed Middle Eastern people drinking a "black drink," *kavah*. Few Europeans sampled it at first, but by the end of the seventeenth century learned treatises on its medicinal properties began to circulate. As Europeans' taste for coffee grew, the colonial powers attempted to break the Arab monopoly on its production. Facing declining profits from its spice trade, the Dutch East India Company introduced coffee plants to Java and other Indonesian islands in the early 1700s. By 1723 the annual crop there reached the staggering figure of 12 million pounds. Coffee production later spread to the French Caribbean, where slaves provided the plantation labor.

Even more than those other novelties, tea and chocolate, coffee created a new pattern of social life because people often drank it in public. The first coffeehouse appeared in

New Societies and the Early Enlightenment, 1690–1740

Jean-Baptiste Chardin,
(detail) **Seated Woman with Book,** *1746*
Economic improvements in the eighteenth century allowed the urban middle classes to develop new avenues of leisure. Many read increasingly popular novels, but religious reading remained important.

London in 1652; by 1700, two thousand coffee-houses had sprung up; and by 1740 every English country town had at least two. The first Parisian cafés appeared at the end of the seventeenth century; before long, hundreds of them flourished, appealing especially to a middle-class clientele. In the Dutch Republic coffee clubs opened everywhere in the early eighteenth century. Berlin got its first coffeehouse in 1714; Bach's Leipzig boasted eight by 1725. Coffeehouses offered conversation, newspapers, and social mixing, in addition to coffee. In England, where newspaper circulation was greatest, thousands of men read newspapers every day in coffeehouses. As a London newspaper explained in 1737, "There's scarce an Alley in City and Suburbs but has a Coffee-house in it, which may be called the School of Public Spirit, where every Man over Daily and Weekly Journals, a Mug, or a Dram . . . devotes himself to that glorious one, his Country."

Coffee symbolized many eighteenth century changes. The spread of coffee drinking meant that Europeans had more disposable income for "extras," that both international and domestic politics had stabilized (international trade was less disrupted

William Hogarth, **White's Coffee House**, *1735*
Coffeehouses offered more than coffee. They served as political and social clubs, especially in England.

and coffeehouses no longer feared as hotbeds of political conspiracy by the police), and that the plantation production of new products had become well entrenched. The culture of coffee also expressed the gender differences of the age; in England and France, as in Leipzig, women could drink coffee at home, but coffeehouses and cafés were for men only. In Amsterdam and Rotterdam, men and women had separate coffee clubs.

Increasing coffee consumption signaled the advent of an era of economic improvement. Rising production and growing populations in the early eighteenth century ended the economic crisis of the seventeenth century. European countries extended their control overseas by establishing new trade outposts and developing plantations to produce new foodstuffs. In Europe innovative English agricultural techniques were altering rural social relations and making it possible to feed larger city populations. Urban growth in turn brought important changes for the middle classes. An increasingly literate society acquired new tastes in music, art, and literature as well as in food and drink. As the public grew more confident, works criticizing absolutism began to be published and discussed. Even women's participation in public life became a subject open to debate. These first challenges to the status quo opened the door to the critical movement that would be known later in the century as the Enlightenment.

Coffee culture and all that it implied depended on a relatively stable state system. By the end of the seventeenth century, strong states developed all over Europe. Compared to their seventeenth-century predecessors, eighteenth-century rulers faced little armed resistance from either the lower classes or the great nobles until the 1780s. Once the wars of Louis XIV's reign ended, an increasingly elaborate diplomatic system kept European dynastic power struggles in a rough equilibrium until 1740. War did not cease, but a balance of power helped prevent military conflict on the scale of the Thirty Years' War. Even though western Europe did not suffer the devastations of war during this time, however, international tensions remained, as new powers emerged in eastern Europe and colonial powers began to clash with each other overseas. The arena for war was broadening rapidly.

The Development of a World Economy

In the half-century between 1690 and 1740, European control of the rest of the world took on distinct characteristics, based on a combination of settler colonies and trading outposts. Europeans seized territories overseas, which provided new goods for European markets and new bases of international power. European colonization was part of a general economic upsurge that began in some places at the end of the 1600s and became general after 1720. The immense impact of European colonization caused economist Adam Smith to proclaim in 1776: "The

discovery of America, and that of a passage to the East Indies by the Cape of Good Hope, are the two greatest and most important events recorded in the history of mankind." Smith overlooked the great achievements of the eastern and Islamic civilizations, but his remark nevertheless captures the enormous importance of the discovery of new worlds—both east and west—for the Europeans. The eighteenth-century extension of European power prepared the way for western global domination in the nineteenth and first half of the twentieth centuries.

The New Economic Environment

The European economy was not transformed all at once. In "the seven ill years" (1691–1697) poor harvests and high grain prices resulted in disease and starvation from Spain to Finland. The winter of 1709 was so cold that most of the fruit and olive trees in France died, sending grain prices to dizzying heights once again. A French archbishop described the situation as "one great hospital" in which people were dying of hunger. Yet after 1720 no general famines and few widespread bad harvests occurred, and food was relatively plentiful and cheap.

Harvests improved because the weather apparently became more favorable after 1700, with winters warmer on average until the late 1700s. Just as the glaciers had advanced in the seventeenth century, bringing colder winters and wetter summers, they now receded. Although historians still debate the causes and exact timing of the eighteenth-century turnaround, no one disputes that conditions grew better. Most trade indicators improved, and international commerce expanded. Trade in coffee, tobacco, and sugar increased dramatically. English imports of tobacco doubled between 1672 and 1700; at Nantes, the center of the French sugar trade, imports quadrupled between 1698 and 1733.

By the 1690s the social effects of the new economic environment became apparent in England. The East India Company began to import huge quantities of cheap, colorful Indian fabrics. This marked the onset of a consumer revolution that would accelerate throughout the eighteenth century. In the English economic literature of the 1690s, writers began to express a new view of humans as consuming animals with boundless appetites. Such opinions gained a wide audience with the appearance of Bernard Mandeville's poem *Fable of the Bees* (published in various versions between 1705 and 1724). Born in the Dutch Republic, Mandeville (1670–1733) worked most of his life as a physician in England. His poem argued that private vices might have public benefits. In the poem a hive of bees abolishes evil in society, only to discover that society has also disappeared. Mandeville insisted that pride, self-interest, and the desire for material goods (all Christian vices) in fact promoted economic prosperity: "Every part was full of Vice, Yet the whole mass a Paradise." Within five years of the poem's definitive publication in 1724, ten books in English had been written to attack it, and France officially condemned it. But Mandeville had captured the essence of the new market for consumption.

With fewer widespread destructive wars, improvements in agriculture, and the retreat of the plague, Europe's population surged by about 20 percent between 1700 and 1750. The gap between a fast-growing northwest and a more stagnant south and central Europe now diminished, as regions that lost population during the seventeenth-century crisis recovered. Cities, in particular, grew. Between 1600 and 1750, London's population more than tripled and Paris's more than doubled.

By mid-century the foundations for a new economy had been laid. Both states and markets established new kinds of powers in local economies. Although in many countries land still could not be bought and sold freely because it was encumbered by legal obligations, many rural economies fitfully yet rapidly commercialized. This process happened most quickly in England and the Dutch Republic, but in other countries too the pressure of state demands for taxes forced peasants to participate in the money economy. The more they found themselves producing for a market, however limited, the more contact they had with people outside their immediate communities. The traditional view of both the economy and the social structure was one of stability, even immobility, and this view was cracking apart. Peasants now sold goods in markets for money. Prospects of better lives lured their children into towns and cities. This migration speeded up after mid-century, but the trend had begun earlier, especially in areas with the most active market economies.

World Colonization Through Trade and Settlement

Although their ships had been circling the globe since the early 1500s, Europeans did not draw most of the world into their orbit until the 1700s. European trade patterns would profoundly affect Africa, Asia, and the Americas, but the effects would differ in each region. The few efforts to found white settlements in Africa, for example, had largely failed by 1700, with the exception of a few Portuguese trading posts in Angola and East Africa (which declined in the eighteenth century) and Dutch farmers on the Cape of Good Hope. But government-backed trading companies from England, France, Portugal, the Dutch Republic, Denmark, and Prussia successfully exploited the thirty-five-hundred-mile coastline of West Africa for slaves. Europeans had less contact with East Africa and almost none with the continent's vast interior.

European trade with Asia also increased, despite resistance from Japan and China. The Chinese emperors had welcomed Catholic missionaries at court in the seventeenth century, but the priests' credibility diminished as they squabbled among themselves and associated with European merchants, whom the Chinese considered pirates. "The barbarians [Europeans] are like wild beasts," the Chinese concluded, "and are not to be ruled on the same principles as citizens." The greatest western economic success in Asia was the phenomenal growth in coffee production on Java and nearby Dutch-claimed islands.

Despite earlier contacts, India came under European influence only in the eighteenth century. English, French, Dutch, Portuguese, and Danish companies all competed for its spices, cotton, and silk, but by the 1740s the English and French had become the leading rivals, just as in North America. They had both extended their power because India's Muslim rulers had been losing control to local Hindu princes, rebellious Sikhs, invading Persians, and their own provincial governors. Europeans who visited India were especially struck by what they viewed as exotic religious practices. In a book published in 1696 of his travels to western India, an Anglican minister described the fakirs (religious mendicants or beggars of alms): "some of whom show their devotion by a shameless appearance, and walking naked, without the least rag of clothes

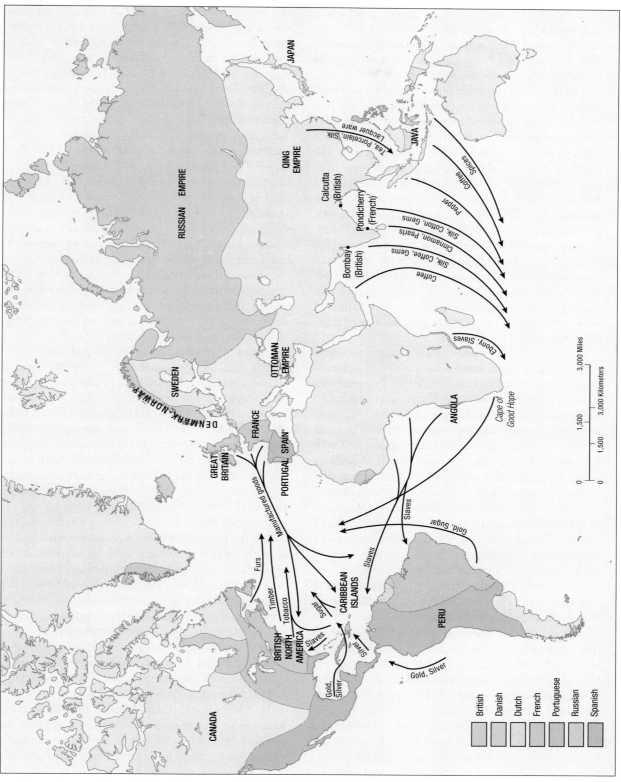

European Trade Patterns, c. 1740

to cover them." Such writings served ambivalent purposes: they increased European interest in the outside world, but they also fed a European sense of superiority that helped excuse the more violent forms of colonial domination.

In the Americas lively competition for colonial lands still involved Spain. The Portuguese and the Spanish disputed boundaries in the new settlements of the southern half of South America, and English settlers came to blows with the Spanish over the territory between the Carolinas, which were English, and Florida, which was Spanish. In 1739, Great Britain went to war with Spain over trade in the colonies. The War of Jenkins's Ear got its name from a Captain Jenkins, who appeared in the House of Commons brandishing his ear preserved in brandy. He claimed Spanish seamen who had boarded his ship to search for contraband cut it off in a swordfight. Jenkins's story provoked violent anti-Spanish feeling, and the war that followed soon became part of the more general War of Austrian Succession (1740–1748).

Patterns of European trade and colonization varied greatly from region to region. Few Europeans lived in the Far East and Africa. For example, in 1720 only one thousand Europeans resided in Guangzhou (Canton), the sole place where Chinese and foreigners could legally trade. In terms of value of imports, however, the eastern trade was still very lucrative; the Europeans paid South American silver and gold for eastern spices, coffee, tea, silk, dyes, and other luxury goods. A few thousand Europeans lived in India, though many thousand more soldiers were stationed there to protect them. The staple of the trade with India in the early 1700s was calicoes—lightweight, brightly colored cotton cloth that caught on as a fashion in Europe.

In contrast to the sparsely inhabited trading outposts in the Far East and Africa, the colonies in the Americas bulged with settlers. The British North American colonies contained about 1.5 million nonnative (that is, white settler and black slave) residents by 1750. North America and the Caribbean islands exchanged a wide variety of staples for European textiles, hardware, tools, paper, glass, and other manufactured goods. Furs and fish came from Canada, tobacco from Virginia and Maryland, rice and indigo from South Carolina and Georgia, sugar and some coffee and cotton from the islands. The New England colonies exported very little, besides fish, though they offered a profitable market for English manufactured goods.

The volume of European trade with Latin America was smaller than with North America or the West Indies. Although the Spanish colonies exported wood, hides, and dyes, the primary export remained precious metals. Silver from Mexico, Peru, and present-day Bolivia supplemented the declining gold supply, and from the 1730s, Portuguese Brazil sent diamonds to Europe. European merchants used the gold and silver to buy goods in the Far East. The Spanish forced the Indians to toil in the silver mines, though they paid them for their skills, and they brought in black slaves to do the unskilled labor. Large ranches owned by American-born Spaniards and worked by Indians provided the meat and supplies for towns and mining communities. The major export crop in Brazil at the end of the seventeenth century was sugar, which (as in the Caribbean islands) was grown on plantations that used African slaves.

Local economies shaped colonial social relations; men in French trapper communities in Canada, for example, had little in common with the men and women of the plantation societies in Barbados or Brazil. Racial attitudes also differed from place to place. The Spanish and Portuguese tolerated intermarriage with the native populations in both America and Asia. Sexual contact, both inside and outside marriage, fostered greater racial variety in the Spanish and Portuguese colonies than among the French or the English (though mixed-race people could be found everywhere). By the end of the eighteenth century, *mestizos,* children of Spanish men and Indian women, accounted for more than a quarter of the population in the Spanish colonies, and many of them aspired to join the local elite. Greater racial diversity seems not to have improved the treatment of slaves, however, which was probably harshest in Portuguese Brazil.

Efforts to impose western Christianity proved most successful in areas where intermarriage between colonials and natives was common, especially in Latin America. Although the Indians of Guatemala, for example, continued to believe in owls who spoke to them in voices, they had come to consider themselves devout Catholics by the early eighteenth century. Indian carpenters and artisans in the villages produced innumerable altars, retables (painted panels), and sculpted images to adorn their local churches, and individual families put up domestic shrines. Yet the clergy remained overwhelmingly Spanish. The church hierarchy concluded that the Indians' humility and innocence made them unsuitable for the priesthood.

The position of women in the colonies depended on race, social origins, the legal system, local customs, and even the male-female ratio. In the early years of settlement many more men than women emigrated from Europe. Although the sex imbalance began to decline at the end of the seventeenth century, it remained substantial; two and one half times as many men as women were among the immigrants from Liverpool (England) leaving between 1697 and 1707, for example. Women who left to become indentured servants ran great risks: if they did not die of disease during the voyage, they might end up giving birth to illegitimate children (the fate of at least one in five servant women in Maryland) or being virtually sold into marriage.

Reactions to the scarcity of women varied. Portuguese colonists in Brazil kept upper-class women in seclusion, but one wealthy widow, Maria da Cruz, nonetheless led a rebellion in the backlands against the colonial government in 1736–1737. As in Europe, white colonial women's positions were closely tied to their marital status; a married woman was legally and customarily viewed as her husband's adjunct, and her husband's position determined her social standing.

The Slave Trade and the Atlantic Economy

Under the new economic conditions of rapidly expanding international trade, commercial empires remained viable only if they could compete in the transatlantic economy. Spain, France, Great Britain, and the Dutch Republic all oriented their mercantilist government policies toward success in international commerce. Realizing that plantation economies producing staples for Europeans could bring fabulous wealth, the European powers grew less interested in the dwindling trade in precious metals and more eager to colonize.

In the last half of the seventeenth century the British, Dutch, French, and Danish set up sugar and tobacco plantations in the Caribbean islands, and state-chartered private companies shipped in slaves from Africa to do the work. Before 1675 most blacks taken from Africa had been sent to Brazil, but by 1700 half of the African slaves landed in the Caribbean. Thereafter, the plantation economy began to expand on the North American mainland. The numbers were staggering. Before 1650 only about seven thousand slaves were annually transported across the Atlantic; this doubled to fourteen thousand between 1650 and 1675, and nearly doubled again in the next twenty-five years; reached forty-three thousand a year between 1701 and 1720; and climbed again to sixty thousand *a year* from 1741 to 1760. The number of slaves taken to the North American colonies increased from fifty thousand between 1721 and 1740 to one hundred thousand (that is, five thousand per year) from 1741 to 1760. In all, over 11 million Africans were forcibly uprooted from their homes and scattered across the seas before the slave trade ended around 1870. Despite the spectacular wealth some individuals gained, the profits the companies carrying slaves and goods between Europe, Africa, and the New World made were often small or even nonexistent in the long term. The English Royal African Company, for example, delivered one hundred thousand slaves to the Caribbean, imported thirty thousand tons of sugar to England, and yet lost money consistently after the first profitable years following its founding in 1672.

The slaves suffered unimaginably terrible experiences. Most slaves were sold to the Europeans by Africans from the west coast who acquired them through warfare, kidnapping, or tribute. The vast majority were between fourteen and thirty-five years old. Before being crammed onto the ships for the two-month trip, their heads were shaved and some were branded. Stripped naked, the men and women were separated. The men were shackled with leg irons. Sailors and officers raped the women whenever they wished and beat those who refused their advances. In the cramped and appalling conditions of the voyage, as many as one-fourth of the slaves died in transit.

Once they landed, slaves were forced into degrading and often horrible lives. As soon as masters bought slaves, they gave them names, often

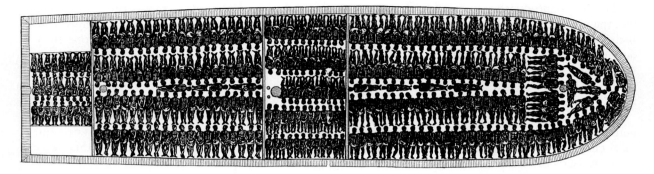

An Eighteenth-Century Slave Ship
*Although the perspective is distorted so that the viewer cannot tell if the slaves are
lying down or standing, this drawing nevertheless conveys the cramped and
crowded conditions endured by slaves on the Atlantic crossing.*

only first names; slaves had no social identities of their own. In some colonies, slaves were branded. Masters expected their slaves to learn their language, to pray to a Christian God (though conversion was discouraged in North America until the end of the eighteenth century), and to do any job assigned to them, whether in a mine, on a plantation, or in a city. Slaves were expected to work fifteen- to seventeen-hour days. Their owners generally fed slaves enough to keep them on their feet, though their diet was unvaried. Brazilian slaves, for example, consumed more calories than poor Brazilians in the twentieth century, but such a diet caused near starvation for pregnant or nursing mothers. At times, however, there was simply not enough food for everyone. The manager of a plantation in Barbados insisted in 1711, "It is the greatest misfortune in this island that few planters give [the slaves] . . . a bellyful" of corn.

The death rate among slaves was high, especially in Brazil, where quick shifts in the weather, lack of clothing, and squalid living conditions made them susceptible to deadly illness. Not surprisingly, slaves sometimes ran away. In Brazil slaves hid in *quilombos* (hideouts) in the forests or backcountry. When it was destroyed in 1695, the *quilombo* of Palmares had thirty-thousand fugitive slaves who had formed their own social organization complete with elected kings and councils of elders.

Outright revolt was uncommon, especially before the nineteenth century, but other forms of resistance included stealing food, breaking tools, and feigning illness or stupidity. Slaveholder para-

noia about conspiracy and revolt lurked beneath the surface of every slave-based society. In 1710 the governor of Virginia reminded the legislature of the need for unceasing vigilance: "The Tryals of Last *Aprill* Court may shew that we are not to Depend on Either their Stupidity, or that Babel of Languages among 'em; freedom Wears a Cap which Can Without a Tongue, Call Togather all Those who Long to Shake off the fetters of Slavery. . . ." Masters defended whipping and other forms of physical punishment as essential to maintaining discipline. Laws called for the castration of a male slave who struck a white person or ran away.

Eighteenth-century slaveholders justified their actions by denigrating the mental and spiritual qualities of those they enslaved. One of the great paradoxes of this time was that talk of liberty and self-evident rights, especially prevalent in Great Britain and its North American colonies, coexisted with the belief that some people were meant to be slaves. Although Christians believed in principle in a kind of spiritual equality between blacks and whites, the churches often defended or at least did not oppose the inequities of slavery. As a leading New England Puritan asserted about the slaves, "Indeed their *Stupidity* is a *Discouragement*. It may seem, unto as little purpose, to *Teach*, as to *wash an Aethiopian*." White Europeans and colonists described black slaves as animal-like, akin to apes.

The balance of white and black populations in the New World colonies depended on the staples produced. New England merchants and farmers bought few slaves because they did not own large agricultural estates. Slaves there were usually domestic servants. Blacks made up only 3 percent of the population in New England, compared to 60 percent in South Carolina. In fact, the British North American colonies contained a higher proportion of African-Americans from 1730 to 1765 than at any other time in U.S. history. In the West Indies (Caribbean islands), English and French emigrant farmers originally worked the land with one or two servants, but once sugar was introduced in the mid-seventeenth century, the small farmers disappeared, and their rough-and-ready, egalitarian community of pioneers gave way to a highly stratified structure of large planters employing indentured servants and large workforces of slaves. In the early 1700s the English sugar islands, for example, had a population of about one hundred fifty thousand people, only thirty thousand of them Europeans. The rest were African slaves.

The slave trade affected Europe more subtly. Wealthy slave traders in English and French port cities built opulent mansions and gained influence in local and national politics. Plantation owners often left their land in the care of agents and collected the revenue to live as wealthy landowners back home. William Beckford, for example, had been sent home to school in England from Jamaica as a young boy. He inherited sugar plantations and shipping companies from his father and older brother, but he moved the headquarters of the family business to London in the 1730s to be close to government and the financial markets. His holdings formed the single most powerful economic interest in Jamaica, but he preferred to live in England where he could collect art for his many luxurious homes, hold political office (he served as lord mayor of London and in Parliament), and even lend money to the government.

The slave trade permanently altered consumption patterns for ordinary people. Sugar had been prescribed as medicine before the end of the sixteenth century, but the development of plantations in Brazil and the Caribbean made it a standard food item. Although sugar was still a luxury for many, the taste for it helped drive colonial expansion. By 1700 the British sent home 50 million pounds of sugar a year, a figure that doubled by 1730. By the time of the French Revolution of the 1790s, sugar shortages would become a cause for rioting in Paris. Equally pervasive was the spread of tobacco, which

Columbus had seen the natives smoking in Cuba when he arrived in 1492. At first most governments prohibited the use of tobacco, but these laws were ignored, and governments came to appreciate the financial advantages offered by state monopolies and taxes (the French tobacco monopoly had been established in 1674). By the 1720s, Britain imported two hundred shiploads of tobacco from Virginia and Maryland every year, and men of every class, including peasants, and country smoked pipes or took snuff.

New Social and Cultural Patterns

The impact of world trade and colonization was most apparent in the cities, where people had more money for the new goods. But rural changes would also have significant long-term influence, as a revolution in agricultural techniques in England made it possible to feed more and more people with a smaller agricultural workforce. As population increased and agricultural techniques improved, more people moved to the cities. When they did, they found themselves caught up in new urban customs such as gathering in coffeehouses. The culture that such congregating fostered helped create a public that responded to new writers and artists. These trends were not uniform across Europe, however; as usual, people's experiences varied depending on whether they lived in wealth or poverty, in urban or rural areas, or in eastern or western Europe.

Agricultural Revolution

Agricultural innovations helped spur demographic recovery in the first half of the eighteenth century and promoted even faster growth in the second half. In Great Britain, as the population increased by 70 percent over the course of the 1700s, agricultural output increased 43 percent. The British imported grain to feed the growing population, but they also benefited from a number of new techniques that together constituted an agricultural revolution. No new machinery propelled this revolution—just new, more aggressive attitudes toward investment and management. The Dutch and the Flemish had pioneered many of these tech-

---

NEW PATTERNS OF CONSUMPTION, 1690–1740

1691 First printed directory of addresses for Paris

1700 Dutch grow coffee on Java and soon take over the world market

1710 Porcelain factory set up at Meissen, Saxony

1719 First cricket match held in Great Britain

1724 Gin drinking becomes popular in London

1727 Coffee first planted in Brazil

1730 Dr. Thomas Smart, a Scottish physician, publishes *A Dissertation upon Tea*, complaining of its deleterious effects on health

1731 Benjamin Franklin founds a subscription library in Philadelphia

1738 First cuckoo clocks made in German states

1739 First camellias arrive in Europe from the Far East

---

niques in the 1600s, but the British took them further.

Three major changes occurred in agriculture. First, farmers increased the amount of land under cultivation by reclaiming wasteland and by growing crops on previously uncultivated common lands. Second, those farmers who could afford it consolidated smaller, scattered plots into larger, more efficient units. Third, livestock raising became more closely linked to crop growing, increasing the yields of each. Farmers planted fodder crops such as clover and turnips in fields that had traditionally lain fallow for a year at a time. Carefully chosen fodder crops added nitrogen to the soil, thereby eliminating the need to leave a field fallow every two or three years. For centuries most farmers had rotated their fields in and out of production to replenish the soil. With more fodder now available, more livestock could be raised, which in turn produced more manure to fertilize grain fields. New crops had only a slight impact; potatoes, for example, were introduced to Europe in the 1500s but not grown in quantity until the late 1700s. Until then, people feared this new vegetable from Latin America might cause leprosy, tuberculosis, or fevers.

Small farmers often resisted the big landlords' efforts to increase their profits from grain by intensifying cultivation using new methods. Villagers defended their common lands (used by everyone in the village) and the customary pattern of dispersed and scattered landholdings. The enclosure movement, by which landlords sought to expand farm size, entailed both dividing common lands into private parcels and fencing off the new larger units. Enclosure frequently sparked a struggle between the big landlords and villagers, and in Great Britain it normally required an act of Parliament. Such acts became increasingly common in the second half of the eighteenth century, and by the century's end 6 million acres of common lands had been enclosed and developed. The effects of the enclosure movement were revolutionary: "improvers" could produce food more efficiently and thus support a growing population that could turn its energies to manufacturing. Already by the 1730s and 1740s, agricultural output had increased rapidly and prices had fallen thanks to such cost-cutting innovations as rotating fodder crops.

Contrary to the fears of contemporaries, small farmers and cottagers (those with little or no land) were not forced off the land all at once. But most villagers could not afford the litigation involved in resisting enclosure, and small landholders consequently had to sell out to landlords or farmers with larger plots. Landlords with large holdings leased their estates to tenant farmers at constantly increasing rents, and the tenant farmers in turn employed salaried agricultural workers. Villagers who could not find jobs as agricultural workers had to move to the towns or new manufacturing areas in search of work.

In this way the English peasantry largely disappeared, replaced by a more strictly hierarchical society of big landlords, enterprising tenant farmers, and poor agricultural laborers who owned little or no land. The land-rich estate owners included wealthy city merchants as well as old gentry families. In the early years of the eighteenth century, the English writer Daniel Defoe noted that "in this part of the country [Essex], there are several very considerable estates purchas'd, and now enjoy'd by citizens of London, merchants and tradesmen. . . . I mention this, to observe how the present increase of wealth in the city of London, spreads itself into the country." Urban influence reached even rural areas.

The new agricultural techniques spread slowly from Great Britain and the Low Countries (the Dutch Republic and the Austrian Netherlands).

Russian Peasants
This view of Russian peasants, an illustration from an English history book of 1693, stresses their exotic look rather than the difficulties of their daily lives.

But outside a few pockets in northern France and the western German states, subsistence agriculture (producing just enough to get by rather than for the market) continued to dominate farming in France, Spain, Scandinavia, the German countries, and the Italian states. In southwestern Germany, for example, 80 percent of the peasants produced no surplus because their plots were too small. Outside the highly urbanized Low Countries, where half the people lived in towns and cities, most Europeans, western or eastern, eked out their existence in the countryside, including seven out of ten people in England and four out of five in France.

In eastern Europe the condition of peasants actually worsened in the areas where landlords tried hardest to improve their yields. To produce more for the Baltic grain market, aristocratic landlords in Prussia, Poland, and parts of Russia forced peasants off lands they worked for themselves, increased compulsory labor services (the critical element in serfdom), and began to manage the estates directly. Many landowners drained wetlands, cultivated moors, and built dikes. In some areas lands were just being reclaimed from the devastation caused by the Thirty Years' War. In parts of Poland and Russia the serfs hardly differed from slaves in status, and their "masters" ran their huge estates much like American plantations. Some eastern landowners were fabulously wealthy. The Potocki

family in the Polish Ukraine, for example, owned 3 million acres of land and had one hundred thirty thousand serfs. The Eszterházy family of Hungary owned 7 million acres; and the Lithuanian magnate Karol Radziwiłł controlled six hundred villages.

Population Growth, Urbanization, and Public Health

The switch from population stagnation to growth in the eighteenth century still puzzles historians and demographers. Beginning first in Britain, then in France and the Italian states, and finally in eastern Europe, population inched up until midcentury, and then began to surge. Although contemporaries could not have realized it then, this was the start of the modern "population explosion." A decline in the death rate rather than a rise in the birth rate apparently fueled the turnaround. Several factors contributed to this decline: better weather and hence more bountiful harvests and fewer famines, improved agricultural techniques, and the plague's disappearance after 1720.

The general population increase certainly did not signal a health-care revolution, however: the state of individual health care continued to be dismal. Hospitals cared for the poor, but patients were as likely to die of diseases caught in the hospital as to be cured of what brought them there in the first place. The wealthy preferred treatment at home, sometimes by private physicians. The medical profession, with nationwide organizations and licensing, had not yet emerged, and no clear line separated trained physicians from quacks. For example, if a woman of the prosperous classes had breast cancer, she could have a doctor remove the breast tumors in a short, painful operation without anesthesia; but many opted instead to use folk remedies such as potions made of warts sliced off a horse's foreleg or a plaster of mutton suet, beeswax, and flaxseed. Unfortunately, neither the surgery nor the concoctions proved successful.

Health care was an economic free-for-all in which physicians competed with bloodletters, itinerant venereal-disease doctors, bonesetters, druggists, midwives, and "cunning women," who specialized in home remedies. Physicians often followed popular prescriptions for illnesses because they had nothing better to offer. Recipes for cures were part of most people's everyday conversation. The various "medical" opinions about childbirth highlight the confusion people faced. Midwives delivered most babies, though they sometimes encountered criticism, even from other midwives. One consulting midwife complained that ordinary midwives in Bristol, England, made women drink a mixture of their husband's urine and leek juice during labor. By the 1730s midwives faced competition from male midwives, who were known for using instruments such as forceps (developed in the eighteenth century) in difficult births. Women rarely sought a physician's help in giving birth, however; they preferred the advice and assistance of trusted local midwives. In any case, trained physicians were few in number and almost nonexistent outside cities.

During the eighteenth century, hospitals underwent a major transformation. Founded originally as charities concerned above all with the moral worthiness of their various inmates, hospitals gradually evolved into medical institutions that defined patients by their diseases. Unlike physicians (who still trained at the universities), surgeons began to learn their trade in the hospital rather than in private instruction as apprentices. Even the process of diagnosis changed as medical men began to use specialized Latin terms for illnesses rather than the language they had previously shared with quacks and cunning women, as well as with the patients themselves. The gap between medical experts and their patients increased, as physicians now emphasized postmortem dissections in the hospital, a practice most patients' families resented. All through the eighteenth and into the nineteenth century, the press reported stories of body snatching and grave robbing by surgeons and surgeon apprentices eager to learn their trade.

Public and private hygiene improved only gradually. Hardly any infectious diseases could be cured, though inoculation against smallpox spread from the Middle East to Europe in the early eighteenth century, thanks to the efforts of Lady Mary Wortley Montague, who learned about the technique while living in Constantinople. Physicians developed successful procedures for wide-scale vaccination only after 1750, and even then many resisted the idea. Diseases spread quickly in the unsanitary conditions of daily life. Ordinary people washed or changed clothes rarely, lived in overcrowded housing with poor ventilation, and got their water from contaminated sources, such as refuse-filled rivers.

Until the mid-1700s, most people considered bathing dangerous. In the sixteenth and seventeenth centuries, public bathhouses had disappeared from cities because they seemed a source of disorderly behavior and epidemic disease. But even private bathing came into disfavor because people feared the effects of contact with water. In the early eighteenth century, fewer than one in ten newly built private mansions in Paris had bathrooms. Baths were hazardous, physicians insisted, because they opened the body to disease. Some believed women could become pregnant by sperm left floating in a warm bath. One manners manual of 1736 admonished, "It is correct to clean the face every morning by using a white cloth to cleanse it. It is less good to wash with water, because it renders the face susceptible to cold in winter and sun in summer." The upper classes associated cleanliness not with baths but with frequently changed linens, powdered hair, and perfume. Perfume was thought to strengthen the body and refresh the brain by counteracting corrupt and foul air.

Urban growth made hygiene problems more acute. Cities were the unhealthiest places because excrement (animal and human) and garbage accumulated where people lived densely packed together. A traveler described the streets of Madrid in 1697 as "always very dirty because it is the custom to throw all the rubbish out of the window." Paris seemed to a visitor "so detestable that it is impossible to remain there" because of the smell; even the facade of the Louvre palace in Paris was soiled by the contents of night-commodes that servants routinely dumped out of windows every morning. Only the wealthy could escape walking in the mucky streets—they hired sedan chairs or coaches.

Still, because of immigration from the countryside cities were growing. Between 1650 and 1750, cities with at least ten thousand inhabitants increased in population by 44 percent. Urban growth from the eighteenth century onward would be continuous. An important south-to-north shift occurred in the pattern of urbanization. Around 1500, half of the people in cities of at least ten thousand residents could be found in the Italian states, Spain, or Portugal; by the eighteenth century, the urbanization of northwestern and southern Europe was roughly equal. Eastern Europe, despite the huge cities of Constantinople and Moscow, was still less urban than western Europe. London was by far the most populous European city, with six hundred seventy-five thousand inhabitants in 1750; Berlin had ninety thousand people, Warsaw only twenty-three thousand. Urbanization was never sudden or spontaneous. Populations usually grew modestly, and the growth rates varied from region to region. But in the long run, urbanization profoundly affected European culture and social life.

Urban Life and the Literate Public

People from an amazing variety of social stations inhabited Europe's cities and towns. The landed nobles topped urban society in much of Europe. These elites maintained at least two residences— one on the family's country estate and the other in town, either in the national or provincial capital or at a fashionable spa such as the English town of Bath, which in the eighteenth century revived its Roman reputation as a recreation and health center. (At Bath, contrary to its name, visitors drank the water rather than bathing in it.) Some nobles filled their lives only with conspicuous consumption of fine food, extravagant clothing, coaches, books, and opera; others held key political, administrative, or judicial offices. However they spent their time, these rich families employed thousands of artisans, shopkeepers, and domestic servants. Many English peers (highest-ranking nobles), for example, had thirty or forty servants at each of their homes.

The middle classes of officials, merchants, professionals, and landowners occupied the next rung down on the social ladder. Some of these people owned small country estates but resided primarily in their urban homes. In this period the middle classes began to develop distinctive ways of life. London's population included about twenty thousand middle-class families (comprising at most one-sixth of the city's population). For breakfast they ate toast and rolls and, after 1700, drank tea. Dinner, served at one o'clock, consisted of roasted or boiled beef or mutton, poultry or pork, and vegetables. Supper at the end of the day was a light meal of bread and cheese, cake, or pie. The amount of meat a family consumed often indicated their social status. Middle-class families in London had meat four or five days a week; a peasant on the Continent rarely ate meat. Beer was the main drink in London, and many families brewed their own.

Jean-Baptiste Chardin, **The Food Supplier,** *1739*
Chardin often depicted scenes from daily life and faithfully reproduced the clothing of ordinary people.

Middle-class houses had about seven rooms, including four or five bedrooms and one or two living rooms. New household items reflected society's increasing wealth and its exposure to colonial imports: by 1700 the middle classes of London typically had mirrors in every room, a coffeepot and coffee mill, numerous pictures and ornaments, a china collection, and several clocks.

Below the middle classes came the artisans and shopkeepers (most of whom were organized in professional guilds), then the journeymen, apprentices, servants, and laborers. At the bottom of the social ladder were the unemployed poor, who survived by casual labor and through charity. Women married to artisans and shopkeepers often kept the accounts and supervised employees, as well as running the household. Women from poorer families usually worked as domestic servants until they married. Every household from the middle classes up employed servants, and artisans and shopkeepers frequently hired them too. Four out of five domestic servants in the city were female. In large cities such as London, the servant population grew faster than the city as a whole.

Social status in the cities was readily visible. Wide, spacious streets graced rich districts; the houses had gardens and the air was relatively fresh. In poor districts the streets were narrow, dirty, dark, humid, and smelly, and the houses damp and crowded. The poorest people were homeless, sleeping under bridges or in abandoned homes. A Neapolitan prince described them as "lying like filthy animals, with no distinction of age or sex." In some districts, rich and poor lived in the same buildings, with the poor having to clamber to the shabby, cramped apartments on the top floors. Clothing was always a reliable social indicator. The poorest working women in Paris wore woolen skirts of dark colors over petticoats, an apron, a blouse, a bodice, and a corset. They also donned caps of various sorts, cotton stockings, and shoes (they probably had only one pair). Working men dressed even more drably. Many occupations could be recognized by dress; no one would confuse lawyers in their dark robes with masons or butchers in their special aprons, for example. People higher on the social ladder were more likely to sport a variety of fabrics, colors, and unusual designs in their clothing.

The basic skills of reading and writing also reflected social differences. People in the upper classes were more likely than lower-class people to know how to read and write; city people were more literate than peasants. In France literacy doubled in the eighteenth century thanks to the spread of parish schools, but it still remained very low for women. Only one in four women could read and write at the end of the eighteenth century, compared to one in two men. Protestant countries appear to have been more successful at promoting education and literacy than Catholic countries because of the Protestant emphasis on Bible reading. Widespread popular literacy was first achieved in the Swiss cantons and in Presbyterian Scotland, and literacy rates were very high in New England and the Scandinavian countries. Some Protestant states, such as Württemberg, Saxony, and Prussia, encouraged primary education by trying to make attendance compulsory, but we have no way of knowing whether people obeyed. Even in Protestant England, male literacy did not exceed 60 percent; female literacy was about 40 percent at the end of the 1700s. Primary schooling was woefully inadequate: few schools existed; teachers received low wages; and no national system of control or supervision was in place.

Despite the deficiencies of primary education and the pronounced stagnation of university life (enrollments and academic standards dropped wherever the clergymen in charge resisted new teachings in science and mathematics), a new literate public arose. More books and periodicals were published than ever before. England and the Dutch Republic led the way in this outpouring of printed words, but the growth of the reading public was a general western European (and New England) phenomenon. Like so many social developments in this time, the trend began in the 1690s and accelerated after 1740. The English government allowed the licensing system for controlling publications to lapse in 1695, and new newspapers and magazines appeared almost immediately. The first London daily newspaper came out in 1702. Joseph Addison and Richard Steele published the first literary magazine, *The Spectator*, in 1709. They devoted their magazine to the cultural improvement of the increasingly influential middle class. By the 1720s, twenty-four provincial newspapers were published, and by the 1730s the new *Gentleman's* magazine enjoyed a large national circulation. In the London coffeehouses, an edition of a single newspaper might reach ten thousand readers.

Newspapers on the Continent lagged behind and often consisted mainly of advertising with little critical commentary of any sort. France had no daily paper until 1777, and outside Great Britain and the Dutch Republic serious political criticism was not tolerated. Tsar Peter the Great founded the first Russian newspaper in 1703, but it was simply a government propaganda organ. Of the titles published during Peter's reign, 60 percent were official pronouncements; less than 1 percent dealt with philosophy or literature. In most of eastern Europe the literate public remained tiny and isolated, but in the West, a growing number of avid readers began to make their voices heard.

New Tastes

The new public influenced the arts and literature as well. In music, urban audiences began to replace rulers' courts as the chief patrons for musical performances. Opera continued to spread in the eighteenth century, attracting a middle-class clientele. Venice had sixteen public opera houses by 1700. Covent Garden opera house opened in London in 1732. The first public music concerts were performed in England in the 1670s, but they became much more regular and frequent in the 1690s. Concert halls typically seated about two hundred, and the relatively high price of tickets limited attendance to the upper classes. In the provinces music clubs provided the only sources of public musical entertainment outside the taverns. On the Continent, Frankfurt organized the first regular public concerts in 1712; Hamburg and Paris began holding them within a few years. With concert halls came the beginnings of printed music criticism.

The establishment of a public who appreciated and supported music had much the same effect as the extension of the reading public; like authors, composers could now begin to liberate themselves from court patronage and work for a paying audience. This development took time to solidify, however, and court or church patrons still commissioned much eighteenth-century music. Bach, a German Lutheran, wrote his *St. Matthew Passion* for Good Friday services in 1729 while he was organist and choirmaster for the leading church in Leipzig. He composed secular works (like the "Coffee Cantata") for the public and a variety of private patrons.

George Frideric Handel
The German composer made his reputation writing music for the English court.

The composer George Frideric Handel (1685–1759) was among the first to grasp the new directions in music. He began his career playing second violin in the Hamburg opera orchestra but moved to England in 1710 and wrote for the English court. After distinguishing himself in his early career as a composer of operas and of such court music as coronation anthems, celebrations of military victories, and funeral music, he turned to composing oratorios, a form he introduced in England. His most famous oratorio, *Messiah* (1741), reflected his personal, deeply felt piety but also his willingness to amalgamate earlier musical materials into a dramatic form that captured the enthusiasm of the new public.

Developments in painting reflected the tastes of the new public, as the rococo style challenged the hold of the baroque and classical schools. Like the baroque, the rococo style emphasized irregularity and asymmetry, movement and curvature, but it did so on a smaller, subtler scale. Many rococo paintings depicted scenes of intimate sensuality

(above) **Antoine Watteau, Gersaint's Shopsign,** *1721*
*Painted originally as a shop sign for an art merchant,
this painting captures the new urban market for art
and a sense of passing times; a portrait of the recently
deceased Louis XIV is being packed away on the left-
hand side of the painting.*

(left) **François Boucher, The Breakfast,** *1738*
*Although known as a painter of erotic mythological
scenes, Boucher also painted scenes from ordinary life,
including this one of a meal. Notice the toys held by
the child on the left.*

rather than the monumentality and emotional
grandeur favored by classical and baroque painters.
Portraits and pastoral paintings took the place of
heroic landscapes and grand, ceremonial canvases.
Adorning homes as well as palaces, rococo paintings complemented newly discovered materials
such as stucco and porcelain and new influences
such as Chinese art, which showed the impact of
the new world economy.

Rococo, like *baroque,* was an invented word
(from the French word *rocaille,* meaning "shell-
work"). Also like the term *baroque* before it,
rococo was originally a derogatory label, meaning
frivolous decoration. But the great rococo painters,
such as Antoine Watteau (1684–1721) and François

Boucher (1703–1770), were much more than mere decorators. With his *fêtes galantes* (mostly scenes of high-society picnics), Watteau captured the spirit of French aristocratic life at the beginning of the eighteenth century. In his painting *Gersaint's Shopsign* (1721), Watteau showed the new consumer culture for art, in which aristocrats and middle-class people replaced the court as the chief supporters of artists. Boucher also painted for the newly rich and for the aristocrats who wanted to patronize art outside the court. Usually highly erotic, his paintings at times also represented middle-class life and values.

Nothing captured the imagination of the new public more than the novel, the literary genre whose very name underscored the taste for novelty. Over three hundred French novels appeared between 1700 and 1730, for example, and the numbers increased even more rapidly after 1730. During this unprecedented explosion the novel took on its modern form, as it became more concerned with individual psychology and social description. Closely tied to the expansion of the reading public, novels were available in serial form in periodicals or from the many booksellers.

Women figured prominently in novels as characters, and women writers abounded. The English novel *Love in Excess* (1719) by Eliza Heywood (1693?–1756) quickly reached a sixth printing, and she earned a living turning out a stream of novels with titles such as *Persecuted Virtue, Constancy Rewarded,* and *The History of Betsy Thoughtless*—all showing a concern for the proper place of women as exemplars of virtue in a changing world. Heywood had first worked as an actress when her husband deserted her and her two children, but she soon turned to writing plays and novels. In the 1740s she would begin publishing a magazine, *The Female Spectator,* which argued in favor of higher education for women.

Heywood's male counterpart was Daniel Defoe (1660?–1731), a merchant's son who had a diverse and colorful career as a manufacturer, political spy, novelist, and social commentator. Defoe wrote about schemes for national improvement, the state of English trade, the economic condition of the countryside, the effects of the plague, and the history of pirates, as well as such novels as *Robinson Crusoe* (1719) and *Moll Flanders* (1722). The story of the adventures of a shipwrecked sailor,

---

> ## THE TAKE-OFF OF LITERARY AND CULTURAL LIFE IN ENGLAND
>
> **1652** First coffeehouse appears in London
>
> **1670s** First public music concerts in London
>
> **1695** Licensing Act allowed to lapse by English Parliament, ending government control over publication
>
> **1702** First daily newspaper published in London
>
> **1709** Joseph Addison and Richard Steele found the first literary magazine, *The Spectator*
>
> **1719** Daniel Defoe, *Robinson Crusoe*
>
> **1722** Daniel Defoe, *Moll Flanders*
>
> **1732** Covent Garden opera house opens in London
>
> **1741** George Frideric Handel, *Messiah*

Robinson Crusoe portrayed the new values of this time: to survive, Crusoe had to meet every challenge with fearless entrepreneurial ingenuity. He had to be ready for the unexpected and able to improvise in every situation. He was, in short, the model for the new individual in an expanding economy. Crusoe's patronizing attitude toward the black man Friday shows the negative side of this individualism.

Male novelists were also very concerned with women's roles in the new society. Defoe's *Moll Flanders* told the story of a girl born in prison and sent to work as a servant. Like many other male authors, Defoe wrote his novel in the form of female autobiography. Seduced by the older son of the family she works for, Moll ends up marrying the younger son instead. Four marriages and many adventures later, she turns to a life of theft, which leads her back to prison. Her death sentence is commuted to transportation to the colonies, and after several years in Virginia and Maryland, she returns to England a prosperous woman. Moll was the model of female survival in the difficult new world of money and social ambition. She was able to overcome even "the hellish Noise, the Roaring, Swearing and Clamour, the Stench and Nastiness" she experienced in Newgate prison. Similar strong female characters, like Moll in their lower class or unknown social origins, showed up in many other novels of the time.

Religious Revivals

Despite the novel's growing popularity, religious books and pamphlets still sold in huge numbers, and most Europeans remained devoutly religious, even as their religions were changing. At the end of the seventeenth century and the first half of the eighteenth, a Protestant revival known as Pietism rocked the complacency of the established churches in the German Lutheran states, the Dutch Republic, Scandinavia, and as far as away as British North America. Pietists believed in a mystical religion of the heart; they wanted a more deeply emotional, even enthusiastic religion. They urged intense Bible study, which in turn promoted popular education and contributed to the increase in literacy. Many Pietists attended catechism instruction every day and also went to morning and evening prayer meetings in addition to regular services.

As a grass roots movement, Pietism appealed to both Lutherans and Calvinists, some of whom left their churches to form new sects. One of the most remarkable disciples of Pietism was the English woman Jane Leade (1623–1704), who founded the sect of Philadelphians, which soon spread to the Dutch Republic and the German states. Leade's visions and studies of mysticism led her to advocate a universal, nondogmatic church that would include all reborn Christians. Philadelphic societies maintained only loose ties to each other, however, and despite Leade's organizational aims they soon went off in various directions.

Catholicism also had its versions of religious revival, especially in France. A French woman, Jeanne Marie Guyon (1648–1717), attracted many noblewomen and a few leading clergymen to her own Catholic brand of Pietism known as Quietism. Claiming miraculous visions and astounding prophecies, she urged a mystical union with God through prayer and simple devotion. Despite papal condemnation and intense controversy within Catholic circles in France, Madame Guyon had followers all over Europe.

Even more influential were the Jansenists, who gained many new adherents to their austere form of Catholicism despite Louis XIV's persecution. In 1713 the pope once again condemned Jansenist doctrine in a papal bull, provoking a series of quarrels that continued until the end of the 1700s. Under the pressure of religious and political persecution, Jansenism took a revivalist turn in the 1720s. At the funeral of a Jansenist priest in Paris in 1727, the crowd who flocked to the grave claimed to witness a series of miraculous healings. Within a few years a new cult formed around the tomb. Clandestine Jansenist presses reported new miracles to the reading public, demonstrating the power of the new public even in matters of religion.[*] Some believers fell into frenzied convulsions, claiming to be inspired by the Holy Spirit through the intercession of the dead priest. Although the Catholic church, the French state, and even many leading Jansenists ultimately repudiated the new cult, its remarkable emotional power showed that popular expressions of religion could not be easily contained. After mid-century, Jansenism became even more politically active as its adherents joined in opposition to crown policies on religion.

Consolidation of the European State System

In the long run all European rulers had to respond to the new public's demands, but at the end of the seventeenth and beginning of the eighteenth centuries, only the western European states faced immediate challenges from this quarter. For most monarchs war was a greater threat than internal opposition. Between 1688 and 1715, Europeans were at war in every year except one (1699–1700). The aims and numbers of belligerents varied from conflict to conflict, but three main questions emerged between 1690 and 1740: Would France dominate western and central Europe? Would the Turks advance or retreat? and, Would Sweden or Russia dominate the northeast? Settling these issues resulted in a more balanced diplomatic system, in which warfare became less frequent and less widespread. States could then spend resources establishing and extending control over their own populations, both at home and in their colonies. By 1740, Great Britain, Russia, and Prussia had joined France and Austria as great powers.

---

[*]When the French government tried to suppress the cult, one wit placed a sign at the tomb that read, "By order of the king, God is forbidden to work miracles here."

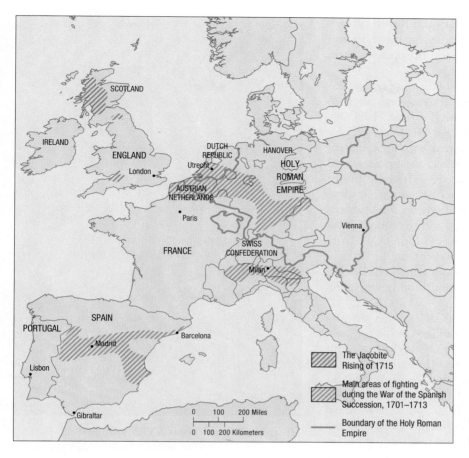

The Jacobite
Rising of 1715

Main areas of fighting
during the War of the Spanish
Succession, 1701–1713

Boundary of the Holy Roman
Empire

**Western Europe
in 1715**

The Limits of French Absolutism

When the seventy-six-year-old Louis XIV lay on his deathbed suffering from constipation and gangrene in 1715, he must have felt depressed by the unraveling of his accomplishments. Not only had his plans for territorial expansion been thwarted, but his incessant wars had exhausted the treasury, despite new taxes. Louis's rival William III, prince of Orange and king of England (*1689–1702), had forged a European alliance that included England, the Dutch Republic, the Austrian Habsburgs, and the Spanish Habsburgs. In 1697 the War of the League of Augsburg ended in a stalemate, but hostilities resumed shortly afterward in the War of the Spanish Succession (1701–1713).

The Spanish succession could not help but be a burning issue, given Spain's importance in European dynastic struggles. The last Habsburg king of Spain, Charles II (*1665–1700), had no heirs. The Austrian emperor Leopold I and Louis XIV both

had Spanish mothers and wives, and so each could claim a dynastic right to the Spanish crown. A crisis erupted when Leopold refused to accept Charles's deathbed bequest of the entire Spanish empire to Louis XIV's Bourbon grandson, Philip, the duke of Anjou.

The war proved disastrous for the French because most of Europe allied against them. The French lost several major battles and had to accept disadvantageous peace terms that perpetuated the stalemate between the Bourbons and the Habsburgs and gave the English many advantages. Although Philip was recognized as king of Spain in the Peace of Utrecht (1713–1714), he had to renounce any future claim to the French crown, thus barring unification of the two kingdoms. The Spanish crown under its first Bourbon ruler, Philip V (*1700–1746), surrendered its territories in present-day Italy and Belgium to the Austrian Habsburgs and Gibraltar to the English; France ceded Newfoundland, the Hudson Bay area, and most of

Nova Scotia to England. Until the Revolutionary and Napoleonic Wars nearly a century later, France would have to work within the European system of nearly equally balanced states.

At home, Louis's policy of absolutism had fomented bitter hostility. Nobles resented his promotions of commoners to high office. The Duke of Saint-Simon complained that "Falseness, servility, admiring glances, combined with a dependent and cringing attitude, above all, an appearance of being nothing without him, were the only means of pleasing him." Even some of the king's leading servants, such as Archbishop Fénelon, who tutored the king's grandson, began to call for monarchical reform. An admirer of Madame Guyon's Quietism, Fénelon criticized the court's excesses: the "steady stream of extravagant adulation, which reaches the point of idolatry"; the constant, bloody wars; and the misery of the people.

On his deathbed, Louis XIV gave his blessing to his five-year-old great-grandson and successor, Louis XV (*1715–1774): "My child, you are about to become a great King. Do not imitate my love of building nor my liking for war." Squabbling over control of the government began immediately. The Duke of Orléans (1674–1723), nephew of the dead king, was named regent. He revived some of the parlements' powers and tried to give leading nobles a greater say in political affairs as a way to restore confidence and appease aristocratic critics. The regent also moved the court back to Paris and away from the atmosphere of moral rigidity and prudery Louis had enforced in his last years at Versailles.

Financial problems plagued the Regency government as they would beset all succeeding French regimes in the eighteenth century. In 1719 the regent appointed the Scottish adventurer and financier John Law to the paramount financial position of controller-general. Law founded a trading company for North America and a state bank, which issued paper money and stock. A state bank would presumably offer lower interest rates and thus cut the cost of financing the state debt. The value of the stock rose rapidly in a frenzy of speculation, only to crash a few months later. With it vanished any hope of establishing a state bank or paper money for nearly a century.

France finally achieved a measure of financial stability under the leadership of the aging but still mentally vigorous Cardinal Hercule de Fleury (1653–1743), the most powerful member of the

Hyacinthe Rigaud, **Louis XV as a Child**
The accession of a child always created problems for royal authority.

Royal Council after 1726. Fleury aimed to avoid adventure abroad and keep social peace at home. Under his leadership state budgets were balanced, the government carried out a large project for road and canal construction, and colonial trade boomed. Although the lower classes still paid disproportionately high taxes, the government maintained political stability by suppressing Jansenist writings and exiling dissident members of the Paris Parlement.

British Rise and Dutch Decline

By 1700, England dominated the seas; but three critical issues remained to be resolved before English imperial power could be fully secured: the line of succession of the monarchy, relations with Scotland and Ireland, and management of Parliament. A succession problem arose because William and

Mary had no children. Parliament ruled that Mary's sister, Anne, would succeed them and that the Protestant House of Hanover in Germany would succeed her if she had no surviving heirs. Catholics were excluded. When the Stuart line ended with the death of Queen Anne (*1702–1714), the elector of Hanover, a Protestant great-grandson of James I, consequently became King George I.*

Obtaining support for the proposed succession required years of maneuvering and even military force. The problem necessarily involved Scotland and Ireland. The Act of Union drawn up in 1707 abolished the Scottish Parliament. The Scots officially recognized the Hanoverian succession and agreed to obey a parliament of Great Britain, which would include Scottish members for the House of Commons and the House of Lords. Nevertheless, both Scotland and Ireland remained potential trouble spots because of their willingness to rebel in favor of the deposed James II and his son. Support from either Spain or France for the Catholic "Pretenders" could threaten national security. A Jacobite (from the Latin Jacobus, or James) rebellion in Scotland in 1715, aiming to restore the Stuart line, received some backing from the English Tories but was suppressed. The threat of Jacobitism nonetheless continued into the 1740s.

The Irish proved even more difficult. When James II had gone to Ireland in 1689 to try to raise a Catholic rebellion against the new monarchs of England, William III himself had taken command of the joint English and Dutch forces and defeated James's Irish supporters. James fled to France again, and the Catholics in Ireland faced yet more confiscations and legal restrictions. Irish Catholics, who in 1640 had owned 60 percent of the land of Ireland, now owned just 14 percent. The Protestant-controlled Irish Parliament passed a series of laws limiting the rights of the Catholic majority (only 10 percent of the Irish were Protestant): Catholics could not bear arms, send their children abroad for education, establish Catholic schools at home, or intermarry with Protestants. Catholics could not sit in Parliament, nor could they vote for its members unless they took an oath renouncing the key tenets of Catholic doctrine. These and a host of other laws reduced Catholic Ireland to the status of a colony; as one English official commented in 1745, "The poor people of Ireland are used worse than negroes." Most of the Irish were peasants who lived in primitive housing and subsisted on potatoes, supplemented by milk, a few vegetables, and perhaps some fish.

Under Queen Anne and her Hanoverian successors George I (*1714–1727) and George II (*1727–1760), the Whigs came to dominate parliamentary politics. In Britain's constitutional system the monarch ruled with Parliament. The crown chose the ministers, directed policy, and supervised administration. Parliament raised revenue, passed laws, and represented the interests of the people to the crown. The powers of Parliament were reaffirmed by the Triennial Act in 1694, which provided that parliaments meet at least every three years; this was extended to seven years in 1716, once the Whigs had established their ascendancy. Only two hundred thousand propertied men could vote, out of a population of more than 5 million people, and not surprisingly, most members of Parliament came from the landed gentry. In fact, a few hundred families controlled the important political offices.

The partisan division between Whigs, who supported the Hanoverian succession and the rights of dissenting Protestants, and the Tories, who backed the Stuart line and the Anglican church, did not hamper Great Britain's pursuit of trading, colonial, and military power. In this period, Great Britain became a great power on the world stage by virtue of its navy and its ability to finance major military involvement in the wars against Louis XIV. The founding of the Bank of England in 1694 enabled the government to raise money at low interest for foreign wars and tied the great merchants and financiers to the government. The bank's success can be measured by the amount of money borrowed in wartime: by the 1740s the government could borrow more than four times what it could in the 1690s.

George I (who did not speak English) and George II relied on one man, Sir Robert Walpole (1676–1745), to help them manage their relations with Parliament. From his position as First Lord of the Treasury, Walpole made himself into first or "prime" minister of state, leading the House of Commons from 1721 to 1742. Although appointed initially by the king, Walpole established an enduring pattern of parliamentary government in which

---

*The House of Hanover still occupies the British throne, though it was renamed the House of Windsor during World War I.

a prime minister from the leading party guided legislation through the House of Commons. Walpole built a vast patronage machine that dispensed government jobs to win support for the crown's policies. Some complained that this patronage system corrupted politics, but Walpole successfully used his political skills to convince the ruling class not to rock its own boat. George II described him as "the most able man in the kingdom . . . he understood the revenue, and knew how to manage that formidable and refractory body, the House of Commons." His successors would extend the patronage system and engender opposition not only from the Tories but also from the popular classes in London and eventually from the North American colonies.

While British influence increased, Dutch imperial power declined, even though the Dutch still controlled a sizable portion of the world's commerce. The Dutch gained little from the Peace of Utrecht and thereafter participated minimally in European wars. When William of Orange (William III of England) died in 1702, he had no heirs, and for forty-five years the Dutch lived without a stadholder. The merchant ruling class of some two thousand families dominated the Dutch Republic more than ever. In some areas, Dutch decline was only relative: the Dutch population was not growing as fast as others, for example, and the Dutch share of the Baltic traffic decreased from 50 percent in 1720 to less than 30 percent by the 1770s.

In other areas, however, Dutch losses were catastrophic. The republic's consul at Smyrna (today Izmir, Turkey) complained in 1721 that trade there "has declined more and more and now seems to be lapsing into total decay." After 1720 the countries of northern Europe—Prussia, Russia, Denmark-Norway, and Sweden-Finland—began to ban imports of manufactured goods, and Dutch trade in particular suffered. The output of Leiden textiles dropped from over twenty thousand pieces a year in 1700 to only seven thousand by 1740. Shipbuilding, paper manufacturing, tobacco processing, salt refining, and potteries all dwindled as well. The Dutch East India Company saw its political and military grip loosened in India, Ceylon, and even Java. The biggest exception to the general downward trend was trade with the New World, which increased with escalating demands for sugar and tobacco.

Russia's Emergence as a European Power

Capping a drive that began under sixteenth- and seventeenth-century rulers, Russia's emergence as a great power in this period owed much to the remarkable leadership of Tsar Peter I (*1689–1725), known as Peter the Great. This influential and controversial figure in Russian history faced a difficult beginning. Like Louis XIV, he came to the throne while still a minor (on the eve of his tenth birthday) and grew up under the threat of a palace coup. With little formal education, the nearly seven-foot-tall tsar spent most of his youth tinkering or playing soldiers with the household staff. In 1697 he left for an eighteen-month trip to western Europe, where he traveled incognito as Peter Mikhailov and worked in Dutch and English shipyards in order to observe firsthand the methods of western military and industrial technology. When he returned, Peter determined to transform public life in Muscovy and establish a state on the western model. His westernization efforts ignited a debate that continues in Russia to this day: Did Peter set Russia on a course of inevitable westernization required to compete with the West, or did he forever and fatally disrupt Russia's natural evolution into a distinctive Slavic society?

Peter reorganized government and finance on western models, and like other absolute rulers, he emphasized strengthening his army. He streamlined the ministries and assigned each a foreign adviser. With ruthless recruiting methods, which included branding a cross on every recruit's left hand to prevent desertion, he forged an army of two hundred thousand men and equipped it with modern weapons. He created schools for artillery, engineering, and military medicine, and built up the first navy in Russian history. Not surprisingly, taxes tripled. The tsar allowed nothing to stand in his way. He did not hesitate to use torture and execute thousands. He allowed a special guards regiment unprecedented power to expedite cases against those suspected of rebellion, espionage, pretensions to the throne, or just "unseemly utterances" against the tsar. Opposition to his policies reached into his own family. Because his only son, Alexei, had allied himself with his critics, Peter threw him into prison, where the young man mysteriously died.

To control the often restive nobility, Peter insisted that all noblemen engage in state service. A Table of Ranks (1722) classified them into military, administrative, and court categories, thereby codifying social and legal relationships in Russia for nearly two centuries. All social and material advantages now depended on serving the crown. Because the nobles lacked a secure independent status, the tsar could control them to a degree that would have been the envy of any western absolutist ruler. State service was not only compulsory but also permanent. Moreover, the male children of those in service had to be registered by the age of ten and begin serving at fifteen. To gain similar dominion over the Russian Orthodox church, Peter allowed the office of patriarch to remain vacant, and in 1721 he relaced it with the Holy Synod, a bureaucracy of laymen under his jurisdiction. For many Russians this made Peter seem the Antichrist incarnate.

As part of his program, Peter insisted on westernizing Russian culture. He set up the first greenhouses, laboratories, and technical schools, and founded the Russian Academy of Sciences. He ordered translations of western classics and hired a German theater company to perform the French plays of Molière. He replaced the traditional Russian calendar with the western one,* introduced Arabic numerals, and brought out the first public newspaper. He ordered his officials and the nobles to shave their beards and dress in western fashion, and he even issued precise regulations about the suitable style of jacket, boots, and cap (generally French or German). He himself published a book on manners for young noblemen and experimented with dentistry on his courtiers.

Peter did not undertake these reforms alone. Those elites who were eager for social mobility and willing to adopt western values cooperated with him. Foreigners were encouraged to move to Russia to offer their advice and skills, especially for building the new capital city, St. Petersburg, meant to symbolize Russia's opening to the West. Construction began in 1703 in a Baltic province that

Chopping off the Russian Beard
Peter the Great ordered his nobles to conform to western European style; in this caricature he wields the scissors over a nobleman's protests.

had been recently conquered from Sweden. By the end of 1709, forty thousand recruits a year were assigned to the work. Skilled workers were required to move to the new city, and all landowners possessing more than forty serf households were ordered to build houses there. By 1710 the permanent population of St. Petersburg was eight thousand; at Peter's death in 1725, it had grown to forty thousand. In the 1720s a German minister described the city "as a wonder of the world, considering its magnificent palaces, sixty odd thousand houses [an exaggeration!] and the short time that was employed in the building of it."

As a new city far from the Muscovite heartland, St. Petersburg represented a decisive break from Russia's past. Peter widened that gap by carrying his westernization into every possible corner of Russian life. At his new capital he tried to improve the traditionally degraded, secluded status of women by ordering them to dress in European styles and appear publicly at his dinners for diplomatic representatives. Imitating French manners, he decreed that women attend his new social

---

*Peter introduced the Julian calendar, then in use in Protestant but not Catholic countries. Later in the eighteenth century, Protestant Europe abandoned the Julian for the Gregorian calendar. Not until 1918 was the Julian calendar abolished in Russia, at which point it had fallen thirteen days behind Europe's Gregorian calendar.

A. Zubov, The Winter Palace in St. Petersburg, begun in 1711, *1717*
This engraving shows one of the first buildings erected in the new city of St. Petersburg. Because of its canals and western-style buildings, St. Petersburg was called the "Venice of the North."

"assemblies" of officials, officers, and merchants for conversation and dancing. A foreigner headed every one of Peter's new technical and vocational schools, and for its first eight years the new Academy of Sciences included no Russians. Such changes affected only the very top of Russian society. Although the upper classes learned to speak foreign languages (eventually even at home and in preference to Russian), the mass of the population had no contact with the new ideas. Tied to the land, serfs had no prospect for social mobility, and their noble lords completely controlled their lives. Peter's projects had a high human cost, not only in terms of ruinous taxation but also in lives lost. Thousands died building St. Petersburg and digging a canal east of the city.

Unfortunately, Peter could not ensure his succession. In the thirty-seven years after his death in 1725, Russia endured six different rulers: three women, a boy of twelve, an infant, and an imbecile. Recurrent palace coups weakened the monarchy and enabled the nobility to loosen Peter's rigid code of state service. In the process the serfs' status worsened. They ceased to be counted as legal subjects; the criminal code of 1754 listed them under the heading of property. They were not only bought and sold like cattle but also had become legally indistinguishable from them.

The Balance of Power in the East

Russia under Peter the Great eventually emerged as the leading power in the Baltic region, replacing Sweden, which had dominated the area since the Thirty Years' War. In 1700, Peter joined an anti-Swedish coalition with Denmark, Saxony, and Poland. Sweden's Charles XII (*1697–1718), still in his teens, proved to be a first-rate military commander when he defeated Denmark, then destroyed the new Russian army, and quickly marched into Poland and Saxony. After defeating the Poles and occupying Saxony, Charles invaded Russia. Here Peter's rebuilt army finally defeated him at the Battle of Poltava (1709). The Russian victory resounded everywhere. The Russian ambassador to Vienna reported, "It is commonly said that the tsar will be formidable to all Europe, that he will be a kind of northern Turk." Prussia and other German states joined the anti-Swedish alliance, and war resumed. Charles XII died in battle in 1718, and complex negotiations finally ended the wars. The Treaty of Nystad (1721), which ended the Great Northern War, forced Sweden to cede its eastern Baltic provinces—Livonia, Estonia, Ingria, and southern Karelia—to Russia. Sweden also lost territories on the north German coast to Prussia and the other allied German states. An aristocratic reaction to Charles XII's incessant demands for war supplies swept away Sweden's absolutist regime,

Russian Expansion to 1725

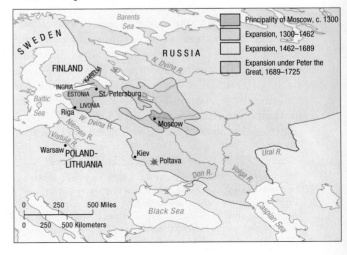

essentially removing Sweden from great power competition.

The siege of Vienna in 1683 had marked the end of the Ottoman Turks' westward expansion. Although no one then realized it, the Ottoman Empire had begun a long process of decay that would eventually culminate in its final dismantling after World War I. Throughout the 1690s, and periodically in the first half of the eighteenth century, the Turks nevertheless continued to fight as the Habsburg armies pushed them back into the Balkans. By 1699, Austria had forced the Turks to recognize Habsburg rule over all of Hungary and Transylvania; by 1717, Austrian troops occupied Belgrade. In the 1730s, however, the Habsburgs lost Belgrade forever, and Russia began to take a more important role in fighting the Turks.

In the reconquered regions of Hungary, language, customs, and ethnic identity separated even the noble elite from the German officials sent by the government in Vienna. The Hungarian nobles, many of them Calvinist and Lutheran, believed fervently in Hungarian autonomy—a belief that occasionally boiled up into revolt against Austrian rule. In 1703 the wealthiest Hungarian noble landlord, Ferenc Rákóczi (1676–1735), led a combined noble and peasant revolt against the Austrians. Rákóczi raised an army of seventy thousand men pledged to fight for "God, Fatherland, and Liberty." Although the rebels did not win the ensuing war, which lasted until 1711, they forced the Habsburgs to recognize local Hungarian institutions, grant amnesty, and restore confiscated estates, in exchange for confirming hereditary Habsburg rule. The nobles were the chief beneficiaries of this agreement. The serfs, who had once been promised freedom by Rákóczi in exchange for fighting, got nothing. Rákóczi died an exile in the Ottoman Empire.

Poland-Lithuania's decline led to its defeat by Sweden's Charles XII and to its withdrawal from meaningful participation in the Turkish wars. Paralyzed politically by the system of the *liberum veto*, the commonwealth had become a mere battleground for power rivalries. A crisis over the Polish succession erupted when Augustus II died in 1733. He had reigned as hereditary king of Saxony since 1694 and as elective king of Poland since 1696. A brief war (1733–1735) pitted France, Spain, and Sardinia against Austria and Russia, each side supporting rival claimants to the Polish throne. France

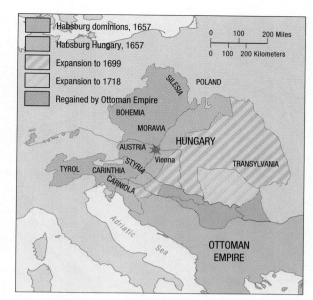

The Habsburg Conquest of Hungary

and Austria resolved the war by direct negotiation without much regard for Polish wishes. France agreed to accept the Austrian candidate, Augustus III, the old king's son; in exchange, Austria gave Lorraine to the French candidate, the father-in-law of Louis XV, with the promise that it would pass to France on his death. Russia manipulated the noble factions within Poland, reducing it to a virtual satellite state.

The consolidation of ever-larger military establishments constantly threatened the balance of power. By building up his armies, Peter the Great had made Russia into a European power. The Prussian kings followed a similar policy, which would bring them clout in the second half of the eighteenth century. King Frederick William I (*1713–1740) doubled the size of the Prussian army, and though much smaller than the French armies, it was the best-trained and most up-to-date force in Europe. The five-foot-five-inch-tall Frederick William was so obsessed with his soldiers that he formed a regiment of "giants," the Grenadiers, composed exclusively of men over six-feet tall. Royal agents scoured Europe trying to find such men and sometimes kidnapped them right off the street.

The army so dominated life in Prussia that the country earned the label, "a large army with a small state attached." Frederick William, the "Sergeant

Frederick William I of Prussia
The military organizer, whose work helped to lay the foundations for the expansion of Prussia, is shown in one of his favorite poses on this painted plate.

King," was one of the first rulers to wear a military uniform as his everyday dress. He created a General Directory to operate the entire domestic administration and subordinate it to the army's needs. He also installed a system for recruiting soldiers by local district quotas. Frederick William financed the army's growth by subjecting all the provinces to an excise tax on food, drink, and manufactured goods and by increasing rents on crown lands. By 1740, Prussia had Europe's highest proportion of men at arms (1 of every 28 people, versus 1 in 157 in France and 1 in 64 in Russia) and the highest proportion of nobles in the military (1 in 7 noblemen, as compared to 1 in 33 in France and 1 in 50 in Russia).

The Power of Diplomacy

No single power emerged from the limited wars of the first half of the eighteenth century clearly superior to the others, and the idea of a balance of power guided both military and diplomatic maneuvering. The Peace of Utrecht had explicitly declared that a balance of power was crucial to maintaining peace in Europe, and in 1720 a British pamphleteer wrote that "There is not, I believe, any doctrine in the law of nations, of more certain truth . . . than this of the balance of power." Forty years later another writer insisted, "What gravity or attraction is to the system of the universe, the balance of power is to Europe." The balance of power often rested on military forces, such as the leagues formed against Louis XIV or the coalition against Sweden. All states counted on diplomacy, however, to resolve issues even after fighting had begun.

To meet the new demands placed upon it, diplomacy, like the military and financial bureaucracies before it, had to develop regular conventions and contacts. The French set a pattern the other European states imitated, and the French diplomatic service was more extensive than any other. By 1685, France had embassies in all the important capitals. Nobles of ancient families served as ambassadors to Rome, Madrid, Vienna, and London, whereas royal officials were chosen for Switzerland, the Dutch Republic, and Venice. Most held their appointments for at least three or four years, and all went off with elaborate written instructions that included explicit statements of policy as well as full accounts of the political conditions of the country to which they were posted. The ambassador selected and paid for his own staff. This practice could make the journey to a new post very cumbersome, because the staff might be as large as eighty people, and they brought along all their own furniture, pictures, silverware, and tapestries. It took one French ambassador ten weeks to get from Paris to Stockholm.

By the early 1700s the French were writing manuals on diplomatic methods that were read everywhere. François de Callières's manual, *On the Manner of Negotiating with Sovereigns* (1716), captured the new techniques of diplomacy. He insisted that sound diplomacy was based on the creation of confidence, rather than deception: "The secret of negotiation is to harmonize the real interests of the parties concerned." Callières believed that the diplomatic service had to be professional—that young attachés should be chosen for their skills, not their family connections. These sensible views did not prevent the development of a dual system of diplomacy, in which rulers sent secret instructions that often negated the official instructions their own foreign offices sent. Secret diplomacy had some advantages because it allowed rulers to break with past alliances, but it also led to confusion and, sometimes, scandal, for the rulers often employed unreliable adventurers as their confidential agents. Still, the diplomatic system in the early eighteenth century proved successful enough to ensure a continuation of the principles of the Peace of Westphalia; in the midst of every crisis and war, the great powers would convene and hash out a written agreement detailing the requirements for peace.

Political Arithmetic

Because a state's strength depended largely on the size of its army, the growth and health of the population increasingly entered into government calculations. As one writer claimed, "The public health is the vigour, the strength, the wealth, and the prosperity of a state." A new school of practical thought called *political arithmetic* reflected these interests. Beginning at the end of the seventeenth century, the political arithmeticians developed new statistical techniques for studying the causes of population growth. Following the lead of the Englishman William Petty, students of population all over Europe tried to estimate total population and rates of births, deaths, marriages, and fertility. A large, growing population could be as vital to a state's future as access to silver mines or overseas trade. In the German states government interest in increasing population size, industrial production, trade, and agriculture took the form of *cameralism,* a specifically German form of mercantilism. In 1727, Frederick William I of Prussia founded two university chairs of cameral studies, and soon textbooks and handbooks systematically advocated state intervention to improve the population's health and welfare.

Physicians used the new population statistics to explain the environmental causes of disease, another new preoccupation in this period. Petty devised a quantitative scale that distinguished healthy from unhealthy places largely on the basis of air quality, an early precursor of our environmental studies. Based on their studies of specific cities, German medical geographers urged government campaigns to improve public sanitation. Everywhere, burgeoning environmentalists gathered and analyzed data on climate, disease, and population, searching for correlations to help direct policy. As

a result of these efforts, local governments undertook such measures as draining low-lying areas, burying refuse, and cleaning wells, all of which eventually helped lower the death rates from epidemic diseases.

The Birth of a Critical Spirit

The efforts of political arithmeticians and cameralists reflected a growing optimism about the future and human potential. Increasingly shared by educated people in Europe and America, this confidence helped generate a new intellectual and cultural movement known as the Enlightenment, a term used to describe the belief that humans can improve their lot by applying reason to each of their problems. Although not called the Enlightenment until later in the eighteenth century, the new secular, scientific, and critical attitude first appeared in western Europe in the late seventeenth and early eighteenth century. Briefly, the Enlightenment was the scientific revolution applied to society and social problems. Skeptics adept in Biblical criticism, popularizers of science, and critics of absolutism in politics joined to vaunt the critical spirit as the solution to society's ills. As part of the general reevaluation of all customs and traditions that ensued, even women's role in society inevitably came under scrutiny, a process that made even many of the most advanced critics of the time uncomfortable.

Rise of the New Skepticism

Most menacing to established authority was a skeptical attitude toward religion and all political attempts to enforce religious conformity. Neither Galileo nor Newton had directly contested the established churches' authority in religious matters. A French Huguenot refugee from Louis XIV's persecutions, Pierre Bayle (1647–1706), launched an internationally influential campaign against religious intolerance from his safe haven in the Dutch Republic. His *News from the Republic of Letters* (first published in 1684) bitterly criticized Louis XIV's policies and was quickly banned in Paris and condemned in Rome.

After attacking Louis XIV's anti-Protestant policies, Bayle took a more general stand in favor of religious toleration. No state in Europe officially offered complete religious toleration, although the Dutch Republic came closest with its tacit acceptance of Catholics and dissident Protestant groups. In 1697, Bayle published a *Historical and Critical Dictionary* that cited all the errors and delusions he could find in past and present writers of all religions. No one and no doctrine was spared the test of reason, for as Bayle claimed, "Any particular dogma, whatever it may be, whether it is advanced on the authority of the Scriptures, or whatever else may be its origins, is to be regarded as false if it clashes with the clear and definite conclusions of the natural understanding." Rome had condemned Galileo's hesitant steps in this direction in the 1620s and 1630s as heretical.

Bayle's reliance on rational investigation rather than faith seemed to lead to skepticism in most religious matters, because faith was the crucial aspect of religion. As one critic complained, "It is notorious that the works of M. Bayle have unsettled a large number of readers, and cast doubt on some of the most widely accepted principles of morality and religion." Bayle asserted, for example, that atheists might possess moral codes as effective as those of the devout. Bayle's *Dictionary* became a kind of bible of critical thought in France, England, and America. The French writer Voltaire (François-Marie Arouet, 1694–1778), perhaps the most influential Enlightenment figure, praised Bayle's influence with biting irony: "He gives facts with such odious fidelity, he exposes the arguments for and against with such dastardly impartiality, he is so intolerably intelligible, that he leads people of only ordinary common sense to judge and even to doubt."

Religion was a burning issue for many other critics too. Books on Biblical criticism used philological and historical techniques to challenge the notion that the Bible offered a complete and unerring revelation of God's truth. New discoveries in geology in the early eighteenth century showed that marine fossils dated immensely further back than the Biblical flood would allow. Investigations of miracles, comets, and oracles, like the growing literature against belief in witchcraft, urged the use of reason to combat superstition and prejudice. Comets, for example, should not be considered evil omens just because such a belief had been passed on from generation to generation. But defenders of church and state published books warning of the dangers of the new skepticism. The spokesman for Louis XIV's absolutism, Bishop Bossuet, warned that "Reason is the guide of their choice, but reason only brings them face to face with vague conjectures and baffling perplexities." Humans, the traditionalists held, were simply incapable of subjecting everything to reason, especially in the realm of religion.

State authorities found the new skepticism particularly unsettling because it threatened to undermine state power. The extensive literature of controversy was not limited to France and criticism of the French state, but much of it was published in French, and the French government took the lead in suppressing the more outspoken books and pamphlets. Forbidden books were then often published in the Dutch Republic, England, or Switzerland and smuggled back across the border to a public whose appetite was only whetted by official censorship. Publication in French also assured a wide audience in the rest of Europe, for many in the literate European public knew French.

Popularization of Science

In the search for a standard of truth that would replace the Bible and tradition, many intellectuals seized on science as a model. Following in the footsteps of Galileo, the French writer Bernard de Fontenelle (1657–1757) popularized the Copernican view of the universe in his *Conversations on the Plurality of Worlds* (1686). Presented as a series of conversations between an aristocratic woman and a man of the world, the book made Copernicanism available to the literate public. By the end of the seventeenth century, mathematics and science had become fashionable in high society. In Paris one mathematician made a name for himself by lecturing to crowds of gentlemen. Journals complained that geometry had become the passport to female affection: "There were two young ladies in Paris whose heads had been so turned by this branch of learning that one of them declined to listen to a proposal of marriage unless the candidate for her hand undertook to learn how to make telescopes." Such writings poked fun at women with intellectual interests, revealing that many men had difficulty accepting the idea that women could be as intelligent and rational as men, but they also demonstrated that women now participated in discussions of science.

Voltaire first presented Newton's discoveries to a popular European audience. The son of a Parisian notary, Voltaire, in addition to becoming a world-famous writer of poetry, drama, novels, histories, and criticism, also made a private fortune in financial speculation. His long career of tangles with church and state began in the early 1730s, when he published his *Letters Concerning the English Nation* (the English version appeared in 1733), in which he devoted several chapters to Newton and Locke and used the virtues of the English to attack French customs. Already impressed by English toleration of religious dissent (at least among Protestants), Voltaire spent two years in exile in England when he published the book, and its publication was greeted by yet another order for his arrest in France.

When he finished his *Elements of the Philosophy of Newton*, Voltaire could not get a French license to publish it, so it appeared in Amsterdam instead (1738). The French state and many European theologians considered Newtonianism threatening because it glorified the human mind and seemed to reduce God to an abstract, external, rationalistic force. So sensational was the success of Voltaire's book on Newton that a hostile Jesuit reviewer reported, "The great Newton, was, it is said, buried in the abyss, in the shop of the first publisher who dared to print him. . . . M. de Voltaire finally appeared, and at once Newton is understood or is in the process of being understood; all Paris resounds with Newton, all Paris stammers Newton, all Paris studies and learns Newton." The success was international. Before long, Voltaire was elected a fellow of the Royal Society in England and in Edinburgh as well as to twenty other scientific academies.

Interest in science spread in literate circles because it offered a model for all forms of knowledge. Enlightenment writers concentrated on collecting all available information and disseminating it as widely as possible. As a result the movement was inherently encyclopedic and propagandistic. Because science appeared able to unlock the secrets of nature, it provided a very positive assessment of human capacities; by observing, collecting, and ap-

plying reason to data, humans could achieve a new understanding of their world. The Enlightenment writers analyzed every social question of the day using these methods: they wanted to reexamine the foundations of morality, religion, aesthetics, systems of government, and social relations. Like the new skepticism, their criticisms of long-held assumptions threatened the entrenched interests of both church and state.

Travel Literature and Relativism in Morals

Critical to the project of reexamination was the relativism that came from widely diffused accounts of travel. Travel literature was not new in the early eighteenth century; Europeans had eagerly followed narratives of the New World written during the voyages of discovery in the fifteenth and sixteenth centuries. In the seventeenth century such works proliferated and took on a new tone. The earliest travel literature simply recorded exotic new sights. In the 1600s, travel writers intended to influence views of their home society by contrasting the utopian conditions of exotic societies with European customs. "Savages" (native peoples) appeared to live in conditions of great freedom and equality; they were "naturally good" and "happy" without taxes, lawsuits, or much organized government.

European accounts of the Chinese, in contrast, emphasized their prosperity and the ancient virtues of their civilization. The "uncivilized savages" might have resisted Christianity out of ignorance, but this could not be said of the Chinese. Christian missionaries made little headway in China in the seventeenth century, and visitors had to admit that China's well-developed religious systems had flourished for four thousand or five thousand years. The basic lesson of travel literature, then, was that customs varied: justice, freedom, property, good government, religion, and morality—all depended on the place. Could any universal truths exist amid this diversity?

Europeans from all countries began to travel more, though most of it was limited to Europe. English gentlemen often traveled to cap their university educations. Philosophers and scientists visited each other to exchange thoughts; even monarchs such as Peter the Great traveled in search of new ideas. The great writers of the Enlightenment journeyed around Europe, partly to escape persecution at home, partly to share ideas with other thinkers, and partly to visit foreign courts to spread their views more widely. One critic complained that travel encouraged free thinking and the destruction of religion: "Some complete their demoralization by extensive travel, and lose whatever shreds of religion remained to them. Every day they see a new religion, new customs, new rites."

Two of the most influential works of the early Enlightenment used travel writing to criticize the customs of European society: Montesquieu's *Persian Letters* (1721) and Voltaire's *Letters Concerning the English Nation* (1733). Charles-Louis de Secondat, Baron of Montesquieu (1689–1755), was the son of an eminent judicial family and himself a high-ranking magistrate in a provincial French court. In 1721 he published the *Persian Letters* anonymously in the Dutch Republic, and the book went into ten printings in just one year—a true best-seller for the times. The paradox of a judge publishing an anonymous work attacking the regime demonstrates the complications of the intellectual scene in this period of ferment. Montesquieu's anonymity did not last long, and Parisian society soon lionized him. In the late 1720s, Montesquieu sold his judicial office to raise money and traveled extensively in Europe, including an eighteen-month stay in England. In 1748 he would publish his authoritative work on comparative government, *The Spirit of Laws*. The Vatican soon listed both *Persian Letters* and *The Spirit of Laws* in its index of forbidden books.

The *Persian Letters* are a novelistic parody of travel accounts. Two Persians, Rica and Usbek, leave their country "for love of knowledge" and journey to Europe. The book is set in the last years of Louis XIV's reign. They write of the king: "He has a minister who is only eighteen years old, and a mistress of eighty . . . although he avoids the bustle of towns, and is rarely seen in company, his one concern, from morning till night, is to get himself talked about." Beneath the obvious satire, however, was a serious investigation into the foundations of good government and morality. Montesquieu chose Persians for his travelers because they came from what was widely considered the most despotic of all governments, in which rulers had life and death power over their subjects.

Portrait of Montesquieu
The French author of Persian Letters *and* The Spirit of Laws *has been painted to look Roman—he wears no wig, and his clothes are draped liked a Roman toga.*

Voltaire's *Letters Concerning the English Nation* praised English tolerance as a way of attacking Catholic bigotry and government rigidity in France: "If one religion only were allowed in England, the government would very possibly become arbitrary [a clear reference to France]; if there were but two, the people would cut one another's throats; but as there are such a multitude, they all live happy and in peace." Throughout his life, Voltaire attacked the injustices committed in the name of religious orthodoxy, but he also devoted many of the letters in this work to the subject of government itself: "No one is exempted in this country [England] from paying certain taxes because he is a nobleman or a priest [unlike France]." Both Montesquieu and Voltaire analyzed society via their travel accounts, presenting the traveler as the unbiased observer who could examine a society without preconceived views. This technique and the observations these writers presented became the basis for scathing criticisms of French practices. Eventually, especially in the 1750s and 1760s, these critical comparisons would be used to develop more general principles about liberty, morality, and good government.

Raising "The Woman Question"

Feminist ideas about the status of women were not entirely new after 1690, but they were presented systematically for the first time and represented a fundamental challenge to the ways of traditional societies. Women writers now went beyond earlier defenses of their sex to argue concrete proposals for changing their status. The most systematic of them was the English writer Mary Astell (1666–1731), the daughter of a businessman and herself a conservative supporter of the Tory party and the Anglican religious establishment. In 1694 she published *A Serious Proposal to the Ladies,* in which she proposed founding a private women's college to remedy women's lack of education. Addressing women, she asked, "How can you be content to be in the World like Tulips in a Garden, to make a fine *shew* [show] and be good for nothing?" Astell advocated intellectual training based on Descartes's principles, in which reason, debate, and careful consideration of the issues took priority over custom or tradition. Her book was an immediate success, and five printings appeared by 1701. In later works, Astell criticized the relationship between the sexes within marriage: "If absolute sovereignty be not necessary in a state, how comes it to be so in a family? . . . If all men are born free, how is it that all women are born slaves?" Her critics accused her of promoting subversive ideas and of contradicting the Scriptures.

Astell's work inspired other women to write in a similar vein. An anonymous *Essay in Defence of the Female Sex* (1696) attacked "the Usurpation of Men; and the Tyranny of Custom," which prevented women from getting an education. In 1709, Elizabeth Elstob published a detailed account of the prominent role women had in promoting Christianity in English history. She criticized men who "would declare openly they hated any Woman who knew more than themselves." Other women wrote poetry about the same theme. In the introduction to the work of one of the best known, Elizabeth Singer Rowe, a friend of the author,

complained of the "notorious Violations on the Liberties of Freeborn English Women" that came from "a plain and an open design to render us meer [mere] Slaves, perfect Turkish Wives."

Enlightenment writers also explored this worry about Turkish wives. Many of Montesquieu's *Persian Letters,* for example, focused on women, marriage, and the family because he considered the position of women indicative of the nature of government and morality. Political despots invariably exercised despotic authority over their wives as well as their subjects. Usbek's harem, for example, showed despotism at work in the family, and one of the major plots of the book tells of the growing revolt of Usbek's wives against the eunuchs who guard them. In the final letter, Usbek's favorite wife, Roxana, writes to him to announce her revolt and her impending suicide: "How could you have thought me credulous enough to imagine that I was in the world only in order to worship your caprices? . . . No: I may have lived in servitude, but I have always been free. I have amended your laws according to the laws of nature, and my mind has always remained independent." The book and its tragic ending showed Montesquieu's own ambivalence about women and power; the Persian visitors criticized the women at the French court for their corrupting influence on monarchical power, yet at home they themselves treated women tyrannically. Later in the eighteenth century other writers would try to answer the question posed by Montesquieu (and by Mary Astell before him) about the proper place for women and the proper form of government in general.

Montesquieu may have been ambivalent about "the woman question," but other male writers unequivocally stuck to the traditional view. Throughout the 1700s, male commentators complained about women's interest in reading novels, which they thought encouraged idleness and corruption. The French theologian Drouet de Maupertuis published an essay, *Dangerous Commerce Between the Two Sexes* (1715), in which he harped once again on the traditional theme of the dangers of women's sexuality: "Women love neither their husbands nor their children nor their lovers," he concluded. "They love themselves."

Such opinions about women often rested on an understanding or misunderstanding of their biology.

In the absence of precise scientific knowledge about reproduction, for example, scientists of the time argued heatedly with each other about women's biological role. In the long-dominant Aristotelian view, only the male seed carried spirit and individuality. At the beginning of the eighteenth century, more physicians and surgeons began to champion the doctrine of ovism—that the female egg was essential in making new humans. Although the French writer François Poullain de la Barre (1647–1723) had asserted the equality of women's minds in a series of works published in the 1670s, most men resisted this idea. Bayle argued, for example, that women were more profoundly tied to their biological nature than were men; by nature they were less capable of discernment but for this very reason were more inclined to conform to God's wishes. During the Enlightenment decades that were to follow, male writers would continue to debate women's nature and appropriate social roles.

The Idea of Progress

Believing as they did in the possibilities of improvement (even improvement in the status of women), Enlightenment writers helped spread a fundamentally new idea about the meaning of human history. They challenged the long-standing Christian notion that Original Sin condemned humans to unhappiness in this world and offered instead the idea that human nature was inherently good and progress was possible if human capacities were developed to the utmost. Science and reason could achieve happiness in this world. For the first time, as a consequence, Europeans began to imagine that they could surpass all those who preceded them in history. They could go beyond the recovery of Greek and Roman ideas that were so important to the Renaissance and make their own discoveries. They could construct a new, better future by applying reason. The idea of novelty or newness itself seemed positive rather than threatening.

More than an intellectual concept, the idea of progress marked a sharp departure from tradition on many fronts. It amounted to nothing less than a new conception of historical time itself and of the Europeans' place within world history. Europeans stopped looking back, whether to a lost Garden of Eden or to the monuments of Greek and Roman antiquity. Instead they oriented themselves toward the future, which they now viewed optimistically. The radical changes in the material world—growing prosperity, increasing population, European dominance overseas—and the transformation of the intellectual world by the scientific revolution combined to set Europeans on a new course. They began to call their epoch "modern" to distinguish it from the ancient period and the Middle Ages (a new term) that came before, and they considered their modern period superior in achievement and certainly in prospects. We still see ourselves within that new framework of time and history first invented in the late seventeenth and early eighteenth century.

CONCLUSION

Between 1690 and 1740, European society changed in many ways. Improvements in the European economy created greater wealth, a longer life span, and higher expectations for the future. People could now spend money on newspapers, novels, and political tracts as well as on coffee, tea, and cotton clothes. In these better times for many, a spirit of optimism prevailed, and the growing literate public avidly followed the latest trends in novels, religious polemics, art, and music. A tide of criticism and new thinking about society swelled in Great Britain and France and began to spill throughout Europe. Politics changed too, although more slowly. Experts urged government intervention to improve public health, and many international disputes were now settled by diplomacy, which itself became more regular and routine. Many Europeans, however, were cut off from these developments or any brighter hopes for their future by illiteracy and poverty. For them, the battle had just begun.

SUGGESTIONS FOR FURTHER READING

Source Materials

Hill, Bridget, ed. *The First English Feminist: Reflections upon Marriage and other Writings by Mary Astell.* 1986. A collection of Astell's major feminist writings that includes an indispensable introduction to her life and times.

Montesquieu. *Persian Letters.* Translated by C. J. Betts. 1973. A classic, published in 1721, that is part political commentary, part novel, and part travel description; includes many passages on eighteenth-century views of women.

Many novels from this period provide fascinating insights into the development of new social attitudes and customs. Possibilities include Daniel Defoe's *Robinson Crusoe* and *Moll Flanders,* the many novels of Eliza Heywood, and Antoine François Prévost's *Manon Lescaut* (1731), a French psychological novel about a nobleman's fatal love for an unfaithful woman.

Interpretive Studies

Besterman, Theodore. *Voltaire.* 1969. A thorough, interesting one-volume biography of the great French writer.

Black, Jeremy, ed. *Britain in the Age of Walpole.* 1984. A useful collection of essays on the various aspects of politics, including popular politics, in the age of Walpole.

Brewer, John. *War, Money, and the English State, 1688–1783.* 1990. Analyzes the most basic foundation of the modern state: its ability to raise money for war.

Cracraft, James. *Peter the Great Transforms Russia.* 3d ed. 1991. The most up-to-date collection of essays on all aspects of this tsar's reign, including an important section on his historical reputation.

Davis, Natalie Zemon, and Arlette Farge, eds. *A History of Women in the West.* Vol. 3, *Renaissance and Enlightenment Paradoxes.* 1993. Essays covering many responses to the "woman question."

De Queirós Mattoso, Katia M. *To Be a Slave in Brazil, 1550–1888.* Translated by Arthur Goldhammer. 1986. A bit abstract in presentation, but filled with interesting information about slavery in Brazil.

De Vries, Jan. *European Urbanization, 1500–1800.* 1984. A sophisticated, quantitative study of the patterns of urbanization over three centuries.

Earle, Peter. *The Making of the English Middle Class: Business, Society, and Family Life in London, 1660–1730.* 1989. A detailed account of the daily life in the middle classes in the most populous European city.

Frey, Linda, and Marsha Frey. *Societies in Upheaval: Insurrections in France, Hungary, and Spain in the Early Eighteenth Century.* 1987. Compares three major early eighteenth-century insurrections; challenges the notion that the early eighteenth century was a time of stability.

Hampson, Norman. *The Enlightenment.* 1968. A sometimes difficult but informative overview of the Enlightenment as a philosophical movement.

Hauser, Arnold. *The Social History of Art.* Vol. 3, *Rococo, Classicism, Romanticism.* Translated by Stanley Godman. 1958. Despite criticism that it emphasizes the middle-class public too much, a pioneering work that still makes interesting connections between the arts and social history in the eighteenth and nineteenth centuries.

Hazard, Paul. *The European Mind, 1680–1715.* 1963. Still the best available guide to the Enlightenment's origins.

Johnston, Edith Mary. *Ireland in the Eighteenth Century.* 1974. A very readable, short history of Ireland that includes good sections on economic and social history.

Jordan, Winthrop D. *The White Man's Burden: Historical Origins of Racism in the United States.* 1974. An abridgment of the author's classic work *White Over Black* (1968); includes an excellent discussion of early attitudes toward blacks in the American colonies.

Krieger, Leonard. *Kings and Philosophers, 1689–1789.* 1970. An excellent introduction to the period that focuses on political and intellectual history.

Parry, J. H. *Trade and Dominion: The European Overseas Empires in the Eighteenth Century.* 1971. A good general history of eighteenth-century colonization patterns.

Price, Richard. *Alabi's World.* 1990. A fascinating account of runaway slaves in Dutch Surinam.

Raeff, Marc. *Understanding Imperial Russia: State and Society in the Old Regime.* Translated by Arthur Goldhammer. 1984. Includes useful chapters on the general context of Peter the Great's reforms.

Raynor, Henry. *A Social History of Music, from the Middle Ages to Beethoven.* 1972. A fast-moving and informative account of changes in music and their relationship to social history.

Reynolds, Edward. *Stand the Storm: A History of the Atlantic Slave Trade.* 1985. A brief synthesis of research on the Altantic slave trade.

Roche, Daniel. *The People of Paris: An Essay in Popular Culture in the Eighteenth Century.* Translated by Marie Evans. 1987. A social history of ordinary people of Paris that includes interesting sections on housing, clothing, and reading habits.

Rothkrug, Lionel. *The Opposition to Louis XIV: The Political and Social Origins of the French Enlightenment.* 1966. Examines the various strains in late seventeenth- and early eighteenth-century France that contributed to the development of the Enlightenment.

Smith, Hilda L. *Reason's Disciples: Seventeenth-Century English Feminists.* 1982. A useful survey of feminist writers in England.

Treasure, Geoffrey. *The Making of Modern Europe, 1648–1780.* 1985. A useful survey of the period.

Van Oss, Adrian C. *Catholic Colonialism: A Parish History of Guatemala, 1524–1821.* 1986. A scholarly study of Catholicism's impact in this Latin American country.

Woloch, Isser. *Eighteenth-Century Europe: Tradition and Progress, 1715–1789.* 1982. A review with a strong emphasis on social history.

In the summer of 1766, Empress Catherine II of Russia (who would later be known as Catherine the Great) wrote to the French Enlightenment figure Voltaire one of the many letters she exchanged with him over a fifteen-year period. The German-born Catherine had seized power in 1762 when her husband, Tsar Peter III, was murdered, quite likely with her cooperation. She wrote to the now-famous, aging Voltaire and, in the tone of a close friend, praised his campaigns for justice:

> *It is a way of immortalizing oneself to be the advocate of humanity, the defender of oppressed innocence. . . . You have entered into combat against the enemies of mankind: superstition, fanaticism, ignorance, quibbling, evil judges, and the powers that rest in their hands. Great virtues and qualities are needed to surmount these obstacles. You have shown that you have them: you have triumphed.*

When Voltaire read this letter, he might well have thought Catherine intended to incorporate some of the Enlightenment's notions about individual rights into her governing of Russia. Catherine made some gestures toward legal reform, but she also jealously guarded her power and did nothing to help the downtrodden serfs. During her reign, in fact, the serfs' plight worsened, and more often than not Catherine harshly suppressed the few feeble efforts to criticize her policies. Yet Voltaire never wavered in his enthusiasm for Catherine, a ruler he likened to an ancient Babylonian queen.

Despite the discrepancies between her professed esteem for Voltaire's virtues and her failure to exhibit qualities she supposedly

The Promise of a New Order, 1740–1787

Wedgwood Jasperware Vase
Wedgwood capitalized on the eighteenth-century taste for neoclassical style in both his crockery lines and more specialized vases. This vase was designed by John Flaxman in neoclassical style around 1780.

valued so highly in her own tenure as ruler, Catherine's long, admiring correspondence with Voltaire shows how influential Enlightenment ideals had become by the middle of the eighteenth century. No one in the educated public could ignore their impact. In encyclopedias and political tracts, in learned treatises about crime and punishment and education, and even in novels, Enlightenment writers advocated social improvement and the legal guarantee of individual rights. The ideas of a relatively small group of social critics spread across Europe and the Atlantic via a variety of new forms of urban social life. In provincial academies and masonic lodges, in coffeehouses and the sophisticated salons of upper-class women, provocative new works were read and debated. Within a remarkably short time, even the most absolute monarchs felt the pressure of this intellectual and social movement. By the 1770s and the 1780s, reform-minded rulers were trying to open new schools, revise penal codes, remove trade restrictions, and extend religious toleration.

The peasants and urban lower classes of Europe, the bulk of the population, had little contact with the new ideas and often did not benefit directly from reforms. The continuing rise in population and new forms of economic growth, some of which had very disruptive effects, shaped their lives more. Occasionally, villagers and townspeople joined resistance movements opposing local lords or rebellions against the state. Many of these popular rebellions were reactions to the extension of grain markets. Whenever grain prices rose, villagers attacked granaries, merchants' stores, or convoys of grain for the armies, insisting that merchants were hoarding grain in order to drive up prices. Local people expected officials to intervene to set prices when grain supplies fell, and they rioted when officials refused to act in the old ways in the name of "free trade." The most successful rebellion of this period, the American War for Independence, had different causes: Americans revolted for national autonomy. Their leaders incorporated Enlightenment ideas such as "self-evident truths" into their movement, and these ideas profoundly influenced the writing of a constitution that many Europeans regarded as the practical realization of all the Enlightenment represented.

The Enlightenment Triumphs

After emerging as a movement in the half-century before 1740 out of the criticism of absolutism and the popularization of science, the Enlightenment developed into a systematic inquiry into the human condition. Enlightenment writers were known as *philosophes* (French for "philosophers"), but their interests ranged far beyond philosophy into politics, economics, history, psychology, aesthetics, and above all, social problems and prospects. In the second half of the eighteenth century the Enlightenment acquired its name, a label its proponents chose to convey the idea of light pushing back the darkness of ignorance and superstition.

Throughout Europe, Enlightenment writers professed a commitment to scientific inquiry and reasoned argument based on empirical study—that is, study founded on observation or experience—rather than reliance on tradition, custom, or dogmatic religion. One Enlightenment manifesto, the French *Encyclopedia* (published from 1751 to

1772), declared its aim to "overturn the barriers that reason never erected" and to "give back to the arts and sciences the liberty that is so precious to them." The German philosopher Immanuel Kant described the Enlightenment as "man's leaving his self-caused immaturity," and he advocated a new intellectual freedom that would lead people to discard their prejudices and use their reason to question traditional ideas.

France was the center of this new critical spirit, and together with London and Amsterdam, Paris formed a kind of intellectual triangle from which the Enlightenment radiated outward. With the encouragement of the hostesses of Paris's dazzling salons, the *philosophes* developed ideas that brought them into conflict with church and state officials, both of which regularly censored writings that threatened established authority. In 1759, for example, the Parlement of Paris condemned the *Encyclopedia* for trying to destroy religion and corrupt morals. Many writers faced the prospect of imprisonment or exile. In the midst of this strife, however, Enlightenment ideas gradually won converts everywhere in the top sectors of society, even among the clergy and state bureaucrats.

Men and Women of the Republic of Letters

The best-known Enlightenment writers were French: Montesquieu, Voltaire, and the French-speaking Swiss writer, Jean-Jacques Rousseau (1712–1778), who lived much of his life in France. Although the most famous books of the movement were written in France (many had to be published elsewhere because of censorship) and most hotly debated there, the new ideas were not provincial but in fact very cosmopolitan. The French *philosophes* considered themselves translators of the great scientific and philosophical breakthroughs of their English predecessors, Bacon, Newton, and Locke; they applied to society and politics the apparent truths about human reason that science had first made evident. The French writers had counterparts in England, Scotland, the German and Italian states, and even as far away as the British North American colonies, Poland, and Russia. Across Europe the Enlightenment spawned a common intellectual culture based on the new urban institutions of public opinion rather than on the now intellectually rigid and generally backward universities (Scotland's universities were the major exception).

The *philosophes* considered themselves part of a grand "republic of letters" that transcended national political boundaries. They were not republicans in the historical sense, that is, people opposed to monarchy in any form. Some, such as Voltaire, warmly endorsed reform programs within the monarchy. What did unite the *philosophes* in their republic of the mind were common beliefs and a network of shared communications through salons, personal visits, printed works, and the exchange of letters. Most were men from the upper classes or even the clergy, yet the careers of others showed how much social mobility was possible in this era. Rousseau's father was a watchmaker of modest means in Geneva, and Denis Diderot (1713–1784), one of the editors of the *Encyclopedia*, was the son of a small-town cutlery maker. Although rare, some women were *philosophes*, such as the French noblewoman Emilie du Châtelet (1706–1749), who wrote extensively about the mathematics and physics of Leibniz and Newton. Despite their social differences, all these writers shared a set of broad beliefs in reform, opposed "superstition," and believed the systematic application of reason could improve the human condition. Enlightenment writings covered a wide range of subjects, from commentary on current affairs to art criticism, from novels and operas to political tracts, and even some clandestine, pornographic novels (most notably by Diderot).

The collective project of the *Encyclopedia* gave the French *philosophes* a common focus. Designed as a compilation of all known knowledge, the *Encyclopedia* aimed to be "a rational dictionary of the sciences, arts, and crafts." Its topics and volumes of illustrative plates reflected Diderot's interest in technology, invention, and efficient production. Individual authors frequently mocked and criticized established institutions, especially the Catholic church. But the *philosophes*' intellectual networks extended far beyond this project. Visits back and forth; letters that were hand copied, circulated, and sometimes published; salon readings of manuscripts; letters to the editor and book reviews in periodicals —all these kept the lines of communication humming from Philadelphia to Moscow, despite govern-

Anicet Charles Lemonnier, **An Evening at Madame Geoffrin's in 1755,** *1812*
Although painted many years later, this painting represents a typical salon scene from the Enlightenment. Lemonnier was alive in 1755 but too young (12 years old) to have participated in the event. Madame Geoffrin is the figure in blue on the right facing the viewer.

ment censorship in many states. Commenting on the exchanges found in newspapers in France and Italy, one writer exclaimed, "Never have new ideas had such rapid circulation at long distance."

If the Enlightenment had an institutional base outside these lines of communication, it would have been in the Paris salons, run almost exclusively by upper-class women. The best known, however, was the salon of Madame Marie-Thérèse Geoffrin (1699–1777), a wealthy middle-class widow, who had been raised by her grandmother and married off at fourteen to a much older man. Creating a salon was her way of educating herself. She brought together the most exciting thinkers and artists of the time; her social gatherings provided a forum for new ideas and an opportunity to establish new intellectual contacts. Madame Geoffrin corresponded extensively with influential people across Europe, including Empress Cather-

ine II of Russia and King Stanislaw August Poniatowski of Poland-Lithuania. One Italian visitor explained, "There is no way to make Naples resemble Paris unless we find a woman to guide us, organize us, *Geoffrinize* us."

Just as some men had ridiculed salon women for their intellectual ambitions in the seventeenth century, so too did certain men resent what they saw as the growing power of women during the Enlightenment. Rousseau railed against their corrupting influence: "Every woman at Paris gathers in her apartment a harem of men more womanish than she." Male writers were divided in their attitudes toward women. Although many argued for more education for women and for women's equality with men in marriage, others still insisted on the natural weakness of women and their unsuitability for public affairs. Voltaire, the devoted lover of Emilie du Châtelet, confessed to a friend, "I frequently wish she were less learned and her mind less sharp." The *Encyclopedia* ignored the contributions of salon women and praised women who stayed at home; in the words of one typical contributor, women "constitute the principal ornament of the world. . . . May they, through submissive discretion and through simple, adroit, artless cleverness, spur us [men] on to virtue." Nevertheless, women's salons helped galvanize reform movements all over Europe. Wealthy Jewish women created nine of the fourteen salons in Berlin at the end of the eighteenth century, and in Warsaw, Princess Zofia Czartoryska gathered around her the reform leaders of Poland-Lithuania. At the other end of Europe, middle-class women in London used their salons to raise money to publish women's writings.

Conflicts with Church and State

Madame Geoffrin did not approve of discussions that were too hostile to the Catholic church in her salon, but elsewhere voices critical of organized religion could be heard. Attacks on religion required daring because the church, whatever its denomination, wielded enormous power in society, and most influential people considered religion an essential foundation of good society and government. In the face of such opinion, the Scottish philosopher David Hume (1711–1776) boldly argued in *The Natural History of Religion* (1755) that belief in God rested on superstition and fear rather than on reason. Hume soon met kindred spirits. Visiting Paris, he attended a dinner party consisting of "fifteen atheists, and three who had not quite made up their minds."

In earlier times *atheist* had been a contemptuous term for someone who (allegedly) lived a "godless" life, disregarding piety and conventional morality. But before the scientific revolution, virtually every European believed in God. After Newton, however, and despite Newton's own deep religiosity, people could conceive of the universe as an eternally existing, self-perpetuating machine, in which God's intervention was unnecessary. Atheists, such as the French *philosophe* Julien de La Mettrie, took just such a position. He insisted that "the weight of the universe . . . far from crushing a real atheist, does not even shake him."

Deists continued to believe in a benevolent, all-knowing God who had designed the universe and set it in motion. But deists usually rejected the idea that God directly interceded in the functioning of the universe, and they faulted all forms of dogmatic religion. Voltaire was a deist, and in his popular *Philosophical Dictionary* (1764) he attacked most of the claims of organized Christianity, whether Catholic or Protestant. Christianity, he argued, had been the prime source of fanaticism and brutality among humans. Throughout his life, Voltaire's motto was *Ecrasez l'infâme*—"crush the infamous thing" (the "thing" meaning bigotry and intolerance). The authorities publicly burned his *Philosophical Dictionary* and other books considered threatening to organized religion.

Criticism of religious intolerance involved more than simply attacking the churches. Critics also had to confront the states to which churches were closely tied. In 1761 a judicial case in Toulouse provoked an outcry throughout France that Voltaire soon joined. When the son of a local Calvinist was found hanged (he had probably committed suicide), local authorities accused the father, Jean Calas, of murdering him to prevent his conversion to Catholicism (it was illegal to practice Calvinism publicly in France). The all-Catholic Parlement of Toulouse found the father guilty and sentenced him to a horrible death—all his bones were broken on the wheel. Voltaire launched a successful crusade to rehabilitate Jean Calas's good name and to restore the family's properties confiscated after his death. Voltaire's efforts eventually helped bring about the extension of civil rights to French Protestants and encouraged campaigns to make the penal system more humane.

Voltaire, like other critics of church and state, was a reformer, not a revolutionary. Although in his early years he had suffered arrest, imprisonment, exile, and even beating by an enraged aristocrat's lackey, Voltaire ended his life within the establishment, thereby showing the growing influence the Enlightenment had on public opinion. He made a fortune in financial speculations, wrote a glowing history of *The Age of Louis XIV* (1751), and lived to be celebrated in his last years as a national hero even by many former foes. Other *philosophes* also lived respectably, believing that published criticism (rather than violent action) would bring about necessary reforms. As Diderot said, "We will speak against senseless laws until they are reformed; and, while we wait, we will

Major Works of the Enlightenment

1748 Charles-Louis de Secondat, Baron of Montesquieu, *Spirit of Laws*

1751 Beginning of publication of the French *Encyclopedia*

1755 David Hume, *The Natural History of Religion*

1762 Jean-Jacques Rousseau, *The Social Contract* and *Emile*

1764 Voltaire, *Philosophical Dictionary*

1770 Abbé Guillaume Raynal, *Philosophical and Political History of European Colonies and Commerce in the Two Indies*

1776 Adam Smith, *An Inquiry into the Nature and Causes of the Wealth of Nations*

1781 Immanuel Kant, *The Critique of Pure Reason*

orators marshaled detailed descriptions of exotic native customs, slavery, and the destruction of native populations by Europeans and denounced the inhumanity and irrationality of European ways. The book strongly opposed slavery and called for a Black Spartacus to lead a rebellion of slaves, "who would be a vehicle for nature asserting her rights against the blind avarice of European and American colonists." The Enlightenment belief in natural rights led many to denounce slavery. An article in the *Encyclopedia* proclaimed, "There is not a single one of these hapless souls . . . who does not have the right to be declared free . . . since neither his ruler nor his father nor anyone else had the right to dispose of his freedom." Some Enlightenment thinkers, however, took a more ambiguous view; Montesquieu, for example, seemed to portray slavery as "natural" to tropical climates.

The Individual and Society

Although Enlightenment writers addressed a wide range of social and political problems, one central theme underlay most of their concerns: the relationship between the individual and society. Never before had the individual's relationship to society and the structure of society itself been the focus of so much attention. The *Encyclopedia*, for example, included information about such disparate aspects of society as religious beliefs and artisans' trade secrets. Scottish treatises on the economy, Italian writings about the penal system, and German philosophizing about morality all shared the same basic concern for defining the best relationship between the individual and society.

To explore the tension between individual and social concerns, the *philosophes* used various methods. Montesquieu advocated extensive comparative study of different civilizations and customs; Voltaire relied most often on explicit comparisons between an unjust France and a more tolerant England; and Rousseau offered hypothetical speculations about the societies established by the first people on earth. Despite different approaches, the *philosophes* shared the belief that humans could improve their condition by drawing on their own resources of reason, experience, and, in some cases, feelings. Adam Smith and Rousseau, though both devoted *philosophes*, examined the relationship between the individual and society from two very different vantage points and came away with conflicting

abide by them." Those few who lived long enough to see the French Revolution resisted its radical turn, for the *philosophes* generally regarded the lower classes—"the people"—as ignorant, violent, and prone to superstition, hence in need of leadership from above. They pinned their hopes on educated elites and enlightened rulers.

Even though most Enlightenment political writers were themselves reformers rather than revolutionaries, in the long run their books often had a revolutionary impact. For example, Montesquieu's widely reprinted *Spirit of the Laws* (1748) warned against the dangers of despotism, opposed the divine right of kings, and favored republican government (government without a monarch). In his somewhat rosy view, England was "the one nation in the world which has political liberty as the direct object of its constitution." His analysis of English constitutionalism inspired French critics of absolutism and greatly influenced the American revolutionaries.

Political criticism extended to scrutiny of European colonization and slavery. One of the most popular books of the time was the *Philosophical and Political History of European Colonies and Commerce in the Two Indies* by Abbé Guillaume Raynal (1713–1796), which appeared in 1770 and in seventy subsequent versions. He and his collab-

conclusions about how people could coexist in harmony.

A highly optimistic view of the relationship between the individual and society permeated the work of the Scottish philosopher Adam Smith (1723–1790), who in 1776 published the first great modern work in economics, *An Inquiry into the Nature and Causes of the Wealth of Nations*. Smith endorsed *laissez-faire* ("leaving alone") policies, in which the economy would be freed from the old ways of mercantilist state intervention and control. He urged governments to eliminate all restrictions on the sale of land, remove restraints on the grain trade, and abandon duties on imports. He believed free international trade would stimulate efforts everywhere and thus ensure the growth of national wealth. Smith's arguments for free markets established him as the father of modern capitalist economics, and when modern commentators refer to classical economics, they mean the writings of Adam Smith and his followers.

Smith rejected the prevailing views that national wealth could best be accumulated through agriculture or by hoarding gold and silver. Instead he argued that the division of labor in manufacturing was the key to increased productivity and would generate wealth for society and well-being for the individual. By performing a task over and over again in the broader system of manufacturing, the individual functioned as a part in a well-running machine. Like Bernard Mandeville before him but much more systematically, Smith insisted that individual self-interest—even greed—was compatible with the society's best interest; the laws of supply and demand served as an "invisible hand," ensuring that individual interests would be harmonized with those of the whole society. As Smith claimed, "The study of his own [the individual's] advantage necessarily leads him to prefer what is most advantageous to the society."

Rousseau was more pessimistic than most other *philosophes* about the fit between individual self-interest and the good of society. In his view, "Man is born free, and everywhere he is in chains." Society threatened natural freedoms. Rousseau's analysis of the tension between the individual and society caught the imagination both of his own time and of succeeding generations. Rousseau first gained fame by writing a prize-winning essay in 1749 in which he argued that the revival of science and the arts had contributed to the corruption of social morals. This startling conclusion was the opposite of most Enlightenment writers' arguments. Rather than improving society, he claimed, science and art raised artificial barriers between people and their natural state. Rousseau's works extolled the simplicity of rural life over the false sophistication of urban society. Although he participated in the salons and contributed to the *Encyclopedia*, Rousseau always felt uncomfortable in high society, and he periodically withdrew to live in solitude far from Paris. Paradoxically, his "solitude" was often paid for by wealthy upper-class patrons, who lodged him on their estates, even as his writings decried the upper-class privilege that made his efforts possible.

Rousseau's most widely read works at the time were the novel *The New Heloïse* (1761) and the educational tract *Emile* (1762). In *The New Heloïse*, Rousseau's heroine, Julie, dies after she gives up her penniless lover, Saint Preux, to marry someone else to please her father. Rousseau completely transformed the medieval story of Heloïse and Abelard in order to focus on the conflict between social demands for virtue in marriage and Julie's intensely personal feelings. Julie transgresses by giving herself to Saint Preux when she has been promised by her father to someone else, but she then learns to live a righteous, married, domestic life with her husband, Wolmar. She still harbors intense feelings for Saint Preux, however, and in a tragic ending, she drowns while boating on a lake. Both female and male readers identified intensely with Julie, as a model of a woman who felt deeply but tried to live a virtuous life in marriage. "You have driven me crazy about her," wrote one retired army officer to Rousseau. "Imagine then the tears that her death must have wrung from me. . . . Never have I wept such delicious tears."

In *Emile*, Rousseau tried to find a different solution to the tragic possibility of conflict between the individual and society, but here he emphasized what he saw as the necessary differentiation between the sexes. The book tells the story of the boy Emile, who works alone with his tutor to develop practical skills and independent ways of thinking, without relying solely on books, and free from the supervision of the clergy, who controlled most schools. Education through nature and experience are exalted as the true sources of masculine knowledge; education, according to Rousseau, should be designed to develop the innately good qualities in a child rather than to repress a sinful nature.

Emile's wife-to-be, Sophie, has an entirely different kind of education, based on what Rousseau thought suited women. "Woman is made to please and to be subjugated to man," he claimed. Sophie is trained for the domestic roles of wife and mother, and like Julie in *The New Heloïse*, she is taught to be obedient, always helpful to her husband and family, and removed from any participation in the public world. Despite his insistence on the necessary differences between men's and women's roles, many women enthusiastically embraced Rousseau's ideas, for he emphasized maternalism, child rearing, and breast-feeding. In the eighteenth century, children attracted more systematic attention than they had previously, and women, as childbearers, could claim a new, special role as society's educators and nurturers. Many women adopted Rousseau's ideas about raising children, and some began to publish their own manuals for mothers. Rousseau's own children, however, suffered the contradictions that characterized his life. By his own admission, he abandoned to a foundling hospital all the children he had with his lower-class common-law wife because he did not think he could support them properly. If their fate was like that of most deserted children of the day, they died young.

Many of Rousseau's writings had extensive impact in the eighteenth century, and even his lesser-known works of the 1760s and 1770s became profoundly important for Europeans in the following decades. *The Social Contract* (1762), for example, inspired the leaders of the French Revolution of 1789, and it continued to exert great influence throughout the nineteenth century. In it, Rousseau proposed an abstract model for government that had no connection to history, tradition, or the Bible. Authorities banned it in both Geneva and Paris. Individual moral freedom (presumably limited to men), according to Rousseau, could be achieved only by learning to subject one's own individual interests to a social contract that represented the good of the community, that is, the "general will." Rousseau's rather mystical concept of a general will resided not in the mind of a ruler but in the collective consciousness of all male citizens. Some modern commentators view Rousseau as the father of totalitarianism because his philosophy provides no protection for the individual against the general will. All must comply with the general will for their own good; if necessary they must "be forced to be free," to obey the laws made in accord with the general will. Others see him as an advocate of democracy who emphasized the underlying equality of all men and tried to reconcile individual liberty with the necessary restraints of society.

Spreading the Enlightenment

Conflicts between the *philosophes* and their opponents in the church and state placed the writers at a distinct disadvantage. Censorship and official harassment sometimes drove them from their homes. Rousseau, for example, had to flee France to escape arrest after the publication of *Emile*, but he was no more welcome in Geneva, his Protestant hometown. (He did, however, return to France once the controversy had died down.) In most European countries state and clerical censors tightly controlled publishing. In Catholic Spain the Inquisition still operated courts in the leading cities and banned books such as Montesquieu's *Spirit of the Laws*. Books could be published in France only by royal permission, and a government censor had to certify each as inoffensive to religion, morals, or the state. Enlightenment views about individual rights and good government threatened too many established authorities.

The persecution of writers proved haphazard, however, because many rulers themselves adopted the new ideas for reform. By the 1760s the French government regularly ignored the publication of many works once thought offensive or subversive. More important, a growing flood of works printed abroad poured into France and circulated underground. In the Dutch Republic and Switzerland, especially, private companies made fortunes smuggling illegal books into France over mountain passes and back roads. Foreign printers provided secret catalogs of their offerings and sold their products through booksellers who were willing to market forbidden books for a high price. Among such books were not only the philosophical treatises of the Enlightenment but also satires of the Catholic church and pornographic pamphlets lampooning leading members of the court. The satires and pornography made up a *low Enlightenment* in contrast to the *high Enlightenment* of Voltaire, Montesquieu, and Rousseau. In the 1770s and

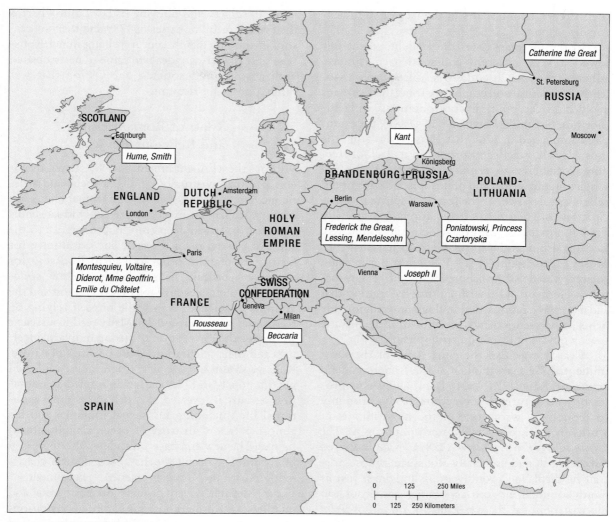

Centers of the Enlightenment

1780s lurid descriptions of sexual promiscuity at the French court helped undermine the popularity of the throne.

The spread of the Enlightenment followed a distinct geographic and social pattern; it was most evident in places where a growing middle class provided an eager audience for ideas of constitutionalism and individual rights. France was the home of the movement because the public there was ready for such ideas and frustrated by the French government's reluctance to accept them. Where constitutionalism and individual rights were most advanced, as in Great Britain and the Dutch Re-

public, the movement had less of an edge, because in a sense there was less need for it. Yet Scotland, joined with England to form the United Kingdom in 1707, had its own version of the Enlightenment, inspired by Hume and Smith and centered in the universities of Edinburgh and Glasgow. In British North America, Enlightenment ideas helped stiffen growing colonial resistance to British rule after 1763. In places with small middle classes, such as Spain and Russia, governments successfully suppressed Enlightenment writings. Italian *philosophes*, such as the Milanese penal reformer Cesare Beccaria (1738–1794), got moral support from their French counterparts in the face of stern censorship at home.

In the German states the Enlightenment followed a very different course than in France. Whereas the French *philosophes* often took a violently anticlerical and combative tone, the Germans avoided direct political confrontations with authorities. Gotthold Lessing (1729–1781), for example, complained in 1769 that Prussia was still "the most slavish society in Europe" in its lack of freedom to criticize government policies. As a playwright, literary critic, and philosopher, he promoted religious tolerance for the Jews and spiritual emancipation of Germans from foreign, especially French, models of culture, which still dominated. Lessing also introduced the German Jewish writer Moses Mendelssohn (1729–1786) into Berlin salon society. Mendelssohn labored to build bridges between German and Jewish culture by arguing that Judaism was a rational and undogmatic religion. He believed persecution and discrimination against the Jews would end as reason triumphed.

Reason was also the chief focus of the most influential German thinker of the Enlightenment, Immanuel Kant (1724–1804). Kant, a university professor who lectured on everything from astronomy to economics, wrote one of the most important works in the history of Western philosophy, *The Critique of Pure Reason* (1781). Kant admired Adam Smith and especially Rousseau, whose portrait he displayed proudly in his lodgings. Just as Smith founded modern economics and Rousseau modern political theory, Kant's *Critique of Pure Reason* set the foundations for modern philosophy. In this difficult book, Kant established the doctrine of "idealism," the belief that true understanding can come only from examining the ways in which ideas are formed in the mind. Ideas are shaped, Kant argued, not just by sensory information (a position central to empiricism, a philosophy based on Locke's writings), but also by the operation of autonomous mental categories such as space and time on that information. In Kant's philosophy these "categories of understanding" were neither sensory nor supernatural; they were entirely ideal and abstract and located in the human mind. For Kant the supreme philosophical questions—Does God exist? Is personal immortality possible? Do humans have free will?—were unanswerable by reason alone. But like Rousseau, Kant insisted that true moral freedom could be achieved only by

living in society and obeying its laws. But whereas the French revolutionaries of 1789 and their successors in the nineteenth century championed Rousseau's ideas, German idealism came to be associated with abstract philosophical speculation that was rarely politically relevant.

Roots of Romanticism and Religious Revival

Within the Enlightenment itself, new trends emerged that eventually kindled a social and artistic movement called *romanticism* in the nineteenth century. Romanticism emphasized individual genius and creative spark, deep emotion, resistance to the rules of classicism in the arts, and an affinity for history. Romantics often looked to Rousseau for inspiration because he scolded his fellow *philosophes* for their excessive reliance on reason and the example of science (even while himself relying on reason and scientific models). Many read Rousseau's works for their evocation of strong individual feelings and their celebration of the beauties of nature. Rousseau's autobiographical *Confessions*, published posthumously in 1782, caused an immediate sensation because it revealed so much of his inner emotional life, including his sexual longings and his almost paranoid distrust of other Enlightenment figures. The new emphasis on feelings also increased interest in the occult by the 1780s. Thus a charismatic Austrian physician turned "experimenter," Franz Mesmer, awed crowds of aristocrats and middle-class admirers with his Paris demonstrations of "animal magnetism." He passed a weak electrical current through tubs filled with water or iron filings, around which groups of his disciples sat, holding hands, and with this process of "mesmerism" he claimed to cure their ailments. (Our word *mesmerize*, meaning "hypnotize" or "hold spellbound," is derived from Mesmer's name.)

A novel by the young German writer Johann Wolfgang von Goethe (1749–1832) captured the early romantic spirit with its glorification of emotion. *The Sorrows of Young Werther* (1774) told of a young man who resembled Rousseau's Julie in many respects: he loved nature and rural life and was unhappy in love. When the woman he loved married another, he feel into deep melancholy and eventually killed himself. Reason could not save him. The book spurred a veritable Werther craze: there were Werther costumes, Werther engravings and embroidery, medallions, a perfume called "Eau de Werther," and unfortunately, a few imitations of Werther's suicide. The young Napoleon Bonaparte, who was to build an empire for France, claimed to have read Goethe's novel seven times.

Religious revivals underlined the limits of reason in a different way. Much of the Protestant world experienced an evangelical awakening in the 1740s. In the German states, Pietist groups founded new communities; in the Scottish highlands, many converted to a more evangelical religion; and in the British North American colonies, revivalist Protestant preachers drew thousands of fervent believers in a movement called the Great Awakening. In North America bitter conflicts between revivalists and their opponents in the established churches prompted the leaders on both sides to set up new colleges to support their beliefs. These included Princeton, Columbia, Brown, and Dartmouth, all founded between 1746 and 1769.

Revivalism also stirred east European Jews at about the same time. Israel ben Eliezer (c. 1700–1760), later known as Ba'al Shem Tov (or the Besht, from the initials), founded the Hasidic sect in the 1740s and 1750s. Teaching outside the synagogue system, Ba'al Shem Tov traveled the Polish countryside offering to cure men of their evil spirits. He invented a new form of popular prayer, in which the believer aimed to annihilate his own personality in order to let the supernatural speak through him. His followers, the Hasidim (Hebrew for "most pious" Jews), scorned the formalism of the regular synagogues in favor of their own prayer houses, where they gathered in rustic clothing and broad fur hats to emphasize their piety and simplicity. They often prayed at the top of their lungs, joyfully swaying and clapping their hands. Their practices soon spread all over Poland and into Lithuania.

Most of the waves of Protestant revivalism ebbed after the 1750s, but in England the movement known as Methodism continued to grow through the end of the century. John Wesley (1703–1791), the Oxford-educated son of an Anglican cleric, founded Methodism, a term evoked by Wesley's insistence on strict self-discipline and a methodical approach to religious study and observance. In 1738, Wesley had a mystical experience in which he felt the need to submit his life totally to Christ. Immediately afterward, he began to travel all over the British Isles, preaching a new brand of Protestantism that emphasized an intense personal experience of salvation and a life of thrift, abstinence, and hard work. In meadows and brickyards, in mine pits and copperworks, wherever ordinary people played or worked, Wesley would mount a table or a box to speak or begin a hymn. He slept in his followers' homes, ate their food, and treated their illnesses with various remedies, including small electric shocks for nervous diseases (Wesley eagerly followed Benjamin Franklin's experiments with electricity). In fifty years, Wesley preached forty thousand sermons, an average of fifteen a week. Not surprisingly, his preaching disturbed the Anglican authorities, who refused to let him preach in the churches. In response, Wesley began to ordain his own clergy. Nevertheless, during Wesley's lifetime the Methodist leadership remained politically conservative; Wesley himself wrote many pamphlets urging order, loyalty, and submission to higher authorities. He denounced political agitation in the 1770s because it threatened to make England "a field of blood" ruled by "King Mob."

Society and Culture in an Age of Improvement

By the mid-1700s the European economy had embarked on a course of steady growth. Population growth accelerated, agricultural production increased, prices and wages rose gradually, and the volume of trade expanded. England and some places on the Continent began to undergo a "consumer revolution," in which people found themselves able to buy more and more goods. Optimism about the future spread; people believed social conditions could and would improve. New institutions of urban social life created an extended public for Enlightenment ideas of reform, attracting nobles and middle-class people alike. Innovations in the organization of manufacturing eroded old customs and laid the foundation for the remarkable changes in energy use and production called the Industrial Revolution in the nineteenth century. Social change, however, was neither uniform nor painless. Most peasants remained tied to the land and their lords, and those who moved to the cities in search of work did not always find their situation better.

Disparities in Social Change

Although the Enlightenment and economic change had indisputable effects on European society, the social structure did not change overnight. Many aristocrats insisted on maintaining their traditional separateness from commoners. The male court nobility everywhere continued to sport swords, plumed hats, makeup, and powdered hair, while middle-class men wore simpler and more somber clothing. Aristocrats had their own seats in church and their own quarters in the universities. Noblemen monopolized the highest ranks in the army, and in many countries, including Spain and France, the law forbade aristocrats from engaging directly in retail trade. In Austria, Spain, the Italian states, Poland-Lithuania, and Russia, most nobles knew little about Enlightenment ideas.

Overall, nobles made up about 3 percent of the European population, but the proportion and way of life of the nobility varied greatly from country to country. At least 10 percent of the population in Poland was noble and 7 to 8 percent in Spain, in comparison with only 2 percent in Russia and between 1 and 2 percent in the rest of the western Europe. Despite (or perhaps partly because of) their greater numbers, Polish and Spanish nobles in particular often lived in poverty. The wealthiest European nobles luxuriated in almost unimaginable opulence. Many of the English peers, for example, owned more than ten thousand acres of land, invested widely in government bonds and trading companies, kept several country residences with scores of servants as well as houses in London, and occasionally even had their own private orchestras as well as greenhouses for exotic plants, kennels of pedigreed dogs, and collections of books, antiques, and scientific instruments.

In the face of economic change, European elites aggressively defended their privileges and continued to expect the lower orders to defer to them. As agriculture became more commercialized in western Europe and inflation began to eat away at noble fortunes, aristocrats converted their remaining seigneurial rights into money payments and used them to support an increasingly expensive life. Peasants felt the squeeze as a result. French peasants, for example, paid taxes to the government on salt, an essential preservative, and on the value of their land; customs duties if they sold produce

or wine in town; the tithe (or tenth tax) on their grain to the church; and a wide range of dues to their landlords, including payments to mill grain at the lord's mill, bake bread in his oven, press grapes at his winepress, and various inheritance taxes on the land. In addition, peasants had to work without compensation for a specified number of days every year on the public roads (*corvée*, or labor duty).

In eastern Europe the state eventually either helped the aristocracy increase its control over enserfed populations or, in the case of Poland-Lithuania, did nothing to protect its peasants from their lords. Catherine II of Russia (*1762–1796) granted the nobility vast amounts of land, the exclusive right to own serfs, and exemption from personal taxes and corporal punishment. Her Charter of the Nobility of 1785 codified these privileges in exchange for the nobles' political subservience to the state. In Prussia, Frederick II (*1740–1786) made sure that the nobility would dominate both the army officer corps and the civil bureaucracy. Only in Austria did the state try—unsuccessfully—to ease the burdens of serfdom.

In England less rigid lines separated nobles and commoners, but the landed gentry tenaciously defended their privileges, most notoriously their exclusive right to hunt game. The game laws kept the poor from eating meat and helped protect the social status of the rich. The gentry enforced the game laws themselves by hiring gamekeepers who hunted down poachers and even set traps for them in the forests. By law, anyone who poached deer or rabbits while armed or disguised could be sentenced to death. After 1760 the number of arrests for breaking the game laws in England increased enormously. In most other countries, too, hunting was the special right of the nobility and a deep cause of popular resentment.

Although the ranks of the nobility remained very small, those of the middle classes or the *bourgeoisie* grew steadily. In France, for example, the overall population grew by about a third in the 1700s, but the *bourgeoisie* nearly tripled in size. Being *bourgeois* or a member of the *bourgeoisie* had several meanings. A *bourgeois*, originally, was merely someone who lived in town (a *bourg*), but the term could also identify people living from investments in land, trade, or manufacturing rather than working with their hands, like artisans or

Thomas Gainsborough, **Conversation in the Park**
The English painter excelled in depicting the life of the English gentry, caught in their moments of relaxation at their country estates.

peasants. Despite their good incomes, *bourgeois* men and women were very conscious that they were not part of the nobility; they had no special pew in church, no tax exemptions, and no special courts to hear their cases. They dressed more soberly than nobles and often earned their living in some professional capacity, as doctors, lawyers, or lower-level officials. Unlike the lower classes, the *bourgeois* could read and write and thus participate directly in the Enlightenment. Yet the middle classes had an odd perception of their station in the eighteenth century. The rapid growth of trade and manufacturing had allowed many of them to raise their standard of living markedly and to have an unprecedented confidence about their future financial and social well-being. They also had many reasons to resent the nobles. But instead of resenting them, most *bourgeois* men and women had one overwhelming ambition: to become nobles themselves—that is, to make enough money in commerce to buy themselves a title or somehow join the ranks of the gentry or the nobility.

The number of poor people increased everywhere in the 1700s. Although relative prosperity limited food shortages and outbreaks of famine, millions of peasants and agricultural workers lived on the edge of dire poverty, and when they lost their land or work, they either migrated to the cities or wandered the roads in search of food and work. Their numbers swelled as the population grew and wages failed to keep up with inflated prices. France alone had two hundred thousand workers who left their homes every year to look for seasonal employment elsewhere. At least 10 percent of Europe's urban population depended on some form of poor relief.

The growing numbers of poor overwhelmed local governments. In some countries beggars and vagabonds had been subject to incarceration in workhouses since the mid-1600s. But the expenses for running these overcrowded institutions increased 60 percent in England between 1760 and 1784. Most German towns created workhouses after 1740 that were part workshop, part hospital, and part prison. Such institutions also appeared for the first time in the North American cities of Boston, New York, and Philadelphia. To supplement the inadequate system of alms, poor offices, public workshops, and workhouse-hospitals, the French government created official *dépôts de mendicité*, or beggarhouses, in 1767. The government sent people to these new workhouses supposedly to work in manufacturing, but most were too weak or sick to do much work, and 20 percent of them died within a few months of incarceration. The ballooning number of poor people created fears about rising crime. To officials, beggars seemed more aggressive than ever. The handful of police assigned to keep order in each town or district found themselves confronted with increasing incidents of rural banditry and crimes against property.

Enlightenment ideas rarely touched the lives of the lower classes. About one in four Parisians owned books, but wage earners read much less than middle-class professionals and less even than servants. Although the number of book owners rose in the eighteenth century, people still read the same kinds of books as they had in the past. For example, more than 90 percent of the books owned by the Parisian lower classes were religious works. Whereas the upper classes might attend salons, concerts, or art exhibitions, peasants enjoyed their traditional forms of popular entertainment, such as fairs and festivals, and the urban lower classes relaxed in cabarets and taverns. Sometimes pleasures were cruel. In England, bullbaiting, bearbaiting, dogfighting, and cockfighting were all common forms of entertainment and provided arenas for organized gambling. Even "gentle" sports had their violent side. Cricket matches, whose rules were first set down in 1744, were often accompanied by brawls among fans (not unlike soccer matches today, although on a much smaller scale). Many Englishmen enjoyed this "battle royal with sticks, pebbles and hog's dung." Even the theater district in London was sometimes the scene of rioting.

The Shaping of a New Elite

Those attracted to Enlightenment ideas included both aristocrats and middle-class people. Intermarriage, the spread of businesslike attitudes among the nobility, and middle-class emulation of noble ways all helped break down traditional barriers between the aristocracy and the middle classes. New urban social institutions fostered the same mixing. Salons had existed in the 1600s but were then less devoted to serious intellectual discussion and the spread of new ideas. Entirely new in the 1700s were masonic lodges, which began as social clubs with elaborate secret rituals. Although not explicitly political in aim, the lodges encouraged equality among members, and both aristocrats and middle-class men could join. Freemasonry arose in Great Britain as an offshoot of the mason's guild; a Grand Lodge was set up in 1717. The first French and Italian lodges opened in 1726. Frederick II of Prussia founded a lodge in 1740, and after 1750, freemasonry gained influence in Poland, Russia, and British North America. Some lodges included women, and women occasionally formed sisterhoods with their own distinctive rituals. Despite the papacy's condemnation of freemasonry in 1738 as subversive of religious and civil authority, lodges continued to multiply throughout the eighteenth century.

Nobles and middle-class professionals also met in coffeehouses and learned societies, at art exhibitions and in concert halls. Local learned societies, which greatly increased in number in this period, brought together nobles, clergymen, physicians, and lawyers, who met to discuss such issues as scientific innovation and how to eliminate poverty.

The barriers between nobles and commoners also came down in more informal ways. For example, the upper and middle classes shared a taste for "grand tours" of cultural sites, such as the newly discovered Greek and Roman ruins at Pompei, Herculaneum, and Paestum in Italy.

The findings in these excavations influenced the spread of the relatively austere neoclassical style in architecture and painting, which pushed aside the rococo and the long-dominant baroque. The emphasis on purity and clarity of line and form in neoclassicism was especially evident in urban residences and new government buildings. As one German writer noted, with considerable exaggeration, "Everything in Paris is in the Greek style." In the 1760s and 1770s in England the upper classes began erecting magnificent houses in the neoclassical style called Georgian (after England's king, George III), and pottery, furniture, fabrics, cutlery, and even wallpaper reflected the renewed interest in classical themes.

This period also supported artistic styles other than neoclassicism. The new emphasis on emotion and family life, represented in Rousseau's *The New Heloïse*, was reflected in a growing taste for moralistic family scenes in painting. The paintings of Jean-Baptiste Greuze (1725–1805), much praised by Diderot, depicted ordinary families at moments of great emotion. Such subjects appealed to a middle-class public, which now attended the official painting exhibitions in France that were held regularly every other year after 1737. Court painting nonetheless remained much in demand. Marie-Louise-Elizabeth Vigée-Lebrun (1755–1842), who painted portraits at the French court, reported that in the 1780s "it was difficult to get a place on my waiting list. . . . I was the fashion."

The clients as well as the subject matter of artists were socially various. The work of English engraver and painter William Hogarth (1697–1764) ranged from noble portraits to popular moralistic print series. He sold his engravings to the middle-class public but still hoped to have his work taken seriously as high art. The English potter Josiah Wedgwood (1730–1795) almost single-handedly created a mass market for domestic crockery by appealing to middle-class desires to emulate the rich and royal. His designs of special tea sets for the English queen, for Catherine the Great of Russia, and for leading aristocrats allowed him to advertise his wares as fashionable; as he said, "Few

Marie-Louise-Elisabeth Vigée-Lebrun, **Marie Antoinette**
Vigée-Lebrun painted many figures at the French court, including this 1778 portrait of the queen herself, for whom she served as official painter after 1779.

ladies dare venture at anything out of the common stile 'till authorized by their betters." By 1767 he claimed that his Queensware line had "spread over the whole Globe," and indeed by then his pottery was being marketed in France, Russia, Venice, the Ottoman Empire, and British North America.

The relaxing of cultural boundaries between the aristocracy and the middle classes affected music, too, as new classical forms began to replace the early eighteenth-century baroque style. Melody replaced complex polyphony, making the music more accessible to ordinary listeners. The violin's tone became stronger and more resonant, helping it overcome a reputation as fit only for village dances. Mass sections of string instruments became the backbone of professional orchestras, playing to large audiences of well-to-do listeners in sizable concert halls. London, Paris, and even the small German princely town of Mannheim became the centers for such musical life. Two supreme masters of this new, so-called classical musical style emerged by 1775; the Austrians Franz Joseph Haydn (1734–1809) and Wolfgang Amadeus Mozart (1756–1791). Incredibly prolific (Haydn wrote more than a hundred symphonies, for example), both excelled in combining lightness, clarity, and profound emotion. Both also wrote numerous operas, a genre whose popularity continued to grow (in the 1780s

Jean-Baptiste Greuze, **The Beloved Mother, *1765***
Having just breast fed one of her many children, this was the idealized happy mother of sentimental painting.

the Papal States alone boasted forty opera houses). Mozart remains one of the greatest opera composers of all time; the dramatic irony, wit, psychological depth, and melodic richness of such operas as *The Marriage of Figaro* (1786) and *Don Giovanni* (1787) are still fresh after two centuries. Almost all this music was sponsored by wealthy patrons, on whom composers depended. Thus Haydn spent most of his career working for the Eszterházys, a Hungarian noble family. Asked why he had written no string quintets (at which Mozart excelled), Haydn responded simply, "No one has ordered any."

Reading, Education, and Child Rearing

The expansion of the audience for Enlightenment and social reform ideas depended on the spread of print culture. In Catholic France the literacy rate for men (measured by those who could sign their names on public documents) had risen from about 30 percent in the 1680s to nearly 50 percent by the 1780s. The rates for women also increased markedly but still reached only 27 percent by the 1780s. The rates in Protestant countries were higher than in France, in eastern Europe much lower. By the end of the eighteenth century, six times as many books were published in the German states, for example, as in 1714. Although religious books were still the most important category in publishing, books on history, the arts, and the sciences proliferated. At the end of the eighteenth century, Louis-Sebastien Mercier (1740–1814) claimed that "people are certainly reading ten times as much in Paris as they did a hundred years ago." According to Mercier, the taste for print had spread to the lower classes: "These days, you see a waiting-maid in her backroom, a lackey in an anteroom reading pamphlets. People can read in almost all classes of society." Provincial towns in England, France, the Dutch Republic, and the German states published their own newspapers; by 1780, thirty-seven English towns boasted local newspapers. Circulating libraries multiplied, and in England, especially, even small villages had secular book clubs.

The novel became a respectable and influential genre of writing. Among the most widely read novels were those by Samuel Richardson (1689–1761), who as the son of a carpenter and a suc-

cessful printer was part of the middle class whose values were explored in most contemporary popular novels. In *Clarissa Harlowe* (1747–1748), Richardson told the story of a young woman from a heartless upper-class family who was torn between her family's choice of a repulsive suitor and her attraction to Lovelace, an aristocratic rake. Although she ran off with Lovelace to escape her family, she resisted his advances; Clarissa soon died of a broken heart after being drugged and raped—this despite the frantic pleas of readers of the first volumes to spare her. One woman complained to Richardson, "I verily believe I have shed a pint of tears, and my heart is still bursting." The French writer Diderot compared Richardson to Moses, Homer, Euripides, and Sophocles.

Novels still aroused criticism, however, especially for their sympathetic portrayals of characters from the lower classes. Even Richardson attacked his fellow novelist Henry Fielding:

> *I found the characters and situations so wretchedly low and dirty, that I imagined I could not be interested for any one of them . . . it is beyond my conception, that a man of family, and who had some learning, and who really is a writer, should descend so excessively low, in all his pieces. Who can care for any of his people?*

Novels were caught in an enduring paradox. Although Richardson wrote *Clarissa* as a kind of manual of virtuous female conduct, critics worried that novels undermined morals with their portrayals of low-life characters, the seductions of virtuous women, and other examples of immoral behavior.

Novels did not appear in the school curriculum. In secondary school, whether lay- or church-run, boys studied Latin, Greek, philosophy, and logic but spent little time on mathematics, science, history, or modern languages. Although university education was necessary for men entering some fields, especially law and medicine, the universities in most countries appeared hopelessly rigid and behind the times. As an Austrian reformer complained about universities in this period, "Critical history, natural sciences—which are supposed to make enlightenment general and combat prejudice—were neglected or wholly unknown."

Girls learned domestic skills, some music, and foreign languages, but they did not get the classical education considered essential for government service or intellectual life. Despite these limitations (and the general exclusion of women from university study), some women from the elites advanced to prominent positions. Laura Bassi (1711–1778) became professor of physics at the University of Bologna, and Catherine Macaulay (1731–1791) published best-selling scholarly histories of England. In France, Stéphanie de Genlis (1746–1830) wrote books specifically for children—a growing genre that reflected middle-class parents' increased interest in education. Women actively participated in some scientific academies, and many middle-class women benefited from the spread of circulating libraries. As one Englishman observed, "By far the greatest part of ladies now have a taste for books."

Yet many more women than men were still illiterate, and even queens rarely learned more than the rudiments of reading and writing. A writer in the *London Chronicle* in 1759 captured the prevailing view when he explained that daughters of tradesmen should be taught "submission and humility to their superiors, decency and modesty in their own dress and behaviour. That they should be very well instructed in all kinds of plain work, reading, writing, accounts, pastry, pickling, preserving and other branches of cookery. . . ." Catherine II of Russia and Madame Geoffrin in France were unusual in their ability to hold their own with the greatest minds of their age.

Outside the elite classes, primary education was very spotty, despite efforts by some states, especially the Protestant German ones, to introduce compulsory education. The Prussian school code of 1763, for example, required all children between the ages of five and thirteen to attend school, but the law was not enforced. Catholic religious orders, lay teachers hired by the churches and individual sects, and many private schools taught reading and writing. One sign of the consumer revolution in England was the increase in newspaper advertising for local schools that taught, at relatively low prices, everything from arithmetic to dancing and drawing.

Even though the lower classes could still acquire only a rudimentary education, children as a group claimed more attention, especially in the middle and upper classes. Sometime around the mid-1700s attitudes toward children began to change. Educators no longer viewed children exclusively as little sinners in need of harsh discipline, and corporal punishment lessened. Paintings now showed individual children playing at their favorite activities rather than formally posed with their families. Books about and for children became popular. *The Newtonian System of the Universe Digested for Young Minds*, by "Tom Telescope," was published in 1761 and reprinted many times afterward. In 1730 no shops in England specialized in children's toys; by 1780 they could be found everywhere. In 1762 the jigsaw puzzle was invented to teach children geography. Baby clothes and children's clothing now differed in style from those for adults, reflecting the notion that childhood was a separate stage of life; children were no longer considered miniature adults.

Attitudes Toward Sexuality

Not everything about children was viewed positively. The Enlightenment's emphasis on reason, self-control, and childhood innocence made parents increasingly anxious about children's sexuality. Moralists and physicians alike wrote books about the evils of masturbation, "proving" that it led to physical and mental degeneration and even madness. One English writer linked masturbation to debility of body and mind; infertility; epilepsy; loss of memory, sight, and hearing; distortions of the eyes, mouth, and face; a pale, sallow, and bluish complexion; wasting of limbs; idiotism; and even death.

Worries about sexual behavior also extended to adults. As men and women began to move to the cities in search of work, the rates of births out of wedlock soared, from less than 5 percent of all births in the seventeenth century to nearly 20 percent at the end of the eighteenth. Historians have disagreed about the causes and meaning of this change. Some detect in this pattern a sign of sexual liberation and the beginnings of a modern sexual revolution; as women moved out of the control of their families, they began to seek their own sexual fulfillment. Others view this change more bleakly, as a story of seduction and betrayal; family and community pressure had once forced a man to marry a woman pregnant with his child, but now a man could abandon a pregnant lover more easily, just by moving away.

Women who came to the city as domestic servants had little recourse against masters or fellow servants who seduced or raped them. The result was a startling rise in abandoned babies. Most European cities established foundling hospitals in the 1700s, but in them infant and child mortality was 50 percent higher than for children brought up at home. Some women tried herbs, laxatives, or crude surgical means of abortion; a few, usually domestic servants who would lose their jobs if their employer discovered they had borne a child, resorted to infanticide. Increased mobility brought freedom for some, but it also aggravated the vulnerability of women from the countryside, newly arrived in cities. For them, desperation, not reason, often ruled their choices.

States had not yet developed clear policies for repressing illicit sexuality. Some of the oldest forms of sexual entertainment for men, such as houses of prostitution, developed in new ways during this period, suggesting a continuing commercialization of sex. The growing number of London brothels became more specialized, including well-known flagellation clubs and bagnios (a combination brothel and bathhouse) for upper-class men. Physicians commonly taught that retention of semen was unhealthy, thus encouraging a double standard, according to which women must vigilantly maintain their virtue (except prostitutes) while men were permitted, even expected, to lose theirs. References to sex could be found in many public places. John Cleland's pornographic novel *Fanny Hill* (1748) made its publisher a fortune, and newspapers advertised sexual services, cures for venereal disease, and abortifacients. In his diaries, James Boswell (1740–1795) detailed his sex life with his wife, mistresses, and prostitutes. Often tormented by guilt about his behavior, he nonetheless contracted "Signor gonorrhoea" at least seventeen times.

Homosexuals developed networks and special meeting places. European courts had long punished sodomy with harsh and sometimes gruesome sentences, and in the eighteenth century, outbreaks of persecution of "sodomites," as homosexuals were called, occurred in various western European countries. The stereotype of the effeminate, exclusively homosexual male seems to have appeared for the first time in the late seventeenth and early eighteenth centuries, perhaps as part of a growing emphasis on separate roles for men and women.

The Beginnings of Industrialization

Changes in sexual relations were one effect of the continuing rise of population in the second half of the eighteenth century. Overall the population of Europe increased by nearly 30 percent, with especially striking growth in England, Ireland, Prussia, and Hungary. Population increased by more than half in England, where the agricultural revolution had gathered momentum and made it possible to feed many more people. Parliament passed hundreds of enclosure acts in the 1760s and 1770s, affecting millions of acres of land. Prices went up in many countries after the 1730s and continued to rise gradually until the early nineteenth century; wages in many trades rose as well but less quickly than prices. Shortages and crises still occurred periodically, but almost all sectors of the economy generally improved.

The volume of trade expanded most notably, partly because of the continuing growth of the colonial economies. In both France and Britain foreign trade quadrupled in the eighteenth century; trade with the colonies increased even more rapidly. While the slave-based colonial economies boomed—a tenfold increase in French colonial trade in the 1700s, for example—significant though less obvious developments also changed the domestic economies. Textile manufacturing had long been a staple in the European economy, and woolen cloth dominated production almost everywhere. Woolens accounted for three-fourths of English exports, for example, in the seventeenth and early eighteenth centuries. All over Europe, textile production increased because of the spread of the "putting-out system," or "domestic system." Hundreds of thousands of workers, many of them women, worked in cloth manufacturing in every country from England to Russia.

Under the putting-out system, the manufacturer supplied the workers with raw materials, such as wool or cotton fibers. Women and children working at home generally cleaned, combed, and spun yarn. Men, assisted by their wives and children, wove the cloth, also at home. The manufacturer then supervised the finishing of the cloth in a large workshop located either in town or in the countryside. This system had existed in some form for hundreds of years, but in the eighteenth century it burgeoned, expanding to include such prod-

Joseph Wright of Derby, The Iron Forge, 1771
As a member of a local scientific society, Wright avidly followed new scientific and industrial experiments. His depiction of an iron forge demonstrates his interest in the effect of light and in the work of industry, but it also shows that families could be found together in what seem to us the most unusual places!

ucts as glassware, baskets, nails, and guns as well as textiles.

In many places, thousands of people who had once worked in agriculture became part- or full-time textile workers. The spread of the domestic system of manufacturing is sometimes called "proto-industrialization" to signify that in some countries the process helped pave the way for nineteenth-century industrialization. Peasants turned to putting-out manufacturing work because they did not have enough land to support their families. Men labored off-season and women often worked year-round to augment their incomes. At the same time, population growth and the general economic improvement meant that demand for cloth increased because more people could afford it. By the end of the eighteenth century, working-class men in Paris began to wear underclothes, something rare at the beginning of the century. Men and women now bought night-clothes; before, Europeans had slept naked. Studies of wills left by working-class men and women

in Paris at the end of the eighteenth century show that people owned more clothes of greater variety; white, red, blue, yellow, green, and even pastel shades now replaced the black, gray, or brown of traditional dress.

While the rest of Europe, even the most advanced areas, continued to grow moderately, England began an industrial "take off" in the 1770s and 1780s that included rapid population growth, a dramatic increase in the use of machines, and a tendency for manufacturing to concentrate in factories employing hundreds if not thousands of workers. One of the most striking results was a staggering jump in the production of manufactured goods. The production of cotton goods—which now began to overtake woolens because they were lighter, washable, and more versatile—increased tenfold, that of iron fourfold just between 1760 and 1787. This combination of machines, factories, rapid population growth, and stunning increases in production together constituted the beginnings of the Industrial Revolution,

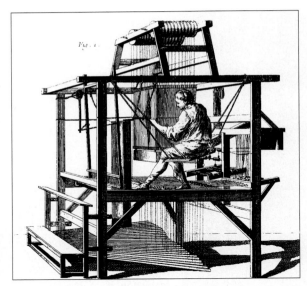

The Drawloom, *from Diderot's* **Encyclopedia**
Fancy fabrics with elaborate patterns were handwoven on looms preset to repeat intricate designs.

which would change the face of Europe—indeed the entire world—in the nineteenth century.

A set of interrelated changes in the technology of cotton manufacturing initiated the process of industrialization. Cotton textiles replaced woolens in popularity not only because of their superior qualities for clothing but also because the supply of raw cotton increased rapidly after it was introduced into the plantation economies of North America and the Caribbean. In 1733, John Kay had developed the flying shuttle, which enabled weavers to "throw" yarn across the loom rather than draw it back and forth by hand. When the flying shuttle came into widespread use in the 1760s, weavers' capacity quickly outran the amount of yarn traditional spinning could supply. The shortage of spun thread propelled the invention of machines to speed up the process of spinning: the spinning jenny and the water frame, a power-driven spinning machine, were introduced in the 1760s. In the following decades water frames replaced thousands of women spinners working at home by hand. In 1776, James Watt developed an improved steam engine, and in the 1780s, Edward Cartwright designed a mechanized loom, which

when perfected could be run by a small boy and yield fifteen times the output of a skilled adult weaver working a handloom. Soon all the new power machinery was assembled in large factories that hired semiskilled men, women, and children to replace skilled weavers.

Historians have no clear-cut explanation for why England led the Industrial Revolution. Some have emphasized England's large internal market, increasing population, supply of private investment capital from overseas trade and commercial profits, or natural resources such as coal and iron. Others have cited England's greater opportunities for social mobility or the pragmatism of the English and Scottish artisans who developed the necessary inventions. These early industrialists hardly had a monopoly on ingenuity, but they did come out of a tradition of independent capitalist enterprise. They also shared a developing culture of informal scientific education through learned societies and popular lectures (one of the prominent forms of the Enlightenment in England). For whatever reasons, the combination of improvements in agricultural production, growth in population and foreign trade, and willingness to invest in new machines and factories appeared first in this relatively small island.

The State and Enlightened Reform

Competition with England and growing awareness of the need to modernize prompted many European rulers to attempt reforms in their states. Historians have often called this phenomenon "enlightened despotism" because many of the reforming rulers continued to exercise absolutist powers; they offered reforms to maintain the state's power in a period of economic and social as well as intellectual changes. The eighteenth-century European state system depended above all on the balance of military power, which could always be upset by dynastic rivalries over territory, shifts in alliances, colonial conflicts, and changes in military technology. Many monarchs promoted internal reforms to compete more effectively for trade and territory throughout the world. Their efforts to improve the conditions of the peasantry, introduce freer markets in grain, extend education, and grant greater religious freedom aroused controversy and powerful opposition from privileged elites, whose resistance eventually limited the reform movement's impact.

War and Diplomacy

The reform efforts of European rulers only made sense within the context of unstable diplomatic alliances and the changing balance of power on the Continent and in the colonies. In military and diplomatic terms three major trends marked the years from 1740 to 1787, trends that had originated in the preceding period: Prussia's rise to great-power status and the resulting conflicts between it

and Austria for dominance in the German states; British and French competition for overseas colonial territory; and the continuing decline of Poland and the Ottoman Empire, together with the advance of Russia in the East.

The difficulties over the Austrian succession typified the dynastic complications that repeatedly threatened the balance of power. In 1740 the Holy Roman Emperor Charles VI died without a male heir. The other European powers maneuvered to secure their own advantage, even though most had already recognized the emperor's chosen heiress, his daughter Maria Theresa, by acknowledging Charles's Pragmatic Sanction of 1713, which had given a woman the right to inherit the Habsburg crown lands. The new king of Prussia, Frederick II, who had just succeeded his father a few months

Martin van Meytens, **Empress Maria Theresa and her Family**
This painting depicts Maria Theresa with her husband Francis I and eleven of their sixteen children. Their eldest son eventually succeeded to the Austrian throne as Joseph II, and their youngest daughter, Maria Antonia, or Marie Antoinette, became the queen of France.

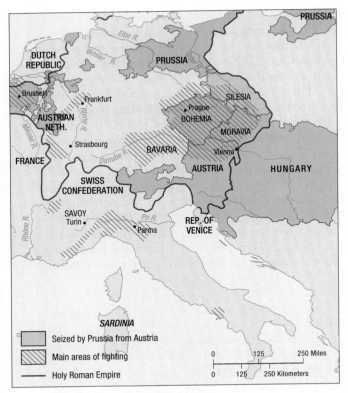

War of the Austrian Succession

Map legend:
- Seized by Prussia from Austria
- Main areas of fighting
- Holy Roman Empire

0   125   250 Miles
0   125   250 Kilometers

earlier in 1740, saw his chance and immediately invaded the rich Austrian province of Silesia. Before long, France, Spain, and Bavaria had joined Prussia against Austria and Great Britain in the War of the Austrian Succession (1740–1748). The struggle soon sucked in the British and French overseas colonies as well. Maria Theresa (*1740–1780) survived only by conceding Silesia to Prussia in order to split the Prussians off from the coalition and take on her other enemies one by one. The peace treaties recognized Maria Theresa as the heiress to the Austrian lands, and her husband Francis I received the title of Holy Roman Emperor.

The fighting between France and Great Britain in Europe during the War of the Austrian Succession quickly extended to India, where a series of naval battles left the British in control of the seas. The Peace of Aix-la-Chapelle in 1748 failed to resolve the colonial conflicts, and English and French trading companies continued to fight unofficially for domination in India. French and English colonials in North America fought each other all along their boundaries, enlisting Native American auxiliaries. Britain tried but failed to isolate the French Caribbean colonies during the war, and hostilities and suspicions continued unabated.

In the mid-1750s a major reversal of alliances—the Diplomatic Revolution—caused a reshuffling of relations among the major powers. To isolate Frederick the Great and regain Silesia, Austria set aside its traditional hostility to France and allied with it against Prussia, an alliance that eventually included Russia and Sweden as well. Meanwhile, Great Britain became Prussia's ally. Each power had different aims, but the realignment was soon tested by another outbreak of war on the Continent. The Seven Years' War (1756–1763) began with undeclared hostilities between Great Britain and France over colonial boundaries (in the opening move, colonial troops led by the Virginia Colonial George Washington invaded French territory near modern Pittsburgh), but war became official when Prussia invaded Saxony, an ally of Austria.

Fighting raged around the world. The French and British battled on land and sea in North America (where the conflict was called "the French and Indian War"), the West Indies, and India. The two coalitions skirmished in central Europe. At first, Frederick the Great surprised Europe with a spectacular victory at Rossbach in Saxony over a much larger Franco-Austrian army (1757). But in time, Russian armies in the east and Austrian armies to the south had encircled his troops. Frederick despaired: "I believe all is lost. I will not survive the ruin of my country." A fluke saved him. Empress Elizabeth of Russia (*1741–1762) died and was succeeded by the mentally unstable Peter III, a fanatical admirer of Frederick and all things Prussian. Peter withdrew Russia from the war. (This was practically his only accomplishment as tsar. He was soon overthrown and mysteriously murdered, probably at the instigation of Catherine II who replaced him.)

The Anglo-French colonial conflicts ended more decisively. British naval superiority, achieved only in the 1750s, enabled British regulars and North American colonial troops to rout the French from Canada, the Ohio Valley, and the Great Lakes. The British also turned back the French in India and, most dramatically, in the West Indies. Although

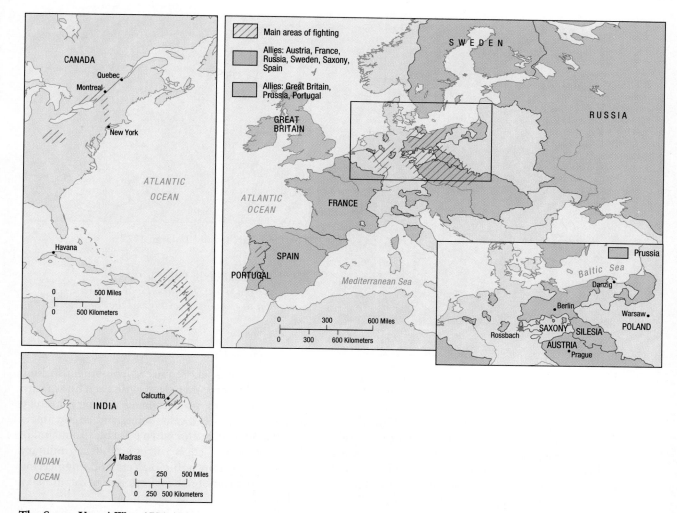

The Seven Years' War, 1756-1763

the various coalition partners had entered the war together, they made peace separately and restored the status quo on the Continent. Frederick kept all his territory, including Silesia. In the Treaty of Paris (1763), France ceded Canada to Britain and agreed to remove its armies from India, in exchange for keeping its rich West Indian islands. French eagerness to avenge their worldwide defeat at British hands would motivate them to support the Americans in the War for Independence just fifteen years later.

When Catherine II seized power from her husband Peter, she pushed Russia into more di-

rectly opposing the Ottoman Empire. During a war with the Turks (1768–1774), Catherine's agents promoted rebellion by the Greeks and Balkan peoples against their Ottoman rulers. Russian ships appeared in Italian and Greek ports. Although the revolts failed, Russian successes in battle against the Turks and fears of Russian influence in the Balkans prompted Prussia and Austria to agree with Russia on the first Partition of Poland in 1772. The idea was to block Russia from gaining complete control over the Polish commonwealth, which it had unofficially dominated for half a century. Despite the Austrian empress Maria

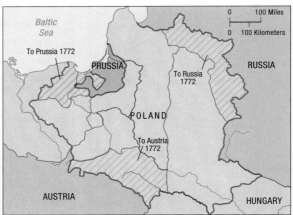

The First Partition of Poland, 1772

(left) **The Situation of Poland,** *1773*
*Catherine the Great, Joseph II, and Frederick II
each point to the portion of Poland they plan to
take.*

Theresa's protests that the division would spread
"a stain over my whole reign," she agreed to split
one-third of Poland-Lithuania's territory and half
of its people among the three powers. Disorder in
Poland ostensibly justified this territorial grab.
Protestants and Orthodox Christians had rebelled
against the Catholic majority, and a virtual civil
war erupted when Catholic nobles organized to resist foreign intervention. What was left of the kingdom remained dependent on Russia until the late
1780s.

War and Enlightened Reform

Militarization accelerated in this period, further
straining state resources. During the Seven Years'
War, France had five hundred thousand men in
arms, at least one hundred thousand more than the
largest armies of Louis XIV, and the Prussian army
nearly tripled in size between 1740 and 1786. The
armies jumbled together peasant and artisan conscripts, volunteers, and foreign mercenaries, ham-
mering them into unified fighting forces by incessant drilling and harsh discipline. Soldiers,
Frederick the Great insisted, must be more afraid
of their sergeant than of the enemy. Widespread use

of flintlock muskets required deployment in long
lines, usually three men deep, with each line in turn
loading and firing on command. Military strategy
became cautious and calculating, and commanders
avoided pitched battles when possible. To maintain
their competitive edge, rulers established military
academies to train noble officers and engineering
schools to promote the development of military
technology.

The peace of 1763 left the crowned heads of
Europe with pressing postwar problems of recovery. For example, when trade resumed, too many
goods flooded the market, prices collapsed, and
many businesses went bankrupt. The growth of
armies, the need for navies to wage overseas conflicts, and the eventual return of inflation combined
to increase states' needs for money. Rather than
simply responding to the short-term needs of the
moment, many monarchs undertook far-reaching
reforms that reflected the Enlightenment's impact
on official circles. Frederick II in Prussia, Catherine II in Russia, Louis XV (*1715–1774) and Louis
XVI (*1774–1793) in France, Maria Theresa and
Joseph II (*1780–1790) in Austria, and a host of
minor rulers all proposed similar programs to establish state independence from the church, to

appoint reforming ministers, to standardize tax collection and administration, to inventory the country's resources, and, in many instances, to extend education and religious toleration. They aimed to increase economic and military power by modernizing society. As one adviser to Joseph II put it, "A properly constituted state must be exactly analogous to a machine . . . and the ruler must be the foreman, the mainspring . . . which sets everything else in motion." Such reforms always threatened the interests of traditional groups, however, and the spread of Enlightenment ideas aroused sometimes unpredictable desires for more change.

The reforming monarchs did not invent government bureaucracy, but in Austria and Prussia especially they insisted on greater attention to merit, hard work, professionalism, and routines that made bureaucrats more like modern civil servants. As Joseph II explained, government must be organized according to "uniform principles," and it must unite "a single mass of people all subject to impartial guidance." According to this view, the ruler should be a benevolent, enlightened administrator who works for the general well-being of his or her people. Frederick II of Prussia, who drove himself as hard as he drove his officials, established new government departments (Commerce and Industry, War Supplies, and so on) and supervised the institution of a uniform civil procedure for the whole country, making Prussian justice the most consistently administered and efficient in Europe. "I am the first servant of the state," boasted Frederick.

Legal reform, both of the judicial system and of the often disorganized and irregular law codes, was central to the work of many reform-minded monarchs. Frederick the Great and Joseph II ordered the compilation of unified law codes, projects that required many years to complete. Catherine II of Russia began such an undertaking even more ambitiously. In 1767 she called together a Legislative Commission of 564 deputies and asked them to consider a long document called the *Instruction*, which represented her hopes for legal reform based on the ideas of Montesquieu and Beccaria. The *Instruction* insisted on absolute government but called for equality of all people before the law, religious toleration, and the elimination of torture and cruel punishments. Despite much dis-

cussion and hundreds of petitions and documents about local problems, little came of the meeting because Catherine herself was not very committed to government reforms. Her efforts in other areas resulted in some changes. Catherine tried to expand elementary education—and the education of women in particular—and founded engineering schools. She encouraged the growth of the publishing industry, which increased rapidly despite limited freedom of the press. She herself wrote for some of the new journals, but she also condemned her leading critics to prison.

Rulers everywhere wanted more control over church affairs. In Catholic countries many government officials resented the influence of the Jesuits (Society of Jesus), the major Catholic teaching order. The Jesuits trained the Catholic intellectual elite, ran a worldwide missionary network, enjoyed close ties to the papacy, and amassed great wealth. Critics mounted campaigns against the Jesuits in many countries, and by the early 1770s the Society of Jesus had been dissolved in Portugal, France, and Spain (only to be welcomed to Russia by Catherine). In 1773, Pope Clement XIV (∗1769–1774) agreed under pressure to disband the order (it was restored in 1814).

Joseph II not only applauded the suppression of the Jesuits but also required Austrian bishops to swear fidelity and submission to him. Under Joseph the Austrian state supervised seminaries, reorganized diocesan boundaries, and abolished monastic orders devoted to the contemplative life, confiscating their property to pay for education and poor relief. Austria launched the most ambitious educational reforms of the period. In 1774, once the Jesuits had been officially disbanded, a General School Ordinance ordered state subsidies for local schools, which the state would regulate. In France, by contrast, the Catholic church resisted state efforts to wrest control of its resources, and the availability of primary education continued to be very spotty. Only the French Revolution of 1789 would change the church-state balance in France.

Toleration for religious minorities gained ground in most countries. Again, the leader was Joseph II of Austria, who had become Holy Roman Emperor and co-regent with his mother, Maria Theresa, in 1765. Joseph was able to carry out his most radical policies only when he ruled alone after 1780, and then he acted swiftly and sometimes brutally. His own brother described him as "imbued with arbitrary, brutal principles and the most severe, brutal and violent despotism." These qualities nevertheless enabled Joseph to push through reforms that might otherwise have been resisted. In 1781 he granted freedom of religious worship to Protestants, Orthodox, and Jews. For the first time these groups were allowed to own property, build schools, enter the professions, and hold political and military offices.

Limits of Reform

Most European states limited the rights and opportunities available to Jews. In Russia only wealthy Jews could hold municipal office, and Polish Jews in the territory incorporated into Russia had to live in certain places. In Prussia, Frederick the Great called the Jews "useless to the state" and imposed special taxes on them. Even in Austria the laws forced Jews to take German-sounding names, and in the Papal States the pope encouraged forced baptism. The leading *philosophes* had opposed persecution of the Jews in theory but often treated them with undisguised contempt. Diderot's comment was all too typical: the Jews, he said, bore "all the defects peculiar to an ignorant and superstitious nation." The situation for other religious minorities was similarly difficult and only beginning to change for the better. The French state regarded Protestants as heretics until 1787, when Louis XVI signed an edict of toleration restoring their civil rights—but they still could not hold political office. Great Britain continued to deny Catholics freedom of open worship and the right to sit in Parliament. In general, toleration in practice remained an elusive goal.

Nowhere were the limits of reform more evident than in agricultural policy, and nowhere were the differences in policy more striking than in eastern Europe. Joseph II tried to remove the burdens of serfdom in the Habsburg lands, a program that contrasted markedly with Frederick II's and Catherine II's granting of greater privileges to their respective nobilities. In 1781, Joseph abolished the personal aspects of serfdom: serfs now could move freely, enter trades, or marry without their lord's permission. Joseph ordered a survey of all lands,

abolished the tithe to the church, shifted more of the tax burden to the nobility, and converted peasants' labor services into cash payments. The nobility reacted to these far-reaching reforms with fury and resistance. When Joseph died in 1790 his brother Leopold had to revoke most provisions to appease the nobles. On his deathbed, Joseph recognized the futility of many of his efforts; as his epitaph he suggested, "Here lies Joseph II, who was unfortunate in all his enterprises." Frederick II, like Joseph, encouraged such agricultural innovations as planting potatoes and turnips (new crops that could help feed a growing population), experimenting with cattle breeding, draining swamplands, and clearing forests. But Prussia's noble landlords, or Junkers, continued to expand their estates at the expense of poorer peasants, and Frederick did nothing to ameliorate serfdom except on his own domains.

Reforming ministers also tried to stimulate agricultural improvement in France. Unlike most other west European countries, France still had about one hundred thousand serfs; though their burdens weighed less heavily than those in eastern Europe, serfdom did not entirely disappear until 1789. A group of economists called the *physiocrats* urged the French government to deregulate the grain trade and make the tax system more equitable to encourage agricultural productivity. In the interest of establishing a free market, they also insisted that urban guilds be abolished because they prevented free entry into the trades. Their proposed reforms applied the Enlightenment emphasis on individual liberties to the economy. The French government took some of this advice and deregulated the grain trade in 1763, but it had to reverse this decision in 1770 when grain shortages caused a famine.

French reform efforts did not end there. To break the power of the parlements, the thirteen high courts of law that had led the way in opposing royal efforts to increase and equalize taxation, Louis XV appointed a reform-minded chancellor who replaced the parlements with new courts, in which the judges no longer owned their offices and thus could not sell them or pass them on as an inheritance. Justice would then be more impartial. Nevertheless, the judges of the displaced parlements aroused widespread opposition to what they portrayed as tyrannical royal policy. The furor calmed down only when Louis XV died in 1774 and his successor, Louis XVI, yielded to aristocratic demands and restored the old parlements. Louis XV died one of the most despised kings in French history. Resented both for his high-handed reforms and his private vices, underground pamphlets lampooned Louis, describing his mistress Madame Du Barry as a prostitute who pandered to the elderly king's well-known taste for young girls. This often pornographic literature linked despotism to the excessive influence of women at court.

Louis XVI tried to carry out part of the program suggested by the physiocrats, and he chose one of their disciples, Jacques Turgot (1727–1781), as his chief minister. A contributor to the *Encyclopedia*, Turgot pushed through several edicts that again freed the grain trade, suppressed many guilds, converted corvée service by peasants into a money tax payable by all landowners, and reduced court expenses. He also began making plans to introduce a system of elected local assemblies, which would have made government much more representative. Faced with broad-based resistance led by the parlements and his own court, as well as with riots against rising grain prices, Louis XVI dismissed Turgot, and one of the last possibilities to overhaul France's government collapsed.

The failure of reform in France reflected the contradictions of late eighteenth-century French politics. The nobles in the parlements blocked the French monarchy's reform efforts using the Enlightenment language spoken by the crown's ministers. But unlike Austria, the other Great Power that faced persistent aristocratic resistance to reform, the Enlightenment in France had attracted a large middle-class public that was increasingly frustrated by this failure to institute social change, a failure that ultimately helped undermine the monarchy itself. Where Frederick II, Catherine II, and even Joseph II used reform to bolster the efficiency of central government, attempts at change in France backfired. French kings found that their ambitious programs for reform succeeded only in arousing unrealistic hopes. A critical difference between France and most of the other great powers had arisen: unlike Great Britain, Prussia, and Russia, in France the crown and the nobility did not establish an enduring pattern of cooperation.

Opposition to and Rebellion Against State Power

The failure of French reform programs showed that trying to blend new and old elements in this period was sometimes like attempting to mix oil and water. Applying Enlightenment ideas of free trade immediately ran into the opposition of consumers, who resented the rise in prices and serious shortages that often resulted. Ordinary people had always been concerned with the price and availability of food, especially grain, and they often rioted when they perceived the government as failing to protect them against shortages. The spread of Enlightenment notions in newspapers, magazines, and coffeehouses, however, did change some of the rules of the game in national politics. Monarchs now appealed directly to public opinion to justify their policies. The growth of informed public opinion had its most significant consequences in the North American colonies, where a struggle over Parliament's right to tax turned into a full-scale war for independence. In Great Britain and its North American colonies, a portion of the public began to organize to force the abolition of the slave trade; for them, Enlightenment ideas of personal liberty and religious beliefs in human dignity were incompatible with the continuation of slavery. These efforts would crystallize into a full-fledged abolition movement only after 1800.

Food Riots and Peasant Uprisings

Population growth, inflation, the extension of the market system, and the increase in enclosures put added pressure on the already beleaguered poorest classes of people. Seventeenth-century peasants and townspeople had rioted to protest new taxes. In the eighteenth century they reacted violently when they feared officials might fail to protect them from food shortages, either by freeing the grain market, which would benefit big farmers, or by requisitioning grain for the armies or the big cities. Other eighteenth-century forms of collective violence included riots against religious minorities, against militia recruiting, against turnpikes and toll gates, against attempts to arrest smugglers, and against enclosures of common fields. Riots sometimes even erupted to express fear and anger in reaction to unexplained epidemics or to protest the execution of criminals who had captured the popular imagination.

In the last half of the eighteenth century the food supply became the focus of political and social conflict. The poorer people in the villages and the towns believed it was the government's responsibility to ensure enough food for them, and in fact many governments did stockpile grain to make up for the occasional bad harvest. At the same time, in keeping with Adam Smith's and the French physiocrats' laissez-faire economic proposals, governments wanted to allow grain prices to rise with market demand, because higher profits would motivate producers to increase the supply of food to the big cities and to the armies. They believed deregulating the grain trade would spur production and thus ultimately benefit everyone. Free trade in grain meant selling to the highest bidder, even if that bidder was a foreign merchant. In the short run, in times of scarcity, big landowners and farmers could make huge profits by selling grain outside their home towns or villages. This practice enraged poor farmers, agricultural workers, and city wageworkers, who could not afford the higher prices. Lacking the political means to affect policy, they could enforce their desire for old-fashioned price regulation only by rioting. Most did not pillage or steal grain but rather forced the sale of grain or flour at a "just" price and blocked the shipment of grain out of their villages to other markets. Women often led these "popular taxations," as they were called in France, in desperate attempts to protect the food supply for their children.

Such food riots occurred regularly in England and France in the last half of the eighteenth century. One of the most turbulent was the so-called Flour War in France in 1775. Turgot's deregulation of the grain trade in 1774 caused prices to rise in several provincial cities. Rioting spread from there to the Paris region, where villagers attacked grain convoys heading to the capital city. Local officials often ordered merchants and bakers to sell at the price the rioters demanded, only to find themselves arrested by the central government for overriding free trade. The government brought in troops to restore order and introduced the death penalty for rioting.

Pugachev
The Russian rebel is shown here in a nineteenth-century rendition.

Uprisings also rocked countries less affected by the commercialization of agriculture. Peasants rebelled in Bohemia in 1775. The revolt had been preceded by years of sporadic unrest caused by harvest failures and epidemic diseases. When Joseph II traveled through the Czech lands in 1771, rumors of reform began to circulate, including the belief that an imperial instruction written in gold would liberate the serfs. Bands of hundreds and sometimes thousands of peasants attacked castles and churches. The army routed them when they marched on Prague.

Large as this uprising was, it paled in comparison with the Pugachev rebellion in Russia that began in 1773. An army deserter from the southeast frontier region, Emelyan Pugachev claimed to be Tsar Peter III, the dead husband of Catherine II. Pugachev's appearance seemed to confirm peasant hopes for a "redeemer tsar" who would save the people from oppression. He rallied around him Cossacks like himself, who resented the loss of their old tribal independence. Now increasingly enserfed or forced to pay taxes and endure army service, these nomadic bands joined with Old Believers, peasants who resented increases in seigneurial obligations, rebellious mine workers, and Muslim minorities. Catherine dispatched a large army to squelch the uprising, but Pugachev eluded them and the fighting spread. Nearly 3 million people eventually participated, making this the largest single rebellion in the history of tsarist Russia. When Pugachev urged the peasants to attack the nobility and seize their estates, hundreds of noble families perished. Foreign newspapers called it "the revolution in southern Russia" and offered fantastic stories about Pugachev's life history. Finally, the army captured the rebel leader and brought him in an iron cage back to Moscow, where he was tortured and executed. In the aftermath, Catherine tightened the nobles' control over their serfs and harshly punished those who dared to criticize serfdom.

Public Opinion and Political Opposition

Peasant uprisings might briefly shake even a powerful monarchy, but enduring changes in European politics often evolved more subtly and less violently. Across much of Europe and in North American colonies, demands for broader political participation reflected Enlightenment notions about individual rights. Aristocratic bodies such as the parlements in France insisted that the monarch consult them on the nation's affairs, and the new, educated elite wanted more influence too. With the rise of public opinion as an independent force in politics, newspapers began to cover daily political affairs, and the public learned the basics of political life, even in countries with strict limits on political participation.

Monarchs turned to public opinion to seek support against aristocratic groups that opposed reform. Gustavus III of Sweden (✶1771–1792) called himself "the first citizen of a free people" and promised to deliver the country from "insufferable aristocratic despotism"—that is, the oligarchic domination that had succeeded the downfall of absolutism after about 1720. Shortly after coming to the throne, Gustavus proclaimed a new constitution that divided power between the king and the legislature, abolished the use of torture in the judicial process, and assured some freedom of the press.

In France both the parlements (which had no legislative role like that of the British Parliament) and the monarch appealed to the public through the printed word. The crown hired writers to make its case; the magistrates responded with their own. French newspapers published in the Dutch Republic, which provided many people in France with detailed accounts of political news, also represented the pro-parlement position. One of the new French newspapers printed in France, *The Women's Journal*, was published by women and mixed short stories and reviews of books and plays with attacks on the regime and demands for more women's rights.

The stakes of political conflict increased as the role of public opinion became more prominent. During the reign of George III (✶1760–1820), the British Parliament provoked a great public outcry when it tried to deny a seat to one of its members, John Wilkes (1727–1797). In 1763, Wilkes attacked the government in his newspaper, the *North Briton*, and sued the crown when he was arrested. He won his release as well as damages. Wilkes cleverly manipulated his reputation as a flamboyant dresser and sexual libertine to establish himself as a popular hero. When he was reelected, Parliament denied him his seat, not once but three times.

The Wilkes episode soon escalated into a major campaign against the corruption and social exclusiveness of Parliament, complaints the Levellers had first raised during the English Revolution of the late 1640s. Newspapers, magazines, pamphlets, handbills, and cheap editions of Wilkes's collected works all helped promote his cause. Those who could not vote demonstrated for Wilkes. In one incident eleven people died when soldiers broke up a huge gathering of his supporters. The slogan "Wilkes and Liberty" appeared on walls all over London, and crowds broke the windows of those who would not display lights in his honor. Middle-class voters formed a Society of Supporters of the Bill of Rights, which circulated petitions for Wilkes; they gained the support of about one-fourth of all the voters. The more determined Wilkesites proposed sweeping reforms of Parliament, including more frequent elections, more representation for the counties, elimination of "rotten boroughs" (election districts so small that they could be controlled by one big patron), and restrictions of pensions used by the crown to gain support. These demands would be at the heart of agitation for

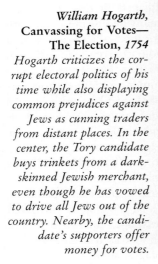

William Hogarth,
**Canvassing for Votes—
The Election,** *1754*
Hogarth criticizes the corrupt electoral politics of his time while also displaying common prejudices against Jews as cunning traders from distant places. In the center, the Tory candidate buys trinkets from a dark-skinned Jewish merchant, even though he has vowed to drive all Jews out of the country. Nearby, the candidate's supporters offer money for votes.

parliamentary reform in Britain for decades to come.

Popular demonstrations did not always support reforms. In 1780 the Gordon riots devastated London. They were named after the fanatical anti-Catholic crusader Lord Gordon, who helped organize huge marches and petition campaigns against a bill the House of Commons passed to grant limited toleration to Catholics. The demonstrations culminated in a seven-day riot that left fifty buildings destroyed and three hundred people dead. Despite the continuing limitations on voting rights in England, British politicians were learning that public opinion could be ignored only at their peril.

Political opposition also took artistic forms, particularly in countries where governments restricted organized political activity. A striking example of a play with a political message was Pierre-Augustin Caron de Beaumarchais's *The Marriage of Figaro* (1784). Beaumarchais (1732–1799) worked as a watchmaker, a judge, a gunrunner in the American War for Independence, and a French spy in England. *The Marriage of Figaro* was first a hit at court, when Queen Marie Antoinette had it read for her friends. But when her husband, Louis

XVI, read it, he forbade its production on the grounds that "this man mocks at everything that should be respected in government." When finally performed publicly, the play caused a sensation. The chief character, Figaro, is a clever servant who gets the better of his noble employer; when speaking of the count, he cries, "What have you done to deserve so many rewards? You went to the trouble of being born, and nothing more." Two years later, Mozart based an equally famous but somewhat tamer opera on Beaumarchais's story.

Revolution in North America

Oppositional forms of public opinion came to a head in Great Britain's North American colonies. There the end result was American independence and the establishment of a republican constitution that stood in stark contrast to most European regimes. The successful revolution was the only blow to Great Britain's increasing dominance in world affairs in the eighteenth century, and as such it was another aspect of the ongoing power rivalries of the time. Yet many Europeans saw the American Revolution as a triumph for Enlightenment ideas. As one German writer exclaimed in

1777, American victory would give "greater scope to the Enlightenment, new keenness to the thinking of peoples and new life to the spirit of liberty."

The British colonies remained loyal to the crown until Parliament's encroachment on their autonomy and the elimination of the French threat at the end of the Seven Years' War transformed colonial attitudes. Unconsciously, perhaps, the colonies had begun to form a separate nation; their economies generally flourished in the eighteenth century, and between 1750 and 1776 their population almost doubled. With the British clamoring for lower taxes and the colonists paying only a fraction of the tax rate paid by the Britons at home, Parliament passed new taxes, including the Stamp Act in 1765, which required a special tax stamp on all legal documents and publications. After violent rioting in the colonies the new tax was repealed, but in 1773 a new Tea Act caused renewed colonial resistance, which culminated in the famous Boston Tea Party of 1773. Colonists dressed as Indians boarded English ships and dumped the imported tea (by this time an enormously popular beverage) into Boston's harbor. The English government tried to clamp down on the unrest, but British troops in the colonies soon found themselves fighting locally organized militias.

The American revolutionary leaders had been influenced by a common Atlantic civilization; they participated in the Enlightenment and shared political ideas with the opposition Whigs in Britain. Supporters demonstrated for Wilkes in South Carolina and Boston, and the South Carolina lower house donated a substantial sum to the Society of Supporters of the Bill of Rights. In the 1760s and 1770s both English and American opposition leaders became convinced that the British government was growing increasingly corrupt and despotic, and both were concerned with the lack of representation in Parliament. English radicals wanted to reform Parliament so the voices of a broader, more representative segment of the population would be heard. The colonies had no representatives in Parliament, and colonists claimed "no taxation without representation" should be allowed. Indeed they denied that Parliament had any jurisdiction over the colonies, insisting that the king govern them through colonial legislatures and recognize their traditional English liberties. The failure of the "Wilkes and Liberty" campaign to produce concrete results convinced many Americans that Par-

Portrait of Benjamin Franklin, 1777
Franklin, shown here in his rustic beaver hat, stood for all the inventiveness and boldness of the New World. He inspired great enthusiasm for American independence among the French.

liament was hopelessly tainted and that they would have to stand up for their rights as English subjects.

Political opposition in the American colonies turned belligerent when Great Britain threatened to use force to maintain control. In 1774 the First Continental Congress convened, composed of delegates from all the colonies, and unsuccessfully petitioned the crown for redress. The next year the Second Continental Congress organized an army with George Washington in command. After actual fighting had begun, in 1776, the congress proclaimed the Declaration of Independence. An eloquent statement of the American cause written by Thomas Jefferson, the Declaration of Independence was couched in the language of universal human rights, which enlightened Europeans could be expected to understand. George III denounced the American "traitors and rebels," calling them "misled by dangerous and ill-designing men." But European newspapers enthusiastically reported on every American response to "the cruel acts of oppression they have been made to suffer." In the ensuing War for American Independence (1775–1783), France boosted the American cause by entering on the colonists' side in 1778. Spain too saw an opportunity to check the growing power of Britain, though without actually endorsing American independence out of fear of the response of its Latin American colonies. Spain declared war in 1779; Great Britain declared war on the Dutch Republic in 1780 in retaliation for Dutch support of the rebels. Thus another worldwide conflict resulted, which this time proved more than Britain could handle. The American colonies achieved their independence in the peace treaty of 1783.

The newly independent states still faced the challenge of republican self-government. The Articles of Confederation, drawn up in 1777 as a provisional constitution, proved weak because they gave the central government few powers. In 1787 a constitutional convention met in Philadelphia to draft a new constitution. Ratified the next year, it established a two-house legislature, an indirectly elected president, and an independent judiciary. The Constitution's preamble insisted explicitly, for the first time in history, that government derived its power solely from the people and did not depend on divine right or on the tradition of royalty

or aristocracy. The new educated elite of the eighteenth century had now created government based on a "social contract" between male, property-owning, white citizens. It was not a democracy in the modern sense, and women and slaves were excluded completely. But the new government still represented a radical departure from European models. In 1791 a Bill of Rights was appended to the Constitution; it outlined the essential rights (such as freedom of speech) that the government could never overturn. Although slavery continued in the new American republic, the climate of opinion about it had changed fundamentally since the 1750s; many American leaders now joined the Wilkesites in England and Enlightenment thinkers in France in opposing it.

Interest in the new republic was greatest in France. The United States Constitution and various state constitutions were published in French with commentary by leading thinkers. Even more important in the long run were the effects of the American war. Dutch losses to Great Britain aroused a widespread movement for political reform in the Dutch Republic, and debts incurred by France in supporting the American colonies would soon force the French monarchy to the edge of bankruptcy and then to revolution. Ultimately, the entire European system of royal rule would be challenged.

CONCLUSION

The American Revolution was the most profound practical result of the general European movement known as the Enlightenment. What began as a cosmopolitan movement of a few intellectuals in the first half of the eighteenth century reached a relatively wide audience among the educated elite of men and women. The spirit of reform with its promise of a new order swept from the salons and coffeehouses into the halls of government. Reasoned, scientific inquiry into the causes of social misery and laws defending individual rights and freedoms gained adherents everywhere. For most Europeans, however, the new order remained a promise rather than reality. Rulers had every intention of retaining their full, often unchecked, powers.

Often as not, reformers found themselves thwarted by the resistance of privileged groups, by the priorities rulers gave to waging wars, or by the resistance of the popular classes to changes in trade that stripped away protection against the uncertainties of the market. Yet even the failure of reform contributed to the ferment in Europe after 1770. Peasant rebellions in eastern Europe, the "Wilkes and Liberty" campaigns in Great Britain, the struggle over reform in France, and the revolution in America all occurred at about the same time, and their conjunction convinced many Europeans that the world was in fact changing. Just how much it had changed, and whether it was for better or for worse, would become more evident in the next ten years.

SUGGESTIONS FOR FURTHER READING

Source Materials

Equiano's Travels. Edited by Paul Edwards. 1967. A fascinating autobiography of a slave who was eventually freed by his master.

Gay, Peter, ed. *The Enlightenment.* 1985. A panoramic collection of documents.

Ménétra, Jacques Louis. *Journal of My Life.* Translated by Arthur Goldhammer. Introduction by Daniel Roche. 1986. A rare autobiography of an ordinary man, a glassworker, during the Enlightenment. Includes an account of his meeting with Rousseau in Paris.

Voltaire. *Candide.* Translated by Lowell Blair. 1959. Although not mentioned in the text, an excellent example of French Enlightenment writing.

Interpretive Studies

Blanning, T. C. W. *Joseph II and Enlightened Despotism.* 1970. A short history of Joseph's reforms that includes a selection of interesting documents.

Brewer, John. *Party Ideology and Popular Politics at the Accession of George III.* 1976. A lively history of the Wilkes movement in the context of the political opposition in late eighteenth-century England.

Darnton, Robert. *The Great Cat Massacre and Other Episodes in French Cultural History.* 1984. A wide-ranging collection of essays on cultural and social life during the Enlightenment.

Gay, Peter. *The Enlightenment: An Interpretation.* 2 vols. 1966, 1969. Still one of the liveliest histories of the movement in all its diversity. Overemphasizes the antireligious character.

Goodman, Dena. *The Republic of Letters: A Cultural History of the French Enlightenment.* 1994. Emphasizes the role of salons run by women.

Gullickson, Gay L. *Spinners and Weavers of Auffay: Rural Industry and the Sexual Division of Labor in a French Village, 1750–1850.* 1986. A study of proto-industrialization and its effects on women as well as men in textile manufacturing.

Hufton, Olwen. *Europe: Privilege and Protest, 1730–1789.* 1980. A useful general history of the eighteenth century, especially strong on state growth.

Jacob, Margaret C. *Living the Enlightenment: Freemasonry and Politics in Eighteenth-Century Europe.* 1991. An account that ties freemasonry in Great Britain, the Dutch Republic, and France to constitutional practices and Enlightenment ideas.

Jarrett, Derek. *England in the Age of Hogarth.* 1986. A social history of Hogarth's England.

McKendrick, Neil, John Brewer, and J. H. Plumb. *The Birth of Consumer Society: The Commercialization of Eighteenth-Century England.* 1982. A fascinating collection of essays on the consumer revolution in England that links jigsaw puzzles and pottery as well as popular politics to commercialization.

McManners, John. *Death and the Enlightenment.* 1981. A very readable account of the ways people thought about and experienced death from suicide to execution.

Palmer, R. R. *The Age of Democratic Revolution: A Political History of Europe and America, 1760–1800.* Vol. 1, *The Challenge.* 1959. Still the classic history of the confrontation between aristocrats and democrats in the decades preceding the French Revolution.

Stone, Lawrence. *The Family, Sex, and Marriage in England, 1500–1800.* Abridged ed. 1979. A one-volume introduction to the issues of family and children.

Venturi, Franco. *The End of the Old Regime in Europe, 1768–1776: The First Crisis.* Translated by R. Burr Litchfield. 1989. A remarkably learned and wide-ranging study of European (especially Italian) public opinion about the major political crises of the period.

On October 5, 1789, a crowd of several thousand women marched in a drenching rain twelve miles from the center of Paris to Versailles, the residence of the French king and his court. When the thoroughly soaked and tired women arrived, they demanded to see the king so they could ask him for help in securing more grain for the hungry Paris populace. The seventeen-year-old flower girl who had been chosen to speak for the women was so frightened by the prospect of meeting the king that she fainted. Others proved more hardy; they demanded an audience with the deputies who were meeting in a National Assembly to consider reform. Before the evening was over, thousands of men who had also marched from Paris joined the women. Early the next morning an angry crowd forced its way into the palace grounds and began breaking into the royal family's private apartments. To prevent further bloodshed—the mob had already killed two royal bodyguards and paraded their heads on pikes—the king agreed to move his family back to Paris. A huge procession set off with the "baker [the king, who should provide bread to his people], the baker's wife, and the baker's son" and thousands of men and women. The people had forced the monarch to respond to their grievances. The traditional political forms would soon crumble.

The October Days, as they were called, offered one of many extraordinary examples of ordinary people's intervening into the events of the decade-long upheaval known as the French Revolution. The Revolution had its immediate origins in a constitutional crisis provoked by a growing government deficit, traceable partly to French involvement in the American War

CHAPTER

20

The Age of Revolutions, 1787–1799

The Execution of Louis XVI, January 21, 1793
As shown in an engraving in the Revolutions of Paris *newspaper, the executioner held out Louis's severed head to the thousands of guardsmen and soldiers present.*

of Independence. It erupted on July 14, 1789, with the Parisians' assault on the Bastille, a royal fortress and prison in the center of Paris. Events then unfolded with astonishing rapidity. In the next few years, revolution transformed France and much of Europe. France's king and queen were beheaded by the guillotine, along with many thousands of others; titles of nobility were abolished; and a republican form of government replaced the monarchy in France. This new government pledged "liberty, equality, and fraternity," in the words of the most famous revolutionary slogan.

Many Europeans greeted 1789 as the dawn of a new era; an enthusiastic German wrote, "One of the greatest nations in the world, the greatest in general culture, has at last thrown off the yoke of tyranny." The violence that accompanied the dramatic events horrified others. In 1790, Edmund Burke, the British politician who had defended the American Revolution, denounced the "vilest of women" and the "cruel ruffians and assassins" who participated in the October Days. The French Revolution might have remained a strictly French affair if war had not enveloped the rest of Europe. As a growing counterrevolutionary army made up of aristocratic émigrés formed across the border, the new French republic declared war on Austria in 1792. Although virtually every other power eventually joined the crusade against France, the republic survived and soon marched across Europe, promising liberation from traditional monarchies but often delivering old-fashioned conquest and annexation. The French republican armies' success ultimately made possible the rise of Napoleon Bonaparte, a remarkable young general who brought France more wars, more conquests, and to the verge of military dictatorship.

The Late Eighteenth-Century Revolutions

The events of the French Revolution still provoke intense controversy, in part because the terms of much modern political debate originated in them. The modern meanings of some of our most important political labels and concepts—*Left* and

---

IMPORTANT DATES

1787 Dutch Patriot revolt is stifled by Prussian invasion

1788 Beginning of resistance of Austrian Netherlands against reforms of Joseph II

1789 French Revolution begins

1790 Internal divisions lead to collapse of resistance in Austrian Netherlands

1792 Beginning of war between France and the rest of Europe

1793 Second Partition of Poland by Austria and Russia

1794 France annexes the Austrian Netherlands

1797–1798 Creation of "sister" republics in Italian states and Switzerland

---

Right, terrorist, propaganda, and even *revolution* itself—come from the French Revolution. The *Left,* for example, designated those deputies who sat in the seats to the speaker's left in the French assembly and favored extensive revamping of the political and social order. *Revolution* had previously meant cyclical change that brought life back to a starting point, as a planet makes a revolution around the sun. Now *revolution* came to mean a self-conscious attempt to reshape society, politics, and even the human personality. Nothing escaped the revolutionary challenge: the king was tried and executed; the nobles were stripped of their titles, power, and privileges; the Catholic church was relieved of much of its authority; babies, streets, and even the months of the year were given new revolutionary names; and the symbols of liberty, equality, and fraternity were stamped on everyday objects from stationery to snuffboxes to chinaware. The French, moreover, made every effort to impose these changes on other countries.

The breathtaking succession of regimes in France and the failure of the republican experiment after ten years of upheaval raised disturbing questions about the relationship between rapid political change and violence. Do all revolutions inevitably degenerate into terror or wars of conquest? How can the French Revolution be seen as the origin of both modern democracy and modern totalitarianism? Can a country with a long tradition of monarchy be transformed into a republic almost overnight? Is a regime democratic if it does not allow poor men, women, or blacks to vote? The French Revolution raised these questions and many more. They resonated in many countries because the French Revolution seemed like only the most extreme example of a much broader political and social movement at the end of the eighteenth century.

Europe on the Eve of Revolution

From Philadelphia to Warsaw, people demanded more participation in the political decisions that shaped their lives. In 1787, at the same time the recently independent United States of America was preparing a new constitution, a broad-based Dutch Patriot movement challenged the powers of the Dutch stadholder. In the Austrian Netherlands (present-day Belgium and Luxembourg), nobles and lawyers resisted in the name of constitutional liberties the reforms of Emperor Joseph II of Austria. In distant Warsaw, patriotic reformers prepared to attack the abuses that had led Poland-Lithuania into humiliating political impotence, dependence on Russia, and large territorial losses. All these movements included calls for more representative government, but only the French revolt developed into a full-fledged revolution.

In the early spring of 1787, few felt the tremors forewarning a coming cataclysm. The Europeans greeted enthusiastically the American experiment in republican government but most did not consider it a likely model for their much more populous and traditional states. Similarly, the Enlightenment had spread into most of the circles of high society in western Europe without affecting the social prominence of aristocrats or the political control of kings and queens. In fact, the European monarchies seemed more securely established than ever, and the French monarchy appeared as sturdy as any of them. The French had regained international prestige by supporting the victorious Americans, and the monarchy had shown its eagerness to promote reforms. In 1787, for example, the French crown abolished torture and granted civil rights to Protestants.

Europeans in general were wealthier, healthier, more numerous, and better educated than they had ever been before. They had more newspapers and books to read, more concerts to attend, and more coffeehouses to enjoy, all subtle signs of economic growth and development. Ironically, political agitation would be most dramatic in some of the wealthiest and best-educated societies within Europe, such as the Low Countries. The eighteenth-century revolutions were a product of long-term prosperity and high expectations, but also of short-term downturn and depression, made all the more disappointing by the preceding decades of robust growth.

Historians have sometimes referred to the revolts of the 1780s as the *Atlantic Revolutions* because so many protest movements arose in countries on both shores of the North Atlantic in the late 1700s. Most scholars agree now, however, that the French Revolution differed greatly from the others: not only was France the richest, most powerful, and most populous state in western Europe, but its revolution was also more violent and more comprehensive. Its example threatened all European rulers and had repercussions as far away as South America and Egypt.

Many different explanations for the French Revolution have been offered. The Marxist interpretation, presented by the nineteenth-century revolutionary philosopher Karl Marx and his modern followers, was one of the most influential. Marx saw the French Revolution as the classic example of a *bourgeois,* that is, middle-class revolution. According to the Marxist interpretation, the *bourgeoisie* (middle class) overthrew the monarchy because of its association with the remnants of feudalism. French revolutionaries used the term *feudalism* to refer to everything that seemed outdated in their nations' economic and social systems, particularly the legal privileges long held by the aristocracy and the seigneurial rights of landowners, such as the many dues landlords levied on their tenants. Marxists believed the remains of the feudal order needed to be swept away to facilitate the development of capitalism.

Recent historians have successfully challenged many aspects of the Marxist interpretation, especially the link between revolution and capitalism. They argue that the French Revolution did not foster the development of capitalism and that a capitalist middle class composed of merchants and manufacturers did not lead the revolt. A kind of middle class did play an important role in the protest movements of the 1780s, but this middle class comprised lawyers, journalists, intellectuals, and lower-ranking officials. In the 1780s they did not act alone. Protest movements began only when aristocratic elites themselves challenged the rulers' powers. Once the uprisings began, the participation of both men and women from the urban lower classes propelled the movements, just as it had during the English Revolution of the mid-seventeenth century. The volatility of this combination of aristocrats, middle class, and lower classes ultimately defeated each revolution. At issue according to this more recent interpretation was the nature of democracy as a form of government rather than capitalism as an economic system. The appeal to "the people" as the source of legitimacy pitted one group against another and opened the way to new and sometimes dangerous forms of political mobilization.

Patriots and Protesters in the Low Countries

If the eighteenth-century revolutions began in America with the War for American Independence, they took their next step in the Dutch Republic. Political protests there attracted European attention because Dutch banks still controlled a hefty portion of the world's capital at the end of the eighteenth century, even though the Dutch Republic's role in international politics had diminished. Government-sponsored Dutch banks owned 40 percent of the British national debt, and by 1796 they held the entire foreign debt of the United States. Relations with the British became strained during the American War for Independence, however, and by the middle of the 1780s, agitation in favor of the Americans had boiled over into an attack on the Dutch stadholder, the prince of Orange, who as the chief executive of the Dutch Republic favored close ties with the British.

The Patriots, as they called themselves, began their agitation in the relatively restricted circles of middle-class bankers, merchants, and writers who supported the American cause. They soon gained a more popular audience by demanding political reforms in a petition campaign and forming armed citizen militias of men, called Free Corps. Parading under banners that read "Liberty or Death," they forced local officials to set up new elections

Orangist Revenge Against the Patriots
After the Prussians invaded, supporters of the prince of Orange plundered the houses of the leaders of the Patriot revolt.

to replace councils that had been packed with Orangist supporters through patronage or family connections. The future American president John Adams happened to be visiting Utrecht when such a revolt occurred. He wrote admiringly to Thomas Jefferson that "In no instance, of ancient or modern History, have the People ever asserted more unequivocally their own inherent and unalienable Sovereignty."

In 1787 the protest movement coalesced when a national assembly of the Free Corps joined with a group of Patriot Regents (the upper-class officials who ran the cities) to demand "the true republican

The Low Countries in 1787

form of government in our commonwealth," that is, the reduction of stadholder powers. The Free Corps fought the prince's troops and soon got the upper hand. In response, Frederick William II of Prussia, whose sister was the princess of Orange and actively involved in trying to rally her husband's supporters, intervened with tacit British support. Thousands of Prussian troops soon occupied Utrecht and Amsterdam, and the House of Orange regained its former position.

The Patriots fell to the fatal combination of outside intervention and their own internal social divisions. Many of the Patriot Regents from the richest merchant families resisted the growing power of the Free Corps, which agitated for a more democratic form of government. They feared the kinds of political disturbances that would soon crop up in France: pamphlets and cartoons attacking the prince and his wife, the rapid spread of clubs and societies made up of common people, and crowd-pleasing public ceremonies, such as parades and bonfires, that sometimes turned into riots. As divisiveness within the Patriot ranks increased, the prince of Orange was able to muster his own popular support. One of his most colorful supporters was Catherina Mulder, a mussels vendor known for her ability to gather crowds, shout slogans, and hand out Orangist songs. The Patriots sent her to prison. In the aftermath of the Prussian invasion, the Orangists got their revenge: lower class mobs pillaged the houses of prosperous Patriot leaders, forcing many to flee to the United States, France, or the Austrian Netherlands. Those Patriots who remained nursed their grievances until the French republican armies invaded in 1795.

Like the Dutch, the Belgians of the ten provinces of the Austrian Netherlands held firmly to their historic rights and liberties. If Emperor Joseph II had not tried to introduce reforms, the Austrian Netherlands might have remained tranquil. Yet Joseph, inspired by Enlightenment ideals, made changes that both extended civil rights and enhanced his own power. He abolished torture, decreed toleration for Jews and Protestants (in this resolutely Catholic area), and suppressed monasteries. His 1787 reorganization of the administrative and judicial systems and elimination of many offices that belonged to nobles and lawyers appeared to attack the elites' traditional rights and privileges. The upper classes felt their power was being usurped.

Belgian resistance to Austrian reforms was thus essentially reactionary, intended to defend historic liberties against a reforming government that seemed to run roughshod over property rights and local privileges. Moreover, the elites—nobles, judges, and lawyers—initiated the resistance. The Countess of Yves, a resistance leader, wrote pamphlets against Joseph's reforms and provided meeting places for the rebels. At the end of 1788 a secret society formed armed companies to prepare an uprising. By late 1789 each province had separately declared its independence, and the Austrian administration had collapsed. Delegates from the various provinces declared themselves the United States of Belgium, a clear reference to the American precedent.

Once again, however, internal squabbling doomed the rebels' movement. Those who wanted a more representative government organized clubs and wrote pamphlets denouncing the authority a minority of aristocrats and monks wielded. These democrats insisted that sovereignty resided in the people. "The nobles have no acquired right over the people," one writer proclaimed. To retain their control of the situation, the more conservative leaders of the provinces encouraged the Catholic clergy and peasants to aid them. Every Sunday in May and June 1790, thousands of peasant men and women led by their priests streamed into Brussels carrying crucifixes, nooses, and pitchforks to intimidate the democrats and defend the church. Faced with the choice between the Austrian emperor and "our current tyrants," the democrats chose to support the return of the Austrians under Emperor Leopold II (*1790–1792), who had succeeded his brother.

The Polish Revival

A reform party calling itself the Patriots also arose in Poland-Lithuania, which had been shocked by the loss of a third of its territory in the First Partition of 1772. The Patriots sought to overhaul the weak, almost anarchistic commonwealth along modern western European lines. Reformers included a few magnate families; some middle-level gentry, prosperous burghers, and clergy who espoused Enlightenment ideas; and King Stanislaw August Poniatowski (∗1764–1795). A nobleman who owed his crown solely to the dubious honor of being Catherine the Great's discarded lover, and a favorite correspondent of the Paris salon leader Madame Geoffrin, Poniatowski was a sophisticated cosmopolitan who saw in moderate reform the only chance for his country to escape the consequences of a century's misgovernment and cultural decline. Ranged against the Patriots stood most of the magnates and their entourages of dependent petty gentry—and the formidable Catherine the Great, determined to uphold imperial Russian influence by guaranteeing the noble "liberties" that kept Poland-Lithuania weak.

Watchful, but not displeased to see Russian influence waning, Austria and Prussia allowed the reform movement to proceed. Also standing aside were the commonwealth's enserfed peasantry, most of its townsfolk, and almost all of its large, impoverished Jewish population. The nonparticipation of these groups of commoners deprived the Patriots of a vital social base. For years after the First Partition, reforms were modest. The most important Patriot success came in revamping the national educational system after the dissolution of the Jesuit order, which hitherto had dominated Polish schooling at all levels.

In 1788 the Patriots got their golden chance. Bogged down in a war with the Ottoman Turks, Catherine could not block the summoning of a reform-minded diet (*Sejm*), which with royal aid outmaneuvered the antireform magnates. Amid much oratory denouncing Russian overlordship, this so-called Four-Year *Sejm* of 1788–1792 enacted some significant reforms, much influenced by the ideas of Montesquieu. The process culminated in the constitution of May 3, 1791, which established a hereditary monarchy with somewhat strengthened authority, at last freed the two-house legislature from the *liberum veto,* granted townspeople limited political rights, and vaguely promised future Jewish emancipation. Abolishing serfdom was hardly mentioned.

Modest though they were, the Polish reforms did not endure. Catherine II could not countenance the spread of revolutionary "radicalism" into eastern Europe and soon engineered the downfall of both the Patriots and the Polish-Lithuanian state. Yet the commonwealth's belated, fleeting regeneration was one more sign of how widely the impulse to reform had spread in the West and how dangerous it seemed to established interests. Once the currents of change reached the powerful kingdom of France, the outcome was sure to be unsettling.

The Origins of the French Revolution, 1787–1789

The French Revolution began with a fiscal crisis provoked by the expense of French support of the Americans against the British in the American War for Independence. About half of the French national budget went to paying interest on the debt that had accumulated. In contrast to Great Britain, which had a national bank to facilitate raising loans, the French government lived off relatively short-term, high-interest loans from private sources.

For twenty years the French government had been trying unsuccessfully to modernize the tax system to raise more revenue and respond to widespread criticism that the tax system was unfair. The peasants bore the greatest burden of taxes, whereas the nobles and clergy were largely exempt. Tax collection was far from systematic; private contractors collected many taxes and pocketed a large share of the proceeds. Neither were tax rates uniform; they varied by region and social group. Yet the multitude of exemptions and exceptions had many tenacious defenders. The failure of the crown's various reform efforts left it at the mercy of its creditors, who with the growing support of public opinion, demanded a clearer system of fiscal accountability.

In a monarchy the ruler's character is always crucial. Louis XVI (∗1774–1793) was the model of a virtuous husband and father, but he took a limited view of his responsibilities in this time of crisis. Many complained that he showed more interest in hunting or his hobby of making locks than in the problems of government. His wife, Marie-Antoinette, was blonde, beautiful, and much criticized for her extravagant taste in clothes, elaborate hairdos, and supposed indifference to popular misery. "The Austrian bitch," as underground writers called her, had been the target of an increasingly violent and often pornographic pamphlet campaign in the 1780s. By 1789 the queen had become an object of popular hatred; when confronted by the inability of the poor to buy bread, she was mistakenly reported to have replied heartlessly, "Let them eat cake." The king's ineffectiveness and the queen's growing unpopularity helped undermine the monarchy as an institution.

Faced with a mounting deficit and resistance to higher taxes from the parlements, in 1787 Louis called a special meeting of leading notables (hand-picked nobles, clergymen, and officials) to consider proposals for tax reform put forward by the chief financial minister, Charles-Alexandre de Calonne. Calonne advocated a more uniform land tax, the abolition of internal tariffs, and the establishment of a state bank. The Assembly of Notables refused to cooperate, and Calonne fled to London in the face of rising opposition. Next the king tried his old rival, the Parlement of Paris. When it too refused to agree to the crown's proposals, he ordered the judges into exile in the provinces. Overnight, the judges (members of the nobility because of the offices they held) became popular heroes for resisting the king's "tyranny"; in fact, they, like the notables, wanted reform only on their own terms. Leading nobles and officials saw an opportunity to make themselves partners in running France. Louis gave in to their demands that he call a meeting of the Estates-General, which had last met 175 years before, in 1614.

In this fluid and uncertain situation, middle-class leaders—lawyers, lower-ranking officials, and urban merchants—saw an opportunity to make their own voices heard. Like many nobles, middle-class men (and some middle-class women) had read Voltaire and Rousseau, joined masonic lodges, and cheered on the American cause. The boom in international trade and domestic textile production had made many merchants and manufacturers very wealthy and much more self-confident. Middle-class critics, such as Abbé Emmanuel-Joseph Sieyès, charged that the nobility and the clergy contributed nothing to the nation's well-being; as Sieyès remarked in his influential pamphlet, *What Is the Third Estate?* the privileged orders were like "a malignant disease which preys upon and tortures the body of a sick man."

The middle classes began to take a leading role as thousands of men (along with a few women) met throughout France to elect deputies and write down their grievances, all by invitation of the king. The effect of such meetings was electric. The humblest peasants were asked to state their views for the first time in their lives, and the result was a massive outpouring of complaints, especially about taxes. As one villager lamented, "The last crust of bread has been taken from us." Educated men from the middle and upper classes dominated the meetings at the regional level. The long series of meetings raised expectations that the Estates-General would help the king solve all the nation's ills.

These new hopes soared just at the moment France experienced an increasingly rare but always dangerous food shortage. Bad weather had damaged the harvest of 1788, and bread prices rose in many places in the spring and summer of 1789, threatening starvation for the poorest people. To make circumstances worse, a serious slump in textile production had been causing massive unemployment since 1786, when France signed a free-trade treaty with Great Britain that opened the door to the more rapidly industrializing—and therefore cheaper—British suppliers. In the biggest French cities thousands of workers were out of work and hungry, adding another volatile element to an already tense situation.

Excitement greeted the long-awaited opening of the Estates-General in May 1789, but a crucial procedural issue remained unresolved: Would the deputies vote by order or by head? As in 1614, deputies had been chosen to represent each of the three orders, or estates: the First Estate, the clergy; the Second Estate, the nobility; and the Third Estate, everyone else, at least 95 percent of the population. In 1614 each order, or estate, voted separately, and each therefore had veto power. Before the elections to the Estates-General in 1789 the king had agreed to double the number of deputies for the Third Estate (making them equal in number to the other two combined), but he had not decided whether the deputies would vote as orders or as individuals. Although most nobles insisted on voting by order, the deputies of the Third Estate refused to proceed on that basis. After six weeks of stalemate, on June 17, 1789, the deputies of the Third Estate took unilateral action and declared

The Opening of the Estates-General at Versailles, May 5, 1789
*The formal ceremony could only paper over already deepening divisions between
the nobility and the Third Estate.*

themselves and whomever would join them "the
National Assembly." Two days later the clergy
voted by a narrow margin to join them. A constitutional revolution was under way, for now the
elected deputies of "the nation" were taking power
for and by themselves. As one new revolutionary
newspaper asserted, "The day of the seventeenth
will be forever memorable." Barred from their
meeting hall on June 20, the deputies swore an oath
in a nearby tennis court not to disband until they
had given France a constitution that reflected their
newly declared authority.

In the next days the reaction of the king and
his court seemed hesitant. At first the king appeared to agree to the new representative assembly, but
he also ordered thousands of soldiers to march to
Paris. The deputies in Versailles feared a plot to arrest them and disperse the assembly. "Everyone is
convinced that the approach of the troops covers
some violent design," one deputy wrote home.
Their fears were confirmed when on July 11 the
king fired Jacques Necker, the Swiss Protestant

finance minister and the one high official thought
to be sympathetic to the deputies' cause.

The popular reaction in Paris to Necker's dis-
missal and the threat of military force changed the
course of the French Revolution. When the news
spread, the common people in Paris began to arm
themselves and attack places where either arms or
grain were thought to be stored. A deputy in Versailles reported home: "Today all of the evils overwhelm France, and we are between despotism, carnage, and famine." On July 14, 1789, an armed
crowd marched on the Bastille, a fortified prison
with walls five feet thick located in the middle of
the working-class district of eastern Paris. The
crowd wanted the cannon and gunpowder stored
at the prison, whose overweening size and notorious history made it a prime symbol of tyranny. After a confusing battle in which over a hundred
armed citizens outside died, the Bastille fell. After
the prison officials surrendered, the angry crowd
hacked to death the governor of the prison and
flaunted his head on a pike.

Lesueur Brothers, **Demolition of the Bastille,** *c. 1789*
After the attack on the Bastille, Parisians spontaneously began tearing down the prison stone by stone. Entrepreneurs sold the ruins as souvenirs. During the Revolution artists such as the Lesueur brothers produced engravings and gouaches detailing revolutionary events for a middle-class public.

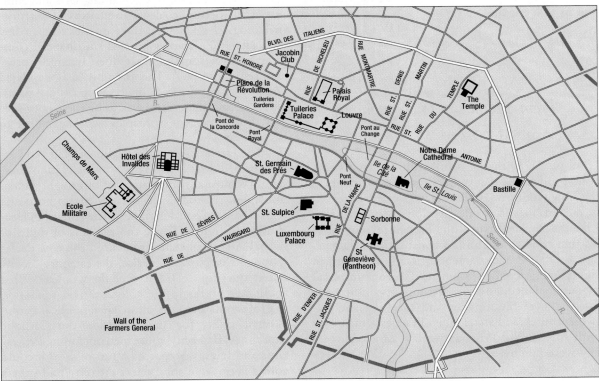

Paris During the Revolution

The fall of the Bastille (an event now commemorated as the French national holiday) set an important precedent. The common people showed themselves willing to intervene violently at a crucial political moment. All over France, food riots turned into local revolutions. The officials in one city wrote of their plight: "Yesterday afternoon [July 19] more than seven or eight thousand people, men and women, assembled in front of the two gates to the city hall. . . . We were forced to negotiate with them and to promise to give them wheat . . . and to reduce the price of bread." Local governments were forced out of power and replaced by committees of "patriots" loyal to the revolutionary cause. The patriots relied on newly formed National Guard units composed of civilians. One of their first duties was to calm the peasants in the countryside, who feared the beggars and vagrants crowding the roads might be part of an aristocratic plot to starve the people by burning crops or barns. In some instances, the Great Fear, as it was called, turned into peasant attacks on aristocrats or on seigneurial records kept in the lord's château. The king's government began to crumble. One of Louis XVI's brothers and many other leading aristocrats fled into exile. In Paris the Marquis de Lafayette, a hero of the American Revolution and a nobleman sympathetic to the French Revolution, became commander of the new National Guard. The Revolution thus had its first heroes, its first victims, and its first enemies.

From Monarchy to Republic, 1789–1793

Until July 1789 the French Revolution followed a course much like that of the protest movements in the Low Countries. Over the next years, however, it moved in directions previously unimagined. Like the Polish Patriots, the French revolutionaries first tried to establish a constitutional monarchy on the Enlightenment principles of human rights and rational government. The constitutional monarchy failed, however, because of conflicts between the revolutionaries and the king and between church and state; when France went to war with Austria and Prussia, the days of the monarchy were numbered.

The Revolution of Rights and Reason

For two years after July 1789 the deputies of the National Assembly strove to establish an enlightened, constitutional monarchy. The National Assembly now included the lawyers and officials who had represented the Third Estate in 1789 as well as most of the deputies from the clergy and a sub-

stantial number of nobles. Their first goal was to write a constitution, but they faced more immediate problems. In the countryside peasants refused to pay seigneurial dues to their landlords, and the persistence of the Great Fear raised alarms about the potential for a general peasant insurrection.

In response the National Assembly decided to make sweeping changes. On the night of August 4, 1789, noble deputies announced their willingness to give up their traditional privileges and dues, thereby freeing the peasants from some of their most pressing burdens. By the end of the night, amid general enthusiasm, dozens of deputies had come to the podium to relinquish the tax privileges of their own professional groups, towns, or provinces. The National Assembly decreed the abolition of what they called "the feudal regime"; that is, they freed the few remaining serfs and eliminated all special privileges in matters of taxation, including all seigneurial dues on the land (a few days later the deputies insisted on financial compensation for some of these dues, but most peasants refused to pay). The assembly also mandated equality of opportunity in access to official posts. Talent, rather than birth, was to be the key to success. Enlightenment principles were beginning to become law.

The Declaration of the Rights of Man and Citizen, passed three weeks later, was the National Assembly's most stirring statement of Enlightenment principles. It proclaimed that "Men are born and remain free and equal in rights." The American Declaration of Independence and the bills of rights of several American states influenced the new declaration. As in North America, the category "men" raised questions. Did it include women? What about free blacks in the colonies? Did toleration of Protestants and Jews mean equal political as well as civil rights for those outside the Catholic church? At first only white men, including Protestants and Jews, who passed a test of wealth could vote. (They were the "active citizens"; all others were "passive.") After 1792 almost all men would get full voting rights, including (eventually) former slaves. Women, however, never received the right to vote. They were theoretically citizens under civil law but without the right to full political participation.

Some women did not accept their exclusion, viewing it as a betrayal of the promised new order.

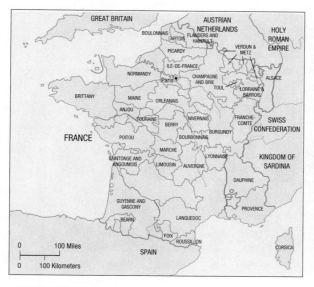

FRENCH PROVINCES IN 1789

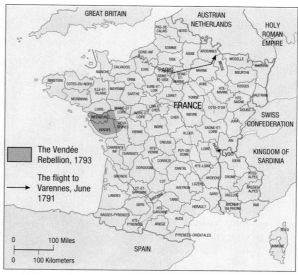

FRENCH DEPARTMENTS, 1791

Redrawing the Map of France, 1789–1791

Women wrote petitions, published tracts, and organized political clubs to demand more participation. In her Declaration of the Rights of Women of 1791, Olympe de Gouges played on the language of the official declaration to make the point that women should also be included. In article I she announced, "Woman is born free and lives equal to man in her rights." She also insisted that since "woman has the right to mount the scaffold," she must "equally have the right to mount the rostrum." De Gouges linked her complaints to a program of social reform in which women would have equal rights to property and public office and equal responsibilities in taxes and criminal punishment.

Unresponsive to calls for women's equality, the National Assembly turned to preparing a constitution that would make France a constitutional monarchy in which the king was simply the state's leading functionary. The change in the king's status had momentous effects. Since the Middle Ages, the monarch had embodied the nation and his will had been law. His every move had been a matter of national policy, and his person had a sacred aura. Now the legislature would have nearly equal powers, and the nation would be an entity separate from the king.

Although the constitution limited the right to vote and the right to hold office to male property owners, in many other respects it produced funda-

mental changes based on the Enlightenment principles of uniform justice and standardized administration. The deputies abolished all the old administrative divisions of the provinces and replaced them with a uniform national system of eighty-three departments with identical administrative and legal structures. All officials were elected; no offices could be bought and sold. The assembly abolished the old taxes and replaced them with new ones that were supposed to be uniformly levied. The new government had difficulty collecting taxes, however, because many people had expected a substantial cut in the tax rate. The new administrative system survived, however, and the departments are still the basic units of French government today.

When the deputies turned to reforming the Catholic church, they created conflicts that would erupt again and again over the next ten years. Following a long tradition of state involvement in church affairs but with the new aim of countering aristocratic domination of high church offices, the National Assembly sought to subject the Catholic church to tighter state control. In a state where Catholicism had always been dominant, virtually no one considered separating church and state (they were not separated in France until 1905). Motivated partly by the ongoing financial crisis, the National Assembly confiscated all the church's property and

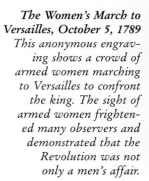

The Women's March to Versailles, October 5, 1789 *This anonymous engraving shows a crowd of armed women marching to Versailles to confront the king. The sight of armed women frightened many observers and demonstrated that the Revolution was not only a men's affair.*

promised to pay clerical salaries in return. The impounded property served as a guarantee for the new paper money the government issued, which soon became subject to inflation. To raise revenues, the new government began to sell church lands to the highest bidders in state auctions, thereby increasing the holdings of wealthy city-dwellers and prosperous peasants.

The government's offensive on the church did not stop there. Convinced that monastic life encouraged idleness and a decline in the nation's population, the deputies outlawed any future monastic vows and encouraged monks and nuns to return to private life on state pensions. Many monks took the opportunity, but few nuns did. As the Carmelite nuns of Paris responded, "If there is true happiness on earth, we enjoy it in the shelter of the sanctuary." To regulate the affairs of the nonmonastic clergy, the National Assembly passed a Civil Constitution of the Clergy in July 1790, which set pay scales for the clergy and provided that the voters elect their own parish priests and bishops just as they elected other officials. In November 1790 the National Assembly required all clergy to swear an oath of loyalty to the Civil Constitution of the Clergy. Pope Pius VI in Rome condemned this constitution, and half of the French clergy refused to take the oath.

The oath of allegiance permanently divided the Catholic population, which had to choose between loyalty to the old church and commitment to the Revolution with its own "constitutional" church. Many people felt intensely devoted to their local priests, who provided solace and direction at all the major life events, from birth to death. The government lost many supporters by passing laws against the clergy who refused the oath and by forcing them into exile, deporting them forcibly, or executing them as traitors. Riots and demonstrations greeted many of the oath-taking priests who showed up to replace those who refused; women almost always led these outbursts. The assault on the Catholic church intensified under the republic.

War and the End of Monarchy

Louis XVI was understandably reluctant to recognize the new limits on his powers, and the reorganization of the Catholic church particularly offended him. On June 20, 1791, the royal family escaped in disguise from the Tuileries palace in Paris and fled to the eastern frontier, where they hoped to gather support to overturn the Revolution. The plans went awry when a postmaster recognized the king from his portrait on the new French money, and the royal family was arrested at Varennes. The National Assembly tried to depict this "flight to Varennes" as a kidnapping, but the incident touched off demonstrations in Paris against the royal family, whom some now re-

Que ce jour est heureux mes Soeurs, oui les doux nom
de mere et d'épouse est bien preferable à celui de nom
il vous rend tous les droits de la Nature ainsi qu'à nous

Decret de l'Assemblée National qui Supprime les Ordres Religieux et Religieuses.

Anonymous, Decree of the National Assembly Suppressing the Religious Orders, 16 February 1790 *In this satirical, anti-Catholic engraving, nuns and monks are depicted as overjoyed at being released from their religious vows and encouraged to marry. Although many younger sons and daughters had been forced into religious orders by their families, the nuns and monks often resisted the destruction of their way of life. Actions taken against the Catholic Church alienated many French people from the Revolution.*

garded as traitors. Cartoons circulated depicting the royal family as animals being returned "to the stable."

Voters chose a new Legislative Assembly in late August and early September 1791. In a rare act of self-denial, the deputies of the National Assembly declared themselves ineligible for the new assembly, thus opening the door to men with no previous experience in national politics. The status of the king might have remained uncertain if war had not intervened, but by early 1792 all factions seemed intent on war. The deputies of the new Legislative Assembly who wanted to push the Revolution toward a republic hoped war would aid their cause by revealing the treachery of the king and the aristocracy. The king and queen thought war might end in the defeat of the revolutionaries and a restoration of absolute monarchy. Thousands of aristocrats, including two-thirds of the army officer corps, had already emigrated from France, including both the king's brothers, and they were gathering on France's eastern border. They wanted to involve the other crowned heads of Europe, including Marie-Antoinette's brother, Leopold II, the Holy Roman Emperor. On April 21, Louis declared war on Leopold. Prussia immediately entered on the Austrian side.

When fighting broke out in 1792, all the powers expected a brief and relatively contained war. But the revolutionaries' crusading spirit and their attempt to mobilize the entire French population led to a very different outcome. As early as December 1789, two and one-half years before war was even declared, one deputy proclaimed, "Each citizen should be a soldier, and each soldier a citizen, or we shall never have a constitution." In other words, many revolutionaries linked revolution to war against the other monarchies. Yet the French were hardly prepared for war, and in the first battles the Austrians promptly routed the French armies, joking that the new French motto was "Conquer or Run." Despite the departure into exile of so many aristocratic officers, the French had the advantage of previous military improvements the monarchy had carried out, which made French artillery one of the most effective in Europe. The emigration of noble officers opened positions to skilled commoners, who rapidly moved up to positions of command.

In the first year or two of the war, as the French frantically reorganized their armies, disaster threatened. When in June 1792 an angry crowd invaded the hall of the assembly in Paris and threatened the royal family, Lafayette left his command on the eastern front and came to Paris to insist on punishing the demonstrators. His appearance only fueled distrust of the army commanders, which increased to a fever pitch when the Prussians crossed the border and advanced on Paris. The Prussian commander, the duke of Brunswick, issued a manifesto announcing that Paris would be totally destroyed if the royal family suffered any violence. Faced with this threat of retaliation and growing fears of conspiracy, on August 10, 1792, leaders of the local district governments of Paris (called *sections*) organized an insurrection and attacked the Tuileries palace, where the king resided. The king and his family had to escape into the meeting room of the Legislative Assembly, where the frightened deputies ordered new elections—this time by universal manhood suffrage—for a National Convention that would write a new constitution. The convention suspended the king's functions, and a new phase of the Revolution began. Lafayette and other liberal aristocrats who had supported the constitutional monarchy fled into exile. The next stage of the Revolution would be marked by growing popular demands for equality and by escalating violence.

Violence soon exploded again. Early in September 1792, as the Prussians approached Paris, hastily gathered mobs stormed the overflowing prisons to seek out traitors who might help the enemy. In an atmosphere of near hysteria, eleven hundred inmates were killed, including many ordinary and completely innocent people. The princess of Lamballe, one of the queen's favorites, was hacked to pieces and her mutilated body displayed under the windows where the royal family was kept under guard. These "September massacres" showed the dark side of popular revolution, in which the common people demanded instant revenge on supposed enemies and conspirators.

The National Convention faced a dire situation. It attempted to write a new constitution while fighting a war with external enemies and confronting increasing resistance at home. The Revolution had divided the population; for some it had not gone far enough toward providing food, land, and retribution against enemies; for others it had gone too far by dismantling the church and the monarchy. The French people had never known

any government other than monarchy. Eighty percent of the French were peasants, and only half the population could read and write at even a basic level. In this situation symbolic actions became very important. The republic announced on September 22, 1792, not only replaced monarchy (noble titles had gone in 1791) but also aimed to root out any reminders of it. Any public sign of the former regime was at risk, and revolutionaries soon pulled down statues of kings and burned seigneurial documents.

The fate of Louis XVI and the future direction of the republic now divided the deputies elected to the National Convention. The Girondins (named after one of the departments, the Gironde, which provided some of the convention's leading orators) met regularly at the salon of Madame Roland, the wife of a minister. They had eagerly supported the war but were determined to prevent Paris from dominating the new republic. The Mountain (so-called because its deputies sat in the highest seats) was closely allied with local militants in Paris, who had directed the insurrection against the king. At a time when everyone considered political parties or organized factions destructive to republican and national unity, political groups could be only loosely organized around common interests. Most of the deputies in both factions were middle-class lawyers and professionals who had been members of the Jacobin Club (named after the former monastery in Paris where it met). With its affiliates throughout the provinces, the Jacobin Club was the closest thing to an organized political movement. After the fall of the monarchy in August 1792, the Girondins began to distance themselves from the Jacobins.

The first showdown between the Girondins and the Mountain occurred during the trial of the king in December 1792. Although the Girondins agreed that the king was guilty of treason, many of them argued for clemency, exile, or a popular referendum on his fate. After a long and difficult debate, the convention supported the Mountain and voted by a very narrow majority to execute the king. Louis XVI went to the guillotine on January 21, 1793, sharing the fate of Charles I of England in 1649. "We have just convinced ourselves that a king is only a man," wrote one newspaper, "and that no man is above the law." Outside France,

Anonymous,
The Purifying Pot of the Jacobins, *1793*
In this satirical engraving, the artist makes fun of the Jacobin Club's well-known penchant for constantly examining the political correctness of its members. Those who failed the test often suffered fatal consequences.

however, the execution profoundly shocked most people. The guillotine had been introduced just a few months before as a way of making capital punishment more humane and more uniform; in the past only aristocrats had been beheaded—common people were hanged.

The Terror and the Republic of Virtue, 1793–1794

The execution of the king did not end the new regime's problems. The introduction of a national draft soon provoked massive resistance in some parts of France, and the war required ever more men and money. In response to growing pressures, the National Convention set up a highly centralized government designed to provide food, direct the war effort, and punish counterrevolutionaries. Thus began the Reign of Terror, in which the guillotine became the most terrifying instrument of a

government that suppressed almost every form of dissent. Policies aimed at creating a Republic of Virtue spawned attacks on Christianity, especially Catholicism. These only fueled divisiveness, which in the end proved fatal for republican government.

Robespierre and the Committee of Public Safety

The conflict between the Girondins and the Mountain over the direction of national policy ended when an armed crowd from Paris invaded the National Convention on June 2, 1793, and forced the deputies to order the arrest of their twenty-nine Girondin colleagues. The common people had intervened again, but this was no formless mass. Most were Paris artisans or shopkeepers who avidly followed politics in local political clubs and district committees. They were known as *sans-culottes* because they wore long trousers rather than the knee breeches of the upper classes. Women from the popular classes participated in many of their meetings and in the attack on the convention. In response to popular pressure the convention agreed to *sans-culottes* demands for

Pierre Roch Vigneron, **Robespierre in 1791**
This painting presents the deputy as he looked during the National Assembly (1789–1791), wearing a somber jacket and his customary powdered wig.

price controls and harsher measures against the enemies of the Revolution.

Setting the course for government and the war now fell to the Committee of Public Safety, composed of twelve deputies from the convention. The chief spokesman of the committee was Maximilien Robespierre (1758–1794), a lawyer from northern France known as "the incorruptible" for his stern honesty and fierce dedication to republican ideals. Because of his association with the Terror, he remains one of the most controversial figures in world history. One of his opponents admitted his "unassailable popularity" but declared that he "combined cunning with pride, envy, hatred and vindictiveness" and demonstrated "an unquenchable thirst for the blood of his colleagues." Robespierre was a follower of Rousseau and believed that any sincere, reasonable person ought to support the republic—the incarnation of the general will—in its time of need. Although he originally opposed the

death penalty and the war, he was convinced that the emergency situation of 1793 required severe measures, including death for those who opposed the committee's policies.

Robespierre was the theorist of the Terror and the chief architect of the Republic of Virtue. Like many other educated eighteenth-century men, he had read all the classics of republicanism from Tacitus and Plutarch to Montesquieu and Rousseau. But he took them a step further. He spoke eloquently about "the theory of revolutionary government" as "the war of liberty against its enemies." He defended the people's right to democratic government, while in practice he supported many emergency measures that restricted their liberties. He personally favored a free-market economy, as did almost all middle-class deputies, but in this time of crisis he was willing to enact price controls and requisitioning. Like Rousseau, he believed the republic would have to reform its citizens by establishing a new civic religion. In a famous speech to the convention, he insisted that "The first maxim of your policies must be to lead the people by reason and the people's enemies by terror . . . without virtue, terror is deadly; without terror, virtue is impotent." *Terror* was not an idle term; it seemed to imply that the goal of democracy justified what we now call totalitarian means.

Through a series of desperate measures, the Committee of Public Safety set the machinery of the Terror in motion. It sent deputies out "on mission" to purge unreliable officials, work with local leaders of the Jacobin clubs and other popular societies to uncover dissidents, and organize the war effort. In the first universal draft of men in history, every unmarried man and childless widower between the ages of eighteen and twenty-five was declared eligible for conscription into the army. Revolutionary tribunals set up in Paris and provincial centers tried political suspects. In October 1793 the revolutionary tribunal in Paris convicted Marie-Antoinette of treason and sent her to her death. The Girondin leaders and Madame Roland were also guillotined, as was Olympe de Gouges, one of the first defenders of women's rights. To satisfy the economic demands of the *sans-culottes,* the convention decreed a maximum, or ceiling, on essential food prices but also set one on wages. The government confiscated all the property of convicted traitors.

The Terror won its greatest success on the battlefield. As of April 1793, France faced war with the Holy Roman Empire, Prussia, Great Britain, Spain, Sardinia, and the Dutch Republic—all fearful of the impact of revolutionary ideals on their own populations. The execution of Louis XVI, in particular, galvanized European governments; according to one Englishman, it was "the foulest and most atrocious act the world has ever seen." The French republic tapped a new and potent source of power, nationalist pride, in decrees mobilizing young and old alike:

> *The young men will go to battle; married men will forge arms and transport provisions; women will make tents and clothing and serve in hospitals; children will make bandages; old men will get themselves carried to public places to arouse the courage of warriors and preach hatred of kings and unity of the republic.*

Scientists contributed improvements in iron production; forges were set up in the parks and gardens of Paris to produce thousands of guns; and citizens everywhere helped collect saltpeter for gunpowder. By the end of 1793 the French nation in arms had stopped the advance of the allied powers, and in the summer of 1794 it invaded the Austrian Netherlands and crossed the Rhine River. The army was ready to carry the gospel of revolution and republicanism to the rest of Europe.

The Republic of Virtue

The program of the Terror went beyond political and economic measures to include efforts to "republicanize everything," in other words, to effect a cultural revolution. The government utilized every possible means to transform the old subjects of the monarchy into virtuous republican citizens. The end of censorship in 1789 had resulted in the appearance of hundreds of newspapers. Overnight a country with few real newspapers was inundated with news and commentary, some of it written by women. Beginning in 1792, however, the government instituted a policy of censoring writings deemed counterrevolutionary.

Refusing to tolerate opposition, the republic left no stone unturned in its endeavor to get its message across. Songs—especially the new anthem, *La Marseillaise*—placards, posters, pamphlets, books, engravings, paintings, sculpture—even everyday crockery, chamberpots, and playing cards—conveyed revolutionary slogans and symbols. Foremost among them was the figure of Liberty (an early version of the Statue of Liberty now in New York harbor), which appeared on coins and bills, letterheads and seals, and as statues in festivals. Hundreds of new plays were produced, and old classics revised. To encourage the production of patriotic and republican works, the government sponsored state competitions for artists. Works of art were supposed to "awaken the public spirit and make clear how atrocious and ridiculous were the enemies of liberty and of the Republic."

At the center of this elaborate cultural effort were the revolutionary festivals modeled on Rousseau's plans for a civic religion. The festivals first emerged in 1789 with the planting of liberty trees in villages and towns. The Festival of Federation on July 14, 1790, marked the first anniversary of the fall of the Bastille. Under the convention, Jacques-Louis David, France's most famous painter and a deputy and follower of Robespierre, took over festival planning. David aimed to destroy the mystique of monarchy and to make the republic sacred. His Festival of Unity on August 10, 1793, for example, celebrated the first anniversary of the overthrow of the monarchy. In front of the statue of Liberty built for the occasion, a bonfire consumed the crowns and scepters of royalty while a cloud of three thousand white doves rose into the sky. This was all part of preaching the "moral order of the Republic . . . that will make us a people of brothers, a people of philosophers."

Some revolutionaries hoped the festival system would replace the Catholic church altogether. They initiated a campaign of "de-Christianization" that included closing churches (Protestant as well as Catholic), selling many church buildings to the highest bidder, and trying to force even those clergy who had taken the oath of loyalty to abandon their clerical vocations and marry. Some of the greatest churches in Christendom became storehouses for arms or grain, or their stones were sold off to contractors. The medieval statues of kings on the facade of Notre Dame cathedral were beheaded. Church bells were dismantled and church treasures melted down for government use.

In the ultimate step in de-Christianization, extremists tried to establish a Cult of Reason to sup-

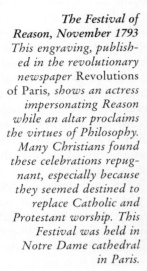

The Festival of Reason, November 1793 This engraving, published in the revolutionary newspaper Revolutions of Paris, *shows an actress impersonating Reason while an altar proclaims the virtues of Philosophy. Many Christians found these celebrations repugnant, especially because they seemed destined to replace Catholic and Protestant worship. This Festival was held in Notre Dame cathedral in Paris.*

plant Christianity. In Paris in the fall of 1793 a goddess of Liberty, played by an actress, presided over a Festival of Reason in Notre Dame cathedral. Many provincial cities copied the festival, which alarmed deputies in the convention, who were wary of turning rural, devout populations against the republic. The Committee of Public Safety halted the de-Christianization campaign, and Robespierre tried to institute his own new religion, the Cult of the Supreme Being, in June 1794. Robespierre objected to the de-Christianization campaign's atheism; he favored a Rousseau-inspired deistic religion without the supposedly superstitious trappings of Catholicism. Neither cult attracted many followers, but they show the depth of the commitment to overturning the old order and all its traditional institutions.

In principle the best way to ensure the future of the republic was through the education of the young. The deputy Georges-Jacques Danton, Robespierre's main competitor as theorist of the Revolution, maintained that "After bread, the first need of the people is education." The convention voted to make primary schooling free and compulsory for both boys and girls. It took control of education away from the Catholic church and tried to set up a system of state schools at both the primary and secondary levels, but it lacked the trained teachers needed to replace those the Catholic religious orders provided. As a result, opportunities for learning how to read and write may have diminished. In 1799 only one-fifth as many boys enrolled in the state secondary schools as had studied in church schools ten years earlier.

Although many of the ambitious republican programs failed, almost all aspects of daily life became politicized. Already in 1789 the colors one wore had political significance. The tricolor—the combination of red, white, and blue that was to become the flag of France—was devised in July 1789, and by 1793 everyone had to wear a little ribbon with the colors. Using the formal forms of speech (in French the *vous* form for "you") or the title Monsieur or Madame might identify someone as an aristocrat; true patriots used the informal *tu* and Citizen instead. Some people changed their names or gave their children new kinds of names; Biblical and saints' names such as Jean, Pierre, Joseph, or Marie gave way to names recalling heroes of the ancient Roman Republic (Brutus or Gracchus), revolutionary heroes, or flowers and plants. Such changes symbolized adherence to the republic and to Enlightenment ideals rather than to Catholicism.

Even the measures of time and space were revolutionized. In October 1793 the convention introduced a new calendar to replace the Christian one. Its basis was reason and republican principles. Year I dated from the beginning of the republic on September 22, 1792. Twelve months of exactly thirty days each received new names derived from nature: Pluviôse (roughly equivalent to February), for example, recalled the rain of springtime (*la pluie* is French for "rain"). Instead of seven-day weeks, ten-day *décades* provided only one day of rest every ten days and pointedly eliminated the Sunday of the Christian calendar. The five days left at the end of the calendar year were devoted to special festivals. The calendar remained in force for twelve years despite continuing resistance to it. More enduring was the new metric system based on units of ten that was invented to replace the hundreds of local variations in weights and measures. Other countries in Europe and the rest of the world eventually adopted the metric system. (The United States is one of the few places that still has not accepted the metric system.) In some places in France even the clocks were "decimalized"—divided into ten hours instead of twelve.

Revolutionary legislation also changed the rules of family life. The state took responsibility for all family matters away from the Catholic church and restricted the powers of fathers. Birth, death, and marriage registration now happened at city hall, not the parish church. Marriage became a civil contract and as such could be broken. The new divorce law of September 1792 was the most far-reaching in the western world: a couple could divorce by mutual consent or for reasons such as insanity, abandonment, battering, or criminal conviction. Thousands of men and women took advantage of the law to dissolve unhappy marriages, even though the pope had condemned the measure. In 1816 the government revoked the right to divorce, and not until the 1970s did French divorce laws return to the principles of the 1792 legislation. The government also limited fathers' rights over their children; they could not imprison them without cause or control their lives after the age of twenty-one. In one of its most influential actions, the revolutionary government passed a series of laws that created equal inheritance among all children in the family, including girls. The father's right to favor one child, especially the oldest male, was considered aristocratic and hence antirepublican.

The Forms of Resistance

By politicizing so many aspects of daily life, from the way people talked to the patterns on their china, the republic enforced its distinctive kind of conformity. Thus new forms of resistance sprang up: shouting curses against the republic, uprooting liberty trees, carrying statues of the Virgin Mary in procession, hiding a priest who would not take the oath, singing a royalist song—all these expressed dissent with the new symbols, rituals, and policies.

Many women, in particular, suffered from the hard conditions of life that persisted in this time of war, and they had their own ways of voicing discontent. The long bread lines in the cities exhausted the patience of women already overwhelmed by the demands of housekeeping, child rearing, and working as shop assistants, fishwives, laundresses, and textile workers. Police spies reported their constant grumbling, which occasionally turned into spontaneous demonstrations or riots over high prices or food shortages. Aristocratic women were often left behind by husbands who joined the emigration; other women had to bear the uncertainties of sons and husbands away at war. Everywhere women inspired efforts to defend the Catholic church.

Violent resistance broke out in many different parts of France and for various reasons. In the early years of the Revolution, Catholics rioted in places with large Protestant or Jewish populations, which tended to support the Revolution and the religious toleration and civil rights it promised. The arrest of the Girondin deputies in June 1793 sparked insurrections in several departments. After the government retook the city of Lyon, one of the centers of the revolt, the deputy on mission ordered sixteen hundred houses demolished. Special courts sentenced almost two thousand people to death. The name of the city was changed to Ville Affranchie (Liberated Town).

Other forms of resistance were more individual. One young woman, Charlotte Corday, assassinated the journalist and deputy Jean-Paul Marat in July 1793. Corday fervently supported the Girondins, and she considered it her patriotic duty to kill the deputy who, in the columns of his paper *The Friend of the People,* had constantly demanded more heads and more blood. Marat was immediately eulogized as a great martyr; Corday went to the guillotine vilified as a monster but con-

***Jean Jacques Hauer,* Portrait of Charlotte Corday**
Charlotte Corday was guillotined for assassinating the deputy Marat in his bath. This respectful, later portrait shows a very different woman from the one portrayed in disdainful terms in the pro-government press of the time.

fident in her own mind that she had "avenged many innocent victims."

Nowhere was resistance to the republic more persistent and violent than in the Vendée region of western France. Between March and December 1793, peasants, artisans, and weavers joined together under noble leadership to form a "Catholic and Royal Army." One rebel group explained their motives: "They [the republicans] have killed our king, chased away our priests, sold the goods of our church, eaten everything we have and now they want to take our bodies [in the draft]." The uprising took two different forms: in the Vendée itself a

The Vendée

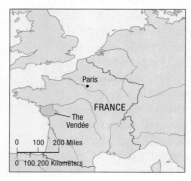

counterrevolutionary army organized to fight the republic; in nearby Brittany resistance took the form of guerrilla bands who united to attack a target then quickly melt into the countryside. Great Britain provided money and underground contacts for these attacks, which were almost always aimed at towns. Town officials sold church lands, enforced measures against the clergy, and supervised conscription. In many ways this was a civil war between town and country, for the townspeople were the ones who supported the Revolution and bought church lands for themselves. The peasants had gained most of what they wanted in 1789 with the abolition of seigneurial dues, and they resented the governments' demands for money and manpower and actions against their local clergy.

For several months in 1793 the Vendée rebels stormed the largest towns in the region. Both sides committed horrible atrocities. At the small town of Machecoul, for example, the rebels massacred five hundred republicans, including administrators and National Guard members; many were tied together, shoved into freshly dug graves, and shot. By the fall, however, republican soldiers had turned back the rebels. A republican general wrote to Paris claiming, "There is no more Vendée, citizens, it has perished under our free sword along with its women and children. . . . Following the orders that you gave me I have crushed children under the feet of horses, massacred women who at least . . . will engender no more brigands." "Infernal columns" of republican troops marched through the region to "pacify" it; military courts ordered thousands executed, and republican soldiers massacred thousands of others. In retaliation for the rebellion the government planned "to coordinate the means of exterminating the Vendeans." Even today, controversy still rages about the rebellion's death toll; estimates of rebel deaths alone range from about twenty thousand to two hundred fifty thousand and higher. Many thousands of republican soldiers and civilians also lost their lives. Even the low estimates reveal the carnage of this catastrophic confrontation between the republic and its opponents.

The Terror in Paris and Robespierre's Fall

Robespierre and the Committee of Public Safety maneuvered ceaselessly to retain control of the National Convention and Parisian politics. Resistance

Lesueur brothers, **The Patriotic Women's Club** *The artists depict the club president urging the members to contribute funds for poor patriot families. Women's clubs focused on philanthropic work but also discussed revolutionary legislation and the debates in the national assemblies.*

from such places as the Vendée only confirmed their suspicion that internal enemies lurked everywhere. Even their allies among the common people had to be held in check. The government prohibited the *sans-culottes* from meeting every day in their sections in Paris and made local officials strictly accountable to the committee and the convention. In exchange for price controls and prompt repression of opponents of the republic, the government demanded political conformity from its lower-class supporters.

The rift between middle-class leaders such as Robespierre and militants among the common people began to widen as the Committee of Public Safety consolidated its power. In the fall of 1793 the convention cracked down on popular clubs and societies. First to be suppressed were women's political clubs. Founded in early 1793, the Society of Revolutionary Republican Women played a very active part in *sans-culottes* politics. The society agitated for harsher measures against the republic's enemies and insisted that women have a voice in politics even if they did not have the vote. Women set up their own clubs in many provincial towns and also attended the meetings of local men's organizations. The closing of women's clubs marked an important turning point in the Revolution. From then on the *sans-culottes,* or common people, and their political organizations came increas-

ingly under the thumb of the Jacobin deputies in the National Convention.

The convention severely limited women's participation in the public sphere because they associated it with political disorder and social upheaval. As one deputy stated, women's clubs consisted of "adventuresses, knights-errant, emancipated women, amazons." Another deputy continued, "Women are ill suited for elevated thoughts and serious meditations." In subsequent years physicians, priests, and philosophers amplified such opinions by formulating explanations for women's "natural" differences from men to justify their inferior status.

The Committee of Public Safety then moved against male opposition. In the spring of 1794 a group labeled "ultra-revolutionaries"—in fact a motley collection of local Parisian politicians—were arrested and executed. Next came the other side, the "indulgents," so-called because they favored a moderation of the Terror. Included among them was the deputy Danton, himself once a member of the Committee of Public Safety and a friend of Robespierre, despite the striking contrast in their personalities. Danton was the Revolution's most flamboyant orator and, unlike Robespierre, a high-living, high-spending, excitable politician. At every critical turning point in national politics, his booming voice had swayed opinion in the National Convention. Now, under government pressure, the

Revolutionary Tribunal convicted him and his friends of treason and sentenced them to death.

With the arrest and execution of these leaders in Paris, the prophecies of doom for the Revolution seemed about to be realized. "The Revolution," as one of the Girondin victims of 1793 had remarked, "was devouring its own children." The middle-class leaders were killing each other. Even after the major threats to the committee's power had been eliminated, the Terror continued and even worsened. A law passed in June 1794 denied the accused the right of legal counsel, reduced the number of jurors necessary for conviction, and allowed only two judgments: acquittal or death. The category of political crimes expanded to include "slandering patriotism" and "seeking to inspire discouragement." Ordinary people risked the guillotine if they expressed any discontent. The rate of executions in Paris rose from five a day in the spring to twenty-six a day in the summer. The political atmosphere darkened even though the military situation improved. At the end of June the French armies decisively defeated the main Austrian army and advanced through the Austrian Netherlands to Brussels and Antwerp. The emergency measures for fighting the war were working, yet Robespierre and his inner circle had made so many enemies that they could not afford to loosen the grip of the Terror.

Across the country the official Terror cost the lives of at least forty thousand French people, most of them living in the regions of major insurrections or near the borders with foreign enemies, where suspicion of collaboration ran high. The Terror hardly touched many parts of France. But overall the experience was undeniably traumatic. As many as three hundred thousand people went to prison as suspects between March 1793 and August 1794 (that is, one out of every fifty French). The toll for the aristocracy and the clergy was especially high. Many leading nobles perished under the guillotine, and thousands emigrated. Thirty thousand to forty thousand clergy who refused the oath emigrated, at least two thousand (including many nuns) were executed, and thousands were imprisoned. The clergy were singled out in particular in the civil war zones: 135 priests were massacred at Lyon in November 1793 and 83 shot in one day during the Vendée revolt. Yet many victims of the Terror were peasants or ordinary working people.

The final crisis of the Reign of Terror came in July 1794. Conflicts within the Committee of Public Safety and the National Convention left Robespierre isolated. On July 27, 1794 (the ninth of Thermidor, Year II, according to the revolutionary calendar), Robespierre appeared before the convention with yet another list of deputies to be arrested. Many feared they would be named, and they shouted him down and ordered him arrested along with his followers on the committee, the president of the Revolutionary Tribunal in Paris, and the commander of the Parisian National Guard. Although initially defended by an armed uprising led by the Paris city government, the whole group, along with their supporters in city hall, went to the guillotine.

The men who led the attack on Robespierre did not intend to reverse all his policies, but that happened nonetheless. Newspapers attacked the Robespierrists as "tigers thirsting for human blood." The new government released hundreds of suspects and arranged a temporary truce in the Vendée. It purged Jacobins from local bodies and replaced them with their opponents. It arrested some of the most notorious "terrorists" in the National Convention—such as Carrier, who had drowned boatloads of priests and other counter-revolutionaries in the Loire River—and put them to death. Within the year the new leaders abolished the Revolutionary Tribunal and closed the Jacobin Club in Paris. Popular demonstrations met severe repression. In the southeast of the country, in particular, a "White Terror" replaced the Jacobins' "Red Terror." Former officials and local Jacobin leaders were harassed, beaten, and often murdered by paramilitary bands who had tacit support from the new authorities. Those who remained in the National Convention prepared yet another constitution in 1795, which set up a two-house legislature and an executive body, the Directory, headed by five Directors.

The Directory regime held tenuously onto power for four years, all the while trying to balance demands from the Left (the Jacobins) and the Right (the royalists). The puritanical atmosphere of the Terror gave way to hedonism—low-cut dresses of transparent materials, the reappearance of prostitutes in the streets, fancy dinner parties, and "victims balls" where guests wore red ribbons around their necks as reminders of the guillotine. Bands of young men dressed in knee breeches and rich fabrics picked fights with known Jacobins and disrupted theater performances with loud antirevolutionary songs. All over France people banded together and petitioned to reopen churches closed during the Terror. If necessary they broke into the church to hold services with a priest who had been in hiding or a lay schoolteacher who was willing to say Mass.

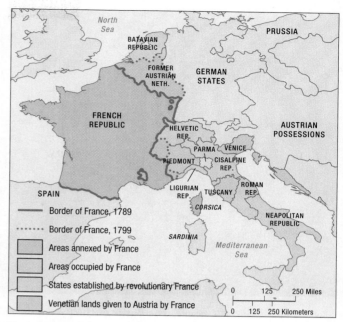

French Expansion, 1791–1799

The Revolution on the March

Beginning in 1792, war raged almost constantly until 1815. At one time or another, and sometimes all at once, France faced every principal power in Europe. The French republic—and later the French Empire under its supreme commander, Emperor Napoleon Bonaparte—proved an even more formidable opponent than the France of Louis XIV. New means of mobilizing and organizing soldiers enabled the French to dominate Europe for a generation. The influence of the Revolution as a political model and the threat of French military conquest combined to challenge the traditional order in Europe.

Arms and Conquests

The allied powers had a chance to defeat France in 1793, when the French armies verged on chaos because of the emigration of noble army officers and the problems of integrating new draftees. At that moment, however, Prussia, Russia, and Austria were preoccupied with clamping down on Poland. For France this diversion meant a reprieve.

Because of the new national draft, the French had a huge and powerful fighting force of seven hundred thousand men by the end of 1793. But the army faced many problems in the field. As many as a third of the recent draftees deserted before or during battle. Uniforms fashioned out of rough cloth constricted movements, tore easily, and retained the damp of muddy battlefields, exposing the soldiers to the elements and the spread of disease. At times the soldiers were fed only moldy bread, and if their pay was late, they sometimes resorted to pillaging and looting. At the top, the

tenure of generals depended on their political reliability; defeat made them suspect, and they might face the guillotine. Military discipline became nearly impossible to enforce consistently under such conditions. France nevertheless had one overwhelming advantage: its soldiers, drawn largely from the peasantry and the lower classes of the cities, fought for a revolution that they and their brothers and sisters had helped make. The republic was their government, and the army was in large measure theirs too; many officers had risen through the ranks by skill and talent rather than by inheriting or purchasing their positions. One young peasant boy wrote to his parents, "Either you will see me return bathed in glory, or you will have a son who is a worthy citizen of France who knows how to die for the defense of his country."

When the French armies invaded Belgium and crossed the Rhine in the summer of 1794, they proclaimed a war of liberation. But as they annexed more and more territory, "liberated" people in many places began to view them as an army of occupation. Those in the territories on the northern and eastern frontiers reacted most positively to the French. In Belgium (the Austrian Netherlands), Mainz, Savoy, and Nice, French occupation meant the organization of Jacobin clubs by French offi-

Louis-François Lejeune, **The Battle of the Pyramids,** *1806*
The painter reconstructs one of the most glorious moments (July, 1798) of an otherwise disappointing military campaign in Egypt and the Middle East.

cers and reliable, middle-class locals. The clubs petitioned for annexation to France, and French legislation was then introduced, including the abolition of seigneurial rights and dues. Despite resistance, especially in Belgium, these areas remained part of France until 1815, and the legal changes were permanent. Like Louis XIV a century before, most deputies in the National Convention considered the annexed territories within France's "natural frontiers"—the Rhine, the Alps, and the Pyrenees.

The Directory government that came to power in 1795 was torn between defending the new frontiers and launching a more aggressive policy of creating semi-independent "sister" republics wherever the armies succeeded. When Prussia declared neutrality in 1795, the French armies moved into the Dutch Republic, abolished the stadholderate, and with the revolutionary penchant for renaming, created the new Batavian Republic, a satellite of France. In Italy the brilliant young general Napoleon Bonaparte defeated the Austrian armies and created the Cisalpine Republic in northern Italy in 1797. Next he invaded Venice and then handed it over to the Austrians in exchange for a peace agreement. Twice the French tried to orga-

nize invasions of Ireland on the promise of local support in the country long oppressed by English rule, but both attempts failed miserably.

Yet the redrawing of the map of Europe continued. When the French invaded the Swiss cantons in 1798, they set up the Helvetic Republic and curtailed many of the Catholic church's privileges. They conquered the Papal States in 1798 and installed a Roman Republic; the pope fled to Siena. The same year, Bonaparte took a great army, originally raised to attack England, across the Mediterranean Sea to Egypt. The Directory government hoped that an occupation of Egypt would strike a blow at British trade by cutting the route to India and thus compensate France for its losses there years before. Once the army disembarked, however, the British admiral Horatio Nelson destroyed the French fleet while it was anchored in Aboukir Bay. In the face of determined resistance and an outbreak of the bubonic plague, Bonaparte's armies retreated from a further expedition in Syria. But the French occupation of Egypt lasted long enough for that largely Muslim country to experience the same kinds of Enlightenment-inspired legal transformations that had been introduced in Europe: the French abolished torture, introduced equality before the law, eliminated religious taxes, and proclaimed religious toleration.

The revolutionary wars had an immediate impact on European life at all levels of society. Thousands of men died in every country involved, with perhaps as many as two hundred thousand casualties in the French armies alone in 1794 and 1795. Although we have no accurate statistics documenting casualties in these wars, we do know that more soldiers died in hospitals as a result of their wounds than on the battlefields. Constant warfare hampered world commerce and especially disrupted French overseas shipping. (The abolition of slavery in 1794 also cut off one lucrative market for the French port cities.) Times were hard almost everywhere, with constant shortages because of the dislocations of internal and external commerce.

European Reactions to Revolutionary Change

The French Revolution profoundly transformed European politics and social relations. At first, many thrilled to "the most glorious event, and the happiest for mankind, that has ever taken place since human affairs have been recorded," as one Englishman put it. The governing elites of Europe became alarmed, however, when the revolutionaries abolished monarchy and nobility and encouraged popular participation in politics. Democrats and reformers from many countries flooded to Paris to witness events firsthand. One of the best known was Thomas Paine (1737–1809), the English agitator who in 1775 and 1776 had played a vital role in mobilizing American support for independence. He was elected deputy to the French National Convention in 1793 and nearly lost his head as a "moderate" during the Terror.

Paine had initially won the hearts of the French by defending the French Revolution in a debate with Edmund Burke (1729–1799). Burke's *Reflections on the Revolution in France* of 1790 had warned his fellow countrymen against the dangerous abstractions of the French. Denouncing the "new conquering empire of light and reason," he argued the case for tradition, continuity, and gradual reform based on practical experience. In his reply, *The Rights of Man* (1791), which sold two hundred thousand copies in two years, Paine defended the idea of reform based on reason, advo-

cated a concept of universal human rights, and attacked the excesses of privilege and tradition in Great Britain.

Other Britons soon joined in. Mary Wollstonecraft (1759–1797) wrote *A Vindication of the Rights of Man* (1791) and then *A Vindication of the Rights of Woman* (1792), in which she argued against Rousseau for equal education for women. She insisted that women could not become virtuous, even as mothers, unless they won the right to participate in economic and political life on an equal basis with men. Supporters of the French Revolution in Great Britain, like the earlier reformers of the 1760s and 1770s, joined constitutional and reform societies that sprang up in many cities. The most important of these societies, the London Corresponding Society, founded in 1792, corresponded with the Paris Jacobin Club and served as a center for reform agitation in England. The British government quickly suppressed the societies and harassed their leaders, charging that their ideas and their contacts with the French were seditious.

Pro-French feeling ran even stronger in Ireland. Catholics and Presbyterians, both excluded from the vote, came together in the Society of United Irishmen, which eventually pressed for secession from England. In 1798 the society timed a rebellion to coincide with a French invasion, but when the landing failed to take place, the British mercilessly repressed the revolt. Twice as many regular British troops (seventy thousand) as fought in any of the major continental battles were required to put down the Irish rebellion of 1798. In response to the rebellion, the British Parliament passed the Act of Union of Great Britain and Ireland, which remained in force until the early twentieth century.

Those countries near France with a substantial middle class and access to newspapers and other publications generally sympathized the most with French ideas. Yet even countries close to France sometimes fiercely resisted French occupation, often in the form of banditry. In the German Rhineland, for example, gangs of bandits preyed on the French and the Jews. One German traveler reported, "It is a characteristic of the region in which the bandits are based that these two nations [the French and the Jews] are hated. So crimes against them are motivated not just by a wish to rob them but also by a variety of fanaticism which is partly political and partly religious."

Many leading intellectuals in the German states, including the philosopher Immanuel Kant, initially supported the revolutionary cause, but after 1793 most of them turned against the popular violence and military aggressiveness of the Revolution. One of the greatest writers of the age, Friedrich Schiller, typified the turn in sentiment against revolutionary politics:

> *Freedom is only in the realm of dreams*
> *And the beautiful blooms only in song.*

The German states, still run by many separate rulers, experienced a profound artistic and intellectual revival, which eventually linked up with anti-French nationalism. This renaissance included a revived intellectual life in the universities, a thriving press (1, 225 journals were launched in the 1780s alone), and the multiplication of masonic lodges and literary clubs.

Not surprisingly, the countries farthest from France—Russia, the Ottoman Empire, the Balkans, Austria, Hungary, and the Scandinavian states—were generally least affected by the French Revolution. One exception was the United States, where opinion fiercely divided on the virtues of the French Revolution. Sweden was a second exception; Gustavus III (*1771–1792) was assassinated in Stockholm by a nobleman who claimed that "The king has violated his oath . . . and declared himself an enemy of the realm." The king's murder changed little in Sweden's power structure though; the king's son Gustavus IV Adolphus was convinced that the French Jacobins had sanctioned his father's assassination, and he insisted on avoiding "licentious liberty." Although just across the border from France, Spain too staunchly resisted the new ideas. The Spanish government suppressed all news from France. When French armies invaded in 1793, they met a crusade for "Religion, King and Country," which won widespread support from all sectors of the population.

Poland Extinguished

Poland was a third exception to the rule that distance from Paris diminished the influence of the French Revolution. "I shall fight Jacobinism, and defeat it in Poland," vowed Catherine the Great in 1792. Paranoid at reports of a few friends of the French Revolution cropping up throughout east-

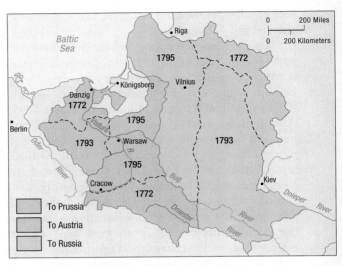

The Partitions of Poland, 1772, 1793, and 1795

ern Europe—even in St. Petersburg—the tsarina determined to smite the moderate reformers in Warsaw. She had the willing cooperation of reactionary Polish magnates who foolishly thought they could thus defend aristocratic "Golden Freedom." Prussia joined her, fearing a regenerated, pro-French Poland. While Prussian and Austrian troops battled the French in the West, a Russian army easily crushed Polish resistance. In effect for barely a year, Poland's May Third Constitution was abolished, and Prussia and Russia helped themselves to generous new slices of Polish territory in the Second Partition of 1793.

Poland's reform movement, however, simply became even more pro-French. Some leaders fled abroad, including Tadeusz Kościuszko (1746–1817), an officer who had been a foreign volunteer in the War of American Independence and who now escaped to Paris. Newly radical nobles and burghers formed conspiratorial groups within Poland. Exiles and the domestic underground alike saw in revolutionary France, embattled against all Europe, a powerful inspiration.

In the spring of 1794, Kościuszko returned from France as "dictator," empowered by his fellow conspirators to lead a national revolt. He incited an uprising at Cracow, which then spread to Warsaw and the old Lithuanian capital, Vilnius. Nobles formed the backbone of these insurgencies, but middle-class burghers, artisans, and Jews also lent significant aid. Yet Kościuszko faced an immediate, insoluable dilemma. He could win only if the peasants joined the struggle—highly unlikely unless villagers could be convinced that serfdom would end. But such a drastic step risked alienating the nobles who had started the revolt. So Kościuszko compromised. In his proclamation of May 7, 1794, he summoned the peasantry to the national cause and promised a reduction of their obligations as serfs, but not freedom itself. He received an equally equivocal response. Armed with scythes, a few peasant bands joined the insurrection, but most let their lords fight it out alone. Urban workers displayed more enthusiasm; at Warsaw, for example, a mob hanged several Russian collaborators, including an archbishop in his full regalia.

The uprising failed. Kościuszko led his troops to a few victories over the surprised Russians, but when Catherine's forces regrouped they routed the Poles. Kościuszko and other Patriot leaders languished for years in Russian and Austrian prisons. Taking no further chances, Russia, Prussia, and Austria wiped Poland completely from the map in the Third Partition of 1795. "The Polish Question" would plague international relations for more than a century as Polish rebels flocked to any international upheaval that might undo the partitions. Beyond all this maneuvering lay the unresolved problem of Polish serfdom, which isolated the nation's gentry and townspeople from the rural masses.

The Revolution in the Colonies

The Caribbean colonies lay far from France, but inevitably they felt the effects of upheaval. From the beginning of the Revolution, political leaders in Paris feared the potential for conflict in the colonies, as aspirations for broader political rights might threaten French authority. The Caribbean colonies were crucial to the French economy. Twice the size in land area of the neighboring British colonies, they also produced nearly twice as much revenue in exports. The slave population had doubled in the French colonies in the twenty years before 1789. Saint Domingue[*] was the most

important French colony, with its approximately 465,000 slaves, 30,000 whites, and 28,000 free people of color, who were employed primarily to apprehend runaway slaves and assure plantation security.

Like many of their North American counterparts, most French revolutionaries did not consider slavery a pressing problem, but they could not avoid the question of rights for free people of color. A Paris club called The Friends of Blacks agitated in the National Assembly for civil rights for free people of color, which were granted in May 1791, only to be rescinded four months later. As one deputy explained, "This regime [in the colonies] is oppressive, but it gives a livelihood to several million Frenchmen. This regime is barbarous but a still greater barbarity will result if you interfere with it without the necessary knowledge."

The discussions in Paris aroused new hopes among the blacks, both free and slave. In August 1791 the slaves in northern Saint Domingue organized a large-scale revolt with the slogan "Listen to the voice of Liberty which speaks in the hearts of all." To restore authority over the slaves, the Legislative Assembly in Paris granted civil and political rights to the free blacks—an action that alienated the white planters and merchants, who in 1793 signed an agreement with Great Britain, now France's enemy in war, declaring British sovereignty over the island. To complicate matters further, Spain, which controlled the rest of the island and had joined Great Britain in the war, offered freedom to individual slave rebels who joined them as long they agreed to maintain the slave regime for the other blacks.

The few thousand French republican troops on the island were outnumbered, and to prevent complete military disaster the French commissioner freed all the slaves in his jurisdiction in August 1793 without permission from the government at home. In February 1794 the National Convention formally abolished slavery and granted full rights to all black men in the colonies. These actions had the desired effect. One of the ablest black generals allied with the Spanish, the ex-slave François Dominique Toussaint L'Ouverture (1743–1803), changed sides and committed his troops to the French. The French eventually appointed Toussaint governor of Saint Domingue as a reward for his efforts. The vicious fighting (many

---

[*]Saint Domingue occupied the western third of the island of Hispaniola, where in 1493, Columbus had created Spain's first New World colony. Today this territory is known as Haiti; the rest of the island consists of the Dominican Republic.

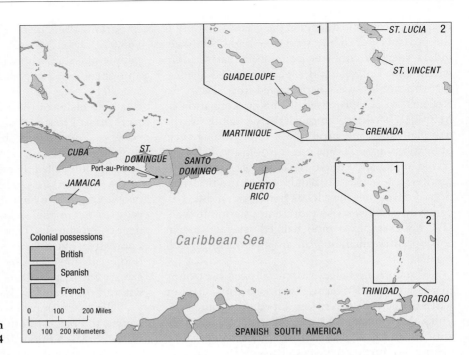

Colonial Possessions in the Caribbean, 1791–1794

colonists were killed) and flight of whites left the island's economy in ruins; in 1800 the plantations produced one-fifth of what they had in 1789. In the zones Toussaint controlled, army officers or officials took over the great estates and kept all those working in agriculture under military discipline. The former slaves were bound to their estates like serfs and forced to work the plantations in exchange for an autonomous family life and the right to maintain personal garden plots.

Toussaint remained in charge until 1802, when Napoleon sent French armies to regain control of the island. They arrested Toussaint and transported him to France, where he died in prison. The English poet Wordsworth wrote, "Though fallen thyself, never to rise again, Live and take comfort. . . . There's not a breath of the common wind That will forget thee; thou hast great allies; Thy friends are exultations, agonies, and Love, and man's unconquerable mind." Toussaint became a hero to abolitionists everywhere, a potent symbol of black struggles for freedom. Napoleon attempted to restore slavery, sending Polish volunteers to do much of the grueling work, but the remaining black generals defeated his armies and in 1804 proclaimed the Republic of Haiti.

Toussaint L'Ouverture
A picture in Marcus Rainsford's Hist. Acc. of the Black Empire of Hayti *(London, 1805) shows the black general and hero of the Haitian struggle for independence from France and from slavery.*

MAJOR EVENTS OF THE FRENCH REVOLUTION

1789

May 5 The Estates-General opens at Versailles

June 17 The Third Estate decides to call itself the National Assembly

July 14 Fall of the Bastille

August 4 Night session of the National Assembly abolishes "feudalism"

August 26 National Assembly passes Declaration of the Rights of Man and the Citizen

October 5–6 The "October Days," during which a large crowd marches from Paris to Versailles to bring the royal family back to the capital

1790

July 12 Civil Constitution of the Clergy

1791

June 20 King attempts to flee in disguise and is captured at Varennes

1792

April 20 Declaration of war on Austria

August 10 Insurrection in Paris and attack on Tuileries palace lead to suspension of the king

September 2–6 Murder of prisoners in "September Massacres" in Paris

1793

January 21 Execution of Louis XVI

March 11 Beginning of uprising in the Vendée

May 31–June 2 Insurrection leading to arrest of the Girondins in the Convention

October 16 Execution of Marie-Antoinette

1794

February 4 Slavery abolished in the French colonies

March 13–24 Arrest, trial, and executions of so-called ultra-revolutionaries

March 30–April 5 Arrest, trial, and executions of Danton and his followers

July 27 "The Ninth of Thermidor" arrest of Robespierre and his supporters (executed July 28–29)

April 1796–October 1797 Succession of Italian victories by Bonaparte

May 1798–October 1799 Bonaparte in Egypt and Middle East

1799 November 9–10 Bonaparte's coup of 18–19 Brumaire

The Rise of Napoleon Bonaparte

Toussaint had followed Napoleon's rise to power in France with interest; he once wrote to Bonaparte "From the First of the Blacks to the First of the Whites." He was not alone in his fascination, for the story of the rise of Napoleon Bonaparte (1769–1821) is one of the most remarkable in Western history. It would have seemed astonishing in 1795 that the twenty-six-year-old son of a noble family from the island of Corsica would within four years become the supreme ruler of France and one of the greatest military leaders in world history. In 1795 he was a penniless artillery officer, only recently released from prison as a presumed Robespierrist. Thanks to some early military successes and links to Parisian politicians, he was named commander of the French army in Italy in 1796.

Bonaparte's astounding success in the Italian campaigns of 1796 through 1797 launched his meteoric career. With an army of fewer than fifty thousand men, he defeated the Piedmontese and the Austrians. In quick order he established client republics dependent on his own authority; he negotiated with the Austrians himself; and he molded the army into his personal force by paying the soldiers in cash taken as tribute from the newly conquered territories. He mollified the Directory government at home by sending back wagonloads of great Italian masterpieces of art, which were added to Parisian museum collections after being paraded in victory festivals. (Most are still there.) Even the failures of the Egyptian campaign did not dull his luster. Bonaparte had taken France's leading scientists with him on the expedition, which had given him a reputation as a man of culture. When his troops were pinned down, he slipped out of Egypt and made his way secretly across the Mediterranean to southern France.

In October 1799 he arrived home at just the right moment. The war in Europe was going badly; the Belgian departments had revolted against new conscription laws; deserters swelled the ranks of the rebels in western France; a royalist army had tried to take the city of Toulouse in the southwest; and many government leaders wanted to revise the Constitution of 1795. Amidst increasing political instability, generals in the field had become virtually independent, and the troops felt more loyal to their units and generals than to the republic. As one army captain wrote, "In a conquering people the military spirit must prevail over other social conditions." Its victories had made the army a parallel and rival force to the state.

Disillusioned members of the government saw in Bonaparte's return an occasion to overturn the Constitution of 1795. On November 9, 1799 (18 Brumaire, Year VIII by the revolutionary calendar), the conspirators persuaded the legislature to move out of Paris to avoid an imaginary Jacobin plot. But when Bonaparte marched into the meeting hall the next day and demanded changes in the constitution, he was greeted by cries of "Down with the dictator." His quick-thinking brother Lucien, president of the Council of Five Hundred (the lower house), saved him by summoning troops guarding the hall and claiming that the deputies had tried to assassinate the popular general. The soldiers ejected the deputies, and a hastily assembled rump voted to abolish the Directory and establish a new three-man executive called the Consulate. Bonaparte became First Consul, a title revived from ancient Rome. In short order a new constitution was submitted to the voters; millions abstained, and the government falsified the results to give an appearance of even greater support to the new regime. Although not a very auspicious beginning, within five years Bonaparte would crown himself Napoleon I, Emperor of the French. A new order would rise from the ashes of the republic, and the French armies would recover from their reverses of 1799 to push the frontiers of French influence even farther eastward.

CONCLUSION

In 1799 no one knew what course Napoleon Bonaparte would follow. Inside France, political apathy had overtaken the original enthusiasm for revolutionary ideals. Yet for most Europeans the political landscape had been permanently altered. One of the most powerful monarchies in the world had been overthrown and replaced with a republic in which civil and political rights had been dramatically extended. Titles of nobility had been abolished and the powers of the Catholic church severely curtailed. At the height of their power, the Jacobins had tried to institute not only a new, more democratic republic but also a republican culture, complete with a new calendar, state festivals, and a civic religion. Future revolutionaries would emulate this model.

The achievements and failures of the French Revolution still provoke debate. The divisions created by the Revolution within France endured in many cases until 1945. Even now, French public-opinion surveys ask if it was right to execute the king in 1793. The French proclaimed human rights and democratic government as a universal goal, but the revolutionary leaders explicitly excluded women, even though they admitted Jewish, Protestant, and black men. They used the new spirit of national pride to inspire armies that could conquer other peoples. Their ideals of universal education and art for the people paled in the face of new forms of government terror to persecute dissidents. The French Revolution ironically sowed the seeds for both totalitarianism and democracy.

Suggestions for Further Reading

Source Materials

Baker, Keith Michael, ed. *University of Chicago Readings in Western Civilization.* Vol. 7, *The Old Regime and the French Revolution* 1987. The most up-to-date collection of documents on France.

Burke, Edmund. *Reflections on the Revolution in France;* and Paine, Thomas. *The Rights of Man.* 1973. The two opposing sides in England on the merits or defects of the French Revolution.

Gay Levy, Darline, Harriet Branson Applewhite, and Mary Durham Johnson, eds. *Women in Revolutionary Paris, 1789–1795.* 1979. Documents chronicling women's participation in the French Revolution.

Interpretive Studies

Applewhite, Harriet B. and Darline G. Levy, eds. *Women and Politics in the Age of the Democratic Revolution.* 1990. Essays on women's participation in France, Great Britain, the Dutch Republic, the Austrian Netherlands, and the U.S.

Barton, H. Arnold. *Scandinavia in the Revolutionary Era, 1760–1815.* 1986. A thorough narrative of a region often overlooked in histories of this period.

Blackburn, Robin. *The Overthrow of Colonial Slavery, 1776–1848.* 1988. Includes excellent chapters on the Haitian revolution and abolitionist movements in America, Britain, France, and Spain.

Blanning, T. C. W. *The French Revolution: Aristocrats Versus Bourgeois?* 1987. A brief and useful overview of historians' views about the Marxist interpretation.

———. *French Revolution in Germany: Occupation and Resistance in the Rhineland, 1792–1802.* 1983. An account of the resistance to the French invasion and occupation of neighboring German territories.

Cobb, Richard. *The Police and the People: French Popular Protest, 1789–1820.* 1970. Lively essays by an eminent historian of popular reactions and resistances to the French Revolution.

Elliott, Marianne. *Partners in Revolution: The United Irishmen and France.* 1982. An analysis of the origins of Irish republicanism in the revolutionary decade.

Forrest, Alan. *Soldiers of the French Revolution.* 1990. A comprehensive overview of the army's crucial role.

Furet, François. *Interpreting the French Revolution.* Translated by Elborg Forster. 1981. A difficult but important interpretation emphasizing the ambiguities of democracy during the Revolution.

Hunt, Lynn. *Politics, Culture, and Class in the French Revolution.* 1984. An account of the development of a revolutionary tradition through festivals, speeches, and symbols.

Jordan, David P. *The King's Trial: The French Revolution Versus Louis XVI.* 1979. A very readable history of the trial and execution of the king.

Landes, Joan. *Women and the Public Sphere in the Age of the French Revolution.* 1988. Traces the links between republicanism and the exclusion of women from politics.

Lefebvre, Georges. *The Coming of the French Revolution.* Translated by R. R. Palmer. 1947. A classic statement about the origins of the French Revolution that traces the participation of the aristocrats, bourgeoisie, and peasantry.

Lyons, Martyn. *France Under the Directory.* 1975. An overview of every aspect of the period from 1795 to 1799, when France tried to establish a liberal republic.

Palmer, R. R. *The Age of the Democratic Revolution: A Political History of Europe and America, 1760–1800.* Vol. 2, *The Struggle.* 1964. Still one of the few comprehensive surveys of the changes throughout Europe during the revolutionary epoch.

Polasky, Janet L. *Revolution in Brussels, 1787–1793.* 1987. The resistance of the Austrian Netherlands as seen from its biggest city, Brussels.

Schama, Simon. *Citizens: A Chronicle of the French Revolution.* 1989. A lively but one-sided narrative of the last years of the Old Regime and the first years of the French Revolution.

———. *Patriots and Liberators: Revolution in the Netherlands, 1780–1815.* 1977. A narrative history of the different phases of the Dutch revolution.

Soboul, Albert. *The Sans-Culottes: The Popular Movement and Revolutionary Government, 1793–1794.* Translated by Remy Inglis Hall. 1980. An abridgement and translation of the classic Marxist work on the popular movement during the French Revolution.

Sutherland, D. M. G. *France, 1789–1815: Revolution and Counterrevolution.* 1986. An excellent but detailed synthesis of recent research on the entire revolutionary period, 1787–1799, in France; emphasizes local resistance to the revolutionary government.

When Napoleon Bonaparte came to power in France, one question preoccupied everyone: Would he continue the Revolution or turn his back on it? Even after Napoleon disappeared from the scene, the specter of revolution continued to haunt Europe's rulers, who ignored it at their peril. Napoleon's own attitude was mixed; he carried forward the Revolution's heritage in some areas but recast it in others. No act captured this division more dramatically than his self-coronation as Emperor Napoleon I in 1804. On the surface the coronation was decidedly backward-looking, reviving the memory of Roman emperors and Charlemagne.* But Napoleon had no interest in resuscitating the French monarchy; he aimed for something new. He invited the pope to attend the ceremony, yet he reserved the important roles for himself.

As the spectators watched transfixed, Napoleon raised Charlemagne's crown and placed it on his own head. Moments later he crowned his wife, Josephine. The ceremony underlined Bonaparte's image as a self-made man, one who could even crown himself emperor. His was the ultimate success story of the Revolution, which had opened careers to those with talent. Napoleon did not have a royal bloodline to guarantee his accession, like the kings of old; he earned his title of emperor after his victories on the battlefield had won him the confidence of the French people.

Napoleon's self-coronation is only one example of his dominance of European affairs between 1799 and 1815. The short,

---

*Charlemagne ruled the Franks in the ninth century and revived the Roman Empire in the West.

Napoleon, the Restoration, and the Revolutionary Legacy, 1799–1832

Jacques-Louis David, Napoleon in His Study
David, who as a deputy during the National Convention voted for the king's death, painted for Napoleon when he came to power. This 1812 painting underscores Napoleon's military leadership as well as his administrative skills.

physically unprepossessing officer from Corsica, who spoke French with an Italian accent, made an unlikely hero and symbol of French imperialism. But he successfully transformed himself into both hero and emperor, and his life is the stuff of legend even today. Eventually, resistance to the French armies and the ever-mounting costs of military glory toppled Napoleon. The powers allied against him rearranged the borders within Europe once again and pledged to uphold governments that restored the Old Regime to some degree. Many changes effected by the French Revolution endured nonetheless, and established conservative governments collided repeatedly with people eager for reform or even a new revolution. Riots shook Paris in 1830, and revolution soon spread to Belgium, Poland, and some of the Italian states. By then the spread of industry, growing awareness of social problems, and aspirations for national self-determination had added new force to the revolutionary legacy.

IMPORTANT DATES

1799 Coup against Directory government in France; Napoleon named First Consul

1801 Napoleon signs a concordat with the pope, ending a decade of church-state conflict

1802 A plebiscite makes Napoleon First Consul for life

1804 Napoleon crowned as emperor of France

1805 British naval forces defeat the French at the Battle of Trafalgar

1806 Continental System implemented to blockade British commerce

1808–1814 Peninsular War in Spain and Portugal ties down French troops

1812 Napoleon invades Russia

1813 French defeat at the Battle of Nations at Leipzig

1814 Napoleon abdicates and goes into exile on the island of Elba

1815 Napoleon defeated at Waterloo and exiled to island of Saint Helena, where he dies in 1821

From Consulate to Empire: The New Authoritarian State

In his first few years of rule, Napoleon created a strong bureaucratic state oriented toward conquest abroad and ensuring order at home. Personally directing the most important government affairs, the emperor came to embody the glory of France. He dreamed of European integration in the tradition of Alexander the Great, Julius Caesar, and Charlemagne, but he also mastered the details of practical administration. To achieve his goals, he compromised with the Catholic church and with exiled aristocrats willing to return to France. He also offered young men of the peasantry and urban working classes the prospect of social mobility through military service. His most enduring accomplishment, the new Civil Code, tempered the principles of the Enlightenment and the Revolution with an insistence on the powers of fathers over children, husbands over wives, and employers over workers.

The Disappearance of the French Republic

Even Napoleon could not create an empire all at once, and at the beginning he had to work within the framework of the republic. The *coup d'état* of November 1799 established three provisional consuls (the title drew on the ancient Roman precedent) to oversee the drafting of yet another constitution—the fourth since 1789. Napoleon immediately asserted his leadership. In his view, "Constitutions should be short and obscure." The new constitution made Napoleon the First Consul with the right to pick the Council of State, which drew up all laws. Government was no longer representative in any real sense: the new constitution eliminated direct elections for deputies and granted no independent powers to the three houses of the legislature. Napoleon and his advisers chose the legislature's members out of a small pool of "notables." In 1802, Napoleon had himself proclaimed First Consul for life; in 1804 he crowned himself emperor. Almost all men over twenty-one could vote, but their only option was to choose "Yes" or "No" in referendums written by the state. The arena of political contest and debate shriveled to almost nothing.

Napoleon continued the centralization of state power that had begun under the absolutist monarchy of Louis XIV and resumed under the Terror. As First Consul he appointed department prefects who resembled the intendants of the Old Regime in their broad powers of supervision over local affairs. He created a Bank of France to facilitate government borrowing and relied on gold and silver coinage rather than paper money. The government directly managed every aspect of education: the books, the subjects for examination, and even the grading system. The new *lycées*, the state-run secondary schools for boys from better-off families, were designed to be "nurseries of patriotism." Students wore military uniforms, and drum rolls signaled the beginning and end of classes. (Without the military trappings, the *lycées* are now coeducational and still the heart of the French educational system.) Napoleon took little interest in girls' education, believing that they should spend most of their time at home learning religion, manners, and such "female occupations" as sewing and music.

This was government from the top down, yet it was government based on law. All the previous revolutionary governments had tried to unify and standardize France's multiple legal codes, but only Napoleon successfully established a new one, partly because he personally presided over half the sessions of the commission that drafted the new Civil Code. Like previous revolutionary projects for legal reform, the code guaranteed religious liberty, a uniform system of law with no social or regional distinctions, the supremacy of a secular state, and the right of men to choose their professions. The code defined property rights in detail. It also, however, sharply curtailed women's rights in almost every aspect of public and private life. The French code was imitated in many European and Latin American countries and Louisiana (once a French colony).

Although the Civil Code assured property rights and equal treatment before the law for males, the Napoleonic regime severely limited political expression. Napoleon promised order and an end to the upheavals of ten years of revolutionary turmoil. He never relied on mass executions to achieve control, but he refused to allow those who opposed him to meet in clubs, influence elections, or publish newspapers. A decree reduced the number of newspapers in Paris from seventy-three to thirteen (and then finally to four), and the newspapers that remained became government organs. Censors had to approve all operas and plays, and they banned "offensive" artistic works just as they had under the Old Regime. The ex-terrorist Joseph Fouché, now the minister of police, could impose house arrest, arbitrary imprisonment, and surveillance of political dissidents. When a bomb attack on Napoleon's carriage failed in 1800, Fouché suppressed the evidence of a royalist plot and instead arrested hundreds of former Jacobins. Over one hundred of them were deported and seven hundred imprisoned.

Napoleon was determined to gain the support of Catholics, who had been alienated by revolutionary policies toward the church. Although nominally Catholic, Napoleon was a deist without deep religious convictions. "How can there be order in the state without religion?" he asked cynically. "When a man is dying of hunger beside another who is stuffing himself, he cannot accept this difference if there is not an authority who tells him: 'God wishes it so.'" In 1801 a concordat with Pope Pius VII (*1800–1823) ended a decade of church-state conflict. The pope validated all sales of church lands, and the government agreed to pay the salaries of bishops and priests who would swear loyalty to the state. Catholicism was officially recognized as the religion of "the great majority of French citizens." The pope thus brought the huge French Catholic population back into the fold—but at the cost of ceding considerable control over church affairs to the French state. The state also paid Protestant pastors' salaries. Napoleon encouraged Jewish assimilation, and in 1808 his government decreed that Jewish regulatory bodies set up by the government would control Jewish religious affairs.

Imperial Rule

Napoleon dominated the new regime with his charismatic personality. As First Consul he worked hard at establishing his reputation as an efficient

Jacques-Louis David, **The Coronation of Napoleon and Josephine,** *1805–1807*
David chose to represent the moment during the coronation in 1804 when Napoleon crowned his wife Josephine, while the pope looked on. Napoleon had crowned himself just moments before.

administrator with broad intellectual interests: he met frequently with scientists, jurists, and artists, and stories of his unflagging energy abounded. He set an example by rising at 2:00 A.M., after only four or five hours of sleep, and working for several hours before going back to bed from 5:00 to 7:00 A.M. When not on military campaigns, he worked on state affairs, usually until 10:00 P.M., taking only a few minutes for each meal. "Authority," declared his advisor Sieyès, "must come from above and confidence from below."

As emperor, Napoleon cultivated personal symbolism to enhance his image as a hero. His visage and name adorned coins, engravings, histories, paintings, public monuments, and even the Civil Code, called the *Code Napoléon*. His favorite painters embellished his legend by depicting him as a warrior-hero of mythic proportions. In his imperial court, Napoleon staged his entrances carefully to maximize his personal presence: his wife and courtiers would all be dressed in regal finery, and he would be announced with great pomp—but dressed in a simple military uniform with no medals, personifying the simple soldier called to rule a people.

Napoleon's imprint appeared everywhere in France. The government lent money to French industries, and engineers built or repaired some fifty thousand miles of roads to facilitate communication and marketing. Government-commissioned architects built the Arc de Triomphe, the Stock Exchange, fountains, and even slaughterhouses. Believing that "what is big is always beautiful" and trying to make Paris "the most beautiful city one can imagine," Napoleon embarked on ostentatious building projects that would outshine even those of Louis XIV. Most of his new construction reflected his neoclassical taste for monumental buildings set in vast empty spaces. Old, winding streets with their cramped houses were demolished to make way for these improvements.

Despite appearances, Napoleon did not rule alone. Among his most trusted officials were men who had served with him in Italy and Egypt. His chief of staff Alexandre Berthier, for example, became minister of war, and the chemist Claude Berthollet, who had organized the scientific part of the expedition to Egypt, became vice president of the Senate in 1804. Napoleon fostered links with the great scientists of the day, preferring them to men and women of letters. Pierre Laplace, the most influential scientist of his generation and designer of the metric system, served as the first minister of the interior under the Consulate and later held high posts in the Senate. Such personal connections illustrate a general tendency in the Napoleonic regime: the bureaucracy was based on a patron-client relationship, with Napoleon as the ultimate patron. Some of Napoleon's closest associates married into his family.

The Senate crowned the patronage system as the most socially prestigious legislative body. Over time, Napoleon took control of naming senators, selecting the nation's most illustrious generals, ministers, prefects, scientists, rich men, and former nobles. According the Senate such eminence was part of Napoleon's plan to reinstitute a social hierarchy in France by rewarding merit and talent, regardless of social origins. By choosing a new elite, he intended to replace both the old nobility of birth and the republic's strict emphasis on equality. In 1802, Napoleon took the first step toward creating a new nobility by founding a Legion of Honor, a way of combining public recognition with social privilege. (Members of the legion received lifetime pensions along with their titles.) By 1814, the legion had thirty-two thousand members, only 5 percent of them civilians. Napoleon usually equated honor with military success.

In 1808, Napoleon introduced a complete hierarchy of noble titles, ranging from princes down to barons and chevaliers. Titles could be inherited but had to be supported by wealth—a man could not be a duke without a fortune of 200,000 francs, or a chevalier without 3,000 francs. Napoleon combined the Old Regime idea of hereditary nobility with the revolutionary ideal of service and talent:

his nobles had all served the state, came from varied social backgrounds, and would lose their status if they lost their wealth. Economic power was thus tied explicitly to political power. The Napoleonic nobility was only one-seventh the size of the Old Regime nobility, with 60 percent of the new nobles rising from the military. Napoleon gave his favorite generals huge fortunes, often in the form of estates in the conquered territories, as well as titles, and they bought sumptuous Parisian townhouses and magnificent country manors.

Napoleon's own family reaped the greatest benefits. His older brother, Joseph, became first king of Naples (1806) and then king of Spain (1808). He named his younger brother, Louis, king of Holland in 1806. At age twenty-three his stepson Eugène de Beauharnais was proclaimed viceroy of Italy, and his sister Caroline and brother-in-law General Murat became king and queen of Naples in 1808. Napoleon wanted to establish an imperial succession, but he lacked an heir. In thirteen years of marriage his wife Josephine had borne no children, so in 1809 he divorced her and in 1810 married the eighteen-year-old Princess Marie-Louise of Austria. The next year she gave birth to a son to whom Napoleon immediately gave the title King of Rome.

The New Paternalism

Although Josephine had enlivened Parisian salon life before their marriage, Napoleon wanted to restrict women to the private sphere of the home. One of his leading jurists remarked, "There have been many discussions on the equality and superiority of the sexes. Nothing is more useless than such disputes. . . . Women need protection because they are weaker; men are free because they are stronger." The framers of the Civil Code used women's supposed innate weakness as justification for limiting their participation in public life and for legally protecting their separate, domestic roles to help ensure their wifely and motherly virtues. The law obligated husbands to support their wives, who in return had to relinquish control of their property and economic transactions. The husband alone controlled any property held in common; a wife could not sue in court, sell or mortgage her own property, or contract a debt without her husband's consent. Not until 1965 did

French wives gain legal status equal to that of their husbands.

The Civil Code took the male revolutionary ambivalence about women's political participation a step farther, modifying even those few revolutionary laws that had been favorable to women and in some instances denying rights women had under the monarchy. Divorce was still possible but severely restricted, especially for women. Adultery was an acceptable grounds for divorce, but the law considered a wife's infidelity more contemptible than a husband's. A wife could petition for divorce only if her husband brought his mistress to live in the family home! In contrast, a wife convicted of adultery could be imprisoned for up to two years. The code's framers saw these discrepancies as a way to reinforce the family and make women responsible for private virtue, while leaving public decisions to men.

The Civil Code not only reasserted a patriarchal system of male domination, but also established a new paternalism in which a father's control of his children became the model for other social relations, much as under the Old Regime. In addition to reinforcing the authority of husbands, the code restored most paternal powers, which revolutionary legislation had limited. For example, fathers could send their children under sixteen to prison for up to a month with no hearing of any sort. At the same time, the code insisted on fathers' responsibilities to provide for their children's welfare. Napoleon himself encouraged the foundation of private charities to help indigent mothers, and one of his decrees made it easier for women to abandon their children anonymously to a government foundling hospital. Napoleon hoped such measures would discourage abortion and infanticide, especially among the poorest classes in the fast-growing urban areas.

In periods of economic crisis the government opened soup kitchens, but in time-honored fashion it also arrested beggars and sent them to newly established workhouses. The state even intervened in prostitutes' lives. Migration from the countryside and wartime upheavals had caused a surge of prostitution in French cities. The authorities arrested prostitutes who worked on their own, but they tolerated and even regulated brothels, requiring the women to have monthly medical examinations for venereal disease.

The new paternalism extended to relations between employers and employees, whose status resembled that of children. The state required all workers to carry a *livret*, or work card,[*] attesting to their good conduct, and it prohibited all workers' organizations. The police considered workers without a *livret* as vagrants or criminals and could send them to workhouses or prison. Arbitration boards settled labor disputes after 1806, but they took employers at their word yet treated workers as minors, demanding that foremen and shop superintendents represent them. Strikes occasionally occurred, led by secret, illegal journeymen's associations, or *compagnonnages*, but wage workers generally lived under the thumb of their employers, many of whom laid off employees when times were hard, deducted fines from their wages, and dismissed them without appeal for being absent or making errors. These limitations on workers' rights won Napoleon the support of French business.

Patronage of Science and Intellectual Life

Napoleon did everything possible to promote French scientific inquiry, especially that which could serve practical ends. As he insisted, "The most honorable occupation and the most useful to nations is to contribute to the extension of human ideas." He closely monitored the research institutes established during the Revolution, sometimes intervening personally to insist on political conformity. He had been elected a member of the Institute of France, whose most important section studied mathematics and physical and natural sciences. The scientists in the institute collected regular stipends and were expected to hold sessions to inform the public about recent scientific activity. Scientists dominated the teaching in the College of France, the Polytechnical School, and the Museum of Natural History, and some even assumed government posts. One of the chemists who taught in the museum, for example, became head of public education. Scientists also met informally in learned societies such as the Society for the Encouragement of National Industry.

---

[*]Work cards had been used in the Old Regime, but the system had not been uniform or national.

An impressive outpouring of new theoretical and practical scientific work rewarded the state's efforts. Experiments with balloons led to the discovery of laws about the expansion of gases, and research on fossil shells prepared the way for new theories of evolutionary change later in the nineteenth century. One of Napoleon's leading officials, the chemist Antoine Chaptal, organized the gathering of public health statistics, promoted technical education, oversaw public works construction, and after his retirement experimented with sugar-beet cultivation on his model farm. The surgeon Dominique-Jean Larrey developed new techniques of battlefield amputation and medical care during many of Napoleon's wars, winning an appointment as an officer in the Legion of Honor and a baron with a pension.

As in so many areas of Napoleon's regime, the intellectual balance sheet was ambiguous. Napoleon had his own forward-looking vision for modernizing French society through science and central administration, but he had to confront both the inertia of the old order and the energy unleashed by the Revolution. To maintain his control he stifled dissent. Napoleon considered most writers useless or dangerous, "good for nothing under any government." Some of the most talented French writers of the time had to live in exile. The best-known expatriate was Germaine de Staël (1766–1817), the daughter of Louis XVI's minister Jacques Necker and a leading novelist and essayist. When explaining his desire to exile her, Napoleon exclaimed, "She is a machine in motion who stirs up the salons." While exiled in the German states, Madame de Staël wrote a novel, *Corinne* (1807), about a brilliant woman whose love is thwarted by a patriarchal system, and *On Germany* (1810), an account of the important new literary currents east of the Rhine. Her books were banned in France.

Although Napoleon restored the strong authority of state and religion in France, many royalists and Catholics still criticized him. Reacting against revolutionary changes and what they saw as the failures of Enlightenment ideals, royalist émigrés such as Joseph de Maistre (1753–1821) and Louis de Bonald (1754–1840) defended absolutism and the close alliance of throne and altar. François-René de Chateaubriand (1768–1848), a royalist but also an admirer of Napoleon as "the strong man who has saved us from the abyss," ex-

Madame de Staël
The writer and Napoleonic opponent helped bring romanticism to France.

alted the *Genius of Christianity* (1802) and argued against excessive reliance on reason. He claimed, "It is to the vanity of knowledge that we owe almost all our misfortunes. . . . The learned ages have always been followed by ages of destruction." Chateaubriand's book reflected a general revival of interest in the Middle Ages and in religion. A Museum of the Monuments of France opened in 1801 with a collection of medieval masterpieces, and composers who once wrote revolutionary music turned to masses and requiems.

Napoleon's personal taste in art, music, and even furniture had an enormous influence because he directly patronized many artists. In art as in architecture he preferred the neoclassical; for example, he hired the former revolutionary artist David to paint his coronation. Furniture makers turned out empire-style chests, tables, and desks made out of dark woods with elaborate hand carvings and expensive gold ornamentation. Napoleon voraciously read such popular eighteenth-century novels as Richardson's *Pamela*, and his personal library of a thousand books went along on his military campaigns.

Napoleon's Conquest of Europe

Napoleon left an indelible stamp on French institutions and political life, yet his fame and much of his power rested on his military conquests. Building on innovations introduced by the republican governments before him, Napoleon revolutionized the art of war with tactics and strategy based on a highly mobile army. By 1810 he ruled an empire more extensive than any since the time of ancient Rome. Yet within two years that empire had begun to crumble, and with it went Napoleon's power at home. Scholars still debate the causes of this remarkable rise to dominance and equally dramatic fall. Was war (and eventual defeat) inevitable given Napoleon's ambition? Was it necessary because the other mighty powers feared an even stronger France? Or was it simply an extension of the French republic's plan to spread the Revolution's ideals throughout Europe? What we know for certain is that Napoleon ensured that the French Revolution had a worldwide impact.

The Grand Army

Napoleon attributed his military success "three-quarters to morale" and the rest to leadership and having more soldiers at the point of attack. Conscription provided the large numbers: 1.3 million men aged twenty to twenty-four were drafted between 1800 and 1812, another million in 1813–1814.

Europe in 1810

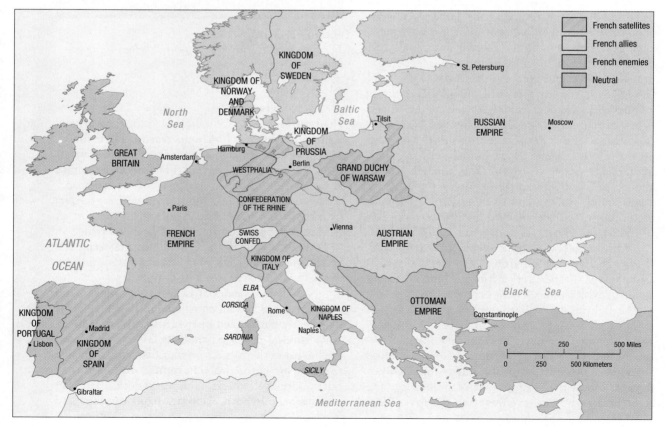

Jean-Louis-Ernest Meissonier, **French Campaign of 1814,** *1864*
In a work completed some years after the fact, the painter depicted Napoleon at the head of his armies.

So many agreed to go because the republic had taught them to identify the army with the nation. Military service was both a patriotic duty and a means of social ascent. The new men who rose through the ranks to become officers were young, ambitious, and accustomed to the new ways of war. Consequently, the French army had higher morale than the armies of other powers, most of which rejected conscription as too democratic and continued to restrict their officer corps to the nobility. Only in 1813–1814 did French morale plummet, as Napoleon's insatiable demands for more men despite military defeat destroyed French enthusiasm for war.

When Napoleon came to power in 1799, France had been at war for almost seven years, and its military position was precarious. Desertion was rampant, and the various republican armies vied for predominance. Napoleon ended this squabbling by uniting all the armies into one Grand Army under his command. By 1812 he personally commanded

seven hundred thousand troops; while two hundred fifty thousand soldiers fought in Spain, others remained garrisoned in France. Between seventy thousand and one hundred eighty thousand men, not all of them French, fought for France in any given battle. Life on campaign was no picnic—ordinary soldiers slept in the rain, mud, and snow, and often had to forage for food—but Napoleon nonetheless inspired almost fanatical loyalty. A brilliant strategist who carefully studied the demands of war, he outmaneuvered virtually all his opponents. He fought alongside his soldiers in some sixty battles and had nineteen horses shot from under him. One opponent said that Napoleon's presence alone was worth 50,000 men.

Napoleon's command was personal and highly centralized. He essentially served as his own operations officer: "I alone know what I have to do," he insisted. This style worked as long as Napoleon could be on the battlefield, but he failed to train independent subordinates to take over in his absence. He also faced constant difficulties in supplying a rapidly moving army, which could not always live off the land. When civilian contractors failed to deliver promised goods in 1806, Napoleon put the military in charge of the transport system and introduced a network of staging areas. Supply would nevertheless remain one of the army's weak points, especially as it ranged farther from France.

Napoleon had a pragmatic and direct approach to strategy: he went for the main body of the opposing army and tried to crush it in a lightning campaign. He gathered the largest possible army for one great and decisive battle, then followed with a relentless pursuit to break enemy morale altogether. In the early years of Napoleon's rule this strategy worked as well as or better than it had in Italy in 1796–1797. His armies' victories at Marengo and Hohenlinden in 1800 forced the Austrian emperor to sue for peace. Britain agreed to the Treaty of Amiens soon after (1802), but peace lasted only until 1803. During this time, Napoleon sent an expeditionary force to Saint Domingue and captured Toussaint l'Ouverture, the leader of the slave revolt. Continuing resistance among the black population and an epidemic of yellow fever forced Napoleon to withdraw his troops from Saint Domingue and abandon his plans to extend his empire to the western hemisphere. As part of his retreat, he sold the Louisiana Territory to the United States in 1803.

Napoleon considered the peace with Great Britain merely a truce and used the time to consolidate his position before again taking up arms. When hostilities resumed, the British navy once more proved its superiority by blocking an attempted French invasion and by defeating the French and their Spanish allies in a huge naval battle at Trafalgar in 1805. France lost many ships; the British lost no vessels, but their renowned admiral, Lord Nelson, perished. On land, however, Napoleon remained invincible. He captured twenty-five thousand Austrian soldiers at Ulm in Bavaria in 1805. After marching on to Vienna, he again trounced the Austrians, who had been joined by their new Russian ally. The Battle of Austerlitz, often considered Napoleon's greatest victory, was fought on December 2, 1805, the first anniversary of his coronation.

Prussia had waited too long to end its decade of neutrality. In 1806 the French destroyed the Prussian army at Jena and Auerstadt. Frederick William III (∗1797–1840) fled Berlin. In 1807, Napoleon defeated the Russians at Friedland. Personal negotiations between Napoleon and the young tsar Alexander I (∗1801–1825) resulted in a humiliating settlement for Frederick William III; the treaties of Tilsit turned Prussian lands west of the Elbe River into the kingdom of Westphalia under Napoleon's brother Jerome, and Prussia's Polish provinces became the duchy of Warsaw attached to the kingdom of Saxony. Alexander recognized Napoleon's conquests in central and western Europe and promised to help him against the British in exchange for Napoleon's support against the Turks. Neither party kept the bargain. Austria took up arms again in 1809—this time alone—and lost yet another battle, at Wagram.

Napoleonic Battles

New National Boundaries and Internal Reforms

Wherever the Grand Army conquered, Napoleon's influence soon followed. In 1803 he began to consolidate the tiny German states by abolishing some of them and attaching them to larger units. In July 1806 he established the Confederation of the Rhine, which soon included almost all the German States except Austria and Prussia. The Holy Roman Emperor gave up his title and became simply the emperor of Austria, ending the Holy Roman Empire that had lasted a thousand years, since the coronation of Charlemagne in 800. In a similar move toward unification, Napoleon partitioned Italy into three main parts: the territories annexed to France, the kingdom of Italy, and the kingdom of Naples. Italy had not been so unified since the Roman Empire. National unification, however, was not Napoleon's goal. He brought the disparate Italian and German states together in order to rule them more effectively and to exploit their resources for his own ends.

Napoleon's victories forced defeated rulers to rethink their political and cultural assumptions. Prussia's Frederick William III appointed a reform commission after the crushing defeat of 1806. On the commission's urging, the king abolished serfdom and allowed nonnobles to buy and enclose land. Peasants gained their personal independence from their noble landlords, who could no longer sell them to pay their gambling debts, for example, or refuse them permission to marry. Yet the lives of the former serfs remained bleak; they were left without land and indebted to their landlords, who no longer had to care for them in hard times. The king's advisers also overhauled the army to make the high command more efficient and to open the way to the appointment of middle-class officers. Prussia instituted these reforms to try to compete with France, not to promote democracy. As one reformer wrote to Frederick, "We must do from above what the French have done from below."

Reform received lip service in Russia. Tsar Alexander I had gained his throne after an aristocratic coup deposed and killed his autocratic and capricious father, Paul (*1796–1805), and in the early years of his reign the remorseful young ruler felt a vague desire to do good. Reform commissions studied abuses; Alexander created western-style ministries, lifted restrictions on importing foreign books, and founded six new universities; he encouraged nobles to free their serfs voluntarily (a few actually did so); and even drafting a constitution was discussed. But none of these reform currents touched beneath the surface of Russian life, and by the second decade of his reign, Alexander began to reject the Enlightenment spirit his grandmother, Catherine the Great, had instilled in him.

The lands that Napoleon had conquered adopted French-style reforms most directly. Annexed territories became departments with administrations identical to those in France. There and in the satellite kingdoms, French reforms included abolishing serfdom, eliminating seigneurial dues, introducing the Napoleonic Civil Code, suppressing monasteries, and subordinating church to state, as well as extending civil rights to Jews and other religious minorities. The experience in the kingdom of Westphalia was typical of a French satellite. When Jerome Bonaparte and his wife Catherine arrived as king and queen in 1807, they relied on French experts who worked with a hand-picked committee of Germans to write a constitution and install legal reforms. The Westphalian army had the first Jewish officers in the German states, and the army, administration, and judiciary all opened to the middle classes. As time passed, however, the German subjects began to chafe under French rule. German officials enforced French decrees only half-heartedly, and the French army had to forbid its soldiers to frequent local taverns and shops because their presence often started fights.

As the example of Westphalia shows, reactions to Napoleonic innovations were always mixed. Napoleon's chosen rulers often made real improvements in roads, public works, law codes, and education, yet almost everyone had some cause for complaint. Republicans regretted Napoleon's conversion of the sister republics into kingdoms after his coronation. In the kingdom of Italy, at least, the Italians soon became used to the hybrid form of half-French, half-Italian government. Most officials were Italian, but the French viceroy made the final decisions with the advice of his French cabinet. Tax increases and ever-rising conscription quotas fomented discontent even in this most successful of the satellites. Historians estimate that the various conquered territories paid half the French war expenses. The removal of internal tariffs, on the other hand, often fostered the growth of factory production. By 1814, Bologna had five hundred factories and Modena four hundred.

Almost everywhere conflicts arose between Napoleon's desire for central government and standard administration and the locals' insistence on maintaining customs and traditions. Sometimes his own relatives sided with their new countries. Louis would not allow conscription in Holland, for example, because the Dutch had never had compulsory military service. He established a National Council for Public Health, enforced vaccination for smallpox, and tried to encourage breast-feeding for babies. When Napoleon tried to introduce an economic policy banning trade with Great Britain, Louis's lax enforcement prompted the frustrated emperor to complain that "Holland is an English province." In 1810, Napoleon annexed the kingdom because his brother had become too sympathetic to Dutch interests.

The one power standing between Napoleon and total dominance of Europe was Great Britain. In an effort to bankrupt this "nation of shopkeepers" by choking its trade, Napoleon inaugurated a Continental System in 1806 that prohibited all commerce between Great Britain and France, as well as France's dependent states and allies. At first the system worked: British exports dropped 20 percent in 1807 and 1808, and industrial production declined 10 percent, creating unemployment and igniting a strike of sixty thousand workers in northern England. In the midst of continuing wars, however, the system proved impossible to enforce, and widespread smuggling brought British goods into the European market. The British retaliated by declaring open season on neutral ships that sailed to or from ports from which the British were excluded—a ban that eventually contributed to causing the War of 1812 between Great Britain and the United States. British industrial growth continued, despite some setbacks, right through the period of the Continental System, partly by opening up new markets in Latin America; calico-printing works, for example, quadrupled their production, and imports of raw cotton increased 40 percent. French and other continental industries benefited from their temporary protection from British competition.

Resistance to French Rule

Smuggling British goods was only one way of opposing the French. Napoleonic domination aroused resentment among defenders of the old governments, nationalists, and most ordinary people. Each had their reasons, from defense of the traditional alliance of throne and altar to dislike of onerous levies of money and men. Peasant societies in which populations understood the costs of new

taxes much better than the benefits of universal rights resisted the most vigorously. In southern Italy gangs of bandits harassed the French army and local officials; thirty-three thousand Italian bandits were arrested in 1809 alone. But resistance remained possible via a network of secret societies, the *carbonari*. (In the mid-nineteenth century the *carbonari* would play an important role in Italian unification.) In Westphalia a colonel rebelled under the banner "Victory or Death in the Cause of the Nation." His army of five thousand unarmed men was easily dispersed, but his protest showed how French rule provoked an increasingly strong nationalist backlash.

The patriotic reaction to Napoleonic conquest also took literary and artistic forms. German intellectuals wrote passionate defenses of the virtues of the German people and of the superiority of German literature. Collections of popular German folk songs glorified independent German culture in the Middle Ages. The poet Friedrich Schiller wrote *William Tell* (1804) to celebrate a hero of Swiss resistance against foreign invasion. Ludwig van Beethoven (1770–1827), whose work presaged nineteenth-century musical romanticism, had originally entitled his Third Symphony *Bonaparte* in tribute to the republican First Consul. Furious when Napoleon named himself emperor in 1804, Beethoven crossed out the title and the symphony became known as the *Eroica*—"in memory of a hero."

No nations bucked Napoleon's reins more than Spain and Portugal. In 1807, Napoleon sent one hundred thousand troops through Spain to invade Portugal, Great Britain's ally. The Portuguese royal family fled to Brazil, but fighting continued, aided by a British army. In an incredibly complex set of political maneuvers, Napoleon managed to get his brother Joseph named king of Spain in place of the senile Charles IV (*1788–1808) and his heir, Prince Ferdinand. An uprising in Madrid in May 1808 brought out thousands of ordinary people who fought against the French with tools, sticks, roof tiles, and even chamber pots. A few of Napoleon's elite Muslim Mameluke soldiers beheaded men, women, and children in their homes, inflaming Spanish sentiment. The Spanish clergy and nobles raised guerrilla bands who proved impossible to squelch. Even Napoleon's taking personal command of the

Francisco de Goya y Lucientes, **The Third of May 1808,** *1814*
Goya's painting is a powerful rendition of French atrocities against the Spanish during the French occupation.

French forces failed to quell the Spanish, who for six years fought a war of independence that pinned down thousands of French soldiers far from the eastern front. Madame de Staël commented that Napoleon "never understood that a war might be a crusade. . . . He never reckoned with the one power that no arms could overcome—the enthusiasm of a whole people."

More than a new feeling of nationalism was aroused in Spain. Peasants hated French requisitioning of their food supplies and sought to defend their priests against French anticlericalism. Joseph's attempts to foster a free economy by dismantling royal monopolies and selling off royal industries only raised unemployment and destroyed foreign investment, fanning discontent.

Spanish nobles feared revolutionary reforms and were willing to defend the old monarchy in the person of the young Ferdinand VII, even while Ferdinand himself was congratulating Napoleon on his victories. The Spanish church spread anti-French propaganda that equated Napoleon with heresy. As the former archbishop of Seville wrote to the archbishop of Granada in 1808, "You realize that we must not recognize as king a freemason, heretic, Lutheran, as are all the Bonapartes and the French nation." In this tense atmosphere, and assisted by the British, the Spanish peasant rebels countered every French massacre with atrocities of their own. They tortured their French prisoners (they boiled one general alive) and lynched collaborators.

From Russian Winter to Final Defeat

Despite opposition, Napoleon had patched together an extensive empire by 1810. The empire had three parts: France and the territories now directly annexed to it (the Dutch Republic, the Austrian Netherlands, parts of Italy, and German territories along the Rhine); the satellite kingdoms of Italy, Naples, Westphalia, and Spain; and the allied states, which were forced to provide troops to the French in wartime (Prussia and Austria both fell into this category for a while, as did Saxony and Bavaria). Only two major European states remained fully independent: Great Britain and Russia. Peace would be possible, Napoleon calculated, only if Britain could find no allies on the Continent. Accordingly, he must crush Russia. Tsar Alexander I wanted war, too: the Continental System was wrecking his economy, and he refused to tolerate continuing insults from the "crowned Jacobin." In preparation for war, Alexander made peace with Turkey and allied himself with Great Britain and Sweden. By June 22, 1812, Napoleon was ready to invade Russia with a host of at least two hundred fifty thousand horses and six hundred thousand men, including contingents of Italians, Poles, Swiss, Dutch, and Germans.

Napoleon followed his usual strategy of trying to strike quickly, but the Russian generals avoided confrontation and retreated eastward. In September, on the road to Moscow, Napoleon finally engaged the main Russian force in the gigantic battle of Borodino. French casualties were thirty thousand men, including forty-seven generals; the Russians lost forty-five thousand, either killed or wounded. The French soldiers had nothing to celebrate around their campfires; "Everyone . . . wept for some dead friend." Once again the Russians retreated, leaving Moscow undefended. Napoleon entered the deserted city, but the victory turned hollow because the departing Russians set the wooden city on fire. Within a week, three-fourths of it had burned to the ground. Still Alexander refused to negotiate, and French morale plunged with worsening problems of supply. Weeks of constant marching in the dirt and heat had worn down the foot soldiers, who were dying of disease or deserting in large numbers. In October, Napoleon began his retreat; in November came the cold. Napoleon himself reported that on November 14 the temperature fell to −4 degrees Fahrenheit. A German soldier in the Grand Army described trying to cook fistfuls of raw bran with snow in order to make something like bread. For him the retreat was "the indescribable horror of all possible plagues." Within a week the Grand Army lost thirty thousand horses and had to abandon most of its artillery and food supplies. Russian forces harassed the retreating army, now more pathetic than grand. By December only one hundred thousand troops remained, one-sixth the original number, and the retreat had turned into a rout: the Russians had captured two hundred thousand soldiers, including forty-eight generals and three thousand other officers.

Napoleon had made a classic military mistake: fighting a war on two distant fronts simultaneously. The Spanish war tied down two hundred fifty thousand troops and forced him to bully Prussia and Austria into supplying soldiers of dubious loyalty. But even without the war with Spain and Portugal, the logistical and communications problems of marching to Moscow were simply too overwhelming given early nineteenth-century conditions. With such a large army to command, Napoleon's insistence on making all decisions himself proved disastrous. Time and again his generals failed to coordinate their efforts. Even if they had, however, enormous obstacles blocked their success.

Spain and Russia were the beginning of the end, but Napoleon was not yet finished. By the spring of 1813 the French emperor had mustered another two hundred fifty thousand men. In response the other powers formed a coalition against him. With British financial support, Russian, Austrian, Prussian, and Swedish armies (the latter un-

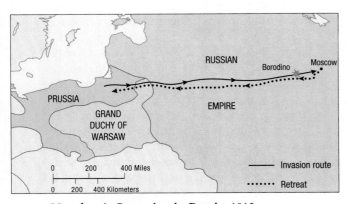

Napoleon's Campaign in Russia, 1812

der Napoleon's former general, now Crown Prince Bernadotte) met the French outside Leipzig in October 1813, and they defeated Napoleon in the Battle of the Nations. One by one, Napoleon's German allies deserted him to join the German "War of Liberation." Napoleon's French Empire began to disintegrate. The Confederation of the Rhine dissolved, and the Dutch revolted and restored the prince of Orange. Joseph Bonaparte fled Spain, and a combined Spanish-Portuguese guerrilla army under British command invaded France. In only a few months the allied powers crossed the Rhine and marched toward Paris. The French Senate deposed Napoleon, who abdicated when his remaining generals refused to fight. Napoleon went into exile on the island of Elba off the Italian coast.

Napoleon had one last chance. The allies restored the Bourbon monarchy to postrevolutionary France: Louis XVI's brother, the count of Provence, became King Louis XVIII* (*1814–1824). The new king tried to steer a middle course by "giving" France a charter that established a British-style monarchy with a two-house legislature and guaranteed civil rights. Discontent was nonetheless widespread. The rank and file of the army were happy to come home, but many professional officers lost their jobs. Those who had supported Napoleon or the republic before him felt uncertain about their futures. Sensing an opportunity, Napoleon escaped from Elba in early 1815 and landed in southern France, making swift and unimpeded progress to Paris. Louis XVIII fled across the border, and the period known as the Hundred Days began.

Napoleon promised free elections and called his veterans back into service, while the allies outlawed him as "an enemy and disturber of the tranquility of the world." Napoleon moved his armies quickly into present-day Belgium. At first it seemed that he might succeed in separately fighting the two armies arrayed against him—a Prussian army, and a joint force of Belgian, Dutch, German, and British troops led by Sir Arthur Wellesley (1769–1852), duke of Wellington. But the Prussians evaded him and joined with Wellington at Waterloo. Completely routed, Napoleon had no choice but to abdicate again. This time the victorious allies banished him permanently to the remote South Atlantic island of St. Helena.

Napoleon spent his last six years (he died in 1821) writing his version of his impact on history. He presented himself as a martyr to the cause of liberty whose goal was to create a European "federation of free people." Few were convinced by this "gospel according to St. Helena," having seen how Napoleon clamped down on political freedom wherever he ruled. But no one could deny the force of the legend of "the Eagle," who had soared to the heights of glory and was brought down only by a coalition of all Europe. Historians still debate his significance. Was he the last of the enlightened eighteenth-century monarchs, or the first modern military dictator? Did he successfully implement reform from above, or did he institute changes in a sinister attempt to create an authoritarian state? The cost of his rule was high: seven hundred fifty thousand French and four hundred thousand soldiers from annexed and satellite states died between 1800 and 1815. Yet no other military figure since Alexander the Great had made such an impact on world history. His plans for a united Europe, his insistence on spreading the legal reforms of the French Revolution, his social welfare programs, and even his inadvertent awakening of national sentiment set the agenda for European history in the modern era.

The "Restoration" of Europe

Even while Napoleon was making his last desperate bid for power, his enemies were meeting to decide the fate of postrevolutionary Europe in the Congress of Vienna (1814–1815). Although interrupted by the Hundred Days, the Congress of Vienna settled the boundaries of European states, determined who would rule each nation, and established a new framework for international relations based on periodic meetings or congresses between the Great Powers. The Congress system helped prevent another major war until the 1850s, and no conflict comparable to the Napoleonic wars would occur again until 1914. Many of Europe's rulers hoped to nullify revolutionary and Napoleonic reforms and thus "restore" their old

---

*Louis XVI's son was known as Louis XVII even though he died in prison in 1795 without ever ruling.

regimes. Some of the returning rulers so abominated revolutionary and Napoleonic innovations that they tore French plants out of their gardens and threw French furniture out of their palaces. Sometimes even reading or café-going might be dangerous. The most successful rulers, however, compromised between old traditions and new ideas. Total negation of the revolutionary legacy might work for a time, but in the long run, accommodation would prove unavoidable.

The Congress of Vienna

Like the Peace of Westphalia, which ended the Thirty Years' War in 1648, the Vienna settlement established a balance of power that endured for decades. All subsequent international conferences followed its procedures. With its aim to establish a permanent, negotiated peace endorsed by all parties, it provided a model for the League of Nations and the United Nations in the twentieth century. Even before the congress opened in 1814, Great Britain, Russia, Austria, and Prussia had agreed to remain allied for twenty years and to enforce French compliance with the peace terms. Austria's chief negotiator at the Congress of Vienna, Prince Klemens von Metternich (1773–1859), not only took the lead in devising the settlement but also went on to become one of the longest-serving chief ministers in history, holding office from 1809 until 1848. Although his penchant for womanizing made him a security risk in the eyes of the British Foreign Office (he even had an affair with Napoleon's younger sister), he worked with the British representatives to ensure a moderate agreement that would both check French aggression and still include France as a full-fledged participant in the forthcoming new order—and thus serve to balance the ambitions of the Prussians and Russians. The French representative was Prince Charles Maurice de Talleyrand (1754–1838), an aristocrat and former bishop who had embraced the Revolution, served as Napoleon's foreign minister, and ended as foreign minister to Louis XVIII after helping to arrange the emperor's overthrow. Napoleon called him "excrement in silk stockings." Through skillful maneuvering, Talleyrand managed to defend many French interests. Although French failure to oppose Napoleon's return to power in the Hundred Days caused the allies to take away all territory conquered since 1790 and to require

France to pay an indemnity and support an army of occupation until it had paid, the allies also recognized that the restored monarchy could succeed only if it retained its great-power status.

The Congress of Vienna imposed postwar stability either by restoring traditional rulers or by rearranging territory to benefit the major powers and balance their interests. The powers established a new Polish kingdom based on a shrunken version of the Napoleonic duchy of Warsaw, but they made the tsar of Russia its king; Poland would not regain its independence until 1918. The former Dutch Republic and the Austrian Netherlands united as the new kingdom of the Netherlands under the restored stadholder. Prussia gained territory in Saxony and on the left bank of the Rhine, and the kingdom of Sardinia (which included Piedmont) took Genoa, Nice, and part of Savoy. Wellington had already restored Ferdinand VII to the Spanish throne. Austria reclaimed the Italian provinces of Lombardy and Venetia and the Dalmatian coast. Other Italian rulers regained their thrones. The Congress established a Germanic Confederation that included Austria and Prussia along with many other smaller German states. Austria presided over the Germanic Confederation, which replaced the defunct Holy Roman Empire. Sweden obtained Norway from Denmark but had to accept Russia's conquest of Finland. Great Britain gave up almost all recent colonial conquests. In return the Congress agreed to condemn in principle the slave trade, abolished by Great Britain in 1807. Nevertheless, the abolition of the slave trade would remain ineffective without international cooperation.

To impart spiritual substance to this very calculated settlement of political affairs, and under the influence of various calls for religious revival, Tsar Alexander proposed a Holy Alliance to ensure divine assistance in upholding religion, peace, and justice. Prussia and Austria signed the agreement, but Great Britain refused to accede to what the British foreign minister called "a piece of sublime mysticism and nonsense." Pope Pius VII also refused on the grounds that the papacy needed no help in interpreting Christian truth. No one asked the Ottoman sultan to join. The Holy Alliance signaled the intent of the Great Powers in central and eastern Europe to resist any new movements for change, but is also showed that Great Britain was ready to stand aloof.

Jean-Baptiste Isabey, **The Congress of Vienna,** *1815 The French diplomat Talleyrand commissioned this sketch of a scene from the negotiations at the Congress of Vienna.*

Conservatism

The French Revolution and Napoleonic domination of Europe had shown that government could be changed overnight, that the old hierarchies could be overthrown in the name of reason, and that even Christianity could be written off or at least profoundly altered with the stroke of a pen. The potential for rapid change raised many questions. What should be the source of authority? What was the standard of belief? Kings and churches could be restored and former revolutionaries locked up or silenced, but the old order no longer commanded automatic obedience. The old order was now merely *old*, and no longer "natural" and "timeless." It had been ousted once and therefore might fall again. People insisted on reasons to believe in their "restored" governments. The answer was *conservatism*, the doctrine that change could not be based on reason alone but must include a proper respect for tradition and history. If change occurred at all, it should happen slowly.

Conservatives benefited from the disillusionment that permeated Europe. In the eyes of most Europeans, Napoleon had become a tyrant who ruled in his own interests. Conservatives believed it crucial to analyze the roots of such tyranny so established authorities could use their knowledge of history to prevent its recurrence. They saw a logical progression in recent history: the Enlightenment based on reason led to the French Revolution, with its bloody guillotine and horrifying Terror, which in turn spawned the authoritarian and militaristic Napoleon. Conservative intellectuals therefore either rejected Enlightenment principles or at least subjected them to scrutiny and skepticism.

Edmund Burke, the British critic of the French Revolution, founded conservatism. As early as 1790 he had laid out its rationale: the French revolutionaries erred in thinking they could construct an entirely new government based on reason, and as they persisted, they inevitably relied on force to ensure their rule. Government, Burke said, had to be rooted in long experience, which could only evolve over generations. "The science of constructing a commonwealth, or renovating it, or reforming it, is, like every other experimental science, not to be taught *a priori*." All change must be gradual and must respect national and historical traditions.

Like Burke, later conservative critics of the French Revolution and Napoleon believed religion to be an essential foundation for any society and a legitimate source of authority. Conservatives blamed the revolutionary attack on religion on the skepticism and anticlericalism of such Enlightenment thinkers as Voltaire, and they defended both

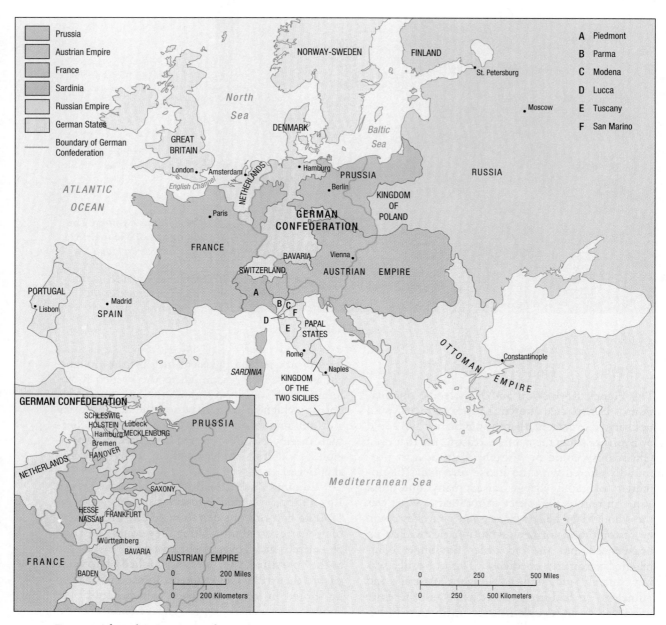

Europe After the Congress of Vienna, 1815

hereditary monarchy and the authority of the church, whether Catholic or Protestant. The "rights of man," according to conservatives, could not stand alone as a doctrine based simply on nature and reason. The community too had its rights, more important than those of any individual, and established institutions best represented these rights. The church, the state, and the patriarchal family would provide an enduring social order for everyone. Faith, sentiment, history, and tradition must fill the vacuum left by the failures of reason and excessive belief in individual rights. These views, developed by the French exiles Maistre and Bonald, were taken up and elaborated by government advisers, professors, and writers across Europe. Not surprisingly, they had their strongest appeal in ruling circles and guided the politics of men such as Metternich in Austria and Alexander I in Russia.

The restored monarchy in France provided a major test for conservatism because the returning Bourbons had to confront the legacy of twenty-five years of upheaval. Louis XVIII tried to ensure a measure of continuity by maintaining Napoleon's Civil Code. He also guaranteed the rights of ownership to church lands sold during the revolutionary period, and he created a parliament composed of a Chamber of Peers nominated by the king, and a Chamber of Deputies elected by very restricted suffrage (less than one hundred thousand voters in a population of 30 million). In making these concessions, the king tried to follow a moderate course of compromise, but the Ultras (ultraroyalists) pushed for complete repudiation of the revolutionary past. When Louis returned to power after Napoleon's final defeat, armed royalist bands attacked and murdered hundreds of Bonapartists and former revolutionaries. In 1816 the Ultras insisted on abolishing divorce and set up special courts to punish opponents of the regime. More extreme measures were to come.

The Revival of Religion

According to conservative doctrine, established churches provided crucial support to restored rulers. The restored monarchy in France hoped to benefit directly from Catholic revivalism. The Catholic church sent out missionaries to hold open-air meetings in an atmosphere of intense emotion. These meetings often included "ceremonies of reparation" to express repentance for the outrages of the Revolution. Such ceremonies sometimes backfired, however, when local opponents of the church's increased presence insisted on staging Molière's famous seventeenth-century play, *Tartuffe,* which attacked religious hypocrisy. Such conflicts sometimes led to rioting. In Rome the papacy reestablished the Jesuit order as an arm of its power. In the Italian states and Spain, governments used religious societies of laypeople to combat the influence of reformers and nationalists such as the Italian *carbonari.*

Revivalist movements, especially in Protestant countries, could also challenge the status quo. In parts of Protestant Germany and Britain, religious revival had begun in the eighteenth century with the rise of Pietism and Methodism, movements that stressed individual religious experience rather than reason as the true path to moral and social reform. In the Napoleonic period, Pietism sometimes took a millenarian* form, as Pietist prophets in the German states and northern European courts predicted the arrival of a man who would overthrow the Antichrist (Napoleon, according to many) and prepare the way for the Second Coming of Christ. A Russian noblewoman, Baroness Julie von Krüdener, was converted to these views in Germany. Her ecstatic prayer meetings drew such leading intellectuals as Chateaubriand and Tsar Alexander I, "the elect of God," according to the baroness. While in Paris the tsar held nightly prayer-séances with her, and her influence is evident in his Holy Alliance. Perhaps one-fourth of the middle- and lower-class Protestants in the German states adhered to some kind of millenarian belief. They believed the three decades after 1800 would be the most crucial ones in the history of humankind, and a few tried to move to Palestine, where they expected the Second Coming to occur. Because Palestine was closed to immigration, thousands of German millenarians moved to Ukraine and southern Russia as the next-best place.

The English Methodists followed John Wesley, who preached an emotional, morally austere, and very personal "method" of gaining salvation. The Methodists, or Wesleyans, gradually separated from the Church of England, and in the early decades of the nineteenth century attracted thousands of members in huge revival meetings that lasted for days. Shopkeepers, artisans, agricultural laborers, miners, and workers in cottage industry, both male and female, flocked to the new denomination, which at first seemed to emphasize conservative political views. Methodist statutes of 1792 had insisted that "None of us shall either in writing or in conversation speak lightly or irreverently of the government." In their hostility to rigid doctrine

---

Millenarian refers to the thousand-year reign of peace (the *millennium*) that according to Christian tradition would follow the overthrow of the Antichrist and precede the end of the world. Millenarian hopes have influenced many religiously tinged protest movements in the Western world.

and elaborate ritual and their encouragement of popular prophecy and preaching, however, the Methodists fostered a sense of democratic community, and even a rudimentary sexual equality. From the very beginning, women preachers traveled on horseback to preach in barns, town halls, and textile dye-houses. The Methodist Sunday schools that taught thousands of poor children to read and write eventually helped create greater demands for working-class political participation.

The religious revival was not limited to Europe. In the United States the second Great Awakening began around 1800 with huge camp meetings that brought together thousands of worshipers and scores of preachers. Men and women danced to exhaustion, fell into trances, and "spoke in tongues." During this same period, Protestant sects began systematic missionary activity in other parts of the world, with British and American missionary societies taking the lead in the 1790s and early 1800s. They were followed by the continental Protestants in the 1810s and 1820s, and later by Roman Catholics. Missionary activity would become one of the arms of European imperialism and cultural influence later in the nineteenth century.

Challenges to the Conservative Order

The lid Metternich hoped to clamp on European affairs kept threatening to fly off. In 1819 a disgruntled German student murdered the playwright August Kotzebue, who had ridiculed the student movement for German national unity. In France in 1820 an assassin killed Louis XVIII's nephew, the duke of Berry, inspiring a like-minded group to try, unsuccessfully, to blow up Britain's Tory cabinet. Revolts in Spain and the kingdom of Naples were followed by uprisings in Greece and Russia. Challenges to the conservative order also came from more subtle, long-term trends; rapid urban growth and the spread of industry created new social tensions and inspired novel doctrines to explain the meaning of economic and social changes. Then in 1830 a startling series of revolts compromised the entire Vienna settlement. Across Europe, many sought constitutional guarantees of individual liberties and the right of national self-determination.

Gradual change could not satisfy their longing for immediate and far-reaching solutions. The proponents of reform and revolution shared few common goals, however, and despite many anxious moments, Metternichian conservatism survived.

Industrial Growth in Britain

In the long run the set of social and economic changes termed *industrialization* profoundly transformed the life of every European. In Britain the Industrial Revolution, which began in the late eighteenth century, ran well ahead of industrialization on the Continent. By the first decades of the nineteenth century, new factories and steam-powered machinery dotted the British landscape. Machines and the factories that housed them would eventually destroy a traditional way of life in which work had been largely agricultural, home-based, and driven by human and animal power. In the early nineteenth century, however, these changes still affected only a relatively small segment of the population.

The textile industry pioneered the new methods of production, first for spinning cotton (imported from the colonies) into thread, and then for weaving cloth. Larger, steam-driven machines made possible the production of more cotton cloth. As supply increased, cotton goods became cheaper. Middle- and lower-class Britons could now purchase more cotton clothing, including underwear (still a novelty for many). The new machines increasingly brought workers together in factories. More than 1 million people in Britain depended on the cotton industry for employment in 1830, and cotton cloth constituted 50 percent of the country's exports.

By the early nineteenth century, factories were springing up in urban areas, where the growing urban population provided a ready source of labor. The population surge in the cities, which began in the eighteenth century, now accelerated. The reasons for urban growth are not entirely clear, however. The population of such new industrial cities as Manchester and Leeds increased 40 percent in the 1820s alone. Historians long thought the factory workers came from the countryside, pushed off the land by the field enclosures of the 1700s. But recent studies have shown that the number of agricultural laborers actually increased during industrialization in Britain, suggesting that a growing birthrate created a larger population and fed workers into the new factory system.

The new workers came from the families of farmers who could not provide land for all their children, soldiers demobilized after the Napoleonic Wars, artisans displaced by the new machinery, and children of the earliest workers who had moved to the factory towns. A system of family employment that resembled family labor on farms or in cottage industry also developed in the new factories. Entire families came to toil for a single wage, although family members performed different tasks. Work days of twelve to seventeen hours were typical and the work was grueling, but parents could maintain contact with and control their children, much as they had always done. Community ties also remained important as workers migrated from rural to urban areas. Many new arrivals joined friends, relatives, and neighbors, often working for subcontractors who provided a service for a manufacturer and thus hired and supervised the workers needed for the job. New Irish arrivals in northern English industrial cities frequently found work in this way, filling the mills after economic decline and population growth in Ireland forced great numbers to migrate.

As urban factories grew, their workers gradually came to constitute a new socioeconomic class with a distinctive culture and traditions. Like *middle class*, the term *working class* came into use only in the first decades of the nineteenth century. It referred first to the laborers in the new factories. Thousands of people working for daily wages had always lived in European cities; in Paris in 1791, for example, such workers and their families made up about half the population. But these people had worked in isolated trades: water and wood carrying, gardening, laundry, and building. In contrast, factories brought working people together with machines, under close supervision by their employers. They soon developed a sense of common interests and organized for mutual help and political reform.

The new factories and new technology threatened some people's very existence, especially in hard times. In Britain, when the effects of Napoleon's wars were compounded by bad harvests, the resulting unemployment and rising food prices struck hard at the lower classes, especially textile workers. To protect livelihoods menaced by the introduction of new technology, bands of skilled workers called Luddites* wrecked new machinery and burned mills in the Midlands, Yorkshire, and Lancashire. To restore order and protect industry, the government sent in an army of twelve thousand regular soldiers and made machine wrecking punishable by death.

Other workers focused their organizing efforts on reforming Parliament, whose members were chosen in elections dominated by the landowning elite. In his *Black Book: or Corruption Unmasked* of 1819, John Wade denounced the aristocracy for "usurping the power of the state." They "patronise a ponderous and sinecure church establishment; they wage long and unnecessary wars . . . create offices without duties, grant unmerited pensions." Another reformer complained that the members of the House of Commons were nothing but "toadeaters, gamblers, public plunderers, and hirelings." Reform clubs held large open-air meetings, and ordinary people eagerly bought cheap newspapers that clamored for change. In August 1819, sixty thousand people attended an illegal meeting held in St. Peter's Fields in Manchester. When the local authorities sent the cavalry to arrest the speaker, panic resulted; eleven people were killed and many hundreds injured. Punsters called it the Battle of Peterloo or the Peterloo Massacre, but an alarmed government passed the Six Acts, which forbade large political meetings and restricted press criticism, suppressing the reform movement for a decade.

Even as reform agitation subsided, a new mode of transportation—the railroad—appeared. The idea of a railroad was not new. Iron tracks were first used to haul coal from mines in wagons pulled by horses or a stationary engine. A railroad system as a mode of transport, however, developed only after the invention of a steam-powered locomotive. In the 1820s, English engineer George Stephenson perfected an engine to pull wagons over rail tracks. Suddenly, railroad building became a new industry. New companies manufactured rails and laid track, with Parliament's permission.

In 1830 the new Liverpool and Manchester Railway line opened to the cheers of crowds and the congratulations of government officials, in-

---

*They got their name from a fictitious figure named Ned Ludd, whose signature appeared on many of their manifestos.

The Opening of a New English Railway Line, 1830 The opening of a new railway line was cause for general celebration.

cluding the Duke of Wellington, the hero of Waterloo and now prime minister. In the excitement some of the dignitaries gathered on a parallel track. Another engine, George Stephenson's famous "Rocket," approached at high speed. Most of the gentlemen scattered to safety, but former cabinet minister William Huskisson fell and was hit. In a few hours he died, the first official casualty of the new-fangled railroad. Despite the tragedy, the line was an immediate success, carrying up to 110 passengers and freight in each direction. One of the many commentators described it as "a kind of miracle exhibited before my astonished eyes."

Railroads were dramatic and expensive—the most striking symbol of the new industrial age—but the key to industrial development was the steam engine itself. Placed on the new tracks, steam-driven carriages could transport people and goods to the cities and link coal and iron deposits to the new factories. As the steam engine had gradually replaced horses and water wheels as sources of power, so now it could begin to replace barges and wagons for transportation. Steam engines helped concentrate workers in factories. Towns then sprouted around the factories; tools and machinery became heavier, more automatic, more precise, and easier to operate; and more goods could be produced quickly and cheaply. As the Scottish

essayist Thomas Carlyle wrote in 1831, "Nothing is done now directly, or by hand; all is rule and calculated contrivance."

Historians today use the term *Industrial Revolution* to describe the set of changes that brought steam-driven machinery, large factories, and a new working class first to Britain, then to the rest of Europe, and eventually to the rest of the world. French and English writers of the 1820s introduced the term to capture the drama of contemporary change and to draw a parallel with the French Revolution. But we should not take the comparison too literally. Unlike the French upheaval, the Industrial Revolution was not over in a decade. From Great Britain in the second half of the eighteenth century it had spread slowly, and by the 1830s it still had little effect on the Continent outside of northern France, Belgium, and the Rhineland. Most Europeans were still peasants working in the old ways.

New Social and Political Doctrines

Although traditional ways of life still prevailed in much of Europe, new modes of thinking about the social and political order arose in direct response to what some have called the "dual revolution" of the French Revolution and the Industrial Revolution. The 1820s and 1830s were an era of "isms"—

conservatism, romanticism, nationalism, liberalism, and newest on the scene, socialism. Even conservatives now had to articulate and justify their vision of a proper social order. The French Revolution had caused people to ask questions about the best possible form of government, and its effects had made clear that people acting together could change their political system. The events of the 1790s and the decades that followed, however, also produced enormous differences of opinion over what constituted the ideal government. Similarly, the Industrial Revolution, first in Britain and then in western Europe, posed fundamental questions about changes in society and social relations: How did the new social order differ from an earlier one, less urban and less driven by commercial concerns? Who should control this new order? Should governments try to moderate or accelerate the pace of change? Answers to these questions about the social and political order were called *ideologies*, a word coined during the French Revolution. An *ideology* is a coherent doctrine about the way a society's social and political order should be organized. In the 1830s and 1840s, ideologies served as the unifying force in new political and social movements induced by the gradual industrialization of Europe.

Many modern ideologies originated between 1799 and 1830, as industrial change surged in Britain and began to spread to the Continent. We have already seen how conservatism developed in reaction to the Enlightenment and the French Revolution. Conservatives also deeply distrusted the new urban, industrial order. Liberals, unlike conservatives, generally applauded the changes and believed greater liberty in politics and economic matters would promote social improvement and economic growth. The leaders of the bourgeoisie, that rapidly expanding middle group in society (neither aristocrats nor wage workers) composed of manufacturers, merchants, and professionals, favored liberalism. As a doctrine, liberalism first appeared in the writings of Locke in the seventeenth century and the Enlightenment philosophy of the eighteenth. Liberals' demands varied from country to country. In divided countries like Italy, liberals allied with movements for national unification. In France and Britain, liberals agitated largely for parliamentary reforms, including more middle-class representation, but also wanted economic changes: they wanted free trade because they believed lifting tariffs would lower prices, increase consumption, and consequently stimulate economic activity. Economic liberalism was much less important in countries, such as Spain, where commercial and industrial change had not yet affected much of society.

The foremost exponent of early nineteenth-century liberalism was the English philosopher and jurist Jeremy Bentham (1748–1832). He advocated the doctrine called *utilitarianism*, which held that the best policy is the one that produces "the greatest good for the greatest number," thus the most useful, or utilitarian. Such views clearly challenged aristocratic values with their emphasis on bloodlines and privilege. Bentham's criticisms spared no institution; he railed against the injustices of the British parliamentary process, the abuses of the prisons and the penal code, and the bad educational system. In his zeal for social engineering he proposed elaborate schemes for managing the poor by placing them in *industry-houses* run by private enterprise and model prisons that would emphasize rehabilitation through close supervision rather than corporal punishment. British liberals like Bentham wanted government reforms, including deregulation of trade, but they shied away from any association with revolutionary violence.

Bentham and many other liberals joined the antislavery movement that intensified between the 1790s and 1820s. One English abolitionist put the matter in these terms: "[God] has given to us an unexampled portion of civil liberty; and we in return drag his rational creatures into a most severe and perpetual bondage." The contradiction between calling for more liberty at home and maintaining slavery in the West Indies seemed intolerable to liberals and to many religious groups, especially the Quakers, who since the 1780s had taken the lead in forming antislavery societies in both the United States and Great Britain. Agitation by such groups as the London Society for Effecting the Abolition of the Slave Trade eventually succeeded, at least in gaining a first victory, when in 1807 the British House of Lords voted to abolish the slave trade. Throughout the 1820s, antislavery activism expanded in the United States, Great Britain, and France because the slave trade still continued in some countries and because slavery itself had not been abolished. As one disappointed British abolitionist explained in 1830:

We supposed that when by the abolition of the slave trade the planters could get no more slaves, they would not only treat better those whom they then had in their power, but that they would gradually find it to their advantage to emancipate them. . . . We did not sufficiently take into account the effect of unlimited power.

The newest ideology of the 1820s, socialism, responded even more directly than liberalism to the challenges prompted by industrialization. New industries provided new jobs, but many workers lived in appalling conditions in cramped, dark, and dank housing near factories that spewed out clouds of dangerous smoke. The early socialists, who came from diverse backgrounds, agreed with liberals in hailing progress and supporting individual liberty. But they sought to reorganize society totally rather than to reform it piecemeal through political measures. They were *utopians* who believed ideal communities are based on cooperation rather than competition.* Socialists criticized the new industrial order for dividing society into two classes: the new middle classes, or capitalists, who owned the wealth; and the toiling workers, their downtrodden and impoverished employees. Such divisions tore the social fabric; the socialists, as their name suggested, aimed to restore harmony and cooperation through social reorganization. Robert Owen (1771–1858), a successful manufacturer, founded British socialism. In 1800 he bought a cotton mill in New Lanark, Scotland, and began to set up a model factory town, where workers labored only ten hours a day (instead of seventeen, as was common) and children between the ages of five and ten years attended school rather than working in the factory. Out of his experiments and writings, such as *The Book of the New Moral World* (1820), would come the movement for cooperative communities, cooperative stores, and a national trade union. Mov-

ing to the United States, in the 1820s he took over an existing community in Indiana and renamed it New Harmony in accordance with his principles. The experiment collapsed, however, after three years.

Owen's counterparts in France were Claude Henri de Saint-Simon (1760–1825) and Charles Fourier (1772–1837). Saint-Simon was a noble who had served as an officer in the American War for Independence and lost a fortune speculating in national property during the French Revolution. Fourier traveled as a salesman for a Lyon cloth merchant. Both shared Owen's alarm about the effects of industrialization. Saint-Simon believed that work was the central element in the new society and that it should be controlled not by politicians, but by scientists, engineers, artists, and the industrialists themselves. Saint-Simon coined the terms *industrialism* and *industrialist*. To correct the abuses of the new industrial order, Fourier urged the establishment of phalanxes or phalansteries that were part garden city and part agricultural commune; all jobs would be rotated to maximize happiness. Fourier hoped that a network of small, decentralized communities would replace the state. The emancipation of women was essential to Fourier's vision of a harmonious community: "The extension of the privileges of women is the fundamental cause of all social progress." Fourier's projects sometimes included outlandish predictions: he envisioned a world in which the oceans would turn into lemonade and the population would include 37 million poets equal to Homer, 37 million mathematicians equal to Newton, and 37 million dramatists equal to Molière—more or less!

Utopianism always has its fringe elements, and the socialists were no exception. After Saint-Simon's death in 1825, some of his followers established a quasi-religious cult with bizarre robes and strange rituals, a "he-pope" and "she-pope," or ruling father and mother. Saint-Simonians lived and worked together in cooperative arrangements and scandalized some by advocating free love. They set up branches in the United States and Egypt. In 1832, Saint-Simonian women founded a feminist newspaper, *The Free Woman*, asserting that "With the emancipation of woman will come the emancipation of the worker." These early utopian social-

---

*The word *utopian* comes from Thomas More's sixteenth-century work *Utopia*, a depiction of an ideal society based on reason, in which private property did not exist. The ultimate origin of such "utopian" plans lay in Plato's *Republic.*

ists, however, were lonely voices. Their emphasis on community and cooperation gained more adherents after 1830.

New Nationalist Aspirations

Unlike liberalism and socialism, nationalism offered no specific social remedies. But in the right circumstances it could appeal to all social classes. People who shared a language, ethnic traditions, and a cultural heritage had long felt national solidarity, but this feeling suddenly became more intense in reaction to Napoleonic domination. Once Napoleon and his satellite rulers departed, nationalist sentiment turned against other outside rulers—the Ottoman Turks in the Balkans, the Russians in Poland, and the Austrians in Italy. Intellectuals took the lead in demanding unity and freedom for their peoples. They collected folk tales, poems, and histories and prepared grammars and dictionaries of their native languages. Students, middle-class professionals, and army officers formed secret societies to promote national independence and constitutional reform.

Nationalist aspirations were potentially explosive for the Austrian Empire, which included a variety of peoples united only by their enforced allegiance to the Habsburg emperor. The empire included three main national groups: the Germans, who made up one-fourth of the population; the Magyars of Hungary (which included Transylvania and Croatia); and the Slavs, who together formed the largest group in the population but were divided into such nationalities as Poles, Czechs, Croats, and Serbs. The empire also included Italians in Lombardy and Venetia and Romanians in Transylvania. Efforts to govern such diverse peoples preoccupied Metternich, chief minister to the weak emperor, Francis I (＊1792–1835). Metternich's domestic policy aimed to restrain nationalist impulses, and it largely succeeded until the 1840s.

As a conservative, Metternich believed the experience of the French Revolution proved the superiority of monarchy and aristocracy as forms of government and society. But he did not hesitate to use new methods of governing when necessary. Consequently, he set up a secret police on the Napoleonic model. The secret police opened letters of even the highest officials, reported any "suspicious" conversations, and followed travelers. Censorship in the Italian provinces was so strict that even the works of Dante were expurgated, and Metternich announced that "the Lombards must forget that they are Italians." In reaction, novelists, playwrights, and poets used their pens to arouse nationalist sentiment. Membership in secret societies such as the *carbonari* grew; before the fall of Napoleon, many had been clerical and anti-French, but now the societies turned anti-Austrian and supported political rights and national self-determination. The societies had no common program across Italy and no central organization, but they attracted tens of thousands of members, including physicians, lawyers, officers, and students.

The new Germanic Confederation had a federal diet, or assembly, but it largely functioned as a tool of Metternich's policies. Some rulers in the smaller German states granted constitutions, but always with extremely limited political participation. Returning rulers and those who had kept their thrones usually had little interest in sharing power. The landed aristocracy continued to control the important positions in the army and in the government bureaucracy. The only sign of resistance in the German states came from university students, who formed nationalist student societies, or *Burschenschaften*. By 1816, sixteen German universities had such fraternities, and in 1817 they held a mass rally at which they burned books they did not like, including Napoleon's Civil Code. One of their leaders, Friedrich Ludwig Jahn, spouted such xenophobic slogans as, "If you let your daughter learn French, you might just as well train her to become a whore." Metternich was convinced that the *Burschenschaften* in the German states and the *carbonari* in Italy were linked in an international conspiracy, and in 1820, after the assassination of Kotzebue, he convinced the leaders of the biggest German states to pass the Karlsbad Decrees dissolving the student societies and more strictly censoring the press. Continuing secret-police surveillance failed to uncover any plots.

Tsar Alexander faced similar problems in his "Congress Kingdom" (so-called because the Congress of Vienna had created it) of Poland, which in 1815 was one of Europe's more liberal states. The

The Wartburg Rally of 1817
In October 1817, German student societies held a festival at which they burned anti-patriotic books and such un-German items as French corsets.

tsar reigned in Poland as a limited monarch, having bestowed a constitution that provided for an elected parliament, a national army, and guarantees of free speech and a free press. But by 1818, Alexander had begun retracting his concessions. Falling under the influence of religious mysticism, the tsar strengthened religious control of education and established complex censorship regulations throughout Russian lands. Polish students and military officers responded by forming secret nationalist societies to plot for change by illegal means. The government then cracked down, arresting student leaders and dismissing professors who promoted reforms. By the 1820s, Polish nationalists and the Russian imperial government were on a collision course.

Liberal and Nationalist Movements on the Periphery

The new social and political doctrines offered more than ideas; they could galvanize large populations into action. Liberal and nationalist demands fueled political upheavals in the 1820s in Spain, Italy, Russia, and Greece, and across the Atlantic, in the Spanish and Portuguese colonies. Most of these up-

risings failed because they lacked widespread popular support and because Metternich's Congress system of great-power collaboration sustained existing monarchs on their thrones. But where national self-determination provided additional leverage and the Congress powers could not agree on a common policy, as in Greece, nationalist movements sometimes succeeded.

When Ferdinand VII regained the Spanish crown in 1814, he first accepted the liberal constitution of 1812. But then he moved quickly to restore the prerevolutionary nobility, church, and monarchy. He had foreign books and newspapers confiscated at the frontier and allowed the publication of only two newspapers. Not surprisingly, such reactionary policies disturbed the middle classes and the army officers who had encountered French ideas. Many responded by joining secret societies. Ferdinand also faced a liberation movement in Latin America that had begun during Napoleon's occupation of Spain. In 1820 an army contingent headed for Latin America demanded that Ferdinand first proclaim his adherence to the Constitution of 1812, which he had abolished in 1814. When the revolt spread from the army to Spanish cities, Ferdinand agreed to call the Cortes (parliament), which passed several measures against the church before being crippled by internal disagreements. Ferdinand bided his time, and in 1823 a French army invaded and restored him to absolute power. The French acted with the con-

Revolutionary Movements of the 1820s

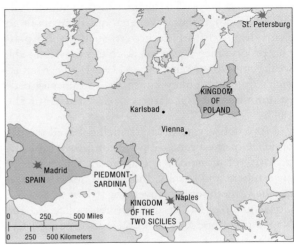

sent of the Congress of Vienna powers, who had convened another conference to discuss the Spanish situation and determine a common course of action. The restored Spanish government hanged the rebel leader and hacked his body into five parts, which were exhibited in the five towns where he had been best known. Hundreds were tortured and executed; thousands were imprisoned or forced into exile.

The uprising in Spain proved contagious. Hearing of the Spanish constitutional struggles, rebellious soldiers in the kingdom of Naples (part of the Kingdom of the Two Sicilies) joined forces with the *carbonari* and demanded their own constitution. When a new parliament met, it too was stymied by struggles over the form the new government should take. Meanwhile the promise of reform sparked rebellion in the north Italian kingdom of Piedmont, where rebels urged the young heir to the throne, Charles Albert, to fight the Austrians for Italian unification. He vacillated; but in 1821, after the rulers of Austria, Prussia, and Russia met and agreed on intervention, the Austrians defeated the rebels in Naples and Piedmont. Liberals were arrested in many Italian states, and the pope condemned the secret societies as "at heart only devouring wolves." Despite the opposition of Great Britain, which condemned the "indiscriminate" suppression of revolutionary movements, Metternich had used the Congress system to obtain diplomatic sanction for his suppression of the Italian revolts.

Aspirations for constitutional government surfaced in Russia when Alexander I died suddenly in 1825. His two equally reactionary brothers, Nicholas and Constantine, each proclaimed the other as tsar, and in the uncertainty, military secret societies planned an uprising called the Decembrist Revolt. On the December day that the troops in St. Petersburg assembled to take an oath of loyalty to Nicholas, rebel officers insisted that the crown belonged to Constantine. Their men raised the cry "Long live Constantine, long live the Constitution." (Some troops apparently thought that "Constitution" was Constantine's wife.) Soldiers loyal to Nicholas easily suppressed them. The Decembrists were so outnumbered that they had no realistic chance of success, but their subsequent trial created a legend for future Russian revolutionary movements. Of their imprisonment at hard

labor, Alexander Pushkin (1799–1837), the supreme Russian poet, wrote:

> The heavy-hanging chains will fall,
> The walls will crumble at a word,
> And Freedom greet you in the light,
> And brothers give you back the sword.

The day of liberation would be long in coming, however. Nicholas I (✳1825–1855) for the next thirty years used a new political police, the Third Section, to spy on potential opponents and quash any hint of rebelliousness.

The Greek movement for independence succeeded, largely because it was a nationalist movement against the Ottoman Turks, who lacked support in Christian Europe and whose authority had been declining steadily. Bosnians, Montenegrins,

Eugène Delacroix, **Massacre at Chios,** *1824*
Delacroix used the techniques of romanticism—vivid colors, emotional scenes, depiction of exotic places—to capture European sympathies in favor of the Greek struggle for independence from the Turks.

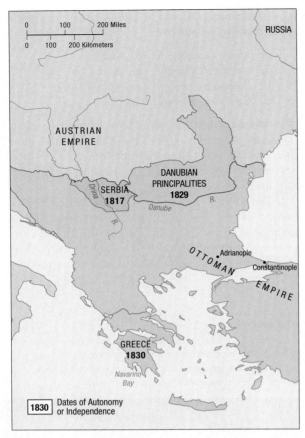

Nationalist Movements in the Balkans, 1815–1830

and Serbs all revolted against Turkish rule in the Balkans, and the Serbs won de facto independence by the 1820s. As the French ambassador explained to Chateaubriand when the writer visited Constantinople in 1807, "To make an alliance with Turkey is the same as putting your arms around a corpse to make it stand up!" The sultans of the Ottoman Empire relied on the intermittent cooperation of local Muslim authorities in northern Africa, while in the Christian Balkans, Greeks controlled the administrative system. In addition to their vital positions in the Ottoman administration, Greeks dominated much of the commerce in the Near East and had access to fashionable nationalist ideas as well as to European sympathy for the home of Western civilization. The sons of Greek merchant families studied abroad, where they learned to organize secret societies dedicated to nationalist goals. A secret society, *Hetairia Philike*, soon included most Greek leaders in Constantino-

ple, and in 1820 a Greek general in the Russian army, Prince Alexander Ypsilanti, became its leader. His revolt in 1821 failed when the tsar, urged on by Metternich, who feared rebellion even by Christians against Turks, disavowed him.

The *Hetairia's* second revolt, this time by Greek peasants in one of the provinces, sparked a wave of atrocities. The Greeks killed every Turk who did not escape to a walled town; in retaliation the Turks hanged the Greek patriarch of Constantinople, and in the areas they still controlled systematically pillaged churches, massacred thousands of men, and sold the women into slavery. Western opinion turned against the Turks. While the diplomats of the Great Powers negotiated, public opinion surged in support of the Greek nationalists. Greeks and pro-Greece committees around the world sent food and military supplies; a few enthusiastic European and American volunteers came to fight, among them the English poet Byron, who died in Greece in 1824.

The Greeks held on until the Great Powers were willing to intervene. In 1827 a combined force of British, French, and Russian ships destroyed the Turkish fleet at Navarino Bay; and in 1828, Russia declared war on Turkey and advanced close to Constantinople. The Treaty of Adrianople of 1829 gave Russia a protectorate over the Danubian principalities in the Balkans and provided for a conference among representatives of Britain, Russia, and France, all of whom had broken with Austria in support of the Greeks. In 1830, Greece was declared an independent kingdom under the guarantee of the three powers; in 1833 the son of King Ludwig of Bavaria became Otto I of Greece. Nationalism, with the support of European public opinion, had made its first breach in Metternich's system.

Across the Atlantic, national revolts also succeeded after a bloody series of wars of independence. Taking advantage of the upheavals in Spain that began under Napoleon's rule, restive colonists from Mexico to Argentina rebelled. Their leader was Simon Bolívar, son of a slaveowner, who was educated in Europe on the works of Voltaire and Rousseau. Although Bolívar fancied himself a Latin American Napoleon, he had to acquiesce to the formation of a series of independent republics between 1821 and 1823, even in Bolivia, which is named after him. At the same time, Brazil (then still a monarchy) separated from Portugal. The

Latin American Independence, 1804–1830

United States recognized the new states, and in 1823, President James Monroe announced his Monroe Doctrine, closing the Americas to European intervention—a prohibition that depended on British naval power and British willingness to declare neutrality.

Revolution and Reform in Western Europe

Liberal and nationalist revolts broke out again in 1830, this time threatening the established order in western Europe more seriously. In most places students, journalists, and professionals spearheaded these uprisings. The signal for rebellion flared in Paris, the home of the revolutionary tradition. Louis XVIII's younger brother and successor, Charles X (✴1824–1830), brought about his own downfall by steering the monarchy in an in-

creasingly reactionary direction. In 1825 a Law of Indemnity compensated nobles who had emigrated during the Revolution for the loss of their estates, and a Law of Sacrilege (1825) imposed the death penalty for such offenses as stealing religious objects from churches. Those excluded from political participation resented the close alliance between monarchy, nobility, and church, and they began to form political societies and newspapers to promote reform. Charles enraged liberals when he dissolved the legislature, removed many wealthy and powerful voters from the rolls, and imposed strict censorship. Spontaneous demonstrations in Paris led to fighting on July 26, 1830. After only three days of street battles in which five hundred citizens and one hundred fifty soldiers died, a group of moderate liberal leaders, fearing the reestablishment of a republic, agreed to give the crown to Charles X's cousin, Louis-Phillipe, duke of Orleans. Charles X went into exile in England, and the new king extended political liberties and voting rights. Although the number of voting men nearly doubled, it remained minuscule—approximately 170,000 in a country of 30 million. Such reforms did little for the poor and working classes, who had manned the barricades in July. Dissatisfaction with the 1830 settlement boiled over in Lyon in 1831, when a silk-workers' strike over wages turned into a rebellion that died down only when the army arrived. Discontent ran high throughout the early 1830s.

The success of the July Revolution in Paris ignited the Belgians, who had been annexed to the kingdom of the Netherlands in 1815. Differences

Revolutions of 1830

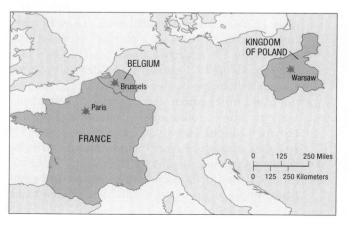

in traditions, language, and religion separated the Dutch from the largely Catholic Belgians. An opera about a seventeenth-century insurrection in Naples provided the spark, and students in Brussels rioted, shouting "Down with the Dutch." The riot turned into revolt. King William of the Netherlands appealed to the Great Powers to intervene; after all, the Congress of Vienna had established his kingdom. But Great Britain and France opposed intervention and invited Russia, Austria, and Prussia to a conference that guaranteed Belgium independence in exchange for Belgian neutrality in international affairs. After much maneuvering, the crown of the new kingdom of Belgium was offered to a German prince, Leopold of Saxe-Coburg, in 1831. Belgium, like France and Britain, would have a constitutional monarchy.

The Russian tsar and the Austrian emperor would have supported intervention in Belgium had they not been preoccupied with their own revolts. Anti-Austrian uprisings erupted in a handful of Italian states, but they fizzled without the hoped-for French aid. The Polish revolt was more serious. Once again, in response to news of revolution in France, students raised the banner of rebellion, this time in Warsaw in November 1830. Polish aristocrats soon formed a provisional government, but they were divided between those who wanted to negotiate with the tsar and others who refused all compromise. Despite some victories on the battlefield, and lacking aid from the liberal powers, the Poles lost. In reprisal, Nicholas abolished the Polish constitution Alexander had granted and ordered thousands of Poles executed or banished. He had completely suppressed the revolt by early 1832. The wave of revolution in the 1830s subsided relatively quickly, but the issues that inspired it remained.

Great Britain, too, reached a fever pitch in the early 1830s over the perennial issue of electoral reform. Earlier, in the 1820s, popular agitation had focused on the Queen Caroline Affair. In 1820, George IV (∗1820–1830) succeeded his father George III. When he came to the throne, the unpopular former prince regent tried to divorce his German wife Caroline, and he refused to have her crowned queen. The divorce trial provoked massive demonstrations, part melodrama and part serious politics, in support of the queen. Women's groups gathered thousands of signatures on petitions supporting the queen, and popular songs and

> ## Restoration Europe
>
> **1814–1815** The Congress of Vienna settles the boundaries of Europe
>
> **1819** The "Battle of Peterloo" in Manchester, England, pits the police against a large crowd of demonstrators for political reform
>
> **1820** Robert Owen, in *The Book of the New Moral World,* lays out a program for cooperative communities; revolt of liberal army officers against the Spanish crown; the Karlsbad Decrees abolish German student societies and tighten press censorship
>
> **1825** Russian army officers demand constitutional reform in the Decembrist Revolt
>
> **1830** The Manchester and Liverpool Railway opens in England; Greece gains its independence from Ottoman Turks; rebels overthrow Charles X of France and install Louis-Philippe; revolt leads to the independence of Belgium from the Kingdom of the Netherlands; Polish revolt against Russian rule eventually fails
>
> **1832** English Parliament passes the Reform Bill, extending voting rights to more men

satires portrayed George as a fat, drunken libertine. The monarchy seemed endangered. The scandal quieted only when Caroline died a few months after George's coronation.

The 1820s had brought into British government new men who were at least open to change. Sir Robert Peel (1788–1850), the secretary for home affairs, revised the criminal code to reduce the number of crimes punishable by death and introduced a municipal police force in London, called the *Bobbies* after him. In 1824 the laws prohibiting labor unions were repealed, and though restrictions on strikes remained, workers could now organize themselves legally to confront their employers collectively. The appointment of the national hero, the Duke of Wellington, as prime minister in 1828 kept the Tories in power, and his government pushed through a bill in 1829 for Catholic emancipation, which allowed Catholics to sit in Parliament and hold most public offices.

When in 1830 and again in 1831 the Whigs in Parliament proposed an extension of the right to

A

BILL

To deprive Her MAJESTY Caroline Amelia Elizabeth of the Title, Prerogatives, Rights, Privileges, and Pretensions of Queen Consort of this Realm, and to dissolve the Marriage between His MAJESTY and the said Queen.

Popular Propaganda During the Queen Caroline Affair This print shows the purported attempt to whitewash George IV while blackening the reputation of his wife Caroline.

vote, Tory diehards, principally in the House of Lords, dug in their heels and predicted that even the most modest proposals would doom civilization itself. This conservative recalcitrance led middle-class reformers once again to encourage the development of political organizations. Even though the proposed law would not grant universal male suffrage, mass demonstrations in favor of it took place in many cities. One supporter of reform described the scene: "Meetings of almost every description of persons were held in cities, towns, and parishes; by journeymen tradesmen in their clubs, and by common workmen who had no trade clubs or associations of any kind." In this "state of diseased and feverish excitement" (according to its opponents), the Reform Bill of 1832 passed, when the king threatened to create enough new peers to obtain its passage in the House of Lords.

Although the Reform Bill altered the political structure in significant ways, the gains were not revolutionary. One of the bill's foremost backers, the historian and Parliament member Thomas Macaulay, explained, "I am opposed to Universal Suffrage, because I think that it would produce a destructive revolution. I support this plan, because

I am sure that it is our best security against a revolution." Although the number of male voters increased by about 50 percent, only one in five Britons could now vote, and voting still depended on holding property. Nevertheless, the bill gave representation to new cities in the industrial north for the first time and set a precedent for further widening the right to vote. Exclusive aristocratic politics now gave way to a more mixed, middle-class and aristocratic structure that would prove more responsive to the problems of a fast-growing, industrial society.

Romanticism

Cutting across and drawing on the turmoil in society and politics was romanticism, a new international movement in the arts and literature that glorified emotionalism and opposed the rationalism of eighteenth-century classicism. Where the Enlightenment had emphasized classical reason, harmony, and modern progress through science and rational knowledge, the romantics turned to nature, history, folklore, and their own feelings. The romantics glorified the individual, the hero, the genius, and the free flights of the imagination that inspired creativity. As the young and dashing English poet George Gordon Byron (1788–1824) explained in his own poetry,

> *For what is Poesy but to create*
> *From overfeeling, Good and Ill, and aim*
> *At an external life beyond our fate,*
> *And be the new Prometheus of new man.*

The "new man" of romanticism was created by poetry, not politics, as in the revolutionary legacy. Like Prometheus, the mythological figure who brought fire from the Greek gods to humans, romantic heroes or heroines risked everything for their creative impulses, their "overfeeling," and their willingness to aim beyond the mundane circumstances of daily life.

Romantics shared no single political view, and some avoided politics to focus exclusively on artistic concerns. The aristocratic Byron supported liberal and nationalist causes; "I have simplified my politics," he announced, "into a detestation of all existing governments." The French novelist and essayist Chateaubriand, in contrast, was an ardent royalist and Catholic. The English poets William Wordsworth (1770–1850) and Samuel Taylor Coleridge (1772–1834) eventually turned against the "excesses" of the French Revolution, which they had once supported. The French writers Alphonse de Lamartine (1790–1869) and Victor Hugo (1802–1885) backed the restored monarchy but turned to republican ideals after 1830. In the midst of this cacophony of beliefs, most romatics shared one lament: they bemoaned the ugly conformity brought by the growth of industry.

If romantics had any common political thread, it was the support of nationalist aspirations. In the German states, the Austrian Empire, Russia and other Slavic lands, and Scandinavia, romantic poets and writers collected old legends and folk tales that expressed a cultural and linguistic heritage stretching back to the Middle Ages. This romantic nationalism permeated the enormously popular historical novels of Sir Walter Scott (1771–1832) in Great Britain and *The Betrothed*, a novel by Alessandro Manzoni (1785–1873) that constituted a kind of Bible for Italian nationalists. Romantic nationalism received support from the most prominent philosopher of the time, Georg W. F. Hegel (1770–1831), who argued that the conservative Prussian state represented the highest development of humankind's reason, though he also unsettled the establishment when he stressed a *dialectical* pattern of change in which old institutions continually gave way to new ones. Deeply influenced by the French Revolution and the rise and fall of Napoleon, whom he dubbed "world history on horseback," Hegel insisted that history itself revealed the inner meaning of human life. Like a surrogate religion, history divulged the operation of the world spirit, which was none other than reason itself. The ambiguity of Hegel's doctrine allowed for contradictory interpretations, either as a support for the status quo or as a promise of greater changes to come.

The most influential arts in the romantic movement were poetry, music, and painting because they captured the deep-seated emotion characteristic of romantic expression. Beethoven's music, according to one leading German romantic, "sets in motion the lever of fear, of awe, of horror, of suffering, and awakens just that infinite longing which is the essence of Romanticism." Beethoven's towering presence in early nineteenth-century music helped set the course for musical romanticism. He transformed the symphony into a connected work with recurring and evolving musical themes. Romantic symphonies conveyed the impression of growth, a metaphor for the organic process and emphasis on the natural that the romantics held dear. For example, Beethoven's Sixth Symphony, the *Pastoral*, used a variety of instruments to represent sounds heard in the country. Beethoven's work showed remarkable diversity, ranging from religious works to symphonies, sonatas, and concertos. Some of his work was explicitly political. His opera *Fidelio* (1807), based on French revolutionary models, exalted a wife who rescued her husband from political imprisonment; his Ninth Symphony (1824) employs a chorus to sing Schiller's verses in praise of universal human solidarity. Romantic influences, however, did not permeate all music written in this period. Most Italian operas, for example, retained familiar classical forms and continued to draw large crowds.

Romanticism in painting broke almost completely with classical models. Classical painters insisted on universal standards of beauty and focused on the human figure; romantics replied that beauty varied from century to century and from nation to nation, and they idealized nature, not human forms, giving it an almost supernatural or spiritual quality. To classicists this was "painting

J. M. W. Turner, **Newark Abbey,** *1807*
Turner combines the Romantic interest in medieval ruins and the play of light and color in this early painting.

with a drunken broom." The English artist J. M. W. Turner (1775–1851) depicted his cosmic vision of nature in mysterious and misty settings, anticipating later impressionist painters by blurring the outlines of objects. The French painter Eugène Delacroix (1798–1863) chose contemporary as well as medieval scenes of great turbulence to emphasize light and color, striving to break away from "the servile copies repeated *ad nauseum* in academies of art." His daring use of vibrant colors as well as his liberal political convictions are evident in his *Liberty Leading the People*, which celebrated the aspirations of the July days of 1830 in Paris.

Their emphasis on authentic self-expression at times drew romantics to exotic, mystical, or even reckless experiences. Such transports drove one

leading German poet to the madhouse and another to suicide and sent Byron to his death in Greece. Some proponents of romanticism depicted the artist as necessarily possessed by demons and obsessed with hallucinations and nightmares. The hyperindividualist side of romanticism was implicitly criticized by the novelist Mary Shelley (1797–1851), the daughter of women's rights advocate Mary Wollstonecraft and wife of the romantic poet Percy Bysshe Shelley. Her novel *Frankenstein* (1818) tells the story of creativity gone awry. The scientist Frankenstein is a technological genius who creates a humanlike monster that evokes horror and wreaks destruction on Frankenstein's own family. The tale represents the negative potential of scientific innovation in a society experiencing the pangs of revolutionary upheaval.

CONCLUSION

The aged German poet Goethe, who obstinately rejected all doctrines, denounced the extremes of romanticism, calling it "everything that is sick." He died in 1832, having just completed the two-part drama *Faust*, which he had begun in 1775. In Goethe's retelling of a sixteenth-century legend, Faust offers his soul to the devil in return for a chance to taste all human experience—from passionate love to the heights of power, where he struggles to reshape nature for humanity's benefit. *Faust* captured the revolutionary and romantic age's thirst for power, glory, and redeeming love. But *Faust*'s message was equivocal: the hero's striving leaves a wake of suffering and destruction, particularly for Gretchen, the seamstress whose life is ruined by Faust's treachery. Countless Europeans came to see Faust as Western humanity personified, for Faust's career illustrated the drive for progress through scientific understanding and industrial development, as well as the clash of contending ideologies under way in Europe by 1832.

Eugène Delacroix, **Mephistopheles Confronts Faust** *In this engraving, the artist shows the scholar Faust making his fatal bargain with the devil.*

The French romantic artist Delacroix captured a similar mood when he wrote, "Try as one will, one always sees within oneself a gulf, an abyss that is never filled. One is always longing for something that never comes." This romantic yearning took several forms: dissatisfaction with the present, repressive regime; dislike for the signs of a new industrial order; dreams of a greater artistic future; and perhaps even a nostalgia for the glory days of Napoleon, whatever their price in terms of human suffering. During the three decades at the beginning of the nineteenth century, people had witnessed the emergence of many new ideas as well as the spectacular rise and fall of one man who dominated the lives and thoughts of Europeans for a generation. The memory of Napoleon lingered well into the final decades of the nineteenth century. Yet the challenges posed by urban and industrial growth and the new aspirations that accompanied them in many ways overshadowed his legacy. Romanticism, liberalism, socialism, and especially nationalism would profoundly affect the decades to come. Although conservative politics had been enshrined in the settlement of the Congress of Vienna, waves of revolution in the 1820s and again in 1830 had shown that the revolutionary legacy of change through political violence was very much alive. Europeans had made a kind of Faustian bargain with scientific development and competing political ideologies. Now these dynamic forces would shape European history.

Suggestions for Further Reading

Source Materials

Arnold, Eric A., Jr., ed. *A Documentary Survey of Napoleonic France.* 1994. Includes treaties and letters as well as documents concerning internal French affairs.

Bruun, Geoffrey. *Napoleon and His Empire.* 1972. A diverse selection of documents about Napoleon.

Hugo, Howard E., ed. *The Romantic Reader.* 1957. The best one-volume overview of romanticism.

Germaine de Staël's novel *Corinne* (1807) tells the story of a tragic romantic heroine. Stendahl's (Marie Henri Beyle) novel *The Red and the Black* (1830) analyzes the psychology of a young man's social rise in post-Napoleonic France.

Interpretive Studies

Artz, Frederick B. *Reaction and Revolution, 1814–1832.* 1934. Still the best one-volume treatment of the restoration.

Beecher, Jonathan. *Charles Fourier: The Visionary and His World.* 1986. A long but fascinating biography that puts one of the early socialists into his historical context.

Bergeron, Louis. *France Under Napoleon.* Translated by R. R. Palmer. 1981. An excellent survey of social and institutional history in France during Napoleon's regime.

Clark, Anna. "Queen Caroline and the Sexual Politics of Popular Culture in London, 1820." *Representations,* 31 (1990): 47–68. A fascinating account of the gender significance of popular reactions to the Queen Caroline Affair in England.

Colley, Linda. *Britons: Forging the Nation, 1707–1837.* 1992. A thematic analysis of the rise of British nationhood.

Connelly, Owen. *Blundering to Glory: Napoleon's Military Campaigns.* 1987. Contains excellent maps and descriptions of Napoleon's major battles.

———, ed. *Historical Dictionary of Napoleonic France, 1799–1815.* 1985. Includes articles by experts on various aspects of Napoleon's rule.

———. *Napoleon's Satellite Kingdoms.* 1965. A lively description of Napoleon's control over France's satellite kingdoms.

Davis, David Brion. *The Problem of Slavery in the Age of Revolution, 1770–1823.* 1975. A wide-ranging and thorough study of British and American antislavery thought.

Johnson, Paul. *The Birth of the Modern: World Society, 1815–1830.* 1991. Although remarkably long and detailed, a very readable account of the rise of early democracy and of the momentous social and cultural changes of a little-appreciated period.

Kafker, Frank A., and James M. Laux. *Napoleon and His Times: Selected Interpretations.* 1989. A useful collection of brief articles exploring different facets of Napoleon's regime; includes translations from the French that would be difficult to obtain individually.

Markham, Felix. *Napoleon.* 1964. A good biography that includes a balanced analysis of Napoleon's military successes and failures.

Mazour, Anatole G. *The First Russian Revolution, 1825: The Decembrist Movement, Its Origins, Development, and Significance.* 1937. Still a useful study of a key event in modern Russian history.

Poovey, Mary. *The Proper Lady and the Woman Writer: Ideology as Style in the Works of Mary Wollstonecraft, Mary Shelley, and Jane Austen.* 1984. Brings together historical and literary analysis of three important writers in early nineteenth-century England.

Spitzer, Alan B. *The French Generation of 1820.* 1987. An essay showing the common concerns of the writers, politicians, and professors in France in the 1820s.

Talmon, J. L. *Romanticism and Revolt: Europe, 1815–1848.* 1967. A beautifully illustrated essay that emphasizes the development of ideology.

Thompson, E. P. *The Making of the English Working Class.* 1964. A now-classic history of the beginnings of working-class organization in England.

In April 1832 a series of riots rocked Paris. The cause of the outbursts was not politics, but rather a cholera epidemic that had gripped the city. As the deadly disease spread, the terrified people became convinced of a plot. A crowd of workers attacked a central hospital, believing the doctors were actually poisoning the poor but using the claim of cholera as a hoax to cover up their conspiracy. Government orders prohibiting visitors to the cholera wards and military guards posted outside hospitals seemed to confirm popular fears. Accounts of attacks on doctors and merchants led newspapers to characterize Paris as a "little outpost of savages." The crisis bared many tensions of the age: the threat of disease, fears of overpopulation, class hatred, and popular resentment against the state and its growing bureaucracy.

In 1830–1832 and again in 1847–1851, outbreaks of cholera swept across Asia and Europe (touching the United States too). No one then understood the disease (we now know a waterborne bacterium causes it), which induced vomiting and diarrhea and left skin blue, eyes sunken and dull, and hands and feet ice cold. Cholera particularly ravaged the crowded, filthy quarters of rapidly growing cities, but it also claimed many rural and some well-to-do victims. In Paris, eighteen thousand people died in the 1832 epidemic, and twenty thousand in that of 1849; in London, seven thousand died in both epidemics; in Russia, two hundred fifty thousand in 1831–1832 and a million in 1847–1851 perished. Rumors and panic followed in the epidemic's wake. Everywhere the downtrodden imagined conspiracies: while the Parisian poor rioted against doctors and state-run hospitals, eastern

CHAPTER

22

Industrialization, Urbanization, and Revolution, 1832–1851

Honoré Daumier, Cholera Morbus, *1840*
Every figure in this engraving, even the dog, testifies to the epidemic's horrors.

European peasants burned estates and killed physicians and officials. Although devastating, cholera did not kill as many people as tuberculosis, Europe's number-one deadly disease; typhus epidemics, another scourge, also broke out every five to ten years.

Such raging epidemics spurred concern for public health. When news of the cholera outbreak in eastern Europe reached Paris in 1831, the city set up commissions in each municipal district to collect information about lower-class housing and sanitation. (Physicians thought the putrid air emanating from garbage piles spread the disease.) In Great Britain, reports on sanitary conditions among the working class led to the passage of new public health laws.

Fear of epidemics was just one of many forces that drove change in the early 1800s. Despite diseases, Europe's population surged. Industrial development, although fitful, caused profound social, economic, cultural, and technological transformation. Middle classes, workers, artisans, and even some women demanded a greater say in

IMPORTANT DATES

1832 Cholera epidemic sweeps across Europe

1833 Factory Act regulates work of children in Great Britain; abolition of slavery in the British Empire

1834 German customs union *(Zollverein)* established under Prussian leadership

1835 Belgium opens first continental railway built with state funds

1836 Charles Dickens publishes *Oliver Twist*

1839 Invention of photography; beginning of Opium War between Britain and China

1844 Hungarian Louis Kossuth forms association to boycott Austrian goods

1846 Famine strikes Ireland; Corn Laws repealed in England; peasant insurrection in Austrian province of Galicia (once part of Poland)

1848 Last great wave of Chartist demonstrations in Britain; Karl Marx and Friedrich Engels, *The Communist Manifesto;* revolutions of 1848 throughout Europe

The Spread of Cholera, 1826–1837

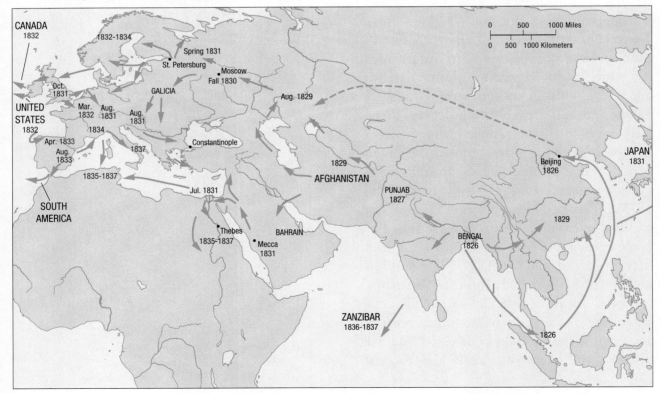

political affairs. Suppressed nationalities and ethnic groups also raised their voices. Men and women everywhere formed organizations devoted to achieving their goals. In response to new requirements, European states rapidly expanded their bureaucracies. For example, in 1750 the Russian government had employed approximately 10,500 functionaries; a century later it needed almost 114,000. In Great Britain a swelling army of civil servants produced a cascade of parliamentary studies on industrialization, foreign trade, and colonial profits, while new agencies such as the British urban police forces (ten thousand strong in the 1840s) intruded increasingly in ordinary people's lives.

In 1848, changes in European society combined to churn up a new wave of revolution, the most powerful since 1789. Food shortages, constitutional crises, class tensions, and nationalist impulses coalesced to produce outbreaks in many European capitals. Some revolutionaries saw this as the beginning of a new age of class warfare, much more international than the uprisings in 1789 and 1830. But the revolutionaries of 1848 went down to defeat, and their failure inaugurated a different, more calculating form of nationalist politics after 1851.

Industrialization and Social Change

A population explosion unprecedented in Western civilization had begun in the eighteenth century and continued unchecked in the nineteenth. Outstripping the rest of the world, Europe's population soared by 42 percent in the first half of the century and by 51 percent in the second. Scholars still debate whether this population growth caused or was caused by industrialization. The most rapid demographic expansion occurred in the British Isles; the populations of England and Wales doubled between 1800 and 1851. But populations increased even in the least-industrialized areas of Europe: in Denmark, for example, from 1 million to 1.5 million. Everywhere, greater numbers of people created a tremendous demand for manufactured goods and foodstuffs—and made possible a burgeoning of the workforce. Industrialization could not have occurred without these demographic changes.

Industrialization had startling and disturbingly paradoxical effects. Industry created unheard-of riches and new forms of poverty simultaneously. "From this foul drain the greatest stream of human industry flows out to fertilize the whole world," wrote the French social critic Alexis de Tocqueville (1805–1859) after visiting the new English industrial city of Manchester in the 1830s. "From this filthy sewer pure gold flows. Here humanity attains its most complete development and its most brutish, here civilization works its miracles and civilized man is turned almost into a savage."

Railroads and Steam

Great Britain, the leader in industrial development since the late eighteenth century, continued to build factories and railroads. By 1835, Parliament was authorizing more money for new railroad lines than had been spent on all the canals combined. In the 1840s railroad track mileage more than doubled in Great Britain. The British also began constructing railroads in India. Canal building waned in the 1840s: the railroad had won out.

Seeing the advantages of rail transportation, other countries soon began their own railway projects. Railroads grew spectacularly in the United States in the 1830s and 1840s. Belgium, newly independent in 1830, opened the first continental European railroad, financed with state bonds (backed by British capital), in 1835. The German states, France, and Russia followed. By 1848–1850, France had 2,000 miles of railroad tracks, and the German states nearly twice as many; Great Britain had 5,127 miles, and the United States 9,000 miles. The world boasted 23,500 miles of rails by mid-century.

Railroad building spurred both industrial development and the growth of state power. Governments everywhere participated in railroad construction, which depended on private and state capital for the necessary massive inputs of iron, coal, heavy machinery, and human labor—and money. Driven above all by the needs of railroad builders, demand for iron products accelerated industrial development. Until the 1840s, cotton production had led the way, increasing 450 percent in Great Britain between 1816 and 1840. But in the 1830s and 1840s, coal and iron production also jumped significantly; from 1830 to 1850, Britain's output of iron and coal tripled.

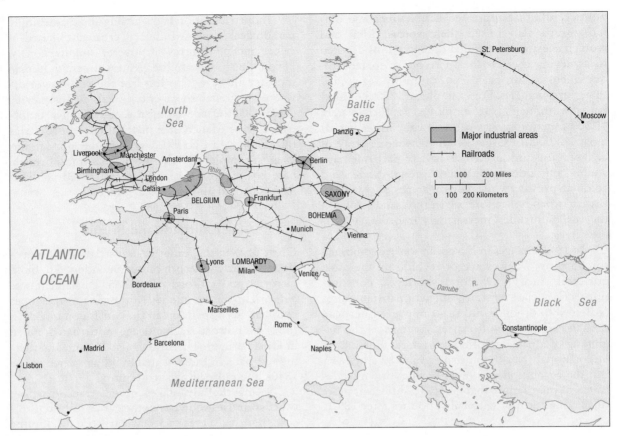

Industrialization in Europe, c. 1850

As railroads created new transportation networks for raw materials and finished goods, the steam engine provided power for textile factories, mining, and locomotives. Already between 1840 and 1850, steam-engine power doubled in Great Britain, and it increased even more rapidly elsewhere in Europe, as those adopting British inventions strained to catch up. Steam-powered engines made Britain the leader in manufacturing. By mid-century more than half of Britain's national income came from manufacturing and trade (35 percent and 17 percent, respectively).

Industrial development in turn hastened urban growth. Half the population of England and Wales lived in towns by 1850, while in France and the German states the urban population was about a quarter of the total. Less than one-fourth of British male workers now engaged in agriculture; in Belgium, the most industrialized nation on the Continent, the comparable figure was 50 percent.

Industrialization occurred much more slowly in eastern Europe but took off in certain areas. Cotton production in the Austrian Empire tripled between 1831 and 1845, with Bohemia accounting for half the empire's mechanized cotton spinning and three-fourths of its cotton weaving. By 1847 coal production, also concentrated in Bohemia, had quadrupled, in just over twenty years. Serfdom, which still survived in eastern Europe, impeded industrialization by hindering labor mobility and tying up investment capital. The problem was worst in Russia. A mid-century commentator there remarked, "We cannot be blind to the fact that most of our iron-masters, reposing on the cushion of protection, long neglected to follow the progress of this industry in foreign countries: any improvements introduced have been very recent and very exceptional." As a result, iron products cost more in Russia than elsewhere in Europe, and Russian firms could not compete in export markets. Nevertheless, industrialization was under way: raw cotton imports (a sign of a growing textile industry) increased sevenfold between 1831 and 1848, and the number of factories doubled, as did the size of the industrial workforce.

Although Great Britain consciously strove to ensure its industrial supremacy, thousands of British engineers defied laws against the export of machinery or the emigration of artisans. The best-known such entrepreneur, John Cockerill, set up a machine works in Belgium that was soon selling its products as far east as Poland and Russia. Cockerill claimed to know of every innovation within ten days of its appearance in England. Only slowly, thanks to pirated British methods and to new technical schools, did most continental countries begin closing the gap. Belgium became the fastest growing industrial power on the Continent: between 1830 and 1844 the number of steam engines quadrupled, and Belgians exported seven times as many steam engines as they imported. Even so, by 1850 continental Europe still lagged a generation behind Great Britain.

The Formation of the Working Class

As industrialization proceeded, factories increasingly became the workplace of laboring people, replacing the dispersed households of preindustrial artisans. Thus the advent of factories caused a migration from rural areas to the cities. Some people moved from one region of the country to another in search of better jobs. In the German states, where the peasantry was gaining its freedom from serfdom between 1807 and 1850, peasants who could not make ends meet moved from the agricultural east to the more industrial west. Urban immigrants unable to find work sometimes joined the charity rolls and thus raised "poor rates" paid by more affluent city-dwellers. German cities tried to block entitlement to resources with legislation preventing the unpropertied from holding artisan jobs and from marrying. In some parts of Europe city leaders banned factories, hoping to insulate their towns from the disorder of immigration. The British government sought to control public welfare costs by passing a new poor law in 1834, called by its critics "the Starvation Act." The act required all able-bodied persons receiving relief to live in workhouses, with husbands separated from wives and parents from children. Workhouse life was designed to be as unpleasant as possible so poor people would seek higher-paying employment.

Despite industrial growth, factory workers remained a minority among laboring people. In the 1840s factories employed only 5 percent of England's workers; in France, 3 percent; in Prussia, 2 percent. In most places a factory with a thousand workers was considered gigantic. Many peasants kept their options open by combining factory work with agricultural labor. From Switzerland to Russia, people worked in agriculture during the spring and summer, and in manufacturing in the fall and winter. In this way workers and their families ensured their food supply, but they also maintained the rhythms of life on the land. Unstable industrial wages made such arrangements essential. Some new industries idled periodically: for example, iron forges stopped for several months when the water level in streams dropped, and blast furnaces shut down for repairs several weeks every year. In hard times factory owners simply closed their doors until demand for their goods improved.

Although factories provided new ways of working, more workers continued to toil at home in the old-fashioned putting-out, or cottage, industries. In the 1840s, for example, two-thirds of the manufacturing workers in Prussia and Saxony labored for contractors or merchants who supplied raw materials and then sold the finished goods. Women worked in the putting-out system as much as or even more than men—they plaited straw and embroidered in Hungary, made pots in Denmark, fashioned lace in the British Isles and France, and spun cotton almost everywhere.

Some of the old forms of putting-out work changed during this period, even when factories did not supplant the cottage industry. Little or no technological innovation prompted the change; instead labor was organized in a different way. Tailoring in the big cities, for example, was no longer the exclusive province of men who produced whole garments themselves or with their families' help; entrepreneurs now gave piecework (parts of the garment in this case) directly to women who toiled either in large shops or at home, often for long hours. Women were hired to do piecework (and much of the lighter factory work) at much lower wages than skilled men; manufacturers profited from the assumption that women should earn less than men because their wages only supplemented those of their menfolk. Skilled male workers' efforts to keep better-paying jobs for themselves only increased the gender segregation of work, with the result of lower wages for everyone.

Dangerous Cities, Dangerous Classes

Both old and new cities teemed with people in the 1830s and 1840s. In the 1830s, London grew by about 130,000 people, Manchester by 70,000, and Birmingham by 40,000. Paris's population increased by approximately 120,000 just between 1841 and 1846, Vienna by 125,000 between 1827 and 1847, and Berlin by 180,000 between 1815 and 1848. Urban growth followed a push-pull pattern: people were pushed off the land and pulled toward cities. Agricultural improvements introduced since the eighteenth century had increased the food supply and hence the rural population; the new surplus population fled the land under the threat of hunger and poverty that accompanied a swollen population. Meanwhile, just as in the developing countries today, the opportunities of city life beckoned that surplus population. Settlements sprang up outside the old city limits but gradually became part of the urban area. City walls came down; they were no longer useful for defense and instead inhibited growth and trade. At the same time, cities incorporated parks, cemeteries, and zoos, all imitations of the countryside, which was being industrialized by railroads and factories. "One can't even go to one's land for the slightest bit of gardening," grumbled a French citizen, "without being covered with a black powder that spoils every plant that it touches."

Many migrants from country to city brought traditions of rural life with them, but they also enjoyed new forms of leisure. Beer halls, pubs, cafés, and coffeehouses, once the meeting places of the elite, provided a haven for conversation. Hungary's twin cities of Buda and Pest (later united as Budapest) had 800 beer and wine houses for the working classes alone by the 1830s. In Great Britain the Beer Act of 1830 made it easy for pubs to obtain licenses. One London street boasted 23 pubs in 300 yards. Here songs about the joys and miseries of working-class life—and sometimes satirical attacks on the government—were written and passed on. In the coffeehouses working-class men could read the latest newspapers, which an ordinary family still could not afford.

Yet the influx of rural people caused serious problems. Nineteenth-century cities faced severe overcrowding, which increased the risk of epidemics. Housing was inadequate everywhere. Whereas Vienna's population rose by 42 percent, the housing stock expanded by only 11 percent. In Paris thirty thousand workers lived in lodging houses, eight or nine to a room, with no separation of the sexes. Observed one contemporary: "The difficulty of finding lodgings is for the worker a constant ordeal and a perpetual cause of misery." In St. Giles, the Irish quarter of London, 461 people lived in twelve houses in 1847. Men, women, and children huddled together on rotting straw or potato peels because they had no money for fuel.

Crowding only worsened already dire urban sanitation problems. Garbage and refuse littered the unpaved streets of poor districts, and smog, smoke, and putrid smells fouled the air. Water was scarce and had to be fetched daily from nearby fountains. Despite the diversion of water from provincial rivers to Paris and a tripling of the number of public fountains, Parisians had only enough water for two baths annually (the upper classes enjoyed more baths, of course; the lower classes fewer). In London private companies that supplied water turned on pumps in the poorer sections for only a few hours a week. Sewage removal was practically nonexistent. Residents dumped refuse into streets or courtyards, and human excrement collected in cesspools under apartment houses. London's approximately 250,000 cesspools (in 1850) were emptied only once or twice a year. In rapidly growing British industrial cities such as Manchester, perhaps one-third of the houses contained no privies. Human waste ended up in the rivers that supplied drinking water. The horses that provided transportation inside the cities left droppings everywhere, and city-dwellers often kept chickens, ducks, goats, pigs, geese, and even cattle, as well as dogs and cats. The result was a "universal atmosphere of filth and stink."

Daguerreotype of Paris
Broad, tree-lined boulevards defined the city's most desirable parts.

Such conditions made cities breeding grounds for disease; those with fifty thousand people or more had twice the death rates of rural areas. A doctor in the Prussian town of Breslau reported on living conditions in working-class districts there:

> *Several persons live in one room in a single bed, or perhaps a whole family, and use the room for all domestic duties, so that the air gets vitiated. . . . Their diet consists largely of bread and potatoes. These are clearly the two main reasons for the scrofula* which is so widespread here; the diet is also the cause of the common malformation of limbs.*

A French physician in the eastern town of Mulhouse described the "pale, emaciated women who walk barefooted through the dirt" to reach the factory. The young children who worked in the factory were "clothed in rags which are greasy with the oil from the looms and frames." Physicians set the life expectancy of workers in Manchester at just seventeen years (partly because of high rates of infant mortality), whereas the average in England was forty years in 1840.

*Scrofula is a disease related to tuberculosis.

The middle and upper classes soon viewed these squalid conditions as a threat to their ways of life. The more prosperous classes lived in apartments or houses with more light, more air, and more water. But the urban lower classes lived near the upper classes, sometimes in the cramped upper floors of the same apartment houses.

To combat the menace of declining public health, local governments encouraged doctors and new health boards to gather volumes of statistics. The amassed information conveyed a dreary and fearsome picture. A report in Lille, France, in 1832 described "dark cellars" inhabited by cotton workers, where "the air is never renewed, it is infected; the walls are plastered with garbage. . . . If a bed exists, it is a few dirty, greasy planks; it is damp and putrescent straw." The immensely popular novels of Charles Dickens and Honoré de Balzac dramatized these conditions, intensifying the sense of a class gulf between the well-off and the "dangerous" classes below them.

Many middle-class reformers associated the circumstances of the poor with moral degeneration. In their view overcrowding led to sexual promiscuity, illegitimacy, and crime. Commentators characterized the lower classes as lacking in sexual self-control. A physician visiting Lille in 1835 wrote of

> *individuals of both sexes and of very different ages lying together, most of them without nightshirts and repulsively dirty. . . . The reader will complete the picture . . . his imagination must not recoil before any of the disgusting mysteries performed on these impure beds, in the midst of obscurity and drunkenness.*

Police officials estimated that London was home to 70,000 thieves and 80,000 prostitutes. One-third to one-half of the babies born in the big European cities were illegitimate, and alarmed medical men wrote about thousands of infanticides. In France, 33,000 babies were abandoned at foundling hospitals every year between 1815 and the mid-1830s. By collecting statistics, physicians and administrators in the public health movement hoped to promote legislation to improve workers' conditions; but at the same time they contributed to the stereotype of workers as helpless and out-of-control people.

Everywhere reformers warned of a growing separation between rich and poor, as the Parisian cholera riots demonstrated. The French poet Amédée Pommier wrote of "These leagues of laborers who have no work, These far too many arms, these starving mobs." Clergy joined the chorus of physicians and humanitarians in making dire predictions. In his Easter sermon of 1843, the archbishop of Paris denounced the subjugation of workers to "the new slavery of pauperism." And a Swiss pastor noted, "A new spirit has arisen among the workers. Their hearts seethe with hatred of the well-to-do; their eyes lust for a share of the wealth about them; their mouths speak unblushingly of a coming day of retribution."

Agricultural Perils and Prosperity

Profound changes were not confined to cities. Insatiable demand spurred crop production across the Continent and augmented landowners' prosperity. Rural people everywhere planted fallow land, chopped down forests, and drained marshes. Still, Europe's ability to feed its expanding population remained questionable, as the Irish famines of 1846–1851 would show. Although agricultural yields increased by one-third to one-half in the first half of the nineteenth century, population was nearly doubling. Nowhere did population grow more rapidly than in Ireland. Railroads and canals improved food distribution in many areas, but much of Europe—particularly in the East—remained isolated from markets and vulnerable to famines.

Most people still lived on the land, and the upper classes still dominated rural society. Successful businessmen bought land avidly, seeing it not only as the ticket to respectability but also as a buffer against hard times. Yet hard-working, crafty, or lucky commoners sometimes saved enough to purchase holdings that they had formerly rented or slowly acquired slivers of land from less fortunate neighboring peasants. In France at mid-century almost 2 million economically independent peasants tended their own small properties. Even in Russia the proportion of peasant and middle-class land ownership increased.

The struggle to expand production hastened rural social change. As agricultural prices rose, landowners pushed for legislation to allow them to continue converting common land to private property. Occasional but severe price swings forced marginal families to sell out. Wringing a living from the soil sometimes required the reversal of traditional gender roles. For example, men often migrated seasonally to earn cash in factories or as village artisans, while their wives, sisters, and daughters did the traditional "men's work" of tending crops. Peasants who managed to enrich themselves a little became customers for such luxuries as soap, sugar, and factory-made textiles.

In turn, rural economic changes directly affected human reproduction. Wherever industry drew people away from agricultural labor, farmers would happily absorb illegitimate children into the rural workforce. (In general, however, illegitimacy was an urban phenomenon; in 1850, 4 percent of the rural births in France were illegitimate, compared to 12 percent in cities and 27 percent in Paris.) Sometimes legal requirements for property division among heirs pressured families to reduce their family size. In France, for example, Napoleon's Civil Code provided for an equal distribution of inheritances among all heirs; as a result, land became so subdivided that less than 25 percent of all French landowners could support themselves. Ordinary families thus began to practice birth control.

In the past, population growth had been contained by postponing marriage (leaving fewer years for childbearing) and by high rates of death in childbirth and of infant mortality. Now, as child mortality declined and people without property began marrying earlier, Europeans became more aware of birth-control methods. Contraceptive techniques improved; for example, the vulcanization of rubber in the 1840s increased the availability and use of condoms. When such methods failed and population increase left no options open at home, people emigrated, often to the United States. Some eight hundred thousand Germans moved out of central Europe by 1850, while in the 1840s famine drove tens of thousands of Irish abroad.

Despite these challenges to established ways of life, rural political power remained remarkably constant. Insecurities, struggle, displacement, and migration took place under the watchful eye of the traditional village notable or lord. Economically, he dominated tenants and sharecroppers, often demanding a greater yield without contributing to improvements that would enhance productivity. Politically, he alone participated in national or regional assemblies. Representatives to the French and English parliaments and to the newly established assemblies in German states were all wealthy and generally landed, and these men often chose the parish clergy and civil servants. Such power provoked resentment. As one Italian critic wrote, "Great landowner is often the synonym for great ignoramus." Nowhere did the old rural social order seem more impregnable than in Russia. Most serfs remained tied to the land, and the middle classes were too tiny to demand reform. Troops easily suppressed serfs' uprisings in 1831 and 1842. By midcentury, peasant emancipation remained Russia's great unresolved problem.

Reforming the Social Order

The changes brought by industrialization and urbanization attracted widespread attention, from novelists and artists, public officials and social reformers. Among the most dedicated reformers were women, especially of the middle and upper classes. In the early nineteenth century many commentators emphasized women's special domestic responsibilities: providing men with a refuge in a heartless world, and children with moral and religious instruction. Women were assigned a separate, private sphere, distinct from the male public sphere. Nevertheless, many women left their homes to carry the message of virtue, morality, and responsibility to the downtrodden.

Depiction of the Social Question

The "social question," an expression reflecting the deeply shared concern about social changes, pervaded all forms of art and literature. Painters and poets did not become propagandists, but their portrayals did underline the worry many in society felt. The English poet Elizabeth Barrett Browning (1806–1861), best known for her love poems, decried child labor in "The Cry of the Children" (1843):

> For, all day, we drag our burden tiring
> Through the coal-dark, underground,
> Or, all day, we drive the wheels of iron
> In the factories, round and round

Playwrights attracted huge audiences to melodramas depicting the antagonism between social classes, as well as divorce, adultery, illegitimacy, and prostitution. Popular theaters in big cities drew thousands from the lower and middle classes every night; in London, for example, some twenty-four thousand people attended eighty "penny theaters" nightly.

The advent of photography in 1839 provided an amazing new medium for artists. Daguerreotypes, named after their inventor, French painter Jacques Daguerre (1787–1851), prompted one artist to claim that "From today, painting is dead." Although this prediction was obviously inaccurate, photography did open up new ways of portraying reality. Visual images, whether on the stage, in painting, or in photography, heightened the public's awareness of the effects of industrialization and urbanization.

In the 1830s and 1840s, painting remained the most important visual art. As museums opened to the public across Europe (the French revolutionaries opened the first state-run museum in the 1790s when they converted the Louvre from a royal

J. M. W. Turner, **Rain, Steam, and Speed: The Great Western Railway,** *1844*
Using techniques that foreshadowed those of impressionism a generation or two later,
Turner explored the effects of light in this depiction of the steam locomotive and its speed.

palace to a public gallery), the number of painters and sculptors mushroomed, and the middle classes began collecting art for themselves. Estimates suggest that the number of painters and sculptors in France, the undisputed center of European art, grew sixfold between 1789 and 1838.

Although no one style of painting dominated in this period, and artists still favored mythological, exotic, and historical themes, painters such as the Englishman J. M. W. Turner (1775–1851) fused romantic styles with an awareness of social issues. Among Turner's best paintings of the 1840s are *Slavers Throwing Overboard the Dead and Dying—Typhoon Coming On* (1840), a portrayal of a slave ship threatened by a menacing storm, and *Rain, Steam and Speed—The Great Western Railway* (1844), which depicted a train confronting inclement weather. Both reflected contemporary

social concerns but within a romantic style that emphasized color and light. Even more socially relevant was the work of French painter and engraver Honoré Daumier (1808–1879), who developed caricature to mock urban types and to criticize economic inequalities. An unflattering caricature of Louis-Philippe as a money-grubbing monster landed Daumier in prison, but in the 1830s and 1840s he nonetheless contributed scores of caricatures to the daily paper *Charivari*.

The novel was the art form best suited to presenting social problems. Thanks to increased literacy, the spread of reading rooms and lending libraries, and serializations in newspapers and journals, novels reached a large reading public. In the German states, for example, the production of new literary works doubled between 1830 and 1843, as did the number of periodicals and newspapers. The great novels of the period piqued interest in the social question by creating a range of characters representing all social classes. Manufacturers, financiers, starving students, workers, bureaucrats, prostitutes, underworld figures, thieves, and aristocratic men and women filled the pages of works by such popular authors as Honoré de Balzac, Charles Dickens, and Nikolai Gogol. The French writer Balzac (1799–1850) portrayed the endless varieties of what he called "The Human Comedy." Almost all his twenty-four full-length novels—grouped together under this general title—had as their chief theme a craving to climb higher in the new social order.

Novels by women often revealed bleak aspects of women's situations. *Jane Eyre* (1847), a novel by Charlotte Brontë (1816–1855), described the difficult life of an orphaned girl who becomes a governess, the only occupation open to most middle-class, single women. Although in an economically weak position, Jane Eyre refuses to marry as a way of achieving respectability and security.

Domesticity

Most women had little hope of economic independence; their lives were bound within the domestic sphere. The notion of women's separate sphere prevented women from pursuing higher education, working in professional careers, or voting, all deemed appropriate only for men. The English poet Alfred, Lord Tennyson (1809–1892) captured the traditional view in a popular poem of 1847: "Man for the field and woman for the hearth; Man for the sword and for the needle she. . . . All else confusion." Although this view had a long history, the question of women's place gained new urgency with industrialization and urbanization. The entry of thousands of women into factories and the movement of millions of people from rural villages to the big cities threatened to make the celebration of domesticity an ideal with little relationship to reality.

Both men and women wrote about the question of women's proper roles, for many saw the right ordering of the private domain as critically important to the maintenance of social order in general. Advice books written by women detailed the many tasks women undertook in the home: cleaning, cooking, maintaining household accounts, supervising servants, organizing social events. Performing these duties kept middle- and upper-class women far from idle. The greatest emphasis fell, however, on developing a distinctive female character. In her popular 1838 guide, Albertine Necker de Saussure urged mothers to rear their daughters to be feminine, sensitive, and gentle: "Docility, that internal disposition which naturally leads to the fulfillment of [obedience], may well be the object of peculiar cultivation in young girls."

Family responsibilities weighed most heavily on working-class women, whose lives bore little resemblance to the ideals of the advice literature and medical manuals. Families crammed into one room had no time or energy for "separate spheres." Working-class women supported their families and also performed the duties expected of wives and mothers. In 1849 one Englishwoman described how she worked every day from eight in the morning until midnight, sewing lace on coats to support three sons.

Distinctions between men and women were most noticeable in the privileged classes. Whereas boys attended secondary schools, most upper-class girls still received their education at home or in church schools, where they were taught to be religious, obedient, and accomplished in music and languages. As men began to wear practical clothing—long trousers and short jackets of somber colors, no makeup (previously common for aristocratic men), and simply cut hair—women continued to dress for decoration, now with tightly corseted waists that emphasized the differences between female and male bodies. Upper-class women had long hair that required hours of work and they wore long, cumbersome skirts.

Laws everywhere codified the subjugation of women. Many countries followed the model of Napoleon's Civil Code, which had classified married women as legal incompetents along with children, the insane, and criminals. In Great Britain, which had no national law code, the courts upheld the legality of a husband's complete control. For example, in 1840 a court ruled that "There can be no doubt of the general dominion which the law of England attributes to the husband over the wife." In some countries, such as France and Austria, unmarried women enjoyed some rights, but elsewhere laws defined them as perpetual minors under paternal control.

Eugène Delacroix, **The French Novelist George Sand**
*Sand refused to be held by the bonds of domesticity.
Here she is shown in her notorious men's dress.*

Scientists reinforced stereotypes. Once considered disorderly because of their presumed sexual insatiability, women were now described as incapacitated by menstruation and largely disinterested in sex, an attitude many equated with moral superiority. Thus was born the "Victorian woman," a figment of the largely male medical imagination. Physicians and scholars also considered women mentally inferior to men. In 1839, Auguste Comte, an influential French sociologist, wrote, "As for any functions of government, the radical inaptitude of the female sex is there yet more marked, even in regard to the most elementary state, and limited to the guidance of the mere family."

Some women denounced domestic ideology: according to the English writer Ann Lamb, for example, "The duty of a wife *means* the obedience of a Turkish slave." Middle-class women who did not marry, however, had few options for earning a living. They often worked as governesses or ladies'

companions for the well-to-do. A few women openly defied society's expectations. The female novelist George Sand (Amandine-Aurore Dupin, 1804–1876) announced her independence to the Parisian world in the 1830s when she dressed like a man and smoked cigars. Like many other women writers of the time, she published her work under a male pseudonym while creating female characters who prevail in difficult circumstances through romantic love and moral idealism. Sand's novel *Indiana* (1832), about an unhappily married woman, was read all over Europe. Eventually she became involved in socialist politics. Her notoriety made the term *George-Sandism* common in several countries to express disdain for independent women.

Religion, Women, and Social Reform

Upper-class women had long been involved in charity efforts. Many women viewed charitable work as the extension of their domestic roles; they promoted virtuous behavior and morality and thus improved society. In one widely read book, Sarah Lewis suggested in 1839 that "Women may be the prime agents in the regeneration of mankind." Their endeavors often focused on the welfare of mothers and children. Women in Lille, France, for example, operated the Society for Maternal Charity to help poor women who had recently given birth. Maternal associations were also common in the United States. In Britain they developed a political edge after the 1834 Poor Law resulted in mothers being separated from their children in workhouses; throughout the country, women from all classes helped form anti–Poor Law societies.

As religious observance became associated with women's sphere, women eagerly formed religiously oriented charitable and reform organizations. British and American women established Bible, missionary, and female reform societies by the hundreds. Chief among their concerns was prostitution, and many dedicated themselves to rehabilitating "fallen women" and castigating men who visited prostitutes. As the Boston Female Moral Reform Society explained, "Our mothers, our sisters, our daughters are sacrificed by the thousands every year on the altar of sin, and who are the agents in this work of destruction: Why, our fathers, our brothers, and our sons."

Women also actively participated in established churches. By mid-century, Catholic religious orders enrolled many more women than men. These women did much of the work in schools, hospitals, leprosaria, insane asylums, and old-age homes. Protestant women also promoted education and health. Elizabeth Fry, an English Quaker minister, toured Europe in the 1830s helping set up institutions for female prisoners modeled on the school and manufacturing shop she had organized at Newgate Prison in London. Amalie Sieveking founded the Female Association for the Care of the Poor and the Sick in Hamburg in 1832.

Women's participation fueled a continuing religious revival. New Catholic orders, especially for women, were founded, and missionary activity overseas increased. The appearance of cholera in 1832 reactivated the medieval cult of St. Roch, who was believed especially powerful against disease, in France. Medals of the "Radiant Virgin," struck to commemorate a novice's vision of the Virgin Mary in Paris in 1832, were thought to have similar power, and merchants sold millions of them all over the world. In Great Britain the growth of nonconformist Protestant denominations such as the Methodists reached its high point in this period, and Roman Catholicism began a revival. Traveling female preachers, once prominent, became rarer as emphasis shifted to building churches and chapels.

Although religion remained important in most rural communities, organized churches fared less well with the new industrial working class. Protestant and Catholic clergy complained that workers had no interest in religion; less than 10 percent of urban workers attended religious services. A report on the state of religion in England and Wales in 1851 commented, "The masses of our working population . . . are *unconscious secularists.* . . . These are never, or but seldom seen in our religious congregations." To combat such indifference, British religious groups launched the Sunday school movement, which reached its zenith in the 1840s. By 1851 more than half of all working-class children between five and fifteen attended Sunday school, even though very few of their parents regularly went to services. The Sunday schools taught children how to read at a time when few working-class children could go to school during the week.

Even though factories employed only a small percentage of the population, they attracted the attention of reformers because they seemed to threaten families. The differentiation of tasks between men, women, and children separated family members at the factory door. Reformers portrayed factories and mines as degrading places, and they agitated for government restrictions on child and female labor. British government efforts to regulate child labor went unheeded until the Factory Act of 1833 outlawed the employment of children under age nine in textile mills (except in the lace and silk industries) and limited the workdays of children aged nine to thirteen to nine hours a day and those aged thirteen to eighteen to twelve hours. As these figures indicate, all factory workers labored during most of their waking hours.

Reports on conditions in other industries prompted further legislation. When investigating commissions reported that women and young children, sometimes under age six, were hauling coal trucks through low, cramped passageways in coal mines, Parliament passed a Mines Act in 1842, which prohibited women and girls from working underground. One nine-year-old girl, Margaret Gomley, described her typical day in the mines as beginning at 7:00 A.M. and ending at 6:00 P.M.:

> *I get my dinner at 12 o'clock, which is a dry muffin, and sometimes butter on, but have no time allowed to stop to eat it, I eat it while I am thrusting the load. . . . They flog us down in the pit, sometimes with their hand upon my bottom, which hurts me very much.*

In 1847 the Central Short Time Committee, one of Britain's many social reform organizations, successfully pressured Parliament to limit the workday of women and children to ten hours. The continental countries followed the British lead; Prussia restricted child labor in 1839, France in 1841, Piedmont in 1843, and Russia in 1845. Unlike Britain, however, most continental countries did not insist on government inspection, so enforcement was lax.

Social reformers in many countries saw education as one of the main prospects for uplifting the poor and the working class. In addition to setting up Sunday schools, churches in Great Britain founded organizations such as the National Society for the Education of the Poor in the Principles of the Established Church, and the British and

Child Labor in British Coal Mines *Depictions of scenes like this one prompted the passage of the first child labor laws.*

Foreign School Society. Most of these emphasized Bible reading. More secular in intent were the Mechanics Institutes, which provided intellectual life for workers in the big cities.

In 1833 the French government passed an education law that required every town to maintain a primary school, pay a teacher, and provide free education to poor boys. Girls schools were optional; even so, hundreds of women taught at the primary level, most of them in private, often religious, schools. The law required every region to set up a teacher-training school for male teachers. As the law's author argued, "Ignorance renders the masses turbulent and ferocious." Despite these efforts, only one out of every thirty children went to school in France, much fewer than in northern Italy or German states such as Prussia, where 75 percent of children were enrolled in primary school by 1835. Popular education remained woefully undeveloped in most of eastern Europe. Peasants were specifically excluded from the few primary schools in Russia, because Tsar Nicholas I blamed the Decembrist Revolt on education; he also made every effort to exclude nonnobles from secondary schools.

Stronger calls for social reform echoed through western Europe. In 1844, for example, four hundred fifty different relief organizations were active in London. Temperance societies were among the most vocal. In Ireland, England, the German states, and the United States, temperance societies organized to fight the "pestilence of hard liquor." The first societies had appeared in the

United States as early as 1813, and the American Temperance Society had 1.5 million members by 1835. The London-based British and Foreign Temperance Society, established in 1831, matched its American counterpart in its opposition to alcohol. Temperance advocates saw drunkenness as a sign of moral weakness and a threat to social order; industrialists blamed it for the loss of worker productivity. Efforts to promote temperance often reflected middle- or upper-class fears of lower-class unruliness. Yet temperance societies also attracted working-class people who shared the desire for respectability.

The temperance movement won the support of Frederick William III of Prussia, who in 1837 ordered local authorities to promote temperance societies. In Prussia clergymen dominated the movement, and many liberals dismissed it as a tool of government ministers and the church. But in other north German states, temperance societies drew in the middle and working classes. By 1846, six hundred thousand adult German men had pledged abstinence. Almost everywhere enthusiasm for temperance was closely associated with religious revivalism and the new awareness of social problems. Most "respectable" people who joined temperance associations agreed with a German temperance advocate who insisted, "One need not be a prophet to know that all efforts to combat the widespread and rapidly spreading pauperism will be unsuccessful as long as the common man fails to realize that the principal source of his degradation and misery is his fondness of drink."

By encouraging restraint, the elite sought to impose discipline and order on working people. Popular sports, especially blood sports such as cockfighting and bearbaiting, suggested a lack of control, and long-standing efforts in Great Britain to eliminate these recreations now gained momentum through such organizations as the Society for the Prevention of Cruelty to Animals. By the end of the 1830s, bullbaiting had been abandoned in Great Britain. "This useful animal," rejoiced one reformer in 1839, "is no longer tortured amidst the exulting yells of those who are a disgrace to our common form and nature." The other blood sports died out more slowly, and efforts in other countries generally lagged behind those of the British.

Abuses and Reforms Overseas

Industrial growth at home made the major European states less dependent on colonies for their wealth in the early nineteenth century. Overseas rivalries affected international relations much less than they had earlier—or would at the end of the century. France and Britain thus managed to avoid coming to blows while each expanded its colonial holdings. France conquered Algeria and settled it with more than one hundred thousand French, Italian, and Maltese colonists by 1850, and also imposed a protectorate over the South Pacific island of Tahiti. Meanwhile, the British retreated somewhat from direct colonial rule by granting Canada greater self-determination in 1839, although they annexed Singapore (1819) and New Zealand (1840). They also extended their control in India, the base from which they set about establishing a regular trade with China in opium, which was legally grown in India.

The Chinese imperial government did its best to keep the highly addictive drug away from its people, both by forbidding western merchants to venture outside the southern city of Guangzhou (Canton) and by banning the export of precious metals and the import of opium. These measures failed. By smuggling opium into China and bribing local officials, British traders established a flourishing market, and by the mid-1830s they were pressuring the British government to force an expanded opium trade on the Chinese. When in 1839 the Beijing authorities expelled British merchants from southern China, Britain retaliated by bombarding Chinese coastal cities. In 1842 it dic-

tated to a defeated China the Treaty of Nanking, by which the British forced the opening of four more Chinese ports to Europeans, received the island of Hong Kong and a substantial war indemnity—and were assured of a continuation of the opium trade. The humiliation thus inflicted on the weakened Chinese empire helped touch off a cataclysmic civil war in China known as the Taiping Rebellion.

Few European reformers protested the opium traffic, but the international slave trade did stir western consciences. By now plantation agriculture was waning economically in the European colonies (although cotton cultivation by slave labor in the southern United States was thriving). As a result, slave labor was no longer intrinsically linked to European commerce. Many writers denounced colonial expansion as a waste of resources. Missionary and evangelical groups condemned the conquest, enslavement, and exploitation of native populations; missionary groups successfully opposed British annexations in central and southern Africa in the 1830s. British reformers finally obtained the abolition of slavery in the British Empire in 1833 (the slave trade had been abolished there in 1807). Antislavery petitions to Parliament bore 1.5 million signatures, including those of three hundred fifty thousand women on one petition alone.

The antislavery movement had spread slowly but decisively after both the British and the Dutch withdrew from the slave trade. The transatlantic trade in slaves actually reached its peak numbers in the early 1840s, however, though reform sentiment against it had won many converts. In France the Society of Christian Morality, composed of leading liberals, had agitated against the slave trade since the 1820s (slavery had been abolished during the French Revolution but reinstituted under Napoleon), and the new government of Louis-Philippe took strong measures against clandestine slave traffic, virtually ending French participation during the 1830s. But slavery itself survived in the remaining French Caribbean colonies until 1848. The new Latin American republics abolished slavery in the 1820s and 1830s after they defeated the Spanish with armies that included many slaves.

Human bondage continued unabated in Brazil, Cuba (still a Spanish colony), and the United States. Some American reformers supported abolitionism, but it remained very much a minority move-

Orientalism

As the Europeans became more involved in their various "eastern" colonies (from French Algeria to British India), artists began to depict exotic oriental scenes for Western audiences. Jean-Auguste-Dominique Ingres's 1839 painting Odalisque and Slave *is typical of the genre that emphasized eastern sensuality and eroticism.*

ment. Like serfdom in Russia, slavery in America involved a quagmire of economic, political, and moral problems that only worsened over time.

The Ferment of Ideologies

In the 1830s and 1840s, Europeans organized to reform almost every aspect of life, from religion to science, from the fight against alcohol to struggles for extending male suffrage. Many of these associations were the direct product of new ideologies—

doctrines and beliefs about the way the world is or should be—that had begun taking shape after the French Revolution. Nationalists forged identities based on common languages and customs. Liberals looked for expanded individual rights and sought economic growth through free trade. Socialists developed new organizations among the working classes. These movements offered new forms of identity in a rapidly changing world.

The Spell of Nationalism

Nationalists sought political autonomy for their ethnic group—a people linked by language and

Languages of Nineteenth-Century Europe

shared traditions from a common past. Renewed interest in cultural heritage helped fan resentment against "foreign occupation." Yet nationalism had an unpredictable quality: it pitted different ethnic groups within the Austrian Empire against each other, for example, and it did not always lead to a consistent political position, such as the demand for constitutional government. Although nationalism was still nascent among the peasants and workers of most countries, ethnic heritage was increasingly a major determinant of personal identity. Being Magyar or Slovak, for example, might matter more than whether one was a landowner or a merchant, especially if resistance to the Austrians was at stake. Nationalism now showed its capacity to arouse passionate feelings about ethnic identity.

Polish nationalism came in the baggage of the ten thousand émigrés (mostly noble army officers and intellectuals) who fled Poland after the revolt against Russian domination in 1830 and 1831 had collapsed. Most of them took up residence in west European capitals, especially Paris, where they mounted a successful public relations campaign for worldwide support. Their intellectual hero was the poet Adam Mickiewicz (1798–1855), whose mystical writings portrayed the Polish exiles as martyrs of a crucified nation with an international Christian mission: "Your endeavors are for all men, not only for yourselves. You will achieve a new Christian civilization." Mickiewicz formed a Polish legion to fight for national restoration, but rivalries and divisions among the Polish nationalists prevented united action.

One of those most touched by Mickiewicz's vision was Giuseppe Mazzini (1805–1872), the fiery Italian nationalist and republican journalist. He believed the Italians were the chosen people. Exiled in 1831 for his opposition to Austrian rule, Mazzini founded Young Italy, a secret society that attracted thousands with its message that Italy would touch off a European-wide revolutionary movement. The conservative order throughout Europe felt threatened by Mazzini's charismatic leadership and conspiratorial scheming, but he lacked both European allies against Austria and widespread support among the Italian masses. His projects for a Young Europe never succeeded, as countless conspiracies fizzled out in the Italian states while Mazzini himself remained safe in London. Yet by 1848 nationalism provided a sense of identity for many educated Italians ready to revolt against the Austrians.

Nationalism was a volatile issue in the Austrian Empire. The 1830s and 1840s saw the spread of cultural nationalism among Magyars, Czechs, Slovaks, Serbs, Slovenes, Croats, and Romanians, in addition to Poles and Italians. Each of these peoples produced leaders who called for a cultural revival in language, literature, and education, as well as political rights. Scholars compiled dictionaries and created a standard literary language to replace peasant dialects; writers used the rediscovered vernacular instead of Latin or German; and historians glorified the national past.

In the German states, teachers of German language, literature, law, and history also embraced nationalism. University professors started a newspaper, *The German Gazette* (1847), which urged the creation of a constitutional government and linked nationalist goals to the cause of individual rights. German economic unification took a step forward with the foundation in 1834, under Prussian leadership, of the *Zollverein,* or Customs Union, of most of non-Habsburg Germany. Economist Friedrich List argued for tariffs that would promote industrialization and cooperation across the boundaries of the German states, so that an economically united Germany might compete with the rest of Europe. German nationalists sought a government uniting German-speaking peoples, but they could not agree on its boundaries. Would it include both Prussia and the Austrian Empire? If it included Austria, what about the non-German

Giuseppe Mazzini
The Italian nationalist is shown in a typical romantic pose.

Habsburg territories? And could the powerful and conservative kingdom of Prussia coexist in a unified German state with other more liberal but smaller states?

The Irish had struggled for centuries against English occupation, but Irish nationalists developed strong organizations only in the 1840s. In 1842 a group of writers founded the Young Ireland movement that aimed to recover Irish history and preserve the Gaelic language (spoken by at least one-third of the peasantry). Young Ireland operated first in conjunction with Daniel O'Connell's Catholic Association and then with his Loyal National Repeal Association. A Catholic lawyer and landowner who sat in the British House of Commons, O'Connell (1775–1847) hoped to force Parliament to repeal the Act of Union of 1801, which had made Ireland part of Great Britain. By the end of 1842, repeal had become the focus of Irish nationalism, with "repeal wardens" and "repeal reading rooms" leading the way. "Monster meetings" in support of repeal often drew crowds of three hundred thousand in 1843. In response to these actions the British government arrested O'Connell and convicted him of conspiracy. Although his sentence was overturned, O'Connell withdrew from politics, partly because of a terminal brain disease. More radical leaders, who preached insurrection against the English, replaced him.

Currents of national revival also touched the Scandinavian countries. High schools emphasizing nationalism were founded in Denmark in the late 1840s, and in Norway scholars compiled historical archives and collected local fairy tales and songs. In 1848 a new Norwegian grammar and dictionary assisted people in distinguishing themselves from Danes.* Finland, before its annexation by Russia in 1809, had been ruled for centuries by Sweden, so cultural nationalism took an anti-Swedish turn. Here too intellectuals helped foster national pride by collecting oral folk epics and establishing literary societies.

In Russia nationalism was characterized by its opposition to western ideas. Russian nationalists, or "Slavophiles" (lovers of the Slavs), opposed the "Westernizers," who wanted Russia to follow western models of industrial development and constitutional government. The Slavophiles favored maintaining rural traditions infused by the values of the Russian Orthodox church. For them, "The entire West is wrapped in the shroud of death," and only a return to Russia's basic historic principles could protect the country against the corrosion of rationalism and materialism. Slavophiles sometimes criticized the regime, however, because they believed the state exerted too much power over the church.

Tsar Nicholas I (*1825–1855) rigidly maintained Russian traditions. He allowed only the upper classes to attend school, and government closely monitored the church-controlled educational system. The schools taught Nicholas's three most cherished principles: autocracy (the unlimited power of the tsar), orthodoxy (obedience to the church in religion and morality), and nationality (devotion to Russian traditions). Nicholas's political police had virtually unchecked powers of surveillance and censorship. Western liberal and socialist writings were banned, as were all books about the United States. Nearly ten thousand people a year were exiled to Siberia, often without knowing what offenses they had allegedly committed. The

---

*Norway and Denmark had formed a united monarchy until 1815, when Norway was united with Sweden. Until the mid-nineteenth century, Danish served as the literary language of Norway.

Russian writer Alexander Pushkin commented on the situation in 1836:

> *We must admit that our social life is a sad affair, that the absence of public opinion, the indifference toward everything that spells* duty, justice, *and* truth, *the cynical disdain for thought and for the dignity of man, are truly desolating.*

As the case of Russia shows, nationalists did not necessarily advocate constitutional government.

Liberalism in Economics and Politics

In principle the economic and political programs of liberalism intertwined. The guarantee of property rights and entrepreneurial freedom seemed to depend on constitutional government and individual legal rights. In practice, however, some liberals stressed economic freedom more than political freedom whereas others did the opposite. Economic liberals were most vociferous in Great Britain, because they already enjoyed constitutional guarantees and industry no longer needed direct government protection. On the Continent political liberalism held sway. In general, liberalism influenced eastern Europe much less than it did western Europe.

British liberals wanted government to limit its economic role to such areas as maintaining the currency, enforcing contracts, and financing major enterprises like the military and the railroads. As Thomas Macaulay (1800–1859) explained in 1830:

> *Our rulers will best promote the improvement of the nation by strictly confining themselves to their own legitimate duties, by leaving capital to find its most lucrative course, commodities their fair price, industry and intelligence their natural reward, idleness and folly their natural punishment, by maintaining peace, by defending property, by diminishing the price of law, and by observing strict economy in every department of the State.*

Liberals of the 1830s sought to lower or eliminate British tariffs, especially through repeal of the Corn Laws, which benefited aristocratic landowners by preventing the import of cheap foreign grain. They also advocated noninterference in employer-employee relations. This hands-off policy caused workers to feel ambivalent about liberalism: although food would cost less if tariffs on imports were cut, they would face unemployment and low wages should the government not protect them.

Liberals had widely supported the Reform Bill of 1832, hoping to gain more votes in Parliament for their economic program. When landholders in the House of Commons thwarted efforts to lower grain tariffs, two Manchester cotton manufacturers set up an Anti–Corn Law League. They appealed to the middle classes against the landlords—"a bread-taxing oligarchy" and "blood-sucking vampires"—and attracted working-class backing by promising lower food prices. The league established local branches, published newspapers and the journal *The Economist* (founded in 1843 and still in existence), and campaigned in elections. Their message grew more urgent as famine spread after Ireland's potato crop failed in 1845, and they eventually won the support of the Tory prime minister Sir Robert Peel, whose government repealed the Corn Laws in 1846.

Dissatisfaction with the Reform Bill of 1832 helped stimulate a new movement for parliamentary reform. Called *Chartism* because the groups behind it all endorsed a document known as the People's Charter, the new movement brought together thousands of workers, poor people, and middle-class radicals who wanted a democratic government. They demanded universal manhood suffrage, vote by secret ballot, the elimination of property qualifications for and the payment of stipends to members of Parliament, equal electoral districts, and annual elections. They denounced their opponents as seeking "to keep the people in social slavery and political degradation." Many women took part by founding female political unions, setting up Chartist Sunday schools, organizing boycotts of unsympathetic shopkeepers, and joining Chartist temperance associations. Nevertheless, the People's Charter refrained from calling for female suffrage because the movement's leaders feared that doing so would alienate potential supporters.

The Chartists organized a massive campaign during 1838 and 1839, with large public meetings, fiery speeches, and torchlight parades. Presented with petitions for the People's Charter signed by more than a million people, the House of Commons refused to act. In response to this rebuff

from middle-class liberals, the Chartists allied themselves in the 1840s with working-class strike movements in the manufacturing districts and associated with various European revolutionary movements. Chartist newspapers denounced "the indifference of the middle classes" to popular interests and concluded that "the most bitter and virulent enemies of the labouring class are found amongst the middle classes." Continuing agitation and organization prepared the way for a last wave of Chartist demonstrations in 1848, but property owners proved unwilling to extend the franchise to the working class, whom they feared would support "social leveling." Liberalism and the defense of property went hand in hand.

Unlike their British counterparts, continental liberals did not focus on economic reform. Free trade was in fact unthinkable in most other European countries because the British, dominant in technology and industrial production, could swamp rivals unprotected by tariffs. Landowners, iron and steel manufacturers, and sugar interests fiercely resisted a French free-trade association founded in 1845. Liberals on the Continent did not oppose a strong state or state intervention in the economy; they usually supported freeing internal trade while maintaining tariffs against imports.

Before 1848, continental liberals failed to win political reforms, opening the way to more radical groups. In France, for example, Louis-Philippe's increasingly restrictive governments thwarted liberals' hopes for reforms after the successful Revolution of 1830 by suppressing many political organizations and reestablishing censorship. The regime antagonized all manner of opponents: supporters of the old monarchy, nostalgic Bonapartists, diehard republicans, and newly organizing workers and artisans. The government brutally repressed working-class and republican insurrections in Lyon and Paris in the early 1830s, the republican opposition went underground, and Louis-Philippe survived ten assassination attempts in the first decade of his rule. Napoleon's nephew, Louis-Napoleon Bonaparte, tried to seize power in a pathetic coup attempt but was quickly arrested and imprisoned until he escaped to England in 1846. All these factions would rise again in 1848.

Repression muted criticism in most other European states as well. Nevertheless, the rulers of Prussia, the smaller German states, and the Austrian Empire all encountered reform movements. In the pockets of industrialization in those countries, workers demanded better conditions, and industrialists wanted more political clout. Landless ex-serfs in many German states constituted a new, increasingly unhappy, class of agricultural laborers. Nationalist sentiment drew intellectuals, journalists, students, and military officers into societies that often pressed for both constitutional reform and national unity.

Metternich's government allowed liberal societies to form. In the Austrian Empire even some state bureaucrats favored economic liberalism, especially university-trained middle-class officials. Such men scrutinized British institutions and economic writings, hoping to apply their ideas at home. The British example also attracted noble landowners, as the remarkable career of the Hungarian Count Stephen Széchenyi (1791–1860) illustrates. As an army officer, Széchenyi had spent years abroad, where he had come into contact with English liberalism. Back in Hungary, he introduced English agricultural techniques on his own lands and wrote books criticizing the social system. He advocated eliminating seigneurial burdens and equalizing taxation. In the 1830s he helped establish projects to start up steamboat traffic on the Danube, to import machinery and technicians for steam-driven textile factories, and to construct Hungary's first railway line, from Budapest to Vienna.

In the 1840s, however, Széchenyi's efforts paled before those of the flamboyant Magyar nationalist Lajos Kossuth (1802–1894). After spending four years in prison for sedition, Kossuth grabbed every opportunity to publicize American democracy and British political liberalism, all in a fervent nationalist spirit. In 1844 he founded the Protective Association, whose members bought only Hungarian products; to Kossuth, boycotting Austrian goods was crucial to ending "colonial dependence" on Austria. Born of a lesser landowning family without a noble title, Kossuth did not hesitate to attack "the cowardly selfishness of the landowner class."

Even in Russia, feared or scorned in the West as corrupt, lifeless, and dominated by "regimented Tatars," signs of liberal, even socialist, opposition appeared in the 1830s and 1840s. Small "circles" of young noblemen serving in the army or bureaucracy met in cities, especially Moscow, to discuss the latest western ideas and to criticize the Russian state: "The world is undergoing a transformation, while we vegetate in our hovels of wood and clay," wrote one. Out of these groups came such future revolutionaries as Alexander Herzen (1812–1870), described by the police as "a daring free-thinker, extremely dangerous to society." Exiled to the provinces, Herzen nonetheless enthusiastically pursued his studies of German philosophy, French socialism, and programs for social change. Leaving Russia in 1847, Herzen became an influential expatriate voice for Russian revolutionary elements.

Socialism and the Early Labor Movement

Socialism had many variants in the 1830s and 1840s, but all railed against the inequalities caused by industrialization and considered liberalism, with its emphasis on parliamentary reform, an inadequate response to the new industrial society. Liberalism seemed incompatible with their visions of a future society in which workers would share a harmonious, cooperative, and prosperous way of life. Socialists built upon the theoretical and practical ideas laid out in the early nineteenth century by Count Henri de Saint-Simon, Charles Fourier, and Robert Owen, whose moralistic reform fervor they shared. They saw the positive potential of industrialization and hoped that economic planning and working-class organization would solve the problems brought by industrial growth, including the threat of increasingly mechanical, unfeeling social relations.

Given the focus on reconstructing social relationships, women not surprisingly participated actively in the socialist movements of the day, even though socialist men often shared the widespread prejudice against women's political activism. In Great Britain many women joined the Owenites and helped form cooperative societies and unions. They defended women's working-class organizations against the complaints of men in the new societies and trade unions. As one woman wrote, "Do not say the unions are only for men . . . 'tis a wrong impression, forced on our minds to keep us slaves!" Women's influence in the Owenite movement, as that among the Saint-Simonians, helped turn it toward community experimentation. Socialism no longer concentrated exclusively on work and consumer organization; Owenites now became interested in free religious thought, women's rights, marriage reform, and popular education. Rousing speakers such as Emma Martin (1812–1851) forcefully put the case: "One great evil is, the depraved and ignorant condition of woman; this evil can only be removed by Socialism." Martin's speeches often stirred turbulent opposition as clergymen urged their congregations to shout her down. Occasionally, she was jeered, chased, and even stoned by mobs, so much did her ideas and very presence challenge conventional expectations.

The French activist Flora Tristan (1801–1844) devoted herself to reconciling the interests of male and female workers. She had seen the "frightful reality" of London's poverty and made a reputation reporting on the Chartists and English working conditions. Before dying young of typhus, she published a stream of books and pamphlets urging male workers to address women's unequal status. She argued that "The emancipation of male workers is *impossible* so long as women remain in a degraded state." Influenced by Fourier and Owen, Tristan advocated a charter of Universal Union of Men and Women Workers that called for workers' unions and for workers' palaces to educate children and care for aged and injured laborers. Despite police harassment, she traveled around France speaking out for her beliefs and attempting to organize workers.

After 1840 some socialists began to call themselves communists, emphasizing their desire to replace private property by collective ownership. The Frenchman Etienne Cabet (1788–1856) first used the word *communist*. In 1840 he published *Travels in Icaria,* a novel describing a communist utopia in which a popularly elected dictatorship efficiently organized work and reduced the workday to seven hours and made work tasks "short, easy, and attractive." More influential in practical terms was Louis Blanc (1811–1882), whose book *Organization of Labor* (1840) advocated the establishment of workers' associations. The thinker who had the most impact on the subsequent labor movement in France was Pierre-Joseph Proudhon (1809–1865), whose 1840 book asked *What Is Property?* Property is theft, he replied: labor alone was productive, and rent, interest, and profit unjust. Blanc and Proudhon moved the focus of socialism away from utopian projects by concentrating on the need for working-class associations. Like many later socialists, Proudhon vilified women who involved themselves in the public arena.

French socialist ideas circulated throughout Europe, from Belgium and Germany to Russia. One extremely influential German socialist was Wilhelm Weitling (1808–1871), a tailor whose brand of socialism had deeply religious overtones. His book *Guarantees of Harmony and Freedom* (1842) argued for a communal society but also emphasized faith as necessary to life. In his view, "Jesus, too, was a communist." He made a profound impression on workers' societies in the western German states.

Out of this churning of socialist ideas came Marxism and, more immediately, an upsurge in working-class organization in western Europe. British workers founded cooperative societies, local trade unions, and "friendly societies" for mutual aid, associations that frightened the middle classes. One newspaper exclaimed in 1834 that "The trade unions are, we have no doubt, the most dangerous institutions that were ever permitted to take root." Even when not unionized, British workers joined together in the political campaigns of the huge Chartist movement.

Continental workers were less well organized because trade unions and strikes were illegal everywhere. Nevertheless, artisans and skilled workers in France formed mutual aid societies that provided insurance, death benefits, and education. Workers in new factories rarely organized, but artisans in the old trades, such as the silkworkers of Lyons (France), created societies to resist mechanization and wage cuts. (Recall that in 1831 and 1834, government forces defeated Lyons silkworkers' insurrections.) More rarely, workers joined secret societies that included middle-class radicals, but these carried relatively little influence. The new workers' press, such as the Saint-Simonian *People's Beehive* (1839), spread the ideas of socialist harmony and economic reform among the working classes. In eastern and central Europe, however, socialism and labor organization—like liberalism—had less impact. Guild-based organizations survived in the German states, for example, but cooperative societies and workers' newspapers appeared only in 1848. Farther east, the working classes were even smaller, and labor organizing reached few people.

The New Historical Imagination

In an age of competing ideologies, history became a kind of common language among the reading public, enjoying unparalleled prestige in the 1830s and 1840s. No mere academic exercise, history writing was also a literary and political pursuit in which historians explicitly sought to explain the past so as to identify the causes of change and support their political positions, especially those of national reaffirmation. The politicization of history was especially evident in France, where politicians, poets, and professors wrote competing histories of the French Revolution. The most influential French writer, Jules Michelet (1798–1874), portrayed "the people" as "the principal actor" of the French Revolution and concluded that the people were "worth much more than its leaders." His approach proved contagious, inspiring, for example, Romanian students in Paris to translate and distribute a chapter on national identity from one of his books.

Nationalism and enthusiasm for history complemented each other: history substantiated claims for a common national identity. German nationalists, for example, avidly read such massive books as Friedrich C. Schlosser's eighteen-volume *General History for the German People* (1844–1856). In Great Britain the equally famous histories by Thomas Macaulay described the British people as "the greatest and most highly civilized people that the world ever saw." Like Michelet, Macaulay aimed to broaden history to include everyday life as well as elite actions. By underlining the role of the common people, these writers made history accessible to a broader public.

History entered the lifeblood of literature and painting as well. Romanticism had given history a special glamor, opening the way for a commercially successful genre, the historical novel. Readers devoured novels like Alexander Dumas's *The Three Musketeers* (1844) and *The Count of Monte Cristo* (1844). Governments appreciated the value of history paintings in reinforcing their own legitimacy. To link himself to the growing cult of Napoleon, Louis-Philippe commissioned four paintings of the emperor's victories for the new Gallery of Battles at Versailles, now transformed into a museum. This effort culminated in 1840 when the government, led by the new prime minister Adolphe Thiers (one of the many historians of the French Revolution), arranged to return Napoleon's ashes to the Invalides church in Paris. Although the spectacular public funeral showed Louis-Philippe's eagerness to establish his connections to Napoleonic history, it did not succeed in its goal of stifling demands for reform.

Nationalism and the new historical imagination also influenced musical romanticism. The Polish composer and pianist Frédéric Chopin became a powerful champion in the West for the cause of his native land. Opera, which of all forms of music depended most on public tastes, abruptly transformed about 1830. Before this time, operatic plots had generally derived from classical mythology or had been contemporary social satires; but now the public demanded passionate tragedy, usually with a picturesque medieval or Renaissance setting. The young Italian Giuseppe Verdi (1813–1901) composed operas on nationalist and historical subjects, thinly disguised to evade Austrian censorship. In all popular operas the portrayal of heroines as sexually pure, noble-minded, emotionally vulnerable, and tragic victims mirrored the redefinition of women's character in contemporary middle-class opinion.

Alongside the burst of interest in the political and artistic uses of history came a new tradition of academic historical writing. The foremost practitioner of this scholarship was Leopold von Ranke (1795–1886), a professor at the University of Berlin who trained many of the leading German historians of the nineteenth century. He taught in small seminars and concentrated on the close study of documents. Ranke tried to understand the past objectively, on its own terms, rather than as lessons for present-day purposes. His reliance on source materials instead of legend or tradition helped reshape the study of history into a discipline based on critical methods. The most immediate response to this approach came in the history of religion. In 1835 the German scholar David Friedrich Strauss published a two-volume *Life of Jesus*, in which he argued that the Gospels were not history but only imaginative stories that reflected Jewish myths in Roman times. Widely reprinted, Strauss's book caused a storm of controversy. In the 1840s a series of new books followed Strauss's lead; some of them ended with proclamations that Jesus never existed.

The study of geology prompted the examination of other religious doctrines. A three-volume work published in 1830–1833 by the British geologist Charles Lyell (1797–1875) with the innocuous title *Principles of Geology* ignited controversy. Lyell argued that the earth was much older than the dating of the Biblical story of Creation (assumed by many to be 4004 B.C.). Questioning religious assumptions enraged those whose beliefs rested on Biblical certainty. But Lyell insisted that scientific analysis required an open mind:

> *Confined notions in regard to the quantity of past time have tended more than any other pre-possessions [presuppositions] to retard the progress of geology, and until we habituate ourselves to contemplate the possibility of an indefinite lapse of ages . . . we shall be in danger of forming most erroneous views in geology.*

Many readers saw in Lyell's work another confirmation of the certainty of progress and the virtues of gradual change. Under Lyell's influence, Charles Darwin began sketching out the essentials of his theory of evolution by natural selection.

The Mid-century Revolutions

The growing ferment of ideologies alarmed Europe's entrenched regimes. Talk of reform conjured up visions of violence, revolution, and the downfall of traditional rule. Conservative governments desired order above all and defended longstanding social hierarchies and aristocratic privileges, even as economic change and new doctrines were challenging these prerogatives. Fear of social upheaval ran rampant, for whereas some segments of society flourished, others suffered misery; tens of thousands actually starved. During times of economic peril, people parading, celebrating, or demanding better working conditions could unpredictably turn revolutionary—as they did in 1848.

The Hungry Forties

In 1845 an airborne blight destroyed Europe's potato crop. The next year other crops failed when drought gripped southern Europe and excessive rain poured onto northern Europe. Farmers who could produce something got higher prices, but marginal cultivators and farm laborers starved. Disasters piled up as urban workers lost their jobs because rural people could no longer afford industrial goods, and meanwhile faced escalating food prices. (In the best of times urban workers paid 50 to 80 percent of their income for a diet consisting largely of bread; now even bread was beyond their means.) Such circumstances fueled political unrest. A Silesian aristocrat described the desperate condition of weavers there in 1847, three years after a wave of riots hit the region: "As long as there was a sure, and honest livelihood, none of the Silesian weavers paid any attention to communistic agitation . . . despair was aroused among them by hunger."

Overpopulation hastened famine in some places, especially Ireland, where even in years of good harvest subsistence had barely kept pace with population growth. Potatoes were the principal food for Irish peasants, and the poor ate little else. Potatoes yielded more food value per acre than grains: a family of four might live off one acre of potatoes but would require at least two acres planted with grain. As potato cultivation increased, greater food production in turn spurred population growth as peasants, assured of a food supply, had more children. Lacking any share in profits from the land (owned by English landlords), Irish peasants often sought security in large families, trusting that their children might help work the land and care for them in old age. Thus Irish population growth outstripped that of the rest of Europe. By the 1840s, Ireland was especially vulnerable to the potato blight, which returned in 1846, 1848, and 1851. Out of a population of 8 million, as many as 1 million people died of starvation and disease. Tens of thousands more emigrated to England, the United States, and Canada. Corpses lay unburied on the side of the road, and whole families were found dead in their cottages, half-eaten by dogs.

Throughout Europe famine jeopardized social peace. In age-old fashion, rumors circulated about large farmers selling to other localities or hoarding grain to drive up prices. Believing that governments should ensure a fair price that would make food accessible, crowds took over village and town streets to protest, often attacking markets or bakers. In villages across Europe they threatened officials with retribution. "If the grain merchants do not

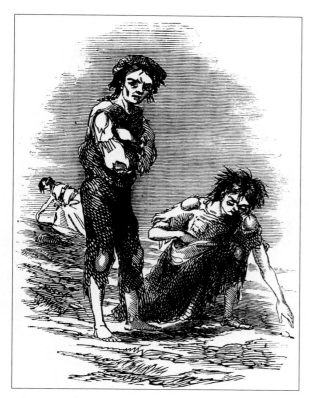

The Irish Famine of the 1840s
Such scenes of desperation were common in Ireland during the "potato famine."

increases. Seasonal work and regular unemployment were already the norm when the crisis of the late 1840s exacerbated the uncertainties of urban life. "The most miserable class that ever sneaked its way into history" is how the future communist leader Friedrich Engels described the combination of underemployed artisans and starving urban immigrants in 1847. Decades of paternalist government regulation, which limited workers' ability to organize for relief, encouraged laborers to look to the government to help them. Should relief not appear, the hungry might well explode in anger.

Liberal, Nationalist, and Socialist Responses

The specter of hunger tarnished the image of established rulers and amplified voices critical of them. Beginning in 1847, opposition leaders in France sponsored banquets at which they denounced government corruption and demanded liberalization of Louis-Philippe's by now conservative regime. Short of funds, Frederick William IV of Prussia (∗1840–1860) convened a parliament in 1847—but promptly dissolved it when liberals demanded a constitution and refused to approve the loans he requested. Hunger and economic instability made these conflicts all the more dangerous for those struggling to maintain power.

Nationalist sentiment escalated everywhere. Thinking their day had arrived, in 1846, Polish exiles in Paris tried to foment a coordinated insurrection for Polish independence. Poles in the free city of Cracow responded, and in a manifesto the rebels proclaimed that "All free nations of the world are calling on us not to let the great principle of nationality fail." Plans for an uprising in the Polish province of Galicia in the Austrian Empire collapsed, however, when the peasants instead revolted against their noble Polish masters. Slaughtering some two thousand aristocrats, a desperate rural population served the Austrian government's end by containing a nationalist challenge. Metternich opportunistically seized the occasion to warn the Magyars that "The example of the justice meted out [in Galicia] could easily turn against the upper classes in Hungary." The Austrian government could not contain all nationalist sentiment, however, as Lajos Kossuth redoubled his efforts to gain Hungarian autonomy, and in many parts of Italy people made their demands for independence clear.

cease to take away grains . . . we will go to your homes and cut your throats and those of the three bakers . . . and burn the whole place down." So went one threat from French villagers in the hungry winter of 1847. Although harvests improved in 1848, by then many people had lost their land or become hopelessly indebted, causing resentment against those who had prospered from high prices.

Had the crisis affected only the food supply, rural and urban people might have found outwork such as spinning, weaving, or other artisan-type production to make up for what the land failed to yield. Yet when high food prices also drove down the demand for manufactured goods and increased unemployment, urban workers began to feel competition from a continuing flood of migrants looking for work. Industrial workers' wages had been rising—in the German states, for example, wages rose an average of 5.5 percent in the 1830s and 10.5 percent in the 1840s—but the cost of living rose about 16 percent each decade, canceling out wage

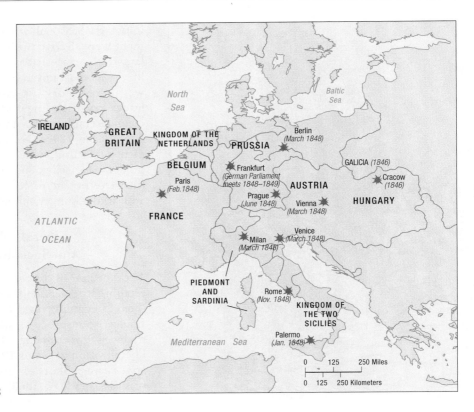

The Revolutions of 1848

The Milanese followed the Hungarian example by refusing to buy certain Austrian products, creating an immediate shortfall in the revenue for occupying Austrian troops.

Out of the growing agitation of the 1840s emerged two men whose collaboration would change the definition of socialism and remake it into an ideology that for one hundred fifty years would shake the world. Karl Marx (1818–1883) and Friedrich Engels (1820–1895) seemed unlikely revolutionaries. Both were the sons of prosperous German-Jewish families that had converted to Christianity. Studying philosophy at the University of Berlin, Marx allied himself with the radical wing of Hegel's followers. Shunning an academic career, he edited a liberal German paper until the government suppressed it. He then left for Paris, where he met Engels. While managing his wealthy family's cotton mill in Manchester, Engels had been shocked into writing *The Condition of the Working Class in England* (1844), a sympathetic depiction of industrial working people's horrible circumstances. Marx and Engels threw

themselves into organizing German workers living outside the German states. Marx read voraciously, especially histories of the French Revolution, and promptly earned a reputation as a fearsome critic of other socialists and would-be reformers. He attacked the Christian socialist Weitling, destroyed much of his influence, and set up the Communist League, in whose name he and Engels published the *Communist Manifesto* (1848). In declaring himself a communist, Marx wanted to differentiate his ideology from that of what he called "utopian socialists," whom he considered mere fanciful dreamers.

Negligible as was Marx's and Engels's influence in the 1840s, they had already begun their lifework of scientifically understanding the "laws" of capitalism and fostering revolutionary organizations. Their principles and analysis of history were in place: communists, they declared, must aim for "the downfall of the bourgeoisie [capitalist class] and the ascendency of the proletariat [working class], the abolition of the old society based on class conflicts and the foundation of a new society without classes and without private property." To them the proletariat and bourgeoisie were mortal enemies; in the long run the progressive logic of history (a Hegelian concept) would bring on the proletarian revolution and abolish exploitation, private property, and class society.

As Marx and Engels issued their *Manifesto*—which ended with the words "Workers of the world, unite!"—several decades of accumulated tensions in Europe erupted in revolutionary outburst. Sporadic violence and strikes over economic issues turned into a sustained demand for social justice, part of a matrix of continentwide protest for political reform, national unity, and guarantees of work and food. Europeans everywhere felt the presence of a renewed revolutionary force. Out of tune with the needs of an increasingly urban, industrial, nationalistic Europe, the conservative regimes, in power in many places since the restoration of 1814–1815, crumbled. Paris supplied the spark that set off the explosion.

Another French Revolution

On the rainy, chilly morning of February 22, 1848, the people of Paris thronged the streets. Stealing time from work, or out of work, they marched to the place where, despite an official ban, liberal opposition groups had scheduled a banquet to criticize the government and foster reform. Although many opposition deputies wanted to cancel the event because they feared violence, leading opposition newspapers and activists insisted it take place. A swelling crowd of students, workers, and the unemployed built barricades to fight the police and army, but this first demonstration was easily dispersed.

Louis-Philippe's government had blocked all moves for electoral reform that might challenge the oligarchy. Aspirations for political change combined with discontent bred by economic crisis to create a volatile situation. By February 23 the crowd had become more aggressive, and the middle-class National Guard began siding with the rioters. Forty or fifty people died when a panicky contingent of regular troops opened fire on the crowd. On February 24, faced with 1,500 barricades and a furious populace, the king abdicated and fled to England. A hastily formed provisional government declared France a republic once again. Its most noteworthy leader was Alphonse de Lamartine (1790–1869), a romantic poet, eloquent orator, and historian of the French Revolution. Lamartine's conviction that he was destined to lead the people enabled him to face down the crowds who now demanded immediate action.

The provisional government issued liberal reforms—an end to the death penalty for political crimes, the abolition of slavery in the colonies, and freedom of the press—and agreed to universal manhood suffrage despite misgivings about political participation by peasants and unemployed workers. For middle-class liberals these measures more than sufficed. Many in the lower classes, however, wanted more. To address the gnawing problem of unemployment and to appease Louis Blanc (the one socialist in the provisional government), the government agreed to let Paris organize a system called the *national workshops* to provide the unemployed with work and wages of two francs a day. This was not a living wage, but the workshops did attract many desperately poor men to Paris. When women protested their exclusion, the city set up a few workshops for women workers, at even lower pay levels. To meet a mounting deficit, the provisional government then levied a 45 percent surtax on property taxes, alienating many peasants and landowners.

The establishment of the republic politicized much of the population. Outside Paris, city after city announced support for the reforms and set up workshops for the unemployed. Priests showed solidarity with the new government by blessing hundreds of liberty trees. Scores of newspapers and political clubs inspired grass roots democratic fervor. Meeting in concert halls, theaters, and government auditoriums, clubs became a regular evening attraction for the citizenry. Women, too, formed clubs, published women's newspapers, and demanded representation in national politics. In a twist on domestic ideology, some argued that political activity followed naturally from motherhood. "This holy function of motherhood," one activist claimed, "gives women the right to intervene not only in all acts of civil life, but also in all acts of political life." A group called the Vésuviennes formed paramilitary groups and insisted that "female citizens furnish their share in the army and navy." Very few women adopted this more radical stance, however.

The Vésuviennes, *1848*
One of the Paris newspapers ridiculed the women who went off to fight.

With everyone organizing, tensions rose. The national workshops enrolled men into squads, brigades, and companies where constant discussion heightened political awareness. To ensure its control, the new government created a paid civilian army in Paris, the mobile guard, which soon had its own rituals, uniforms, and barracks and provided unemployed youth a new occupation and sense of purpose. Exercising the newly won right of assembly, members of some groups banded together by the thousands to support or oppose particular government policies; the communist Etienne Cabet led one demonstration of one hundred fifty thousand workers. Street-corner activism threatened to dictate the new republic's politics.

The new National Assembly, elected in April 1848, wanted to proceed with cautious reform and maintain law and order. Of the 900 elected representatives to the new assembly, less than half were confirmed republicans; at most, seventy-five to eighty leaned toward left-wing republicanism or socialism. Most deputies were lawyers; others were landowners or businessmen; and only twenty-five

were workers. Suspicious of all demands for rapid change, the deputies dismissed a petition to restore divorce, and it voted down women's suffrage by 899 to 1. The assembly immediately appointed a five-man executive committee and pointedly excluded known supporters of workers' rights. By mid-May mass street demonstrations had become profoundly disturbing to most of the French, as well as to the deputies, and as the numbers enrolled in the national workshops rocketed in Paris, from a predicted ten thousand to one hundred ten thousand, this huge group of working people began to appear menacing. Fearing violence, the government on May 24 closed the Paris workshops to new workers, and on June 21 it directed those already enrolled to the provinces or to the army.

On June 23 the Parisian workers responded by taking to the streets in the tens of thousands. In the June Days, as the ensuing week came to be called, the government summoned the army, the National Guard, and the newly recruited mobile guard to fight the workers. Fierce street fighting lasted for several days, while provincial volunteers arrived to help put down the workers, who had been depicted to them as lazy ruffians intent on destroying order and property. Middle-class supporters of political reform who feared the consequences of workers' rights also took up arms. One observer breathed a sigh of relief: "The Red Republic [red being associated with demands for drastic social change] is lost forever; all France has joined against it. The National Guard, citizens, and peasants from the remotest parts of the country have come pouring in." When the June Days ended, more than ten thousand had been killed or injured, twelve thousand arrested, and four thousand were eventually convicted and deported.

Later in 1848 the assembly adopted a new constitution calling for an American-style president elected by universal manhood suffrage. The electorate chose Louis-Napoleon Bonaparte, nephew of the emperor, whom leading politicians dismissed as a harmless halfwit. Lamartine's moment of glory had passed; he came in fifth with less than eighteen thousand votes. (Bonaparte got more than 5.5 million votes out of some 7.4 million cast.) Bonaparte had wide appeal, especially to the peasantry. In uncertain times his name offered the promise of reconciling reform with law and order, and memories of past glory.

Revolt and Reaction in Central Europe

News of the February revolution in Paris touched off popular demonstrations in many German cities and states. "My heart beat with joy. The monarchy had fallen. Only a little blood had been shed for such a high stake, and the great watchwords Liberty, Equality, Fraternity were again inscribed on the banner of the movement." So responded one Frankfurt woman to Louis-Philippe's overthrow. All over central Europe, opposition groups seized the opportunity to force long-desired changes. Monarchs appeared to lose their nerve in the face of popular pressure.

Austria, bastion of central European conservatism, succumbed to a combination of economic crisis and the political challenge of liberalism and nationalism. Just as Magyar nationalists were demanding political autonomy for Hungary, on March 13 a student-led demonstration in Vienna turned into rioting, looting, and machine breaking. Metternich resigned, escaping to England in disguise. The dim-witted emperor Ferdinand promised a constitution, an elected parliament, and the end of censorship. The beleaguered authorities in Vienna could not refuse Magyar demands for home rule, and Széchenyi and Kossuth both became ministers in the new Hungarian government. Meanwhile, demonstrators insisted on comparable concessions in the Habsburgs' Italian lands.

At the same time, Prussia and many western German states witnessed numerous protests, not only by liberals and nationalists but also by unemployed artisans and workers. Peasants burned landlords' records and occasionally attacked Jewish moneylenders. In Bavaria students marched to the "Marseillaise" and called for a republic.

At first the German revolutions looked much like the French, with different social groups joining in giant protests to demand political liberalization. But nationalism complicated the German situation: revolutionaries wanted not only liberty but also national unification. The Prussian army's efforts to clear the square in front of Berlin's royal palace on March 18, 1848, provoked panic and street fighting around hastily assembled barricades. The next day the crowd paraded wagons loaded with dead bodies under King Frederick William IV's window, forcing him to salute the people killed by his own army. In a state of near collapse, the king promised to call an assembly to draft a constitution and adopted the national black, red, and gold flag, whose colors a popular patriotic song of 1848 described: "The Black betokens death to tyrants. . . . Red's the blood we poured as offering/For justice and for liberty. . . . Gold is freedom's blessing. . . . The sacred German colors three."

In March and April most German states agreed to elect delegates to a federal parliament at Frankfurt that would attempt to unite Germany. Local princes and even the more powerful kings of Prussia and Bavaria seemed to totter. Yet the revolutionaries' weaknesses soon became apparent. The 800 delegates to the Frankfurt parliament had little practical political experience: "A group of old women," one socialist called them; a "Professors' Parliament" was the common sneer. Nor did these parliamentarians—mostly lawyers, journalists, and professors—command an army.

The advantage lay with the princes, who retained legal authority and control over the armed forces. The most powerful German states (Prussia and Austria) expected to determine whether and how Germany should unite. The Frankfurt parliament proceeded slowly to write a liberal constitution for a united, federal Germany. Guaranteeing civil liberties and universal male suffrage, the parliament also underscored its nationalistic attitude by denying self-determination to Czechs, Poles, and Danes within their proposed state. Self-determination would be only for Germans.

As early as the summer of 1848, divisions appeared among the groups who had revolted. In Hungary, fears of peasant insurrection prompted the noble Magyar nationalists around Kossuth to abolish serfdom and institute equal rates of taxation. These measures alienated the largest landowners. In Prague, Czech nationalists convened a Slav congress as a counter to the Germans' Frankfurt assembly and called for a federal reorganization of the Austrian Empire. Such assertiveness by non-German peoples provoked German nationalists in Austria to protest on behalf of German-speaking people in areas with a Czech or Magyar majority.

Within the Austrian Empire, the revolutionaries' last success came when Viennese rioters forced the emperor himself to flee the capital. Hoping to quell peasant discontent and appease liberal reformers, the Austrian government abolished all remaining peasant obligations to the nobility in March 1848. Rejoicing country folk soon lost interest in the revolution. Class conflicts flared in Vienna, where the middle classes who had welcomed liberal political reforms had no sympathy for the starving artisans and workers flooding the city. Meanwhile, the new Hungarian government alienated the other nationalities when it imposed the Magyar language on Slovaks, Serbs, Croats, and Romanians living in Hungary. In the Habsburgs' Polish and Czech lands, similar divisions made national unity hard to maintain.

The military forces of the established powers bided their time while revolutionary unity frayed. The first blow fell in Prague, where in June 1848, students organized demonstrations and parades, launched newspapers, and demanded arms. General Prince Alfred von Windischgrätz, the military governor, bombarded the city into submission when a demonstration led to violence (including the shooting death of his wife, watching from a window). After another uprising in Vienna a few months later, Windischgrätz marched seventy thousand soldiers into the capital and shored up his military control. In December the Habsburg monarchy revived when the eighteen-year-old Francis Joseph (*1848–1916), unencumbered by promises extracted from his now feeble uncle Ferdinand, assumed the crown after intervention by leading court officials. In the spring of 1849, General Count Joseph Radetsky defeated the last Italian challenges to Habsburg power in northern Italy, and his army moved east, joining with Croats and Serbs to take on the Hungarian rebels. This extensive military operation succeeded only when Tsar Nicholas I invaded with more than three hundred thousand Russian troops. Hungary was put under martial law. Széchenyi went mad, and Kossuth found refuge in the United States.

A newly assertive Prussian army played a similar role in the German states. After first crushing the revolution in Berlin in the fall of 1848, Prussian troops intervened to help other local rulers squelch the last wave of democratic and nationalist insurrections in the spring of 1849. By now the Frankfurt parliament had concluded its work, offering the emperorship of a constitutional, federal Germany to the king of Prussia. But it was too late for liberal nationalism to shape events in central Europe. Contemptuously, the king refused this "crown from the gutter."

A Failed Revolution in Italy

Revolution in the Italian states followed a long series of uprisings in the 1830s and 1840s. Italian nationalists hoped to unite the territories now divided among the Kingdom of Piedmont and Sardinia, under King Charles Albert; Lombardy and Venetia under Austrian control; the principalities of central Italy, including areas ruled by the papacy; and the Kingdom of the Two Sicilies, comprising Naples and Sicily and ruled by a branch of the Bourbons. The election of Pius IX in 1846 promised change; Pius released political prisoners and instituted political reforms in his territories. Hopeful reformers aimed to encourage unification through railroads and customs unions. Yet the Austrians only reinforced their garrisons and began occupying trouble spots.

Bread riots and worker agitation had intensified during 1847, as the economic crisis heightened nationalist sentiment among the hungry and unemployed. When Verdi's opera *Macbeth* was performed in Venice in 1847, audiences leaped to their feet at the words, "The fatherland has been betrayed . . . brothers we must hasten to save it." In January 1848 an uprising broke out in Palermo, Sicily, against the Bourbon ruler. Then came the electrifying news of the February revolution in Paris. In Milan a huge demonstration quickly degenerated into battles between Austrian forces and armed demonstrators. In Venice a popular uprising drove out the Austrians. Peasants in the south occupied large landowners' estates. Across central Italy uprisings mobilized the poor and unemployed against local rulers. Peasants demanded more land, and artisans and workers called for higher wages, restrictions on the use of machinery, and unemployment relief.

Longing for unity, Italians were divided by class. Property owners, businessmen, and professionals wanted liberal reforms and national unification under a conservative regime; democrats and republicans dreamed of universal manhood suffrage and social reforms in the interests of peasants and artisans as well. Civic guards, like the National Guard in Paris, generally enrolled well-to-do men who resisted lower-class cries for sweeping social changes. Such social divisions intensified differences over the form unification should take. Many favored a loose federation; others wanted a monarchy under Charles Albert of Piedmont and

Anonymous,
Fighting at the Tosa Gate
*This painting depicts
scenes from the 1848 uprising
in Milan against the Austrians.*

Sardinia; still others urged rule by the pope; a few hoped for a republic with a strong central government.

As king of the most powerful Italian state, Charles Albert inevitably played a central role. After some hesitation caused by fears of French intervention, he led a military campaign against Austria. It soon failed, partly because of dissension over goals and tactics among the nationalists. Determined republicans in Milan, for example, wanted an independent Lombard republic, not union with conservative, monarchical Piedmont. The pope refused to join the war on Austria, and Charles Albert proved unwilling to press beyond his initial successes.

Although Austrian troops defeated the rebels in the north in the summer of 1848, democratic and nationalist forces prevailed in the south in the fall when the Romans drove the pope from the city and declared Rome a republic. For the next few months republican leaders, such as Mazzini and Giuseppe Garibaldi (1807–1882), congregated in Rome to establish and extend the new republic. These efforts eventually faltered in the face of upper-class fears of revolution and foreign intervention. The new

president of republican France, Louis-Napoleon Bonaparte, sent an expeditionary force to secure the papal throne for Pius IX. Mazzini and Garibaldi fled. The chance for an international republican alliance evaporated. Although revolution had been defeated in Italy, as elsewhere, the memory of the Roman Republic and the commitment to unification remained, and they would emerge again with new force in a few years.

Aftermath to 1848

The defeat of the largely urban revolutions marked a resounding triumph for landed interests. Workers and unemployed artisans would not be allowed to set the social or political agendas. Even freedom for serfs in the Austrian Empire benefited landowners, who now treated freed serfs as agricultural workers—mere employees to whom they had few obligations. Large landowners had demonstrated their loyalty to kings and empires, and as army officers they put down revolutionary forces challenging their interests and their control of parliamentary bodies. Aristocratic landlords had held on to their political power. As one Italian princess

REVOLUTIONS OF 1848

1848

January Uprising in Palermo, Sicily

February Revolution in Paris

March Insurrections in Vienna, German cities, Milan and Venice; autonomy movement in Hungary; Charles Albert of Piedmont and Sardinia declares war on Habsburg empire

May Frankfurt Parliament opens

June Revolutionary movement in Prague suppressed by General Windischgrätz; June Days end in defeat of workers in Paris

July Charles Albert and Italian forces defeated by Austrians

October Revolution defeated in Vienna

November Insurrection in Rome

December Francis Joseph becomes Habsburg emperor; Louis-Napoleon elected president in France

1849

February Rome declared a republic

April Frederick William of Prussia rejects crown of united Germany offered by Frankfurt Parliament

July Roman Republic overthrown by French intervention

August Hungarian forces finally defeated by combined Russian and Austrian armies

explained, "There are doubtless men capable of leading the nation . . . but their names are unknown to the people, whereas those of noble families . . . are in every memory."

Peasants, too, often supported conservatism. In France, Bonaparte's election owed much to backing from independent peasants, who feared the chaos of urban and industrial life and resisted any change that might reduce their already meager prosperity. The Slavs who joined armies to oppose Kossuth's nationalist reformers were small farmers and former serfs who preferred Habsburg rule to Magyar domination. Italian farmers whose sons were conscripted for the Piedmontese army of Charles Albert often aided the invading Austrians; nationalism was too vague an ideal for them.

Nationalism did not disappear, however. In the Habsburg empire the government incited national-ism among its various ethnic groups to keep them at one another's throats rather than united against imperial forces. In the German states, nationalists dissociated themselves from the failed liberalism of the Frankfurt parliament and looked for other solutions. They would eventually find an answer in military might—armies had gained prestige in defeating revolutionary forces. Overcoming initial setbacks, the Prussian army had crushed rebels in Berlin and other German cities; the Habsburg army had defeated the Italians and restored order in the imperial cities; and the Russian army had intervened to restore Austrian rule in Hungary. National unification in central and eastern Europe would henceforth depend on what the Prussian leader Otto von Bismarck called "blood and iron," not speeches and parliamentary resolutions.

The reassertion of conservative rule hardened gender definitions. Women everywhere had taken up arms, especially in the Italian states, where they joined armies in the tens of thousands and applied household skills toward making bandages, clothing, and food. Schoolgirls in Prague had thrown desks and chairs out of windows and helped build students' barricades. Many women in Paris had supported the new republic and seized the occasion of greater political openness to demand women's rights, only to experience isolation as most republican men denied their claims. Men in the revolutions of 1848 almost always defined universal suffrage as a male right. But when working men gained the vote and women did not, the notion of separate spheres penetrated even into working-class life: political participation became one more way to distinguish masculinity from femininity. As conservatives returned to power, all signs of women's political activism disappeared. The French feminist movement, the most advanced in Europe, fell apart when the government forbade women to form political clubs after the June Days and eventually arrested and imprisoned two of the most outspoken women leaders.

In May 1851, Europe's most important female monarch presided over a mid-century celebration of peace and industrial growth that helped dampen the still-smoldering fires of revolutionary passion. Queen Victoria (*1837–1901), who herself promoted the notion of domesticity as women's sphere, opened an international "Exhibition of the Works of Industry of All Nations" in London on May 1. "This miracle which has so suddenly ap-

The Crystal Palace Exhibition of 1851
British organizers hoped to inaugurate a new age of industrial magnificence.

peared to dazzle the inhabitants of our globe," as one German visitor described it, portrayed all the wonders of industry and reinforced for its visitors the virtues of social order and political peace (including women's proper place). All admired the building itself—a monument of modern iron and glass architecture, more than a third of a mile long and so tall that it was merely built *over* the trees of its Hyde Park site. Soon people referred to their visit to the Crystal Palace; its nine hundred tons of glass created an aura of fantasy, and the abundant goods from all nations inspired satisfaction and pride. In the place of revolutionary fervor, the Crystal Palace offered a government-sponsored spectacle of what industry, hard work, and technological imagination could produce.

CONCLUSION

The 6 million people who visited the Crystal Palace display of industrial machinery, consumer goods, and artistic works had probably not forgotten the threat of disease, fears of overpopulation, popular resentments, and political upheavals that had characterized the 1830s and 1840s. Overcrowding in the cities, workers' organizations, nationalist demands, even cholera, still loomed, and the state's capacity to intervene in everyday life would only continue to grow in the decades to come. Many expected the revolutions of 1848 to mark a turning point, for some inaugurating a socialist future, for others accomplishing national dreams of self-determination. Even in 1851 some critics of the Crystal Palace exhibition warned that it would bring communists and other foreign troublemakers to London. Yet 1848 was not a watershed in social and political development. Although the revolutions demonstrated the profound tensions within a European society in transition toward industrialization and modernization, they resolved none of the conflicts. In many ways, contrary to the expectations of Marx and Engels, 1848 marked the beginning of the end of a revolutionary tradition based on mass uprising rather than the start of a true proletarian revolutionary movement. In future years, workers' aspirations, nationalists' hopes, and even women's ambitions would take very different paths.

SUGGESTIONS FOR FURTHER READING

Source Materials

Mather, F. C., ed. *Chartism and Society: An Anthology of Documents*. 1980. A wide-ranging collection that emphasizes the diversity of the Chartist movement in England.

Murray, Janet Horowitz. *Strong-Minded Women and Other Lost Voices from Nineteenth-Century England*. 1982. Stresses women's reactions to some of the most important nineteenth-century developments.

Pollard, S., and C. Holmes. *Documents of European Economic History*. Vol. 1, *The Process of Industrialization, 1750–1870*. 1968. Covers most aspects of the economic and social history of industrialization.

Walker, Mack. *Metternich's Europe*. 1968. A collection of documents from many countries that focuses on the more traditional topics of political and diplomatic history.

Interpretive Studies

Agulhon, Maurice. *The Republican Experiment, 1848–1852*. Translated by Janet Lloyd. 1983. A comprehensive account of the French revolution of 1848 and the difficulties of the new republic.

Coleman, William. *Death Is a Social Disease: Public Health and Political Economy in Early Industrial France*. 1982. An excellent study of the origins of the public health movement in France.

Corbin, Alain. *The Lure of the Sea: The Discovery of the Seaside in the Western World, 1750–1840*. Translated by Jocelyn Phelps. 1994. Examines how the beach became a place for holidays and became more accessible by railroad.

Davidoff, Leonore, and Catherine Hall. *Family Fortunes: Men and Women of the English Middle Class, 1780–1850*. 1987. An integrated treatment of men's and women's roles in shaping middle-class culture and values.

Deak, Istvan. *The Lawful Revolution: Louis Kossuth and the Hungarians, 1848–1849*. 1979. An outstanding study of this revolutionary hero.

Himmelfarb, Gertrude. *The Idea of Poverty: England in the Early Industrial Age*. 1984. Examines various responses to poverty in England, including reactions to the Poor Law of 1834.

Hobsbawm, E. J. *The Age of Revolution, 1789–1848*. 1962. A Marxist essay on the legacy of the French Revolution and the Industrial Revolution.

Langer, William L. *Political and Social Upheaval, 1832–1852*. 1969. A remarkably fresh, detailed account of the major events and issues, except women's history.

Lincoln, W. Bruce. *Nicholas I: Emperor and Autocrat of All the Russias*. 1978. A thorough biography and analysis of the reign of one of Russia's most important tsars.

Lynch, Katherine A. *Family, Class, and Ideology in Early Industrial France: Social Policy and the Working-Class Family, 1825–1848*. 1988. Examines the social reformers' ideas about and state policy toward the family in France.

Maurois, André. *The Life of George Sand*. Translated by Gerard Hopkins. 1953. Still a lively account of one of the most fascinating writers of the nineteenth century.

Moses, Claire Goldberg. *French Feminism in the Nineteenth Century*. 1984. Includes detailed coverage of French feminists in the 1830s and the 1840s and in the revolution of 1848.

O'Grada, Cormac. *The Great Irish Famine*. 1989. A brief review of recent debates about the causes and consequences of the Irish famine.

Roberts, James S. *Drink, Temperance, and the Working Class in Nineteenth-Century Germany*. 1984. An in-depth analysis of the temperance movement in the German states from its beginnings to the end of the century.

Sewell, William H., Jr. *Work and Revolution in France: The Language of Labor from the Old Regime to 1848*. 1980. A comprehensive study of working-class language and organization.

Stadelmann, Rudolf. *The Social and Political History of the German 1848 Revolution*. Translated by J. G. Chastain. 1975. An account of the German revolutions.

Stearns, Peter. *1848: The Revolutionary Tide in Europe*. 1974. A useful comparative overview of 1848.

Taylor, Barbara. *Eve and the New Jerusalem: Socialism and Feminism in the Nineteenth Century*. 1983. A path-breaking study of women's contributions to Owenite socialism in Great Britain.

Late in the 1850s, before Italy was united, people of the Italian peninsula began scrawling the name "VERDI" on city walls, yelling it in the streets, and shouting it at musical performances. Giuseppe Verdi, whose name they seemed to worship, wrote operas, many with political themes: for example, *Rigoletto* (1851) explored the abuses of power, and *Don Carlo* (1867) portrayed the trials of leadership. Although the Verdi graffiti were a sign of his operas' popularity, "VERDI" also formed an acrostic for *Vittorio Emmanuele Re* (King) *d'Italia*. Scribbling "VERDI" in public places was thus a call for the Italian states to free themselves from Austrian domination and unite under the king of Sardinia and Piedmont, Victor Emmanuel II.

Nationalist Italians finally got their wish, although their defeat in the revolutions of 1848 had fatally wounded the romantic nationalism of a generation earlier. Instead, political realists devised the major political achievements (such as Italian unification) of these years. Cultural life, including opera, popular science, art, and literature, expressed the mood of political realism. In the 1840s, Verdi operas had depicted idealistic political heroes such as Charles V, the Holy Roman Emperor and a staunch defender of Catholicism. After the revolutions, however, his works gave a bleaker picture of political rule. In the wake of the failed revolutions of 1848–1849, European statesmen and the politically conscious public increasingly based their decisions on *Realpolitik*—a politics of "tough-minded realism" aimed at strengthening the state and improving its order. Claiming to distrust the romanticism and high-minded ideologies of the revolutionaries and hoping to control nationalism and other movements

CHAPTER

23

Politics and Culture of the Nation-State, 1851–1871

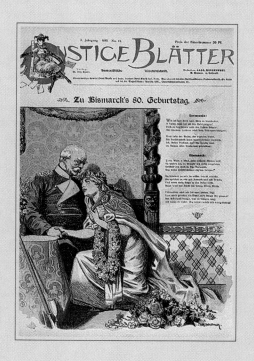

German Nationalism
Otto von Bismarck was a giant even among other nation-builders of the age. After his retirement from politics he remained a cultural icon of German nationalism; here Germania, a mythical figure representing the nation, expresses her devotion on Bismarck's 80th birthday.

for reform, these politicians believed in playing power politics, estblishing a strong government, and repressing revolutionary fervor. Two practitioners of Realpolitik, the Italian Camillo di Cavour and the Prussian Otto von Bismarck, succeeded in unifying Italy and Germany, respectively, not by consensus politics but by war and diplomacy.

Many ingredients went into forging modern nation-states and empires during these momentous decades. The strategy of Realpolitik did not extinguish the appeal of liberal economic programs, even though political liberals were so many thorns in the side of the era's high-handed rulers. Industrial prosperity—boosted by the discovery of gold in California and Australia, and spreading now from England to the Continent—won support from nation builders. Two very different autocrats, Alexander II in Russia and Napoleon III in France, promoted economic reform. The new Habsburg emperor, Francis Joseph, tried to restore political absolutism but did not revive serfdom; his ministers supported programs of economic development. Most towering figures of these decades, enmeshed like Verdi's heroes in political maneuverings, advanced state power by harnessing the forces of nationalism and liberalism that had earlier led to political revolt.

Wealth and power alone do not guarantee the success of the modern nation-state or empire. For a nation-state to thrive, ordinary people must have a sense of belonging and common purpose, and during this period feelings of national identification welled in many European countries. As productivity and wealth increased, governments took vigorous steps to improve the urban environment, monitor public health, and promote national sentiment. State support for cultural development ranging from public schools to opera productions helped establish a common fund of knowledge and even shared political beliefs. Economic growth and public programs did not affect the lives of all people, most notably those in eastern Europe, but where social conditions improved, these changes meshed with the aims of Realpolitik. Leaders such as Bismarck and Napoleon III believed that a better quality of life would calm revolutionary impulses, ensure social order, and build state power, all the while keeping political liberals at bay.

IMPORTANT DATES

1852 The Second Empire begins in France

1854-1856 Britain and France clash with Russia in the Crimean War

1861 Victor Emmanuel declared king of a unified Italy; abolition of serfdom in Russia

1861-1865 Civil War in the United States

1867 Second Reform Bill, increasing the ranks of male voters, passed by English Parliament; Austro-Hungarian monarchy established to stabilize Habsburg rule

1868 The Mejii Restoration begins in Japan

1870 Bismarck manipulates the Ems telegram and sparks the Franco-Prussian War; Third Republic declared in France

1871 Franco-Prussian War ends; German Empire proclaimed at Versailles; Parisians form a commune in March to oppose the central government; the French army crushes the commune in May

---

The Quest for National Power

Rulers desperately sought social order after 1848. In contrast to the relative calm that had followed the French Revolution and the Napoleonic era, however, volatility in international politics distinguished the quest for national power during the 1850s and 1860s. Political ambition sparked risky expansionist policies and wars of national unification; the ensuing tumult weakened some states and led others to forge new alliances to preserve European stability. The age of Realpolitik brought unification in Germany and Italy but the loss of diplomatic clout and the risk of political turmoil to the Russian and Austrian empires, despite their attempts to stamp out revolutionary impulses by executing, exiling, or imprisoning activists.

The era publicized national politicians as great men. A hungry reading public devoured biographies of political leaders, past and present. The well-financed press and politically ambitious historians turned these men into heroes and credited them with creating the triumphant nation-state. The lore that cast these men as legends obscured the democratic and utopian ideals of the revolutionary era. Energetic and commanding figures such as the Italian Garibaldi ultimately served as substitutes for both the divine-right king and the active citizen with democratic aspirations. Biographies, monuments, and public holidays celebrating heroic achievements fed nationalist sentiment and cohesion.

Napoleon III and the Quest for French Glory

Louis-Napoleon Bonaparte encouraged the resurgence of French grandeur and the cult of the national hero as part of nation building. "There are certain men who are born to serve as a means for the march of the human race," he had written. "I consider myself to be one of these." On December 2, 1851, the anniversary of Napoleon I's coronation in 1804, he staged a political coup that allowed him to revise the constitution and declare himself eligible for a second presidential term, provided a plebiscite of male voters approved. Bonaparte won easily, partly because he promised not to restrict voter eligibility, as monarchists in the assembly had proposed. Exactly one year later he declared himself Emperor Napoleon III (∗1852–1870) and proclaimed the Second Empire. A plebiscite also ratified this act, even though Napoleon employed authoritarian tactics to ensure victory, placing loyal allies in key government positions and manipulating the press. Thus the French traded in political liberty for a strong man's promises of order and national glory.

Napoleon III acted as Europe's "schoolmaster," showing its leaders how to combine economic liberalism and nationalism with authoritarian rule. Under the banner of "Order and Progress," he ruthlessly repressed opposition in small towns and cities alike, deporting thousands of Parisians who appeared suspect. For example, Pauline Roland, a former Saint-Simonian who had become a newspaper editor, was convicted of opposing the coup in Paris and sent to a penal colony even though she had been far from the capital in early December.

Prorepublican professors were thrown out of work, a school gardener was fired for growing red flowers, cafés where men might discuss politics were closed, and a rubber-stamp legislature (the *Corps législatif*) reduced representative government to a facade. Imperial style replaced republican rituals. Napoleon's opulent court dazzled the public, and the emperor cultivated a masculine image of strength and majesty by wearing military uniforms (like his namesake) and conspicuously maintaining mistresses. Meanwhile, Empress Eugénie appealed to middle-class conventions such as separate spheres for men and women by serving as a devoted mother to her only son and supporting many volunteer charities.

Authoritarian order satisfied many peasants, while a strong economy, public works programs, and jobs lured the middle and working classes away from radical politics. International trade fairs, artistic expositions, and the magnificent rebuilding of Paris helped sustain French prosperity as Europe recovered from the hard times of the late 1840s. Empress Eugénie wore lavish gowns, encouraging French silk production and keeping Paris at the center of the lucrative fashion trade. The emperor helped promote commerce, most notably in a free-trade agreement with England, the Cobden-Chevalier Treaty (1860). The regime promoted a major financial innovation by backing an investment bank, the Crédit Mobilier. Such new institutions led the way in financing railroad expansion, and railway mileage increased fivefold during Napoleon III's imperial reign.

When an economic recession struck in the late 1850s the regime was once again subject to criticism, forcing Napoleon III to seek new alliances. Conservatives opposed Napoleon's free-trade and foreign policies, so he tried to woo political liberals by introducing democratic features into his governing methods. He encouraged the formation of working-class organizations and in the following years allowed the *Corps législatif* more power of deliberation, causing people to contrast this "liberal empire" of the late 1860s with the authoritarian one of the preceding decade and a half. Although historians have judged Napoleon III to be enigmatic and shifty, his maneuvers were pragmatic responses to the rapidly changing economic and political demands of the time.

Napoleon III's overriding goals were to overturn the changes enacted by the Congress of Vienna, realign continental politics to benefit France, and acquire international glory. Postrevolutionary Europe was one stage he wanted to dominate. For two decades he played a prominent part, pitting France first against Russia in the Crimean War, then Austria in the War of Italian Unification, and finally Prussia in the Franco-Prussian War of 1870. Like his more successful uncle, his ambitions extended beyond Europe. The army continued to enforce French rule in Algeria and southeast Asia, but it was defeated in trying to install Francis Joseph's brother, Maximilian, as ruler of Mexico and ultimately of all Central America. Although Napoleon III's disastrous assault on Mexico ended with the execution of Maximilian, his encouragement of projects like the Suez Canal to connect the Mediterranean and the Red seas proved visionary. His foreign policy transformed relations among the Great Powers by causing a breakdown in the international system of peaceful diplomacy established at the Congress of Vienna. In the long run, however, this policy destroyed him: the emperor's diplomatic appetite tarnished his reputation abroad and ended in his overthrow after Prussia easily defeated the French army in 1870.

The Crimean War, Alexander II, and Reform in Russia

Napoleon first flexed his diplomatic muscle in the Crimean War (1854–1856), a short, vicious conflict that had long-lasting consequences. The war severed the alliance between the Habsburgs and Russia, the two reactionary powers on which the Congress of Vienna peace settlement had rested since 1815. It also forced the Russian autocracy to abolish serfdom and embark on long-overdue internal reforms. The issue that precipitated war was whether the Ottomans would honor Russia's right under eighteenth-century treaties to protect Orthodox Christians within the Ottoman Empire and Christian holy places such as the Ottoman-controlled city of Jerusalem (a holy city for Muslims and Jews as well). Napoleon III had already ensured that France would serve as a protector of Catholics, and when the Ottomans resisted Russian claims on behalf of the Orthodox Christians, Russia invaded the Danubian provinces of Moldavia and Walachia—both under Ottoman rule. A Russo-Turkish war erupted between the two empires in October 1853.

Behind the conflict lay much larger issues pertaining to the European balance of power. The other Great Powers feared that growing Russian authority in Ottoman-controlled southeastern Europe would adversely affect their interests. Tsar Nicholas I wanted to liquidate the Ottoman Empire, fast becoming known as "the sick man of Europe," because of its disintegrating authority. To protect its Mediterranean routes to the Far East, Britain prodded the Turks to stand up to Russia. The Austrian government still resented its dependence on Russia in putting down Hungarian revolutionaries in 1849 and felt threatened by continuing Russian expansion into the Balkans. This anxiety helped Napoleon III gain a promise of Austrian neutrality during the war, thus fracturing the conservative coalition that had quashed French ambitions since 1815. In the fall of 1853 the Russians blasted the wooden Turkish ships to bits at the Ottoman port of Sinope on the Black Sea; in 1854, France and Great Britain, enemies in war for more than a century, declared war on Russia to defend the Ottoman Empire's sovereignty and territory. Austria, much to Nicholas's chagrin, actually kept its promise to France and declared neutrality but acted favorably toward the British and French allies.

The use of the telegraph and increased press coverage meant that home audiences received news from the front lines at Crimea more rapidly and in more detail than ever before, a phenomenon that resulted in unprecedented outpourings of public opinion. Distaste for autocratic Russia and a desire to avenge the "massacre at Sinope" roused the British public. France was divided among those who had seen enough bloodshed during the recent revolution, those who wanted a new Catholic crusade against "infidels," and those who shifted with the winds of the emperor's own policy—sometimes conciliatory, at other times bellicose. But the war ultimately stunned even those who longed for the excitement of battle: it was spectacularly bloody; generals on both sides demonstrated their incompetence; and governments failed to provide combatants with even minimal supplies, sanitation, or medical care. Russian military leadership proved most inept, but the befuddled British commander in chief (a veteran of Waterloo who like many of his soldiers would die of cholera during the war) still harangued his troops to beat "the French."

The Crimean War

Florence Nightingale in the Crimean War
Before the Crimean War, women from the lowest ranks of society served as nurses, and hospitals were ill-kept places where the poor went to die. Nightingale not only aimed to save soldiers in the Crimea, but to transform nursing and sanitary practices in general.

Faced with attacking the massive Russian empire, the allies eventually settled for limited military goals focused on capturing the Russian naval base at Sevastopol. British and French troops landed in the Crimea in September 1854 and waged a long siege of the fortified city, but it fell only after a year of savage and costly combat. The most famous battle came at Balaklava in October 1854, where Lord Raglan ordered the British Light Brigade to charge through a valley controlled from the heights by Russians. "It is madness," a French general muttered as he watched some 673 men ride into gunfire. Fewer than 200 returned unscathed; bodies of the rest, along with their fallen horses, covered the battlefield.

Some historians have called the Crimean War one of the most senseless conflicts in modern history, because except for Napoleon's driving ambition competing claims in southeastern Europe could have been settled by diplomacy. Yet this "avoidable" war claimed a massive toll and resulted in far-reaching consequences. Three-quarters of a million men died, more than two-thirds from disease and starvation. Reports of incompetence and poor sanitation outraged the public. Only one admirable figure rose above the carnage—Florence Nightingale. She seized the moment to escape the confines of middle-class domesticity, improve sanitary conditions of the troops through her tough-minded organization of nursing units, and spearhead the postwar campaign for military reform. Technology such as the railroad, shell-fired cannon, breech-loading rifles, the telegraph, and steam-powered ships was introduced in this war, though its use was not yet perfected. The war also accomplished Napoleon III's goal of ending Austria's and Russia's conservative grip on European affairs and undermined their ability to contain the forces of liberalism and nationalism. And Russia's defeat left that mighty giant reeling.

In 1855, Alexander II (*1855–1881) ascended the Russian throne in the midst of this unfolding catastrophe. The new tsar hoped for some minimal Russian triumph so he could negotiate peace from a position of strength, but as the casualties mounted and the possibility of victory dwindled, he yielded. As a result of the Peace of Paris, signed on March

30, 1856, Russia lost rights to base its navy in the Straits of Dardanelles and the Black Sea, which were declared neutral waters. Moldavia and Walachia (which soon merged to form Romania) became autonomous Turkish provinces under allied protection, and Russia ceded southern Bessarabia to Moldavia.

Defeat not only thwarted Russia's territorial ambition but also forced it on the path of reform. Internal troubles were already brewing when Nicholas I died in 1855. Hundreds of peasant insurrections had erupted during the decade before the Crimean War; serf defiance ranged from malingering while at forced labor to boycotting vodka to protest its heavy taxation. "Our own and neighboring households were gripped with fear," one aristocrat reported, because everyone expected "a serf rising at any minute, a new Pugachev revolt." Although industrial development and liberal ideology spread in eastern Europe, the Russian economy stagnated compared with western Europe's. Old-fashioned farming techniques led to depleted soil and food shortages, and the nobility were often contemptuous of ordinary people's suffering. Nonetheless, through such sympathetic portrayals of serfs and frank depictions of brutal masters found in Ivan Turgenev's *A Hunter's Sketches* (1852), the spirit of reform grew. A Russian translation of Harriet Beecher Stowe's antislavery novel, *Uncle Tom's Cabin,* also appeared in the 1850s and struck a responsive chord. When Russia lost the Crimean War, the educated public (including some government officials) found the poor performance of serf-conscripted armies a disgrace and the system of serf labor an intolerable liability.

Confronted with the need for change, Alexander proved more flexible than his father. Well educated and more widely traveled, he ushered in an age of "Great Reforms," granting Russians new rights "from above" as a way of ensuring that change would not be extorted violently from below. The most dramatic reforms included the emancipation of 22 million privately owned serfs in 1861 and 25 million state-owned peasants a few years later. Other important innovations included the creation of a judicial system that limited landowners' rights to mete out justice arbitrarily and the establishment of regional self-governing councils, or *zemstvos,* in 1864 to promote local government. Realistic officials knew, however, that these "great reforms"

were not designed to introduce democracy but rather to preserve the social hierarchy. One large landowner described the serfs' emancipation as "even more necessary for the welfare of our class than for the serfs."

By the terms of emancipation, communities of former serfs, headed by male village elders, received grants of land. The community itself, called the *mir,* had full power to allocate this land among individuals and to direct their economic activity. Thus, although emancipation partially laid the groundwork for a modern labor force in Russia, communal landowning and decision making prevented unlimited mobility and the development of a pool of free labor. The string attached to these so-called land grants was that peasants were not *given* land along with their personal freedom: they were forced to "redeem" the land they farmed by paying the government, which in turn compensated the original landowners. Most peasants ended up owning less land than they had tilled as serfs. These burdens blunted Russian agricultural development for decades. But idealistic reformers believed the emancipation of the serfs, once treated by owners as virtual livestock, produced miraculous results: "The people are without any exaggeration transfigured from head to foot. . . . The look, the walk, the speech, everything is changed."

As with serf emancipation in Prussia (1810) and Austria (1848), landowners benefited most from the change because they received the best land. Fearing it would alienate the nobility, the tsar's government compensated them not only for land but also for the loss of peasant services. The *zemstvos* provided aristocrats with an institution through which they could provide considerable leadership in such neglected local matters as education, public health, and welfare. Generally dominated by the nobility, *zemstvos* were essentially a conservative political structure, but their members also served as a countervailing political force to the distant central government. Some nobles profited from the relaxation of censorship, of restrictions on travel, and of controls on university teaching, even coming to agree with liberals in western Europe that the Russian system of political autocracy and religious orthodoxy had grave disadvantages.

Another reform swept away much of Russia's abuse-ridden judicial system. One conservative

Emancipation of the Russian Serfs
The emancipation decree of February 19, 1861, which burdened peasants with debt and tied them to the village, proved a mixed blessing for many liberated serfs. In this photo peasants gather for a reading of the terms of the decree.

writer exclaimed, "At the mere recollection of it [the old court] one's hair stands on end and one's flesh begins to creep." Judicial reform gave Russians access to modern civil courts. Rather than leave his subjects at the mercy of a landowner's version of justice, military tribunals, or the old court system, Alexander II implemented new judicial procedures to replace secret, arbitrary, and blatantly preferential practices. The Western principle of equality of all persons before the law, regardless of social rank, was introduced in Russia for the first time.

Military reform followed in 1874 when the government ended the twenty-five-year period of conscription that kept the army both inefficient and too small for modern needs. A six-year term, a subsequent period in the reserves, attention to education and efficiency, and an end to inhumane treatment of recruits made the Russian army competitive once again with those in western Europe. Service in the army had formerly been so like a lifetime sentence that villages had held funerals for its conscripts. Soldiers returned home from the reduced term somewhat more educated and patriotic.

Alexander's reforms assisted modernizing and market-oriented landowners just as enclosures and emancipation had done much earlier in western

Europe. Other landowners, unprepared for modern competition, mortgaged or sold their estates and remained confined within the traditional mindset of provincial life. The changes diminished the personal prerogatives of the nobility, leaving their authority weakened and sparking intergenerational rebellion. "An epidemic seemed to seize upon [noble] children . . . an epidemic of fleeing from the parental roof."

Youthful rebels from the upper class stressed practicality and sometimes identified with peasants and workers. Some formed communes where they hoped to do humble manual labor or start small businesses, whereas others turned to higher education, especially the sciences. Rebellious daughters of the nobility flouted parental expectations by cropping their hair short, wearing black, and escaping from home through phony marriages so they could study in European universities. This repudiation of traditional society led Turgenev to label radical youth as *nihilists,* a term that implied a lack of belief in any values whatsoever.

The atmosphere of reform also produced serious resistance among some nationalities under Russian rule and an uprising by the Poles. Although Alexander II had begun extending his reforms to the Congress Kingdom of Poland, aristocratic and middle-class nationalists there wanted full independence. The January Rising of 1863 erupted in Warsaw after the tsarist government tried to draft restive students into the army. Some two hundred thousand organized rebels—a mix of landowners, bureaucrats, merchants, and workers, often supported by secret societies and nationalist revolutionaries across Europe—attacked army bases and waged guerrilla warfare for over a year. The Russian authorities responded by emancipating the Polish serfs on better terms than they gave Russian peasants, thus encouraging Polish peasants as a whole to remain loyal to the tsar. Alexander II's army regained control of the former Russian section of Poland by 1864, and many conspirators fled abroad or were captured. Alexander responded to national unrest in the Caucasus and elsewhere with repression and programs of intensive Russification—a tactic meant to reduce the threat of future rebellion by national minorities within the empire by forcing them to adopt Russian language and culture. Meanwhile, Russia continued to build state supremacy by relentless expansion into central and eastern Asia, a process that brought still more peoples and ethnic interests under the control of the central government.

In this era of "Great Reforms" the tsarist regime only partially succeeded in transforming itself into a modern authoritarian state. After someone tried to assassinate him in 1866, Alexander II became more cautious; the seeds of economic liberalism and political radicalism germinated nonetheless. Some peasants in the *mir* experimented with new methods of farming and modern trade practices, while students, intellectuals, and some officials urged further political change. Political pragmatism in Russia produced a hybrid: economic growth and the spread of liberal ideas accompanied the evolution of a bureaucratic autocracy ruling over a multinational state.

Cavour, Garibaldi, and the Process of Italian Unification

Even though the disunited states of the Italian peninsula were tiny compared to Russia and France, the Crimean War and the disintegrating concert of Europe allowed a unified Italy to emerge in 1861 as a significant power. Despite the failure of the revolutions of 1848, the issue of *Risorgimento* (Italian unification) continued to percolate. The architect of the new Italy was the pragmatic Camillo di Cavour (1810–1861), prime minister of the Kingdom of Piedmont and Sardinia from 1852 until his death. A rebel, economic liberal, and gambler in his youth, the young Cavour also conducted agricultural experiments on land his aristocratic father owned, organized steamship companies, played the stock market, and inhaled the heady air of modernization during his travels to Paris and London. Verdi, who shared Cavour's interest in agriculture, visited his farm in 1859 to see the latest farming techniques and to converse with "the man whom every Italian will call the father of his country."

Cavour, who did not speak Italian (he spoke Piedmontese, a dialect), had begun his quest for a united Italy in the late 1840s as a moderate who saw economic progress rather than a democratic uprising as the means to his end. As prime minister to the capricious and scheming king, Victor Emmanuel (*1861–1878), Cavour capitalized on favorable economic conditions to develop a healthy Piedmontese economy, a modern army, and a liberal political climate through such reforms as freedom of the press. Gradually, he focused most of his immense energy on plotting the expansion of Piedmont so it would dominate the unification process.

To unify Italy, however, Piedmont would have to confront Austria, which governed the provinces of Lombardy and Venetia and exerted strong influence over almost all the rest of the peninsula. Cavour turned to Napoleon III for help. He admired French success in advancing the liberal economic goals he saw as essential for Italian independence, and the emperor seemed to champion the cause of national self-determination. More bizarrely, Napoleon had become committed to Italian unification after a conspirator who had tried to assassinate the emperor and empress in January 1858 made a last-minute plea on his way to execution that his would-be victim become Italy's savior. In the summer of 1858 at a meeting in the French mountain spa of Plombières, Cavour promised Napoleon the city of Nice and the region of Savoy in exchange for French help in driving the Austrians out of Italy. "Only by showing one is ready to fight can one prove one's worthiness to become a nation," Napoleon maintained. He envisioned a successful war to produce an enlarged Piedmont governing the north, a central Italian state governed by one of his relatives, and an Italian confederation under the nominal presidency of the pope. All this, Napoleon III expected, would ensure permanent French influence in the region. Sure of French help, Cavour provoked the Austrians to invade northern Italy in April 1859, and using the newly built Piedmontese railroad, the French joined Victor Emmanuel's army in soundly defeating the Habsburg forces at Solferino, Magenta, and San Martino in June.

Napoleon III was never a reliable ally, however. Hoping to prevent a sweeping Piedmontese victory that might lessen his own control, he signed a peace treaty with Francis Joseph at Villafranca in July 1859. Its terms gave Lombardy but not Venetia to Piedmont, but the rest of Italy remained disunited. The treaty, which enraged Cavour, allowed both France and Austria to avoid the financial and political losses a prolonged war would entail. Events proved that Napoleon's anxiety over growing Piedmontese strength was well founded. Once the war had broken out, the cause of Piedmont became the cause of nationalist Italians everywhere, even those who had formerly supported the republicanism of Mazzini. The promise of Italian renewal helped romantic ideologies die easily: "Arms are needed, not Mazzinian pratings," an old-time rebel decided. Putting aside their traditional aspirations, political liberals in Tuscany and other central Italian states rose up on the side of Piedmont. "During the war of independence, I do not want liberty," said one, "but dictatorship: the dictatorship of a soldier."

Napoleon III's plans for controlled liberation and a partitioned Italy were derailed as support for Piedmont swelled inside Italy and as a financially strapped Austria stood helplessly by. Ousting their rulers, citizens of Parma, Modena, Tuscany, and the Papal States (except Rome, which French troops occupied) elected to join Piedmont. As elections to an expanded Piedmontese parliament were taking place in May 1860, Giuseppe Garibaldi (1807–1882), committed republican and inspired guerrilla fighter, set sail from Genoa with an army of a thousand volunteers (many of them teenage boys) to liberate Sicily, where peasant revolts against their landlords and the corrupt government were under way. Garibaldi's rallying cry was "Italy and Victor Em-

Garibaldi and the Red Shirts
The popular Italian leader is shown here landing with "the thousand," Garibaldi's liberation army, in Sicily in 1860. Ultimately more than twenty thousand Italian volunteers participated in the unification drive in the southern part of the peninsula.

manuel," but he was also known as a democratic populist. Garibaldi's expedition to Sicily forced Cavour to expand his vision of Piedmont's leadership to include poor and agrarian southern Italy. Rapid victories on the island followed by the "Red Shirts" invasion of the southern mainland alarmed Cavour, who dispatched the Piedmontese army south to keep Garibaldi from reaching Rome, where he would surely confront the French. In the autumn of 1860 the forces of King Victor Emmanuel and Garibaldi finally met. Although some of his supporters still clamored for social reform and a republic, Garibaldi threw his support to the king, and the two unlikely allies rode together through the streets of Naples to the wild cheering of the crowd. Like the growing chain of public celebrations and holidays, this parade bound rulers and ruled in support of the nation-state. In 1861 the Kingdom of Italy was proclaimed.

Exhausted by a decade of overwork, Cavour died within months of his victory, leaving lesser

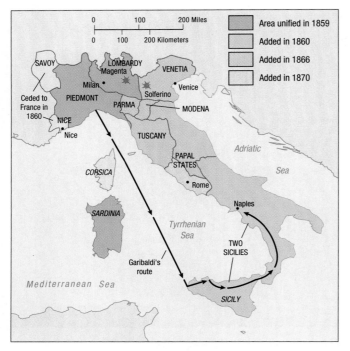

The Unification of Italy, 1859-1870

states of him dotted Italy. National myth making glorified military struggle; heroes emerged such as the dying Garibaldian who urged mercy for royalists "because they were Italians too."

Bismarck and the Realpolitik of German Unification

The creation of a united Germany in 1871 was the most momentous act of nation building for the future of Europe and of the world. Its architect, Otto von Bismarck (1815–1898), the Prussian minister-president, picked his way through the wreckage of the European concert and put together what by the end of the century would become the foremost European power. Bismarck came from a traditional Junker (Prussian landed nobility) family on his father's side, but his mother's family included high-ranking bureaucrats and literati. Obeying his mother's wishes, the young Bismarck had gone to the university, but he spent his time there gambling and womanizing. Only a course on the economic foundations of politics interested him academically. After failing in the civil service he took up the life of a Junker, working to modernize operations on his landholdings and reading widely but by his own admission leading a loutish life. Such was his preparation for becoming the arbiter of European diplomacy and a titanic figure in German history.

In 1846, Bismarck experienced a religious conversion, married a pious Lutheran woman, and acquired a seriousness of purpose. With the post-1848 counterrevolution victorious, in 1851 he became the Prussian representative to the restored diet of the German Confederation. There the Habsburg domination of German affairs and Prussia's impotence repelled him. He learned a formative lesson in Realpolitik: despite ideological similarities between the Prussian and Austrian monarchies and past alliances to contain revolutionary France, the multinational Habsburg empire with its overbearing diplomacy blocked the path for the full flowering of the Prussian state. Thus Bismarck not only tried to thwart Austrian actions in the diet, often by offensive and boorish posturing, but he also urged the Prussian government to take a consistently anti-Austrian stand. Along the way, Bismarck came to admire Napoleon III for maintaining his autocracy through mass plebiscites, social spending

men to organize the new Italy. First among these was Victor Emmanuel, who continued to rule by the constitution grudgingly accorded during the revolution of 1848. This constitution declared him ruler by the grace of God *and* by parliament, an ambivalent settlement that left him room to maneuver against elected representatives by invoking monarchical, even divine, privilege. Moreover, consensus among Italy's elected political leaders was often elusive. The wealthy north and impoverished south remain at odds even today. Many southern peasants continued to rebel against the old, inequitable patterns of landholding, whereas the northern politicians who dominated the government concentrated economic benefits in their own area. For the moment, Italian borders did not yet seem final because Venetia and Rome remained outside them, under Austrian and French control, respectively. But the legend of an Italian struggle for freedom symbolized by the figure of Garibaldi and his Red Shirts papered over these defects and spiritualized the hard-headed pragmatism and even monarchical egoism that also made unification possible. Every town had its square named after Garibaldi, and

on cities, and economic development. Bismarck's second lesson was that liberal political measures, such as extending suffrage, could aid Prussia if the monarchy carefully controlled them. For Bismarck's ultimate goal was Prussian supremacy.

In 1862, King William I (king of Prussia *1861–1871; German emperor *1871–1888) appointed Bismarck prime minister in hopes that he would quash the growing power of the liberals in the Prussian Landtag or parliament. Here was a major test of Bismarck's Realpolitik methods against the force of political ideas. These liberals, representing the prosperous professional and business classes, had gained parliamentary strength during the decades of industrial expansion at the expense of conservatives. Indeed the wealth they engendered was crucial to the Prussian state's ability to augment its power. Desiring to emulate western governments, they advocated extending political rights, increasing civilian control of the military, and other liberal reforms as the key to Prussia's future. William I along with members of the traditional Prussian elite saw western Europe as no model at all. For example, rather than subordinating the military, William wanted to consolidate it by ending the civilian militia system, integrating it into the regular army, and lengthening the term of military service. The issue of the military, on which Prussian bureaucratic and political strength had depended, gave Bismarck his first critical victory. When the liberals rejected the tax increase these measures required, Bismarck announced that the king's agents would collect taxes despite parliamentary disapproval, and he proceeded to build up the military. He also articulated his own appraisal of contemporary politics, specifically his view of liberal ideas: "Germany looks not to Prussia's liberalism, but to its power," he preached to the Landtag. "The great questions of the day will not be settled by speeches and majority decisions—that was the great mistake of 1848 and 1849—but by blood and iron."

After his triumph over the Landtag, Bismarck led Prussia into a series of wars, against Denmark in 1864, Austria in 1866, and finally, France in 1870. Using war as a political tactic, he obstructed the disunited German states from choosing Austrian leadership, the so-called *grossdeutsch* solution to the national question, and instead united them around Prussia, forcing what was known as a *kleindeutsch,* or small German, alternative. The war with Denmark was a prelude to forcing this choice and finally resolving the Austro-Prussian dualism that had existed since the eighteenth century. When the Danish king suggested incorporating the provinces of Schleswig and Holstein, with their mixed Danish and German populations, Bismarck drew Austria into a joint war with Prussia against Denmark in 1864 to prevent two equally distasteful alternatives: that competing national claims inflame international politics or that the two provinces be ruled independently by a liberal, German prince. The allied victory resulted in an agreement that Prussia would administer Schleswig, and Austria, Holstein. Such an arrangement stretched Austria's geographic interests far from its central European base.

Austria proved a weak rival to Prussia. By the time France and Piedmont defeated the Habsburgs in 1859, the Austrian state debt had swollen to five times its annual revenues, and because economic development did not grow at the same pace, Austria could not afford Prussian-style military modernization. Internally the empire had to contend with disaffected nationalities, particularly the Magyars, whose oppression after 1849 fueled their nationalism. Yet the Austrian government still behaved as if it had the same power and prestige as in the days of Metternich. Bismarck encouraged these pretensions. Then, fomenting disputes over the administration of Schleswig and Holstein and assuring Russian, French, and Italian neutrality through a combination of flattery, territorial promises, and other diplomatic maneuvers, he goaded Austria into declaring war on Prussia itself. Austria went to war in the summer of 1866 with the support of most small states in the German Confederation. Within seven weeks the modernized Prussian army, using railroads and breechloading rifles against the outdated Austrian military, had won decisively at Königgrätz (Sadowa). Austria ceded Venice to the new Italian state, but most important, victory allowed Bismarck to drive Austria from the German Confederation, to annex the states of Hesse-Cassel and Hanover and the city of Frankfurt that had allied themselves with Austria, and to create a North German Confederation led by Prussia. This confederation subsequently adopted a common political and economic program, permitting it to compete better in the burgeoning industrial marketplace and to spearhead reform. Bavaria and the other independent south German states found themselves clients of Prussia, and some clamored for annexation.

Bismarck next moved to entrap France in a war with Prussia. He had suggested to Napoleon III that his neutrality during the Austro-Prussian War should bring France territory. Bismarck thus made Napoleon III his foil. Desperate for a foreign-policy victory because of the sudden appearance of a united Italy adjacent to France in the south, the expansion of Prussian influence to the east, and the public folly of his Mexican misadventure, the emperor announced expansionist ambitions that whipped up German nationalism.

In 1868 an issue arose that would precipitate war: a military coup in Spain sent that country's leaders shopping for a new king from among Europe's royal families. They chose the German prince Leopold of Hohenzollern-Sigmaringen, a Catholic member of the minor branch of the Prussian ruling family. His candidacy offended French pride and threatened them with Hohenzollern rulers on two of their borders. King William withdrew his relative's candidacy. The French government, however, was not satisfied. In the summer of 1870 the French ambassador accosted William I at the German spa of Ems and demanded both an apology and promises that Prussia would never again try to put a Hohenzollern on the Spanish throne. "If he refuses, it's war," the French foreign minister remarked. When in the famous "Ems telegram" William related the incident with the French ambassador to Bismarck, the latter saw his opportunity. Bismarck stirred up the German nationalist press against the French as he had done on the eve of other wars. Although William's message really contained only complaints about the French ambassador's public harangue, Bismarck edited the telegram to make it look as if the king had insulted France and then released this revised version to journalists. The inflamed French public demanded war, and on July 19, 1870, the parliament gladly declared it.

The French declaration of war set in motion the alliances Prussia had created with all the German states. France's sword-rattling had isolated it from such potential allies as Austria, Russia, and Great Britain, and all three states sat by as the Prussian army captured Napoleon III with his army on September 2, 1870. "Thank God," remarked Alexander II of Russia on hearing of Napoleon III's defeat at Sedan. "Sevastopol is now avenged." The Second Empire fell on September 4, though guerrilla attacks against the Germans persisted. In the spring of 1871 civil war racked France; Parisians revolted against the provisional government because it seemed yet another vast, centralized apparatus unresponsive to local needs. With German forces still besieging Paris, in January 1871 in the Hall of Mirrors at Versailles, Grand Duke Friedrich of Baden proclaimed William the kaiser of a new, imperial Germany. Without French protection for the papacy, Rome became part of Italy. The terms of the peace signed in May 1871 required France to cede the rich industrial provinces of Alsace and Lorraine to Germany and to pay a multibillion-franc indemnity. Germany was now poised to dominate continental politics.

Prussian military might served as the foundation for German state building, and a complex constitution gave predominance to aristocratic forces. The kaiser, who remained Prussia's king, appointed Bismarck to the powerful position of chancellor and controlled the military. Bismarck provided special consideration to Bavarian, Saxon, and other powerful princes who joined the federation. The German states offset imperial authority somewhat through the Bundesrat, a body composed of representatives from each state. The Reichstag, an assembly elected by universal male suffrage, ratified all budgets. In framing this constitutional settlement, Bismarck accorded such rights as suffrage in the belief that the masses would uphold autocracy out of their fear of "the domination of finance capital" —shorthand for "liberal power."

Bismarck had little to fear from the liberals, who became dizzy with German military success. The new National Liberal party came to blend its belief in economic progress and constitutionlism with the Prussian social hierarchy Bismarck represented and militaristic nationalism. Once associated with demands for political rights and constitutional reform to protect ordinary people from abuses by monarchs and aristocrats, German nationalism came more to connote military superiority. Bismarck, who instituted real social-welfare programs to benefit the German people, nonetheless did nothing to discredit a vision of Prussia as a nation at arms led by powerful heroes like himself: "The old women, when they hear my name, fall upon their knees and

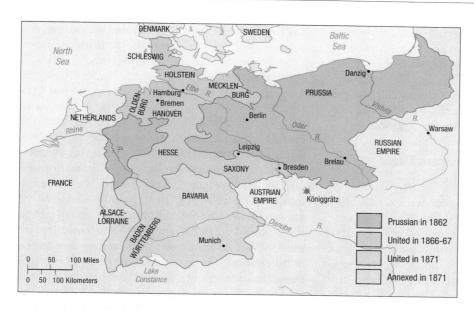

German Unification Under Bismarck

Map legend:
- Prussian in 1862
- United in 1866-67
- United in 1871
- Annexed in 1871

National Grandeur

Royal entries of a monarch and troops into cities, which once served dynastic interests exclusively, now fostered a broader, nationalist allegiance. Here, Emperor William I and his troops parade through the Brandenburg Gate in Berlin, June 1871.

beg me for their lives," he wrote to his wife during one of his wars. "Attila was a lamb compared with me." However, the next decades of stunning German ascendancy under Bismarck's leadership depended on a far more complex political vision, the continuing expansion of industry, and enormous efforts by Germans of all classes.

The Habsburg Empire Faces the Realities of Change

The Austrian Empire emerged from the revolutions of 1848 and 1849 renewed by the ascension of Francis Joseph (*1848–1916), who on New Year's Eve 1851 abruptly declared the restoration of absolutist rule. His chief minister, Felix zu Schwarzenberg, was a self-proclaimed absolutist but one who saw the monarchy as advancing "liberal and popular institutions [and] constitutional monarchy sincerely and unreservedly." He thus maintained some of the reforms of 1848. After Schwarzenberg's premature death in 1852, however, Francis Joseph took charge of the government, working tirelessly on policies and documents and enhancing his authority through stiff, formal court ceremonies. Because the emperor insisted on grandeur and decorum, the Viennese became expert in recognizing degrees of nobility according to insignia on carriages and position in funeral processions. Francis Joseph ruled by playing to the popular fascination with the trappings of power; he also stubbornly resisted change, compromising only under duress.

Francis Joseph was no crafty practitioner of Realpolitik; his rigid adherence to absolutism often frustrated the modernizing bureaucrats. Young middle-class Slavs and Germans (led by interior minister Alexander Bach, an ex-liberal from 1848) staffed the government. Official standards of honesty and efficiency improved, and the regime promoted local education. Although the administration used the German language and the schools all taught it, the regime respected national minorities' rights to receive education and to communicate with officials in their native tongue. Above all, the government abolished most internal customs barriers, freed trade with Germany, and sold off most of the state railway system, giving impetus to a boom in private railway construction. Foreign capital flowed into Austria, especially after the formation of the great Creditanstalt Bank in 1855; the

city of Vienna underwent extensive rebuilding; and people found jobs in new manufacturing ventures.

Economic hard times in 1857 and a series of military defeats and diplomatic setbacks eroded the support for the monarchy these reforms had generated. Prosperous liberals resented the swarm of police informers, the virtually free hand of the Catholic church, and their own lack of representation in such important policy matters as taxation and finance. Money for military modernization and warfare dried up, and Francis Joseph was forced to modify his absolutist system. In an 1860 document known as the October Diploma, he decentralized the empire somewhat and agreed to consult with an assembly of aristocrats. This action so enraged middle-class Germans, on whom the government depended for credit, that in February 1861 the emperor created a more modern parliament (the Reichsrat) in which German liberals predominated and which almost immediately imposed rigid economies on the military similar to those Prussian liberals in Berlin were demanding. However, Austria lacked a Bismarck to override the liberals. When Prussian and Habsburg forces clashed in 1866, Bismarck's military machine swiftly humiliated Francis Joseph's scaled-back armies.

After the defeat, Francis Joseph's most disaffected land, Hungary, became the key to stabilizing the empire. Leadership of the wealthy Hungarian agrarian elites passed from the exiled rebel Kossuth to Ferenc Deák, who as the nationalists' chief spokesman made a simple demand: Magyar home rule over an undivided Hungarian kingdom. Negotiating from a position of strength, the Magyar leadership forced the emperor to accept an agreement called the *Ausgleich*, which restored the Hungarian parliament, gave it control of internal policy (including the right to decide how to treat Hungary's national minorities), and made the Hungarian contribution to the joint army a matter of negotiation every decade. Although Francis Joseph was crowned King of Hungary and Austro-Hungarian foreign policy was coordinated from Vienna, the Hungarians mostly

The Austro-Hungarian Monarchy

ruled themselves after 1867 and hammered out any policies of joint interest, such as taxation and tariffs, in cumbersome and acrimonious negotiations with Vienna.

The so-called Dual Monarchy of Austria-Hungary was designed specifically to address the Hungarian problem, but in so doing it strengthened the voices of Czechs, Slovaks, and at least a half dozen additional national groups wanting the same kind of consideration and self-rule. Although the Poles received a relatively free hand to run Galicia and to oppress the local Ukrainians, the Czechs failed to gain Hungarian-style liberties and no one had achieved the full range of reforms desired by the middle class of every nationality. For some of the dissatisfied ethnic groups, Pan-Slavism became a rallying cry. Instead of looking toward Vienna, they turned to the largest Slavic country—Russia. Thus from 1867 on, the Austro-Hungarian monarchy encountered both the problems of a developing industrial society and the internal competition among its many peoples for reform and nationalist recognition. Few expected dualism to work smoothly or to last very long, but the monarchy itself served as a powerful unifying institution that endured until 1918, despite these extraordinary strains. Any alternative solution to the region's tangled claims would have aroused even more opposition, as the bloody history of central and eastern Europe in the twentieth century amply demonstrates.

Political Stability Through Gradual Reform in Great Britain

In contrast to the turmoil on the Continent, Britain appeared a model of liberal progress. By the 1850s its ruling family symbolized domestic tranquility and propriety. Contemporaries considered Queen Victoria and Prince Albert, unlike their predecessors, models of morality who were emblematic of British stability. Britain's parliamentary system incorporated new ideas and steadily brought more men into the political process. Economic prosperity fortified ongoing political reform, which helped different classes to cohere and resulted in relative social peace.

Whereas some countries were powder kegs of myriad, antagonistic political interests and others (such as Italy and Germany) were just being born,

Great Britain was united under a single government, despite a growing movement for reform in Ireland. Lord Palmerston, a Whig with few definable political loyalties, dominated politics in these decades, building confidence in "progressive improvement." Palmerston promised to share power with the upper and middle classes, and eventually with workers. Factionalized by the repeal of the Corn Laws in 1846, the Tory party evolved into the Conservatives, who favored a more status-oriented politics but still went along with the developing liberal consensus. The Whigs changed names, too, and became the Liberals; the inclusion of radical members of Parliament in Palmerston's ministries built new levels of support for liberalism. In 1867 the Conservatives, led by Benjamin Disraeli (1804–1881), passed the Second Reform Bill, which made a million more men eligible to vote. After 1867 the Conservatives and Liberals developed into more efficient organizations with recognized platforms that targeted a wider variety of voters.

The government also addressed family and marital issues with the Matrimonial Causes Act of 1857, which facilitated divorce, and the Married Women's Property Act of 1870, which allowed married women to own property and keep the wages they earned. Political parties supported these reforms because pressure groups now influenced the modern party system. The Law Amendment Society and the Social Science Association, for example, lobbied for laws to improve social conditions, and groups like the Reform Union and the Reform League worked for a broader franchise. Reformist activism, much of it by the middle class, added to the political process a continuous and extensive network of groups that rejected the revolutionary politics common on the Continent and instead pressed for change from within the structure of the British political system.

Not everyone favored reform, especially the expansion of the electorate. All one found in lower-class voters, charged an angry critic, was "block-headism, gullibility, bribeability, amenability to beer and balderdash." But the government overlaid liberalism with royal ceremonies that united critics and activists, and more important, different social classes. Whereas previous monarchs' sexual infidelities had incited crowds to riot and inspired bawdy songs, the monarchy of Queen Victoria and Prince Albert, with its celebrations of royal marriages, anniversaries, and births, drew respectful, though still exuberant crowds. Recalling the royal past, the aristocracy began building gigantic country houses in such traditional English architectural styles as Queen Anne and Georgian. Other building projects used a refurbished design of the thatched-roof cottage associated with the rural countryside. These symbols of Merrie Olde England evoked a common past to forge a united future:

> *Forget the spreading of the hideous town;*
> *Think rather of the pack-horse on the down,*
> *And dream of London, small, and white,*
>   *and clean.*

Politicians in Britain and throughout Europe fashioned a modern state around economic development, improved constitutions or reformed legal institutions, and a common culture. Britain's robust industry and liberal consensus underwrote its special success.

Civil War and Nation Building in the United States and Canada

Increasing nationalism and powerful economic growth characterized the nation-building experiences in North America. The United States entered a period of upheaval with a more democratic political culture than Europe had. Virtually universal white male suffrage, a rambunctiously independent press, and mass political parties endorsed the accepted view that sovereignty derived from the people. Between 1861 and 1865, however, a devastating civil war tore apart the United States, and at the end the northern states imposed their vision of the nation-state on the defeated South.

In 1848 the United States won a war with Mexico and as a result almost doubled its territory; Texas was officially annexed, and large portions of California and the southwest extended U.S. borders into former Mexican land. Both politicians and citizens argued about the settlement of these new western lands. Many expected the government to ban the native Indian peoples from the land and open it to agricultural development. Complicating matters was the issue of slavery. Would the West be settled by free white farmers, or could southern slaveholders bring in their slaves, against whose unpaid labor white farmers could not compete?

The issue polarized the country. In the North the new Republican party emerged to demand "free soil, free labor, free men," although few Republicans endorsed the abolitionists' demand to end slavery. When in 1860 the Republican Abraham Lincoln won the presidency (with northern votes alone), most of the slaveholding states seceded to form the Confederate States of America.

Under Lincoln's leadership the North fought to uphold the Union. Lincoln did not initially aim to abolish slavery, but in January 1863 his Emancipation Proclamation came into force as a wartime measure, officially freeing all slaves in the Confederate states and turning the war into a fight not only for union but also for liberation from slavery. This transformation of the Civil War, along with belated Union military victories, helped deter Britain and France from intervening on the Confederate side—something they had seriously contemplated both to weaken the United States and to ensure a resumption of southern cotton exports to their textile factories. After the summer of 1863 the North's superior industrial strength and military might overpowered the South, forcing Confederate retreat and bringing destruction throughout the region. By April 1865 the North had prevailed over a now prostrate South, even though a Confederate sympathizer had assassinated Lincoln. Constitutional amendments ended slavery and promised free African-American men full political rights.

Even though Northerners hailed their victory as the triumph of American values, racism had not been uprooted. By 1871 northern interest in promoting African-American political rights was waning, and southern whites began regaining control of state politics, often by organized violence and intimidation. The end of northern occupation of the South in 1877 put on hold for nearly a century the promise of rights for blacks.

The North's triumph had profound effects elsewhere in North America. It allowed the reunited United States to contribute to Napoleon III's defeat in Mexico. The United States had also demanded the annexation of Canada in retribution for Britain's partiality to the Confederacy. The British government allowed Canadians to form a united, self-governing dominion to head off this threat and also to answer both Canadians' own appeals for home rule and domestic opposition to

Britain's owning Canada in the first place. The United States' only territorial acquisition immediately after the Civil War was the 1868 purchase of Alaska from Russia, which was eager to sell the distant colony for much-needed cash.

Alternative Paths to Constructing Order

In this age of nation building, government officials developed mechanisms to forge social unity by means less dramatic than war. Confronted with growing populations and crowded cities, governments intervened in more areas of everyday life. Many liberal theorists advocated a laissez-faire government that left social and economic life largely to private enterprise. But recent waves of revolution and epidemics required the state to guard social peace by attending to personal safety and public health. Along with continuing industrial development, expanding public institutions in

Europe during the 1850s and 1860s affected the psychological, physical, and social life of ordinary citizens. Confident in the benefits of European institutions in general, bureaucrats, missionaries, and explorers pressed European influence beyond the nation-state's boundaries into the farthest reaches of the globe.

The Power of Cities

Dramatic changes in the urban environment made many European cities the backdrop for displays of state power and national solidarity. In 1857, Francis Joseph ordered the destruction of the old Viennese city walls, which were replaced by concentric boulevards lined with major public buildings such as the opera house and government offices. Napoleon III initiated similar embellishment of Paris, making it the symbol of his regime's grandeur. Even noncapital cities acquired handsome parks, widened streets, stately museums, and massive city halls. Yet governments understandably focused their refurbishing efforts on their capital cities. Opera houses and ministries tangibly represented wealth and national power, and the broad

Vienna Opera House, 1864
The opera house, first of the grand public buildings in reconstructed Vienna, stood in the center of affluent neighborhoods, parks, and avenues. Like other newly built public monuments across Europe, it testified to the cultural magnificence of the state.

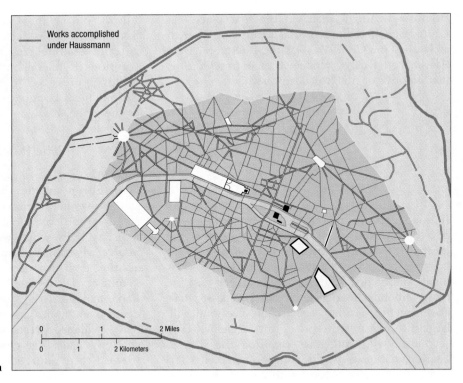

Paris: The Haussmann Plan

boulevards allowed crowds to observe royal pageantry. These wider roads were also easier for troops to navigate than the twisted, narrow medieval streets of cities like Paris and Vienna, which in 1848 had concealed insurrectionists. The dangerous city, strung with barricades and crammed with diseased and threatening people, now became more open and airy; the wide streets allowed troops easier access if they were called on to quell the disorderly. The revamped city inspired awe for the nation-state or empire.

Refashioned cities also highlighted class differences. Construction first required destruction; buildings and entire neighborhoods of housing for the poor disappeared, thus dislocating thousands of city-dwellers. The boulevards often served as boundaries marking rich and poor sections of the city. In Vienna wealthy inhabitants even suggested walling off major streets so they might obtain a more secure separation from the poor.

In Paris the process of urban change was called *Haussmannization,* named for the prefect Georges-Eugène Haussmann, who implemented a grand design for change that included eighty-five miles of new city streets. London experienced more piecemeal urban development. British city planners nonetheless saw advantages in rebuilding for an industrial nation, and large commercial streets replaced torn-down slums and lower-class neighborhoods. Other improvements in London seemed only decorative: old building facades, for example, were given a new look with graceful plaster work and pillars. Those who undertook these embellishments, which often strike twentieth-century observers as manifestations of Victorian bad taste, believed that ornamentation would blot out the ugliness of commerce and industry. Public beauty would enhance pedestrians' lives and lift their spirits. Moreover, the size and spaciousness of the many new banks and insurance companies built in London "help[ed] the impression of stability of the concern," as an architect put it. Private entrepreneurs participated in urban development across Europe with a liberal commitment both to making money and to fostering social harmony.

Sanitation as Order

Amid signs of economic prosperity, the devastation caused by repeated epidemics of such diseases as cholera debilitated city-dwellers and gave the strong impression of social decay. In December 1861, Britain's Prince Albert died of typhoid, commonly known as a "filth disease." Poor sanitation allowed typhoid bacteria to spread through sewage and into water supplies, infecting rich and poor alike. Unregulated urban slaughterhouses and tanneries; heaps of animal excrement in chicken coops, pigsties, and stables; human waste alongside buildings; open cesspools; and garbage everywhere facilitated the spread of disease. The many corpses that had to be buried during epidemics also posed health problems. As society grew more prosperous, the stench, disease, and "morbid air" of cities indicated such a degree of failure, disorder, and danger that sanitation became a government priority.

Scientific research, increasingly undertaken in public universities and hospitals, provided the means to promote public health and control disease. Initial efforts to improve public sanitation relied on the miasmatic theory of disease, which traced sickness to breathing in putrid odors. The germ theory advanced by France's Louis Pasteur, whose three young daughters had died of typhoid fever, was not only more accurate but also had widespread sanitary application. Seeking a method to prevent wine from spoiling, Pasteur began his work in the mid-1850s by studying fermentation. He found that the growth of living organisms caused fermentation, and he suggested that certain organisms—bacteria and parasites—might be responsible for human and animal diseases. Pasteur further demonstrated that by heating such foods as wine and milk to a certain temperature, a process that soon became known as *pasteurization,* these organisms could be killed and the food made safe. In the mid-1860s the English surgeon Joseph Lister applied the germ theory in medicine. He connected Pasteur's theory of bacteria to infection and developed antiseptics for treating wounds. Advocating the use of carbolic acid for sterilization, Lister's findings hastened the decline of puerperal fever, a condition caused by the dirty hands of physicians and midwives that killed innumerable women in childbirth.

Even though the germ theory proved that "bad air" did not cause disease, air pollution still bothered city-dwellers, prompting the most fastidious to move to elegant suburbs, where they could also escape the sight of their poorer neighbors. Land development and new roads also gave workers displaced by urban renewal a chance to live outside the city. By the mid-1860s the Viennese, like residents of other capitals, could travel the city and reach rings of inner and outer suburbs by streetcar or horsedrawn *omnibuses,* although the latter as conveyances of the lower classes were denigrated as "horrible, bulging, dirty, [and] damp."

Meanwhile, governments undertook projects to improve sewer systems and drainage. In Paris huge underground collectors provided a watertight terminus for the accumulated sewage. In addition, Haussmann was determined to provide fresh water for every Parisian dwelling. To do so he piped in water from less contaminated sources in the countryside. Such ventures were imitated throughout Europe: the Russian empire's port city Riga (now in Latvia), for example, organized its first water company in 1863 and also tore down its old city walls. Improved sanitation testified to progress and a more active role for the state. Modernization of the city also encouraged new values. Citizens came to prize these material improvements, leading to a deeper feeling of national and local pride.

Although government-mandated upgrades could especially burden taxpayers in small towns, higher taxes did not prevent ordinary people from supporting better public works. Shopkeepers agitated for paved streets to end the difficulties of transporting goods along muddy or flooded roadways. When public toilets for men became a feature of modern Paris, women petitioned the government unsuccessfully for decades for similar facilities. On the lookout for disease and sanitary dangers, the average person became more aware of smells and the foul air that had been an accepted part of daily life for thousands of years. A citizen of Voronezh in central Russia reported to the Moscow papers "an enormous cloud of white dust [hanging] constantly over the city" that injured the lungs and eyes. To show that they were becoming more "civilized," the middle and lower middle

The Great Paris Sewer
Once popularly believed to be the haunt of criminals and the source of devastating epidemics, the modernized sewers of Paris became the symbol of urban order.

classes bathed more regularly and even perfumed themselves, something aristocrats had been doing for centuries.

The Expanding Realm of Bureaucracy

The drive to improve sanitation and create a modern urban environment occurred in the midst of government expansion. The new nation-state required citizens to follow a growing catalog of regulations, as government authority reached farther into the realm of everyday life. The regular censuses that Britain, France, and the United States had begun early in the nineteenth century became routine in most other countries as well. Censuses provided the state with such personal details as age, occupation, marital status, residential patterns, and fertility. Governments then used these data for a variety of endeavors, ranging from setting quotas for military conscription to predicting needs for new prisons. Reformers like Florence Nightingale, who gathered copious statistics to support military reform, felt that such quantitative information made government less susceptible to corruption, special deals, and inefficiency. In 1860, Sweden introduced taxation based on income, which opened an area of private life—one's earnings from work or investment—to government scrutiny. The extension of

bureaucracy pleased those who thought centralized policies would help society operate more fairly and efficiently than could capricious rule of local notables, but those who believed in laissez-faire often opposed such "intrusions."

Most governments, including those of Britain, Italy, Austria, and France, also expanded their regulation and investigation of prostitution. Venereal disease, especially syphillis, was another scourge of the era, infecting individuals and whole families. Officials blamed prostitutes for its spread. The police picked up any "suspicious" woman on the street and passed her to public health doctors who examined her for syphillis. If the woman was infected with the disease she was sent to a medical institution for obligatory treatment, which usually meant a period of incarceration. To control prostitution in cities, French public planners stipulated that brothels could be built only in designated neighborhoods. As states began monitoring prostitution and other social matters like public health and housing, they had to add new departments and agencies. In 1867 Hungary's bureacracy handled less than two hundred fifty thousand individual cases, ranging from health to poverty issues; twenty years later it dealt with more than a million.

As government bureaucracies grew, new jobs opened. The looming question was who would get these influential, relatively secure, and higher-status positions. Would the old aristocracy and their clients fill them? Or would the government hire people based on merit and skill? In the Habsburg empire various nationalities demanded that their language become the official language of local administration, because replacing German would open bureaucratic posts to native speakers. The middle classes in the empire lobbied to eliminate the stranglehold aristocrats held on the top positions and to keep civil service jobs from becoming a reward for political loyalty. In Britain a civil service law passed in 1870 required competitive examinations for government posts. The push for reform in Sweden transformed the bureaucracy from an aristocratic bastion to a civil service in which more than two-thirds of all jobs went to members of the middle class. Not only did government impose new standards of order, but citizens also insisted that the state itself conform to middle-class ideas of competence and opportunity.

Schooling Society

Ongoing expansion of the electorate along with lower-class activism prompted one British aristocrat to exclaim, "We must now educate our masters!" Reformers called for radical changes in the scope, curriculum, and personnel of schools from kindergarten to university to make the general population more fit for citizenship and useful in furthering economic progress. The growth of commerce and the state were partly behind a craze for learning that made traveling lecturers, public forums, reading groups, and debating societies popular among the middle and working classes. Governments also introduced compulsory schooling to reduce illiteracy (which was more than 70 percent in Italy and Spain in the 1870s). Educational reformers believed that even a few hours of lessons each day would teach important social habits and the responsibilities of citizenship, along with practical knowledge. The impulse to strengthen the educational system came from a variety of quarters: liberals, nationalists, conservatives, and radicals all believed in bettering educational opportunities, but often for different ends, from training people for the civil service or industry, to encouraging civic loyalty, to instilling patterns of obedience, to developing "modern" attitudes.

Primary education had traditionally emphasized religious instruction, with church doctrine, Biblical maxims, and obedience at the core of the curriculum. Initially, various denominations had supervised schools and charged tuition, making primary education an option chosen only by prosperous or very religious parents. Curricular changes in the 1850s and 1860s aimed at introducing secular and scientific instruction: "The mind," reported one enthusiast of modern education, "should be brought into direct relation with fact." Instead of the Bible, an English commission on education concluded in 1861 that, "The knowledge most important to a labouring man is that of the causes which regulate the amount of his wages, the hours of his work, the regularity of his employment, and the prices of what he consumes." For many, liberal rationalism supplanted religiosity as a guiding principle.

The Netherlands and Switzerland had fully functioning systems of public primary schools in the 1830s, and Sweden ordered towns and parishes to provide primary schooling after 1842. School attendance was virtually impossible to enforce, however. Rural parents depended on their children to perform crucial farm chores and believed that they would gain useful knowledge in the fields or the household. Urban homemakers needed their children to help with domestic tasks such as fetching water, disposing of waste, tending the younger children, and scavenging for household necessities such as stale bread from bakers or soup from local missions. Secondary and university education was even more of a luxury, reserved for the top echelons of society, and officials argued endlessly about the curriculum of higher education. In Russia, for example, the government considered teaching technical subjects and science potentially subversive and so closely monitored university professors. In many countries people debated whether future leaders should have traditional education in religion, a classical education based on Latin and Greek, or a liberal education grounded in science, mathematics, and modern languages.

Amidst the controversy over what kind of education constituted the best education, the secondary school became more systematized, reflecting the demands of both an industrial society and a bureaucratic state. In Prussia a system of secondary schools *(Gymnasia)* offered a classical curriculum that trained students for diverse careers. Those who left after a few years entered the lower ranks of the bureaucracy; higher-level positions were reserved for degree holders. In the 1860s, however, new *Realschulen,* comparatively less prestigious at the time, emphasized math, science, and modern languages for those who would not attain a *Gymnasium* degree or attend the university. Typically, those trying for a business or technical career pursued such an education. Like many other countries, Prussia ultimately developed an intricate educational system to track the various career paths and social strata of the pupils.

Educational systems also developed for girls and young women, who were educated separately from boys, just as they were prepared for separate spheres in their adult lives. Reformers pushed for more advanced and more complex courses for young women. In France and Russia, for example, government leaders themselves saw (as the Russian minister of education wrote to Tsar Alexander II in 1856) that, "Public education has had in view only half the population—the male sex." Both Napoleon III and Alexander II sponsored secondary- and university-level courses for women as part of their program to control the modernization of society. Nonetheless, higher education for women remained a hotly contested issue. Reformers from across the political spectrum generally concurred that well-educated mothers would rear their children better and prove more satisfactory companions to their husbands.

Young women who attended universities in Zurich and Paris in the 1860s—where medical training was open to them—often aspired to an education that would qualify them to move into social roles other than those of mother and wife. The expansion of the medical profession and the opportunities in public health appealed to women's reforming zeal. These women appeared to weaken the system of separate domains by joining a profession only men had previously entered. Yet many women wanted to practice medicine to protect female patients' modesty and to bring feminine values to health care. For example, these doctors claimed to perform examinations and treatments with more discretion and concern for women patients than shown by traditional doctors. In Britain the founders of two women's colleges, Girton (1869) and Newnham (1871) at Cambridge,

believed that exacting standards in women's higher education would provide an example of a modern curriculum in this stronghold of traditional learning. Reformers maintained that the low standards of scholarship still prevalent at Cambridge and Oxford reinforced the gentlemanly ideal that education served primarily as a mark of social status. Rewarding merit and competition in women's education, they hoped, would lead to improved education for men too. As in primary-school reform, better education for women served a variety of ends.

The expansion of preschool education offered an opportunity for large numbers of women to enter teaching, a field once dominated by men. Influenced by the reformer Friedrich Froebel, hundreds of women founded nurseries, kindergartens, and day-care centers. Education in many of these institutions was based on Enlightenment belief, which held that instruction and supervision from an early age by mothers started developmental processes on the right footing. In Italy, women founded schools as a way to expand knowledge and teach civic lessons, thus providing a service to the fledgling state. Yet the idea of women theorizing about educational development and teaching citizenship also aroused intense opposition: "I shudder," said one critic of female kindergarten teachers, "at philosophic women." Seen as radical because it enticed middle-class women out of the home, the cause of early childhood education, or the "kindergarten movement," was as controversial as most other educational reform.

Improving the Globe, Rethinking State Power

During the 1850s and 1860s, countries debated the issues of the social role of government in a time of rapid change and the role of European states in the colonies in the context of growing trade. Before the 1850s, British liberals desired the commercial opportunities offered by colonies, but believing in laissez-faire, they also wanted to spend as little of public resources as possible. Some even envisioned that colonies might gain their independence. Thus political involvement, especially the development of national bureaucracies for colonial affairs, remained minimal, whereas trading treaties multiplied. In India, for example, the

British exercised political control through the East India Company, but many regional rulers maintained their thrones by awarding commercial advantages to Britain.

Gaining strategic advantages remained an important motivation for some European ventures overseas. As the Crimean War showed, the Mediterranean basin interested the Great Powers because of its pivotal role in European trade. Napoleon III, remembering his uncle's campaign in Egypt, took an interest in the project of building the Suez Canal, which would dramatically shorten the route to Asia. The canal was completed in 1869 and formally opened by Empress Eugénie with a gala celebration. Canal fever spread: Verdi composed the opera *Aïda* (set in ancient Egypt), but the Franco-Prussian War of 1870 delayed its premiere.

After mid-century, Great Britain, France, and Russia revised their colonial policies by instituting direct rule, expanding colonial bureaucracies, and in many cases providing a wider array of social and cultural services such as schools. In the 1850s and 1860s, provincial governors and local officials promoted the extension of Russian borders to gain control over many nomadic tribes in central and eastern Asia. The French government established its dominion over Cochin China (today southern Vietnam) in the 1860s. Pushing into the North African hinterland, the French army occupied all of Algeria by 1870; Napoleon's government decided to convert Algeria into French territory and colonize it with French immigrants. French rule in Algeria, as European rule in many other parts of the non-European world, was aided by the attraction of European goods, technology, and institutions to merchants and local leaders, who cooperated in building railroads, sought bank loans and trade, and sent their children to schools that provided a European education.

Britain, the era's mightiest colonial power, faced challenges at home and abroad over the changes it imposed during these decades. Since the eighteenth century, the East India Company had expanded its dominion over various kingdoms on the Indian subcontinent whenever a regional throne fell vacant. Lord Dalhousie, governor-general of the East India Company from 1848 to 1856, used this authority to conquer more territory and to build more railroads throughout the countryside. At the same time, contrary to strict laissez-faire beliefs,

British institutions gradually arose in India, inspired in part by the historian Macaulay, who two decades earlier in the House of Commons had called for an activist colonial policy to form "a class of persons, Indians in blood and colour, but English in taste, in opinion, in morals, and in intellect."

An expanding British bureaucratic and economic presence allowed some Indian merchants to grow wealthy and other natives to enlist in the British-run Indian army. But resistance and resentment also grew. In 1857, Indian troops, both Muslim and Hindu, violently rebelled against regulations that violated their religious practices. Ignoring the Hindu ban on beef and the Muslim prohibition on pork, the British forced Indian soldiers to use cartridges greased with cow and pig fat. The infuriated soldiers stormed and conquered Delhi and declared the independence of the Indian nation in the so-called Sepoy Mutiny. Simultaneously in Jhansi in central India, the Rani Lakshmibai led a separate military revolt when the East India Company tried to take over her country after her husband died. Brutally put down, the Sepoy Mutiny and the Jhansi revolt gave birth to Indian nationalism. They also persuaded the British government to take direct control of India rather than working through the East India Company. "Despotism is a legitimate mode of government . . . with barbarians, provided the end be improvement," the liberal thinker John Stuart Mill proclaimed after the rebellions. The Government of India Act of 1858 redefined India as the concern of the British cabinet in London, and the resulting colonial civil service expanded British institutions still further. In the context of global politics, some liberals revised their previous view of government's limited responsibility in shaping global order.

In China, missionaries, carrying their message of Christian salvation, provided an opening for Western powers to enhance their position there. Reaching a population that had almost doubled during the preceding century and now numbered about 430 million, missionaries spread Christianity among people already disturbed by demographic growth, defeat in the Opium War, and economic pressures. These contacts with the West helped generate the mass movement known as the Taiping, or Heavenly Kingdom. The leader, Hung Hsui-ch'uan (Hong Xiuquan), believed himself the younger brother of Jesus Christ and attracted millions of followers by preaching an end to the ruling Qing dynasty, the reform of morals, the elimination of foreigners, more equal treatment of women, and land reform. By the mid-1850s the Taiping controlled half of China. Its dynasty threatened, the Qing regime promised the British and French greater economic and political influence in exchange for aid. The result was a bloody civil war that finally ended in 1864 with some 30 million to 60 million Chinese killed (compared to six hundred thousand dead in the U.S. Civil War). When peace finally came, Western governments controlled much of the Chinese customs service and had virtually unlimited access to the country.

Almost alone, Japan was able to escape European domination. Through Dutch traders at Nagasaki, the Japanese had become keenly aware of the rising Western challenge to China but also of the important industrial, military, and commercial innovations of European society. Thus in 1854, when American Commodore Perry supposedly "opened" Japan to trade, it already had a healthy appetite for Western goods and knowledge. Curiosity, ambition, and fear that the United States would attack its cities with superior technology motivated the trade agreements that followed Perry's arrival, but relations with the West became increasingly tense. In 1867 the ruling Tokugawa *shogun* (the dominant military leader) abdicated under pressure from reformers, who restored the emperor to full power. The goal of the Meiji Restoration was to establish Japan as a modern, technologically powerful state free from Western control. It ultimately inspired other countries under the intensifying pressure of Europeans.

Artistic and Intellectual Visions of Order

Some artists and writers felt ambivalent about the rising nation-state, its institutions of social order, and its expanding reach. After 1848 many had profound grievances, notably about the brutal repression of revolutionary activists, and real concerns about the effect of enfranchising working-class men. Infused with commercial values and organized by officials, daily life seemed tawdry and hardly bearable to many artists. Unlike the romantics of the first half of the century, however, artists of the 1850s, 1860s, and 1870s often had difficulty depicting an alternative heroism or recapturing an ideal past. "How tired I am of the ignoble workman, the inept bourgeois, the stupid peasant, and the odious priest," wrote the French novelist Gustave Flaubert, frustrated by his inability to romanticize these figures as previous generations had done. Such disenchantment promoted the style called *realism,* and the concerns of intellectuals caused them to develop *positivism* and *Darwinism*—theories that starkly explained how society functioned.

The Art of Modern Life

As literacy spread through schooling, all classes of readers responded to the mid-nineteenth-century novel. The novels of Charles Dickens (1812–1870), for example, appeared in serial form and each new installment attracted crowds eager to buy the newspaper that carried the latest plot twist. A popular, humorous, and essentially optimistic writer in the 1830s and 1840s, Dickens adopted an increasingly pessimistic tone in such later novels as *Bleak House* (1852), *Hard Times* (1854), and *Great Expectations* (1860–1861). His characters came from contemporary English society and included starving orphans, grasping lawyers, heartless bankers, and ruthless opportunists. *Hard Times* (1854) depicted the difficult life of sensitive members of the middle class, as well as the grinding poverty and ill health of workers. *Bleak House,* like many of Dickens's other novels, used dark humor to portray the judicial bureaucracy's intrusion into private life, while the character Mrs. Jelleby, a caricature of the reforming spirit of the time, spent so much energy worrying about the fate of Africans that she largely ignored her own children. Dickens linked social ills to the power of poorhouses and other bureaucratic institutions, but as a writer dependent on sales of his work and eager to become rich, he resembled bureaucrats in his work habits, producing exactly so many pages each week so that he could get paid regularly.

Like Dickens, the novelist George Eliot (the pseudonym of Mary Ann Evans; 1819–1880) examined contemporary moral values and deeply probed private dilemmas. Her works, including such classics as *The Mill on the Floss* (1860) and *Middlemarch* (1871–1872), showed heroines vacillating between a world of imagination and the "real" world of family. Eliot also wrote for money, and she lived as a social outcast with a married man. Thus she fully experienced Victorian life's constraints. Characterized as a realist, Eliot nonetheless depended on drownings, untimely deaths, and other forms of primitive, mythical violence to underscore her characters' moral duties and dilemmas. In this vision of social order, Eliot showed the instability of such institutions as the family and marriage—conventionally upheld as the bulwark of order.

French writers equally scorned dreams of political utopias and ideals of transcendent beauty, preferring instead to show the world as it was. In *Madame Bovary* (1857), Gustave Flaubert (1821–1880) told the story of a bored doctor's wife, who full of romantic longings and eager for distraction, has one love affair after another and becomes so hopelessly indebted that she commits suicide. Serialized in a Paris journal, *Madame Bovary* scandalized French society for its ugly depiction of marriage and frank picture of women's sensuality. The poet Charles-Pierre Baudelaire (1821–1867) in *Les Fleurs du mal* (Flowers of Evil) (1857) expressed sexual passions and visions of evil with a clear intent to attract his readership with sensual images. Aware that writers now depended on middle-class audiences rather than princely patrons, Baudelaire gained shocked attention with his explicit writing about sex. Both Flaubert and Baudelaire attacked a range of social conventions, but the French authorities fought back, prosecuting the two writers on obscenity charges. The issue was social and artistic order: "Art without rules is no longer art," the prosecutor maintained.

During the era of the "Great Reforms," Russian writers responded to the perception that European values were insidiously transforming their culture. Ivan Turgenev (1818–1883) created a powerful novel of Russian life, *Fathers and Sons* (1862), a story of nihilistic children espousing science and rejecting the older, romantic generation's spiritual values. Popular in the West, Turgenev aroused anger in Russian readers for the way he criticized both romantics and the new generation of "materialists." Fyodor Dostoevsky (1821–1881) satirized Turgenev's writing in *The Possessed* (1871–1872) and other works by showing the dark, ridiculous, and

---

THE GREAT BOOKS

1851 Auguste Comte, *System of Positive Politics*

1852 Harriet Beecher Stowe, *Uncle Tom's Cabin*

1857 Gustave Flaubert, *Madame Bovary*
Charles Baudelaire, *Les Fleurs du mal*

1859 Charles Darwin, *The Origin of Species*
John Stuart Mill, *On Liberty*

1865-1869 Leo Tolstoy, *War and Peace*

1867 Karl Marx, *Das Kapital*

1869 John Stuart Mill, *On the Subjection of Women*

1871-1872 George Eliot, *Middlemarch*

---

neurotic side of nihilists and thus holding up Turgenev as a soft-headed romantic. Dostoevsky was exiled to Siberia late in the 1840s for participating in a political study group; there his contact with many common criminals provided him models for his brand of literary antihero featured in *Notes from the Underground* (1864) and *Crime and Punishment* (1866). These highly intelligent characters are often personally tormented and condemned to lead absurd lives. Dostoevsky used these antiheroes, however, to emphasize spirituality and traditional Russian values and to combat leanings toward an Enlightenment faith in rational behavior.

Whereas Dostoevsky's eccentric heroes had some kinship to romantic types, Leo Tolstoy's were initially modeled from realist clay. Tolstoy (1828–1910) gained national fame with *Sevastopol Stories* (1855–1856), the report of his soldiering in the Crimean War. Returning to his estate after the war, he ran schools for peasants in which he followed a Rousseauian method of useful lessons and instilled Russian patriotism in his pupils. A huge panorama of Russian life during the Napoleonic invasion, his masterwork *War and Peace* (1865–1869) portrays aristocratic society's quest to defend Russian values against incursions by the French and their revolutionary views.

Painting and sculpture were not part of the same mass market as literature; artists depended on government commissions and exhibitions. Prince Albert of England was an active patron of the arts, purchasing works for official collections and for himself until his death in 1861. The art world

Gustave Courbet, **The Sleeping Spinner,** *1853 Courbet often depicted workers more harshly, but this gentle portrait shows his interest in working-class life. Hand spinning, a typical employment for women, faced intense competition from mechanization and the spread of mills.*

centered in Paris. Having one's work displayed at government-sponsored exhibitions (*salons*) was the best way for an artist to gain prominence and earn a living. Officially appointed juries selected works of art to appear in the *salon* and then chose prize winners from among them. By the Second Empire thousands of paintings were shown annually, with hundreds of thousands of people from all classes in attendance. At the international exposition held in Paris in 1855, nearly a million people visited the art exhibit.

The repression of political disorder after 1848 lessened the romantic glorification of workers, country folk, and nature. Instead of idealizing, artists followed novelists in realistically depicting society. French painter Gustave Courbet (1819–1877) portrayed groaning laborers at backbreaking work because he believed an artist should "never permit sentiment to overthrow logic." Art could foster "democracy" by showing the world as it was and hiding neither the shabbiness nor the depravity of life.

Courbet's philosophy, shared by some other artists, led to the so-called art wars of the Second Empire. In 1853, Courbet submitted paintings en-

titled *The Wrestlers* and *The Bather* to that year's *salon.* Critics, expecting the idealized female nude that patrons were accustomed to, scorned the bather as fat and ugly, and saw the wrestlers as "fighting to see which is the dirtiest. The victor will receive a four-cent bath ticket." Painters whose work was declared inappropriate for the official *salon* ultimately started a *Salon des refusés* (a *salon* for rejected paintings), where the most innovative art was displayed.

These innovative painters also rejected grand historic scenes and instead depicted social change, particularly the reconstruction of cities. Paris, artists found, had become a visual spectacle, a place of grand boulevards where urban residents displayed themselves as part of the cityscape. The artist's canvas showed the renovated city as a stage for individual ambition and exhibition. *Universal Exhibition* (1867) by Edouard Manet (1823–1883) used a world's fair in the background; figures in the foreground were separated from one another by the planned urban spaces as they promenaded, gazing at the Paris scene. In promenading the classes were also watching one another to learn the new social rules of modern life.

Edouard Manet, Dejeuner sur l'herbe *(Luncheon on the Grass), 1863*
Painters during this period broke with the tradition of producing idealized versions of historic scenes and highly romanticized nudes. In this painting Manet's juxtaposition of the nude and a depiction of everyday life, complete with picnic lunch and discarded clothing, both helped to inspire a new art and irritated polite society.

Manet's work took off the rose-colored glasses through which polite society seemed to view women and sexuality. His famous *Dejeuner sur l'herbe* (Luncheon on the Grass) (1863) was deemed scandalous because of the two women, one naked and the second half undressed, on a picnic in a woods with fully clothed contemporary men. *Olympia* (1865) depicted a white courtesan lying on her bed, attended by a black woman. Both nudes proved shocking because instead of mythologizing and romanticizing women's bodies they appeared in realistic settings. This disregard for the traditions of the fine arts was too much for the critics: "A sort of female gorilla," one wrote of *Olympia;* "her greenish, bloodshot eyes appear to be provoking the public," wrote another. Shocking at first, graphic portrayals that shattered comforting illusions became a feature of modern art.

By contrast, opera was commercially profitable, accessible to most strata of society, and thus an effective artistic vehicle for reaching the nineteenth-century public. The great Italian composer Giuseppe Verdi (1813–1901) used musical theater to contrast noble ideals with the corrosive effects of power. His *La Traviata* (1853) nonethe-

less stunned audiences with the tragedy of a tubercular Parisian courtesan who falls in love with a respectable middle-class man. The lax morals and political corruption of the Second Empire also inspired the sardonic satire of Jacques Offenbach (1819–1880), a German Jew who made his career composing and producing operettas (amusing, light operas) in Napoleon III's Paris.

The German Richard Wagner (1813–1883) was the most flamboyant and musically innovative composer of this era. Exiled from most German states because of his revolutionary activities in 1848, Wagner spent much of the 1850s working on a gigantic four-part group of operas, *Der Ring des Nibelungen,* that reshaped ancient German myths into a modern, nightmarish allegory of a world doomed by its obsessive pursuit of money and power and redeemable only through unselfish love. Wagner hoped to revolutionize opera, fusing music and drama to arouse the audience's fear, awe, and commitment. His music was lush and harmonically daring, and it strove for overpowering emotional climaxes. Despairing of seeing the *Ring* actually staged, Wagner produced other operas, most notably the comedy *Die Meistersinger*

(1862–1867), a nationalistic tribute to German art. Only completing the *Ring* in 1874, Wagner was sustained by unrepaid loans and generous gifts he extracted from his friends so he could surround himself with the silks, fine clothing, and artworks he deemed necessary for inspiration. His flair for publicity and musical innovation ultimately made him a major force in philosophy, politics, and the arts.

A New Order for Religion and the Natural Sciences

Organized religion formed a bulwark of traditional order after the revolutions of 1848. Thus in the 1850s many politicians supported religious institutions and attended public church rituals. But many nation builders, intellectuals, and economic liberals eventually rejected the competing jurisdiction and religious world view of established churches, particularly Roman Catholicism. "Do not interfere with what we teach and write," one intellectual proposed to the clergy, "and we will not question your control over the people." Protestant churches claimed limited authority over secular life, though they inspired social reform. The Roman Catholic church, however, insisted on its political influence and explicitly attacked nineteenth-century visions of progress.

The Catholic church felt assaulted by intellectual critiques of its doctrine and by the state building of Italy and Germany that jeopardized its temporal rule. Rulers of these new countries found that the competing loyalty demanded by the Catholic church drained patriotism. Nation building had resulted in the extension of liberal rights to Jews, whom Christians and particularly the Catholic church considered enemies. Provocatively attacking modernity in all its forms, Pope Pius IX (✶1846–1878) issued *The Syllabus of Errors* (1864), which denied that the church and its pontiff should come to terms "with progress, with liberalism and with modern civilization." In 1870 the First Vatican Council approved a declaration of papal infallibility. This teaching proclaimed that the pope, under certain circumstances, must be regarded by Catholics as speaking divinely sanctioned truth on issues of morality and faith. Liberal-minded Catholic intellectuals and clergy found themselves obliged either to submit to the new dogma or be excommunicated.

Religious doctrine had powerful popular appeal. Although church attendance declined among workers and artisans, many in the upper and middle classes and most of the peasantry remained faithful. The Orthodox church fostered nationalism among Serbs, as other churches did for ethnic minorities in rural areas. Women's spiritual beliefs became more intense, causing an increase in both Roman Catholic and Russian Orthodox women's religious orders. In 1854 the pope announced the doctrine of the Immaculate Conception, stating that Mary (alone among all humans) had been born without original sin. This announcement was followed by an outburst of popular religious fervor. In 1858 a peasant girl from Lourdes in southern France, Bernadette Soubirous, began having visions of the Virgin Mary. Calling herself "the Immaculate

Pilgrims at Lourdes
The site of Bernadette Soubirous's visions of the Virgin Mary, Lourdes rapidly attracted sick people hoping to be cured. The Church first resisted this burst of religious fervor but soon organized pilgrimages to the site and established a vast complex there of churches, shrines, and hostels.

Conception," Mary told Bernadette to drink from the ground, at which point a spring appeared. Crowds of women besieged the area to be cured of ailments by the waters of the Immaculate Conception. In 1867, less than ten years later, a railroad track was laid to Lourdes, which from then on was visited by millions of pilgrims on church-organized trips. The Catholic church thus came to rely on such modern means as railroads, medical verifications of miraculous cures, journalism, and political parties.

Almost contemporaneously with Bernadette's vision, the English naturalist Charles Darwin (1809–1882) published *The Origin of Species* (1859), a challenge to the entire Judeo-Christian world view that humanity represented a unique creation of God. Darwin argued that life had taken shape over countless millions of years before humans existed, and that human life was but the result of evolutionary change. Evolutionary theory was in the air before Darwin's book appeared: Charles Lyell's *Principles of Geology* (1832–1834) had cautiously suggested that the earth's geological structure had developed over an immense span of time. As a young scientist on an expedition aboard the *Beagle* in 1831 through 1836, Darwin had read Lyell's work and begun to consider various scientific puzzles in the environments he visited. Why, he pondered, did species of animals vary from one tropical island to another even though climate and other natural conditions were roughly the same? As early as the 1840s, Darwin was applying theories of evolution to biological life and suggesting that new biological forms arise from older ones as the most fit survive and reproduce. *The Origin of Species* pulled together his insights on evolution and almost immediately raised a storm of controversy.

Darwin's thought also reflected the gloomy predictions of Thomas Malthus that population growth would outstrip the food supply unless checked by famine or disease. Instead of the Enlightenment vision of nature and society as harmonious, Darwin saw the constant turmoil of all species—including humans—struggling to survive. In this fight only the hardiest prevailed, and by sexual selection passed their natural strength to the next generation. That generation in turn might face harsh conditions. In this perpetual challenge to meet the forces of nature, Darwin suggested, some species died out whereas those with better-

The Challenge of Evolution
Charles Darwin's theories suggested that humankind had not descended from angels but instead had evolved from other species in the animal kingdom. Such ideas were frequently lampooned, as in this satirical drawing of Darwin holding up a mirror to a monkey.

adapted characteristics would survive in a new environment.

Darwin's theories shocked adherents of traditional Christianity because they undercut the story of Creation described in Genesis by maintaining that species evolved from one another. Instead of God miraculously bringing the universe and all life into being in six days, life developed from lower forms through a primal battle for survival. An eminently respectable Victorian, Darwin announced that the Bible gave a "manifestly false history of the world." Darwin's theories also undermined certain liberal, secular beliefs. Enlightenment principles, for example, had glorified nature as tranquil and noble and had viewed human nature as essentially rational. The theory of natural selection suggested a different kind of human society, one based in a hostile environment where combative individuals and groups constantly fought one another. The mechanisms by which characteristics were passed from generation to generation eluded Darwin, but the Austrian monk and botanist Gregor Mendel (1822–1884) was laying the foundations for this understanding in Darwin's lifetime. Working in obscurity on plants in his monastic garden, Mendel discovered the principles of heredity in the 1860s; his discoveries received little attention until 1900.

Darwin's findings and other innovative biological research provoked further studies and influenced contemporary beliefs. Investigation into the female reproductive cycle led German scientists to discover the principle of spontaneous ovulation—the automatic release of the egg by the ovary whether sexual intercourse took place or not. This discovery caused theorists to conclude that men had strong sexual drives because reproduction depended on their sexual arousal, but that the spontaneous and cyclical release of the egg independent of arousal was a sign of women's lack of sexual feeling.

Darwin, who shared the stereotypical social assumptions of his age, used his findings to explain Victorian society. The legal, political, and economic privilege of white European men in the nineteenth century derived from their being more highly evolved than white women or people of color, he maintained. "The chief distinction in the intellectual powers of the two sexes," Darwin declared, "is shewn by man's attaining to a higher eminence in whatever he takes up." As others applied Darwin's theories to explain social life, a school of Social Darwinism arose to lobby for public policy based on evolution and natural selection.

From Natural Science to Social Science

An enthusiasm for hard-edged scientific methods shaped social thought after 1850 as concerned intellectuals scrambled to find alternatives to the religious vision of social order. Even before *The Origin of Species* appeared, select members of the

English middle class had formed the National Association for the Advancement of Social Science in 1857, and in 1872 the French Society for Sociology was founded. The impulse for such new organizations came partly from the theories of the French philosopher Auguste Comte (1798–1857), whose ideas formed the base for a "positive science" of society and politics. *Positivism* claimed that careful study of facts would generate accurate, or "positive," laws of society. Comte's *System of Positive Politics, or Treatise on Sociology* (1851) proposed that social scientists construct the political order as they would construct an understanding of the natural world, that is, according to informed investigation. This idea inspired people to believe they could deal with the incredible problems spawned by economic and social change. Comte also prompted women's participation in reform because he deemed "womanly" compassion and love as fundamental as scientific public policy for restoring social harmony. Positivism in the form of social science thus opened a new road to order. The fields of anthropology, psychology, economics, and sociology developed during this period, largely under the banner of positivism.

The English philosopher John Stuart Mill (1806–1873) confronted the many problems in modern society and quickly became an enthusiast of Comte. Mill broke with his father's utilitarian thought to embrace many features of positivism, to espouse widespread reform and mass education, and to support the complete enfranchisement of women. His famous *On Liberty* (1859) couched his aspiration for general social improvement in a concern that superior people not be brought down or confined by the will of the masses. *On Liberty* also argued for individual liberties protected from state intrusion and for freedom of expression for those whose views ran counter to state interests. Mill's writings reflected anxiety for the status of the individual in a nation with a growing electorate of differing interests and a multi-racial empire.

Stretching liberal principles to embrace an array of issues, Mill became notorious for extending the concept of rights and freedom to women. Here Mill felt the profound influence of his wife, Harriet Taylor Mill (1808–1858), with whom he studied marriage, women's rights, and divorce. After his wife's premature death, Mill intensified his activities on behalf of women's rights, notably by introducing a women's suffrage bill into the House of Commons. The bill's defeat prompted Mill to publish *The Subjection of Women* (1869), a work recapitulating his studies with his wife. Translated into many languages and influential in eastern Europe, Scandinavia, and the western hemisphere, *The Subjection of Women* discussed the family as maintaining an older kind of politics devoid of modern concepts of rights and freedom. Mill also proposed that the aura of women's voluntary obedience and love in marriage were necessary to mask gross marital inequality. According to Mill, to create "not a forced slave, but a willing one," women were raised "from the very earliest years in the belief that their ideal of character is the very opposite to that of men; not self-will and government by self-control, but submission and yielding to the control of others." Critiquing the century's most basic beliefs about men's and women's roles, *The Subjection of Women* became a bible for a growing women's movement committed to expanding liberal rights.

The fundamental decency of much of Mill's social thought was soon lost in the flood of Social Darwinist theories. Even before *The Origin of Species,* Herbert Spencer's *Social Statics* (1851) advocated the study of society from many intellectual perspectives to arrive at a true picture of its workings. Spencer promoted laissez-faire and unadulterate competition, and his claim that the "unfit" should be allowed to perish in the name of progress was greatly reinforced by Darwin's work. His opposition to public education, social reform, and any other attempt to soften the harshness of the struggle for existence struck a receptive chord, contributing to the surge of Social Darwinism in the next decades.

Contesting the Political Order of the Nation-State

By the end of the 1860s the unchecked growth of the state and the ongoing process of economic change had led to palpable tensions in many segments of society. In the context of defeat in the Franco-Prussian War, these tensions led to bitter if brief civil war. In the spring of 1871 the people of Paris, blaming the French surrender to the Germans on the centralized state, declared Paris a *commune,* a community of equals without bureaucrats and pompous politicians. Hearing of the bloody struggle between the people of Paris and the new republican government while living in safety in England, the economist and philosopher Karl Marx produced his *Civil War in France* (1871). Translated along with his other writings, it provided workers with a popular and politically galvanizing account of events. From the 1870s on, these two phenomena—the writings of Karl Marx and the fury of working people—renewed fear among the middle classes that their carefully constructed national order might be violently destroyed.

Marxist Ideas and the Working-Class Movement

After a period of repression in the 1850s, workers' organizations slowly reemerged as a political force. Like other interest groups, worker organizations were part of a pattern of *horizontal allegiances* in which people with similar backgrounds or with similar goals joined together to shape the political process. Such horizontal allegiances replaced or coexisted with the *vertical allegiances* that reflected not similarity and equality but hierarchy and subordination. The family was one example of a vertical structure increasingly displaced as a source of social identity by peer groups in schools, factories, and clubs. Worker organizations were a part of this development.

In the 1850s governments often outlawed unions, fearing they would challenge the established political order. Those that existed were thus secret, poorly coordinated, and shaped by a wide range of programs for change, including the ideas of former printer Pierre-Joseph Proudhon (1809–1865). In the 1840s, Proudhon had coined the explosive phrase "Property is theft," suggesting that ownership robbed propertyless people of their rightful share of the earth's benefits. He opposed the centralized state and proposed that society be organized instead around natural groupings of men (but not women) in artisanal workshops. These workshops and a central bank crediting each worker for his labor would replace government and lead to a "mutualist" social organization. Proudhon heartily opposed any mingling of men and women in political life; he believed the mutualist organization of men in public should be matched by the seclusion of the wife laboring at home for her husband's comfort.

Another theorist and politician who had a working-class following across Europe was expatriate Russian nobleman Mikhail Bakhunin (1814–1876), who advocated the destruction of all state power. The slightest infringement on freedom, especially by the existence of the central state and its laws, Bakhunin argued, was unacceptable. The notion that the mere existence of the state was the root of social injustice was the fundamental tenet of *anarchism,* a political theory born in this age of nation building.

In 1864 a London meeting of German, Italian, British, and French workers formed the International Workingmen's Association. Besides Bakhunin, another of the new organization's sponsors was Karl Marx, who believed that social theory required political action from groups like the International. From the first, he sought to steer the association toward Marxist principles and constantly battled mutualism and anarchism. These doctrines, Marx insisted, were emotional and wrongheaded, lacking a sound, scientific basis.

Marx's analysis, expounded most notably in *Das Kapital (Capital)* (1867–1894), saw the march of the working class toward socialism as scientifically inevitable. Shaped by philosophical questions, Marx adopted the liberal idea (dating back to Locke in the seventeenth century) that human existence was defined by the basic need to work as a way of sustaining life. He held that the fundamental organization of any particular society, including its politics and culture, arose from the relationships growing from work or production. This idea, known as *materialism,* meant that the foundation of a society rested on class relationships—such as those between serf and medieval lord, slave and master, or worker and capitalist—growing out of the social organization of productive systems or "modes of production" such as slavery, feudalism, or capitalism. Rejecting the liberal focus on individual rights, he emphasized the unequal class relations caused by slaveholders, feudal lords, and the bourgeoisie, who took control of the "means of production" in the form of the land, tools, or factories necessary to sustain life. Only in the socialist mode of production would this control disappear, yielding a classless society of workers.

Karl Marx, His Three Daughters, and Friedrich Engels
Marx (on the right), whose theories had such a revolutionary impact on politics and society, followed many conventions of middle-class life, including fathering a child by the family servant. His daughter Eleanor became an important activist. Engels provided financial support to allow Marx to carry out his research and writing.

Economic liberals saw the free market ultimately producing balance and a harmony of interests, but Marx saw social organization and productive life not as harmonious but as full of conflict. He argued that those who controlled the means of production took their profit from workers, who thereby literally lost some of their "being" or were "alienated." He expected that awareness of this condition of "alienation" would produce class consciousness among large numbers of workers in the same predicament and ultimately lead to their revolt against their exploiters. Whatever the form of rebellion, it would, according to Marx, bring about a more advanced mode of production. For example, the overthrow of the aristocracy in the English and French revolutions had allowed the capitalist mode of production to rise, which Marx saw as a vast improvement over feudalism. Capitalism, in turn, would be overthrown by the proletariat to bring socialism into being. The clash of classes led to a higher mode of production, and this progression Marx called the *dialectic.* (In the twentieth century, Marx's complex theory was boiled down into *dialectical materialism.*) Theories of social conflict and the passage to higher forms of existence were common to Marx and Darwin.

Never precise about what socialism would entail, Marx nonetheless said that it would involve workers' control of production in large factories. He envisioned a utopia based on ending private ownership of the means of production, which would in turn end class conflict and the state that supported the propertied classes. Like many male intellectuals at mid-century, Marx accorded inequalities based on race and sex little analytical importance, concluding, for example, that the condition of women would automatically improve in a socialist utopia. The possibility of this socialist utopia continued to inspire men to organize, and in France, Napoleon III by the 1860s had come to recognize that unions could render worker protests more predictable and more controllable.

Although the emperor legalized workers' associations in 1864, the rigors of workers' industrial life remained unrelieved, and a wave of strikes erupted in the late 1860s. In France alone, forty thousand workers participated in strikes in 1869, more than eighty-five thousand in 1870. The strikers included not just artisans but industrial workers who felt overworked and underpaid because of the continuing pace and expense of technological innovation that lowered their wages. More often than not, these strikes focused on economic issues. But at times, such as in the Paris Commune, protest questioned the entire political system.

The Paris Commune Versus the French State

The bloody and bitter struggle over the Paris Commune developed from mutualist and socialist goals that churned to the surface in Paris as the Franco-Prussian War ended. The French state's weakness first became apparent in the late 1860s when Napoleon III was forced to grant liberal reforms such as freedom of the press and a more independent legislature. But the Haussmannization of Paris, which had displaced many Parisian workers from their homes in the heart of the city, embittered the population against the state. Crowded together in working-class neighborhoods to the north, their painful memories of 1848 festered and their condition appeared to deteriorate in relation to middle-class prosperity.

The French press and populace had welcomed the war. As the Prussians pressed on to Paris and inflicted harsh peace terms on the provisional government that replaced Napoleon III, the besieged Parisians demanded a continuation of the war, new republican liberties, and a more balanced distribution of power between the central government and localities.

By the winter of 1870–1871 the Parisian population was suffering from the siege, the harsh winter, and the lack of sufficient food to feed more than 2 million people. As rumors of coups filled the air, they demanded to elect their own local government to handle the emergency. Adolphe Thiers, who headed the government during the negotiations with Bismarck, called the Parisians a "vile multitude" and refused. Claiming that anarchy threatened, he sent the army into Paris in mid-March to disarm the local National Guard and particularly to retrieve the cannons placed in the middle of the city for its defense. For Parisians this was the last straw, a sign of the utter despotism of the centralized government. Fraternizing with the troops and massacring their general, Parisians declared themselves a self-governing commune on March 28, 1871. They called on all other French municipalities to do the same and form a decentralized France of independent, confederated units.

In the Paris Commune's two months of existence, its forty-member council, its National Guard, and its many other improvised offices found themselves at odds. Trying to maintain "communal" values while administering a complex city, the Commune ultimately failed. Nonetheless, Parisians quickly developed a rich array of political clubs, communal ceremonies, and self-managed, cooperative workshops. Women workers, for example, banded together to make National Guard uniforms on a cooperative rather than a profit-making basis. Beyond mere liberal political equality, the Commune proposed to liberate the worker and ensure "the absolute equality of women laborers." Thus a *commune* in contrast to a *republic* was

The Women Incendiaries of the Commune Burn Paris

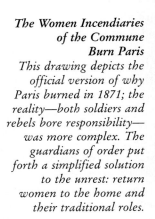

This drawing depicts the official version of why Paris burned in 1871; the reality—both soldiers and rebels bore responsibility— was more complex. The guardians of order put forth a simplified solution to the unrest: return women to the home and their traditional roles.

meant to entail a social revolution. But Communards often disagreed on what specific route to take to change society: mutualism, anticlericalism, feminism, international socialism, and anarchism were but a few of the proposed avenues to social justice.

In the meantime the provisional government at Versailles struck back. It quickly stamped out similar uprisings that had followed in other French cities. On May 21 the army entered Paris. In a week of fighting, both Communards and the army set the city ablaze (the Communards did so to slow the progress of government troops). Both sides executed hostages, and in the wake of victory the army shot tens of thousands of citizens it found on the streets. Just to be in the city meant treason: Parisian insurgents, one citizen commented, "deserved no better judge than a soldier's bullet." The Communards had fatally promoted a kind of antistate in an age of growing national power, and the French establishment saw all Parisians as traitors.

This reaction soon succumbed to a different interpretation of the Commune as the work of the *pétroleuse,* or woman incendiary. Adolphe Thiers roused the French to battle by describing the Commune as basically a case of women run mad, crowding the streets in frenzy and fury. Other writers portrayed women of the Commune as sexually depraved: "They tossed much more than their caps over windmills . . . soon all the rest of their cloth-

ing followed." Within a year the burning of Paris was blamed on women—"shameless slatterns, half-naked women, who kindled courage and breathed life into arson." Revolutionary men often became heroes in the history books, but women in political situations were characterized as "sinister females, sweating, their clothing undone, their bosoms almost bare, [who] passed from man to man."

Defeat in the Franco-Prussian War, the Commune, and the civil war were all horrendous blows from which the French state struggled to recover. A key to restoring order in France after 1870 was instilling family virtues, fortifying religion, and claiming that the Commune had resulted from the collapsed boundaries between the male political sphere and the female domestic sphere. Karl Marx disagreed: he analyzed the Commune as a class struggle of workers attacking bourgeois interests, which were embodied in the centralized state. Later socialists saw the Commune as a disorganized mess run by anarchists—an example of how not to overthrow the state. Still later the French government claimed the uprising was the work of Marxist labor leaders, although few had any major part in the Commune. Executions and deportations by the thousand virtually shut down the French labor movement and kept resentment smoldering. The French would spend the next decades struggling to rebuild political and social unity.

CONCLUSION

By 1871, ambitious politicians, resilient monarchs, and determined bureaucrats had transformed very different countries into modern and powerful states. Nation building was most dramatic in Germany and Italy, where states had unified through military force and where people of many political tendencies had ultimately agreed that nationalism surpassed most other causes. Compelled by military defeat to shake off centuries of tradition, the Austrian and Russian monarchs instituted reforms as a way of remaining viable. In eastern Europe the middle class was far less powerful than in western Europe, and reform came from above to preserve autocratic power rather than from popular agitation to democratize it.

Nineteenth-century liberalism, which had little to do with its twentieth-century namesake, envisioned a severely restricted role for the state and maximum economic competition as the key to ensuring progress. As the consequences of unregulated competition and the challenge of increasingly democratized politics intensified, liberals and progressives came to enlist the state as their ally. This contributed to the evolution of the state's social role in sponsoring schools, sanitation, and other institutions that improved the lives of average citizens. But nationalism and imperialism were also becoming important unifying forces. When the ordinary people of the Paris Commune rose up to protest the loss of French power and prestige but also to defy the trend toward state building, their actions raised difficult questions. How far should the power of the state extend in both domestic and international affairs? Would nationalism be a force for war or peace? As these issues ripened, the next decades saw extraordinary economic advance and an unprecedented surge in European global power.

SUGGESTIONS FOR FURTHER READING

Source Materials

Darwin, Charles. *Autobiography.* 1969. A great scientific theorist's view of his life and work.

Michel, Louise. *Memoirs of the Red Virgin.* 1985. The memoirs of a woman who actively participated in the Paris Commune.

Turgenev, Ivan. *A Hunter's Sketches.* 1852. Includes vivid depictions of serfs and their masters before emancipation.

Interpretive Studies

Clark, T. J. *The Painting of Modern Life: Paris in the Art of Manet and His Followers.* 1984. A path-breaking study of cultural representations.

Devlin, Judith. *The Superstitious Mind: French Peasants and the Supernatural in the Nineteenth Century.* 1987. Examines religion and popular beliefs in the French countryside.

Engel, Barbara Alpern. *Between the Fields and the City: Women, Work, and Family in Russia, 1861–1914.* 1994. Explores the complex and varied impact of emancipation on women's work and family lives.

Field, Daniel. *The End of Serfdom: Nobility and Bureaucracy in Russia, 1856–1861.* 1976. A careful and interesting study.

Fieldhouse, David. *Economics and Empire, 1830–1914.* 1973. Looks at changing economic and political relationships between Europe and the rest of the world.

Hobsbawm, E. J. *The Age of Capital, 1848–1875.* 1979. A detailed and highly interpretive overview.

Homans, Margaret. *Bearing the Word: Language and Female Experience in Nineteenth-Century Women's Writing.* 1986. A revisionist view of English women writing fiction.

Jarausch, Konrad H., and Larry Jones. *In Search of a Liberal Germany: Studies in the History of German Liberalism.* A wide-ranging group of essays that consider the fate of liberals and their values.

Johanson, Christine. *Women's Struggle for Higher Education in Russia, 1855–1900.* 1987. An interesting and detailed investigation.

Kingston-Mann, Esther, and Timothy Mixter, eds. *Peasant Economy, Culture, and Politics of European Russia,*

1800–1921. 1991. Essays on the family, village life, political protest, and migration.

Lebra-Chapman, Joyce. *The Rani of Jhansi: A Study in Female Heroism in India*. 1986. Describes the fate of an Indian head of state as imperialism unfolded.

Lepenies, Wolf. *Between Literature and Science: The Rise of Sociology*. Translated by R. J. Hollingdale. 1988. A useful study of sociology's place in modern thought.

McClellan, David. *Karl Marx: His Life and Thought*. 1978. The standard intellectual biography.

McPherson, James M. *Battle Cry of Freedom: The Civil War Era*. 1988. A prize-winning investigation of the war that brings together military, social, and political perspectives.

Mueller, Detlef K., Fritz Ringer, and Brian Simon, eds. *The Rise of the Modern Educational System*. 1987. Includes important essays on education in Europe.

Nord, Philip. *The Republican Awakening: Civil Society and Democratic Politics in France, 1851–1885*. 1995. An innovative study of the ways in which the arts, university life, and middle-class institutions developed republicanism during the Second Empire.

Olsen, Donald J. *The City as a Work of Art*. 1986. An informative and beautiful treatment of the development of European cities.

Paul, Harry. *From Knowledge to Power: The Rise of the Science Empire in France, 1860–1939*. 1986. An excellent study of the institutional power of science.

Pflanze, Otto. *Bismarck*. 3 vols. 1990. An exhaustive study of Bismarck's policies and strategies.

Reid, Donald. *Paris Sewers and Sewermen: Representations and Realities*. 1991. A lively treatment of sanitation work and people's perceptions of it.

Robinson, Paul. *Opera and Ideas*. 1985. Examines opera and its depiction of historical issues.

Shapiro, Ann-Louise. *Housing the Poor of Paris, 1850–1902*. 1985. Discusses the impetus toward rebuilding and the effect housing reform had on the working classes.

Sked, Alan. *The Decline and Fall of the Habsburg Empire, 1815–1918*. 1989. A more positive appraisal of Habsburg accomplishments.

Smith, Denis Mack. *Cavour*. 1985. A detailed biography of Cavour's life and politics.

Sutcliffe, Anthony. *Towards the Planned City: Germany, Britain, and the United States, 1789–1914*. 1981. An important comparative work.

Wohl, Anthony. *Endangered Lives: Public Health in Victorian Britain*. 1983. Explores how Victorian England viewed and came to grips with health issues.

"I am sometimes called Empress of India," Queen Victoria complained to one of her ministers in 1876. "Why have I never officially assumed this title?" Since the British government had taken control of India from the East India Company in 1858, Queen Victoria had fondly regarded the region, its inhabitants, and its exotic goods. She gave out Indian shawls as presents, surrounded herself with Indian attendants, and eagerly received luxurious gifts from Indian princes. But critics suggested that as a constitutional monarch of the world's most prosperous industrial society, Victoria envied the imperial title of Kaiser William I, who had once been simply king of Prussia. Whether a fascination with the East or ambition provoked her, Victoria got her wish later in 1876 when the Royal Titles Act proclaimed her Empress of India. Thereafter she signed her name "Victoria Queen and Empress," sat for a new portrait in imperial garb, and insisted on personally approving major policies for the massive subcontinent.

Britain's formalized relationship with India was part of the vast expansion of European power in the nineteenth century. The advance of industry brought Europe wealth and confidence enough to annex areas in Asia and Africa, formerly bound only economically to Europe as markets for finished goods and suppliers of raw materials. Europeans ultimately controlled 80 percent of the globe; their predominance ensured continued financial benefit and also promoted the expansion of state power in this *new imperialism*. Following two decades of diplomatic turmoil, government leaders throughout Europe feared that Darwin's message about "the survival of the fittest" could also apply to their nations. Thus they raced to

Empire, Industry, and Everyday Life, 1871–1894

Queen Victoria as Empress of India
The Queen coveted her dominion over India, and thousands of Europeans in the late nineteenth century flocked to Africa and Asia in search of fame and fortune. Many identified themselves as the bearers of Western civilization to inferior peoples.

build empires but also worked to maintain peace among themselves through a proliferation of international conferences and alliances.

The new imperialism fired people's imagination. Stimulating both national rivalry and the popular fascination with foreign lands, imperialism was something that rich and poor alike could appreciate. Expansion caught the attention of the masses, who often watched the race for empire as if it were an athletic contest; to some degree the interest in empire building distracted workers from the hardships of their lives. Nationalist enthusiasm entered the blood of mass politics, giving people common aspirations and helping them cope with the uneven prosperity that accompanied industrial progress.

Common national goals could not obscure the turbulence brought on by accelerating industrialization, which had a decidedly mixed impact on people from all walks of life. Technological advances increased upper-class wealth and brought new levels of comfort into people's daily lives. Business people took steps to improve management, to boost consumption, and to become more competitive. Yet many Europeans remained discouragingly poor, and millions of the less fortunate, aided by breakthroughs in communications and transportation, migrated in search of a better life. Members of the working class who remained in their native countries banded together in close-knit, forceful organizations; their growing political voice prompted governments to pass social-welfare laws. Moreover, groups of middle-class Europeans, awakened to humanitarian concerns, committed themselves to relieving the misery of the poor. Thus in spite of widespread social turmoil and economic uncertainty, the peoples of Europe brimmed with confidence in their ability to shape the future—both at home and in the world beyond their borders.

The Advance of Industrial Society

Continuing industrial development formed the backdrop to European expansion, but national economies also periodically suffered long, painful recessions. Initially, the end of the Franco-Prussian War and the Paris Commune in 1871 brought a burst of prosperity. Paris, Berlin, Vienna,

---

IMPORTANT DATES

1860s–1890s Impressionism flourishes in the arts

1872 Bismarck begins the *Kulturkampf* against Catholic influence

1873 Extended economic recession begins; the impact is global

1876 Invention of the telephone

1882 The Triple Alliance formed between Germany, Austria-Hungary, and Italy

1882–1884 Bismarck sponsors social welfare legislation

1884 British Parliament passes the Second Reform Act, doubling the size of the male electorate

1884–1885 European nations carve up Africa at the Berlin Conference

1889 Socialists meet in Paris and establish the Second International

1892 The Meline Tariff enacted in France

---

and Rome experienced a frenzy of building, and many workers' wages increased. Industry turned out a cornucopia of products that improved people's material well-being. Beginning in 1873, however, a series of downturns in business threatened entrepreneurs with falling profits and bankruptcy. Workers lost their jobs. Industrialists scrambled all the harder to remain competitive by manufacturing new products and improving management practices.

Innovation Takes Command

Industrial and commercial innovation characterized the last third of the nineteenth century. Such products as the bicycle, typewriter, freestanding stove, telephone, internal combustion engine, mass-produced soap, portable camera, and gramophone (phonograph) provided dizzying proof of industrial progress. Many independent tinkerers or inventor-manufacturers created new products, but sophisticated engineers, on whom innovation would increasingly depend, also produced revolutionary inventions. For example, in 1885 the German engineer Karl Benz devised a workable gasoline engine; six years later France's Armand

Peugeot constructed a car and tested it by chasing a bicycle race. Electricity became more widely used after 1880, providing power to light everything from public trams to the British House of Commons. The Eiffel Tower in Paris, constructed for the International Exhibit of 1889, stood as a monument to the age's engineering wizardry; visitors rode to its summit in electrical elevators.

The leading industrial nations also mined and produced massive quantities of coal, iron, and steel during the 1870s and 1880s. The output of the major iron-producing countries grew from 11 million to 23 million tons in these decades. (Even in relatively underdeveloped Spain, iron-ore mining unearthed a total of 130,000 tons in 1861 but 6 million tons in 1890—an almost 5,000 percent increase.) Steel output grew just as impressively in the industrial nations, increasing from 500,000 tons to 11 million tons in the 1870s and 1880s. Manufacturers used massive quantities of metal to produce the more than 100,000 locomotives that pulled trains during these years, which transported 2 billion people annually.

Historians have often contrasted this "second" Industrial Revolution, with its concentration on heavy industrial products, to the "first" revolution, in which innovations in textile making and the use of steam energy predominated. But some historians now believe this distinction applies mainly to Britain. Numerous textile mills were installed on the Continent later than in Britain, often simultaneously with the construction of blast furnaces. Although industrialization led to the decline of cottage production in traditional crafts like weaving, home industry persisted in garment making, metal work, and such "finishing trades" as porcelain painting and button polishing.

Industrial innovations transformed agriculture. Chemical fertilizers boosted crop yields, and reapers and threshers mechanized harvesting. In the 1870s, Sweden produced a cream separator, a first step toward mechanizing dairy farming. Wire fencing and barbed wire simplified farm work; and the development of refrigeration allowed fruits, vegetables, and meat to be transported without spoiling, thus diversifying and increasing the urban food supply. Finally, tin from colonial trade facilitated large-scale commercial canning, which made urban people more reliant on canned food.

During these decades, Britain's rate of industrial growth slowed, as its entrepreneurs remained wedded to older technologies with a successful track record. Although Great Britain maintained its high output of industrial goods and profited from a multitude of worldwide investments, two impressive newcomers began surpassing it in research, technical education, innovation, and rate of growth.

In the aftermath of the Franco-Prussian War, Germany received the territories of Alsace and Lorraine, with their textile industries and rich iron deposits, and a monetary indemnity that aided industrial development. Investing heavily in research, German businesses rapidly devised and applied new processes and mass-produced products that other countries had originally manufactured. Germany also spent as much money on education as on its military in the 1870s and 1880s. This investment resulted in highly skilled engineers and technical workers whose work enabled Germany's electrical and chemical engineering capabilities to soar.

The United States began an intensive exploitation of its vast natural resources, including coal, ore, gold, and oil. The value of U.S. industrial goods produced spurted from $5 billion in 1880 to $13 billion two decades later. Whereas German accomplishments rested more on state promotion of industrial efforts, U.S. growth often involved daring entrepreneurs, such as Andrew Carnegie and John D. Rockefeller. Challenging Britain's dominance, Germany and the United States entered a three-way industrial rivalry that would soon have political and diplomatic repercussions.

Other countries trailed these leaders in the pervasiveness of industry, except Belgium, the first continental country to industrialize. French industry grew steadily but French businesses remained smaller than those in Germany and the United States. Although France had huge mining, textile, and metallurgical establishments, some businessmen retired early to imitate the still-enviable aristocratic way of life. Industrial development in Spain, Austria-Hungary, and Italy was primarily a local phenomenon. Austria-Hungary had densely industrialized areas around Vienna and in Styria and Bohemia, but the rest of the country stayed tied to traditional, unmechanized agriculture. Italy's economy was urban and industrial in the north, rural and agricultural in the south. The Italian government spent more on building Rome into a grand

Swedish Sawmill in the 1880s
Surging population and industrialization spawned further economic development to house, clothe, feed, and otherwise provision the burgeoning work force.

capital than it invested in economic growth. For example, a mere 1.4 percent of Italy's 1872 budget went to education and science, compared with 10.8 percent in Germany. The commercial use of electricity finally allowed Scandinavians, who were poor in coal and ores, to industrialize. Sweden and Norway became leaders in the use of hydroelectrical power and the development of electrical products; Denmark developed a major commercial sector in animal and dairy products. Despite these innovations, however, Scandinavia retained its mostly rural character.

Russia's road to industrialization was tortuous, slowed partly by its relatively small urban labor force. Many Russian peasants who may have wished to take advantage of the opportunities industrialization offered were tied to the *mir* by the terms of the serf emancipation. Some villages sent men and women to cities, but on the condition that they return for plowing and harvesting. Nevertheless, by the 1890s, Moscow, St. Petersburg, Baku, and a few other cities had substantial working-class populations. Under Minister of Finance Sergei Witte (✳1892–1903), Russia attracted foreign capital, entrepreneurs, and engineers; it focused on railroad construction, including the trans-Siberian railway, which upon completion stretched 5,787 miles from Moscow to Vladivostok. The burgeoning of the railroads combined with growth in metallurgi-

Growth of Railways in Europe

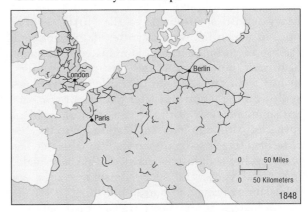

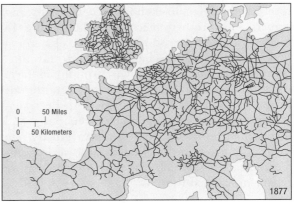

cal and mining operations lifted Russia as an industrial and military power; in the 1890s it rose to fourth in iron production and fifth in steel output. The peasants bore much of the burden of financing Russia's industrial growth, especially in the form of higher taxes on vodka. Thus neither they nor the underpaid Russian workers could afford to buy the goods their country produced. Russia was a prime example of the halting spread and heavy costs of industrialization.

Facing Economic Crisis

Although innovations and business expansion often conveyed a sense of optimism, economic conditions were far from rosy throughout the 1870s and 1880s. Within two years after the Franco-Prussian War ended, prosperity abruptly gave way to a severe economic downturn, or depression, in many industrial countries. The crisis of 1873 was followed by almost three decades of economic fluctuations, most alarmingly a series of sharp downturns in 1882, 1884 (United States), 1890, 1893 (United States), and 1899, whose severity varied from country to country. People of all classes lost their jobs or businesses and faced consequences ranging from long stretches of unemployment to bankruptcy. American economists have recently interpreted these three decades as an extended recession, but for generations this period of economic instability was called the "Great Depression." Economists of the day were stunned by the relentlessness of the slump: one expressed his dismay at the depression's "universality, affecting nations . . . which have a stable currency based on gold, and those which have an unstable currency . . . ; those which live under a system of free exchange of commodities and those whose exchanges are more or less restricted." Because economic ties bound industrialized western Europe to international markets, recession affected the economies of such diverse regions as Australia, South Africa, California, Newfoundland, and the West Indies.

These dramatic fluctuations differed from economic cycles that were the rule before 1850, in which failure on the land led to higher food prices and then to failure in manufacturing. Although suffering problems of its own, agriculture was no longer so dominant that its fate determined the welfare of other sectors of the economy. By the 1870s industrial and financial setbacks were sending businesses into long-term tailspins. In France, for example, the textile industry slumped early in the 1870s and revived only late in the 1880s; the vital silk industry did not recover until 1892. One steel plant with business transactions of almost 40 million francs a year in 1883 shut down five years later. Innovation created new or modernized industries on an unprecedented scale, but economic disaster constantly loomed. Politicians, economists, and bureaucrats struggled in vain to understand this paradox and control its impact.

As industrialization advanced, entrepreneurs encountered fundamental problems. First, the start-up costs of new enterprises had skyrocketed. Textile mills had required relatively modest amounts of capital, but factories producing steel and iron cost millions. Industrialization had become what modern economists call *capital-intensive* rather than *labor-intensive*—purchasing expensive machinery rather than hiring more workers contributed to growth. Second, the distribution and consumption of goods were inadequate to sustain industrial growth. Increased productivity in both agriculture and industry led to rapidly declining prices. Wheat, for example, dropped to one-third its 1870 price by the 1890s. Consumers, however, did not always benefit from this deflation; nor could they afford many of the new goods. Industrialists had made their fortunes by emphasizing production, not consumption. They had paid workers barely subsistence-level wages. Furthermore, their distribution networks often proved inefficient. The slump refocused entrepreneurial policy on finding ways to enhance sales and distribution and to control markets and prices.

Encouraged by business interests and seeking social stability in the wake of the Paris Commune, governments took steps to foster economic prosperity. For example, new laws in various countries spurred the development of the limited-liability corporation, which protected investors from personal responsibility for the firm's debt. Before limited liability, businesses drew the large amounts of necessary capital primarily from their own family assets and from partners, and financial backers were individually responsible should the firm have financial difficulty, with potentially ruinous results. In one case in England a former partner who had failed to have his name removed from a legal document after leaving the business remained responsible to creditors when the company went bankrupt. He lost everything he owned except a watch and $100. The end of personal liability greatly increased investor confidence about financing business ventures.

Public financing in stocks and bonds promised wider opportunity to gain high profits. Stock markets had existed prior to the changes in liability laws, but they had dealt mainly in trading of government bonds and government-sponsored enterprises such as railroads. By the end of the century, stock markets traded heavily in industrial corporate stock, and so investors raised money from a larger pool of private capital than before. The London Stock Exchange in 1882 traded industrial shares worth £54 million, a value that surged to £443 million by 1900. At the center of an international economy linked by telegraph, telephone, railways, and steamships, the London Stock Exchange successfully offered a wide range of services to attract domestic and foreign investors. Banks competed with the stock exchange by increasing their financing of industry. As this system of external investment expanded, individual firms were compelled to create new financial departments to manage the flow of money; thus financing and production became distinct aspects of the same business.

Less personal financial liability and new sources of capital did not eliminate business difficulties, however. In another adaptive move, individual firms in the same industry banded together in cartels and trusts to control prices and competition. Cartels flourished particularly in German chemical, iron, coal, and electrical industries. For example, the Rhenish-Westphalian Coal Syndicate, founded in 1893, eventually dominated more than 95 percent of coal production in Germany. Although businessmen might continue to advocate free trade, they broke with its practices by restricting output and setting prices. Smaller businesses trying to compete and consumers had no effective means of resisting these new business techniques.

Powerful trusts appeared first in the United States. In 1882, John D. Rockefeller created the Standard Oil Trust by acquiring stock from many different oil companies and placing it under the direction of trustees. The trustees then controlled so much of the companies' stock that they could set prices and even dictate to the railroads the rates for transporting the oil. Trusts and cartels also over-saw the *vertical integration* of industries, in which, for example, a steel company acquired mining operations in ore and coal, and railroads to distribute output. Such acquisitions ensured access to raw materials, lower production costs, and greater control of product distribution. The spectacular growth of trusts in the United States sparked *muckraking* journalists who charged that these new businesses were evil predators who preyed on hardworking people.

The emergence of trusts and cartels testified to industrialists' declining faith in classical liberal economics, and government imposition of tariffs expressed similar disillusionment. Much of Europe had adopted free trade after mid-century, but during the recession huge trade deficits—in which imports exceeded exports—had soured many Europeans on the concept. A country with a trade deficit had less capital available to invest internally; fewer jobs were created, and the chances of social unrest increased. Farmers in many countries were hurt when improvements in transportation made it possible to import perishable food, such as grain from the United States and Ukraine. France was particularly vulnerable to trade deficits in the last three decades of the century, and Germany saw its exports drop steadily in 1879, 1883–1889, and 1891–1894. In response, governments in both countries approved tariff legislation throughout these decades, including France's famous Meline Tariff of 1892, which included stiff duties on imported agricultural products. In the same period, Italy, Portugal, Spain, Russia, and the United States set barriers to free trade. Farmers, capitalists, and even many workers supported tariffs; all of them worried about the costs of foreign goods and thus gave added impetus to nationalist appeals and imperial competition. By the early 1890s, Belgium, Britain, and the Netherlands were the only industrialized countries that had rejected protectionism in international commerce.

The Birth of Management, Rise of the Service Sector, and Advance of Consumer Society

Industrialists tried to minimize the damage of business cycles by ensuring that their firms operated smoothly. A generation earlier a factory owner was directly involved in every aspect of his business and often learned to run the firm through trial and error. In the late 1800s, industrialists began to hire managers to run the company's day-to-day operations. Few people had the expertise to compete successfully in an international market of highly technological firms single-handedly. By the late nineteenth century, managers who specialized in sales and distribution, finance, and procuring raw materials made decisions and oversaw the implementation of their policies. Lower-level managers kept worker productivity high through uninterrupted supervision. One German steel magnate told his managers to hire "supervisors and supervisors of supervisors to watch what our men are doing." Every facet of industrial life—from technology to cost accounting—became more complex and required more specialized knowledge, and the managerial class formed a useful layer between owners and workers.

The rise of the manager was accompanied by the emergence of a service sector that supported the production of goods. Businesses employed secretaries, file clerks, and typists to guide the flow of business information. Banks that accepted savings from the general public and that invested heavily in business needed tellers and clerks, and railroads, insurance companies, and government-run telegraph and telephone companies all hired veritable armies of white-collar employees. New service workers entered the labor market with mathematical skills and literacy acquired in public primary schools.

The service sector provided clean work for educated, middle-class women; in fact, female employees eventually predominated in service jobs. In Paris the number of women in white-collar work tripled between 1866 and 1886. For several generations since the time early in the century when middle-class women had tended businesses with their husbands, the ideology of domesticity had dictated that middle-class women should not work outside the home. But by the late nineteenth century, the costs of middle-class family life, especially children's education, were becoming onerous. Many middle-class people could not even afford to marry. So whether to help pay family expenses or to support themselves, many "surplus" or unmarried women of the respectable middle class took jobs. Employers claimed to see a "quickness of eye and ear, and the delicacy of touch" essential to office work in the new women workers. By hiring women

for newly created clerical jobs, business and government perpetuated a dual labor market in which certain categories of jobs were predominantly male and others were overwhelmingly female. In the absence of competition, businesses in the service sector enjoyed lower costs by paying women chronically low wages—much less than they would have had to pay men for the same work.

Female service workers supported the growth of consumer society in Europe by working as salesclerks in department stores. Entrepreneurs developed spectacular department stores to begin solving the problem of underconsumption. Founded after mid-century in the largest cities, department stores gathered such an impressive variety of goods in a centralized place that they were called "marble palaces" or "the eighth wonder of the world." Created by daring entrepreneurs such as Aristide and Marguerite Boucicaut of the Bon Marché in Paris and John Wanamaker of Wanamaker's in Philadelphia, department stores eventually replaced the single-item stores that people entered knowing clearly what they wanted to purchase.

These modern palaces sought to stimulate consumer whims and desires with luxurious fabrics, delicate laces, and richly embellished tapestries. The items spilled over railings and counters, not in the calculated order inherent in rational ideals of the nineteenth century, but in disarray. Shoppers no longer bargained over prices; instead they reacted to sales, a new marketing technique that could incite a buying frenzy. Most men lacked the time required for shopping expeditions. Instead department stores drew women out of their domestic sphere into the public. Women rationalized their forays outside the home, however, as necessary to enhance their home and family lives. Attractive salesgirls were supposed to inspire customers to buy. Shopping was not only an urban phenomenon: glossy mail-order catalogs arrived regularly in rural areas, replete with all the luxuries and household items contained in the exotic, faraway dream world of the city. The department store revealed the enormous impact consumer demand could have on industrial prosperity.

Changes for Traditional Laborers

As the commercial economy spread, even rural people needed cash to pay rents and taxes. In eastern Europe, more and more peasants migrated to

John Wanamaker's Department Store, Philadelphia, 1876 Lights, bright colors, and expansive spaces of department stores revolutionized consumer buying, as shoppers were lured in by the variety of goods for sale in glamorous surroundings.

cities to work as masons, cab drivers, or factory hands to supplement declining income for agricultural produce; in the winter off-season, others manufactured shawls, bricks, pottery, sieves, lace, locks, and samovars in their cottages. In Russia, to keep up with the payments on their land, many families sent some of their sons and daughters to work at least part of the year in the city. Thus ongoing modernization meant that peasants had to adapt to survive and to preserve their village life.

During these decades the purchasing power of many urban workers rose as prices dropped and wages remained steady. At the same time, changes in technology and management practices eliminated outmoded jobs and often made the work of those who survived job cuts more difficult. Workers often complained that new machinery sped up the pace of work to an unrealistic level. For example, new furnaces at a foundry in suburban Paris required workers to turn out 50 percent more metal per day than they had produced using the old furnaces. Moreover, stepped-up productivity demanded much more physical exertion, but workers did not receive additional pay for their extra efforts. Workers also grumbled about the proliferation of managers; many believed that foremen, engineers, and other supervisors interfered with their

work. For women, new supervision sometimes brought on-the-job harassment, as in the case of female workers in a German food-canning plant who kept their jobs only in return for granting sexual favors to the male manager.

As new machines replaced old in factories, managers established a more formal range of skill levels, from the most knowledgeable machinist to the untrained person who carried supplies and raw materials. Inventions such as metal-stamping machines had contradictory effects on skill requirements. On the one hand, the introduction of machinery "deskilled" some jobs—traditional craft ability was not a prerequisite for operating many new machines. Employers could increasingly use untrained workers, often women, and pay them less. On the other hand, inventions always demanded and helped create new skills, especially among those who had to understand work processes or repair machinery. Employers began to use the concept of skill (based in the old craft traditions) to segment the labor force, designating some groups as skilled and others unskilled, sometimes arbitrarily.

Already prevalent in such trades as garment making, the trend toward breaking down and separating work processes into discrete tasks continued. For example, builders employed excavators, scaffolders, and haulers to do the "dirty work," thereby spending less on highly paid carpenters. Those filling unskilled jobs formed a pool of "casual" labor. These people could not count on regular employment and spent much of their time searching out temporary jobs. On the other end of the scale, a foreman was no longer the most skilled worker laboring alongside the less adept, but a supervisor chosen for the "pushing powers that he has of driving fellow men."

Many in the urban labor force continued to do outwork, even for the most highly technological industries. Every branch of industry, from metallurgy to toy manufacturing to food processing, employed women at home. They painted tin soldiers, wrapped chocolate, made cheeseboxes, decorated porcelain, and polished metal—and this work was essential to the family economy. Factory owners liked to employ outworkers because their low piece rates made them desperate for work under any conditions, and their isolation made them less likely than factory workers to strike. Their far lengthier workdays made organizing virtually impossible: a German seamstress at her new sewing machine reported that she "pedaled at a stretch from six o'clock in the morning until midnight. . . . At four o'clock I got up and did the housework and prepared meals." Women at home could be laid off during slack times and rehired when they were needed again without fear of protest. But economic change and the periodic recurrence of hard times ultimately had real consequences for people's everyday lives—and thus for politics.

The Political Foundations of Mass Society

In the uneven prosperity of late nineteenth-century society, Marx's predictions that capitalism would soon collapse gained credibility among working people, many of whom were drawn to socialist organizations in these years. At the same time, western European governments continued to bring men into electoral politics, and even high-ranking politicians such as William Gladstone, the prime minis-

ter of Great Britain, had to campaign by railroad to win votes from an expanded electorate. Although only men profited from electoral reform, the era's expanded franchise marked the beginning of mass politics—a hallmark of the twentieth century. Even in the autocratic monarchies to the east, struggles for political representation and reform erupted, leading to increased violence and ethnic conflict.

Workers, Politics, and Protest

Strikes and political activism came in reaction to industrial and commercial innovation and an uneven economy. Some historians believe that community bonds forged by homemakers and home workers were necessary for worker solidarity. School officials or police looking for truant children and delinquents met a phalanx of housewives ready to hide the children or to lie for their neighbors. When landlords evicted tenants, women would gather in the streets and replace household goods as fast as they were removed from the rooms of the ousted family. Meeting on doorstoops or at fountains, laundries, pawnshops, and markets, women initiated rural newcomers in urban ways and developed a unity paralleling that of factory workers. Before strikes could occur, workers had to know that these support networks were in place.

The uncertainties of the work experience and the perils of economic life also led workers to organize formal unions and their own political parties in the 1870s and 1880s. As the nineteenth century entered its final decades these groups attracted the allegiance of millions. The organization of workers frightened many political and business leaders, who feared it would cause social unrest and thereby undermine industrial growth and productivity. Unlike the mutual aid societies of earlier times, some of these new unions built on the utopian socialist, mutualist, and Marxist ideologies of the preceding four decades; others were based on traditions of craft or religious solidarity. Instead of simply gathering worker contributions and paying out assistance in hard times, as the old societies had done, unions demanded a say in working conditions and aimed, as one French union's rule book put it, "to ensure that wages never suffer illegitimate reductions and that they always follow the rises in the price of basic commodities." Strikes had

The Dock Strike, London 1889
Along with the matchgirls' strike, this one by dock workers marked the beginning of the "new unionism" in which mass organizations were established for unskilled workers.

occurred before the late nineteenth century, but in the wake of the Revolution of 1848 and the Paris Commune, businesses and governments viewed massive numbers of striking workers as not only unproductive but the first step to political unrest and destructive violence. Even so, strong unions appealed to some industrialists because a union could make strikes more predictable (or even prevent them), present worker demands more coherently, and provide a liaison for labor-management negotiations.

From the 1880s on, the pace of collective action for more pay, lower prices, and better working conditions accelerated. In 1888, for example, hundreds of young women who made matches, the so-called London matchgirls, struck to end the fining system, under which they could be penalized an entire day's wage for being a minute or two late to work. This system, striking matchgirls maintained, helped match companies rake in profits of more than 20 percent. Newspapers and philanthropists picked up the strikers' story, helping them win their case. Soon after, London dockworkers and gasworkers protested their precarious working conditions. In France the number of strikes among textile workers, coal miners, and others jumped from 188 in 1888 to 289 in 1890. On May 1, 1890, sixty thousand workers took to the streets of Buda-

pest to agitate for suffrage and safer working conditions. Day laborers on Hungarian farms struck in 1891. Housewives, who often demonstrated in support of strikers, carried out their own protests against high food prices because they were responsible for stretching meager family funds. They confiscated merchants' goods and sold them at what they considered a just price. "There should no longer be either rich or poor," said organized Italian peasant women. "All should have bread for themselves and for their children. We should all be equal." Fearing threats to industrial and agricultural productivity, governments increasingly responded with force: French troops shot into a crowd of workers and their families celebrating May Day, 1891, in the industrial town of Fourmies, killing seven children and one adult and wounding dozens more.

Craft-based unions of skilled artisans, such as carpenters and printers, were the most active and cohesive, but from the mid-1880s on, a *new unionism* attracted transport workers, miners, matchgirls, and dockworkers. These new unions were nationwide groups with salaried managers who could plan massive general strikes across the trades, focusing on such common goals as the eight-hour workday, and thus paralyze an entire nation. Although they never totally eliminated vibrant local or single craft unions or religiously affiliated organizations, the large unions of the industrialized countries of western Europe, like cartels and trusts, increasingly influenced business practices and society's views of workers.

New political parties also engaged the masses in political life by addressing working-class issues. Working men helped create the Labour party in England, the Socialist party in France, and the Social Democratic parties of Sweden, Hungary, Austria, and Germany. Germany was home to the largest socialist party in Europe after 1890. Historians attribute the extraordinary strength of the German Social Democratic party, with its millions of voters, to the conservative social and political atmosphere. Both French and German worker organizations were far more radical than those in reformist Britain.

Working women joined these parties but in much smaller numbers than men. Not able to vote in national elections and usually responsible for housework in addition to their paying jobs, they had little time for party meetings. Furthermore, their low wages hardly allowed them to survive, much less to pay party or union dues. Many working men opposed their presence, fearing women would dilute the union's masculine camaraderie. Contact with women would mean "suffocation," one Russian working man believed, and end male union members' sense of being "comrades in the revolutionary cause." The shortage of women's voices in unions and political parties paralleled women's exclusion from government; it helped make the middle-class belief in separate spheres a part of a working-class ideology that glorified the heroic struggles of a male proletariat against capitalism. Marxist leaders continued to maintain that injustice to women was caused by capitalism and would melt away in the socialist society following the coming revolution. As a result, the new political organizations, although they encouraged women's support, downplayed women's concerns about lower wages and sexual coercion. One women's issue they did debate was the merits of legislation that would bar women from certain occupations. In conservative countries working-class parties sometimes advocated a greater measure of equality for women than did middle-class feminists.

Socialist parties attracted working men because they promised the triumph of new male voters who could become a powerful collective force in national elections. Those who accepted Marx's assertion that "working men have no country," however, wanted an international movement that could address workers' common interests. In 1889 some four hundred credentialed socialists from across Europe (joined by many onlookers and unofficial participants) met in Paris to form the Second International, a federation of working-class organizations and political parties. In disarray after the bloody end to the Paris Commune and the outlawing of socialist parties in Germany between 1878 and 1890, socialists had nonetheless gained enormous strength from the growth of working-class organizations. Participants presented many varieties of socialism during the spirited meetings of the Second International, where some of the most engaged followers of Marx tried to articulate what his writings had meant and what the future held. Unlike the First International, this meeting adopted a Marxist revolutionary program from the start, but it also advocated suffrage where it still did not exist and better working conditions in the immediate future. Thus the Second International accommodated Marxists, who anticipated the triumph of working people through mass revolution, but it also harbored reformers, who eventually challenged Marxist revolutionary tactics by seeking allies among nonsocialist, activist forces.

Members of the Second International determined to rid the organization of anarchists, who based their program solely on a vision in which associations among individuals or groups with similar interests would replace all governments. Anarchism, which lacked Marxism's detailed theories of social and historical change, seemed additionally suspect to Marxists because it flourished in the less industrial parts of Europe—Russia, Italy, and Spain. In these countries anarchism attracted some industrial workers, but it got heavy support from peasants, small property owners, and agricultural day laborers, for whom the industrially based theories of Marx had less appeal. In an age of crop failures and stiff international competition in agriculture, many rural people looked to the possibility of life without the domination of large landowners and government. Like trade unionists, anarchists acted against the powerful, but many advocated more extreme tactics, including physical violence, even murder. "We want to overthrow the government . . . with violence since it is by the use of violence that they force us to obey," wrote one Italian anarchist. In the 1880s anarchists bombed stock exchanges, parliaments, and businesses. "There are no innocents in bourgeois society," said one. But members of the Second International felt such random violence was simply counterproductive.

While struggling against competing political groups, organizers tried to forge worker solidarity. Socialist politics "gave the worker the weapons of self-awareness and self-consciousness . . . very different from the old world of priestly and economic authority where the worker was merely an object of domination and exploitation!" a German clay miner explained. But worker organizations also sponsored popular community activities that intertwined politics with everyday life. The gymnastic and choral societies that had once united the Germans in nationalistic fervor now served working-class goals. Songs emphasized worker freedom, progress, and eventual victory. "Out of the dark past, the light of the future shines forth brightly," went one Russian workers' song. Socialist gymnast, bicycling, and marching societies rejected competition and prizes as middle-class preoccupations, but they valued physical fitness for what it could do to the "outer and inner organism" and for helping workers in the "struggle for existence"—a reflection of the prevailing thinking about "the survival of the fittest" that factory production presumably demanded of workers. Workers also held festivals and gigantic parades, most notably on May 1, proclaimed by the Second International as a labor holiday. Like religious processions of an earlier time, parades were rituals that fostered unity. Although historians now see these events as part of a burgeoning working-class culture, European governments at the time frequently prohibited such public gatherings, fearing they were tools for agitators.

Expanding Political Participation in Western Europe

In the industrial countries of western Europe, politicians of various parties sought to incorporate more people into the political process. In the fall of 1879, William Gladstone (1809–1898), leader of the British Liberals, whose party was then out of power, waged an experimental campaign in northern England and in Scotland for a seat in the House of Commons. During this so-called Midlothian Campaign, Gladstone spoke before thousands of working men and women, denouncing foreign adventurism in India and Africa and summoning his audiences to "honest, manful, humble effort" in the middle-class tradition of "hard work." Newspapers around the country highlighted his trip, and journalism and mass meetings fueled public interest in politics. Queen Victoria bristled at Gladstone's speaking tour and at his attacks on her empire and vowed that he would never again serve as prime minister. However, Gladstone's Liberals won, and he again headed the cabinet.

Gladstone's Midlothian Campaign exemplified the trend toward expanded participation in Britain's political life. The process began with the Reform Bill of 1832, which extended the franchise to middle-class men. The Ballot Act of 1872 made voting secret, a reform supported by those who wished to limit the influence of landlords and employers. (Opponents argued that it would encourage irresponsible voting.) Most significant, the Reform Act of 1884 doubled the electorate, to around 4.5 million men. These new conditions diminished traditional aristocratic influence in the countryside by enfranchising many urban workers and artisans. As many British men entered political life as voters for the first time, Liberals and Conservatives alike found it necessary to establish national political clubs as a means to gain party loyalty. These national clubs competed with the insular groups of parliamentary elites, who ruled through "wirepulling," as one member of House of Lords put it. Interest groups such as unions, businessmen's associations, and national political clubs began to direct politics just as cartels directed economics.

British political reforms immediately affected Irish politics—a mass display of nationalism erupted. The political situation in Ireland was ready to explode, mainly because of the repressive tactics of absentee landlords, many of them English and Protestant. These landlords evicted not only starving Catholic tenants who failed to bring them any profit; they also evicted *successful* tenants and leased the property to land-hungry newcomers, jacking up the rent in the process. Opponents formed the Irish National Land League in 1879 and launched protests that further charged the tense political atmosphere. Armed with the secret ballot,

William Gladstone Campaigns by Train
British Prime Minister Gladstone established the "whistle stop speech" as a staple of mass politics; in the process he offended the Queen's sense of electoral propriety.

Irish tenants elected a solid block of nationalist representatives to the British parliament; their leader was Charles Parnell (1846–1891), a Protestant who nonetheless hated the English.

The Irish members of Parliament, voting as a group, had sufficient strength to defeat legislation proposed by either the Conservatives or the Liberals, and Parnell demanded support for home rule—a system giving Ireland its own parliament—in return for Irish votes. Gladstone, who served several terms as prime minister in these years (*1868–1874, 1880–1885, 1886, and 1892–1894), accommodated Parnell with bills on home rule and tenant security. But Conservatives had a different view of home rule, calling it "a conspiracy against

the honor of Britain," and a "monstrous mixture of imbecility, extravagance and political hysterics" to "gratify the ambition of an old man." When Conservatives held the reins of power (1885–1886 and 1886–1892), they cracked down on Irish activism. Scandals reported in the press ultimately ended Parnell's political career. The first came late in the 1880s, when journalists at the London *Times* fabricated letters implicating Parnell in the assassination of English officials. Parnell was cleared of this charge, but in 1890 the news broke of his affair with a married woman, and he died in disgrace soon after. In his wake, home rule remained as divisive an issue as ever—it finally split the Liberal party in 1894. The influence of the press on British politics was firmly established.

The same breath of intrigue and scandal infused popular politics of the Third Republic in France, where universal manhood suffrage already existed. Replacing the Second Empire of Napoleon III, the republic began with monarchist political factions—Bonapartist, Orléanist, and Bourbon—struggling for control of the National Assembly and to restore their respective families to power. Using their clout to get Adolphe Thiers dismissed as head of the government, these groups by 1873 had agreed among themselves that the Bourbons under the Comte de Chambord would assume a restored throne. But the republican form of government, which the French had been trying to solidify for almost a century, held firm when the Comte de Chambord stubbornly refused to accept the tricolored flag. In 1875 a new constitution created a ceremonial presidency and a premiership dependent on support from a Chamber of Deputies; an alliance of businessmen, shopkeepers, professionals, and rural property owners hoped the new system would prevent the kind of strong-arm politics that had ended previous republics.

Fragile constitutional compromises put the Third Republic on shaky ground in the midst of destabilizing economic downturns, widespread corruption, and growing antisemitism. Support for the government was rocked by newspaper stories about members of the Chamber of Deputies selling their votes to business interests, and the press contributed to unrest by linking economic swings to the machinations of Jewish businessmen. Thereafter, public sentiment blamed Jews for the failures of republican government and the economy. Confidence in republican politics plummeted in 1887 when the president's son-in-law was discovered to have sold memberships in the Legion of Honor, and the republic almost fell when politicians of both the Left and the Right backed a coup attempt by General Georges Boulanger. But Boulanger lacked the stomach to carry out his mission: he escaped to Belgium in 1889 just as the coup was supposed to occur and eventually committed suicide. France was left to rebuild a republican consensus rather than resort once again to authoritarian solutions.

Government leaders attempted to coalesce the country by establishing civic institutions, most notably compulsory and free public education. Secular, republican-minded teachers supplanted Catholic clergy, who often favored monarchy, in public schools; and a centralized curriculum featured patriotic primers and courses in French geography, literature, and history. Mandatory military service for men replaced regional and rural identities with pride in France's imperial conquests, and educated draftees about current domestic and international events. In short, it turned peasants into Frenchmen.

Although many western European leaders believed in economic liberalism, constitutionalism, and efficient central government, these ideals did not always translate into universal suffrage. Spain abruptly awarded suffrage to all men in 1890; Belgium, in 1893. Denmark and Sweden continued to limit political participation, and reform in the Netherlands in 1887 and 1896 only boosted manhood suffrage to 14 percent. An 1887 law in Italy enfranchised all men who had a primary school education, but this affected only 14 percent of the men. In Italy the accession of liberals to power under the constitutional monarchy ushered in decades of political and economic insecurity. The process of unification left a towering debt and massive pockets of discontent, including Catholic supporters of the pope and impoverished citizens in the south, where the north's policy of free trade ruined budding industries and agriculture. Disenfranchised, the average Italian groaned under the weight of petty regulations and feared the devastating effects of national taxes and the draft on the family economy.

Whatever the size of the electorate, the rise of mass journalism that occurred after 1880 gave the populace ready access to information (and misinformation) about politics. The invention of automatic typesetting and the production of newsprint from wood pulp lowered the costs of printing; the telephone allowed reporters to communicate news almost instantly. Once philosophical and literary in content, daily newspapers now emphasized the sensational, using banner headlines, dramatic pictures, and gruesome or lurid details—particularly about murders and sexual scandals—to sell papers and stimulate interest. A series of articles in 1885 in London's *Pall Mall Gazette* on the "White Slave Trade" warned the innocent not to read further: the author then proceeded to describe how young women were "snared, trapped" and otherwise forced into prostitution through sexual violation and drugs. In the hustle and bustle of industrial society, one editor wrote, "You must strike your reader right between the eyes." Papers used the excitement of scandalous stories to help sell their political point of view, whether it was liberal, conservative, or socialist.

Journalism created a national community of up-to-date citizens, whether they could vote or not. Stories of crime and corruption appealed to the growing body of publicly educated, critical readers. Newspapers were not meant for quiet reflection at home or in the upper-class club but for quick reading on mass transportation and on the streets. Elites grumbled that the sensational press symbolized social decay. But for up-and-coming people from the working and middle classes it provided an avenue to success. As London, Paris, Vienna, Berlin, and St. Petersburg became centers not only of politics but of news, a number of European politicians got their start working for daily newspapers.

Power Politics in Central and Eastern Europe

Russia, Austria-Hungary, and Germany diverged from the political paths taken by western European countries. Bismarck had upset the European balance of power—first by humiliating France in the Franco-Prussian War and then by creating a powerful, unified Germany—and he now desired stability and a respite from war. Fearing France would soon seek revenge against the new Reich, he attempted to appear pacified by pronouncing Germany "satisfied," meaning that it sought no new territory. Bismarck also wanted to ensure Germany's long-term security in Europe and in 1873 forged an alliance with the other conservative powers, Austria-Hungary and Russia, called the Three Emperors' League. All three countries shared a strong interest in maintaining the political status quo. In addition, Austria-Hungary owed Bismarck a debt of gratitude for his lenient peace terms after the Austro-Prussian War of 1866, and Tsar Alexander II had received precious aid from Prussia in suppressing the Polish revolt of 1863. Feared as a fomenter of war, Bismarck now pursued diplomacy to consolidate the German empire.

At home, Bismarck, who owned land and invested heavily in industry, joined with the liberals to create a central bank, a unified monetary system, a standardized judiciary, and other institutions that would make Germany powerful and rich. Made chancellor in 1871, Bismarck aggressively combated the Catholic church because its influence, especially in southern Germany and among ethnic minorities, impeded the growth of nationalist sentiment. Watching with alarm as the new Catholic Center party made overtures to workers, he mounted a full-blown *Kulturkampf* (culture war) that embodied a liberal cultural vision and that resembled French republican tactics against Catholic authority. Bismarck was initially more direct than the French: the government expelled the Jesuits in 1872; passed the May Laws in 1873, which increased state power over the clergy in Prussia; and introduced obligatory civil marriage in 1875. Aided and urged on by German liberals, Bismarck had devised these measures believing that the Catholic church had been weakened by the divisive issue of papal infallibility. For once, he had grossly miscalculated his chosen enemy and his own ability to manipulate politics. The conservative establishment and Catholics both rebelled against policies of religious repression.

The *Kulturkampf* ended during the pontificate of Leo XIII (*1878–1903), a cultured scholar and humanist who regrouped Catholic forces to address a social and political scene inhospitable to Catholicism and to religion in general. First, Leo confronted the skeptical intellectual climate, especially as it was affected by Darwin's findings, by encouraging up-to-date scholarship in Catholic institutes and universities. Second, he tried to develop an effective niche for Catholic politics by accepting aspects of democracy while opposing socialism. Because Catholicism had identified itself so strongly with monarchism, this about-face marked a dramatic turn. His encyclical *Rerum Novarum* (1891) articulated his political principles and exhorted Catholics to develop a social conscience that would allow for a rebirth of religious and political unity among the classes. During these dark days of war on Catholic culture, Leo's pontificate was fortuitous for beleaguered Catholics across Europe.

In a climate of economic crisis after the mid-1870s, Bismarck reevaluated Germany's situation and decided that the most pressing problems came from social unrest and liberal economic policies. He left off persecuting Catholics and turned to blocking socialists and liberals. He used unsuccessful assassination attempts on Emperor William as a pretext to outlaw the Social Democratic party in 1878. Simultaneously, hoping to wean the working class from socialism, Bismarck sponsored an accident and disability insurance program—the first of its kind in Europe and an important step in broadening the mandate of government to encompass social welfare. In 1879 he assembled a conservative Reichstag coalition that put through tariffs, thus protecting German agriculture and industry from foreign competition but also raising the prices of consumer goods. Ending his support for laissez-faire economics, Bismarck also severed his working relationship with political liberals.

Like Germany, Austria-Hungary frequently relied on liberal economic policies and for a time in the 1870s even had political liberals in government. In the 1860s liberal businessmen had succeeded in industrializing parts of the empire; they had also financed the construction in Vienna of huge parliamentary buildings, built in a classical style that evoked ancient democracy. The prosperous middle classes erected conspicuously large homes, giving themselves a prominence in urban life that rivaled the aristocracy's. They persuaded the government to enact free-trade provisions in the 1870s and to search out foreign investment to build up the infrastructure, such as railroads.

Yet despite such influences, Austria-Hungary remained resolutely monarchist and authoritarian. The Hungarian Magyars had gained privileges in 1867, but much of their parliamentary legislation still required Francis Joseph's approval. Furthermore, liberals in Austria—most of them ethnic Germans—saw their influence eroded under the leadership of Count Edouard von Taaffe, Austrian prime minister from 1879 until 1893. Taaffe built a coalition of clergy, conservatives, and Slavic parties—the so-called Taaffe ring—and used its power to weaken the liberals. In Bohemia, for example, he designated Czech as an official language of the bureaucracy and school system, thus breaking the German-speakers' monopoly on office holding and also reinforcing the Catholic church's power in the Czech-speaking countryside. "The irrepressible parliamentary conflict between slavery and anti-slavery parties [in the United States] was not waged with more acrimony" is how a diplomat characterized the German-Czech split. Reforms outraged people at whose expense other ethnic groups received benefits, and those who won concessions continued to clamor for even greater autonomy. In this way the government played nationalities off against one another and ensured the monarchy's predominance as the central mechanism for holding competing interest groups together in an era of rapid change.

Despite the success of these divide-and-rule tactics, Francis Joseph and his ministers feared the influence of the most powerful Slavic nation—Russia—on the ethnic minorities living within Austria-Hungary. Following its defeat in the Crimean War, Russia wanted to refurbish its tattered reputation as a Great Power, and to accomplish this goal it stirred up the emotions of discontented Slavs living in Austria-Hungary and in the Balkans under Ottoman rule. Slavophile Russian officials and journalists spread the gospel of Pan-Slavism, which could mean anything from loose cultural cooperation among Slavs to outright political union under Russian aegis. In either case, Francis Joseph considered the Pan-Slavic movement dangerous to the stability of his empire, and he opposed Russian attempts to undermine Ottoman rule.

The Balkans, where the competing forces of modernization and Ottoman decay aroused political ambition, nevertheless became the scene of the next European struggle. Slavs of Bulgaria and Bosnia-Herzegovina revolted against Turkish rule in 1876, killing Ottoman officials. As the Ottomans slaughtered thousands of Bulgarians, two other small Balkan states, Serbia and Montenegro,

rebelled against the sultan. Russian Pan-Slavic organizations sent aid to the Balkan rebels and so pressured the tsar's government that Russia declared war on Turkey in 1877, supposedly to protect Orthodox Christians. With help from Romania and Greece, Russia defeated the Ottomans and by the Treaty of San Stefano (1878) created a large, pro-Russian Bulgaria.

The Russo-Turkish War and the ensuing treaty sparked an international uproar that almost resulted in general war. Austria-Hungary and Britain feared that an enlarged Bulgaria would become a Russian satellite and that this development would enable the tsar to dominate the Balkans. British Prime Minister Disraeli moved warships into position against Russia, while Gladstone (then leader of the opposition) inflamed the atmosphere by accusing the Jewish-born Disraeli (who had converted to Christianity as a young teenager) of wantonly ignoring the Turkish massacre of Christians. The public was drawn into foreign policy as the music halls of England echoed a new *jingoism* throbbing with sentiments of war: "We don't want to fight, but by Jingo if we do, We've got the ships, we've got the men, we've got the money too!"

The other Great Powers, however, did not want a European-wide war, and in 1878 they attempted to revive the Concert of Europe by meeting at Berlin under the auspices of Bismarck, who saw *this* potential war as inopportune. The Congress of Berlin rolled back the Russian victory by partitioning the large Bulgarian state that Russia carved out of Ottoman territory and denying any part full independence from the Ottomans. Austria occupied (but did not annex) Bosnia and Herzegovina as a way of gaining clout in the Balkans, and Britain received the island of Cyprus. Serbia and Montenegro became fully independent. Nonetheless, the Congress failed to resolve the question of Slavic movements and Russian influence over them, and the Balkans remained a site of political unrest and great-power rivalries.

Following the Congress of Berlin, the European powers attempted to guarantee stability through a complex series of alliances and treaties. Anxious about Balkan instability and Russian aggression, the Austro-Hungarian foreign minister, the Hungarian Count Gyula Andrássy, forged a defensive alliance with Germany in 1879. The Dual Alliance, as it was called, offered protection against

The Russo-Turkish War
This war in the Balkans inflamed the political emotions of western Europeans and generated intense diplomatic maneuvering over the question of who would gain advantage from the dissolution of the Ottoman Empire. Pictured here are children aiding Ottoman forces by dragging a cannon to the front.

Russia, whose threat to Hungarian control of its Slavic peasantry (a German diplomat wrote) "was on [Andrássy's] mind day and night." In 1882, Italy joined this partnership (henceforth called the Triple Alliance), largely because of its imperial rivalries with France. Trying to rebuild monarchical solidarity, Bismarck convinced both Austria-Hungary and Russia to join Germany in a revived Three Emperors' League, which lasted from 1881 to 1887. Because tensions between Russia and Austria-Hungary remained high, Bismarck signed a Reinsurance Treaty (1887) with Russia to stifle Habsburg illusions about having a free hand against its rival.

Although Russia enjoyed some international success during these decades, its internal affairs were a mess. By 1871 the era of "Great Reforms" had run its course, and Russia remained almost alone in Europe without a constitutional form of government. The debt-burdened peasantry was unhappy, and reform-minded youth increasingly turned to revolutionary groups for solutions to political and social problems. One such group, the Populists, wanted to rouse the peasantry to revolt. Other people formed tightly coordinated terrorist bands with the goal of assassinating public officials and thus forcing change. The secret police, relying

The Balkans in 1878

Russian Girl Student
Women's education was a hotly debated issue throughout Europe in the nineteenth century. In Russia the administration of Alexander II accomplished reforms, but many women felt that they learned little but good manners in their schooling.

on informers among the peasantry and the revolutionaries, rounded up hundreds of members of one of the largest groups, Land and Liberty, and subjected them to torture, show trials, and imprisonment. When in 1878 a young radical, Vera Zasulich, tried unsuccessfully to assassinate the chief of the St. Petersburg police, the people of the capital city applauded, so great was their horror at the brutal treatment of young radicals from respectable families. Zasulich's act and subsequent acquittal by a jury inspired future revolutionaries to idealize her.

Writers added to the intense debate over Russia's future. Tolstoy and Dostoevsky both opposed the revolutionaries' desire to overturn the social order; they believed that Russia above all required spiritual regeneration. Tolstoy's novel *Anna Karenina* (1877) told the story of an impassioned, adulterous love affair, but it also wove in the spiritual quest of Levin, a former "progressive" landowner who, like Tolstoy, eventually rejects modernization and idealizes the peasantry's tradition of stoic endurance. Dostoevsky satirized Russia's radicals in *The Possessed,* a novel in which a group of revolutionaries carries out one central act: the murder of one of its own members. In Dostoevsky's view the radicals could only act destructively and were incapable of offering any positive solution to Russia's ills. His final novel, *The Brothers Karamazov* (1881), followed the fortunes of three brothers, including an Orthodox monk and a scientific atheist, both deadly serious, and the third, an exuberant lover of life who is accused of murdering his father. This framework allowed Dostoevsky to enlarge the public debate about social issues by exploring his favorite subjects: the existence of God, the nature of religious faith and regeneration, the nobility of the ordinary Russian, and the fate of Russia.

The more radical revolutionary groups did not share the moral vision of Tolstoy and Dostoevsky. They sought to change Russia by violent action rather than persuasion. In 1881 the People's Will, a splinter group of Land and Liberty impatient with its failure to mobilize the peasantry, killed Alexander II in a bomb attack. His death, however, failed to provoke the general uprising the terrorists expected. Instead the peasants thought the assassination of the "tsar liberator" was directed against them. Alexander III (*1881–1894), rejecting further liberal reforms that his father had proposed on the eve of his death, unleashed a new wave of oppression against religious and ethnic minorities. In addition to imposing strict censorship and giving the police virtually unchecked power to do as they pleased, Alexander pursued a rigorous policy of "Russifying" the empire's numerous minorities. Poles, Lithuanians, Ukrainians, Caucasian and Baltic peoples, and Germans faced new regulations requiring them to use Russian in education, church services, newspapers, and nearly every other aspect of public life. Not only did Russification aggravate old grievances among such oppressed nationalities as the Poles, but it also turned the once-loyal German middle and upper classes of the Baltic provinces against Russian rule, with serious long-term consequences.

The 5 million Russian Jews endured particularly severe oppression. Local officials instigated outbursts of organized mob violence (pogroms) against Jews, whose distinctive language, dress, and isolation in ghettos made them easy targets in an age when the Russian government was enforcing cultural homogenization and a uniform national identity. Government officials encouraged ordinary people to blame Jews for escalating taxes and living costs—though the true cause was the policy of making the peasantry pay for industrialization.

As the tsar responded to internal turmoil with ever greater repression, Bismarck's delicate alliance of the three conservative powers was unraveling because of the empires' competing interests. A brash but deeply insecure young kaiser, William II (*1888–1918), mounted the German throne in 1888. William chafed under Bismarck's tutelage, and his advisers flattered the young man into thinking that his own personal talent made Bismarck expendable, even a rival. William dismissed Bismarck in 1890 and, because he ardently supported German nationalism, let the Reinsurance Treaty with Russia lapse in favor of a strong relationship with the supposedly kindred Austria-Hungary. Fatefully, he had opened the door to a realignment of the Great Powers. Between 1891 and 1894, tsarist Russia and republican France entered a series of defensive alliances, ending French diplomatic isolation and threatening Germany with the two-front war that Bismarck had always sought to avoid. In his enforced retirement, Bismarck predicted disaster. By 1894, internal politics in eastern Europe and the Balkans remained unsettled, the international scene had grown more dangerous and unpredictable, and imperial rivalries intensified antagonisms among the European nation-states and empires.

Russia: The Pale of Settlement

The Race for Empire

In the last third of the nineteenth century, the contest to acquire territory in Africa and Asia became an integral component of European nation building and national identity. "Nations are not great except for the activities they undertake," declared a French advocate of huge imperial acquisitions in 1885. Empire building was one way of reestablishing French national grandeur after the Franco-Prussian War, and indeed, Bismarck encouraged France's overseas ambitions, hoping these ventures would help the French forget their loss of Alsace and Lorraine. Many other European governments found the new imperialism an exciting prospect. Conquering foreign territory heaped glory on the nation-state, although it brought conflict with local peoples and ominously intensified discord among the European powers.

Imperialism was more than just government policy: it infected everyday life, providing both consumer goods and gripping stories of adventure. In 1871 the *New York Herald* sponsored British explorer Henry Stanley's expedition to find the noted missionary David Livingstone, supposedly lost in Africa. The newspaper reeled in a huge readership by playing up Stanley's travails in locating

Livingstone. The published reports of their eventual meeting, in which Stanley, upon "finding" his man, uttered the polite and understated words, "Dr. Livingstone, I presume?" sold in record numbers. Imperialism was a political and military undertaking, but the press helped involve the entire national community in the excitement of global expansion.

Taming the Mediterranean, Conquering Africa

The European powers eyed the African and Asian shores of the Mediterranean for reasons based on the old imperialism: the chance to profit through trade. Great Britain and France were especially eager to do business with Egypt, where the combined value of imports and exports had jumped from 3.5 million Egyptian pounds in 1838 to 21 million in 1880 (and would grow to 60 million in 1913). European capital investment in the region also rose, first in ventures such as the Suez Canal and then in the laying of thousands of miles of railroad track and creation of telegraph systems. Improvement-minded rulers paid dearly for modernization: whereas European bankers charged 5 percent interest on loans at home, non-Europeans paid rates of 12 percent and higher, a difference European financiers justified by determining foreign investments to be a greater risk. High rates of return on loans, however, made foreign investments very attractive, and the completion of harbors, dams, canals, and railroads increased the Middle East's desirability as a market for European exports and as an intermediate stop on the way to trade with Asia.

Britain and France had pursued a stake in Egypt since the Napoleonic Wars, and in 1875, Disraeli bought a massive share in the Suez Canal for Britain. This purchase gave the beleaguered Khedive Ismail (*1863–1879), Egypt's profligate ruler, money to make payments on high-interest loans to European creditors. In 1879 the British and the French took over the Egyptian treasury in the name of securing their own financial investments. Nationalist groups protested this heavy-handed encroachment on Egyptian sovereignty, and in 1881 they revolted. Fear of a nationalist victory and of a subsequent default on Egyptian loans led British troops to invade the country in August 1882. (Although France kept its fleet ready in the Mediterranean, it ultimately refused to join the invasion.)

The Suez Canal
Inaugurated in 1869, the canal allowed Europeans swifter access to Asia and thus promoted imperialism, as the crush of European ships in this photograph attests.

After defeating the nationalist forces, however, the British did not restore the khedive's independent rule but instead stayed to run the government from behind the scenes. Despite heated parliamentary opposition at home, the British reshaped the Egyptian economy to their own needs. In keeping with the demands of modernization, they brought in new agricultural machinery, created irrigation systems, and abolished forced labor. They also reorganized agriculture, changing the system from one based on multiple crops that maintained the country's self-sufficiency to one that emphasized the production of a few crops—mainly cotton, raw silk, wheat, and rice—for European manufacturing and processing. Colonial powers, local landowners, and moneylenders profited from these agricultural changes, while the bulk of the rural population continued to eke out an existence.

The rest of the Mediterranean and Ottoman Empire felt the heightened presence of the European powers. With Algeria increasingly dominated by the French military, French settlers now moved onto land cleared of native Algerians. As a further guarantee of their Mediterranean claims, the French occupied neighboring Tunisia in 1881. Elsewhere, businessmen from Britain, France, and Germany flooded Asia Minor with cheap goods, driving artisans from their trades and into low-paid work building railroads or processing tobacco. Instead of basing wage rates on gender (as they did at home), Europeans used ethnicity and religion, paying Muslims less than Christians, and Arabs less than other ethnic groups. Such practices, as well as contact with European technology and nationalism, planted the seeds for anticolonial movements.

Sub-Saharan Africans also experienced the new wave of European ambition, which was most evident after the British takeover of the Egyptian government. Economic relationships between Africans and Europeans were not new, but contact between the two continents had principally involved the trade of slaves by African dealers to Europeans in exchange for manufactured goods. The intercontinental slave traffic had drastically diminished by this time, and Europeans' principal objective was expanding trade in Africa's raw materials, such as palm oil, cotton, diamonds, cocoa, and rubber. Additionally, with its industrial and naval supremacy and its empire in India, Britain hoped to keep the southern and eastern coasts of Africa secure as a series of ports on the route to Asia. Except for French conquest of Algeria, commerce had rarely involved direct political control in Africa.

Yet in the 1880s, European influence turned into direct control as one African territory after another fell to European military force. The French, Belgians, Portuguese, Italians, and Germans jockeyed for national advantage in controlling peoples, land, and resources. King Leopold II of Belgium claimed the Congo region of central Africa, thereby initiating competition with France for that territory. Bismarck, who saw colonies mostly as political bargaining chips, sent out explorers in 1884 and established German control over Cameroun and a section of East Africa. Faced with this competition, the British poured millions of pounds into preserving their position by dominating the region "from Cairo to Capetown," and the French cemented their hold on large portions of western Africa.

The scramble for Africa escalated tensions in Europe and prompted the calling of a conference at Berlin in 1884–1885. The fourteen nations at the meeting agreed that settlements along the African coast guaranteed rights to internal territory. This agreement led to the strictly linear dissection of the continent, as geographers and diplomats cut across indigenous boundaries of African culture and tribal life. The Berlin conference also banned alcohol and controlled arms sales to native peoples. In theory the meeting was supposed to reduce bloodshed and temper ambitions in Africa, but utterly rapacious individuals like King Leopold continued to plunder the continent and abuse its people. The news from Berlin only whetted the popular appetite for more imperialist ventures.

Domination depended on the technological strength that Europeans had been developing over the past century. The gunboats that forced the Chinese to open their borders also played a part in forcing Africans to give up their tribal independence. Quinine and guns were also an important factor in African conquest. Before the development of quinine prophylaxis in the 1840s and 1850s, the spread of deadly malaria had threatened to decimate any European party embarking on exploration or military conquest. The extraction of quinine from cinchona bark for the prevention and treatment of malaria set death rates from the disease plummet-

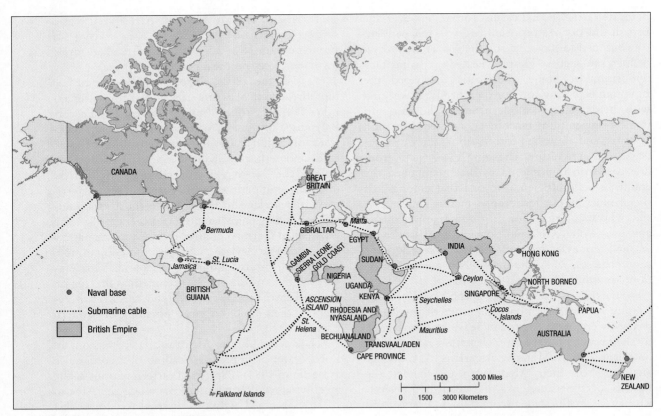

The British Empire, c. 1900

ing. Missionaries, adventurers, traders, and bureaucrats traveled with their supply of quinine, and a Dutch cartel, successfully experimenting with cinchona cultivation in Indonesia, broke the South American hold on quinine production and cornered the market until World War II. Meanwhile, the development of the breech-loading rifle and the machine gun, or "repeater," drastically improved European firepower. Europeans carried on a brisk trade selling inferior guns to Africans on the coast, but peoples of the interior used bows and arrows. Muslim slave traders and European Christians alike crushed African resistance with blazing gunfire: "The whites did not seize their enemy as we do by the body, but thundered from afar. . . . Death raged everywhere—like the death vomited forth from the tempest."

Nowhere did this destructive capacity have greater effect than in southern Africa, where civilian farmers and prospectors rather than military personnel battled the Xhosa, Zulu, and other peoples for control of the frontier regions of Transvaal,

Natal, the Orange Free State, Rhodesia, and the Cape Colony. Although the Dutch had originally settled the area in the seventeenth century, the British had gained control by 1815. Thereafter descendants of the Dutch, called Boers, were joined by British immigrants in their fight to wrest farmland and mineral resources from natives. Cecil Rhodes (1853–1902), sent to South Africa for his health just as diamonds were being discovered in 1870, cornered the diamond market and claimed a huge amount of African territory with the help of official charters from the British government. Pushing hundreds of miles into the interior of southern Africa, Rhodes moved into gold mining too. His ambition for Britain and for himself was boundless: "I contend that we are the finest race in the world," he explained, "and that the more of the world we inhabit the better it is." Although notions of European racial superiority had been advanced before, racist attitudes now justified converting trade with Africans to conquest and political control of their lands.

Wherever necessary to ensure profit and domination, Europeans destroyed African economic and political systems or transformed them into instruments of their rule. A British governor of the Gold Coast put the matter succinctly in 1886: the British would "rule the country as if there were no inhabitants," as if local traditions of political and economic life did not exist. Indeed most Europeans considered Africans barely civilized despite the wealth local rulers and merchants accumulated in their international trade in cotton, tobacco, palm oil, cloves, and other products, and despite individual African peoples' accomplishments in dyeing, road building, and architecture. Unlike the Chinese and Indians, whom Europeans credited with a scientific and artistic heritage, Africans were seen as valuable only for manual labor. By confiscating land and imposing taxes on Africans, Europeans forced native peoples to work for them to obtain the money to pay revenues and support themselves. Subsistence agriculture, often performed by women and slaves, thus declined in favor of mining and farming cash crops. Standards of living often dropped for Africans who lost their lands to the invading whites without realizing the Europeans were claiming permanent ownership. Systems of family and community unity provided support networks for Africans during this upheaval, while many Europeans truly saw imperialism as bringing these people the benefits of economic modernization, Christianity, and civilization.

Acquiring Territory in Asia

Britain justified the invasion of Africa and the conquest of Asian countries as strategically necessary to preserve control of India's quarter of a billion people. Unlike Africa, close to a half million Indians ran the country under the supervision of a few thousand British men, and Indians also collected taxes and distributed patronage. Like Africans, ordinary Indians benefited in some places from improved sanitation and medicine, which allowed the population to surge. Upper-class Indians attended British-style schools and served in a British-style bureaucracy, often coming to reject Indian customs such as infanticide, child marriage, and a wife's self-immolation on her husband's funeral pyre. British notions of a scientific society were attractive to these upper classes, while the unity that British rule gave to what were once small localities and prince-

Imperial and Indigenous Rulers
Imperial powers often maintained local rulers in place, using them to maintain order. In this photograph, the British Viceroy's real supremacy over the Indian Maharaja is disguised by the apparent equality of the two men sitting together.

doms with separate allegiances promoted nationalism among this new, Western-educated elite. Aside these advantages were drawbacks: British policy forced the end to indigenous production of such finished goods as cotton textiles that would compete with its own manufactures. Instead the British wanted cheaper raw materials such as wheat, cotton, and jute to supply its industries. Enclaves of British civil servants, who sought prosperity and status for governing the vast subcontinent, enforced segregation and discrimination against all classes of Indians. Discriminated against but educated, the Indian elite in 1885 founded the Indian National Congress, which challenged Britain's right to rule.

To the east, British military forces took control of the Malay peninsula in 1874 and of the interior of Burma in 1885. In both areas political instability often threatened secure trade. The British depended on the area's tin, oil, rice, teak, and rubber, but the region was also crucial for Britain's access to the interior trade routes of China. The presence of British troops guaranteed the order

Russian Annexations in Asia

necessary to expand railroads for more efficient export of raw materials and the development of Western systems of communication. Once secured, the relative tranquility also allowed the British to build factories and from there to create an industrial base in China.

The British rapidly added to their holdings in Asia partly to counter Russian and French annexations. Since 1865, Russia had been absorbing the small Muslim states of central Asia, including Turkestan and provinces of Afghanistan. Besides extending into the Ottoman Empire, Russian tentacles reached Persia, India, and China, often encountering competing British ambition. In the 1880s, France acquired territories in Cochin China and established protectorates in neighboring areas of Southeast Asia through favorable treaties backed by the threat of military action. In 1887, France created the Union of Indochina from the ancient states of Cambodia, Tonkin, Annam, and Cochin China (the latter three now constitute Vietnam). Laos was added to Indochina in 1893.

French Indochina

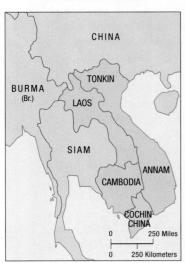

Like the British, the French brought Western ways to the conquered societies. Modern pro-

jects in the Mekong Delta, for example, increased the amount of cultivated land and spurred rapid growth in the food supply; the French also improved sanitation and public health in Indochina. Such changes proved a mixed blessing, however, because they led to population growth that strained limited resources. Furthermore, landowners and French imperialists siphoned off most of the profits from economic improvement. The French also undertook a cultural mission to transform Saigon and other cities into centers of French civilization. Tree-lined boulevards that emulated Paris were constructed in an urban building program. French literature, theater, and art diverted not only colonial officials but also upper-class Vietnamese. Contact with Western culture eventually spawned Vietnamese nationalism, based on a Western model but rejecting Western rule.

The Rise of Japan

For Japan the new imperialism brought not Western domination but the rise of a modern industrial nation with its own imperial agenda. A Japanese print of the 1880s illustrated both traditional ways and the Western influence behind Japan's burgeoning power. The picture's costumed women, strolling with their parasols amidst flowering cherry trees, might have been rendered centuries earlier; but a steaming locomotive in the background symbolized change. The Japanese embraced foreign trade and industry under the leadership of the Satcho Hito clan, whose accession to power in 1868 was called the Meiji Restoration. "All classes high and low shall unite in vigorously promoting the economy and welfare of the nation," ran one of the first pronouncements of the new regime. The Japanese had long acquired knowledge from other countries, so unlike China, Japan endorsed the challenge from the West.

In the 1870s, Japanese government officials traveled to Europe and the United States to study technological and industrial developments. Western dress became the rule at the imperial court, and when Tokyo burned in 1872 a European directed the rebuilding, creating a city reminiscent of Western architecture. Opposition to such changes was not tolerated, as the new central government, led by some individuals of the old samurai, or warrior elite, crushed massive rebellions by others in the elite who resisted modernization. The Japanese

Westernization in Japan
In this woodcut the editor of the first Japanese newspaper is depicted as a Western-style self-made man. As the Japanese incorporated Western styles, so European artists used the palette, flat surfaces, and spatial arrangements found in Asian art.

adapted samurai traditions to a large, technologically modern military, which was filled by universal conscription. By 1894, Japan had become powerful enough to force traders to accept its terms for commerce and diplomatic relations.

The Japanese government instigated the turn toward industry. Japanese legal scholars, following German models, helped draft a constitution in 1889 that emphasized state power rather than individual rights. The state also stimulated economic development by building railroads and shipyards and establishing financial institutions. Then in the 1880s, when the cost of modernization had drained resources, the government auctioned off its businesses to the highest bidder, thereby collecting

essential revenue to stabilize its finances. State support led daring innovators like Iwasaki Yataro, founder of the Mitsubishi firm, to develop heavy industries. Technology borrowed from the West influenced such ventures, but in Japan, unlike the rest of Asia, the adaptation of Western-style enterprises became a patriotic goal. Motivated by such ambitions, Japan started intervening in nationalist and imperialist struggles elsewhere in Asia, ultimately provoking war with its traditionally more powerful neighbors—China and Russia.

The Paradoxes of Imperialism

Imperialism ignited constant, sometimes heated debate because of the many paradoxes in its meaning and scope. For example, although it was meant to stabilize great-power status, imperialism intensified distrust in international politics. New countries vied with old ones for a share of world influence, bringing clashes around the globe. Securing Indian borders, for example, the English faced Russian expansion in Afghanistan and confronted it again along the borders of China. Moreover, imperial competition made areas of Europe, such as the Balkans, more volatile than ever as states sought status and national security in the control of disputed territory.

The need for the international conference at Berlin suggested that the imperial powers had grabbed more than they could afford to hold onto. The search for new markets often proved more costly than profitable to society. Britain, for example, spent enormous amounts of tax revenues to maintain its empire amidst its relative industrial decline. Yet for certain businesses the colonies provided crucial markets: late in the century, French colonies bought 65 percent of French exports of soap and 41 percent of France's metallurgical exports. Although many adventurers failed, colonies allowed investors to diversify in uncertain times. Imperialism also benefited the inhabitants of European port cities, even though taxpayers in all parts of a nation paid for colonial armies and administrators. Despite the unevenness of the benefits, the new imperialism took an ever-growing amount of national revenues to maintain.

Motives for imperialism were equally paradoxical. Goals such as civilizing "heathen" peoples, fostering national might, and boosting national loyalty often proved unattainable or difficult to measure. Many believed that through imperialist ventures, "A country exhibits before the world its strength or weakness as a nation." Governments worried that imperialism—because of its expense and the constant possibility of war—would weaken rather than strengthen them. As one French politician put it, France "must keep its role as the soldier of civilization." But it was unclear if imperialists should emphasize soldiering—that is, conquest and conflict—or the more pacific goal of exporting civilization.

Hoping to Christianize colonized peoples, European missionaries flooded Africa and Asia. A woman missionary working among the Tibetans reflected a common view when she remarked that the native peoples were "going down, down into hell, and there is no one but me . . . to witness for Jesus amongst them." Europeans were confident in their own religious and cultural superiority. In the judgment of many, Asians and Africans were a class beneath Europeans, variously characterized as lying, lazy, self-indulgent, or irrational. One English official pontificated that "Accuracy is abhorrent to the Oriental mind." At the height of imperialism, such beliefs explained conquest and dominion as a civilizing process whereby people of the conquered colonies would eventually be grateful for what Europe had brought them. Viewing other races as somehow "degenerate" helped promote Western notions of progress, but in feeling compelled to foster these stereotypes, Europeans also revealed some hesitation, however slight, about Western dominance and national cohesion.

Western scholars and travelers had long gathered ideas and knowledge about Asian and African languages and cultures, and they claimed during these years to have garnered a totally objective and scientific knowledge about history and society. Yet even the best scholars generally viewed foreign cultures in terms of their own biases, characterizing Islam's Muhammad as a pale imitation of Jesus, for example. Alternatively, some Europeans—from novelists to military men—considered conquered peoples better than Europeans because they were unspoiled by civilization. "At last some local color," enthused one colonial officer, fresh from industrial cities of Europe, on seeing Constantinople. "What a dream out of the *Thousand and One Nights*." This romantic and misinformed vision of an ancient center of culture, similar to

THE NEW IMPERIALISM

1840s–1890s Russian expansion in central and western Asia

1874 Britain gains control of Malay peninsula

1876 Queen Victoria declared Empress of India

1879 Partition of West Africa begins

1880s Germany takes control of parts of East Africa

1882 The British invade and take control of Egypt

1885 British control Burma; Indian National Congress founded; Berlin Conference

1887 France creates Union of Indochina

1890s Partition of East Africa

1910 Union of South Africa established

eighteenth-century condescension toward the "noble savage," had little to do with the reality of conquered peoples' lives. Other Europeans paradoxically questioned their own accomplishments: "It is we who have the air of barbarians," the same officer reported on reaching the European settlement in Algiers. European civilization appeared grand because of its international reach and simultaneously bland because of its growing industrial uniformity.

The Complexities of Imperial Society

The paradoxes of imperialism and the spread of industry were powerful ingredients shaping everyday life in the late nineteenth century. European society prospered because of advancing industrialization that made the world an interconnected marketplace. Success in industry and empire created millionaires, and the development of a professional and service sector resulted in more people affluent enough to own property, see some of the world, and educate their children. Price deflation allowed consumers to purchase goods that poured into both urban and rural areas. Coffee, tea, sugar, tobacco, cocoa, cola, and other stimulants from the colonies became more available and their consumption more widespread. The tons of palm oil from Africa were turned into margarine, adding fat to the European diet. Whereas colonial societies lost much of their former prosperity and self-sufficiency, many Europeans grew healthier, partly because of improved diet and partly because government programs aimed at promoting the strength and fitness necessary for citizens of imperial powers. Yet this prosperity did not touch everyone, and millions of Europeans emigrated to the United States, Canada, Australia, Argentina, Brazil, and Siberia. Others in these complex societies came to grips with some of the paradoxes of imperial life. In particular the elites tried to puzzle out and reform the problems of poverty amidst growing plenty, and artists tried to portray society's intricate workings and values.

The European Exodus

Industrial prosperity did not extend to many areas of rural Europe, and hungry people by the millions were driven not only to cities that were relatively near but even to other continents. In parts of Europe the land simply could not produce enough to feed a rapidly expanding population. In Sicily, for example, the vast forests that had in ancient times supplied the Greek navy wood to build ships had been replaced by nearly worthless, eroded soil, and hundreds of thousands of Sicilians left to save themselves from starvation. The British Isles, especially Ireland, yielded one-third of all European emigrants between 1840 and 1920, first because of the potato famine and then because of uncertain farm tenancy and periodic economic crises. The Scandinavian countries also had more people than the land could support: half a million Swedes out of a population of 4.75 million left their country between 1886 and 1900. Millions of rural Jews, especially those of eastern Europe, also left their villages for economic reasons, but Russian Jews fled in the face of vicious antisemitism. Mobs brutally attacked Jewish communities, destroying homes and businesses and even murdering some Jews. "People who saw such things never smiled any more, no matter how long they lived," recalled one Russian Jewish woman who emigrated to the United States early in the 1890s.

Most of the emigrants went to North and South America, Australia, and New Zealand, from which news of opportunity poured into Europe. For example, the U.S. government had promised cheap land to homesteaders—people willing to improve and cultivate previously undeveloped territory. Moreover, the railroad and steamship made the trip from Europe more affordable, more comfortable, and faster, even though most made their way in ships' steerage compartments where they traveled with baggage and supplies and with few amenities. Once established elsewhere, migrants frequently sent money back home and thus remained part of the family economy; European farm families often received a good deal of their income from migrating sons and daughters. Emigrants also appreciated the chance to begin anew without the deprivation and social deference of the old world. One settler in the United States was relieved to escape the meager peasant meal of rye bread and herring: "God save us from . . . all that is Swedish," he wrote home sourly.

Migration often meant the end to an older way of life. Men immediately had to learn new languages and civic ways and to compete for jobs in growing cities where they formed the cheapest pool of labor. Women who worked found the same need to adapt to meet the needs of the workplace, often a factory or sweatshop. Women who stayed at home, however, tended to associate with others like themselves, preserving traditional ways. More insulated at home, they might never learn the new language, never put their peasant dresses away. Their children and husbands more often devalued their past as they were forced to build a life in schools and factories of the new world.

More frequent than intercontinental migration was internal migration from rural areas to cities within Europe itself. Cities of one hundred thousand and over grew the most, but every urban area attracted migrants seeking employment. Despite this intense migration, more people still lived in rural areas of under two thousand people than lived in towns and cities. The most urbanized countries were Great Britain and Belgium, followed by Germany, France, and the Netherlands. In Russia only 7 percent of the population lived in cities of ten thousand people or more; in Portugal the figure was 12 percent. But migration to the city, as a place of opportunity and escape, continued unabated even in those predominantly rural countries.

The "Best" Circles

At the other end of the social scale were the "best" circles, so called because of their members' wealth, education, and social status. People in the best circles often came from the aristocracy, which retained much of its power and was still widely emulated. Increasingly, however, aristocrats had to share their social position with new millionaires from the ranks of the bourgeoisie. In fact, the very distinction between aristocrat and bourgeois became blurred, as monarchs gratefully endowed millionaire industrialists and business people with aristocratic titles, in thanks for their contributions to the national wealth. Moreover, down-at-the-heels aristocrats were only too willing to offer their children in marriage to families from the newly rich. Such arrangements brought a necessary infusion of funds to old, established families, and upstart families acquired the cachet of an aristocratic title. Thus the Jewish-American heiress Winaretta Singer (of Singer sewing machine fame) married the French Prince Edmond de Polignac, and Jeanette Jerome, daughter of a wealthy New York financier, married England's Lord Randolph Churchill (their son, Winston, later became prime minister). Even millionaires without official connections to the aristocracy discarded the modest ways of a century earlier to build palatial country homes and villas, engage in conspicuous displays of wealth, and wall themselves off from the poor in suburbs or new sections of town inhabited only by the rich. To justify their success, the wealthy often appealed to Social Darwinist principles, which seemed to indicate that the great accumulation of money demonstrated the natural superiority of the rich over the poor.

Sport and leisure brought upper-class men together in their favorite activity—hunting. Fox and bird hunting had been aristocratic pastimes in parts of Europe for centuries, but big-game hunting in Asia and Africa now became the rage. Stags' heads, elephant tusks, and animal skins decorated European homes. In Africa, European hunters wrested control from natives, who had depended on hunting to produce income or food and to serve as a unifying tribal ritual. Forcing natives to work as guides, porters, and domestics on these hunts instead, Europeans demonstrated their influence on the conquered region's social as well as political life. Collectors on these hunts brought exotic specimens back to Europe for zoological exhibits, natural history museums, and traveling displays, all of which flourished during this period.

Those fortunate enough to have made it into the upper class, whether for reasons of birth or of accumulated wealth, did their best to exclude others by overseeing marriages and regulating their children's social life. Marriageable women in the upper and middle classes remained closely watched to preserve their chastity and to keep them from socializing with lower-class men. Upper-class men had frequent liaisons with lower-class women—part of the double standard that saw men's promiscuity as normal and women's as immoral—but few thought of marrying them. Parents still arranged marriages directly, but other marriages were initiated during *visiting days*. On these occasions prominent hostesses held an open house under rather formal conditions, and such regular social contact sometimes provided the foundation for matrimonial decisions.

Ritualistic visits filled the everyday lives of upper-class women. Instead of working for pay, they devoted themselves to reproducing children, directing staffs of servants, maintaining standards of etiquette and social conduct, and pursuing fashion in clothing and home furnishing. The latter activity took on imperial motifs in these decades, featuring Oriental carpets, wicker furniture, and Chinese porcelains. Being an active consumer of fashion was a time-consuming task. In contrast to men's plain garments, upper-class women's costumes were elaborate, ornate, and dramatic, featuring constricting corsets, long voluminous skirts, and accentuated décolletage for evening wear. Wealthy men admired women of their class as symbols of elite leisure, and these women fervently tried to offset the drabness of industrial life with the rigorous practice of art and music: one observer wrote, "The piano mania has become almost an epidemic in Budapest as well as Vienna." Women also took their role seriously by keeping detailed accounts of their expenditures and monitoring their children's religious and intellectual development. Some women were quite active outside the home, engaging in religious and philanthropic activities and taking a particular interest in the welfare of lower-class women.

Below the richest "ten thousand," or "upper crust," the "solid" middle class was expanding, most notably in western and central Europe. Growing numbers of doctors, lawyers, managers, professors, and successful journalists found their positions enhanced by the increased prestige of science and information, and they established their position as masters of a complex body of knowledge. Government legislation began to allow people engaged in such work to determine who would and who would not be admitted to "the professions." Such legislation had both positive (allowing groups to set professional standards) and negative (prohibiting otherwise qualified people from engaging in work because they lacked the necessary credentials) effects. Germany's Lawyer Code of 1878 encouraged the formation of a bar association and lifted traditional restrictions on the numbers of people who could become lawyers. The German medical profession was also granted authority to control licensing, which led to more rigorous, university training for future doctors but also pushed midwives out of medicine and made it possible for healers not trained in medical school to be arrested. Professional standards regarding modern scholarship and teaching were introduced for professors, and scholarly societies formed to advance and monitor these standards. Science, too, became more the province of the trained specialist than the amateur genius; scientists were now likely to be employed by universities and institutes, funded by the government, and provided with equipment and a variety of assistants. Like other members of the middle class, professors were intensely patriotic, often interpreting their work as part of an international struggle for prestige and excellence. Without more staff and equipment, one French scientist threatened in 1880, "We will be far behind the German and Dutch laboratories."

Although professionals could sometimes mingle with those at the apex of society, their lives remained more modest. They employed at least one servant, which distinguished them from the working classes and which allowed their wives and daughters to participate in charitable activities and attend church. In industrial society many in the middle class took their social and political values from the rich but were also concerned about the condition of the poor. They feared the consequences of uneven prosperity and upheaval caused by migration and massive urbanization. Growing working-class solidarity, unsafe city life, and the sight of human misery alarmed the middle classes about the direction of imperial society despite the advantages they themselves experienced.

Approaches to Reforming Society

Thousands of reform organizations were formed in the late nineteenth century to attack social problems. Impelled by a Social Darwinist fear that Europeans would lack the fitness to survive in a competitive world, settlement houses, clinics, halfway houses, and maternal and child wellness societies became common in cities. Young men and women, often from universities, flocked to staff these new organizations, where they strove to make the population fit for industrial and imperial competition. Many of these young people believed in the scientific approach to social problems, thinking that study would uncover the causes of social ills and point the way to solutions. One famous group devoted to this enterprise was the Fabian Society in London, a small organization founded in 1884. Committed to a socialism based on reform and state planning rather than revolution, the Fabians helped found the Labour party in 1893 as a way of incorporating social improvement into politics. Still other reformers felt not only horror at the plight of the poor but a strong religious impulse that had motivated earlier charity efforts. "There is Christ's own work to be done," wrote one woman who volunteered to inspect workhouse conditions. Religious fervor sometimes added a moral component to reform efforts, as in the case of Prime Minister Gladstone, who regularly walked the streets of London seeking to convert prostitutes to a life of purity.

Philanthropists, industrialists, and government agencies intervened more and more in the lives of working-class families. They sponsored health clinics and milk centers to provide good medical care and food for children; mothers were instructed in child-care techniques, and some even received prizes for breast-feeding—an important way, reformers maintained, to improve infant health. Some schools distributed free lunches, medicine, and clothing, and inspected the health and appearance of their students. These attempts to improve urban life had their downside, however, as when government officials or private reformers deemed themselves the overseers of the working-class family and entered apartments with impunity. Such intrusions pressured already overworked, poor mothers to conform to standards for their children that they often could not afford.

To counteract the burdens facing the working-class family, some professionals began to make available birth-control information, in the belief that small families were more likely to survive the rigors of urban life. In the 1880s, Aletta Jacobs (1851–1929), a Dutch physician, opened the first birth-control clinic, which specialized in promoting the new, German-invented diaphragm. Jacobs was moved to act by the plight of women in Amsterdam slums who were worn out by numerous pregnancies and whose lives, she believed, would be greatly improved by limiting their fertility. Jacobs had also been inspired by the English Malthusians Annie Besant and Charles Bradlaugh, who preached the doctrine of voluntary motherhood and spread birth-control information.

Reproductive issues framed another significant government reform common to these decades: legislation that would "protect" women from certain kinds of work. In such cases the fear was not that families were too large but that women were not producing healthy enough children and were stealing jobs from men. Moreover, protective legislation was considered crucial to national development; as one French official put it, such laws provided the foundation on which a nation could "achieve the plenitude of its economic and political power." Thus women across Europe were barred from night work and from such "dangerous trades" as pottery work. In England, for example, women were kept from the better-paying jobs in the pottery trade allegedly for health reasons, even though medical statistics demonstrated that women became sick on the job *less* often than men. But lawmakers and working men claimed that women's work in potteries endangered reproduction, and those who had worked in the trade were forced to find other, lower-paying jobs or remain at home. Protection further defined and limited women's sphere, as work was once again divided into jobs for men (that paid more) and jobs for women. The new laws did not prevent women from earning their livelihood, but they made the task harder by limiting their access to higher-paying jobs. The fledgling welfare state was taking shape around such programs as Bismarck's social insurance plans and protective legislation for women.

Professional Sports and Organized Leisure

As nations competed with one another for territory and economic markets, male athletes banded together to organize sport for more serious competition than had existed in the past. Team sports such as soccer, rugby, and cricket drew mass followings. The new emphasis on competition also found favor with the reading public, as newspapers reported the results of all sorts of contests, including the Tour de France bicycle race, sponsored by tiremakers who wanted to prove the superiority of their products. Industrially based tests of speed and the use of machines replaced older forms of competition such as cockfighting and sack racing. Competitive sports began to be seen as valuable to national strength and spirit, for middle- and lower-class men alike. "The Battle of Waterloo was won on the playing fields of Eton" ran the wisdom of the day, suggesting that the games played in school could mold the strength and character of an army.

Team sports—like military service—helped differentiate male and female spheres and thus promoted social order based on distinction between the sexes. Some women found individual sports invigorating: "Riding improves the temper, the spirits and the appetite," wrote one sportswoman. "Black shadows and morbid fancies disappear from the mental horizon." Rejecting the idea of women's natural frailty, reformers introduced exercise and gymnastics into schools for girls, often with the idea that this would strengthen them for motherhood and thus help the nation-state. Hardy types even took to team sports such as soccer, field hockey, and rowing. Although these remained segregated, young women gained a sense of parity with their brothers and male neighbors.

The middle classes believed their leisure pursuits should be edifying as well as fun. Thus mountain climbing became a popular middle-class hobby. As the editor of a Swedish publication of 1889 explained, "The passion for mountain-climbing can only be understood by those who realize that it is the step-by-step achievement of a goal which is the real pleasure of the world." The working class adopted middle-class habits by

Women Bicycle Racers in France
Improvements in the bicycle made it useful for competitive sports, recreation, and transportation. The opportunity it allowed the young to travel on their own weakened social conventions, especially those that limited young women's freedom.

joining, for example, bicycle, touring, and hiking clubs in which they were not just fans but participants. Laborers and their families also sought the benefits of fresh air and exercise by visiting beaches, taking the train into the countryside, and enjoying day trips on river steamships. Clubs that sponsored trips often had such names as The Patriots or The Nationals, again associating physical fitness with the nation's strength. The new emphasis on healthy recreation also gave individuals a greater sense of freedom and power. A farmer's son in the 1890s boasted that with a bicycle, "I was king of the road, since I was faster than a horse."

Social Consciousness and Imperial Culture

The arts in these years explored the consequences of global expansion, scientific progress, and economic innovation. The tone of art changed. Fiction writers, for example, rejected the sentimentality and idealism of the preceding generation's realistic works. Instead, they depicted life pessimistically, sometimes in Darwinian terms. The French writer Emile Zola (1840–1902), influenced by fears of social degeneration prompted by Darwin's work, produced a series of novels set in industrializing France about a family plagued by alcoholism and madness. Zola's protagonists, who led violent strikes and once even castrated an oppressive grocer, raised real

anxieties in his readers about the future of civilization. Zola had less concern for exploring character than for describing the effects of industrial society on individuals: his *Au bonheur des dames* (Women's Happiness, 1883) describes the frenzy produced in supposedly refined upper-class women by the pleasures of shopping in the new department stores of Paris.

Other writers envisioned a widespread degeneration that threatened all of society: men and women, aristocrats and peasants, rural folk and urbanites, peasants and imperialists. Emilia Pardo Bazán (1859–1921) penned dramas of incest and murder among wealthy landowning families in rural Spain. In *The Mayor of Casterbridge* (1886), English novelist Thomas Hardy followed the path of a common man who sells his wife at a country fair and later rises to a position of power and respect, only to find that he cannot escape his murky past. Hardy's vision was fatalistic; his characters battle forces beyond their control. Writers had already brought attention to working class lives, and now authors like Hardy examined rural conditions under the realist microscope. In contrast to Hardy's story of the wife-selling mayor, Norwegian playwright Henrik Ibsen (1828–1906) created the character of Nora, a woman who shocked audiences of *A Doll's House* (1879) by leaving a loveless and oppressive marriage. Olive Schreiner (1855–1920) went even further: in *The Story of an*

African Farm (1889), the heroine rejects the role of submissive wife and describes the British Empire as a "dirty little world, full of confusion." By questioning British institutions, Schreiner helped launch a critical, turn-of-the-century mindset about a range of social issues.

While writers described social decay, ordinary people looked for relief from industrialization in tradition. Paradoxically, country people used mass-produced textiles to design traditional-looking costumes, and they developed ceremonies based on a mythical past: such new "customs" amused city-dwellers and brought tourist business to villages. Folkways and folk motifs interested urban architects and industrial designers, who turned to local artistic styles for models of household goods, decorative objects, and clothing. Architects copied Swiss chalets or Russian country homes to achieve a rustic look. English designers William Morris (1834–1896) and his daughter May Morris (1862–1938) designed fabrics, wallpaper, and household items from such natural styles as the silhouettes of plants so that, replacing the "dead" and ornate styles of the past, "living flowers should inspire a

Wallpaper from Morris & Co.
Morris aimed to raise the standards for consumer goods, which industrialization had debased. The Morrises revolutionized design by creating well-crafted products without the ostentation of luxury goods.

living ornament," as May Morris explained. Some designers were inspired by socialist ideas and hoped the enthusiasm for hand-crafted products would improve conditions for struggling artisans and help preserve unique styles in an age of increasing mass production.

Painters and sculptors, although patronized by wealthy collectors, continued to depend on the fancies of official taste. Government purchases of art for museums and government-sponsored exhibits of new works still determined an artist's success. But even artists in the government's good graces felt intense competition from a popular industrial invention—the camera. Photographers could produce cheap copies of paintings and create more realistic portraits than painters could, at affordable prices. In response, painters altered their style, at times trying to make their work look as different from photographs as possible. As a result much of it became incomprehensible to ordinary people.

Art also reflected the increasingly managed and leisurely ways of an imperial and industrial society in which a growing segment of service workers did less physical work and had more energy for leisure. The works of French painter Georges Seurat (1859–1891), for example, depicted the newly created parks with their walking paths and Sunday bicyclers; white-collar workers in their store-bought clothing, carrying books or newspapers, paraded like the well-to-do. Another French artist, Edgar Degas (1834–1917), focused on portraying women in various states of exertion and fatigue, in subjects ranging from ballet dancers to laundry women. Such fatigue marked almost a romantic nostalgia for a past that was seen to require relentless physical labor from sunrise to sunset. The city of Paris itself inspired artists such as Camille Pisarro (1831–1903) and Claude Monet (1840–1926), who represented its monuments, bridges, churches, railroad stations, and other focal points. When depicting the bleak outskirts of cities where industries were often located and where the desperately poor lived, Dutch-born Vincent Van Gogh (1853–1890) avoided the intense colors he typically used for the countryside.

These avant-garde artists were known after 1870 as *impressionists*—a term Edouard Manet used to emphasize the artist's attempt to capture a single moment by focusing on the ever-changing light and color found in everyday vision. Using splotches and dots, impressionists moved away

(left) *Berthe Morisot,* **Edouard Manet and His Daughter** *Morisot was one of the women artists who helped advance impressionist style by depicting ordinary people in public scenes or land-scapes. Her model is her brother-in-law, the painter Manet, for whom she also modeled.*

(below) *Vincent Van Gogh,* **Portrait of Père Tanguey,** *Like many other Western artists, Van Gogh borrowed techniques from Asian printmakers. In this por-trait he has incorporated copies of prints themselves into the background.*

from the precise realism of earlier painters. Claude Monet, for example, was fascinated by light's trans-formation of an object and often portrayed the same place—a bridge or a railroad station—at dif-ferent times of day. Van Gogh used vibrant colors in great swirls to capture sunflowers, corn stacks, and the starry evening sky. Such distortions of re-ality made the impressionists' visual style seem outrageous to those used to realism, but others enthusiastically greeted impressionism's luminous quality. Industry contributed to the new style, as chemicals were used to produce a range of pigments that allowed artists to express a wider, more intense spectrum of colors.

In both composition and style, impressionists showed the influence of Asian art and architecture, now more readily available. Photography captured the forms of Asian architecture for impressionists to portray, and the color, line, and delicacy of Japanese art is evident, for example, in Monet's later paintings of water lilies, his studies of wisteria, and even his creation of a kind of Japanese garden as the subject for artistic study. Similarly, the American expatriate Mary Cassatt (1845–1926) used the two dimensionality of Japanese art in her *Woman in Black at the Opera* (1880). Other artists, like Degas, imitated the Far East's use of wandering and conflicting lines to orchestrate space on a canvas, and Van Gogh filled the background of portraits with copies of intensely colored Japanese prints.

Whereas the visual arts absorbed stylistic influences from around the world, music expressed cultural nationalism and even patriotism. Czech composer Antonín Dvořák (1841–1904) employed popular national melodies in his *Moravian Duets* (1876) and *Slavonic Dances* (1878), and Norwegian composer Edvard Grieg's (1843–1907) music for Ibsen's play *Peer Gynt* (1875) integrated rural legends into music for urban audiences. Transcending nationalism, however, were the classical musical forms of Johannes Brahms (1833–1897), a German composer who carried on the tradition of Beethoven in symphonies, chamber music, and other works that glowed with the warm harmonies

of late romanticism. Brahms's expression of general musical themes was counteracted by the works of the most important operatic composer of the day, the antisemitic and increasingly reactionary Richard Wagner. In 1876, Wagner's monumental cycle of four music dramas, *Der Ring des Nibelungen,* received its first complete performance in the festival theater built to his design at Bayreuth, Germany. The *Ring* was hailed as a triumphal celebration of German nationalism, and the aging Wagner did little to contradict such interpretation. Everywhere, even in France—where the *Ring* was periodically banned—both Wagner's often extremist pronouncements on social and political matters and his intoxicatingly powerful music aroused intense interest. His work foreshadowed the disturbing currents lurking beneath the surface as imperial and industrial Europe reached the end of the nineteenth century.

CONCLUSION

This period has been called the age of industry and empire because Western society pursued both these ends in a way that rapidly transformed Europe and the world. Industrial innovation and national growth caused much of Europe to thrive and become more populous and urban. Europeans proudly and eagerly spread their "superior" culture globally. The Great Powers undertook a new imperialism. Political reformers drew lower-class men into active citizenship by extending the suffrage; humanitarian commitment prompted the development of philanthropic agencies and promoted the welfare state. Yet as workers struck and the impoverished migrated, it was clear that all was not perfect in this civilization. While newspapers, novels, and the arts helped inform people of profound social and international changes, they also raised questions about the state of society. By 1894, events were starkly revealing the paradoxes of economic advance and empire, forcing Europeans to confront the consequences of their progress, prosperity, and modernity.

SUGGESTIONS FOR FURTHER READING

Source Materials

Bonnell, Victoria, ed. *The Russian Worker.* 1983. Includes extracts from autobiographies of workers depicting the horrid conditions many faced.

Cullwick, Hannah. *Diaries.* 1984. Details the life of a Victorian maid.

Verga, Giovanni. *The House by the Medlar Tree.* 1881. A fascinating novel of Italian village life that describes how ordinary people come to feel the effect of the new nation-state.

Interpretive Studies

Accampo, Elinor. *Industrialization, Family Life, and Class Relations: Saint Chamond, 1815–1914.* 1989. A study of how family life and work intersected in an industrial town.

Adams, Carole. *Women Clerks in Wilhelmine Germany:*

Issues of Class and Gender. 1988. A close-up view of the service revolution and the changes it entailed.

Baumgart, Winfried. *Imperialism: The Idea and Reality of British and French Colonial Expansion.* 1989. Features the political side of imperial ventures.

Berlanstein, Lenard R. *The Working People of Paris, 1871–1914.* 1984. An interesting analysis of the changes in work and how people reacted to them.

Callen, Anthea. *Women Artists of the Arts and Crafts Movement, 1870–1914.* 1979. The story of May Morris and other craft innovators.

Davis, Lance, and Robert Huttenbach. *Mammon and the Pursuit of Empire.* 1988. Demonstrates statistically that imperialism was unprofitable.

Franzoi, Barbara. *At the Very Least She Pays the Rent: Women and German Industrialization.* 1985. An excellent look at women's outwork role in the family economy and women's activism.

Good, David. *The Economic Rise of the Habsburg Empire.* 1984. An important survey of Habsburg industry, finance, and trade.

Headrick, Daniel R. *The Tools of Empire: Technology and European Imperialism in the Nineteenth Century.* 1981. An engaging story of how technology ensured conquest and built empires.

Jones, Gareth Stedman. *Outcast London.* 1984. A major study of transformations in labor and in the lives of working men.

Lidtke, Vernon. *The Alternative Culture: Socialist Labor in Imperial Germany.* 1985. An innovative history of working people's organizations from singing groups to gymnastic societies.

MacKenzie, John. *The Empire of Nature: Hunting, Conservation, and British Imperialism.* 1988. A lively work on a much neglected aspect of imperialism as sport and recreation.

Miller, Michael. *The Bon Marché: Bourgeois Culture and the Department Store, 1869–1920.* 1981. A classic study that gives an inside look at how department stores functioned.

Moch, Leslie Page. *Moving Europeans: Migration in Western Europe Since 1650.* 1993. A major survey of migratory patterns.

Pilbeam, Pamela M. *The Middle Classes in Europe, 1789–1914: France, Germany, Italy, and Russia.* 1990. An overview of interpretations of middle-class life in four very different historical settings.

Robinson, Ronald, John Gallagher, and Alice Denny. *Africa and the Victorians: The Official Mind of Imperialism.* 1981. The revised version of a classic account of the "scramble for Africa."

Rodney, Walter. *How Europe Underdeveloped Africa.* 1981. A revisionist study of the ways in which imperialism affected Africa over the long term—and for the worse.

Rogger, Hans. *Jewish Policies and Right-Wing Politics in Imperial Russia.* 1986. Examines government decision making about the pograms and the reaction to them.

Ross, Ellen. *Love and Toil: Motherhood in Outcast London, 1870–1918.* 1993. A sensitive and detailed exploration of family life and women's roles.

Rotberg, R. I. *The Founder: Cecil Rhodes and the Pursuit of Power.* 1988. A psychologically oriented biography of a towering imperialist.

Schirokauer, Conrad. *Modern China and Japan: A Brief History.* 1981. An indispensable survey that provides good detail on the economy and culture as well as on political transformation.

Trebilcock, Clive. *The Industrialization of the Continental Powers.* 1981. A detailed, comparative exploration that attempts to see European industrialization apart from the British model.

Walkowitz, Judith. *City of Dreadful Delight.* 1993. A fascinating and innovative history of the world's most powerful city, including its scandals, murderers, and eccentric characters.

Weiner, Joel H., ed. *Papers for the Millions: The New Journalism in Britain, 1850s to 1914.* 1988. Discusses the newspaper revolution and its relation to mass politics.

Worobec, Christine D. *Peasant Russia: Family and Community in the Post-Emancipation Period.* 1991. Describes social and economic organization and survival strategies in rural Russia.

Laura Knight, A Balloon Site Coventry, *England, 1943*

PART
IV

*The Crisis
of the West,
1894–Present*

The West's "crisis" of the twentieth century has not been its problem alone because the West—defined since the late 1800s as Europe and its offshoot settlements in North America, Australia, and New Zealand—had created a "global," interconnected world. The process had begun with the voyages of discovery of the 1400s, and it slowly intensified between the 1500s and the 1800s. Now, late in the twentieth century, globalization has penetrated into the most ordinary aspects of everyday life. New communication technologies from the radio and television to the computer and live video by satellite have made the world, it seems, into one global village. In living rooms around the world, viewers can follow wars, revolutions, ethnic conflicts, ecological disasters, and daily international market reports. Such events almost invariably produce international repercussions.

In the 1800s, most Westerners believed in progress. The secular ideologies of the "rights of man," including the right of national self-determination, of progress through science and education, and of politics based on mass participation, had steadily undermined the traditional old regimes in Europe and the Americas. Constitutional, representative governments held power in most of western Europe and North America by the 1880s, though women were excluded from the vote until after World War I. Central and eastern Europe, however, remained in the grip of autocratic, dynastic rulers. Much of the turmoil of the twentieth century can be traced to the difficulties of making the transition to democracy in formerly autocratic countries.

Developments in the 1900s sorely tested the belief in progress. By the 1890s Western imperialism had already created dangerously interlocking international conflicts. Confrontations over imperial possessions and an escalating arms race helped to bring about World War I, which broke out when a Bosnian Serb nationalist assassinated the heir to the Austrian throne in 1914. Mass armies, led on both sides by aristocratic officers, fought the war from deep trenches separated by narrow strips of territory. Millions of men died battling for a few yards of barren, desolate landscape. Improved military technology only ensured the killing of much of a young generation of Western men. Their deaths produced the first major crisis of confidence in Western values. The very meaning of civilization came into question.

Political events of the 1920s and 1930s exacerbated the pervasive sense of crisis. The peace treaties that settled World War I left widespread resentments in Germany and deep strains elsewhere. The experience of defeat in World War I, with the resulting Russian Revolution of 1917, destroyed the autocratic governments in place in eastern and central Europe, but their successor regimes confronted immense obstacles in establishing democratic nation-states. Newly enfranchised men—and eventually, newly enfranchised women—often voted for racist, antisemitic, or xenophobic parties or authoritarian dictators. The economic depression of the 1930s heightened tensions and contributed to the outbreak of World War II, an even more global, more deadly war in which tens of millions of combatants and civilians died. Mass education that had been devised to eliminate ignorance and intolerance failed to prevent the systematic persecution and killing of millions of Jews, gypsies, and homosexuals by one of the West's most "civilized" countries, Germany. Technology that had been intended to liberate humans from their burdens was used to organize concentration camps to torture and kill. Mass politics, nationalism, and even science revealed their menacing—indeed, nightmarish—possibilities.

The United States' atomic bombings of the Japanese cities of Hiroshima and Nagasaki in 1945 ended World War II but ushered in an age of anxiety about the real possibility of nuclear annihilation. The twentieth century divides quite decisively at 1945. Replacing the system of multipower competition that had governed Western politics since at least the mid-1600s was a much starker division of the entire world into two major armed camps led by two superpowers, the United States and the Soviet Union. International relations took a new turn as many countries embraced the model of communist revolution held up by those who had seized power in the USSR. A nineteenth-century ideology created by the German Karl Marx out of his studies of the French Revolution and the growth of capitalist industry—that is, a quintessentially Western ideology—now had world-wide impact, usually in the places that Marx himself would have least expected. For most of the twentieth century, the question of communism—of its prospects and eventually its horrendous failures—dominated world politics.

Another western ideology, the belief in the right to national self-determination, galvanized the remaining European colonies in Africa and Asia, most of which had gained their independence by 1963. Forced to choose between capitalism and communism, many of them opted for a "third way" for the "Third World," but in fact that third way all too often meant one-man rule, suppression of dissent, and economic stagnation. Westerners had believed that they could reshape Africa in their own self-image by importing Western technology, education, and economic and political practices. In reality, however, they created artificial political units (nation-states on the Western model) that bore little relationship to the African past.

The right to national self-determination, a right officially proclaimed by United States president Woodrow Wilson at the end of World War I but generally accepted since the mid-1800s, created problems even in Europe. After World War I the Ottoman and Austrian empires were carved up into smaller nation-states. But the new boundaries always encompassed more than one ethnic group, more than one language, and more than one culture. The resulting tensions and instabilities had helped to bring about both world wars, and with the collapse of communism after 1989, they have sprung up once again, kindling ethnic clashes and all-out ethnic wars. When more than one "nation" shares a territory, claims for national self-determination inevitably provoke violence. Thus one of the factors that most contributed to the "rise" of the West to world hegemony—its political organization into nation-states—has proved the undoing of many who would emulate that model of success.

Changes in other aspects of Western life proved equally complex. World War I and the Russian Revolution definitively ended the centuries-old grip of aristocracies on politics and the economy. New elites, however, arose within growing government bureaucracies and in industry and finance. The power and loyalties of corporate chiefs ultimately transcended national boundaries, as industry became increasingly global. While political and financial leaders propounded social scientific theories based on Enlightenment faith in rational and predictable behavior, cultural leaders including scientists, artists, and writers increasingly challenged the firm belief in absolute knowledge and rationality. Uncertainty in the sciences, anti-realism in the arts, and relativism in disciplines like history infiltrated twentieth-century thought. Finally, work, family life, and gender roles all underwent profound metamorphoses.

Even as the world, and the West within it, struggles with the legacies of the violent twentieth century, some causes for hope remain. Western Europe, the cradle of the West for more than a thousand years, has continued to change. When France, Germany, and Great Britain lost their great-power status in the aftermath of World War II and decolonization, they regrouped with their neighbors into a new supranational unit, the Common Market, now the European Union. Recognizing that power is now inescapably located in a global context and is as much economic as military in foundation, the Europeans have tried to reconcile their national differences with new supranational institutions dedicated to a common European welfare. Since 1945 the European democracies have not made war on each other. At the same time, they individually and in different fashions have developed welfare systems for the protection of their populations that are the envy of the rest of the world. Human rights, democracy, and national self-determination have consequently taken on new meanings that include rights for children and the elderly and protection from disease and technologically induced ecological problems. The interdependency of globalization has magnified the effect of every problem we face, but such connections may also offer us new solutions in the future.

In the autumn of 1900 an eighteen-year-old Austrian woman made her first visit to Sigmund Freud, a Viennese physician who practiced a new therapy called psychoanalysis. Freud's patient suffered from periodic vomiting, inability to speak, abdominal pains, and other symptoms of hysteria—a condition psychoanalysts attributed to strict Victorian morality, which denied that women were capable of sexual feelings. Freud's cure for the woman, whom he fictitiously named Dora, required her to talk about her family, the substance of her dreams, and the way in which her physical symptoms might be produced by sexual feelings for her father and for adults close to her family. Freud's scandalous suggestions about Dora's incestuous impulses led her to walk out of the analysis by the year's end. He went on to publish her story in *Dora* (1905), a classic of psychoanalysis.

Freud's analysis of Dora arose from his belief in the constant progress of scientific enlightenment. This faith also inspired discoveries in physics at the turn of the century that matched Darwin's revolution in biology a generation earlier. Science even influenced the arts, as musicians and painters drew upon psychological findings and technological changes. Advances in public health and the social sciences prompted governments to enact social programs, extend democracy, and encourage urban improvement, thus building on the reforms of previous decades. Feminists and other activists believed reform would make society more rational by ending traditional forms of injustice. Living amidst growing abundance, reformers, statesmen, and scientists were confident in Western civilization's capacity to understand and change the world.

CHAPTER

25

Modernity and the Road to War, 1894–1914

Sigmund Freud and His Daughter Anna Freud, 1912
Although bourgeois in appearance and habit, Freud's work on the irrational components of the psyche formed a central part of modernity's critique of conventional thought. His daughter later became famous in her own right as a child analyst.

Despite such conviction, European society experienced extraordinary strains at the turn of the century. Many in the middle class felt tremendously anxious about the rapid changes in values and technology. Although Freud believed in scientific progress, he saw society riddled with mental torment, much of it stemming from the very family relations Victorians cherished. Moreover, the spiraling development of communication, transportation, and sprawling cities overwhelmed some observers with a sense of chaos and impending doom. Artists of this period expressed cultural pessimism forcefully. "Ours is a society ceaselessly racked," Emile Zola wrote in 1896: "We are sickened by our industrial progress, by science; we live in a fever, and we like to dig deeper into our sores." British novelist H. G. Wells had a more apocalyptic vision, claiming that he saw "humanity upon the wane . . . the sunset of mankind" in this era. As intellectuals such as Freud, Zola, and Wells gathered information about modern life, they confronted a disturbing specter of irrationality and decay.

In part, violent politics contributed to this pessimism. Contrary to liberal expectations, expanded suffrage had brought disharmony to political life. In Freud's Vienna a mayoral candidate whipped up antisemitism and ethnic chauvinism—and won a resounding victory. Soon politicians throughout Europe had learned that in an age of mass politics, extreme appeals to militant nationalism could combine with racist rhetoric to produce electoral success. In France, traditional home to political liberalism, the false espionage conviction of a Jewish army captain in 1894 led to the Dreyfus Affair and ultimately made violent antisemitism a factor in French political life. A liberal ethos of tolerance receded before a wave of political assassinations and public brutality. At the same time, imperial competition by the Great Powers and colonial resistance to European dominance fueled an arms race that threatened to turn Europe into a battleground.

Historians have often applied the term *modern* to this period, in which the pace of life accelerated and traditional, agrarian society continued to erode. Historians also refer to the response by intellectuals and artists to this rapid change as modern. The celebrated art of this period, which often both rejected and endorsed technology, was as chaotic

IMPORTANT DATES

1894–1895 Japan defeats China in the Sino-Japanese War

1894–1899 Dreyfus Affair lays bare antisemitism in France after the conviction for treason of a Jewish army captain

1899–1902 Boer War fought between Dutch descendants (Boers) and the British in South African states

1900 Sigmund Freud publishes *The Interpretation of Dreams*

1901 Irish National Theater established by Maud Gonne and William Butler Yeats; death of Queen Victoria

1903 Emmeline Parkhurst founds the Women's Social and Political Union to fight for women's suffrage in Great Britain

1904–1905 Japan defeats Russia in the Russo-Japanese War

1905 Revolution erupts in Russia; violence forces Nicholas II to establish an elected body, the Duma; Albert Einstein publishes his "Special Theory of Relativity"

1906 Women receive the vote in Finland

1907 Pablo Picasso launches cubist painting with *Les Demoiselles d'Avignon*

1908 Young Turks revolt against rule by the sultan in the Ottoman Empire

1911–1912 Revolutionaries overthrow the Qing dynasty and declare China a republic

1914 Assassination of the Austrian Archduke and Archduchess by a Serbian nationalist precipitates World War I

and disturbing as the weakening of traditional social values. The advent of mass politics has also been characterized as modern, in contrast with the rule of traditional elites. Uncertainty reigned in international relations, too. The nation-state had reached the height of its power, but without any guarantee of security. During these decades the nations of Europe lurched from one diplomatic crisis to the next, international tensions flared, and finally a deadly world war erupted, sparked by national hatreds and dreams of military glory. Was this the price of being modern?

Private Life in an Age of Modernity

Transformations in private life, a by-product of industrialization, provoked intense debate by the turn of the century. A falling birthrate, a rising number of divorces, and growing activism for marriage reform affected relations between men and women. Some imagined that distinct gender roles were disappearing. With women out in public more than ever before, one songwriter in the late 1890s wrote:

> Rock-a-bye baby, for father is near
> Mother is "biking" she never is here!
> Out in the park she's scorching all day
> Or at some meeting is talking away!

Some saw women's emergence as progress, others as decay. Some adults rejected traditional stereotypes altogether and formed homosexual subcultures. Depending on one's point of view, this trend was seen as a sign of either modern enlightenment or sin. Freud and other scientists tried to study these phenomena dispassionately; they eventually formulated new theories of the human personality. Public discussions of private life—which often found their way into political rhetoric and programs—demonstrated the interwined nature of private and public concerns.

Population Control and Warnings of Social Decay

Contemporary Western leaders, influenced by Social Darwinist warnings of racial decay, feared that urbanization, migration, social turmoil, and other products of advanced industrial life were sapping European strength. Whereas earlier social critics had focused on filthy urban conditions and economic deprivation, mental deterioration in individuals and a falling birthrate were now seen as the most menacing problems. In 1895 one physician noted that industrial society was responsible for the "brutalization of the individual," a situation that in turn led to "the lowering of the intellectual level and depopulation." United States president Theodore Roosevelt (1858–1919) viewed the falling birthrate among middle-class families as the source of social decay. Women's refusal to have large families, he complained, "forms one of the most unpleasant and unwholesome features of modern life."

For all this concern, population had not stopped soaring, and thousands migrated from rural areas to swell the size of cities. Germany increased in size from 41 million people in 1871 to 64 million in 1910; tiny Denmark, from 1.7 million in 1870 to 2.7 million in 1911. Such growth resulted from improvements in sanitation and public health that extended longevity and reduced infant mortality. As people lived longer, cities adapted to cope with their burgeoning populations. Urban building, which disrupted the day-to-day life of millions, had consumed Paris and Vienna in the 1880s, and now Berlin, Budapest, and Moscow were torn apart. William II pulled down eighteenth-century Berlin and rebuilt the city, featuring modern business and government buildings; the completion of new roadways and mass-transport systems helped push Berlin's population to over 4 million people. In Moscow, an estimated one hundred thousand immigrants arrived each year, and the Russian government undertook massive renovations. "Moscow has been transformed," reported a guidebook in 1903; it had become "overstimulating," too full of "bright colors that strike the eye and involuntarily attract attention." The hustle and bustle of life in these rebuilt metropolises could overwhelm people who longed for continuity and tradition, but fear of modern life did not stem the tremendous expansion of cities.

Thus although the *absolute* size of the population was rising in much of the West, what concerned social critics and politicians was the falling birth*rate*, which suggested to some observers a whole set of potential problems. Whereas the birthrate had been decreasing in France since the eighteenth century, other European countries began experiencing the decline late in the nineteenth century. The Swedish rate dropped from thirty-five births per thousand people in 1859 to twenty-four per thousand in 1911 and would fall even more in the next two decades. England and Wales suffered a similar slump, and even populous Germany went from forty births per thousand in 1875 to twenty-seven per thousand in 1913. The spread of birth-control practices that would encompass most of the globe by the end of the twentieth century brought about this ebbing birthrate.

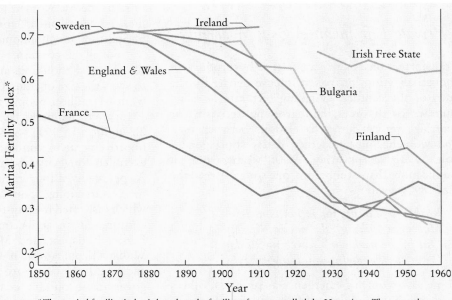

Marital Fertility in Europe

*The marital fertility index is based on the fertility of a group called the Hutterites. These people, who marry young and practice no contraception, are thought to have the highest possible fertility. Other groups tend to measure lower on this scale.

Community norms had traditionally regulated family limitation. But individual couples practiced modern birth control. For example, early modern communities often called for couples to postpone marriage until they were too old to produce large numbers of children. Abstinence was thus a common form of birth control. In modern cities, however, pamphlets and advice books for those with enough money and education spread information about coitus interruptus or the withdrawal method of preventing pregnancy. Technology also played a role in curtailing reproduction: diaphragms and condoms, improved after the vulcanization of rubber in the 1840s, proved fairly reliable in preventing conception. Abortions were legion in cities, with the most conservative figures showing that in France some one hundred thousand were performed annually during these decades.

The wider use of birth control stirred controversy. Critics accused middle-class women, whose fertility was falling most rapidly, of holding a "birth strike." Others thought women were creating an identity "independent of love"—independent of men, motherhood, and separate spheres. Anglican bishops, meeting early in the twentieth century,

deplored family limitation, especially by artificial means, as "demoralizing to character and hostile to national welfare." In France, where fertility decline was startling, politicians worried about a crisis in masculinity. They suggested that men of the respectable classes were failing to produce new generations of leaders, and in the race for national power many feared that a declining population would keep France from competing militarily with Germany. As schools and industry took over the father's role of teaching sons a trade, moreover, critics charged that men had abandoned the family hearth for taverns or radical political activism. In response to these apparent problems, physicians, statisticians, and reformers founded the National Alliance for Increasing the French Population in 1896. German activists, concerned about the declining birthrate in their country, started the German League for the Preservation of the People.

Social Darwinist language converted the debate on family issues into anxieties over class and race. In an age of agricultural industrialization, farm families needed fewer hands and limited their family's size as a rational way to deal with economic change. But what especially struck leaders such as Theodore

European Family Setting Out by Train
With only three children, the family in this photograph took part in the revolution in fertility. Rising costs of maintaining a comfortable life encouraged the limitation of family size.

Roosevelt was that the middle and upper classes had smaller families to curb the rising costs of rearing children and keeping up appearances. If the "best" classes had fewer children, politicians asked, what would society look like when peopled mostly by the "worst" classes? The decline in fertility, one German nationalist warned, would make the country a "conglomerate of alien peoples, above all Slavs and probably East European Jews as well." The fear that one's nation or "race" was being polluted by the presence of "aliens," the mentally ill, the severely disabled, and "nonproductive" elderly people was a feature of *eugenics,* a pseudoscience popular among educated Europeans. Applying Darwin's idea of the survival of the fittest to humans, eugenicists favored increased fertility for "the fittest" and limitations on the fertility of "degenerates." Middle-class reformers, aspiring to perfect the outcome of human reproduction, promoted these pseudoscientific goals throughout society, and politicians worked eugenicist and racial rhetoric into electoral campaigns, thus inflaming fears of ethnic minorities and the poor.

Reforming Marriage

An array of activists, liberal politicians, feminists, and population experts believed that marriage reforms would help address the problems of declining birthrates and a potentially "degenerate" population. To win support for the passage of new laws, activists pointed out that for more than a century outmoded relationships such as those of master and slave or serf and lord had been eliminated, but that married women still lacked basic rights in contrast to their husbands. Even so, women were not refusing to marry: France maintained a steady rate of marriage (approximately fifteen per thousand from the beginning of the nineteenth-century to World War I) and illegitimacy declined across Europe. But the conditions of marriage were the subject of debate: "Give birth, give birth, without stopping," one French woman complained, "but if married, your child will be the *property* of its father."

Feminist groups and reform-minded men successfully lobbied to change the legal relationships of married men and women by giving women more rights. Across most of Europe new laws allowed married women a legal right to their wages and to own property. Sweden, which made men's and women's control over property equal in marriage, allowed women to work without their husband's permission. Such changes made marriage more egalitarian legally, but because of the dual labor market, women's economic status remained low—and thus still unequal in practice. The German law code of 1900 eliminated phrases about women's owing obedience to their husbands and about men's paternal power, although it limited divorce more than the earlier laws of some individual German states. Other countries, among them France, legalized divorce (1884) and made it less complicated, and thus less costly, to obtain.

Reformers believed these legal changes would result in an upswing of the birthrate. Women, they felt, would be more inclined to reproduce if the shackles in the traditional system of marriage were removed and wives were no longer treated as second-class citizens. Given the current constraints of motherhood—no financial resources to leave the home, no legal rights to their own children, little recourse in the event of an abusive or miserable marriage—women were reluctant to have more than two or three, if any, children. Divorce would allow unhappy couples to separate and undertake a new, more loving, and thus more fertile marriage. Greater financial parity in marriage was seen as a way to promote better health and a higher standard of living for women and their children. Swedish reformer Ellen Key (1849–1926) thought financially secure motherhood was a basic right of all women—married and single. Key, one of the most widely read reformers of the time, appealed both to "populationists" and to feminists in her advocacy of better living conditions for mothers and their children. By the early twentieth century, several countries had passed legislation that provided government subsidies to needy mothers. Great Britain, for example, mandated small maternal allowances in 1913. Like the earlier development of social-security legislation in Germany and other countries, the system of subsidizing indigent mothers helped lay the foundations of the modern welfare state.

The conditions of marriage and motherhood varied throughout Europe. In eastern Europe the father's power over the extended family remained almost dictatorial. According to a survey of family life in eastern Europe in the early 1900s, fathers married off their children so young that 25 percent of women in their early forties had been pregnant more than ten times. A woman in Russia could obtain a divorce only if witnesses would testify that they had seen her husband having sex with another woman. Yet as in western Europe, the sentimental aspects of marriage seemed to flourish. For instance, in some Balkan villages, a kind of extended-family system called the *zadruga* survived from earlier times, in which all the nuclear families shared a common great house and individual couples had a degree of privacy in surrounding one-room sleeping dwellings. Many children in the middle and upper classes of eastern Europe were coming to believe they had a right to select a marriage partner, not just to accept the spouse their parents chose for them based on economic or social reasons.

New Women, New Men, and the Politics of Sexual Identity

Rapid economic and institutional change set the stage for bold new behaviors among some middle-class women. The increasing availability of white-collar

Swedish Woman Ice Sailing, 1900
Active participation in sports characterized the "new woman." It shocked polite society that refined women would experience such intense bodily sensations as speed and exertion.

jobs for educated women meant that more women could afford to adopt an independent way of life. So-called new women dressed more practically, with fewer petticoats and looser corsets, biked and hiked through city streets and down country lanes, lived apart from the family in women's clubs or apartments, and supported themselves. Many women of accomplishment acted in ways that challenged accepted views of women's economic dependence in the traditional middle-class family. Italian educator Maria Montessori (1870–1952), for example, went to medical school and secretly gave birth to an illegitimate child. Artists like Gabriele Münter not only drove modernist innovation but also lived openly with their lovers. Some writers portrayed these unconventional women sympathetically. Norwegian novelist and Nobel laureate Sigrid Undset (1882–1940) in *Jenny* (1911) described an unmarried woman's reflections on her pregnancy. But in this time of social transformation, others protested the threat to gender roles: the new woman, German philosopher

Friedrich Nietzsche wrote, had led to the "*ugli-fication* of Europe."

Journalists wrote many articles that helped make sexual life, including male homosexuality, a public issue. In the spring of 1895, reporters covered the trial of Irish playwright Oscar Wilde (1854–1900), who was sentenced to two years in prison for indecency—a charge that referred to his sexual affairs with young men. After Wilde's conviction one newspaper rejoiced, "Open the windows! Let in the fresh air!" The reading public lapped up such sensational stories. Beyond the infamous Wilde case, journalists revealed that married men of the ruling classes sometimes had sexual relations with other men, perhaps with those they had known since their days together in all-male boarding schools. Between 1907 and 1909, German newspapers publicized the courts-martial of men in Kaiser William's closest circle, who were condemned for homosexuality and transvestism. In a case involving adultery, the French on the eve of World War I were gripped by revelations of sexual promiscuity in the murder trial of Henriette Caillaux, who had killed a prominent newspaper editor to protect the honor of her husband, a high-ranking government official.

Books in the new field of "sexology," which studied sex scientifically from a clinical and medical point of view, encouraged public discussion of sexual issues. *Sexual Inversion* (1894) by Havelock Ellis (1859–1939) was more popular than any of Freud's writings at the time. Ellis postulated that the homosexual was a personality type identifiable by such traits as effeminate behavior and a penchant for the arts in males, and physical passion for members of their own sex in both males and females. Homosexuals joined the discussion, calling for recognition that they composed a legitimate and natural "third sex" and were not just people behaving sinfully. Much of this debate remained confined to physicians, psychologists, and intellectuals, but it began the trend toward seeing sexuality in general as a fundamental part of human identity.

Attention to sexual behavior raised concerns about falling birthrates and the solidity of the family. During the scandals over the kaiser's entourage, the public received assurances that William II's own family life "provides the entire country with a fine model." In a time of growing nationalism, sexuality took on patriotic overtones: the accused homosexual elite in Germany were said to be out

to "emasculate our courageous master race. . . ." Although these cases paved the way for growing sexual openness in the next generations, early twentieth-century demagogues often incited the masses by connecting sexual behavior to politics.

Sciences of the Modern Mind

Scientists believed the hectic pace of industrial society produced a host of physical complaints such as fatigue and irritability. By the end of the nineteenth century, doctors had expanded their specialties to include the treatment of maladies stemming from the stresses and strains of everyday life. Many nervous illnesses, they reasoned, resulted from too many rapid changes and the demands of urban living.

Social Darwinists labeled nervous pathology as yet another cause of national decline, and a rash of books in the 1890s expounded on this subject. The most widely translated of them, *Degeneration*, written by Hungarian-born physician Max Nordau (1849–1923), blamed overstimulation for both individual and national deterioration. According to Nordau, increasingly bizarre modern art, male lethargy, and female hysteria were all symptoms of overstimulation and reflected a general downturn in the human species. The standard Social Darwinist cure for modern debilitation was imperial adventure, renewed virility, and increased childbearing.

Medical scientists promised new and better approaches to these nervous ailments. Some researchers attempted to classify and quantify mental characteristics. Italian psychiatrist Cesare Lombroso (1836–1909) devised typologies for criminal minds, which he reached by evaluating the physical features of deviants, and created the "science" of criminology. The French psychologist Alfred Binet (1857–1911) designed intelligence tests that he maintained could measure the capacity of the human mind more accurately than schoolteachers could. In Russia, physiologist Ivan Pavlov (1849–1936) proposed that behavior could be modified by conditioning reflexes. His most famous case involved a dog that would begin to salivate after hearing a bell and seeing his food. Having established the connection between the dog's food and the sound of the bell, Pavlov withdrew the food and found that the dog would still salivate when the bell rang. Such experiments formed the basis of modern psychology, which eventually modified religious and moral evaluations of the human personality.

Sigmund Freud (1856–1939) devised an approach to modern anxieties that, he claimed, avoided traditional moral evaluations of human behavior. He became convinced that the human psyche was far from rational. Dreams, as he explained in *The Interpretation of Dreams* (1900), revealed a repressed part of personality—the "unconscious"—where all sorts of desires were more or less hidden. These desires appeared only involuntarily, in the form of dreams, symptoms of physical illness, and abnormal behavior. Freud also believed that human personality was made up of competing parts: an ego, which was concerned with reality; an id (or libido), which contained drives and sexual energies; and a superego, which served as the force of conscience. Like Darwin's ideas, Freud's notions challenged accepted liberal belief in a unified, rational self that acted in its own interest. They also undermined the social implications of this belief, namely, that society would move in a consistently progressive direction.

Freud shocked many contemporaries in insisting that all children had sexual drives from the moment of birth, but he also believed that many of these sexual impulses had to be repressed for children to attain maturity and for society to remain civilized. Attaining one's adult sexual identity was always a painful process because it depended on repressing infantile urges, including bisexuality and incest. Freud's insights that boys and girls reached different adult identities by a variety of psychic paths was extraordinary, first because it made gender more complicated than simple biology. Although Freud claimed that certain gender roles were normal and that women generally achieved far less than men, he believed adult gender identity was never predetermined but the result of life experiences acting on biological tendencies. Finally, psychoanalytic theory maintained that girls and women had powerful sexual feelings, rupturing Victorian ideas of women's passionlessness.

The influence of psychoanalysis became pervasive in the twentieth century. For example, psychoanalysis, or the talking cure, gave rise to a general acceptance of talking out one's problems. (Incidentally, Freud, who always had his patients lie on a couch facing away from him, could not stand to be looked at by his patients when they spoke.) As psychotherapy became a respected means of recovering mental health, terms such as a *neurosis, the unconscious,* and *libido* came into widespread usage. But Freud's theory that girls' complaints about unwanted sexual advances or abuse were mere fantasy influenced members of the new profession of social work to believe that most instances of such abuse had not actually occurred. Psychoanalysis thus partook of the many contradictions at work in turn-of-the-century Europe. On the one hand, Freud was a meticulous scientist, examining symptoms, urging attention to the most minute evidence from everyday life, and demanding that sexual life be regarded with a rational rather than a religious eye. On the other hand, he had abandoned the optimism of the Enlightenment and pre-Darwinian science by claiming that humans were motivated by irrational drives toward death and destruction and that these shaped society's collective mentality. A pessimistic vision of instinctual destructiveness began crowding beliefs in the nobility of human nature and the inevitability of progress. Freud later interpreted World War I's vast devastation of humanity as bearing out his bleak conclusions.

Modernism and the Revolt in Ideas

From ideas about a modern family and a modern mind-set to those about modern art and music, the term *modern* relentlessly clings to the period from the end of the nineteenth century on, even though historians still struggle with the word's precise meaning. In the realm of ideas and the arts, scholars use *modern* to describe a set of changes brought about by elite groups of intellectuals and artists, people who reacted to the turmoil in turn-of-the-century society by rejecting much of the past, especially traditional values and artistic forms. Thus philosophers who emphasized the irrational and the accidental in day-to-day life challenged the belief that fundamental social laws could be discovered. In science, theories that time was relative and that energy and mass interchangeable rocked established truths about time, space, matter, and energy. Art and music became unrecognizable from anything they had looked or sounded like before; much modern art and music appalled the public. Many artists deliberately produced shocking, lurid works, but like Freud they were heavily influenced by advances in science and critical thinking. Within this contradictory frame, artists helped launch a disorienting revolution in the forms of creative expression that we now identify collectively as modernism.

The Challenge to Positivism

Late in the nineteenth century, many philosophers and social thinkers rejected the century-old faith that in science one could discover enduring social laws based on rationally determined principles. This belief had come to be called *positivism,* and it motivated reformers' attempts to perfect legislation based on studies of society. Challenging positivism, the philosophers Wilhelm Dilthey in Germany and John Dewey in the United States declared that human understanding was founded on the conditions of day-to-day existence. Ever-changing experience and information precluded theories and standards from being constant or enduring. Just as scientific theory always changed, so must social theories and practice always evolve with changing circumstances. American philosopher and psychologist William James (1842–1910) claimed that people did not act according to principles, but instead reacted pragmatically to the immediate conditions at hand. Whereas Enlightenment thinkers had emphasized the permanent nature of fundamental laws—either natural or political—turn-of-the-century theorists explored the limits of certainty in making social judgments. These critics, called *relativists* and *pragmatists,* influenced thinking about society throughout the twentieth century.

In the same vein, German sociologist and political theorist Max Weber (1864–1920) was pessimistic about the ability of government bureaucracy—once seen as a rational alternative to the rule of a whimsical monarch—to deal effectively with all the variables of modern society. Watching government expand, he maintained that the sheer numbers involved in policy making would often make decisive action, especially in times of crisis,

impossible. Although Weber favored constitutional government, he nonetheless believed that in certain situations a charismatic leader might usurp power because his flexible and instinctual reactions would allow him to react better to a crisis. Thus the development of impartial forms of government such as bureaucracy was not steady or sure but carried within it the potential for undermining the rule of law and eroding the modern commitment to constitutional procedures in government. Most famously, Weber saw a direct connection between economic progress and religious feeling. In *The Protestant Ethic and the Spirit of Capitalism* (1905) he discussed how the Calvinist doctrine of predestination had advanced capitalism by inspiring entrepreneurs with self-confidence. Weber's work applied the spiritual and irrational to phenomena that had once been seen as inevitable products of progress and rationality.

German philosopher Friedrich Nietzsche (1844–1900) was far more explosive and radical than these other scholars. Early in his career he developed one of his most challenging ideas, based on the distinction between the "Apollonian," or rational, side of human existence and the "Dionysian" moments when humans expressed more primal urges. Nietzsche believed that people generally clung to the rational, Apollonian explanations of life because Dionysian expressions of nature, death, and love such as those found in Greek tragedy were too disturbing. From the scientific revolution on, people had come to rely on the certitude of scientific findings, but Nietzsche maintained that all assertions of scientific fact and theory were mere illusions. Knowledge of nature had to be expressed in mathematical, linguistic, or artistic representation; truth thus existed only in the representation itself, for humans could never escape it to some unfiltered knowledge of nature or reality. Since Nietzsche's time, thinkers have had to confront the challenge this philosophy posed to the possibility of exact scientific truth.

Much of Nietzsche's writing took the form of aphorisms or short, disconnected paragraphs—a form that broke with the logical rigor of traditional philosophy. Nietzsche used aphorisms to convey the impression that his ideas were a single individual's unique perspective, not universal truths. Nietzsche was convinced that late nineteenth-century

Europe was witnessing the decline of all dogmatic truths, especially the decline of religion—hence his announcement that "God is dead, we have killed him." Far from arousing dread, the death of God was to give birth to a joyful quest for a constantly changing array of new "poetries of life."

Nietzsche, who taught sporadically in Switzerland, was so intense that his first students thought they were hearing another Socrates. But like many in the 1800s, he contracted syphilis, which often left him unable to teach; he suffered from insanity for the last eleven years of his life. After Nietzsche went mad, his sister endeavored to spread his fame. Most important for twentieth-century politics, she edited Nietzsche's diatribes against middle-class values into attacks on Jews. She revised his concepts about each individual's "will to power" and of "supermen" so as to advocate military conquest and displays of power.

The highly popular teachings of French philosopher Henri Bergson were often intertwined with the distorted version of Nietzsche to counter pessimistic views that the West might be facing an inevitable decline or savage defeat. Bergson proposed the existence of an *élan vital,* or intuitive creative force, that, like an electrical charge, could spark individuals and nations to superior accomplishment. Racists, nationalists, and militarists reduced these very complicated philosophies into simple-minded creeds that justified violent antisemitism and competition for empire.

Revolutionizing Science

While philosophers questioned the ability of science to provide timeless truths, scientific inquiry itself flourished. Improvements in hygiene and a steady stream of technological advances, moreover, earned science great prestige with the public. The scientific method gained authority beyond the traditional sciences, especially in fields such as history and psychology, and many people still held to positivist assumptions that natural laws could be understood and the universe consequently mastered. Technological breakthroughs and the fruits of applied science seemed to confirm this kind of confidence. Around the turn of the century, however, discoveries by pioneering researchers shook the foundations

of traditional scientific certainty and challenged accepted knowledge about the nature of the universe.

Some scientists' findings undermined the principles of time, space, matter, energy, and the immutability of physical entities on which science had rested since Newton. In 1896, Antoine Becquerel (1852–1908) discovered radioactivity and suggested that elements could be changed from one to another by the rearrangement of their components. French chemist Marie Curie (1867–1934) and her husband, Pierre Curie (1859–1906), isolated polonium and radium, which were more radioactive than the uranium Becquerel used. From these and other discoveries, scientists concluded that atoms were composed of subatomic particles moving about a core. Instead of being solid, as scientists had believed since ancient times, atoms were largely empty space and acted less like a concrete substance than like the intangible electromagnetic field. German physicist Max Planck (1858–1947) announced his famous quantum theorem in 1900; it demonstrated that energy was emitted in irregular packets, not in a steady stream.

New research transformed astronomy as well as physics. Scientists had already demonstrated that light had the same velocity no matter which direction it traveled from earth and was not relative to the motion of the earth; thus neither the wave character of light nor the hypothesis that the universe was filled with an "ether" (on which scientists had relied to accommodate so-called light waves) was tenable. It was in this anomalous situation that physicist Albert Einstein (1879–1955) published his "Special Theory of Relativity" in 1905. Einstein, who had been expelled from high school as disruptive and a bad influence on other students, had later studied physics with teachers ignorant of the intellectual transformation taking place in scientific thought. But on his own, working in a Swiss patent office, he proclaimed in his 1905 paper that space and time were not absolute categories. Instead they varied according to the vantage point of the observer; only the speed of light was constant. That same year he also suggested that the solution to problems in Planck's quantum theorem lay in considering light both as the little packets *and* as waves. These theories continued to undercut Newtonian physics as well as commonsense understanding, for example, that space was a uniformly measurable entity. Einstein later proposed yet another blurring of two distinct physical properties, mass and energy. He expressed this equivalence in the formulation of $E = mc^2$, or energy equals mass times the square of the speed of light.

The findings of this scientific avant-garde would eventually revolutionize the physical sciences, but these theories were often not accepted immediately. Einstein struggled against mainstream science and its professional institutions, and conservative scientists resisted his concepts because they destroyed time-honored Newtonian physics. Established power was also at stake. Just as the Catholic church centuries earlier had controlled scientific doctrine and opposed change, so many university professors entrenched in their positions now flatly opposed the new findings. Even Planck, who had excellent university positions because of family connections, tried desperately for years to get senior researchers to approve his findings. Marie Curie faced such resistance that she was forced to work for years in a shed where the temperature sometimes dipped below 40 degrees. After her husband's death in 1906, she refused the widow's pension the government offered her and demanded a job instead; in 1908 she became the first woman to teach at the Sorbonne. Even then and even after she became the first person ever to receive a second Nobel Prize (1911), the prestigious Academy of Science turned down her candidacy for membership that year.

These prejudices ultimately broke down. Max Planck institutes were established in German cities, streets across Europe were named after Marie Curie and other scientific pioneers, and Einstein's name became synonymous with genius. These scientists achieved what historians call a *paradigm shift*—that is, in the face of understandable resistance they transformed the foundations of science. Einstein's publication of his "General Theory of Relativity" (1916) connected the force, or gravity, of an object with its mass and postulated a "fourth" mathematical dimension to the universe. Human society still had to assimilate the meaning of *relativity*. Ordinary perceptions of the workings of the universe were more divergent than ever from a scientific view if space and time were, as Einstein maintained, a single continuum. Moreover, agreed-upon standards

of time gave way to individualized standards proposed in Einstein's equations. Much more lay ahead, once Einstein's theories of energy were developed: television, nuclear power, and, within forty years, nuclear bombs.

Christianity Faces Science and Secularism

A growing acceptance of scientific and secular accounts of human society led to a continuing decline in religious fervor among urban elites and the working class alike. Extreme religious attacks on scientific findings, such as Darwin's, paradoxically did much to undermine religious belief: "The educated middle class, especially the young people, are losing touch altogether with the House of God," one Protestant clergyman wrote in 1911. Wealthy Catholic men often tended their businesses or played sports rather than observing Mass.

Some theologians wanted to modernize religion by applying scholarly methods to the Bible, and although many Protestant and Catholic churches did not liberalize their theological claims, they did counter secular challenges to their authority through increased missionary efforts abroad and among the urban poor. Pope Leo XIII's call for a more active ministry among the working classes led the church in Hungary to channel some of its efforts away from its traditional constituency in villages and toward ministering to workers in cities. In France, Leo finally gave papal endorsement to the republic despite its secularism and antimonarchism, prompting some Catholic elites to abandon their obstructionist politics. Small cohorts of educated men revived their interest in religion: some of Bergson's youthful disciples hoped that a rebirth of Catholic spirituality—a surge of religious élan vital—would redirect the French away from materialism and godless sciences.

Many opposed liberalization to meet scientific claims, especially papal policy makers. Pius X (*1903–1914) condemned Catholic "Modernists" who wanted Catholicism to reconcile with scientific claims. In Austria-Hungary, Francis Joseph and his officials, faced with mounting political discontent, strictly observed the rituals of their Catholic faith hoping that they would draw the masses away from spectacles such as the annual workers' May Day parade. In Orthodox Russia the reactionary policies of Alexander III and his son, Nicholas II (＊1894–1917), opposed free thinking in both intellectual and religious matters. They equated the Orthodox religion with political loyalty.

Art Transformed

The same conflicts between traditional values and new ideas raged in the arts, as artists distanced themselves from classical norms and from the conventions of polite society, believing them passé. Their rebellion, however, was far more disorganized than the impressionist revolt a generation earlier. Various artistic splinter groups challenged the historic and realistic scenes still favored, for example, by the powerful German monarchy and by some buyers for museums and important collections. Such schools as fauvism, cubism, and expressionism coexisted or followed one another in rapid succession because of the many visions of how art should be made modern.

Abandoning the soft colors of impressionism as too subtle for a dynamic industrial society, a group of Parisian artists exhibiting in 1905 combined blues, greens, reds, and oranges so intensively that they were called *fauves,* or "wild beasts." A leader of this short-lived group, Henri Matisse (1869–1954), soon struck out in a new direction, targeting the expanding class of white-collar workers in creating his canvases. Matisse dreamed of "an art . . . for every mental worker, be he businessman or writer, like an appeasing influence, like a mental soother, something like a good armchair in which to rest from physical fatigue." Thus Matisse believed modern art should both challenge and comfort urbanites caught up in the rush of modern life.

Most modern styles were indebted to French painter Paul Cézanne (1839–1906), who had broken with the impressionist emphasis on color and fleeting images to focus on structure in painting. Cézanne used rectangular daubs of paint in his scenes of nature and portraits of people to capture a geometric vision of his subjects. Accentuating the lines and planes found in nature, Cézanne's art, like science, was removed from the realm of ordinary perception. The dishes, fruit, and drapery of his still lifes of the 1890s took geometric form, as did the human body in *Boy in a Red Vest* (1893–1895).

Spanish artist Pablo Picasso (1881–1973), following in Cézanne's footsteps, initiated *cubism,* a radical departure in painting that also emphasized planes and surfaces while presenting bizarre, inhuman, and almost unrecognizable forms. Picasso's painting *Les Demoiselles d'Avignon* (1907) depicted the bodies of the demoiselles, or young ladies, as fragmented and angular, with their heads modeled on African masks. Like impressionism and fauvism, Picasso's work incorporated features of Asian, African, and South American art that imperialism had made the artist aware of, but his depiction of these features was less decorative and more brutal. Shown secretly to his painter friends at first, the work so enraged the public when it was finally exhibited that the French Chamber of Deputies heatedly debated how to prevent cubism from corrupting the people.

Picasso had a political critique in mind when he painted. "Show the people how hideous is their actual life, and place your hands on the causes of its ugliness" was the anarchist challenge at the time, and Picasso had spent his youth in the heart of working-class Barcelona, a hotbed of anarchist thought. Picasso's radical art aimed to speak the truth about industrial society instead of seeking an idealized and thus, to his mind, false beauty. In *Les Demoiselles d'Avignon* the nude was no longer a matter of pleasurable delectation. *Demoiselles* can mean "prostitute" in French, and the grotesque poses of the women were as offensive to the standards of art as prostitution was to the standards of polite society.

In 1912, Picasso and French painter Georges Braque (1882–1963) devised a new kind of collage that incorporated bits of newspaper, string, and other artifacts. The effect was a canvas that appeared to be cluttered with refuse. The newspaper clippings Picasso included described battles and murders, suggesting the shallowness of Western pretensions to high civilization. Modernism in painting aimed to register the hideous features of turn-of-the-century life by eschewing the sentimental art favored by the middle classes. It expressed its concerns, however, in a far more abstract, nonrepresentational way than previous forms of art engaging in social criticism.

Although Paris was still the center of the art world, artists in the thriving cities of central and eastern Europe and Scandinavia formed

Art Nouveau Ceramic Design
Art nouveau styles appeared on objects for everyday use, such as lamps and vases. This design relies on flowers, flowing lines, and a female figure—all intrinsic to concepts of the beautiful in the new style.

associations ("secessions") to express their own rebellion against officially approved styles. Such groups as the Berlin Secession and the Vienna Workshop were at the forefront in experimenting with form and in portraying the psychological complexity of the self. Their joint exhibits of work by ethnically diverse artists criticized the growing nationalism that determined official purchases of sculpture and painting. "The whole empire is littered with monuments to soldiers and monuments to Kaiser William of the same conventional type," one artist complained.

Practitioners of *art nouveau,* or "new style," responded to industrial society by creating commercially successful artistic products for the masses. Creating everything from advertising posters to streetlamps to dishes and even entire buildings in this new style, continental designers manufacturered beautiful things for the general public. As one French official said about the first version of art nouveau coins issued in 1895, "Soon even the most humble among us will be able to have a masterpiece in his pocket." Like the earlier arts and crafts movement in Britain, art nouveau, or *Jugendstil* (in German),

featured intertwined vines and flowers; women with long, wavy hair; and other motifs to counteract the effects of mechanization on human society. The organic and natural elements of *Jugendstil* were meant to offset the atomization of factory and office work with images depicting the unified forms of nature; the impersonality of machines was replaced by softly curving bodies of female nudes that would psychologically soothe the individual viewer—an idea that directly contrasted with Picasso's artistic vision. Gustav Klimt (1862–1918), son of a Czech goldsmith, flourished in Viennese high society because his paintings captured the psychological essence of dreamy, sensuous women, their bodies Eastern-inspired mosaics liberally dotted with gold.

Scandinavian and east European artists produced more anguished works; their understanding of psychological reality was less optimistic than practitioners of *Jugendstil.* Norwegian painter Edvard Munch (1863–1944), who participated in German exhibitions, aimed "to make the emotional mood ring out again as happens on a gramophone." His painting *The Scream* (1895) used twisting lines and a depiction of a tormented skeletal human form to convey the horror of modern life that many artists perceived. German avant-garde artist Gabriele Münter (1877–1962) and Russian painter Wassily Kandinsky (1866–1944) opened their "Blue Rider" Exhibit in Munich, featuring "expressive" work that made use of geometric forms and striking colors. Kandinsky, who employed these forms and colors to express an inner, spiritual truth, is often credited with producing the first abstract paintings. The artists of the Blue Rider group imitated the paintings of children and the mentally ill and experimented with forms such as primitive images painted under glass to achieve their representation of psychological reality. The expressionism of Oskar Kokoschka (1886–1980) was even more intense, displaying ecstasy, horror, and hallucinations. Explicitly erotic, his *Bride of the Wind* (1914) used swirling colors to announce the sensuality of his liaison with Alma Mahler, widow of the composer Gustav Mahler. Kokoschka's bizarre paintings earned him the name "the talented terror," and he was forced to leave Vienna at least once because of the violent reaction to his work.

As was the case for many expressionists and cubists before World War I, Kokoschka's work was

Oskar Kokoschka, Bride of the Wind, *1914*
Kokoschka's paintings sought to capture animated spirit, the psyche, and the luminescence of life. The overlay of torment, despair, and sexual rawness made much of his work hated at the time.

a commercial failure, whereas impressionist art sold well to international collectors through a system of dealerships. Sponsoring exhibits of "their" artists' work, dealers relied on favorable reviews by professional art critics. With styles changing rapidly, the "old masters" of Renaissance and baroque art gained status as classics, selling for ever higher prices. Experts in authenticating and judging these older works of art, among them the American Bernard Berenson (who set himself up outside Florence as the ultimate arbiter for an international clientele), made it possible for buyers from around the world to purchase with confidence. Meanwhile, collectors of modern art, such as the experimental writer Gertrude Stein and her brother Leo, held open houses to show their collection and thus give experimental styles publicity. The struggle by artists to gain public acceptance and the proliferation of

schools, tastes, and styles were part of a clash over traditional norms.

Musical Iconoclasm

"Astonish me!" was the motto of modern dance and music, both of which shocked audiences in the concert halls of Europe. American dancer Isadora Duncan (1877–1927) took Europe by storm at the turn of the century when, draped in a flowing garment, she danced barefoot in the first performance of modern dance. Her primitive style "lifted from their seats people who had never left theater seats before except to get up and go home." Similar experimentation with forms of bodily expression animated the Russian Ballet's performance in 1913 of *Rite of Spring* by Igor Stravinsky (1882–1971), the tale of an orgiastic dance to the death that was done to ensure fertile soil and a bountiful harvest. The star, Vaslav Nijinsky (1890–1950), was noted for his grace and meticulous execution of classical ballet steps, but his choreography of the *Rite of Spring* created a scandal. Nijinsky and the troupe struck awkward poses and danced to what were supposed to be primitive rhythms. "The audience began shouting its indignation. . . . Fighting actually

London Theater, 1899
Theaters brought modern drama to educated audiences at the turn of the century and staged plays on many of the most controversial topics of the day.

The Rite of Spring, 1913
The costumes and movements of the dancers in this Russian production departed from the traditions of classical ballet. Many in the audience were incensed by the new forms of art wrought by modernity.

broke out among some of the spectators." Such controversy made the *Rite of Spring the* ballet to attend, although its choreographer was called a "lunatic" and the music itself "the most discordant composition ever written."

Austrian composer Richard Strauss (1864–1949), influenced by Wagner, upset tonalities by using several keys simultaneously in his compositions. Like cubism, atonality or several tonalities at once distorted familiar perceptual patterns for the audience. Strauss's operas *Salome* (1905) and *Elektra* (1909) took Biblical and classical heroines and expressed through them the modern fascination with violence and obsessive passion. A newspaper critic claimed that Strauss's dissonant works "spit and scratch and claw each other like enraged panthers." The Hungarian pianist Béla Bartók (1881–1945) was so impressed by Strauss's innovations that he took up composing himself. Fascinated by central European folk tales, he incorporated their melodies into his compositions as Grieg and other nationalist composers had before him. Bartók's aim was to elevate the virtues of Hungarian ethnicity above the Habsburg empire's unifying cosmopolitanism. His music, however, disturbed some audiences because of its nationalism and oth-

ers because of its dissonance (he composed so that two folk melodies could be played simultaneously in different keys).

Strauss and Bartók disturbed the concertgoing public because their work diverged so much from the usual diet of Mozart and Beethoven, but the early work of Arnold Schoenberg (1874–1951), who also wrote cabaret music to earn a living, shocked even Strauss. In *Theory of Harmony* (1911) he proposed eliminating tonality altogether; ultimately he devised his twelve-tone scale. "I am aware of having broken through all the barriers of a dated aesthetic ideal," Schoenberg wrote of his music.

Modernists in music, like modernists in other arts, felt they were shattering old norms and values with their concern for abstract forms. But new aesthetic models distanced artists from their audiences, separating high from low culture even more and ending the support of many in the upper classes, who found this music not only incomprehensible but unpleasant. The artistic elite and the social elite parted ranks. "Anarchist! Nihilist!" shouted Schoenberg's audiences, showing their contempt for modernism and bringing the language of politics into the arts. Pushing rational critiques of traditional arts to their extremes, modern culture both reflected and helped create the tense political situation in turn-of-the-century Europe.

Politics in a New Key

New political challenges accompanied the revolution in intellectual life. To some observers, Queen Victoria's death in 1901 after a reign of more than sixty years symbolized the uncertainties that lay ahead in European politics. "It isn't only the Queen who has disappeared," commented a diplomat's wife. "It is the century." The Crystal Palace exhibit Queen Victoria had opened in 1851 had exemplified people's unshakable faith in progress. Now, less than fifty years later, that optimism had been tempered by an apprehensive, even pessimistic feeling about the future, especially among the upper classes. Cracks in the political consensus and changing political tactics had undermined upperclass control of politics. Liberalism had opened the door to mass politics by espousing tolerance for diverse opinions and had expanded political representation. A growing number of governments recognized the political rights of the working class, and socialists won elections to parliaments. Political activists, however, were no longer satisfied with the liberal rights sought by radical reformers a century earlier. Militant nationalists, antisemites, socialists, suffragists, and many others demanded changes that often alarmed old-fashioned liberals. Traditional agrarian elites joined in feeding the jingoistic press and contributed to a politics of hatred. Mass politics soon threatened social unity, especially in central and eastern Europe, where governments often responded to reformers' demands with repression and a refusal to budge.

The Growing Power of Labor

European leaders watched the rise of working-class political power late in the century with dismay. Unions and labor parties gained members, parliamentary representation, and organizational strength. After dismissing Bismarck in 1890, Kaiser William II allowed antisocialist laws to lapse. Through continuous grass roots organizing, moreover, the Social Democratic party (SPD), founded by socialists in 1875, became the largest parliamentary group in the Reichstag by 1912. In France separate labor unions formed the General Confederation of Labor (CGT) early in the twentieth century. In 1905 the socialist Jean Jaurès, who favored reform rather than revolution, and the more orthodox Marxist Jules Guesde merged their competing political parties into the French Section of the Workers' International (SFIO). These massive workers' parties in central and western Europe voted representatives favorable to labor into parliaments, where they focused on passing legislation that benefited laborers and their families.

Many labor politicians, however, felt uncomfortable sitting cheek by jowl with the upper classes in parliaments. Socialists worried that their participation in ministerial cabinets would compromise their ultimate goal of revolution, especially after the late 1890s, when renewed prosperity seemed to preclude Marx's prediction that capitalism would collapse. Socialist cabinet members did have an opportunity to influence government even more than they had within parliaments. But socialist cabinet ministers appeared to endorse rather than to oppose capitalism. Party bureaucracies became more concerned in maintaining their members as an electoral force than as a revolutionary one. Socialist leaders' cooperation with established powers, called *reformism,* seemed antithetical to Marxist and anarchist doctrine.

Between 1900 and 1904 the Second International wrestled with the issue of reformism. The International hotly debated the "revisionist" theories of Eduard Bernstein, who in 1898 had criticized many Marxist tenets and proposed that socialism be achieved by evolutionary rather than revolutionary means. German Marxist Karl Kautsky responded that reformism only buttressed capitalism. Other delegates sought a middle ground, urging that socialists collaborate with liberals only when the existence of a socialist party was threatened. The topic touched off stormy discussions, sometimes pitting delegates from France, England, and Belgium who had attained some political authority and thus favored reform against more intransigent German socialists who were denied ministerial posts by military and aristocratic statesmen.

Russian socialists had even less political legitimacy than their German counterparts and could gain no ground against a rigidly authoritarian government. Most of these socialists operated in exile because the Russian government outlawed political parties until 1905 and persecuted activists. The foremost activist, V. I. Lenin (1870–1924), became a radical after his brother was executed for plotting to assassinate the tsar. Jailed and sent to Siberia during the 1890s for his left-wing politics, Lenin migrated to western Europe after his release and earned his reputation among Russian Marxists there with his hard-hitting journalism and political intrigue. He fought with his comrades—over whether the party should admit sympathizers or remain a tight band of orthodox Marxist revolutionaries, and over the kind of society that would replace autocratic Russia after the revolution. Lenin advanced the theory that a highly disciplined party elite would lead a lightly industrialized Russia immediately into socialism. At a 1903 party meeting of Russian Marxists, he briefly gained the upper hand when a group of his opponents walked out of the proceedings. In ensuing votes, Lenin's supporters eked out slim victories for control of the party. Thereafter his faction of Bolsheviks, so named after the Russian word for *majority,* which they had *temporarily* formed, constantly struggled to suppress the Mensheviks, the dominant voice in Russian Marxism. Neither of these groups, however, had as large a constituency within Russia as the Socialist Revolutionaries, whose objective was to politicize not industrial workers but peasants. Socialist Revolutionaries saw organizing the peasantry as the prelude to a populist revolution. All these groups prepared for the revolutionary moment through study, propaganda efforts, and organizing.

During this period anarchists and trade union members known as syndicalists kept Europe in a panic with terrorist acts; they also antagonized Marxists. Anarchists assassinated Spanish premier Antonio Canovas del Castillo in 1897, Empress Elizabeth of Austria-Hungary in 1898, King Umberto of Italy in 1900, and President William McKinley of the United States in 1901, to name a few famous victims. Syndicalist ideas were set forth most clearly in French engineer Georges Sorel's *Reflections on Violence* (1908), which explained how a general strike of workers could paralyze the industrial economy and how widespread violence could transform society. By the time of that book's publication, syndicalists had aroused some worker support for their goals. In Italy, for example,

sporadic strikes among agricultural and industrial workers in the 1890s were followed by a general strike in 1904. Elsewhere anarchist plots, strikes, and protests over the high cost of living revealed rising worker activism.

Working people's voices had never been so powerful as in these two decades, and that power caused the upper and middle classes grave anxiety. Despite growing acceptance of representative institutions, most people in the "best circles" still believed that they alone should hold political power. Urban workers and peasants might be better educated, better informed politically, and even appear healthier and more civilized than in earlier generations, but many in the upper and middle classes did not consider them fit to rule. Politicians from the old landowning and military elites of eastern and central Europe were often the most adamant in their rejection of mass politics, and many of them hoped to reverse the trend toward constitutionalism, worker activism, and reform.

Rights for Women and the Battle for Suffrage

Women did not benefit from the gains of liberalism such as parliamentary representation and equal access to the free press. They often could not vote, exercise free speech, or own property. In Austria and Germany they could not attend political meetings or belong to political groups. In France during the Third Republic, the police often prohibited women's political meetings and talks, citing laws dating from the French Revolution that forbade women to gather publicly in groups. British women could serve on school councils but were deprived of most other representation.

In response to such restrictions the movement committed to gaining rights for women grew stronger. Throughout the nineteenth century, women singly and in groups had struggled for rights, and by this time their efforts involved millions of activists with a variety of goals. German women, influenced by the ideal of *Bildung* (the belief that proper education can build strength of character), agitated to reform education and to acquire teaching positions more forcefully than they sought the vote. They met in educational organizations because the law banned women's outright political activism. Women in various countries continued to monitor the regulation of prostitution. Their goal was to prevent prostitutes from being imprisoned on suspicion of having syphilis when men with syphilis faced no such incarceration or inspection. Other women took up pacifism as their special cause. Bertha von Suttner, who influenced Alfred Nobel to institute a peace prize and then won the prize herself in 1903, had written an increasingly popular book on peace, *Lay Down Your Arms* (1889). This work emphasized the terror inflicted on women and families by the ravages of war.

By the 1890s, however, many activists concluded that only the vote would right the assortment of wrongs they were combatting in piecemeal fashion. Thus they launched a suffrage movement with the express purpose of reducing male privilege by giving women an equal say in society. They argued that men had promised to protect disenfranchised women but that this system of supposed chivalry had led to exploitation and abuse. Power and privilege—no matter how couched in expressions of goodwill—worked to the detriment of those without it. "So long as the subjection of women endures, and is confirmed by law and custom, . . . women will be victimized," a leading suffragist claimed. Other suffragists believed women had attributes needed to counterbalance masculine qualities in the running of society. The characteristics that came from mothering should shape a country's destiny as much as qualities that stemmed from work in industry and trade.

Women's rights activists were predominantly, though not exclusively, middle class. Those whose husbands or fathers could afford servants and other conveniences simply had more time to be activists, and a higher level of education allowed them to read the works of feminist theorists such as Harriet Taylor and John Stuart Mill. Working-class women, especially socialists, felt conflicted over whether to engage in women's rights campaigns. Most distrusted middle-class men and women and saw suffrage for women as subordinate to economic concerns. Although some working women, such as those in the textile industries of Manchester, England, put together a vigorous suffrage movement connecting the vote to improved working conditions, socialists and suffragists differed over issues of class and gender.

In the 1890s major suffrage organizations with

Finnish Woman Voting, 1913
Finnish women were the first in Europe to win the national franchise.

paid officials and permanent offices emerged out of the voluntary reform groups and women's clubs that had existed earlier in the century. From charity work performed as part of their "mission," women had acquired skills in fund-raising, public speaking, and organization building. They also devoted their lives to "the Cause" for personal reasons. Millicent Garrett Fawcett, the British suffrage leader, had endured such humiliation at having her stolen purse officially labeled her husband's property that she vowed to change things. Fawcett pressured members of Parliament for the vote, recruited new members, and participated in national and international congresses on behalf of suffrage. Similarly, Susan B. Anthony (1820–1906) traveled throughout the United States, organized suffrage societies, edited a newspaper, raised money for the movement, and founded the International Women's Suffrage Association in 1904.

In 1906 in Finland suffragists achieved their first major victory when the Finnish parliament granted women the vote. "The miracle has happened," rejoiced a Finnish activist. But the failure of parliaments elsewhere in Europe to enact similar legislation provoked some suffragists to violence and bold public activism. Part of the English suffragist movement adopted a militant political style when Emmeline Pankhurst (1858–1928) and her daughters founded the Women's Social and Political Union (WSPU) in the belief that women would accomplish nothing unless they threatened men's property. Starting in 1907, members of the WSPU held parades in English cities, and in 1909 they began a campaign of violence, blowing up railroad stations, slashing works of art, and chaining themselves to the gates of Parliament. Easily disguising themselves as ordinary shoppers, they carried little hammers in their muffs to smash the plate-glass windows of department stores and shops. Parades and demonstrations made suffrage a public spectacle, inciting violent attacks on the marchers by outraged men. Arrested for disturbing the peace, the marchers went on hunger strikes in prison. Like workers, these women were willing to use confrontational tactics to obtain rights. As politicians dithered over the question of the vote for women, militant suffragists added to the tensions of conflict-ridden urban life.

Liberalism Modified in Britain and Italy

Governments in western Europe, where liberal institutions were seemingly well entrenched, handled late nineteenth-century industrialization, urbanization, and mass politics with pragmatic policies that often struck at liberalism's very foundations. After ending laissez-faire in trade by instituting protective tariffs, some reformers and politicians decided government needed to intervene in society to maintain social peace. The scope of social-welfare programs broadened, giving government officials more access to information about the family, public health, and domestic relations so they could devise protective legislation, administer disability plans, and establish food and medical programs for needy children. Officials hoped these policies would guarantee a contented work force and better productivity, which in turn would counter economic uncertainty and political unrest. Although many programs addressed urban needs insufficiently, they added to the growing apparatus of the welfare state in which government actively promoted social well-being.

In 1905 the British Liberal party won a solid majority in the House of Commons and seemed determined to enact social legislation to gain working-class support. "We are keenly in sympathy with the representatives of Labour," one Liberal politician announced. "We have too few of them in the House of Commons." Liberal chancellor of the exchequer David Lloyd George (1863–1945) wanted to make a "new departure" in social policy and initiated a system of relief for the unemployed in the National Insurance Act of 1911. Conservatives in the House of Lords resisted higher taxation on the wealthy to pay for this and other social programs, leading to a Liberal threat to create more peers (lords) who could be counted on to vote for reform. Under this threat the lords approved the Parliament Bill (1911), which eliminated their veto power, but many wealthy businessmen who had formerly been Liberals deserted their party because of its alliance with Labour.

A modified liberalism advanced in Britain on these issues, but the Irish question tested British commitment to such values as self-determination and individual rights. The House of Lords had blocked previous bills granting home rule to Ireland, and after the fall of Parnell the Irish needed to rebuild their organization. In the 1890s groups formed to foster Irish culture. In 1901 the circle around the modernist poet William Butler Yeats (1865–1939) and the charismatic patriot and actress Maud Gonne (1865–1953) founded the Irish National Theater. Gonne took Irish politics into everyday life by opposing British efforts to woo the young. Every time an English monarch visited Ireland, he or she held special receptions for children. Gonne and other Irish volunteers sponsored competing events, handing out candies and other treats for patriotic youngsters. "Dublin never witnessed anything so marvelous," enthused one home rule supporter, "as the procession . . . of thirty thousand school children who refused to be bribed into parading before the Queen of England."

Singing Gaelic songs, speaking Gaelic instead of English in unprecedented numbers, using Catholicism as a rallying point, and generally reconstructing an "Irish way of life," the promoters of Irish culture affected Irish political life in two ways. First, the movement aroused intense resistance to Irish independence from a new sector—Irish Protestants, who set out to stop home rule. Second, the new value placed on Irish heritage threw into question the educated class's preference for everything English and made their contempt for the language and customs of the peasantry seem unpatriotic. This cultural agenda took political shape with the founding in 1905 of Sinn Fein ("We Ourselves"), a group that strove for complete Irish independence. In 1913, Parliament approved home rule for Ireland, but it was not put into effect because of the outbreak of World War I.

While British liberals modified their policies to enhance social cohesion, their Italian counterparts drifted more rapidly from liberalism's moorings. Corruption plagued Italy's constitutional monarchy, which had not yet developed either the secure parliamentary system of England or the authoritarian monarchy of Germany to guide its growing industrial economy. To forge a national consensus in the 1890s, Prime Minister Francesco Crispi (*1887–1891, 1893–1896) used patriotic rhetoric, bribes to gain press support, and imperial adventure, culminating in an attempt to conquer Ethiopia in 1896 after an earlier failure to do so. But at the battle of Adowa the spirited Ethiopian army delivered a humiliating defeat and forced the Italians out. Crispi's attempts to unite the public behind him through imperialism failed and led instead to riots and strikes, followed by armed government repression.

A new prime minister, Giovanni Giolitti (1842–1928), who held office for three terms between 1903 and 1914, followed a policy known as *traformismo,* by which he used bribes, public works programs, and other benefits to localities to influence their deputies in parliament in the absence of well-developed political parties. Political opponents called Giolitti "the Minister of the Underworld" and accused him of preferring to buy the votes of local bosses rather than to spend money to develop the Italian economy. Despite his attempts to achieve consensus by greasing the political machinery with money and favors, Giolitti encountered unrest in the rapidly industrializing cities of Turin and Milan and in the depressed agrarian south. Urban and rural workers alike demanded change, especially of the restricted suffrage that allowed only 3 million out of more than 8 million adult men to vote. Giolitti appeased the protesters by adopting French and British policies. Thus he instituted social-welfare programs and introduced virtually complete manhood suffrage in 1912.

Antisemitism and Nationalism in Mass Politics

In the two decades before the outbreak of World War I, nationalism and antisemitism provided pat answers to complex questions. Leaders invoked these themes to maintain interest-group support, to direct hostility away from themselves, and to win elections. The public responded vehemently, coming to see Jews as villains responsible for the perils of modern society, and the nation-state as the hero in the struggle to survive. In both republics and monarchies, antisemitism and nationalism played a key role in giving mass politics a radical Right increasingly committed to combatting the radical Left of social democracy. Liberals had hoped that voting by the masses would make politics more harmonious as parliamentary debate and compromise smoothed out class differences. But antisemites and nationalists, scorning tolerant liberal values as effete, often preferred fights in the street to consensus building in parliaments.

The Russian autocrat Nicholas II confronted modern life with an unswerving belief in orthodoxy in religion, autocracy in politics, and antisemitism and Russification in social policy. In this he followed the lead of Alexander III, whose reign had opened after the 1881 assassination of his father with an outbreak of vicious attacks, called *pogroms,* against the Jews. Taught as a child to hate Jews, Nicholas II did not stop Jewish persecution, and in his reign many high officials eagerly endorsed antisemitism to gain his favor. Pogroms became a regular feature of the Easter holiday in Russia, and Nicholas increasingly limited where Jews could live and how they could earn a living. He tightened restrictions on other groups and supported Russification, under which Poles, Ukrainians, Tatars, and people in the Baltic states were coerced into learning and speaking Russian, converting to the Russian Orthodox religion, and ignoring, at least publicly, their own cultural heritage.

Violence toward Russian Jews shocked liberals in western Europe, but antisemitism was worming its way into mass politics throughout Europe. In France in 1894 a Jewish army captain, Alfred Dreyfus, was charged with spying for Germany. Dreyfus had attended the elite Ecole Polytechnique and become an officer in the French military, whose upper echelons were traditionally aristocratic, Catholic, and monarchist. Evidence that documents were being passed to Germany led the military command to fix on the one Jew in the general staff—Dreyfus. His conviction and harsh exile to Devil's Island (French Guiana in South America) failed to stop the espionage, but his plight aroused little immediate notice, either in the Jewish community or the public at large. For several years the Dreyfus case was barely more than an individual tragedy.

Dreyfus's family protested his innocence, but the republican government took the word of the ministry of war, whose old guard maintained that "There is no Dreyfus Affair." Then several newspapers received proof that the army had used perjury and fabricated documents to convict Dreyfus. In 1898 the celebrated French novelist Emile Zola published "J'Accuse" ("I accuse") on the front page of a Paris daily. Zola cited a list of military lies and cover-ups perpetrated by highly placed government officials to create an illusion of Dreyfus's guilt. The article was explosive because it named names; but it was also a ringing defense of liberal principles in government—"I have but one passion, that of Enlightenment," wrote Zola. "J'Accuse" caused the public to become violently divided over the question of Dreyfus's guilt or innocence.

Public riots, quarrels among families and friends, and denunciations of the army eroded public confidence in the republic and in French institutions. While republicans and the conservative opposition fought out the Dreyfus Affair, socialists made inroads into local government, winning control of mayoralties and city councils in elections. The government finally pardoned Dreyfus and then ousted from office the aristocratic and Catholic officers held responsible for what increasingly appeared a humiliation of the republic. Early in the twentieth century it ejected religious teaching orders to ensure that education was secular and republican and raised anticlericalism to a high pitch. When the smoke cleared, liberal republicans had firmly taken charge and gained civilian control over the army. They had secured that control, however, by fanning the flames of anticlericalism and hatred. The Dreyfus Affair made antisemitism a standard tool of politics by producing invective that would be used repeatedly to blame

A Crowd Attacks a Pro-Dreyfus Official
The conviction of Captain Alfred Dreyfus on trumped-up spying charges galvanized French politics, making it the stuff of passion, antisemitism, and street violence.

Jews for various dissatisfactions, whether social, economic, or political.

The ruling elites in Germany also used antisemitism as a political weapon to garner support from those who feared the consequences of Germany's sudden and overwhelming industrialization. These elites, unlike French conservatives, still controlled the highest reaches of government and influenced the kaiser's policy. But the basis of their power was rapidly eroding, as agriculture, from which they drew their fortunes and social prestige, declined as a percentage of gross national product from 37 percent in the 1880s to only 25 percent early in the 1900s. As new opportunities lured the subservient rural population away from the land and as industrialists grew wealthier than they, these elites came to loathe industry and the working class. As a Berlin newspaper noted, "The agrarians' hate for cities . . . blinds them to the simplest needs and the most natural demands of the urban population." In contrast to Bismarck's astute wooing of the masses through social programs, William II's aristocracy often encouraged antisemitism, both in the corridors of power and in the streets.

Conservatives and a growing radical Right claimed Jews, who made up less than 1 percent of the population, were responsible for the disruption of traditional society and saw them as the main beneficiaries of economic change. In the 1890s nationalist and antisemitic pressure groups flourished, spewing forth diatribes against Jews but also against Social Democrats, whom they branded as internationalist and unpatriotic. In the German elections of 1893 the new Agrarian League played to the fears of small farmers, whom vast quantities of foreign grain on the market had adversely affected, by accusing Jews of causing agricultural booms and busts. Candidates from other parties noted the popular response to these charges and made antisemitism a regular feature of their campaigns, too. The Pan-German League whipped up patriotic sentiment by calling on citizens to unite around making German ethnicity triumphant worldwide, and members of the National Union of Commercial Employees, a powerful organization of white-collar workers, faced their insecure future by attacking Social Democrats and feminists. In an age when a changing economy threatened to flatten social distinctions, they hoped to maintain their status against both the old kind of manufacturing worker and the competitive "new women" workers. Although not primarily antisemitic, both groups used antisemitism to make points: "The rejection of all Jewish influence presents itself as the complement of the conscious cultivation of German national ways."

Ultimately these groups, with their antiliberal rhetoric and their extraparliamentary intrigues, profoundly affected German political life. First, instead of working for parliamentary compromise among various interests, "the politics of the irrational"—as this ultranationalist and antisemitic phenomenon is often called—fueled extremist hatreds and violent feelings of nationalism. Second, instead of meeting the problems of rapid economic

change with some measure of social unity and a rational program, these movements created classes of enemies whose defeat would allegedly cure all modern ills. Finally, the other Great Powers, facing severe economic competition from Germany for the first time and watching the increased saber-rattling of its politicians, began to fear an outbreak of war at German hands and to prepare for it.

People in the Austro-Hungarian empire also expressed their political and economic discontent in militantly nationalistic and antisemitic terms, but here nationalism had a different effect because of the presence of many competing ethnic groups. Foremost among the nationalists were the Hungarians, who wanted autonomy for themselves while forcibly imposing Hungarian language and culture (Magyarizing) on all other national groups in Hungary. The demands for greater Hungarian influence, if not outright independence, seemed only just to them: Budapest was a thriving industrial city, and the export of Hungarian grain from the vast estates of the Hungarian nobility balanced the monarchy's foreign trade deficit. With vociferous nationalism and separatism mounting, the three-day funeral of Louis Kossuth in 1894 became a nationalist spectacle. Led by Kossuth's son, Ferenc, and Gyula Andrássy, the Independence party in the Hungarian Parliament provoked a series of crises for the Dual Monarchy by refusing to approve budgets, army call-ups, and revisions to the Compromise of 1867, which was scheduled for review every ten years.

Although capable of causing trouble for the empire, Hungarian nationalists, who mostly represented agrarian wealth, were vulnerable both to the resistance of other nationalities and to the demands of a growing industrial proletariat. On the land the policy of Magyarization resulted in the formation of strong political groups among Slovaks, Romanians, and Ruthenians. Workers insisted on an end to horrendous labor conditions: a strike of railway employees in 1904 shut down transport for a week until the military crushed it; in 1905, thirty thousand metal workers struck for several months, and they were joined by rural workers. In the fall of 1905, one hundred thousand activists demonstrated in front of the Hungarian parliament for the vote. In the face of this resistance, Hungarians intensified Magyarization, even decreeing that tombstones be engraved in Magyar. Francis Joseph temporarily brought the Hungarian nationalists to bay by threatening them with the introduction of universal manhood suffrage that would allow the Magyars' lower-class opponents to vote. Although numerous nationality groups and the many Jews who settled in Budapest assimilated Magyar ways, the uncompromising and chauvinist nature of Hungarian policies toward both Vienna and different ethnic groups within the country made for instability throughout the Austro-Hungarian monarchy.

The insurgency of Hungary further changed the course of Habsburg politics after 1867 by arousing other nationalities within the empire to intensify their demands for rights. Croats, Serbs, and other Slavic groups in the south organized and called for parity with the Hungarians. The central government gave more privileges to the Czechs and allowed them to increase the proportion of Czech officials in the government simply because growing industrial prosperity in their region gave them more influence. But every step toward recognition of Czech ethnicity provoked outrage from the traditionally dominant ethnic Germans, causing more tensions in the empire. When in 1897 the Austro-Hungarian government decreed that government officials in the Czech region of the empire would have to know Czech as well as German, riots erupted among the Germans.

Tensions mounted as politicians in Vienna linked the growing power of Hungarian and Czech politicians to Jews. A prime instigator of this politics of hate was Karl Lueger (1844–1910), who as a member of Parliament in the 1880s had voted to restrict Jewish immigration and who at election time could whip the public up into a frenzy against Jews—especially the "Judeo-Magyars" that he claimed ran Hungary. Operating from the newly formed Christian Social party that attracted members from among the aristocracy, Catholics, artisans, shopkeepers, and white-collar workers, Lueger built a mass following. He appealed to those groups for whom modern life meant a loss of privilege and security, and in 1895 he was elected mayor of Vienna after using rough language and verbal abuse against Jews and ethnic groups in his campaign.

Francis Joseph refused to ratify the victory, however, because Lueger's nationalism and antisemitism contradicted the cosmopolitanism on which the Dual Monarchy and its capital depended. As a result, Lueger ruled unofficially for two years, until Francis Joseph approved his election in 1897. By that time the franchise had been increased, granting the vote to men lower on the social ladder. The regime far preferred workers to support Lueger rather than the Social Democrats, a sentiment shared by many wealthy Europeans who provided financial support for antisemitic opponents of social democracy. By the 1890s a radical right had gained substantial power by mutating liberal values such as nationalism into militant chauvinism and by making antisemitism a volatile and central political issue.

By the turn of the century, influential parties built on aggressive nationalism and antisemitism had appeared in Austria-Hungary and Germany. Although their visibility declined after the 1890s with the return of better economic times, these two causes had entered public life for good. The Jews had been made to represent the "sucking vampire" of modernity, the unevenness of economic wellbeing, and just about anything else people did not like. From then on, Jewishness became a symbol Austrian and German politicians often harped on in their election campaigns. Rabid nationalism also inflamed the atmosphere, making politics a thing of the streets, bloated with hateful rhetoric and racism.

The Jewish Response to Modernity

Throughout the nineteenth century, Jews in western Europe had responded to the spread of legal emancipation by adopting liberal political and cultural values, intermarrying with Christians, and in some cases converting to Christianity. By contrast, Jews in Russia and Romania were increasingly singled out for persecution, legally disadvantaged, and forced to live in ghettos. For these Jews the cities of central and eastern Europe provided both a refuge and an opportunity to succeed. They often adopted the cosmopolitan culture of Vienna or Magyar ways in Budapest. By 1900, Jews were cultural and economic leaders in cities across the Continent.

Historians have debated why Jews made such significant contributions to almost all fields of cultural and professional endeavor. Using the case of Jews in central Europe, some scholars maintain that in German culture such professions as medicine, law, and the arts offered Jews a chance to demonstrate their acquisition of *Bildung,* which Germans prized above political participation. Many Jews also favored the German empire because classical German culture seemed more appealing than the Catholic ritual they saw promoted by the Dual Monarchy. Even escalating antisemitism did not stop Jews from dominating cultural achievement in Vienna, Budapest, and Prague. The celebrated composer Mahler, the budding writer Franz Kafka, and the pioneer of psychoanalysis Freud were shaped in the crucible of Habsburg society.

Most Jews, however, were not so accomplished or prosperous as these cultural giants, and their migration, in reaction to both pogroms and economic change, filled towns and cities with poor day laborers and struggling artisans. Amidst this vast migration and persecution, a spirit of Jewish nationalism arose: "Why should we be any less worthy than any other . . . people," one leader asked. "What about our nation, our language, our land?" Jews began organizing resistance to pogroms and antisemitic politics, and intellectuals drew upon Jewish folklore, philology, and history to establish a national identity parallel to that of other Europeans.

In the 1880s, Odessa physician Leon Pinsker, seeing the Jews' lack of national territory as fundamental to the persecution heaped upon them, advocated the migration of Jews to Palestine. In 1896, Theodor Herzl (1860–1904), strongly influenced by Pinsker, published the *Jewish State,* which called not simply for migration but for the creation of a Jewish nation-state. A Hungarian-born Jew, Herzl experienced antisemitism firsthand as a Viennese journalist and a writer in Paris during the Dreyfus Affair. He became driven to found a Jewish state, searching Europe for financial backing, technical advice, and a political structure for the venture. His constituency should have been prosperous Jews, but many of them had assimilated and thought his ideas mad. However, with the support of poorer east European Jews, he succeeded in calling the first International Zionist Congress (1897), which endorsed settlement in Palestine and helped gain financial backing from the Rothschild banking family. By 1914 some eighty-five thousand Jews had resettled there.

European Imperialism Challenged

Individual nations might ultimately have calmed domestic politics and the traumas of modern industrial life had colonial and diplomatic relations not deteriorated. In 1897 the poet Rudyard Kipling marked the Diamond Jubilee of Queen Victoria with "Recessional," a somber poem comparing the British Empire to ancient cities whose glory had long since faded:

> *Far-called our navies melt away—*
> *On dune and headland sinks the fire—*
> *Lo, all our pomp of yesterday*
> *Is one with Ninevah and Tyre.*

Kipling had gained an enormous following for his homey verse, often written in the Cockney dialect of soldiers cheering the blood and thunder of empire. His turn to pessimistic sentimentalism in "Recessional" was nonetheless apt, first because holding imperial territory was aggravating relations among the European powers and second because colonized peoples were challenging European control. Japan had become an Asian power, and nationalist movements for independence were gaining strength, a development that eventually led to open rebellion against European rule.

The Trials of Empire

Imperial adventure had soured for Britain and France as the twentieth century opened, and being an imperial power proved difficult for such newcomers as Italy and Germany. "Where thirty years ago there existed one sensitive spot in our relations with France, or Germany, or Russia," the British economist J. A. Hobson wrote in 1902, "there are a dozen now; diplomatic strains are of almost monthly occurrence between the Powers." Hobson's statement referred to new developments in imperialism: increasing competition among a greater number of nations for colonies and escalating tensions between the French and British in Africa and elsewhere had raised serious questions about imperialism's future.

Accustomed to imperial victories, the British experienced a bloody defeat in 1896, when Cecil Rhodes, prime minister of the Cape Colony in southern Africa, inspired Dr. Leander Jameson to lead a raid into the neighboring territory of the Transvaal. The foray was intended to stir up trouble between the descendants of early Dutch settlers, called Boers, and the more recent immigrants from Britain and elsewhere who had come to southern Africa in search of gold and other riches. Rhodes hoped the raid would justify a British takeover of the Transvaal and the Orange Free State, which the Boers independently controlled. The Boers, however, easily routed the raiders, forcing Rhodes to resign in disgrace. The defeat was even more of a blow to the British public, whose patriotism featured imperial pride as a cornerstone. Many Europeans gloated over the British loss. Kaiser William II telegrammed his congratulations to Transvaal president Paul Kruger for "maintaining the independence of the country against attacks from without." Hobson drew his critique of imperialism, as did a growing number of British citizens, from the humiliation of the Jameson raid. This ignominious defeat led to the three-year-long Boer War, in which the British fought the Transvaal and Orange Free State outright. Britain annexed the area after defeating the Boers in 1902, but the cost of war caused many Britons to see imperialism as a burden.

Almost simultaneously, Spain lost Cuba, Puerto Rico, and the Philippines as a result of its defeat in the Spanish-American War of 1898. Instigated in the United States by the ambitious Theodore Roosevelt and the inflammatory daily press, this war showed the fragility of established European empires and the unpredictability of imperial fortunes. Even the triumphant United States, encourged by Kipling to "take up the white man's burden" by bringing the benefits of Western civilization to those whom it had liberated from Spain, had to wage a bloody war against the Filipinos, who wanted independence, not just another imperial ruler. Reports of American brutality in the Philippines further soured the European public, who liked to imagine natives joyously welcoming the bearers of civilization.

Dispite these setbacks, imperialism still seemed so vital to national prestige that emerging powers had an emotional stake in gaining colonies. In the early twentieth century, Italian public figures, among them the popular writer Gabriel D' Annunzio, bragged about the Italians' becoming

The Boer War, 1899–1902
This prolonged struggle contributed to the development of pessimistic attitudes about imperialism and about the fate of Western civilization.

Nietzschean supermen by conquering Africa and restoring Italy to its ancient position of world domination. After the disastrous war against Ethiopia in 1896, Italy won a costly victory over Turkey in Libya. But these wars roused Italian hopes for easy national grandeur, only to dash them.

Germany likewise demanded "a place in the sun" and an end to the virtual British-French monopoly of colonial power. Foremost among the new competitors for empire, German bankers and businessmen were ensconced throughout Asia, the Near East, and Latin America. Colonial skirmishes Germany had once ignored became matters of utmost concern. But Germany, too, instead of winning unalloyed glory, met humiliation and constant problems, especially in its dealings with Britain and France, and setbacks tortured this hungry newcomer to the imperial table. As Italy and Germany aggressively pursued new territory, the rules set for

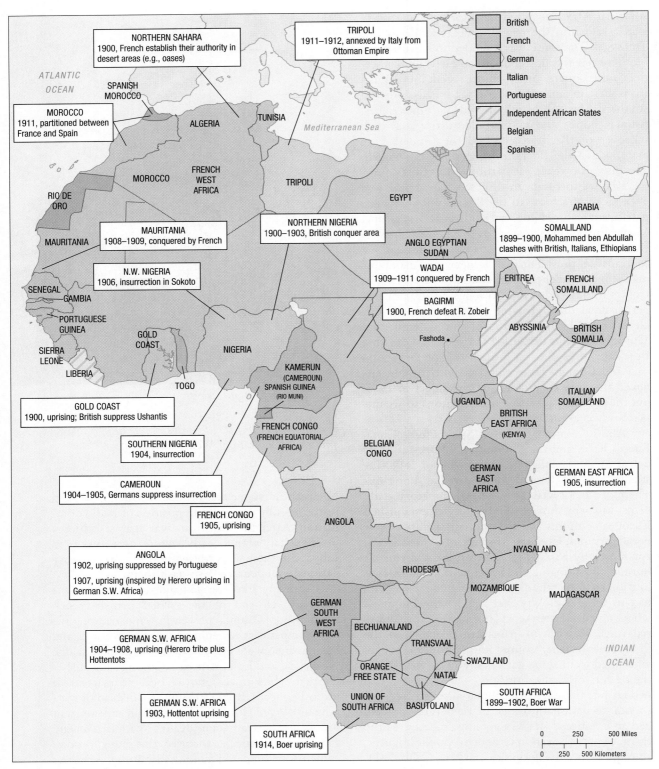

NORTHERN SAHARA
1900, French establish their authority in desert areas (e.g., oases)

TRIPOLI
1911–1912, annexed by Italy from Ottoman Empire

British
French
German
Italian
Portuguese
Independent African States
Belgian
Spanish

ATLANTIC OCEAN

SPANISH MOROCCO

MOROCCO
1911, partitioned between France and Spain

ALGERIA

TUNISIA

Mediterranean Sea

RIO DE ORO

MOROCCO

FRENCH WEST AFRICA

TRIPOLI

EGYPT

Nile R.

ARABIA

MAURITANIA

MAURITANIA
1908–1909, conquered by French

NORTHERN NIGERIA
1900–1903, British conquer area

ANGLO EGYPTIAN SUDAN

SOMALILAND
1899–1900, Mohammed ben Abdullah clashes with British, Italians, Ethiopians

N.W. NIGERIA
1906, insurrection in Sokoto

WADAI
1909–1911 conquered by French

ERITREA

FRENCH SOMALILAND

SENEGAL
GAMBIA

BAGIRMI
1900, French defeat R. Zobeir

Fashoda

ABYSSINIA

BRITISH SOMALIA

PORTUGUESE GUINEA

GOLD COAST

SIERRA LEONE

NIGERIA

LIBERIA

TOGO

KAMERUN (CAMEROUN)
SPANISH GUINEA (RIO MUNI)

ITALIAN SOMALILAND

UGANDA

BRITISH EAST AFRICA (KENYA)

GOLD COAST
1900, uprising; British suppress Ushantis

SOUTHERN NIGERIA
1904, insurrection

FRENCH CONGO (FRENCH EQUATORIAL AFRICA)

BELGIAN CONGO

GERMAN EAST AFRICA

GERMAN EAST AFRICA
1905, insurrection

CAMEROUN
1904–1905, Germans suppress insurrection

FRENCH CONGO
1905, uprising

ANGOLA

ANGOLA
1902, uprising suppressed by Portuguese

1907, uprising (inspired by Herero uprising in German S.W. Africa)

NYASALAND

RHODESIA

MOZAMBIQUE

MADAGASCAR

GERMAN SOUTH WEST AFRICA

BECHUANALAND

GERMAN S.W. AFRICA
1904–1908, uprising (Herero tribe plus Hottentots

TRANSVAAL

SWAZILAND

INDIAN OCEAN

GERMAN S.W. AFRICA
1903, Hottentot uprising

ORANGE FREE STATE

NATAL

SOUTH AFRICA
1899–1902, Boer War

UNION OF SOUTH AFRICA

BASUTOLAND

SOUTH AFRICA
1914, Boer uprising

0   250   500 Miles

0   250   500 Kilometers

Africa Before 1914

imperialism at the Congress of Berlin a generation earlier gave way to increasingly heated rivalry and nationalist fury.

Europeans' confident approach to imperialism was also eroded by the rise of Japan as a power and its stunning defeat of Russia in 1904–1905. The Japanese had started building an empire by invading the island of Formosa (present-day Taiwan) in 1874 and continued by forcing trading treaties on Korea in 1876. In 1894, Japan sparked a war with China. As a result of its resounding victory, Japan received an indemnity, formal cession of Formosa and the Pescadores islands, and an agreement that China would end its domination of Korea. The alarmed European powers, however, forced Japan to relinquish other gains, a move that outraged and affronted the Japanese. Japan's insecurity had risen with Russian expansion to the east and south in Asia. Pushing into eastern Asia, the Russians had built the trans-Siberian railroad through Manchuria and sponsored anti-Japanese groups in Korea, making the peninsula appear to Japanese military leaders like "a dagger thrust at the heart of Japan." Russia's establishment of a naval base at Port Arthur outraged the Japanese still more because they had taken the port from China in 1894, but the Great Powers had forced them to return it. Angered by the continuing presence of Russian troops in Manchuria, the Japanese attacked tsarist forces at Port Arthur in 1904.

The conservative Russian military proved inept in this war, even though it often had better equipment or strategic advantage. In an astonishing display of poor leadership, Russia's Baltic Fleet sailed halfway around the globe only to be completely destroyed in the Battle of Tsushima Straits (1905). The ensuing peace treaty turned Manchuria over to Japanese influence and gave Japan part of Sakhalin Island, a provision that became an ongoing source of conflict between Russia and Japan. Opening an era of Japanese domination in East Asian politics, the victory was the first by a non-European nation over a European Great Power in the modern age, and it gave the West an additional reason to fear the future. As one English general ominously observed of the Russian defeat: "I have today seen the most stupendous spectacle it is possible for the mortal brain to conceive—Asia advancing, Europe falling back."

Empire Threatened: The Russian Revolution of 1905

Russia, a mighty empire that concealed its weaknesses well, tottered on the brink of chaos in 1905 as revolution erupted alongside military defeat. State-sponsored industrialization in the 1890s had made the country appear modern to outside observers, and the Russification policy imitated Western-style state building by attempting to impose a unified, national culture on Russia's diverse population. Industrialization, however, also produced urban unrest as Marxist and union activists incited workers to demand better workplace conditions. In 1903, skilled workers led strikes in Baku, where the predominant Armenians united with Tatar oil workers in a demonstration that showed how urbanization and Russification could facilitate political action among the lower classes. These and other worker protests challenged the autocratic regime. Russia's defeat at the hands of the Japanese added to the hardships of everyday life, already made difficult by the high cost of industrialization. The secret police kept a lid on discontent by spying on the people and by organizing its own unions staffed by police informants. In January 1905 a crowd led by one of these informants, an orthodox priest named Father Gapon, gathered outside the tsar's Winter Palace in St. Petersburg to try to make Nicholas aware of their brutal working conditions. Instead of allowing the demonstration to pass, troops guarding the palace shot into the crowds, killing hundreds and wounding thousands.

Thus began the Revolution of 1905, and news of Bloody Sunday spurred other urban workers to rebel. In almost a year of turmoil across Russia, workers struck over wages, hours, and factory conditions and demanded political representation in the government. Delegates from revolutionary parties such as the Social Democrats and the Socialist Revolutionaries encouraged more direct blows against the central government, but workers rejected their leadership and organized their own councils, called *soviets*. In February the tsar's brother, Grand Duke Sergei, was assassinated; in June sailors on the battleship *Potemkin* mutinied; in October a massive railroad strike ground rail transportation to a halt and the Baltic states and Transcaucasia rebelled; and in November uprisings broke out in Moscow. The tsar's Cossack troops kept killing strikers across the country, but their deaths only fueled the protest.

Because Nicholas II, almost alone among European monarchs, ruled his empire as an absolutist unhampered by a constitution, the revolution coalesced the discontent of many social groups, including artisans and industrial workers, peasants, professionals, and the upper classes. These groups saw that the Russian nobility, especially those who profited from markets in grain to feed urban areas, enjoyed a far more privileged way of life than even their western European counterparts. Using the unrest to press their goals, liberals from the *zemstvos* and intelligentsia demanded political reform, in particular the replacement of autocracy with a constitutional monarchy and representative legislature. They believed the reliance on censorship and the secret police that was characteristic of Romanov rule relegated Russia to the ranks of the most backward states. Impelled by the continuing violence, the tsar announced the formation of a representative body (called the Duma) with only advisory powers; but fledgling political parties protested, and skilled and white-collar workers continued fighting in the streets in the fall of 1905. The tsar's inadequate response, in the words of one protestor, turned "yesterday's benighted slaves into decisive warriors."

Nicholas, who preferred a military solution to the problem of revolution, nonetheless had to face reality and offer some concessions: he announced in his October Manifesto that he would give the Duma minimal powers, notably the right to approve certain parts of the budget. In principle the manifesto also supported freedom of speech and assembly. Although very few could vote for representatives to the Duma, its mere existence, coupled with the right of public political debate, liberalized government and allowed people to present their grievances to a responsive body. During this time political parties took shape, with professional organizations and *zemstvo* leaders forming the liberally minded Constitutional Democratic (or Kadet) party that pushed for a full program of reform. Another party, the Octobrists, was more conservative and took its platform from the October Manifesto, which provided enough change for its tastes. After these constitutional parties threw their support to the reorganized government, revolutionary activity died down and troops crushed the remaining pockets of resistance.

People soon began to wonder, however, if anything had really changed. From 1907 to 1917 the Duma convened, but twice when the tsar disliked its recommendations he sent the delegates home and forced new elections. Conservative representatives were satisfied with the Duma's severely limited prerogatives and willingly let some grievances fester, especially because industrialization continued to bring prosperity. Nevertheless, Prime Minister Pyotr Stolypin (1863–1911), a successful administrator and landowner, was determined to eliminate the sources of discontent by reforming landholding and ending the system of communal farming and taxation represented by the *mir*. He cancelled the land redemption payments that had burdened the peasants since their emancipation in 1861, thereby liberating them from their bondage to the land and to the state. He also made government loans available to peasants, who were then able to purchase land and to own individual farms outright. Although these reforms did not eradicate rural poverty, they did allow people to move to the cities in search of jobs and created a larger group of independent peasants. On the eve of the Russian Revolution in February 1917, some two-thirds of the peasantry had taken steps to gain title to their land, and 10 percent had acquired consolidated holdings.

Stolypin succeeded only partially in his other goal of restoring law and order. He clamped down on revolutionary organizations, executing their members by hanging them with "Stolypin neckties." The government channeled general frustration by urging more pogroms and stifled ethnic unrest by stepping up Russification. But rebels continued to assassinate government officials—four thousand were killed or wounded in 1906–1907—and Stolypin himself was assassinated in 1911. Moreover, Stolypin's reforms had promoted peasant well-being, which encouraged what one historian has called a "new peasant assertiveness." The industrial proletariat also grew, and another round of strikes broke out in the gold mines, oilfields, textile factories, electric works, and rubber companies. A general strike erupted in St. Petersburg in 1914. Despite the creation of a Duma, the imperial government and the conservative nobility had no solutions to the ongoing social turmoil and felt little inclination to share power. From the defeat by Japan through the period of reform, Russia nurtured the seeds of revolution.

Growing Resistance to Colonial Domination

Japan's defeat of two important dynasties—the Qing and the Romanov—within a single decade had repercussions in the colonies, further eroding the security Westerners had once found in imperialism. The Japanese victories and the ability of Russian revolutionaries to force a great European power to reform inspired nationalist-minded activists who opposed European imperialism. The success of a non-Western, constitutional government fed protest virtually everywhere, beginning with China. Uprisings there increased after their 1895 defeat by Japan forced the ruling Qing dynasty to concede rights to ports and railroads and to make other economic concessions to Western powers. Humiliated by these events, peasants organized into secret societies to restore Chinese integrity; but unlike subsequent activists, they did not imitate the constitutional and modernizing Japanese model. One organization, based on beliefs in the spiritual values of boxing, was the Society of the Righteous and Harmonious Fists (or Boxers), whose members maintained that ritual boxing would protect them from a variety of evils, including bullets. Encouraged by the Qing ruler Dowager Empress Tz'u-hsi (Cixi) (1835–1908), and desperate because of worsening economic conditions, the Boxers rebelled in 1900, massacring the missionaries and Chinese Christians to whom they attributed China's troubles. The colonial powers put down the Boxer Rebellion and encouraged the Chinese troops in their service to ravage the areas in which the Boxers operated. Defeated once more, the Chinese were compelled to pay a huge indemnity, to destroy many of their defensive fortifications, and to allow more extensive foreign military occupation.

The Boxer Rebellion thoroughly discredited the Qing dynasty, and in 1911 a successful group of revolutionaries finally overthrew the dynasty and declared China a republic the next year. Their leader, Sun Yat-Sen (1866–1925), who had been educated in Hawaii and Japan, used Western concepts to express traditional Chinese goals and values. Sun took Western slogans for his platform of "nationalism, democracy, and socialism," but he made this into a palatable stew of traditional and new aspirations: freedom from the Qing dynasty, Chinese-style correctness in behavior between governors and the governed, and modern economic reform. Despite Sun's stirring leadership, the revolution stalled because warlords, an economic and military elite, quickly assumed the reins of power. Nonetheless, changes brought about by China's revolution upset the course of Western imperialism because they threatened channels of trade and domination.

In India, meanwhile, the Japanese victory over Russia and the Revolution of 1905 stimulated politicians to take a more radical course than that offered by the Indian National Congress. A Hindu leader, B. G. Tilak (1856–1920), fervently anti-British and less moderate than Congress reformers, preached blatant noncooperation: "We shall not give them assistance to collect revenue and keep peace. We shall not assist them in fighting beyond the frontiers or outside India with Indian blood and money." Tilak promoted Hindu customs, asserted their distinctiveness from British ways, and inspired violent rebellion in his followers. This brand of nationalism broke with that based on assimilating to British culture and promoting gradual change. Trying to repress Tilak, the British sponsored the Muslim League, a rival nationalist group favored for its restraint and its potential to divide Muslim nationalists from Hindus in the Congress. Faced with political activism on many fronts, however, Britain conceded the right to vote based on property ownership and to representation in ruling councils. Because the independence movement had not fully reached the masses, these small concessions temporarily maintained British power by appeasing the best-educated and most influential dissidents among the upper and middle classes. But the empire's hold on the subcontinent was weakening.

Revolutionary nationalism was simultaneously sapping the Ottoman Empire, which for centuries had controlled much of the Mediterranean. In the nineteenth century several rebellions had plagued Ottoman rule, and more erupted early in the twentieth century because of growing resistance to the

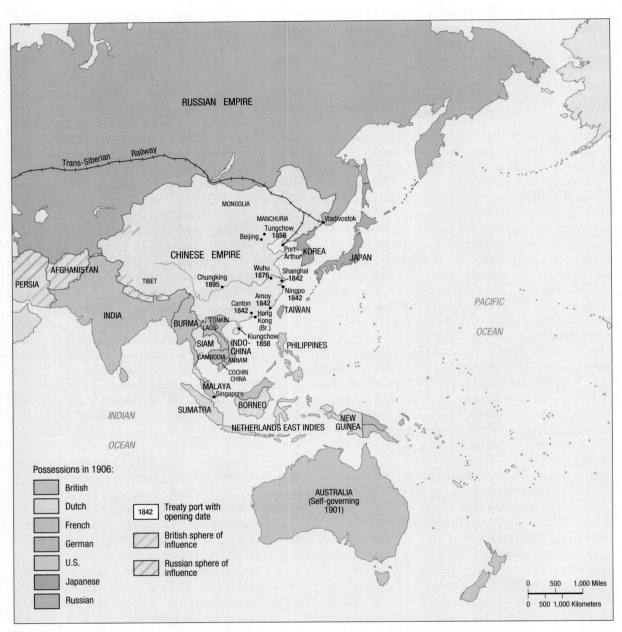

Imperialism in Asia

empire and to European influence. Governing a multiethnic territory like that of the Habsburgs, Sultan Abdulhamid II (*1876–1909) tried to revitalize the empire by using Islam as a unifying force to counteract the rising nationalism of the Serbs, Bulgarians, and Macedonians. Instead he unwittingly provoked a burgeoning Turkish nationalism in Constantinople itself. Turkish nationalists rejected the sultan's pan-Islamic solution and built their movement on the uniqueness of their culture, history, and language, as many European ethnic groups were doing. Using the findings of Western scholarship, they first traced the history of the group they called Turks to change the word *Turk* from one of derision to one of pride. Nationalists also tried to purify their language of words from Arabic and Persian, and they popularized the folklore of rural Turkish peoples scattered across territories from eastern Europe through Asia. The events of 1904--1905 electrified these nationalists with the vision of a modern Turkey becoming "the Japan of the Near East." In 1908 a group of them called the Young Turks took control of the government in Constantinople, which had been fatally weakened by nationalist agitation and by the empire's economic dependence on Western financiers and businessmen.

The Young Turks' triumph motivated other groups in the Middle East and the Balkans to demand an end to Ottoman domination in their regions as well. These groups adopted Western values and platforms, and some, such as the Egyptians, even had strong contingents of feminist-nationalists who mobilized women to work for independence. But the Young Turks, often aided by European powers with financial and political interests in the region, brutally tried to repress uprisings in Egypt, Syria, and the Balkans that their own success had encouraged.

These rebellions became part of the tumult facing the Great Powers in the decade before World War I. Empires, whether old or young, were the scene of growing resistance in the wake of Japanese, Russian, and Turkish events. In German East Africa colonial forces countered native resistance with a scorched-earth policy, eventually killing more than one hundred thousand natives after their 1905 uprising. The French closed the University of Hanoi, executed Indochinese in-

tellectuals, and deported thousands of suspected nationalists merely to maintain a tenuous grip on Indochina. A French general stationed there summed up the fears of many colonial rulers in the new century: "The gravest fact of our actual political situation in Indochina is not the recent trouble in Tonkin [or] the plots undertaken against us but in the muted but growing hatred that our subjects show toward us more and more."

Roads to War

International developments aggravated competition among the Great Powers and caused Western nationalism to swell. In the spring of 1914, U.S. president Woodrow Wilson (1856–1924) sent a trusted adviser abroad to assess the tensions among the European powers. "It is militarism run stark mad," the adviser reported, adding that he foresaw an "awful cataclysm" ahead. Government spending on what people called the "arms race" had stimulated European economies; but arms were not stockpiled only for economic growth. By 1914, the Great Powers were brandishing their weapons over their competing claims to global power. As early as the mid-1890s, the socialist Eduard Bernstein had called the situation a "cold war" because the hostile atmosphere made physical combat seem imminent. By the twentieth century, the air was even more charged, with militant nationalism in the Balkan states and conflicts in domestic politics also setting the stage for war. Although historians have long debated whether World War I could have been avoided, they have never reached a consensus. Considering the feverish background of prewar change, they have had to content themselves with tracing the steps Europeans took along a fatal course toward mass destruction.

Competing Alliances and Clashing Ambitions

As the twentieth century opened, the Triple Alliance that Bismarck had negotiated between Germany, Austria-Hungary, and Italy confronted an opposing alliance between France and Russia, created in the 1890s. The wild card in the diplomatic scenario was Great Britain, traditional enemy of France, and nowhere more so than in the contest for colonial power. Constant rivals in Africa, Britain and France edged to the brink of war in 1898 at Fashoda in the Sudan. The French government, however, backed away from the imminent clash, and both governments were frightened into rapprochement for reasons of mutual self-interest. To prevent another Fashoda, they concluded secret agreements, the first of which (1904) guaranteed British claims in Egypt and French claims in Morocco. This agreement marked the beginning of an alliance called the *Entente Cordiale.*

A secret truce between Britain and France could not alone end international tensions, as Germany—which counted on British support because of a shared antipathy to France—became increasingly aggressive in its imperial demands. From being a "satisfied" nation under Bismarck, who had worked to balance great-power interests and had spared Germany from the draining fight for colonies, Germany under William became dissatisfied with its international status and inflamed rather than calmed the diplomatic atmosphere. Convinced of British hostility toward France and emboldened by Germany's growing industrial might, the kaiser used the opportunity presented by the defeat of France's ally Russia to contest French claims to territory in Morocco. A man who boasted and blustered and was easily prodded to rash actions by his advisers, William landed in Morocco in 1905, thus challenging French sovereignty in the First Moroccan Crisis. To resolve the situation, an international conference met at Algeciras, Spain, in 1906, at which Germany confidently expected to gain concessions and new territories. Instead the powers, now including the United States, decided to support the status quo of French rule. The French and British military, faced with German aggression in Morocco, drew closer together, even coordinating their planning.

Germany found itself weak diplomatically and strong economically, a situation that made its leaders more determined to compete for territory abroad. When the French finally took over Morocco in 1911, Germany triggered the Second Moroccan Crisis by sending a gunboat to the port of Agadir and demanding concessions from the French. This time no power—not even Austria-Hungary—backed the German move. No one acknowledged this dominant country's might, nor did the constant demands for recognition make anyone want to do so. The British and French now made binding military provisions for the deployment of their forces in case of war, thus strengthening the bonds of the Entente Cordiale. Smarting from its setbacks on the world stage, Germany refocused its sights on its role on the Continent and on its own alliances.

Germany's shifting territorial claims along with public uncertainty about the binding force of alliances unsettled Europe. Some historians have placed a heavy responsibility for the eventual outbreak of world war on the alliance system. In particular they have criticized the diplomats themselves for conducting a foreign policy fundamentally out of date in the industrial age. The diplomats—who came from the aristocracy, the old military elite, and the highest ranks of landed nobility—employed inept spies and leaked partial and unreliable information to reporters, further confusing government officials throughout Europe. In the conditions of the early twentieth century, the alliance system the diplomats had engineered destabilized Europe and set the stage for war.

The destabilizing effects of the alliance system became particularly evident in the Balkans as German statesmen envisioned the creation of a *Mitteleuropa* that included central Europe, the Balkans, and Turkey under their sway. The Habsburgs, now firmly backed by Germany, judged that expansion into the Balkans would weaken the claims for the improved status of any single ethnic minority in the Dual Monarchy. Russia, however, saw itself as the protector of Slavs in the region and wanted to replace the Ottomans as the dominant Balkan power, especially after Japan had crushed its hopes for expansion to the east. Austria's swift annexation of Bosnia during the Young Turk revolt in 1908 thus enraged not only the Russians but the Serbs as well, because these southern Slavs wanted Bosnia as part of an enlarged Serbia.

Tensions smoldered until the First Balkan War in 1912, when Serbia, Bulgaria, Greece, and

Punch Cartoon, 1912
European rulers try to keep the lid on Balkan conflicts.
Competing interests and ambitions made these efforts
unsuccessful.

The Balkans in the Early Twentieth Century

Montenegro joined forces to drive out the Ottomans. Conquering Albania and Macedonia, these small powers divided up their booty, with Bulgaria gaining most territory. The victors soon turned against one another. Serbia, Greece, and Montenegro joined forces in a Second Balkan War in 1913 to contest Bulgarian gains. Much to Austrian dismay, these allies won a quick victory. Austria-Hungary lost Novi Pazar, a territory adjacent to Serbia where it had garrisoned troops in the past, but Austria-Hungary prevented Serbia from annexing parts of Albania. Grievances between the Habsburgs and Serbs now seemed irreconcilable. Moreover, the peace conditions did not demilitarize the region, allowing Balkan peoples, especially angry Slavs who continued to look to Russia for help, to imagine further challenges to Austria-Hungary. The Balkans had become a perilous region along whose borders both Austria-Hungary

as ruler of many Slavs, and Russia as their protector, stationed increasing numbers of troops.

The Race to Arms

Between the Napoleonic Wars of the early nineteenth century and World War I a hundred years later, technology, nationalism, and imperialism transformed the practice of and rationale for war. During that period global rivalries, aspirations for national greatness, and in some cases even the struggle for independence made constant readiness for war seem necessary. On the seas and in foreign lands the colonial powers battled to establish their control, and they developed railroad, telegraph, and telephone networks everywhere to bolster their military conquests. Governments began to conscript ordinary citizens for periods of two to six years into large standing armies, whereas eighteenth-century forces had been smaller, in keeping with the more limited military goals of the time. By 1914 escalating tensions in Europe boosted the annual intake of conscripts: Germany, France, and Russia called up two hundred fifty thousand or more each year; Austria-Hungary and Italy about one hundred thousand. The per capital expenditure on the military rose in all the major powers between 1890 and 1914; the proportion of national budgets devoted to defense in 1910 was lowest in Austria-Hungary at 10 percent and highest in Germany at 45 percent.

The modernization of weaponry also transformed warfare. Swedish arms manufacturer Alfred Nobel patented dynamite and developed a kind of gunpowder that improved the accuracy of guns by keeping their barrels clean. The industrial revolution in chemicals affected long-range artillery, which by 1914 could fire on targets as far away as six miles. Greater accuracy and heavy firepower made an offensive war more difficult to win than in the past because neither side could overcome such weaponry by attacking on foot or on horseback. Military leaders devised strategies to protect their armies from overwhelming firepower; in the Russo-Japanese War, trenches and barbed wire blanketed the front around Port Arthur. New weapons were used in that conflict and in the Boer War, including howitzers, Mauser rifles, and Hotchkiss machine guns. Vickers in Britain, Creusot in France, Krupp in Germany, and Skoda in Austria-Hungary manufactured ever-growing stockpiles of these rifles, machine guns, and cannons.

Naval construction played a more sensational role in nationalist politics. As a result of more powerful, accurate weaponry, ships were constructed out of metal rather than wood after the mid-nineteenth century. In 1905 the English launched the H.M.S. *Dreadnought,* a warship with unprecedented firepower, and initiated a period of intense competition among the Great Powers for naval superiority. The launching of the *Dreadnought* was part of a program to update the navy by constructing at least seven battleships per year. Germany followed British naval building step by step and made itself not just a land but a sea power. Grand Admiral Alfred von Tirpitz encouraged the insecure kaiser to see the navy as the essential ingredient to making Germany a world power and oversaw the modernization and immense buildup

Good Friends, Trusted Neighbors, 1909
This cartoon predicts an outbreak of destructive war from the arms race, or keeping up with one's neighbors militarily.

of the fleet. Tirpitz admired the American naval theorist Alfred Thayer Mahan and planned to build bases as distant as the Far East, following Mahan's conclusion that command of the seas had historically been the key factor in determining international power. German ambitions, especially Tirpitz's drive to build battleships, alarmed the British and motivated them to ally with France. Under the *new navalism,* Britain raised its naval spending from $50 million per year in the 1870s to $130 million in 1900; Germany, from $8.75 million to $37.5 million; France from $37 million to $62.5 million. The Germans announced the fleet buildup as "a peaceful policy," but like the British buildup it led only to a hostile international climate and the manufacture of more weapons.

Because the arms race had domestic ramifications, military policy was made with an eye to internal politics. Military buildup could help a country's social and economic stability by providing jobs and profit. When a temporary "naval holiday" was suggested to stop British and German building, officials opposed the moratorium by warning that it "would throw innumerable men on the pavement." Colonial leagues, pan-German organizations, and other patriotic groups lobbied for military spending, while enthusiasts in government publicized large navies as beneficial to international trade and domestic industry. The question of who would pay for arms, however, was proving divisive in Germany and indicative of unresolved political and social questions.

Public relations campaigns helped generate popular support for the arms race as they had for colonial expansion. When Tirpitz wanted to enlarge the German fleet, he made sure the press connected the buildup to the cause of national power and pride. The press accused Social Democrats, who wanted a tax system more proportionate to wealth, of being unpatriotic. The Conservative party in Great Britain, eager for more dreadnoughts, made popular the slogan "We want eight and we won't wait." Despite the massive expenditures needed to establish military might in 1914, most of the public was convinced of the relationship between national prestige and military power

and believed war was on its way to settle lingering international tensions. The remarks of the French Marshall Joseph Joffre typified the sentiments of many military men of the time. When asked in 1912 if he thought about war, he said that he did constantly. "We shall have war," he maintained. "I will make it. I will win it."

War Finally Arrives

On June 28, 1914, a Serbian nationalist assassinated the heir to the Habsburg throne, Archduke Franz Ferdinand, and his wife Sophie as they visited Sarajevo in Bosnia. The assassin, Gavrilo Princip, was a Bosnian student who had dreamed of freeing his homeland from the Austrians and uniting it with Serbia. Many Austro-Hungarian diplomats actually breathed a sigh of relief at Franz Ferdinand's assassination because they disliked his abrasive style and his lenient policies toward most nationality groups except the powerful Hungarians. Other world leaders anticipated a measured response, because death by murder had become a kind of occupational hazard for major political figures over the past decades.

Archduke Franz Ferdinand and his wife Sophie in Sarajevo, June 1914
Minutes after this photograph was taken, the Crown Prince (heir to the Habsburg throne) and his wife were assassinated. The murders precipitated diplomatic and military maneuvering that led to World War I.

Yet some in the Habsburg government, especially General Franz Conrad von Hoetzendorf, who had long opposed Franz Ferdinand's conciliatory policy toward the Slavs, saw an opportunity to put down the Serbians once and for all. Evidence showed that Princip had received arms and information from Serbian officials, who directed the terrorist organization Black Hand from within the government. German statesmen and military leaders urged the Austrians to be unyielding and reiterated promises of support in case of war. After the state funeral for the archduke and his wife and while many heads-of-state and politicians were vacationing, the Austrians sent an ultimatum to the Serbian government, demanding public disavowals of terrorism, suppression of terrorist groups, and the inclusion of Austrian officials in an investigation of the crime. Austrian diplomats timed the ultimatum to reach Belgrade just after President Raymond Poincaré and Prime Minster René Viviani of France had left a meeting with Nicholas II, to delay a joint response from Russia and France. Those who saw the ultimatum were stunned by its severity: "You are setting Europe ablaze," the Russian foreign minister remarked of the humiliating demands Austrians made of Serbia. Yet the Serbs were conciliatory, answering within the forty-eight hours given them and accepting all the terms except the interference of Austrian officials in the commission. Kaiser William was pleased: "A great moral success for Vienna! All reason for war is gone." His relief proved misguided. Austria-Hungary, confident of German backing, used the Serbs' single limitation of the ultimatum's terms as its pretext for declaring war against Serbia on July 28.

Complex and ineffectual maneuvering now consumed statesmen. The tsar and the kaiser sent pleading letters to one another not to start a European war. Sir Edward Grey, foreign secretary of Great Britain, proposed an all-European conference to no avail. The German chancellor as well as the kaiser displayed firm support for Austria in hopes of convincing the French and British to shy away from war. The failure of either to fight, German officials believed, would subsequently keep Russia from mobilizing. At the same time, German military leaders had become fixed on fighting a short preemptive war that would provide territorial gains and simultaneously justify arresting the leadership of the Social Democratic party, so threatening to conservative rule.

Meanwhile, the European press caught the war fever of the pan-German, imperialist, and other prowar organizations. Military leaders, especially in Germany and Austria-Hungary where there was less supervision by the civilian government, promoted mobilization rather than diplomacy in the last days of July. The Austrians, urged on by General Conrad, declared war and then ordered mobilization on July 31 without fear of a Russian attack. They did so in full confidence of German military aid, because as early as 1909 the German chief of staff Helmuth von Moltke had assured Conrad that his government would defend Austria-Hungary not only if it were attacked but also if it *started* a war against Serbia. Under the circumstances, Austria-Hungary believed Russia would not dare intervene. Nevertheless, Nicholas II ordered the Russian army to mobilize in defense of Russia's Slavic allies, the Serbs. Encouraging the Austrians to attack Serbia, the German General Staff mobilized on August 1.

German strategy was based on the Schlieffen Plan, named after its author, a former chief of the general staff. The plan essentially outlined for German forces a way to combat antagonists on two fronts by concentrating on one foe at a time. It called for a rapid and concentrated blow against France that would lead to that nation's defeat in six weeks, accompanied by a light holding action to the east. The western armies would then be deployed against Russia, which, it was believed, would mobilize far more slowly. But German strategy hit an unexpected snag in the form of Belgian resistance. On August 2 the Belgian government rejected an ultimatum to allow the uncontested passage of the Germany army through the country. The subsequent violation of Belgian neutrality brought Britain into the war on the side of Russia and France, which had also mobilized

The Schlieffen Plan

against Germany on August 1. Although the kaiser at the last minute demanded a war limited to Russia to avoid fighting the British, the military vetoed him because of its unalterable plan for a two-front war. "Who's in charge in Berlin?" one statesman wondered upon viewing the German government's plan for peace and the military's push toward war.

CONCLUSION

Rulers soon forgot their last-minute hesitations in the general celebration that erupted with the war. "Old heroes have reemerged from the books of legends," wrote a Viennese actor after watching the troops march off. "A mighty wonder has taken place, we have become *young*." Both sides exulted, believing in certain victory for themselves. A short conflict, people maintained, would resolve tensions ranging from the rise of the working class to political problems caused by global competition for empire.

The arms race had stimulated militant nationalism and brought many Europeans to favor war over peace. The crisis of modernity had helped blaze the path to war: the *Rite of Spring* ballet that opened in Paris in 1913 had taken as its theme the ritualistic attraction of death. Facing continuing violence in politics, incomprehensibility in the arts, and problems in the industrial order, Europeans had come to believe war would set events back on course and save them from the perils of modernity. "Like men longing for a thunderstorm to relieve them of the summer's sultriness," wrote one Austrian official, "so the generation of 1914 believed in the relief that war might bring." Such a possibility caused Europeans to rejoice. But tragically, their elation was short-lived. Instead of bringing the refreshment of summer rain, war opened an era of political turmoil, widespread suffering, and massive human slaughter.

SUGGESTIONS FOR FURTHER READING

Source Materials

Fenyvesi, Charles. *When the World Was Whole.* 1990. The memoirs of a Jewish family in Hungary over three centuries, but especially focused on the late Habsburg empire.

Mann, Thomas. *Buddenbrooks.* 1901. A novel tracing the decline of the traditional middle class when confronted by industrialization and the other forces that made Germany a world power at the turn of the century.

Pruitt, Ida. *A Daughter of Han: The Autobiography of a Chinese Working Woman.* 1945. A fascinating account of Chinese life under imperialism.

Interpretive Studies

Ascher, Abraham. *The Revolution of 1905: Russia in Disarray.* 1988. A judicious study of the movements and events of this volatile year.

Burns, Michael. *Dreyfus: A Family Affair.* 1992. Sets Dreyfus's plight in the context of social, family, and economic history.

Chickering, Roger. *We Men Who Feel Most German: A Cultural Study of the Pan-German League, 1886–1914.* 1984. An important investigation of a crucial extraparliamentary political organization.

Dube, Wolf-Dieter. *The Expressionists.* 1987. Discusses the social and political origins of modern art in central and eastern Europe.

Duberman, Martin, Martha Vicinus, and George Chauncey, Jr. *Hidden from History: Reclaiming the Gay and Lesbian Past.* 1989. An innovative collection about sexual orientation in historical perspective.

Eksteins, Modris. *Rites of Spring: The Great War and the Birth of the Modern Age.* 1989. Describes how turn-of-the-century art and culture forecast the outbreak and shape of war.

Fischer, Fritz. *The War of Illusions: German Policies from 1911–1914.* 1975. A classic revisionist study that places enormous responsibility on the German government for the outbreak of war.

Hoensch, Jörg K. *A History of Modern Hungary, 1867–1986.* 1988. Examines politics and society in this crucial part of the Dual Monarchy.

Hull, Isabell. *The Entourage of Kaiser Wilhelm II, 1888–1918.* 1982. An analysis of the emperor, his closest advisers, and German policy.

Jelavich, Peter. *Munich and Theatrical Modernism: Politics, Playwriting, and Performance, 1890–1914.* 1985. Explores how popular culture influenced the development of modernism.

Kern, Steven. *The Culture of Space and Time, 1880–1918.* 1983. An interesting look at the social and cultural significance of changing notions of time in this crucial era.

Kornberg, Jacques. *Theodor Herzl: From Assimilation to Zionism.* 1993. A modern biography that features Herzl's intellectual evolution.

Lambi, Ivo. *The Navy and German Power Politics.* 1984. A discussion of military build-up and policy decisions in the Wilhelmine period.

Manning, Roberta. *The Crisis of the Old Order in Russia.* 1982. Describes changing relations among nobility, peasants, and the government before 1917.

Meyers, Ramon H., and Mark R. Peattie, eds. *The Japanese Colonial Empire, 1895–1945.* 1984. Includes essays on the rise of Japan and its expanding empire.

Nehamas, Alexander. *Nietzsche: Life as Literature.* 1985. A revisionist interpretation of the great philosopher.

Nord, Philip G. *Paris Shopkeepers and the Politics of Resentment.* 1986. Shows Paris commercial life in all its complexity as a source of republicanism.

Quataert, Donald. *Social Disintegration and Popular Resistance in the Ottoman Empire, 1881–1908.* 1983. A pioneering study of this pivotal period.

Rewald, John. *Cézanne and America: Dealers, Collectors, Artists, and Critics.* 1989. Examines how the international art market functioned to build reputations and make profits.

Schorske, Carl E. *Fin-de-Siècle Vienna: Politics and Culture.* 1981. Contains pioneering essays on political culture and cultural politics.

Silverman, Debora L. *Art Nouveau in Fin-de-Siècle France: Politics, Psychology, and Style.* 1989. Describes the ways in which psychology and attitudes toward politics affected art.

Stavrianos, L. S. *A Global Destiny: The Human Heritage.* 1983. An important survey of world history that shows the complex place of Western culture and politics.

Tech, Mikuláš, and Roy Porter, eds. *The National Question in Europe in Historical Context.* 1993. Presents essays on ethnicity and nationalism, with extensive coverage of the Balkans and eastern Europe.

Tickner, Lisa. *The Spectacle of Women: Imagery of the Suffrage Campaign, 1907–1914.* 1988. A richly illustrated history of radical suffragism in Britain and its relationship to mass politics.

Williamson, Samuel. *Austria-Hungary and the Origins of the First World War.* 1991. Discusses the interests, reasons, weaknesses, and misjudgments behind Habsburg policy.

World War I opened in a blaze of enthusiasm. War, according to one German soldier, was "our dream of greatness, power, and glory. It was a man's work." Despite massive casualties and the general futility of all offensive thrusts, such sentiments persisted for the first eighteen months of the war. "I don't loathe war," one English soldier wrote to his wife in January 1916. "I love 95 percent of it, and hate the thought of it being ended too soon." The costly yet indecisive battles of Verdun and the Somme in 1916, however, and the endless months in wretched trenches dampened the spirit of even the heartiest. The German soldier's dream of greatness had turned into the "stench of thousands upon thousands of decaying bodies." One Englishman wrote to his mother: "It is not fit for men to be here, where men die and are left to rot because of snipers and the callousness that War breeds. 'It might be me tomorrow. Who cares?' "

World War I is known as the Great War not only because of its staggering human toll—40 million wounded or killed in battle—but also because of its transforming impact on politics, society, and the human spirit. As military technology blasted away soldiers' fantasies of heroism, so too did it obliterate politicians' hopes of decisive victory and postwar glory. Instead the war produced political cataclysm and social upheaval, ruining lofty empires. In Russia revolutionaries overturned the tsarist regime even before the war ended. In Germany defeat forced the kaiser to abdicate, leaving that once haughty nation starving, demoralized, and buffeted by the winds of political extremism. The Ottoman and Austro-Hungarian empires were dismembered at the war's end. The crushing burden of war

War, Revolution, and Reconstruction, 1914–1929

War Propaganda, c. 1915
"Never Forget!" the headline screams, suggesting that the magazine will describe German war atrocities, including the murder of babies, assault on women, and wanton destruction of homes and property.

on the European powers accelerated the rise of the United States as a competitor for global leadership, largely against its will.

On a moral level, many Europeans wondered what one could believe in after such an orgy of death. For some, nineteenth-century optimism, already tinged with a sense of decline, gave way to a more pervasive postwar cynicism. Others found reason for hope in the new political systems the war had made possible: Soviet communism and Italian fascism. Many turned away from politics and attacked life with frenzied gaiety in the Roaring Twenties. Europeans snapped up new consumer goods, drank in entertainment provided by films and radio, and enjoyed personal freedoms that Victorianism had forbidden. Social controls that had been easy to justify and enforce before the war now seemed superfluous.

Paradoxically, the consolidation of prewar tendencies to expand institutions in government, industry, and labor threatened the new personal liberty. Moreover, postwar political disarray weakened people's belief in parliamentary solutions to public problems, promoted antidemocratic sentiments, and glorified militaristic leaders. World War I, long anticipated and ardently welcomed, destabilized Europe and the world far into the 1920s and 1930s.

IMPORTANT DATES

1914 August World War I begins

1916 Irish nationalists stage Easter Rebellion against British rule; Austria's Francis Joseph dies after 68-year reign

1917
March Revolution in Russia overturns tsarist autocracy
April The United States enters World War I
November Bolshevik Revolution in Russia

1918 November The signing of an armistice ends the fighting of World War I; the Kaiser abdicates; revolutionary turmoil throughout Germany; a republic established at Weimar

1918–1922 Civil war in Russia

1919 The Paris Peace Conference redraws the map of Europe

1922 Ireland is split in two: the independent Irish Free State in the south and British-affiliated Ulster in the north; Fascists march on Rome; Mussolini becomes Italy's prime minister; T. S. Eliot publishes "The Wasteland"; James Joyce publishes *Ulysses*

1924 Lenin dies; Stalin and Trotsky contend for power

1924–1929 Period of general economic prosperity and stability

1929 October stock market crash in United States

The Great War

How could educated and experienced Europeans not sense the impending disaster, and why did they not halt the war once they saw the cost in lives? First, military planners were blind to anything but a short war. Their knowledge of war came from history lessons about the swift, decisive triumphs of Bismarck or the distant, exciting campaigns of Napoleon. Ignoring the bloody precedent the Boer and Russo-Japanese wars had set, they were mostly unprepared for what World War I came to be: filthy, destructive, and prolonged, involving civilians as well as soldiers. At the beginning of August 1914, generals mobilized their armies and soldiers marched off to war, their rifles adorned with flowers, expecting a brief, heroic experience and a holiday from the humdrum of everyday life.

As the casualties mounted, the second question often arose: Why not stop the madness? But by then it was too late: quitting short of victory had become tantamount to admitting that all the suffering had been in vain.

On the Offensive

The first months of the war squelched expectations of quick victory. All the major armies mobilized rapidly. The German army, guided by the Schlieffen Plan, reached Luxembourg on August 2 and Belgium on August 4, 1914. The plan counted on unchallenged passage through these small countries. Meanwhile, the main body of French troops, sucked in by German diversionary tactics, attacked the Germans in Alsace and Lorraine instead of meeting the invasion from the north. The French offensive depended heavily on fighting spirit and Bergsonian élan, inspired by lavishly decorated, colorful uniforms and the jaunty music of military bands.

Yet in the heat of August and the Indian summer that followed, both the Schlieffen Plan and the French offensive disintegrated because of bad planning and worse luck. The Belgians unexpectedly resisted at the fortress of Liège, slowing the German advance with guerrilla sniping and sabotaging of railroad lines and thus buying time for British and French troops to reach the northern front. Moreover, because German reservists were not up to endless miles of summer marching under fire, their generals directed the armies to the east of Paris rather than taking the longer and slower way to encirclement from the west. But the German detour ground to a bloody halt as the British and French armies engaged their enemy along the Marne River in France. Neither side could defeat the other, and the fighting continued late into the autumn of 1914 along the Marne and up to Ypres in Belgium.

The casualties of the Battle of the Marne rose as high as 40 percent, as in the first three months more than 1.5 million men fell on the Western Front alone. What was supposed to be an offensive war of movement changed into a stationary, defensive one, with the two sides facing off along a line that stretched from the North Sea through Belgium and northern France to Switzerland. Soldiers dug in: they excavated parallel lines of trenches up to thirty feet deep that would serve—for the next four years and for millions of men—as nightmarish homes.

On the Eastern Front the "Russian steamroller" drove far more quickly than expected, into East Prussia on August 17 and into parts of the Austro-Hungarian empire, while the Russian-allied Serbs repulsed Francis Joseph's troops. The Russians arrogantly believed that no army could stand up to their massive numbers. The old-fashioned Russian commanders were "slow-witted men who did what they were told," and they scoffed at suggestions that they modernize communications and transportation: "If the War Minister himself boasted that he had not read a single military textbook in . . . thirty-five years . . . why should anyone else?"

Russian success was short-lived. The Germans, aided by intercepted messages that the Russians failed to send in code, crushed the tsar's army in East Prussia on August 29 at Tannenberg and in campaigns around the Masurian Lakes in September. The German armies then turned south to Galicia where Russian and Austro-Hungarian armies were fighting costly battles. Although the Russian army was capable of fighting the Dual Monarchy's armed forces, the technologically superior German army usually stopped it cold. Victory boosted German morale and made heroes of the military leaders Paul von Hindenburg and Erich Ludendorff, who thereupon demanded more troops for the Eastern Front. Their efforts against a poorly led foe, however, helped wreck the Schlieffen Plan, which had called for only light holding action to the east until the Western Front had been won. By year's end, German triumphs in the east had failed to knock out the Russians, and the lack of a decisive victory brought trench warfare to the Eastern Front too.

War at sea proved equally indecisive. Confident in Britain's superior naval power, the Entente—also known as the Allies, and led by Britain, France, and Russia—blockaded the entry to the Mediterranean and North seas as a way of preventing supplies from reaching the Central Powers—Germany and Austria-Hungary. Nonetheless, neutral countries, notably the Netherlands, Switzerland, Sweden, and Norway, kept trading with the Central Powers. German losses in several early battles soon forced neutral ships back to port. William II and his advisers planned a massive submarine, or U-boat (*Unterseebot*), campaign against Allied and neutral shipping around Britain and France. In May 1915, German submarines sank the passenger ship *Lusitania* and killed 1,198 people, including 124 Americans. Although the atmosphere in the United States crackled with outrage, President Woodrow Wilson maintained a policy of neutrality. The Germans, not willing to provoke Wilson any further, called off unrestricted submarine warfare. In May 1916 the navies of Germany and Britain finally clashed in the great Battle of Jutland. Although inconclusive, the battle demonstrated that the German fleet could not dislodge the British as rulers of the sea.

Fighting became global in late August 1914, when Japan, eager to expand its empire in the Far East, declared war on Germany. In the fall, Turkey entered on the side of the Central Powers and prevented much-needed Allied supplies from reaching Russia via the Black Sea. Ottoman armies forced the Entente to shift troops from Europe to protect

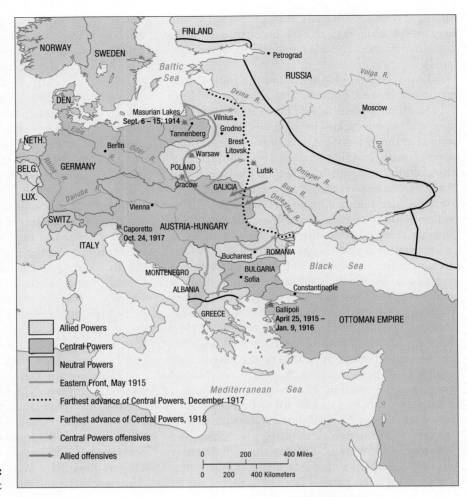

**World War I:
The Eastern Front**

its oil interests in the Near East, which Turkey threatened to seize. In 1915, Italy, which had been allied with Austria-Hungary, sold its support to the Entente. Under the terms of the Treaty of London (1915), Italy was promised territory in Africa, Asia Minor, the south Tyrol, the Balkans, and elsewhere in return for opening a third front against the Central Powers. Bulgaria, hoping to defeat Serbia and to annex Macedonia, joined the Central Powers in October 1915. Finally, the colonies provided assistance. Britain deployed Indian regiments to meet the German advance on the Western Front in the first days of the war and enlisted Arabs against the Turks. The French relied heavily on Senegalese and North African recruits.

The European powers waged war with the same hunger for territory and prestige that had in-

spired imperialism. Despite the stalemate, each side envisioned a triumph followed by territorial gains that would justify the bloodshed. While German troops sat mired in trenches, the General Staff, many high-ranking politicians, leading industrialists, respected university professors, and groups such as the Pan-German League continued to foresee a far-flung empire. Germany aspired to annex Russian territory, to incorporate parts of Belgium and an industrialized slice of France and Luxembourg, and to turn the Netherlands and the rest of Belgium into a satellite zone. Some German leaders hoped to annex Austria-Hungary as well. The Dual Monarchy sought victory to consolidate its control of the Serbs, Germans, Hungarians, Croats, Czechs, Poles, and other nationalities who lived together uneasily under the Habsburg crown.

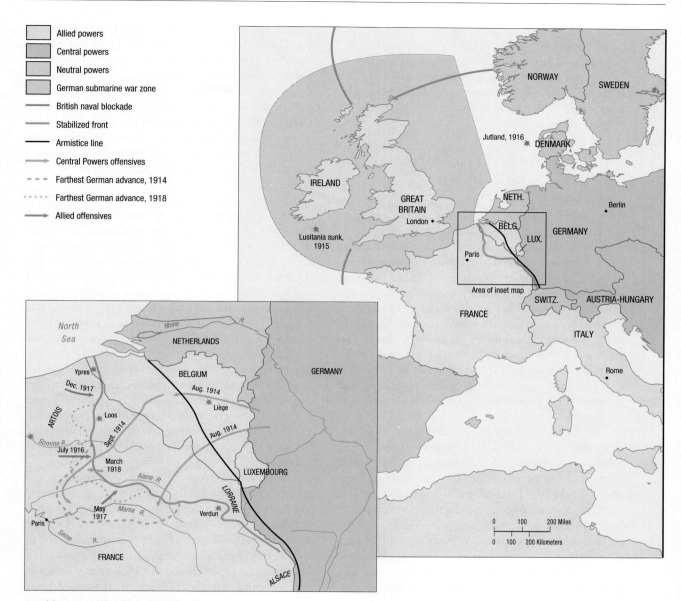

Legend:

- Allied powers
- Central powers
- Neutral powers
- German submarine war zone
- British naval blockade
- Stabilized front
- Armistice line
- Central Powers offensives
- Farthest German advance, 1914
- Farthest German advance, 1918
- Allied offensives

World War I: The Western Front

On the other side, Russia wanted to reassert its status as a Great Power and as the Slavs' protector by adding a reunified Poland to the Russian empire, annexing Habsburg territory peopled by Ukrainians, and reorganizing the rest of Austria-Hungary into a triple monarchy that recognized Slavic political claims. France and Britain fed Russian dreams of expansion by promising it Constantinople and the long-desired Dardenelles at the end of the war. The French too craved territory, especially the return of Alsace and Lorraine, taken from them after the Franco-Prussian War, and desperately wanted new boundaries with Germany that would, they thought, guarantee their security. The British sought to keep the North Sea coast from falling to another Great Power and to cement their hold on Egypt and the Suez Canal, as well as to secure the rest of their world empire.

The particulars of each country's vision varied, but all powers wanted security and prosperity in a postwar world that promised to be competitive, even predatory. Thus even as the death toll mounted, ideas of a negotiated peace were discarded. "No peace before England is defeated and destroyed," the kaiser railed against his cousin King George V. "Only amidst the ruins of London will I forgive Georgy." Georges Clemenceau (1841–1929), who would become premier of France in 1917, called for a "war to the death."

Mobilizing the Home Front for Total War

In the summer of 1914, before reaching the front, many officers had proudly sharpened their swords; but such preparations for individual military heroics would prove futile. Soldiers in World War I were mere cogs in a mass war machine driven by technology. Most soldiers reached the front by train, truck, and even taxi. Quickly bogged down in their trenches and shredded by the millions by artillery and machine-gun fire, they were trapped helplessly before an awesome military technology that industrialization had produced. Barbed wire kept them from advancing, as did the new heavy firepower and poisonous gas—technological enemies against which swords and individual bravery were equally useless.

Reliance on industrial technology extended the conflict from the trenches to the home front, where civilian industry supplied weapons, transport, and other matériel. Civilian involvement made World War I a total war—one that depended on government overseeing factories, transportation systems, and resources ranging from food to coal and steel to textiles. Such control of economic matters would have been anathema to many liberals before the war. Governments also passed sedition laws that made it a crime to criticize official policies, and propaganda encouraged civilians to endure longer working hours and shortages of consumer goods. Some countries conscripted people into the labor force, blurring the distinction between military and civilian life. Total war severely tested the stamina of civilians and soldiers alike.

At the outset many socialists and working-class people who had formerly criticized the military buildup announced their support for the cause. For decades socialist parties had preached that the "worker has no country" and that nationalism was an artificial ideology meant to keep workers dis-united and subjected to the will of their employers. Socialists of the Second International envisioned that their deputies would vote against military budgets and that their members would refuse to fight. But workers had become increasingly nationalistic before the war, and in August 1914 the socialist rank and file, along with most of the party leaders, were as patriotic as the rest of society. Their eager support of wartime governments ended the Second International's role as the vanguard of socialist leadership.

Political parties also put aside their differences, leading to all-party solidarity known in Germany as the *Burgfriede* (domestic peace) and in France as the *union sacrée* (sacred union). Feminists divided over whether to maintain their traditional condemnation of militarism or to support the war. Whereas many feminists actively opposed the conflict, the Pankhursts became militant nationalists, even changing the name of their suffrage paper to *Britannia*. Still other women flocked to philanthropic organizations assisting the war effort. Parties representing the middle classes shelved their distrust of the socialists and working classes in the interests of social peace at home. National leaders wanted to end political division: "I no longer recognize [political] parties," William II declared on August 4. "I recognize only Germans."

Maintaining national unity became more and more difficult as the lack of long-range planning hampered armies across Europe and tested civilian resolve. As early as mid-November 1914, German artillery on the Western Front had been reduced to a four-day supply of ammunition. All countries lacked ready replacements for their heavy losses of weapons and matériel. Governments soon stepped in to ensure steady production of war supplies and their timely arrival at the front. War ministries set up boards that allocated labor on home- and battle-fronts, sponsored efficiency studies of individual industries, oversaw the regulation of factory work, and gave industrialists financial incentives to encourage productivity. In the Dual Monarchy the Hungarian Emergency Measures Act allowed the drafting of both men and women. In 1916 the National Service Act made all British citizens eligible for industrial or military service. In Germany all men between the ages of seventeen and sixty could be conscripted.

Countries mobilized the home front with varying degrees of success. The Russian bureaucracy only reluctantly and ineffectively cooperated with industrialists and other groups that could aid the war effort. Desperate for factory workers, the Germans forced Belgian citizens to move to Germany, housing them in prison camps until they could be rotated into factory work. In Germany, Austria, France, and Britain officials eventually controlled food allocations through rationing. Municipal governments arranged for local workshops to organize sewing and other essential tasks; they also set up canteens and day-care centers to provide for family needs so men and women could focus fully on war production. Rural Russia, Austria-Hungary, Bulgaria, and Serbia, where youths, women, and old men struggled to sustain farms, had no relief programs. Simultaneously, governments and industrialists retreated from the trend toward protective legislation by ignoring laws that limited the length of women's workday, the kind of work they were allowed to do, and their performance of dangerous tasks.

To ensure civilian acceptance of the extra hours at work and the shortages of food and consumer goods, governments created agencies to tout the war as a patriotic mission to resist villainous enemies. British propagandists fabricated many of the atrocities the German "Huns" supposedly committed against Belgians, and they invented statements—for example, the kaiser's remark that British soldiers formed a "contemptible little army"—to incite the troops. German propaganda warned that French African troops would rape German women if Germany were defeated. In Russia, Nicholas II changed the German-sounding name of St. Petersburg to the Russian "Petrograd" in 1914. But propaganda sometimes backfired. Worried about the loyalty of their many ethnic minorities, the Russians plastered Polish towns with posters promising national independence if the Poles would help fight the Germans. But by printing the Polish flag upside down on the posters, the Russians weakened rather than strengthened their cause. In Britain soldiers ridiculed the film *Battle of the Somme* (1916), with its staged scenes of war obviously filmed in a studio. The film, however, drew packed civilian audiences, and its fake screen images bolstered their desire to smash the Germans. Playing on fears and arousing hatred, propaganda rendered a compromise peace unlikely.

Artists saturated public space with colorful posters that depicted working women, loyal to their absent men. In fact, propaganda was not what first spurred women to do war work. In the war's early days many women had lost their jobs when luxury shops, textile factories, and other low-priority establishments closed. With men at the front, many women headed households with little support and few opportunities to work. Some were reduced to desperate measures: a photo taken in Berlin early in the war shows women lined up to sell their long hair. Only after governments and businesses realized the magnitude of the war did they recognize the amount of labor the struggle would take. As more and more men left for the trenches, women took over higher-paying jobs in formerly restricted munitions and metallurgical industries. In Warsaw they drove trucks, and in London they conducted streetcars. Some young women drove ambulances and nursed the wounded near the front lines.

The press praised women's patriotism in adopting new roles, but women's assumption of men's jobs also suggested social disorder, even to some women. "The feminine in me decreased more and more, and I did not know whether to be sad or glad about this," wrote one Russian nurse about learning to wear rough male clothing near the battlefield. Men returned home wounded and weak, but women demonstrated uncustomary strength and enthusiasm for war: "Oh, it's you that have all the luck, out there in the blood and muck," went one woman author's jingle. Working men commonly protested that women, in the words of one metalworker, were "sending men to the slaughter." Men feared that when the war was over women would remain in the workforce, robbing men of work and usurping their role as breadwinners. Others objected to women's loss of femininity. Working long hours, the typical factory woman "makes you afraid, with her hands and face turned yellow, her colourless hair and the corpse-like look which the handling of explosives gives her." Some criticized young female munitions workers for squandering their pay on ribbons, furs, and jewelry. These wartime tensions over traditional gender roles echoed prewar changes in relations between the sexes and presaged further rifts to come.

Trench Warfare

Despite the heavy casualties of 1914, the military wisdom of the day dictated that armies take the offensive again in 1915. In theory a major offensive drive would inspire both soldiers and civilians, and so general staffs prepared fierce attacks several times a year. Campaigns opened with heavy artillery pounding enemy trenches and gun emplacements. Troops then scrambled "over the top" of their trenches, usually to be mowed down by machine-gun fire from defenders secure in their own trenches.

On the Western Front the French desperately wanted to oust the Germans from their northern industrial regions. Throughout 1915 they assaulted the enemy at Ypres, Loos, and Artois; but they accomplished little, and casualties of one hundred thousand and more for a single campaign became commonplace. The next year, however, was even more disastrous. When the Germans judged that a definitive blow against the French would induce the British to withdraw from the war, they turned their attention in early 1916 to the fortress at Verdun. The fall of the fortress, they calculated, would cripple French morale. Launching massive assaults from February through April, the Germans fired as many as a million shells in a single day. Combined French and German losses totaled close to a million men. Nonetheless the French held.

Like the Germans at Verdun, the British command still believed in taking the offensive. Hoping to relieve their allies, the British unleashed an artillery pounding of German trenches in the Somme region in June 1916 that was supposed to ensure a bloodless victory for Britain. But on July 1, twenty thousand British soldiers died going over the top—the artillery had failed to penetrate the deeply dug German fortifications. In several months of battle at the Somme, 1.25 million men were killed or wounded, but the end result was stalemate.

By the end of 1916 the French had absorbed more than 3.5 million casualties. With the German army firmly entrenched in French soil, many French people remained more committed than ever to Clemenceau's "war to the death." In Germany people were beginning to express doubts. Failure to win by late 1916 had severely diminished the country's resources and begun to undermine morale.

On the Eastern Front troops on both sides fared no better than their counterparts in Belgium and France, as the decaying empires traded severe body blows. In the spring of 1915, Russian armies captured Przemysl in Galicia and lumbered toward Hungary. The Central Powers struck back, taking Warsaw, Brest-Litovsk, and Vilnius later that year and bringing the front perilously close to Petrograd. The Austro-Hungarian armies successfully routed the Serbs in 1915, conquered Montenegro and parts of Albania, and then engaged the newly mobilized Italian army. In 1916, to help out the Allies engaged at Verdun and the Somme, the Russians struck again, driving once more into the Carpathians, recouping territory, and menacing the Habsburg empire. Only the German army stopped its advance. Amidst the huge losses, the Habsburg army recruited men in their mid-fifties and the German General Staff was impelled to take over its military operations. As would happen again in World War II, however, Russia sustained the greatest number of casualties—7.5 million by 1917. Slaughter on the Eastern Front drove hundreds of thousands of peasants into the Russian interior, where officials were unprepared to deal with the refugees' hunger, homelessness, and disease.

Officer in Trenches
Trenches became 'homes' for men at the front and accumulated some domestic comforts. Many war photos, however, were staged for propaganda purposes.

Firing Line of the French Army in World War I
The dead and wounded filled trenches, and battlefields were littered with body parts. Here a soldier shelters a wounded comrade while getting better support for his rifle.

Whereas governments and officers tended to see war as "kill or be killed," troops at the front often put into effect their own practice of "live and let live." Some battalions went for long stretches with hardly a casualty, a far cry from the common picture of relentless bloodshed. Diaries show that these low rates stemmed from agreements among troops to avoid battles. Opposing trenches were close enough at some points to be reached by grenades, and so troops were vulnerable at mealtime, when they were not on alert. Yet enemies facing each other across the trenches frequently ate their meals in peace. A German soldier described trenches where "friend and foe alike go to fetch straw from the same rick to protect them from cold and rain—and never a shot is fired." On both fronts soldiers fraternized. They played an occasional game of soccer, yelled across the trenches, sang together at Christmas and Easter, exchanged mementos, and made gestures of agreement not to fight. A British veteran of the trenches explained to a new recruit that the Germans "don't want to fight any more than we do, so there's a kind of understanding between us. Don't fire at us and we'll not fire at you." Burying enemy dead in common graves with their own fallen comrades, ordinary soldiers came to feel more warmly toward enemies who shared the trench experience than toward civilians back home: "It is only on the home front that the atmosphere is still warlike. . . . At the front there is far too much mutual understanding of one for the other." Despite such understandings, life in the trenches was miserable because of the presence of disease, rats, choking dust in the summer, and endless mud in the winter.

Newly forged bonds of male camaraderie alleviated some of the misery of trench life. Sharing the danger of death and the deprivations of the front-line experience weakened traditional class distinctions. Upper-class officers and working-class draftees became friends in that "wholly masculine way of life uncomplicated by woman," as one man put it. According to diaries and letters, soldiers picked lice from one another's bodies and clothes, worshiped section leaders who tended their blistered feet, and came to love one another, sometimes even passionately. Positive memories of this front-line community survived the war and influenced postwar politics.

When the fighting resumed, men in trenches lived in a veritable hell of shelling and sniping, flying body parts, rotting cadavers, and blinding gas. Some were reduced to hysteria or succumbed to shell shock through the sheer stress and violence of battle. Under these conditions soldiers felt their separation from civilization intensely, despite the regular arrival from home of daily newspapers, letters, and packages. They periodically became disillusioned by a war that was "so damned impersonal" and depended less on swords and heroism than on wire cutters, artillery shells, gas masks, and tanks. Having gone to war initially to escape ordinary life in industrial society, they learned, as one German put it, "that in the modern war . . . the triumph of the machine over the individual is carried to its most extreme form."

On February 1, 1917, the German government, hard-pressed by the public clamor over mounting casualties and by the military's growing control over decision making, resumed unrestricted submarine warfare. Although Chancellor Theobald von Bethmann-Hollweg wanted to avoid total war at sea for fear of bringing in the United States, Ludendorff and Hindenburg, whose prestige was on the rise, bullied the kaiser into unleashing the U-boats. The military made the irresistible promise to end the war in six months by cutting off imported food and military supplies to Britain and thus forcing the island nation to surrender before the United States could come to its rescue. The British responded to the initial devastation the U-boats caused in the spring of 1917 by mining harbors and the seas and by developing depth charges. But the most effective measure was the convoy system of shipping, in which a hundred or more warships and freighters traveling the seas together could drive off the submarines. As predicted, unrestricted submarine warfare brought in the United States in April 1917 after German U-boats had sunk several U.S. ships. The submarine gamble had also utterly failed to thwart the British.

Revolt Amidst War

With the loyalties of its multiethnic citizenry divided, the United States was initially unprepared for total war and sent massive military reinforcements to France only in the spring of 1918. Meanwhile, political opposition to the war increased in Europe, and deteriorating living conditions sparked outright revolt by civilians. "We are living on a volcano," warned an Italian politician in the spring of 1917.

On Easter Monday, 1916, a group of Irish nationalists attacked government buildings in Dublin in a poorly coordinated effort to wrest Irish independence from Britain. The rebels, a band of between one thousand and two thousand, held out for some six days against government forces. When the Easter Rebellion was over, the British, who could not tolerate sedition amidst the mounting problems of war, dealt harshly with the participants, executing fifteen and incarcerating many more. Nevertheless the Easter Rebellion took the Irish farther along the road to partitioning of their island and to independence.

Elsewhere people protested increasing prices and food shortages: "Wages are not rising [but] food prices have risen by 100 and 200 percent," a Budapest paper complained in the summer of 1915. "We cannot bear this any longer!" In the fall of 1916 the symbol of old Europe, Francis Joseph of Austria, died after a reign of sixty-eight years, but failed harvests left his subjects with more pressing worries than his death. Food shortages in cities of Italy, Russia, and Germany as well as in Vienna provoked women, unable to feed their families, to riot. As inflation mounted, tenants conducted rent strikes, factory hands and white-collar workers alike walked off the job, and female workers protested the skyrocketing cost of living and their fatigue from overwork. Despite pockets of unrest, the majority of ordinary Europeans stoically endured the war's hardships.

Although many soldiers from different social backgrounds felt bonds of solidarity in the trenches, wartime conditions increasingly pitted civilians against one another along class lines. While workers toiled longer hours on less food, many in the upper classes bought abundant food and fashionable clothing on the black market and lived conspicuously well. Governments allowed many businesses high rates of profit, a step that resulted in a surge in the cost of living and thus contributed to social strife. In 1918 a German roof workers' association pleaded for relief: "We can no longer go on. Our children are starving. . . . It is simply beyond our strength." Craftspeople producing nonessential consumer goods suffered the most. In some countries white-collar employees, accustomed to being a notch above manual workers, endured falling real wages in comparison to munitions workers. Civilians held governments responsible for these everyday difficulties; ultimately some of this bitterness sometimes festered into revolution.

Other protest concentrated on shattering the nationalist consensus supporting the war. For example, activists in the international women's movement met in The Hague in 1915, determined to end the war. "We can no longer endure . . . brute force as the only solution of international disputes," declared Dutch physician Aletta Jacobs in her opening speech. Governments on both sides prevented many women from attending, because the slightest public move toward a negotiated peace was seen as "defeatism." Activists who reached The Hague, however, spent the remainder of the war urging statesmen to work out a peace settlement.

In Austria-Hungary nationalist groups agitating for self-determination hampered the empire's war effort. The Czechs undertook a vigorous anti-Habsburg campaign at home, while in Paris, Thomas Masaryk (1850–1937) and Edouard Beneš (1884–1948) established the Czechoslovak National Council from which they lobbied the Western powers for recognition of their rights. For Poles the war had finally split the powers that had partitioned their country in the eighteenth century. Jozef Pilsudski (1867–1935) set up the Polish Military Organization in Austrian Galicia, which he trained to form the basis for an independent Polish army; groups such as the People's party (representing peasants) and the National Union of Workers developed an underground political movement. In the Balkans the Croats, Slovenes, and Serbs had competing approaches to independence; many Serbs favored complete independence from other South Slavs. Yet a committee representing all three groups envisioned a South Slav nation carved from Habsburg possessions and other Balkan territory. Nationalists in central and eastern Europe were buoyed by Wilson's public support in January 1917 for self-determination by ethnic groups, and from then on the Allies encouraged independence movements as part of their strategy to defeat the Habsburgs.

As war continued a few socialists who maintained the Second International's original antiwar commitment also began meeting. In the spring of 1915, Marxist women, at the instigation of the exiled Bolsheviks Inessa Armand, Nadezhda Krupskaya, and Lenin, convened at Berne, Switzerland, to oppose the killing of workers by workers. Other meetings followed at Zimmerwald, Switzerland, in 1915 and 1916; leaders urged the working classes to renew their internationalism and "begin the struggle for peace." Lenin was one of the leaders of this so-called Zimmerwald Movement that denounced the Second International for having brought about a "class truce" with its support for the war.

Revolution in Russia

The most consequential overturning of prowar national unity came at the tsar's doorstep. In February 1917[*] crowds of working women demanding relief from harsh conditions swarmed the streets of Petrograd. The protests began as a commemoration of International Women's Day, but the women and children turned to looting shops for food. They enlisted support from soldiers guarding the streets and drew other citizens into widespread rioting. A comparatively backward nation, Russia lacked the commercial and industrial base to provision its citizens in a total war. Peasants, unable to exchange their produce for consumer goods, withheld crops from the market and sent the price of food in cities soaring by 800 percent. In the midst of this deprivation many in the army, instead of remaining steadfastly loyal to the tsar, were embittered by the massive casualties caused by their inferior weapons and their leaders' foolhardy tactics. The politicization that had evolved since the Revolution of 1905 combined with the tsar's incompetence during the war to raise the voice of protest to a crescendo—and in the process to topple the 300-year-old Romanov dynasty.

The Russian monarchy commanded little respect by 1917 because Nicholas stubbornly refused to reform his autocratic government. He was not much of a leader in the best of circumstances. The tsar was exceptionally devoted to his family, and this inclination ironically contributed to his downfall. Grigori Rasputin, a combination of holy man and charlatan, held Nicholas and his wife Alexandra in his thrall by claiming to control the hemophilia of their son and heir. When government

---

[*]Until February 1/14, 1918, Russian and other European calendars differed by 13 days, so the February Revolution occurred in March according to the European calendar.

Nicholas II, Alexandra, and Their Children, 1914
*This devoted family lived in splendor and privilege, but
the tsar was fatally incapable of meeting the incredible
tests posed by modernization and total war. The entire
family would be executed four years later by a group of
Bolshevik revolutionaries, an event that brought three
centuries of Romanov rule to a bloody close.*

ministers challenged Rasputin's influence on state
matters, Nicholas sided with Rasputin and dismissed his officials. "Is this stupidity or treason?"
one member of the Duma asked of the impotent
wartime administration. Educated and influential
leaders withdrew their support from the feckless
dynasty. As the riots erupted in February 1917,
Nicholas was headed for the front to rally his
forces; but when railway workers diverted his train
and virtually held him prisoner, he knew the situation was hopeless. He abdicated, and he and his
family were taken into custody.

Politicians from the old Duma formed a new
ruling entity called the Provisional Government,
but continuing hardships and the competing aspirations of many groups—workers, homemakers,
students, liberal politicians, and soldiers—made it
difficult for the new body to govern. Yet at first
hopes were high, even utopian, that under the Provisional Government, as one revolutionary poet
put it, "our false, filthy, boring, hideous life should

become a just, pure, merry, and beautiful life."
Composed essentially of moderates, the Provisional Government had to pursue the war successfully, manage internal affairs better, and set government on a firm constitutional footing to establish
its credibility. However, it did not rule alone: spontaneously elected soviets—councils of workers and
soldiers—competed with the government for
political support and often challenged its policies.
Soviets had sprung up during the Revolution of
1905 and quickly revived in 1917 to press for improved conditions and a speedy resolution of the
war. Lively and informal, the soviets contrasted the
people's needs with the privileges of the upper-class
men in the Provisional Government. In the first
euphoric rush of revolution, the soviets ended def-
erential treatment for industrialists and officers,
urged respect for workers and the poor, and temporarily gave an air of celebration and carnival to
this political cataclysm. The peasantry constituted
another competing force for power. Peasants began
to confiscate gentry estates and continued to with-
hold produce from the market, thus intensifying
urban food shortages.

In hopes of further destabilizing Russia, the
Germans in April 1917 provided safe rail transportation for Lenin and other prominent Bolsheviks to return to Petrograd through German
territory. Lenin, described at the time as "humor-
less, uncompromising, and detached," had devoted
his entire existence to bringing about socialism
through the force of his small band of Bolsheviks.
As a political exile he had no parliamentary experience, but he had developed his position by
maneuvering among socialist factions, by writing
propaganda and theoretical works, and through the
sheer strength of his will. Upon his return
to Petrograd, Lenin issued the April Theses, a
document that called for Russia to withdraw from
the war, for the soviets to seize power on behalf of
workers *and* poor peasants, and for all private land
to be nationalized. The Bolsheviks challenged the
legitimacy of the Provisional Government with the
slogans "All power to the soviets" and "Peace,
Land and Bread." Definitively breaking with the
heritage of social democracy in the Second International, they adopted the name *Communists.*

By early summer the Provisional Government
saw a military victory as the only way to ensure its
position against competitors at home and to bar-

Demonstration During the Russian Revolution, 1917
Soldiers joined working people during the early days of the Revolution, thus fortifying food and antiwar protests.

gain with the Central Powers for an advantageous peace. On July 1 the Russian army attacked the Austrians in Galicia but fell to defeat once again. The new prime minister, the Socialist Revolutionary Aleksandr Kerensky (1881–1970), used his commanding oratory to arouse patriotism, but he lacked the political skills needed to fashion an effective wartime government. In Petrograd groups of workers, soldiers, and sailors—many of them Bolsheviks—agitated for the soviets to replace the Provisional Government. To restore order, the government rounded up Bolshevik leaders and accused them of being German agents, forcing many others into hiding. By the end of the month, however, the government needed the Bolsheviks to head off a coup led by General Kornilov, described by one of his fellow generals as having "the heart of a lion and the brains of a sheep." Kornilov, an announced backer of the revolution, hoped to bring it under control with a military dictatorship.

As Bolshevik popularity in the cities rose, the stature of other politicians fell. By fall 1917 the Provisional Government which now included members of the Socialist Revolutionary and Men-

shevik parties, was thoroughly discredited. The government had failed both to call a constituent assembly and to enact a well-defined land reform. Some found it complicit in the Kornilov coup attempt, and its conduct of the war had been disastrous, leaving the army "a huge crowd of tired, poorly clad, poorly fed, embittered men." The soviets, led by the Mensheviks and Socialist Revolutionaries and associated with the plight of soldiers and workers, had also failed to solve the problems of rampant unemployment and urban misery. Despite their rivals' waning credibility, Bolsheviks were divided over whether to proceed against the Kerensky government. Only in October 1917 did the leadership, cajoled by Lenin, decide to stage an uprising against Kerensky to prevent him from holding the promised elections that might have stabilized the Provisional Government. The Bolsheviks seized key facilities (including the Winter Palace), drove out Kerensky's government, and presented supreme power to a congress of soviets while claiming the right to form a government. As opponents of the Bolsheviks marched out of the meeting in protest, the communist Leon Trotsky,

REVOLUTION IN RUSSIA

1917

March 8 International Women's Day, strikes and demonstrations

March 12 Establishment of Provisional Government

March 15 Nicholas II abdicates

April 17 Lenin and other Bolshevik leaders return to Russia

May 14 Resignation of Milyukov, first head of Provisional Government

May 16 Provisional Government run by Socialists, dominated by Kerensky

Late June–early July Russian offensive against Germany fails

Mid-July Attempted popular uprising fails

September 9–14 Kornilov coup d'état fails

November 6–7 Bolshevik seizure of power

November 25 Constituent Assembly elections held

1918

January 18 Constituent Assembly closed down by Bolsheviks

1918–1922 Civil war

1924 Union of Soviet Socialist Republics formally established

a former Menshevik, predicted that enemies of communism would become "refuse [on] the garbage-heap of history."

In January 1918 a freely elected Constituent Assembly, made up of representatives from a variety of political parties, first convened. Having failed to carry the elections, the Bolsheviks used troops to disperse the assembly and place themselves at the head of the government. They took over town and city administrations, closing down the *zemstvos* and other institutions in the countryside where Socialist Revolutionary support was keen. Soon after the Bolshevik takeover, Lenin asked Germany for peace. The Germans agreed but imposed the Treaty of Brest-Litovsk, which placed Poland, the Baltic lands, Finland, the Ukraine, and other regions of the old Russian empire under German occupation. The treaty partially realized the German ideal of a central European region, or *Mitteleuropa,* under its control. It

also showed the remaining Allied powers how tough the Germans were as victors and how unreliable the Russians were as allies. Because the loss of millions of square miles put Petrograd at future risk, the Bolsheviks relocated the capital to Moscow. Lenin agreed to these draconian terms not only because he had promised to bring peace to Russia but also because he believed that the rest of Europe would soon rebel against war and overthrow the capitalist order.

The Great War Ends

Lenin's prediction of imminent revolution across the Continent was not completely far-fetched. Combatant countries were rife with dissension and conflicting goals. By mid-1917 the war had strengthened nationalist movements in the Habsburg empire, and the new emperor, Karl (*1916–1918), secretly asked the Allies for a negotiated peace to avoid a total collapse of his empire. In the summer of 1917, the German Reichstag passed a resolution announcing its desire for a "peace of understanding and permanent reconciliation of peoples." Outraged, Ludendorff and Hindenburg incited the formation of a Fatherland Party to whip up antisemitic and pan-Germanic sentiment in support of the war. President Wilson further weakened civilian resolve in Germany and Austria-Hungary in January 1918 by issuing his Fourteen Points, which held out the promise of a nonvindictive peace settlement to war-weary citizens of the Central Powers. The Allies faced dissent too. In the spring of 1917, French soldiers had mutinied, refusing to participate in any more bloody and fruitless offensives. General Henri Philippe Pétain (1856–1951) crushed the uprisings, but he also instituted reforms that ended the foolhardy commitment to offense at any cost.

The German High Command continued to put its faith in offensives despite the groundswell of discontent. Indeed the generals had developed a new strategy to break the stalemate in the trenches. Instead of attacking along a front extending for miles, concentrated forces would pierce single points of the enemy's relatively thin defense lines and then wreak havoc from the rear. In the fall of 1917 the Central Powers had overwhelmed the Italian army at Caporetto using these tactics. In the spring of 1918 they made one final attempt to smash through the Allied lines, but the offensive ground to a bloody halt within weeks. By then the British and French had started making limited but effective use of tanks supported by airplanes. Although the first tanks were cumbersome, their ability to withstand machine-gun fire made offensive attacks possible. In the summer of 1918 the Entente, now fortified by the Americans, pushed back the Germans all along the Western Front and headed toward Germany. The German armies, suffering more than 2 million casualties between spring and summer, rapidly disintegrated.

By October 1918 the desperate German command helped create a civilian government, led by the liberal Prince Max of Baden, expressly to take responsibility for the defeat and to sue for peace. This change acknowledged growing pressures for constitutionalism in Germany but also served to deflect blame from the military, whose generals proclaimed themselves still fully capable of winning the war. Weak-willed civilians had dealt the military a "stab in the back" and were, in the words of the half-demented Ludendorff, "largely responsible for things having turned out as they have. . . . They must now eat the soup they have served us." Amidst this political flux, naval officers called for a final sea battle. As rumors of the proposed sorties leaked, sailors at the naval base at Kiel mutinied against what they saw as a suicide mission. Their rebellion capped years of indignities from high-ranking officers whose champagne-filled diet contrasted with their meager fare of turnips and "barbed-wire" soup. The sailors' revolt spread to working people, who demonstrated in Berlin and other cities. The uprisings provoked the declaration of a German republic in an effort to prevent revolution. On November 9 the kaiser fled.

The Central Powers were collapsing on all fronts. Since the previous winter, Austria-Hungary had kept many combat divisions at home simply to maintain civil order. By the fall of 1918, crowds in Prague and other disaffected parts of the empire were vandalizing imperial insignia on public buildings. At the end of October, Czechs and Slovaks declared an independent state, and the Croatian parliament simultaneously announced its independence.

Finally, on November 11, 1918, at 5:00 A.M., an armistice was signed. The guns fell silent on the Western Front six hours later. At noon in Vienna, Emperor Karl abdicated, the third European emperor to fall. In the course of four years, European civilization had been sorely tested, if not shattered.

Otto Dix, The War
Like many artists, the former soldier Dix was obsessed by the horrors of World War I. In addition to this oil painting expressing the chaos of war and the destructiveness of modern weaponry, he drew repulsive sketches of dead soldiers with their faces eaten by insects.

Conservative figures put the battlefield toll at a minimum of 10 million deaths and at least 30 million wounded, many of them permanently disfigured, incapacitated, or eventually to die of their wounds. In every European combatant country, industrial and agricultural production had plummeted from prewar output. Moreover, much of the reduced output had been put to military use, and food and supplies for civilians had often fallen below subsistence levels. Asia, Africa, and the Americas, which depended on European trade, felt the painful impact of Europe's declining production.

From 1918 to 1919 the weakened global population suffered another devastating blow when an influenza epidemic rampaged around the world, leaving at least 20 million more dead.

Besides illness, hunger, and death, the war also provoked tremendous moral questioning. Soldiers returning home in 1918 and 1919 flooded the book market with their memoirs, trying to give meaning to their experience. People had expressed a range of feelings about the Great War in prose and verse almost from the start: some twenty-five hundred war poets published in Britain alone. Whereas many had begun by emphasizing heroism and glory, others were cynical and bitter by war's end. They insisted the fighting had been absolutely meaningless. Total war had drained society of resources and population, challenged prewar values, and inadvertently sown the seeds of future catastrophes.

Revolution, Counterrevolution, and Peace

In the aftermath of unprecedented bloodshed, the question of what Europe would be like in the postwar era loomed large. Revolutionary fervor swept the Continent, especially in the former empires of Germany and Austria-Hungary. In Moscow, Lenin welcomed the emperors' downfall as a stage of world revolution that would usher in an age of working-class internationalism. Indeed until 1921 the triumph of socialism seemed plausible. Immediately following the war, many of the newly independent peoples of eastern and central Europe fervently supported socialist principles, and the lower classes in Germany were in a revolutionary mood. Yet as revolutionaries attempted to realize their political program, they faced liberal and right-wing opponents. Many of the latter hoped for a political order based on military authority. Faced with a volatile mix of revolution and counterrevolution, diplomats from around the world arrived in Paris in January 1919 to negotiate the terms of peace. For eighteen months they planned Europe's reconstruction according to their own competing interests, often without rec-

ognizing the magnitude of the changes brought about by the war.

Toward World Revolution

Lenin and his followers believed that the Russain Revolution was the spark that would light a revolutionary fire throughout Europe and then the world. In January 1919 the red flag flew from city hall in Glasgow, Scotland, while in cities of the collapsing Austro-Hungarian empire workers set up councils to direct factory production and to influence political events. As in Russia, many soldiers did not disband at the armistice but formed volunteer armies or paramilitry bands, making Europe ripe not for parliamentary politics but for revolution by brute force. The key to socialist success, in Lenin's view, lay in Germany's hands. If workers took control in that pivotal nation, the socialist movement would be unstoppable.

In November 1918, Germany was politically unstable, partially because of the terrible shock of defeat. Germans initially took to the streets en masse to rally around the civilian politicians who were ending the war. Cracks in this unified facade soon developed: by December independent socialist groups and workers' councils were vying with the dominant Social Democrats for control of the government. The masses, suffering under the Allies' continuation of the wartime blockade, cried out for help. At demonstrations in December and January crowds demanded economic policies that would assuage workers' misery and give veterans their back pay. Whereas revolutionaries in 1848 marched to city hall or the king's residence, these protesters took over newspapers and telegraph offices, thus controlling the flow of information. Some were inspired by one of the most radical socialist factions, the Spartacists, led by confounders Karl Liebknecht (1871–1919) and Rosa Luxemburg (1870–1919). Contrary to Lenin, the two Spartacist leaders favored *spontaneous* political uprisings and *direct* worker control of institutions, but they shared his dislike for parliamentary politics. In the winter of 1919 they judged that the moment was not right for a large-scale socialist victory and thus tried to restrain the demonstrations.

Social Democratic leader Friedrich Ebert (1871–1925), who headed the new government, believed that the parliamentary republic would best realize Social Democratic objectives. To achieve such goals, Ebert compromised his principles by meeting violence with violence. Splitting with his former socialist allies, he called on the German army and the Freikorps—a roving paramilitary band of students, demobilized soldiers, and others—to suppress the workers' councils and demonstrators. He thus gave official credence to the idea that political differences could be settled in the streets, with guns. "The enthusiasm is marvelous," wrote one young soldier. "No mercy's shown. We shoot even the wounded. . . . We were much more humane against the French in the field." Police rounded up an array of known political activists. Luxemburg and Liebknecht were hunted down and murdered while in government custody. After the violence a measure of calm returned to Berlin and other cities.

In February a constituent assembly met in the city of Weimar, where it approved a constitution and founded a parliamentary republic. Despite public support for the new order, powerful elements sneered at the republic from its very beginnings. Officers dreamed of a restored monarchy and renewed military prestige of imperial days. "As I love Germany, so I hate the Republic . . ." wrote an officer who helped Ebert quell the worker opposition.

Contempt for republican institutions motivated an attempted military coup called the Kapp *Putsch* in the spring of 1920, when Freikorps officers supported by the regular army announced they were taking over the government. Ludendorff voiced his support, for he thought the new republic was "un-German" and brought only "chaos, bolshevism, and terror." The military command refused to crush the coup: "Soldiers do not fire on soldiers." So Ebert called for a general strike to prevent the return of "military dictatorship," and the strike's effectiveness in closing down essential services showed the military that it could not rule legitimately. Ebert refused to punish the conspirators, however, leaving Germany deeply divided between those who supported the republic and those who hated it. Although revolutions from both the Right and the Left failed, the Weimar government's grip on power was far from solid, and it had set the dangerous precedent of relying on street violence, paramilitary groups, and protests to solve political problems.

Civil War in Russia and Eastern Europe

In the winter of 1918–1919, Bolshevik attention was riveted on Germany. The belief that revolution would spread to industrialized Europe invigorated Lenin and his colleagues as they began to shore up their unstable hold on power and make Russia a communist country in the face of economic collapse and counterrevolution. In keeping with Marxist doctrine, the Bolshevik government abolished private property. At the same time it allowed peasants to work the land they had seized to shift their allegiance away from the Socialist Revolutionary party. The government nationalized factories. It desperately needed to restore production, which had fallen precipitously under the control of workers' councils. Under the Provisional Government, both men and women had received the vote, making Russia the first Great Power to legalize universal suffrage. However, this soon became a hollow privilege once slates were limited to candidates from the Communist party.

Resistance to Bolshevik policies mushroomed. The tsarist military leadership, composed of many landlords and supporters of aristocratic rule, took whatever troops it could muster to the field. Many non-Russian nationality groups, formerly incorporated into the empire, fought because they saw their chance for independence. Before World War I ended, Russia's former allies, notably the United States, Britain, France, and Japan, landed troops in the country. Motives for the invasion varied. Some wanted to keep Entente supplies out of German hands; others fought to help tsarist loyalists overturn the communists. All these forces made extraordinary inroads; one came within thirty miles of Petrograd in October 1919, and others controlled large sections of eastern and southern Russia. Yet the various counterrevolutionary groups competed with one another, offended civilians, and desperately needed unified goals. Some called for a new Russia "one and indivisible," but such a goal alienated those aspiring to nation-state status, such as the Ukrainians, Estonians, and Lithuanians. Ultimately, without a common purpose, the opponents of revolution could not sustain their battlefield victories. In short, they lacked the leadership of a Lenin.

They also lacked the disciplined genius of Leon Trotsky (1879–1940), disliked by many of his

The Russian Civil War

colleagues for his arrogant, dictatorial manner. As Bolshevik commissar of war, Trotsky rebuilt the Red Guard into a highly disciplined army by ending democratic procedures, such as the election of officers, that had originally attracted soldiers to bolshevism. Lenin and Trotsky introduced the policy of War Communism, whereby urban workers and troops moved through the countryside, brutally confiscating grain from the peasantry to feed the army and workforce during the period of civil war and ultimately to achieve the centralization of agricultural production.

The Bolsheviks repressed any resistance to their policies. In December 1917 they had instituted the Cheka (secret police), which, led by Felix Dzerzhinsky, set up detention camps for "hooligans," black marketeers, and political opponents. Dzerzhinsky did not hesitate to have suspected enemies shot without trial. The expansion of the size and strength of the Cheka and Red Army—the latter eventually numbered 5 million men—accompanied the expansion of the bureaucracy, making government more authoritarian and undermining the promise of Marxism that revolution would bring a "withering away" of the state.

As the Bolsheviks clamped down on opposition during the bloody civil war, they organized

their supporters to foster revolutionary Marxism across Europe. In March 1919 they founded the Third International, also known as the Comintern, for the explicit purpose of replacing the old International with a centralized organization dedicated to promoting communism. The Bolsheviks had cause for optimism in the late winter of 1919, when leftists proclaimed soviet republics in Bavaria and Hungary. The Hungarian regime, led by Béla Kun (1885–1937), gained some middle-class nationalist support by resisting Allied plans to reduce the size of Hungary drastically. But Kun's zeal to nationalize production and his secret police's brutality alienated most Hungarians, and the soviet republic was overthrown in August. Meanwhile in Bavaria, German revolutionaries fell before the assault of the volunteer armies and government troops.

The Bolsheviks tried to establish a Marxist regime in Poland. In the spring of 1920 a newly independent Poland struggled to recapture its eighteenth-century territory, which prompted the Red Army to invade in the belief that its people wanted a workers' revolution. Instead the Poles resisted and drove the Red Army back, while the Entente powers rushed supplies and advisers to Warsaw and warned Russia not to cross the Curzon Line (the line, named for the British foreign secretary, marked Poland's eastern ethnic border).

As the possibility of world revolution collapsed, the Red Army shored up bolshevism in Russia. Although Poland, Estonia, Lithuania, and Latvia had established their independence, the army and Bolshevik agents secured the Crimea, Caucasus, and the Muslim borderlands by the spring of 1921. When the Japanese withdrew from Siberia in 1922, civil war ended in the Far East. In Europe Communist parties splintered off from the old Social Democratic and Socialist parties and followed the dictates of Moscow in shaping party policy. Despite such loyalty, the hoped-for global revolution never materialized.

Peacemaking, 1919–1923

As political turmoil engulfed peoples from Berlin to Moscow, the Paris peace conference opened in January 1919. Visions of bolshevism spreading westward haunted the assembled statesmen, but the desperation of millions of war-ravaged citizens, the status of Germany, and the reconstruction of a secure Europe topped their agenda. Such leaders as French Premier Georges Clemenceau also had to appease their angry citizens, who demanded revenge or, at the very least, compensation for their suffering. France had lost 1.3 million dead—almost an entire generation—and more than a million buildings, six thousand bridges, and thousands of miles of railway lines and roads had been destroyed while the war was fought on its soil. Great Britain's representative, Prime Minister David Lloyd George, caught the mood of the British public by campaigning in 1918 with such slogans as "Hang the kaiser." Italians arrived on the scene unconditionally demanding the territory promised to them in the Treaty of London of 1915.

The stance of the United States further complicated the remaking of Europe. This new world power had helped make the Allied victory possible, and its presence at the conference indicated a drastic realignment of power away from any individual European country. In preparation for the peacemaking sessions at Paris, President Wilson triumphantly toured the Western capitals in December 1918. Like other heads-of-state, Wilson had a special agenda: incorporating his conciliatory Fourteen Points, on which the truce had been based, into the final settlement. Steeped in the language of security and freedom, the Fourteen Points called for open diplomacy, arms reduction, an "open-minded" settlement of colonial issues, evacuation of France and Belgium, the return of Alsace and Lorraine to France, and the self-determination of peoples. This was no small ambition, for on top of the death and destruction on both sides, Allied propaganda had made the Germans seem inhuman—like monsters. Many citizens demanded a harsh peace.

Moreover, some experts feared that Germany was only using the armistice to regroup for more warfare. Indeed, Germans widely refused to admit that their army had lost the war. Eager for army support, Ebert had given returning soldiers a rousing welcome: "As you return unconquered from the field of battle, I salute you." Thus conservative leaders among the president's former allies campaigned to make Wilson look utterly naive and deluded. "Wilson bores me with his Fourteen Points," Clemenceau complained. "Why the good Lord himself has only ten."

Nevertheless, Wilson's Fourteen Points appealed to European moderates and had convinced Germans that the settlement would not be vindictive. In fact, Wilson's commitment to *settlement* as opposed to *surrender* contained tough-minded stipulations, for he recognized that Germany was still the strongest state on the Continent. He merely pushed for a treaty that balanced the strengths and interests of the powers. Many of the historians, ethnographers, economists, and other experts accompanying Wilson to Paris agreed that, harshly dealt with and humiliated, Germany might soon become vengeful and chaotic—a lethal combination that could lead to the growth of unsavory political sects.

After six months the statesmen and their teams of experts produced the Peace of Paris, which comprised the Treaty of Versailles for Germany, the Treaty of St. German for Austria, the Treaty of Trianon for Hungary, the Treaty of Neuilly for Bulgaria, and the Treaty of Sèvres for Turkey. These treaties shocked the countries that had to accept them. They separated Austria from Hungary, reduced Hungary by almost two-thirds of its inhabitants and three-quarters of its territory, and treated Germany severely. The treaties replaced the Habsburg empire with a group of small, internally divided, and relatively weak states. The terms established the boundaries of the new states of Czechoslovakia, Poland, and the Kingdom of the Serbs, Croats, and Slovenes (later renamed Yugoslavia). Cutting 3 million Germans away from Austria, the treaties clustered these Germans in Czechoslovakia and reduced Austria's economic base. Many Austrians, their empire gone, desperately wanted to merge with Germany, but the settlement expressly forbade such a union. After a century and a half of partition, Poland was reconstructed from parts of Russia, Germany, and Austria-Hungary, with one-third of its population ethnically non-Polish. The statesmen in Paris also created a Polish corridor that connected Poland to the Baltic Sea; the corridor separated East Prussia from the rest of Germany, although the city of Danzig was granted the status of a free city. The Allies had high hopes that the region would be stable; however, many of the new states became rivals and appeared not only weak, but vulnerable to takeover.

The Treaty of Versailles only partially quenched the French thirst for revenge. France recovered

Europe After the Peace Settlements of 1919–1921

what it called a *Diktat,* or dictated peace. Article 231 allowed the victors to collect reparations from economically viable Germany rather than from decimated Austria, which had deployed the first troops. Suggesting war guilt also made Germany an outcast in the community of nations.

Finally, the Peace of Paris set up the League of Nations, whose deliberations and collective security were to replace the divisive secrecy of prewar power politics. The League would guide the world toward disarmament, arbitrate its members' disputes, and monitor labor conditions. Returning to prewar isolationism, the United States Senate failed to ratify the peace settlement and refused to join the League. Moreover, both Germany and Russia were excluded from the League and were thus blocked from acting in legal concert with other nations. The wartime mentality of allies and enemies, of victors and losers, haunted the interwar years.

The covenant of the League of Nations administered the colonies and territories of Germany and the Ottoman Empire through a system of mandates. The European powers exercised political control over mandated territory, but local leaders retained limited authority. In the Near East, Great Britain acquired a mandate over Mesopotamia and Palestine; France received a mandate over Lebanon

Mandated Territory in the Middle East After World War I

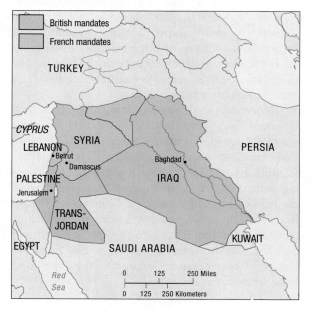

Alsace and Lorraine; Belgium also received a strip of German land. The victors would temporarily occupy the left, or western, bank of the Rhine and the coal-bearing Saar basin. Wilson accepted his allies' expectations that Germany would pay substantial reparations for the civilian damage. The specific amount was established not by the peacemakers in 1919 but by Allied commissions, which only in 1921 agreed on the sum of 132 billion gold marks. Germany also had to surrender the largest ships of its merchant marine, reduce its army, almost eliminate its navy, stop manufacturing offensive weapons, and deliver a large amount of free coal each year to Belgium and France. Furthermore, it was forbidden to have an air force.

The average German saw in these terms an unmerited humiliation that was compounded by Article 231 of the Treaty of Versailles. It spoke of Germany's "responsibility" for damage done during a conflict "imposed on [the Entente] by the aggression of Germany and her allies." The outraged German people interpreted this as a "war guilt" clause, and the government set up a special propaganda office to refute it and to contest the terms of

Senegalese Soldier and Red Cross Nurse, 1918
Asian and African soldiers served the Entente during the war. This Senegalese veteran lost his arms and received artificial limbs.

and Syria. Germany's territories in Africa were mandated to Great Britain, South Africa, France, and Belgium. Japan, Australia, and New Zealand held mandates over Germany's former colonies in the Pacific. The League covenant justified the mandate system as providing governance by "advanced nations" over territories "not yet able to stand by themselves under the strenuous conditions of the modern world." The war, however, had depleted the Great Powers' financial resources and mental resolve for imperialism. Colonized and other people of color, many of whom had served as "cannon fodder" at the front, had come to challenge the claims of their European masters. "Never again will the darker people of the world occupy just the place they had before," the African-American leader W. E. B. Du Bois predicted in 1918. Thus, although the mandate system continued the practice of apportioning the globe among European powers, the next decades saw increasingly heated struggles against this domination.

A Decade of Recovery: Europe in the 1920s

Treaties settling the war did not bring immediate peace to Europe or end the wartime spirit. Words and phrases from the battlefield punctuated speech. Once the word *lousy* had meant "lice-infected"; English-speaking soldiers returning from the trenches now applied it to anything bad. Civilians quickly adopted wartime phrases. Raincoats became *trenchcoats,* and *trench mouth, bombarded,* and *rank and file* all entered peacetime usage. Many feared the "bolshies" and the "reds" and wondered when rationing would end and they would have enough to eat. Maimed, disfigured veterans were present everywhere, and those without limbs were sometimes carried in baskets—hence the expression *basket case.* They overflowed hospitals, rest homes, and mental institutions, and family life centered on their care.

The war also lived on in diplomacy, the economy, and social relations. The key question was how to restore civilian government and peacetime prosperity when total war had generally strengthened military values, authoritarian government, and a controlled economy. Although people referred to the 1920s as the Roaring Twenties and the Jazz Age, the sense of cultural release masked the serious problem of restoring social stability and implementing democracy. Three autocratic governments had collapsed as a result of the war, but their fall did not secure either representative institutions or prosperity.

Diplomatic and Economic Consequences of the Peace

Western leaders worried deeply about two intertwined issues in the 1920s. The first was economic recovery and its relationship to war debts, the conditions of international trade, and German reparations. France, the hardest hit by wartime destruction and billions of dollars in debt to the United States, estimated that Germany owed it at least $200 billion. The British, by contrast, worried about maintaining their empire and restoring trade with Germany, not about exacting huge reparations. Nevertheless, both these powers depended on some monetary redress to pay their war debts to the United States because Europe's share of world trade had plunged during the war. Although the United States wanted the debts paid, it used a soft tone toward the fragile Weimar Republic and a harsh one toward its Allied debtors, for whom U.S. sympathy had dwindled.

Germany claimed that the demand for reparations strained its government, already beset by political upheaval. Because the kaiser had refused to raise wartime taxes, especially on the rich, to pay for the war, the new republic had to deal with the resulting inflation, to pay reparations, and to finance the staggering domestic war debt. Moreover, as an experiment in democracy the Weimar Republic needed to woo the citizenry, not alienate it by hiking taxes. In 1921, when Germans refused to present a realistic payment scheme, the French occupied several cities in the Ruhr. Germany then accepted a payment plan that appeared for the sake of voters in receiver countries to amount to $33 billion but that really came only to $12.5 billion over thirty-six years.

Embroiled with powers to the west, the German government deftly sought economic and diplomatic ties in eastern Europe. It reached an economic agreement with Russia, desperate for Western trade, in the Treaty of Rapallo (1922, renewed in the Treaty of Berlin of 1926). The relationship with powers to the west, however, deteriorated. In 1923, after a default on coal deliveries, the French and Belgians sent troops into the Ruhr basin, planning to use its abundant resources to recoup their wartime expenditures. Urged on by the government, Ruhr citizens fought back, shutting down industry and services by staying home from work. The German government printed trillions of marks to support them, to provide funds to the closed industries, and to pay its own war debts with practically worthless currency. Soon Germany was in the midst of a staggering inflation that demoralized many of its citizens and gravely threatened the international economy: at one point a single U.S. dollar cost 4.42 trillion marks, and wheelbarrows of money were required to buy a turnip. The inflation wiped out people's savings and ruined those living on fixed incomes.

The spirit of the League of Nations was invoked to resolve this economic chaos through negotiations. The Dawes Plan (1924) and eventually the Young Plan (1929) diminished payments to the victors and restored the value of German currency. These plans also evened the balance of Germany's trade between east and west, a balance the Treaty of Rapallo had threatened. Only the French were unhappy, but their postwar weakness forced them to accept the reductions.

Statesmen faced a second pressing issue: ensuring peace. It took hard diplomatic bargaining outside the League to produce two agreements in Germany's favor. At the Washington Conference in 1921 the United States, Great Britain, Japan, France, and Italy agreed to cut back their existing battleships and to stop constructing new ones for ten years. Four years later the Legaue sponsored a meeting of the Great Powers, including Germany, at Locarno, Switzerland. The German diplomat Gustav Stresemann, who claimed that the Versailles Treaty unfairly penalized Germany, negotiated a treaty at Locarno that provided Germany with a seat in the League of Nations as of 1926. In return, Germany agreed not to violate the borders of France and Belgium and to keep the nearby Rhineland demilitarized. Moreover, Italy and Great Britain promised their help should any "flagrant violation" of the Rhineland's demilitarized status occur.

To the east the door seemed open to a German attempt to regain territory lost to Poland or to some kind of merger with Austria. Czechoslovakia, Yugoslavia, and Romania had already formed the "Little Entente" to coordinate their collective security vis-à-vis their two powerful neighbors—Germany and Russia—and against Hungarian expansionism. Between 1924 and 1927, France allied itself with the Little Entente and with Poland to replace its prewar alliance with Russia. Finally, the relaxation of diplomatic tensions symbolized by the "Spirit of Locarno" helped produce the Kellogg-Briand Pact (1928), in which the nations of the world formally rejected international violence. The nations failed, however, to commit themselves to concrete action to prevent its outbreak.

The publicity and planning that yielded the international agreements during the 1920s sharply contrasted with old-style diplomacy, conducted in secret and subject to little public scrutiny or democratic influence. The new openness suggested a diplomatic revolution and promised a peaceful age in international relations. Historians both praise and fault this era of apparent international cooperation. They praise it for promoting solid negotiations among the Great Powers, launching a system of collective security, reintegrating Germany into the community of nations, and showing an awareness that international politics and economics are related. Other scholars denounce the "amateur" diplomats of this era who fed the press reports calculated to arouse the masses. For example, much of the German populace was lashed into a nationalist frenzy whenever Germany's diplomats, who were actually working to undo the Treaty of Versailles, seemed to compromise. Although meetings such as the one at Locarno appeared to promote the goal of collective security, they also exposed the diplomatic process to demagogues who could rekindle nationalist hatreds.

The Promise of Democratic Rebirth in the 1920s

The threat of revolution and demagoguery coexisted with a sense of democratic rebirth because of the League of Nations, the emergence of new nations from the Habsburg empire, and the formation of a democratic German republic. The extension of suffrage to women in many countries, granted to reward them for their war efforts and to make revolution less tempting, also suggested the beginnings of a more democratic political order. In the first postwar elections, women were voted into parliaments, and the impression grew that they had also made extraordinary gains in breaking down barriers in the workplace. French men pointedly denied women the vote, insisting they would vote to bring back the rule of kings and priests. Governments continued building the welfare state by expanding insurance programs for workers and family allowances. New government benefits attested to a spreading belief that economic democracy was important to stability in postwar society.

In addition to bringing about political and economic changes, the war had blurred class distinctions. The massive casualties had generated social mobility by allowing commoners to move up to the rank of officer, a position often monopolized by the prewar aristocracy. Members of all classes had rubbed shoulders in the trenches. The identical, evenly spaced crosses of military cemeteries made all the dead seem equal, as did the mass "brothers' grave" where rich and poor lay side by side in a single, commonly shared burial pit. Away from the battlefield, middle-class daughters worked outside the home; their mothers did

WOMEN GAIN SUFFRAGE IN THE WEST	
1906	Finland
1913	Norway
1915	Denmark, Iceland
1917	The Netherlands, Russia
1918	Czechoslovakia, Great Britain (limited suffrage)
1919	Germany
1920	Austria, United States
1921	Poland
1925	Hungary (limited suffrage)
1945	Italy
1946	France

their own housework because servants could earn more money in factories. The "servant problem," born of wartime opportunities, made middle-class and working-class households more similar. Moreover, the income of the leisure class fell because of inflation, and fewer people could afford the services of professionals such as lawyers in wartime. Finally, Soviet refusal to honor prewar Russian bonds hurt thousands of European investors, adding to the social leveling of war.

The slow trend toward economic democracy was not easy to maintain, however, because the cycles of boom and bust that had characterized the late nineteenth century reemerged. A short postwar boom prompted by rebuilding war-torn areas and filling consumer needs was followed by an economic downturn that was most severe between 1920 and 1922. Skyrocketing unemployment led some to question the effectiveness of their governments and the fairness of society. By the mid-1920s many of the economic opportunities for women had disappeared; they often made up a smaller percentage of the workforce than in 1913. Hard times especially corroded the new democracies of eastern Europe, once part of the economically balanced Habsburg empire but now unprepared for independence in the sophisticated world market. Intensely nationalistic and competitive with one another, none but Czechoslovakia had a mature industrial sector, and agricultural techniques were often primitive. Like late nineteenth-century politicians, leaders in these new countries reacted to adversity by erecting tariff barriers to protect manufacturing and domestic markets.

The development of Poland exemplified eastern Europe's problems. Two-thirds of the population lived by subsistence farming. The new democratic government, run by the *Sejm* (parliament), tried to legislate the redistribution of large estates

National Minorities in Postwar Central Europe

Western Slavs	Southern Slavs	Eastern Slavs	
Polish	Serbian*	Great Russians	German
Czech	Croatian	Belarusan	Estonian
Slovak	Slovenian	Ukranian	Latvian
	Bosnian		Lithuanian
* Serbian and Serbian-speaking Muslims	Bulgarian		Magyar
	Macedonian		Albanian
			Romanian

to the peasantry, but declining crop prices and over-population made life in the countryside difficult. Urban workers were better off compared to the peasantry but worse off compared to laborers across Europe. The economic downturn brought strikes and violence in 1922–1923, and the inability of coalition parliaments to effect economic prosperity led to a coup in 1926 by strongman General Jozef Pilsudski. Pilsudski brought order to a country choked by the endless debates of dozens of political parties and impaired by ethnic strife. Poland was not the only country to reject liberal government: Admiral Miklós Horthy (1868–1957), after putting down Béla Kun, ruled Hungary during the interwar years as the leader of the nationalists determined to repress Jewish and other minorities. Economic hardship and strong-arm solutions went hand in hand in east central Europe.

To the west the industrially sophisticated Weimar Republic confronted daunting challenges to making Germany democratic, even after putting down the postwar revolution. Although consumer spending revived and Germany became a center of experimentation in the arts, German political life remained precarious because so many felt nostalgia for imperial glory and loathed the Versailles treaty's restrictions. On the surface, Weimar's political system—a bicameral parliament and a chancellor responsible to the lower house—appeared similar to the parliamentary system in Britain and France, but extremist politicians heaped daily abuse on Germany's leaders. Contempt for parliamentary politics was widespread. Anyone who cooperated with "the parliamentary system," wrote a wealthy newspaper and film magnate, "is a moral cripple." Right-wing parties, supporting the defunct monarchy or envisioning a new authoritarian state, constituted a threat to democracy instead of a loyal opposition. They favored violence rather than consensus building, and nationalist thugs murdered democratic leaders. One prominent victim was industrialist and foreign minister Walter Rathenau, who had streamlined the German economy during the war; Rathenau, as a Jew, was part of a group increasingly blamed for all Germany's woes. Support for the far Right came from wealthy landowners and businessmen, white-collar workers whose standard of living had dropped during the war, and members of the lower-middle and middle classes hurt by inflation. In the forefront of these contentious groups strutted bands of disaffected youth and veterans like Adolf Hitler's "Brown Shirts."

In the wake of the Ruhr occupation of 1923, many plotted Weimar's overthrow. In November, Ludendorff and Hitler (1889–1945) with his storm troopers (the *Sturmabteilung*, or SA) launched a putsch from a beer hall in Munich. Government troops suppressed the coup, but Hitler spent less than a year in jail and Ludendorff was acquitted. Weimar judges, like most bureaucrats, were prewar holdovers and therefore reluctant to jail right-wing antirepublicans; those who plotted coups from the Left were either executed or imprisoned for life. In an age of violent politics practiced on both ends of the political spectrum, the 13 murders allegedly committed by leftists between 1919 and 1921 were punished with 8 executions and prison sentences totaling 176 years. By contrast, the 314 murders attributed to rightists during this same period drew a single life sentence and a mere 31 years in prison. For conservative bureaucrats the Freikorps were national heroes. After the mid-1920s, as the German economy surged, violent tactics and extreme political movements temporarily lost some of their appeal.

In Britain and France parties of the Right had less effect because parliamentary institutions were better established and the influential "best circles" were not plotting to restore an authoritarian monarchy. In France politicians from the conservative Right and moderate Left successively formed coalition governments whose major tasks focused on rebuilding war-torn regions and on ensuring the Germans came up with reparation money to pay for the reconstruction. Hoping to stimulate population growth after the devastating loss of life, the French parliament made distributing birth-control information illegal and abortion a capital crime.

Britain encountered a series of political problems. Postwar boom and bust and continuing strife in Ireland tarnished Lloyd George's Liberal government, and in 1924 the electorate voted in Ramsey MacDonald (1866–1937), the first Labour prime minister, in the belief that Labour could better promote international understanding and a fair deal for working people than could the Conservatives. An appealing orator at the head of a Labour-Liberal coalition, MacDonald proved inept as the

standard-bearer of Labour, for like Ebert in Germany he worried more about gaining respectability among upper-class Liberals than about serving his working-class constituency. Unable to please either group, MacDonald was defeated within a few months by the Conservative Stanley Baldwin (1867–1947), who charged his rival with being "soft on communism."

Postwar British leaders had to swallow the incredible fact that although Britain had the largest world empire, many of its industries were obsolete or in poor condition. In the ailing coal industry, prices fell and British wages plummeted once the Ruhr mines reopened. On May 3, 1926, transport, gas and electrical, printing, building, and other industrial workers joined miners in a nine-day general strike against wage cuts and dangerous conditions in the mines. The strike provoked extraordinary middle-class resistance. University students, homemakers, and businessmen drove trains, worked on docks, and replaced workers in other jobs. The strike failed to help the miners, who continued to protest alone for months after the general strike had ended. Instead, Baldwin passed antiunion laws, and some of the national unions fragmented once more into weak, local units.

The British government met bloody confrontation in Ireland over the continuing failure to implement home rule. In January 1919, leaders of the Sinn Fein movement announced Ireland's independence from Britain and created a separate parliament called the Dail Eireann. In response the government sent in the Black and Tans, an army of demobilized soldiers, who volunteered to crush the rebellion. Terror reigned in Ireland, as both the Sinn Fein and the Black and Tans—so-called because the color of their uniforms made them look like a pack of hounds—waged guerrilla warfare, taking hostages, blowing up buildings, and even shooting into crowds at soccer matches. By 1921 public outrage forced the British to negotiate a treaty declaring the Irish Free State a self-governing dominion. Ulster, a group of six counties containing a majority of Protestants, gained a

The Irish Free State and Ulster

separate status: it was self-governing but still had representation in the British Parliament. This division of Ireland, though acceptable at the moment, subsequently led to renewed violence when Irish Catholics tried to unite Ulster with independent Ireland.

European empires also encountered rebellion overseas. Colonized peoples who had fought in the war expected more rights and even independence. Fearful of losing India, British colonial forces massacred protesters at Amritsar in 1919 and put down revolts against the mandate system in Egypt and Iran early in the 1920s. The Dutch jailed political leaders in Indonesia; the French punished Indochinese nationalists. European statesmen simultaneously began seeking compromises that would allow them to keep their empires intact. For many Western politicians, maintaining empires abroad was crucial to ensuring democracy at home, for any hint of declining national prestige fed antidemocratic forces.

The Science of Labor

Along with the global political struggles, worldwide economic competition intensified. The European economy had lost many of its international markets to India, Canada, Australia, Japan, and the United States during the war. Nonetheless the war had forced European manufacturing to become more efficient and had expanded the demand for automotive and air transport, electrical products, and synthetic goods. The prewar pattern of mergers and cartels continued after 1918, giving rise to gigantic food-processing firms such as Nestlé and petroleum enterprises such as Royal Dutch Shell. Owners of large manufacturing conglomerates wielded more financial and political power than entire small countries and hired rafts of public relations officials to perform a kind of industrial diplomacy. In the 1920s many European manufacturers adopted U.S. innovations such as Henry Ford's automobile assembly line. By 1929 a Ford rolled off the line in the Ford Motor Company in Detroit every ten seconds. Ford touted this miracle of productivity as a way to lower the cost of living and better the lot of workers.

Scientific management, sometimes called the science of work, also aimed to raise productivity. By timing a variety of methods workers used to

accomplish tasks, the American efficiency expert Frederick Taylor demonstrated that people worked inefficiently. He developed methods to streamline workers' tasks and motions. American industrial psychologist Dr. Lillian Gilbreth and her husband, engineer Frank Gilbreth, pioneered more precise studies of work by filming workers fitted with electric lights. The projection then transformed the movement into paths of light by which experts could determine more "efficient" motions workers should use. European industrialists adopted Taylor's methods during the war and after, but many of them were also influenced by European psychologists who emphasized the mental aspects of productivity. Their studies illuminated the need for balanced workdays and leisure activities, such as cinema and sports, for both workers and managers.

Many industrial experts feared that bolshevism would inspire class conflict, and they believed that increased productivity would bind workers and management together. In theory, managers would reap enhanced output and profits, and workers would be rewarded with shorter hours and higher wages. In practice, workers argued, the emphasis on efficiency was inhuman. Often they were allowed to use the bathroom only on a fixed schedule. "When I left the factory, it followed me," wrote one. "In my dreams I was a machine." In German mines conveyor belts ended the backbreaking work of hauling but made miners' jobs more monotonous and psychologically stressful. Streamlining did, however, help reduce hours in many industries.

The managerial sector in industry had expanded during the war and continued to do so thereafter. Managers reorganized work procedures and classified workers' skills; workers' initiative became devalued, with managers alone seen as creative and innovative. They categorized "female" jobs as those requiring less skill and therefore deserving of lower wages, thus adapting the old segmentation of the labor market to the new working conditions. With male workers' jobs increasingly threatened by labor-saving machinery, unions usually agreed that women should receive lower wages to keep them from competing with men for scarce well-paying jobs.

Union bureaucracy had ballooned during World War I to help monitor labor's part in the war. Union leaders cooperated with their former antagonists in management and government to settle questions ranging from the creation of a lighter, less potent beer to plans for the reintegration of veterans into industry. Union membership grew in many areas: the Italian farm workers' union doubled in size to nearly five hundred thousand in 1919 and then almost doubled again to more than nine hundred thousand in 1920. Union bureaucracies became specialized, composed of negotiators, membership organizers, educators and propagandists, and political liaisons. They often used ruthless tactics to control smaller, maverick groups. When local activists set up workers' councils in imitation of the Bolsheviks, national labor leaders encouraged government officials to root out troublemakers. Unions could mobilize masses of people, as they demonstrated during the 1920 coup attempt against the Weimar government and in the 1926 general strike in Great Britain. Although their lobbying efforts were often less successful than those of manufacturers' associations, unions played a key role in mass politics.

Homes for Heroes

With combined joy and trepidation, postwar society welcomed the returning millions of brutalized, incapacitated, and shell-shocked veterans. Many veterans harbored enormous hostility toward those who had remained home. Civilians had rebelled against wartime conditions, some soldiers charged, instead of patriotically enduring them. The world the veterans returned to differed from the home they left: women had cut their hair, wore clothes with a streamlined cut, smoked, held jobs, and had money of their own. In contrast, veterans often had no jobs; and some soldiers found that wives and sweethearts had abandoned them—a wrenching betrayal for those who had risked their lives to protect the homeland.

United in exhilaration when the war erupted, civilians, especially women, sometimes felt estranged from these returning warriors, who had inflicted so much death and who had lived daily with filth, rats, and decaying animal and human flesh. Their anxieties were often valid. Tens of thousands of German, central European, and Italian soldiers refused to disband; a few British veterans even vandalized university classrooms and assaulted women streetcar conductors and factory workers. Women who

had served on the front could empathize with the soldiers' woes, but they were the exception. Many suffragists in England, who had fought for an end to separate spheres before the war, now embraced sex segregation, so shocked were they by the vision of brutalized veterans. Social Democratic women in Germany worked less for political integration with men and more for welfare organizations for women and families. Many activists eliminated rights for working and professional women from their agendas in favor of fighting for a separate, protected sphere in the family. This switch in emphasis caused many to believe that feminism was dead as a political issue.

Fearing bolshevism, governments tried to make civilian life more comfortable as a way of reintegrating men into society and preventing revolution. Believing in the stabilizing power of traditional family values, politicians supported social programs as a way of alleviating pent-up anger and rewarding society for its endurance. These programs included pension plans for veterans, stipends for war widows, and benefits for out-of-work men. Building housing—"homes for heroes," politicians called them—addressed another civilian need neglected in wartime.

The new housing was a vast improvement over nineteenth-century working-class tenements. In Vienna, Frankfurt, Berlin, and Stockholm, modern housing projects furnished collective laundries, day-care centers, and rooms for group socializing. Often benefiting the more highly paid skilled workers, the new housing featured gardens, terraces, and balconies to provide a soothing, country ambience that offset the hectic nature of industrial life. The houses boasted modern kitchens, indoor plumbing, central heating, and electricity, and avoided the moldings, plaster work, and curlicues of old-fashioned dwellings. Architects for these projects became part of a "planning mania," and by the late 1920s some worked on a gigantic scale to cut costs and to deal with the problem of urban crowding. German architect Ludwig Hilbersheimer and Swiss-born Le Corbusier favored "high rise" apartments that adopted the principles of New York's skyscrapers and arranged them according to criteria of "urban planning" that called for an efficient use of space.

War had dissolved many middle-class conventions, among them attempts to keep unmarried young men and women apart. Freer relationships and more open discussions of sex occurred in the 1920s. Unmarried women of wealthy families no longer needed chaperones when on the streets or in the company of young men. Middle-class youth of both sexes visited jazz clubs together, attended movies, and began keeping company in cars. Revealing bathing suits, short skirts, and body-hugging clothing publicized women's sexuality, seeming to invite men and women to join together and replenish the postwar population. Still, the context for sexuality remained marriage. In 1918, Marie Stopes published the best-seller *Married Love,* which featured frank discussions of sexual relations. In 1927 the wildly successful *Ideal Marriage: Its Physiology and Technique* by Dutch author Theodor van de Velde appeared. Translated into dozens of languages, van de Velde's book, as Stopes's had, described sex in rhapsodic terms and offered precise information about birth control and sexual physiology. Changing ideas about sex were not limited to the middle and upper classes: a Viennese reformer described working-class marriage as "an erotic-comradely relationship of equals," rather than the economic partnership of past centuries. The flapper, a sexually liberated working woman, replaced the household drudge as the image of the ordinary woman. Meanwhile such writers as D. H. Lawrence and Ernest Hemingway glorified men's sexual vigor. Images of sexually compatible men and women served to bridge the gap between home- and battlefront that had caused such anxiety as the war ended.

As standard images of men and women changed, people paid more attention to bodily improvement. The increasing use of toothbrushes and toothpaste, safety and electrical razors, and deodorants reflected new standards for personal hygiene and grooming. For women a multibillion-dollar cosmetics industry sprang up almost overnight. Women went to beauty parlors regularly to maintain their short hair and to have it set, dyed, conditioned, straightened, or permanently curled. They also tweezed their eyebrows, applied makeup, and even submitted to cosmetic surgery. Ordinary women painted their faces as formerly prostitutes alone had done and competed in beauty contests that judged facial and bodily appearance. Instead of wanting to look plump and prosperous, people dieted or embraced vegetarianism to become

Italian Magazine Cover in the Jazz Age, 1921
Snappy dancing to lively music was one form of postwar release in the West.

thin. The proliferation of boxers, hikers, gymnasts, and tap dancers spurred people to exercise and to participate in amateur sports. The consumer focus on bodily health coincided with modern industry's need for a physically fit workforce. Moreover, women found release and a whole new pastime in the public world of shopping—a role some saw as a poor substitute for the "angel in the house" of Victorian times.

As prosperity returned, people could afford to buy more consumer goods, thanks to a gradual postwar increase in real wages. The middle and upper classes bought sleek modern furniture, washing machines, and vacuum cleaners; thousands of other items such as electric irons, iceboxes, and stoves became standard in better-off working-class families. Installment buying, popularized from the 1920s on, helped ordinary people finance these purchases. Household work became more mechanized, and family intimacy increasingly depended

Postwar Fashions for Women
Women wore streamlined clothing, bobbed their hair, and left more of their bodies exposed after the war. Whereas the "new woman" of the 1880s was middle class, now working women adopted these modern styles and habits.

on machines like the radio, phonograph and inexpensive automobiles.

Culture for the Masses

Wartime propaganda had aimed to unite all classes against a common enemy. In the 1920s developments in education and the media continued the process of incorporating diverse groups into a homogeneous culture. War bulletins had whetted the public's craving for news and real-life stories, and sales of nonfiction books soared. After years of deprivation, people were driven to achieve material success, and they snapped up books that advised how to gain it. Henry Ford's biography, a story of social mobility and technological accomplishment, became a best-seller in Germany. With postwar

readers avidly pursuing practical knowledge, institutes and night schools became popular, and school systems promoted reading in geography, science, and history. Photographs, the radio, and movies also contributed to the formation of national culture. Films of literary classics and political events developed people's sense of a common heritage. The British government sponsored documentary films that articulated national goals. Bolshevik leaders also supported filmmaking, underwriting the work of director Sergei Eisenstein. His films *The Battleship Potemkin* (1925) and *Ten Days That Shook the World* (1927–1928) presented a Soviet view of history to Russian and international audiences.

Films incorporated familiar elements from other cultural forms. The piano accompaniment that went along with the action of silent films derived from music halls; comic characters, farcical plots, and slapstick comedy were borrowed from street or burlesque shows and from new trends in postwar living. Thus popular domestic comedies of the 1920s satirized men and women who botched the job of achieving emotional intimacy. Comedies and romances featured the flapper and made her more visible to the masses. Movies attracted some 100 million weekly viewers, the majority of them women. Popular books and films crossed national borders easily, in the process creating a culture that reached an international audience.

Cinematic portrayals also played to postwar fantasies and fears. In Germany, where filmmakers used expressionist sets and costumes to make films more frightening, the influential hit *The Cabinet of Doctor Caligari* (1919) used events in an insane asylum as horrifying symbols of state power. Fritz Lang's classic *Metropolis* (1926) showed technological forces in modern life as wildly and destructively out of control. Popular detective and cowboy films portrayed heroes who could restore the disordered world of murder, crime, and injustice to wholeness. Depictions of the plight of gangsters appealed to war veterans, who had been exposed to the cheap value of life in the modern world. The films of director G. W. Pabst awakened anxieties about cross-class sexual attraction; they also presented complex women characters, who did not fit such simple stereotypes as the flapper. Comedian Charlie Chaplin's "Little Tramp" won international popularity as the defeated hero, the anonymous modern man, trying to keep his dignity in a mechanical world.

In the 1920s filmmaking changed from an experimental medium to a big, international business. Pioneering filmmakers had written, directed, produced, and starred in their own movies and hired little-known performers. The war years, when the U.S. film industry began to outstrip the European, gave rise to the specialization of cinematic function in which directors, producers, marketers, photographers, film editors, and many others subdivided the process. A star system turned film personalities into celebrities, highly admired and living like royalty. Stars and directors worked within a "studio," or large corporate structure, that set up theater chains and marketed films worldwide. To help sell films, fan magazines and paraphernalia like dolls, dishes, and decorative objects bearing stars' faces made movies part of daily life.

Nightmares from the Past, Bold Visions of the Future

Despite all efforts to reestablish social and economic order, the age of recovery was also an age of dissatisfaction with the very idea of returning to "normalcy." After the experience of war, some saw in normalcy a return to effete democracy and submission to mass culture. Thinkers like the Spanish poet José Ortega y Gasset urged artists to form an experimental avant-garde that refused to cater to "the drab mass of society." Elite modern art, inaccessible to the masses, prepared the ground for avant-garde politics, in which authoritative and visionary leaders directed rather than heeded the voice of the people.

By the end of the 1920s, strongmen had come to power in Hungary, Poland, Romania, the Soviet Union, and Italy by exploiting popular discontent and the glamor attached to bold, militaristic leadership. Regimes in Poland and Hungary resembled old-fashioned dictatorships. By contrast, Italian fascism under Benito Mussolini (1883–1945) and bolshevism under Lenin and Joseph Stalin (1879–1953) deliberately aimed to look dynamic and modern, even utopian. These undemocratic movements employed outright violence to maintain power and thus reversed the century-old trend toward democratization and consensus politics. Many Westerners were impressed by the tough efficiency of the fascists and communists in curing the postwar malaise; they overlooked the brutality because compared with the war it seemed tame. From the 1920s on, these cultural and political programs profoundly weakened democratic principles.

Disillusionment and Dreams in the Arts

Whereas the mass media often depicted the return to the comfortable middle-class values of the belle époque, or good old days, artists recalled the war in all its brutality. Germany's Kaethe Köllwitz (1867–1945), whose son died in the war, portrayed bereaved parents, starving children, and other heart-wrenching, pacifistic images in her woodcuts. Other artists employed satire, irony, and flippancy to express postwar rage and revulsion at civilization's apparent failure. George Grosz, stunned by the carnage like so many other German veterans, joined the *dada* movement, which was committed to savage expressions of alienation. His paintings and cartoons of maimed soldiers, brutal capitalists, and grotesque women reflected his psychic wounds and his desire "to bellow back." Dadaist bellowing continued the modernist tradition of shocking the audience, only the shocks were more savage and often more hateful of ordinary people. Avant-garde portrayals of seediness and perversion in everyday life flourished in cabarets and theaters in the 1920s and reinforced veterans' visions of civilian decadence.

A battle erupted in Germany over the war's lessons, that is, over the conflict's meaning for postwar life. Popular writers such as Ernst Jünger glorified life in the trenches and called for the militarization of society to restore order. Erich Maria Remarque (1898–1970) cried out for an end to war in his controversial *All Quiet on the Western Front* (1928). This international best-seller depicted the common life shared by enemies on the battlefield, thus dampening the national hatred stoked by wartime propaganda. For the British, World War I was the Great War, but the battle over the war's meaning in German novels paralleled the Weimar Republic's contentious politics.

Kaethe Köllwitz,
The Survivors
Depicting the plight of ordinary people before the war, the work of Köllwitz took on a special poignancy afterward. It showed starving children, wounded veterans, and bereaved families.

Poets reflected on postwar conditions in more general terms, using styles that rejected the comforting rhymes or accessible metaphors of earlier verse. T. S. Eliot (1888–1965), an American-born poet who for a time worked as a banker in Britain, portrayed postwar life as petty and futile in "The Wasteland" (1922) and "The Hollow Men" (1925). The Irish nationalist poet William Butler Yeats joined Eliot in bemoaning the replacement of traditional society's moral conviction and religious values by a new, superficial generation gaily dancing to jazz and engaging in promiscuous sex and vacuous conversation. Yeats's "Sailing to Byzantium" (1928) starts:

*That is no country for old men. The young
In one another's arms, birds in the trees
—Those dying generations . . .*

Both poets had an uneasy relationship with the modern world and at times advocated authoritarianism rather than democracy.

The arts produced utopian and dystopian fantasies of life in postrevolutionary Europe. Russian intellectuals, temporarily entranced by Soviet utopianism, optimistically wrote novels about cement factories, plays about robots, and ballets about steel. Franz Kafka (1883–1924), an employee of a large insurance company in Prague, saw the world as a vast, impersonal machine. His novels *The Trial* (1925) and *The Castle* (1926) evoked both the hopeless condition of the individual confronting a relentless, coglike society and the personal guilt provoked by the presence of authorities ranging from fathers to the modern corporation or the state. Kafka's bizarre stories, for example of a salesman who wakes up one morning and discovers he has turned into a gigantic insect, resonated as nightmarish fables of postwar modernity.

Some novelists abandoned the social themes of nineteenth-century writers and concentrated on the intense and complex inner life of individuals. Marcel Proust (1871–1922), in his multivolume novel *Remembrance of Things Past* (1913–1927), explored the workings of memory, the passage of time, and sexual modernity through the life of a narrator who at the outset of the first book is obsessed with his mother's company as he tries to fall asleep at night. The narrator witnesses progressively more disturbing obsessions, such as violent sexuality and personal betrayals of love. At the end the narrator, moved by remembered sensations from his past, such as those induced by drinking tea and eating a kind of French cake called a madeleine, decides to write a novel about his past. For Proust redemption lay in producing beauty from the raw material of life, not in promoting outmoded conventions of decency and morality.

Irish writer James Joyce (1882–1941) and British writer Virginia Woolf (1882–1941) shared Proust's vision of an interior self built on memories and sensations. Joyce's *Ulysses* (1922) and Woolf's *Mrs. Dalloway* (1925) illuminate the complex inner lives of their characters in the course of a single day. In one of *Ulysses'* most celebrated passages, a pages-long interior monologue traces a woman's lifetime of erotic and emotional sensations. For Woolf the war had dissolved the solid society from which absorbing stories and fascinating characters were once fashioned. Her characters experience fragmented conversations, momentary sensations, and incomplete relationships. Woolf's strange novel *Orlando* (1928) portrays a hero who participates in centuries of history and eventually changes from a man into a woman.

Woolf lived with a group of upper-class intellectuals in the Bloomsbury section of London. Like the Parisian circle headed by the American writer Gertrude Stein (1874–1946), the Bloomsbury group of writers and artists saw themselves as part of an unconventional avant-garde devising new artistic forms and setting future standards. Although many of these artists pondered aesthetic questions that seemed totally irrelevant to ordinary people's concerns, others wanted to redirect postwar arts toward rationality, science, and technology. The aim of art, observed one of them, "is not to decorate our life but to organize it." The group of German artists called the Bauhaus (after the idea of a craft association, or *baühutte*) created streamlined office buildings and designed functional furniture, utensils, and decorative objects. Many artists worked in large collectives where, under the guidance of intellectuals such as the Bauhaus's Walter Gropius (1883–1969), they staged shows of modern products that also turned a profit.

Artists fascinated by technology and machinery were drawn to the most modern of all countries—the United States. Hollywood films, glossy advertisements, and the modern metropolis of New York attracted careworn Europeans. They were especially attracted to jazz, the improvisational music that emanated from Harlem. African-American jazz musicians showed a resiliency of spirit in the face of racial discrimination that inspired Europeans, and performers like Josephine Baker (1906–1976) and Louis Armstrong (1900–1971) became international sensations when they toured Europe's capital cities. Like jazz, the New York skyscraper pointed to the future. Skyscrapers seemed to show how engineering and architectural genius could break the bounds of city space instead of being confined by it. Europeans found in New York a potent example of avant-garde expression that rejected a terrifying past and boldly shaped the future.

The Communist Vision

Communism also promised a shining future, but despite ending the civil war, the Bolsheviks encountered powerful obstacles to consolidating their rule. Although the Red Army and Cheka tried to crush opposition as quickly as it cropped up, peasant bands called Green Armies revolted in the early 1920s against War Communism and prohibitions on private trade in agricultural produce. Other circumstances further complicated Bolshevik plans: industrial production stood at only 13 percent of its prewar output; the civil war had produced massive casualties; shortages of crops, livestock, and housing affected the entire population; and millions of refugees desperately sought food and shelter. In the early spring of 1921, workers in Petrograd and sailors at the naval base at Kronstadt revolted, calling for "Soviets without Communists." Workers protested their short rations and the privileged standard of living Bolshevik supervisors enjoyed; the sailors, whose Kronstadt community was a model of cooperative socialism, wanted a return to the early promises of the Bolsheviks for a worker state and an end to "Commissarocracy."

Lenin raged that the sailors were merely reactionary "petty bourgeois" and Trotsky had many of the rebels shot, but Kronstadt pushed Lenin to institute reform. During the Kronstadt revolt he announced the first steps in the New Economic Policy (NEP), substituting a fixed tax on production for requisitions of grain. Subsequent laws returned parts of the economy to the free market, a temporary compromise with capitalist methods that allowed peasants to control their grain sales and to profit from free trade in consumer goods. Although the state still controlled large industries and banking, the NEP encouraged people to produce, to sell, and even, in the words of one leading communist, to "get rich." Goods to buy and more food to eat soon became available. Some peasants and merchants did indeed get rich, but many more remained impoverished. The rise of "NEPmen," who bought and furnished splendid homes and who cared only about improving their standard of living, belied the Bolshevik credo of a classless utopia.

Bolsheviks were not immune to protest from within. At the 1921 party congress a group called the Worker Opposition objected to the Party's usurpation of economic control from worker organizations. The group favored trade-union leadership of industry and pointed out that the NEP was an agrarian program, not a proletarian one. Because of the NEP, other critics charged, prostitutes, criminals, and bourgeois capitalists thrived. In response to such criticism of growing bureaucratization, Lenin put down the Worker Opposition faction in 1921 and set up procedures for purging dissident Bolsheviks.

As the Bolshevik leaders tightened their grip on politics, they also drove the revolution to become a cultural reality that would inform people's daily lives and reshape their thoughts. Lenin called for widespread participation in creating the Soviet utopia: "Take over all state affairs. Get to work right there, at the grass roots, without waiting for orders." Party leaders invaded the countryside to set up classes, and volunteers harangued the public about the importance of literacy—only 40 percent on the eve of World War I. To facilitate social equality between the sexes, the state made birth control, abortion, and divorce readily available. As commissar for public welfare, Aleksandra Kollontai (1872–1952) promoted birth-control education and programs to offer day care for children of working parents as well as those to provide housing, medical care, and pensions for soldiers and workers. The ravages of civil war, however, prevented many of these programs from having much practical or long-lasting effect.

Lenin's wife and co-worker in the Bolshevik movement, Nadezhda Krupskaya, hoped that the spread of education would thwart growing bureaucratization: "Let us not be afraid of the people. . . . Our job is to help the people . . . to take their fate into their own hands." During the early years of improvised rule, the bureaucracy nonetheless swelled, spawning such agencies as the Zhenotdel (Women's Bureau), which sought to teach women about their rights under socialism and about modern hygienic practices. Semiofficial institutes and associations brought the methods of Ford and Taylor into factories, the army, the arts, and everyday life. *Timeists,* as efficiency experts were called, aimed to replace tsarist backwardness with technological modernity.

Journalists, writers, and artists organized dozens of associations that received government support for cultural activities. The short-lived Proletkult aimed to develop proletarian culture through such undertakings as worker universities, a workers' encyclopedia, workers' theater, and workers' publishing. Its members argued heatedly about whether the old elite culture could be integrated into the socialist one, a strategy Lenin favored, or whether it had to be thrown out, as avant-garde intellectuals like the "futurists" believed. In the 1920s, Soviet culture maintained the rebelliousness of prewar experimental theater, abstract art, and free verse.

Many Soviet artists experimented with blending high art, technology, and mass culture. Composers punctuated their music with the sound of train or factory whistles. Other artists stressed the artistic value of such crafts as textile design, printed posters, and woodworking. The poet Vladimir Mayakovsky edited a journal advocating utilitarian art, wrote poetry praising his Soviet passport and essays promoting toothbrushing, and staged uproarious farces for ordinary citizens. Aleksandra Kollontai's novels about love and work in the new socialist society employed a simple style so less-educated women might read them. The Bolsheviks confiscated mansions and imperial buildings and turned them into galleries that displayed works of art to the masses. Some artists despaired at the political turn art was taking and went into exile; a few even committed suicide.

As with War Communism, many resisted the reshaping of culture. Early communist theories of

E.L. Lissitzky, **Design for the Lenin Tribune,** *1920*
Lissitzky was an avant-garde artist who caught the revolutionary fever, seeing in a marriage of communism and the arts a way to "affirm the new."

In the spring of 1922, Lenin suffered a debilitating stroke, and in January 1924, amidst ongoing experimentation, turmoil, factional fighting, and repression, he died. The Party congress declared the day of his death a permanent Soviet holiday and changed the name of Petrograd to Leningrad. Lenin's funeral, stunning for its pomp, gave a new direction to Soviet political life by elevating the deceased leader into a sort of secular god. After Lenin's death, no one was allowed to criticize anything associated with Lenin's name, a situation that paved the way for future abuses of power by Soviet leaders.

Stalin, who served in the powerful post of general secretary of the Communist party, led the deification of Lenin. Both organizing the Lenin cult and dealing with thousands of local Party officials gave him enormous national patronage, and his welding of non-Russian regions into the Union of Soviet Social Republics (1924) gave him a claim to executive accomplishment. Lenin had become wary of Stalin's growing influence and ruthlessness and asked in his last will that "the comrades find a way to remove Stalin." Stalin, however, prevented Lenin's will from being publicized to the Party. He proceeded to discredit his chief rival, Trotsky, by emphasizing the necessity of building socialism in the Soviet Union alone and thus making Trotsky look like an unpatriotic internationalist who was unwilling to concentrate on the tough job of modernizing the USSR. Stalin even made Trotsky's revolutionary eminence appear disrespectful or "un-Leninist" at a time when Leninism was becoming the test of orthodoxy. Next Stalin took on the so-called Right—those who had supported the NEP compromise—and then advanced his power by bringing in several hundred thousand new Party members, called the "Lenin enrollment." These new members owed their position to Stalin, and they contributed to his march toward complete dictatorship.

Fascism on the March

A second figure promising an efficient utopia was the fascist leader Mussolini, brought to power on a wave of postwar discontent and political chaos. Italian ire was first aroused when the Allies at Paris refused to honor the Treaty of London's territorial promises. Domestic unrest swelled when peasants, who had made great sacrifices at the front,

education were often progressive and Western and thus seemed immoral and lax to traditional educators. Bolsheviks also threatened everyday customs and the distribution of power within the family. As Zhenotdel workers moved into the countryside, for example, they attempted to teach women to behave as men's equals. Peasant families were still strongly patriarchal, however, and Zhenotdel activists threatened gender relations. In Islamic regions, Bolsheviks urged Muslim women to remove their veils and change their way of life, but the native people murdered or assaulted both Zhenotdel workers and women who followed their advice.

protested their serflike status in Italian society. Workers demanded the right to organize; some even seized factories to draw attention to their cause. Finally, the economic slump of the early 1920s increased misery in everyday life, and Italians blamed the parliamentary government. Mussolini, a socialist journalist who turned to the radical Right, had long hated parliamentarism, and he built a personal army of veterans and the unemployed to overturn it. In 1922, his supporters, known as Fascists, started a March on Rome, thus threatening a coup. King Victor Emmanuel III (*1900–1946) asked the dynamic Mussolini to become prime minister and revive the country.

The Fascist movement flourished in the soil of poverty, social unrest, and wounded national pride. It attracted to its bands of "Black Shirts" many young men who felt cheated of glory by the Allies and veterans who missed the vigor of military life. The *fasces,* an ancient Roman symbol depicting a bundle of sticks wrapped around an ax handle with the blade exposed, served as the movement's emblem; it represented both unity and force to Mussolini's supporters. Fascism offered a less-developed ideology than Marxism but fashioned its rejection of theory into a virtue. "Fascism is not a church," Mussolini announced upon taking power in 1922. "It is more like a training ground." Fascism depended on an elite minority to smash the antinationalist socialist movement and to destroy the impotent parliament and bureaucracy.

Mussolini consolidated his power by putting himself at the head of government departments, by making criticism of the state a criminal offense, and by steamrolling parliamentary opposition. His Fascist bands demolished Socialist newspaper offices, attacked striking workers, and used their favorite tactic of forcing castor oil (which caused diarrhea) down the throats of Socialists. They even murdered certain powerful opponents such as the moderate Socialist parliamentary deputy Giacomo Matteotti.

Mussolini's Black Shirts
The war helped militarize politics, making obedience, wearing uniforms, and violence valued aspects of political behavior.

Despite their brutality, the sight of the Black Shirts marching through the streets like disciplined soldiers seemed a signal to many Italians that social order would be restored. Large landowners and businessmen approved Fascist attacks on strikers, and they generously supported the movement. This ample funding allowed Mussolini to build a large staff by hiring the unemployed and thus made it look as if Fascists could spark the economy when no one else could.

In addition to violence, Mussolini used mass propaganda and the media to foster support. Peasant men huddled around radios to hear him call for a "battle of wheat" to enhance farm productivity. Peasant women, hearing his praise for maternal duty, adulated him. In the cities the government launched modernist architectural projects, designed new statues and public adornments, and used public relations promoters to advertise its achievements. Some modernist intellectuals liked the Fascists' avoidance of debate in favor of action and clamored to take part in Mussolini's promotion of avant-garde culture. Mussolini claimed that he had made the trains run on time, and this one triumph of modern technology persuaded people to think that other victories would follow.

Mussolini added a strong dose of traditional values and prejudices to his modern order. Although an atheist, he recognized the importance of Catholicism to most Italians. In 1929 he signed the Lateran Agreement with the church, which resolved tensions with the papacy that dated from the wars of unification. The Lateran Agreement regularized the borders of Vatican City and put it under papal sovereignty. The government recognized the church's right to determine marriage and family doctrine and endorsed its role in education. In return the church ended its criticism of Fascist tactics. Next Mussolini introduced a "corporate" state in which individual political rights were denied in favor of a system that emphasized people's duty to the state. Corporatist decrees in 1926 organized employers, workers, and professionals into groups or corporations that would settle grievances and determine conditions of work through state-controlled channels. These decrees outlawed independent labor unions and eliminated peasant political groups, effectively ending political or workplace activism. Mussolini drew more applause from business leaders when he cut women's wages by decree; and then late in the 1920s won the approval of civil servants, lawyers, and professors by banning women from those professions. Mussolini did not want women out of the workforce altogether but wanted to ensure their relegation to low-paying jobs.

Mussolini's admirers included Adolf Hitler, who throughout the 1920s had been building a paramilitary group of storm troopers and a political organization called the National Socialist German Workers' Party, or Nazis. Hitler was fascinated by the March on Rome, by Mussolini's legal accession to power, and by his ability to thwart Socialists and trade unionists. But the austere conditions that had allowed Mussolini to rise to power in 1922 no longer existed in Germany. Although Hitler was welding the Nazi party into a strong political instrument, parliamentary government in Weimar was actually working as the decade wore on, bringing relative prosperity, and the future for authoritarian movements there was uncertain.

CONCLUSION

Just as 1914 had been, 1929 was to prove a fateful year. The Great War had begun amidst certainty that it would resolve international tensions and social problems. Instead it had wrought unbelievable suffering, socialist revolution, and a fundamental questioning of traditional values. The 1920s was a decade devoted almost exclusively to coming to terms with the consequences of the war, whether economic, diplomatic, political, or cultural. The variety of responses—from utter despair to utopian hopes for international peace or more efficient political order—hung heavily in the air when the United States stock market crashed in 1929. The economic depression and renewed desperation that would unfold in the 1930s made authoritarian solutions look even more appealing. Capitalizing on the anxieties and discontent unleashed by war and revolution, modern dictators attacked civilized values and unleashed a catastrophe even more devastating than World War I.

SUGGESTIONS FOR FURTHER READING

Source Materials

Brittain, Vera. *Testament of Youth.* 1933. An English woman's tale of war both as a civilian and as a war nurse.

Hasek, Jaroslav. *The Good Soldier Schweik.* 1920. Describes the misadventures of a soldier in the Austro-Hungarian army.

Kollontai, Aleksandra. *Love of Worker Bees.* 1923. Tells the story of a Russian woman resolving the tensions between love and work in a new, communist way.

Interpretive Studies

Ellis, John. *A Social History of the Machine-Gun.* 1986. Explains how one particular weapon and other technology changed the face of war.

Fitzpatrick, Sheila. *The Russian Revolution.* 1982. A concise and readable summary.

Green, Christopher. *Cubism and Its Enemies: Modern Movements and Reaction in French Art, 1916–1928.* 1987. Relates how surrealism and dadaism challenged more abstract forms of art.

Gruber, Helmut. *Red Vienna: Experiment in Working-Class Culture, 1919–1934.* 1991. Discusses one example of housing, recreational, and other social-welfare activities in the interwar years.

Harsch, Donna. *German Social Democracy and the Rise of Nazism.* 1994. Discusses Weimar social and economic policy, especially as it paved the way for Nazism.

Hayman, Ronald. *Kafka: A Biography.* 1981. Explores the life and works of a disturbed genius.

Higgonet, Margaret Randolph, Jean Jenson, Sonya Michel, and Margaret Collins Weitz, eds. *Behind the Lines: Gender and the Two World Wars.* 1987. A major collection of interpretive essays showing the ways in which gender affects the course of war.

Hynes, Samuel. *A War Imagined: The First World War and English Culture.* 1991. A rich depiction of how the war was changed from a horrible frontline experience into an exciting story for mass consumption.

Jelavich, Barbara. *History of the Balkans: Twentieth Century.* 1983. An important and scholarly study of a conflicted area.

Kent, Susan. *Making Peace: The Reconstruction of Gender in Postwar Britain.* 1994. An innovative interpretation of the experience of war and its effect on interwar society.

Kitchen, Martin. *Europe Between the Wars: A Political History.* 1988. A lively account of domestic and international policy in troubled times.

Kocka, Jürgen. *Facing Total War: German Society, 1914–1918.* 1984. Examines the unprecedented mobilization of an entire people and its institutional results.

Leed, Eric J. *No Man's Land: Combat and Identity in World War I.* 1979. Looks at what war meant in human terms to soldiers.

Lyttleton, Adrian. *The Seizure of Power: Fascism in Italy, 1919–1929.* 1987. A classic treatment of Mussolini's brutal triumph.

Maier, Charles. *Recasting Bourgeois Europe: Stabilization in France, Germany, and Italy in the Decade After World War I.* 1975. An important analysis of how social power was restored after the transformations of war.

Neuberger, Joan. *Hooliganism: Crime, Culture, and Power in St. Petersburg.* 1994. An innovative study of prewar life that leads to a reinterpretation of wartime protest.

Petro, Patrice. *Joyless Streets.* 1989. A major study of film in Germany in the 1920s.

Rabinbach, Anson. *The Human Motor: Energy, Fatigue, and the Origins of Modernity.* 1990. An impressive study of theories of work, motion, and leisure, as well as an account of their implementation in the workplace.

Roberts, Mary Louise. *Civilization Without Sexes: Reconstructing Gender in Postwar France, 1917–1927.* 1994. A reinterpretation of French cultural and social life in the Jazz Age.

Schmitt, Bernadotte E., and Harold C. Vederler. *The World in the Crucible, 1914–1919.* 1984. A military, political, and diplomatic overview of the world at war.

Schwabe, Klaus. *Woodrow Wilson, Revolutionary Germany, and Peacemaking, 1918–1919: Missionary Diplomacy and the Realities of Power.* 1985. Surveys the difficulties of peace making given the political complexities of the war and the horrors it had generated.

Smith, Leonard. *Between Mutiny and Obedience: The Case of the French Fifth Infantry Division During World War I.* 1994. A fascinating account of one division's role in the mutiny and its reasons for disobedience.

Stites, Richard. *Revolutionary Dreams: Utopian Vision and Experimental Life in the Russian Revolution.* 1989. A positive evaluation of utopian plans in revolutionary times.

Travers, Tim. *The Killing Ground: The British Army, the Western Front, and the Emergence of Modern Warfare, 1900–1918.* 1987. A study of British military leaders' failure to grasp the changing aspects of warfare.

Willett, John. *The New Sobriety, 1917–1933: Art and Politics in the Weimar Period.* 1978. A well-illustrated comparative discussion of the arts in postwar Europe.

Winter, J. M., and R. M. Wall. *The Upheaval of War: Family, Work, and Welfare in Europe, 1914–1918.* 1988. An important social history of the home front.

When Etty Hillesum left home in the early 1930s to attend law school in Amsterdam, an economic depression gripped the world. A resourceful young woman, Hillesum pieced together a living as a housekeeper and part-time language teacher. The pressures and pleasures of everyday life kept her from fully comprehending the anti-semitism around her, as Adolf Hitler and other demagogues blamed her fellow Jews for the economic slump. World War II, however, ruptured her normal existence. After the German army conquered the Netherlands in 1940, Dutch Jews suffered severe deprivation and persecution, a development that forced Etty Hillesum to the shattering realization she noted in her diary in July 1942: "What they are after is our total destruction." The Nazis occupied the Netherlands and started relocating Jews to camps in Germany and Poland. Hillesum went to work for Amsterdam's Jewish Council, which was compelled to organize the transportation of Jews to the east. Changing from self-absorbed student to heroine, she did what she could to help other Jews and minutely recorded the deportation. "I wish I could live for a long time so that one day I may know how to explain it." When she was taken prisoner, she smuggled out letters witnessing the brutal treatment in the camps, serving as "the ears and eyes of a piece of Jewish history." Etty Hillesum never fulfilled her ambition of becoming a professional writer: she died in the Auschwitz death camp in November 1943.

The economic misery of the 1930s, triggered by the U.S. stock market crash of 1929, intensified social grievances that had festered in Europe since the end of World War I and helped propel brutal politicians to power.

An Age of Catastrophes, 1929–1945

Concentration Camp Life
Everyday existence in camps throughout Europe was a living hell. The use of technology and bureaucracy to exterminate millions of Jews, Slavs, gypsies, and other groups deemed inferior by the Nazis was only the most unspeakable atrocity in this age of catastrophes.

Hitler roused the German masses to poisonous outpourings of antisemitism, nationalist frenzy, and rage against the Peace of Paris. Authoritarian and fascist regimes in Portugal, Spain, Poland, and Hungary trampled on representative institutions and democratic aspirations in the name of national rejuvenation. In the Soviet Union, Stalin oversaw the USSR's rapid industrialization but in the process justified killing millions of workers, military personnel, and ordinary people who opposed his plans as the necessary price of Soviet growth.

Fearful of another massive war, concerned for their own well-being, and sometimes even lured by the authoritarian rhetoric that promised power and social order, the democracies reacted ineffectually to these menacing leaders in the 1930s. In 1939, World War II erupted as the German army overran Poland; in 1941 and 1942 Japanese forces stormed the Pacific. By late 1941 the United States and Britain had allied themselves with the Soviet Union to stop fascism in Europe and were confronting Japanese imperialism in the Far East. Tens of millions of people would perish in World War II, often civilians like Etty Hillesum. The growth of national bureaucracies and advances in technology that were supposed to improve modern life had made war even more lethal. Dictators who glorified war as the path to social order and national greatness used big government and industrial know-how to attack humane values and to set the world ablaze.

IMPORTANT DATES

1929 The U.S. stock market crashes; global depression begins; Soviet leadership initiates war against prosperous farmers, the "kulaks"; Germany's Thomas Mann wins the Nobel Prize for Literature

1930 Marlene Dietrich stars in *The Blue Angel*

1933 Hitler comes to power in Germany

1936 Show trials begin in the USSR; Stalin purges top Communist party officials and military leaders; the Spanish Civil War begins

1938 Virginia Woolf publishes *Three Guineas*

1939 Germany invades Poland; World War II begins; the Spanish Civil War ends

1940 France falls to the German army

1940–1941 The British air force fends off German attacks in the Battle of Britain

1941 Germany invades the Soviet Union; Japan attacks Pearl Harbor; the United States enters the war

1941–1945 The Holocaust

1944 Allied forces land at Normandy, France

1945 U.S. drops atomic bombs on Hiroshima and Nagasaki; World War II ends

---

The Great Depression

In 1929, with the crash of the U.S. stock market, the relative prosperity of the preceding five years ended and an era of economic depression began that would continue until the outbreak of World War II. The collapse brought financial failure, industrial breakdown, and unprecedented unemployment. As government resources for relief stretched thin, popular protests erupted throughout Europe and strikes broke out in industrial areas. Governments worried that the declining birthrate among the middle and working classes would jeopardize national vitality. The Great Depression had social and political repercussions that threatened both individual morale and democratic institutions.

Economic Disaster

For several years some 9 million Americans had recklessly "played the market." Using readily available credit, they invested with complete confidence in economists' predictions that the stock market was on a "permanently high plateau." When the Federal Reserve Bank, hoping to stabilize the market, tightened the availability of credit, brokers demanded that their clients immediately pay back the money they had borrowed to buy stock. As people sold their stocks and turned their earnings into cash to pay their brokerage bills, the market plummeted. Between early October and mid-November 1929 the value of business listed on the

Italian Newspaper Depicts the Crash on Wall Street
The Fascist press depicted the crash as bringing utter civilian chaos in contrast to Mussolini's social order. The collapse of the U.S. stock market withdrew capital from markets that depended on it around the world, with severe economic, political, and psychological repercussions.

U.S. stock market dropped from $87 billion to $30 billion.

The crash spawned a global depression because the United States, a leading international creditor, had financed the economic growth of the past five years. Suddenly strapped for credit, U.S. financiers cut back on loans and called in short-term debts, undermining banks and industry internationally but especially in central Europe. The fact that the United States had become the leading industrial power, producing 45 percent of the world's manufactured goods, compounded the collapse; Japanese industry also took business that had formerly been Europe's. From the decrepit industries of Britain to the fledgling factories of eastern Europe, a decline in consumer buying and overproduction further eroded the European economy. Despite its po-

sition as the world's leading manufacturer, the United States also reeled. By 1932, U.S. steel production had slumped to only 12 percent of its level before the crash. Consumer purchases were especially low because U.S. worker productivity had increased by 55 percent during the 1920s, whereas industrial wages had risen by only 2 percent. The Great Depression left no sector of the world economy unscathed.

The depression worsened as governments turned to orthodox methods for spurring the economy, cutting their budgets and enacting huge tariffs against foreign goods. These policies dampened trade, employment, and spending in the great industrial powers even more. In 1933 an estimated 14 million U.S. workers were unemployed, and the failure of more than five thousand banks had wiped out savings and reserves. In Germany almost 6 million workers, or about one-third of the workforce, were out of work, and many others were underemployed. France had a more self-sufficient economy, but by the mid-1930s more than eight hundred thousand French people had lost their jobs. Great Britain, with its textile, steel, and coal industries near ruin because of out-of-date techniques and foreign competition, had close to 3 million unemployed in 1932, for many the worst year of this "devil's decade."

In the agricultural sector, where prices had been declining for several years because of abundant harvests and technological innovation, creditors confiscated farms and equipment. Moreover, millions of small farmers had no money to buy the chemical fertilizers and motorized machinery they needed to remain competitive, and they too went under. Eastern and southern European peasants, who had pressed for the redistribution of land after World War I, especially suffered because they could not afford to operate their newly acquired farms. The Polish *Sejm* awarded more than 6 million acres from the vast estates of the Catholic church and nobility during the interwar years. Much of this land went to existing small landowners, but more than seven hundred thousand new farms were created. Many of these new landowners fell into debt trying to make their farms viable. Eastern European governments often ignored the farmers' plight and instead used the scarce capital to start new industries in hopes that industrial prosperity would improve the entire economy. Most of the agricultural population were left to fend for themselves in these desperate times, a situation that rent the fabric of rural society.

Social Dimensions of the Crash

Because the Great Depression affected communities unevenly, modernization proceeded in some sectors. Bordering English slums, one traveler in the mid-1930s noticed, was an "England of arterial and by-pass roads, of filling stations and factories that look like exhibition buildings, of giant cinemas and dance halls and cafés, bungalows with tiny garages, cocktail bars, Woolworth's, . . . factory girls looking like actresses, . . . [and] swimming pools." In the 1930s municipal and national governments continued electrification, road construction, and sanitation projects. Running water and sewage pipes were installed in many ordinary homes for the first time. New factories manufactured synthetic fabrics, electrical products, and other consumer goods that were still in demand. With government assistance, eastern European industry developed; Romanian industrial production, for example, increased by 55 percent between 1929 and 1939. Later in the decade munitions production soared and helped create jobs. Thus despite the depression, service workers, managers, and business magnates often enjoyed considerable prosperity in the 1930s. Some members of the old aristocracy were able to maintain their high standard of living in expensive cities by selling their country estates and castles. Lower on the social scale, people with steady employment benefited from a drastic drop in prices.

The unemployed, however, barely eked out a miserable existence. In towns with heavy industry, sometimes more than half the population was out of work. This circumstance created an atmosphere of dread: the unemployed wondered how they would stay alive, and the employed feared that they might soon join the bread lines. In England in the mid-1930s close to 20 percent of the population lacked adequate food, clothing, or housing. "We was like animals, we was like animals at home, all of us hungry. . . ," a day laborer recalled life in the 1930s. "I used to sit eating cabbage stalks cos I was that hungry." The depression also eroded self-confidence, as a German youth described in a school assignment in 1932: "My father has been out of work for two-and-a-half years. He thinks that I'll never find a job because there are 700,000 young people alone unemployed in Germany." The good life eluded many. After her pay was slashed in half, a woman in the hard-hit north of England wrote that young workers "could afford to adorn their ears with gold earrings in my mother's youth," but that in the 1930s parents talked only about "how long it would be before their offspring were able to bring in a wage packet." A thundercloud of fear and resentment settled over Western society.

Economic catastrophe upset social life, strained gender relations, and dashed expectations of a better future. Unemployment was unusually high among men under age twenty-one. Restlessness and enforced idleness led many of these young men to form gangs that rode the subways or loitered in parks all day. They intruded in areas usually frequented by mothers and their children and old people during the day, and their presence often unsettled the traditional denizens of these spaces. Sometimes unemployed men stayed home all day, increasing the tension in small, overcrowded apartments. Women could often find low-paying jobs doing laundry and cleaning house for others. While these women were out working, men who stayed at home sometimes took over housekeeping chores but often felt that this "women's work" demeaned their masculinity. This blurring of gender roles made many uncomfortable. In the past, men had defined themselves as the family breadwinners. Now women often earned the money the family lived on, and men could be seen standing on street corners, begging. This skewed version of the way things were supposed to be fueled the discontent of unemployed men throughout Europe. Men who lived in rural areas saw their traditional roles erode as well. The percentage of farm workers in the western European population decreased, causing patriarchal authority, once central in overseeing farm labor and allocating property among inheritors, to continue its decline. Demagogues berated parliamentary politicians for their failure to stop this collapse of traditional values. The climate was thus primed for Nazi and fascist politics.

Demagogues and parliamentary politicians did agree on one issue: the falling birthrate alarmed them. After a brief postwar upturn, the birthrate

The Unemployed in Britain
The Depression had an uneven impact on occupational groups and industries. It frequently made women the sole breadwinners in families because they could continue to find menial or part-time work.

plummeted; in many industrial countries by the early 1930s, it stood at half or less than half of turn-of-the-century levels. In difficult economic times, people chose to have fewer children. A British scientist calculated that given the 1930 birthrate, England and Wales would have only 2 million inhabitants in 1985. Mandatory education and more required years of schooling, both enforced more strictly than before World War I, resulted in greater expenses for workers. Children no longer brought in wages to supplement the family's income; the cost of feeding, clothing, and sheltering them while they went to school proved a financial liability for their already strapped parents. Also at this time, pioneers in family planning were spreading knowledge of birth control to the working and lower-middle classes. By 1939, Britain's Family Planning Association, founded by Marie Stopes and others, numbered more than sixty clinics. In the United States, Margaret Sanger, working with the medical profession, led a similar organization to make birth-control devices accessible.

In eastern Europe the overall birthrate dropped even though the population in rural areas rose, a phenomenon that worsened economic conditions. More sophisticated medical knowledge caused the infant mortality rate to decrease and life expectancy to increase—mirroring what had happened earlier in the west. Overpopulation and economic catastrophe compounded the burdens of eastern European farm families, and people who lived off the land faced an unprecedented struggle for survival. Rural unrest weakened the fragile new states created after World War I. Early in the 1930s, Polish peasants refused to pay new taxes and blockaded debt-laden farms about to be confiscated. Hundreds of casualties followed as peasants and police collided. Financial woes helped infect peasant political parties with antisemitism. The parties blamed Jewish bankers for farm foreclosures and Jewish civil servants for new taxes and inadequate relief programs. They maintained that the good jobs Jews held should be filled by Christians. Other minority peoples fared little better; the dominant nationality groups in Hungary, Yugoslavia, Romania, and elsewhere purged ethnic minorities from jobs. Economic misery, in tandem with demographic changes, elicited antisemitism, ethnic chau-

Gypsies in Romania in the 1930s
*Gypsies fared badly in eastern Europe in this decade.
During the Holocaust they were one of the groups tar-
geted by the Nazis for extermination.*

vinism, and rural violence and sapped social stability in the new eastern European states.

Global Challenges

Britain and France believed their colonies were
critical to maintaining their international prestige
and restoring their economic viability. Because
protectionism had caused trade among the most
industrialized powers to decline, the rich nations
looked increasingly to colonized or less-developed areas for new markets for their manufactured goods. World War I and postwar investment
had generated economic growth in Asia, Africa,
and Latin America. Economic expansion had
brought profound demographic alterations, rural
emigration, and explosive urban growth. Between
1920 and 1940, Shanghai ballooned from 1.7 million to 3.75 million residents, Calcutta from 1.8

million to 3.4 million, and Cairo from 865,000 to
1.5 million.

Colonial city-dwellers chafed more under
foreign domination than did inhabitants of isolated
agricultural areas. When the Great Depression affected fledgling enterprises in developing areas, it
added to other, smoldering grievances. Millions of
African and Asian colonial troops had fought for
Britain and France in World War I, and these veterans deeply resented British and French indifference and ingratitude. Especially offensive to non-
white colonial leaders, the League of Nations
charter had pointedly omitted any reference to the
principle of racial equality. Furthermore, the growing economic power of Japan continued to provide
colonized peoples a model of non-European success.
Moved by the Wilsonian ideal of self-determination
and inspired by Japan's example, colonial people
increasingly set their sights on winning Western-style
autonomy—at exactly the time Western powers
most wanted to keep their allegiance *and* the profits of their economic development.

The British government loosened its formal
political ties to the *dominions* (Canada, New
Zealand, Australia, the Irish Free State, and the
Union of South Africa) with the Statute of West-
minster (1931), which instituted the British Commonwealth of Nations. The commonwealth's tariffs against outsiders effectively created a group of
trading partners. India was not included in the
commonwealth, however, and became the arena
for a momentous struggle against colonial domination. Upper-class Indians, who had organized to
reform in the late nineteenth century, were joined
in the 1930s by millions of ordinary people, including hundreds of thousands of returning soldiers, in a nationalist movement demanding an end
to British rule. Mohandas ("Mahatma," or "great-
souled") Gandhi (1869–1948) emerged as the
charismatic leader for Indian independence. Of
privileged birth and trained as a Western-style
lawyer, Gandhi embraced Hindu self-denial, rejecting the elaborate trappings of English life in
favor of simple clothing made of thread he had
spun. He advocated civil disobedience, which he
professed to model on British suffragists' tactics.
In 1930 he led a march to India's salt flats to protest
the British monopolies in salt and other products,
important sources of colonial revenue. He encouraged all Indians to wear homespun clothing

and thus boycott British-made textiles. Such "non-cooperation" contrasted significantly with the deference Indians had traditionally shown the British.

Gandhi's tactics and leadership proved devastatingly effective in the long run, but the British did not surrender without a struggle. The colonial government jailed Gandhi repeatedly and tried to split the independence movement by encouraging the Muslim League. The league, led by Mohammed Ali Jinnah, feared the power of Gandhi's Hindu-dominated movement and took the slogan "Islam is in danger" as its motto. Hindu-Muslim violence, which served British imperial interests, formed a counterpoint to Gandhi's campaign. By 1935 many people within Great Britain sympathized with Gandhi's moralistic appeal, and public pressure led Parliament to pass the Government of India Act, which granted much of India internal self-government. The drive for complete independence was momentarily checked.

In the Middle East the economic and political ambitions of peoples of the old Ottoman Empire made headway. Turkey, which had been a republic led by the Westernizer Mustafa Kemal (1881–1938) (or Atatürk, meaning "first among Turks") since 1923, curtailed British and Greek influence and developed a capitalist economy. In an effort to nationalize and modernize Turkish culture, Kemal moved the capital from Constantinople to Ankara, changed the ancient Greek *Constantinople* to the Turkish *Istanbul* in 1930, mandated Western dress for both men and women, introduced the Latin alphabet, and abolished polygamy. In 1936, women received the vote and were eligible to serve in the parliament. Persia similarly loosened the Great Power grip on its economy by forcing the renegotiation of oil contracts; at the same time it updated its government and changed its name to Iran. Persistent uprisings compelled Britain to end its mandate in Iraq in 1930, although it retained crucial oil concessions. In 1936, Britain agreed to end its military occupation of Egypt (though not the Suez Canal), fulfilling the promise of the self-rule granted in 1922. Conflict escalated in Palestine despite British efforts both to make a safe home for Zionist immigrants and to protect the rights of native Arabs. Although the area of Transjordan (today the Kingdom of Jordan) was to be a settlement for indigenous Arabs alone, the swelling tide of Jewish immigration to Palestine intensified Arab opposition to the British mandate.

Obsessed by rising trade barriers in Europe and their own population decline, the French made fewer concessions to the demands of colonized people. Their trade with the colonists increased as that with Europe lagged, and the demographic surge in Asia and Africa bolstered French optimism; as one official put it, "One hundred and ten million strong, France can stand up to Germany." Western-educated native leaders such as Ho Chi Minh, founder of the Indochinese Communist Party, contested their people's subjection, but in 1930 the French government brutally crushed the peasant uprising he led. In Algeria, French settlers resisted a nationalist movement inspired by liberal values as well as Islamic and pan-Arab revival advocated by other reform groups.

In general, British and French pursuit of economic recovery through empire split these two nations from their former allies in World War I by seeming to oppose self-determination. Thus preoccupied and divided, they let authoritarian and totalitarian forces make unchecked inroads during the crisis-ridden 1930s.

Totalitarian Triumph

Representative government collapsed in many countries under the sheer weight of social and economic crisis. After 1929, Italy's Benito Mussolini and the Soviet Union's Joseph Stalin consolidated their power, and the hate-spewing Nazi leader Adolf Hitler became chancellor of Germany. Prominent U.S. citizens, among them carmaker Henry Ford, admired Mussolini and Hitler for the discipline they brought to social and economic life, and they overlooked the brutal side of dictatorship. Cultural leaders and working people respected Stalin's administration in the USSR because it promised full employment, free social services, and education for the masses. Their hopes for utopia in an age of crisis blinded them to the violence Stalin inflicted on the Soviet people in the process of industrialization and to his ruthlessness in eliminating opposition.

The Birth of Stalinism

In 1931, British playwright George Bernard Shaw went on a pilgrimage to the Soviet Union, seeking to observe firsthand how socialism worked. At the border he threw away a packet of food he carried as insurance against hunger, for he was convinced that Stalin had created a utopian society. Despite this not uncommon optimism about life in the new USSR, the reality was far more complex—and troubling.

By 1929, Stalin had taken firm control of the Soviet Union and had made himself Lenin's heir. Confronted with ongoing economic crises, Stalin ended the New Economic Policy (NEP), Lenin's temporary compromise between Marxism and capitalism. He transformed the USSR into a formidable industrial power—in the process presiding over the deaths of leaders of the various nationalities, most of the important pre-Revolution Bolsheviks, and millions of peasants. Within a decade the Soviet Union had become an industrial nation directed by technocrats with few connections to prewar socialist aspirations. The costs were staggering. Besides the millions dead in the Revolution, civil war, and famine, tens of millions more starved, were executed, or were worked to death in labor camps during the 1930s. Stalin became the unquestioned leader of a single-party state.

Stalin manipulated Marxist theory to justify converting the USSR into a highly industrialized country—Marx had scorned agricultural utopias and the "idiocy of rural life." In the spring of 1929, Stalin had presented his first Five-Year Plan to the Communist Party Congress. Outlining a program for massive increases in the output of coal, ore, steel, and industrial goods, Stalin called the plan an emergency measure to end Soviet backwardness. He warned that without it, "The advanced countries . . . will crush us." Central planning of the economy—a policy gaining credence among Western economists and industrialists—and forced industrialization helped make the USSR a leading industrial nation. Between 1928 and 1940, the number of workers in industry, construction, and transport rose from 4.6 million to 12.6 million. The bureaucracy overseeing industrial output grew, and production figures soared; from 1927 to 1937, production in metallurgy and machinery rose 1,400 percent. Central planning allowed the Party to dominate Soviet workers by limiting their ability to change jobs or move from place to place. It also enabled the state to focus on industrialization and to produce only minimal consumer goods. Finally, the Five-Year Plan (and the others that followed) ended public debate and experimentation. Stalin shoved the USSR into the modern industrial world, although without the benefits of private property, which had traditionally inspired innovation, entrepreneurship, and industrial growth.

Skilled workers and bureaucrats benefited substantially from the redistribution of privileges that accompanied industrialism and central planning. Compared with people working the land, those in industry and especially those with mechanical skills received better housing, higher wages, and access to the limited consumer goods. Unskilled workers, however, faced a grim plight. Newcomers from the countryside were often herded into barracklike dwellings and subjected to dangerous factory conditions. Many, however, eventually took pride in the skill they acquired: "We mastered this profession—completely new to us—with great pleasure," a women lathe operator recalled. Communist officials, meanwhile, enjoyed perquisites such as country homes, better health care, special foods unavailable to the masses, and luxurious vacations. Like industrial managers in the West, these officials asserted that statistics, planning, and other aspects of social engineering (which, of course, only they could provide) were indispensable to high productivity. Yet almost everyone, from workers and managers to inspectors and government overseers, falsified production figures and other supposedly scientific data to protect their jobs—and in some cases their lives. Workers often lacked the technical education and even the tools necessary to accomplish goals prescribed by the Five-Year Plan. But because fulfilling the plan had top priority as a measure of Communist success, official lying, inequity, and corruption became ingrained in the productive system.

The industrialization of the Soviet Union was an extraordinary achievement, but it entailed far more suffering than the Industrial Revolution of the West. Many Soviet citizens willingly endured their burden because they believed in the ethos of "constant struggle, struggle, and struggle" to achieve a communist society. Youth in particular accepted the hardships of Stalin's industrialization as a heroic challenge. After the romance of the Revolution and civil war, wrote one youth, "The older generation had left to our lot only a boring, prosaic life that was devoid of struggle and excitement." For workers, the NEP diminished revolutionary egalitarianism. They were willing to accept the consumer shortages industrialization brought because "ahead of us lay the route to the complete victory of socialism."

The Five-Year Plan caused unprecedented hardships for the peasantry. Under the NEP many farmers had prospered, but Stalin's government did not think these *kulaks* (prosperous farmers) produced enough for the state's needs. Stalin demanded more grain to feed the urban workforce, and he also wanted to export grain to earn hard currency; both these steps were necessary to industrialize rapidly. Peasants resisted government demands by cutting production or withholding produce from the market. Faced with such recalcitrance, Stalin announced in 1929 the end of private farming and the beginning of huge state-dominated agricultural enterprises known as *collective farms.* Stalin also called for the "liquidation of the kulaks," which in theory referred only to prosperous peasants but in practice meant anyone who opposed his plans for collectivization.

Stalin generated enthusiasm for the attack on the peasantry by presenting it as a revolutionary challenge. Tens of thousands of volunteers and Party officials eagerly spread Stalin's brand of communism to the countryside. In the winter of 1929–1930, Party workers armed with quotas scoured villages for produce; Communist officials soon arrived and forced villagers to identify the kulaks among them. Stalin ordered these "enemies of the state" evicted, imprisoned, exiled, or murdered. Whole families and even entire villages were robbed of their possessions and left to starve. "In the station square," one writer recalled, "Ukrainian kulaks . . . lay down and died. One got used to seeing the dead there in the morning, and the hospital stable-boy . . . would come along with his cart and pile the corpses in." Propaganda units instilled hatred for anyone connected with kulaks. One Russian remembered believing they were "bloodsuckers, cattle, swine, loathsome, repulsive: they had no souls; they stank." Confiscated kulak land formed the basis of the *kolkhoz,* or collective farm, where peasants were to create a socialist

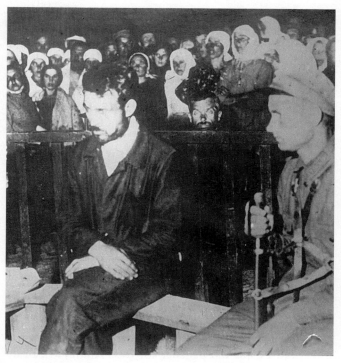

Trial of a Kulak in the Soviet Union, 1932
The prosecution charged this farmer with stealing grain. The death of millions of peasants came without such legal formalities through eviction, forced labor, and starvation.

agricultural system using cooperative farming and modern machinery. Collectivization provoked resistance: some country men formed guerrilla bands, and women on the kolkhoz hid barnyard animals and preserved rural traditions that the modernizers detested. Many peasants deserted communism for good in the 1930s.

Stalin's war against the kulaks left 5 million to 10 million peasants dead. In areas, such as the Ukraine, where anti-Soviet feeling ran high, attacking kulaks became the pretense for suppressing nationalism, which was strongly rooted in the Ukrainian countryside. Party ignorance of agriculture and lack of equipment and scientific personnel made collectivization an utter disaster. Soviet citizens starved as the grain harvest declined from 83 million tons in 1930 to 67 million in 1934.

Stalin blamed the famine on "wreckers," saboteurs of communism, and he instituted purges to rid society of these villains. Bourgeois engineers were the first group condemned for being the cause of low productivity. Soviet citizens expressed their relief that the wreckers had been punished, and they searched their own workplaces for "concrete bearers of evil . . . workers guilty of foul-ups, breakdowns, defects." Trials of increasingly prominent figures followed. When in 1934, Sergei Kirov, the popular first secretary of the Leningrad Communist party, was murdered, Stalin used his death (which he may have instigated) as the pretext to try former Bolshevik leaders Grigori Zinoviev and Lev Kamenev. The secret police soon claimed they had uncovered a massive conspiracy led by Trotsky to overthrow Soviet rule. At a series of "show trials" held in 1936, 1937, and 1938, old Bolsheviks, beginning with Zinoviev and Kamenev, were coerced to confess, despite a lack of evidence, that they had corresponded with the exiled Trotsky. Most of those found guilty were shot.

The trials, public confessions, and executions spread panic everywhere: "Great concert and lecture halls were turned into public confessionals . . . People did penance for [everything] . . . Beating their breasts, the 'guilty' would lament that they had 'shown political short-sightedness' and 'lack of vigilance' . . . and were full of 'rotten liberalism.'" Accusations of crimes ranging from treason to industrial sabotage led to purges of hundreds of thousands of local bureaucrats. Purges went on in universities, technical schools, and other training grounds for political and technological jobs. As international tensions developed, Stalin convinced hesitant Party members to accept more purges by pleading the dangers from "German-Japanese agents of Trotskyism." In 1937 and 1938, military leaders were arrested and executed without public trials, many of their names being drawn from Nazi forgeries. In some ranks every officer was killed. From industry and education to the Party and the army, no segment of the Soviet power structure escaped the great purges.

This bloody period of Soviet history has provoked intense historical debate. Were the purges carefully planned and directed solely by Stalin, who watched the trials from a secret booth in the courtroom? How much support and initiative came from the Communist party's rank and file? Some historians view the purges as the machinations of a psychopath, whereas others see them as a clear-headed attempt to eliminate barriers to Stalin's total con-

trol of the state and society. Recently, historians have judged the purges as discrete events that emanated from power struggles between Party officials and were fueled by the treachery of those looking for a quick route to the top. People in the lower ranks denounced their superiors to cover the way they themselves had falsified statistics, been lenient on kulaks, or lacked the proper vigilance.

The purges had an air of necessity and authenticity. To suspect the trials as fake was, in the words of the gullible U.S. ambassador to Moscow, to suspect "the creative genius of Shakespeare." As millions perished, Stalin was elevated to the USSR's single "Great and Wise Ruler." People who benefited from the purges, such as those who took over the jobs of the "purged," believed communism had finally achieved its egalitarian goals; but not everyone was taken in by the show trials. Arthur Koestler's *Darkness at Noon* (1940) portrayed the psychological debasement and physical battering that led innocent people to confess their guilt.

Under Stalin, bureaucrats renounced the political and cultural experimentation of the 1920s. In education, Communist political values superseded scientific knowledge, even at the cost of much-needed technical expertise. Much like the rest of Europe, the Soviet Union experienced a rapid decline in its birthrate. This drop, combined with famine and disease, a multitude of orphans roaming the streets, and the need to replace the millions slaughtered since 1914, motivated Stalin to end the reproductive freedom of the early revolutionary years and turn state policy toward increasing the birthrate. Abortions and birth-control information became difficult to obtain. Gold wedding rings and more lavish wedding ceremonies came back into fashion, and people were forced to remain married and encouraged to reproduce. The state condemned homosexuality and touted motherhood not only as a joy but a patriotic duty.

Propaganda now referred to the family as a "school for socialism"—that is, a miniature of the Soviet state—whereas Bolsheviks had once derided it as "bourgeois." As in some Western countries, the government provided subsidies based on the number of children in a family; even so, the birthrate did not rise much. The campaign for more children accompanied increased participation of women in the industrial workforce. Women who

of socialism. As "engineers of the soul," writers were expected to foster a growing cult of Stalin, who was worshiped as much as the tsar had been. Many artists, such as the poets Anna Akhmatova and Boris Pasternak, refused to accept this system:

> *Stars of death stood above us, and Russia,*
> *In her innocence, twisted in pain*
> *Under blood-spattered boots . . .*

wrote Akhmatova in those years. Others, such as the composer Sergei Prokofiev (1891–1953), found ways to accommodate their talents to the state's demands. Prokofiev composed the score for Eisenstein's 1938 film *Alexander Nevsky,* a work that transparently compared Stalin to the legendary medieval ruler as a great leader of the Russian people. When his ballet *Romeo and Juliet* was censored, Prokofiev wrote children's music, including the delightful *Peter and the Wolf.* Aided by adaptable artists, workers, and bureaucrats, Stalin stood triumphant as the 1930s drew to a close.

Hitler's Rise to Power

Hitler ended German democracy. Mass interest in his hate-filled antisemitism and German racism, featured in *Mein Kampf* (*My Struggle,* 1925), a book Hitler wrote while in prison, grew after the Great Depression struck Germany. In the midst of financial collapse and unemployment some big businessmen, notably Alfred Hugenberg, who owned film and press conglomerates, joined forces with Hitler to protest the Young Plan. Hugenberg's press relentlessly attacked the Weimar government, blaming it for the disastrous economy, and picked at wounded German pride over the defeat in World War I. In the panicky atmosphere of 1929, Hugenberg and Hitler used the media to brand the Young Plan, which actually reduced German reparations, a humiliation agreed to by traitorous republican politicians.

In 1930, reactionary and monarchist politicians took over the chancellorship from conservative republicans and Social Democrats. Chancellor Heinrich Brüning (1885–1970) proposed to stabilize the economy with a balanced budget, reduced government expenditures, and increased taxes and protective tariffs. Called the "Hunger Chancellor" because of his austere policies, Brüning failed to get Reichstag approval for his emergency plans and

Anna Akhmatova, 1936
Akhmatova kept secret much of her poetry about the purges of the Communist party and Soviet army leadership. Her patriotic verse written during World War II served Stalin's ends; later he had her detained in horrid conditions in a hospital.

worked long hours and who also stood in long lines for scarce consumer goods were supposed to have large families for the Fatherland.

Stalinism signaled the end of diversity in the arts. Writers who wished to publish had to join the Union of Soviet Writers. The union took control of matters such as foreign publication and translations. It assigned housing, office space, supplies, equipment, and secretarial help and even determined the type of books authors could write. In return, the "comrade artist" adhered to the official style of "socialist realism," derived from the 1920s focus on the common worker as a type of social hero. This mandated style infused such monumental works as Mikhail Sholokhov's *And Quiet Flows the Don* (1928–1940), which explored the consciousness of a rural hero and his work on behalf

Nazi Parade
Minutely planned for the maximum emotional effect, parades, rallies, and spectacles
emphasized Nazi power and national military might in an attempt to mold individual
Germans into obedient followers of the Führer.

called for new elections. The Nazis, however, made the government look totally unable to maintain order; they smashed windows of stores owned by Jews and beat up Communists and Social Democrats. By targeting Social Democrats and Communists as a single, monolithic group of "Bolshevik" enemies, the Nazis won the approval of the middle classes, who feared revolution and the loss of their property.

Benefiting from the publicity Hugenberg's media showered on it and from its own street tactics, Hitler's National Socialist German Workers' party, which had received little more than 2 percent of the vote in 1928, won almost 20 percent in the Reichstag elections of 1930 and in 1932 more than doubled its representation. As newspapers vilified the Weimar Republic for its failures, favorable press reports, brass-knuckles politics, and storm-trooper parades gave the illusion of Nazi vigor. Hitler's supporters, like Stalin's, were young and idealistic. In 1930, 70 percent of Party members were under forty, and they contrasted the image of Weimar politicians as aged and ineffectual. Although businessmen provided substantial sums of money, every class supported the Party. The largest number of supporters came from the

industrial working class, but white-collar workers and the lower-middle class joined in percentages out of proportion with their numbers in the population.

The elections of 1930 and 1932 stunned conservatives like Brüning because they showed the rising appeal of radicals—both Nazis and Communists made gains. Hitler's propaganda techniques had served him well against old-fashioned contenders. His propaganda chief, Joseph Goebbels, sent thousands of recordings of Hitler's speeches to the countryside and provided Nazi mementos to the citizenry. Teenagers painted their fingernails with swastikas, a symbol used by the Nazis, and in that bastion of traditional conservatism, the German army, soldiers flashed metal match covers with Nazi insignia. Nazi rallies were masterpieces of political display in which Hitler mesmerized the crowds. He began talking slowly until he had a sense of the audience; then, as one witness reported, "Suddenly he bursts forth. His words go like an arrow to their target; he touches each private wound on the raw, liberating the mass unconscious, expressing its innermost aspirations, telling it what it most wants to hear." Although Hitler appealed to the masses, he viewed them only as tools. In

Mein Kampf he discussed his philosophy of how to deal with them:

> The receptivity of the great masses is very limited, their intelligence is small. In consequence of these facts, all effective propaganda must be limited to a very few points and must harp on those in slogans until the last member of the public understands what you want him to understand.

After the Communist and Nazi success in the 1932 elections, the leader of one of these parties was the logical choice as chancellor. Germany's conservative elites—from the military, industry, and the state bureaucracy—loathed the Communists and favored Hitler as a common type they could easily control. In any case they wanted to reestablish an authoritarian order in Germany. Since 1930 they had been able to undermine Reichstag authority by excluding Socialists and Communists with their mass constituencies from the cabinet, and Hindenburg had constantly invoked emergency powers to bypass the parliament. As a result, by the end of 1932 the Reichstag had met only thirteen days, and it passed only five pieces of legislation. Antirepublican chancellors during these years often looked the other way when Nazi brutality was directed at their own political enemies. The government, for example, reprieved Nazi thugs who tortured a young Communist to death in front of his mother in the summer of 1932. Ultimately, elite leaders persuaded the aging Hindenburg that the army could not merely stage a coup against the Weimar Republic, because Hitler's supporters combined with the Communists would overpower the army. Hindenburg thus invited Hitler to become chancellor in January 1933.

The Nazification of Germany

Vowing to uphold the Weimar constitution, Hitler took office amidst jubilation in Berlin, as tens of thousands of storm troopers holding blazing torches paraded through the streets. Millions celebrated Hitler's ascent to power. A dressmaker rejoiced that "servants would no longer have to eat off the kitchen table." A businessman remembered, "My father went down to the cellar and brought up our best bottles of wine. . . . And my mother wept for joy. 'To think that I should live to see this!' she said. 'Now everything will be all right.'" Hitler

moved immediately to cement his power and silence opposition. When the Reichstag building was gutted by fire in February 1933, Hitler blamed the Communists and used the fire as the excuse for declaring press censorship, prohibiting meetings of opposition writers and artists, and disrupting the work of other political parties. Old-fashioned conservatives in the cabinet agreed to this curtailment of rights but warned that Hitler's control of the media might diminish their own electoral chances. Hitler, however, had made clear throughout his career that *all* political parties except the NSDAP were his enemies: "Our opponents complain that we National Socialists, and I in particular, are intolerant and intractable. They say we refuse to cooperate with other parties. . . . They are right, we are intolerant! I have set myself one task, namely to sweep those parties out of Germany." Within a month of Hitler's taking power, the elements of Nazi domination were in place.

New elections were held in March. The Nazis won 288 Reichstag seats, but Social Democrats and Communists still retained more than 200 seats, and right and center parties claimed another 158. Storm troopers lashed out violently at this political failure, beating up opponents and destroying property. They prevented Communist delegates from attending Reichstag sessions and had so intimidated the others that at the end of March, Hitler was able to pass the Enabling Act—only the Social Democrats voted against it. The act suspended the constitution for four years, in order, Hitler promised, to boost Germany out of crisis. His activities in these first months in office ended the political potential of Socialists and Communists. Once this popular opposition was quelled, any other dissent was easily eliminated, even that of his former allies.

Solid middle-class Germans approved the Enabling Act as a way of pulling the country out of its morass, but the law gave Hitler unprecedented power over the workings of everyday life. In June 1933 a bill that encouraged Aryans (people defined as racially German) to marry took effect. The bill provided for loans to Aryan newlyweds, but only to those couples in which the wife left the workforce. The loans were forgiven on the birth of the pair's fourth child. Nazi marriage programs enforced a nineteenth-century ideal of femininity; females were supposed to be subordinate so men would feel tough and industrious despite military defeat and economic depression. Although some women complained about having to forfeit their jobs, others, remembering the miserable war and postwar years, believed Hitler would elevate Nazi women, rewarding one "who joyfully sacrifices and fulfills her fate." Nazi military and marriage programs promised to increase Germany's birthrate, restore its economy, and strengthen the nation.

Proposing to promote the German *Volk,* or people, Nazism in fact impoverished ordinary life. Although Minister of Propaganda Goebbels ensured that by 1938, 70 percent of households had "people's radios," the programming broadcast was severely censored. Books like Remarque's *All Quiet on the Western Front* were banned, and in May 1933 a huge book-burning ceremony rid libraries of works by Jews, socialists, homosexuals, and modernist writers out of favor with the Nazis. Modern art in museums and private collections was either destroyed or confiscated. Under the policy of *Gleichschaltung* ("bringing into line"), civil servants, teachers, and other government officials were forced to adhere to Nazi practices. Another law took jobs from Jews and women and bestowed them on Party members as rewards. In 1936 membership in the Hitler Youth, an organization that indoctrinated the young, became mandatory for all boys and girls over age ten. These children learned to report the names of adults they suspected of disloyalty to the regime, even their own parents. In public, citizens had to worry about the presence of informers—more than one hundred thousand were on the Nazi payroll—and so they employed what was called the "German look," a surreptitious glance around a public space for spies or the Party faithful.

The avowed purpose of Hitler's program was to create a *Volksreich* ("people's empire"); from the beginning, violence and forced uniformity were its glue. The first concentration camp opened at Dachau near Munich in March 1933. The Nazis filled it with socialists, homosexuals, and Jews. They touted these camps as places where "antisocial" elements would be housed so that they could no longer interfere with the *Volksgemeinschaft* ("people's community"). Heinrich Himmler, who headed the elite SS (*Schützstaffel*) organization that protected Hitler and other Nazi leaders, commanded the Reich's political police system. The Gestapo, organized by Hermann Goering, and the

Order of the Death's Head also enforced complete obedience to Nazism. In the muscular logic of the Nazis, rights interfered with the *Volksgemeinschaft.* One Nazi leader proclaimed:

> *[National Socialism] does not believe that one soul is equal to another, one man equal to another. It does not believe in rights as such. It aims to create the German man of strength, its task is to protect the German people, and all . . . must be subordinate to this goal.*

Hitler deliberately blurred authority among the agencies of order and terror so that confusion and bitter competition reigned within the government as well as among the population at large.

In Hitler's first year and a half in power these rivalries threatened his regime. Businessmen and army leaders, whose support Hitler wanted, complained about the constant destruction wrought by the SA, Hitler's storm troopers, under the leadership of Ernst Roehm. In turn, Roehm called for a "Second Revolution" to end the corrupt influence of these elites on the Nazi leadership, especially Hitler. He hoped to make the SA the germ of a new German army. Despite their long-standing collaboration, Hitler ordered the assassination of Roehm, hundreds of SA leaders, individual enemies, and innocent civilians. The bloody Night of the Long Knives (June 30, 1934) eroded the SA's challenge to the army and the SS and led conservative business and military leaders to support Hitler's assumption of a new title—*Reichsführer*—after Hindenburg died on August 2, 1934.

Putting people back to work was also crucial to the survival of Hitler's regime. Economic revival built popular support, strengthened military industries, and provided the basis for German expansion. The Nazi government pursued economic *pump priming,* that is, stimulating the economy through government spending. Under the guise of making farm equipment, Germany built tanks and airplanes; the Autobahn highway system also had a military purpose. From farms to factories the government demanded high productivity and set economic independence and self-sufficiency as goals. Skilled workers prospered in the drive to rearm; and unemployment had declined to 1.6 million by 1936. As labor shortages began to appear in certain areas, the government conscripted single women into service as farmworkers and domestics.

The Nazi party reorganized work life to curtail labor activism. Government officials classified jobs, determined work procedures, and in May 1933 closed down labor unions and seized their property. Industrial managers set pay levels, rating jobs women performed lower no matter what level of expertise the work required. All workers, from those in lowly unskilled jobs to top professionals, were compelled to join the Nazi-controlled German Labor Front. The Labor Front snuffed out worker independence. It also enacted the proposals of industrial psychologists through its *Kraft durch Freude* ("strength through joy") program that rewarded Labor Front members with vacation trips and other benefits.

Imitating Stalin, Hitler announced a Four-Year Plan in 1936 with the secret aim of preparing Germany for war by 1940. Government officials allocated raw materials, sponsored the production of synthetics, and intensified labor management; defense spending soared to 50 percent of all government expenditures by 1938. The Four-Year Plan produced large trade deficits, and the Nazi government negotiated agreements with eastern European countries to boost exports and gain raw materials. Hitler believed the spoils of future conquests would eliminate the deficits caused by remilitarization.

Hitler partially fulfilled his promise to create a well-ordered national community. People boasted that they could leave their bicycles out at night without fear of robbery. But many of his promises were empty. Although he attacked big business in his speeches, his military buildup caused big industry to thrive. Unemployment, emigration, and attacks on so-called non-Aryan Germans still remained. However, the generally improved economy led people to believe that Hitler was working "an economic miracle" while restoring pride in Germany, the prewar sense of authority, and the harmonious community of an imaginary past.

Nazi Racism

The idea of *community* implies not only belonging but also exclusion—the exclusion of outsiders, strangers, and enemies. In the 1920s, Hitler's oratory revived the emotional hatred of the enemy of World War I, directing it against those he designated as enemies of the German race. Although Hitler attacked many ethnic and social groups, he propelled the nineteenth-century politics of antisemitism to new and frightening depths. In the rhetoric of Nazism, Jews were "vermin," "abscesses," "parasites," and "Bolsheviks," which the Germans would have to eliminate to become a true *Volksgemeinschaft.* Hitler deviously fashioned an enemy that most sections of the population could passionately hate; he defined the Jews both as evil financiers and businessmen and as working-class Bolsheviks. The Nazis convinced the public that Jews were at the root of all Germany's problems and that German greatness could be restored with forceful political measures against Jews.

In 1935 the government enacted the Nuremberg Laws, legislation that deprived Jews of citizenship, defined Jewishness according to one's ancestry, ended special consideration for Jewish war veterans, and prohibited marriage between Jews and other Germans. Culled from such prewar sciences and pseudosciences as Social Darwinism, criminal psychology, genetics, and eugenics, these laws transformed people that shared a religious and cultural heritage into a biological race and suggested to the German people that "science" would solve the "Jewish problem." To hold jobs, workers had to present their baptismal certificates and other evidence of their Aryan heritage. Whereas women defined as Aryan had increasing difficulty obtaining abortions or even birth-control information, these were readily available to the outcast groups. By 1939 special courts forced Jews and other so-called inferior groups, such as gypsies, to undergo sterilization and reproductive experiments performed by Nazi doctors. In the name of racial improvement, doctors helped organize the T4 project—the execution of some two hundred thousand handicapped and aged people. The T4 project used carbon monoxide poisoning and other means to kill masses of people, thus preparing the way for the Holocaust.

Some Jews thought the Nuremberg Laws would regularize their status and end street violence; instead the persecution escalated. One young Jewish woman fled her home in 1936 after being warned that the Gestapo had scheduled her arrest for daring to work in broadcasting, but her parents greeted this news with disbelief: "My mother thought I must be depressed over an unhappy love affair." In 1938 a Jewish teenager, reacting to the harassment of his parents, killed a high German official. In retaliation for this single murder, Nazis attacked some two hundred synagogues, smashed windows of Jewish-owned stores, and threw more than twenty thousand Jews into prisons and camps. The night of November 9–10 became known as *Kristallnacht,* or "the night of broken glass," which refers to the thousands of shattered windows.

By the outbreak of World War II, over half of Germany's five hundred thousand Jews had emigrated, often leaving behind all their possessions and paying huge emigration fees for the privilege. In the 1930s, Hitler's policies favored the migration of Jews rather than their extermination, and many emigrants—such as physicist Albert Einstein, filmmaker Fritz Lang, and architect Mies van der Rohe—advanced the scientific, cultural, and scholarly accomplishments of their adopted countries, especially England and the United States.

Emigrant intellectuals contributed to developing the concept of *totalitarianism* to describe the Fascist, Nazi, and Communist regimes of the 1930s. The term identifies highly centralized systems of government that attempt to control society and ensure conformity through a single party and police terror. Forged in the crucible of war and its aftermath, totalitarian governments broke with humane liberal principles to wage war on its own citizens. Many scholars find this term useful, but others claim it discounts the considerable popular support these governments enjoyed, as demonstrated by the masses cheering for Hitler and Mussolini or the cult of Stalin. Still others emphasize the differences rather than the similarities among these regimes. Nazi ideology condemned the Communists; and the socialized and centralized economy of the Soviet Union differed from the economies of both Nazi Germany and Fascist Italy. Moreover, these parties had different intellectual roots. Nationalism was key in the rise of fascism and Nazism, whereas communism began as an international workers' movement. Antisemitism also infected totalitarian societies in varying degrees: in Italy, Jews were rarely persecuted (and frequently protected from Nazis) and anti-Jewish laws were often ignored; Stalin purged individual Jews without singling out the entire race for extermination; but Hitler's and the Nazis' hatred of Jews infused their rhetoric, motivated their political strategies, and shaped their vision of a future German society. Finally, the totalitarian countries, like the democracies and authoritarian governments, intervened more and more in daily life through welfare programs, such as those to encourage population growth.

Democracies on the Defensive

Stalin, Mussolini, and Hitler projected themselves as dynamic leaders, modeling their personas on World War I military heroes. In comparison, some Western leaders seemed confused: they consulted parliaments, allowed the media to criticize them, and reacted hesitantly to the rise of dictators. Despite appearances, western European and U.S. politicians undertook notable experiments to solve social and economic crises and still maintain democratic politics. In eastern Europe, however, the appeal of nationalism and authoritarianism overwhelmed many fledgling democracies.

Meeting the Crisis of the 1930s

In the United States, where the Great Depression had struck first, President Herbert Hoover (1874–1964) confidently predicted that the economic downturn was only temporary because of the fundamental health of American business. When his rosy forecast proved false, Hoover, an advocate of government planning, directed municipalities to hire the unemployed and urged businessmen not to fire or lay off workers. As the economy slumped, his administration lent money to businesses and financial institutions. But the conservative Hoover opposed direct help to the unemployed, believing that such "handouts" would weaken the nation's moral fiber. In June 1932 some ten thousand World War I veterans marched on Washington, D.C., demanding relief, and two thousand of them set up a shantytown on the edge of the city. Hoover ordered the army to drive them away with tanks, thus discrediting his humanitarian reputation.

Hoover was defeated in the 1932 election by a bolder politician, Franklin Delano Roosevelt (1882–1945), the patrician governor of New York. In the tense atmosphere of his administration's first Hundred Days, Roosevelt pushed through a torrent of legislation: relief for businesses and instructions for firms to cooperate in stabilizing prices; price supports for hard-pressed farmers; public works programs for unemployed youth; and refinancing agencies for homeowners' mortgages. These were just a few of FDR's government remedies that were collectively called the New Deal. When the economy had not recovered by 1934, critics charged that Roosevelt's economic directives were turning the country toward socialism. However, the president still had enough political muscle to expand his program, most notably with the Social Security Act of 1935, which set up a fund to which employers and employees contributed. It provided retirement benefits for workers, unemployment insurance, and payments to dependent mothers and children and people with disabling physical conditions.

Like Mussolini, Hitler, and other charismatic politicians of the 1930s, Roosevelt was an expert at using the mass media. He, however, used radio (his "fireside chats") and public speeches to sustain faith in popular government at a time when authoritarians were denouncing democratic rights. "The only thing we have to fear is fear itself," he asserted to the nation at his inauguration. Americans, he exhorted, should not focus only on their present miseries but on the greatness that lay before them: "This generation of Americans has a rendezvous with destiny." Ably advised by his wife, Eleanor, FDR insisted that justice, human rights, and liberal values must not be surrendered in difficult times. "We Americans of today . . . are characters in the

living book of democracy," he told a group of teenagers in 1939. "But we are also its author. It falls upon us now to say whether the chapters that are to come will tell a story of retreat or a story of continued advance." Having overcome a crippling disease—polio, which left him unable to walk—Roosevelt seemed the most vigorous democratic leader battling the Great Depression.

Sweden, although a neutral power that had profited from World War I, suffered from the postwar inflation, depression, and population decline. Its government instituted economic planning and social welfare. The government devalued the kronar to make Swedish exports more attractive on the international market. Using pump-priming programs to maintain consumer spending and to encourage modernization, the Social Democratic leaders saw Swedish productivity rise 20 percent between 1929 and 1935, a time when other democracies were still experiencing decline.

Inspired by new theories of government planning, the Swedish administration concluded that in an industrial, urban society the national government had to encourage reproduction to ensure prosperity. Alva Myrdal (1902–1986), a social scientist and leading member of parliament, believed fertility rates were dependent on the economy and individual well-being. It was undemocratic, she maintained, "that the bearing of a child should mean economic distress to anybody in a country . . . that wants children." Acting on

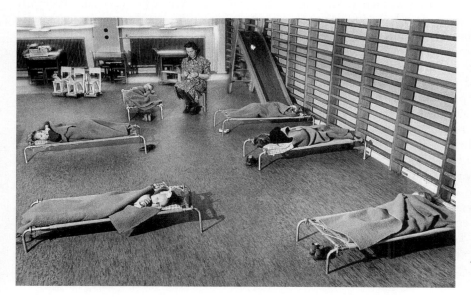

Kindergarten in a Cooperative Apartment House in Stockholm, 1940 *The Swedish government met the declining birthrate with an array of social programs, among them child care and subsidies to mothers.*

Myrdal's advice to promote "voluntary parenthood," the government started a loan program for married couples in 1937 and introduced prenatal care, free childbirth in a hospital, a food relief program, and subsidized housing for large families. Although projected to aid ten thousand women, by the end of the decade more than forty-five thousand women, almost 50 percent of all mothers, received government aid. Care of families, which had long been a feminist and social reform issue, became integral to the modern welfare state.

British and French leaders reacted uncertainly to the crisis because of their societies' moral and financial exhaustion after World War I. They felt torn between the apparent need for government direction of social and economic life and the tenets of liberal individualism. Officials had to relieve people's suffering, restore economic competitiveness, and maintain a healthy international financial position while also bolstering democracy. Because the most powerful democracy, the United States, had withdrawn from world leadership after the war, Britain and France had to bear a burden heavier than their resources could sustain. Their response to the world economic crisis—and later to the totalitarian challenge—proved woefully inadequate.

Britain was already mired in economic difficulties when the Great Depression hit. The prime minister in 1929, Ramsay MacDonald, though a leader of the Labour party, agreed with Conservatives on economic orthodoxy. Faced with falling government revenues, he cut payments to the unemployed. At a time when married women were the first to be laid off and were often barred from holding any job, Parliament in 1931 effectively denied unemployment insurance to such women even though they had contributed to the unemployment fund. To protect jobs and domestic markets, the government imposed huge protective tariffs, setting duties on some goods at 100 percent of their value. The tariff discouraged a revival of international trade and did not relieve British misery.

Only in 1933, with the economy continuing to worsen, did the government begin to take effective steps. A massive program of slum clearance and new-housing construction not only alleviated some distress, but also provided employment and infused money into the economy. These measures sparked signs of recovery by 1935 when a new government, that of Conservative prime minister Stanley Bald-

win, took office. By 1938 an extension of the National Insurance Act was providing minimal health benefits to 20 million workers and their families. As in the United States, however, the depression finally ended only with rearmament on the eve of World War II.

Battered by the economy and by vivid memories of wartime loss, the British were dazed by a scandal that, had the outcome been different, might have rocked the political system. In 1936 the new king, Edward VIII (∗January 20–December 10, 1936), announced his intention to marry a twice-divorced American woman. Baldwin and the government opposed the marriage and persuaded the king to abdicate in favor of his younger brother. Edward VIII's political opinions—he criticized parliamentary government and publicized his respect for Nazi ideas—and unseemly personal behavior made him unacceptable as the symbolic head of state. The closing of ranks against him prevented the affair from destabilizing British politics.

Depression struck later in France, but the country endured a decade of public strife in the 1930s. By 1932 severe postwar demoralization and stagnant population growth had joined with wage cuts and rising unemployment to create social and political turmoil. Deputies with opposing views on the economic crisis frequently came to blows in the Chamber of Deputies, and governments were voted in and out with dizzying rapidity. Each successive premier looked "profoundly irresolute," like someone who switched policies "according to passing incidents and visits which he received." Parisians took to the streets to protest the government's belt-tightening policies, and the press trumpeted the disorderly mass rallies, antigovernment leafleting, and demonstrations by shopkeepers and workers in banner headlines. Right-wing paramilitary groups mushroomed. Combining nineteenth-century royalism or Catholic fervor with more up-to-date admiration for Mussolini and Hitler, such groups as *Camelots du Roi* ("King's Henchmen") and *Croix de Feu* ("Fiery Cross") attracted the unemployed, students, and veterans. They aimed to end representative government, which in their eyes was a "bastion of corruption."

Matters boiled over early in 1934. A shadowy swindler, Serge Stavisky, committed suicide, leaving a trail of unanswered questions about his connections with influential politicians and judges.

When the government censored press reports about the scandal and refused to authorize a special investigation, the right-wing press incited an attack on the government. On February 6, 1934, these paramilitary groups joined Communists and other outraged citizens, who were simply fed up with official corruption, in riots around the parliament building. "Let's string up the deputies," chanted the crowd. "And if we can't string 'em up, let's beat in their faces, let's reduce 'em to a pulp." The police lines barely held as hundreds of demonstrators were wounded and killed; inside the Chamber of Deputies democratic representatives hurled ink bottles at one another. But the Right lacked both substantial support outside Paris and a leader, like Hitler or Mussolini, capable of unifying its various groups, and the republic survived the night. Thus France escaped the fate of Germany and Italy, but the lure of the antirepublican Right foreshadowed the fall of the Third Republic in 1940.

Shocked into action by this narrow escape, liberals, Socialists, and Communists rallied in support of democracy; by 1936 they had evolved into an antifascist coalition known as the Popular Front. Until that time such a coalition (which might have saved the Weimar Republic) had been impossible in democratic countries because of Stalin's strict opposition to Communist collaboration with liberals and Socialists. As fascism spread throughout Europe, Stalin reversed course and sanctioned the inclusion of Communists in popular front governments.

For just over a year in 1936–1937 and again very briefly in 1938, the French Popular Front had enough electoral support to form a government, with the Socialist leader Léon Blum (1872–1950) as premier. Like the American New Dealers and the Swedish Social Democrats, the Popular Front instituted long-overdue reforms. It conciliated labor unions to end the strikes that had been staged when workers' wages failed to reflect increased productivity. Blum extended family subsidies, state services, and welfare benefits, and he appointed women (though they still were not allowed to vote) to his government. In June 1936 the government guaranteed workers two-week paid vacations, a forty-hour work week, and the right to collective bargaining. The Popular Front also nationalized the armaments industry and directed the Bank of France to expand its board of governors to represent all segments of society, not just the privileged. Working people would long remember Blum as the man who improved their living standards and provided them with benefits and vacations.

In its brief life the Popular Front seemed to reinvigorate French republicanism. "In 1936 everyone was twenty years old," one man recalled, evoking the atmosphere of idealism that had been kindled. Local cultural centers for activities such as popular theater sprang up. Inspired to express their opposition to fascism, citizens celebrated democratic holidays, such as Bastille Day, with new enthusiasm. Speakers at these events contrasted their spontaneous solidarity and good humor with fascist militarism and abuse of human rights.

Despite support from workers, the Popular Front governments were politically weak. Fearing for their investments, bankers and industrialists greeted Blum's appointment by sending their capital out of the country, leaving France financially strapped. "Better Hitler than Blum" was the slogan of the upper classes. Blum tried to win support from powerful financial interests by holding down taxes on the wealthy, in effect forcing the lower levels of society to pay for Popular Front programs. He appeased the French Right by denying active support to the Spanish Republic during their civil war. In protest, Blum's Communist coalition partners withdrew parliamentary support. Blum's inability to do more than just talk about fascism epitomized the dilemmas that faced western Europe's democracies in the 1930s. Many opposed attacks on democracy, whether in Spain, Germany, eastern Europe, or elsewhere. But the memories of World War I provoked fear of another war. Thus these powers withheld crucial support to foreign democratic forces and also kept their own military budgets small as a way of ensuring peace. The collapse of the antifascist Popular Front late in June 1937 showed the difficulties of pluralistic and democratic societies in crisis-ridden times.

Eastern European societies, hit hard by the depression, welcomed authoritarian government. In 1932, Engelbert Dollfuss (1892–1934) came to power in Austria; two years later he dismissed the parliament and ruled briefly as a dictator. Despite his authoritarian stance, Dollfuss would not submit to the Nazis, who assassinated him in 1934. In Hungary, where outrage over the Peace of Paris remained intense, two successive conservatives had followed tight-money policies in an attempt to revive the crippled Hungarian economy. Their failure, combined with continuing outrage over the terms of the Peace of Paris, resulted in the coming to power of General Gyula Gömbös (1886–1936) in 1932. Gömbös admired fascism and reoriented his country's foreign policy toward Mussolini and Hitler. He stirred up antisemitism and ethnic hatreds, enacting laws against Jews and leaving more than a residue of pro-Nazi feeling after his fall in 1936. In democratic Czechoslovakia the depression hit the German population of the industrialized Sudeten region especially hard. As a result the Nazi physical education teacher Konrad Henlein gained an enthusiastic following. The Slovaks, who were both poorer and less well-educated than the urbanized Czechs, built a strong Slovak Fascist party. In Poland, Romania, Yugoslavia, and Bulgaria, ethnic tensions simmered and the appeal of fascism grew as the Great Depression lingered.

Cultural Vision in Hard Times

Writers, filmmakers, and artists responded vigorously to the depression in the midst of ongoing economic modernization. Some portrayed the situations of factory workers, homemakers, and shopgirls struggling to support themselves or their families, and the ever-growing number of unemployed and destitute. In 1931, French director René Clair's (1898–1981) *A nous la liberté* (*Give Us Liberty*) related prison life to work on a factory assembly line. Charlie Chaplin's film *Modern Times* (1936) showed the Little Tramp again, this time as a worker in a modern factory who is so molded by his monotonous job that he assumes anything he can see, even a co-worker's body, needs mechanical adjustment. Other movies showed the rhythms of modern work through chorus lines and tap dancing, which depicted bodies moving with machinelike precision. Like the body of an assembly line employee, the dancer's body was disciplined, working at peak intensity. Chorus girls were interchangeable and indistinguishable, their faces often reshaped by plastic surgery to create a glamorous look. These representations of the modern factory illuminated life in the 1930s with humor, mimicry, satire, and sympathy.

Films presented down-and-out types familiar in everyday life—the tramp, the organ-grinder, and the criminal—and used gender stereotypes to explain modern conditions. *The Blue Angel* (1930), a German film starring Marlene Dietrich, showed how a vital, modern woman could destroy men—and civilization. A woman's power was contrasted to the figure of an impractical professor, who appears a bumbling failure. Although in dramas unemployment and the population crisis were blamed on overpowering women, in comedies and musicals heroines behaved bravely, pulling their men out of the depths of despair and setting things right again. The British comedienne Gracie Fields portrayed spunky working-class women who kept on smiling despite hard times. The camera made both heroism and degradation bigger than life for millions of moviegoers.

Like many filmmakers, intellectuals confronted the crisis through *engagement*—a word that describes their turn away from the aestheticism of earlier generations. Popular Front writers created realistic studies of human misery and the threat of war that shaped life in the 1930s. The Soviet system inspired many writers and artists, whether Communist or not, to adopt socialist realism for their depictions of working people. American novelist John Steinbeck (1902–1968) interpreted the desperate migration of ruined Dust Bowl farmers in *The Grapes of Wrath* (1939). The British writer George Orwell (1903–1950) described his experiences among the poor of Paris and London, wrote investigative pieces about the unemployed in the north of England, and published an account of atrocities committed by both sides during the Spanish Civil War.

Authors found it crucial to reaffirm their belief in Western values. German writer Thomas Mann (1875–1955) won the Nobel Prize in 1929, in part for his *Magic Mountain* (1924), the story of tuberculosis patients in a Swiss sanitarium whose doomed condition mirrored that of postwar Europeans struggling to find meaning and hope. Even though he did not face persecution as a Jew, Mann went into exile when Hitler came to power and began a series of novels based on the Old Testament hero Joseph to convey the struggle between humanist values and barbarism. The fourth volume, *Joseph the Provider* (1944), eulogized Joseph's welfare state, in which the granaries were full and

Charlie Chaplin, **The Great Dictator,** *1940*
In this film, Chaplin used his formidable skills to depict a maniacal Hitler.

the rich paid taxes so the poor might live decent lives. One of the last works of English writer Virginia Woolf, *Three Guineas* (1938), directly attacked militarism, the oppression of women, and poverty, claiming they were interconnected parts of a single, devastating ethos undermining Europe in the 1930s.

While writers rekindled moral concerns, scientists in research institutes and universities continued to point out limits to human understanding—limits that seemed at odds with the megalomaniacal pronouncements of dictators. Although sophisticated findings could be popularized, in fact most scientific work was beyond an amateur's understanding. Astronomer Edwin Hubble (1889–1953) in California determined in the early 1930s that the universe was an expanding entity. Czech mathematician Kurt Gödel (1906–1978) maintained that any mathematical system contains some propositions that are undecidable. The German physicist Werner Heisenberg developed the "uncertainty," or "indeterminacy," principle in physics. Scientific observation of atomic behavior, according to this theory, actually disturbed the atom and thereby made precise formulations impossible. Even scientists, Heisenberg asserted, had to settle for statistical probability. The attempt to

learn the secrets of the universe led to doubts about human understanding itself. Viennese-born philosopher Ludwig Wittgenstein (1889–1951) explored the limits of what language can say. He also questioned the traditional philosophical quest to find the essence of such terms as thought, knowledge, and belief.

Religious leaders also emphasized the limitations of human competence and spurred many to recommit to religious activism. This impulse contested the violent secularization in Germany and the Soviet Union and helped foster a spirit of resistance to dictatorship among religious people. The Swiss theologian Karl Barth (1886–1968) taught that the faithful had to take Scriptural justifications of resistance to oppression seriously. In his Barmen Declaration he encouraged rebellion against the Nazis. Pope Pius XI's (*1922–1939) encyclical *Quadragesimo Anno* (1931) condemned the failure of modern societies to provide their citizens with a decent life and supported government intervention to create better moral and material conditions. The encyclical might have seemed an endorsement of the heavy-handed intervention of the fascists, but it also inspired some theologians and pastors on the Continent to ally themselves with the poor and politically oppressed. German

Catholics frequently opposed Hitler, and religious commitment inspired many other individuals to resist fascism through the churches.

The Road to World War II

During the 1930s, Hitler, Mussolini, and Japan's military leaders marched the world toward another catastrophic war. Initially many ordinary people and statesmen in Britain and France hoped that the League of Nations would be able to contain aggression through collective security. Others believed that the powers had rushed into World War I and counseled the appeasement of Mussolini and Hitler. By the 1930s, Western public opinion outside of France viewed the Treaty of Versailles as too harsh on Germany, and many statesmen accepted Hitler's wish to change its provisions. The desire for peace in the 1930s is hardly surprising given the fresh and painful memories of World War I, the chaos of the 1920s, and the social and economic turmoil of the Great Depression; but it left people foolishly blind to Hitler's professed expansionist goals. By early 1938, Fascists were fighting to overthrow the Spanish Republic, and Hitler was menacing eastern Europe. Some historians claim that World War I, the violent interwar years, and World War II make up a single "Thirty Years' War" of the twentieth century. According to this view, the dramatic events of the 1930s, traditionally seen as the prelude to World War II, were actually the middle years of this conflict.

Japan Strikes in Asia

In September 1931 a railroad train in the Chinese province of Manchuria blew up, and Japanese army officers used the explosion, which they had actually set, as an excuse to invade the territory. The invasion aimed to overcome China's resistance to Japan's economic penetration. The moment looked opportune because of power struggles among U.S.-backed modernizers led by Jiang Jieshi (Chiang Kai-shek, 1887–1985), warlords controlling large tracts of land, and a growing Communist movement. Like Hitler and Mussolini, Japanese leaders pursued a policy of regionalism, in which their thorough domination of much of Asia would guarantee their self-sufficiency.

China and the West
In this photograph, Generalissimo Jiang Jieshi, his American-educated wife Mei-ling Soong, and British and American officers inspect Chinese troops. The Jiangs attempted Westernization in China, including U.S. training of the Chinese army.

Japanese leaders also believed that their society had chafed long enough under Western imperialism. During the difficult years of the Great Depression, the press aroused public sentiment against the kind of Western interference that had occurred at the Washington Conference, at which Japan had agreed to keep its fleet smaller than Western navies. Journalists called for aggressive expansion to restore the economy. Businessmen wanted new markets and resources for their burgeoning but wounded industries. In this uncertain time the military extended its influence in the government, advocating Asian conquest as part of Japan's "divine mission." By 1936–1937, Japan was spending 47 percent of its budget on arms.

The situation in East Asia had international repercussions. Great Power economic interests were threatened, as Japanese aggression compounded the effect of the growing market in Japanese goods. China asked the League of Nations to adjudicate the question of Manchuria. The League condemned the Japanese invasion, but it imposed no sanctions that would have put economic teeth into its condemnation. Meanwhile, the rebuff goaded Japan to ally with Hitler and Mussolini. In 1933, China and Japan agreed to a truce, with Japan occupying territory on the Asian mainland. In 1937, however, Japan attacked China again, justifying its offensive as a first step toward "A New Order in East Asia" that would liberate the region from Western imperialism. Chinese nationalists and Communists announced a joint effort to defend the country, and the United States enforced stringent economic sanctions on the crucial raw materials that drove Japanese industry. Although Japan responded by claiming more land and resources in the Pacific rim, the Western powers and the Soviet Union did not effectively resist its territorial expansion.

Stamping Out the Legacy of Versailles

Like Japanese leaders, Mussolini and Hitler called their countries "have-nots." The Allies had reneged on their promise to hand over territories to Italy after World War I, and Mussolini threatened "permanent conflict" to right that wrong by expanding Italy's borders. Hitler's agenda, as stated in *Mein Kampf*, included reestablishing control over the Rhineland, breaking free from the Versailles treaty's military restrictions, and bringing Germans living in other nations into the Third Reich's orbit. The dictators portrayed themselves as peace-loving men who resorted to extreme measures only to benefit their country and humanity. Moreover, their anticommunism appealed to statesmen across Europe.

In the autumn of 1933, Hitler announced Germany's withdrawal from the League of Nations and from the international disarmament conference then meeting. He swiftly concluded a Non-Aggression Pact with Poland in January 1934, which reassured Western statesmen that Germany would not threaten Poland's boundaries or the free city of Danzig (populated by ethnic Germans). Hitler also tried to unify Germany and Austria, but Dollfuss resisted this attempted *Anschluss* (unification) and was assassinated for his obstruction. In 1935, Hitler loudly rejected the clauses of the Treaty of Versailles that limited German military strength; he

Italians Celebrate the Conquest of Ethiopia, 1936
Building on wartime dreams of glory, Mussolini promised Italians national greatness through military conquest. His army's victory built patriotism and allegiance to his regime.

reintroduced military conscription and publicly started rearming. Rearmament, however, had been going on for years in secret.

Mussolini also chose 1935 as the year in which to assert Italian power: he invaded Ethiopia. The attack was intended to demonstrate his regime's youth and vigor and to raise Italy's standing among the colonial powers. "A new cycle is beginning for our country," one soldier exclaimed. "The Roman legionnaires are again on the march." The poorly equipped Ethiopians resisted but could not withstand the Italian army, and their capital fell in the spring of 1936. The League of Nations voted sanctions against Italy, and although the sanctions were ineffective—both French and British leaders secretly undermined League policy—they succeeded in driving Mussolini into Hitler's arms. The British public was outraged at this attack on a country and monarch that had been Christianized.

Meanwhile in March 1936, Hitler had defiantly sent his troops into what was supposed to be a permanently demilitarized Rhineland. The inhabitants greeted his troops with wild enthusiasm, and the French, whose security was most endangered by this act, protested to the League of Nations. Without the support of the British, who accepted the fait accompli, the French general staff, committed to a strategy of defense, counseled against a military attack on Germany. The two dictators thus appeared not just as political leaders but as powerful military heroes, in contrast to the tentative politicians of France and Great Britain.

The Spanish Civil War

In what seemed like an exception to the trend toward authoritarian government, Spanish republicans overthrew their king in 1931. For centuries, Spain had declined compared with the rest of Europe; large landowners and the Catholic clergy, who had the impoverished peasantry at their mercy, continued their domination. The republicans hoped to modernize Spain, but they had neither a practical domestic policy nor the will to confront reactionary forces, especially in hard economic times. The government failed to enact land redistribution, which might have ensured popular loyalty and diminished the power of landowners and the church. This failure was all the more damaging because the antimonarchist forces were divided. Left and right republicans, anarchists, Communists, Socialists, Trotskyites, and other splinter groups vied for power and constantly harassed one another. Meanwhile, right-wing forces acted in concert and drew on their substantial financial backing.

In 1936 prorepublican forces temporarily banded together in a Popular Front coalition to win elections and prevent the republic from collapsing. With the Popular Front victory, euphoria swept the country: prisoners were set free, unemployment abated, and coveted municipal jobs were doled out. But the Right recovered and revolted under the leadership of General Francisco Franco (1892–1975). Franco had the support of a host of right-wing groups, including monarchists, clergymen, landowners, and ultimately the fascist Falange party.

The military uprising led to the Spanish Civil War, which pitted the republicans, or *Loyalists,* against the rebel *Falangists* and the rest of the Right. In a war of ever shifting battle lines, republicans held Madrid, Barcelona, and other commercial and

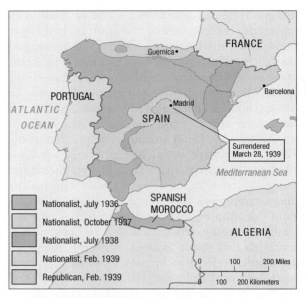

The Spanish Civil War

industrial areas, whereas the rebels found most support in the agricultural west and south. Like World War I, the struggle sometimes bogged down into trench warfare. It became a rehearsal for World War II when Hitler and Mussolini sent military personnel to test new weapons and to practice new tactics, particularly the terror bombing of civilians. In 1937 the German Condor Legion of aviation aces, who entered the country on tourists visas, attacked the town of Guernica with low-flying planes, mowing down civilians in the streets. This gratuitous slaughter inspired Pablo Picasso's memorial mural to the dead, *Guernica* (1937), in which the intense suffering is starkly displayed in monochromatic grays and whites to capture a sense of moral decay as well as physical death.

The Spanish government appealed everywhere for assistance. Only the Soviet Union answered, but Stalin withdrew his troops and tanks in 1938 as the republican forces floundered. Britain and France were wary of war and refused to provide aid despite the outpouring of popular support for the cause of democracy. Instead a few thousand volunteers from a variety of countries—including many students, journalists, and artists—fought for the republic. For these volunteers, "Spain was the place to stop Fascism," and refugees from Mussolini's Italy found hope in thinking, "Today in

Spain, tomorrow in Italy." Besides being dependent on male and female volunteers and less well supplied, the republican ranks soon splintered into competing groups of liberals, Trotskyites, anarchists, and Communists. In this bitter contest both sides committed widespread atrocities against civilians. The aid Franco received ultimately proved decisive, and his nationalist troops defeated the republicans in 1939. The ensuing repressive dictatorship reinforced the European trend toward authoritarian government.

Central Europe Falls to Hitler

Hitler's intervention in Spain was relatively spontaneous and officially secret, but his annexation of Austria in 1938 gave Germany access to assets Hitler had long coveted. Many Austrians had hoped for such a merger after the Paris peace settlement stripped them of their empire, whereas Nazi racial ideology called for a union of Aryans. A proposed customs union in 1931 and the attempted coup in 1934 were followed by several years during which Hitler bullied the Austrian government to accede to Nazi policies. In March 1938, Austrian Chancellor Kurt von Schuschnigg (1897–1977), hoping to maintain his country's independence, announced a plebiscite in which Austrians would vote for or against merging with the Third Reich. Fearing a negative result, Hitler ordered an invasion.

His troops entered Austria as easily as tourists. The country was in chaos, and the Nazis represented themselves as guardians of law, order, and racial pride. Austria was declared a German province, the Ostmark, and Hitler's thugs ruled once-cosmopolitan Vienna. An observer later commented on the scene:

> *University professors were obliged to scrub the streets with their naked hands, pious white-bearded Jews were dragged into the synagogue by hooting youths and forced to do knee-exercises and to shout "Heil Hitler" in chorus. Innocent people in the streets were trapped like rabbits and herded off to clean the latrines in the S.A. barracks.*

The *Anschluss* enhanced the image of German omnipotence, advancing Hitler's plan to "keep Europe gasping."

THE ROAD TO WORLD WAR II

1929 Global depression begins with U.S. stock market crash

1931 Japan invades Manchuria

1933 Hitler comes to power in Germany

1935 Italy invades Ethiopia

1936 Civil war breaks out in Spain; Hitler remilitarizes the Rhineland

1937 Japan invades China

1938 Germany annexes Austria; European leaders converge in Munich to negotiate with Hitler

1939 Germany takes control of Czechoslovakia; Hitler and Stalin sign a nonaggression pact; Germany invades Poland; Britain and France declare war on Germany

---

Hitler turned immediately to Czechoslovakia and its resources. Overpowering this democracy did not appear as simple a task as seizing Austria. Czechoslovakia had a large army and formidable border defenses and armaments factories, and most Czech citizens were prepared to fight for their country. Hitler, who loathed the Czech people, gambled that Czechoslovakia's noisy, pro-Nazi German minority could create a crisis and that the Western powers would not interfere. Many in the West thought that Czechoslovakia, a creation of the postwar peace settlement, unjustly denied Germans and other national minorities their right to self-determination. Throughout the spring and summer of 1938, therefore, Hitler and his propaganda machine poured tremendous abuse on Czechoslovakia and its president, Edouard Beneš, for "persecuting" the German minority. He wooed Czechoslovakia's neighbors into accepting his claims, partly by convincing the Poles and Hungarians that they had something to gain from the country's dismemberment. By October 1, 1938, he warned, Czechoslovakia would have to grant autonomy (amounting to Nazi rule) to the German-populated border region, the Sudetenland, or face German invasion.

As Hitler's deadline approached, British Prime Minister Neville Chamberlain (1869–1940), eager to keep the peace, made three trips to Germany. At the last of these meetings, on September 29, 1938,

Germany in 1933
Remilitarized in 1936
Annexed in 1938- April 1939
Satellite state, March 1939
Conquered by Germany, September 1939
Annexed by Soviet Union, September 1939
International boundaries, 1936

The Growth of Nazi Germany

Mussolini and French Premier Edouard Daladier (1884–1970) joined Hitler and Chamberlain in Munich and agreed to cede the Sudetenland to Germany. Hitler topped off the Munich Conference by signing an agreement that Germany would never go to war with Great Britain. Amidst great publicity, crowds lined the streets of European capitals and hailed their returning leaders for keeping the peace. Appeasement was seen as a noble act, and the agreement between Germany and England prompted Chamberlain to announce that he had secured "peace in our time." By contrast, the Czech ambassador to Germany wept. Stalin, excluded from the Munich deliberations, learned from the conference that the democracies were not going to fight to preserve eastern Europe.

Hitler, meanwhile, was disgruntled that the agreement had thwarted his ambition to invade Czechoslovakia. Having portrayed himself as a man of peace, he waited another six months, until March 1939, and then sent German troops over the border. Britain and France responded by promising military support to Poland, Romania, Greece, and Turkey in case of Nazi invasion. In May 1939, Hitler and Mussolini countered by signing their Pact of Steel.

Historians have sharply criticized the Munich Pact because it bought Hitler time to build his army, provided him with additional resources, and seemed to give him the green light for further aggression. Some historians believe a confrontation might have stopped Hitler and that even if war had resulted the democracies would have triumphed. According to this view, each military move by Germany, Italy, and Japan should have been met with stiff opposition, and the Soviet Union should have been made a partner to this resistance. Others counter that appeasement provided France and Britain precious time to beef up their own armies and to prepare their citizens for another war. Support for war was almost nonexistent, and even statesmen who knew of Hitler's ambitions respected, sometimes even admired, and almost always sought to pacify him in the confused belief that even though he was "mad" he could be dealt with rationally.

Such thinking received a final jolt on August 23, 1939, when Germany and the USSR signed a nonaggression agreement. The Nazi-Soviet Pact was astonishing, given Hitler's promise to wipe the Bolsheviks off the face of the earth and official Soviet abhorrence of fascism. It provided that if one country became embroiled in war, the other signatory would remain neutral. Moreover, by secret protocols the two dictators agreed to divide the Baltic states and Poland at some future date, with Hitler claiming western Poland and Stalin the Baltic states, Finland, and eastern Poland. The Nazi-Soviet Pact ensured that should war come, the democracies would be fighting a Germany with no fear of attack on its eastern borders. In any case, Hitler believed that Great Britain and perhaps even France would not fight, for his aggression had met no resistance so far. He now aimed his forces at Poland.

World War II

The six-year catastrophe that quickly came to be called the Second World War opened when Hitler launched an all-out attack on Poland on September 1, 1939. The Poles had rejected his demand that they return the free city of Danzig and yield to Germany a strip of land to connect East Prussia with the rest of the Reich. Hitler had couched the ultimatum in nationalistic terms, claiming that Germans in Polish territory were in danger. "I needed an alibi," Hitler blatantly admitted, "especially with the German people." In contrast to 1914, no jubilation in Berlin accompanied the invasion; when Britain and France declared war two

days later, the mood in other capitals was similarly grim. World War II began with dire predictions about its ultimate consequences: the British Home Office had estimated in 1938 that the first two months of war would produce 1.8 million casualties and that London would be bombed daily by at least seven hundred tons of bombs. Although Japan, Italy, and the United States did not join the battle immediately, their participation eventually spread the fighting throughout the world. By the time World War II ended in 1945, many Europeans were starving, much of the Continent lay in ruins, and unparalleled atrocities and genocide had killed 6 million Jews and countless others.

The German Onslaught

Invading in a two-pronged attack, German ground forces quickly encircled the ill-equipped Polish troops, and the air force bombed transportation networks and strafed the infantry. The Polish army fought back, but they confronted an overpowering *Blitzkrieg* (lightning war), in which the Germans concentrated airplanes, tanks, and motorized infantry to defeat a surprised defender with overwhelming speed. Drawing on military insights gained late in World War I and in Spain, German strategists allowed individual units to charge once they had crashed through to the rear of the enemy's lines. This reliance on human initiative and speed proved extraordinarily successful in allowing an army to adapt to conditions and in conserving German supplies. *Blitzkrieg* also assured Germans at home that the human costs of gaining *Lebensraum*, that is, sufficient "living space" for the full flowering of the Aryan races, would be low.

On September 17 the Soviets invaded too. By the end of the month, the Polish army was in shambles. Having divied up the country according to Nazi-Soviet protocols, Hitler then issued a peace initiative in October to make future clashes look like the fault of the democracies. Their refusal to negotiate an immediate end to the conflict allowed Hitler to sell the war within the Reich as one of self-defense. Meanwhile, the USSR attacked Finland for refusing to provide a base for the Soviet military. As sympathy for the valiant Finns mounted, the League of Nations expelled the Soviet Union.

Hitler ordered an attack on France for November 1939, but his generals, who feared that

Germany was ill-prepared for total war, were able to postpone the offensive until the spring of 1940. During the "phony war" of November to April, the combatants engaged in little direct conflict. Then in April 1940 the *Blitzkrieg* crushed Denmark and Norway; the battle for Belgium, the Netherlands, and France followed in May and June. As German planes strafed them mercilessly, thousands of civilians fled south to escape the invasion.

In France panic and defeatism infected the army. On June 5, Mussolini, eyeing future spoils for Italy, invaded France from the southeast. Much to the shock of the rest of the world, the French defense rapidly collapsed. Nor could the British army withstand the German onslaught. Trapped on the beaches of Dunkirk in northern France, 370,000 British and French soldiers were rescued in a heroic effort by an improvised fleet of naval ships, fishing boats, and pleasure craft. Led by a dejected and resigned government, France surrendered on June 22, 1940, leaving Germany to rule the northern half of the country, including Paris. In the south, named Vichy France after the spa town where the government sat, the reactionary and aged World War I hero, Henri Philippe Pétain, was allowed to govern. Preparing propaganda footage from the capitulation ceremony, British film editors made it look as if Hitler were dancing a celebratory jig in a railroad car where the Germans had surrendered in 1918. Meanwhile, Stalin used the diversion in western Europe to annex the Baltic states and to seize Bessarabia and Bucovina from Romania.

Britain now stood alone. Blaming Germany's rapid victories on Chamberlain's policy of appeasement, the British swept him out of office and installed Winston Churchill (1874–1965), an early advocate of resistance to Hitler. After Hitler ordered the bombardment of Britain in the summer of 1940, Churchill rallied the nation by radio to undo the pacifist spirit and resist. In the "Blitz," as the bombardment was called, the German air force struck at public buildings and monuments, harbors and weapons depots, and military bases and industry. Refusing to negotiate and scorning surrender, the British people held fast as the government poured resources into developing its advantage in radar (a technique it had perfected in the 1930s) and anti-

aircraft weapons. By the end of the year the British air industry was outproducing the Germans by 50 percent.

By the fall of 1940, German air losses forced Hitler to abandon his plan for a naval invasion of Britain. He consoled himself by attacking British bases in the Mediterranean, Near East, and North Africa and by forcing Hungary, Romania, and Bulgaria to join the Axis, thus gaining access to more food and oil for his armies. He concluded a Tripartite Pact with Italy and Japan in 1940 and a Non-Aggression Pact with Turkey in 1941. He also made his fatal decision to attack the "center of judeobolshevism"—the Soviet Union—in the spring of 1941. However, the German army first came to the aid of the floundering and overextended Italian armies in Yugoslavia and Greece, which Mussolini had foolishly decided to attack in jealous imitation of his northern ally. In June 1941, Operation Barbarossa began when German armies crossed the Soviet border. Hitler declared himself "happy to be delivered from [the] torment" of allying with Bolsheviks and promised to "raze Moscow and Leningrad to the ground."

Deployed along a two-thousand-mile front, 3 million German troops quickly penetrated Soviet lines. Scornful of intelligence of troops massed on his border, Stalin refused to believe that the Germans had invaded and simply disappeared for several days. Then he rallied to direct the defense; by July, however, the Wehrmacht (German armed forces) had rolled to within two hundred miles of Moscow and would eventually reach its suburbs. The German armies, using a strategy of rapid encirclement, had killed, captured, and wounded more than half the 4.5 million Soviet soldiers defending the borders. Now Hitler blundered. Considering himself a military genius and the Slavs inferior, he proposed attacking Leningrad, the Baltic states, and the Ukraine simultaneously, whereas his generals wanted to concentrate on Moscow. Following this cumbersome strategy allowed precious time to slip away, and the German armies got bogged down in the autumn rains. Driven by Stalin, Party bureaucrats, and rising patriotic resolve, the Soviet people fought back in the winter, turning Nazi soldiers to frostbitten wretches, "weak as dogs." In these early years of the war, Hitler feared that equipping his armies for the

Russian winter would suggest the truth: the limits of *Blitzkrieg* had been reached and a prolonged campaign lay in store. Meanwhile his ill-supplied armies besieging Moscow, Leningrad, and other major cities succumbed to the weather and disease. "What is all this for?" one German wrote in his diary in December 1941. "When will we ever get back home?"

War Expands: The Pacific and Beyond

As the German Army entrenched, a stunning attack ignited war in the Pacific. On Sunday, December 7, 1941, Japanese navy planes bombed targets at Hawaii's Pearl Harbor and then decimated a fleet of airplanes in the Philippines. Roosevelt pronounced it "A day that will live in infamy" and summoned Congress to declare war on Japan the next day. For a decade the United States and Japan had been edging toward war because of their competing interests in the Pacific. Japanese invasions in the Far East had provoked more American anger than had Hitler's aggression. Despite threats of economic sanctions from the United States, Japan acquired control of parts of the British Empire, bullied the Dutch in Indonesia, and in 1940 invaded Indochina to procure raw materials for its industrial and military expansion. After the invasion of Indochina, the United States restricted commerce in oil and scrap metal, on which the Japanese depended. Under the leadership of Hideki Tojo (1884–1948), the militarist Japanese government decided it should settle matters once and for all; Japan would forcefully unite Asians in a regional "coprosperity sphere." By spring 1942 the Japanese had conquered Guam, the Philippines, Malaya, Burma, Indonesia, Singapore, and much of the southwest Pacific.

On December 11, 1941, Hitler, faithful to the Tripartite Pact, declared war on the United States—an appropriate enemy, he proclaimed, as it was "half Judaized and the other half Negrified." Mussolini followed suit. The United States was not prepared for a prolonged struggle, even though Roosevelt had shifted the country's foreign policy from isolation to intervention by increasing defense spending, supporting the institution of a draft in 1940, and endorsing a program called lend-lease to provide equipment for the British military. American aid was crucial in the battle of the Atlantic—the struggle to protect vital British shipping from constant German attack. In August 1941, on a warship off Newfoundland, Roosevelt and Churchill had forged the Atlantic Charter, which condemned aggression and renewed the ideal of collective security. But isolationist sentiment remained strong, U.S. armed forces numbered 1.6 million, and no plan existed for producing the necessary guns, tanks, and airplanes. Moreover, many U.S. and British leaders and a good part of the general public hated the thought of joining forces with the USSR; Stalin himself remained profoundly mistrustful of his new allies. The Grand Alliance of Great Britain, the Free French (an exile government led by Charles de Gaulle and based in London), the Soviet Union, and the United States evolved slowly over the course of the war through diplomatic negotiations and meetings of its leaders. Given the urgency of war and the partners' competing interests, the Grand Alliance and the larger coalition with twenty other countries had much to overcome in the struggle against the Axis—Germany, Italy, and Japan.

The Holocaust

As it stomped through eastern Europe, the German army slaughtered Jews, Communists, Slavs, and others it deemed enemies. In Poland the SS murdered the nobility, clergy, and intellectuals and relocated hundreds of thousands of Polish citizens to work as slaves. Across the Continent, the army rounded up civilians to work on German farms, in German industry, and in concentration and labor camps throughout the Reich—all to feed the voracious Nazi war machine. Herded into urban ghettos and living on minimal rations, eastern European Jews were forced to work for the Nazis. The Jews became special targets of SS violence. Around Soviet towns, Jews were usually shot in pits, some of which they had been forced to dig themselves. After shedding their clothes and putting them in ordered piles for later Nazi use, ten thousand or more would be killed at a time, often with the help of Ukrainian or Lithuanian antisemites. More than thirty thousand were massacred at Babi Yar after the fall of Kiev at the end of September 1941. However, the "Final Solution"—the Nazis' diabolical

**Concentration Camps and
Extermination Sites in Europe**

1 Auschwitz-Birkenau
2 Belzec
3 Bergen-Belsen
4 Buchenwald
5 Chelmno
6 Dachau
7 Flossenbürg
8 Gross Rosen
9 Majdanek
10 Mauthausen
11 Mittelbau
12 Natzweiler
13 Neuengamme
14 Ravensbrück
15 Sachsenhausen
16 Sobibor
17 Stutthof
18 Theresienstadt
19 Treblinka

Principal German concentration
and extermination camp

0   100   200 Miles

0   100 200 Kilometers

plan to exterminate all of Europe's Jews—had not yet begun.

Compared to the initial massacres, the Final Solution was a bureaucratically organized and efficient technological system for rounding up Jews and transporting them to extermination sites. On the eve of war in 1939, Hitler had predicted "the destruction of the Jewish race in Europe." In 1942 he exploded in rage before mass audiences: "There was a time when the Jews in Germany also laughed at my prophecies. . . . But take my word for it: they will stop laughing everywhere." Historians have demonstrated that although no clear order written by Hitler exists, he discussed the Final Solution's progress and issued oral directives for it. It went into effect in 1942, as the Soviets turned back the Germans at Stalingrad and inflicted more than a million casualties.

Six camps in Poland were developed specifically for the purposes of mass extermination—Auschwitz, Majdanek, Chelmno, Belzec, Sobibor, and Treblinka. Some, like Auschwitz, served both as extermination and labor camps; inmates produced synthetic rubber and fuel for the chemical firm I. G. Farben. Others existed solely for exter-

mination. SS troops supervised all the camps. Improvising with sealed-up houses and trucks and using techniques developed in the T4 project, Nazis and collaborators at Chelmno first gassed Christian Poles and Soviet prisoners of war. The Nazis burned the corpses in huge pits until the specially designed crematoria for mass burning started functioning in 1943. By then, Auschwitz had the capacity to burn 1.7 million bodies per year. About 60 percent of new arrivals—particularly children, women, and older people—were sent directly to the gas chambers; the other 40 percent labored until the Nazis determined that weakness or disease rendered them expendable.

Extermination camps received their victims from across the Continent. In the ghettos, councils of Jewish leaders, such as the one in Amsterdam where Etty Hillesum worked, were ordered to determine those to be "resettled in the East," and many of them did so in the belief that life outside the ghetto could hardly be worse than life within. Effective resistance was nearly impossible, as Jews in the ghettos were weakened by hunger and disease and could not obtain enough necessary weapons. Any kind of resistance meant certain death. When Jews rose up against their Nazi captors in Warsaw in 1943, they were mercilessly butchered. The Nazis took pains to cloak their true purposes in the extermination camps. Bands played when trainloads of victims arrived; some were given postcards with reassuring messages to mail home. Then the selection process began, with men and women segregated. Many mothers, unaware that their children were automatically doomed, refused to be separated from them and thus went directly to the gas chamber. Those who avoided immediate selection had their heads shaved, were showered and disinfected, and were then given prison garments. So began life in "a living hell."

Overworked inmates usually took in less than five hundred calories per day and experienced unimaginably bleak physical conditions, leaving them vulnerable to the typhus and other diseases that swept through the camps. The brutality of inspections and roll calls, of sick-minded and criminal prison guards, and of inhumane medical experiments failed to crush the spirit of those like Etty Hillesum. Women observed religious holidays, celebrated birthdays, and re-created other sustaining

Jews from the Warsaw Ghetto to be Transported for Extermination
The Nazis built allegiance by arousing hatred for a variety of religious, ethnic, and other groups and often confined them to ghettos to make extermination easier. In 1943 Jews in the Warsaw Ghetto rebelled against the Nazis but were mercilessly crushed.

aspects of domestic life. Language lessons or story-telling sessions maintained human culture in an inhumane setting. Prisoners forged new friendships that helped in the struggle for survival. An onion or part of a turnip could serve as a precious gift to someone sick with typhus. Thanks to someone sharing a bread ration and doing him favors, wrote the Auschwitz survivor Primo Levi, "I managed not to forget that I myself was a man."

Historians debate what the Allies should have done about the Holocaust during the war. Some fault them for delaying the invasion of Europe or for failing to bomb the death camps. After the war, Jews questioned why their own leaders cooperated in the deportation. Others have asked how much ordinary Germans knew of the genocide and why

so few protested. No one has been able to answer how the Holocaust could have been carried out in a society so proud of its cultural accomplishments and its high level of civilization. Six million Jews, the vast majority from eastern Europe, along with gypsies, Slavs, and countless others perished. Activists still search for surviving perpetrators of the Holocaust.

Society at War

Even more so than World War I, the outcome of the Second World War depended on industrial productivity. The Axis countries remained at a disadvantage throughout the war despite their vast conquests. Although the war accelerated economic production some 300 percent between 1940 and 1944 in all belligerent countries, the Allied powers produced twice the armaments of the Axis powers in 1941 and more than three times Axis output in 1943. Even while its lands were occupied and many of its cities besieged, the Soviet Union increased its production of aircraft 40 percent between 1942 and 1943; by the spring of 1943 it was turning out 2,000 tanks per month.

Both Japan and Germany maneuvered around their lower capacity, most notably in the strategy of *Blitzkrieg*. Hitler had to avoid imposing wartime austerity because he had come to power promising an end to economic suffering, not more of it. The use of laborers and resources from occupied areas improved the German standard of living, but those benefits disappeared after *Blitzkrieg* failed in the Soviet Union. Although Japan's government had built public support for the war, it maintained the erroneous belief that a few costly attacks would discourage Americans from pursuing war so far from home. Neither country took the resources and morale of its enemies into full account.

Allied governments were overwhelmingly successful in generating civilian participation, especially among women. In the Axis countries, where government policy encouraged large families and motherhood was particularly exalted, women followed the fascist doctrine of separate spheres, avoiding paid work even though they were desperately needed in offices and factories. In contrast, Soviet women constituted more than half the workforce by war's end, and eight hundred thousand volunteered for the military, even serving as pilots. They dug massive antitank trenches around Moscow and other threatened cities. In the Soviet Union, however, civilians were treated like soldiers, with holidays eliminated, workdays set at twelve hours or more, and rations cut to starvation levels. Muslims and minority ethnic groups were uprooted and relocated as potential Nazi collaborators. As the Germans invaded, Soviet citizens moved entire factories eastward; some five hundred were moved from Moscow in the single month of October 1941. Stalin encouraged a revival of Russian nationalism, allowing religious services because the Orthodox church provided people with hope and inspired patriotism and sacrifice.

The democracies used propaganda to mobilize loyalty; even more than in World War I, it saturated society in movie theaters and on the radio. Accustomed to listening to politicians on the air, people were glued to their radios for war news. Films depicted aviation heroes and infantrymen as well as the working women and wives left behind. Government agencies monitored filmmaking and allocated supplies to approved films. In the United States the military loaned authentic props only if they could censor the scripts. Advertisers of consumer goods connected their products to the war effort: "If your dealer doesn't have your favorite LIFE SAVERS," read one advertisement, "please be patient. . . . It is because the shipment he would have received has gone to the Army and Navy."

Between 1939 and 1945, people lost much of their privacy as governments organized many more aspects of everyday life. Bureaucrats regulated the production and distribution of food, clothing, and household products, all of which became scarce and generally of lower quality. In England the wartime Ministry of Food employed thirty-nine thousand people by 1943 just to manage what people ate. It taught that women and children should embrace deprivation so their fighting men would survive. Governments hired more businessmen, economists, statisticians, and other specialists to influence civilian thought and behavior.

With governments standardizing such items as food, clothing, and entertainment, World War II furthered the development of mass society. Millions took up canning or grew "Victory Gardens" with government-sponsored media direction. On the home front homogenized news reports instilled hatred for the enemy. Since the early 1930s the German government had drawn ugly caricatures of Jews. Allied propaganda during the war depicted Germans as sadists and perverts and the "Japs" as uncivilized insectlike fanatics. Soldiers and civilians on both sides were preoccupied with enemies, sharply depicted in stereotypical racial and ethnic terms.

From Resistance to Allied Victory

Professional armies ultimately defeated the Axis powers, but civilian resistance in Nazi-occupied areas also contributed to the Allied triumph. General Charles de Gaulle (1890–1970) directed the Free French forces from his haven in England;

"Long Live King Haakon VII," 1942
This graffiti symbolized hatred for Nazi control of Norway by celebrating the exiled monarch and constituted one form of civilian resistance to totalitarianism.

many more French resisters fought in Communist-dominated groups like "Combat." Some in these groups gathered information to aid the Allied invasion of the Continent. The Polish resistance was unified against the Nazis, whereas in Yugoslavia, Serbs and Croats often attacked each other (or Communists) as much as they did the fascists. Rural groups known as partisans, or the *maquis*, planned assassinations, disrupted communications, and bombed important war facilities and matériel.

People also fought back through everyday activities. Homemakers circulated newsletters telling how to foil the plans of the occupying powers through demonstrations at prisons where civilians were detained and marketplaces where food was rationed. In central Europe hikers smuggled Jews and others over dangerous mountain passes. Danish villagers created vast escape networks. Resisters played on stereotypes of femininity: women often carried weapons to assassination sites in the cor-

rect belief that Nazis would rarely suspect or search them; they also seduced and assassinated enemy officers. In Paris a woman chemist made explosives for the resistance in her university laboratory. Other actions, even though not violently resistant, subtly undermined the demands of Fascist leaders. Couples in Germany and Italy limited family size in defiance of pronatalism. German teenagers danced the forbidden American jitterbug, thus defying the Nazis and forcing the police to monitor their groups. Resistance helped rebuild community solidarity and the liberal ideal of political participation that authoritarian rule had fractured.

The spirit of resistance produced real heroes such as Swedish diplomat Raoul Wallenberg (1912–1947?), whose machinations with Nazi officials saved thousands of Hungarian Jews. But villains abounded—collaborators who contributed to the initial Nazi victories and who cooperated with them during the occupation for personal advantage.

The Battle of Stalingrad
*German and Soviet troops
fought tenaciously in
the rubble of this city
until the Soviets finally
gained the upper hand.
The defeat marked the
turn in Nazi fortunes.*

From Vidkun Quisling, a Norwegian promoter of Nazism and prime minister during the occupation of his country, to countless ordinary citizens who betrayed Jews in hiding or informed on resistance networks, Nazi Germany profited from the services of these traitors.

Nonetheless, starting in late 1942, the Allies started tightening a noose around the Axis. A major turning point came at Stalingrad. In the summer of 1942, in an effort to capture Soviet oil and to bisect the country, the German army rapidly took Sevastapol and Rostov; on August 22 it began the siege on Stalingrad. Months of ferocious fighting led to house-to-house combat, as neither side would surrender despite massive casualties. Finally, the Soviet army began a pincer movement from the north and south, slowly entrapping and capturing the ninety-thousand German survivors in February 1943. Meanwhile, the British army in North Africa held against the Germans in Egypt and Libya and together with U.S. forces invaded Morocco and Algeria in the autumn of 1942 and landed on Sicily in July 1943. A quick victory over Italy seemed possible, especially after the king ousted Mussolini in July 1943. However, the Germans rescued the Duce, occupied northern Italy, and fought bitterly for the peninsula until April

1945. After Italy's liberation, partisans shot Mussolini and his mistress and hanged their dead bodies for public display.

The victory at Stalingrad marked the beginning of the costly Soviet drive westward. As the Americans and British invaded North Africa and Europe and pounded German cities with strategic bombing to demoralize civilians and destroy war industry, coordination among the Allies became imperative. In November and December 1943, Roosevelt, Churchill, and Stalin met at Teheran, Iran, to agree on the opening of a western front, for which Stalin had been pressing and Churchill had resisted. At Teheran, Churchill put aside his mistrust of Stalin and his misgivings about armies crossing the English Channel to set a date for the invasion at Normandy, France. On June 6, 1944, the combined Allied forces under the command of U.S. general Dwight Eisenhower reached the heavily fortified French coastline. The Nazis had been deceived into concentrating their forces to the north. After taking the beaches, Allied troops fought their way through the Norman hedgerows as the air force pummeled the cities of western France. In late July, Allied forces broke through German defenses and a month later helped liberate Paris, where rebellion had erupted against the Nazis. British, Canadian,

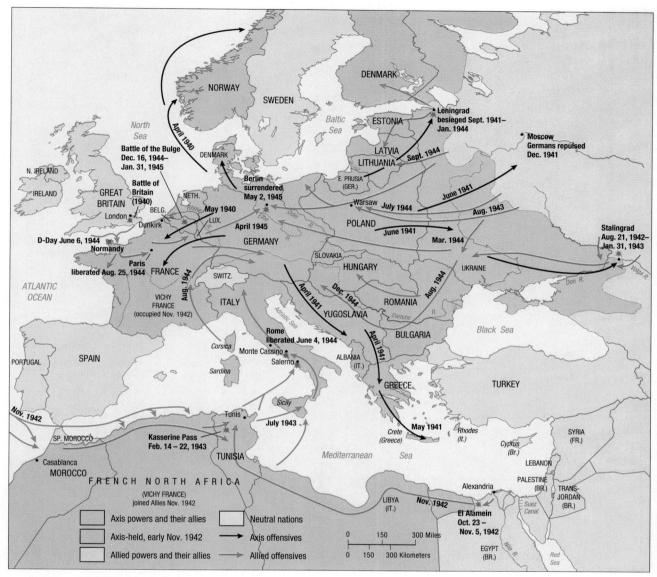

World War II in Europe and Africa

U.S., and other Allied forces fought their way eastward to join the Soviets in squeezing the Third Reich to its final end.

In July 1944 a group of German military officers, fearing their country's military humiliation, attempted to assassinate Hitler by exploding a bomb at a meeting. Only wounding the führer, the conspirators and many hundred others were cruelly tortured and slowly strangled, their dead bodies filmed hanging from wire attached to meathooks for Hitler's entertainment. Despite crushing military defeat, Hitler continued to preach German victory, maintaining that the Allies were merely "stumbling into their ruin." He based his faith on the development of the V-2 rocket—the prototype of the ballistic missile. Driven by his demented ideology, he nonetheless believed that Germans were proving themselves unworthy of his greatness and deserved to perish in a cataclysmic conflagration. He thus refused all negotiations that

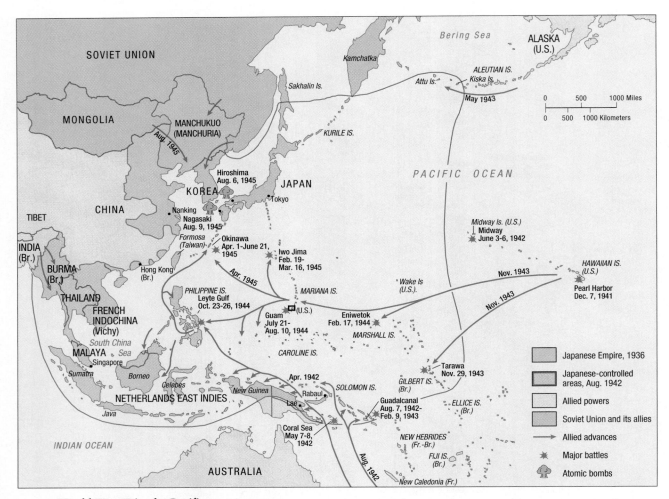

World War II in the Pacific

might have spared Germany. The Soviet armies entered Poland, pausing only to allow the Germans to put down a spontaneous uprising of the Polish resistance in August 1944. The elimination of the Polish resistance would allow the Soviets a freer hand after the war. Facing more than twice as many troops as on the western front, Stalin's forces entered Romania at the end of August and continued to roll toward Germany, although they met fierce German fighting in Hungary during the winter of 1944–1945. Hitler's refusal to surrender resulted in massive bombing of Germany. As the Soviet army took Berlin, he committed suicide with his wife, Eva Braun. Their bodies were burned in the courtyard of the German chan-

cellery. Although many soldiers remained committed to the Third Reich, Germany finally surrendered on May 8, 1945.

In keeping with their "Europe first" strategy, the Allies were now free to focus solely on the Pacific war. Turning points in the war had occurred as far back as 1942, when the U.S. forces beat the Japanese in battles at Coral Sea and Midway island. The Americans relied on submarines and aircraft carriers in beating the vastly overextended Japanese, whereas the Japanese had relied on battleships too long. The Allies stormed one Pacific island after another, gaining more bases from which to cut off supplies and launch bombers. The Japanese ruled out surrender even after the fall of Saipan in 1944 delivered a blow to the military government. Japan's press actively tried to toughen up public opinion, as did media in the West, but its factories were unable to approach U.S. output. The Japanese resorted to *kamikaze* tactics, in which pilots deliberately crashed their planes into American ships. The United States stepped up its bombing raids on the Japanese mainland. In the spring of 1945 its firebombing of Tokyo killed more than one hundred thousand civilians. Meanwhile a U.S.-based international team of more than 100,000 scientists, technicians, and other workers engaged in the Manhattan Project had succeeded in developing the atomic bomb. On the sixth and ninth of August, U.S. pilots dropped them on Hiroshima and Nagasaki, inflicting hundreds of thousands of casualties. Fulfilling its promise to join the war against Japan, the USSR invaded Manchuria. Even then diehards in the Japanese military wanted to continue the war, but a week later, at the emperor's behest, the country accepted defeat.

Uncertain Victories

The Grand Alliance was composed of nations with vastly different political and economic systems, and wartime agreements reflected continuing differences about the shape of postwar Europe. In October 1944, Churchill and Stalin met again to plan the postwar distribution of territories. The Soviet Union would control Romania and Bulgaria, Britain would control Greece, and they would jointly look after Hungary and Yugoslavia. These agreements went against Roosevelt's faith in collective security and seemed to threaten American commitments to self-determination and open doors in trade. At the next meeting of the "Big Three," in the Crimean town of Yalta in February 1945, Roosevelt advocated the institution of the United Nations to serve as a global peace mechanism. He also underwrote future Soviet influence in Korea, Manchuria, and the Sakhalin and Kurile islands in return for promises of Stalin's help against Japan. The last meeting of the Allied leaders took place at Potsdam, Germany, in the summer of 1945. By this time, Harry S Truman (1884–1972) had succeeded Roosevelt, who had died in April; Clement Attlee (1883–1967), whose Labour party had just won the British elections, replaced Churchill. At Potsdam the leaders agreed to give the Soviets control of eastern Poland, to cede a large stretch of eastern Germany to Poland, and to adopt a temporary four-way occupation of Germany that included France as one of the supervising powers.

Although victory brought declarations of a common purpose from the Allies, many haunting questions accompanied the defeat of Hitler, Mussolini, and Japan's military leaders. People sensed that the trauma of war and the institutions it had created had unalterably changed society. Sometime in 1943, George Orwell began to write his novel *1984,* (1949) and although it was set some decades in the future, the novel used wartime England as its inspiration. Poor food and worn clothing, grimy streets and dwellings, people prematurely aged and careworn—all characterized both London of the 1940s and Orwell's fictional state, Oceania. Like his hero, Winston Smith, Orwell worked for the wartime Ministry of Information (called the Ministry of Truth in the novel) and churned out doctored news for wartime audiences. Information and truth hardly mattered, in the language called "Newspeak," where old words were replaced by sanitized ones. As in Orwell's novel, words took on new meaning during the war: *disengagement* replaced *retreat, battle fatigue* substituted for *insanity,* and *liberating* a country could mean invading it and slaughtering its army and civilians. The integrity of language and the accurate reporting of events were casualties of this war, even more so than in the Great War.

Parts of Asia and the South Pacific and much of Europe lay in ruins in 1945 as Orwell revised his manuscript of *1984.* He saw the routinization of work, the deadening of creativity, the intrusion of big government into everyday life, and the replacement of democracy by the rule of bureaucratic managers as part of war's legacy. For Orwell, bureaucratic power depended on the perpetuation of conflict, and fresh conflict was indeed brewing in the race for Berlin and Japan even before the war ended. As Allied powers competed for territory, a new struggle called the *Cold War* was taking root. In the midst of the perpetual war experienced by Winston Smith in *1984,* the screen in his room blares out the national anthem—"Oceania 'tis of thee"—predicting the replacement of democracy by a culture of obedient patriots despite the defeat of the Nazis and Fascists.

CONCLUSION

The Great Depression brought massive social dislocation and fear and thus provided a setting in which dictatorship thrived. Seeking a brighter future and enticed by the mass media, people turned from representative institutions toward dynamic, if brutal, leaders. Memories of World War I permitted Hitler and Mussolini to menace Europe unimpeded throughout the 1930s. When a coalition to stop them formed, it was an uneasy one among the industrial giant the United States, the imperial powers France and Britain, and the Stalinist Soviet Union. The costs of a bloody war taught these powers different lessons. The United States, Britain, and France were convinced that a minimum of civilian well-being was necessary to prevent the recurrence of fascism. As the death camps were liberated, many people renewed their commitment to tolerance, pluralism, and democracy. Meanwhile, Soviet citizens hoped that life would become easier and more open for them. The devastation of the USSR's population and resources, however, had made Stalin increasingly obsessed with national security and reparations. Britain and France confronted the final eclipse of their global might, underscoring Orwell's insight that the war had transformed society irrevocably. Backed by vast arsenals of sophisticated weaponry, the competing visions of former Allies on how to deal with Germany and eastern Europe led them to threaten one another—and the world—with yet another war.

SUGGESTIONS FOR FURTHER READING

Source Materials

Dawidowicz, Lucy S. *A Holocaust Reader.* 1976. Includes documents showing the organization of the Holocaust and the daily lives of its victims.

Ginzburg, Natalia. *Family Sayings.* 1964. A prize-winning story of life under Italian fascism.

Orwell, George. *1984.* (1949) A grim fantasy based on Britain during the war that predicted what Orwell imagined the world would be like later in the century.

Vassiltchikov, Marie. *Berlin Diaries, 1940–1945.* 1988. A fascinating look at the destruction of German society and at the development of the plot against Hitler.

Interpretive Studies

Bridenthal, Renate, Atina Grossmann, and Marion Kaplan, eds. *When Biology Became Destiny: Women in Weimar and Nazi Germany.* 1984. Contains excellent essays on women in unforgettable times, including the organization and remuneration of work by Nazi managers.

Conquest, Robert. *The Harvest of Sorrow: Soviet Collectivization and the Terror-Famine.* 1986. A stirring popular account of the brutal war against the peasantry.

Dower, John W. *War Without Mercy: Race and Power in the Pacific War.* 1986. Discusses the development of race hatred both sides used to rouse citizens to a fighting mood.

Evans, Richard J., and Dick Geary. *The German Unemployed: Experiences and Consequences of Mass Unemployment from the Weimar Republic to the Third Reich.* 1987. Includes analytic essays on the social and political consequences of unemployment. Especially interesting on youth culture in bad times.

Fest, Joachim. *Hitler.* 1974. A thorough and detailed portrait of the man and his policies.

Fitzpatrick, Sheila, ed. *Cultural Revolution in Russia, 1928–1931.* 1978. An exciting collection of articles on socialist culture.

Fussell, Paul. *Wartime: Understanding and Behavior in the Second World War.* 1989. Takes the unorthodox view that the war was less meaningful than most historians claim and reveals many of its less than noble aspects.

Hilberg, Raoul. *The Destruction of the European Jews.* 1985. A detailed examination of the bureaucratic and human history of the Holocaust.

Hildebrand, K. *The Third Reich.* 1984. A concise survey of the internal workings of Nazi Germany.

Iriye, Akira. *The Origins of the Second World War in Asia and the Pacific.* 1987. An expert overview of internal politics, economic issues, and diplomatic maneuverings.

Jackson, Julian. *The Politics of Depression in France, 1932–1936.* 1985. Describes how the French dealt with economic disaster.

———. *The Popular Front in France: Defending Democracy, 1934–1938.* 1988. A fresh look at the cultural politics of antifascists and the many rituals they created to undermine their enemy morally.

James, Harold. *The German Slump: Politics and Economics, 1924–1936*. 1986. A detailed study of why the slump occurred and how business and government reacted.

Kalvemark, Ann-Sofie. *More Children or Better Quality? Aspects of Swedish Population Policy*. 1980. Examines the development of social-welfare programs in a country that created the first, most comprehensive system.

Koonz, Claudia. *Mothers in the Fatherland: Women, the Family, and Nazi Politics*. 1987. Details the many ways in which Nazism appealed to German women and deceived many who thought it would give them influence.

Kuromiya, Hiroaki. *Stalin's Industrial Revolution: Politics and Workers, 1928–1932*. 1988. An investigation of the support for and resistance to Soviet industrialization under Stalin.

Lewis, Peter. *A People's War*. 1986. Explains how the British home front mobilized for daily battle during World War II.

Mayer, Arno. *Why Did the Heavens Not Darken? The "Final Solution" in History*. 1988. A controversial look at how the "unthinkable"—the Holocaust—came about.

Medvedev, Roy. *Let History Judge: The Origins and Consequences of Stalinism*. 1989. The revised interpretation of Stalin's impact by a famous Russian intellectual.

Rhodes, Richard. *The Making of the Atomic Bomb*. 1986. A detailed popular account of the international cast of characters and goverment policies behind the bomb.

Thomas, Hugh. *The Spanish Civil War*. 1987. The classic history of an important and gripping prelude to World War II.

Tucker, Robert C. *Stalin in Power*. 1990. An up-to-date look at the excesses of Stalin's rule in the 1930s.

Von Laue, Theodore H. *The World Revolution of Westernization: The Twentieth Century in Global Perspective*. 1987. A well-argued treatment of Europe's revolutionary relationship to the rest of the world.

Weinberg, Gerhard. *A World at Arms: A Global History of World War II*. 1994. An encyclopedic work that links the political and military aspects of the war.

In 1955 the Soviet Union exploded its first hydrogen bomb. After the test a banquet honored those involved with the project. Andrei Sakharov, the scientist who had guided the effort, proposed the first toast: "May all our devices explode as successfully as today's, but always over test sites and never over cities." Sakharov's toast met a stony silence: "as if I had said something indecent." The next speech, by Marshall Nedelin, military director of the test, featured a vulgar, dirty joke that mocked Sakharov's pacifist comment—and captured the aggressive mood of the times. By 1955 the world had been polarized for nearly a decade, as the Soviet Union and the United States menaced each other with nuclear weapons. In this supercharged atmosphere the fate of ordinary citizens and the concerns of privileged elites like Sakharov mattered little.

Within a few years of the defeat of Germany and Japan in World War II, the United States and the Soviet Union had become mortal enemies: "like two scorpions in a bottle, each able to kill the other, but only at the risk of its own life." Victorious in the war, the two superpowers now competed fiercely for global power in a "bipolar" world. The United States, whose territory was virtually untouched in the war, had emerged as the world's economic giant. The Soviet Union, despite suffering gruesome devastation, retained its formidable military might. These two nations drew the entire world into a diplomatic battle of nerves that became known as the Cold War.

A measure of optimism, however, accompanied the war's grim aftermath. Heroic efforts had crushed fascism, raising hopes that a new age of democratic humanitarianism

The Atomic Age, 1945–1962

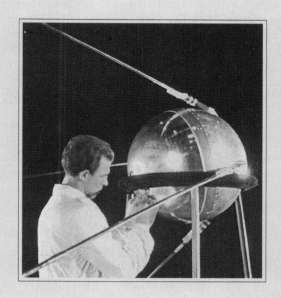

Soviet Scientist Works on Sputnik I
The superpower rivalry that followed World War II led to threats of nuclear war. It also motivated space exploration and technological advance.

would begin. Atomic science promised advances in medicine, and nuclear energy was trumpeted as a revolutionary replacement for coal and oil. The creation of the United Nations heralded an era of international cooperation. Around the globe, colonial peoples won independence from European dominion. Not only did the welfare state expand, but support for basic human rights also gained momentum in the West. Finally, by the end of the 1950s, economic rebirth, stimulated partly by the Cold War, had made much of Europe more prosperous than ever before.

Yet as Europe began its recovery, its peoples' political future was uncertain. In the former fascist regimes, political leaders tried to regain authority after years of military government. For Eastern Europeans the price of recovery was submission to Soviet authority. In the late 1940s the USSR imposed Communist rule throughout most of Eastern Europe and in the 1950s quashed all rebellions against its dominance. Western Europeans found themselves at least partially constricted by U.S. economic power. Some, moreover, resented and feared American anticommunism and interference in European affairs. Anxieties reached a climax in 1962, when the two superpowers came to the brink of war in the most ominous confrontation of the nuclear age.

Reconstruction in an Age of Uncertainty

Europe's future looked bleak at the end of World War II. Much of Europe lay in ruins by the summer of 1945, and conditions would deteriorate before they got better. Nearly 50 million people had perished during the war, and millions more were near starvation, barely scratching out an existence. Restoring basic social and political order was difficult because of the collapse of the bureaucracies needed to govern and to provision a complex industrial society. Compared to the sophisticated military tactics of wartime, the methods of reconstruction were initially crude and backbreaking. Revival was further complicated by competition and disagree-

IMPORTANT DATES
1945 The Cold War begins
1947 India and Pakistan win independence
1948 State of Israel established
1949 Mao Zedong leads Communist Revolution in China; Simone de Beauvoir publishes *The Second Sex*
1950 The Korean War begins
1953 Stalin dies; the Korean War ends
1954 *Brown vs. Board of Education* overturns segregated schools in the U.S.; Vietnamese forces defeat the French at Dien Bien Phu
1956 Egyptian leader Gamal Abdel Nassar nationalizes the Suez Canal; uprising in Hungary
1957 Boris Pasternak publishes *Doctor Zhivago;* USSR launches Sputnik
1958 Fifth Republic begins in France
1962 The U.S. and the USSR face off in the Cuban missile crisis

ment between the Soviet Union and the United States over the way to restore Europe.

Europe Prostrate

In contrast to World War I, in which the devastation was limited to France and the Eastern Front, World War II was a war of movement that leveled thousands of square miles of territory. In eastern and central Europe whole cities were clogged with rubble; homeless survivors wandered the streets. In Sicily and on the Rhine River almost no bridge remained standing; in France motorized vehicles lacked the necessary parts to operate. In the Soviet Union seventy thousand villages and more than a thousand cities lay in shambles.

Everywhere people were starving. In the Netherlands, where both the Nazi occupation and the struggle for liberation had been unusually severe, the Dutch faced imminent death until an airlift of food provided relief. In Britain soap and other basic commodities were difficult to obtain, and many died in the bitterly cold winter of 1946–1947 because of fuel shortages. Italian bakers sold bread by the slice, and people often bartered instead of using money. When Allied troops passed through German towns, the famished inhabitants lined the roads in hopes that someone would toss them something to eat. "To see the children fighting for food," one British soldier observed, "was like watching animals being fed in a zoo." Unlike the last war, military occupation combined with human exhaustion prevented a general uprising.

The tens of millions of refugees suffered the most. Many had been inmates of prisons and death camps; others, especially ethnic Germans, had fled the victorious but vengeful Red Army. Soviet troops—human bulldozers—pushed people from east to west. After Nazi atrocities became public, fleeing Germans were despised; moreover, native Germans in the western-occupied zones viewed refugees as competitors for food and work. "Unwanted, even hated," they were treated "like dirt," one journalist reported. Many refugees ultimately found homes in countries that had endured only minimal war damage, from Denmark and Sweden to Canada and Australia. Following the exodus of refugees from the east, Western Europe became one of the world's most densely populated regions.

The USSR drove many people from Eastern Europe and lobbied hard for the repatriation of millions of Soviet prisoners of war and forced laborers. Although many of the prisoners and laborers fought attempts to return them to the Soviet Union, the Allies transported the majority back to the USSR within a year after the war ended. Once home they were usually sent into forced labor or executed for being "contaminated" by Western ideas. As stories of the executions filtered out, the Allies slowed down the process of returning them; hundreds of thousands of Soviet troops consequently remained in Western Europe for several years.

The suffering of concentration-camp survivors did not end with Germany's defeat. In *The War*, (1986) French author Marguerite Duras, drawing on her diary, described the returnees' arrival at Paris train stations: skeletal, diseased, and disoriented. Jews often had no home to return to, as entire Jewish communities had been annihilated. Nor had the Holocaust eradicated antisemitism. In the summer of 1946, a vicious crowd in Kielce, Poland, killed at least 40 of the 250 Jewish residents. Elsewhere in Eastern Europe, pogroms against returning Jews

were common. Some Jewish survivors were not even released from death camps for more than a year after the liberation because no one knew what to do with them. Meanwhile, a few officials in Europe denied that systematic atrocities had been committed, and wanted to refuse Jews any help.

Jews sought safety in various places. Some hoped to settle in the United States, but President Harry S Truman feared the response of U.S. anti-semites. He let only some twelve thousand Jews into the country. Many survivors crammed into the port cities of Italy and other Mediterranean countries, eventually to wend their way to places unassociated with antisemitism, notably Palestine. As they had in the 1930s, the British balked at the vast migration to the Middle East, for they saw their interests threatened by a likely Arab-Jewish conflict over control of the region.

The Superpowers Forge the Future

The turmoil of wartime and the postwar years ended the global leadership of France, Great Britain, and Germany. The United States was now the richest country in the world. Its industrial output had increased an incredible 15 percent annually between 1940 and 1944, a growth rate that was reflected in American workers' wages. By 1947 the United States controlled almost two-thirds of the world's gold bullion and more than half of its commercial shipping, up from 17 percent of the total in the 1930s. (Other countries had also profited from the war: Norwegian electrical output and Swedish exports had risen dramatically because of German demand. India, Egypt, and Australia had made so much money supplying British war needs that they were able to buy out many British firms.) Continuing to spend heavily on industrial and military research, the United States enhanced its postwar economic position still more.

A euphoric mood swept the United States at the end of the war. Although some feared a postwar depression, a new wave of suburban housing development and the release of pent-up consumer demand kept the economy buoyant. Temporarily reversing the trend toward a lower birthrate, a "baby boom" exploded from the late 1940s through the early 1960s as couples responded to economic abundance by having more children.

U.S. Atom Bomb Test in Bikini Lagoon
The superpowers carried out atmospheric and underground testing of increasingly power-
ful nuclear weapons. In the 1950s and thereafter civilians protested the release of radia-
tion and other dangerous consequences of these tests.

Only growing awareness of pervasive racial discrimination and the unfolding knowledge of the
Holocaust muted the country's optimism.

Casting aside the post–World War I policy of
nonintervention, Americans embraced their position as world leaders. Many had learned about
the world while tracking the war's progress in the
popular media; hundreds of thousands of soldiers,
government officials, and relief workers had served
personally in Europe and Asia. Leaders in the
United States expressed confidence in their ability
to guide the rest of the world. "America must be
the elder brother of nations in the brotherhood of
man," *Life* magazine advised.

The Soviets also emerged from the war with
a well-justified sense of accomplishment. Despite
horrendous losses, they had resisted the most
massive onslaught ever launched against a modern
nation and thus earned an influential position in
world affairs. Instead of international isolation,
Soviet leaders expected parity in decision making
with the United States. Ordinary citizens believed

that a victory that had cost the USSR as much as
25 million lives would bring some improvement in
the conditions of everyday life and a continuation
of the war's relatively relaxed politics. "Life will
become pleasant," one writer prophesied. "There
will be much coming and going, and a lot of contacts with the West." Others foresaw the opening
of private shops and restaurants as well as the distribution of plots of land to individual farmers.
The Stalinist goals of industrialization and defense
against Nazism had been achieved, and thus many
Soviets expected decades of hardship to end.

Soviet leader Joseph Stalin took a different
view. As returning soldiers realized, he chose to
step up repression. Mobilization for total war had
dispersed power and responsibility, and Stalin
moved ruthlessly to reassert his personal control.
In 1946 his new Five-Year Plan raised production
goals and mandated more stringent collectivization
of agriculture. Although industrial production had
doubled by 1950, per capita gross national product
was still less than one-third that of the United

States. Stalin cut back the army by two-thirds to expand the labor force and also turned his attention to the low birthrate, the result of wartime male casualties and women's long, arduous days working without consumer conveniences. He introduced an intensive propaganda campaign emphasizing that working women should not only hold down jobs but also fulfill their "true nature" by producing many children.

Looking beyond his own borders, Stalin continued to see a world hostile to Soviet interests. Despite the Red Army's resounding triumph in the war, he anticipated future invasions from the west. A "buffer zone" of European states loyal to the USSR would safeguard its great-power status as well as the socialist revolution. Stalin prepared to take the necessary steps to create such a zone. Across the Atlantic, Truman opposed Soviet intervention in Europe, believing it heralded an era of Communist expansion.

Meanwhile, in June 1945 a new international organization, the United Nations, met for the first time. Hopes ran high as the Cold War developed that the United Nations would be more effective than the League of Nations in settling international disputes. The U.N. Charter provided for a collective global authority to adjudicate conflicts and offer military protection to member nations threatened with outside aggression. Yet at the center of the United Nations was the Security Council of five powers—the United States, the Soviet Union, Britain, China, and France—each empowered to veto decisions. Fearing his former allies, Stalin had successfully imposed this veto power. In addition, he obtained separate representation in the larger General Assembly for two Soviet republics, the Ukraine and Byelorussia, thus securing control of three votes. Seeing the United Nations as a tool of the United States, Stalin attempted to manipulate it by constantly wielding the veto and his two "extra" votes in the General Assembly. In response, the United States tried to organize new administrative mechanisms within the United Nations to bypass the Soviets in the representative bodies.

In the years immediately following World War II the United States and the Soviet Union were like two world-class chess players sizing each other up. Their battles of rhetoric and disagreements in the United Nations and over what to do with defeated Germany were more subtle than outright war, but with the specter of nuclear bombs lurking on the horizon, potentially more lethal than any war in history. This power struggle between the two superpowers, which would be carried out not only on European territory but throughout the world, would soon develop into a cold war that would transform the rebuilding of a war-ravaged Europe and cast an ominous cloud over global politics for more than four decades.

The Political Restoration of Europe

In May 1945 Europeans lived under overlapping systems of political jurisdiction: local resistance leaders, Allied armies of occupation, and entrenched bureaucrats often worked at cross-purposes to restore society. All had a stake in replacing Nazi and Fascist political structures, but they disagreed on how to accomplish this common goal. For example, whereas prewar bureaucrats considered civilian provisioning a top priority, some resistance fighters wanted to purge Nazis from politics immediately, often by violent means.

The discovery of the death camps' emaciated survivors and the remnants of the hundreds of thousands killed in the camps as the Soviet army approached fueled the desire for revenge against Nazis. Swift vigilante justice released pent-up rage and aimed to punish collaborators and fascist sympathizers for their complicity in the Holocaust and other war crimes. Angry mobs shaved the heads of French women suspected of willingly associating with the Germans who had occupied France and then paraded them naked through local streets. Members of the resistance did not wait for courtroom justice but executed tens of thousands of Nazi officers and collaborators on the spot. Amidst such an atmosphere of revenge and purge, crowds descended on village and town halls to obtain certification that they had worked in the resistance. The celebration of resistance heroes—some of them self-proclaimed—and the simultaneous purge of evildoers became the founding acts of a reborn European political community.

Newly empowered government officials and representatives of the Allies undertook a more systematic *denazification.* Belgium investigated seven hundred thousand people (out of a total population of 8 millon) suspected of collaboration. These

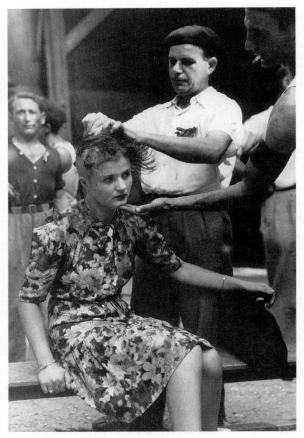

Punishment of Civilians in France
*Citizens often ignored legal procedures and determined
the guilt of accused Nazi collaborators on their own.
Women charged with having relations with German
soldiers had their heads shaved and were paraded
(sometimes naked) through villages and cities.*

investigations often showed how difficult it was to
draw a line between acts of collaboration with totalitarianism and acts of cooperation in the name
of survival. At a different level, the Nuremberg trials in the autumn of 1945 provided a horrifying
panorama of crimes by Nazi leaders. The Allies
contributed their most esteemed legal experts to
conduct this unusual trial, which underscored the
need to uphold principles of justice and accountability for crimes even in wartime. Although international law lacked a precedent for defining genocide as a crime, the judges at Nuremberg found
sufficient cause to sentence twelve of twenty-four
defendants to death and the remainder to prison

terms. Goering escaped execution by committing
suicide in his prison cell.

After Nuremberg, the Allies continued to
prosecute Nazi and Fascist leaders but they never
succeeded completely in that huge task. Some of
the leaders most responsible for war crimes disappeared. Patriotic Germans, many of them brutalized by invading Soviet armies, were skeptical
about denazification. They interpreted the trials
as the characteristic retribution of victors rather
than the punishment of the guilty. Allied officials,
anxious to restore government services, often relied on the expertise of high-ranking Fascist and
Nazi bureaucrats, many of whom kept their jobs
in the new system. The pragmatics of putting
Europe back together often took precedence over
punishing all former Nazis.

In Western Europe reform-minded civilian
governments reflecting the coalitions that had
opposed the Axis took shape. These governments
contrasted conspicuously with totalitarian regimes.
In France, Charles de Gaulle governed briefly as
chief of state, but quit over limitations on the
president's power that he judged as too reminiscent of the Third Republic. The French approved
a constitution in 1946 that established the Fourth
Republic and finally granted French women the
vote. Meanwhile, Italy abolished its monarchy. A
resistance-based Socialist government was replaced
late in 1945 by the more conservative Christian
Democrats, a coalition that included Communists
and Socialists. They pursued liberal economic programs and democratic reform. In Britain the
Labour government of Clement Attlee focused
on fulfilling promises to ensure that prosperity
would be shared more equally among the classes
by expanding social-welfare programs.

As reform proceeded in Western Europe, the
Soviet Union repressed democratic government in
Central and Eastern Europe between 1945 and
1948. Coalition, or Popular Front, governments,
comprising liberals, Socialists, and Communists,
initially predominated in these regions. However,
Stalin almost immediately imposed Communist
rule in Bulgaria and Romania. In Romania, Moscow cited civil violence in 1945 as the reason they
were ousting all non-Communists from the civil
service and cabinet. When the Allies protested, a
single member of the Peasant party and another
from the Liberal party were allowed to join eigh-

teen Communists in the government. In response to these events, Party membership in Romania soared from two thousand in 1945 to more than eight hundred thousand a year later. In Poland the Communists fixed the election results of 1945 and 1946 to create the illusion of approval for communism. Nevertheless, the Communists had to share power between 1945 and 1947 with the popular Peasant party of Stanisław Mikołajczyk, which had a large constituency of rural workers and peasant landowners.

The United States acknowledged Soviet influence in areas it occupied, but West European leaders worried that Communist power would spread even farther. The difficult conditions of postwar life made communism increasingly attractive to West European workers. Concern mounted when Communist insurgents threatened to overrun the right-wing monarchy the British had installed in Greece in 1944. The British propped up this repressive government until the terrible winter of 1946–1947 made it financially impossible for them to keep sending aid. As Communist guerrillas continued to make inroads with strong support from Yugoslav Partisans, U.S. leaders feared that Europe was on the brink of "going Communist."

In March 1947, Truman reacted to the threat, announcing what became known as the *Truman Doctrine*. The president requested $400 million in aid for Greece and Turkey, which the Soviets were also pressuring. Fearing that the American people wanted no more to do with Europe, U.S. congressmen would agree to the program only if Truman would "scare hell out of the country." He accommodated them, publicizing the aid program as crucial to preventing a wave of Soviet conquest from engulfing the world. In the autumn of 1948 the United States supplied the Greek government with 10,000 transport vehicles, close to 100,000 rifles, and 140 planes. The show of U.S. support convinced the Yugoslavs to back off, and in 1949 the Greek rebels declared a cease-fire. More generally, Truman had set a precedent for countering political crises with economic aid.

"The seeds of totalitarian regimes are nurtured by misery and want," Truman warned in the speech that introduced his doctrine. His linkage of poverty to the rise of dictatorship led to the *Marshall Plan,* a program of massive U.S. economic aid to Europe. Secretary of State George C. Marshall announced the plan in a Harvard commencement address in June 1947. He cited the breakdown in economic exchange during the war as a threat to political stability. By the early 1950s the United States had sent Europe more than $12 billion in food, equipment, and services.

The Marshall Plan claimed nonpartisanship, directed not "against any country or doctrine but against hunger, poverty, desperation, and chaos." Stalin, however, saw it as a U.S. political ploy because he knew the United States was aware that the USSR could not offer similar economic aid. The Soviet Union reacted by suppressing the remaining coalition governments and assuming political control in Central and Eastern Europe. In Poland, where the government found the possibility of Marshall Plan aid attractive, Stalin purged Mikołajczyk in 1947 in the name of creating a "people's government"—the code name for a Communist-controlled state. In Hungary the prime minister and head of the popular Small-Holders party was forced out while on a trip to Switzerland in 1947. Czechoslovakia, which by Eastern European standards had prospered under a Communist-led coalition, welcomed the Marshall Plan as the beginning of East-West rapprochement. This illusion ended, however, during a purge of non-Communist officials that began in the autumn of 1947. Two government ministers, including the anticommunist foreign minister Jan Masaryk, the son of the country's first president, were found to have "fallen" from windows to their deaths. By June 1948 the Socialist president, Edouard Beneš, had resigned and been replaced by a Communist figurehead. Nonetheless, the populace remained so passive that leaders likened the takeover to "cutting butter with a knife." The Soviet Union had successfully created a buffer of satellite states in Eastern Europe by crushing representative institutions. In the autumn of 1947, Stalin capped his victory by organizing the Comin-form, a centralized association of Communist parties from around the world directed by Moscow.

The only exception to the Soviet sweep in Eastern Europe came in Yugoslavia, under the Communist Tito (Josip Broz) (1892–1980), leader of the powerful anti-Nazi Partisans during the war. Drawing on support from Serbs, Croats, and Muslims alike, the Partisans triumphed in a Communist revolution after the war. Yugoslavia

German Poster for the Marshall Plan
The plan poured billions of dollars into Western-bloc countries to promote economic growth and political stability.

emerged from the revolution a federation of six socialist republics and two autonomous provinces within Serbia. This settlement recognized the country's cultural diversity but was based on the belief that only tough measures would quell ethnic and religious animosities. Tito's forceful personality held these groups together, a feat he sustained until he died in 1980. He had also developed such a strong organization by war's end that he was able to resist Soviet control. Eager for Yugoslavia to develop industrially rather than simply to serve Soviet needs, he remarked: "No matter how much each of us loves the land of Socialism, the USSR, he can, in no case love his country less. . . . We study and take as an example the Soviet system, but we are developing socialism in our country in somewhat different forms." Furious, Stalin ejected

Yugoslavia from the Cominform. To Stalin, commitment to communism meant obedience to him.

Moscow also dominated the Communists in Western Europe. In the summer of 1947, Communist leaders met in Poland, where those from Italy and France were accused of "parliamentary cretinism" for failing to capitalize on economic discontent by seizing power. These leaders returned home with a militant message. Maurice Thorez, the French Communist chief, called the French Fourth Republic a "reactionary dictatorship" and summoned the French people to struggle against it. De Gaulle responded by creating a new anticommunist party, Rally of the French People (RPF). In other countries all cooperation between ruling Christian Democrats and Communists abruptly ceased. Before Marshall Plan aid took hold, the political climate was so tense that Western Europe looked, said one observer, as if "blood was going to flow."

The Cold War Fragments Germany

Postwar Germany had lost its sovereignty. The terms of the Yalta agreement had divided it into four zones, each occupied by troops from one of the four principal victors in World War II—the United States, Britain, the Soviet Union, and France. The growing postwar rivalry between East and West further clouded Germany's political status. As both sides took a firm stand over the future of this once-rich and still potentially powerful country, the Cold War escalated. At issue was not a small nation but the heart of the Continent.

After two world wars and the Holocaust, many Americans had concluded that something was inherently wrong with the Germans' character. At the height of the war, Roosevelt had often spoken of using desperate means to end their apparent militaristic tendencies. After the war the U.S. military occupation forces began a plan to reprogram German life culturally, controlling the press and determining the content of all the media. They allowed German filmmakers, for example, to make only four films in the first years after the war. Allied censors reviewed scripts to verify that they did not express fascist or authoritarian values. Stalin took a different tack to suppress the "evils" of German society in the Soviet-occupied zone. He believed

Nazism had been spawned by monopoly capitalism and therefore confiscated and redistributed the estates of wealthy Germans.

The occupying powers disagreed about how to develop Germany's economic potential. American leaders hoped that all four occupation zones would coordinate economic activity to the mutual benefit of each zone. For example, they envisioned that surplus produce from the Soviet-controlled zone would feed the urban populations in western Germany; in turn, German industrial goods would be sent to the USSR. They believed reciprocal arrangements such as these would best benefit both the occupying countries and Germany itself. The Soviets threw a wrench into this plan. They immediately dismantled industries in their zone and sent machinery, vehicles, and other equipment to the Soviet Union. They also transported skilled workers, engineers, and scientists to the USSR to work as virtual slave laborers. Not only did Stalin pillage the Soviet zone, but he manipulated its currency, enabling the USSR to buy German products at unrealistically low prices. These actions certainly did not foster trade and cooperation. Instead they generated economic chaos in the divided Germany during 1946 and 1947 and fueled animosity.

In 1947, foreign ministers of the four occupying powers met to decide on currency reform and on a plan for rebuilding Germany. The Soviet minister's demands for an increased share of reparations from Germany halted negotiations at an impasse. Meanwhile, the three Western allies merged their sectors and embarked on an economic buildup under the Marshall Plan to make West Germany their own buffer against extending Soviet power. Notions of a permanently weakened Germany came to an end. To make the western zone self-supporting and to block Soviet expansion as rapidly as possible, the United States enlisted many former Nazi officials as spies and rechanneled the hatred of bolshevism that was a keystone of Nazism.

Stalin struck back on July 24, 1948, when Soviet troops blockaded Germany's capital, Berlin. Like Germany as a whole, the city had also been divided into four occupation zones—but it was located more than a hundred miles into the Soviet zone and was thus cut off from Western territory.

The Soviets declared that they now controlled all of Berlin, and they refused to allow vehicles to travel through their occupation zone to reach the city. Stalin expected the Western bloc to capitulate to the new situation, as it had done in Hungary, Romania, and elsewhere in Eastern Europe.

Instead the United States responded decisively, flying in millions of tons of provisions to the cut-off city. During the winter of 1948–1949 the Berlin airlift—"Operation Vittles"—even funneled coal to the city to warm the isolated Berliners. Reports of people's suffering, of pilots' valiant deeds, and of Soviet belligerence transformed the Cold War in the popular imagination, as citizens of the Western bloc increasingly came to see the conflict as a moral crusade. By the time the Soviets ended the blockade on May 12, 1949, the fate of Germany and especially of a divided Berlin had become a public barometer of the Cold War. The Soviet Union would risk war to maintain its security and prerogatives, and the United States would do no less.

The Berlin Airlift

To counter further threats, the Western nations formed the North Atlantic Treaty Organization (NATO) in April 1949. NATO provided a unified military force for the member countries: Britain, France, Belgium, the Netherlands, Luxembourg, Italy, Denmark, Portugal, Iceland, Norway, the United States, and Canada. The membership of the United States and Canada marked the serious involvement of North America in Western Europe. NATO constituted the kind of massive regional alliance on which both sides in the Cold War were coming to depend.

By the end of 1949, the establishment of rival regional alliances, the division of Germany into hostile sectors, the Soviet Union's explosion of its own atomic bomb, and the reconversion of public opinion from a peacetime to a wartime mentality had fractured the Grand Alliance of World War II. Citizens prepared themselves emotionally for war again, as the world now split into two hostile camps.

East Versus West

The ideological clash between East and West, brought into millions of households by the popular media, loomed large in everyday life. Many people in Eastern Europe, the Soviet Union, and even the Western democracies expressed strong faith in Marxist-Leninism. That confidence was often genuine, but in Communist-dominated countries such professions of loyalty were often obtained by force. Moreover, the state controlled all media, and public dissent, which the Party could find in simple disagreement, was not tolerated. Most Westerners supported liberal values such as free speech, private property, and human rights. Yet many Western Europeans resented what they saw as too much U.S. clout and interference in Europe and held anti-American sentiments even as they accepted U.S. aid. European recovery proceeded in this sizzling ideological atmosphere. Western Europe revived its democratic political structures, its individualistic culture, and its productive capabilities. Eastern Europe restlessly endured a far less prosperous existence under Stalinism.

Cold War Mentalities

The radio played a significant role in shaping Cold War attitudes. In 1946, people tuned in as Winston Churchill warned of the Soviet entrapment of Eastern Europe in its "iron" grip: "From Stettin in the Baltic to Trieste in the Adriatic, an iron curtain has descended across the Continent." During World War II, people had been glued to their radios for news updates. Government officials and resistance forces alike had recognized the importance of controlling the airways and thus the information received during the war. After the war the number of radios in homes grew steadily, and the 1950s marked a high tide of radio's influence.

As the Cold War intensified, radio's propaganda function increased. The Voice of America, with its main studio in Washington, D.C., broadcast in 38 languages from 100 transmitters during the late 1940s and early 1950s and provided an alternative source of news for Eastern Europeans. The Soviet counterpart broadcast in Russian around the clock but initially spent much of its wattage jamming U.S. programming. Russian pro-

The Cold War in Europe

grams stressed a uniform "Communist" culture and set of values; the United States, by contrast, promoted more open debate over current affairs. In Western Europe governments controlled much of the programming and news, and thus the independent Radio Luxembourg became popular because of its less predictable editorial stance. The influence of Western radio even reached Asia and Africa where new radio transmitters thrust into the sky. The English and French built them, hoping to use radio to regain native allegiance.

Conveyed by radio and other media, Cold War tensions became a part of the daily life of millions of ordinary people. The news featured reports of nuclear testing, military buildups, and hostile diplomatic incidents. The public heard tests of emergency power facilities that sent them scurrying for cover; schoolchildren, in addition to fire drills, now had drills to rehearse what to do in case of nuclear war—the precautions usually involved crawling under their desks and covering their heads. Word of Soviet and American leaders' facing one another down heightened feelings of nuclear fear. Amid constant news stories of the possibility of nuclear annihilation, English mathematician and philosopher Bertrand Russell (1872–1970) reported living daily in "confused agitation."

The Cold War mushroomed as a cultural phenomenon. George Orwell's novel *1984* was claimed by ideologues on both sides as a vindication of their beliefs. Ray Bradbury's popular *Fahrenheit 451* (1954), whose title indicated the temperature at which books would burn, condemned Cold War curtailment of intellectual freedom. In the USSR official writers (those who belonged to the Union of the Soviet Writers) churned out spy stories; espionage novels topped best-seller lists in the Western bloc. *Casino Royale* (1953), written by British author Ian Fleming, introduced James Bond, a British secret agent who survived tests of wit and physical prowess at the hands of Communist and other villains. Traveling to exotic locales, Bond, also known as Agent 007, brilliantly improvised with sophisticated weaponry provided by government scientists—themselves employed in the Cold War. Daily papers meanwhile fired people's passions with stories of real-life spies. The execution of Ethel and Julius Rosenberg in 1953 after

their conviction for passing atomic secrets from the United States to the Soviet Union created a public furor about their guilt or innocence that has yet to die down completely.

West European Economic Miracles

Fears of nuclear catastrophe did not impede Western Europe's economic rebirth. In the first months after the war, the job of rebuilding often involved rude kinds of labor that mobilized entire populations. With so many men dead, wounded, or detained as prisoners of war, German housewives, "women of the ruins," earned their living clearing rubble by hand. The task was vast: up to 95 percent of major cities had been bombed to bits. Neighborhoods set up survival networks to pro-

Women Clear Rubble in Berlin after World War II
Sophisticated weaponry pulverized European cities during the war. Personal survival and urban rebuilding depended on back-breaking, manual labor.

vide daily necessities; grass roots activism, so at odds with Nazi practices, influenced German politics in the decades to come.

Europe diverted labor and capital into reconstructing the infrastructure—transportation, communications, and industrial capacity—but the scarcity of goods sparked unrest and made communism politically attractive. Thus although West European economies had started to revive by 1947, the Marshall Plan poured in American dollars and goods to sustain recovery in the capital *and* consumer sectors. Food and consumer goods became more plentiful, and demand for automobiles, washing machines, and vacuum cleaners boosted economies. The growth in all kinds of production wiped out most unemployment. Labor-short northern Europe even arranged for "guest" workers to migrate from impoverished regions such as Sicily to help restore cities. The outbreak of war in Korea in 1950 spurred defense expenditures and further stimulated the European economy.

The 1950s witnessed astonishing rates of economic growth. The West German economy grew at an unmatched 8.2 percent annually between 1950 and 1954. France's economy jumped 8 percent each year in the second half of the 1950s. Late in the 1950s, Italy likewise rebounded with new ventures in the production of oil and synthetic products. Because Britain's annual growth was only 3 percent, it played the part of the comparatively poor relation. Not facing massive reconstruction, it repaired but did not modernize its basic industries. More important, although Britain's immediate postwar capital investment was very high, its trade was oriented toward the less vigorous Commonwealth economies. Thus it missed out on some of the opportunities the West European trade boom offered.

The postwar recovery also featured the conversion of wartime technology to consumer industry and the introduction of new industrial processes. Advances in aircraft construction during the war fed an expanded global network of civilian travel, and nations organized their own airline systems. Synthetic goods that had been developed to relieve wartime shortages now became part of peacetime civilian life. Factories churned out a vast assortment of plastic goods, ranging from pipes to shoes and rainwear. Striking innovation revolutionized the production of electronic com-

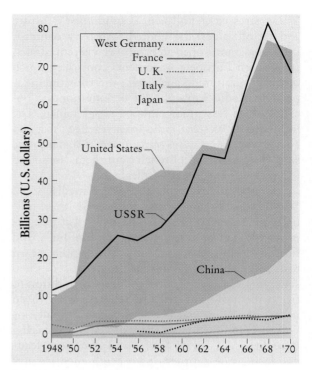

Postwar Arms Race

ponents, glass and steel, and even earth-lifting machinery.

As the Cold War replaced the world war, military spending continued to pump up national economies. In the late 1940s, for example, Britain and France, respectively, spent 6.5 and 5.7 percent of their gross national product on the military. Governments ordered bombs, fighter planes, tanks, and missiles; they also sponsored military research. Spending for armaments helped stabilize the economy by creating jobs, as it had in Germany and the United States in the late 1930s. After World War I, decreased military expenditures caused instability, and in 1947, strikes and protests in Western Europe threatened a return to those tumultuous times. Marshall Plan aid and other Cold War spending calmed the social and political climate.

International cooperation and planning provided a final ingredient in recovery and would become a permanent feature of economic life. The Bretton Woods Agreement of 1944, eventually signed by forty-four nations (with the Soviet Union a notable exception), envisioned a world bank and devised the International Monetary Fund (IMF). The IMF was to ensure the stability of international currencies by using pooled monies to prop up any weak national currency, and thus aimed to promote trade. Marshall Plan assistance went only to countries that agreed to cooperate economically and financially both to stimulate free trade still more and to move toward the political unification of Western Europe. In this way the plan ambitiously intended to destroy the economic and political nationalism that had caused war.

Changing Political Horizons in the West

The United States had a strong stake in European recovery. Europe's revival, American statesmen recognized, would open up trade with a vast market. They also believed that prosperity would dull the allure of postwar European authoritarian movements. Most West European leaders agreed on the political desirability of a rapid economic revival; but they differed over the issue of Germany's reintegration into the postwar world. Whereas Scandinavia and the Low Countries wanted their traditional trading partner restored as quickly as possible, the French, and to a lesser extent the British, advocated the division of Germany into smaller administrative units. Pressed by the U.S. government to rebuild Germany for reasons of trade and Western-bloc security in the face of the Cold War and to consider attempting their own political unification, West Europeans devised plans for economic coordination based on national self-interest and the hard-headed resolution of mutual animosities. The resulting economic consortia brought a surprising end to almost a century of Franco-German rivalry.

In 1949, delegates from most West European countries began meeting regularly in a Council of Europe. Two years later, Italy, France, West Germany, Belgium, Luxembourg, and the Netherlands formed the European Coal and Steel Community (ECSC). This organization cooperatively managed coal and steel production and set prices, and, most important, distributed West German output throughout Western Europe as a whole. According to the ECSC's principal architect, Robert Schuman, the economic unity the organization created would reduce the competition for resources and economic tensions and make another war "materially impos-

sible." Simply put, the bonds of common productivity and trade would keep the traditional enemies —France and Germany—from another cataclysmic war.

"The six," as the ECSC members were called, took another giant step toward ensuring regional prosperity in 1957 when they signed the Treaty of Rome. This pact established an agreement for sharing atomic resources through a commission called EUROCOM, as well as a trading partnership called the European Economic Community (EEC), known more popularly as the Common Market. The EEC reduced tariffs among the six partners and worked to develop common trade policies. According to one of its founders, the EEC aimed to "prevent the race of nationalism, which is the true curse of the modern world." Increased cooperation reaped economic rewards for the six members. Italy's economy, which had lagged behind that of France and West Germany, boomed. Britain, which pointedly refused to join the EEC because membership would have required it to surrender certain imperial trading rights—and because participation in any continental trading block would make it "just another European country," as one British statesman put it—continued its relative decline. The future lay with the new Western Europe joined in the Common Market.

The Soviet Union also formed regional organizations, among them the Council for Mutual Economic Assistance (COMECON), charged with coordinating economic relations among the satellite countries and Moscow. Then in 1955, after West Germany was invited to join NATO, the Soviet Union retaliated by establishing a similar organization, the Warsaw Treaty Organization, more commonly known as the Warsaw Pact. Joining the Soviet Union in this alliance were Albania, Bulgaria, Czechoslovakia, East Germany, Hungary, Poland, and Romania. The Soviet Union dominated its alliances through coercion, whereas U.S. economic leadership provided the cohesive force for the Western alliances. On both sides the regional coordination of policies marked the end of single-nation management of economic and military resources.

Such regional coordination and planning reflected Europe's past as well as its future. The general staff of Hitler and, before him, William II had planned regional economic coordination. The bureaucrats of Vichy, France, the satellite of the Third Reich, had developed a technocratic vision of how to run society. Less ominously, resistance leaders had hoped that international cooperation would arise from the ashes of World War II. Thus the head of the ECSC, Jean Monnet, who also inspired and helped create the Common Market, believed rational administration by supranational agencies composed of disinterested experts reduced the potential for irrationality and violence in politics—both domestic and international. Finally, cooperation and expert planning had an American aura that had also drawn Europeans to jazz and skyscrapers a generation earlier. Monnet attacked socially conservative practices in favor of down-to-earth American manners that suggested U.S. innovation and success. In summertime meetings with high-ranking leaders he encouraged them to take the daring step of removing their jackets and rolling up their sleeves, telling them, "It's a habit I picked up in America."

Bureaucrats and planners increasingly dominated European political and economic life, and the moderates held sway over the extremes of Right and Left. France, Norway, and the Netherlands developed planned economies that reduced the influence of parliamentary politicians by forcing them to heed bureaucratic expertise. In France the Fourth Republic shuffled cabinets at a rapid pace, but because the economy grew, the shifts seemed inconsequential. According to one observer, France was no longer run by the top 200 families, but by 200 technocrats. In Italy the Christian Democrat Alcide De Gasperi (1881–1954) strongly supported the Common Market. He was also influential in keeping Spain and Portugal out of the EEC. Although Spain's Franco and Portugal's Antonio Oliviera Salazar invoked common Catholic culture in their bid to join, De Gasperi emphasized the difference in political values: the EEC supported democracies, not dictatorships.

In 1949, a variety of West German experts acting with centrist politicians created a new state, the German Federal Republic. Its first chancellor was seventy-three-year-old Catholic anticommunist, Konrad Adenauer (1876–1967), a man Hitler had sacked as mayor of Cologne in 1933. Working with other democrats, Adenauer drafted a constitution that would prevent the emergence of a dictator and guarantee individual rights. Adenauer

also allied himself with Ludwig Erhard (1897–1977), an economist who had stabilized the post-war German currency so that commerce could resume. Erhard used his academic expertise and commitment to the free market to "turn a lunar landscape into a flourishing beehive," in one commentator's words. The politician and the economist successfully guided Germany away from both fascism and communism. Adenauer delegated Erhard wide-ranging authority to revive business and himself assumed control of the Christian Democrats. Unlike Britain and France, where the Labour government nationalized many private businesses, West Germany offered incentives to privately owned companies so they would prosper. It simultaneously forced businesses into a "co-partnership," or cooperative relationship, with workers to avoid prewar antagonisms that had put management and labor at odds. Union leaders served on managerial boards, where they helped determine policies on wages, automation, and worker retraining.

These events unfolded in an era of unprecedented U.S. activism in world affairs. In the 1950s the Western giant negotiated dozens of bilateral treaties with countries around the globe, built air bases outside the United States, doled out massive foreign aid, and took part in foreign wars and territorial occupation. In contrast to the extreme partisanship within the United States over America's role after World War I (Republican congressmen, pushing isolationism, refused to ratify the League of Nations, Democratic president Woodrow Wilson's beloved brainchild), broad, bipartisan domestic support bolstered the nation's assumption of world leadership by the 1950s. Truman helped build this consensus by fanning Americans' fears of Soviet expansion. The concerted effort against the Nazis had required Soviet-American cooperation, and during the war U.S. government propaganda had portrayed the Soviets as abandoning their Marxism for American values. In 1947, however, Truman reemphasized the great gap between the "free institutions" of the United States and the "terror" and "suppression" of the Soviet Union. The Marshall Plan, so vital to future U.S. trade, was sold to the American public as crucial to the fight against communism. By the mid-1950s most Americans believed in a massive Soviet plot to take over the world and in the necessity of global military preparedness to prevent freedom's imminent collapse.

In February 1950, after the Soviets had exploded their first nuclear weapon and after the Communist Revolution in China, U.S. senator Joseph McCarthy, who needed a sensational issue to latch onto to win reelection, dropped a "bomb" of his own. In a public speech he claimed to know of a great Communist conspiracy to overthrow the United States from within. McCarthy purported to have uncovered a Communist plot in the State Department: "I have here in my hand a list of 205 names," McCarthy warned, "a list of names known . . . as being members of the Communist party and who nevertheless are still working and shaping policy." McCarthy had no names, but his accusations aroused a hysteria that curtailed free speech in the United States.

Claiming to have evidence from patriotic "informers," McCarthy launched a campaign against the "card-carrying Communists" and "pinkos" who he alleged were trying to subvert the American government and indeed America itself. His denunciations led to the investigation of more than 6 million people by various government agencies by 1952. Many of those investigated for "un-American" behavior, from members of the clergy to filmmakers to government bureaucrats and even members of the army, had their careers and lives ruined, even though no evidence of wrongdoing surfaced. Rumor, insinuation, and a "witch-hunt" mentality poisoned American culture. McCarthy had books he deemed subversive removed from government shelves and actually sponsored book burnings. McCarthyites championed themselves as protectors of America; paradoxically, they adopted fascist tactics to preserve a democracy.

In the 1952 presidential election the war hero Dwight D. Eisenhower teamed up with another Communist hunter, Republican Richard M. Nixon, to defeat the Democrat Adlai E. Stevenson, branded by some opponents as an appeaser and protector of Communists. Eisenhower himself remained "above politics" and refused to attack McCarthy's excesses directly. The Senate finally voted to censure McCarthy in the winter of 1954. Nonetheless, anticommunism escalated. Eisenhower's secretary of state, John Foster Dulles, denounced mere "containment" of the Soviets on the grounds that "We shall never have a secure peace

or a happy world so long as Soviet communism dominates one-third of all the peoples. . . ." Despite suffering through four recessions in the 1950s, the American people were more unified than ever by their common fears of a Soviet menace.

A Humanitarian Revival in the West

Meanwhile, in Western Europe postwar cultural currents reemphasized morality, spiritual values, and political choice after the wartime bloodbath. In the early postwar years people proclaimed the triumph of a Western heritage, Western civilization, and Western values over fascism. "We have felt that our war is a war to defend civilization [from] a conspiracy against man," a British critic wrote. The first U.S. Western civilization textbooks had appeared late in the 1930s to document the superiority of Western culture, then threatened by fascists and by nationalist movements in Asia and Africa. University courses in Western civilization flourished after the war to reaffirm those values.

Churches actively participated in restoring Western values, making a commitment to "re-Christianize" Europe. Despite instances of accommodating dictators, many Catholic priests had preached sermons challenging totalitarian practices, and Protestant pastors in Germany had worked against Hitler during the Third Reich. In France the worker-priest movement sent the clergy into factories as missionaries to minister to the common laborer. Fascist ideology had emphasized the physically strong, but the church embraced the unfortunate. Pope John XXIII's (*1958–1963) encyclical *Mater et Magistra* (1961) officially summoned world rulers to care for the disadvantaged. Nevertheless, the churches' success in postwar re-Christianization was only partial, and the trend toward a more secular culture continued.

Memoirs of the death camps became popular reading material. Rescued from the Third Reich in 1940, Nelly Sachs (1891–1970) won the Nobel Prize for Literature in 1966 for her poetry about the Holocaust. Anne Frank's *Diary of a Young Girl* (1947), the poignant record of a teenager hidden away with her family in the back of an Amsterdam warehouse, became emblematic of the survival of Western values in the face of Nazi persecution. Faced with the small miseries of daily life and the grand evils of Nazism, Anne never stopped believing that "people are really good at heart." Although some admirers of the Nazis denied that a Holocaust had occurred, the postwar flood of memoirs confirmed the grim truth. For many readers, this literature instilled a new commitment to tolerance and pluralism.

Histories of the resistance tapped into the public's desire for inspiration after the wartime orgy of savagery. Governments marked spots where resisters had been killed; their biographies filled magazines and bookstalls. Organizations of resisters commemorated their role in winning the war. Although resistance efforts were publicized, discussing collaboration with Nazis was tacitly forbidden. French filmmakers, for example, avoided the subject for decades after the war for fear of reopening wounds. Whereas stories of resistance became the stuff of legends, the behavior of the victors was considered off limits to critics. After the war it appeared that the Allied peoples had been united against fascism from the start, but the truth was quite different. The questioning of motives that occurred after World War I was avoided: this had been a "good war," one in which the sacrifices (caused, for example, by the massive bombing of the civilian population in Germany and Japan) occurred on behalf of clear, humane values.

On a theoretical level, existential philosophy explored the meaning (or lack of meaning) of human existence in a world where evil flourished. Two existentialist leaders, Albert Camus (1913–1960) and Jean-Paul Sartre (1905–1980), had written for the resistance during the war, although Nazis censors had also allowed the production of Sartre's plays. Taking as their starting point the work of the German philosophers Friedrich Nietzsche and Martin Heidegger, existentialists confronted the question of what "being" was about, given the absence of God and the breakdown of morality. The answer was that "being," or existing, was not the automatic process either of God's creation or of birth into the natural world. One was not *born* with spiritual goodness in the image of a Creator, but instead, through action and choice, one *created* an "authentic" existence. Such Camus novels as *The Stranger* (1942) and *The Plague* (1947) dissected the evils of a corrupt political order and pondered human responsibility

in such situations. Whereas Camus focused on mental attitudes and choices in the face of evil, Sartre's writings emphasized political activism. Sartre's idea of an activist existence validated resistance under totalitarianism. Despite the fact that they had never faced the enormous problems of making choices while living under fascism, young people in the 1950s found existentialism compelling and made it the most fashionable philosophy of the day. A decade later the spirit of existentialism became part of the inspiration for students who sought to reform society through political confrontation.

In 1949, Simone de Beauvoir (1908–1986), Sartre's lifetime companion, published the twentieth century's most important work on the condition of women, *The Second Sex*. Beauvoir believed that most women had failed to take the kind of action necessary to lead authentic lives. Instead they lived in the world of "necessity," devoting themselves exclusively to reproduction and motherhood. Failing to create an authentic self through considered action and accomplishment, they had become the opposite—an object, or "Other." Moreover, instead of struggling to define themselves and assert their freedom, women passively accepted their own "Otherness" and lived as defined by men. In the 1960s Beauvoir's theory would guide the women's movement beyond struggles for legal and political reform and underscore the powerful cultural and psychological components of women's condition.

Beauvoir's book was a smash hit, in large part because people thought Sartre had written it. Both Beauvoir and Sartre became celebrities, for the intellectual world increasingly attracted media attention. The media spread the new humanitarianism just as it had roused support for the war. A steady barrage of glossy magazine photos, newspaper articles, and radio interviews built a cohesive, enlightened public sector fascinated by the new ecumenism in the church, by the death-camp literature and stories of the resistance, and by the latest trends in philosophy.

The new humanitarianism did not deal only with high-minded ethical issues. It also addressed matters that polite society wanted to avoid. In Italy *neorealist* filmmakers produced such classics as Roberto Rossellini's *Open City* (1945) and Vittorio De Sica's *Bicycle Thief* (1948). These movies

The Bicycle Thief, *1948*
Filmmakers in the postwar era explored the struggle of ordinary people to live with dignity and humanitarian values. In this film, a man and his son fight for a better life in post-fascist Italy.

replaced glamorous characters, flashy sets, and elegant costumes with ordinary characters living in devastated, impoverished cities. By depicting such stark conditions, directors conveyed their distance both from middle-class prosperity and from fascist bombast. As one Italian director described the new realist challenge:

> *We are in rags? Let's show everyone our rags. We are defeated? Let's look at our disasters. How much are we obligated to the Mafia? to hypocritical bigotry? to conformity. . . ? Let's pay all our debts with a ferocious love of honesty.*

Down-and-out characters represented a return to morality and ethical values after more than a decade of fascist dishonesty and evil.

In the United States the African-American struggle for civil rights pushed many Americans toward a greater commitment to racial equality. In 1954 the Supreme Court declared segregated education unconstitutional in *Brown* v. *Board of Education,* a case initiated by well-organized activists in the National Association for the Advancement of Colored People (NAACP). The drive for rights was taken up by ordinary people, especially black veterans and civilians who had contributed to the victorious American war effort. On December 1, 1955, in Montgomery, Alabama, Rosa Parks, an African-American seamstress and part-time secretary for the local branch of the NAACP, boarded a bus and took the first available seat in the so-called white section. When a white man found himself without a seat, the driver screamed at her: "Nigger, move back." Sitting in the front violated Southern laws, which encompassed a host of inequitable, even brutal policies toward African Americans. Parks had confronted that system by practicing civil disobedience, and her act led to what would become a year-long mass boycott of public transportation by Montgomery's blacks. The protest pushed the civil rights movement into the African-American community as a whole.

Led by a host of groups, blacks and some white allies boycotted discriminatory businesses, "sat in" at segregated facilities, and registered black voters disenfranchised by local regulations. Many talented leaders emerged, foremost among them Martin Luther King, Jr., a Georgia minister whose oratorical power galvanized activists to uphold nonviolence in the face of brutal retaliation that included bombings, arson, and murder.

Blacks' pursuit of civil rights spread to other disadvantaged groups, who heeded the message of pluralism. Early in the 1960s, César Chávez, a California farm worker, began unionizing migrant laborers, most of them Hispanics from Mexico and Puerto Rico. Native Americans also took political action. In 1961 they drew up a Declaration of Purposes, detailing the injustices of centuries of white rule. The postwar renewal of humanitarianism pushed issues of pluralism and rights to the forefront of politics in the West.

Behind the Iron Curtain

A far different political climate prevailed in Eastern Europe. Stalin approached reconstruction by using the crushing methods that had served him throughout his career. In Eastern Europe he enforced agricultural collectivization and an industrial buildup through the nationalization of private property. In Hungary, where a mere 1,000 families owned more than 25 percent of the arable land, Communists seized and reapportioned all estates of more than 1,200 acres. Having gained the support of the poorer peasants through this redistribution, the Communists later pushed them into cooperative farming. In the Transylvania region of Romania, Communists seized the land of the German minority and redistributed it to poorer Romanian farmers. Then the property of wealthier peasants (the equivalent of kulaks) was converted into collective farms. The process took time: only late in the 1950s did the majority of peasants join cooperative farm organizations and did the Communist bureaucracy gain control of the food supply to sustain industrialization. Rural Romanians looked back on the 1950s as dreadful times and found management of collective farms a scandal. Still, many of these same people felt that their lives had improved overall. "Before we peasants were dirty and poor, we worked like dogs. . . . Was that a good life? No sir, it wasn't. . . . I was a miserable sharecropper and my son is an engineer."

Stalin prodded all the socialist economies in the Eastern bloc to match U.S. productivity. An admirer of American industrial know-how, he once claimed that "the union of Russian revolutionary drive with American business ability" was "the essence of Leninism." Modernization of produc-

tion in the Eastern bloc opened new technical and bureaucratic careers; but like Soviet industrialization in the 1930s, it also brought repression.

Science and culture were the building blocks of Stalinism, and the Soviet leader manipulated them to serve his ends. Thus the crackpot genetic theories of T. D. Lysenko, the biologist whom Stalin elevated to a scientific "dictator," were given credence over solid European and American findings. The *Great Soviet Encyclopedia,* started in 1949, celebrated Russian forerunners in every field of endeavor from automobile technology to early atomic physics. In the satellite countries an intense program of Russification and de-Christianization began. The Soviets forced Eastern European students to read histories of the war that ignored native resistance and gave the Red Army sole credit for fighting the Nazis. They replaced revered national symbols with Soviet emblems. On a new Hungarian flag, for example, a red Soviet star beamed its rays onto a hammer and sickle; the traditional Hungarian colors covered only a small band. The Communist regimes' historical distortion, revivified antisemitism, and rigid censorship resulted in what one staunchly socialist writer characterized as a "dreary torrent of colorless, mediocre literature.

In the USSR itself, new Stalinist purges ensured obedience and conformity. Marshall Georgi Zhukov, a popular leader of the armed forces, and the great poet Anna Akhmatova were among the first victims. Akhmatova, whose popular writing had emphasized perseverance and individual heroism during the war, refused to churn out poems on Communist themes and to celebrate Stalin's life; for this crime she was confined to a crowded hospital room. Composer Dmitri Shostakovich suffered censure for writing music considered critical of Communist politics. Secretary of the Party Central Committee Andrei Zhdanov instigated this cultural impoverishment. Under his direction, Soviet agents rooted out "Jewish influences" and "bourgeois decadence" in the arts: they put writers and artists out of work, evicted them from their apartments, and denied them the privileges traditionally accorded to artists.

In March 1953, while planning more purges, Stalin died. As people openly mourned this man whom they considered their savior from Nazism, troubles were already boiling up in the empire he had ruled so tyrannically. Political prisoners in the labor camps who had started rioting late in the 1940s now pressed their demands for reform. Consumer goods had become much scarcer than in the Western bloc because of the government's high military spending and the enormous cost of recovery. Amid deprivation and discontent, Soviet leaders enjoyed country homes, luxury goods, and plentiful food, but many of them had come to distrust Stalinism and were ready for change. The Stalinist system thus faced daunting challenges.

Within the Soviet Union a power struggle for control of the Communist empire erupted, claiming as its first victim Stalin's secret police chief, Lavrenti Beria, who was executed allegedly for advocating liberal policies. A coalition headed by Georgi Malenkov assumed power and soon made overtures to the Western bloc to lessen tensions. On June 17, 1953, however, demonstrations broke out in East Germany against the administration of Communist Party boss Walter Ulbricht (1893–1973). Workers gathered in front of government buildings in East Berlin, demanding a relaxation of industrial speedups. Urged on by a loudspeaker van circuiting the city, the demonstrators widened their protests, but the Soviets put them down a few days later. As authorities quelled other uprisings across the Soviet empire, labor-camp inmates went on strike for better food and the right to receive letters. Ultimately, Malenkov rehabilitated some labor-camp inmates, approached the United States with inconclusive results once again, and boosted the production of consumer goods—a policy later called "goulash Communism" because in part it emphasized more food for ordinary people.

In 1955, Nikita Khrushchev (1894–1971), an illiterate coal miner before the Revolution, outmaneuvered Malenkov and other rivals to emerge as the Soviet Union's undisputed leader. The next year, addressing the Twentieth Party Congress, he attacked Stalin's "perversions" of the Communist revolution, denounced the "cult of personality" that Stalin had encouraged, and announced that Stalinism did not equal socialism. The "secret speech"—it was not published in the USSR but became widely known—sent tremors through Communist parties around the world and signaled that Stalin's death might bring change. But even as Stalin's remains were removed from their honored

place in Red Square, the cult of Lenin flourished and was used to support continuing minority rule while discrediting Stalin. Thus the effects of Khrushchev's speech remained unclear.

Protest erupted in the Soviet sphere again in early summer 1956, when discontented railroad workers in Poland struck for better wages. Popular support for their cause forced the return to power of Wladislaw Gomułka (1905–1982), a Communist victim of an earlier Stalinist purge, who now initiated a more liberal Communist program. Inspired by Polish success, Hungarians rebelled against forced collectivization in October 1956—the golden October, they would call it. As in Poland, economic issues, especially announcements of reduced wages, sparked some of the first outbreaks of violence, but the protest soon targeted the entire Communist system. Intellectuals and students turned universities into beehives of political activity. Residents of Budapest filled the streets and smashed the city's huge statue of Stalin. As the protest swelled to tens of thousands of people, the Hungarian army, sent to disperse the mob, instead joined the rebellion, which returned a popular hero, Imre Nagy (1896–1958), to power. Nagy brought non-Communists into his government and even announced that Hungary might withdraw from the Warsaw Pact. At that threat, Soviet troops moved in early in November, killing thousands and driving hundreds of thousands more into flight to the Western bloc. Nagy was hanged. Eisenhower's refusal to intervene showed that, despite a rhetoric of "liberation," the United States would not risk World War III by militarily challenging the Soviets in their sphere of influence. Hungary's new leader, János Kádár, firmly steered the country back toward Communist political orthodoxy.

The failure of Eastern European uprisings overshadowed significant changes in Soviet policy. In the process of defeating his rivals, Khrushchev ended the Stalinist purges and the pattern of "liquidating" political enemies in the Party. He also reformed the courts so that they functioned according to procedures rather than the whim of a dictator. With some exceptions, political offenders and criminals received more limited sentences than during Stalin's time. Some prisoners were released from labor camps, and the conditions of those who remained improved. In addition, the secret police

Hungarians Pull Down a Statue of Stalin, 1956
From the Reformation to the fall of the Soviet Empire in 1989, icon-smashing has been a tool of resistance in the West. Note the "W.C." (the European abbreviation for water-closet or toilet) on Stalin's face.

lost many of their arbitrary powers. These changes contributed to producing what came to be called the *thaw.*

The thaw, however, was tenuous. It depended on a sense of security among the Soviet leadership, acquired from increased productivity, military buildup, and stunning successes in aerospace development. In 1957 the USSR successfully launched the first artificial Earth satellite, *Sputnik,* and in 1961 the Soviets put the first cosmonaut, Yuri Gagarin, in orbit around Earth. The Soviets' edge in space technology shocked the Western bloc and motivated the creation of the United States' National Aeronautics and Space Administration (NASA). These successes indicated that the Soviets were on the way to achieving Stalin's goals of Westernization and modernization. But despite these outward successes, Khrushchev continued to fear and bully dissidents. He forced writer Boris Pasternak, for example, to refuse the Nobel Prize in 1958 because his novel *Doctor Zhivago* (1957) cast doubt on the glory of the Revolution and affirmed the value of the individual.

Khrushchev made several trips to Western bloc countries and appeared in public far more than Stalin had. More confident and more affluent, the Soviets took steps to reduce their diplomacy's paranoid style and concentrated their efforts on spreading their message of Leninism and socialist progress to the emerging countries of Asia, Africa, and Latin America.

Beyond the West: The Ambiguities of Independence

World War II dealt a crippling blow to the ability of European powers to maintain their vast empires and their global influence. During the war the Allies had encouraged anti-Axis independence movements, but in the postwar world they attempted to stamp out the nationalist groups that had formed. Often led by individuals steeped in Western values, people in Asia, Africa, and the Middle East embraced the cause of independence. In revolting against imperialist control, many nations clashed with the West in bloody warfare.

The goal of developing a modern nation-state, however, did not always fit the needs of peoples whose identity came from local or tribal living arrangements. In Africa, a continent whose peoples spoke more than five thousand languages, regional designations such as Rhodesia and Nigeria had been marked off by European conquerors to arrange convenient administrative units. Religion also played an ambiguous role in independence movements. In India, Hindus and Muslims, both desiring independence, battled with one another even though they shared the goal of eliminating the British. In the Middle East and North Africa, pan-Arab and pan-Islamic movements seemed bonded together. Yet many Muslims were not Arab, not all Arabs were Muslim, and Islam itself encompassed many competing beliefs and sects. Allegiances to religion, ethnic group, and tribe overlapped and undermined political divisions. Despite these complications, peoples in the emerging Third World* succeeded in throwing off the imperial yoke imposed by Britain, France, Belgium, and the Netherlands.

Loss of empire threatened Europe's economy and upset a European sense of identity constructed out of a belief in Western superiority. At the same time, the wave of decolonization offered a new field for competition between the United States and the Soviet Union, thus increasing the possibility of nuclear war and magnifying the drama of the process. Many leaders of newly independent nations turned a cold shoulder to the two global giants: they envisioned a consortium of non-aligned countries exerting its own leverage in world affairs.

Communist Revolution in Southeast Asia

In 1949 a Communist takeover in China brought in a government that was no longer the plaything of the traditional colonial powers. Mao Zedong (Mao Tse-tung, 1893–1976) led his army of Communists to victory over Jiang Jieshi's unpopular, corrupt government, which the United States had bankrolled. Chinese communism emphasized

above all the welfare of the peasantry rather than the industrial proletariat and was thus distinct from Stalinism, Leninism, and Marxism. Mao instituted such social reforms as civil equality for women, but at the same time copied Soviet collectivization, industrialization, and brutal repression of the privileged classes. Although China began to distance itself from the USSR in the mid-1950s, the Western bloc saw only monolithic red from Leningrad to Beijing.

The United States and the Soviet Union were both deeply interested in East Asia—the United States because of the region's economic potential; the USSR because of its geopolitical importance. Thus the Chinese Revolution spurred both superpowers to increase their involvement in Asian politics. They faced off indirectly in Korea, which had been split in two at the thirty-eighth parallel after the war. In 1950 the North Koreans, supported by the Soviet Union, invaded U.S.-backed South Korea. The United States maneuvered the U.N. Security Council into approval of a "police action" against North Korea. Eventually, the United States deployed four hundred thousand troops to help the South Korean army repel the invaders. The combined military forces quickly pushed far into North Korean territory—almost to China's border—where they were met by the Chinese rather than the Soviet army. After a two-and-a-half-year

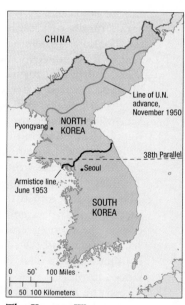

The Korean War

stalemate, the opposing sides agreed to a settlement in 1953: Korea would remain divided at its prewar border, the thirty-eighth parallel.

The United States lost more than fifty thousand men in the conflict—almost as many as would die in the Vietnam War—and paid a huge financial price for this limited victory. American military spending leaped from $10.9 billion in 1948 to almost $60 billion in 1953 in this effort to hold the

---

*A French statesman coined the term *Third World* in the 1950s to distinguish the emerging nations of Africa and Asia in economic terms. The *First World* referred to the capitalist democracies of the West; the *Second World* encompassed the socialist bloc.

line on Communist expansion. From 1951 to 1960 U.S. military spending outpaced Soviet expenditures by $10 billion to $20 billion annually. The potential for communism to take root in decolonizing areas led American statesmen to characterize Asian countries as a row of dominoes: "You knock over the first one and what will happen to the last one is that it will go over [to communism] very quickly." The expansion of the Cold War to Asia prompted the creation of an Asian counterpart to NATO. Formed in 1954, the Southeast Asia Treaty Organization (SEATO) included Pakistan, Thailand, the Philippines, Britain, Australia, New Zealand, France, and the United States.

The Cold War spread to Indochina, where nationalists fought the revival of French imperialism. Their leader, the European-educated Ho Chi Minh, preached both nationalism and socialism. Building a powerful organization, the Viet-Minh, to struggle against colonial rule, Ho advocated the redistribution of land held by big landowners, especially in agriculturally rich southern Indochina, where some six thousand owners possessed more than 60 percent of the land. Armed with promises of land, the Viet-Minh mobilized poor peasants to serve in a liberation army. After they captured Hanoi on August 19, 1945, and Saigon on August 25, the Viet-Minh declared the creation of the Democratic Republic of Vietnam in September.

Swiftly, France landed troops there in October, determined, in the words of Charles de Gaulle, to "recover [France's] sovereignty over Indochina." The army first aimed to reclaim the south, where the big landowners and prosperous peasants welcomed the French return. After a brief period of accommodation between the opposing sides, open conflict erupted. The Viet-Minh's tenacious resistance surprised the French. Peasant guerrillas forced the technologically advanced French army to withdraw after the bloody battle of Dien Bien Phu in 1954.

The Geneva Convention of 1954 carved out an independent Laos and divided Vietnam into northern and southern regions, each free from French control. The Viet-Minh were supposed to retreat north of the seventeenth parallel. But superpower intervention undermined the peace treaty. President Harry S Truman, viewing the Indochinese conflict as part of the anticommunist crusade rather than as a nationalist issue, had begun providing aid to the French well before their defeat at Dien Bien Phu. The advisers of Truman's successor, President Dwight D. Eisenhower, had urged that the United States drop an atomic bomb on the Viet-Minh. After Vietnam's partition, Eisenhower helped southern landowners in their efforts to rid the south of guerrillas loyal to Ho and justified the aid by invoking the domino theory. At the same time, China, a would-be superpower bordering Vietnam, tried to build influence in the north. Thus, like Korea, Vietnam cast off imperialism, only to attract superpower meddling on Asian soil.

The Struggle for Identity in the Middle East

Growing reliance on oil as an energy source heightened foreign interest in the Middle East. As in the rest of the world, however, colonial peoples' new aspirations to independence provoked resistance to the attempted reassertion of imperial control after World War II. Furthermore, the Cold War allowed Middle Eastern leaders to bargain with the superpowers, playing them off one another, for resources to develop their countries. Western powers pursued their commitment to secure the Jews a homeland in the Middle East after the Holocaust. This commitment furthered Arab determination to gain their economic and political control of the region.

When World War II broke out, six hundred thousand Jewish settlers resided in British-controlled Palestine, which was also home to twice as many Arabs. In 1947 the British ceded the area to the United Nations to forge an agreement between the Jews and the Arabs. In the aftermath of the Holocaust, the United Nations voted to partition Palestine into an Arab sector and a Jewish zone. Conflicting claims, however, led to war. Jewish military forces prevailed, and on May 14, 1948, the state of Israel came into being. "The dream had come true," Golda Meir (1898–1978), its future president later remembered—but "too late to save those who had perished in the Holocaust." Israel opened its gates to immigrants, and by the end of 1949 another three hundred fifty thousand refugees had found homes there. The more populous Israel grew, the more its ambitions clashed with those of its Arab neighbors.

Symbols for a New Nation
Modern states commemorated the citizen-soldier lost in national struggles. Here Israeli women— obliged to serve in the armed forces along with men—take part in a ceremony at a monument to those who died during Israel's war for independence.

One of those neighbors, Egypt, had gained its independence from Britain at the end of World War II. Britain meanwhile retained control of other oil-rich Middle Eastern states, of the island of Cyprus, and of the Suez Canal. Owned and operated by a British company, the canal dominated shipping from the Mediterranean to Asia. In 1952, Colonel Gamal Abdel Nasser (1918–1970) became the country's new president, taking the reins of government after the ouster of Egypt's king. Nasser had great dreams for Egypt that included economic modernization and true national independence. An obvious goal was reclaiming the Suez Canal, "where 120,000 of our sons had lost their lives in digging it [by force] and for the foundation of which we paid 8 million pounds, [but which is now] a state within a state." In July 1956, Nasser nationalized the canal.

Britain immediately demanded the canal's return and won support from Israel and France. In October, Israel, which regarded Nasser's actions as menacing, attacked Egypt. The British and French followed, bringing the crisis over the Suez to a head. British prime minister Anthony Eden (1897–1977) branded Nasser another Hitler and called on the United States for help, but the Eisenhower administration declined, fearing that U.S.

involvement might trigger a military conflict with the Soviet Union, which also had its eye on the Hungarian revolt. In refusing support, the United States struck an anti-imperialist posture to impress developing nations whose partnership it sought. American opposition made the British back down from what one of their own diplomats called "a squalid and most humiliating episode."

Nasser's triumph inspired confidence that the Middle East could confront the West and win. Syria, Jordan, Lebanon, and Iraq, all of which had become independent at the end of World War II, were attracted to the pan-Arab nationalism that Nasser embodied. But unity proved elusive. Nasser failed to eradicate his country's poverty, and some Arab states, angered by U.S. support for Israel, drifted into the Soviet camp for military and economic assistance. Few in the Middle East, however, were inclined to accept socialism or Soviet domination. Meanwhile, Iran—populated by Persians rather than Arabs—drove Communist rebels out of the north just after World War II and prospered under the repressive, pro-American regime of the Shah Reza Pahlavi (1919–1980). By the early 1960s, Middle Eastern development was based on an ever-changing and uncertain mixture of Zionism, pan-Arabism (and anti-Zionism), pan-Islam, and nationalism, all of them shaped by Cold War competition.

The End of Empire

By World War II's end other leaders in Asia and Africa were mobilizing the mass discontent that had bubbled up during the war, and sought to drive out foreign rulers. The biggest loser would be Britain. Within two decades of its victory in World War II, Britain would decline from a global imperial power to a small island nation. After the war, British politicians initially divided over the best course to take regarding their empire. Winston Churchill was determined not to let the colonies go their own way, but the victorious Labourites, under Clement Attlee, promoted decolonization as key to social justice. Such debate became moot as colonies increasingly took matters into their own hands.

The British had promised to grant India its independence in the 1930s, but they had postponed implementation when war had broken out, and they had even declared war against the Nazis on the Indians' behalf. During the war, Indian business interests further developed local industry and bought out British entrepreneurs short of cash. In these years of internal economic growth, political fissures between India's Hindus and Muslims widened. After the war, when Britain's Labour government sent its statesmen to preside over the demise of the Indian empire, they therefore decreed that *two* countries should be carved from the old colony. Thus in 1947, India was created for Hindus, and Pakistan for Muslims. During the independence year, political tensions exploded between opposing members of the two religions. Hundreds of thousands were massacred in a great shift of populations between the two nations. In 1948 a radical Hindu assassinated Gandhi, who had continued to champion religious reconciliation. "The light had gone out of our lives and there is darkness everywhere," lamented the Hindu leader Jawaharlal Nehru (1889–1964), India's first prime minister.

Confronting nationalist movements elsewhere, Britain retained control of Hong Kong but granted independence to Ceylon (Sri Lanka) and Burma in 1948, Malaya and Singapore in 1957, and Borneo in 1963. Before two decades of the postwar era had passed, almost half a billion Asians had gained their freedom from the rule of 50 million British.

In sub-Saharan Africa nationalist leaders likewise roused their people to challenge British rule. During World War II, Europeans had needed more resources than ever from the colonies. "The European Merchant is my shepherd, and I am in want," went an African version of the Twenty-third Psalm. Disrupted in their traditional agricultural patterns, Africans had flocked to urban shantytowns during the war, where they had survived by scavenging, doing craft work, and performing menial labor for whites. Such underemployed city-dwellers formed a power base for politicians committed to decolonization.

Kwame Nkrumah (1909–1972) led the diverse inhabitants of the relatively prosperous West African Gold Coast to passive resistance, in imitation of Gandhi's methods. After years of arresting and jailing the resisters, the British withdrew, allowing the state of Ghana to come into being in 1957. Nigeria, the most populous African region, became independent in 1960 after the leaders of its many tribes, regional groupings, and political organizations finally agreed on a federal-style government. In these and other African states where the population was mostly black, independence came less violently than in mixed-race territories.

In contrast, the eastern coast and southern and central areas of Africa had numerous European settlers, who mercilessly fought independence movements. In the 1950s violence rocked British East Africa, for example, where white settlers lived in debt-ridden splendor while blacks lacked both land and economic opportunity. African men, almost all of whom had assisted the British as soldiers in World War II, responded to their plight by forming rebel groups called the Land Freedom Army but known as Mau Mau. They maintained their solidarity through ceremonies, oaths, and rigid discipline. With women serving as provisioners, messengers, and weapon stealers, Mau Mau bands tried to recover land from whites. The British slaughtered some ten thousand to fifteen thousand Kikuyu tribespeople, who headed the native armies, but in the long run could not afford the costs of this repression. In 1964 an independent Kenya was born, under the presidency of Jomo Kenyatta (1894–1978); in the words of the British colonial secretary, "Any other policy would have

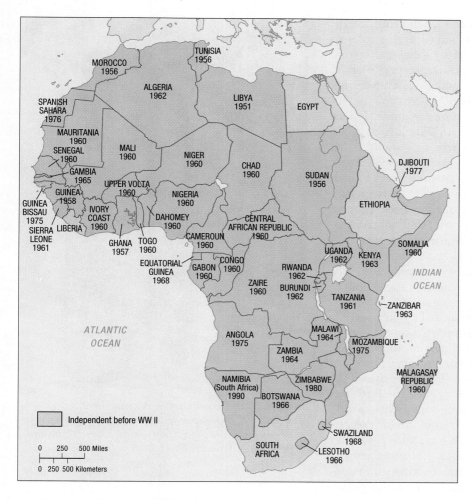

MOROCCO 1956
TUNISIA 1956
ALGERIA 1962
LIBYA 1951
EGYPT
SPANISH SAHARA 1976
MAURITANIA 1960
SENEGAL 1960
MALI 1960
NIGER 1960
CHAD 1960
SUDAN 1956
DJIBOUTI 1977
GAMBIA 1965
GUINEA 1958
UPPER VOLTA 1960
NIGERIA 1960
ETHIOPIA
GUINEA BISSAU 1975
IVORY COAST 1960
DAHOMEY 1960
CENTRAL AFRICAN REPUBLIC 1960
SIERRA LEONE 1961
LIBERIA
GHANA 1957
TOGO 1960
CAMEROUN 1960
SOMALIA 1960
EQUATORIAL GUINEA 1968
GABON 1960
CONGO 1960
RWANDA 1962
UGANDA 1962
KENYA 1963
ZAIRE 1960
BURUNDI 1962
INDIAN OCEAN
TANZANIA 1961
ZANZIBAR 1963
ATLANTIC OCEAN
ANGOLA 1975
MALAWI 1964
MOZAMBIQUE 1975
ZAMBIA 1964
NAMIBIA (South Africa) 1990
ZIMBABWE 1980
BOTSWANA 1966
MALAGASAY REPUBLIC 1960
SWAZILAND 1968
SOUTH AFRICA
LESOTHO 1966

☐ Independent before WW II

0   250   500 Miles
0   250   500 Kilometers

Decolonization of Africa

led to terrible bloodshed." In 1948 in South Africa, meanwhile, the Dutch-speaking Afrikaners had taken control of the government and formalized the white supremacist policies of segregation into the brutal system of *apartheid* (apartness). Pressured to reform its racist system in keeping with the British government's policy of civil rights, South Africa seceded from the Commonwealth in 1961, refusing to abandon apartheid.

The French, humiliated by defeat and occupation in World War II, hoped to regain status by retaining their African empire; the French military hoped to rehabilitate its reputation by restoring peace to areas in rebellion. Like the British, the French readily acquiesced to certain colonies' demands for independence, among them Tunisia, Morocco, and West Africa, where fewer French settlers lived, economic stakes were more limited, and military involvement was minimal. Elsewhere, French struggles against independence movements were costly, prolonged, and bloody.

The ultimate test of the French empire came in Algeria. When Algerian nationalists resisted the restoration of French rule in the final days of World War I, the French army massacred tens of thousands of them. The slaughter squelched the liberation movement until 1954, when it resurfaced as the Front for National Liberation. The Front attacked not only European settlers but the Arabs who supported them with ferocious intensity. Meanwhile, the French dug in. Asked what would happen were Algerian independence granted without a fight, one French general replied, "The army would rebel." Increasing its troops in the region to more than four hundred thousand, the French army fought back savagely. Neither side played by the rules of warfare: the French tortured civilians; Algerian women (shielded by gender stereotypes) planted bombs in European clubs and cafés and carried weapons to assassination sites.

Shedding other colonies at a rapid rate, France had drawn the line at Algeria. "The loss of Algeria," warned one French statesman, "would be an unprecedented national disaster." Although many agreed, the Algerian war itself threatened French social stability as fierce protests in Paris greeted reports of the army's barbarous practices. In turn, French settlers in Algeria and the military responded to the antiwar movement with terrorism against citizens in France. They threatened coups, set off bombs, assassinated politicians, and promoted other kinds of violence in the name of "Algérie Française" (French Algeria).

France's Fourth Republic collapsed over Algeria. In 1958, de Gaulle, supported by the French army and approved by the Chamber of Deputies, resumed power. In return for leading France out of the Algerian quagmire, de Gaulle demanded the creation of republican government—the Fifth Republic—with a strong president who would choose the prime minister and could exercise emergency power. The result was a plan for a government somewhere between a parliamentary and a presidential system. "Mutts are often more intelligent than thoroughbreds," one French politician quipped, and French voters agreed, approving a constitution in 1958 by a four-to-one margin.

From the strengthened presidential office of the Fifth Republic, de Gaulle led the French out of Algeria and toward a new, noncolonial identity. Having portrayed himself as above the fray, he had ambiguously invoked images of French grandeur and the legacy of French culture. Although army leaders had thought de Gaulle opposed Algerian independence, he ultimately did not support the military's interest in preserving the empire. By 1962 de Gaulle had negotiated independence with the Algerian nationalists. Hundreds of thousands of *pieds noirs* ("black feet"), as Europeans in Algeria were called, fled to France, choosing "a suitcase instead of a coffin."

The empires controlled by smaller countries, notably the Netherlands and Belgium, also disintegrated in these years. Frightened by nationalist

Independence Ceremonies in Algeria, 1962
The struggle for independence from the French enlisted all segments of the population—men, women, and children—in a bitter war. This soldier is fourteen years old.

insurgency, Belgian rulers pulled out of the Congo in south-central Africa without warning in 1960. The power vacuum thus created plunged the region into a four-year civil war. Portugal resisted letting go of its colonies and for more than a decade bitterly opposed a struggle for the independence of Angola in southwestern Africa that broke out in 1961. In the Netherlands East Indies (the Indonesian Islands), the Dutch empire had been undermined by Japanese occupation during World War II. In 1949, Indonesian statesman Achmed Sukarno reached a formal agreement on Indonesian independence with the Dutch; six years later he sponsored the Bandung Convention of twenty-nine nonaligned nations representing more than one-half the globe's population, to set a common policy for achieving modernization and dealing with the superpowers. By the 1960s, Third World nations faced the difficult task of political, economic, and social restructuring as newly independent states.

The Return of Prosperity on the Brink of Nuclear War

By 1960 the world's industrial countries had left behind the poverty of the Great Depression, and Europeans had emerged from wartime deprivation to enjoy a higher living standard than ever before in human history. Indeed an economic miracle had invigorated Western Europe. Even in the Eastern bloc, the material conditions of everyday life had improved as peasant societies were forced to modernize. In both Western and Eastern Europe the state took increasing responsibility for citizens' health and well-being. With prosperity came more leisure time as well as new forms of cultural consumption, both of which affected gender roles and attitudes. But people enjoyed this rising economic security in a tense international atmosphere. In Berlin in 1961, Cold War conflict again flared. Then, in October 1962, the world's peoples collectively held their breath as leaders of the Soviet Union and the United States took dangerous steps toward a nuclear conflagration.

The Welfare State and Conditions of Everyday Life

In the postwar world, governments intervened forcefully to ameliorate social conditions. The growth of the *welfare state* revealed that nations were no longer interested solely in maintaining internal order and augmenting their power. Despite the new currency of the term, the concept of the welfare state had been taking form for almost a century. In Britain a national health-care system had provided 20 million workers with medical benefits during the Great Depression. After World War II, other governments opened their purse strings to fund more and more social programs, and the effects on everyday life were more easily gauged.

The welfare state directly encouraged population growth. The European population had declined during the war. Consequently, almost all countries now urged couples to reproduce. In France, where fertility had been dropping for more than a century, de Gaulle called on women to produce "twelve million healthy babies." Imitating the sweeping Swedish programs of the 1930s, nations expanded or created family allowances, health-care and medical benefits, and programs for pregnant women and new mothers. The French gave larger allowances for each subsequent birth after the first; for many French families, this allowance provided as much as a third of the household income. Britain's maternity benefits and child allowances, announced in a 1942 report, favored women who did not work outside the home and provided little coverage of any kind to working women. The West German government passed strict legislation that discouraged employers from hiring women. In fact, West Germans bragged about removing women from the workforce, saying it distinguished democratic practices from communist ones that were said to demand women's work outside the home. In Eastern Europe and the Soviet Union, where wartime loss of life had been enormous, women worked nearly full time and usually outnumbered men in the labor force. Child-care programs, family allowances, and maternity benefits were designed to encourage full-time working women to have children. The scarcity of consumer goods and the lack of household conveniences in the Eastern bloc, however, discouraged working women from having large families. Because women were responsible for onerous domestic duties on top of their paying jobs, their already heavy workload increased with the birth of each additional child.

Other welfare-state programs aimed to improve people's health. State medical insurance and subsidized medical care covered health-care needs everywhere except in the United States. Countries as diverse as Great Britain and the Soviet Union developed nationalized health-care systems in which doctors and hospital employees worked for the state; these programs covered a country's entire population. In other nations, citizens' medical expenses were reimbursed through social-security plans. The combination of better material conditions and state provision of health care dramatically extended life expectancy and lowered rates of infant mortality. Contributing to the overall progress, the number of medical doctors and

Postwar Housing in Poland
Wartime devastation made massive rebuilding imperative and nowhere more so than in Eastern-bloc countries. These one-family units were less usual than apartment buildings.

dentists more than doubled between the end of World War I and 1950, and vaccines greatly reduced the death toll from such diseases as tuberculosis, diphtheria, measles, and polio. In England, school-children stood on average an inch taller than children of the same age a decade before. As people lived longer into old age, governments established programs for that segment of the population. All in all, per capita expenditures on welfare programs shot up after the war. Belgium, for example, which had spent $12 per capita in 1930, led West European countries with $148 per capita in 1956; Britain, which had led in 1930 with welfare expenditures of $59, now lagged behind with $93 because of its near bankrupt condition.

Government initiatives not only in health care but in other areas played a role in the higher standard of living. A growing network of government-built atomic power plants brought electricity to Eastern Europe and the Soviet Union. Governments legislated better workplace conditions and more leisure time for workers. Beginning in 1955, Italian workers received twenty-eight paid holidays annually; Swedish workers enjoyed twenty-nine vacation days, and the number grew in the 1960s. Government programs also increased the variety and abundance of food: meat, fish, eggs, cheese, milk, and fresh fruit replaced the older

grain-based diets. In Czechoslovakia annual per capita consumption of meat was 125 pounds in 1960 and in Hungary, 105. In the new, consumerist atmosphere, Western Europeans, emulating Americans, were driving some 40 million motorized vehicles, including motorbikes, cars, buses, and trucks by the 1950s. The demand for cars made the automobile industry a leading economic sector. The young spent their money on hi-fi equipment, records, clothing, and cigarettes. Many Eastern European women worked a full day and then did housework without benefit of indoor plumbing. Most West Europeans in major cities had toilets and running water, adequate heating, and an array of household appliances that drastically reduced the time necessary to perform domestic tasks like laundry.

Housing shortages posed a daunting challenge for both governments and individuals. After three decades of war and depression, people had trouble finding a decent place to live. Because the war had been so destructive and had diverted resources into military needs, postwar Europeans often lived with three generations of their family sharing a single room or two. East Europeans faced the worst conditions, whereas Germans and Greeks fared better because the war had ruined only between 20 and 25 percent of prewar housing. Britain, which had not been invaded, had lost less than 10 percent. Existing urban flats, particularly in Eastern Europe, had often degenerated into slums, and apartment dwellers shared toilets, often located on stairway landings.

Governments sponsored a postwar housing boom. In the Western bloc, they provided tax rebates and other incentives to private builders. In the Eastern bloc the state undertook building projects. New cities formed around the edges of major urban areas. Many buildings went up slap-dash, giving restored towns a uniform look and leading to their constant deterioration; Westerners labeled the new housing in Poland "environmentally horrible." Modern engineering and U.S. styles often set the pattern. The construction of prefabricated buildings, already advanced in the United States, speeded up the availability of millions of units in both Eastern and Western Europe. Even with the building frenzy, housing shortages had not disappeared by the 1960s. Nevertheless, the modernized appearance of many European cities suggested that the century's two cataclysmic wars had definitively swept away a good deal of the old Europe.

Angry Young Men and "New Look" Women

Government spending on reconstruction, productivity, and welfare helped prevent the kind of social and political upheaval that had followed World War I. The immense task of rebuilding prevented unemployment from threatening most people's well-being, and some European countries even experienced labor shortages. Nor did the same tensions prevail among men and women, because governments worked to demobilize and reintegrate veterans into the workforce rapidly. Men felt less frustration than they had in the 1920s because of the decisive nature of World War II. No Freikorps developed in Germany; and in England, for example, where veterans had wrecked university classrooms and attacked working women after World War I, faculty were surprised at how docilely World War II veterans returned to their studies.

The young men who had not been old enough to fight in the war, however, adopted a martial style. The 1920s had seen the streets filled with paramilitary bands such as the Freikorps; in the 1950s young

"delinquents" merely posed as tough military types. Their delinquency did not necessarily involve crime but rather the swaggering control of urban space and the display of rebellious attitudes. Groups such as the "teddy boys" in England (named after their Edwardian style of dressing of the early twentieth century) and the *gamberros* in Spain took their cues from new forms of pop culture in music and film.

The leader of rock-and-roll style and substance was the American singer Elvis Presley. Sporting slicked-back hair and an aviator-style jacket, Presley's gyrating hips and sexual lyrics attracted screaming and devoted fans. In a German nightclub late in the 1950s, members of a band of Elvis fans called The Quarrymen performed, fighting and yelling at each other as part of their show. They would soon become known as The Beatles. Rebellious young American film stars like James Dean in *Rebel Without a Cause* (1955) and Marlon Brando in *The Wild One* (1954) added to the beginnings of a conspicuous postwar youth culture.

The rebellious masculine style appeared in a variety of literary genres. In a classic autobiography explaining how he and Francis Crick had discovered the molecular structure of DNA in 1953, James Watson portrayed himself as a fanatic bad boy. His book, *The Double Helix* (1968), described how he had rifled people's desk drawers (among other dishonest acts) to become a scientific hero. The aspiring young professor in British novelist Kingsley Amis's *Lucky Jim* (1954) found it impossible to imitate the genteel manners of his senior colleagues and their families. The formality of etiquette, after the wartime experience, seemed antiquated.

Some artists challenged the prevailing humanitarianism as unthinkable after the Holocaust. Samuel Beckett's (1906–1989) *Waiting for Godot* (1952) features two tramps standing around talking nonstop while trusting that something—or someone—good would eventually come along. Beckett proposed that such hope was absurd. In the revival of West German literature, Günter Grass's *The Tin Drum* (1959) presented the world of madness as the only one that made sense in the light of the Nazi experience. His compatriot Heinrich Böll published *The Clown* (1963), a novel whose young hero takes to performing as a clown and begging in a railroad station. Böll protested that

The Beatles, 1960
Before the group traveled to play in Hamburg, Germany, John Lennon took this picture of the band and their manager at a British memorial to World War I soldiers. Paul McCartney is seated at center; George Harrison is second from the right.

West Germany's postwar goal of respectability had allowed the resurgence of precisely those groups of people who had produced Nazism. Across the Atlantic, American "beat" poets, such as Allen Ginsberg and Lawrence Ferlinghetti, who looked dirty, bearded, and sometimes crazy, critiqued traditional ideals of the upright and rational male achiever.

Society promoted a different postwar model for women than it had in the 1920s. Late in the 1940s the French fashion house of Christian Dior launched a clothing style called the "new look." It featured a pinched waist, tightly fitting bodices, and voluminous skirts. This restoration of the nineteenth-century female silhouette invited a renewal of clear gender roles. Women's magazines publicized the "new look" and urged a return to domesticity to indicate that women and men had recovered their proper social roles. Clad in crinolines, hats, gloves, and dainty shoes, and reshaped by an array of constricting undergarments, "feminine" women represented the return to normalcy. In Europe and especially the United States Freudian psychoanalytic theories were used to prove that fulfillment of maternal duties was a sign of individual health. New household products such as refrigerators and washing machines raised standards for women's accomplishment in the home by giving them the means to be more "perfect" housewives.

"New look" propaganda did not mesh with reality, however. Dressmaking fabric was still rationed in the late 1940s; even in the 1950s one could not get enough of it to make voluminous skirts. Furthermore, the underwear needed for "new look" contours simply did not exist. Instead consumers had access only to standardized undergarments available with ration tickets. Finally, European women continued to work outside the home after the war; in the West mature women and mothers were working more than ever before. The female workforce was going through a profound revolution as it gradually became less youthful and instead consisted of a greater number of wives and mothers who would work outside the home all their lives. Nonetheless, heroines in Soviet fiction were portrayed as ready to embrace maternal subservience: "I can't be the boss forever," one woman says to her husband, trying to encourage him to resume his prewar authority. "I'll be having children." Despite cultural paeans to domesticity, Soviet women, like those across Europe, worked to support their families. Regularly employed, modern women nonetheless lived in a culture that bombarded them with images of nineteenth-century femininity.

Because both men and women were working outside the home, gender definition came less from

The "New Look" in Women's Fashion
Postwar women were supposed to look thin, and models were tightly corseted to reduce their waists from two up to five or more inches. Some suggest that wartime deprivation and the skeletal survivors of the camps influenced this trend.

the reality of separate spheres than from portrayals in the mass media. In 1953 the first issue of *Playboy* magazine appeared on the U.S. market, and European versions were published soon after. *Playboy* differed from standard pornographic magazines: along with pictures of nude women, it also featured serious articles, especially on the topic of masculinity. According to *Playboy* and its imitators, masculinity no longer depended on filling the role of breadwinner for a wife and children. This segment of the media presented modern man as sexually aggressive and independent of dull domestic life, which only destroyed his freedom and sense of self. (An acknowledgment of

sexuality as crucial to human well-being came from a very different quarter when the Swedish government made sex education mandatory in schools in 1953.) The notion of human liberty had come to include not just political and economic rights but freedom of sexual expression; this definition would become increasingly integrated into politics by movements seeking rights for varying sexual orientations.

The advertising business presided over the creation of cultural messages such as those found in *Playboy*. Advertising agencies became symbols of renewed prosperity; they designed publicity campaigns and analyzed markets for everything from household appliances to books. Financed by this advertising, the number of magazines and books proliferated. Guided by marketing analysts, publishers destined books and magazines for distinct sections of the public, from those who sought pornography to readers of novels and comic books. By the 1960s such fine-tuning of selling culture had given rise to a vast network of new jobs: market researchers, account executives, and a multitude of other consultants.

The development and spread of American mass culture provoked diverse kinds of resistance by those who saw increasing homogenization as the result of American influence. On the lowest level, the French, for example, banned Coca Cola for a time in the 1950s. A more widespread strategy involved producing elite things to buy. Thus, French *New Wave* cinema developed in reaction to the mass-market Hollywood films. Directors like François Truffaut and Jean-Luc Godard focused on the "maker," or *auteur,* of a film to contrast their work with movies formulated by anonymous studio executives. The auteur produced New Wave films much as an author created a literary work. In addition, New Wave directors tried to integrate the history of film into their work by developing common film themes and symbols that had been used over the decades. In literature, French writers pioneered the "new novel" as an antidote to bestsellers that glutted the mass market. Although the first in this genre, Natalie Sarraute's *Tropismes,* was written in 1939, most "new novels" appeared in the 1950s and thereafter. Sarraute wrote in terms of human "gestures," "subconversations," and fleeting glimpses of the interior of the human psyche.

Willem de Kooning, **Abstraction,** *1949–1950*
Trained by the Dutch avant-garde, de Kooning still incorporated recognizable objects like the skull, nail, doors, windows, and ladder on the right side of this early abstract expressionist painting. His reliance on objects to provide three-dimensionality disappeared in later paintings.

New novelists rejected the idea of plot and clearly defined characters.

Changing the novel's format, however, further segmented the market by creating highbrow work for an elite audience. The "new novel" was read by a much smaller public than had bought up Dickens, for example, a century earlier. The same could be said for the visual arts, where *abstract expressionism,* practiced by U.S. artists such as Jackson Pollock (1912–1956), substituted a technique of dripping, spattering, and pouring paint in abstract forms for works that still had elements of realism, such as those of Picasso. Abstract expressionists spoke of the importance of the artist's self-discovery, spiritual growth, and sensations in the process of painting: "If I stretch my arms next to the rest of myself and wonder where my fingers are, that is all the space I need as a painter," commented Willem de Kooning (b. 1904) on the relationship he had with his canvas.

The fight against mass culture began to lose ground as a new instrument for communicating with the masses—television—was becoming popular. The development of television in the 1920s and 1930s was interrupted by the war, but peacetime saw its rapid spread in the United States, which had 20 million sets by 1953. In Britain only 20 percent of the population owned TVs in the early 1950s, but 75 percent of all households there owned one by 1961. Britain, however, was an exception: the French had only sixty thousand sets in the mid-1950s; the Italians, only five thousand. Only in the 1960s did television become an important consumer item for most Europeans. In the 1950s, radio still predominated. In the United States, some Americans rejected television in favor of finding their authentic roots in European culture: they traveled more extensively to Europe, attended European films, and bought classical music. New fears of cultural crisis led to renewed interest in Europe as the birthplace of the West.

Kennedy, Khrushchev, and the Atomic Brink

The 1960 election of John Fitzgerald Kennedy (1917–1963) heralded a new era. Kennedy, a Democrat of Irish descent, was the first Roman Catholic ever elected president. Although he had served in World War II, he seemed to usher in a new generation of leadership that replaced that of Churchill, Stalin, Roosevelt, and Eisenhower. Kennedy was youthful and eager to travel in Europe—and a man whose relaxed good looks were enhanced by the medium of television. Kennedy's media advisers and ghostwriters recognized that their candidate was a perfect match for television. His poise in televised debates helped him squeak through to victory over the perspiring and uneasy vice president Richard Nixon.

Amidst U.S. prosperity, Kennedy intensified the arms race and faced an escalation of the Cold War. In 1959 a revolution in Cuba, just off the coast of Florida, had brought to power Fidel Castro, who allied his government with the Soviet Union. In the spring of 1961, Kennedy launched a feeble invasion of Cuba at the Bay of Pigs that failed miserably and humiliated the United States. A few months later, Kennedy had a chilling meeting with Khrushchev in Vienna, at which the Soviet leader brandished the specter of nuclear holocaust over the continuing U.S. presence in Berlin.

THE COLD WAR

1945–1949 The USSR establishes satellite states in Eastern Europe

1947 The Truman Doctrine announces American commitment to contain communism; the U.S. provides massive aid to rebuild Europe in the Marshall Plan

1948–1949 Soviet troops blockade Berlin; the U.S. airlifts provisions to Berliners

1949 Western democracies form the North Atlantic Treaty Organization (NATO); the Soviet bloc establishes the Council for Mutual Economic Assistance (COMECOM); USSR tests first nuclear weapon

1950–1953 The Korean War

1950–1954 U.S. Senator Joseph McCarthy leads hunt for American communists

1953 Stalin dies

1955 The USSR and East-bloc countries form a military alliance, the Warsaw Pact

1956 Khrushchev denounces Stalin in so-called Secret Speech to Soviet Communist Party Congress; Hungarian's revolt against Soviet domination

1959 Castro comes to power in Cuba

1961 Berlin Wall erected

1962 Cuban missile crisis

In the summer of 1961, East German workers, supervised by police and army, stacked bales of barbed wire across miles of border to begin construction of the Berlin Wall. The divided city had served as an escape route whereby some 3 million people had fled to the West. As a wall replaced the barbed wire, people jumped through apartment windows to freedom; when the windows were blocked, they jumped from roofs. Kennedy responded at home with a call for more weapons and an enhanced civil defense program, but he made no move toward tearing down the wall, indicating an acceptance of Soviet control in Eastern Europe and an end to Dulles's argument about rolling back the USSR.

In October 1962, matters came to a head when the CIA reported the installation of Soviet medium-range missiles in Cuba. Kennedy now responded decisively, calling for a blockade of ships headed for Cuba and implicitly threatening to reply with military force if the missiles were not removed. For several days the world trembled on the edge of utter disaster. Then, between October 25 and 27, Khrushchev and Kennedy negotiated an end to the crisis. The Soviets promised to

remove the missile installations. Kennedy spent the remainder of his short life working to improve nuclear diplomacy. Khrushchev, too, began bringing the Eastern bloc closer to a policy of *detente*. The two leaders, who had looked deeply into the nuclear abyss, clearly feared what they saw.

CONCLUSION

The postwar reconstruction of Europe occurred in the context of growing antagonism between the United States and the Soviet Union. Divided virtually in half into an Eastern bloc dominated by the Soviets and a freer Western bloc mostly allied with the United States, Europe recovered almost miraculously. To the east, where wartime devastation was greatest, recovery was less dramatic and achieved at greater human cost than in Western Europe. Each bloc, however, saw its postwar revival as necessary to preserve distinctive values against a belligerent enemy, priming itself for attack. The dwindling freedom that accompanied postwar recovery behind the Iron Curtain provoked civilian resistance to Soviet rule and a backing away from Stalinism. The United States, in contrast, stood at the apex of its influence early in the 1960s. Western Europe rebuilt, shed colonies, and adopted new technologies that delivered a higher standard of living, changed the social structure, and promised an ever brighter future. In the midst of this recovery many came to wonder whether Cold War was really worth the threat of nuclear annihilation.

SUGGESTIONS FOR FURTHER READING

Source Materials

Beauvoir, Simone de. *The Mandarins.* 1956. A novel about politics and intellectuals in postwar France.

Pasternak, Boris. *Doctor Zhivago.* 1958. An epic novel of the turmoil in early twentieth-century Russia, which the Soviet government banned.

Young, Michael, and Peter Willmott. *Family and Kinship in East London.* 1957. Includes accounts of talks working men and women had with sociologists about life in the 1950s.

Interpretive Studies

Brown, L. Carl. *International Politics and the Middle East.* 1984. A historical survey of the Middle East and its role in world politics beginning in the eighteenth century.

Chaliand, Gerard. *Revolution in the Third World: Currents and Conflicts in Asia, Africa, and Latin America.* 1989. A major survey of the process of decolonization.

Cohen-Solal, Annie. *Sartre.* 1987. An expert biography of the leader of the French existentialists.

Ehrenreich, Barbara. *The Hearts of Men.* 1983. Discusses how people coped with postwar society and argues that men, not women, were the first to desert family roles.

Flaphan, Simha. *The Birth of Israel: Myths and Realities.* 1987. A revisionist look at Israelis and Palestinians.

Hargreaves, J. D. *Decolonization in Africa.* 1989. Describes how Africans shaped their nations.

Hosking, Geoffrey. *A History of the Soviet Union.* 1985. Includes good coverage of the move away from Stalinism and the thaw in the Cold War.

Lapidus, Gail. *Women in Soviet Society: Equality, Development, and Social Change.* 1978. Explores how women fared in the difficult postwar years.

Laqueur, Walter. *Europe in Our Times: A History, 1945–1992.* 1992. A wide-ranging and expert overview.

Leffler, Melvyn P. *A Preponderance of Power: National Security, the Truman Administration, and the Cold War.* 1993. A new perspective on the complex unfolding of the Cold War.

Marcus, Millicent. *Italian Film in the Light of Neorealism.* 1986. A new interpretation of the brilliant postwar Italian cinema.

Marrus, Michael. *The Unwanted: European Refugees in the Twentieth Century.* 1985. Examines the experiences of millions of migrating European refugees, including those created by World War II and the Holocaust.

Mayne, Richard. *Postwar: The Dawn of Today's Europe.* 1983. A lively, popular history by someone who watched postwar Europe develop.

Medvedev, Roy. *Khrushchev.* 1983. A Soviet historian's biography of this powerful leader in the post-Stalin era.

Milward, Alan. *The Reconstruction of Western Europe, 1945–1951.* 1984. An important study of the conversion from wartime to peacetime.

Moeller, Robert. *Protecting Motherhood: Women and the Family in the Politics of Postwar West Germany.* 1993. An excellent account of Third Reich attitudes toward women in the postwar German legal system.

Pinder, John. *European Community: The Building of a Union.* 1991. Describes the steps by which the EC developed and analyzes its future.

Stokes, Raymond. *Divide and Prosper: The Heirs of I. G. Farben Under Allied Authority, 1945–1951.* 1988. A case study of how the economic "miracle" developed.

Swann, Abram de. *In Care of the State: Health Care, Education, and Welfare in Europe and the United States in the Modern Era.* 1988. A comparative look at the collectivization of services.

Talbott, John. *The War Without a Name: France in Algeria, 1954–1962.* 1980. A scholarly look at a savage piece of history.

Turner, Henry A. *The Two Germanies Since 1945.* 1987. A significant study of the postwar division of Germany and its consequences for ordinary people and international politics.

Vadney, T. E. *The World Since 1945.* 1987. An informative overview of political developments.

Verdery, Katherine. *Transylvanian Villagers: Three Centuries of Political, Economic, and Ethnic Change.* 1983. A portrait of how communism changed peasant life in Romania based on extensive discussions with villagers.

Wilkinson, James. *The Intellectual Resistance in Europe.* 1981. An important study of resistance and its consequences.

In January 1968 the French minister of youth and culture presided over the opening of a swimming pool at the University of Nanterre, one of the many new institutions of higher learning springing up to educate the scientists, engineers, and technicians needed by advanced industrial economies. Out of the crowd stepped a brash student, Daniel Cohn-Bendit, who asked the minister to light his cigarette. Once he had everyone's attention, Cohn-Bendit launched a harangue about the sexual problems of French students. Why did official publications about student life consider only the curriculum and never such personal matters? Considering the way Cohn-Bendit looked, responded the quick-witted minister, it was no wonder he had problems with women. "Fascist," someone yelled from the crowd, and pandemonium erupted. The incident at the Nanterre swimming pool became part of the legend of 1968, when university students throughout the world revolted against social conformity.

Students, the elite of the "baby-boom" generation, were rebelling against the comfortable life that postwar science, technology, and management had made possible. To young protesters like "Danny the Red" (as the Western press called Cohn-Bendit), neither capitalism nor communism offered much to choose from: both systems stifled freedom and demanded conformity. In their view society would not improve until the last capitalist had been strangled with the guts of the last Soviet-style bureaucrat. The surging anger and hope of 1960s youth fueled the continuing fight against racism and ignited protests against sexism, militarism, and environmental destruction, all of which the young rebels saw as endemic to both capitalism and communism. Only by expanding

Technology, Social Change, and Challenges to Western Dominance, 1962–1979

Student Demonstrations in Paris, 1968
Students throughout the world called for reform on the basis of Maoist, Marxist, Trotskyist, anarchist, and other political theories. Among other things, they protested against racism, sexism, war, and an impersonal technological society.

democracy, they believed, could necessary social change come about in the technological, "post-industrial" world.

While reform groups questioned the conditions of technological society, whole nations challenged the superpowers' monopoly of international power. An agonizing war in Vietnam sapped the United States' will and resources, and China confronted the Soviet Union with increasing belligerence and confidence in its growing power. Faced with a revolt against communism in their own sphere, the Soviets cracked down hard in Czechoslovakia. Western Europe and Japan invested heavily to improve their industrial bases and boost their exports; as a result they overcame the economic dominance the United States had commanded since the end of World War II. In the Third World oil-producing states formed a cartel and cut the flow of oil to the leading industrial nations in the 1970s. The resulting price increases turned a slowdown in the postwar economic boom into a recession. Other Third World countries disdained the use of economic leverage and resorted to terrorism in the 1970s. Even their wealth, military might, and technological leadership could not guarantee that the superpowers would always emerge victorious in this new age of global competition.

IMPORTANT DATES

1962 Forum on "pop art" at the Museum of Modern Art in New York

1962–1965 Vatican II meets to reform Catholic ritual and dogma

1963 U.S. president John F. Kennedy assassinated in Dallas, Texas

1964 Nikita Khrushchev ousted in the USSR; Leonid Brezhnev and Alexei Kosygin replace him

1966 Willy Brandt becomes West German foreign minister and develops *Ostploitik,* a policy designed to bridge tensions between the two Germanys

1967 South Africa's Dr. Christiaan Barnard performs first successful human heart transplant

1968 Revolution in Czechoslovakia against communism; student uprisings throughout Europe and the U.S.

1969 U.S. astronauts walk on the moon's surface

1972 North Vietnam and the U.S. sign treaty ending war in Vietnam; OPEC raises price of oil

1973–1976 Aleksandr Solzhenitsyn publishes *Gulag Archipelago*

1978 The first test-tube baby is born in England

1979 Iranians take U.S. hostages in Teheran

New Machines

Three decades after World War II, continuing technological advances steadily boosted prosperity and changed daily life in industrial countries. In Europe and the United States, people awoke to television news, worked with computers, and used revolutionary new contraceptives to control family size. Satellites orbiting the earth reported weather conditions, relayed telephone signals, and collected military intelligence. Smaller gadgets—electric popcorn poppers, portable radios, automatic garage-door openers, and portable tape players—made life more pleasant. The reliance of humans on machines led one philosopher to insist that people were no longer self-sufficient individuals but rather *cyborgs* who depended on machines to sustain ordinary life processes.

The Information Revolution

Information technology catalyzed social change in the 1960s and 1970s just as innovations in textile making and the spread of railroads had in the nineteenth century. Already mass journalism, film, and radio had helped forge a more homogeneous society based on shared information and images; by the late 1960s, people gravitated to a newer medium—television. With the average viewer tuning in about thirty hours per week, the audience for newspapers and theater eroded. "We devote more . . . hours per year to television than [to] any other single artifact," one sociologist commented in 1969. Virtually every Western home boasted a TV set. As with radio, European governments controlled programming, and they tried to avoid what they perceived as the substandard fare offered by American commercial broadcasting by featuring theater, ballet, concerts, variety shows, and news. Advertising (when used) was not permitted to interrupt European programs and was not attached to a single show. What "sold" was not considered an acceptable programming criterion. Rather, a British official believed this new medium should be used to preserve the humanist tradition by presenting viewers with "choice, the widest possible range of subjects treating the entire field and all the variety of the human conscience and experience." Thus the welfare state assumed a new obligation to fill its citizens' leisure time—and also gained more power to shape daily life. Critics charged that television avoided extremes to prevent offending anyone and in the United States to keep sponsors happy, and instead spoon-fed audiences only "moderate" or "official" opinions. They complained that although TV provided people with more information than ever before available, the shared culture it engendered represented the lowest common denominator.

With the emergence of communication satellites and video recorders in the 1960s, state-sponsored television encountered competition. Satellite technology allowed for the diffusion of sports broadcasts and other programming to a worldwide audience. Feature films on videotape became readily available to television stations, although not yet to individuals, and competed with made-for-television movies. European governments continued to produce high-quality television, but they found themselves outpaced by private pay stations that either churned out American-style "sitcoms" (situation comedies) or bought American comedies and simply dubbed them. What statesmen and intellectuals considered the junk programming of the United States—soap operas and game shows as well as sitcoms—amused a vast Western audience because it dealt with the joys, sorrows, tensions, and aspirations of everyday life.

Eastern-bloc television also exercised a powerful, widespread cultural influence. Even in one rural area of the Soviet Union, 44 percent of the inhabitants watched television every day; another 27 percent tuned in every three or four days; many others still preferred radio. By the end of the 1970s, Soviet announcers were broadcasting government-approved news to some 30 million TV sets in rural and urban areas alike, uniting a far-flung population; educational programming generally consisted

The Age of Television
Television brought national politics and culture into the private sphere with new force in the 1960s, and changed patterns of family life and leisure. The medium's popularity is evident in this scene of antennas dotting the Venetian skyline.

of shows designed to advance Soviet culture. In both the East and the West, the array of communication technology bombarded the everyday worlds of television watchers (and radio listeners) with standardized messages, muting the distinctness of individual experience.

Governments used the media not only to disperse culture but also to achieve political ends. Heads of state could usually preempt regular programming. In the 1960s, French president Charles de Gaulle addressed his fellow citizens frequently, employing grandiose gestures to stir patriotism. As electoral success increasingly depended on cultivating a successful media image, political staffs came to rely on media experts as much as they did policy experts. To ensure political neutrality in West Germany, an official committee regularly

Television and Political Power
French president Charles de Gaulle became a master of the new medium. He used it to make direct appeals to the French people in support of decolonization, a foreign policy independent of the United States, and economic modernization.

monitored state television announcers, watching for subtle signs of bias.

Just as revolutionary as television was the computer, which reshaped work in science, defense, and ultimately the industrial workplace. Computers had evolved dramatically since the first electronic, digital computer, the Colossus, which the British built in 1943 to decode Nazi military and diplomatic messages. Awesome in its day, Colossus was primitive by later standards—gigantic, slow, able only to decode, and so noisy that it sounded like "a roomful of [people] knitting away with steel needles." With growing civilian use after the war, computing machines shrank from the size of a gymnasium in the 1940s to that of a small desk in the late 1970s; by the mid-1980s they would be no larger than an attaché case and fantastically more powerful than Colossus.

The expanding capabilities and tumbling prices of computers depended on the development of increasingly sophisticated digital electronic circuitry implanted on tiny silicon chips, which replaced the clumsy radio tubes used in 1950s computers. Within a few decades the computer could perform hundreds of millions of operations per second and even respond to sound. The price of the integrated circuit at the heart of computer technology would eventually fall to less than a dollar; as a result, businesses and households would gain access to enormous amounts of information and computing ability at a reasonable cost. Interconnected institutional and personal networks of information about individuals, however, would raise troubling concerns. Foremost among them was the question of whether computer technology might result in the violation of an individual's right to privacy.

Computers changed the pace and patterns of work not only by speeding up and easing tasks but also by performing many operations that workers had once done themselves. For example, in garment making experienced workers no longer painstakingly figured out how to arrange patterns on cloth for maximum efficiency and economy. Instead a computer specified instructions for the optimal positioning of pattern pieces, and trained workers, usually women, followed the machine's directions. By the end of the 1970s, the miniaturization of the computer had made possible a rebirth of eighteenth-century "cottage industry." As in earlier times, people could work in the physical isolation of their homes, but now a modem connected them to a business headquarters.

Computers massively transformed human society. Whereas the Industrial Revolution had seen physical power replaced by machine capabilities, the information revolution witnessed brain power augmented by computer technology. Many believed computers would profoundly expand mental life, providing, in the words of one scientist, "boundless opportunities . . . to resolve the puzzles of cosmology, of life, and of the society of man."

The Space Age

When the Soviets launched the satellite *Sputnik* into orbit in 1957, they touched off an intensive "space race" with the United States. Although President Eisenhower had little interest in what he considered merely an expensive attempt to gain global status, John F. Kennedy became obsessed by the idea of "beating" the Soviets in space. He proclaimed it an American goal to put a man on the moon by the end of the 1960s. Throughout the decade increasingly complex space flights tested humans' ability to survive the process of space exploration, including weightlessness. Astronauts walked in space, endured weeks (and later, months) in orbit, repaired malfunctioning equipment, docked with other craft, tried fixing satellites, and carried out experiments for the military and private industry. Meanwhile a series of unmanned rockets filled the earth's gravitational sphere with weather, television, intelligence, and other communication satellites.

The climactic moment in the space age came in July 1969, when a worldwide television audience watched as U.S. astronauts Neil Armstrong and Edwin "Buzz" Aldrin walked on the moon's surface. As Armstrong stepped out of *Apollo 11's* lunar module, he remarked, "That's one small step for a man, one giant leap for mankind." America's success in the space race had fulfilled eons of human longing for contact with something beyond the earth. Astronauts and cosmonauts were perhaps the era's most admired heroes. Beginning with Soviet cosmonaut Yuri Gagarin, these space explorers had to live up to high public expectations. American astronaut John Glenn became a senator and presidential contender. The Soviets promoted the first woman in space, Valentina Tereshkova, as a role model for women—and never more so than when she married another astronaut and became a mother.

The space race grew out of Cold War mentalities, and such attitudes drove Western cultural developments. A whole new fantasy world developed. Children had a new setting—space—in which to imagine their adventures. Science fiction writing, already a popular genre for several decades, reached ever larger audiences. Films portrayed space explorers answering questions about life that were formerly the domain of church fathers. American filmmaker Stanley Kubrick's breathtakingly original 1968 film based on Arthur C. Clarke's *2001: A Space Odyssey* explored human morality and intelligence through a prism of extraterrestrial life and space travel. Likewise, in the internationally popular television series "Star Trek," crew members of the starship *Enterprise* wrestled with the problems of maintaining humane

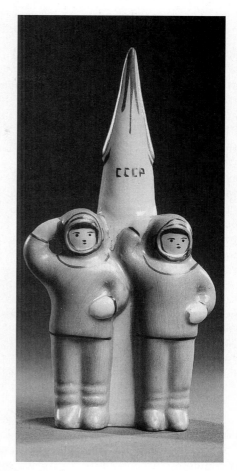

Space Age Kitsch
Porcelain statuettes of cosmonauts served an important role publicizing Soviet expertise in science.

values both as individuals and as members of a collective security community against less developed, often menacing civilizations. In the Eastern bloc, Polish author Stanisław Lem's novel *Solaris* (1971) showed space-age individuals engaged in personal quests. The film version (1972), by Soviet filmmaker Andrei Tarkovsky, was not as dazzling as Kubrick's masterwork.

The space age echoed Cold War concerns, but it also offered the possibility of more global political cooperation because, like the United States' atomic bomb project during World War II, the diffusion of rocket technology resulted from international efforts. From the 1960s on, U.S. spaceflights often involved the participation of such countries as Great Britain and the Netherlands. In 1965,

THE SPACE AGE

1957 Soviet Union launches the first artificial satellite, Sputnik

1961 Soviet cosmonaut Yuri Gagarin orbits the earth in Vostok 1

1961 Capsule carrying Alan Shepard, Jr. makes first U.S. suborbital flight

1965 U.S. launches first commercial communications satellite, Intelsat 1

1969 U.S. astronauts Neil Armstrong and Edwin Aldrich walk on moon's surface

1971 Soviet Union attempts unsuccessfully to put Salyut 1, a space station, into orbit

1973 U.S. puts Skylab, an experimental space station, into orbit

1970s–to present Soviet Union and United States individually and in collaboration with various countries perform space station experiments, lunar probes, and other scientific experiments

1976 Viking spacecraft explores Mars

1979–1986 Spacecraft Voyager makes successful flybys of Jupiter, Saturn, and Uranus

Western European countries established the European Space Research Organization to develop rocket technology in competition with the superpowers. The United States launched the first commercial communication satellite, *Intelsat 1*, in 1965, and by the 1970s more than four hundred stations worldwide and some one hundred fifty countries worked together to maintain global satellite communications. Interlocking television, telephone, computer, and other information technology systems still served Cold War ends, but the international collaboration needed to sustain these systems also countered virulent nationalism.

Lunar landings and experiments in space advanced pure science despite space-race hype. Astronomers, for example, previously dependent on remote sensing for their work, used mineral samples from the moon to calculate the age of the solar system more precisely. Unmanned spacecraft provided data on cosmic radiation, magnetic fields, and infrared sources. *Viking* transmitted stunning pictures of Mars in 1976, and *Voyager*, in its flyby of Saturn, Jupiter, and Uranus beginning in 1979, sup-

plied masses of new data about our solar system. Such findings from outer space reinforced the "big bang" theory of the universe's origins, first posited in the 1930s by American astronomer Edwin Hubble and given crucial support in the 1950s by the discovery of a low level of radiation permeating the universe in all directions.

Although the media touted the human conquerors of space, breakthroughs in space exploration and astronomy were utterly dependent on technology. As the first American astronauts themselves acknowledged, their chief role had been to rouse public interest. Similarly, scientists could gain accurate knowledge of the heavens only with the aid of mathematics and remarkable new instruments such as the radiotelescope, which depicted space by receiving, measuring, and calculating nonvisible rays. The scientific use of sophisticated technologies was not limited to astronomy and physics, moreover, but extended to the life sciences, investigating the origins and evolution of life itself.

The Revolution in Biology

Extraordinary advances in the biological sciences ensued after English scientists Francis Crick and James Watson discovered the configuration of DNA, the material in the chromosomes that carries hereditary information, in 1952. Apparently solving the mystery of the gene and thus of biological inheritance, they had shown how the "double helix" of the DNA molecule split in cellular reproduction to form the basis of each new cell. This genetic material, biologists concluded, provided a chemical pattern for an individual organism's life. Beginning in the 1960s, genetics and the new field of molecular biology progressed rapidly. Growing understanding of nucleic acids and proteins permitted important progress in knowledge of viruses and bacteria and made possible a host of new antibiotics and antiviral serums to combat polio and such dangerous childhood diseases as mumps and measles. Tetanus, syphilis, and tuberculosis no longer ravaged the West.

In the wake of this biological revolution came questions about the ethics of humans' tampering with the natural processes of life. Although scientific progress unraveled the mysteries of many genetic and other diseases and paved the way for their cure, scientists' new ability to intervene in life processes provoked controversy about the appropriate limits of such intervention. For example, understanding how DNA worked allowed scientists to bypass natural animal reproduction by a process called *cloning*—obtaining the cells of an organism and dividing or reproducing them (in an exact copy) in a laboratory. But should scientists be allowed to interfere with so basic and essential a process as reproduction? Similarly, the possibility of genetically altering species and even creating new ones (perhaps to control agricultural pests) led to concern about how the actions would affect the balance of nature. Thus although science functioned on a "pure" and "theoretical" plane, its consequences rippled through the social, cultural, and moral realm as well. Invoking Mary Shelley's *Frankenstein,* one critic noted that people still fear "that our scientists, well-intentioned and decent men and women all, will go on being titans who create monsters."

In 1967, Dr. Christiaan Barnard of South Africa performed the first successful heart transplant, and U.S. doctors later developed an artificial heart that allowed its critically ill recipients to live for several more years, although often severely disabled. Such medical miracles, however, prompted questions and even protests. For example, given the shortage of reusable organs, what criteria should doctors use in selecting recipients? Such quandaries moved medicine farther into the arena of social policy. Commentators also debated whether the enormous cost of new medical technology to save a few people would be better spent on helping the many who lacked even basic medical and health care.

Reproductive Technologies

Technology also influenced the most intimate areas of human relations—sexuality and reproduction. In traditional societies community and family norms dictated marital arrangements and sexual practices, in large part because too many or too few children threatened the crucial balance between population size and agricultural productivity. As Western societies industrialized and urbanized, however, not only did these considerations become less urgent but the growing availability of reliable birth-control devices permitted young people to begin sexual relationships earlier, with

less risk of pregnancy. In the 1960s these trends accelerated. The birth-control pill, first produced in the United States and tested on women in underdeveloped areas, came on the Western market after U.S. and British health authorities approved it in the early 1960s. By 1970 "the pill," which prevents ovulation, provided a more reliable means than condoms and diaphragms for controlling reproduction and spread to all industrialized countries. The intrauterine device (IUD), whose principles had been understood in the nineteenth century, was also widely used—until the discovery of its dangers to women's health. Worldwide, millions sought out voluntary surgical sterilization through tubal ligations and vasectomies, often after having the number of children they wanted. Techniques such as suction brought abortion, traditionally performed by amateurs, into the hands of medical professionals, making it a safe procedure for the first time.

Whereas only a small minority of Western births took place in hospitals in 1920, more than 90 percent did by 1970. Obstetricians took over much of the work midwives had once done, as pregnancy and birth became more of a medical process rather than an at-home experience. Innovative new procedures and equipment now made it possible to monitor women and fetuses throughout pregnancy and labor and delivery. The number of medical interventions rose: cesarean births increased 400 percent in one part of the United States in these decades, and the number of prenatal visits per patient in Czechoslovakia rose 300 percent between 1957 and 1976. In 1978 the first test-tube baby, Louise Brown, was born to an English couple. She had been conceived when her mother's eggs were fertilized in a laboratory dish and then implanted in her mother's uterus. This complex process, called *in vitro fertilization,* ultimately spared many couples the agony of unwanted childlessness. Donor-supplied "banks" provided sperm or eggs for the in vitro method if the couple who wanted to conceive could not produce their own. If a woman could not carry a child to term, the laboratory-fertilized embryo could be implanted in the uterus of a surrogate, or substitute, mother. Researchers even began working on an artificial womb to allow for reproduction entirely outside the body—from storage bank to dish to artificial embryonic environment.

A host of disturbing ethical and political controversies—and some tragedies—accompanied these breakthroughs. In the early 1960s a West German drug firm, without prior testing, distributed the tranquilizer thalidomide, claiming that it safely prevented miscarriages. Pregnant women used the drug widely, with disastrous results: thousands of deformed and retarded children were born. The Catholic church firmly opposed all mechanical and chemical means of birth control as a sinful intervention in a sacred process. Catholics and other opponents of abortion maintained that life begins at conception, and they branded abortion as murder. In vitro fertilization also stirred disapproval, appearing to some as "playing God" with life.

The expanding media and medical professions meanwhile helped democratize knowledge of birth-control procedures after World War II and made public discussions of sexual matters explicit, technical, and widespread. Popular use of birth control allowed Western society to be saturated with highly sexualized music, literature, and journalism without a corresponding rise in the birthrate—impressive evidence of the increasing separation of sexuality from reproduction. Surveys showed a more intense absorption with sexual pleasure and an ever younger age at which regular sexual activity took place. The Western media trumpeted the "commercialization of sex" and announced the arrival of a "sexual revolution."

Postindustrial Society

Reshaped by soaring investments in science, the spread of technology, and growing prosperity, Western countries in the 1960s became what social scientists called *postindustrial.* Coining the term, U.S. sociologist Daniel Bell defined 1960s society as focused less on industrial production than on the distribution of services—health care, education, and consumer benefits. The development of this service sector, Bell believed, meant that intellectual work, not industrial or manufacturing work, had become primary, an essential phase in launching any productive, societal, or political project. Moreover, all parts of society and industry interlocked,

The Postindustrial Workplace
Decorated with art, plants, and modern furniture, this Swedish Volvo factory encouraged its workers to act in teams, direct their own efforts, and make suggestions to management.

forming a system constantly in need of complex analysis. Out of this idea arose systems analysis, based on predictive, statistical calculations. One Soviet scientist characterized his work as "not simply an act of creativity but a complex system of coordinati[on]" that demanded management.

Postindustrial society changed the day-to-day lives and material conditions of millions of workers. Although remnants of an older way of life survived in the countryside, and people in the Soviet bloc had fewer modern conveniences than those in the Western bloc, the look of old-style industrial laborers and agricultural workers was disappearing everywhere. Factory workers often carried their lunch or work clothes in a briefcase, once the sign of executive status. Many working-class people, once cramped in crowded tenements, could now afford to buy their own homes; by the 1970s more than one-third of Western European workers owned homes. Multinational corporations reduced the threat of violent strikes, a common occurrence in the nineteenth century, by boosting worker participation in management decisions and by employing industrial psychologists to alleviate tensions. Instead of factories, corporate headquarters, banks, and university and government buildings dotted urban skylines. Workers and businesses generally flourished in this era, and Western affluence also allowed governments to eliminate some of the worst blemishes of industrialization.

Multinational Corporations

New multinational corporations produced for a global market and conducted business worldwide, but unlike older kinds of international firms, they established major factories in countries other than their home base. For example, by 1970, Standard Oil of New Jersey employed around 150,000 people, about 90,000 of them outside the United States. Of the 500 largest businesses in the United States in 1970, more than 100 did over a quarter of their business abroad; IBM operated in more than 100 countries. Although U.S.-based corporations led the way, European and Japanese multinationals like Volkswagen, Shell, Nestlé, and Sony also broadened their global scope.

Some multinational corporations had bigger revenues than entire nations. They appeared to burst the bounds of the nation-state, as they set up shop in whatever part of the world offered cheap labor. Their interests differed starkly from those of ordinary people with a local or national outlook. In the first years after the war, multinationals preferred European employees, who constituted a highly educated labor pool, had a strong consumer tradition, and eagerly sought secure work. Then in the 1960s, multinationals moved more of their operations into the Third World. This development both drove up sales and afforded new options should labor costs rise or taxes and regulations increase. Although multinational corporations provided jobs in developing areas, profits usually enriched foreign stockholders.

Initially some Europeans denounced what they perceived as a new imperialism in the guise of corporate invasion. However, many European firms realized that they could only stay competitive by expanding, and they adeptly and aggressively reacted to the changing international business climate by stepping up mergers. In chemicals, glass, electrical products, transport, metallurgy, and many

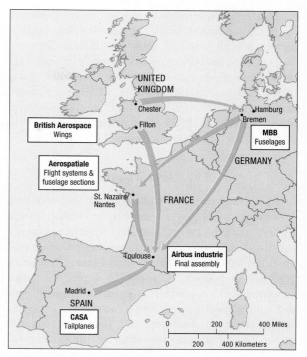

The Airbus Production System

other industries, huge conglomerates came to dominate European production. In France, for example, a massive glass conglomerate merged with a metallurgical company to form a new group specializing in all phases of construction—a wise move given the postwar building boom. Whereas U.S. production had surpassed the combined output of West Germany, Great Britain, France, Italy, and Japan in the immediate postwar years, by the mid-1970s these countries had rebounded to restore the position they had held in the 1930s. By 1972 both the nationalized British Steel company and the privately owned and German-based Thyssen firm were approaching the revenues of U.S. Steel and Bethlehem Steel.

Most crucial to regaining economic strength, European firms, often backed and sometimes even owned by their governments, increased their investment in research and used international cooperation to produce major new products. Ventures like the British-French Concorde supersonic aircraft, which flew from London to New York in under four hours, and the Airbus, a more practical passenger jet produced by a consortium of

European firms, attested to the strong relationship among government, business, and science. Jointly pursuing technological and production innovations, European firms commanded large enough research budgets to compete successfully with U.S.-based multinational giants. "The prime function . . . of an industrial company," said one British executive, "[is] to spend every possible penny it can afford on technical development."

The New Worker

In its formative stage, industrial production had depended on impoverished workers who often labored to exhaustion, endured malnourishment, and lived in a state of discontentment that sometimes led to violence. This scenario changed fundamentally in postwar Europe. To begin with, the proportion of people toiling in factories and mines and on farms dropped. Whereas the farm population had been declining as a percentage of the workforce for almost two centuries, the substantial reduction of the blue-collar workforce was new, resulting from resource depletion in coal mines, the substitution of oil for coal and of plastics for steel, the growth of international competition, and automation in manufacturing processes.

Even manual labor changed, as more workers spent their days simply tending or maintaining machines rather than performing backbreaking jobs. Managers increasingly recognized that old-fashioned hierarchical decision making diminished productivity. Following the lead of Swedish manufacturers, employers started grouping workers into teams that set their own production quotas, organized and assigned tasks, enforced their own quality standards, and competed with other teams to see who could produce more. As workers adopted attitudes and gained responsibilities that had once been managerial prerogatives, traditional definitions of labor became obsolete. Union membership declined along with blue-collar work, although strikes remained important (outside West Germany and the Soviet bloc) for raising labor issues, and unions continued to play a key role in factory organization. If strikes did occur, they were often short-lived and symbolic. Union leaders acted more like bureaucrats than workers.

In both East-bloc and West-bloc countries, a "new working class" emerged, consisting of white-collar service personnel. Its rise undermined old social distinctions based on the way one worked: those who performed service work or had managerial functions were not necessarily better paid than blue-collar workers. As longevity increased and medical technology expanded, the number of health-care and medical workers soared. The ranks of service workers also swelled with researchers, technicians, planners, and government functionaries. Scientists and technicians constituted 3.6 percent of the U.S. workforce in 1965, up 50 percent from a decade earlier. Employment in traditional parts of the service sector—banks, insurance companies, and other financial institutions—also surged, because of the vast sums of money needed to finance technological society. The consumer economy provided jobs in sales and repair, in restaurants and personal grooming salons, and in household work. By 1969 the percentage of service-sector employees had passed that of manufacturing workers in several industrial countries: 61.1 percent versus 33.7 percent in the United States; 49.8 percent versus 41.9 percent in the Netherlands; and 48.8 percent versus 41.1 percent in Sweden.

Postindustrial society had a different configuration in the Eastern bloc. Late in the 1960s, Communist leaders announced a program of "advanced socialism"—more social homogenization, greater equality of salaries, and nearly complete absence of private production—for the Soviet Union. In Poland, however, approximately 25 percent of the workforce engaged in private peasant farming and artisan work. A huge difference between professional occupations and those involving physical work remained in socialist countries. Little mobility existed between the two classifications, and much as in the Western bloc the workforce was distinctly organized by gender. Somewhere between 80 and 95 percent of women worked in socialist countries, but they generally held the most menial and lowest paying jobs. Moreover, consumer spending differed radically in Eastern and Western Europe: socialist families still spent by far the largest percentage of their income on food—55 percent in Poland and 45 percent in East Germany and the Soviet Union. The costs of military buildup and the bloated bureaucratic sector sapped resources and left socialist workers with a paltry variety of consumer goods.

As the postwar boom accelerated, West Germany and other Western nations absorbed immigrant, or "guest," laborers. Coming from Turkey, Greece, southern Italy, Portugal, and North Africa, these workers collected garbage, built roads, and cleaned homes. In an environment where desirable work usually involved mental operations and clean work, these jobs appeared more lowly than before. Although males predominated among migrant workers, female migrants who worked performed similar chores for less pay. Migrants *looked* different from the native population and were thus pegged as lower class, although by the 1980s many had obtained better-paying, higher-status jobs and integrated themselves into the host culture. Despite the announced labor shortage that justified the invitation to guest workers, industrial societies simultaneously developed a stratum of the permanently unemployed.

By the 1970s one could travel for miles in Europe without seeing a farmhouse. Small landowners sold family plots to farmers engaged in *agribusiness.* Governments, farmers' cooperatives, and planning agencies took over from the individual farmer; they set production quotas and handled an array of marketing transactions. Western European agriculture rebounded rapidly from its low productivity of the late 1940s, when refugees did much farmwork without machinery or fertilizer. In the 1960s agricultural output rose an average of 3 percent per year in Greece and Spain and 2.5 percent in the Netherlands, France, and Great Britain. Genetic research and the skyrocketing use of machinery contributed to growth. For example, the number of tractors in Germany went from 384,000 to 1,340,000 and in Spain from 22,000 to almost 250,000. The six Common Market countries used more than 8.3 million tons of chemical fertilizer in 1969. Although politicians continued to invoke the well-being of the family farmer to win elections, such appeals were partially successful exercises in nostalgia.

As farming modernized it required flexibility, even in Italy and France, which had the highest proportion of people employed in agriculture in Europe. For example, in the 1970s a French farmer, Fernande Pelletier, with the help of her husband, son, and daughter-in-law, made a living on her 100-acre farm in southwestern France in the new setting of international agribusiness. Advised by a government expert, Pelletier produced anything from lamb to walnuts or veal—whatever might sell competitively in the Common Market. She also compared interest rates, whether on the purchase of machinery or baby animals; learned how to diversify her labor-intensive farming; and joined with other farmers in her region to buy heavy machinery and to sell produce. Agricultural solvency required as much managerial and intellectual effort as did success in the industrial sector.

Educating Technocratic Society

Education was both the key to running postindustrial society and the means by which nations maintained their economic and military might. "Today one is educated and therefore powerful," one French official put it. "It's the accumulation of knowledge, not of wealth, that makes the difference." Technological progress demanded a multitude of researchers; those corporations and governments that invested the most in research became military and industrial leaders. The United States funneled more than 20 percent of its gross national product into research in the 1960s and consequently siphoned off many of Europe's leading intellectuals and technicians in a so-called brain drain. Complex systems—for example, the many components of nuclear power generation, from scientific conceptualization to plant construction to the publicly supervised disposal of radioactive waste—required intricate professional oversight. Scientists and bureaucrats frequently made more crucial decisions than did elected politicians in the realm of space programs, weapons development, and economic policy. Soviet-bloc nations proved less adept at linking their considerable achievements in science to actual applications because of the bureaucratic red tape involved in getting an innovation approved. In the 1960s some 40 percent of East-bloc scientific findings became obsolete before the government approved them for application to technology.

In the Western world artisanal know-how, hard work, and creative intuition had launched the earliest successes of the Industrial Revolution. By the late twentieth century these qualities alone no longer sufficed. Rather, success in business or government demanded the humanistic or technological expertise of a highly educated manager. Even lower-level jobs required some formal education. The new criteria for success fostered unprecedented growth in education, especially in universities and scientific institutes (where the majority of research was conducted) and other postsecondary institutions. The number of university students in the United States spurted from 1.2 million in 1950 to 7 million in 1969—an increase of nearly 600 percent. In Sweden it rose by 582 percent and in West Germany by 250 percent. Great Britain established a new network of universities and polytechnics to encourage the technical research that elite universities often scorned and to accommodate the baby boomers now coming of age. France set up administrative schools for future high-level bureaucrats. By the late 1970s the Soviet Union had built its scientific establishment so rapidly that the number of its advanced researchers in the natural sciences and engineering surpassed that of the United States. Khrushchev's successors tried to rid Soviet science of such ideological remnants of Stalinism as the commitment to Lysenko's genetic theories. Meanwhile, institutions of higher learning in the United States and Western Europe added courses in business and management, information technology, and systems analysis.

Although education ostensibly made the avenues to success more democratic by basing them on talent instead of wealth, in fact no such societal leveling resulted in most West European countries. During these decades only about 10 percent of university students were the children of workers or peasants; thus to some extent a university degree certified that one was from the right social circles. Moreover, pedagogy often remained rigidly centralized. In France, for example, the national ministry of education determined primary and secondary curricula, including the books students read and the time of year they read them. Although eighteenth-century Europeans had pioneered educational reform, by the 1960s and 1970s new theories influential in the United States for half a century had made little impact. Students reported that teachers lectured even young children, who were required to take notes, and pupils spoke in class only to echo the teacher or to recite homework memorized the night before. At the university level, as one angry writer put it, the professor was "a petty, threatened god," who puffed himself up "on the passivity and dependence of students."

Such judgments combined with the new emphasis on science, engineering, and business to provoke students to rebel late in the 1960s.

The "Hi-Tech" Family

The new technologies of birth control, information and media, and household mechanization changed family life in these decades. In the 1960s the family appeared in new forms: households were now headed by a single parent, by remarried parents merging two sets of unrelated children, by unmarried couples cohabiting, or by traditionally married parents who had fewer children. Households of same-sex partners also became more common. After almost two decades of baby boom the birthrate dropped significantly. The average Belgian woman, for example, bore 2.6 children in 1960 but only 1.8 by the end of the 1970s. Although the birthrate fell, the percentage of children born outside of marriage soared; in Switzerland, for example, it went up by 100 percent during these years. Combined with high rates of abortion—435 per 1,000 live births in Czechoslovakia, and 146 per 1,000 in Sweden—the new conditions of reproduction aroused social concern. At the end of the 1970s the marriage rate had fallen 30 percent from its 1960s level. The average marriage lasted one-third longer than it had a century earlier because of increased longevity. The rate of divorce, especially in areas of northern Europe, nonetheless rose, suggesting yet another change in attitudes toward marriage.

Daily life within the family changed. For one thing, technology saturated domestic space. Machines such as dishwashers, washers, and dryers became more affordable and more widespread, reducing (in theory) the time women had to devote to household work and raising standards of cleanliness. Radio and television filled a family's leisure time and often formed the basis of its common social life. Even more women worked outside the home during these years to pay for prolonged adolescence wherein children did not work until their twenties but instead attended school and cost their parents money. Some social scientists interpreted this phenomenon as women's abandonment of the family. They charged that most social problems and personal disorders were caused by selfish and greedy women who worked.

Whereas the early modern family organized labor, taught craft skills, and monitored reproductive behavior, the modern family seemed to have a primarily psychological mission. Parents were to provide emotional nurture while their children learned intellectual skills in school; spouses offered one another comfort after the grueling discipline of office or factory work. Families did not handle this responsibility alone: psychologists, social workers, and social-service agencies provided counseling and assistance. Television programs portrayed a variety of family experiences, on soap operas, sitcoms, and family-oriented game shows, giving viewers an opportunity to see how other families deal with the tensions of modern life.

Postindustrial society transformed teenagers' lives. A century earlier, teens had been full-time wage earners; now they were students, financially dependent on their parents. The young sometimes remained financial "minors" into their twenties, situation that produced new tensions for both young and old. Advertisers and industrialists saw the baby boomers as a huge market and wooed them with such consumer items as rock music, which became a multibillion-dollar business. Pop music of the previous generation had described the route from youthful attraction to love and finally to adult marriage. In contrast, rock music celebrated youthful rebellion against adult culture in biting, critical, and often explicitly sexual lyrics.

Rockers began in music clubs, slowly building followings and reputations. The Beatles were a little-known band in 1962 when they hired a new manager, Brian Epstein. Epstein remade their image and their music, booked them in major theaters across Europe and the United States, and encouraged them to produce tamer songs. Beatle John Lennon claimed to write two different kinds of music, one a formulaic kind for mass consumption, and another more innovative kind to please himself. "What's your message for American teenagers?" the Beatles were asked. "Buy some more Beatle records," they responded. By the mid-1960s public appearances of the Beatles summoned thousands of screaming fans whose hysteria intensified during the group's performances.

Live concerts featured the spontaneity and blending of forms—gospel, blues, jazz, country—from which rock and roll had originated in the 1950s. In contrast, producing records depended on the electronic abilities of technicians, who usually fashioned records according to the directives of marketers and advertisers. Musicians, the masters of onstage performances, thus surrendered their autonomy in the recording studio. Promoters scoured clubs and schools for young rock musicians who could be packaged and marketed as the Beatles and Rolling Stones had been. Despite the popularity of a few individual women rockers, promotion focused on men, depicted as surrounded by worshiping female "groupies." By the mid-1970s several recording empires that sold billions of records dominated rock music. The proliferation of rock music anchored teenagers to mass consumer culture, but the music's often rebellious message also encouraged them to resist adult values and their parents' demands. Thus a chasm, referred to as a "generation gap," sometimes opened up among members of the same family.

Art, Ideas, and Faith in a Technocracy

Abstract expressionism and the celebration of the artistic ego by Jackson Pollock and the New York School provoked resistance almost from its inception in the 1940s and 1950s. A new generation of challengers revived the tradition of endorsing technology through their art. *Pop art,* whose leading practitioners were Richard Hamilton of Britain and Robert Rauschenberg of the United States, featured images from everyday life and employed the glossy techniques and products of what these artists called "admass," or mass advertising, society. "There's no reason," one of them maintained of modern society's commercialism, "not to consider the world as one gigantic painting." Rauschenberg sold little in the 1950s because his totally white paintings, executed with housepaint, had no appeal; but he saw the reflections appearing in the monochromatic white as a new kind of art that broke down artistic boundaries. He eventually turned to collages made from comics, magazine clippings, and fabric to fulfill his vision that "a picture is more like the real world when it's made out of the real world."

In 1962, New York's Museum of Modern Art held a forum to consider the phenomenon of pop art. This event marked the beginning of this movement's acceptance and commercial success. By then Rauschenberg had been joined by such maverick American artists as Jasper Johns and Andy Warhol

Claes Oldenburg, **Giant Hamburger with Pickle Attached,** *1962*
Pop artists often expressed a "benign or amiable" attitude toward machines and consumer goods. Satire, irony, and humor characterized Oldenburg's approach to postindustrial life.

(c. 1927–1987). Pop art in the 1960s parodied modern commercialism. It showed, for example, how the female body, the classic form that attracted nineteenth-century male art buyers, was used to sell everything mass culture had to offer in the 1960s and 1970s. Swedish artist Claes Oldenburg depicted the grotesque aspects of ordinary consumer products in *Giant Hamburger with Pickle Attached* (1962) and *Lipstick Ascending on Caterpillar Tractor* (1967).

Many of these visual artists were inspired by the work of composers, among them the American John Cage, who were rapidly changing musical forms. Cage worked within the tradition of Debussy and Schoenberg, which highlighted sound images and eliminated the dissonance-consonance distinction, but he added sounds produced by such everyday items as combs and pieces of wood into his musical scores. Buddhist influence led Cage also to incorporate silence in music and to compose by randomly tossing coins and then choosing notes by the corresponding numbers in the ancient Chinese *I Ching* (Book of Changes). Cage's orchestral scores allowed the players themselves to decide when and how they would participate in the musical production. Other composers called *minimalists* simplified music by featuring repetition and sustained notes, as well as rejecting the "masterpiece" tradition of lush classical compositions. Another group stressed modern technology; they introduced tape recordings into vocal pieces and used computers and synthesizers both to compose and to perform their works. Many listeners found it difficult to appreciate these new patterns of sound. At the same time, improved recording technology and mass marketing brought classical music of all varieties to a wider home audience than ever before.

Intellectuals elevated the social sciences to the peak of their prestige during these decades. Sociologists and psychologists produced empirical studies that purported to demonstrate rules for understanding individual, group, and societal behavior. Sociologists, anthropologists, and psychologists also undermined some of the foundations for belief that individuals had any true freedom and for supposing that Western civilization was any more sophisticated or just than non-Western societies. American psychologist B. F. Skinner proposed to modify behavior through a system of rewarding positive behaviors and punishing negative ones. Behaviorists sought to eliminate the study of what they considered ephemeral mental states and values, and they seemed to trample on concepts of human freedom in their advocacy of "social engineering" of ordinary people by so-called experts.

The influential work of French anthropologist Claude Lévi-Strauss questioned his discipline's ability to understand foreign cultures in a Western intellectual framework. Lévi-Strauss's theory, structuralism, insisted that all societies functioned within controlling structures—kinship and exchange, for example—that operated according to coercive rules similar to those of language. Structuralism challenged existentialism's tenet that humans could create a free existence and social science's faith in the triumph of rationality. The findings of the social sciences generally underscored concerns that technology was creating a society of automatons and that complex managerial systems would eradicate individualism and human freedom.

Debates about free will coincided with new Christian answers to changing times. Responding to what he saw as a crisis in faith caused by affluence and secularism, Pope John XXIII (∗1958–1963) in 1962 convened the Second Vatican Council, known as Vatican II. The participants in Vatican II modernized the liturgy, democratized many church procedures, and at the last session in 1965, renounced its dogma that Catholics should regard the Jewish people as guilty of killing Jesus. These new policies countered elitist, authoritarian, and antisemitic aspects of traditional religion that many people interpreted as having buttressed fascism and also opened the Catholic church to new influences. Although Pope John's successor, Paul VI (∗1963–1978), reiterated Catholic opposition to artificial birth control in the encyclical *Humanae Vitae* (1968), he became the first pontiff to visit Africa, Asia, and South America. He also encouraged Catholicism in the Soviet bloc. A Protestant revival occurred in the United States; growing numbers of people joined sects that stressed the literal truth of the Scriptures. In Western Europe churchgoing remained at a low ebb. In the 1970s, for example, only 10 percent of the British population went to religious services—about the same number that attended live soccer matches.

Contesting the Cold War Order

Affluence, scientific sophistication, and military might elevated the superpowers to the peak of their power early in the 1960s. By 1965, however, the six nations of the Common Market had replaced the United States as the largest global merchant, and Communist China, along with countries in Eastern Europe, was contesting Soviet policies. In the decolonizing world the superpowers had difficulty finding suitable and pliable allies. The struggle for Indochinese independence had never ended, and by the mid-1960s Marxist-Leninist ideology, peasant aspirations, and Western technological capitalism converged to produce the devastating war in Vietnam. Rising citizen discontent also challenged Cold War priorities as industrial societies adjusted to the changes brought by technological development.

Politics and Prosperity

In the summer of 1963, less than a year after the shock of the Cuban Missile Crisis, the United States and the Soviet Union signed a test-ban treaty outlawing the explosion of nuclear weapons in the atmosphere and in the seas. Opening an era of reduced international tensions, or détente, the acceptance of the treaty suggested that the superpowers would reduce international tensions to focus on domestic politics. The new Soviet middle class of bureaucrats and managers demanded a better standard of living and a reduction in Cold War animosity, and Western-bloc reformers called for more effective democracy and the more equal distribution of prosperity.

The assassination of John F. Kennedy in November 1963 came amidst increasing demands for civil rights for African Americans and other minorities. White segregationists reacted to sit-ins at lunch counters, efforts to register voters, and freedom marches with extraordinary violence. White racists firebombed churches, schools, homes, and buses, and murdered individual activists. In response, Kennedy had introduced civil rights

The Struggle for Civil Rights
To block integration in the southern United States, some whites committed murder, arson, assault, and bombings. They set fire to this bus of black and white "Freedom Riders" and then attacked passengers as they fled the burning vehicle.

legislation and forced the desegregation of schools and universities, calling civil rights for blacks "a moral issue . . . as old as the Scriptures." He appealed to Americans to end racism "in the Congress, in your state and local legislative body, and, above all, in our daily lives." In a massive rally in Washington, D.C., in August 1963, hundreds of thousands of marchers assembled around the Lincoln Memorial, where they heard the electrifying words of the African-American activist minister Martin Luther King, Jr.:

> I have a dream . . . that all of God's children, black men and white men, Jews and Gentiles, Protestants and Catholics, will be able to join hands and sing in the words of that old Negro spiritual "Free at last! Free at last! Thank God almighty, we are free at last!"

Lyndon B. Johnson (1908–1973), Kennedy's successor, turned rhetoric into reality when he steered the Civil Rights Act through Congress in 1964. This legislation forbade segregation in public facilities and created the Equal Employment Opportunity Commission (EEOC) to fight job discrimination based on "race, color, national origin, religion, and sex." (Southern conservatives had tacked on the provision against sex discrimination

in the vain hope that it would doom the bill.) Modeling himself on his hero Franklin Roosevelt, Johnson envisioned a Great Society in which new government programs would give the 40 million Americans living in poverty some share of American abundance. Johnson simultaneously proposed a tax cut to stimulate economic growth and sponsored myriad reform programs: Project Head Start for disadvantaged preschool children, the Job Corps for training youth, Volunteers in Service to America (VISTA) to support volunteers in poverty-stricken areas, and projects for urban development. These programs brought hope to many Americans, who agreed with black novelist Ralph Ellison (1914–1994) that Johnson was "the greatest American president for the poor and the Negroes."

In West European countries voters elected politicians who promoted similar social programs; a significant minority shifted their votes away from the Christian Democratic coalitions to Socialist and Social Democratic parties. In the autumn of 1964 the British electorate returned the Labour party to power. Support for the Conservatives had eroded when they chipped away at the welfare state and presided over decolonization. Harold Wilson, the Labour prime minister, had refurbished the party's working-class platform by calling for technocratic education and more attention to the needs of the expanding middle class of service workers. Wilson could not reverse the economy's decline, however. British productivity remained the lowest among industrialized powers, and commonwealth trading partners increasingly turned to Japanese and American goods. As unemployment increased, the government restricted immigration to control welfare-state expenditures and devalued the pound to make British goods more competitive.

In 1963, Konrad Adenauer surrendered West Germany's leadership to Ludwig Erhard, who had guided the country's "economic miracle." Although the Christian Democrats had presided over West Germany's political and economic rehabilitation, the lead in 1960s politics passed to Social Democratic politicians who shifted money from defense spending to domestic programs. Willy Brandt (1913–1992), the Socialist mayor of West Berlin, became foreign minister in a coalition government in 1966. Brandt pursued reconciliation with fellow Germans in communist East Germany. This policy, known as *Ostpolitik*, ended frigid relations with the Soviet bloc. With German and other markets saturated by goods from the economic resurgence, West German business leaders wanted, as one industrialist put it, "the depoliticization of Germany's foreign trade"—mainly the opening of the Eastern bloc to consumerism and new business opportunities.

French president Charles de Gaulle also moved to break the Cold War stranglehold on Europe. Although France had but a 4 percent share of the world economy, de Gaulle forcefully advocated the interests of France and of a cooperative Europe in opposition to the superpowers. He poured more money into French nuclear development, and he steered a middle course between the United States and the Soviet Union. Thus he withdrew French forces from NATO (after the United States tried to dissuade him from developing an independent nuclear deterrent) and signed trade treaties with the Soviet bloc. However, he also protected France's good relations with Germany to prevent further encroachments from the Eastern bloc. At home, de Gaulle's government mandated the cleaning of all Parisian buildings and sponsored the construction of modern housing. He described France as "like the princess in the fairy story or the Madonna in the frescoes . . . dedicated to an exalted and exceptional destiny." With his haughty demeanor and stubborn pursuit of French grandeur, de Gaulle offered the European public an alternative to superpower toadying. Following his lead, Western Europe began reasserting itself.

Brandt's *Ostpolitik* and de Gaulle's assertiveness had their echoes in the Eastern bloc, where since 1953 the uneven progress of thaw, detente, and insurgency had stirred the winds of change. Pushing de-Stalinization, Khrushchev took the dangerous course of trying to reduce Communist officialdom's privileges, and he sanctioned the publication of Aleksandr Solzhenitsyn's *One Day in the Life of Ivan Denisovitch* (1962), which revealed firsthand the terrible conditions in the labor camps. Khrushchev's blunders—notably his humiliation in the Cuban Missile Crisis, his ineffectual schemes to improve Soviet agriculture, and his inability to patch the rift with China—became intolerable to his Kremlin colleagues. In 1964 they ousted him in favor of two party bureaucrats, Leonid Brezhnev (1906–1982) and Alexei Kosygin (1904–1980). Nevertheless, attempts at reform continued. As premier, Kosygin decentralized parts of the economy to encourage plant managers to turn a profit. Soviet policy called for ratcheting up the defense budget while producing televisions, household appliances, and cheap housing to alleviate the discontent of better-educated citizens. The government also loosened restrictions to allow cultural and scientific meetings with Westerners, another move that relaxed the Cold War atmosphere in the mid-1960s.

The Soviet satellites in Eastern Europe grasped the opportunity presented by Moscow's less rigid posture. Members of COMECON (the Soviet bloc's economic organization) refused to become agricultural backwaters supporting Soviet growth. Romania promoted industrialization, Poland allowed private farmers greater freedom to make money, and Hungarian leader János Kádár (1912–1989) introduced elements of a market system (the New Economic Mechanism) into the national economy. East Germans, benefiting from economic ties to West Germany, strove to advance technological education.

In the arts, Eastern-bloc writers continued for a time to thaw the frozen monolith of socialist realism. Ukrainian poet Yevgeny Yevtushenko exposed Soviet complicity in the Holocaust in *Babi*

Yar (1961), a passionate protest against the slaughter of tens of thousands of Jews near Kiev during World War II. In East Berlin, Christa Wolf challenged the celebratory nature of socialist art. Her novel *Divided Heaven* (1965) showed a couple divided by the Berlin Wall; the man chooses to escape to the Western bloc but the woman stays behind to support socialism and ultimately commits suicide. Eastern-bloc writers undermined the focus on social progress in socialist literature by examining individual subjectivity and emotions. In 1966 the chill returned to writing in the USSR when two authors were convicted for producing so-called anti-Soviet literature. Thereafter the best writers relied on *samizdat* culture, in which uncensored publications were reproduced by hand or by mimeograph and passed from reader to reader.

Vietnam and Turmoil in Asia

Outside the Eastern and Western blocs, countries looked to the superpowers for military and economic support. Israel and Taiwan unequivocally depended on the United States to protect them; Cuba and certain African states turned to the Soviet Union. Elsewhere during the 1960s, Third World nations increasingly distanced themselves from the superpowers.

China led the way, and even developed its own nuclear weapon in 1967. Mao Zedong, ever hostile to Western capitalism, also detested Soviet bureaucratization. Moreover, he sharply criticized Soviet foreign policy and rebuked Khrushchev for backing down in Cuba. In 1966, Mao unleashed the Cultural Revolution, a movement to remake individual personality according to Mao's vision of socialism. Mao wanted the Chinese to experience revolution on a permanent basis instead of stagnating in Soviet-style bureaucratic corruption. China's youth were empowered to punish former revolutionary leaders, civil servants, and teachers, as well as workers, farmers, and even retired people. Thus young people hauled away their elders for "reeducation"—which translated to personal humiliation, incarceration, or death. Economic goals lost their importance as the Chinese became obsessed with reinventing revolutionary political culture. In foreign policy the Cultural Revolution widened differences with the Soviet Union over support for Communist insurgency.

Both superpowers had interests in East and Southeast Asia, but they were often blind to the complex changes under way in the region. American policy makers did not detect the growing dispute between the two Communist giants because many were influenced by an inflexible vision of monolithic communism. While China plunged into Mao's bloody cultural and economic experiments, the peoples of Southeast Asia were coming to grips with decades of demographic upheaval. Despite war and nationalist revolution, the region's population more than tripled between 1920 and 1970, reaching 370 million by the end of the 1970s. This explosive growth confounded nationalist leaders, typically military men with little experience in governing a booming population. Like the 85 percent of Third World leaders who rose from the military, most East and Southeast Asian rulers were dictators without the technological expertise to make their countries economically viable. Thus superpower intervention in this unstable part of the world often came with an uncertain price tag.

The United States chose to assert itself in this volatile region through Vietnam. In the autumn of 1963 a group of South Vietnamese army officers overthrew the right-wing government of Ngo Dinh Diem, who had ruled since 1954 with increasing U.S. assistance. Thereafter a series of military coups kept the South Vietnamese government unstable, but the United States escalated its commitment to a noncommunist South Vietnam. Although Kennedy beefed up the U.S. military presence in an attempt to steady Saigon's corrupt leadership, a swift triumph over the rebel Vietcong was not forthcoming. Backed by North Vietnam, the Soviet Union, and China, the influence of the Vietcong seemed to grow daily.

After an encounter in the Gulf of Tonkin between North Vietnamese and American battlecraft in August 1964, Lyndon Johnson induced the U.S. Congress to pass a resolution endorsing the bombing of North Vietnam. By 1966 the United States had more than a half-million soldiers in South Vietnam. Before the war ended, the United States would drop more bombs on North Vietnam than the Allies had launched on Germany and Japan combined during World War II. Television reports carried the optimistic predictions of Johnson's advisers that each fresh attack and every new draft call-up revealed a "light at the end of the tunnel." Massive air attacks, some boasted, would "bomb North Vietnam back to the Stone Age." Yet the strategy failed. Despite regular announcements of enormous North Vietnamese "body counts," American casualties also mounted relentlessly. The Vietcong escalated its guerrilla warfare and then melted away into jungles and cavernous hillsides.

Johnson's heart was really in his civil rights legislation and "war on poverty," but his reelection depended on defeating the prowar senator Barry Goldwater. Frustrated but still confident, Johnson offered massive aid to Indochina if the Vietcong and North Vietnamese would stop fighting. After decades of anticolonial struggle, the insurgents rejected a negotiated peace. North Vietnam's leaders calculated that the United States would give in first as the American public recoiled from the horrors of televised slaughter: South Vietnam officials casually executed people in the streets, and children screamed in mortal pain as they were engulfed by flaming napalm, a jellied gasoline that asphyxiated its victims while they burned. Branded as murderers by international opinion, American forces simultaneously looked inept before images of pajama-clad Asians on bicycles who held at bay the technologically advanced Yankees.

By 1968 a swelling American antiwar movement challenged the killing on humanitarian grounds. In an age of ideological war, lack of support at home spelled the beginning of the end for the U.S. war effort. Johnson abandoned his soaring political ambition and announced in March 1968 that he would not run for president again. Swallowing his contempt for antiwar activists, he accepted deescalation and peace talks. As he left office in January 1969, peace remained elusive and the war's social and economic costs to the United States had yet to be tallied.

The Explosion of Civic Activism

In the midst of Cold War, technological advance, and bloody conflict, a new social activism emerged in the West. Students, blacks and other racial minorities, women, antiwar protesters, environmentalists, and homosexuals and lesbians raised their voices to demand that Western reality match its ideals. The civil rights movement in the United States ignited fiery protests in the streets, in universities, and in the halls of government. Behind the Iron Curtain dissident movements demanded political democratization and social change. These movements nearly swept up France and Czechoslovakia in revolution, and they cast doubts on the superpower status of the United States and the Soviet Union.

A broad cross section of Americans led the way in radicalizing civic activism. In 1965, César Chávez (1927–1993) led Mexican-American migrant workers in the California grape agribusiness to strike for better wages and working conditions. Controversy swirled around the protest: "A hoax, a fantasy, a charade," one columnist called the work action and the hunger strikes. Deeply religious and ascetic, Chávez helped Spanish-speaking Americans define their identity and struggle against deportation, inferior schooling, and discrimination. Meanwhile, the civil rights movement veered onto a violent course as riots erupted in Watts, a black district of Los Angeles, in the summer of 1965. In the "long, hot summer" that followed, city after city endured similar outbursts of anger and frustration. Some African-American activists transformed their struggle into a militant affirmation of racial differences. They urged blacks not to push for mere equality but for a celebration of their race under the banner "Black is beautiful." Instead of imitating whites, which amounted to self-hatred, blacks should celebrate their African heritage and work for "black power" by reclaiming rights instead of peacefully begging for them. Some formerly pacifist black leaders turned their rhetoric to violence: "Burn, baby, burn," chanted rioters who destroyed the grim inner cities around them in the belief that civil rights legislation alone offered only slight relief to their plight.

White university students who had participated in the early stages of the civil rights movement found themselves excluded from leadership positions. Many soon joined the swelling protest against the dramatic educational and social consequences of technological change, consumerism, sexual repression, and the Vietnam War. European youth caught the same fever. In Rome university students occupied an administration building after right-wing thugs assassinated one of their number during a protest against the 200-to-1 student-teacher ratio. Polish high school and university

Youth Culture
These young Norwegians, bedecked in flowers at a "hippie" wedding, enacted several special rituals, including baptism to purify them of the sin of war and the "love-in."

students to wake up from the slumbering pace of student life and reform the world. Situationists believed that bureaucratic, mass society numbed people, and they emblazoned challenging slogans on university walls to jolt activists and passersby alike.

Students attacked the traditional university curriculum. They questioned how studying Plato or Dante would help them tend machines after graduation. They also took part in forcing many required humanities courses out of the curriculum. Students turned the defiant rebelliousness of 1950s youth culture into a political style by mocking education: "How to Train Stuffed Geese," the Nanterre students called the way universities taught them. "No professors over forty" and "Don't trust anyone over thirty" were powerful slogans of the day. Long hair, blue jeans, communal living, and a repudiation of personal hygiene announced students' rejection of middle-class values, as did their denunciation of sexual chastity. "The pill" made abstinence unnecessary as a method of birth control, and students made the sexual revolution explicit and public with open promiscuity and experimentation.

The young nourished their revolt with heavy doses of sex, rock and folk music, and drugs. Early in the 1960s then Harvard professor Timothy Leary provided his students with the hallucinogen LSD. Marijuana use became common among student protesters, and "speed" and barbiturates added to the drug culture with its separate rituals, songs, and gathering places. Electronic rock music and body-altering chemicals—produced by the very technology that youth culture scorned—induced new sensations, created a sense of personal creativity, and restored a belief in the individuality of one's experience. Businesses made billions selling blue jeans, dolls dressed as "hippies," natural foods, and drugs, as well as packaging and managing the hard rock stars of the counter culture.

Women active in the civil rights and student movements realized that protest organizations devalued women just as society at large did. Male protesters adopted the leather-jacketed *machismo* style of their film and rock heroes, but women in the movements often judged their own worth by the status of their male-protester lover. "A woman was to 'inspire' her man," African-American activist Angela Davis complained, adding that women aim-

students created Michnik Clubs, named for the outspoken dissident Adam Michnik, to study Western political theory, science, and economics but faced constant harassment by the secret police. In Prague in 1965, students held a carnival-like procession celebrating the American "beat" poet Allen Ginsberg as their May King, and on May Day in 1966 chanted, "The only good communist is a dead one." In commemorating the tenth anniversary of the 1956 uprisings, some students were arrested and expelled from the university. The Federation of [West] German Socialist Students (SDS), led by Rudi Dutschke and the "situationists" in Strasbourg, France, called on

Women's Liberation Activists Demonstrate in London, 1971
Politics in the streets, which had led to increasing violence in the late nineteenth century and interwar years, became a common way for groups to make their programs and grievances public. Governments issued permits for marches, provided police escorts, and often set up public address systems.

ing for equality supposedly "wanted to rob them of their manhood." Such biting criticisms of masculine supremacy among African-American activists elicited a response among white women, who admired the strength of African-American women and also had their own grievances against the youth culture's exploitation of them. "We demand that our problems be discussed substantively," announced a speaker in Frankfurt, West Germany, interrupting a student meeting. "It is no longer enough that women are occasionally allowed to say a few words to which, as good antiauthoritarians, you listen—and then go on with the order of the day."

More conventionally political middle-class women eagerly responded to the international best-seller *The Feminine Mystique* (1963) by American journalist Betty Friedan. Popularizing Simone de Beauvoir's philosophy, Friedan focused on the changes in middle-class women's lives wrought by technology and affluence. Friedan maintained that middle-class women led useless existences, allowing their talents to stagnate while labor-saving devices and the absence of children most of the time reduced them to hollow shells. Her work appeared just as middle-class activists were working on the legal issues of reproductive and civil rights. In

France they helped end the ban on birth control in 1965. In Sweden, where for decades generous welfare benefits and access to birth control had improved women's lives, the Frederika Bremer Association lobbied to make tasks less gender-segregated. The National Organization for Women (NOW) was formed in the United States in 1966 "to bring women into full participation in the mainstream of American society now. . . ."

Whereas these organizations followed official procedures for contesting unequal rights, some middle-class women joined street activists on behalf of such issues as abortion rights or the decriminalization of gay and lesbian sexuality. Many flaunted social conventions in their attire, language, and attitudes. Renouncing brassieres, hair curlers, high-heeled shoes, cosmetics, and other adornments, they spoke openly about taboo subjects such as their sexual feelings, explained the "politics of housework," and even announced that they had resorted to illegal abortions. In France, for example, several hundred prominent women, including Simone de Beauvoir, went public with this information. This brand of feminist activity was meant to shock polite society—and it did. At a Miss America contest, women protesters crowned a sheep the new beauty queen. West German women students tossed tomatoes at male protest leaders in defiance of standards for lady-like behavior. Finally, many women of color broke with feminist solidarity and spoke out against the "double jeopardy" of being "black and female."

1968

The tumultuous activism of the decade converged to make 1968 an epochal year. In January, on the first day of Tet (the Vietnamese New Year), the Vietcong and the North Vietnamese attacked more than a hundred South Vietnamese towns and American bases. The attack took a heavy toll of U.S. casualties and caused many Americans to conclude that the war might be unwinnable. The antiwar movement of students, clergy, intellectuals, and pacifists suddenly gained mainstream support from a disillusioned public. Antiwar senator Eugene McCarthy drew impressive support in early presidential primaries. Then on April 4 a white racist assassinated Martin Luther King, Jr., and more than a hundred cities erupted in violence as African Americans vented their anguish and rage. On campuses strident confrontation over the intertwined issues of war, technology, racism, and sexism closed down classes. At Columbia University in New York City, where the administration proposed destroying a Harlem neighborhood to build a gym, students took over buildings and suffered violent police attacks in order, as one student put it, "to recapture a school from business and war and rededicate it to learning and life."

At Nanterre in France students went on strike, invaded administrative offices, and demanded a say in university governance. They called themselves a proletariat—an exploited working class—and considered themselves part of a New Left. When students at the more prestigious Sorbonne (the University of Paris) showed solidarity with Nanterre in street demonstrations, the police arrested and beat up hundreds of them. The Parisian middle classes reacted with unexpected sympathy to the student uprising because of their own resentment of bureaucracy. They were also horrified at seeing the elite and brutal police force, the CRS, beating middle-class students and passersby who expressed their support.

Throughout May the violence accelerated, with students handing out advice for evading tear gas and fragmentation grenades used by the CRS:

VARIOUS PROTECTIVE MEASURES.
Garbage can cover as a shield. . . .
Lemon—wet a handkerchief with it, suck
on it. Bicarbonate of soda around the eyes,
in diluted form on a handkerchief. Goggles,
motorcycle or ski, or a swimming mask.

Workers joined in: some 9 million went on strike, occupying factories and calling not only for higher wages but also for *la participation* in everyday decision making. For a moment the revolt of youth and workers looked as if might spiral into another French revolution.

The normally decisive president Charles de Gaulle seemed paralyzed at first. Then in June he announced a raise for workers, and management offered them a strengthened voice in industry. Many citizens grew tired of the street violence, the destruction of private property, and the breakdown of social services (for example, garbage was not collected for weeks). Having separated students from the wider population, especially by skillful use of the media, de Gaulle then sent tanks into Paris. Although demonstrations continued throughout June, the student movement had been closed down.

In the mid-1960s, Soviet-bloc students and intellectuals were only slightly less rebellious than in the Western bloc, where the arms of censorship and police repression were much shorter. In January 1968, students at the University of Warsaw protested the closing of a classic nineteenth-century play critical of the Russians. Although the play was a standard of the high school curriculum, live performances allowed the audience to applaud the anti-Russian lines wildly. Other Eastern European universities protested the subsequent expulsion of the Warsaw students and the firing of sympathetic faculty.

Accompanying these cultural protests, the Czechoslovak Communist party had already started distancing itself from the Soviets. In the autumn of 1967 at a Party congress, Alexander Dubček (1921–1992), head of the Slovak branch of the Party, had called for more social and political openness rather than cultural conformity in the face of a shadowy Cold War enemy. Antonin Novotný

***The Soviet
Invasion of Prague***
*Czechoslovaks, who had
become politically engaged
in the 1968 revolution
against Communist domi-
nation, continued face-to-
face protest with the troops
sent to squash the Prague
Spring.*

(1904–1975), who as First Party Secretary had built the largest statue of Stalin anywhere in the Eastern bloc, responded with ridicule: "We've had more than enough of democracy." In a culture where anti-semitism and ethnic prejudice remained formidable political weapons, Novotny taunted Dubček as an inferior Slovak. Yet the call for reform struck a chord among frustrated Party officials, technocrats, and intellectuals, who were collectively strong enough to remove Novotny from power. Czechoslovaks began to dream of creating a new society—one based on "socialism with a human face."

The Prague Spring had begun—"an orgy of free expression," one journalist called it. People bought uncensored publications, packed uncensored theater productions, and engaged in almost nonstop political debate. "Nobody talks about football . . . anymore," one taxi driver complained. Meanwhile, Dubček's new government faced the enormous problem of negotiating acceptable policies. Whereas radicals pressed for fundamental change, those with a vested interest in the system wanted more limited reform. The Polish, East German, and Soviet regimes threatened the reform government daily. Announcing new recognition of civil rights and the separation of the Communist party from government, Dubček warned that democracy demanded "a conscious civic disci-

pline" and "statesmanlike wisdom of all citizens." When Dubček failed to attend a meeting of Warsaw Pact leaders, Soviet threats became intense. Finally on the night of August 20–21, 1968, Soviet tanks rolled into Prague in a massive show of anti-revolutionary force.

Citizens tried to halt the return to Communist orthodoxy by using free expression as sabotage. They painted graffiti on tanks and confused invading troops by removing street signs. Illegal radio stations broadcast testimonials of resistance, accounts of Soviet brutality, and warnings to people about to be arrested. They refused to sell food or other commodities to Soviet troops. Even as the Soviets gradually removed reformers from power, resistance continued. On January 16, 1969, university student Jan Palach immolated himself in Wenceslas Square in Prague; a month later another student did the same. Although pale beside these sacrifices, which ultimately took six student lives, protest of one type or another never stopped, forcing the new Czechoslovak government to maintain repression. Meanwhile, Soviet determination to retain control over the Eastern bloc was expressed in the Brezhnev Doctrine, announced in November 1968. Reform movements, Brezhnev declared, were not merely domestic matters but rather "a common problem and concern of all socialist countries." Thus further moves toward change would meet similar repression.

Protest in 1968 changed the style and direction of high politics in Western societies and challenged superpower dominance. Whether burning draft cards in the United States or scribbling graffiti on public buildings in Europe, students made government less inviolable. Profanity and guerrilla theater gave political discourse a different, less sacrosanct air. Although these protests may not have caused Johnson's decision not to seek reelection in 1968 and de Gaulle's resignation in 1969, they certainly altered the course of politics. Yet change did not necessarily occur in the way reformers had hoped. Governments turned to conservative solutions, while disappointed reformers considered more radical avenues to social transformation.

The Erosion of Superpower Mastery

The 1970s brought an era of detente, a lessening of Cold War tensions, as the United States quit the Vietnam War and as the superpowers negotiated to limit the nuclear arms race. By the early 1970s, student protest evolved into ongoing reform movements, and new, sometimes violent causes sprang up, such as those for Basque independence in Spain and for Catholic rights in Northern Ireland. Although they still controlled the balance of power, the superpowers' grip was loosening because of their own internal corruption, the challenge of terrorism, and competition from the oil-producing states, Japan, and the Common Market.

Detente and Realpolitik

In November 1968 the conservative Richard Nixon was elected president of the United States. Nixon claimed to have a "secret plan" to bring peace to Southeast Asia, but even as peace talks dragged on, warfare continued to ravage Vietnam and to mount up debt in the United States. Although Nixon's chief foreign policy aide, Henry Kissinger, called North Vietnam a "miserable little country," he also pursued Realpolitik in the tradition of nineteenth-century diplomats. In 1970, Nixon ordered U.S. troops to invade Cambodia, the site of

North Vietnamese bases. The campuses erupted again in protest, and on May 4 the National Guard shot dead four students and wounded eleven others at Kent State University in Ohio. Nixon called the victims "bums," and a growing reaction to the years of drugs and demonstrations made many Americans agree that the guardsmen "should have fired sooner and longer." Student radicalism gradually declined as groups were riven by factionalism, harassed by government infiltrators, and often incapacitated by drug use.

The United States and North Vietnam finally signed a peace treaty in the autumn of 1972. By terms of the agreement, Nixon withdrew American troops, but he still continued to supply South Vietnam's forces. The Communists did not relent either, and in 1975, South Vietnam collapsed under a determined North Vietnamese offensive. As Vietnam was forcibly unified, tens of thousands fled, often as "boat people" braving the seas in dangerously inadequate vessels. In Cambodia the communist Khmer Rouge inflicted a horrendous reign of terror in which they slaughtered a million people and drove urban citizens into the countryside for "reeducation." The Vietnam War had cost the United States billions of dollars, more than fifty thousand lives, and its reputation. Many countries now viewed the United States not as a defender of liberty but as an oppressor of Third World

The Vietnam War

people. Moreover the "domino theory" was proven false: although Cambodia and Laos went communist, Thailand did not; and Communist Vietnam became China's enemy.

A small, undeclared Sino-Soviet war opened the way to dramatic global realignment. Unlike analysts a decade earlier, Nixon's cabinet recognized the importance of the fissure between the Communist giants. In 1972, Kissinger secretly visited China to prepare the official visit by President

Richard Nixon in 1972. Pictures of Mao and Nixon shaking hands rocked the world, for they seemed to promise the possibility that diplomatic miracles would end the Cold War. Within China the meeting helped stop the brutality and excesses of the Cultural Revolution, which had left the country prostrate. Gradually, pragmatists interested in technology, trade, and relations with the West replaced hard-line ideologues. Although the locus of power remained uncertain after Mao suffered a stroke in 1972, his death four years later closed the Chinese revolutionary era.

Fearful of the Chinese and of the Cold War's economic toll, Soviet leader Brezhnev made overtures to the Western bloc. With the evolution of detente, Washington was now prepared to listen. In 1972 the superpowers signed the Strategic Arms Limitation Treaty (SALT I), which set a cap on the number of antimissile defenses. In 1975, in the Helsinki accords on human rights, the Western bloc officially acknowledged Soviet territorial gains in World War II in exchange for the Soviet bloc's guarantee of basic human rights. A later treaty, SALT II (1979), further limited armament but failed to win ratification in the U.S. Senate.

While pursuing a degree of mutual reconciliation, the superpowers ruled conservatively at home. In the United States, the enigmatic Nixon focused on reelection at any price. After his landslide victory in the 1972 presidential race, evidence came to light that Nixon's reelection committee had paid several men to wiretap the telephones at Democratic party headquarters in Washington's Watergate building. Congressional hearings revealed that not only had the president's office jeopardized the Constitution's guarantee to free elections but that Nixon himself had attempted to cover up the truth. Between 1968 and 1972, Nixon had forged a powerful conservative consensus based on the idea that activist groups calling for expanded rights were but a minority. The so-called silent majority supported Nixon in all but one state in 1972, but in the summer of 1974 Nixon resigned in disgrace.

By then the hard-liner Brezhnev had eclipsed Kosygin's influence in the Soviet Union; unconstrained by the constitutional safeguards that brought Nixon down, Brezhnev freely clamped down on dissent. Following the events in Czechoslovakia in 1968, the Soviet dissident movement was at a low ebb. "The shock of our tanks crushing the Prague Spring . . . convinced us that the Soviet colossus was invincible," explained one pessimistic liberal. In 1974, Brezhnev expelled Solzhenitsyn from the USSR after the publication of the first volume of the *Gulag Archipelago* (1973–1976) in the Western bloc. Composed from myriad biographies, firsthand reports, and other bits of information about prison camp life, Solzhenitsyn's story of the Gulag (an acronym for the Soviet system of internment and forced-labor camps) documented the brutal conditions Soviet prisoners endured. It appeared at a time when West European *Ostpolitik* was spreading dissatisfaction in the East bloc with the economy and with the repression of free speech. The Soviet hierarchy could not tolerate revelations of the Gulag.

The Kremlin persecuted many ordinary people who did not have Solzhenitsyn's international reputation. Soviet psychologists complying with the government certified the "mental illness" of people who did not play by the rules; thus dissidents wound up as virtual prisoners in mental institutions. The crudest Soviet persecutions, however, involved antisemitism: Jews were subject to educational restrictions (especially in university admissions), severe job discrimination, and constant assault on their religious practice. It was "not dramatic" persecution, as one put it, "but daily . . . always present." A commonplace accusation went that Jews were "unreliable, they think only of emigrating . . . their allegiance is elsewhere. It's madness to give them an education, because it's state money wasted." Ironically, even dissidents blamed Jews for the Bolshevik Revolution, for the terror of Stalinist collectivization, and for supposedly destroying Russian literature. As attacks intensified in the 1970s, Soviet Jews protested and sought to emigrate to Israel or the United States, but the government severely restricted emigration, often claiming that Jews who had finished their compulsory military service could not leave because they knew "state secrets." Many Jews could do no more than join the chorus of ridicule at the self-aggrandizing and increasingly senseless Brezhnev.

To block dissent, Communist parties in satellite countries purged the most reactionary leaders. Wladyslaw Gomułka, whose announcement of price increases during the Christmas season of 1970 triggered strikes and bloody riots in Poland, was replaced by professed economic reformer Edward

Gierek in 1971; East German Walter Ulbricht, who obstructed the detente with West Germany that the Soviets needed for economic reasons, was ousted in 1971. Dissent, however, persisted in Hungary, Poland, and Czechoslovakia. In an open letter to the Czechoslovak Communist party leadership in 1975, playwright Václav Havel accused Marxist-Leninist rule of making people materialistic and indifferent to civic life. The only viable conduct under Communist repression, Havel wrote, was either to disengage from public life or to work for the special privileges awarded to successful technocrats. In 1977, Havel, along with a group of fellow intellectuals and workers, signed Charter 77, a public protest against the Communist regime. The police imprisoned and tormented many of the charter's signatories; philosopher Jan Patocka died after his "interrogation."

East-bloc writers published abroad or emigrated to the United States and West European capitals, where they helped erode any lingering support for communism. In France, for example, a group of "new philosophers" loudly demanded that leftists justify their commitment to Soviet communism in light of the brutal practices revealed by Solzhenitsyn and others. Communist parties in the West broke their last remaining ties to the Soviet Union, but even after declaring an independent path, their success at the polls dwindled.

The West, the Middle East, and the Politics of Energy

While the superpowers wrestled with internal political embarrassments and the intricacies of nuclear diplomacy, other nations focused on developing new economic muscle. Since 1960 the Common Market countries, led by West Germany, had surpassed the United States in percentage of gross world product. This achievement made the Common Market a countervailing power to the Soviet Union and the United States. Although the six countries maintained their lead, their economic ascent slowed; by 1965 the rate of West German economic growth had fallen from a high of 9.4 percent between 1951 and 1955, to less than 5 percent. In the face of this downturn, politicians used pump-priming techniques to stimulate industrial investment and put foreign "guest" laborers and married women out of work in favor of native-born men. The opening of Eastern European markets

helped bolster West European prosperity; by the end of the decade, West European exports to the Eastern bloc totaled some $45 billion annually, producing a burden of debt that Communist countries could ill afford. In 1973, Britain joined the Common Market, followed by Ireland and Denmark. The market's exports now amounted to almost three times those of the United States.

Japan emerged from its postwar reconstruction to challenge the United States and Western Europe as a manufacturing and exporting giant. In the 1960s its rate of growth accelerated from an annual average of 9 percent in the 1950s to over 11 percent. Even without energy and other key natural resources, Japan had become the world's largest shipbuilder, and only the United States and the Soviet Union surpassed it in iron and steel production. Much of Japan's growth came at the expense of Great Britain, as it ate into traditional British trade with New Zealand, Australia, and other commonwealth trading partners.

Meanwhile, the United States, still the leading single producer in most fields, had also become a major debtor. Rising purchases of military and imported goods brought inflation and a trade deficit. Dollars flooded the international currency markets. The Bretton Woods currency system collapsed in 1971, as currency rates—formerly linked to the dollar—were allowed to "float" in relation to each other and as the price of gold was allowed to soar from its artificially fixed low price. The international monetary crisis actually strengthened European integration, as Common Market countries agreed to cooperate to prevent financial chaos. The Common Market's economic clout allowed it to force the United States to relinquish its single-handed direction of Western economic strategy.

Economic and geopolitical power spread beyond the West. In the 1970s the Middle East's oil-producing nations, though caught in a tangle of competing ambitions, dealt Western dominance a critical blow. Tensions between Israel and the Arab world provided the catalyst. On June 5, 1967, Israeli forces, responding to Palestinian guerrilla attacks, seized Gaza and the Sinai peninsula from Egypt, the Golan Heights from Syria, and the West Bank from Jordan. Although Israel won a stunning victory in this Six-Day War, the Arab humiliation helped consolidate Palestinian insurgency against Israel and forced the Arab states to try to forge a common political and economic

Israel After the Six-Day War

strategy. The populist militancy of the defeated Egyptian leader Nasser gradually gave way to more conservative and somewhat more pro-Western leadership in Saudi Arabia. Instead of looking toward the Soviets, the Arab nations increasingly purchased more reliable American and French technology. The Saudis supported pan-Islamic policies, but they downplayed guerrilla warfare and domestic social change. Radical factions of the Palestine Liberation Organization (PLO) continued to employ terrorism against Israel: in 1972, PLO members slaughtered eleven Israeli athletes at the Munich Olympics. In 1973, Egypt and Syria attacked Israel on Yom Kippur, the Jewish day of atonement. Still using inferior Soviet weapons, Egypt initially made headway, but Israel, with material assistance from the United States, stopped the assault and counterattacked.

Having failed militarily, the Arab nations now tried economic coercion. The Organization of Petroleum Exporting Countries (OPEC) quadrupled the price of their oil and cut off all exports of it to the United States in retaliation for its support of Israel's attacks on Palestinian settlements. For the first time since imperialism's heyday, the *producers* of raw materials—not the industrial powers—controlled the flow of commodities and set prices to their own advantage.

Throughout the 1970s oil-dependent Westerners watched in astonishment as OPEC upset the balance of economic power. Instead of being controlled by the Western powers, the oil-producing nations helped provoke a recession that caused unemployment to rise by more than 50 percent in Europe and the United States. Whereas previous recessions had brought falling prices as goods went unsold, this recession resulted in soaring inflation. By the end of 1973 the inflation rate jumped above 8 percent in West Germany, 12 percent in France, and 20 percent in Portugal; in 1974 it reached 13 percent in Britain and Italy and 8 percent in the United States. East-bloc countries, dependent on

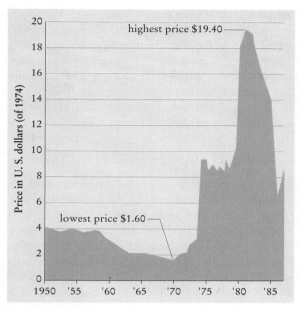

Fluctuating Oil Prices

The Power of Oil
In the 1970s representatives of OPEC met and stunned the West by boosting the price of crude oil and even stopping its export.

Soviet oil, fared little better. Inflation in Yugoslavia soared to 40 percent by the end of the decade. Interest rates in the Western bloc skyrocketed, which discouraged both industrial investment and consumer buying. With prices soaring, a sense of discouragement settled over Westerners as they realized that energy resources were finite and that their economic prosperity had limits.

Political Alternatives in Hard Times

The unprecedented economic situation and the changing global balance of power inspired new waves of citizen activism. A sense of limits to global resources encouraged the formation of environmental political parties. An escapee from Nazi Germany, E. F. "Fritz" Schumacher, produced one of the bibles of the environmental movement, *Small Is Beautiful* (1973), which spelled out how technology and the industrial revolution threatened the earth and its inhabitants. Environmentalists like Schumacher and the American Rachel Carson, author of *Silent Spring* (1962), advocated the immediate rescue of rivers, forests, and the soil from the ravages of factories and chemical farming. Instead of massive agribusiness, which required huge doses of chemical fertilizers and produced single crops for the market, they pleaded for small-scale, diverse, organic (pesticide-free) farming. For industry, environmentalists demanded that factories be scaled back and made more environmentally responsible. These attitudes challenged almost two centuries of faith in industrial growth and in the infinite ability of humanity to extract progress from the natural world.

The environmental movement had its greatest political effect in West Germany. As student protest subsided in the 1970s, environmentalism united members of older and younger generations around the 1960s political tactic called *citizen initiatives,* in which groups of people blocked everything from public transportation fare increases to plans for urban growth. In the 1970s citizen initiative groups targeted nuclear power and nuclear installations; they took their cue from chancellor Willy Brandt, whose *Ostpolitik* sought to extricate West Germany from the threat of nuclear devastation. Demonstrations against nuclear power stations drew crowds in the tens of thousands, often armed with wirecutters to enter fenced-in areas.

In 1979 the Green Party was founded in West Germany and launched candidates for political office. Elsewhere in Western Europe, environmentalists influenced mainstream politics, forcing candidates to voice their concern for the environment and leading governments to establish ministries for the environment. In the Eastern bloc, Communist commitment to industrial development completely blinded governments to environmental destruction or to the effects of pollution on people. In the context of Cold War, the toll in human life from the pollution caused by work in such enterprises as uranium mining for nuclear weapons was seen as justifiable.

Feminist activism also became more mainstream. Ecological parties attracted many women angered at the birth of thalidomide babies and concerned about the chemical contamination of their family's food. Men could escape to the moon or into their careers, a West German ecologist maintained, but not women, "who must give birth to children, willingly or unwillingly, in this polluted world of ours." Other women's activism had notable successes in the 1970s. In Catholic Italy, activists won the right to divorce, birth-control information, and abortion. The demand for these rights as well as for equal pay, job opportunities, and protection from rape, incest, and battering framed the major legal struggles of thousands of women's groups in the 1970s. In the Western bloc, personal change also became a goal. Consciousness-raising sessions in which groups of women shared individual experiences in marriage, with children, and in the workforce became popular. Such sessions alleviated some of the isolation women felt at home; participants realized that females shared many similar experiences. Eastern-bloc women, who often formed the majority of the workforce and shouldered responsibility for all domestic work, received inspiration from feminist stories spread through the *samizdat* network. The new camaraderie among many women, whether in the Western or Eastern bloc, prepared them for political participation.

In 1977, fifteen thousand activist women from around the globe poured into Houston to mark the International Year of Women. The meeting brought together Westerners interested in political and economic rights and cultural equality and Third World women calling for an end to violence, starvation, and disease. The utter poverty afflicting women in less-developed countries called into question the commonality on which Western feminist politics was based. The issue of sexual orientation also challenged many mainstream activists in Houston, as lesbians exposed the greater privileges heterosexual women enjoyed. After Houston the media publicized the "death of feminism," both because of the convention's relative calm and because of the invisible roots sunk into mainstream local, national, and global politics. In 1978, Christa Wolf spoke of a confident new attitude pervading the movement: "[Women] feel that their new role has already begun to solidify; their lust for life is great, their hunger for reality insatiable." Organizing, consciousness raising, and economic gains backed women's entry into local and national government from the 1970s on. The ecology and women's movements had firmly established their political credentials.

Terrorist bands took a radically different path, responding to the conservative political climate and worsening economic conditions with kidnappings, bank robberies, bombings, and assassinations. Disaffected and well-to-do youth, steeped in the most extreme theories of society's decay, often joined these groups. Eager to bring down the Social Democratic coalition that led West Germany throughout the 1970s, the Baader-Meinhof gang assassinated prominent businessmen as well as judges and other public officials. Practiced in assassinations of public figures and random shootings of pedestrians, Italy's Red Brigades kidnapped and then murdered the head of the dominant Christian Democrats, Aldo Moro, in 1978. Terrorists in northern Spain, advocates of independence for the Basque nation, assassinated Spanish politicians and police.

In Britain nationalist and religious terrorism in the 1970s pitted the Catholics in Northern Ireland against the dominant Protestants. Catholics experienced job discrimination and a lack of civil rights. In 1969, Catholic student protest turned into demonstrations on behalf of union with the Irish Republic. As violence in Northern Ireland escalated, the Conservative British government of Edward Heath sent in troops. On "Bloody Sunday" in 1972, British troops fired at demonstrators and killed thirteen, setting off a cycle of violence that left five hundred dead in that single year.

Sorely tried as it was, parliamentary government did score some important successes in the

Violence in Northern Ireland
Northern Ireland, Spain, Italy, West Germany, and other parts of Europe experienced increasingly deadly political violence in the 1970s and thereafter.

1970s. The Iberian peninsula, suffering under dictatorship since the 1930s, regained its freedom and set out on a course of greater prosperity. The death of Spain's Francisco Franco in 1975 ended more than three decades of dictatorial rule. Franco's handpicked successor, King Juan Carlos, surprisingly steered his nation to Western-style constitutional monarchy, facing down threatened military coups. Portugal and Greece also ousted right-wing dictators, thus paving the way for their integration into Western Europe and for substantial economic growth.

Moreover, terrorists failed in their goal of overturning the existing democracies. In Italy, Christian Democrats and Communists managed to govern together; the Communists practiced *Eurocommunism* independently of Moscow and capably administered many cities while restraining union demands. In West Germany the public voted out Willy Brandt in 1974 over the economic downturn and his failure to curb terrorism. They replaced Brandt, however, with another Social Democrat, the more pragmatic Helmut Schmidt. In Britain, Heath's administration spent heavily on domestic programs, but growing crime, economic decline, labor unrest, and violence in Northern Ireland tore at the civic-minded fabric of British life that had made the country so formidable in World War II. In 1974 the Labour party brought down the Tories but fared little better with Britain's deep domestic problems in the remainder of the decade.

In 1976, Jimmy Carter, a wealthy farmer and governor of Georgia, narrowly won the U.S. presidential election by selling himself as an outsider to Washington corruption. Carter's style featured fundamentalist religion and down-home honesty. Although he temporarily brought down the unemployment rate, he could effect few other domestic changes. In foreign policy, Carter championed human rights rather than Nixonian Realpolitik. As with his domestic policy, Carter's good intentions met with some success; but they did little to stem global terrorism. The United States seemed especially paralyzed by turmoil in the Middle East. In Lebanon a deadly civil war erupted in 1975 among Lebanese Christians, Muslim sects, and Palestinian immigrants to Beirut. Syria and Israel intervened substantially, escalating the possibility of another regional war.

In 1979, hoping to defuse Arab-Israeli hostilities, Carter induced the leaders of Israel and Egypt to sign a peace agreement known as the Camp David Accords. Under its terms, Israel gradually withdrew from the Sinai peninsula; Egypt, however, found itself isolated from other Arab states, which continued to support PLO attacks on Israel. Late in the 1970s students, clerics, shopkeepers, and unemployed men in Iran began a religious agitation that forced Shah Reza Pahlavi to leave the country in January 1979. Repressively and brutally ruled by the shah, Iran had enormous but unevenly distributed wealth and a population of discontented, poor Shi'ite Muslims. These people overturned the liberal regime that had sent the shah into exile and installed a fundamentalist Muslim leader, Ayatollah Ruhollah Khomeini (1900?–1989), whose messages criticizing the shah had arrived from his Parisian exile via cassettes. A stern-looking leader dressed in flowing black garments, Khomeini called for a transformation of the region into a truly Islamic society awaiting the coming of the *Mahdi,* or Messiah. Iran, he believed, could lead this transformation if it renounced the Western ways advocated by the shah and followed the strict rule of Islam. In the autumn of 1979, revolutionary supporters of Khomeini took hostages at the American embassy in Teheran. Unable to gain the hostages' release and coping with soaring inflation following another round of OPEC price hikes, Carter in his role as leader of the free world seemed paralyzed as the 1970s drew to a close.

CONCLUSION

The 1960s and 1970s left the West with a sense of emergency. In the 1960s sophisticated technology in industry, communications, biology, and warfare had an enormous impact both on governments and on everyday life. Optimism abounded in the potential of humans to perpetuate progress and affluence. Yet technological change also produced intractable problems: concentrations of bureaucratic and industrial power, social inequality, environmental degradation, even uncertainty about humankind's future. By 1979 war in Vietnam, protests throughout the Soviet bloc, and the power of oil-producing states had weakened superpower preeminence. The Western bloc also confronted rising terrorism; the Soviet Union, long able to repress dissent in a growing economy, now faced the uncertainties generated by a perceptible decline in the standard of living. While the superpowers faltered, society entered a global age—one unified by information, communication, transportation, and the reach of technology. The dual phenomena of globalism and rapid technological advance posed unparalleled challenges to a world on the verge of a new millenium.

Suggestions for Further Reading

Source Materials

Altbach, Edith Hoshino, et al. *German Feminism: Readings in Politics and Literature.* 1984. An anthology of East and West German women's writings from the 1960s and 1970s, including fictional works and political treatises on environmentalism, with good background material on each selection.

Lévi-Strauss, Claude. *Tristes Tropiques.* 1961. Describes the experiences of a French anthropologist in the Brazilian jungle who finds that he has reached the limits of Western cultural understanding.

Solzhenitsyn, Aleksandr. *The Gulag Archipelago.* 1973–1976. A detailed and horrifying account of the Soviet internment system.

Interpretive Materials

Battah, Abdalla M., and Yehuda Lukachs, eds. *The Arab-Israeli Conflict: Two Decades of Change.* 1988. Includes important essays on successive crises in the Middle East.

Caute, David. *Sixty-Eight.* 1988. A readable and detailed survey of activism throughout the world in this important year.

Evans, Christopher. *The Micro Millennium.* 1979. A popular history of how computers evolved into small machines available as consumer items and of the potential for their use as seen in the 1970s.

Firth, Simon. *Sound Effects: Youth, Leisure, and the Politics of Rock and Roll.* 1981. An engaging consideration of the ingredients and development of rock and roll.

Fry, F., and G. Raymond. *The Other Western Europe.* 1980. Explores how the smaller states approached postwar economic and political life.

Giddings, Paula. *When and Where I Enter: The Impact of Black Women on Race and Sex in America.* 1984. A survey of black women's history with good coverage of their participation in activist movements.

Gittings, John. *China Changes Face: The Road from Revolution, 1949–1989.* 1989. Examines the tumultuous and often terrifying transformation of the world's most populous nation.

Heering, George C. *America's Longest War: The United States and Vietnam, 1950–1975.* 1986. A detailed survey that charts growing U.S. involvement and its consequences for domestic and international politics.

Huelsberg, Werner. *The German Greens: A Social and Political Profile.* 1988. Describes the rise and evolution of the most powerful ecology party in Europe.

Kennedy, Paul. *The Rise and Fall of the Great Powers: Economic Change and Military Conflict from 1500 to 2000.* 1987. A persuasive, well-documented, and sweeping interpretation of international power politics with good attention to the economic consequences of the Cold War for the superpowers.

Kramer, Jane. *Unsettling Europe.* 1980. Contains insightful essays on European people in the 1970s by an American journalist.

Lacouture, Jean. *De Gaulle.* Vol 2, *The Ruler, 1945–1970.* 1991. Shows how a great modern statesman forged the Fifth Republic, helped France modernize, and faced defeat.

Laqueur, Walter. *The Age of Terrorism.* 1987. Surveys the rationales for terrorism and its spread as a political tactic in the 1970s and 1980s.

Leaman, Jeremy. *The Political Economy of West Germany, 1945–1985.* 1988. A thorough and readable study of the booming West German economy, its problems, and its connection with both European and domestic politics.

Marks, Elaine, and Isabelle de Courtivon, eds. *New French Feminisms.* 1980. An anthology of sometimes difficult but provocative writing from the French women's movement, mostly dating from the 1970s.

Mazlich, Bruce. *The Fourth Discontinuity: The Co-Evolution of Humans and Machines.* 1994. Argues that humans have always lived with technologies.

Proctor, Robert. *Cancer Wars: The Politics Behind What We Know and Don't Know About Causes and Trends.* 1994. Documents the status of the environment in the West, especially during the Cold War; particularly good on uranium mining, nuclear issues, and debates over rising environmental toxicity.

Sampson, Anthony. *The New Europeans.* 1968. Describes the changes in work and society caused by postwar technological change.

Sinfield, Alan. *Literature, Politics, and Culture in Postwar Britain.* 1989. Contains responses of writers, artists, and other cultural leaders to decolonizing Britain in a time of economic retrenchment.

Sitkoff, Harvard. *The Struggle for Black Equality, 1954–1980.* 1981. Tells the gripping story of civil rights and black power movements in the United States.

Swain, Geoffrey, and Nigel Swain. *Eastern Europe Since 1945.* 1993. Provides a good background to the satellites' relationship to the USSR and to their domestic economic and political policies.

Tarrow, S. *Democracy and Disorder: Protest Politics in Italy, 1965–1975.* 1989. A study of a variety of Italian movements during this surge of political activism.

Wheeler, Daniel. *Art Since Mid-Century, 1945 to the Present.* 1991. An in-depth look at recent developments in art, with close attention to pop art and the international cross-fertilization of styles and the market.

Late in the summer of 1989, thousands of East Germans crowded into Budapest and converged on the West German embassy. Many of these self-styled vacationers arrived with their families, and most had one thing on their mind: escape. In Prague the story was the same—the West German embassy filled with East Germans, who camped out on nearby lawns as they waited to see if the West German government would grant them asylum. They all wanted to partake in the West's economic opportunity, and many also sought freedom from communism's stifling atmosphere, including those who had prospered under the system. An East Berliner underscored the point: "Do you see these townhouses? Empty. All the people left last week. They had everything—houses, cars, money, a *dacha* in the country." In September the stream of migrants looking for freedom and a higher standard of living became a flood. Astonishingly, the Soviet satellite states opened their borders, and masses of East Europeans packed up and headed westward.

The East Germans' migration proved to be the beginning of the end of Communist dominance in Europe. Mikhail Gorbachev's reforms could not reverse the Soviet Union's complete economic failure, but his tolerance of free speech allowed thousands of ordinary people throughout the East bloc to express their dissatisfaction with Communist repression and corruption. When East Europeans massed in the streets in 1989 to protest scarcity of basic goods and the absence of democracy, one Communist government after another tumbled with unexpected ease. In November peaceful demonstrators pulled down the Berlin Wall, symbolically ending nearly half a century of

The West and the New Globalism, 1979 to the Present

Children of Sarajevo, 1992
The collapse of the Soviet empire unleashed ethnic hostilities and made entire countries like the former Yugoslavia into deadly battlefields where ordinary people were killed or struggled for bare survival. Many joined the millions of global migrants seeking opportunity and security.

Cold War and reconnecting the rich culture of a divided Europe. In the final act of this incredible drama, Soviet democrats in August 1991 stood their ground against a last-gasp coup attempt by hard-line Communists. "For the first time in their history . . . not just in the Soviet period but in the centuries before," exclaimed one diplomat, the Russian people "have demanded a voice in the designing of their own society."

The flow of East Europeans to the West highlighted more than communism's failure: it also demonstrated the enormous impact of global connections. Communication technology had penetrated formerly impervious boundaries such as the Berlin Wall; in the age of globalism, East Germans could watch satellite television from West Germany and see for themselves how different life was on the other side. These changes did not just affect Europeans, millions of whom had migrated in the past two centuries in search of a new start. Now tens of millions of people from all corners of the world left their homes with dreams of finding a better life. Even those who stayed behind often found new opportunities as multinational corporations, looking for cheap labor, set up shop outside the West.

Although freedom and prosperity were watchwords of people on the move in the late 1980s, globalism did not always lead to stability. Many inhabitants of the former Eastern bloc, where the established authority had collapsed, found themselves facing the threat or reality of civil war. Resurgent nationalism and ethnic conflict flared throughout the world as the resolution of the Cold War left questions of power open to debate. Environmental catastrophe blew across borders with the wind and floated downstream from one country to the next in great rivers. Western nations, many of which were home to vast numbers of new immigrants, continued to struggle with challenges to their economic dominance. Led by Japan, the nations of the so-called Pacific Rim garnered an increasing percentage of world trade. The Atlantic region thus surrendered manufacturing jobs to the Pacific, but it also lost manufacturing positions when multinationals relocated because of cheaper labor elsewhere. Faced with threats to prosperity, governments and individuals in the West often took a "me first" approach at the expense of those in need.

IMPORTANT DATES

1979 Iranian militants take U.S. hostages in Teheran

1980 An independent trade union, Solidarity, organizes resistance to Polish communism; Prime Minister Margaret Thatcher begins dismantling the welfare state in Britain

Early 1980s AIDS epidemic strikes the West

1981 Ronald Reagan takes office as president of the U.S.

1985 Mikhail Gorbachev comes to power in the USSR

1986 Explosion at Soviet nuclear plant at Chernobyl causes death and local toxic exposure to radiation and raises global radioactivity levels; Spain joins the Common Market

1989 Chinese students revolt in Tiananmen Square and government suppresses them; fall of the Berlin Wall; Gorbachev declares an end to the socialist economy

1990–1991 War in the Persian Gulf

1991 Civil war erupts in the former Yugoslavia

1992 Common Market countries take new step toward unification with the creation of common legal and business practices

1993 Toni Morrison becomes the first African-American woman to win the Nobel Prize

1994 Neo-fascists join government in Italy; post-apartheid elections held in South Africa

As the final years of the millennium unfolded, thinkers began to posit a variety of scenarios for the future. One optimistically foresaw an "end of history," that is, an end to the world's great ideological conflicts and the triumph of liberal democracy. Another predicted a "clash of civilizations" in which religious and cultural factors would provide the impetus for future global strife. Surely the march of democracy has made great strides in recent years; just as certainly, cultural differences have kindled bloody wars. Nevertheless, as we look back from the 1990s on the years since 1979, we can see the world's inhabitants—despite a range of seemingly intractable problems—pursuing a valiant struggle for prosperity, freedom, and dignity.

The Global Predicament

The health of the planet encountered a multi-pronged attack in the 1980s as nuclear disaster, acid rain, and surging population threatened the world's ecosystem. Moreover, economic prosperity continued to elude great masses of people in all corners of the globe, and millions left their native country in search of work and a measure of a comfortable life. In geopolitics a greater number of states than ever before exercised power—a shift from the bipolarism of the Cold War to the multilateralism of the global age. Middle Eastern nations exerted a sometimes violent influence on economics and politics in the 1980s. The West felt intense competition from Japan and other Pacific countries, which were becoming more productive than the Atlantic states. Whereas decolonization and growing prosperity had once satisfied many people outside the West, a new generation of leaders now wanted a larger slice of political power as well.

The Assault on the Earth

Despite the best efforts of the growing ecology movement, technological development continued to threaten the environment. The dangers were laid bare starkly in 1986, when the nuclear plant at Chernobyl in the Soviet Union exploded and spewed radioactive dust into the atmosphere. The reactor, like most in the USSR, had been constructed with the bottom line in mind and thus contained minimal safety features. Many workers at the plant died within the year; others perished more slowly from the effects of radiation. Levels of radioactivity rose for hundreds of miles in all directions, and scientists predicted that the explosion would have long-term consequences on the health of people in the region.

Other attacks on the environment occurred more insidiously but also had devastating global effects. The mixture of fossil-fuel pollutants with atmospheric moisture produced acid rain, a poisonous brew that destroyed forests in industrial areas. Acid rain damaged more than 70 percent of Europe's Norway spruce trees. In Eastern Europe, where fossil fuels were burned with virtually no safeguards, forests looked as if they had been rav-

Nuclear Disaster
The explosion at the Chernobyl nuclear power plant spewed radiation into the atmosphere, with grave consequences for people in the region and still unknown ones for the planet. Here technicians check the fields near Chernobyl for radiation.

aged by fire, and children suffered from a range of ailments such as chronic bronchial disease. In less industrial areas the world's rain forests were hacked down at an alarming rate, as developers and ordinary people sought land to graze cattle or grow cash crops. Clearing the forests depleted the global oxygen supply and threatened the biological diversity of the entire planet. By the late 1980s, scientists had charted yet another possible challenge to the environment. The public's use of chlorofluorocarbons (CFCs), chemicals used in aerosol and refrigeration products, had blown a hole in the ozone layer. Now changes in temperature, rainfall, and the growth of vegetation indicated that a *greenhouse effect* might be permanently warming the earth. Again, some researchers forecast dire effects for the earth's future.

The Western public stepped up pressure on governments to try to keep pollution in check. As

Green Politics in the 1980s
As the effects of industrial advance and population growth became more dangerously apparent, environmental parties—such as West Germany's Green party (Die Grünen)— attracted European voters. Citizens angry at the major, established parties or at powerful leaders also expressed protest by "voting green."

a result some automobile manufacturers, particularly in the United States, began building cars with lower carbon monoxide emissions, and industrialists scaled back on factory pollution of air and waterways. Consumers began recycling such products as newspapers, glass and plastic containers, and cardboard. In Europe municipal governments turned streets into automobile-free pedestrian zones and established more "green" areas in cities. European countries, along with Japan, led the world in providing efficient public transportation, thus reducing the number of polluting automobiles on the streets. The affluent West possessed the resources to begin to undo some of the damage that had accompanied industrialization and technological change.

Less-developed regions struggled with another challenge to the well-being of communities and the environment: surging population. The annual growth rate of world population had been about 2 percent since 1950. In 1987 the globe's population reached 5 billion; it was expected to double by the year 2000. Whereas the population of the most industrialized countries had grown by approximately 40 percent since the 1950s, that

of the least industrialized had jumped more than 120 percent. Much of the change reflected the spread of Western medicine to Asia and Africa. Rural areas could not sustain the growing numbers, however, and desperate people flocked to already overcrowded cities looking for work and food.

The population increased partly because people began to live much longer. In nonindustrial countries life expectancy rose by an average of sixteen years between 1950 and 1980. The superpowers did not fare well by this measure of social health: life expectancy in the Soviet Union fell steadily in the 1970s and 1980s, from a peak of seventy years to sixty-seven years by 1979, and the United States barely ranked in the top twenty by 1990. Meanwhile, fertility rates, which had been dropping in the West for decades, were also declining in the less-developed world by 1985. Women in North Africa, who had reproduced an average of 6.8 children in the 1950s and 1960s, were giving birth to an average of 5.6 by the mid-1980s. In China over the same period, the number had fallen precipitously, from 6.2 to 2.4, but the Chinese population still skyrocketed.

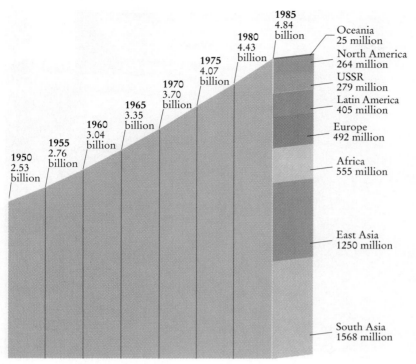

1950
2.53
billion

1955
2.76
billion

1960
3.04
billion

1965
3.35
billion

1970
3.70
billion

1975
4.07
billion

1980
4.43
billion

1985
4.84
billion

Oceania
25 million

North America
264 million

USSR
279 million

Latin America
405 million

Europe
492 million

Africa
555 million

East Asia
1250 million

South Asia
1568 million

World Population Growth

While Western medicine found its way into the underdeveloped world, medical practice in the industrialized nations focused on high-tech solutions to health problems. Specialists performed heart bypass surgery, transplanted organs, and treated cancer with radiation therapy and chemotherapy. Preventive care received little attention; for example, in the late 1970s the Netherlands spent less than 3 percent of its total medical expenditures on preventive medicine. Expensive, technological, in-hospital treatment of the sick became the rule in wealthy nations, and studies showed that a disproportionate amount of these services went to the upper classes, especially men. At the other end of the scale, the unemployed suffered more chronic illnesses than those who were better off, but they received less care. As technological change threatened the environment and contributed to population growth, people began to question whether technological solutions could remedy global problems.

Meanwhile, a provocative new scientific theory suggested the profound global reach of seemingly random natural phenomena. According to *chaos theory,* such behavior as the path of a pinball, the falling of a leaf, or the crashing of a wave on shore conceals deeper patterns of regularity, a sort of "orderly disorder." The theory was first posited by American meteorologist Edward Lorenz, who found that incalculable changes in weather could be triggered by the smallest disturbances. The phenomenon has been dubbed "the butterfly effect" in reference to Lorenz's question: "Does the flap of a butterfly's wings in Brazil set off a tornado in Texas?" Beyond its usefulness to meteorology, chaos theory has applications and implications in physics, chemistry, biology, demography, ecology, and social psychology—indeed in any field exploring apparently unstable and unpredictable systems.

Global Migration Refashions Society

Uneven economic development, political persecution, and warfare (which has claimed as many as 90 million victims since 1945) spurred vast numbers of people to migrate in search of safety and opportunity. Many fled to the West. In the 1970s alone, more than 4.7 million people moved to the United States. West Germany had 5 million foreign residents by 1982; France about half a million less.

The West in the Global Age
In the 1980s people from around the world migrated to Western cities and diversified their societies and cultures. Here a group of Muslim men gather in front of a bakery in France to pray.

Thirteen percent of Sweden's population was composed of immigrants. Not all newcomers went to the West: the oil-producing nations of the Middle East employed 3 million foreign workers, who constituted one-third of the labor force, in 1980. In that same year, 120,000 people moved to Singapore, and in 1981, Nigeria was home to more than 2.5 million foreign-born inhabitants.

Although the turmoil of decolonization produced millions of refugees, most people left their homelands to find work. Migrants often earned desperately needed income for family members who remained in the native country, and in some cases they propped up the economies of entire nations. In the southern African country of Lesotho, where the soil had been ruined by overuse during colonial rule, between 40 and 50 percent of national income came from migrant workers, particularly from those who dug in the mines of South Africa. In countries as different as Yugoslavia, Egypt, Spain, and Pakistan, money sent home from abroad in 1980 constituted between

13 and 60 percent of national income. Often migrant labor had government sanction under a system that allowed foreigners to work in the host country for periods ranging from one or two to ten or more years. In places where immigration was restricted, millions of people nevertheless successfully crossed borders: from Mexico to the United States, over unguarded African frontiers, between European states. Such migrants, unprotected by law, risked exploitation and abuse of their human rights.

As inflation and unemployment hit Europe in the 1980s, foreign workers became a convenient scapegoat for natives suffering from these economic woes. Political parties with racist programs came to life: the National Front party in France, the Progress party in Norway, the Zentrum party in the Netherlands. These groups called for the elimination of blacks and Arabs from Europe in the name of racially and ethnically "pure" nations. Tensions between foreigners and natives often exploded in violence. In Eastern Europe, which had accepted large numbers of Indochinese refugees, economic crisis brought outbursts against Vietnamese and other Asians. In the 1990s young Germans from the less-prosperous eastern half of the newly unified nation took out their frustrations in racial violence that left hundreds dead or wounded. Despite widespread verbal and physical attacks on foreigners and migrants, the phenomenon of multiculturalism made inroads in many corners of the globe. Sweden, for example, welcomed migrants.

Women migrants in Europe had little say in decisions about leaving home; a patriarchal head of the household generally made such choices. Once abroad, migrant women suffered the most from unstable working conditions. West Germany, for example, prohibited them from working during economic crises. Even in prosperous times, foreign-born women usually obtained more menial, lower-paying jobs than migrant men or native Europeans. Moreover, the host society often denigrated their emphasis on nurturing their children as "backward" or "primitive."

The offspring of immigrants also had a difficult time adjusting to their new surroundings. Unemployment hit them especially hard. They also struggled with questions of identity. To advance in school or at work, immigrant youth had to embrace their new society in varying degrees, and they often felt torn between two cultures. Young black immigrants in particular began to forge an international identity, one that combined elements of African, Caribbean, American, and European cultures. As tens of millions of people migrated in the 1980s, the former sense of national identity based on a single culture was losing ground.

Resurgent Islam Confronts the West

The hostage crisis that began in 1979 showed that religion and nationalism could join with the power of oil to make the Middle East an arbiter of international order. The charismatic leaders of the 1980s —Iran's Ayatollah Khomeini, Libya's Muammar Qaddafi, and Iraq's Saddam Hussein—despite important differences, all promoted a pan-Arabic or pan-Islamic world order. According to Muslim intellectuals, the capitalist West had used up "that stock of values which gave it its predominance. . . . The turn of Islam has come." Nor did the Soviet Union offer a useful alternative. Muslims should confront the superpowers, urged Khomeini, by

taking the position, "Neither East, nor West, only the Islamic Republic."

Under Khomeini, Iran rejected all forms of Westernization. The new regime forced women to wear the veil again and restricted their right to divorce. Such changes became a standard component of Islamic revolution. Fundamentalists believed these reversions made women appear less Western and also restored the pride and Islamic identity that imperialism had stripped from Middle Eastern men.

The Shi'ite Muslims were thrilled by the power that accompanied the rebirth of so-called religious fundamentalism. Even though they constituted the majority in many Middle Eastern countries—72 percent of the population in Bahrain, 60 percent in Iraq, and 95 percent in Iran—they had long been ruled by the Sunnis. The tables turned when Khomeini proclaimed the ascendancy of the Shi'ite clergy in Islamic revolutionary society. Even in Saudi Arabia, where the Shi'ite population numbered only several hundred thousand, the ruling family of Saud worried that the spread of revolution might destabilize their control.

The Iranian Shi'ites could best express their newfound power and anti-Western feeling by refusing to release the hostages taken from the U.S. embassy. As the months dragged on, Americans at home endured mounting frustration, and the United States seemed powerless to act. Iranian students chanted defiant slogans against "the Great Satan" and paraded their weary prisoners before television cameras. A botched rescue attempt symbolized to many Americans the failure of President Carter both in domestic and foreign affairs. Ronald Reagan trounced Carter in the 1980 presidential election. Iran finally released the hostages only moments after the new president was inaugurated.

Meanwhile, in September 1980, Iraq's president, Saddam Hussein, launched an attack on Iran. Hussein feared that Iraq's Shi'ite minority might rebel, and he sought to channel their aggression through a patriotic crusade against the non-Arab Iranians. The Iraqi leader also coveted oil-rich territory in Iran. After eight years of combat, however, the war's primary outcome was massive loss of life on both sides.

The Soviet Union became embroiled against the force of Islam when it supported a communist coup in Afghanistan in 1979. The new rulers met with stiff resistance from Afghanis whose tradi-

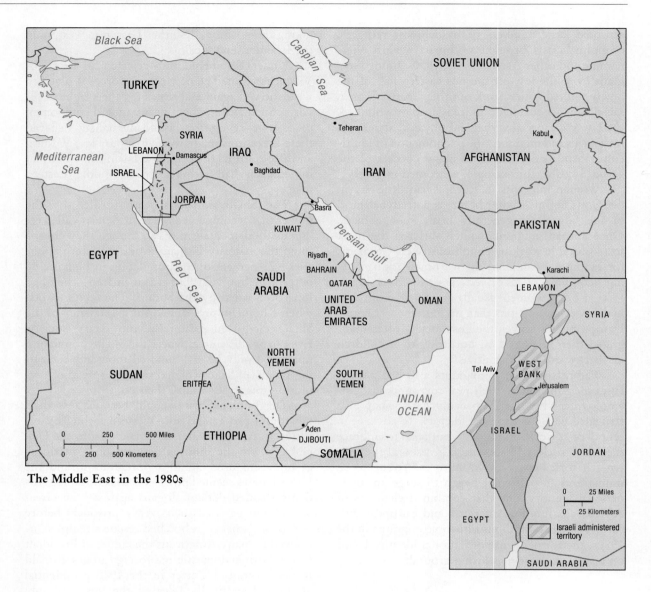

The Middle East in the 1980s

tional way of life was threatened by communism's modernizing thrust. By 1980, tens of thousands of Soviets were fighting in Afghanistan, using the USSR's most advanced missiles and artillery to overcome Muslim tribesmen. Aided by the U.S. Central Intelligence Agency, anticommunist guerrilla forces struck back, and soon the USSR was mired in its own version of the Vietnam War. Furthermore, after nearly two decades of detente, the Cold War flared up again. President Carter cut off grain sales to the Soviet Union, retracted the SALT II nuclear arms treaty from the Senate ratification

process, and led a boycott of many nations against participation in the 1980 Moscow Olympics. For the remainder of the decade, terrorist politics and superpower rivalry would confound efforts to bring peace to the Middle East.

The Rise of the Pacific Rim

While terrorism, oil politics, and war in the Middle East threatened Western stability and reignited the Cold War, quieter challenges from Asia's Pacific region eroded Western economic dominance. Just

The Global Economy
*By the 1980s companies and products from the Pacific
Rim had penetrated both the Western and Eastern
blocs, as this sign in Poland for Japanese-based Hitachi
demonstrates.*

as economic changes in the early modern period
had slowly redirected European affairs from the
Mediterranean to the Atlantic, explosive productivity from Japan to Singapore in the 1980s began
to shift power from the Atlantic region to the
Pacific. In 1982 the Asian Pacific nations accounted
for 16.4 percent of global gross domestic product
(GDP), a figure that had doubled since the 1960s;
analysts predicted that by the end of the century,
Pacific Rim output would equal or surpass that of
other major economic powers, including the
United States, the Soviet Union, and the Common
Market.

Although South Korea, Taiwan, Singapore,
Hong Kong, and even regions of Communist
China contributed to the rise of the Pacific economy,
Japan led the charge. In the process it became an
economic power rivaled only by the United States
and West Germany. Investment in high-tech consumer industries drove the Japanese economy. Thus
in 1982, Japan had 32,000 industrial robots in operation; Western Europe employed only 9,000; the
United States 7,000. In 1989 the Japanese government and private businesses invested $549 billion

to modernize industrial capacity, a full $36 billion
more than American public and private investment
combined. Such spending paid off substantially,
as Japanese companies turned out high-quality
consumer products that found an eager international market. In particular, U.S. buyers snapped
up automobiles, televisions, video cassette recorders
(VCRs), cameras, and computers from Japanese or
other Asian Pacific companies.

As the profits rolled in, Japanese enterprises
bought large sections of American cities and swallowed up Western businesses. Huge financial institutions flourished: by the end of the 1980s, Japan
was home to the world's eight largest banks, as well
as a brokerage house that was twenty times the size
of its nearest American competitor. Furthermore,
whereas Japanese military expenses remained low
by constitutional mandate, the United States
throughout much of the 1980s poured mounting
sums into its Cold War military budget—but failed
to raise taxes to pay for this expenditure. Thus the
Japanese and other Asians purchased the U.S. government bonds that financed America's ballooning
national debt. Forty years after its total defeat in
World War II, Japan was bankrolling its former
conqueror. This state of affairs eventually produced
a backlash: American workers charged that the
Asians were stealing their jobs, and the U.S. government accused Japanese businesses of unfair trade
practices.

Despite rising national prosperity, individual
Asian workers, particularly outside of Japan, often
paid dearly for this newly created wealth. For
example, women in South Korea and Taiwan labored in sweatshops to produce clothing for such
U.S.-based companies as J.C. Penney and Calvin
Klein. Their workdays were nearly twice as long as
those of American workers, and their pay, as in
nineteenth-century Europe, went to a patriarchal
head of the household. Workers in the Pacific could
not always improve their situation through political change. National leaders in a host of countries—
Taiwan and South Korea, for example—strove to
maintain an authoritarian grip by holding prisoners
without trial and torturing dissenters.

Japanese workers reaped some of the benefits
of their country's economic resurgence, but as individuals they were expected to subordinate their
interests to those of the business firm. In turn, the
government tightly coordinated business activity.

Economic Summit, 1987
The new globalism made regular meetings of world leaders imperative for coordination of economic and political policies.

Although a highly successful recipe for economic success, this hierarchical system came into question by the late 1980s. Japanese consumers, who had a high rate of savings in comparison with Westerners, became less willing to postpone their gratification. Resistance to patriarchy developed: in 1989, Japanese women led the way in voting out of office a prime minister who kept a mistress. Women also entered the parliament and cabinet, long a bastion of elderly men. Legislators began to express concern about environmental deterioration and the quality of life in overcrowded cities. Finally, a new emperor succeeded in the throne—the son of Emperor Hirohito, who died in 1989—and he broke with tradition by emphasizing the human rather than the divine aspects of the Japanese imperial past.

For all its success, Japan faced mounting difficulties in the 1990s. Attempts to maintain cultural homogeneity brought charges of racism from abroad. The country also had to deal with the reality that hundreds of thousands of non-Japanese had illegally entered the country to perform the menial labor shunned by native workers. Financial

scandals and widespread corruption, long a problem in postwar Japanese politics, repeatedly brought down the political leadership. The stock market plunged, and unemployment threatened social peace. In the international arena, Japan's relations with its major trading partner, the United States, were often strained. And in the post–Cold War world, Japanese officials became increasingly nervous about the prospect of nuclear weapons in North Korea. Although Japan maintained its economic power, an array of serious challenges confronted this island nation by the mid-1990s.

Western Politics Turns to the Right

Although Western governments had to heed the changing conditions from the Middle East to the Pacific Rim, their first task as the 1980s began was to put their own economic houses in order. In the postwar world, government spending had been the spark that recharged a flagging economy. Now the problems manifested in the energy crisis, soaring unemployment, and double-digit inflation brought calls for new remedies. Voters frustrated by threats of a declining standard of living elected conservative politicians in the hope that they would restore prosperity. In Britain, Prime Minister Margaret Thatcher (*1979–1990) slashed social spending as her cure for "the British disease," that is, the country's slow, steady fall from global economic prominence. In the United States, President Ronald Reagan pushed through a tax cut that benefited the wealthiest Americans above all. As Western-bloc countries reached the depths of recession in 1981 and 1982, tough times intensified feelings that the unemployed and new migrants were responsible for the downturn. Thus the consensus that had helped the West through hard times was undermined by divisive political rhetoric.

Thatcher Reshapes Political Culture

In 1979 the combination of continuing economic decline, revolt in Northern Ireland, and labor unrest brought to power an outspoken leader of the Conservative party, Margaret Thatcher. The combative prime minister eschewed the politics of consensus building, which united competing interest groups to champion a cause, such as Winston Churchill had done during World War II. Instead she vowed to transform Britain through the force of her own ideas. "I don't spend a lifetime watching which way the cat jumps," she announced. "I know really which way I want the cats to go." In parliamentary speeches, Thatcher lashed out at union leaders, Labour politicians, and people who received welfare-state benefits. Her political style alone justified her claim after a few years in power: "I have changed everything."

Thatcher believed that only a resurgence of private enterprise could revive the sluggish British economy. Although her anti-welfare-state policies struck a revolutionary chord, she called herself "a nineteenth-century liberal" in reference to the economic liberalism of that age. In her view business leaders and entrepreneurs were the key members of society. She saw labor unions as a brake on economic growth; she characterized as inferior the unemployed and immigrants from Britain's former colonies, saying that neither group contributed to

national wealth. More than two-thirds of the public read newspapers that advocated part or all of this general attitude; thus even members of the working class blamed labor leaders or newcomers for Britain's trauma.

The policies of "Thatcherism" were based on *monetarist* or *supply side* theories associated most prominently with U.S. economist Milton Friedman. Monetarists contended that inflation resulted when government pumped money into the economy at a rate that was higher than a nation's economic growth rate. Thus they advocated a tight rein on the money supply to keep prices from rising rapidly. Supply-side economists maintained that the economy as a whole throve when business prosperity "trickled down" throughout society. To implement such theories, the British government cut income taxes on the wealthy to spur new investment; it also pushed up sales taxes on necessities to make up for lost revenues from the reduced income levy. Thatcher vigorously pruned government intervention in the economy: she sold such publicly owned businesses and utilities as Britoil, British Airways, and Rolls Royce; refused to prop up what she believed were "outmoded" industries such as coal mining; and slashed education and health programs. The quality of universities, public transportation, highways, and hospitals deteriorated, and leading scholars and scientists left the country in a renewal of the "brain drain." At the same time, the tax cuts led to a dramatic increase in the nation's private wealth, although the benefits fell to the already well-off members of society.

In the first three years of Thatcher's government, the British economy did not respond well to her shock treatment. Social unity fragmented—in 1981, blacks and Asians rioted in major cities—and her popularity sagged. A turning point came in March 1982, when Argentina invaded the British Falkland Islands in the South Atlantic. Thatcher invoked patriotism to unify the nation behind her and refused to surrender the islands without a fight, even though they were thousands of miles away. The British were ecstatic: one newspaper urged its readers to "Rejoice . . . just rejoice" at Thatcher's tough stand. The gambit paid off, as the British armed forces triumphed. The prime minister's public support soared, and in 1984 and 1985 she used her still-high approval rating to denounce a miner's strike as unpatriotic. The appeal to national sentiment had replaced the progress of economic democratization as a unifying social force.

By the mid-1980s inflation had dissipated in Britain. Historians and economists today debate whether the change resulted from Thatcher's policies or from the lack of spending power that burdened the poor and the unemployed. In any case, Thatcher's growing popularity after the mid-1980s serves as testament to her success in creating a brand of conservative political consensus.

Alternatives to Thatcherism

Other West European leaders confronted economic problems with less bombast than Thatcher, but most found some retrenchment of the welfare state necessary. Nevertheless, Sweden retained a broad array of humane programs. For example, the country offered each immigrant a choice of subsidized housing in neighborhoods ranging from all-Swedish to those inhabited primarily by people from the immigrant's native land. Swedish employers by law had to allow their workers 240 hours per year of paid leave for language study. Such programs were expensive: the tax rate on income over $46,000 was 80 percent. When productivity flagged, the government cut taxes, tightened the focus of welfare relief, and denied benefits to unemployed workers who refused retraining or a job offer. The Swedes also reduced their dangerous dependence on foreign oil by cutting consumption in half between 1976 and 1986; to make up some of the shortfall, they decided after much debate to rely on power generated by nuclear plants. By 1987 the inflation rate had fallen to 4 percent, and the high productivity of Swedish workers attracted new business investment.

In West Germany the 1980s began with unions and managers working together to fight inflation by keeping prices and wages down. However, during 1981 and 1982 the West German economy succumbed to the same forces that plagued other Western-bloc states. Support for Helmut Schmidt vanished, and the center-right leader Helmut Kohl took power in 1982 amid revelations of corruption and payoffs. The Kohl administration reduced welfare spending, froze government wages, and cut corporate taxes. By 1984 the inflation rate was only 2 percent, and West Germany had acquired a

10 percent share of world trade. Kohl claimed that his curbing of the welfare state had brought about the *Wende* ("turning") of the economy.

The late 1970s and early 1980s also saw West Germany gripped by domestic terrorism. In an atmosphere of fear, businessmen hired bodyguards and refused to travel by air because of frequent bomb threats. The government responded by making it a crime to "defame the state," curtailing the civil rights of suspected terrorists, and imprisoning their lawyers. Some protested that the terrorists were achieving their ends by inducing the government to diminish human rights, but only after terrorism died down in the mid-1980s did Kohl's government repeal some of the antiterrorist legislation. After German reunification, vicious racist attacks replaced terrorism as a threat to public order.

France took a different political path through the 1980s than either Germany or Britain but ended up in a similar position. The decade began with the conservative Valéry Giscard d'Estaing (*1974–1981) as president, but high unemployment and inflation as well as personal scandals led to his removal from office in 1981. By then more than 1.5 million people were out of work and the economic growth rate stood at an anemic 1.2 percent. Giscard was replaced by a socialist, François Mitterrand, who nationalized banks and certain industries and stimulated the economy by raising wages and social spending. However, French financial leaders reacted by sending capital abroad rather than investing it at home, and Mitterrand was forced to clamp down on welfare expenditures. The economy rebounded but, as elsewhere, political racism emerged as an expression of discontent with changing social and economic conditions. In the 1985 national elections, Jean-Marie Le Pen's National Front party, which promised to deport African and Muslim immigrants and cut French ties with non-white nations, won 10 percent of the vote. Hundreds of thousands of youth responded by rallying against the party and calling for better treatment of immigrants.

Meanwhile, a cluster of smaller states without heavy defense commitments enjoyed increasing prosperity after the recession of the early 1980s ended. In Spain tourist dollars helped rebuild the southern cities of Grenada and Cordoba. Under a moderate Socialist prime minister, Felipe González—who, like Mitterrand and other Socialist leaders, supported the aspirations of the middle class—the country joined the Common Market in 1986. The Italian economy grew despite pervasive political corruption, and Switzerland capitalized on its trading and financial prowess. Austria prospered, too, in part by reducing government pensions and aid to industry and agriculture. Austrian Chancellor Franz Vranitzky summed up the changed focus of government in the 1980s: "In Austria, the shelter that the state has given to almost everyone—employee as well as entrepreneur—has led . . . a lot of people [to] think not what they can do to solve a problem but what the state can do. . . . This needs to change." As the decade closed, the nations of Western Europe had managed to retain their position in a rapidly changing global economy, but they often did so at the expense of society's less fortunate members.

America and the Reagan Revolution

The conservative presidency of Ronald Reagan dominated political life in the United States during the 1980s. Taking office in January 1981, Reagan sought to reawaken American self-confidence after the humiliations of Vietnam and Watergate. The former actor was at his best in carefully planned television appearances. In front of the camera the "great communicator" successfully boosted American esteem by furthering the idea that a so-called moral majority existed in the land that had somehow lost its grip on affairs during two decades of social turmoil and political scandal. Reagan vowed to promote the values of this group, which included commitment to Bible-based religion, dedication to work, sexual restraint, and unquestioning patriotism.

In domestic affairs, Reagan pursued a radical course on a par with Thatcher's. His program of "Reaganomics" produced a whopping income tax cut of 25 percent between 1981 and 1983, combined with massive reductions in federal spending for student loans, school lunch programs, and mass transit. Like Thatcher, Reagan believed that tax cuts would lead to investment and a reinvigorated economy; federal outlays for welfare programs,

which only encouraged sloth, would generally be unnecessary thereafter. The president promoted the concept of state and local responsibility, or federalism, which in practice meant that states and cities would bear more of the financial burden for mandated social programs. Scorning environmentalist groups, Reagan appointed a progrowth secretary of the interior, James Watt. The secretary's belief in imminent apocalypse led him to oppose ecological concerns as futile, and he opened federal lands, particularly in western states, to private development.

In foreign policy, Reagan spent most of his time in office preoccupied with the Communist threat. The long-time Cold Warrior labeled the Soviet Union an "evil empire" and demanded huge military budgets to counter the Soviet arms buildup of the 1970s. The combination of tax cuts and military expansion had pushed the federal budget deficit to $200 billion by 1986. Throughout much of the decade the United States opposed communism verbally, with military aid, and with armed forces, particularly in the western hemisphere. In Nicaragua the administration channeled funds to the so-called contras, a rebel force that opposed the revolutionary Marxist Sandinista government that had come to power in 1979. In 1983, U.S. armed forces invaded the tiny West Indian island of Grenada and overthrew its radical leftist government. Earlier that year, Reagan had announced the Strategic Defense Initiative (SDI; but known popularly as "Star Wars"), a costly plan to put lasers in space to defend the United States against a nuclear attack. Although Reagan tried to sell SDI as a peaceful initiative and even claimed he would eventually share the plan's secrets with the Soviet Union, the Cold War continued until Reagan and future Soviet leader Mikhail Gorbachev began to meet in 1985 to discuss disarmament plans seriously.

The impact of Reagan's military buildup on U.S. global power and domestic health is a topic heatedly debated. However, as historian Paul Kennedy pointed out in his best-selling book *The Rise and Fall of the Great Powers* (1988), nations at the top have always had trouble balancing military commitments with economic resources. Thus although Reagan's administration spent less of the gross national product on the military than

Eisenhower's had (7.5 percent as opposed to 10 percent), it did so at a time when the United States faced stiff competition from such global economic giants as Japan and West Germany. The system of military procurement itself took place outside the bounds of the competitive market system Reagan glorified. Paul Kennedy warned of the danger that the United States, with its vast network of overseas allies, would succumb to the "imperial overstretch" that had weakened Spain in the sixteenth century and Britain in the early twentieth.

At home, critics held Reaganomics accountable for the escalating violence and drug use in cities, the deteriorating roads and schools across the country, and the growing numbers of homeless Americans sleeping on the streets. Others cheered Reagan for the real estate boom and stock market rally of the years 1982 to 1987, two developments that created many new millionaires. His defenders maintained that he had restored national unity and pride. As the 1980s came to a close, the popularity in the West of conservative ideas as put into practice by Reagan and Thatcher remained strong.

The Collapse of Communism

In 1979, Communist leaders in Eastern Europe and the Soviet Union clung firmly to power. The fate of peoples in the USSR rested in the hands of Leonid Brezhnev and a *gerontocracy* of elderly bureaucrats who had matured during Stalin's "construction of socialism" in the 1930s. Although Poland and Hungary experimented with limited economic reform, most East-bloc leaders followed the Soviet line without deviation. Western-bloc analysts found no reason to think that radical change would happen in the near future. In the United States the CIA reported that the bloc was in robust economic health. Yet a mere decade later, communism had begun to disappear from Europe, the Soviet economy lay in ruins, and the Cold War of more than forty years was virtually at an end. By the mid-1990s, observers came back to speak of "Weimar Russia," an epithet suggesting that the former empire's lack of a democratic heritage might make it ripe for dictatorship in hard times.

Solidarity Takes the Lead

Twelve years after the Prague Spring, the Poles launched their own revolt against Communist rule. In the summer of 1980, they reacted furiously to increased food prices by going on strike. As the protest spread, workers at the Gdansk shipyards, led by electrician Lech Wałesa and crane operator Anna Walentynowicz, created an independent labor movement, Solidarity. The organization soon embraced much of the adult population, including a million members of the Communist party.

The Poles had engaged in various forms of resistance to Communist rule for decades. The Catholic church, which numbered 28 million members out of a total population of 35 million, had long opposed socialist secularization. Moreover, worker protest in the 1970s had been common, as steep energy prices, scarce consumer goods, inflation, and government ineptitude worsened the conditions of everyday life. In the summer of 1980, opposition to Poland's rulers coalesced. Intellectuals banded together in the Workers' Defense Committee (KOR) and joined the attack. The defiant Cardinal Stefan Wyszyński (1901–1981) suggested that the government might restore social peace by "giving the censors a good retirement and thanking them for their work." Another church leader, the former archbishop of Cracow, had become Pope John Paul II in 1978, and he lent his authority to the anticommunist cause. Solidarity workers occupied factories and waved Polish flags as well as giant portraits of the pope and the Virgin Mary.

Having achieved mass support at home and worldwide sympathy through media coverage, Solidarity pledged to support moderate economic reform. It insisted, however, that the government recognize it as an independent union—a radical demand. The government again hiked prices and added rationing regulations, but popular resistance only increased, as tens of thousands of women marched in the streets crying, "We're hungry!" Polish officials finally made price concessions and even sanctioned the union by October 1980. Yet as the Party teetered on the edge of collapse, the police and the army, with Brezhnev's support, swept aside Poland's civilian government and in the winter of 1981 outlawed Solidarity.

Polish Strike, 1980
For Poles and many others in the Eastern bloc who hated Soviet domination, religion symbolized the cause of resistance.

Continued efforts by reporters and dissidents, using the global communications network, kept the union alive.

Stern and puritanical, General Wojciech Jaruzelski took over as the head of Poland's new regime. In a 1982 film ostensibly about the French Revolution, *Danton*, Polish filmmaker Andrezej Wajda likened Jaruzelski to Robespierre, the fanatic instigator of the Reign of Terror. Jaruzelski insisted that "the place of People's Poland is and will remain among the socialist powers," but his hope was not so much to revive socialist enthusiasm at home as to ward off Soviet intervention. The general could not push repression too far: he needed new loans from the Western bloc to keep the Polish economy afloat, and in any case neither Solidarity nor the people's religious and nationalist fervor disappeared with martial law. Despite Jaruzelski's ap-

parent grasp on power, the stage had been set for communism's downfall.

Gorbachev Sparks Reform in the Soviet Union

The rise of Solidarity signaled an epidemic of economic woes in the Soviet bloc. Far from insulating people from the ups and downs of capitalism, Soviet-style economies suffered from rampant decay by the early 1980s. Years of stagnant and then "negative" growth led to a deteriorating standard of living. After working a full day, Soviet homemakers stood in long lines to obtain basic commodities, and housing and food shortages necessitated the three-generation household, in which grandparents took over this tedious task from their working children and grandchildren. "There is no special skill to this," a seventy-three-year-old grandmother and former garbage collector remarked. "You just stand in line and wait." Even so, they often went away empty-handed, and one foreign visitor complained that she had never eaten so many varieties of cabbage salad. Basic household supplies like soap disappeared instantly from stores, and the quality of medical care varied according to one's status. One readily available, cheap product—vodka—often formed the center of people's social lives. Alcoholism reached crisis levels, thus diminishing worker productivity and tremendously straining the nation's morale.

Economic stagnation had many ramifications. Ordinary people decided not to have children, and fertility fell below replacement levels throughout the Soviet bloc, except for the Muslim areas of Soviet Central Asia. The country was forced to import massive amounts of grain because 20 to 30 percent of the grain that was produced in the USSR rotted before it could be harvested or shipped to market. Industrial pollution, spewed out by enterprises responsible only for meeting production quotas, reached scandalous dimensions. A massive and privileged Party bureaucracy hobbled industrial innovation and failed to achieve socialism's professed goal of a decent standard of living for working people. To match American military growth, the Soviet Union diverted 15 to 20 percent of its gross national product (more than double the U.S. proportion) to armaments. As this combustible mixture of problems festered, a new

Superpower Détente
Gorbachev's reforms in the USSR contributed to lowering Cold War tensions. Here the Gorbachevs and Reagans depict the new superpower rapport for photographers.

generation was coming of age that had no memory of World War II or Stalin's purges. One observer found them as "cynical, but less afraid." "They believe in nothing," a mother said of Soviet youth in 1984; "they won't be pushed around," added another.

In 1985 a new leader, Mikhail Gorbachev, brought an end to the Soviet gerontocracy. In 1956, Gorbachev, then only twenty-five, had attended the Twentieth Party Congress at which Khrushchev had first condemned Stalin's excesses. Later, as a trusted official, he traveled widely and got a firsthand glimpse of life in the West. The son of peasants, Gorbachev had risen through the Party ranks as an agricultural specialist. After Brezhnev's death in 1982 and the sudden demise of two successors, high Party officials elected Gorbachev to the top spot in the Communist world. He quickly proposed broad plans to reinvigorate the Soviet economy. His program of *perestroika* ("restructuring") aimed to streamline production and management. The economy had depended on labor-intensive production, but falling birthrates meant that the system could not expect an abundant labor supply in the future. Moreover, outmoded machinery hampered Soviet industrial output.

Against the will of managers, who benefited from the status quo, Gorbachev hoped to reverse economic decay by improving productivity, increasing the rate of capital investment, introducing up-to-date technology, and slowly developing such market features as prices and profits.

Along with perestroika, Gorbachev proclaimed a policy of *glasnost* (usually translated as "openness" or "publicity"). For the Soviet leader, glasnost meant speaking "the language of truth," disseminating "wide, prompt, and frank information," and allowing Soviet citizens new measures of free speech. When officials complained that glasnost threatened their status, Gorbachev replaced more than a third of the Party's leadership in the first months of his administration. The pressing need for glasnost became most evident after the Chernobyl catastrophe in 1986, when bureaucratic cover-ups delayed the spread of information about the accident, with lethal consequences for people living near the plant.

After Chernobyl even the Communist party and Marxism-Leninism were opened to public criticism. Party meetings suddenly witnessed complaints about the highest leaders and their policies. Television shows such as "The Fifth Wheel" adopted the outspoken methods of American investigative reporting; one program showed an interview with an executioner of political prisoners and exposed the plight of Leningrad's homeless children. "Work is getting pretty easy around here," remarked TV censor Natalya Strepetova, who had less and less to do at her job. Even academic research fell off as professors spent their time reading newspapers and debating public events. Political camps arose, and in the fall of 1987 one of Gorbachev's erstwhile allies, Boris Yeltsin, quit the Politburo after denouncing perestroika as inadequate for real reform. Yeltsin's political daring, which in the past would have consigned him to oblivion (or Siberia), inspired others to organize in opposition to the crumbling ruling orthodoxy. By the spring of 1989 not a single Communist was chosen for office in Moscow's local elections.

Glasnost and perestroika dramatically affected superpower relations as well. Recognizing how the Cold War arms race was draining Soviet resources, Gorbachev on taking power almost immediately began scaling back missile production. His unilateral actions gradually won over Reagan. The two leaders met at Geneva, Switzerland, in the autumn of 1985 to initiate a personal relationship and begin defusing the Cold War. "I bet the hard-liners in both our countries are bleeding when we shake hands," said the jovial Reagan at the summit's conclusion. Although future meetings did not go as smoothly, a major breakthrough from the U.S. point of view occurred in early 1989, when Gorbachev at last withdrew his country's forces from the debilitating war in Afghanistan. By late 1989 the United States was beginning to cut back its own vast military commitments. Meanwhile, the people of Eastern Europe took glasnost to its logical conclusion by rebelling against Communist rule and bringing a true end to the Cold War.

The Collapse of Marxist-Leninist Government

Tremors in the Communist world shook China's capital, Beijing. Inspired by a visit to the city from Gorbachev, thousands of students massed in Tiananmen Square in the spring of 1989 to demand democracy. They used telex machines and e-mail to rush their messages to the international community and effectively conveyed their goals through the cameras Western television trained on them. China's aged Communist leaders, while pushing economic modernization and even allowing market operations, refused to consider the introduction of democracy. As workers began joining the "Democracy" forces, the government crushed the movement and executed as many as a thousand rebels.

Despite this setback to the forces of democracy, the spirit of revolt advanced in Eastern Europe in 1989 and brought decades of Communist rule to an end. Indeed the year has been designated the twentieth century's *annus mirabilis* ("year of miracles") because of the sudden and unexpected disintegration of Communist power throughout the region. Events in Poland took a dramatic turn first. In the spring the Polish government, weakened by its own bungling of the economy and lacking Soviet support for further repression, again legalized Solidarity and promised free elections. In June parliamentary elections, Solidarity candidates drove out the Communists. "Our defeat," Jaruzelski admitted, "is total." By early 1990, Jaruzelski had been replaced as president by Wałesa, who began Poland's rocky transition to a market economy.

As it became evident that the Soviet Union would not intervene in Poland, the fall of communism repeated itself in country after country. In Hungary, which had experimented with "market socialism" since the 1960s, popular demands for liberalization spread from economics to politics at the beginning of 1989. Critical journals appeared, and the populace boycotted the traditional May Day parade. In June crowds turned out for the ceremonial burial in a national hero's grave of Imre Nagy, the prime minister who had been hanged three decades earlier for his role in the 1956 uprising. In the fall, Parliament dismissed the Communist party as the official ruling institution and people tore down Communist symbols throughout the country.

In Czechoslovakia, which after 1968 had been firmly restored to Soviet-style rule, people watched the progress of glasnost expectantly. Although they could see Gorbachev on television calling for free speech, he never mentioned reform in Czechoslovakia. In the spring of 1989, however, a petition campaign secured the release of dissident leader Václav Havel. Demonstrators protested in the streets for democracy, but the government cracked

Destroying the Berlin Wall, 1989
As soldiers observe impassively, a citizen hammers the wall. Often painted with intricate graffiti and murals, pieces of the wall are now in museums or in private hands as souvenirs of a bygone era.

cape over the wall for decades, despite their country's reputation as having the most dynamic economy in the socialist world. When Austria and Hungary opened their borders in August 1989, thousands of East Germans began taking "vacations" to Hungary and then crossing into the West. The combination of emigration and protest toppled Erich Honecker's antireform regime, unsupported now by Soviet tanks. New Communist leaders offered little hope of a better life to the East German people, who kept pressing for change through mass demonstrations. On November 9 the government conceded to the people's protests and opened the Berlin Wall to free traffic between both halves of the divided city. The Communists tried to make the best of their loss of authority by explaining events with traditional Marxist language: "A revolutionary people's movement has brought into motion a process of great change. The renewal of society is on the agenda." People celebrated the opening of the wall as a festive holiday: West Berliners handed out a consumer good in short supply in the Eastern zone, the banana, and that fruit became the unofficial symbol of reunion. Berliners released years of frustration at their division by assaulting the wall with sledgehammers and bringing home chunks as souvenirs. The government finished the wall's complete destruction in the fall of 1990.

Almost as soon as the Berlin Wall tumbled, the world's attention fastened on the political drama in Romania. Since the mid-1960s, Nicolae Ceauşescu had ruled as the harshest dictator in Communist Europe since Stalin. In the name of modernization he destroyed whole villages; to build up the population he outlawed contraceptives and abortions, a restriction that led to the abandonment of tens of thousands of children. Most Romanians lived in utter poverty and seemed prepared to remain obedient even while the rest of Eastern Europe rebelled. Yet in early December an opposition movement rose up, and when authorities moved to suppress it, the spirit of resistance spread. Most of the army turned against the government and crushed the forces loyal to Ceauşescu. On Christmas Day viewers watched on television as the dictator and his wife were tried by a military court and then executed. Soon after, Western photographers displayed what Ceauşescu had wrought, from orphanages packed with thousands

down by turning the secret police on them. The turning point came on November 24 when Alexander Dubček, leader of the Prague Spring of 1968, addressed the crowds in Prague's Wenceslas Square with a call for the ouster of Stalinists from the government. Almost immediately, hard-line leader Milos Jakeš and the rest of the Politburo resigned. Capping the country's "velvet revolution," the formerly Communist-dominated Parliament elevated Havel to the presidency.

The most potent symbol of a divided Europe stood in the midst of a divided Germany: the Berlin Wall. East Germans had attempted to es-of unwanted, uncared-for children to the mass graves of those who had earlier dared to dissent.

The collapse of communism in Europe paved the way for an event that filled many Westerners with apprehension: the reunification of Germany. Many feared that the sudden change would alter the balance of power and destabilize Central Europe, and possibly the world, once more. In Germany itself, however, unification topped the agenda. Chancellor Kohl seized the opportunity to speed up the process; his plans were facilitated when East Germans, in their first free elections, voted in as prime minister a Christian Democrat, the same party Kohl headed in West Germany. Kohl based the campaign for reunification on the promise of a more comfortable way of life. In July 1990 he arranged for East German currency to be exchanged on a one-to-one basis with West German marks. A shrewd politician, Kohl had a "grass-roots instinct that the East Germans wanted their microwaves now, and not in three years." After the economic foundations were in place, full political union took place on October 3, far earlier than anyone had expected at the end of 1989.

The realities of unification did not live up to the dream. East German industry passed into the hands of West German managers, whose efficiencies caused unemployment to soar, especially among women and youth. As early as September 1990, many social services, such as day-care centers that allowed women to work to support their families, closed down. Although restoration of buildings and industrial modernization proceeded in the nation's former Communist half, social tensions flared. West Germans blamed their new co-citizens for the diversion of resources to the east, and East Germans took out their frustrations through violent attacks or hateful rhetoric against immigrants. Throughout the former East bloc, the transition to democracy and free markets gave rise to social instability, economic upheaval, and nationalist expressions of discontent.

Nationalism Fractures Yugoslavia and the Soviet Union

Populist nationalism brought down the Soviet empire and ripped Yugoslavia into wartorn pieces. Like Hungarians and Czechs in the nineteenth-century Habsburg empire, nationality groups in the USSR began to demand political and cultural autonomy in the 1980s. The empire held together more than a hundred ethnic groups, and the five republics of Soviet Central Asia were home to 50 million Muslims. In the spring of 1990, Lithuania declared its independence from the Soviet Union. In response, Gorbachev placed an embargo on goods vital to the Lithuanian economy and stipulated that future secessions would require approval by a two-thirds majority of voters as well as a two-year waiting period. Unlike the situation in Eastern Europe, the Soviet leadership could not sanction the breakup of the USSR without a fight.

Meanwhile, ethnic tensions erupted in Yugoslavia, where Communist rulers had kept the peace for nearly half a century. Serbs bitterly remembered the massacres of their people by Croat fascists during World War II. In December 1990 a Serb Communist, Slobodan Milošević, won the presidency of his republic and began to assert Serb ascendancy within Yugoslavia. Other nationalities resisted. "Slovenians . . . have one more reason to say they are in favor of independence," warned one observer. In the spring of 1991, first Slovenia and then Croatia seceded, but the Croats soon lost almost a quarter of their territory to the Serb-dominated Yugoslav army. A more ghastly civil war engulfed Bosnia-Herzegovina. In 1991 the republic's Muslim majority tried to create a multicultural state, but most Bosnian Serbs violently rejected participation. In the ensuing conflict the Serb guerrilla army, backed by covert support by Milošević's government, gained the upper hand; the Muslim Bosnians were prevented by a U.N. arms embargo from equipping their forces adequately to resist. Not only did many civilians die, but each competing force also aimed at the cultural heritage of its opponent. Military units destroyed libraries and museums, architectural treasures like the Mostar bridge, and cities with medieval history such as Dubrovnic. Attempts by U.N. peacekeepers to ensure safe havens re-

Division of Yugoslavia as of 1994

peatedly failed, while NATO and the European community watched from the sidelines.

Blood was spilled throughout the disintegrating Communist world in a variety of ethnic conflicts in the early 1990s. With backing from the reform government, newly liberated Romanians attacked their neighbors of Hungarian descent. In the Soviet republic of Tajikistan, native Tajiks rioted against Armenians living there; in Azerbaijan, Azeris and Armenians clashed over contested territory; and in the Baltic states, antisemitism revived as a political tool. In a nonviolent parting of the ways, Czechs and Slovaks peacefully agreed to separate into two nations as of January 1, 1993.

Economic distress brought about by the transition from socialism to capitalism contributed to ethnic unrest and weakened the bonds that held the Soviet Union together. Perestroika had failed to revitalize the Soviet economy; people confronted soaring prices, the specter of unemployment, and even greater scarcity of goods than they had endured in the past. In the autumn of 1990, Gorbachev moved to stave off utter collapse by proposing the complete abolition of the socialist economy. The state would sell off property, gradually end price controls, allow worker collectives to decide their own fate, and devalue the ruble in accordance with its price in world currency markets. Gorbachev announced the absolute necessity of such changes: "There is no alternative to the transition to the market." However, his plan proved a matter of too little, too late. The Soviet republics demanded freedom in the production and distribution of consumer goods; closer to home, Gorbachev faced new political challenges in the summer of 1990 when the Russian parliament elected Boris Yeltsin president of the Russian Republic over a Communist candidate. Despite their differences, the two men eventually negotiated a treaty that would have granted the republics greater autonomy and kept the USSR united in the process.

The signing of the treaty was set for August 20, 1991. On August 19, while Gorbachev was vacationing in the Crimea, a group of eight anti-reform hard-liners, from the Soviet vice president to the head of the KGB, staged a coup. Feebly attempting to legitimize their actions, they declared that Gorbachev was ill and "needs some time to get his health back"; in the meantime the coup leaders would rescue the Soviet Union from the "mortal danger" posed by "extremist forces."

THE END OF SOVIET COMMUNISM IN EUROPE

June 1989 Solidarity defeats Communists in Polish elections

August 1989 Czechoslovakia opens borders to Western Europe

October 1989 Hungary dismisses Communist party as official party; Erich Honecker resigns as head of East German government

November 1989 East German politburo resigns; Berlin Wall opened; Alexander Dubček calls for the ouster of Stalinists and a reform government comes to power in Czechoslovakia

December 1989 Nicholae Ceauşescu driven from power and assassinated in Romania

Spring 1990 Lithuania announces its secession from the USSR and other Baltic states follow suit

October 1990 Germany reunited; Gorbachev announces transition to a market economy; Boris Yeltsin defeats Communist candidate to become president of the Russian Republic

August 1991 After coup attempt in Moscow, operations of Communist party suspended

Yeltsin, however, challenged the so-called State Committee for the State of Emergency. Standing atop a tank outside the Russian Republic's parliament building, he called for mass resistance. Hundreds of thousands of Muscovites and Leningraders filled the streets, the heads of the other republics declared their support for Yeltsin and Gorbachev, and units of the army defected to protect Yeltsin's headquarters. People used fax machines and computers to coordinate internal resistance and send messages to the rest of the world. On the night of August 20–21, several tanks attacked the parliament building and killed three young men who tried to block their way, but the crowds repulsed them with Molotov cocktails, rocks, and guns. By morning the junta was in complete disarray in the face of citizen determination not to allow a return of Stalinism, or indeed of any form of Soviet orthodoxy.

Although a shaken Gorbachev returned to Moscow, the Soviet Union now disintegrated. People tore down statues of the first Soviet secret

Countries of the Former Soviet Union

police chief, Felix Dzerzhinsky; Yeltsin outlawed the party newspaper, *Pravda,* sealed the KGB files, and forced Gorbachev to fire his cabinet. On August 29 the Soviet Parliament suspended operations of the Communist party itself. Gorbachev and his few remaining allies tried to stem the tide, but one republic after another followed the lead of the Baltic states in declaring their independence. The USSR finally dissolved on January 1, 1992. Eleven of the fifteen former Soviet republics now banded together in a Commonwealth of Independent States.

As Gorbachev ceded power to Yeltsin—who in turn had to fight for his political life—the Soviet economy remained in crisis and ethnic battles continued. In Russia the political Right appealed to nationalist sentiments and won increasing support. Political disorder was matched by social disarray, as organized crime interfered in the distribution of goods and services and assassinated legitimate

entrepreneurs. The conditions of everyday life became dire.

The West on the Eve of a New Millennium

The approach of the twenty-first century brought wonderment at human accomplishment but also acute awareness that much work remained to ensure a comfortable life for vast numbers of the world's peoples. Rivals contested the centuries-long dominance of Europe and the United States for a more equitable distribution of the planet's resources. Europeans, though no longer divided by the Iron Curtain, had to reconcile the fact of advancing regional alignment in the western part of the Continent with the problems of political fragmentation and uncertain reform in the eastern half. Although the Cold War's end removed fears of imminent nuclear holocaust, the problems of environmental decay, rapid population growth, hunger, epidemic disease, and economic under-development loomed large on the international agenda. Western culture, developed over the course of several thousand years, continued to adapt to new conditions. Enriched by non-Western culture and altered drastically by the mass media, it promised to offer new avenues to understanding the global age.

A New World Order?

The fall of communism threw the world's distribution of power into question, and the weakening of Cold War rivalries narrowed Third World countries' ability to win financial and other support from one of the two superpowers. Iraqi dictator Saddam Hussein was the first to test the new geopolitical waters. At the end of the Iran-Iraq war in 1988, Iraq staggered under a heavy debt, unresolved territorial disputes with Iran, the bitter loss of hundreds of thousands of soldiers and civilians, and a lowered standard of living. Saddam viewed the annexation of neighboring Kuwait, whose 600,000 citizens enjoyed the world's highest per capita income, as a solution to Iraq's troubles and a means of smothering internal discontent, and he invaded the oil-rich country in August 1990. While stirring fears that he would gobble up other Arab nations, he appealed to the masses as a pan-Arab hero.

Contrary to Hussein's expectations, the deployment of Iraqi troops on the Saudi Arabian border galvanized international resistance. Supported by U.S. diplomatic efforts, the United Nations clapped an embargo on Iraq and accepted a Saudi invitation to send troops to the region to protect against further Iraqi encroachments. Most important, Gorbachev joined the U.N. coalition in warning Hussein to quit Kuwait, signaling a post–Cold War shift in the winds of diplomacy whereby small warring nations would no longer be able to exploit superpower animosities. The multinational force, led by the United States with support from a range of nations, pummeled the Iraqi army. Iraq's defeat heightened pressure on all Middle Eastern countries to negotiate a peaceful solution to their

decades-long disputes. Changes in the region prompted U.S. president George Bush to proclaim the coming of "a new world order." Indeed the progress—though uneven—of peace talks between Israel and the PLO in 1993 and 1994 suggested that people in that part of the globe had reason to hope for the future.

During the 1980s, world leaders tried to address a growing economic schism among the earth's northern regions and southern lands. Although Australians and New Zealanders were exceptions, southern peoples generally suffered lower living standards and measures of health than northerners. Latin American nations grappled with multibillion-dollar debt, government corruption, widespread crime, and grinding poverty. In Brazil bands of homeless children roamed city streets. The drug trade plagued Colombia; the illegal commerce diverted resources that might have been channeled toward investment, social reforms, and the development of democracy. Other countries, prominent among them Mexico, began to strengthen their economies by marketing their oil and other natural resources more effectively.

In sub-Saharan Africa environmental destruction resulted from the conversion of land to the production of cash crops. The region suffered from three years of drought (1982–1985), continuing famine, and civil war. In such lands as Liberia and Rwanda, military rule, ideological factionalism, and tribal antagonism produced a deadly mixture. Hundreds of thousands of Africans perished; others were left starving and homeless. Although African countries began turning away from military dictatorship and toward parliamentary government, global economic advance left most of Africa untouched in the 1980s.

In South Africa native peoples struggled on for political rights and economic opportunity against entrenched white racism. In 1990 the moderate South African leader F. W. de Klerk released the imprisoned Nelson Mandela, who had been held for almost three decades because of his anti-apartheid politics. By then the media had made Mandela's plight a focus of worldwide concern, and multinational corporations had reduced their economic activity in the segregated country. De Klerk's government followed Mandela's release with a gradual dismantling of such aspects of apartheid as segregated parks and beaches. In 1993 the government and the African National Congress

(ANC) agreed to a democratic constitution that granted the nonwhite majority the vote while guaranteeing whites and other minorities civil liberties. The path to reform was complicated by divisions between African tribes, most notably between the ANC-supporting Xhosa and the Zulus. Strong evidence suggested that conflict among Africans was fanned by white supremacists in the police and army and in paramilitary groups, and violence mounted in the spring of 1994 as national elections approached. Nevertheless, in May the ANC won a landslide victory and Mandela, the country's new president, promised a tolerant and multiracial democracy.

Non-Western countries' drive to modernize could serve as a force for political stability, but sometimes internal struggles over national policy ignited turmoil. In India, Rajiv Gandhi, the grandson of Nehru, worked for education, women's rights, and an end to bitter local rivalries; his assassination in 1991 by Tamil nationalists raised questions about whether India would continue to have the strong leadership necessary to attract investment and thus to continue modernization. In Pakistan and the Phillippines, too, the impulse for Westernization was strong, but unstable social conditions and inept political systems discouraged

investment. Nonetheless, because the Third World as a whole continued to increase its share of gross domestic product during the 1980s and 1990s, Western domination eroded proportionately.

The West in a Global Age

"[A united] Europe will not be created at a stroke [of a pen] or according to a single plan," Robert Schumann, an outspoken promoter of European unity, had prophesied in the 1950s. Indeed the further integration of the European Community (EC) in 1992 proved that a unified Europe remained an evolving entity with an unpredictable future. That year the twelve countries of the EC ended national distinctions in the spheres of business activity, border controls, and transportation. Citizens of EC member countries carried a common burgundy-colored passport, and governments, whether municipal or national, had to treat all member nations' firms the same. New rules also prepared the way for a common currency, the European Currency Unit (ECU), as well as for common policies in everything from television regulations on the number of American soap operas aired to pollution controls on automobiles to standardized health warnings on cigarette packages.

Vote "No" to Maastricht
The Maastricht Treaty called for new levels of integration among countries of the European Community. Many people, from these French farmers to members of Communist parties, feared the consequences and lobbied against the treaty.

	Original members of the Common Market
	Became members in 1973
	Became a member in 1981
	Became members in 1986
	Likely members by 1995
	Applying for membership

The European Union

Some national leaders opposed tighter integration as an infringement on national sovereignty. Margaret Thatcher warned that terrorists would pass freely across borders, opposed the use of a common currency, and criticized moves toward closer pan-European unity, but her forceful opposition seemed so out of step with the times that her own party forced her resignation in 1991. Meanwhile, intellectuals across the continent worried that an emerging "Eurospeak" jargon threatened the distinctiveness of national languages and portended a dull standardization of culture. Eventually, the suspicions of ordinary people were registered in votes against the Maastricht Treaty, which codified the new unification measures. After various amendments were added, the treaty went into effect on January 1, 1994, and the EC became the European Union (EU). New countries were scheduled to join "the twelve"—Sweden, Norway, Finland, and Austria; Turkey and Cyprus also pressed for entry. Most former Communist-run nations also sought inclusion in the EU, but West Europeans balked at competing with the lower labor costs to the east and made only vague promises regarding future EU membership.

Its growing global affluence had turned the West itself into a consumer commodity. Tourism had become the largest single industry in Britain and many other countries by the early 1990s. Throngs of visitors from Japan and elsewhere testified to the powerful place the West still held in the world's imagination. Chinese students in Tiananmen Square had rallied around their own representation of America's Statue of Liberty, itself a gift from France to the United States. In Japan business people wore Western-style clothing and watched soccer, baseball, and other Western sports. Ruling families in Asia became Western-style celebrities instead of sacred, godlike figures. Although the Pacific Rim countries had taken over as creditors to much of the world, they had also become heavy borrowers of Western culture. Observers were reminded of the ancient world, when the triumph of Rome had depended on the building blocks laid by Greek civilization.

Despite these successes, the dawning twenty-first century confronted Westerners with gnawing problems about the consequences of the technological and organizational revolution they had unleashed. Would innovation add to or detract from the quality of human work? Technologically sophisticated workers might find meaningful challenges in their productive lives, but would those without such skills be reduced to minimum-wage

ACT UP-PARIS
EN LUTTE
CONTRE
LE SIDA.

The AIDS Crisis
Groups like Act-Up became increasingly vocal in the 1980s and 1990s as governments reacted slowly to the spread of AIDS. Gay-rights activists put the issue of sexual orientation on the political agenda globally.

jobs as clerks, cashiers, and fast-food attendants? Such trends, already apparent in the 1990s, were creating a two-tiered labor market so reminiscent of the way women had traditionally been exploited that critics spoke of a new "feminization" of work. Furthermore, multinational corporations, often seen as out of reach and out of touch, neither inspired nor displayed loyalty, and mounting business scandals—ranging from Wall Street junk-bond scams to the corrupt dealings of much of the Italian elite—eroded confidence in the ethics of capitalism. "I don't care about ethics," said one German "cyberpunker" at his arraignment for infiltrating a variety of national computer banks. "If it's Russian interests or Western interests, I don't care about that stuff." As people questioned which values of Western civilization still held, some Westerners acknowledged their lack of compassion for underemployed immigrants, homeless people, or the destitute in general.

In the late 1970s both Western values and Western technological expertise were challenged by the spread of a global epidemic disease: acquired immune deficiency syndrome, or AIDS. An incurable, highly virulent killer, AIDS initially afflicted heterosexuals in central Africa; its first European victim, Danish physician Grethe Rask, died in 1977 after working among the sick in that region. The disease later turned up in Haitian immigrants to the United States and in gay men worldwide. As researchers focused attention on the mysterious ailment in the early 1980s, they discovered that it effectively shut down the body's entire immune system. By the mid-1990s no cure had yet been discovered, and the mounting death toll made AIDS seem to some like a Black Death of the twentieth century. In many American cities, for example, AIDS had become the leading cause of death among women between 15 and 45. Nevertheless, the circumstances of the disease's transmittal reinforced prejudices and stereotypes about some of its most vulnerable victims.

The failure of corporate and government "megasystems" to deal effectively with the strains of advanced technological society forced people to rely on piecemeal local efforts. The ability of modern nations to satisfy the needs of ethnic minorities was violently challenged by groups ranging from the Basque separatists of northern Spain to the Breton separatists of western France. Separatist parties in different areas of Italy gained strength; in 1994 neo-fascists joined the ruling coalition as the Christian Democrats were linked to Mafia leaders and discredited. On an intellectual level, philosophers of the 1990s called for less reliance on abstract theory and more on "adaptive" or "situational" knowledge; individuals should return to Aristotle's advice and make decisions "as the occasion requires." Commitments to technology, to scientific management of government, and to a rational social order—all heritages of the Enlightenment values that had shaped the West since the eighteenth century—often seemed inadequate to the problems of twenty-first-century society.

The Global Diffusion of Culture

The experience of culture has long transcended political boundaries. In the ancient world the Romans studied the work of Greek philosophers; in the nineteenth century Western scholars immersed themselves in Eastern languages. Over the past two

Rock Concert in Moscow, 1989
Foreign flags, Hard Rock Cafe T-shirts, and rock itself were part of the globalization of culture.

centuries, however, stunning advances in telecommunications and computers have vastly accelerated the diffusion of culture. In the process national cultural distinctions have increasingly blurred.

These remarkable innovations have made the earth seem a much smaller place. In the contemporary world business people and politicians rely on the media to track important developments around the globe. Computer hackers, in the privacy of their own homes and using only a computer and a modem, now enter a vast information "highway" and roam through the world's information systems. Videotapes and satellite-beamed telecasts transport American television shows to Hong Kong and Japanese movies to Europe and North America. American rock music recordings sell briskly in the Soviet Union and elsewhere in the former Eastern bloc. When more than 100,000 Czechoslovakian rock fans, including President Václav Havel, attended a Rolling Stones concert in Prague in 1990, it was clear that despite a half-century of supposedly insular Communist culture, Czechs and Slovaks had tuned into the larger world. Sports stars like the Brazilian soccer player Pelé and the American basketball hero Michael Jordan became better known to countless people than their own national leaders. In today's world millions of people might even, at the same moment, be spectators at a "live" event anywhere on the planet, whether the 1994 Winter Olympics from Lillehammer, Norway, or an Academy Awards broadcast from Los Angeles, California. Despite the strong Western orientation of much of this transmitted culture, critics feared that distinctive Western identities and values might be weakened with the spread of Western culture across the earth.

Because of U.S. success in "marketing" culture and its leadership in multinational business, English became the dominant international language. Such English words as *stop, shopping, parking, okay,* and *rock* infiltrated dozens of non-English vocabularies. With British and American pop music filling the airwaves worldwide, people anywhere could tune their radios to hear songs in English. English was the official language of the Common Market and of the new Central European University in Budapest; unofficially, it was the language of travel. In the 1960s, French president de Gaulle, fearing the corruption of the

French language, had banned such new words as *computer* in government documents; in the mid-1990s the French government updated the ban. Neither directive, however, could stop the influx of English into daily life. Other European countries, however, among them Germany and the Netherlands, built on their polyglot traditions by assimilating the new words.

Western Europe, the United States, and Australia boasted the largest publishing firms. The giant media empire of Australian-born Rupert Murdoch not only published books, magazines, and newspapers but produced movies and television shows through its filmmaking and TV-network subsidiaries. The news media concocted an extremely successful formula for "selling" news broadcasts that combined reports of late-breaking local, national, and international events with slice-of-life stories about ordinary people. Focusing heavily on Third World suffering, whether because of war, famine, disease, or general underdevelopment, contemporary newscasts reinforced the apparent benefits of life in the West.

The publishing behemoths successfully marketed the outpouring of written work by major Third World artists and intellectuals. Such literature not only sold well but also won critical acclaim and exerted a strong influence on European and North American writers. The lush, exotic fantasies of Colombian-born Nobel Prize winner Gabriel García Márquez, for example, attracted a vast Western readership. His novels, including *One Hundred Years of Solitude* (1967) and *Love in the Time of Cholera* (1988), portray people of titanic ambitions and passions who endure war and all manner of personal trials. Whereas European writers of the day often wrote books in a style that was inaccessible to a mass readership, García Márquez's *magical realism* continued an older tradition of comprehensible narrative with larger-than-life characters.

Another Noble Prize recipient (in 1988) who won high regard in the West was Egyptian writer Naguib Mahfouz. Having immersed himself in his youth in the great Western writers, Mahfouz authored more than forty books. His celebrated *Cairo Trilogy,* written in the 1950s, describes a middle-class family—from its practice of Islam and seclusion of women to the business and cultural life of men in the family. British colonialism forms the trilogy's backdrop; it impassions the protagonists and shapes their lives and destinies. In the eyes of many Arab observers, Mahfouz was a "safe" choice for the Nobel Prize, not only because he produced a literature about the history of colonialism but also because he had adopted a European style. "He borrowed the novel from Europe; he imitated it," charged one compatriot and fellow writer. "It's not an Egyptian art form. Europeans . . . like it very much because it is their own form." Thus although non-Western literature reshaped Western taste, it also sometimes provoked charges of inauthenticity in its authors' homelands.

Immigrants to Europe also contributed to the reshaping of Western culture. The popular writer Buchi Emecheta, in her novel *In the Ditch* (1972) and her autobiography *Head Above Water* (1986), explored her experiences as a newcomer to Britain. Her *The Joys of Motherhood* (1979) was an imaginary foray back in time to probe the nature of mothering under colonial rule in her native Lagos in West Africa. While critiquing colonialism and the welfare state from a non-Western perspective, Emecheta, like many writers and politicians from less-developed countries, felt the lure of Western education and Western values. Salman Rushdie, also an immigrant to Great Britain (from India), produced the novel *The Satanic Verses* (1988), which ignited outrage among Muslims around the world because it appeared to blaspheme the prophet Muhammad. From Iran the Ayatollah Khomeini promised both a monetary reward and salvation in the afterlife to anyone who would assassinate the writer. In a display of Western cultural unity, international leaders took bold steps to protect Rushdie. Nigerian playwright and poet Wole Soyinka, who traveled between his homeland and various teaching posts in the West, movingly described the repressive politics that had followed the heady experience of African liberation. In 1986, Soyinka won the Nobel Prize for his plays, poetry, and prison writings, perhaps because his work defended many Western ideals, such as freedom of speech and political rights for all. From within the West, novelist Toni Morrison, the first African-American woman to win the Nobel Prize for Literature, described the experiences and dreams of the descendants of men and women who had been brought as slaves to the United States.

The Pompidou Center, Paris
This center, containing a museum, library, restaurants, and areas for art exhibits, is the height of functional, modernist style. Its placement in the midst of centuries-old buildings rather than in the more contemporary sections of the city makes it part of postmodernist city planning that amalgamates rather than segregates styles.

The writings of Eastern-bloc dissidents enjoyed increasing popularity in the West because of their powerful rearticulation of Western values. Many of these writers first published their works in the West; their writings were eventually smuggled back to their homelands. Milan Kundera left Czechoslovakia in 1975 after Communist police had harassed him for his rebellious writing. Settling in Paris, Kundera produced *The Book of Laughter and Forgetting* (1979) and *The Unbearable Lightness of Being* (1984). In these works he dwelt on the importance of remembering the oppressive climate of the Eastern bloc in the face of the natural human tendency to repress, to forget. In Kundera's fictional world, life often drifted toward immateriality and a quest for ease. The culture of forgetting and an easy attitude toward life, however, were just what repressive governments wanted. Writers who remained in the Eastern bloc were often suspicious of those who found success in the West. In the land of prosperous book contracts, said one Polish writer, there was no such thing as literature; rather, writing was merely a "line of business."

Some dissident writers chose not to leave the Communist world, and they survived by turning out a literature that was acceptable, even if the government did not embrace it wholeheartedly. East German writer Christa Wolf explored subjects—individuality, personal guilt, and the search of self-identify—that went against the grain of East Germany's Communist ideology. Themes she touched on in such works as *The Quest for Christa T.* (1970) appealed deeply to Westerners in the 1970s and 1980s. While probing Western values in the context of communism, however, Wolf never crossed the fine line that would have brought her into open opposition to the government. Consequently, the East German regime allowed her to continue publishing. With the collapse of communism, Wolf was condemned for the privileges she had enjoyed under Communist rule and for her lack of forceful dissent.

Other intellectuals reworked Western culture through a style known as *postmodernism*, which rejected modern nonrepresentational art as too inhuman. Striking examples of postmodernism abounded in Western society, including the AT&T

building in New York City, the work of architect Philip Johnson. Although the structure itself, designed in the late 1970s, looked sleek and modern, its entryway was a Roman arch, and its cloud-piercing top suggested the eighteenth-century Chippendale style. The blueprints of Johnson and other postmodernists, in other words, appealed to the human past and drew from cultural styles that spanned millennia. In Paris the multicolored Pompidou Center was an inside-out building whose brightly hued pipes and supports were on the exterior for all to see. Other postmodernist creations emphasized the anarchic, the faddish, or the ephemeral. Swiss sculptor Jean Tinguey, for example, produced art that would self-destruct over time in the belief that change was the only universal constant.

Postmodern intellectuals cast disillusioned eyes on the eighteenth-century ideals of human rights, individualism, and personal freedom: all this, they suggested, needed adjusting in an age of global technology, mass communication, and international migration. The 1982 American film *Blade Runner*, for example, depicted a dangerous, densely packed Los Angeles patrolled by police with high-tech gear—a metropolis with no place for national or personal identity or human rights. For postmodernists computers had replaced the autonomous self and bureaucracy had rendered representative government obsolete.

Thus French psychoanalyst Jacques Lacan, who deeply influenced Western literary criticism in the 1980s, maintained that people operate in an unfree, predetermined world of language. Patriarchal rules of language exist before we are born, and in becoming social, communicating beings we must bow to these laws. Another prominent French thinker, Michel Foucault, professed to deplore the easy acceptance of such liberal ideas as the autonomous self, the progressive march of history, and the advance of freedom. For him the sexual revolution had not been liberating at all; rather, sexuality was merely a way in which humans expressed power over one another and through which society, by allowing greater sexual expression, actually controlled individuals. Freedom, in short, had lost credibility: even in the most intimate part of human experience, people were locked in a grid of social and individual constraint.

CONCLUSION

Although postmodernists proclaimed an end to centuries of faith in progress, they themselves worked within the Western tradition of constant criticism and reevaluation. Moreover, said their critics, the daunting problems of contemporary life—population explosion, resource depletion, North-South inequities, nuclear power, global pollution, and ethnic hatred—demanded the exercise of humanistic values and the renewal of a rational commitment to progress now more than ever.

The years since 1979 had provided some cause for cautious optimism. The collapse of communism signaled at least the eclipse of an ideology that was perhaps noble in intent but frequently deadly in practice. Events from South Africa to the Middle East to Northern Ireland indicated that certain long-feuding groups were wearying of conflict and groping for peace, even as other peoples took up arms against their neighbors. As the new millennium approached, Western traditions of democracy, human rights, and economic equality were only imperfectly realized in daily life, but people from around the globe recognized the merit of such traditions and often sought to embrace them. At the same time, these non-Westerners challenged, criticized, refashioned, and enriched Western culture. As Western civilization increasingly absorbed values from the rest of the world, it continued to offer useful models for social, political, and economic systems and to influence the course of global change.

SUGGESTIONS FOR FURTHER READING

Source Materials

Emecheta, Buchi. *The Joys of Motherhood.* 1979. A widely acclaimed novel about colonial Africa as imagined by an immigrant novelist to England.

Kundera, Milan. *The Unbearable Lightness of Being.* 1984. A novel about people's personal and public choices under communism.

Philipsen, Dirk. *We Were the People: Voices from East Germany's Revolutionary Autumn of 1989.* 1993. A collection of interviews from East Germans reacting to the "year of miracles."

Interpretive Studies

Appleyard, Reginald, and Charles Stahl, eds. *International Migration Today.* 2 vols. 1988. Discusses trends and issues in global migration.

Ash, Timothy Garton. *The Polish Revolution: Solidarity.* 1983. Describes the early days of the movement.

———. *The Uses of Adversity: Essays on the Fate of Central Europe.* 1989. An Englishman's look at social and political change in the 1980s before the breakup of the Eastern bloc.

Beschloss, Michael, and Strobe Talbott. *At the Highest Levels: The Inside Story of the End of the Cold War.* 1993. Includes inside reports of the relationship between Gorbachev and Bush, who agreed that hardliners in both the USSR and the United States were the biggest threat to the end of the Cold War.

Bialer, Seweryn. *The Soviet Paradox: External Expansion, Internal Decline.* 1986. An expert analysis of the Soviet predicament.

Cracraft, James. *The Soviet Union Today.* 1988. Contains fascinating studies of the many sides of Soviet society in the 1980s, including the military, scientists, and consumers.

Daedalus. 1980s and 1990s. A journal devoted to topics such as Eastern Europe, world development, population, India, and so on.

Gill, Stephen, and David Law. *The Global Political Economy: Perspectives, Problems, and Policies.* 1988. Explains how the international economy functions, with some attempt to predict its future course.

Hughes, H. Stuart. *Sophisticated Rebels: The Political Culture of European Dissent, 1968–1987.* 1988. A brief but helpful overview of a variety of activists and dissidents.

Jarausch, Konrad. *The Rush to German Unity.* 1994. Explores the issues and problems raised by unification.

Jencks, Christopher. *Post-Modernism: The New Classicism in Art and Architecture.* 1987. Describes the arts in the new cultural concept.

Kavanagh, Dennis. *Thatcherism and British Politics: The End of Consensus?* 1987. Explores Margaret Thatcher's revolution and its political meaning.

Keddie, Nikki R. *Roots of Revolution: An Interpretative History of Modern Iran.* 1981. A lively treatment of the political resistance generated by the shah's regime.

Keylor, William R. *The Twentieth-Century World: An International History.* 1992. An excellent survey of global events that rests on a unified vision from 1914 to the present while appreciating the discontinuities since 1989.

Kramer, Jane. *The Europeans.* 1988. Offers fascinating close-ups of both ordinary and famous people.

Lukacs, John. *The End of the Twentieth Century and the End of the Modern Age.* 1991. An interpretation of state authority, internationalism, and populist nationalism at work in contemporary society.

Malia, Martin. *The Soviet Tragedy: A History of Socialism in Russia, 1917–1991.* 1994. A work that links Lenin's policies to current crises in the former Soviet Union.

Medvedev, Zhores. *The Legacy of Chernobyl.* 1990. A detailed look at the nuclear catastrophe, its aftermath, and implications for the future.

Owen, Richard, and Michael Dynes. *The Times Guide to 1992.* 1989. Examines benefits, problems, and other consequences of the next step toward European unity.

Penley, Constance, and Andrew Ross. *Technoculture.* 1991. Includes essays on fax machines, cyberpunk rap, and other technological phenomena of the 1980s and 1990s.

Shilts, Randy. *And the Band Played On: Politics, People, and the AIDS Epidemic.* 1987. A gripping account of the spread of AIDS and medical and political reactions to it.

Smith, Hedrick. *The New Russians.* 1990. A journalist reports on a changing society, but before the onset of many of the real hardships.

Wright, Patrick. *On Living in an Old Country.* 1986. Looks at politics and culture in 1980s Britain.

Wright, Robin. *In the Name of God: The Khomeini Decade.* 1989. Examines the connection between religion, politics, and nationalism under Mullah rule.

EPILOGUE

Textbooks, by their very nature, give the impression that history is a settled matter. Because so much information has to be packed in such a relatively small space, uncertainty, doubt, debate, and controversy rarely break the surface of the seemingly self-evident march of events. But history is never a settled matter; it is always in process, being constantly rewritten, as our sense of the present changes. Even the chronology, supposedly the bedrock of history writing, alters as our sense of the meaning of the flow of time changes in response to transformations in our world. The most immediate example of such change is the disintegration of the Soviet empire after 1989. Suddenly the superpower rivalry of the cold war had a terminus, and the chronology of the preceding decades itself began to shift. Now historians seek the signs of that coming disintegration, whereas previously they focused more on the reasons for the persistence of Soviet power.

History writing in the twentieth century follows the models developed in the eighteenth and nineteenth centuries. Contemporary scholars usually divide Western time into the chronological categories first established between 1500 and 1800: prehistory succeeded by ancient, medieval, early modern, and modern history. This set of categories depends on the sense that the "modern" world is dramatically different from what came before. We have tried not to let this chronology predetermine our narrative because it distorts as much as it illuminates past experiences. Men and women in what we call ancient times did not feel "ancient"; people in the middle ages did not think of themselves as living in a time between ancient and modern times. Before the eighteenth century, few thought that history revealed a steady progression forward into better times; more often Western peoples believed that history showed the effects of inevitable deterioration, disintegration, and decay.

Nevertheless, present-day history scholarship cannot ignore the perspective set up by modernity, with all of its potential for both good and ill. Since the nineteenth century, historians have considered it their task to investigate how the world came to be as it is, and as a consequence, their efforts depend in large measure on their definition of what the old now is, that is, on their definition of modernity itself. Our chapters necessarily reflect some of these presuppositions, for we have chosen to emphasize certain themes in the modern period: the establishment of an international political system based on competition between states defined by their national identities; the development of new economic methods for exploiting resources, including the conquest of overseas territories, the extension of slavery, and industrialization; the growing differentiation of society with increases in education, communications, and economic specialization; and the evolution of new cultural attitudes toward the status of individuals in society, in particular the notion that individuals have inalienable human rights that give all of them (historically first propertied men, then the working classes, religious minorities, freed slaves, and finally women) claims to participate in the various aspects of political, economic, and cultural life.

Although we have tried to avoid giving the impression that such trends can easily be traced back through the past or that they determined Western history in some lockstep fashion, assumptions about modernity influence our views even of the very distant past. Because industrialization, for instance, so profoundly transformed Western life after the eighteenth century, historians now routinely consider economic factors to be very important in shaping past societies. So for each period of time, we have examined the effects of economic structures and changes on the organization of societies. Societies based on hunting and gathering rather than settled agriculture, for example, differed in almost every respect from medieval societies structured by lord-serf bonds, from eighteenth-century plantation societies dependent on slave labor, or from twentieth-century societies shaped by industrialization, automation, and computers.

Similarly, because the modern conception of the individual as an autonomous being with inherent rights has so influenced the development of modern democratic politics, we have looked closely at the cultural presuppositions about the individual in past societies and their political consequences. The individual personality, male and female, depicted in ancient Greek philosophy, poetry, and drama, for example, has inspired many of our own modern notions about the nature of men and women, but Greek culture also differs in some essential respects from our own. The same can be said of medieval and early modern (Renaissance and Reformation) cultural patterns; we have inherited some of their most striking features while at the same time are moving away from them. As a consequence, our narratives always reflect an inherent and inescapable tension between a focus on what we have retained from the past and an emphasis on how much past peoples differed from us. The past is familiar enough for us to understand it and different enough so that we can learn something new from it.

Historians have always debated the relative importance of the diverse factors shaping human life, and in the past, they favored many different kinds of interpretations of those factors. We have tried to present an integrated account in which social and political structures, cultural, religious, and intellectual configurations, and economics and demography all play their part. If there has been one consistent emphasis in our story it has been the focus on power, but as Western history shows, power takes many forms: control over the slave trade or agricultural surplus, dominance through positions of political authority, the ability to raise powerful armies, the right to make decisions in a village or individual household, access to information through reading and writing, special status in relation to the supernatural—all these are forms of power and all of them can involve life-and-death matters. The most significant change in history writing in the last two centuries has been a steadily growing appreciation of the importance of ordinary people and the ordinary things of life (who cooks, who tends the sheep, who gets the property). Generals and statesmen certainly influence the course of affairs in an obvious fashion, but the less obvious decisions—when to marry, how many children to have, where to live, what to believe—weave webs of meaning and influence that enmesh even the generals and statesmen. We need the perspective both from on high and from below to properly understand the past.

Having taken you on this long and complex journey through many centuries of the past, we have only one last reminder. Whatever your own interpretation of how things were—and there is no final interpretive word in history—it is most important to respect the differences of the past. The "modern" view of history, because it has tended to see the modern world as better than what came before, has often encouraged a certain condescension toward people in the past; their customs and traditions often seem strange and "backward." People in the past could no more see into the future than we can; our insight into their lives is made possible solely by the passage of time.

We have probably fallen into this attitude ourselves from time to time, because any retrospective view is bound to introduce some kind of "one-directional" thinking called *teleology;* what comes first seems to prepare the way for what comes after and so to be in some way preliminary, less developed, even immature. So we must always make an effort to overcome this distortion in our hindsight. History should teach us to be humble about ourselves, because in history we see how others have struggled to make and remake their worlds. We see how easily failure met their best efforts and thus can appreciate that even with all we know, we cannot predict or control our own future. In this, we are not that different from those who came before us, and so we can continue to learn from them, as we hope future generations will learn from our efforts, our failures, and our successes.

CREDITS

Text

p. 213, chart, "Roman Imperial Silver Coinage, 27 B.C.–A.D. 272" from *The Archeology of the Roman Empire* by Kevin Greene, published by B. T. Batsford Ltd., London and reproduced with permission.

p. 273, figures from Clive Foss, *Ephesus After Antiquity: A Late Antique Byzantine and Turkish City,* reprinted with the permission of Cambridge University Press.

p. 279, figure adapted from *The Venture of Islam* by Marshall Hodgson, 1974, p. 168. Reprinted by permission of The University of Chicago Press.

p. 286, drawing of Tours c. 600, based on Henri Galinie, "Archeologie et topographie Historique de Tours-IVeme-XIeme Siecle," *Zeitschrift Fur Archolaogie des Mittelalters,* 6 (1978); 33–56, figures 2 and 4. Reprinted by permission of Dr. Rudolf Habelt GmbH.

p. 361, map adapted from *Domesday England* by H. C. Darby, 1977, reprinted with the permission of Cambridge University Press.

p. 371, diagram of Cistercian monastery from *Monasteries of Western Europe* by Wolfgang Braunfels, p. 75, figure 61, Copyright © 1972. Reprinted by permission of Princeton University Press.

p. 390, lines from Frederick Goldin, ed. and trans. *Lyrics of the Troubadours and Trouveres, Original Texts with Translations,* Anchor Press 1973. Reprinted by permission of Doubleday a division of Bantam, Doubleday, Dell Publishing Group, Inc.

p. 391, "Of things I'd rather keep in silence . . . ," from Meg Bogin, *The Women Troubadours,* 1976, p. 85, W. W. Norton Publishers.

pp. 391, 392, lines from Frederick Goldin, ed. and trans. *Lyrics of the Troubadours and Trouveres, Original Texts with Translations,* Anchor Press 1973. Reprinted by permission of Doubleday a division of Bantam, Doubleday, Dell Publishing Group, Inc.

p. 392, from *Raoul de Cambrai: An Old French Feudal Epic,* trans. Jessie Crosland, Cooper Square Publishers, 1966, Rowman & Littlefield Publishers Inc.

p. 860, chart from Ansley J. Coale, "The Decline of Fertility in Europe from the French Revolution to World War II," in S. J. Berhman, Leslie Corsa, and Ronald Freedman, eds., *Fertility and Family Planning,* University of Michigan Press, 1969, 23 (3–24). Reprinted by permission of University of Michigan Press.

p. 882, map based on "Strife in Africa 1899–1914" from *A World Atlas of Military History,* 1978, p. 35, reprinted with permission of Hippocrene Books, Inc.

Photograph

Prologue
p. xxxvii, Erich Lessing/Art Resource, NY; p. xxxix, M. Shostak/Anthro-Photo; pp. xli–xliv, Erich Lessing/Art Resource, NY.

Part I
p. 1, Nimatallah/Art Resource, NY.

Chapter 1
p. 3, The University of Pennsylvania Museum, Philadelphia, neg. # CBS 7051; p. 6, Hirmer Fotoarchiv; p. 7, The University of Pennsylvania Museum, Philadelphia, neg. # T4-28c3; p. 12 (top), Copyright British Museum; p. 12 (bottom), Lila AbuLughod/Anthro-Photo; p. 13, Giraudon/Art Resource, NY; p. 15, Courtesy, Museum of Fine Arts, Boston; p. 18, The National Trust Photographic Library/Art Resource, NY; p. 19, Erich Lessing/Art Resource, NY; p. 27, The Metropolitan Museum of Art, Rogers Fund and Contribution from Edward S. Harkness, 1929 (29.3.2); p. 28, Griffith Institute, Ashmolean Museum, Oxford.

Chapter 2
p. 37, Copyright British Museum; p. 39, British School at Athens. Photo credit: Popham/Sackett; p. 42, Courtesy of the Oriental Institute of the University of Chicago; p. 46, American School of Classical Studies at Athens: Agora Excavations; p. 47, From A. M. Snodgrass: *Archaic Greece* © 1980, J. M. Dent & Sons, Ltd., London; courtesy of the author and The Orion Publishing Group Ltd.; p. 48, Antikensammlungen und der Glyptothek in München; p. 50, Makron, Greek, Attic, Red-figure *Kylix,* (72,55) 480 B.C., wheel thrown, slip decorated earthenware. Ht. 4 11/32 in.; Diam. with handles 14 5/32 in. The Toledo Museum of Art, Toledo, Ohio; Gift of Edward Drummond Libbey; p. 54, The Metropolitan Museum of Art, Rogers Fund, 1911 (11.210.1); p. 55, George Obremski/The Image Bank; p. 58, Hirmer Fotoarchiv; p. 59, The Metropolitan Museum of Art, Purchase, Walter C. Baker Gift, 1956 (56.11.1). Rollout Photograph by Justin Kerr; p. 65, Anne van der Vaeren /The Image Bank.

Chapter 3
p. 75, Scala/Art Resource, NY; p. 82, Photo Deutsches Archäologisches Institut Athens; p. 85, American School of Classical Studies at Athens: Agora Excavations; p. 86, Alberto Incrocci/The Image Bank; p. 87, Guido Alberto Rossi/The Image Bank; p. 88, Copyright British Museum; p. 91, Copyright

British Museum; p. 93, Roberto Valladares/The Image Bank; p. 96, H. L. Pierce Fund. Courtesy, Museum of Fine Arts, Boston; p. 97, The Master and Fellows of Corpus Christi College, Cambridge; p. 105, Staatliche Museen zu Berlin. Photo: Jürgen Liepe, 1990 © Bildarchiv Preussischer Kulturbesitz, Berlin.

Chapter 4

p. 111, Scala/Art Resource, NY; p. 113, Copyright British Museum; p. 114, William Francis Warden Fund. Courtesy, Museum of Fine Arts, Boston; p. 116, Copyright British Museum; p. 125, Erich Lessing/Art Resource, NY; p. 130, Scala/Art Resource, NY; p. 132, Staatliche Museen zu Berlin. © Bildarchiv Preussischer Kulturbesitz, Berlin; p. 135, Copyright British Museum; p. 137, Scala/Art Resource, NY; p. 138 (left), Scala/Art Resource, NY; p. 138 (right), The Metropolitan Museum of Art, Rogers Fund, 1909. (09.39); p. 140, Weinberg-Clark/The Image Bank.

Chapter 5

p. 147, Copyright British Museum; p. 150, Scala/Art Resource, NY; p. 151, Scala/Art Resource, NY; p. 161 (top), Scala/Art Resource, NY; p. 161 (bottom), Scala/Art Resource, NY; p. 163, Alinari/Art Resource, NY; p. 165, Sopr. Archeologica di Pompei (M. Grimoldi); p. 168, Scala/Art Resource, NY; p. 170, From Olaf Höckmann: *Antike Seefahrt,* © 1985, Beck's Archäologishce Bibliothek, Munich; p. 173, Scala/Art Resource, NY; p. 183, Copyright British Museum; p. 184, Museo Capitolino, Rome. S. Rissone (M. Grimoldi).

Chapter 6

p. 187, Scala/Art Resource, NY; p. 190, The American Numismatic Society; p. 192, Scala/Art Resource, NY; p. 194 (left), Scavi Ostia Antica (M. Grimoldi); p. 194 (right), Erich Lessing/Art Resource, NY; p. 195, Art Resource, NY; p. 204, Scala/Art Resource, NY; p. 206, Sopr. Archeologica delle Prov. di Napoli e Caserta (M. Grimoldi); p. 210, Art Resource, NY; p. 214, Lozovet/The Image Bank; p. 217, Scala/Art Resource, NY; p. 221, Scala/Art Resource, NY.

Chapter 7

p. 225, Giraudon/Art Resource, NY; p. 233, Copyright, Martha Cooper/Peter Arnold, Inc.; p. 235, Scala/Art Resource, NY; p. 242, Erich Lessing/Art Resource, NY; p. 246, William Karel/Sygma; p. 248, Archäologisches Landesmuseum, Schleswig; p. 253, Musée du Bardo, Tunisia; p. 258, Alinari/Art Resource, NY; p. 262, Scala/Art Resource, NY; p. 263 (left), Deutsches Archäologisches Institut (M. Grimoldi); p. 263 (right), Art Resource, NY.

Part II

pp. 266–267, Art Resource, NY

Chapter 8

p. 269, By permission of the British Library; p. 273, The Walker Trust, University of St. Andrews Library, Scotland; p. 277, Kurgan-Lisnet/Liaison; p. 278, Bibliothèque Nationale, Paris; p. 282, Copyright British Museum; p. 283, Clive Foss Architectural Photographs, Cambridge; p. 287, Bibliothèque Nationale, Paris; p. 288, Prähistorische Staatssammlung, Munich;

p. 289, Musée Alfred Bonno, Chelles; p. 292, York Castle Museum; p. 293, By permission of the British Library; p. 296, S. Rissone (M. Grimoldi).

Chapter 9

p. 303, Hessische Landes- und Hochschul- Bibliothek, Darmstadt; p. 304, Biblioteca Nazionale Marciana di Venezia; p. 306, Victoria & Albert Museum, London/Art Resource, NY; p. 307, Bibliothèque Nationale, Paris; p. 308, Erzbischöfliches Diözesanmuseum Köln; p. 313, Pro Bibliotheca Academiae Scientiarum Hungaricae; p. 314, Reproduced by kind permission of the Trustees of the Chester Beatty Library, Dublin; p. 321, By permission of the British Library; p. 322, Giraudon/Art Resource, NY; p. 324, Werner Forman Archive/Art Resource, NY; p. 328, KL Weyarn I, Bayerisches Hauptstaatsarchiv; p. 332, Bayerische Staatsbibliothek; p. 333, Ashmolean Museum, Oxford.

Chapter 10

p. 341, Staatsbibliothek Preussischer Kulturbesitz © Bildarchiv Preussischer Kulturbesitz, Berlin; p. 344, Staatliche Museen zu Berlin © Bildarchiv Preussischer Kulturbesitz, Berlin; p. 345, Giraudon/Art Resource, NY; p. 350, The Master and Fellows of Corpus Christi College, Cambridge; p. 358, Owen Franken, Paris; p. 360, Erich Lessing/Art Resource, NY; p. 367, Erich Lessing/Art Resource, NY; p. 368 (right), Foto Marburg/Art Resource, NY; p. 369 (top left), © Caisse Nationale des Monuments Historiques et des Sites/SPADEM; p. 369 (bottom left), Giraudon/Art Resource, NY; p. 369 (right), Erich Lessing/Art Resource, NY; p. 372, © Caisse Nationale des Monuments Historiques et des Sites/SPADEM.

Chapter 11

p. 377, Deutscher Kunstverlag; p. 382, Barb. lat. 2738, fol. 104v-105r, Foto Biblioteca Vaticano; p. 383, Erich Lessing/Art Resource, NY; p. 386, Photo: Bridgeman Art Library/John Bethell; p. 387, By permission of the British Library; p. 389, © Caisse Nationale des Monuments Historiques et des Sites/SPADEM; p. 390, Photo by Jutta Brüdern, courtesy of Der Braunschweiger Dom; p. 392, Biblioteca Ambrosiana, Milano; p. 393, Alinari/Art Resource, NY; p. 400, Bayerische Staatsbibliothek; p. 402, The Master and Fellows of Corpus Christi College, Cambridge; p. 405, National Museum, Copenhagen.

Chapter 12

p. 409, Erich Lessing/Art Resource, NY; p. 410, The Pierpont Morgan Library, New York. M.240, f.8; p. 411, Scala/Art Resource, NY; p. 414, Bibliothèque Nationale, Paris; p. 415, Scala/Art Resource, NY; p. 416, Giraudon/Art Resource, NY; p. 417, Owen Franken; p. 418, Scala/Art Resource, NY; p. 419, Scala/Art Resource, NY; p. 422, Cod. Pal. lat. 1071, fol. iv, Foto Biblioteca Vaticano; p. 427, Public Record Office, London; p. 428, Monique Salaber/Liaison; p. 431, Bibliothèque Nationale, Paris/Photo: Bridgeman Art Library.

Chapter 13

pp. 437, 444, Giraudon/Art Resource, NY; p. 449, The Hulton Deutsch Collection; pp. 450, 453, Giraudon/Art Resource, NY; p. 454, Bridgeman/Art Resource, NY; p. 456, By permission of the Houghton Library, Harvard University; pp. 462, 463, Giraudon/Art Resource, NY; p. 464, Erich Lessing/Art Resource, NY; p. 465, Bridgeman/Art Resource, NY.

Chapter 14

p. 469, Cameraphoto/Art Resource, NY; p. 472, Erich Lessing/Art Resource, NY; p. 473, National Gallery of Art, Washington, DC; p. 475, Giraudon/Art Resource, NY; p. 479, Sovfoto/Eastfoto; pp. 482, 483, Scala/Art Resource, NY; p. 485, Erich Lessing/Art Resource, NY; pp. 487, 490, 491, 492, Scala/Art Resource, NY.

Chapter 15

p. 501, The Metropolitan Museum of Art, Gift of Robert Lehman, 1955. (55.220.2); p. 504, Victoria & Albert Museum, London/Art Resource, NY; p. 505, Art Resource, NY; p. 508, Scala/Art Resource, NY; p. 515, Alinari/Art Resource, NY; p. 517, Snark/Art Resource, NY; p. 521, Erich Lessing/Art Resource, NY; pp. 523, 524, Scala/Art Resource, NY; p. 525, Giraudon/Art Resource, NY; p. 528, Foto Marburg/Art Resource, NY; p. 529, Giraudon/Art Resource, NY.

Part III

pp. 538–539, Alinari/Art Resource, NY

Chapter 16

p. 543, Alinari/Art Resource, NY; p. 545, Scala/Art Resource, NY; p. 548, Private Collection; p. 549, Victoria & Albert Museum/Art Resource, NY; p. 557, North Carolina Museum of Art, Raleigh, Purchased with funds from the State of North Carolina; p. 559, Giraudon/Art Resource, NY; p. 561, Scala/Art Resource, NY; p. 563, Patrimonio Nacional, Madrid; p. 564, Scala/Art Resource, NY; p. 568, *America,* fresco, 1595, Paolo Farinati. Villa Della Torre, Mezzane di Sotto, Verona; p. 570, Giraudon/Art Resource, NY; pp. 571, 574, Erich Lessing/Art Resource, NY.

Chapter 17

p. 577, Scala/Art Resource, NY; p. 579 (right), The Mansell Collection; p. 580, North Wind Picture Archives; p. 587, Art Resource, NY; p. 588, Giraudon/Art Resource, NY; p. 591, Bettmann; p. 593, Erich Lessing/Art Resource, NY; p. 598, Bridgeman/Art Resource, NY; p. 601, Hulton Deutsch Collection; pp. 603, 605 (top), Scala/Art Resource, NY; pp. 605 (bottom), Erich Lessing/Art Resource, NY.

Chapter 18

p. 611, J. B. S. Chardin: *Seated Woman with Book.* Photo: Nationalmuseum, Stockholm; p. 612, By courtesy of the Trustees of Sir John Soane's Museum; p. 618, North Wind Picture Archives; p. 621, By permission of the Houghton Library, Harvard University; p. 623, Giraudon/Art Resource, NY; pp. 625, 626, Scala/Art Resource, NY; p. 630, Giraudon/Art Resource, NY; p. 633, North Wind Picture Archives; p. 634, Sovfoto/Eastfoto; p. 636, Victoria & Albert Museum/Art Resource, NY; p. 640, Giraudon/Art Resource, NY.

Chapter 19

p. 645, Bridgeman/Art Resource, NY; pp. 648, 657, Giraudon/Art Resource, NY; p. 659 (top), Erich Lessing/Art Resource, NY; p. 663, Bridgeman/Art Resource, NY; p. 664, Stock, Montage; p. 665, Art Resource, NY; p. 668 (left), The Mansell Collection; p. 672, Snark/Art Resource, NY; p. 674, Bridgeman/Art Resource, NY; p. 675, Courtesy of The Harvard University Art Museums, Gift of William Gray from the Collection of Francis Calley Gray.

Chapter 20

p. 679, Bibliothèque Nationale, Paris; pp. 686, 687 (top), 690, Giraudon/Art Resource, NY; p. 691, Snark/Art Resource, NY; pp. 693, 694, Giraudon/Art Resource, NY; p. 696, Department of Special Collections, Van Pelt-Dietrich Library, University of Pennsylvania; pp. 698, 699, 702, Giraudon/Art Resource, NY; pp. 706 (bottom), North Wind Picture Archives.

Chapter 21

p. 711, Giraudon/Art Resource, NY; p. 714, Scala/Art Resource, NY; p. 717, North Wind Picture Archives; p. 719, Art Resource, NY; p. 723, Scala/Art Resource, NY; p. 727, Giraudon/Art Resource, NY; p. 732, The Science Museum/Science and Society Picture Library; p. 736 (top), Staatsbibliothek zu Berlin © Bildarchiv Preussischer Kulturbesitz, Berlin; p. 737, Scala/Art Resource, NY; p. 741, Hulton Deutsch Collection; p. 743, Yale Center for British Art, Paul Mellon Collection; p. 744, Giraudon/Art Resource, NY.

Chapter 22

p. 747, Department of Printing and Graphic Arts, The Houghton Library, Harvard University; p. 753, Bayerisches National Museum; p. 756, Art Resource, NY; p. 758, Giraudon/Art Resource, NY; p. 760, Hulton Deutsch Collection; p. 762, Courtesy of The Harvard University Art Museums, Bequest of Grenville L. Winthrop; p. 764, Stock, Montage; p. 771, Hulton Deutsch Collection; p. 774, Bibliothèque Nationale, Paris; p. 777, Scala/Art Resource, NY; p. 779, Department of Printing and Graphic Arts, The Houghton Library, Harvard University.

Chapter 23

pp. 781, 785 (right), Mary Evans Picture Library; p. 787, Hulton Deutsch Collection; p. 789, Collection Bertarelli, Milan. Photo Saporetti; p. 793 (bottom), Hulton Deutsch Collection; p. 797, Hulton Deutsch Collection; p. 800, Bettmann; p. 806, Giraudon/Art Resource, NY; p. 807, Scala/Art Resource, NY; p. 808, North Wind Picture Archives; p. 809, Hulton Deutsch Collection; p. 812, Stock, Montage; p. 814, Hulton Deutsch Collection.

Chapter 24

p. 817, Mary Evans Picture Library; p. 820 (top), Courtesy of Stora; p. 824, The Historical Society of Pennsylvania; pp. 826, 829, 833, Hulton Deutsch Collection; p. 834, N. A. Yaroshenko, *A Girl Student,* 1883. Museum of Russian Art, Kiev; p. 836, Hulton Deutsch Collection; p. 839, By permission of The British Library; p. 841, Jane Voorhees Zimmerli Art Museum, Rutgers University; p. 847, Collection Sally Fox; p. 848, Victoria & Albert Museum/Art Resource, NY; p. 849 (top), Giraudon/Art Resource, NY; p. 849 (bottom), Erich Lessing/Art Resource, NY.

Part IV
pp. 852–853, Laura Knight: *Balloon Site Coventry,* The Imperial War Museum

Chapter 25
p. 857, Mary Evans Picture Library/Sigmund Freud Copyrights/Courtesy of W. E. Freud; p. 861, Bettmann; p. 862, Ice Yachting Scene by Jenny Nyström. Courtesy of Kalmar Läns Museum; p. 869, Amendola/Art Resource, NY; p. 870 (top), Erich Lessing/Art Resource, NY; p. 870 (bottom), Hulton Deutsch Collection; p. 871, Bettmann; pp. 874, 877, Mary Evans Picture Library; pp. 881, 889 (left), Bettmann; pp. 890, 891, Mary Evans Picture Library.

Chapter 26
pp. 895, 902, Mary Evans Picture Library; p. 903, Bettmann; p. 906, Stock, Montage; p. 907, Bettmann; p. 909, Erich Lessing/Art Resource, NY; p. 915, Bettmann; p. 922, Mary Evans Picture Library; p. 923, Ullstein Bilderdienst; p. 925, Art Resource, NY; p. 928, Scala/Art Resource, NY; p. 929, Hulton Deutsch Collection.

Chapter 27
p. 933, Bettmann; p. 935, Mary Evans Picture Library; p. 937, Hulton Deutsch Collection; p. 938, Bettmann; p. 941, Sovfoto/Eastfoto; p. 942, Photo courtesy of Zephyr Press; p. 944, Arthur Lockwood; p. 949, Carl Mydans, Life Magazine © Time Warner; p. 953, Bettmann; p. 954, Hulton Deutsch Collection; pp. 955, 963, 965, Bettmann; p. 966, Hulton Deutsch Collection.

Chapter 28
p. 973, Sovfoto/Eastfoto; p. 976, Wide World Photos; p. 978, Bettmann; p. 980, © Topham/The Image Works; p. 983, Bettmann; p. 989, Museum of Modern Art Film Stills Library; pp. 992, 995, 998, Bettmann; p. 1000, Sovfoto/Eastfoto; pp. 1002, 1003, Hulton Deutsch Collection; p. 1004, Art Resource, NY.

Chapter 29
p. 1009, B. Barbey/Magnum; p. 1011, Tom Bross/Stock, Boston; p. 1012, Bettmann; p. 1013, Shapiro Collection/Cooper-Hewitt Museum; p. 1016, Philippe Ledru/Sygma; p. 1022, Art Gallery of Ontario, Toronto, Purchase, 1967; pp. 1024, 1028, Bettmann; p. 1029, Hulton Deutsch Collection; p. 1031, Bettmann; p. 1035, Henri Bureau/Sygma; p. 1037, James Nachtwey/Magnum.

Chapter 30
p. 1041, Reuters/Bettmann; p. 1043, Gamma Liaison; p. 1044, Régis Bossu/Sygma; p. 1046, Steve McCurry/Magnum; p. 1049, Dennis Chamberlain/Black Star; p. 1050, Reuters/Bettmann; p. 1055, Peter Marlow/Magnum; p. 1056, © Ruelas L.A. Daily News/Sygma; p. 1058, 1063, Reuters/Bettmann; p. 1065, Marc DeVille/Gamma Liaison; p. 1066, Reuters/Bettmann; p. 1068, Ken Ross/Liaison.

INDEX

This index includes a guide to pronouncing proper names and terms that may be unfamiliar to the English-speaking reader. The purpose of the guide is to provide an acceptable indication of pronunciation of selected foreign terms.

Accent marks indicate the syllable to be stressed.

The following symbols are used to indicate the pronunciation of certain vowels, consonants, and letter clusters.

Long vowels

a = ay	as in *date (dayt)*
e = ee	as in *even (ee vn)*
i = ī	as in *size (siz)*
o = o	as in *soap (sop)*
u = oo	as in *flute (floot)*

Short vowels

a	as in *map*
ah	broad a as in *father*
e	as in *met*
uh	as in *but* or *banana*

Other sounds

oy	as in *coin*
zh	as in *vision*
ny	as in *signoria* (si·nyo·ree′·uh)
x	a gutural sound produced at the back of the throat, as in German *Bach* or Russian *Khrushchev*

French and Polish nasal vowels are indicated by *ahn, ehn, ihn, ohn,* and *uhn.*

Page numbers in italic refer to illustrations and captions.
Page numbers followed by "n." refer to footnotes.

House of Windsor, 631n.

Housing: Athenian, 84–87, *85, 86, 87;* in commercial centers, 344–345, *345;* conditions in nineteenth-century factory cities, 734; eighteenth-century middle-class, 624; fourteenth-century, 462; Frankish, 286; late Roman country estates, 253, *253;* neoclassical/Georgian, 658; Neolithic, xlii, xliv; in nineteenth-century cities, 752; Roman, 173, 193–194, 195, *195;* shortages after World War II, 1000–1001, *1000;* suburban, in the U.S. after World War II, 975; Sumerian, 5; for World War I veterans, 921

Howard, Katharine, 519

Hubble, Edwin, U.S. astronomer (1889–1953), 953, 1014

Hubris (hyoo′ • bris), 94

Hugenberg, Alfred, 943

Hugh of St. Victor, 354

Hugo, Victor, French writer (1802–1885), 742

Huguenots: in Brandenburg-Prussia, 596; French religious wars and, 544–548, 590

Hülegü, Mongol ruler, *431*

Humanae Vitae (Pope Paul VI), 1023

Humanism/humanists, 466, 487–488, 504–505, 526–527

Humanitas, 184

Humbert of Silva Candida, 336, 337

Hume, David, Scottish philosopher (1711–1776), 649

Humiliores (hew • mee • lee • or′ es), 204

Humors, 100

Hundred Days, 725

Hundred Years' War (1337–1453), 451–453

Hungarian Diet (1681), 595

Hungary/Hungarians: collectivization in, 990; dissent in the 1960s and 1970s, 1034; fall of communism in, 1057; fifteenth-century, 478; fighting between the Habsburgs and the Ottomans over, 593–595; government during the 1920s, 924; Habsburg conquest of, 635; liberalism during the 1830s and 1840s, 767; Mongols in, 429; nationalism and antisemitism in, during 1894–1914, 878–879; nationalism in the nineteenth century, 771, 775, 776; in the 1930s, 951–952; post–World War I, 918; proclaimed a soviet republic, 912; protests in the 1950s, 991, *992;* Soviet takeover after World War II, 979; twelfth-century, 378–379; in the Warsaw Pact, 985;

World War I peacemaking process and, 913. *See also* Austria-Hungary; Magyars

Hung Hsui-ch'uan (Hong Xiuquan), Taiping leader, 803–804

Huns, Germanic tribes and, 249–250

Hunter-gatherers, knowledge and beliefs of, xl–xli

Hunter's Sketches, A (Turgenev), 786

Hurrian, 25

Hus, Jan (hoos, yon), 446, 448–449, *449,* 513

Hussein, Saddam, president of Iraq, 1047, 1062

Hussitism/Hussites, 446, 448–450, 513

Hydor (hyoo′ • dor), 263

Hydrogen bombs, 973

Hyksos, 26

Hymn to Demeter, The, 92

Hyphasis (hi • fah′ • sis) River, 127

Iaroslav the Wise, prince (✱1019–1054), 310

Iasus (ee′ ah • sus), 134

Iberia/Iberian (ī • beer′ i • a), 52, 53; fifteenth-century, 476–477; fourteenth-century Christian expansion in, 459–460

IBM, 1017

Ibn Rushd, Cordoban philosopher/physician (1126–1193), 412

Ibn Sina, Arab philosopher (980–1037), 314, 366

Ibsen, Henrik, Norwegian playwright (1828–1906), 847, 850

Ice Age, xli

Iconoclasm (ī • kon′ • e • klas′ • m), 275–276, 296–297, 306

Ideal Marriage: Its Physiology and Technique (van de Velde), 922

Ideologies, nineteenth-century, 733–735

Idylls (Theocritus), 136

Ignatius (ig • nay′ • shus), bishop of Antioch (c. A.D. 35–107), 219

Ignatius Loyola (Rubens), *521*

Ignatius of Loyola, saint (1491–1556), 521–522, *521*

Ile-de-France (eel • duh • frahns′), 330

Iliad, The (il′ ee • ad) (Homer), 21, 48, 125, 172, 262

Illidius, saint, 286–287

Illyrians, 124

Imam, 311, 311n.

Imhotep, architect of King Djoser, 14

Immaculate Conception, doctrine of (1854), 808–809

Imperator (im • pe • rah′ • tor), 191

Imperial Diet, definition of, 457

Imperial Diet at Regensburg (ray′ • gens • berk) (1541), 522

Imperial Diet of Worms (1521), 511

Imperialism (1871–1894): conflict and colonial resistance, 880–887; European expansion into Africa, 836–839; European expansion into Asia, 839–841; fight for Egypt, 836–837; impact of, 841–842

Imperium, 156

Impiety, 116

Impressionism, 848–850, *849*

Incas, 530

Independents, conflict with Charles I and, 579

India: Alexander's expedition to, 126–128; British in, 761, 803, 817, 839; British ties with, in the 1930s, 938–939; colonization of through trade and settlement, 614, 616; independence of, 996; in the 1990s, 1063; resistance to colonial domination, 885; Sepoy Mutiny (1857), 803

Indiana (Sand), 758

Indian National Congress, 838

Indochina: Communist takeover of, 994; French, 840, 887; World War II and Japanese invasion of, 961. *See also specific countries*

Indo-Europeans, 18–19

Indonesian islands, 998

Industrialism/industrialist, use of the term, 734

Industrialization/Industrial Revolution: beginnings of, 662–664; in Great Britain during the nineteenth century, 730–732; growth of, during 1871–1894, 818–821; impact of, during 1894–1914, 859–861; impact on religion, 759; post–World War II conversion of weapons to consumer products, 984; railroads and steam, 730–732, 749–750; Second, 818–821; social change and, 749–755; Stalin, during the 1930s, 940–941. *See also* Workplace, postindustrial

Industrial Revolution, use of the term, 732

Inflation: in Germany after World War I, 916; in the 1970s, 1035–1036; in the 1980s, 1046; Roman, 212–213, 229, 253

Influenza epidemic during 1918–1919, 910

Information revolution of the 1960s and 1970s, 1010–1012

Ingres, Jean-Auguste-Dominique (ahn′ • gr), 762

Inheritance, impact of French Revolution on, 697

Innocent III, pope (✱1198–1216), 401, 402, 404, 410–411, *411,* 421